JEREMIAH 21–36

VOLUME 21B

THE ANCHOR BIBLE is a fresh approach to the world's greatest classic. Its object is to make the Bible accessible to the modern reader; its method is to arrive at the meaning of biblical literature through exact translation and extended exposition, and to reconstruct the ancient setting of the biblical story, as well as the circumstances of its transcription and the characteristics of its transcribers.

THE ANCHOR BIBLE is a project of international and interfaith scope: Protestant, Catholic, and Jewish scholars from many countries contribute individual volumes. The project is not sponsored by any ecclesiastical organization and is not intended to reflect any particular theological doctrine. Prepared under our joint supervision, THE ANCHOR BIBLE is an effort to make available all the significant historical and linguistic knowledge which bears on the interpretation of the biblical record.

THE ANCHOR BIBLE is aimed at the general reader with no special formal training in biblical studies; yet it is written with the most exacting standards of scholarship, reflecting the highest technical accomplishment.

This project marks the beginning of a new era of cooperation among scholars in biblical research, thus forming a common body of knowledge to be shared by all.

William Foxwell Albright
David Noel Freedman
GENERAL EDITORS

THE ANCHOR BIBLE

JEREMIAH
21–36

◆

A New Translation
with Introduction and Commentary

JACK R. LUNDBOM

THE ANCHOR BIBLE
Doubleday
New York   London   Toronto   Sydney   Auckland

THE ANCHOR BIBLE
PUBLISHED BY DOUBLEDAY
a division of Random House, Inc.
1745 Broadway, New York, New York 10019

THE ANCHOR BIBLE DOUBLEDAY, and the portrayal of an
anchor with the letters A and B are trademarks of
Doubleday, a division of Random House, Inc.

Library of Congress Cataloging-in-Publication Data

Bible. O.T. Jeremiah XXI–XXXVI. English. Lundbom. 2004.
    Jeremiah 21–36: a new translation with introduction and commentary
By Jack R. Lundbom.—1st ed.
      p. cm. — (The Anchor Bible; v. 21B)
    Includes bibliographical references and indexes.
      1. Bible. O.T. Jeremiah XXI–XXXVI—Commentaries. I. Lundbom,
Jack R. II. Title. III. Series: Bible. English. Anchor Bible. 1964; v. 21B.
BS192.2.A1 1964.G3 vol. 21B
[BS1523]
220.7′7 s—dc21
[224′. 2077]
                                                                97–35473
                                                                CIP

ISBN 0-385-41113-8

First Edition

10 9 8 7 6 5 4 3 2 1

To the Memory of My Father
Carl Russell Lundbom
"who did justice and righteousness"

CONTENTS

◆

INDEXES

PREFACE

◆

The present volume and one to follow on chaps. 37–52 bring to completion my Anchor Bible commentary on the book of Jeremiah. The decision to issue the work in three volumes instead of two allowed for a break at chap. 36, which is fitting in that this chapter—and earlier its expanded colophon in vv 1–8—served to conclude a prose composition that is now embodied in the present Jeremiah book and perhaps was even a book in itself at an earlier time. The "Introduction" contained in *Jeremiah 1–20* can suffice for both volumes, requiring as it does no essential revision now that the entire book has been translated, exegeted, and commented upon. A few texts cited in the Introduction were later altered, but the changes were all very minor.

In *Jeremiah 21–36* and *Jeremiah 37–52* I have made full notation of the section markings in M^A (Aleppo Codex), M^L (Leningrad Codex), and M^P (St. Petersburg Codex of the Prophets); in *Jeremiah 1–20* the sections cited were those of M^L unless otherwise noted. The reader should be advised that the Qumran (Dead Sea Scroll) fragments and major medieval manuscripts (M^P, M^A, and M^L) simply have blank spaces at the beginning, middle, and end of lines, or between lines, which mark the *setumah* (closed section) and *petuhah* (open section). The sigla (ס for a *setumah* and פ for a *petuhah*) came later, their first known appearance being in an edition of Isaiah and Jeremiah published at Lisbon in A.D. 1492 (C. D. Ginsburg 1885 III: xvi). In both of the present volumes I have also included more Greek readings from Aquila (Aq), Symmachus (Symm), and Theodotion (Theod) as they appear in the standard work of Frederick Field, *Origenis Hexaplorum II* (1875), one reason being that they consistently support the MT when the LXX contains an omission. In the present volume I have included a Bibliography Supplement and Abbreviations Supplement that fill out documentation in both *Jeremiah 21–36* and *Jeremiah 37–52*.

Once again, I am indebted to a number of individuals, schools, and granting institutions for making the completion of this large work possible, and wish here to express thanks for all help kindly given. I began work on these last two volumes at the Albright Institute (American School of Oriental Research) in Jerusalem, where I was an NEH Fellow and Albright Fellow for the fall and winter of 1997–98. Work continued in the spring and summer of 1998 at my Cambridge University college, Clare Hall. Research and writing at both institutions were underwritten by a grant from the U.S. National Endowment of the Humanities. In Jerusalem the fine libraries of the Albright and nearby École Biblique proved once again to be invaluable, and in Cambridge the same can be said for the incomparable University Library, as well as the excellent libraries of Oriental Studies, the Divinity School, and neighboring Tyndale House.

In 1998–99 I was privileged to be a member of the Center of Theological Inquiry in Princeton, N.J., which made possible a year of research and writing in the collegial environment of another fine research institution adjacent to Princeton Theological Seminary and its excellent Speer Library. New Covenant Research, Chicago, supported return visits to the Albright Institute in 1999–2000 and 2000–2001, as well as a part-year stay at Clare Hall, Cambridge during 2000–2001. To supporters of this valued foundation I express deep thanks. In 2002 I was awarded a senior research grant from the Fulbright-Kommission to spend the grant period at Universität Tübingen, which enabled me to complete in Germany what I started there fourteen years earlier at Universität Marburg. My thanks to Professor Bernd Janowski for being the kind and generous host he was during my Tübingen stay. The libraries of this fine German university also greatly facilitated my work. Kind thanks go as well to the Executive Director of the Fulbright-Kommission, Dr. Georg Schütte, and to Program Director Dr. Reiner Rohr for the privilege once again of being part of an organization known not only for its commitment to solid academic research, but the creation of better understanding and goodwill among nations of the world.

Thanks once again to my editor, senior colleague, and valued friend, David Noel Freedman, with whom I spent the fall and winter of 2002–2003 as a Visiting Scholar at the University of California, San Diego, getting the manuscript of these two concluding volumes ready for the publisher. Professor Freedman's careful reading of the manuscript, corrections, and judicious editorial comments added substantially to the final product, and I gladly acknowledge my enormous debt to him for all of this and more.

Excursus IV on the "New Covenant in the Literature of Judaism, Including Qumran" and Excursus V on "The New Covenant in the New Testament and Patristic Literature to A.D. 325" are reproduced here with minor change from my "New Covenant" article in the *Anchor Bible Dictionary* (4: 1089–94) and are reprinted with permission from Doubleday.

Finally, my thanks once again to the fine editor at Doubleday, who saw these latter volumes through to publication. Would that every author were privileged to have an editor as able and pleasurable to work with as Andrew R. Corbin.

Jack R. Lundbom
Universität Tübingen, 2002

ABBREVIATIONS SUPPLEMENT

◆

AASOR	The Annual of the American Schools of Oriental Research
ABIU	*Annual of Bar-Ilan University*
ABRL	Anchor Bible Reference Library
AbrNa	*Abr-Nahrain* (continued by *Ancient Near Eastern Studies*)
ADAJ	*Annual of the Department of Antiquities of Jordan*
AfO	*Archiv für Orientforschung*
AION	*Annali dell'Istituto Universitario Orientale di Napoli*
AJBA	*Australian Journal of Biblical Archaeology*
AnBib	Analecta Biblica
ANETS	Ancient Near Eastern Texts and Studies
ANF	Ante-Nicene Fathers (ed. A. Roberts and J. Donaldson, rep. Grand Rapids, 1989)
ANQ	*Andover Newton Quarterly*
AnSt	*Anatolian Studies*
AOS	American Oriental Series
AP	*Aramaic Papyri of the Fifth Century B.C.* (ed. A. E. Cowley; Oxford, 1923)
Ar	Arabic
Aram	Aramaic
ArB	Arabic version of the Bible
ARM	Archives Royales de Mari
ArOd	*Archaeology Odyssey*
ATR	*Anglican Theological Review*
AUM	Andrews University Monographs
BAIAS	*Bulletin of the Anglo-Israel Archaeological Society*
BASS	Beiträge zur Assyriologie und semitischen Sprachwissenschaft
BATAJ	Beiträge zur Erforschung des Alten Testaments und des Antiken Judentums
BFCT	Beiträge zur Förderung christlicher Theologie
BHT	Beiträge zur historischen Theologie
BibO	*Bibbia e Oriente*
BM	The Babylonian Chronicle
BR	*Biblical Research*
BRL²	*Biblisches Reallexikon* (2d ed.; ed. Kurt Galling; HAT 1/1; Tübingen, 1977)
BSt	Biblische Studien
BTA	Bible and Theology in Africa
BTS	Biblisch-Theologische Studien
CAH	The Cambridge Ancient History (2d ed.)
CCen	*The Christian Century*
ChCr	*Christianity and Crisis*

CHI	*The Cambridge History of Iran* (7 vols.; Cambridge, 1968–1991)
CIS	*Corpus Inscriptionum Semiticarum* (Paris, 1881–)
ConJ	*Concordia Journal*
CrCu	*Cross Currents*
CS	*The Context of Scripture I–II* (ed. William W. Hallo; Leiden, 1997–2000)
CTM	*Concordia Theological Monthly*
CuadBib	*Cuadernos bíblicos*
DANE	*Dictionary of the Ancient Near East* (ed. Piotr Bienkowski and Alan Millard; London, 2000)
DSS	Dead Sea Scrolls
EA	El-Amarna tablets. According to the edition of J. A. Knudtzon, *Die el-Amarna-Tafeln.* Leipzig, 1908–1915. Reprint, Aalen, 1964. Continued in A. F. Rainey, *El-Amarna Tablets* 359–379. 2d rev. ed. Kevelaer, 1978
EAT	Estudios del Antiguo Testamento
EncBib	*Encyclopaedia Biblica* (ed. T. K. Cheyne and J. Sutherland Black; London, 1899–1903)
EncIs	*The Encyclopaedia of Islam* (new ed.; ed. C. E. Bosworth et al.; Leiden, 1960–)
EncMiqr	*Entsiqlopedia Miqra'it / Encyclopaedia Biblica* (ed. U. Cassuto et al.; Jerusalem, 1950–1982)
EncRhet	*Encyclopedia of Rhetoric* (ed. Thomas O. Sloane; Oxford, 2001)
EstB	*Estudios bíblicos* (Petropolis)
FAT	Forschungen zum Alten Testament
FRLANT	Forschungen zur Religion und Literatur des Alten und Neuen Testaments
G^A	Codex Alexandrinus
G^B	Codex Vaticanus
G^Q	Codex Marchalianus
G^S	Codex Sinaiticus
GeLe	*Geist und Leben*
HAMNS	*Hymns Ancient and Modern New Standard* (London, 1983)
HDR	Harvard Dissertations in Religion
HTS	*Hervormde teologiese studies*
IMJ	*The Israel Museum Journal*
IOVCB	*The Interpreter's One-Volume Commentary on the Bible* (ed. Charles M. Laymon; Nashville, 1971)
ITS	*Indian Theological Studies*
JAAR	*Journal of the American Academy of Religion*
JBLMS	Journal of Biblical Literature Monograph Series (continued as Society of Biblical Literature Monograph Series)
JBQ	*Jewish Bible Quarterly* (continuing *Dor le Dor*)
JDT	*Jahrbücher für deutsche Theologie*
JEA	*Journal of Egyptian Archaeology*
JESHO	*Journal of the Economic and Social History of the Orient*
JITC	*Journal of the Interdenominational Theological Center*
JJPES	*Journal of the Jewish Palestine Exploration Society*
JRAS	*Journal of the Royal Asiatic Society*
JRT	*The Journal of Religious Thought*

JSP	*Journal for the Study of the Pseudepigrapha*
JSSEA	*Journal of the Society for the Study of Egyptian Antiquities*
K^{OR}	*Ketib in Oriental texts*
LA	*Liber Annuus Studii biblici franciscani, Jerusalem*
LacLe	Lachish Letters
Lane	E. W. Lane, *An Arabic-English Lexicon* (London, 1863–1893)
M^C	Masoretic Text according to the Cairo Codex of the Prophets (Codex C)
MGWJ	*Monatschrift für Geschichte und Wissenschaft des Judenthums*
MHUC	Monographs of the Hebrew Union College
MNTC	Moffatt New Testament Commentary
Mus	*Le Muséon*
MUSJ	*Mélanges de l'Université Saint-Joseph* (Beirut)
MVÄG	Mitteilungen der Vorderasiatisch-ägyptischen Gesellschaft
NAC	The New American Commentary
NEAEHL	*The New Encyclopedia of Archaeological Excavations in the Holy Land* (ed. Ephraim Stern; 4 vols.; Jerusalem, 1993)
NedTT	*Nederlands Theologische Tijdschrift*
NEH	*The New English Hymnal* (Norwich, 1986)
NHS	Nag Hammadi Studies
NIB	The New Interpreter's Bible (ed. Leander E. Keck)
NSKAT	Neuer Stuttgarter Kommentar Altes Testament
NTS	*New Testament Studies*
OAC	Orientis Antiqui Collectio
OEANE	The Oxford Encyclopedia of Archaeology in the Near East (ed. Eric M. Meyers; New York, 1997)
ÖBS	Österreichische biblische Studien
OL	Old Latin
OrAnt	*Oriens Antiquus*
PG	J.-P. Migne, *Patrologiae Graecae* (Paris, 1857–)
PSBF	Pubblicazioni dello Studium Biblicum Franciscanum
RGG^4	Religion in Geschichte und Gegenwart (4th ed.; ed. Hans Dieter Betz et al.; Tübingen, 1998–)
RHPhR	*Revue d'Histoire et de Philosophie Religieuses*
RLA	*Reallexikon der Assyriologie* (ed. Erich Ebeling et al.; Berlin, 1932–)
SBA	Stuttgarter biblische Aufsatzbände
SBB	Stuttgarter biblische Beiträge
SBeT	*Studia Biblica et Theologica*
SEAJT	*South East Asia Journal of Theology*
SeK	*Skrif en Kerk*
SBLSCSS	Society of Biblical Literature Septuagint and Cognate Studies Series
Sem	*Semitica*
St.-B.	H. L. Strack and P. Billerbeck, *Kommentar zum Neuen Testament aus Talmud und Midrasch* (Munich, 1922–1961)
Syr	Syriac
TDNT	*Theological Dictionary of the New Testament* (ed. G. Kittel and G. Friedrich; trans. G. W. Bromiley; 10 vols.; Grand Rapids, 1964–1976)
THAT	*Theologisches Handwörterbuch zum Alten Testament* (ed. Ernst Jenni and Claus Westermann; 2 vols.; Stuttgart, 1971–1976)

TL	*Theology and Life*
Tosef	*Tosefta*
TR	*Theological Review* (continuing *Near East School of Theology Quarterly*)
Trans	*Transeuphratène*
TTK	*Tidsskrift for Teologi og Kirke*
TynB	*Tyndale Bulletin*
TYoma	*Tosefta Yoma*
UM	C. H. Gordon, *Ugaritic Manual* (Rome, 1955)
VAB	*Vorderasiatische Bibliothek*
VH	*Vivens Homo*
VS	Vorderasiatische Studien
Wand	*Die Wandlung*
WHJP	*The World History of the Jewish People* (first series: Ancient Times; ed. E. A. Speiser et al.; Jerusalem, 1964–1979)
WUNT	Wissenschaftliche Untersuchungen zum Neuen Testament
WVDOG	Wissenschaftliche Veröffentlichungen der deutschen Orientgesellschaft
WW	*Western Watch*
YOSR	Yale Oriental Series, Researches
ZA	*Zeitschrift für Assyriologie und Vorterasiatische Archäologie*

JEREMIAH 21–36: A TRANSLATION

◆

I. ON KINGS AND PROPHETS (21:1–23:40)

A. Speaking of Kings (21:1–23:8)

1. Bad News, Good News (21:1–10)

a) Bad News for Zedekiah (21:1–7)

21 ¹The word that came to Jeremiah from Yahweh when King Zedekiah sent to him Pashhur son of Malchiah and Zephaniah son of Maaseiah, the priest, saying: ²'Seek would you Yahweh on our behalf, for Nebuchadrezzar, king of Babylon, is fighting against us; perhaps Yahweh will do for us according to all his extraordinary deeds, and he will go away from us.' ³But Jeremiah said to them, Thus you shall say to Zedekiah:

⁴Thus said Yahweh, God of Israel:

Look I will turn around the weapons of war that are in your hand, with which you are fighting the king of Babylon and the Chaldeans who are besieging you from outside the wall, and I will gather them together into the midst of this city. ⁵And I myself will fight against you with outstretched hand and with strong arm, yes, in anger and in wrath and in great fury. ⁶And I will strike down the inhabitants of this city—both human and beast; by a great pestilence they shall die.

⁷And after this—oracle of Yahweh—I will give Zedekiah, king of Judah, and his servants, and the people, and those remaining in this city from the pestilence, from the sword, and from the famine, into the hand of Nebuchadrezzar, king of Babylon, and into the hand of their enemies, and into the hand of those who seek their lives. And he will strike them down into the mouth of the sword; he will not spare them, and he will not pity, and he will not have mercy.

b) Bad News–Good News for the People (21:8–10)

21 ⁸And to this people you shall say:

Thus said Yahweh:

Look I will set before you the way of life and the way of death. ⁹Whoever stays in this city shall die by sword, and by famine, and by pestilence, but whoever goes out and surrenders to the Chaldeans who are besieging you shall live, and his life will be his booty.

¹⁰For I have set my face against this city for evil, and not for good—oracle of Yahweh. Into the hand of the king of Babylon it shall be given, and he will burn it with fire.

2. Oracles to the Royal House (21:11–14)

a) Execute Justice in the Morning! (21:11–12)

21 ¹¹To the house of the king of Judah: 'Hear the word of Yahweh, ¹²house of
David.'
> Thus said Yahweh:
> Execute justice in the morning
>> and rescue the robbed from the oppressor's hand!
> lest my wrath go forth like fire
>> and burn so none can quench it
>>> on account of their evil doings.

b) Indictment for Royal Pride (21:13)

> ¹³Look, I am against you, sitting one of the valley
>> rock of the tableland—oracle of Yahweh
> Those saying, 'Who can come down upon us
>> and who can enter into our habitations?'

c) Judgment on Royal Deeds (21:14)

> ¹⁴But I will reckon upon you
>> according to the fruit of your doings
>>> —oracle of Yahweh
> And I will kindle a fire in her forest
>> and it will consume everything around her.

3. Once Again, O King: Do Justice and Righteousness! (22:1–5)

22 ¹Thus said Yahweh: Go down to the house of the king of Judah and you
shall speak there this word. ²And you shall say, 'Hear the word of Yahweh, king
of Judah, who sits on the throne of David—you, and your servants, and your
people who come through these gates.'
> ³Thus said Yahweh:
> Do justice and righteousness, and rescue the robbed from the oppressor's
> hand; and the sojourner, the orphan, and the widow do not wrong, do not
> treat violently; and the blood of the innocent do not shed in this place.
> ⁴For if you really do this word, then through the gates of this house shall
> come kings sitting for David on his throne, riding in chariots and with
> horses—he, and his servants, and his people.

> ⁵But if you will not hear these words, I swear by myself—oracle of Yah-
> weh—that this house will come to be a ruin.

4. A Cutting in Lebanon South (22:6–9)

22 ⁶For thus said Yahweh concerning the house of the king of Judah:
> Gilead you are to me
>> the top of Lebanon
> But I will surely make you a wilderness
>> cities that are uninhabited

> ⁷So I am sanctifying destroyers against you
>> each person with his axes
> And they will cut down your choicest cedars
>> and fell them upon the fire.

⁸And many nations will pass by this city, and they will say each person to his fellow, 'Why has Yahweh done thus to this great city?' ⁹And they will say, 'Because they abandoned the covenant of Yahweh their God and worshiped other gods and served them.'

5. Lament Jehoahaz, Not Josiah! (22:10–12)

22 ¹⁰Weep not for the dead
> and condole not for him
>> weep continually for him who goes away
> Because he will not return again
>> and not see the land of his birth.

¹¹For thus said Yahweh to Shallum son of Josiah, king of Judah, who reigned in place of Josiah his father, who departed from this place:
> He will not return there again. ¹²For in the place where they exiled him, he will die, and this land he will not see again.

6. A King with an Edifice Complex (22:13–17)

22 ¹³Woe to him who builds his house without righteousness
> and his upper rooms without justice
He makes his fellow serve for nothing
> his wages he does not give to him
¹⁴Who says, 'I will build for myself a house of dimensions
> with spacious upper rooms'
And he frames for himself windows
> and panels in cedar
>> and paints in vermilion

¹⁵Are you a king because you compete in cedar?
> Your father—Did not he eat and drink
and do justice and righteousness?

Then it went well for him
¹⁶He prosecuted the case of the poor and needy
   then it went well
Is not that knowing me?
   —oracle of Yahweh

¹⁷Indeed your eyes and your heart are on nothing
   except your cut
and for shedding innocent blood
   and for practicing oppression and running.

7. A Non-lament for Jehoiakim (22:18–19)

22 ¹⁸Therefore thus said Yahweh to Jehoiakim son of Josiah, king of Judah:
They shall not lament for him
   'Woe, my brother!
     Woe sister!'
They shall not lament for him
   'Woe lord!
     Woe his majesty!'
¹⁹The burial of an ass he will be buried
   dragged away and cast off
     beyond the gates of Jerusalem.

8. Lebanon South To Be Strangely Favored (22:20–23)

22 ²⁰Go up to Lebanon and scream
   and in the Bashan raise your voice!
And scream from Abarim
   because all your lovers are broken
²¹I spoke to you in your good times
   you said, 'I will not listen'
This has been your way from your youth
   that you have not listened to my voice

²²All your shepherds the wind shall shepherd
   and your lovers into captivity shall go
Indeed then you will be ashamed and disgraced
   from all your wickedness
²³You who dwell in Lebanon
   you who are nested in the cedars
How you will be favored when pangs come upon you
   pain like a woman in labor.

9. Coniah: A Rejected Seal (22:24–27)

22 ²⁴As I live—oracle of Yahweh—even if Coniah son of Jehoiakim, king of Judah, be a seal on my right hand, surely from there I will tear you off. ²⁵And I will give you into the hand of those who seek your life and into the hand of those before whom you are in dread and into the hand of Nebuchadrezzar, king of Babylon, and into the hand of the Chaldeans. ²⁶And I will throw you and your mother who bore you to another land where you were not born, and there you shall die. ²⁷So to the land where they will carry their great desire to return, there they shall not return.

10. Is Coniah a Throwaway Pot? (22:28–30)

22 ²⁸Is an unwanted, smashed pot
    this man Coniah?
      or a jar in which no one takes delight?
So why are he and his offspring thrown
    and cast away to a land that they do not know?

²⁹Land, Land, Land
    Hear the word of Yahweh!

³⁰Thus said Yahweh:
Write this man down childless
    a man who will not prosper in his days
Indeed there shall not prosper from his offspring
    a man to sit upon the throne of David
      and rule again in Judah.

11. The Call Is Out for New Shepherds (23:1–4)

23 ¹Woe to shepherds who destroy and who scatter the flock of my pasture—oracle of Yahweh.
²Therefore, thus said Yahweh, God of Israel, against the shepherds who shepherd my people:
You, you have scattered my flock and dispersed them, and you have not reckoned them. Look I will reckon upon you your evil doings—oracle of Yahweh.

³And I, I will gather the remnant of my flock from all the lands where I dispersed them, and I will bring them back to their pasture, and they shall be fruitful and multiply. ⁴And I will raise up over them shepherds who will shepherd them. And they shall not again be afraid, and they shall not be broken, and they shall not be reckoned with—oracle of Yahweh.

12. For David: A Righteous Shoot (23:5–6)

23 ⁵Look, days are coming—oracle of Yahweh—
　　when I will raise up for David a righteous Shoot
And he shall reign as king and shall succeed
　　and do justice and righteousness in the land

⁶In his days Judah will be saved
　　and Israel will dwell in security
And this is his name by which one will call him:
　　'Yahweh is our righteousness.'

13. New Exodus, New Oath (23:7–8)

23 ⁷Look, hereafter, days are coming—oracle of Yahweh—when they will
no longer say, 'As Yahweh lives who brought up the children of Israel from
the land of Egypt,' ⁸but, 'As Yahweh lives who brought up and who brought
in the offspring of the house of Israel from a land to the north and from all
the lands where I scattered them.' And they shall dwell on their own soil.

B. Speaking of Prophets (23:9–40)

1. Of Adulterers the Land is Full! (23:9–12)

23 ⁹To the prophets:
　　My heart is broken within me
　　　　all my bones waver
　　I have become like a drunken man
　　　　and like a mighty man whom wine has overcome
　　　　　　before Yahweh
　　　　　　and before his holy words.

¹⁰Indeed of adulterers
　　the land is full!

Indeed before the curse the land mourns
　　pastures of the wild are dried up
Yes, their course has become evil
　　and their might is not right

¹¹Indeed even prophet
　　even priest—they are polluted!
Even in my house
　　I have found their evil
　　　　—oracle of Yahweh.

¹²Therefore their way shall become to them
  like slippery ground in thick darkness
    they shall be pushed and fall upon it
Indeed I will bring evil upon them
  in the year of their reckoning
    —oracle of Yahweh.

2. Tale of the Evil Prophets (23:13–15)

23 ¹³Now in the prophets of Samaria
  I have seen a foolish thing:
They prophesied away by Baal
  and led my people Israel astray

¹⁴But in the prophets of Jerusalem
  I have seen a horrible thing:
Committing adultery and walking by the lie
  they even strengthened the hands of evildoers
    so that no person turned from his evil
All of them have become to me like Sodom
  and her inhabitants like Gomorrah.

¹⁵Therefore thus said Yahweh of hosts concerning the prophets:
Look I will feed them wormwood
  and will make them drink poisoned water
Because from the prophets of Jerusalem
  pollution has gone forth to all the land.

3. Prophets with a Vision of Their Own (23:16–17)

23 ¹⁶Thus said Yahweh of hosts:
Do not listen to the words of the prophets who prophesy to you; they make you nothing; a vision of their own heart they speak, not from the mouth of Yahweh, ¹⁷continually saying to those who spurn me, 'Yahweh has spoken, "It will be well for you"'; and to everyone who walks in the stubbornness of his heart they say, 'Evil will not come upon you.'

4. Prophets without Portfolio (23:18–22)

23 ¹⁸For who has stood in the council of Yahweh?
  then let him see and let him hear his word!
    who has hearkened to my word and heard?

¹⁹Look! the tempest of Yahweh
  wrath goes forth

yes, a whirling tempest
Upon the head of the wicked it whirls
[20]the anger of Yahweh does not turn back
until it does and until it fulfills
the purposes of his heart
In the days afterward
you will consider the meaning in this.

[21]I did not send the prophets
yet they, they ran
I did not speak to them
yet they, they prophesied

[22]Now if they had stood in my council
and caused my people to hear my words
Then they would have turned them from their evil way
and from the evil of their doings.

5. Am I a God Nearby and Not a God Far Off? (23:23–24)

23 [23]Am I a God nearby
—oracle of Yahweh—
and not a God far off?

[24]If a person hides himself in secret places
do I myself not see him?
—oracle of Yahweh.

The heavens and the earth
do I not fill?
—oracle of Yahweh.

6. Speaking of Dreams . . . (23:25–32)

23 [25]I have heard what the prophets say who are prophesying a lie in my name: 'I have dreamed, I have dreamed.' [26]How long will there be in the mind of the prophets prophesying the lie—yes, prophets of their deceitful mind, [27]those who plan to make my people forget my name with their dreams, which they recount each person to his fellow, as their fathers forgot my name through Baal? [28]The prophet who has with him a dream, let him recount his dream; and the one who has my word with him, let him speak my word faithfully.

What is the grain to the straw?
—oracle of Yahweh.

^{29}Is it not so—my word is like fire
   —oracle of Yahweh—
      and like a hammer shattering rock?

^{30}Therefore, look I am against the prophets
   —oracle of Yahweh—
      who steal my words each person from his fellow.

^{31}Look I am against the prophets
   —oracle of Yahweh—
      who heed their own tongue and oracle an oracle.

^{32}Look I am against those prophesying lying dreams
   —oracle of Yahweh—
      yes, they recount them and lead my people astray
         with their lies and with their wantonness.

For I, I did not send them
   and I did not command them
      and they are no profit whatever to this people
         —oracle of Yahweh.

7. Speaking of 'Burdens' . . . (23:33–40)

23 ^{33}Now when this people or the prophet or a priest asks you: 'What is the burden of Yahweh?' then you shall say to them: 'You are the burden, and I will cast you off!'—oracle of Yahweh. ^{34}So the prophet or the priest or the people who says, 'the burden of Yahweh,' yes, I will reckon against that person and against his house.

^{35}Thus you shall say each person to his fellow and each person to his brother, 'What has Yahweh answered?' or 'What has Yahweh spoken?' ^{36}But 'the burden of Yahweh' you shall not again remember, for the burden becomes to each person his own word, and you pervert the words of the living God, Yahweh of hosts, our God. ^{37}So you shall say to the prophet: 'What has Yahweh answered you?' or 'What has Yahweh spoken?' ^{38}But if 'the burden of Yahweh' you say:
   Therefore thus said Yahweh:
   Because you have said this word, 'the burden of Yahweh,' when I sent to you saying, you shall not say 'the burden of Yahweh': ^{39}Therefore, look I, yes I will surely lift you up and cast you out—also the city that I gave to you and to your fathers—from my presence. ^{40}And I will put upon you an eternal reproach and an eternal disgrace that will not be forgotten.

II. PREPARE FOR A LIFE IN EXILE (24:1–29:32)

A. Good Figs Gone for Export (24:1–10)

24 ¹Yahweh showed me, and there! two baskets of figs situated in front of the temple of Yahweh—after Nebuchadrezzar, king of Babylon, had exiled Jeconiah son of Jehoiakim, king of Judah, and the princes of Judah and the craftsmen and the smiths from Jerusalem and brought them to Babylon. ²The one basket had very good figs, like the early figs, and the other basket very bad figs, which could not be eaten because they were so bad. ³And Yahweh said to me: 'What do you see, Jeremiah?' And I said: 'Figs! The good figs are very good, and the bad ones very bad, which cannot be eaten because they are so bad.' ⁴And the word of Yahweh came to me:

⁵Thus said Yahweh, God of Israel: Like these good figs, so will I regard the exiles of Judah whom I sent away from this place to the land of the Chaldeans—for good; ⁶and I will keep my eye upon them for good, and I will bring them back to this land, and I will build them up and not overthrow, and I will plant them and not uproot. ⁷And I will give them a heart to know me, for I am Yahweh, and they will be a people to me, and I, I will be God to them, for they shall return to me with their whole heart.

⁸And like the bad figs, which could not be eaten because they were so bad, indeed thus said Yahweh: So will I make Zedekiah, king of Judah and his princes and the remnant of Jerusalem, the ones who remain in this land, and the ones who dwell in the land of Egypt. ⁹Yes, I will make them a fright, a calamity to all the kingdoms of the earth, a reproach and a proverb, a taunt and a swearword, in all the places where I shall disperse them. ¹⁰And I will send against them the sword, the famine, and the pestilence, until they are consumed from upon the soil that I gave to them and to their fathers.

B. Indictment of Judah and the Nations (25:1–38)

1. Nebuchadrezzar: Yahweh's Servant for a Time (25:1–14)

25 ¹The word that came to Jeremiah concerning all the people of Judah in the fourth year of Jehoiakim son of Josiah, king of Judah (that was the first year of Nebuchadrezzar, king of Babylon), ²which Jeremiah the prophet spoke concerning all the people of Judah and to all the inhabitants of Jerusalem, saying: ³From the thirteenth year of Josiah son of Amon, king of Judah, yes, until this day—this is twenty-three years—the word of Yahweh has come to me, and I have spoken to you—constantly I spoke—but you have not listened; ⁴and Yahweh has repeatedly sent to you all his servants the prophets—constantly he sent—but you have not listened, indeed you have not bent your ear to listen.

⁵Return, would you, each person from his evil way and from your evil doings, and dwell on the soil that Yahweh gave to you and to your fathers for all time.
⁶Do not go after other gods to serve them and to worship them, and do not provoke me to anger with the work of your hands, and I will do you no hurt. ⁷But you have not listened to me — oracle of Yahweh — so as to provoke me to anger with the work of your hands, to your own hurt.

⁸Therefore thus said Yahweh of hosts: 'Because you have not listened to my words':
⁹Look I am sending and I will take all the tribes of the north — oracle of Yahweh — also to Nebuchadrezzar, king of Babylon, my servant, and I will bring them against this land and against its inhabitants and against all these nations round about, and I will devote them to destruction, and I will make them a desolation, an object of hissing, and ruins forever. ¹⁰And I will banish from them the voice of joy and the voice of gladness, the voice of the groom and the voice of the bride, the sound of millstones and the light of the lamp. ¹¹And all this land will become a ruin and a desolation, and these nations shall serve the king of Babylon seventy years.

¹²And it will happen when seventy years are fulfilled, I will reckon against the king of Babylon and against that nation — oracle of Yahweh — their iniquity; also against the land of the Chaldeans, and I will make it desolations forever. ¹³And I will bring against that land all my words that I have spoken against it, everything written in this book, which Jeremiah prophesied against all the nations. ¹⁴Indeed many nations and great kings shall make them serve — even them! And I will repay them according to their deeds and according to the work of their hands.

2. A Wrath-Filled Cup of Wine for the Nations (25:15–29)

25 ¹⁵For thus Yahweh, God of Israel, said to me: Take this wrath-filled cup of wine from my hand, and make all the nations to whom I am sending you drink it. ¹⁶And they shall drink and retch and go mad before the sword that I am sending among them. ¹⁷So I took the cup from the hand of Yahweh and made all the nations to whom Yahweh sent me drink: ¹⁸Jerusalem and the cities of Judah, and its kings, its princes, to make them a ruin, a desolation, an object of hissing, and a swearword, as at this day; ¹⁹Pharaoh, king of Egypt, and his servants, and his princes, and all his people, ²⁰and all the mixed races; and all the kings of the land of Uz, and all the kings of the land of the Philistines, that is, Ashkelon, and Gaza, and Ekron, and the remnant of Ashdod; ²¹Edom, and Moab, and the Ammonites; ²²and all the kings of Tyre, and all the kings of Sidon, and the kings of the coastlands that are across the sea; ²³and Dedan, and Tema, and Buz, and all who crop the hair at the temples; ²⁴and all the kings of Arabia, and all the kings of the mixed races who dwell in the desert; ²⁵ and all the kings of Zimri, and all the kings of Elam, and all the kings of Media; ²⁶and

all the kings of the north, those near and those far, one to another; yes, all the world's kingdoms that are on the face of the earth. And the king of Sheshak shall drink after them.

[27]Then you shall say to them:

Thus said Yahweh of hosts, God of Israel:

Drink and be drunk, yes, vomit and fall, and you shall never rise before the sword that I am sending among you.

[28]And it will happen that they will refuse to take the cup from your hand to drink; then you shall say to them:

Thus said Yahweh of hosts:

You shall certainly drink! [29]For look, if I am beginning to work evil in the city upon which my name is called, then for you, shall you assuredly go unpunished?

You shall not go unpunished, for I am calling a sword upon all the inhabitants of the earth—oracle of Yahweh of hosts.

3. Yahweh Will Roar from on High (25:30–31)

25 [30]And you, you shall prophesy to them all these words, and you shall say to them:

Yahweh will roar from on high
 and from his holy abode he will utter his voice
He will roar mightily against his pasture
 a shout like the treaders will ring out
  to all the inhabitants of the earth

[31]The uproar has reached the end of the earth
 for Yahweh has a case against the nations
He has entered into judgment with all flesh
 as for the wicked, he has given them over to the sword
  —oracle of Yahweh.

4. Evil Will Travel (25:32–33)

25 [32]Thus said Yahweh of hosts:
Look, evil shall go forth
 from nation to nation
A great tempest is roused
 from remote parts of the earth.

[33]And they shall be—the slain of Yahweh in that day—from the one end of the earth to the other end of the earth. They shall not be lamented, and they shall

not be gathered, and they shall not be buried; for dung upon the surface of the ground they shall be.

5. Wail, O Shepherds, and Cry Out! (25:34–38)

25 ³⁴Wail, O shepherds, and cry out
   and roll about, O nobles of the flock
Because your days for slaughter are fulfilled
   and you will be scattered
      and you will fall like a vessel of great value
³⁵Flight shall vanish from the shepherds
   escape from the nobles of the flock

³⁶The sound of a scream of the shepherds
   and the wailing of the nobles of the flock
      because Yahweh is devastating their pasturage
³⁷Yes, the peaceful pastures lie silent
   before the burning anger of Yahweh

³⁸Like a young lion he left his lair
   indeed their land became a desolation
Before the oppressive burning
   before his burning anger.

C. The Cost of Prophetic Preaching (26:1–24)

1. The Temple Oracles and Jeremiah's Day in Court (26:1–19)

26 ¹In the beginning of the reign of Jehoiakim son of Josiah, king of Judah, this word came from Yahweh: ²Thus said Yahweh: Stand in the courtyard of the house of Yahweh, and you shall speak concerning all the cities of Judah who come to worship in the house of Yahweh all the words that I command you to speak to them. Do not hold back a word. ³Perhaps they will listen and return each person from his evil way and I will repent concerning the evil that I am planning to do to them on account of their evil doings. ⁴And you shall say to them:

Thus said Yahweh:

If you do not listen to me to walk in my law that I have set before you, ⁵to listen to the words of my servants the prophets whom I am sending to you, constantly I am sending, although you have not listened, ⁶then I will make this house like Shiloh, and this city I will make a swearword for all the nations of the earth.

⁷And the priests and the prophets and all the people heard Jeremiah speaking these words in the house of Yahweh. ⁸And it happened as Jeremiah finished

speaking everything that Yahweh commanded him to speak to all the people, the priests and the prophets and all the people then laid hold of him, saying, 'You shall surely die! ⁹Why have you prophesied in the name of Yahweh saying, Like Shiloh this house shall become, and this city will dry up without inhabitant?' And all the people crowded up to Jeremiah in the house of Yahweh. ¹⁰And the princes of Judah heard these things and came up from the house of the king to the house of Yahweh, and they sat at the entrance of the New Gate of the house of Yahweh. ¹¹And the priests and the prophets said to the princes and to all the people: 'A sentence of death for this man! because he has prophesied to this city according to what you have heard with your ears.'
¹²Then Jeremiah said to all the princes and to all the people:
> Yahweh sent me to prophesy to this house and to this city all the words that you have heard. ¹³And now, make good your ways and your doings, and obey the voice of Yahweh your God; and then Yahweh will repent concerning the evil that he has spoken against you. ¹⁴But I, look I am in your hands. Do to me as seems good and right in your eyes. ¹⁵Only know for sure that if you put me to death, then you will bring innocent blood upon yourselves and to this city and to its inhabitants; for in truth, Yahweh sent me against you to speak in your ears all these words.

¹⁶Then the princes and all the people said to the priests and to the prophets, 'There should be no sentence of death for this man, because in the name of Yahweh our God he has spoken to us.' ¹⁷And men from among the elders of the land stood up and said to the entire assembly of the people:
> ¹⁸'Micah, the Morashtite, was prophesying in the days of Hezekiah, king of Judah, and he said to all the people of Judah:
> > Thus said Yahweh of hosts:
> > Zion shall be plowed a field
> > > and Jerusalem shall become stone heaps
> > And the mountain of the House
> > > high places of a forest.

¹⁹Did Hezekiah, king of Judah, and all Judah indeed put him to death? Did he not fear Yahweh and soften the face of Yahweh? And did not Yahweh repent of the evil that he spoke against them? And we are doing great evil against ourselves!

2. Uriah of Kiriath-jearim: Prophet of Yahweh (26:20–24)

26 ²⁰Also, a man was prophesying mightily in the name of Yahweh—Uriah son of Shemaiah from Kiriath-jearim. And he prophesied against this city and against this land like all the words of Jeremiah. ²¹And King Jehoiakim heard his words, also all his officers and all the princes, and the king sought to put him to death. But Uriah heard of it, and he was afraid and fled, and came to Egypt. ²²So King Jehoiakim sent men to Egypt—Elnathan son of Achbor and men with him to Egypt. ²³And they fetched Uriah from Egypt and brought him to

King Jehoiakim, and he struck him down with the sword and cast his dead body into the graves of the common people.

^{24}But the hand of Ahikam son of Shaphan was with Jeremiah, so as not to give him into the hand of the people to put him to death.

D. Jeremiah and the Yoke Bars (27:1–22)

27 ^{1}In the beginning of the reign of Zedekiah son of Josiah, king of Judah, this word came to Jeremiah from Yahweh. ^{2}Thus Yahweh said to me: Make for yourself straps and yoke bars; then you shall put them upon your neck. ^{3}You shall also send them to the king of Edom, and to the king of Moab, and to the king of the Ammonites, and to the king of Tyre, and to the king of Sidon by the hand of messengers who are coming to Jerusalem, to Zedekiah, king of Judah. ^{4}And you shall command them to their masters:

Thus said Yahweh of hosts, God of Israel:

Thus you shall say to your masters: ^{5}I, I made the earth, human and beast that are on the face of the earth, with my great strength and with my outstretched arm, and I give it to whoever seems right in my eyes. ^{6}And now I, I have given all these lands into the hand of Nebuchadnezzar, king of Babylon, my servant; and even the beasts of the field I have given to him, to serve him. ^{7}So all the nations shall serve him and his son and his grandson until the time of his land comes—even he! Then many nations and great kings shall make him serve!

^{8}And it shall be that the nation or the kingdom who does not serve him, that is, Nebuchadnezzar, king of Babylon, and who will not put its neck into the yoke of the king of Babylon, by sword and by famine and by pestilence I will reckon with that nation—oracle of Yahweh—until I have consumed them by his hand.

^{9}And you, do not you listen to your prophets, and to your diviners, and to your dreamers, and to your soothsayers, and to your sorcerers—they who are saying to you: 'You shall not serve the king of Babylon.' ^{10}Indeed a lie they are prophesying to you, in order to remove you far from your soil, for I will disperse you and you will perish. ^{11}But the nation who does bring its neck into the yoke of the king of Babylon, and serves him, I will then leave it on its own soil—oracle of Yahweh—to work it and dwell upon it.

^{12}And to Zedekiah, king of Judah, I spoke all these words: Bring your necks into the yoke of the king of Babylon, and serve him and his people, and live! ^{13}Why should you die, you and your people, by sword, by famine, and by pestilence according to what Yahweh has spoken to the nation that will not serve the king of Babylon?

^{14}And do not listen to the words of the prophets who are saying to you: 'You shall not serve the king of Babylon.' Indeed a lie they are prophesying to

you, [15]for I have not sent them—oracle of Yahweh—and they are prophesying the lie in my name in order that I should disperse you, and you will perish, you and the prophets who are prophesying to you.
[16]Then to the priests and to all this people I spoke:
Thus said Yahweh:
Do not listen to the words of your prophets who are prophesying to you, saying, 'Look, the vessels of the house of Yahweh will be brought back from Babylon now shortly.' Indeed a lie they are prophesying to you.
[17]Do not listen to them; serve the king of Babylon and live. Why should this city become a ruin? [18]And if they are prophets and if the word of Yahweh is with them, do let them pressure Yahweh of hosts so that the vessels remaining in the house of Yahweh and the house of the king of Judah and in Jerusalem not go to Babylon.
[19]For thus said Yahweh of hosts concerning the pillars, and concerning the sea, and concerning the stands, and concerning the rest of the vessels remaining in this city, [20]which Nebuchadnezzar, king of Babylon, did not take when he exiled Jeconiah son of Jehoiakim, king of Judah, from Jerusalem to Babylon, also all the nobles of Judah and Jerusalem: [21]Indeed, thus said Yahweh of hosts, God of Israel, concerning the vessels remaining in the house of Yahweh, and the house of the king of Judah, and Jerusalem: [22]To Babylon they shall be brought, and there they shall be until the day I attend to them—oracle of Yahweh—and I bring them out and bring them back to this place.

E. Jeremiah Meets Hananiah (28:1–17)

28 [1]And it happened in that year, in the beginning of the reign of Zedekiah, king of Judah, in the fourth year in the fifth month, Hananiah son of Azzur, the prophet who was from Gibeon, said to me in the house of Yahweh in the presence of the priests and all the people:
[2]Thus said Yahweh of hosts, God of Israel:
I have broken the yoke of the king of Babylon. [3]Within two years' time I will bring back to this place all the vessels of the house of Yahweh that Nebuchadnezzar, king of Babylon, took from this place and brought to Babylon.

[4]And Jeconiah son of Jehoiakim, king of Judah, and all the exiles of Judah who came to Babylon, I will bring back to this place—oracle of Yahweh—for I will break the yoke of the king of Babylon.
[5]Then Jeremiah the prophet said to Hananiah the prophet in the presence of the priests and in the presence of all the people who were standing in the house of Yahweh; [6]and Jeremiah the prophet said:
Amen! So may Yahweh do! May Yahweh confirm your words that you have prophesied—to bring back the vessels of the house of Yahweh and all the exiles from Babylon to this place! [7]But do hear this word that I speak in your ears and in the ears of all the people: [8]"The prophets who were before

me and before you, from ancient times, yes, they prophesied to many lands and against great kingdoms of war and evil and pestilence. ⁹The prophet who prophesies peace, when the word of the prophet comes to be, the prophet whom Yahweh has truly sent will be known.'

¹⁰Then Hananiah the prophet took the yoke bar from upon the neck of Jeremiah the prophet and broke it. ¹¹And Hananiah said in the presence of all the people:

Thus said Yahweh:

Even so will I break the yoke of Nebuchadnezzar, king of Babylon, within two years' time from upon the neck of all the nations.

And Jeremiah the prophet went his way.

¹²Then the word of Yahweh came to Jeremiah after Hananiah the prophet broke the yoke bar from upon the neck of Jeremiah the prophet: ¹³Go and you shall say to Hananiah:

Thus said Yahweh:

Yoke bars of wood you have broken, but you have made in their place yoke bars of iron.

¹⁴For thus said Yahweh of hosts, God of Israel:

A yoke of iron I have put upon the neck of all these nations to serve Nebuchadnezzar, king of Babylon, and they shall serve him; even the beasts of the field I have given to him.

¹⁵And Jeremiah the prophet said to Hananiah the prophet: Do listen, Hananiah, Yahweh has not sent you, and you, you have made this people trust in a lie. ¹⁶Therefore thus said Yahweh:

Look I will send you away from off the face of the earth. This year you will die, for you have spoken rebellion concerning Yahweh.

¹⁷And Hananiah the prophet died in that year, in the seventh month.

F. Letters to the Exiles (29:1–32)

1. Bloom Where You Are Planted! (29:1–23)

29 ¹And these are the words of the letter that Jeremiah the prophet sent from Jerusalem to the remnant of the elders of the exile, and to the priests and to the prophets, and to all the people whom Nebuchadnezzar exiled from Jerusalem to Babylon—²after Jeconiah the king, and the queen mother and the eunuchs, the princes of Judah and Jerusalem, and the craftsmen and the smiths had gone out from Jerusalem—³by the hand of Elasah son of Shaphan and Gemariah son of Hilkiah, whom Zedekiah, king of Judah, sent to Nebuchadnezzar, king of Babylon, in Babylon:

⁴Thus said Yahweh of hosts, God of Israel, to all the exiles whom I exiled from Jerusalem to Babylon:

⁵Build houses and live in them; and plant gardens and eat their fruit. ⁶Take wives and beget sons and daughters, and take for your sons wives, and your daughters give to husbands, and let them bear sons and daughters. Yes, multiply there, and do not decrease. ⁷And seek the welfare of the city where I have exiled you, and pray on its behalf to Yahweh, for in its welfare will be welfare for you.

⁸For thus said Yahweh of hosts, God of Israel:
Do not let your prophets who are in your midst or your diviners deceive you; also do not listen to your dreamers whom you cause to dream. ⁹For by a lie they are prophesying to you in my name. I have not sent them—oracle of Yahweh.

¹⁰For thus said Yahweh:
When Babylon has completed seventy years before me, I will attend to you and confirm upon you my good word to bring you back to this place. ¹¹For I, I know the plans that I am planning concerning you—oracle of Yahweh—plans of welfare and not for evil, to give to you a future and a hope. ¹²And you will call me and will come and pray to me, and I will listen to you. ¹³And you will search for me and will find if you seek me with your whole heart.

¹⁴And I will be found by you
   —oracle of Yahweh—
      and I will restore your fortunes.

And I will gather you from all the nations and from all the places where I have dispersed you—oracle of Yahweh—and I will bring you back to the place from which I exiled you.
¹⁵Because you have said, 'Yahweh has raised up for us prophets in Babylon':
¹⁶For thus said Yahweh concerning the king who sits on the throne of David and concerning all the people who sit in this city—your brothers who did not go out with you into exile:
¹⁷Thus said Yahweh of hosts:
Look I am sending against them sword, famine, and pestilence, and I will make them like horrid figs, which cannot be eaten they are so bad. ¹⁸And I will pursue them by sword, by famine, and by pestilence, and I will make them a fright to all the kingdoms of the earth—a curse, and a desolation, and an object of hissing, and a reproach among all the nations where I have dispersed them—¹⁹inasmuch as they have not listened to my words—oracle of Yahweh—which I sent to them by my servants the prophets—constantly I sent—and you did not listen—oracle of Yahweh.
²⁰Now you! Hear the word of Yahweh, all the exiles whom I sent away from Jerusalem to Babylon:

[21]Thus said Yahweh of hosts, God of Israel, concerning Ahab son of Kolaiah and concerning Zedekiah son of Maaseiah, who are prophesying a lie to you in my name:
Look I will give them into the hand of Nebuchadrezzar, king of Babylon, and he will strike them down before your eyes. [22]From them will be taken up a swearword for all the exiles of Judah who are in Babylon: 'Yahweh make you like Zedekiah and like Ahab whom the king of Babylon roasted in the fire,' [23]because they did a scandalous thing in Israel, yes, they committed adultery with the wives of their fellows and have spoken a lying word in my name that I did not command them. But I am he who knows and am witness—oracle of Yahweh.

2. Concerning Shemaiah in Babylon (29:24–32)

29 [24]And concerning Shemaiah, the Nehelamite, you shall say:
[25]Thus said Yahweh of hosts, God of Israel:
Because you, you sent letters in your name to all the people who are in Jerusalem, and to Zephaniah son of Maaseiah, the priest, and to all the priests saying, [26]Yahweh made you priest under Jehoiada, the priest, to be overseers in the house of Yahweh concerning every madman and one prophesying away, and you are to put him into the stocks and into the collar. [27]And now, why have you not rebuked Jeremiah, the Anathothite, who is prophesying away to you? [28]seeing that he sent to us in Babylon saying, 'It will be long! Build houses and live in them; and plant gardens and eat their fruit.'
[29]And Zephaniah, the priest, read this letter in the hearing of Jeremiah, the prophet. [30]And the word of Yahweh came to Jeremiah: [31]Send to all the exiles saying: Thus said Yahweh concerning Shemaiah, the Nehelamite, because Shemaiah prophesied to you when I, I did not send him, and he has made you trust in a lie—
[32]Therefore thus said Yahweh:
Look I will reckon with Shemaiah, the Nehelamite, and with his offspring. There shall not be to him a man dwelling in the midst of this people, and he shall not see the good that I will do for my people—oracle of Yahweh—for he has spoken rebellion against Yahweh.

III. THE BOOK OF RESTORATION (30:1–33:26)

A. Book of the Covenant (30:1–31:40)

1. Superscription and Introductory Oracle (30:1–3)

30 [1]The word that came to Jeremiah from Yahweh: [2]Thus said Yahweh, God of Israel: 'Write for yourself all the words that I have spoken to you into a scroll.'

³For look, days are coming—oracle of Yahweh—when I will restore the fortunes of my people Israel and Judah, said Yahweh, and I will bring them back to the land that I gave to their fathers, and they shall possess it.

2. Yahweh Waits to Be Gracious (30:4–31:22)

a) A Time of Distress for Jacob (30:4–7)

30 ⁴And these are the words that Yahweh spoke to Israel and to Judah:
⁵For thus said Yahweh:
A sound of fright we have heard
    terror, and no peace
⁶Ask, would you, and see
    if a male can bear a child?

So why do I see every man
    his hands on his loins like a woman in labor?
        and all faces turned deadly pale?

⁷Woe! For great is that day
    there is none like it
Yes, a time of distress it is for Jacob
    and from it shall he be saved?

b) Do Not You Be Afraid, Jacob (30:8–11)

30 ⁸And it will happen in that day—oracle of Yahweh of hosts:
    I will break his yoke from upon your neck
        and your straps I will tear away
So strangers shall not again make him serve; ⁹instead they shall serve Yahweh their God and David, their king, whom I will raise up for them.

¹⁰But you, do not you be afraid, Jacob my servant
    —oracle of Yahweh—
    and do not you be broken, Israel
For look I will save you from afar
    and your offspring from the land of their captivity
And Jacob will return and be undisturbed
    yes, be at ease and none will frighten

¹¹For I am with you
    —oracle of Yahweh—
    to save you
For I will make a full end of all the nations
    among which I have scattered you

But of you I will not make a full end
   Yes, I will correct you justly
      but I will by no means leave you unpunished.

c) Your Blow Is Incurable (30:12–15)

30 [12]For thus said Yahweh:
Your brokenness is desperate
   your blow incurable
[13]There is none to diagnose your case of a sore
   a healing scar there is not for you
[14]All your lovers have forgotten you
   you, they care not about

For the blow of an enemy I have struck you
   punishment of a cruel one
Because your iniquity was much
   your sins were numerous

[15]Why do you cry over your brokenness
   your desperate pain?
Because your iniquity was much
   your sins were numerous
      I did these things to you.

d) But from Your Blows I Will Heal You (30:16–17)

30 [16]Hereafter all who consume you shall be consumed
   and all your foes—all of them—into captivity shall go
Those who plunder you shall be for plunder
   and all who despoil you I will give for spoil

[17]For I will bring up new flesh for you
   and from your blows I will heal you
     —oracle of Yahweh—
For they have called you an outcast:
   'That Zion Whom No One Cares About'

e) Rebuilt City, Return to Joy (30:18–22)

30 [18]Thus said Yahweh:
Look I will restore the fortunes of Jacob's tents
   and on his dwellings I will have pity
A city shall be built on its tell
   and a citadel on its rightful place shall sit

[19]And from them thanksgiving shall go forth
   and the sound of merrymakers

And I will multiply them, and they shall not decrease
  I will give them honor, and they shall not be insignificant

²⁰His sons shall be as of old
  and his congregation before me established
I will reckon with all who oppress him
  ²¹and his noble one shall be one of his own

And his ruler from his midst shall go forth
  and I will bring him near, and he will approach me
For who is he that would risk his life
  to approach me?
    —oracle of Yahweh.

²²And you will be a people to me
  and I, I will be God to you.

f) Yahweh's Desert Storm (30:23–24)

30 ²³Look! the tempest of Yahweh
  wrath goes forth
    a sweeping tempest
Upon the head of the wicked it whirls
  ²⁴the burning anger of Yahweh does not turn back
Until it does and until it fulfills
  the purposes of his heart
In the days afterward
  you will understand it.

g) Grace Again in the Wilderness (31:1–6)

31 ¹At that time—oracle of Yahweh—I will be God to all the tribes of Israel,
and they, they will be a people to me.

²Thus said Yahweh:
It found grace in the wilderness
  a people, survivors of the sword
    Going to find his rest is Israel
³From far off Yahweh appeared to me:
  'With an eternal love I have loved you
    therefore I draw you faithfully along
⁴Again I will build you and you shall be built
  virgin Israel
Again you'll deck yourself with your hand-drums
  and go forth in the dance of merrymakers
⁵Again you'll plant vineyards on Samaria's mountains
  planters shall plant and eat the fruit'

⁶For there shall be a day when watchmen will call out
   on Mount Ephraim
'Up, let us go to Zion
   to Yahweh our God!'

h) Yahweh Will Return the Remnant of Israel (31:7–9)

31 ⁷For thus said Yahweh:
Cry with gladness for Jacob
   and scream over The Head of the Nations
Proclaim, praise, and say:
   'Yahweh has saved your people
      the remnant of Israel!'

⁸Look I will bring them
   from the land of the north
And I will gather them from remote parts of the earth
   among them the blind and the lame
the pregnant and woman in labor together
   a great assembly shall return here
⁹With weeping they shall come
   and with supplications I will lead them
I will bring them to streams of water
   on a level path, in which they will not stumble
For I am as a father to Israel
   and Ephraim, my firstborn is he.

i) The One Who Scattered Will Gather (31:10–14)

31 ¹⁰Hear the word of Yahweh, nations
   and declare among the distant coastlands, and say:
He who scattered Israel will gather him
   and will keep him as a shepherd his flock
¹¹For Yahweh has ransomed Jacob
   and redeemed him from a hand stronger than his own

¹²And they shall come and cry for joy on the height of Zion
   and they shall be radiant over the goodness of Yahweh
Over the grain and over the wine and over the oil
   and over the young of the flocks and the herds
And their soul shall become like a saturated garden
   and they shall no longer languish any more
¹³Then shall the maiden be glad in the dance
   yes, young men and old men together

And I will turn their mourning into joy
   and I will comfort them

and I will make them glad from their sorrow
[14]And I will saturate the soul of the priests with abundance
and my people with my goodness will be sated
—oracle of Yahweh.

j) Rachel Weeping in Ramah (31:15)

31 [15]Thus said Yahweh:
The voice of lament is heard in Ramah
bitterest weeping
Rachel is weeping over her sons
she refuses to be comforted over her sons
because they are not.

k) Rachel, Don't You Weep No More! (31:16–17)

31 [16]Thus said Yahweh:
Restrain your voice from weeping
and your eyes from tears

For there is a reward for your labor
—oracle of Yahweh—
and they shall return from the land of the enemy

[17]And there is hope for your future
—oracle of Yahweh—
and sons shall return to their territory.

l) Ephraim Heard Rockin' in Grief (31:18–19)

31 [18]I can indeed hear
Ephraim rockin' in grief
'You disciplined me and I was disciplined
like a young bull not trained
Bring me back so I may come back
for you are Yahweh my God

[19]For after my turning away
I repented
And after I came to understand
I hit upon my thigh
I was ashamed and also disgraced
for I bore the reproach of my youth.'

m) But I Still Remember Ephraim (31:20)

31 [20]Is Ephraim my dear son?
Is he the child of delight?
For more than all my speaking against him

I will assuredly remember him still
Therefore my innards moan for him
 I will assuredly have mercy on him
   —oracle of Yahweh.

n) Return, Virgin Israel! (31:21–22)

31 [21]Set up road-markers for yourself
 make for yourself signposts
Fix your mind on the highway
 the way you have gone
Return, virgin Israel
 return to these, your cities

[22]How long will you waver
 O turnable daughter?
For Yahweh has created a new thing on earth:
 the female protects the man!

3. Look, Days Are Coming! (31:23–40)

a) May Yahweh Bless You, O Holy Mountain! (31:23–26)

31 [23]Thus said Yahweh of hosts, God of Israel:
Again they shall say this word in the land of Judah and in its cities, when I
restore their fortunes:
 May Yahweh bless you
  righteous pasture
   O holy mountain
[24]And Judah and all its cities shall dwell in it together, the farmers and they
who set out with the flock. [25]For I will saturate the thirsty soul, and every
languishing soul I will fill.

[26]At this I awoke and looked around, and my sleep was pleasant to me.

b) Planting, Building, and Accountability (31:27–30)

31 [27]Look, days are coming—oracle of Yahweh—when I will sow the house
of Israel and the house of Judah with the seed of human and the seed of beast.

[28]And it will be, as I have watched over them to uproot and to break down
and to overthrow and to destroy, also to bring evil, so I will watch over them
to build and to plant—oracle of Yahweh.

[29]In those days they shall not again say:
 Fathers have eaten sour grapes
  and children's teeth become set on edge

[30]But each person in his iniquity shall die. Every human who eats the sour grapes, his teeth shall become set on edge.

c) The New Covenant (31:31–34)

31 [31]Look, days are coming—oracle of Yahweh—when I will cut with the house of Israel and with the house of Judah a new covenant, [32]not like the covenant that I cut with their fathers in the day I took them by the hand to bring them out from the land of Egypt, my covenant that they, they broke, though I, I was their master—oracle of Yahweh.

[33]But this is the covenant that I will cut with the house of Israel after those days—oracle of Yahweh: I will put my law in their inward parts, and upon their hearts I will write it. And I will be God to them, and they, they will be a people to me. [34]And they shall not again instruct each person his fellow and each person his brother, saying, 'Know Yahweh,' for they, all of them, shall know me, from the least of them to the greatest of them—oracle of Yahweh—for I will forgive their iniquity, and their sin I will not remember again.

d) Ongoing Creation, Ongoing Covenant (31:35–37)

31 [35]Thus said Yahweh
    who gives the sun for light by day
statutes of the moon and stars
    for light by night
who stirs up the sea so its waves roar
    Yahweh of hosts is his name:

[36]If these statutes depart
    from before me—oracle of Yahweh
Then the seed of Israel shall cease
    from being a nation before me—all the days.

[37]Thus said Yahweh:
If the heavens above can be measured
    and the foundations of the earth explored to the depths
Then I, I will reject all the seed of Israel
    because of all that they have done
        —oracle of Yahweh.

e) Rebuilt City, Reconsecrated Valley (31:38–40)

31 [38]Look, days are coming—oracle of Yahweh—when the city shall be rebuilt for Yahweh from the Tower of Hananel to the Corner Gate. [39]And the measuring line shall go out again, straight over Gareb Hill and turn to Goah. [40]And all the valley land, the corpses and the ashes, and all the terraces up to the

Brook Kidron, up to the corner of the Horse Gate toward the east, shall be holy for Yahweh. It shall not be uprooted, and it shall not again be overthrown—forever.

B. Jeremiah Buys Land in Anathoth (32:1–44)

1. Why Are You Prophesying Thus? (32:1–5)

32 ¹The word that came to Jeremiah from Yahweh in the tenth year of Zedekiah, king of Judah (that was the eighteenth year of Nebuchadrezzar). ²At that time the army of the king of Babylon was besieging Jerusalem, and Jeremiah, the prophet, was confined in the court of the guard, which was in the house of the king of Judah, ³because Zedekiah, king of Judah, confined him saying: 'Why are you prophesying:

Thus said Yahweh:

Look I am giving this city into the hand of the king of Babylon, and he shall take it; ⁴And Zedekiah, king of Judah, will not escape from the hand of the Chaldeans—indeed he will surely be given into the hand of the king of Babylon, and his mouth shall speak with his mouth and his eyes shall see his eyes.

⁵And to Babylon he shall make Zedekiah walk, and there he will be until I reckon with him—oracle of Yahweh—for though you fight the Chaldeans, you shall not succeed?'

2. The Right of Redemption is Yours (32:6–15)

⁶And Jeremiah said, the word of Yahweh came to me: ⁷Look, Hanamel son of Shallum, your uncle, is coming to you to say: 'Buy for yourself my field that is in Anathoth, for the right of redemption to buy is yours.' ⁸And Hanamel, son of my uncle, came to me—according to the word of Yahweh—to the court of the guard, and he said to me, 'Buy, would you, my field that is in Anathoth, that is in the land of Benjamin, for the right of possession is yours and the redemption is yours. Buy it for yourself!' Then I knew that this was the word of Yahweh. ⁹So I bought the field from Hanamel, son of my uncle, that was in Anathoth, and I weighed for him the silver—seventeen shekels of silver. ¹⁰Then I wrote in the deed, and I sealed it, and I called for witnesses, and I weighed the silver on the two scales. ¹¹And I took the sealed deed of purchase—the contract and the conditions—also the open copy, ¹²and I gave the deed of purchase to Baruch son of Neriah, son of Mahseiah, in the presence of Hanamel, son of my uncle, and in the presence of the witnesses who had written on the deed of purchase, and in the presence of all the Judahites who were sitting in the court of the guard. ¹³And I commanded Baruch in their presence, saying:

¹⁴Thus said Yahweh of hosts, God of Israel:

Take these deeds—this sealed deed of purchase and this open deed—and you shall put them in an earthenware jar in order that they may last many days.

[15]For thus said Yahweh of hosts, God of Israel:
Again houses and fields and vineyards shall be bought in this land.

3. Just Why Did I Buy This Field? (32:16–25)

[16]Then I prayed to Yahweh after I had given the deed of purchase to Baruch son of Neriah: [17]Ah, Lord Yahweh! Look, you, you have made the heavens and the earth with your great strength and with your outstretched arm. Nothing is too difficult for you, [18]who shows steadfast love to thousands but who repays the iniquity of the fathers into the lap of their children after them, the great God, the mighty, Yahweh of hosts is his name, [19]great in counsel and mighty in deed, so that your eyes are open upon all the ways of humanity's children, to give to each person according to his ways and according to the fruit of his doings; [20]so that you have shown signs and wonders, in the land of Egypt—up to this day—and in Israel and among humankind, and you made for yourself a name, as at this day. [21]And you brought your people Israel out from the land of Egypt with signs and with wonders and with a strong hand and with an outstretched arm and with great terror; [22]and you gave to them this land that you swore to their fathers to give to them, a land flowing with milk and honey. [23]And they came in and took possession of it, but they did not obey your voice and in your law did not walk; everything that you commanded them to do, they did not do, so you made them meet up with all this evil. [24]Look, the siege ramps have come to the city to take it, and the city has been given into the hand of the Chaldeans who are fighting against it, because of the sword and the famine and the pestilence; and what you have spoken has happened. So look, you are watching! [25]Yet you, you have said to me, O Lord Yahweh, 'Buy for yourself the field with silver and call for witnesses,' but the city has been given into the hand of the Chaldeans!

4. Yahweh's Promised Judgment (32:26–35)

a) Is Anything Too Difficult for Me? (32:26–29)

[26]And the word of Yahweh came to Jeremiah: [27]'Look I am Yahweh, God of all flesh. Is anything too difficult for me?'
    [28]Therefore thus said Yahweh:
    Look I am giving this city into the hand of the Chaldeans and into the hand of Nebuchadrezzar, king of Babylon, and he shall take it. [29]And the Chaldeans who are fighting against this city shall come in and set this city on fire and burn it, including the houses on whose roofs they burned incense to Baal, and poured out drink offerings to other gods, in order to provoke me to anger.

b) Away with This City! (32:30–35)

[30]Indeed, the children of Israel and the children of Judah have been doing only what is evil in my eyes from their youth. Indeed, the children of Israel have only provoked me to anger with the work of their hands — oracle of Yahweh. [31]Indeed, with respect to my anger and my wrath, this city has become to me — from the day that they built it up until this day — in order to remove it from my presence, [32]on account of all the evil of the children of Israel and the children of Judah, which they did to provoke me to anger — they, their kings, their princes, their priests, and their prophets, also the men of Judah and the inhabitants of Jerusalem. [33]They faced me with the back of the neck, and not the face, although I taught them — constantly taught — but they did not listen to take correction. [34]And they set up their wretched things in the house upon which my name is called to defile it. [35]And they built the high places of Baal that are in the Valley of Ben-Hinnom to give over their sons and their daughters to Molech — which I did not command them, nor did it enter my mind for them to do this abomination — in order to make Judah sin.

5. Yahweh's Promised Salvation (32:36–44)

a) The Eternal Covenant (32:36–41)

[36]But now after this, thus said Yahweh, God of Israel, to this city of which you are saying, 'It has been given into the hand of the king of Babylon by sword and by famine and by pestilence':

[37]Look I am going to gather them from all the lands where I dispersed them in my anger and in my wrath and in great fury, and I will bring them back to this place and settle them in security. [38]And they will be a people to me, and I, I will be God to them. [39]And I will give them one heart and one way to fear me all the days, for their own good and for their children after them. [40]And I will cut for them an eternal covenant, in which I will not turn away from them to do good to them; and the fear of me I will put in their hearts so they may not turn away from me. [41]And I will rejoice over them to do them good, and I will truly plant them in this land, with all my heart and with all my soul.

b) Fields Will Again Be Bought and Sold (32:42–44)

[42]For thus said Yahweh:
Even as I brought to this people all this great evil, so I am going to bring upon them all the good that I am speaking concerning them. [43]The field shall be bought in this land, of which you are saying, 'It is a desolation, without human or beast; it has been given into the hand of the Chaldeans.' [44]Fields shall be bought with silver, also writing in the deed and sealing and the summoning of witnesses to witness, in the land of Benjamin and in the regions around Jerusalem and in the cities of Judah, in the cities of

the hill country and in the cities of the Shephelah and in the cities of the Negeb; for I will surely restore their fortunes—oracle of Yahweh.

C. More on Restoration and Covenants (33:1–26)

1. I Will Tell You Great and Hidden Things! (33:1–3)

33 ¹And the word of Yahweh came to Jeremiah a second time, while he was still confined in the court of the guard:
　²Thus said Yahweh who made it
　　Yahweh who formed it to establish it
　　　Yahweh is his name!
　³Call to me and I will answer you
　　and let me tell you great things and hidden things
　　　you have not known.

2. Healed City, Healed People (33:4–9)

33 ⁴For thus said Yahweh, God of Israel, concerning the houses of this city and concerning the houses of the kings of Judah that were broken down toward the siege ramps and toward the sword, ⁵those coming to fight the Chaldeans only to fill them with the corpses of men whom I struck down in my anger and my wrath, and because I hid my face from this city on account of all their evil:
　⁶Look I am going to bring to it new flesh and healing, and I will heal them and I will reveal to them the sweet smell of peace and security. ⁷And I will surely restore the fortunes of Judah and the fortunes of Israel, and I will build them as at first. ⁸And I will cleanse them from all their iniquity by which they sinned against me, and I will forgive all their iniquities by which they sinned against me and by which they rebelled against me. ⁹And it shall be to me a joyful name, a praise, and a glorious decoration before all the nations of the earth who shall hear all the good that I am doing to them; they shall tremble and they shall shake on account of all the good and on account of all the peace that I am doing for it.

3. Two Promises of Return (33:10–13)

a) The Return of Joyful Sounds (33:10–11)

33 ¹⁰Thus said Yahweh:
Again it shall be heard in this place—of which you are saying, 'It is a waste, without human and without beast,' in the cities of Judah and in the streets of Jerusalem that are deserted without human and without inhabitant and without beast—¹¹the voice of joy and the voice of gladness, the voice of the groom and the voice of the bride, the voice of those saying,

Give thanks to Yahweh of hosts
    for Yahweh is good
        for his steadfast love is eternal
and those bringing a thank offering to the house of Yahweh, for I will surely restore the fortunes of the land as at first—said Yahweh.

b) The Return of Pastureland (33:12–13)

33 ¹²Thus said Yahweh of hosts:
Again there shall be in this place of waste, without human or beast, and in all its cities, pasture for shepherds resting the flock. ¹³In the cities of the hill country, in the cities of the Shephelah, and in the cities of the Negeb, and in the land of Benjamin, and in the regions around Jerusalem, and in the cities of Judah, again the flock shall pass under the hands of the one who counts it—said Yahweh.

4. A Righteous King in a Righteous City (33:14–16)

33 ¹⁴Look, days are coming—oracle of Yahweh—when I will confirm the good word that I spoke to the house of Israel and concerning the house of Judah:

¹⁵In those days and at that time
    I will make sprout for David a Shoot of righteousness
        and he will do justice and righteousness in the land

¹⁶In those days Judah will be saved
    and Jerusalem will dwell in security
And this is what one will call her:
    'Yahweh is our righteousness.'

5. Davidic and Levitical Lines to Continue (33:17–18)

33 ¹⁷For thus said Yahweh:
There shall not be cut off for David a man who sits upon the throne of the house of Israel. ¹⁸And for the Levitical priests, there shall not be cut off a man from before me who brings up the burnt offering and who burns the cereal offering and who makes sacrifice—all the days.

6. Two Covenant Promises (33:19–26)

a) Covenants with David and Levi Remain Intact (33:19–22)

33 ¹⁹And the word of Yahweh came to Jeremiah:
    ²⁰Thus said Yahweh:
    If you could break my covenant of the day and my covenant of the night, so daytime and night would not come at their appointed time, ²¹then could

my covenant be broken with David, my servant, so there would not be for him a son reigning on his throne, also with the Levitical priests, my ministers. ²²As the host of heaven cannot be numbered and the sand of the sea cannot be measured, so I will multiply the seed of David, my servant, also the Levites who minister to me.

b) Seed of Jacob and David to Continue (33:23–26)

33 ²³And the word of Yahweh came to Jeremiah: ²⁴"Have you not seen what this people has said: "The two families that Yahweh chose—now he has rejected them," so they have spurned my people from being any longer a nation before them?'
²⁵Thus said Yahweh:
If indeed I have not established my covenant of daytime and night—statutes of heaven and earth—²⁶then the seed of Jacob and David, my servant, I will reject, not taking from his seed rulers unto the seed of Abraham, Isaac, and Jacob, for I will surely restore their fortunes, and I will show them mercy.

IV. FALSE COVENANTS, TRUE COVENANTS (34:1–36:32)

A. Zedekiah's Covenant (34:1–22)

1. A Word on the King's Personal Fate (34:1–7)

34 ¹The word that came to Jeremiah from Yahweh when Nebuchadrezzar, king of Babylon, and all his army, and all the kingdoms of the earth under his dominion, and all the peoples were fighting against Jerusalem and against all its cities: ²Thus said Yahweh, God of Israel: Go, and you shall say to Zedekiah, king of Judah, and you shall say to him:
Thus said Yahweh:
Look I am giving this city into the hand of the king of Babylon, and he will take it and will burn it with fire. ³And you, you will not escape from his hand, but you will surely be captured and into his hand you will be given. And your eyes shall see the eyes of the king of Babylon, and his mouth shall speak to your mouth, and to Babylon you shall go.
⁴But hear the word of Yahweh, Zedekiah, king of Judah:
Thus said Yahweh concerning you:
You shall not die by the sword; ⁵in peace you shall die; and like the burnings for your fathers, the former kings who were before you, so shall they burn for you, and "Woe, lord!" they shall lament for you, for the word I, I have spoken—oracle of Yahweh.
⁶So Jeremiah, the prophet, spoke to Zedekiah, king of Judah, all these words in Jerusalem. ⁷And the army of the king of Babylon was fighting against Jeru-

salem and against all the cities of Judah, the ones remaining to Lachish and to Azekah, for they still remained among the cities of Judah, cities of fortification.

2. The Covenant of Liberty: On Again Off Again (34:8–22)

34 [8]The word that came to Jeremiah from Yahweh after King Zedekiah cut a covenant with all the people who were in Jerusalem to proclaim liberty to them, [9]to send away free each person his male slave and each person his female slave, Hebrew and Hebrewess, so that no person should make them serve a Judahite, his kin. [10]And all the princes and all the people who entered into the covenant gave heed to send away free each person his male slave and each person his female slave, so that he should not make them serve again; and they gave heed and sent them away. [11]Then they turned around after this and took back the male slaves and female slaves that they had sent away free, and subjugated them to being male slaves and female slaves. [12]And the word of Yahweh came to Jeremiah from Yahweh:

[13]Thus said Yahweh, God of Israel:
I, I cut a covenant with your fathers in the day I brought them out from the land of Egypt, from the house of slavery, saying, [14]After seven years' time you shall send away each person his Hebrew kin who was sold to you and served you six years, yes, you shall send him away free from your midst. But your fathers did not listen to me and did not bend their ear. [15]And you, you turned around one day and you did what is right in my eyes, to proclaim liberty each person to his fellow, and you cut a covenant before me in the house upon which my name is called; [16]then you turned around and profaned my name and took back each person his male slave and each person his female slave whom you sent away free according to their desire, and you subjugated them to be for you male slaves and female slaves.

[17]Therefore thus said Yahweh:
You, you have not listened to me to proclaim liberty each person to his kin and each person to his fellow.

Look I am proclaiming liberty to you—oracle of Yahweh—to the sword, to the pestilence, and to the famine, and I will make you a fright to all the kingdoms of the earth. [18]And I will make the men who walked over my covenant, who did not carry out the words of the covenant that they cut before me, the calf that they cut in two and walked between its parts— [19]the princes of Judah and the princes of Jerusalem, the eunuchs and the priests, and all the people of the land who walked between the parts of the calf. [20]And I will give them into the hand of their enemies and into the hand of those who seek their life, and their dead bodies shall become food for the birds of the skies and the beasts of the earth. [21]And Zedekiah, king of Judah, and his princes, I will give into the hand of their enemies and into the hand of those who seek their life, into the hand of the army of the king of Babylon, who have withdrawn from you.

²²Look I am commanding—oracle of Yahweh—and I will bring them back to this city, and they will fight against it and take it, and they will burn it with fire; and the cities of Judah I will make a desolation without inhabitant.

B. What about Those Rechabites? (35:1–19)

1. A Lesson on Obedience (35:1–11)

35 ¹The word that came to Jeremiah from Yahweh in the days of Jehoiakim son of Josiah, king of Judah: ²Go to the house of the Rechabites, and you shall speak to them and bring them to the house of Yahweh, to one of the chambers, and you shall offer them wine to drink. ³So I took Jaazaniah son of Jeremiah, son of Habazziniah, and his brothers and all his sons, indeed the entire house of the Rechabites, ⁴and I brought them to the house of Yahweh, to the chamber of the sons of Hanan son of Igdaliah, the man of God, which was next to the chamber of the princes, which was above the chamber of Maaseiah son of Shallum, the keeper of the threshold. ⁵Then I set before the sons of the house of Rechabites pitchers full of wine and cups, and I said to them, 'Drink wine.' ⁶But they said, 'We will not drink wine, for Jonadab son of Rechab, our father, commanded us saying, "You shall not drink wine—you or your sons—forever, ⁷and a house you shall not build, and seed you shall not sow, and a vineyard you shall not plant, nor shall it belong to you, for in tents you shall dwell all your days, in order that you may live many days on the face of the earth where you are sojourning." ⁸And we have obeyed the voice of Jonadab son of Rechab, our father, in all that he commanded us, so as not to drink wine all our days— we, our wives, our sons, and our daughters, ⁹also so as not to build houses for our dwellings, and vineyard or field or seed not to have for ourselves. ¹⁰So we dwell in tents, and we have heeded and done according to everything that Jonadab, our father, commanded us. ¹¹But it happened when Nebuchadrez-zar, king of Babylon, came up into the land, then we said, "Come, and let us enter Jerusalem because of the army of the Chaldeans and because of the army of the Aramaeans." So we are dwelling in Jerusalem.'

2. Oracles for the Obedient and Disobedient (35:12–19)

¹²And the word of Yahweh came to Jeremiah: ¹³Thus said Yahweh of hosts, God of Israel: Go, and you shall say to the men of Judah and to the inhabitants of Jerusalem:

Will you not take correction to listen to my words—oracle of Yahweh? ¹⁴The words of Jonadab son of Rechab, which he commanded his sons so as not to drink wine have been carried out, and they have not drunk to this day because they have heeded the command of their father. But I, I have spoken to you—constantly I have spoken—and you have not listened to me. ¹⁵And I have sent to you all my servants the prophets—constantly I sent—saying: Return, would you, each person from his evil way and make good your doings and do not go after other gods to serve them and dwell on the soil that I gave to you and your fathers. But you have not bent your ear, and you have not listened to me. [16]Indeed the sons of Jonadab son of Rechab have carried out the command of their father which he commanded them, but this people have not listened to me.

[17]Therefore thus said Yahweh, God of hosts, God of Israel:
Look I am bringing to Judah and to all the inhabitants of Jerusalem all the evil that I spoke concerning them, because I have spoken to them and they have not listened, and I have called to them and they have not answered.
[18]But to the house of the Rechabites Jeremiah said, Thus said Yahweh of hosts, God of Israel: Because you have listened to the command of Jonadab, your father, and you have kept all his commands and you have done according to all that he commanded you,
[19]Therefore thus said Yahweh of hosts, God of Israel:
There shall not be cut off a man belonging to Jonadab son of Rechab who stands before me all the days.

C. A Scroll for Future Days (36:1–32)

1. Baruch and the First Jeremiah Scroll (36:1–8)

36 [1]And it happened in the fourth year of Jehoiakim son of Josiah, king of Judah, this word came to Jeremiah from Yahweh: [2]Take for yourself a writing-scroll, and you shall write on it all the words that I have spoken to you concerning Israel and concerning Judah and concerning all the nations, from the day I spoke to you, from the days of Josiah, until this day. [3]Perhaps the house of Judah will listen to all the evil that I am planning to do to them, in order that they may turn each person from his evil way, and I will forgive their iniquity and their sin. [4]So Jeremiah called Baruch son of Neriah, and Baruch wrote from the dictation of Jeremiah all the words of Yahweh that he had spoken to him upon a writing-scroll. [5]And Jeremiah commanded Baruch, saying: 'I am under restraint; I am not able to enter the house of Yahweh. [6]So you, you shall enter, and you shall read aloud from the roll that you have written from my dictation the words of Yahweh in the hearing of the people in the house of Yahweh on a fast day, yes, also in the hearing of all Judah who come from their cities, you shall read them aloud. [7]Perhaps their petition will be laid before Yahweh, and they will turn each person from his evil way, for great is the anger and wrath that Yahweh has spoken toward this people.' [8]And Baruch son of Neriah did according to all that Jeremiah, the prophet, commanded him, to read aloud the scroll of the words of Yahweh in the house of Yahweh.

2. More on the Scroll's First Reading (36:9–26)

36 [9]And it happened in the fifth year of Jehoiakim son of Josiah, king of Judah, in the ninth month, they called a fast before Yahweh—all the people in Jerusalem and all the people who had come in from the cities of Judah—in Jerusalem. [10]And Baruch read aloud from the scroll the words of Jeremiah in the house of Yahweh—in the chamber of Gemariah son of Shaphan, the scribe, in the upper court at the opening of the New Gate in the house of Yahweh—in the hearing of all the people. [11]And Micaiah son of Gemariah, son of Shaphan, heard all the words of Yahweh from the scroll. [12]And he went down to the house of the king, to the chamber of the scribe, and look! there all the princes were sitting: Elishama, the scribe, and Delaiah son of Shema-iah, and Elnathan son of Achbor, and Gemariah son of Shaphan, and Zede-kiah son of Hananiah, yes, all the princes. [13]And Micaiah told them all the words that he had heard when Baruch read aloud the scroll in the hearing of the people. [14]And all the princes sent Jehudi son of Nethaniah, son of Shelemiah, son of Cushi, to Baruch, saying, 'The roll that you read aloud in the hearing of the people—take it in your hand and come.' So Baruch son of Neriah took the roll in his hand and came in to them. [15]And they said to him, 'Do sit down, and read it aloud in our hearing.' And Baruch read it aloud in their hearing. [16]And it happened when they heard all the words, they turned trembling one to another and said to Baruch, 'We must surely tell the king all these words.' [17]And they asked Baruch: 'Tell us, would you, how did you write all these words, from his dictation?' [18]And Baruch said to them, 'From his dic-tation; he would proclaim all these words to me and I would write upon the scroll in ink.' [19]And the princes said to Baruch, 'Go, hide yourself, you and Jeremiah, so that no one may know where you are!' [20]And they went in to the king, to the court, but the roll they deposited in the chamber of Elishama, the scribe. And they told in the hearing of the king all these words. [21]And the king sent Jehudi to take the roll, and he took it from the chamber of Elishama, the scribe, and Jehudi read it aloud in the hearing of the king and in the hearing of all the princes who were standing beside the king. [22]And the king was sit-ting in the winter house, in the ninth month, and a fire in the stove was burn-ing before him. [23]And it happened as Jehudi proclaimed three or four columns, he would tear it with the scribe's knife and would throw it into the fire that was in the stove, until the entire roll was consumed on the fire that was in the stove. [24]And they did not tremble, and they did not tear their gar-ments—the king and all his servants who were hearing all these words. [25]However, Elnathan and Delaiah and Gemariah strongly urged the king not to burn the roll, but he did not listen to them. [26]And the king commanded Jerahmeel, the king's son, and Seraiah the son of Azriel and Shelemiah son of Abdeel to seize Baruch, the scribe, and Jeremiah, the prophet, but Yahweh hid them.

3. The Scroll Is Rewritten (36:27–32)

36 ²⁷And the word of Yahweh came to Jeremiah after the king burned the roll, that is, the words that Baruch wrote from the dictation of Jeremiah: ²⁸Once again, take for yourself another roll and write on it all the former words that were contained on the first roll, which Jehoiakim, king of Judah, burned.

²⁹And concerning Jehoiakim, king of Judah, you shall say, Thus said Yahweh:

You, you have burned this roll, saying, 'Why have you written on it "The king of Babylon will surely come and destroy this land and make to cease from it human and beast"?'

³⁰Therefore, thus said Yahweh concerning Jehoiakim, king of Judah:

He shall not have one to sit upon the throne of David, and his dead body shall be thrown out to the heat by day and the frost by night. ³¹And I will reckon upon him and upon his offspring and upon his servants their iniquity; and I will bring upon them and upon the inhabitants of Jerusalem and to the men of Judah all the evil that I spoke to them, but they did not listen.

³²So Jeremiah took another roll and gave it to Baruch son of Neriah, the scribe, and he wrote upon it from the dictation of Jeremiah all the words of the scroll that Jehoiakim, king of Judah, burned in the fire. And besides, many words like these were added to them.

BIBLIOGRAPHY
SUPPLEMENT

◆

TEXTS AND REFERENCE WORKS

◆

Abegg, Martin Jr., et al.
  1999   *The Dead Sea Scrolls Bible.* Edinburgh: T. & T. Clark.
Apollodorus
  1967   *Apollodorus: The Library I: Books I–III 9.* Tr. James George Frazer. LCL. Cambridge, MA: Harvard University Press.
Bieberstein, Klaus, and Hanswulf Bloedhorn
  1994   *Jerusalem: Grundzüge der Baugeschichte von Chalkolithikum bis zur Frühzeit der osmanischen Herrschaft I–III.* Wiesbaden: Reichert.
Blackman, Philip
  1977   *Mishnayoth II: Order Moed.* 2d ed. Gateshead: Judaica.
Boardman, John, et al.
  1991   (eds.) *The Assyrian and Babylonian Empires and Other States of the Near East from the Eighth to the Sixth Centuries* B.C. Vol. 3/2 of *The Cambridge Ancient History.* 2d ed. Cambridge: Cambridge University Press.
  1982   (eds.) *The Expansion of the Greek World, Eighth to Sixth Centuries* B.C. Vol. 3/3 of *The Cambridge Ancient History.* 2d ed. Cambridge: Cambridge University Press.
Brenner, Athalya
  1982   *Colour Terms in the Old Testament.* JSOT Supp 21. Sheffield: JSOT Press.
Charlesworth, James H.
  1985   (ed.) *The Old Testament Pseudepigrapha II.* Garden City, NY: Doubleday.
Cyprian
  1972   *Sancti Cypriani Episcopi Opera.* Corpus Christianorum Series Latina 3. Turnhout: Brepols. Contains *De Lapsis.* [English: *St. Cyprian: The Lapsed; The Unity of the Catholic Church.* Tr. Maurice Bévenot. Westminster, MD: Newman, 1957]
Danby, Herbert
  1933   *The Mishnah.* Oxford: Oxford University Press.
Diodorus
  1984   *Diodorus of Sicily XII: Fragments of Books XXXIII–XL.* Tr. Francis R. Walton. LCL. Cambridge, MA: Harvard University Press.
Eusebius
  1862   *Eusebii Pamphili Episcopi Caesariensis Onomasticon Urbium et Locorum Sacrae Scripturae.* Ed. F. Larsow and G. Parthey. Berlin: Friderici Nicolai (G. Parthey).
  1949   *The Ecclesiastical History I.* Tr. Kirsopp Lake. LCL. Cambridge, MA: Harvard University Press.
Florus
  1995   *Epitome of Roman History.* Tr. Edward Seymour Forster. LCL. Cambridge, MA: Harvard University Press. [Original ed., 1929]

Freedman, H.
    1939a   (ed.) *Midrash Rabbah: Genesis II*. London: Soncino.
    1939b   (ed.) *Midrash Rabbah: Leviticus*. London: Soncino.
    1939c   (ed.) *Midrash Rabbah Ecclesiastes*. London: Soncino.
    1939d   (ed.) *Midrash Rabbah: Song of Songs*. London: Soncino.
Gershevitch, Ilya
    1985   (ed.) *The Cambridge History of Iran II*. Cambridge: Cambridge University Press.
Ginsburg, Christian D.
    1871   *The Moabite Stone: A Fac-simile of the Original Inscription*. London: Reeves and Turner.
    1880–85 *The Massorah I–III*. London/Vienna: George Brög (vol. I: 1880); Carl Fromme (vols. II–III: 1883–1885). [Reprinted in 4 volumes with a prolegomenon by Aron Dotan; New York: KTAV, 1970]
Gordon, Cyrus H.
    1955   *Ugaritic Manual*. AnOr 35. Rome: Pontifical Biblical Institute.
Hallo, William W.
    1997   (ed.) *The Context of Scripture I*. Leiden: Brill.
    2000   (ed.) *The Context of Scripture II*. Leiden: Brill.
Homer
    1953   *Homer: The Odyssey II: Books 13–24*. Tr. A. T. Murray. LCL. Cambridge, MA: Harvard University Press.
Horace
    1964   *Horace: The Odes and Epodes*. Tr. C. B. Bennett. LCL. Cambridge, MA: Harvard University Press.
Josephus
    1966   *Josephus I: The Life of Josephus; Against Apion*. Tr. H. St. J. Thackeray. LCL. Cambridge, MA: Harvard University Press.
Kraft, Robert A., and Ann-Elizabeth Purintun
    1972   (eds.) *Paraleipomena Jeremiou*. Missoula, MT: Scholars Press.
Livy
    1961   *Livy I: Books 1–2*. Tr. B. O. Foster. LCL. Cambridge, MA: Harvard University Press.
    1963   *Livy V: Books 21–22*. Tr. B. O. Foster. LCL. Cambridge, MA: Harvard University Press.
    1970   *Livy VII: Books 26–27*. Tr. Frank Gardner Moore. LCL. Cambridge, MA: Harvard University Press.
    1968   *Livy X: Books 35–37*. Tr. Evan T. Sage. LCL. Cambridge, MA: Harvard University Press.
Lust, Johan, et al.
    1996   *A Greek-English Lexicon of the Septuagint II*. Stuttgart: Deutsche Bibelgesellschaft.
Mandelkern, Solomon
    1967   *Veteris Testamenti Concordantiae Hebraicae Atque Chaldaicae*. Jerusalem: Schocken.
May, Herbert G.
    1962   (ed.) *Oxford Bible Atlas*. London: Oxford University Press.

Meyers, Eric M.
>1997   (ed.) *The Oxford Encyclopedia of Archaeology in the Near East.* 5 vols. Oxford: Oxford University Press.

Neusner, Jacob
>1985   *Genesis Rabbah: The Judaic Commentary to the Book of Genesis: A New American Translation I–III.* Brown Judaic Studies 104–6. Atlanta: Brown University and Scholars Press.
>1988   *The Mishnah: A New Translation.* New Haven: Yale University Press.

Ratner, B.
>1897   סדר עולם רבה [*Seder ʿOlam Rabba*]. Vilna: Romm. [Reprint, New York: Talmudical Research Institute, 1966]. Chapter 25 (pp. 110–14); chapter 26 (pp. 115–20).

Sallust
>1965   *Sallust.* Tr. J. C. Rolfe. LCL. Cambridge, MA: Harvard University Press. [Contains *Bellum Iugurthinum* (The War with Jugurtha)]

Sasson, Jack M.
>1995   (ed.) *Civilizations of the Ancient Near East I–IV.* New York: Scribner's.

Stern, Ephraim
>1993   (ed.) *The New Encyclopedia of Archaeological Excavations in the Holy Land.* 4 vols. Jerusalem: Israel Exploration Society. [Hebrew original, 1992]

Strabo
>1967   *The Geography of Strabo VIII: Book 17.* Tr. Horace Leonard Jones. LCL. Cambridge, MA: Harvard University Press.

Thompson, J. David
>2000   *A Critical Concordance to the Septuagint Jeremiah I–II.* The Computer Bible 74. [Wooster, OH]: Biblical Research Associates.

Torrey, Charles C.
>1946   *The Lives of the Prophets.* JBLMS 1. Philadelphia: Scholars Press.

Virgil
>1969   *Virgil II: Aeneid VII–XII, The Minor Poems.* Tr. H. Rushton Fairclough. Rev. ed. LCL. Cambridge, MA: Harvard University Press.

Xenophon
>1914   *Xenophon I: Cyropaedia; I–IV.* Tr. Walter Miller. LCL. New York: Macmillan.
>1914   *Xenophon II: Cyropaedia; V–VIII.* Tr. Walter Miller. LCL. New York: Macmillan.
>1921   *Xenophon Hellenica VI–VII; Anabasis I–III.* Tr. Carleton L. Brownson. LCL. New York: Putnam's.

COMMENTARIES

◆

Fretheim, Terrence E.
    2002   *Jeremiah*. Macon, GA: Smyth and Helwys.
Miller, Patrick D.
    2001   "The Book of Jeremiah" in *NIB* 6. Ed. Leander E. Keck. Nashville:
        Abingdon. Pp. 555–926.
Werner, Wolfgang
    1997   *Das Buch Jeremia*. NSKAT 19/1. Stuttgart: Katholisches Bibelwerk.

BOOKS, MONOGRAPHS, AND ARTICLES

◆

Abramsky, Samuel
    1967   "The House of Rechab" in *E. L. Sukenik Memorial Volume*. [Hebrew with English summary] Ed. N. Avigad et al. Eretz-Israel 8. Jerusalem: Israel Exploration Society. Pp. 255–64, 76.

Abrego, José Maria
    1983a   "El Texto Hebreo Estructurado de Jeremias 36–45." *CuadBib* 8: 1–49.
    1983b   *Jeremías y el Final del Reino*. EAT 3. Valencia: Institución San Jerónimo.

Ackroyd, Peter R.
    1968   "Historians and Prophets." *SEÅ* 33: 18–54.
    1972   "The Temple Vessels—A Continuity Theme" in *Studies in the Religion of Ancient Israel*. VT Supp 23. Leiden: Brill. Pp. 166–81.

Aharoni, Yohanan
    1982   *The Archaeology of the Land of Israel*. Ed. Miriam Aharoni. Tr. Anson F. Rainey. London: SCM Press.

Aitken, Kenneth T.
    1984   "The Oracles against Babylon in Jeremiah 50–51: Structures and Perspectives." *TynB* 35: 25–63.

Albrektson, Bertil
    1994   "Translation and Emendation" in *Language, Theology, and the Bible* [Essays in Honour of James Barr]. Ed. Samuel E. Balentine and John Barton. Oxford: Clarendon Press. Pp. 27–39.

Albright, W. F.
    1924   "Researches of the School in Western Judaea." *BASOR* 15: 2–11.
    1936   "A Supplement to Jeremiah: The Lachish Ostraca." *BASOR* 61: 10–16.
    1938   "The Oldest Hebrew Letters: The Lachish Ostraca." *BASOR* 70: 11–17.
    1941a   "Ostracon No. 6043 from Ezion-Geber." *BASOR* 82: 11–15.
    1941b   "The Lachish Letters after Five Years." *BASOR* 82: 18–24.
    1951   "The Hebrew Expression for 'Making a Covenant' in Pre-Israelite Documents." *BASOR* 121: 21–22.
    1953   "Dedan" in *Geschichte und Altes Testament* [Festschrift für Albrecht Alt]. BHT 16. Ed. Gerhard Ebeling. Tübingen: Mohr (Siebeck). Pp. 1–12.
    1956   "The Nebuchadnezzar and Neriglissar Chronicles." *BASOR* 143: 28–33.
    1969   *Archaeology and the Religion of Israel*. Garden City, NY: Doubleday. Originally 1942.
    1970   "Some Comments on the ʿAmmân Citadel Inscription." *BASOR* 198: 38–40.

Alexander, James Edward
    1879   *Cleopatra's Needle: The Obelisk of Alexandria*. London: Chatto & Windus.

Alonso-Schökel, Luis
    1979   "Jeremias 30–33." *CuadBib* 3: 1–30.
Alt, Albrecht
    1929   "Das Institut im Jahre 1928." *PJB* 25: 5–59.
    1932   "Das Institut im Jahre 1931." *PJB* 28: 5–47.
    1943   "Taphnaein und Taphnas." *ZDPV* 66: 64–68
Althann, Robert
    1988   "*Běrē'šît* in Jer 26:1, 27:1, 28:1, 49:34." *JNSL* 14: 1–7.
    1991   "Does *'et* (*'aet-*) Sometimes Signify 'from' in the Hebrew Bible?" *ZAW* 103: 121–24.
    1997   *Studies in Northwest Semitic*. BetOr 95. Rome: Pontifical Biblical Institute.
Amesz, J. G.
    1997   "Grote stenen en een brief." *Amc* 16: 80–98.
Amiran, Ruth
    1958   "The Tumuli West of Jerusalem." *IEJ* 8: 205–27.
Anbar, Moshé
    1999   "La libération des esclaves en temps de guerre: Jer 34 et ARM XXVI.363." *ZAW* 111: 253–55.
Andersen, Francis I.
    2001   *Habakkuk*. AB 25. New York: Doubleday.
_____ and A. Dean Forbes
    1983   " 'Prose Particle' Counts of the Hebrew Bible" in *The Word of the Lord Shall Go Forth* [Essays in Honor of David Noel Freedman]. Ed. Carol L. Meyers and M. O'Connor. Winona Lake, IN: American Schools of Oriental Research and Eisenbrauns. Pp. 165–83.
_____ and David Noel Freedman
    2000   *Micah*. AB 24E. New York: Doubleday.
Anderson, Bernhard W.
    1964   "The New Covenant and the Old" in *The Old Testament and Christian Faith*. Ed. Bernhard W. Anderson. London: SCM Press. Pp. 225–42.
    1978   " 'The Lord Has Created Something New': A Stylistic Study of Jer 31:15–22." *CBQ* 40: 463–78. [=Perdue and Kovacs 1984: 367–80; B. W. Anderson 1994: 179–94]
    1994   *From Creation to New Creation*. Minneapolis: Fortress.
Anderson, Robert T.
    1960   "Was Isaiah a Scribe?" *JBL* 79: 57–58.
Aufrecht, Walter E.
    1989   *A Corpus of Ammonite Inscriptions*. ANETS 4. Lewiston, NY: Edwin Mellen.
Avemarie, Friedrich, and Hermann Lichtenberger
    1996   (eds.) *Bund und Tora: Zur theologischen Begriffsgeschichte in alttestamentlicher, frühjüdischer und urchristlicher Tradition*. WUNT 92. Tübingen: Mohr (Siebeck).
Avigad, Nahman
    1972   "Excavations in the Jewish Quarter of the Old City of Jerusalem, 1971." *IEJ* 22: 193–200.
    1975   "Jerusalem, the Jewish Quarter of the Old City, 1975." *IEJ* 25: 260–61.

1979   "Hebrew Epigraphic Sources" in *The World History of the Jewish People: The Age of the Monarchies: Political History.* Vol. 4/1. Ed. Abraham Malamat. Jerusalem: Massada. Pp. 20–43, 315–17.
1980   "The Chief of the Corvée." *IEJ* 30: 170–73 + plates.
1983   *Discovering Jerusalem.* Nashville: Thomas Nelson.
1985   "The Upper City" in *Biblical Archaeology Today* [Proceedings of the International Congress on Biblical Archaeology Jerusalem, April 1984]. Ed. Avraham Biran et al. Jerusalem: Israel Exporation Society. Pp. 469–75.
1987   "The Contribution of Hebrew Seals to an Understanding of Israelite Religion and Society" in *Ancient Israelite Religion* [Essays in Honor of F. M. Cross]. Ed. Patrick D. Miller et al. Philadelphia: Fortress. Pp. 195–208.
1989   "The Inscribed Pomegranate from the 'House of the Lord.'" *IMJ* 7: 7–16.
1997   *Corpus of West Semitic Stamp Seals.* Revised and completed by Benjamin Sass. Jerusalem: Israel Academy of Sciences and Humanities.

_____ and Hillel Geva
1993   "Jerusalem: The Second Temple Period" in *NEAEHL* 2: 717–57.

Avi-Yonah, M.
1954   "The Walls of Nehemiah: A Minimalist View." *IEJ* 4: 239–48.

Bach, Robert
1961   "Bauen und Pflanzen" in *Studien zur Theologie der alttestamentlichen Überlieferungen* [Festschrift für Gerhard von Rad]. Ed. Rolf Rendtorff and Klaus Koch. Neukirchen-Vluyn: Neukirchener Verlag. Pp. 7–32.
1962   *Die Aufforderungen zur Flucht und zum Kampf im Alttestamentlichen Prophetenspruch.* WMANT 9. Neukirchen-Vluyn: Neukirchener Verlag.

Badè, William F.
1933   "The Seal of Jaazaniah." *ZAW* 51: 150–56.
1934   *A Manuel of Excavation in the Near East.* Berkeley: University of California Press.

Bader, Johannes B.
1961–62   "ΤΑ ΘΗΛΥΚΑ ΑΠΑΝΔΡΩΘΕΝΤΑ [Clement of Alexandria, *Excerpta ex Theodoto*, 21, 3]." *NTS* 8: 56–58.

Bahat, Dan, and Chaim T. Rubinstein
1990   *The Illustrated Atlas of Jerusalem.* Tr. Shlomo Ketko. Jerusalem: Carta.

Bardtke, Hans
1935   "Jeremia der Fremdvölkerprophet." *ZAW* 53: 209–39.
1936   "Jeremia der Fremdvölkerprophet 2." *ZAW* 54: 240–62.

Barkay, Gabriel, and Amos Kloner
1986   "Jerusalem Tombs from the Days of the First Temple." *BAR* 12/2: 22–39.

Barnett, R. D., and M. Falkner
1962   *The Sculptures of Tiglath-Pileser III (745–727 B.C.).* London: The British Museum.

Barthélemy, Dominique
1986   *Critique Textuelle de L'Ancien Testament II.* OBO 50/2. Fribourg [Suisse]: Éditions Universitaires and Göttingen: Vandenhoeck & Ruprecht.

Bartlett, David L.
1978   "Jeremiah 31:15–20." *Int* 32: 73–78.

Bartlett, John R.
    1990   "From Edomites to Nabataeans: The Problem of Continuity" *Aram* 2: 25–34.
    1999   "Edomites and Idumaeans." *PEQ* 131: 102–14.

Batto, Bernard F.
    1983   "The Reed Sea: *Requiescat in Pace.*" *JBL* 102: 27–35.

Becking, Bob
    1990   "Jehojachin's Amnesty, Salvation for Israel? Notes on 2 Kings 25,27–30" in *Pentateuchal and Deuteronomistic Studies.* BETL 94. Ed. C. Brekelmans and J. Lust. Leuven: Leuven University Press. Pp. 283–93.
    1994a   "Jeremiah's Book of Consolation: A Textual Comparison. Notes on the Masoretic Text and the Old Greek Version of Jeremiah xxx–xxxi." *VT* 44: 145–69.
    1994b   "'A Voice Was Heard in Ramah.'" *BZ* 38: 229–42.
    1998   "The Times They Are A Changing: An Interpretation of Jeremiah 30,12–17." *SJOT* 12: 3–25.

Beckman, Gary
    1996   *Hittite Diplomatic Texts.* Ed. Harry A. Hoffner Jr. SBL Writings from the Ancient World 7. Atlanta: Scholars Press.

Begg, Christopher T.
    1994   "The Gedaliah Episode and Its Sequels in Josephus." *JSP* 12: 21–46.
    1995   "Jeremiah under Jehoiakim according to Josephus (*Ant.* 10.89–95)." *AbrNa* 33: 1–16.

Begin, Ze'ev B.
    2002   "Does Lachish Letter 4 Contradict Jeremiah xxxiv 7? *VT* 52: 166–74.
_____ and Avihu Grushka
    1999   "Where Was Lachish 4 Written?" [Hebrew with English summary] in *Frank Moore Cross Volume.* Ed. Baruch A. Levine et al. Eretz-Israel 26. Jerusalem: Israel Exploration Society and Hebrew Union College. Pp. *13–24, 226–27.

Begrich, Joachim
    1929   *Die Chronologie der Könige von Israel und Juda.* BHT 3. Tübingen: Mohr (Siebeck).
    1934   "Das priesterliche Heilsorakel." ZAW 52: 81–92.

Beit-Arieh, Itzhaq
    1987   *Edomite Shrine: Discoveries from Qitmit in the Negev.* Jerusalem: The Israel Museum.
    1991   "The Edomite Shrine at Horvat Qitmit in the Judean Negev." *Tel Aviv* 18: 93–116.
    1995a   (ed.) *Ḥorvat Qitmit: An Edomite Shrine in the Biblical Negev.* Tel Aviv University Institute of Archaeology, Monograph Series 11. Tel Aviv: Tel Aviv University.
    1995b   "The Edomites in Cisjordan" in Edelman 1995a: 33–40.

Bekel, Heinrich
    1907   "Ein vorexilisches Orakel über Edom in der Klageliederstrophe—die gemeinsame Quelle von Obadja 1–9 und Jeremia 49,7–22." *TSK* 80: 315–43.

Bellis, Alice Ogden
    1995   *The Structure and Composition of Jeremiah 50:2–51:58.* Lewiston, NY: Mellen Biblical Press.

Ben-Barak, Zafrira
    1975   "The Religious-Prophetic Background of the 'Law of the King' in Deuter-
            onomy." [Hebrew with English summary] *Shnaton* 1: viii, 33–44.
Bennett, Crystal-M.
    1966   "Fouilles D'Umm El-Biyara." *RB* 73: 372–403.
    1973   "Excavations at Buseirah, Southern Jordan, 1971: A Preliminary Report."
            Levant 5: 1–11.
    1974   "Excavations at Buseirah, Southern Jordan, 1972: Preliminary Report."
            Levant 6: 1–24 + plates.
    1975   "Excavations at Buseirah, Southern Jordan, 1973: Third Preliminary
            Report." *Levant* 7: 1–19.
    1977   "Excavations at Buseirah, Southern Jordan, 1974: Fourth Preliminary
            Report." *Levant* 9: 1–10.
    1982   "Neo-Assyrian Influence in Transjordan" in *Studies in the History and
            Archeology of Jordan I*. Ed. Adnan Hadidi. Amman: Department of Antiq-
            uities, Hashemite Kingdom of Jordan. Pp. 181–87.
    1983   "Excavations at Buseirah (Biblical Bozrah)" in Sawyer and Clines 1983:
            9–17.
    1984   "Excavations at Tawilan in Southern Jordan, 1982." *Levant* 16: 1–23.
_____ and Piotr Bienkowski
    1995   *Excavations at Tawilan in Southern Jordan*. British Academy Monographs
            in Archaeology 8. Oxford University Press.
Benoit, P.
    1975   "The Archaeological Reconstruction of the Antonia Fortress" in *Jeru-
            salem Revealed*. Ed. Y. Yadin. Jerusalem: Israel Exploration Society.
            Pp. 87–89.
Berkovitz, Eliezer
    1969   "The Biblical Meaning of Justice." *Judaism* 18: 188–209.
Berlin, Adele
    1984   "Jeremiah 29:5–7: A Deuteronomic Allusion." *HAR* 8: 3–11.
Bernhardt, Karl-Heinz
    1960   "Beobachtungen zur Identifizierung moabitischer Ortslagen." *ZDPV* 76:
            136–58.
Bewer, Julius A.
    1925–26 "Nergalsharezer Samgar in Jer. 39:3." *AJSLL* 42: 130.
Beyerlin, Walter
    1978   (ed.) *Near Eastern Religious Texts Relating to the Old Testament*. Tr. John
            Bowden. OTL. London: SCM Press.
Bienkowski, Piotr
    1990a   "Umm El-Biyara, Tawilan and Buseirah in Retrospect." *Levant* 22: 91–
            109.
    1990b   "The Chronology of Tawilan and the 'Dark Age' of Edom." *Aram* 2: 35–
            44.
    1992   (ed.) *Early Edom and Moab: The Beginning of the Iron Age in Southern
            Jordan*. Sheffield Archaeological Monographs 7. Sheffield: J. R. Collins
            and The University of Sheffield.
    1995   "The Edomites: The Archaeological Evidence from Transjordan" in
            Edelman 1995a: 1–11.

_____ and Eveline van der Steen
2001   "Tribes, Trade, and Towns: A New Framework for the Late Iron Age in Southern Jordan and the Negev." *BASOR* 323: 21–47.
Biran [Bergman], Avraham, and Joseph Naveh
1993   "An Aramaic Stele Fragment from Tel Dan." *IEJ* 43: 81–98.
Black, Matthew
1961   *The Scrolls and Christian Origins.* New York: Scribner's.
Blenkinsopp, Joseph
1972   *Gibeon and Israel.* Cambridge: Cambridge University Press.
Boecker, Hans Jochen
1980   *Law and the Administration of Justice in the Old Testament and Ancient East.* Tr. Jeremy Moiser. London: SPCK.
Böhmer, Siegmund
1976   *Heimkehr und neuer Bund: Studien zu Jeremia 30–31.* Göttingen: Vandenhoeck & Ruprecht.
de Boer, P. A.
1948   "An Inquiry into the Meaning of the Term מַשָּׂא." *OTS* 5: 197–214.
1973   "Jeremiah 45, Verse 5" in *Symbolae Biblicae et Mesopotamicae Francisco Mario Theodoro de Liagre Böhl Dedicatae.* Ed. M. A. Beek et al. Leiden: Brill. Pp. 31–37. [=*OTS* 27 (1991) 122–28]
Bogaert, Pierre-Maurice
1990   "La libération de Jérémie et le meurtre de Godolias: Le texte court (LXX) et la rédaction longue (TM)" in *Studien zur Septuaginta—Robert Hanhart zu Ehren.* Ed. Detlef Fraenkel et al. Göttingen: Vandenhoeck & Ruprecht. Pp. 312–22.
1991   "Les trois formes de Jérémie 52 (TM, LXX et VL)" in *Tradition of the Text* [Festschrift Dominique Barthélemy]. OBO 109. Ed. Gerard J. Norton and Stephen Pisano. Freiburg [Schweiz]: Universitätsverlag and Göttingen: Vandenhoeck & Ruprecht. Pp. 1–17.
Booth, Osborne
1942   "The Semantic Development of the Term מִשְׁפָּט in the Old Testament." *JBL* 61: 105–10.
Borger, Riekele [Rykle]
1961   "Zu den Asarhaddon-Verträgen aus Nimrud." *ZA* 54: 173–96.
1972   "Die Waffenträger des Königs Darius." *VT* 22: 385–98.
Borowski, Oded
1987   *Agriculture in Iron Age Israel.* Winona Lake, IN: Eisenbrauns.
Bozak, Barbara A.
1991   *Life 'Anew': A Literary-Theological Study of Jeremiah 30–31.* AnBib 122. Rome: Pontifical Biblical Institute.
Branden, A. van den
1964   "L'inscription phénicienne de Larnax Lapethou II." *OrAnt* 3: 245–61.
Brekell, John
1767   *The Double Question Discussed in a Dissertation on Jeremiah, Chap. xxxi. Ver. 29: Occasioned by a Late Controversy about Children's Suffering for the Crime of Their Parents. . . .* London: Buckland and Wilkie.
Bright, John
1949   "A New Letter in Aramaic, Written to a Pharaoh of Egypt." *BA* 12: 46–52.

Brooke, George J.
1997   "The Book of Jeremiah and Its Reception in the Qumran Scrolls" in *The Book of Jeremiah and Its Reception*. Ed. A. H. W. Curtis and T. Römer. BETL 128. Leuven: Leuven University Press. Pp. 183–205.
Broshi, Magen
1974   "The Expansion of Jerusalem in the Reigns of Hezekiah and Manasseh." *IEJ* 24: 21–26.
_____ and Ada Yardeni
1995   "On *netinim* and False Prophets" in *Solving Riddles and Untying Knots* [Studies in Honor of Jonas C. Greenfield]. Ed. Ziony Zevit et al. Winona Lake, IN: Eisenbrauns. Pp. 29–37.
Brown, Raymond E.
1958   "The Pre-Christian Semitic Concept of 'Mystery.'" *CBQ* 20: 417–43.
Bryan, C. P.
1931   (tr.) *The Papyrus Ebers*. New York: Appleton.
Buber, Martin
1949   *The Prophetic Faith*. Tr. Carlyle Witton-Davies. New York: Macmillan.
1968   "False Prophets (Jeremiah 28)" in *Biblical Humanism*. Ed. Nahum N. Glatzer. London: Macdonald. Pp. 166–71. [= "Falsche Propheten." *Wand* 2 (1947), 277–83]
Budde, Karl
1878   "Ueber die Capitel 50 und 51 des Buches Jeremia." *JDT* 23: 428–70; 529–62.
1883   "Ein althebräisches Klagelied." *ZAW* 3: 299–306.
1906   *Das prophetische Schrifttum*. Tübingen: Mohr (Siebeck).
Budge, E. A. Wallis
1926   *Cleopatra's Needles and Other Egyptian Obelisks*. London: Religious Tract Society.
Bultmann, Rudolph
1951   *Theology of the New Testament I*. Tr. Kendrick Grobel. New York: Scribner's.
Burrows, Eric
1926–27 "Cuneiform and the Old Testament: Three Notes." *JTS* Old Series 28: 184–85.
Burrows, Millar
1962   "Jerusalem" in *IDB* E–J, 843–66.
Butler, Sally A.
1998   *Mesopotamian Conceptions of Dreams and Dream Rituals*. AOAT 258. Münster: Ugarit-Verlag.
Carr, A.
1908   "Sacrificial Cakes." *PEFQS* 168.
Cary, John, and Alastair Fowler
1968   (eds.) *The Poems of John Milton*. London: Longmans, Green.
Cassuto, Umberto
1973c   "The Prophecies of Jeremiah concerning the Gentiles" in Cassuto 1973a: 178–226. Originally 1917.
Cazelles, Henri
1981   "La vie de Jérémie dans son contexte national et international" in P.-M. Bogaert 1981a: 21–39.

Charlesworth, James H.
    1982   *The History of the Rechabites I: The Greek Recension.* SBL Texts and
            Translations 17; Pseudepigrapha Series 10. Chico, CA: Scholars Press.
    1986   "Greek, Persian, Roman, Syrian, and Egyptian Influences in Early Jewish
            Theology" in *Hellenica et Judaica* [Hommage à Valentin Nikiprowetzky].
            Ed. A. Caquot et al. Leuven / Paris: Éditions Peeters. Pp. 219–43.
Charpin, Dominique, et al.
    1988   *Archives Épistolaires de Mari I/2.* ARM 26. Paris: Éditions Recherche sur
            les Civilisations.
Childs, Brevard S.
    1979   *Introduction to the Old Testament as Scripture.* London: SCM Press.
    1985   *Old Testament Theology in a Canonical Context.* London: SCM Press.
Christensen, Duane L.
    1975   *Transformations of the War Oracle in Old Testament Prophecy: Studies in
            the Oracles against the Nations.* HDR 3. Missoula, MT: Scholars Press.
Churgin, Pinkhos
    1907   *Targum Jonathan to the Prophets.* YOSR 14. New Haven: Yale University
            Press.
Clifford, Richard
    1966   "The Use of *Hôy* in the Prophets." *CBQ* 28: 458–64.
Clines, David J.
    1972   "Regnal Year Reckoning in the Last Years of the Kingdom of Judah." *AJBA*
            [2/1]: 9–34.
Cogan, Morton (Mordechai)
    1968   "A Technical Term for Exposure." *JNES* 27: 133–35.
    2001   *I Kings.* AB 10. New York: Doubleday.
_____ and Hayim Tadmor
    1988   *II Kings.* AB 11. [New York]: Doubleday.
Cohen, Mark E.
    1988   *The Canonical Lamentations of Ancient Mesopotamia I–II.* Potomac,
            MD: Capital Decisions Ltd.
Cohen, Rudolph, and Yigal Yisrael
    1995   *On the Road to Edom: Discoveries from ʿEn Ḥaẓeva.* Jerusalem: Israel
            Museum.
Condamin, Albert
    1897   "Le Texte de Jérémie XXXI, 22: Est-Il Messianique?" *RB* 6: 396–404.
Conrad, Edgar W.
    1985   *Fear Not Warrior: A Study of ʾal tîraʾ Pericopes in the Hebrew Scriptures.*
            Brown Judaic Studies 75. Chico, CA: Scholars Press.
Cooke, Francis T.
    1923–24 "The Site of Kirjath-jearim." *AASOR* 5: 105–20.
Cooke, G. A.
    1903   *A Text-Book of North-Semitic Inscriptions.* Oxford: Clarendon Press.
Copher, Charles B.
    1975   "Blacks and Jews in Historical Interaction: The Biblical/African Experi-
            ence." *JITC* 3: 9–16.
    1988–89 "The Bible and the African Experience: The Biblical Period." *JITC* 16:
            32–50.

Corbett, Edward P. J.
    1971   *Classical Rhetoric for the Modern Student*. 2d ed. New York: Oxford University Press.
Cowley, A. E.
    1923   (ed.) *Aramaic Papyri of the Fifth Century B.C.* Oxford: Clarendon Press.
    _____ and A. Neubauer
    1897   (eds.) *The Original Hebrew of a Portion of Ecclesiasticus*. Oxford: Clarendon Press.
Croatto, José S., and J. Alberto Soggin
    1962   "Die Bedeutung von שדמות im Alten Testament." *ZAW* 74: 44–50.
Cross, Frank M. Jr.
    1953   "The Council of Yahweh in Second Isaiah." *JNES* 12: 274–77.
    1956   "A Footnote to Biblical History." *BA* 19: 12–17.
    1970   "The Cave Inscriptions from Khirbet Beit Lei" in *Near Eastern Archaeology in the Twentieth Century* [Essays in Honor of Nelson Glueck]. Ed. James A. Sanders. Garden City, NY: Doubleday. Pp. 299–306.
    1973a   *Canaanite Myth and Hebrew Epic*. Cambridge, MA: Harvard University Press.
    1973b   "Notes on the Ammonite Inscriptions from Tell Sīrān." *BASOR* 212: 12–15.
    1988   "Reuben, First-Born of Jacob." *ZAW* 100 Supp: 46–65.
    _____ and Esther Eshel
    1997   "Ostraca from Khirbet Qumran." *IEJ* 47: 17–28.
    _____ and David Noel Freedman
    1952   *Early Hebrew Orthography*. AOS 36. New Haven: American Oriental Society.
    _____ and J. T. Milik
    1956   "Explorations in the Judaean Buqêʿah." *BASOR* 142: 5–17.
Crown, A. D.
    1963   "Aposiopesis in the OT and the Hebrew Conditional Oath." *AbrNa* 4: 96–111.
Cummings, J. T.
    1979   "The House of the Sons of the Prophets and the Tents of the Rechabites" in *Studia Biblica 1978* [Sixth International Congress on Biblical Studies, Oxford, 3–7 April 1978]. Ed. E. A. Livingstone. JSOT Supp 11. Sheffield: JSOT Press. Pp. 119–26.
Dahood, Mitchell
    1959a   "The Linguistic Position of Ugaritic in the Light of Recent Discoveries" in *Sacra Pagina I*. Ed. J. Coppens et al. BETL 12–13. Gembloux: Duculot. Pp. 267–79.
    1965   *Ugaritic-Hebrew Philology*. BetOr 17. Rome: Pontifical Biblical Institute.
    1976a   "Vocative *kî* and *wa* in Biblical Hebrew" in *Mélanges Offerts au R. P. Henri Fleisch I. MUSJ* 48 (1973–74). Beirut: Imprimerie Catholique. Pp. 49–63.
    1977a   "Word and Witness: A Note on Jeremiah xxix 23." *VT* 27: 483.
    1977b   "The Word-Pair ʾakal/kālāh in Jeremiah xxx 16." *VT* 27: 482.
Dalman, Gustav
    1932   *Arbeit und Sitte in Palästina II*. Gütersloh: Bertelsmann.
    1933   *Arbeit und Sitte in Palästina III*. Gütersloh: Bertelsmann.

Daube, David
    1965   *Collaboration with Tyranny in Rabbinic Law*. London: Oxford University
              Press.
Daviau, Michèle, and Margreet Steiner
    2000   "A Moabite Sanctuary at Khirbat al-Mudayna." *BASOR* 320· 1–21.
Davidson, A. B.
    1895   "The False Prophets." *The Expositor* 5th Series 2: 1–17.
Davies, W. D.
    1969   *The Sermon on the Mount*. Cambridge: Cambridge University Press.
Day, John
    1985   *God's Conflict with the Dragon and the Sea: Echoes of a Canaanite Myth
              in the Old Testament*. Cambridge: Cambridge University Press.
Dearman, J. Andrew
    1989a   (ed.) *Studies in the Mesha Inscription and Moab*. Atlanta: Scholars Press.
    1989b   "Historical Reconstruction and the Mesha⸵ Inscription" in Dearman
              1989a: 155–210.
    1997   "Roads and Settlements in Moab." *BA* 60: 205–13.
de Hoop, Raymond
    1997   "The Meaning of *pḥz* in Classical Hebrew." *ZAH* 10: 16–26.
Deist, Ferdinand E.
    1971   "The Punishment of the Disobedient Zedekiah." *JNSL* 1: 71–72.
Delamarter, Steve
    1999   "'Thus Far the Words of Jeremiah.'" *BiRev* 15/5: 34–45, 54–55.
Delcor, Mathias
    1982   "Le culte de la 'Reine du Ciel' selon Jer 7,18; 44,17–19,25 et ses survi-
              vances" in *Von Kanaan bis Kerala* [Festschrift für J. P. M. van der
              Ploeg]. Ed. W. C. Delsman et al. AOAT 211. Kevelaer: Butzon &
              Bercker and Neukirchen-Vluyn: Neukirchener Verlag. Pp. 101–22.
              [=Delcor 1990: 138–59]
    1990   *Environnement et Tradition de l'Ancien Testament*. AOAT 228. Kevelaer:
              Butzon & Bercker and Neukirchen-Vluyn: Neukirchener Verlag.
Delitzsch, Friedrich
    1881   *Wo Lag das Paradies?* Leipzig: Hinrichs.
de Moor, Johannes C., and Herman F. de Vries
    1988   "Hebrew *hēdād* 'Thunder-Storm.'" *UF* 20: 173–77.
Dentan, Robert C.
    1956   "Malachi" in IB 6. Ed. George A. Buttrick. New York: Abingdon Press.
              Pp. 1117–44.
DeRoche, Michael
    1978   "Is Jeremiah 25:15–29 a Piece of Reworked Jeremianic Poetry?" *JSOT* 10:
              58–67.
Derrett, J. Duncan
    1981   "Mt 23,8–10 a Midrash on Is 54,13 and Jer 31,31–34." *Biblica* 62: 372–86.
Dicou, A.
    1988   "Geen wijsheid Meer in Edom: Jeremia 49,7 en Obadja 7–8." *Amc* 9: 90–
              96.
    1989   "De structuur van de verzameling profetieën over de volken in Jeremia
              46–51." *Amc* 10: 84–87.

Dicou, Bert
1994   *Edom, Israel's Brother and Antagonist: The Role of Edom in Biblical Prophecy and Story.* JSOT Supp. 169. Sheffield: Sheffield Academic Press.

Dietrich, Ernst Ludwig
1925   שוב שבות: *Die Endzeitliche Wiederherstellung bei den Propheten.* BZAW 40. Giessen: Alfred Töpelmann.

Dietrich, M., and O. Loretz
1964–66 "Der Vertrag zwischen Šuppiluliuma and Niqmandu." WO 3: 206–45.

Dimant, Devorah
1973   "Jeremiah 51:55—Versions and Semantics." *Textus* 8: 93–99.
1994   "An Apocryphon of Jeremiah from Cave 4 (4Q385^B = 4Q385 16)" in *New Qumran Texts and Studies.* STDJ 15. Ed. George J. Brooke and Florentino García Martínez. Leiden: Brill. Pp. 11–30.

Diringer, David
1941   "On Ancient Hebrew Inscriptions Discovered at Tell ed-Duweir (Lachish)—II." *PEQ* 73: 89–106.
1943   "On Ancient Hebrew Inscriptions Discovered at Tell ed-Duweir (Lachish)—III." *PEQ* 75: 89–99.

Dobbs-Allsopp, F. W.
1993   *Weep, O Daughter of Zion: A Study of the City-Lament Genre in the Hebrew Bible.* BetOr 44. Rome: Pontifical Biblical Institute.

Dodd, C. H.
1932   *The Epistle of Paul to the Romans.* MNTC. London: Hodder and Stoughton.
1952   *According to the Scriptures.* London: Nisbet.

Donner, H., and W. Röllig
1962–64 *Kanaanäische und Aramäische Inschriften I–II.* Wiesbaden: Harrassowitz. Band I: Texte (1962); Band II: Kommentar (1964).

Dorsey, David A.
1991   *The Roads and Highways of Ancient Israel.* Baltimore: Johns Hopkins University Press.

Dotan, Aron
1991   "*Ka-Te'enim Ha-Sho'arim* (Jer. 29:17)" [Hebrew with English summary] in *Te'uda* 7. Studies in Judaica. Ed. Mordechai A. Friedman. Tel Aviv: Tel Aviv University. Pp. 67–73, ix–x.

Dresner, Samuel H.
1994   *Rachel.* Minneapolis: Fortress Press.

Driver, G. R.
1940   "Hebrew Notes on Prophets and Proverbs." *JTS* Old Series 41: 162–75.
1950a   "Hebrew Roots and Words." WO 1: 406–15.
1964   "Once Again Abbreviations." *Textus* 4: 76–94.
_____ and John C. Miles
1955   *The Babylonian Laws II.* Oxford: Clarendon Press.

Drotts, Wallace D.
1973   "A Study of the Prophet Jeremiah Compared and Contrasted with Martin Luther King Jr., with Guidelines for Prophetic Ministry Today." Unpublished D.Min. Thesis, San Francisco Theological Seminary.

Dürr, Lorenz
 1938   *Die Wertung des göttlichen Wortes im Alten Testament und im antiker Orient.* MVÄG 42/1. Leipzig: Hinrichs.
Dupont-Sommer, André
 1948   "Un papyrus araméen d'époque saïte découvert à Saqqara " *Semitica* 1: 43–68 + plate.
Edelman, Diana Vikander
 1995a   (ed.) *You Shall Not Abhor an Edomite for He Is Your Brother: Edom and Seir in History and Tradition.* SBL and ASOR Archaeological and Biblical Studies 3. Atlanta: Society of Biblical Literature, American Schools of Oriental Research, and Scholars Press.
 1995b   "Edom: A Historical Geography" in Edelman 1995a: 1–11.
Ehrlich, Ernst Ludwig
 1953   *Der Traum im Alten Testament.* BZAW 73. Berlin: Alfred Töpelmann.
Eissfeldt, Otto
 1961   "Jeremias Drohorakel gegen Ägypten und gegen Babel" in *Verbannung und Heimkehr* [Festschrift für Wilhelm Rudolph]. Ed. Arnulf Kuschke. Tübingen: Mohr (Siebeck). Pp. 31–37.
Elat, Moshe
 1983   "The Iron Export from Uzal (Ezekiel xxvii 19)." *VT* 33: 323–30.
 1991   "Phoenician Overland Trade within the Mesopotamian Empires" in *Ah, Assyria . . .* [Studies Presented to Hayim Tadmor]. Scripta Hierosoly-mitana 33. Ed. Mordechai Cogan and Israel Eph'al. Jerusalem: Magnes Press. Pp. 21–35.
Elitzur, Yehuda
 1963   "The Moab Prophecy and the Moabite Stone." [Hebrew with English summary] *Bar-Ilan* 1: 58–65, xviii–xx.
Elliger, K.
 1934   "Josua in Judäa." *PJB* 30: 47–71.
Emmerson, Grace I.
 1984   *Hosea.* JSOT Supp 28. Sheffield: JSOT Press.
Engnell, Ivan
 1943   *Studies in Divine Kingship in the Ancient Near East.* Uppsala: Almqvist & Wiksells.
Eph'al, Israel
 1978   "The Western Minorities in Babylonia in the 6th–5th Centuries B.C.: Maintenance and Cohesion." *Orientalia* 47: 74–90.
 1982   *The Ancient Arabs.* Jerusalem: Magnes Press and Leiden: Brill.
 1984   "The Assyrian Siege Ramp at Lachish: Military and Lexical Aspects." *Tel Aviv* 11: 60–70.
Erbt, Wilhelm
 1902   *Jeremia und seine Zeit.* Göttingen: Vandenhoeck & Ruprecht.
Erman, Adolf
 1894   *Life in Ancient Egypt.* Tr. H. M. Tirard. London: Macmillan.
Everson, A. Joseph
 1974   "The Days of Yahweh." *JBL* 93: 329–37.
Fackenheim, Emil L.
 1990   "The Lament of Rachel and the New Covenant." *CrCu* 40: 341–49.

Feigin, Samuel
1933–34 "The Captives in Cuneiform Inscrptions I." *AJSLL* 50: 217–45.
Fensham, F. Charles
1982 "Nebukadrezzar in the Book of Jeremiah." *JNSL* 10: 53–65.
Ferry, J.
1998 "'Je restaurerai Juda et Israël' (*Jr* 33,7.9.26). L'écriture de *Jérémie* 33." *Trans* 15: 69–82.
Filson, Floyd V.
1943 "The Omission of Ezek. 12:26–28 and 36:23b–38 in Codex 967." *JBL* 62: 27–32.
Finesinger, Sol B.
1926 "Musical Instruments in the O.T." *HUCA* 3: 21–76.
Fischer, Georg
1991 "Jer 25 und die Fremdvölkersprüche: Unterschiede zwischen hebräischem und griechischem Text." *Biblica* 72: 474–99.
1993 *Das Trostbüchlein: Text, Komposition und Theologie von Jer 30–31.* SBB 26. Stuttgart: Katholisches Bibelwerk.
1995 "Aufnahme, Wende und Überwindung dtn/r Gedankengutes in Jer 30f" in *Jeremia und die 'deuteronomistische Bewegung'.* Ed. Walter Groß. BBB 98. Weinheim: Beltz Athenäum. Pp. 129–39.
1998 "Jeremia 52 — Ein Schlüssel zum Jeremiabuch." *Biblica* 79: 333–59.
2001a "Jeremia/Jeremiabuch" in RGG⁴ 4: 414–23.
2001b "Jeremiah 52: A Test Case for Jer LXX" in *X Congress of the International Organization for Septuagint and Cognate Studies* (Oslo, 1998). SBLSCSS 51. Ed. Bernard A. Taylor. Atlanta: Society of Biblical Literature. Pp. 37–48.
Fischer, Leopold
1910 "Die Urkunden in Jer 32 11–14 nach den Ausgrabungen und dem Talmud." *ZAW* 30: 136–42.
Fitzmyer, Joseph A.
1958 "The Aramaic Suzerainty Treaty from Sefire in the Museum of Beirut." *CBQ* 20: 444–76.
1961 "The Aramaic Inscriptions of Sefire I and II." *JAOS* 81: 178–222.
Fleming, Daniel E.
1986 "'House'/'City': An Unrecognized Parallel Word Pair." *JBL* 105: 689–97.
Fohrer, Georg
1972 "Vollmacht über Völker und Königreiche: Beobachtungen zu den prophetischen Fremdvölkersprüchen anhand von Jer 46–51" in *Wort, Lied und Gottesspruch. II: Beiträge zu Psalmen und Propheten* [Festschrift für Joseph Ziegler]. Ed. Josef Schreiner. Würzburg: Echter Verlag Katholisches Bibelwerk. Pp. 145–53. [=Fohrer 1981a: 44–52]
1981a *Studien zu alttestamentlichen Texten und Themen (1966–1972).* BZAW 155. Berlin: de Gruyter.
1981b "Der Israel-Prophet in Jeremia 30–31" in *Mélanges bibliques et orientaux en l'honneur de M. Henri Cazelles.* AOAT 212. Ed. A. Caquot and M. Delcor. Neukirchen-Vluyn: Neukirchener Verlag. Pp. 135–48. [=Fohrer 1991: 56–69]
Fox, Michael V.
1973a "Ṭôb as Covenant Terminology." *BASOR* 209: 41–42.

Freedman, David Noel
       1955   "God Compassionate and Gracious." WW 6: 6–24.
       1963c   "The Second Season at Ancient Ashdod." BA 26: 134–39.
       1976   "The Twenty-Third Psalm" in *Michigan Oriental Studies in Honor of
                 George G. Cameron*. Ed. Louis L. Orlin. Ann Arbor. Braun and Brum-
                 field. Pp. 139–66.
       1993   "Editing the Editors: Translation and Elucidation of the Text of the Bible"
                 in *Palimpsest: Editorial Theory in the Humanities*. Ed. G. Bornstein and
                 R. G. Williams. Ann Arbor: University of Michigan Press. Pp. 227–56.
                 [=Freedman 1997 I: 521–45]
       2000   *The Nine Commandments*. New York: Doubleday.
_____ and Frank M. Cross Jr. *See* Cross and Freedman.
_____ and Jack R. Lundbom
       1999   "Haplography in Jeremiah 1–20" in *Frank Moore Cross Volume*. Ed.
                 Baruch A. Levine et al. Eretz-Israel 26. Jerusalem: Israel Exploration So-
                 ciety and Hebrew Union College. Pp. 28–38.
Freedy, K. S., and D. B. Redford
       1970   "The Dates in Ezekiel in Relation to Biblical, Babylonian and Egyptian
                 Sources." *JAOS* 90: 462–85.
Frick, Frank S.
       1971   "The Rechabites Reconsidered." *JBL* 90: 279–87.
Friebel, Kelvin G.
       1999   *Jeremiah's and Ezekiel's Sign-Acts*. JSOT Supp 283. Sheffield: Sheffield
                 Academic Press.
Fried, Lisbeth S., and David Noel Freedman
       2001   "Was the Jubilee Year Observed in Preexilic Judah?" in Milgrom 2001:
                 2257–70.
Frymer, Tikva Simone
       1977   "The Nungal-Hymn and the Ekur-Prison." *JESHO* 20: 78–89.
Gaballa, G. A.
       1969   "Minor War Scenes of Ramesses II at Karnak." *JEA* 55: 82–88 + plates.
Gadd, C. J.
       1958   "The Harran Inscriptions of Nabonidus." *AnSt* 8: 35–92.
Gall, August von
       1904   "Jeremias 43,12 und das Zeitwort עטה." *ZAW* 24: 105–21.
Galling, Kurt
       1931   "Die Halle des Schreibers: Ein Beitrag zur Topographie der Akropolis von
                 Jerusalem." *PJB* 27: 51–57.
       1936   "Die Nekropole von Jerusalem." *PJB* 32: 73–101.
Garber, Paul Leslie
       1951   "Reconstructing Solomon's Temple." *BA* 14: 2–24.
       1958   "Reconsidering the Reconstruction of Solomon's Temple." With
                 Comments by William F. Albright and G. Ernest Wright. *JBL* 77:
                 123–33.
Gardiner, Alan H.
       1920   "The Ancient Military Road between Egypt and Palestine." *JEA* 6: 99–
                 116 + plates.
       1961   *Egypt of the Pharaohs*. Oxford: Clarendon Press.

Gaster, Theodor H.
  1947   "The Magical Inscription from Arslan Tash." *JNES* 6: 186–88.
  1976   *The Dead Sea Scriptures.* 3d rev. ed. Garden City, NY: Doubleday.
Gehman, Henry S.
  1940–41 "The 'Burden' of the Prophets." *JQR* 31: 107–21.
Gelb, I. J.
  1973   "Prisoners of War in Early Mesopotamia." *JNES* 32: 70–98.
Gelston, A.
  1993   "'Behold the Speaker': A Note on Isaiah xli 27." *VT* 43: 405–8.
Gemser, B.
  1952   "Be῾ēber Hajjardēn: In Jordan's Borderland." *VT* 2: 349–55.
Gerlach, Monica
  1986   "Zur chronologischen Struktur von Jer 30,12–17: Reflexion auf die involvierten grammatischen Ebenen." *BN* 33: 34–52.
Gershenson, Daniel E.
  1996   "A Greek Myth in Jeremiah." *ZAW* 108: 192–200.
Geva, Hillel
  1979   "The Western Boundary of Jerusalem at the End of the Monarchy." *IEJ* 29: 84–91.
Gevirtz, Stanley
  1973   "Evidence of Conjugational Variation in the Parallelization of Selfsame Verbs in the Amarna Letters." *JNES* 32: 99–104.
Gibson, Shimon
  1987   "The 1961–67 Excavations in the Armenian Garden, Jerusalem." *PEQ* 119: 81–96.
Ginsberg, H. L.
  1946   *The Legend of King Keret.* BASOR Supplementary Studies 2–3. New Haven: American Schools of Oriental Research.
Gitin, Seymour
  1990   "The Effects of Urbanization on a Philistine City-State: Tel Miqne–Ekron in the Iron Age II Period" in *Proceedings of the Tenth World Congress of Jewish Studies; Division A: The Bible and Its World.* Jerusalem: The World Union of Jewish Studies, The Hebrew University. Pp. 277–84.
  1993   "Seventh Century B.C.E. Cultic Elements at Ekron" in *Biblical Archaeology Today, 1990* [Proceedings of the Second International Congress on Biblical Archaeology]. Jerusalem: Israel Exploration Society. Pp. 248–58.
  1995   "Tel Miqne–Ekron in the 7th Century B.C.E.: The Impact of Economic Innovation and Foreign Cultural Influences on a Neo-Assyrian Vassal City State" in *Recent Excavations in Israel: A View to the West* [Archaeological Institute of America: Colloquia and Conference Papers No. 1]. Ed. S. Gitin. Dubuque, IA: Kendall / Hunt. Pp. 61–79 + plates.
  1997   "The Neo-Assyrian Empire with Its Western Periphery: The Levant, with a Focus on Philistine Ekron" in *Assyria 1995.* Ed. S. Parpola and R. M. Whiting. Helsinki: Helsinki University Press. Pp. 77–103.
  1998   "The Philistines in the Prophetic Texts: An Archaeological Perspective" in *Hesed ve- Emet: Studies in Honor of Ernest S. Frerichs.* Ed. Jodi Magness and Seymour Gitin. Brown Judaic Studies 320. Atlanta: Scholars Press. Pp. 273–90.

_____ and Amir Golani
2001 "The Tel Miqne–Ekron Silver Hoards: The Assyrian and Phoenician Connections" in *Hacksilber to Coinage: New Insights into the Monetary History of the Near East and Greece.* Ed. Miriam S. Balmuth. New York: The American Numismatic Society. Pp. 27–48.

_____ et al.
1997 "A Royal Dedicatory Inscription from Ekron." *IEJ* 47: 1–16.

Glaser, Eduard
1890 *Skizze der Geschichte und Geographie Arabiens.* 2d ed. Berlin: Weidmannsche Buchhandlung.

Glasson T. F.
1963 *Moses in the Fourth Gospel.* SBT 40. Naperville, IL: Allenson.

Glueck, Nelson
1939 *Explorations in Eastern Palestine, III.* AASOR 18–19. New Haven: American Schools of Oriental Research.
1970 *The Other Side of the Jordan.* Cambridge, MA: American Schools of Oriental Research.

Görg, Manfred
1985 "Zum Titel *BN HMLK* ('Königssohn')." *BN* 29: 7–11.

Goldenberg, Robert
1982 "The Problem of False Prophecy: Talmudic Interpretations of Jeremiah 28 and 1 Kings 22" in *The Biblical Mosaic.* Semeia Studies 10. Ed. Robert M. Polzin and Eugene Rothman. Philadelphia: Fortress and Chico, CA: Scholars Press. Pp. 87–103.

Goldman, Yohanan
1992 *Prophétie et royauté au retour de l'éxil.* OBO 118. Freiburg [Schweiz]: Universitätsverlag and Göttingen: Vandenhoeck & Ruprecht.

Gonen, Rivka
1975 *Weapons of the Ancient World.* London: Cassell.

Gorali, Mosche
1972 "Antike Musikinstrumente." *Ariel* 14: 68–73.

Gorringe, Henry H.
1882 *Egyptian Obelisks.* New York: Gorringe and Putnam's.

Gosse, Bernard
1986 "La malédiction contre Babylone de Jérémie 51,59–64 et les rédactions du livre de Jérémie." *ZAW* 98: 383–99.
1990 "Jérémie xlv et la place du recueil d'oracles contre les nations dans le livre de Jérémie." *VT* 40: 145–51.
1998 "The Masoretic Redaction of Jeremiah: An Explanation." *JSOT* 77: 75–80.

Grätz, Heinrich
1870 "Gedalja Sohn Achikam's Dauer seiner Statthalterschaft und Datum seines gewaltsamen Todes." *MGWJ* 19: 268–75.
1875 *Geschichte der Israeliten II.* Leipzig: Oskar Leiner.

Graham, J. N.
1984 "'Vinedressers and Plowmen': 2 Kings 25:12 and Jeremiah 52:16." *BA* 47: 55–58.

Graupner, Axel
    1991   *Auftrag und Geschick des Propheten Jeremia: Literarische Eigenart,*
              Herkunft und Intention vordeuteronomistischer Prosa im Jeremiabuch. BTS
              15. Neukirchen-Vluyn: Neukirchener Verlag.

Gray, John
    1970   *I and II Kings.* OTL. 2d rev. ed. London: SCM Press.

Grayson, A. Kirk
    1975a   *Assyrian and Babylonian Chronicles.* Locust Valley, NY: Augustin. [Re-
              printed, Winona Lake, IN: Eisenbrauns, 2000]
    1975b   *Babylonian Historical-Literary Texts.* Toronto: University of Toronto Press.
_____ and W. G. Lambert
    1964   "Akkadian Prophecies." *JCS* 18: 7–30.

Greenberg, Gillian
    2001   "Some Secondary Expansions in the Masoretic Text of Jeremiah: Retro-
              version Is Perilous but the Risk May Be Worthwhile" in *Biblical Hebrews,*
              Biblical Texts [Essays in Memory of Michael P. Weitzman]. Ed. Ada Rap-
              oport-Albert and Gillian Greenberg. JSOT Supp 333. London: Sheffield
              Academic Press. Pp. 222–43.

Greenberg, Moshe
    1983   *Ezekiel 1–20.* AB 22. Garden City, NY: Doubleday.
    1997   *Ezekiel 21–37.* AB 22A. New York: Doubleday.

Greenfield, Jonas C.
    1958   "Lexicographical Notes." *HUCA* 29: 203–28.
    1978   "The Meaning of פחז" in *Studies in Bible and the Ancient Near East*
              [Presented to Samuel E. Loewenstamm]. Ed. Yitzchak Avishur and
              Joshua Blau. Jerusalem: Rubinstein's. Pp. 35–40.
    1981   "Aramaic Studies and the Bible," VT Supp 32 [Congress Volume,
              Vienna, 1980]: 110–30.

Gressmann, Hugo
    1929   *Der Messias.* FRLANT New Series 26. Göttingen: Vandenhoeck &
              Ruprecht.

Grether, Oskar
    1934   *Name und Wort Gottes im Alten Testament.* BZAW 64. Giessen: Alfred
              Töpelmann.

Grothe, Jonathan F.
    1981   "An Argument for the Textual Genuineness of Jeremiah 33:14–26 (Mas-
              soretic Text)." *ConJ* 7: 188–91.

Gruber, Mayer I.
    1987   "Hebrew *Daʾăbôn nepeš* 'Dryness of Throat': From Symptom to Literary
              Convention." *VT* 37: 365–69. [=Gruber 1992: 185–92]

Guy, P. L.
    1938   *Megiddo Tombs.* Chicago: University of Chicago Press.

Habachi, Labib
    1977   *The Obelisks of Egypt.* London: Dent.

Haddad, George
    1982   "An Ethiopian Officer Forces the Hand of King Zedekiah: Jeremiah 38:1–
              13." *TR* 5: 58–62.

Hallo, William
    1966   "Akkadian Prophecies." *IEJ* 16: 231–42.

Halpern, Baruch
    1998   "The New Names of Isaiah 62:4: Jeremiah's Reception in the Restoration and the Politics of 'Third Isaiah.'" *JBL* 117: 623–43.

Hals, Ronald M.
    1988   "Some Aspects of the Exegesis of Jeremiah 31:31–34" in *When Jews and Christians Meet*. Ed. Jakob J. Petuchowski. Albany, NY: State University of New York Press. Pp. 87–97.

Hammershaimb, E.
    1966   *Some Aspects of Old Testament Prophecy from Isaiah to Malachi*. Copenhagen: Rosenkilde og Bagger.

Haran, Menahem
    1985c   "Bible Scrolls in Eastern and Western Jewish Communities from Qumran to the High Middle Ages." *HUCA* 56: 21–62.

Harper, William Rainey
    1905   *Amos and Hosea*. ICC. New York: Scribner's.

Hasel, Gerhard F.
    1972   *The Remnant: The History and Theology of the Remnant Ideas from Genesis to Isaiah*. AUM 5. Berrien Springs, MI: Andrews University Press.

Haupt, Paul
    1900   "Babylonian Elements in the Levitic Ritual." *JBL* 19: 55–81.
    1902   "The Hebrew Term שליש." *BASS* 4: 583–87.

Hayes, John H.
    1968   "The Usage of Oracles against Foreign Nations in Ancient Israel." *JBL* 87: 81–92.

_____ and Paul K. Hooker
    1988   *A New Chronology for the Kings of Israel and Judah*. Atlanta: John Knox.

Heaton, E. W.
    1952   "The Root שאר and the Doctrine of the Remnant." *JTS* New Series 3: 27–39.

Heinemann, Joseph
    1982   "A Homily on Jeremiah and the Fall of Jerusalem (*Pesiqta Rabbati, Pisqa 26*)" in *The Biblical Mosaic*. Semeia Studies 10. Ed. Robert M. Polzin and Eugene Rothman. Philadelphia: Fortress and Chico, CA: Scholars Press. Pp. 27–41.

Heltzer, Michael L.
    1968   "The Word ṣṣ in Ugaritic." *AION* 28: 355–61.
    2000   "Some Questions Concerning the Economic Policy of Josiah, King of Judah." *IEJ* 50: 105–8.

Hempel, Johannes
    1938   "Die Ostraka von Lakiš." *ZAW* 56: 126–39.

Herr, Larry G.
    1985   "The Servant of Baalis." *BA* 48: 169–72.
    1993a   "What Ever Happened to the Ammonites?" *BAR* 19/6: 26–35, 68.
    1993b   "The Search for Biblical Heshbon." *BAR* 19/6: 36–37, 68.
    1997   "The Iron Age II Period: Emerging Nations." *BA* 60: 114–83.

Herrmann, Wolfram
    1983   "Jeremia 23,23f als Zeugnis der Gotteserfahrung im babylonischen Zeitalter." *BZ* 27: 155–66.

Hertzberg, H. W.
   1952   "Jeremia und das Nordreich Israel." *TLZ* 77: 595–602.
Hicks, R. Lansing
   1983   "Delet and M^egillāh: A Fresh Approach to Jeremiah xxvi." *VT* 33: 46–66.
Hillers, Delbert R.
   1992   *Lamentations*. AB 7A. 2d ed. Garden City, NY: Doubleday.
Hoffmeier, James K.
   1981   "A New Insight on Pharaoh Apries from Herodotus, Diodorus, and Jeremiah 46:17." *JSSEA* 11: 165–70.
Hoftijzer, J., and G. van der Kooij
   1976   (eds.) *Aramaic Texts from Deir ʿAlla*. Leiden: Brill.
Hogarth, D. G.
   1914   *Carchemish I: Introductory*. Oxford: Trustees of the British Museum and Oxford University Press. [Reprint: London: British Museum, 1969]. Vol. II by C. L. Woolley (1921); Vol. III by Leonard Woolley and R. D. Barnett (1978).
Holladay, William L.
   1966c   "Jeremiah xxxi 22b Reconsidered: The Woman Encompasses the Man." *VT* 16: 236–39.
   1974   *Jeremiah: Spokesman Out of Time*. Philadelphia: Pilgrim.
Holmgren, Fredrick C.
   1999   *The Old Testament and the Significance of Jesus*. Grand Rapids: Eerdmans.
Honeyman, A. M.
   1940   "Observations on a Phonecian Inscription of Ptolemaic Date." *JEA* 26: 57–67 + plate.
   1948   "The Evidence for Regnal Names among the Hebrews." *JBL* 67: 13–25.
Horn, Siegfried H., and L. H. Wood
   1954   "The Fifth-Century Jewish Calendar at Elephantine." *JNES* 13: 1–20.
Hossfeld, F.-L., and I. Meyer
   1974   "Der Prophet vor dem Tribunal: Neuer Auslegungsversuch von Jer 26." *ZAW* 86: 30–50.
Howard, Margaret
   1955   "Technical Description of the Ivory Writing-Boards from Nimrud." *Iraq* 17: 14–20.
Huddlestun, John R.
   1995   " 'Who Is This That Rises Like the Nile?' Some Egyptian Texts on the Inundation and a Prophetic Trope" in *Fortunate the Eyes That See* [Essays in Honor of David Noel Freedman]. Ed. Astrid B. Beck et al. Grand Rapids: Eerdmans. Pp. 338–63.
   f.c.   *"Who Is This That Rises Like the Nile?" A Comparative Study of the River Nile in Ancient Egypt and the Hebrew Bible*. OBO. Fribourg [Suisse]: Univeritätsverlag and Göttingen: Vandenhoeck & Ruprecht.
Huffmon, Herbert B.
   1999   "The Impossible: God's Words of Assurance in Jeremiah 31:35–37" in *On the Way to Nineveh* [Studies in Honor of George M. Landes]. Ed. Stephen L. Cook and S. C. Winter. Atlanta: American Schools of Oriental Research and Scholars Press. Pp. 172–86.

Hultgren, Arland J.
    2000   *The Parables of Jesus: A Commentary.* Grand Rapids: Eerdmans.
Humbert, Paul
    1933   "Die Herausforderungsformel 'hinnenî êlékâ.'" *ZAW* 51: 101–8.
Hunger, Hermann
    1968   *Babylonische und assyrische Kolophone.* AOAT 2. Neukirchen-Vluyn:
                Neukirchener Verlag.
Husser, Jean-Marie
    1999   *Dreams and Dream Narratives in the Biblical World.* Tr. Jill M. Munro.
                Sheffield: Sheffield Academic Press.
Huwyler, Beat
    1997   *Jeremia und die Völker: Untersuchungen zu den Völkersprüchen in Jeremia
                46–49.* FAT 20. Tübingen: Mohr Siebeck.
Hyatt, J. Philip
    1939   "The Deity Bethel and the Old Testament." *JAOS* 59: 81–98.
    1956   "New Light on Nebuchadrezzar and Judean History." *JBL* 75: 277–85.
    1966   "The Beginning of Jeremiah's Prophecy." *ZAW* 78: 204–14. [=Perdue and
                Kovacs 1984: 63–72]
Irwin, William A.
    1931–32 "An Ancient Biblical Text." *AJSLL* 48: 184–93.
Jackson, Kent P.
    1989   "The Language of the Mesha‹ Inscription" in Dearman 1989a: 96–130.
Jacobsen, Thorkild
    1943   "Primitive Democracy in Ancient Mesopotamia." *JNES* 2: 159–72.
                [=Jacobsen 1970: 157–70]
    1970   *Toward the Image of Tammuz and Other Essays on Mesopotamian History
                and Culture.* Ed. William L. Moran. Cambridge, MA: Harvard University
                Press.
Jahnow, Hedwig
    1923   *Das hebräische Leichenlied im Rahmen der Völkerdichtung.* BZAW 36.
                Giessen: Alfred Töpelmann.
James, Frances
    1966   *The Iron Age at Beth Shan.* Philadelphia: Museum of the University of
                Pennsylvania.
Janzen, Waldemar
    1972   *Mourning Cry and Woe Oracle.* BZAW 125. Berlin: de Gruyter.
    1981   "Withholding the Word" in *Traditions in Transformation* [Essays in Honor
                of Frank Moore Cross]. Ed. Baruch Halpern and Jon D. Levenson.
                Winona Lake, IN: Eisenbrauns. Pp. 97–114.
Japhet, Sara, and Robert B. Salters
    1985   (eds.) *The Commentary of R. Samuel Ben Meir* Rashbam *on Qoheleth.*
                Jerusalem: Magnes Press and Leiden: Brill.
Jeremias, Joachim
    1933   "Moreseth-Gath, die Heimat des Propheten Micha." *PJB* 29: 42–53.
    1955   *The Eucharistic Words of Jesus.* New York: Macmillan.
Jirku, Anton
    1921   "Neues keilinschriftliches Material zum Alten Testament." *ZAW* 39: 144–
                60.

Johnson, Aubrey R.
1953   "The Primary Meaning of גאל√" in VT Supp 1 [Congress Volume, Copenhagen, 1953]: 67–77.

Jones, Brian C.
1991   "In Search of Kir Hareseth: A Case Study in Site Identification." *JSOT* 52: 3–24.

Jones, Douglas
1963   "The Cessation of Sacrifice after the Destruction of the Temple in 586 B.C." *JTS* New Series 14: 21–31.

de Jong, C.
1981   "Deux oracles contre les Nations, reflets de la politique étrangère de Joaqim" in P.-M. Bogaert 1981a: 369–79.

Joüon, Paul
1937   "Un parallèle a la 'sépulture d'un ane' de Jérémie (xxii, 19) en arabe moderne de Palmyre." *RSR* 27: 355–56.

Kallai, Zecharia
1986   *Historical Geography of the Bible.* Jerusalem: Magnes Press and Leiden: Brill.

Kaminsky, Joel S.
1995   *Corporate Responsibility in the Hebrew Bible.* JSOT Supp 196. Sheffield: Sheffield Academic Press.

Kartveit, Magnar
2001   "Sions dotter." *TTK*1: 97–112.

Katho, Bungishabaku
2001   "Jeremiah 22: Implications for the Exercise of Political Power in Africa" in *Interpreting the Old Testament in Africa.* BTA 2. New York: Peter Lang. Pp. 153–58.

Katzenstein, H. J.
1983   "'Before Pharaoh Conquered Gaza' (Jeremiah xlvii 1)." *VT* 33: 249–51.
1994   "Gaza in the Neo-Babylonian Period (626–539 B.C.E.)." *Trans* 7: 35–49.

Keel, Othmar
1974   *Wirkmächtige Siegeszeichen im Alten Testament.* OBO 5. Freiburg [Schweiz]: Universitätsverlag and Göttingen: Vandenhoeck & Ruprecht.

Kegler, Jürgen
1980   "Das Leid des Nachbarvolkes: Beobachtungen zu den Fremdvölkersprüchen Jeremias" in *Werden und Wirken des Alten Testaments* [Festschrift für Claus Westermann]. Ed. Rainer Albertz et al. Göttingen: Vandenhoeck & Ruprecht and Neukirchen-Vluyn: Neukirchener Verlag. Pp. 271–87.

Kenyon, Kathleen M.
1967   *Jerusalem: Excavating 3000 Years of History.* [London]: Thames and Hudson.

Kessler, Martin
1966   "Form-Critical Suggestions on Jer 36." *CBQ* 28: 389–401.
1973   "Rhetoric in Jeremiah 50 and 51." *Semitics* 3: 18–35.

Kida, Kenichi
1993   "The Sovereignty of God and the Destiny of the Nations in the Prophecies of Amos, Isaiah and Jeremiah" in *Konsequente Traditionsgeschichte* [Festschrift für Klaus Baltzer]. Ed. Rüdiger Bartelmus et al. OBO 126.

Freiburg [Schweiz]: Universitätsverlag and Göttingen: Vandenhoeck &
Ruprecht. Pp. 169–81.

Kilpp, Nelson
1985   "Eine frühe Interpretation der Katastrophe von 587." *ZAW* 97: 210–20.
1990   *Niederreissen und aufbauen: Das Verhältnis von Heilsverheissung und
          Unheilsverkündigung bei Jeremia und im Jeremiabuch.* BTS 13.
          Neukirchen-Vluyn: Neukirchener Verlag.

King, Leonard W.
1919   *A History of Babylon from the Foundation of the Monarchy to the Persian
          Conquest.* London: Chatto & Windus.

King, Martin Luther Jr.
1959   *The Measure of a Man.* Philadelphia: Pilgrim.

King, Philip J.
1999   "Travel, Transport, Trade" in *Frank Moore Cross Volume.* Ed. Baruch
          A. Levine et al. Eretz-Israel 26. Jerusalem: Israel Exploration Society.
          Pp. 94–105.

Kingsbury, Edwin C.
1964   "The Prophets and the Council of Yahweh." *JBL* 83: 279–86.

Klausner, Joseph
1956   *The Messianic Idea in Israel.* 3d ed. Tr. W. F. Stinespring. London:
          Allen and Unwin. Original editions, 1902 (part III); 1909 (part I); and
          1921 (part II).

Klein, Ralph W.
1980   "Jeremiah 23:1–8." *Int* 34: 167–72.

Kletter, Raz
1996   *The Judean Pillar-Figurines and the Archaeology of Asherah.* Oxford: Tem-
          pus Reparatum.

Kloner, Amos
1982–83   "Rock-Cut Tombs in Jerusalem." *BAIAS*: 37–40.

Knights, Chris H.
1993   "The Nabataeans and the Rechabites." *JSS* 38: 227–33.
1995–96   "Who Were the Rechabites?" *ET* 107: 137–40.
1996–97   " 'Standing Before Me Forever': Jeremiah 35:19." *ET* 108: 40–42.
1997–98   "Jeremiah 35 in the Book of Jeremiah." *ET* 109: 207–8.

Knudtzon, J. A.
1964   *Die El-Amarna-Tafeln I.* VAB 2. Aalen: Zeller. Originally 1915.

Kob, Konrad
1932   "Netopha." *PJB* 28: 47–54.

Kooij, Arie van der
1994   "Jeremiah 27:5–15: How Do MT and LXX Relate to Each Other?" *JNSL*
          20: 59–78.
1998   "The Death of Josiah according to 1 Esdras." *Textus* 19: 97–109.

Kopf, L.
1958   "Arabische Etymologien und Parallelen zum Bibelwörterbuch." *VT* 8:
          161–215.

Kraeling, Emil G.
1953   (ed.) *The Brooklyn Museum Aramaic Papyri.* New Haven: The Brooklyn
          Museum and Yale University Press.

Kramer, Samuel Noah
1951 "The Sumerian School: A Pre-Greek System of Education" in *Studies Presented to David Moore Robinson I*. Ed. George E. Mylonas. St. Louis: Washington University. Pp. 238–45.
1982 "BM 98396: A Sumerian Prototype of the *Mater-Dolorosa*" in *Harry M. Orlinsky Volume*. Ed. Baruch A. Levine and Abraham Malamat. Eretz-Israel 16. Jerusalem: Israel Exploration Society. Pp. 141–46.
1983 "The Weeping Goddess: Sumerian Prototypes of the *Mater Dolorosa*." *BA* 46: 69–80.
Krašovec, Jože
1993 "Vergebung und neuer Bund nach Jer 31,31–34." *ZAW* 105: 428–44.
Kraus, Hans-Joachim
1964 *Prophetie in der Krisis: Studien zu Texten aus dem Buch Jeremia*. BSt 43. Neukirchen-Vluyn: Neukirchener Verlag.
Kremers, Heinz
1953 "Leidensgemeinschaft mit Gott im Alten Testament: Eine Untersuchung der 'biographischen' Berichte im Jeremiabuch." *EvTh* 13: 122–40.
Kselman, John S.
1979 "*RB / KBD*: A New Hebrew-Akkadian Formulaic Pair." *VT* 29: 110–13.
Kuenen, A.
1894 " 'Die Melecheth des Himmels' in c. 7 und 44 des Buches Jeremia" in *Gesammelte Abhandlungen zur biblischen Wissenschaft*. Tr. K. Budde. Leipzig: Mohr (Siebeck). Pp. 186–211.
Kuhrt, Amélie
1995 *The Ancient Near East c. 3000–330 BC Volume II*. London: Routledge.
Kuschke, Arnulf
1961a "Jeremia 48,1–8: Zugleich ein Beitrag zur historischen Topographie Moabs" in *Verbannung und Heimkehr* [Festschrift für Wilhelm Rudolph]. Ed. Arnulf Kuschke. Tübingen: Mohr (Siebeck). Pp. 181–96.
1961b "Das Deutsche Evangelische Institut für Altertumswissenschaft des Heiligen Landes Lehrkursus 1960." *ZDPV* 77: 1–37.
1967 "Horonaim and Qiryathaim." *PEQ* 99: 104–5.
LaBianca, Øystein S., and Randall W. Younker
1995 "The Kingdoms of Ammon, Moab and Edom: The Archaeology of Society in Late Bronze / Iron Age Transjordan (ca. 1400–500 BCE)" in *The Archaeology of Society in the Holy Land*. Ed. Thomas E. Levy. London: Leicester University Press. Pp. 399–415.
Lambdin, Thomas O.
1953 "Egyptian Loan Words in the Old Testament." *JAOS* 73: 145–55.
Lambert, W. G.
1957 "Ancestors, Authors, and Canonicity." *JCS* 11: 1–14.
1970 "History and the Gods: A Review Article." *Orientalia* 39: 170–77.
1972 "Nabonidus in Arabia" in *Proceedings of the Fifth Seminar for Arabian Studies* [Oriental Institute, Oxford, September 1971]. London: Seminar for Arabian Studies. Pp. 53–64.
Lamon, Robert S., and Geoffrey M. Shipton
1939 *Megiddo I*. Chicago: University of Chicago Press.
Lance, H. Darrell
1971 "The Royal Stamps and the Kingdom of Judah." *HTR* 64: 315–32.

Landes, George M.
　1956　　"The Fountain at Jazer." *BASOR* 144: 30–37.
　1961　　"The Material Civilization of the Ammonites." *BA* 24: 66–86.
Landsberger, Franz
　1949　　"The House of the People." *HUCA* 22: 149–55.
Lane, W. H.
　1923　　*Babylonian Problems*. London: Murray.
Lang, Bernhard
　1983　　"Ein babylonisches Motiv in Israels Schöpfungsmythologie (Jer 27,5–6)."
　　　　　BZ 27: 236–37.
Lanham, Richard A.
　1968　　*A Handlist of Rhetorical Terms*. Berkeley: University of California Press.
Lauterbach, Jacob Z.
　1939　　"The Belief in the Power of the Word." *HUCA* 14: 287–302.
Layton, Scott
　1986　　"Biblical Hebrew 'To Set the Face' in Light of Akkadian and Ugaritic."
　　　　　UF 17: 169–81.
Leene, Hendrik
　1992　　"Jeremiah 31, 23–26 and the Redaction of the Book of Comfort." *ZAW*
　　　　　104: 349–64.
Lehmann, Manfred R.
　1953　　"A New Interpretation of the Term שדמות." *VT* 3: 361–71.
Lemaire, André
　1979　　"Note sur le titre *bn hmlk* dans l'ancien Israël." *Sem* 29: 59–65.
Lemche, Niels Peter
　1976　　"The Manumission of Slaves—The Fallow Year—The Sabbatical Year—
　　　　　The Jobel Year." *VT* 26: 38–59.
Lemke, Werner E.
　1966　　"Nebuchadrezzar, My Servant." *CBQ* 28: 45–50.
　1981　　"The Near and Distant God: A Study of Jer 23:23–24 in Its Biblical Theo-
　　　　　logical Context." *JBL* 100: 541–55.
　1983　　"Jeremiah 31:31–34." *Int* 37: 183–87.
Lesko, Leonard H.
　1977　　*King Tut's Wine Cellar*. Berkeley: B. C. Scribe.
　1996　　"Egyptian Wine Production during the New Kingdom" in *The Origins
　　　　　and Ancient History of Wine*. Ed. Patrick E. McGovern et al. Amsterdam:
　　　　　Overseas Publishers / Gordon and Breach. Pp. 215–30.
Levenson, Jon D.
　1976　　"On the Promise to the Rechabites." *CBQ* 38: 508–14.
　1984　　"The Last Four Verses in Kings." *JBL* 103: 353–61.
Levey, Samson H.
　1974　　*The Messiah: An Aramaic Interpretation*. MHUC 2. Cincinnati: Hebrew
　　　　　Union College Press.
Levin, Adina
　1996　　"A Newly Discovered Ammonite Seal." *IEJ* 46: 243–47.
Levin, Christoph
　1985　　*Die Verheißung des neuen Bundes*. FRLANT 137. Göttingen: Vanden-
　　　　　hoeck & Ruprecht.

Lewy, Julius
1958 "The Biblical Institution of *D⁽ᵉ⁾rôr* in the Light of Akkadian Documents" in *Benjamin Mazar Volume*. Ed. M. Avi-Yonah et al. Eretz-Israel 5. Jerusalem: Israel Exploration Society. Pp. 21–31.

Licht, J.
1963 "Paralipomena Jeremiae" [Hebrew with English summary]. *ABIU* 1: 66–80, xxi–xxii.

Lichtheim, Miriam
1980 *Ancient Egyptian Literature Volume III*. Berkeley: University of California Press.

Liebreich, Leon J.
1955–56 "The Compilation of the Book of Isaiah." *JQR* 46: 259–77.

Lindars, Barnabas
1979 "'Rachel Weeping for Her Children'—Jeremiah 31:15–22." *JSOT* 12: 47–62.

Lindsay, John
1976 "The Babylonian Kings and Edom, 605–550 B.C." *PEQ* 108: 23–39.

Lindström, Fredrik
1983 *God and the Origin of Evil*. CB OT Series 21. Lund: CWK Gleerup.

Lipiński, Edward
1970a "באחרית הימים dans les textes préexiliques." *VT* 20: 445–50.
1970b "Se battre la cuisse." *VT* 20: 495.
1972 "The Egypto-Babylonian War of the Winter 601–600 B.C." *AION* 32: 235–41.
1974 "Prose ou Poésie en Jér. xxxiv 1–7?" *VT* 24: 112–13.

Lipschits, Oded
1998 "Nebuchadrezzar's Policy in 'Ḫattu-Land' and the Fate of the Kingdom of Judah." *UF* 30: 467–87.

Lloyd, Seton, and Fuad Sufar
1945 "Tell Hassura: Excavations by the Iraq Government Directorate General of Antiquities in 1943 and 1944." *JNES* 4: 255–89 + figures and plates.

Loader, J. A.
1991 "The Prophets and Sodom: The Prophetic Use of Sodom and Gomorrah Theme." *HTS* 47: 5–25.

Loewenstamm, Samuel E.
1969 "The Expanded Colon in Ugaritic and Biblical Verse." *JSS* 14: 176–96.

Lohfink, Norbert
1981 "Der junge Jeremia als Propagandist und Poet: Zum Grundstock von Jer 30–31" in P.-M. Bogaert 1981a: 351–68. [=Lohfink 1991a: 87–106]
1991a *Studien zum Deuteronomium und zur deuteronomistischen Literatur II*. SBA 12. Stuttgart: Katholisches Bibelwerk.
1991b *The Covenant Never Revoked*. Tr. John J. Scullion. New York: Paulist Press. [German: *Der Niemals Gekündigte Bund*. Freiburg: Herder, 1989]

Lombardi, Guido
1970 "Ḥ. Fārāh-W. Fārāh, presso ʿAnatot e la questione della tomba di Raḥel." *LA* 20: 299–352.
1971 *La Tomba di Raḥel*. PSBF 11. Jerusalem: Franciscan Printing Press.

Long, Burke O.
1971 "Two Question and Answer Schemata in the Prophets." *JBL* 90: 129–39.

Lord, David N.
    1854   *The Characteristics and Laws of Figurative Language.* New York: Franklin Knight.

Loud, Gordon
    1948   *Megiddo II: Plates.* Chicago: University of Chicago Press.
_____ et al.
    1936   *Khorsabad I: Excavations in the Palace and at a City Gate.* Chicago: University of Chicago Press.

Lucas, Alfred
    1934   *Ancient Egyptian Materials and Industries.* 2d rev. ed. London: Edward Arnold.

Luckenbill, Daniel David
    1924–25 "The Black Stone of Esarhaddon." *AJSLL* 41: 165–73.
    1926   *Ancient Records of Assyria and Babylonia I.* Chicago: University of Chicago Press.
    1927   *Ancient Records of Assyria and Babylonia II.* Chicago: University of Chicago Press.

Ludwig, Theodore M.
    1968   "The Shape of Hope: Jeremiah's Book of Consolation." *CTM* 39: 526–41.

Luke, K.
    1992   "Ararat, Minni and Ashkenaz (Jer 51:27)." *ITS* 29: 185–205.

Lundbom, Jack R.
    1975a   "Double-Duty Subject in Hosea viii 5." *VT* 25: 228–30.
    2001   "Hebrew Rhetoric" in *EncRhet*: 325–28.

Luria, Ben-Zion
    1975   "And I Will Make Thee a Burnt Mountain." [Hebrew with English summary] *BeitM* 64: 118–23, 171.
    1982   "ירמיהו כ׳׳ו ומשפחת שפן." *BeitM* 89–90: 97–100.

Lust, Johan
    1981   "'Gathering and Return' in Jeremiah and Ezekiel" in P.-M. Bogaert 1981a: 119–42.
    1994   "The Diverse Text Forms of Jeremiah and History Writing with Jer 33 as a Test Case." *JNSL* 20: 31–48.

Lutz, Henry Ludwig
    1939   *The Concept of Change in the Life and Thought of the Babylonians.* [Berkeley?]: Publisher unknown.

Lys, Daniel
    1979   "Jérémie 28 et le problème du faux prophète ou la circulation du sens dans le diagnostic prophétique." *RHPhR* 59: 453–82.

Macalister, R. A.
    1912   "The Topography of Rachel's Tomb." *PEFQS*: 74–82 + plates.
    1914   *The Philistines: Their History and Civilization.* Schweich Lecture of the British Academy 1911. London: British Academy and Oxford University Press.

MacDonald, Burton
    1999   "Ammonite Territory and Sites" in MacDonald and Younker 1999: 1–19.
_____ and Randall W. Younker
    1999   (eds.) *Ancient Ammon.* Leiden: Brill.

Machinist, Peter
    1982   "Provincial Governance in Middle Assyria and Some New Texts from Yale." *Assur* 3/2: 65–101 + plates.

Malamat, Abraham
    1950–51 "The Historical Setting of Two Biblical Prophecies on the Nations." *IEJ* 1: 149–59. [=Malamat 2001: 370–80]
    1951   "Jeremiah and the Last Two Kings of Judah." *PEQ* 83: 81–87. [=Malamat 2001: 381–86]
    1966   "Prophetic Revelations in New Documents from Mari and the Bible" in VT Supp 15 [Volume du Congrès, Genève, 1965]: 207–27. [Published also in *E. L. Sukenik Memorial Volume* (Hebrew with English summary). Ed. N. Avigad et al. Eretz-Israel 8. Jerusalem: Israel Exploration Society, 1967. Pp. 231–40; 75]
    1968   "The Last Kings of Judah and the Fall of Jerusalem." *IEJ* 18: 137–56.
    1971   "Mari." *BA* 34: 2–22.
    1973   "Josiah's Bid for Armageddon: The Background for the Judean-Egyptian Encounter in 609 B.C." *JANES* 5: 267–79. [=Malamat 2001: 282–98]
    1979   "The Last Years of the Kingdom of Judah" in *The World History of the Jewish People: The Age of the Monarchies: Political History.* Vol. 4/1. Ed. Abraham Malamat. Jerusalem: Massada. Pp. 205–21, 377.
    1990   "The Kingdom of Judah between Egypt and Babylon." *ST* 44: 65–77. [=Malamat 2001: 322–37]
    1995   "A Note on the Ritual of Treaty Making in Mari and the Bible." *IEJ* 45: 226–29.
    1999   "Naamah, the Ammonite Princess, King Solomon's Wife." *RB* 106: 35–40.
    2001   *History of Biblical Israel: Major Problems and Minor Issues.* Leiden: Brill.

Mansoor, Menahem
    1961–62 "The Thanksgiving Hymns and the Massoretic Text (Part II)." *RQ* 3: 387–94.

Marconcini, Benito
    1993   "La novità nell 'alleanza' secondo Geremia 31,31–34." *VH* 4: 207–24.

Martens, Karen
    2001   "'With a Strong Hand and an Outstretched Arm.'" *SJOT* 15: 123–41.

Maspero, G.
    1900   *The Passing of the Empires* 850 B.C. to 330 B.C. Ed. A. H. Sayce. Tr. M. L. McClure. London: Society for Promoting Christian Knowledge.

Matthiae, Paulo
    1980   *Ebla: An Empire Rediscovered.* Tr. Christopher Holme. London: Hodder & Stoughton.

Mattingly, Gerald
    1989   "Moabite Religion and the Mesha⁽ Inscription" in Dearman 1989a: 211–38.

May, Herbert G.
    1935   *Material Remains of the Megiddo Cult.* Chicago: University of Chicago Press.
    1939   "Three Hebrew Seals and the Status of Exiled Jehoiakin." *AJSLL* 56: 146–48.

1942   "Towards an Objective Approach to the Book of Jeremiah: The Biographer." *JBL* 61: 139–55.

1955   "Some Cosmic Connotations of *Mayim Rabbîm*, 'Many Waters.'" *JBL* 74: 9–21.

1961   "Individual Responsibility and Retribution." *HUCA* 32: 107–20.

Mazar [Maisler], Benjamin

1958   "Jerusalem" [Hebrew] in *EncMiqr* 3: 791–837.

1961   "Geshur and Maacah." *JBL* 80: 16–28.

_____ et al.

1993   "Jerusalem: Early Periods and the First Temple Period" in *NEAEHL* 2: 698–716.

McCarter, P. Kyle Jr.

1980   *I Samuel.* AB 8. Garden City, NY: Doubleday.

McCarthy, Dennis J.

1963   *Treaty and Covenant.* AnBib 21. Rome: Pontifical Biblical Institute.

McCown, Chester Charlton

1947   *Tell en-Naṣbeh I: Archaeological and Historical Results.* Berkeley: The Palestine Institute of the Pacific School of Religion and New Haven: The American Schools of Oriental Research.

McKane, William

1980a   "מַשָּׂא in Jeremiah 23, 33–40" in *Prophecy* [Essays Presented to Georg Fohrer]. BZAW 150. Ed. J. A. Emerton. Berlin: de Gruyter. Pp. 35–54.

1995   "Jeremiah and the Wise" in *Wisdom in Ancient Israel* [Essays in Honour of J. A. Emerton]. Ed. John Day et al. Cambridge: Cambridge University Press. Pp. 142–51.

Meek, Theophile J.

1951   "Archaeology and a Point in Hebrew Syntax." *BASOR* 122: 31–33.

Meier, Gerhard

1937   *Die assyrische Beschwörungssammlung Maqlû.* AfO 2. Berlin: Ernst F. Weidner.

Meier, Samuel A.

1988   *The Messenger in the Ancient Semitic World.* HSM 45. Atlanta: Scholars Press.

Mendecki, Norbert

1983   "Die Sammlung und die Hineinführung in das Land in Jer 23,3." *Kairos* 25: 99–103.

1988   "Jer 31,7–9: Berührungen mit der Botschaft Deuterojesajas?" in *Wünschet Jerusalem Frieden* [XII Congress of IOSOT]. Ed. Matthias Augustin and Klaus-Dietrich Schunk. BATAJ 13. Frankfort: Peter Lang. Pp. 323–36.

Mendelsohn, Isaac

1949   *Slavery in the Ancient Near East.* New York: Oxford University Press.

Meshorer, Yaʿakov

1978   "Early Means of Payment and the First Coinage." *Ariel* 45–46: 127–43.

1998   *Ancient Means of Exchange, Weights and Coins.* Haifa: University of Haifa.

Meyer, Martin A.

1907   *History of the City of Gaza.* Columbia University Oriental Series 5. New York: Columbia University Press.

Meyers, Carol L.
1991   "Of Drums and Damsels." *BA* 54: 16–27.
Michel, Ernst
1947–52 "Ein neuentdeckter Annalen-Text Salmanassars III." *WO* 1: 454–75.
Migsch, Herbert
1996   *Jeremias Ackerkauf: Eine Untersuchung von Jeremia 32.* ÖBS 15. Frank-
        furt: Peter Lang.
1997   "Die Vorbildlichen Rechabiter: Zur Redestruktur von Jeremia xxxv."
        VT 47: 316–28.
2001   "Zur Interpretation von *wᵉʾet kål-bêt hārekābîm* in Jeremia xxxv 3." *VT* 51:
        385–89.
Milgrom, Jacob
1998   "The Nature and Extent of Idolatry in Eighth–Seventh Century Judah."
        HUCA 69: 1–13.
2001   *Leviticus 23–37.* AB 3B. New York: Doubleday.
Millard, Alan R.
1999   "Owners and Users of Hebrew Seals" in *Frank Moore Cross Volume.*
        Ed. Baruch A. Levine et al. Eretz-Israel 26. Jerusalem: Israel Explora-
        tion Society. Pp. 129–33.
Miller, James E.
1990   "Dreams and Prophetic Visions." *Biblica* 71: 401–4.
Miller, J. Maxwell
1989   "Moab and the Moabites" in Dearman 1989a: 1–40.
1991   (ed.) *Archaeological Survey of the Kerak Plateau.* ASOR Archaeological
        Reports 1. Atlanta: Scholars Press.
1992   "Early Monarch in Moab?" in Bienkowski 1992: 77–91.
1997   "Ancient Moab: Still Largely Unknown." *BA* 60: 194–204.
_____ and John H. Hayes
1986   *A History of Ancient Israel and Judah.* Philadelphia: Westminster.
Miller, Patrick D. Jr.
1968   "The Divine Council and the Prophetic Call to War." *VT* 18: 100–107.
1970   "Animal Names as Designations in Ugaritic and Hebrew." *UF* 2: 177–86.
1982   *Sin and Judgment in the Prophets: A Stylistic and Theological Analysis.*
        SBLMS 27. Chico, CA: Scholars Press.
1984   "Sin and Judgment in Jeremiah 34:17–19." *JBL* 103: 611–13.
Minns, Ellis H.
1915   "Parchments of the Parthian Period from Auroman in Kurdistan." *JHS* 35:
        22–65.
Mitchell, Hinckley G.
1879   *An Examination of Some of the Final Constructions of Biblical Hebrew.*
        Leipzig: Ackermann & Glaser.
Mittmann, Siegfried
1982   "The Ascent of Luhith" in *Studies in the History and Archeology of Jor-
        dan I.* Ed. Adnan Hadidi. Amman: Department of Antiquities,
        Hashemite Kingdom of Jordan. Pp. 175–80.
Montgomery, James A.
1934   *Arabia and the Bible.* Philadelphia: University of Pennsylvania Press.
1951   *The Book of Kings.* Ed. Henry Snyder Gehman. ICC. Edinburgh: T. & T.
        Clark.

Moore, Carey A.
    1977   *Daniel, Esther and Jeremiah: The Additions.* AB 44. Garden City, NY:
            Doubleday.
Moore, George F.
    1927   *Judaism in the First Centuries of the Christian Era: The Age of the Tannaim
            I–II.* Cambridge, MA: Harvard University Press.
Moran, William L.
    1958   "Ugaritic ṣîṣûma and Hebrew ṣîṣ (Eccles 43,19; Jer 48,9)." *Biblica* 39: 69–
            71.
    1963c   "A Note on the Treaty Terminology of the Sefire Stelas." *JNES* 22: 173–
            76.
Morgenstern, Julian
    1929   "The Gates of Righteousness." *HUCA* 6: 1–37.
    1961   "The 'Son of Man' of Daniel 7 13f.: A New Interpretation." *JBL* 80: 65–77.
Morla Asensio, Victor
    1988   "Dos Notas Filologicas: Jr 29,22 y Eclo 8:10b." *EB* 46: 249–51.
Morris, Nathan
    1929–33 "Jeremiah 25:10." *TGUOS* 6: 68.
Moulton, Wilfrid J.
    1906   "The New Covenant in Jeremiah." *The Expositor* 7th Series 1: 370–82.
Mowinckel, Sigmund
    1956   *He That Cometh.* Tr. G. W. Anderson. Oxford: Blackwell.
Muilenburg, James
    1947a   "The Literary Sources Bearing on the Question of Identification" in *Tell
            en-Naṣbeh I.* Ed. C. C. McCown. Berkeley: The Palestine Institute of the
            Pacific School of Religion, and New Haven: The American Schools of
            Oriental Research. Pp. 23–44.
    1947b   "The History of Mizpah of Benjamin" in *Tell en-Naṣbeh I.* Ed. C. C. Mc-
            Cown. Berkeley: The Palestine Institute of the Pacific School of Religion,
            and New Haven: The American Schools of Oriental Research. Pp. 45–49.
    1955   "Mizpah of Benjamin." *ST* 8: 25–42.
    1960   "Father and Son." *TL* 3: 177–87.
    1962a   "Book of Obadiah" in *IDB* K–Q: 578–79.
Mullo-Weir, Cecil J.
    1929a   "Fragment of an Expiation-Ritual against Sickness." *JRAS*: 281–84.
    1929b   "Fragments of Two Assyrian Prayers." *JRAS*: 761–66.
Myres, John L.
    1948   "King Solomon's Temple and Other Buildings and Works of Art." *PEQ*
            80: 14–41.
Na'aman, Nadav
    1986   *Borders and Districts in Biblical Historiography.* Jerusalem: Simor.
Naveh, J.
    1963   "Old Hebrew Inscriptions in a Burial Cave." *IEJ* 13: 74–92.
Niebuhr, Reinhold
    1935   "Marx, Barth and Israel's Prophets." *CCen* 52: 138–40.
Nielsen, Eduard
    1954   *Oral Tradition.* SBT 11. Chicago: Allenson and London: SCM Press.

Noegel, Scott B.
　1996　　"*Atbash* (אתב״ש) in Jeremiah and Its Literary Significance I–III." *JBQ* 24: 82–89, 160–66, 247–50.

North, Christopher R.
　1958　　"The Essence of Idolatry" in *Von Ugarit nach Qumran* [Festschrift für Otto Eissfeldt]. Ed. Johannes Hempel and Leonhard Rost et al. BZAW 77. Berlin: Alfred Töpelmann. Pp. 151–60.

Noth, Martin
　1966a　　*The Laws in the Pentateuch and Other Studies.* Tr. D. R. Ap-Thomas. Edinburgh: Oliver and Boyd.
　1966b　　*The Old Testament World.* Tr. Victor I. Gruhn. Philadelphia: Fortress.
　1981　　*The Deuteronomic History.* JSOT Supp 15. Sheffield: JSOT Press. Originally 1943.

Olley, J. W.
　1998　　"Texts Have Paragraphs Too—A Plea for Inclusion in Critical Editions." *Textus* 19: 111–25.

Olrik, Axel
　1930　　*Viking Civilization.* Tr. Jacob W. Hartman and Hanna A. Larsen. Revised by Hans Ellekilde. New York: American-Scandinavian Foundation and Norton.

Oppenheim, A. Leo
　1941　　"Idiomatic Accadian." *JAOS* 61: 251–71.
　1955　　"'Siege Documents' from Nippur." *Iraq* 17: 69–89.
　1964　　*Ancient Mesopotamia: Portrait of a Dead Civilization.* Chicago: University of Chicago Press.
　1967　　*Letters from Mesopotamia.* Chicago: University of Chicago Press.

Oren, Eliezer D.
　1984　　"Migdol: A New Fortress on the Edge of the Eastern Nile Delta." *BASOR* 256: 7–44.

Orlinsky, Harry M.
　1939　　"*Ḥāṣēr* in the Old Testament." *JAOS* 59: 22–37.

Orr, Avigdor
　1956　　"The Seventy Years of Babylon." *VT* 6: 304–6.

Ottosson, Magnus
　1969　　*Gilead: Tradition and History.* Tr. Jean Gray. Lund: CWK Gleerup.

Overholt, Thomas W.
　1967　　"Jeremiah 27–29: The Question of False Prophecy." *JAAR* 35: 241–49.
　1968　　"King Nebuchadnezzar in the Jeremiah Tradition." *CBQ* 30: 39–48.

Pagán, Samuel
　1996　　"The Book of Obadiah" in *NIB* 7. Ed. Leander E. Keck. Nashville: Abingdon. Pp. 435–59.

Pardee, Dennis
　1978　　"An Overview of Ancient Hebrew Epistolography." *JBL* 97: 321–46.
　1982　　*Handbook of Ancient Hebrew Letters.* Chico, CA: Society of Biblical Literature and Scholars Press.

Parker, Simon B.
　1978　　"Possession Trance and Prophecy in Pre-Exilic Israel." *VT* 28: 271–85.

Parke-Taylor, Geoffrey H.
    2000   *The Formation of the Book of Jeremiah: Doublets and Recurring Phrases.*
             SBLMS 51. Atlanta: Society of Biblical Literature.
Parrot, André
    1957   *The Temple of Jerusalem.* Tr. B. E. Hooke. London: SCM Press.
    1961   *Nineveh and Babylon.* Tr. Stuart Gilbert and James Emmons. [London]:
             Thames & Hudson.
Parunak, H. Van Dyke
    1975   "A Semantic Survey of NḤM." *Biblica* 56: 512–32.
    1994   "Some Discourse Functions of Prophetic Quotation Formulas in Jere-
             miah" in *Biblical Hebrew and Discourse Linguistics.* Ed. Robert D. Ber-
             gen. Dallas: Summer Institute of Linguistics. Pp. 489–519.
Paton, Lewis Bayles
    1906   "The Meaning of the Expression 'Between the Two Walls.'" *JBL* 25: 1–13.
Paul, Shalom M.
    1969   "Literary and Ideological Echoes of Jeremiah in Deutero-Isaiah" in *Pro-
             ceedings of the Fifth World Congress of Jewish Studies I.* Ed. Pinchas Peli.
             Jerusalem: World Union of Jewish Studies. Pp. 102–20.
    1978   "Amos iii 15—Winter and Summer Mansions." *VT* 28: 358–60.
    1991   *Amos.* Hermeneia. Minneapolis: Fortress.
_____ and William G. Dever
    1973   (eds.) *Biblical Archaeology.* Jerusalem: Keter.
Pedersén, Olof
    1998   *Archives and Libraries in the Ancient Near East 1500–300 B.C.* Bethesda,
             MD: CDL.
Penkower, Jordan S.
    2000   "Verse Divisions in the Hebrew Bible." *VT* 50: 379–93.
Perles, Felix
    1905   *Babylonisch-jüdische Glossen.* Berlin: Wolf Peiser.
Péter, René
    1975   "פר et שׁור: Note de lexicographie hébraïque." *VT* 25: 486–96.
Petit, Thierry
    1988   "L'évolution sémantique des termes hébreux et araméens *pḥh* et *sgn* et
             accadiens *pāḫatu* et *šaknu*." *JBL* 107: 53–67.
Petrie, W. Flinders
    1888   *Tanis, Part II: Nebesheh (Am) and Defenneh (Tahpanhes).* Fourth Memoir
             of The Egypt Exploration Fund. London: Trübner.
    1892   *Ten Years' Digging in Egypt.* [London]: Religious Tract Society.
_____ and Ernest Mackay
    1915   *Heliopolis Kafr Ammar and Shurafa.* London: University College, School
             of Archaeology in Egypt, and Quaritch.
Pettinato, Giovanni
    1976   "The Royal Archives of Tell Mardikh-Ebla." *BA* 39: 44–52.
Pfeiffer, Robert H.
    1926   "Edomite Wisdom." *ZAW* 44: 13–25.
Phillips, Anthony
    1975   "*Nebalah*—A Term for Serious Disorderly and Unruly Conduct." *VT* 25:
             237–42.

Polak, Frank H.
  1984   "Jer. 23:29—An Expanded Colon in the LXX?" *Textus* 11: 119–23.
Polley, Max E.
  1980   "Hebrew Prophecy within the Council of Yahweh, Examined in Its
            Ancient Near Eastern Setting" in *Scripture in Context*. Ed. Carl D.
            Evans et al. Pittsburgh: Pickwick. Pp. 141–56.
Porten, Bezalel
  1974   (ed.) *Jews of Elephantine and Arameans of Syene: Aramaic Texts with
            Translation*. In collaboration with Jonas C. Greenfield. Jerusalem:
            Hebrew University.
  1979   "Aramaic Papyri and Parchments: A New Look." *BA* 42: 74–104.
  1981   "The Identity of King Adon." *BA* 44: 36–52.
Porter, Bertha, and Rosalind L. B. Moss
  1934   *Topographical Bibliography of Ancient Egyptian Hieroglyphic Texts, Re-
            liefs, and Paintings IV*. Oxford: Clarendon Press.
Potter, H. D.
  1983   "The New Covenant in Jeremiah xxxi 31–34." *VT* 33: 347–57.
Press, Ieshayahu
  1953   "The Vision of Jeremiah on the Rebuilding of Jerusalem" in *Zalman Lif
            Volume* [Hebrew]. Eretz-Israel 2. Jerusalem: Israel Exploration Society.
            Pp. 126–28.
Pritchard, James B.
  1956   "The Water System at Gibeon." *BA* 19: 66–75.
  1959   "Gibeon's History in the Light of Excavation" in VT Supp 7 [Congress
            Volume, Oxford, 1959]. Pp. 1–12.
  1964   *Winery, Defenses, and Soundings at Gibeon*. Philadelphia: The Univer-
            sity Museum, The University of Pennsylvania.
Quell, Gottfried
  1952   *Wahre und falsche Propheten*. BFCT 46/1. Gütersloh: Bertelsmann.
Quesnel, Michel
  1989   "Les citations de Jérémie dans l'évangile selon saint Matthieu." *EB* 47:
            513–27.
Raabe, Paul R.
  1996   *Obadiah*. AB 24D. New York: Doubleday.
Rabin, C.
  1958   *The Zadokite Documents*. 2d rev. ed. Oxford: Clarendon Press.
von Rad, Gerhard
  1966   "There Remains Still a Rest for the People of God: An Investigation of a
            Biblical Conception" in von Rad, *The Problem of the Hexateuch and
            Other Essays*. Tr. E. W. Trueman Dicken. Edinburgh and London: Oliver
            & Boyd. Pp. 94–102. [German: "Es ist noch eine Ruhe vorhanden dem
            Volke Gottes" in von Rad, *Gesammelte Studien zum Alten Testament*.
            Munich: Chr. Kaiser, 1971. Pp. 101–8. Originally 1933]
Rainey, A. F.
  1975   "The Prince and the Pauper." *UF* 7: 427–32.
Ramsey, Paul
  1949   "Elements of a Biblical Political Theory." *JR* 29: 258–83.
Raven, Susan
  1984   *Rome in Africa*. New ed. London: Longman.

Reimer, David J.
    1993   *The Oracles against Babylon in Jeremiah 50–51: A Horror among the*
                Nations. San Francisco: Mellen Research University Press.
    1998   "Political Prophets?" in *Intertextuality in Ugarit and Israel.* Ed. Johannes
                C. de Moor. OS 40. Leiden: Brill. Pp. 126–42.
Renaud, Bernard
    1986   "L'alliance éternelle d'Éz 16,59–63 et l'alliance nouvelle de Jér 31,31–34"
                in *Ezekiel and His Book.* Ed. J. Lust. BETL 74. Leuven: Leuven Univer-
                sity Press. Pp. 335–39.
    1999   "L'oracle de la nouvelle alliance. À propos des divergences entre le texte
                hébreu (Jr 31,31–34) et le texte grec (38,31–34)" in *Lectures et Relectures*
                de la Bible [Festschrift P.-M. Bogaert]. Ed. J.-M. Auwers and A. Wénin.
                BETL 144. Leuven: Leuven University Press. Pp. 85–98.
Rendtorff, Rolf
    1960   "Zur Lage von Jaser." ZDPV 76: 124–35.
    1993   *Canon and Theology.* Minneapolis: Fortress.
Renkema, Johan
    1997   "A Note on Jeremiah xxviii 5." VT 47: 253–55.
Rice, Gene
    1975   "Two Black Contemporaries of Jeremiah." JRT 32: 95–109.
Richardson, Alan
    1958   *An Introduction to the Theology of the New Testament.* New York: Harper
                & Row.
Riemschneider, Kaspar K.
    1977   "Prison and Punishment in Early Anatolia." JESHO 20: 114–26.
Rin, Svi
    1963   "Ugaritic=Old Testament Affinities." BZ 7: 22–33.
Roach, Corwin C.
    1941   "Notes and Comments." ATR 23: 347–48.
Robinson, Bernard P.
    2001   "Jeremiah's New Covenant: Jer 31,31–34." SJOT 15: 181–204.
Robinson, Edward
    1874   *Biblical Researches in Palestine and in the Adjacent Regions I–II.* 11th ed.
                Boston: Crocker & Brewster; London: John Murray. Journal of travels in
                the year 1838.
Robinson, H. Wheeler
    1944   "The Council of Yahweh." JTS Old Series 45: 151–57.
Robinson, T. H.
    1917–18 "The Structure of Jeremiah l, li." JTS Old Series 19: 251–65.
Römer, Thomas
    1991   "Les 'anciens' pères (Jér 11,10) et la 'nouvelle' alliance (Jér 31,31)."
                BN 59: 23–27.
Rofé, Alexander
    1989   "The Arrangement of the Book of Jeremiah." ZAW 101: 390–98.
    1991   "The Name YHWH ṢĔBĀʾÔT and the Shorter Recension of Jeremiah"
                in *Prophetie und geschichtliche Wirklichkeit im alten Israel* [Festschrift für
                Siegfried Herrmann]. Ed. Rüdiger Liwak and Siegfried Wagner. Stuttgart:
                Kohlhammer. Pp. 307–16.

1995 "Not Exile But Annihilation for Zedekiah's People: The Purport of Jeremiah 52 in the Septuagint" in *VIII Congress of the International Organization for Septuagint and Cognate Studies, Paris 1992*. Ed. Leonard Greenspoon and Oliver Munnich. Atlanta: Society of Biblical Literature and Scholars Press. Pp. 165–70.

Rogers, John B. Jr.
1988 "Jeremiah 31:7–14." *Int* 42: 281–85.

Rogers, Robert William
1926 (ed.) *Cuneiform Parallels to the Old Testament*. 2d ed. New York: Abingdon.

Ruben, Paul
1899 "Strophic Forms in the Bible." *JQR* Old Series 11: 431–79.

Rubensohn, Otto
1907 *Elephantine-Papyri*. Berlin: Weidmannsche Buchhandlung.

Rubinger, Naphtali J.
1977 "Jeremiah's Epistle to the Exiles and the Field in Anathoth." *Judaism* 26: 84–91.

Sachs, Curt
1940 *The History of Musical Instruments*. New York: Norton.

Saggs, H. W.
1963 "The Nimrud Letters, 1952 — Part VI." *Iraq* 25: 70–80 + plates.
1978 *The Encounter with the Divine in Mesopotamia and Israel*. London: Athlone.

Saleh, Abdel-Aziz
1981 *Excavations at Heliopolis I*. Cairo: Cairo University.

Sanders, James A.
1977 "Hermeneutics in True and False Prophecy" in *Canon and Authority*. Ed. George W. Coats and Burke O. Long. Philadelphia: Fortress. Pp. 21–41.

Sarason, Richard S.
1988 "The Interpretation of Jeremiah 31:31–34 in Judaism" in *When Jews and Christians Meet*. Ed. Jakob J. Petuchowski. Albany, NY: State University of New York Press. Pp. 99–123.

Sarna, Nahum M.
1973 "Zedekiah's Emancipation of Slaves and the Sabbatical Year" in *Orient and Occident* [Essays Presented to Cyrus H. Gordon]. Ed. Harry A. Hoffner Jr. AOAT 22. Neukirchen-Vluyn: Neukirchener Verlag. Pp. 143–49.
1978 "The Abortive Insurrection in Zedekiah's Day (Jer. 27–29)" in *H. L. Ginsberg Volume*. Ed. Menahem Haran. Eretz-Israel 14. Jerusalem: Israel Exploration Society. Pp. 89–96.

Sasson, Jack M.
1977 "Treatment of Criminals at Mari." *JESHO* 20: 90–113.
1983 "Mari Dreams." *JAOS* 103: 283–93.

Sauer, James A.
1985 "Ammon, Moab and Edom" in *Biblical Archaeology Today* [Proceedings of the International Congress on Biblical Archaeology Jerusalem, April 1984]. Ed. Avraham Biran et al. Jerusalem: Israel Exporation Society. Pp. 206–14.

1986   "Transjordan in the Bronze and Iron Ages: A Critique of Glueck's Synthe-
          sis." *BASOR* 263: 1–26.
Sawyer, John F.
1983   "The Meaning of *Barzel* in the Biblical Expressions 'Chariots of Iron,'
          'Yoke of Iron,' Etc." in Sawyer and Clines 1983: 129–34.
_____ and David J. Clines
1983   (eds.) *Midian, Moab and Edom*. JSOT Supp 24. Sheffield: JSOT Press.
Schaeffer, Claude F.-A.
1929   "Les fouilles de Minet el-Beida et de Ras-Shamra (campagne du print-
          emps 1929)." *Syria* 10: 285–97 + plaque LX.
1963   "Neue Entdeckungen in Ugarit." *AfO* 20: 206–15.
Schildenberger, Johannes
1963   " 'Drum schlägt ihm mein Herz—Ich muß mich seiner erbarmen' (Jer
          31,20)." *GeLe* 36: 163–78.
Schmid, Konrad
1996   *Buchgestalten des Jeremiabuches: Untersuchungen zur Redaktions- und
          Rezeptionsgeschichte von Jer 30–33 im Kontext des Buches*. WMANT 72.
          Neukirchen-Vluyn: Neukirchener Verlag.
Schmidt, Carl
1978   (ed.) *Pistis Sophia* . NHS 9. Leiden: Brill.
Schmidt, Kenneth W.
1982   "Prophetic Delegation: A Form-Critical Inquiry." *Biblica* 63: 206–18.
Schmidt, Nathaniel
1901a   "Jeremiah" in *EncBib* 2: 2366–72.
1901b   "Jeremiah Book" in *EncBib* 2: 2372–95.
Schoneveld, J.
1963   "Jeremia xxxi 29,30." *VT* 13: 339–41.
Schottroff, Willy
1966   "Horonaim, Nimrim, Luhith und der Westrand des 'Landes Ataroth.' "
          ZDPV 82: 163–208.
Schumacher, G.
1889   "Der arabische Pflug." *ZDPV* 12: 157–66.
Schwally, Friedrich
1888   "Die Reden des Buches Jeremia gegen die Heiden. XXV. XLVI–LI." *ZAW*
          8: 177–217.
Seitz, Christopher R.
1985   "The Crisis of Interpretation over the Meaning and Purpose of the Exile:
          A Redactional Study of Jeremiah xxi–xliii." *VT* 35: 78–97.
1989   "The Prophet Moses and the Canonical Shape of Jeremiah." *ZAW* 101:
          3–27.
Sekine, Masao
1959   "Davidsbund und Sinaibund bei Jeremia." *VT* 9: 47–57.
Selwyn, E. C.
1915   "The Trial-Narratives Based on the Oracles." *The Expositor* 8th Series 9:
          254–71.
Sendrey, Alfred
1969   *Music in Ancient Israel*. London: Vision Press and New York: Philosophi-
          cal Library.

Shead, Andrew G.
   1999   "Jeremiah 32 in Its Hebrew and Greek Recensions." *TynB* 50: 318–20.
Simons, J.
   1952   *Jerusalem in the Old Testament.* Leiden: Brill.
   1954   "The 'Table of Nations' (Gen. X): Its General Structure and Meaning." *OTS* 10: 155–84.
   1959   *The Geographical and Topographical Texts of the Old Testament.* Leiden: Brill.
Singer, Charles, et al.
   1954   *A History of Technology I.* Oxford: Clarendon Press.
Siqueira, Tércio Machado
   1987   "Conhecer a Deus é Praticar a Justica (Jr 22,13–19)." *EstB* 14: 9–17.
Sivan, Daniel, and William Schniedewind
   1993   "Letting Your 'Yes' Be 'No' in Ancient Israel: A Study of the Asseverative לֹא and הֲלֹא." *JSS* 38: 209–26.
Smelik, Klaas A.
   1987   "De functie van Jeremia 50 en 51 binnen het boek Jeremia." *NedTT* 41: 265–78.
   1989–90 "Jeremia 26 als literarische Komposition." *DBAT* 26: 102–24.
   1992   *Converting the Past: Studies in Ancient Israelite and Moabite Historiography.* OS 28. Leiden: Brill.
   1997   "Mijn knecht Nebukadnessar in het boek Jeremia." *Amc* 16: 44–59, 141.
Smend, Rudolf
   1899   *Lehrbuch der Alttestamentlichen Religionsgeschichte.* 2d rev. ed. Freiburg: Mohr (Paul Siebeck).
Smit, E. J.
   1969   "Jer. 52:28–30: A Chronological Crux?" in *Biblical Essays* [Proceedings of the 12th Meeting of Die Ou-Testamentiese Werkgemeenskap in Suid-Afrika, 28–31 January, 1969]. Ed. A. H. van Zyl. Potchetstroom: Pro Rege-Pers Bpk. Pp. 111–21.
Smith, Morton
   1975   "The Veracity of Ezekiel, the Sins of Manasseh, and Jeremiah 44,18." *ZAW* 87: 11–16.
Smith, W. Robertson
   1892   *The Old Testament in the Jewish Church.* 2d ed. New York: Appleton.
Snaith, John G.
   1971   "Literary Criticism and Historical Investigation in Jeremiah Chapter XLVI." *JSS* 16: 15–32.
Snaith, Norman H.
   1965   "יַם־סוּף: The Sea of Reeds: The Red Sea." *VT* 15: 395–98.
   1967   *Leviticus and Numbers.* CB New Edition. London: Thomas Nelson.
Soggin, J. Alberto
   1975f   "Jeremiah 29,8b" in Soggin 1975a: 238–40. [= "Testo e significato de Ger. 29,8b." *BibO* 16 (1974) 33–34]
Sommer, Benjamin D.
   1999   "New Light on the Composition of Jeremiah." *CBQ* 61: 646–66.
Sparks, H. F.
   1959   "The Symbolical Interpretation of *Lebanon* in the Fathers." *JTS* New Series 10: 264–79.

Speiser, E. A.
    1964   *Genesis*. AB 1. Garden City, NY: Doubleday.
Stade, Bernhard
    1883   "Weitere Bemerkungen zu Micha 4.5." ZAW 3: 1–16.
    1887   *Geschichte des Volkes Israel I*. Berlin: Baumgärtel.
    1892   "Bemerkungen zum Buche Jeremia." ZAW 12: 276–308.
Stager, Lawrence E.
    1975   "Ancient Agriculture in the Judean Desert: A Case Study of the Buqêᶜah
               Valley in the Iron Age." Unpublished. Ph.D. dissertation, Harvard
               University.
    1982   "The Archaeology of the East Slope of Jerusalem and the Terraces of the
               Kidron." *JNES* 41: 111–21.
    1991   *Ashkelon Discovered*. Washington D.C.: Biblical Archaeological Society.
               [Articles reprinted from BAR 17/2: 24–37, 40–43; 17/3: 26–42; 17/4: 34–
               53, 72]
    1996   "Ashkelon and the Archaeology of Destruction: Kislev 604 BCE" in *Joseph
               Aviram Volume*. Ed. Avraham Biran et al. Eretz-Israel 25. Jerusalem: Israel
               Exploration Society. Pp. 61–74.
Steele, David
    1985–86 "Jeremiah's Little Book of Comfort." *ThTo* 42: 471–77.
Steiner, Richard C.
    1996   "The Two Sons of Neriah and the Two Editions of Jeremiah in the Light
               of Two *Atbash* Code-Words for Babylon." *VT* 46: 74–84.
Stipp, Hermann-Josef
    1997   "Linguistic Peculiarities of the Masoretic Edition of the Book of Jere-
               miah: An Updated Index." *JNSL* 23: 181–202.
Stern, Ephraim
    2001   *Archaeology of the Land of the Bible II*. ABRL. New York: Doubleday.
Swanson, Dwight D.
    1994   "'A Covenant Just like Jacob's': The Covenant of 11QT29 and Jeremiah's
               New Covenant" in *New Qumran Texts and Studies*. STDJ 15. Ed. George
               J. Brooke and Florentino García Martínez. Leiden: Brill. Pp. 273–86.
Sweeney, Marvin A.
    1996   "Jeremiah 30–31 and King Josiah's Program of National Restoration and
               Religious Reform." ZAW 108: 569–83.
Swete, Henry Barclay
    1899   *The Old Testament in Greek III*. 2d ed. Cambridge: Cambridge University
               Press.
    1914   *An Introduction to the Old Testament in Greek*. 2d rev. ed. Cambridge:
               Cambridge University Press. Originally 1900.
Swetnam, James
    1965   "Some Observations on the Background of צדיק in Jeremias 23,5a." *Bib-*
               lica 46: 29–40.
Taatz, Irene
    1991   *Frühjüdische Briefe*. Freiburg [Schweiz]: Universitätsverlag and Gött-
               ingen: Vandenhoeck & Ruprecht.
Tadmor, Hayim
    1958   "The Campaigns of Sargon II of Assur: A Chronological-Historical Study
               II." *JCS* 12: 77–100.

1994   *The Inscriptions of Tiglath-Pileser III King of Assyria.* Jerusalem: Israel Academy of Sciences and Humanities.

1995   "Was the Biblical *sārîs* a Eunuch?" in *Solving Riddles and Untying Knots* [Studies in Honor of Jonas C. Greenfield]. Ed. Ziony Zevit et al. Winona Lake, IN: Eisenbrauns. Pp. 317–25.

Tallqvist, Knut L.
1914   *Assyrian Personal Names.* Leipzig: Harrassowitz.

Thelle, Rannfrid I.
1998   "דרש את־יהוה: The Prophetic Act of Consulting YHWH in Jeremiah 21,2 and 37,7." *SJOT* 12: 249–56.

Thomas, D. Winton
1946a   "The Lachish Ostraca: Professor Torczyner's Latest Views." *PEQ* 78: 38–42.

1946b   '*The Prophet*' *in the Lachish Ostraca.* London: Tyndale.

1950   "The Age of Jeremiah in the Light of Recent Archaeological Discovery." *PEQ* 82: 1–15.

1961   "Again 'The Prophet' in the Lachish Ostraca" in *Von Ugarit nach Qumran* [Festschrift für Otto Eissfeldt]. 2d ed. Ed. Johannes Hempel and Leonhard Rost et al. BZAW 77. Berlin: Alfred Töpelmann. Pp. 244–49.

Thompson, J. A.
1977   "Israel's 'Lovers.'" *VT* 27: 475–81.

Toorn, K. van der
1986   "Judges xvi 21 in the Light of the Akkadian Sources." *VT* 36: 248–51.

Torczyner (Tur-Sinai), Harry
1947   "A Hebrew Incantation against Night-Demons from Biblical Times." *JNES* 6: 18–29.

Torrey, Charles C.
1923   "A Few Ancient Seals." *AASOR* 2–3: 103–8.

1928   *The Second Isaiah: A New Interpretation.* New York: Scribner's.

Tov, Emanuel
1975a   "The Contribution of Textual Criticism to the Literary Criticism and Exegesis of Jeremiah—The Hebrew *Vorlage* of the LXX of Chapter 27" [Hebrew with English summary]. *Shnaton* 1: 165–82; xxi.

1975b   (ed.) *The Book of Baruch.* Missoula, MT: Scholars Press.

1999   "The Characterization of the Additional Layer of the Masoretic Text of Jeremiah" [Hebrew with English summary] in *Frank Moore Cross Volume.* Ed. Baruch A. Levine et al. Eretz-Israel 26. Jerusalem: Israel Exploration Society. Pp. 55–63, 229.

Trible, Phyllis
1977   "The Gift of a Poem: A Rhetorical Study of Jeremiah 31:15–22." *ANQ* 17: 271–80. [=*Image-Breaking, Image-Building.* Ed. Linda Clark et al. New York: Pilgrim, 1981. Pp. 104–15]

1978   *God and the Rhetoric of Sexuality.* Philadelphia: Fortress.

Tristram, H. B.
1873   *The Land of Moab.* London: John Murray.

Tsevat, Matitiahu
1962   "Studies in the Book of Samuel." *HUCA* 33: 107–18.

Tsumura, D. T.
1983   "Literary Insertion (AXB Pattern) in Biblical Hebrew." *VT* 33: 468–82.

Turkowski, Lucian
    1969   "Peasant Agriculture in the Judean Hills." *PEQ* 101: 21–33, 101–12.
Tushingham, A. D.
    1972   *The Excavations at Dibon (Dhîbân) in Moab*. AASOR 40. Cambridge,
              MA: American Schools of Oriental Research.
Ullendorff, Edward
    1953   "South Arabian Etymological Marginalia." *BSOAS* 15: 157–59.
Ussishkin, David
    1970   "The Necropolis from the Time of the Kingdom of Judah at Silwan, Jeru-
              salem." *BA* 33: 34–46.
    1978   "Excavations at Tel Lachish 1973–1977." *Tel Aviv* 5: 1–97 + plates.
    1982   *The Conquest of Lachish by Sennacherib*. Tel Aviv: Institute of Archaeol-
              ogy, Tel Aviv University.
Van der Wal, A. J.
    1996   "Opdat Jakob weer Gods dienaar kan zijn: Opbouw en achtergrond van
              Jeremia 30: 5–11." *Amc* 15: 77–93.
Van Selms, A.
    1974   "The Name Nebuchadnezzar" in *Travels in the World of the Old Tes-
              tament* [Studies Presented to M. A. Beek]. Ed. Heerma van Voss et al.
              Assen: Van Gorcum. Pp. 223–29.
Van Zyl, A. H.
    1960   *The Moabites*. POS 3. Leiden: Brill.
de Vaux, Roland
    1933   "Le 'Reste d'Israël' d'après les Prophètes." *RB* 42: 526–39.
    1938   "Exploration de la région de Salt." *RB* 47: 398–425.
    1939   "Les Ostraka de Lachis." *RB* 48: 181–206.
    1941   "Notes d'histoire et de topographie transjordaniennes." *Vivre et Penser*
              1[*RB* 50]: 16–47.
    1969   "Téman, ville ou région d'Édom?" *RB* 76: 379–85.
Villafane, Eldin
    1992   "The Jeremiah Paradigm for the City." *ChCr* 52: 374–75.
Vincent, Louis-Hugues
    1907   "Église byzantine et inscription romaine à Abou-Ghôch." *RB* 4: 414–21.
    1934–35 "Jérusalem Ville Sainte (Jér. XXXI, 38–40)." *JJPES* iii–xvi.
Vogel, Eleanor K.
    1971   "Bibliography of Holy Land Sites." *HUCA* 42: 1–96.
_____ and Brooks Holtzclaw
    1981   "Bibliography of Holy Land Sites II." *HUCA* 52: 1–92.
Wainwright, G. A.
    1956a   "Caphtor-Cappadocia." *VT* 6: 199–210.
    1956b   "The Septuagint's Καππαδοκία for Caphtor." *JJS* 7: 91–92.
Waldman, Nahum M.
    1989–90 "Parents Have Eaten Sour Grapes." *JBQ* 18: 1–5.
Walker, Norman
    1957   "The Masoretic Pointing of Jeremiah's Pun." *VT* 7: 413.
Wallenstein, M.
    1954   "Some Lexical Material in the Judean Scrolls." *VT* 4: 211–14.
Wang, Martin Cheng-Chang
    1972   "Jeremiah and the Covenant Traditions." *SEAJT* 14/1: 3–13.

Wanke, Gunther
1971   *Untersuchungen zur sogenannten Baruchschrift.* BZAW 122. Berlin: de
        Gruyter.
Watson, Wilfred G.
1980   "Gender-Matched Synonymous Parallelism in the OT." *JBL* 99: 321–41.
Watts, James W.
1992   "Text and Redaction in Jeremiah's Oracles against the Nations." *CBQ* 54:
        432–47.
Weidner, Ernst F.
1939   "Jojachin, König von Juda, in babylonischen Keilschrifttexten" in *Mé-
        langes syriens offerts à M. René Dussaud II.* Paris: Geuthner. Pp. 923–35.
1945–51 "Baḥrein." *AfO* 15: 169–70.
1956   "Amts- und Privatarchive aus mittelassyrischer Zeit" in *Festschruft für
        Prof. Dr. Viktor Christian.* Ed. Kurt Schubert et al. Vienna: Notring der
        wissenschaftlichen Verbände Österreichs. Pp. 111–16.
Weinfeld, Moshe
1970   "The Covenant of Grant in the Old Testament and in the Ancient Near
        East." *JAOS* 90: 184–203.
1976a   "The Loyalty Oath in the Ancient Near East." *UF* 8: 379–414.
1990   "Sabbatical Year and Jubilee in the Pentateuchal Laws and Their Ancient
        Near Eastern Background" in *The Law in the Bible and in Its Environ-
        ment.* Publications of the Finnish Exegetical Society 51. Ed. Timo
        Veijola. Helsinki: Finnish Exegetical Society and Göttingen: Vanden-
        hoeck & Ruprecht. Pp. 39–62.
Weippert, Helga
1979   "Das Wort vom neuen Bund in Jeremia xxxi 31–34." *VT* 29: 336–51.
1989   "Schöpfung und Heil in Jer 45" in *Schöpfung und Befreiung* [Fest-
        schrift für Claus Westermann]. Ed. Rainer Albertz et al. Stuttgart: Cal-
        wer. Pp. 92–103.
Weippert, Manfred
1981   "Assyrische Prophetien der Zeit Asarhaddons und Assurbanipals" in *Assyr-
        ian Royal Inscriptions: New Horizons.* Ed. F. M. Fales. OAC 17. Rome:
        Istituto per l'Oriente. Pp. 71–115.
Weiser, Artur
1954   "Das Gotteswort für Baruch Jer. 45 und die sogenannte Baruchbiogra-
        phie" in *Theologie als Glaubenswagnis* [Karl Heim Festschrift]. Ham-
        burg: Furche. Pp. 35–46.
Weiss, Johannes
1959   *Earliest Christianity I.* Tr. Frederick C. Grant et al. New York: Harper.
Weissbach, F. H.
1906   (ed.) *Die Inschriften Nebukadnezars II im Wâdi Brîsā und am Nahr
        El-Kelb.* WVDOG 5. Leipzig: Hinrichs.
Welch, Adam C.
1921a   "Jeremiah's Letter to the Exiles in Babylon." *The Expositor* 8th Series 22:
        358–72.
Wernberg-Møller, P.
1956   "The Pronoun אתמה and Jeremiah's Pun." *VT* 6: 315–16.

Werner, Wolfgang
    1988   *Studien zur alttestamentlichen Vorstellung vom Plan Jahwes.* BZAW 173.
              Berlin: de Gruyter.
Wessels, W. J.
    1989   "Jeremiah 22,24–30: A Proposed Ideological Reading." *ZAW* 101: 232–49.
    1992   "Sosiale geregtigheid: 'n Perspektief uit die Jeremiaboek." *SeK* 13: 80–95.
Westermann, Claus
    1994   *Lamentations: Issues and Interpretation.* Tr. Charles Muenchow. Edin-
              burgh: T. & T. Clark and Minneapolis: Augsburg Fortress. [German: *Die
              Klagelieder.* Neukirchen-Vluyn: Neukirchener Verlag, 1990]
Westhuizen, J. P. van der
    1991–92   "A Stylistic-Exegetical Analysis of Jeremiah 46:1–12." *JBQ* 20: 84–95.
Whitley, C. F.
    1954   "The Term Seventy Years Captivity." *VT* 4: 60–72.
Widengren, Geo
    1951   *The King and the Tree of Life in Ancient Near Eastern Religion.* UUÅ
              1951/4. Uppsala: Lundequist.
Wiebe, John M.
    1987b   "The Jeremian Core of the Book of Consolation and the Redaction of the
              Poetic Oracles in Jeremiah 30–31." *SBeT* 15: 137–61.
Wiedemann, Alfred
    1897   *Religion of the Ancient Egyptians.* London: H. Grevel.
Wiejesinghe, S. L.
    1997   "Tracing the Shorter Version Behind the Short Text (LXX): A New
              Approach to the Redaction of Jeremiah 34,8–22." *Mus* 110: 293–328.
Wiklander, Bertil
    1978   "The Context and Meaning of NHR ʾL in Jer. 51:44." *SEÅ* 43: 40–64.
Wilkinson, J. Gardner
    1878   *The Manners and Customs of the Ancient Egyptians I–III.* Revised by
              Samuel Birch. London: John Murray.
Wilkinson, John
    1975   "The Way from Jerusalem to Jericho." *BA* 38: 10–24.
Wilson, John A.
    1964   *Signs and Wonders upon Pharaoh: A History of American Egyptology.* Chi-
              cago: University of Chicago Press.
Winnett, Fred V., and William L. Reed
    1964   *The Excavations at Dibon (Dhîbân) in Moab.* AASOR 36–37. New
              Haven: American Schools of Oriental Research.
    1970   *Ancient Records from North Arabia.* Toronto: University of Toronto Press.
Wiseman, Donald J.
    1953   *The Alalakh Tablets.* London: The British Institute of Archaeology at
              Ankara.
    1955   "Assyrian Writing-Boards." *Iraq* 17: 3–13.
    1958a   "The Vassal-Treaties of Esarhaddon." *Iraq* 20: 1–99 + plates. [=*The Vassal-
              Treaties of Esarhaddon.* London: The British School of Archaeology in
              Iraq, 1958]
    1958b   "Abban and Alalaḫ." *JCS* 12: 124–29.
    1973   (ed.) *Peoples of Old Testament Times.* Oxford: Clarendon Press.

Wolff, Hans W.
　1977　*Joel and Amos.* Tr. Waldemar Janzen et al. Hermeneia. Philadelphia: Fortress.
Woolley, C. Leonard
　1921　*Carchemish II: The Town Defences.* Oxford: Trustees of the British Museum and Oxford University Press. [Reprint: London: British Museum, 1969]. Volume I by D. G. Hogarth (1914); Volume III by Leonard Woolley and R. D. Barnett (1978).
_____ and R. D. Barnett
　1978　*Carchemish III: The Excavations in the Inner Town and The Hittite Inscriptions.* Oxford: Trustees of the British Museum and Oxford University Press. Volume I by D. G. Hogarth (1914); Volume II by C. Leonard Woolley (1921).
Worschech, Udo, and Ernst A. Knauf
　1986　"Dimon und Horonaim." *BN* 31: 70–96.
Wright, G. Ernest
　1938a　"Some Personal Seals of Judean Royal Officials." *BA* 1/2: 10–12.
　1938b　"Lachish—Frontier Fortress of Judah." *BA* 1/4: 21–30.
　1941　"Solomon's Temple Resurrected." *BA* 4:17–31.
　1947　"Tell En-Nasbeh." *BA* 10: 69–77.
　1952　*God Who Acts: Biblical Theology as Recital.* SBT 8. London: SCM Press.
　1953　"Deuteronomy" in IB 2. Ed. George A. Buttrick. New York: Abingdon. Pp. 311–537.
　1957　*Biblical Archaeology.* Philadelphia: Westminster and London: Gerald Duckworth.
　1971　"The Theological Study of the Bible" in *IOVCB*: 983–88.
Wright, J. Edward
　1996　"Baruch, the Ideal Sage" in *'Go to the Land I Will Show You'* [Studies in Honor of Dwight W. Young]. Ed. Joseph E. Coleson and Victor H. Matthews. Winona Lake, IN: Eisenbrauns. Pp. 193–210.
Wylie, C. C.
　1949　"On King Solomon's Molten Sea." *BA* 12: 86–90.
Yadin, Yigael
　1961　"More on the Letters of Bar Kochba." *BA* 24: 86–95.
　1962a　"The Expedition to the Judean Desert, 1961: Expedition D—The Cave of the Letters." *IEJ* 12: 227–57.
　1983　(ed.) *The Temple Scroll II.* Jerusalem: Israel Exploration Society.
_____ et al.
　1961　*Hazor III–IV: Plates* Jerusalem: Magnes.
　1989　*Hazor III–IV: Text* Ed. Amnon Ben-Tor. Jerusalem: Israel Exploration Society and The Hebrew University.
Yamauchi, Edwin
　1983　"The Scythians: Invading Hordes from the Russian Steppes." *BA* 46: 90–99.
Yeivin, S.
　1948　"The Sepulchers of the Kings of the House of David." *JNES* 7: 30–45.
　1959　"Jachin and Boaz." *PEQ* 91: 6–22 + plates.
Yellin, David
　1933–34　"Paronomasia in the Bible" [Hebrew]. *Tarbiz* 5: 1–17.

Younker, Randall W.
1985   "Israel, Judah, and Ammon and the Motifs on the Baalis Seal from Tell el-ʿUmeiri." *BA* 48: 173–80.
1999   "Review of Archaeological Research in Ammon" in MacDonald and Younker 1999: 1–19.
Zatelli, Ida
1991   "The Rachel's Lament in the Targum and Other Ancient Jewish Interpretations." *RivBib* 39: 477–90.
Zayadine, Fawzi
1973   "Recent Excavations on the Citadel of Amman." *ADAJ* 18: 17–35.
Zeitlin, Solomon
1975   "Dreams and Their Interpretation from the Biblical Period to the Tannaitic Time: An Historical Study." *JQR* 66: 1–18.
Zevit, Ziony
1969   "The Use of עֶבֶד as a Diplomatic Term in Jeremiah." *JBL* 88: 74–77.
Ziegler, Joseph
1950   "Die Hilfe Gottes 'am Morgen'" in *Alttestamentliche Studien* [Festschrift für Friedrich Nötscher]. Ed. Hubert Junker and Johannes Botterweck. BBB 1. Bonn: Peter Hanstein. Pp. 281–88.
Zimmerli, Walther
1965a   *The Law and the Prophets.* Tr. Ronald E. Clements. Oxford: Blackwell.
1979   *Ezekiel 1.* Hermeneia. Tr. Ronald E. Clements. Philadelphia: Fortress.
1983   *Ezekiel 2.* Hermeneia. Tr. James D. Martin. Philadelphia: Fortress.
1995   "From Prophetic Word to Prophetic Book" in Robert P. Gordon 1995: 419–42. [German: "Vom Prophetenwort zum Prophetenbuch." *TLZ* 104 (1979), 481–96]
Zorn, Jeffrey Ralph
1993   *Tell en-Nasbeh: A Re-evaluation of the Architecture and Stratigraphy of the Early Bronze Age, Iron Age and Later Periods.* 4 vols. Unpublished Ph.D. dissertation, University of California, Berkeley.
1997   "Mizpah: Newly Discovered Stratum Reveals Judah's Other Capital." *BAR* 23/5: 28–38, 66.
Zunz, Leopold
1873   "Bibelkritisches I. Deuteronomium." *ZDMG* 27: 669–76.
Zwickel, Wolfgang
1991   "Mōṭāh = Jochhaken." *BN* 57: 37–40.

TRANSLATION, NOTES, AND COMMENTS

◆

I. ON KINGS AND PROPHETS
(21:1–23:40)

◆

A. SPEAKING OF KINGS (21:1–23:8)

1. Bad News, Good News (21:1–10)

a) Bad News for Zedekiah (21:1–7)

21 ¹The word that came to Jeremiah from Yahweh when King Zedekiah sent to him Pashhur son of Malchiah and Zephaniah son of Maaseiah, the priest, saying: ²'Seek would you Yahweh on our behalf, for Nebuchadrezzar, king of Babylon, is fighting against us; perhaps Yahweh will do for us according to all his extraordinary deeds, and he will go away from us.' ³But Jeremiah said to them, Thus you shall say to Zedekiah:

⁴Thus said Yahweh, God of Israel:
Look I will turn around the weapons of war that are in your hand, with which you are fighting the king of Babylon and the Chaldeans who are besieging you from outside the wall, and I will gather them together into the midst of this city. ⁵And I myself will fight against you with outstretched hand and with strong arm, yes, in anger and in wrath and in great fury. ⁶And I will strike down the inhabitants of this city—both human and beast; by a great pestilence they shall die.

⁷And after this—oracle of Yahweh—I will give Zedekiah, king of Judah, and his servants, and the people, and those remaining in this city from the pestilence, from the sword, and from the famine, into the hand of Nebuchadrezzar, king of Babylon, and into the hand of their enemies, and into the hand of those who seek their lives. And he will strike them down into the mouth of the sword; he will not spare them, and he will not pity, and he will not have mercy.

b) Bad News–Good News for the People (21:8–10)

21 ⁸And to this people you shall say:
Thus said Yahweh:
Look I will set before you the way of life and the way of death. ⁹Whoever stays in this city shall die by sword, and by famine, and by pestilence, but

whoever goes out and surrenders to the Chaldeans who are besieging you shall live,[a] and his life will be his booty.

[10]For I have set my face against this city for evil, and not for good—oracle of Yahweh. Into the hand of the king of Babylon it shall be given, and he will burn it with fire.

RHETORIC AND COMPOSITION

Chapters 21–23 form an appendix to the First Edition (1–20), in which is contained various Jeremianic utterances, narrative, and a minimum of added comment concerning 1) Judah's kings (21:1–23:8); and 2) Jerusalem's prophets (23:9–40). In the present book these chapters constitute an entirely new section (Giesebrecht; Streane; Lundbom 1975: 28–30 [= 1997: 42–44]), having no obvious continuity with what precedes. The suggestion by J. D. Michaelis (1793: 137), repeated by Rudolph and others, that the name "Pashhur" in 20:1–6 and 21:1 bridges the division is unlikely. The prose of 20:1–6 and 21:1–10 is not otherwise linked. The core poetry of 21:1–23:8 and 23:9–40, however, does preserve an earlier continuity created by catchwords. Chapters 21–24 do not constitute a literary unit, as is sometimes alleged (see Thiel 1973: 230); chap. 24 begins a new unit terminating now with chap. 36 (see Rhetoric and Composition for 24:1–10).

An earlier "King Collection" was introduced by *lĕbêt melek yĕhûdâ* ("To the house of the king of Judah") in 21:11, just as the "Prophet Collection" now has the introductory *lannĕbi'îm* ("To the prophets") in 23:9. The compositional criterion for the two collections is "audience" (Westermann 1967: 95–96), which is true also in the case of the Foreign Nation Oracles. The discourse—prophetic and otherwise—emanates from different periods, although most of it can confidently be assigned to the reigns of Jehoiakim and Zedekiah (Weiser). It should not be assumed that everything in the King Collection comes from Zedekiah's reign because 21:1–10 records preaching from that time. Some is earlier. The controlling structure of the King Collection is rhetorical, not chronological. Also, in three places within chaps. 21–36, Zedekiah narrative is placed ahead of Jehoiakim narrative: 1) here in 21:1–10; 2) in chap. 24, which precedes earlier material in chaps. 25–26; and 3) in chap. 34, which precedes earlier material in chaps. 35–36.

The outer frame of the King Collection comprises 21:1–10 and 23:1–8. Oracles in these two units, 21:3–7 and 23:5–6, contrast Zedekiah to a messianic king who will be what Zedekiah is not. This future king will be named "Yahweh is our righteousness" (23:6), a play and reversal on the name "Zedekiah," which means "My righteousness is Yahweh." In the frame, then, is an inclusio repeating subtly the point made by the wordplay in 23:6 (Lundbom 1975: 31–32 [= 1997: 45–47]):

---

[a]Reading the Kt *yiḥyeh* ("he shall live"); the Q has *wĕḥāyā* ("then he shall live"); cf. 38:2.

Two *Zedekiah* (*ṣidqîyāhû*) oracles   21:3–7
A '*Yahweh is our righteousness*' (*yhwh ṣidqēnû*) oracle   23:5–6

The whole of the present King Collection can be outlined as follows:

Oracles on King Zedekiah and life for the nation (21:1–10)
   Oracles to the royal house (21:11–22:5)
   "Lebanon-cedar" oracles and royal laments / non-laments (22:6–23)
   Oracle and lament for King Jehoiachin (22:24–30)
Oracles on kings, a future davidic king, and life for the nation (23:1–8)

The present verses contain 1) an introductory narrative, followed by two oracles for King Zedekiah (21:1–7); and 2) a brief one-line introduction, followed by two oracles for the people (21:8–10). The LXX lacks the messenger formula in v 10, but this can be attributed to haplography (see Notes). A comparison can be made here to Huldah's oracles in 2 Kgs 22:16–20, one of which was for the nation (vv 16–17), the other for the king (vv 18–20). But these constituted a single delivery; the oracles here have been assembled by an editor, which is clear from the two introductions. In v 4 Jeremiah instructs messengers to address the king, whereas in v 8 Yahweh instructs Jeremiah to address the people. Both oracle clusters emanate from the same period, however, which is the beginning of the final siege of Jerusalem in 588 B.C. (Weiser).

The unit as a whole is delimited at the top end by a *petuḥah* in M^A, M^L, and M^P, and a *petuḥah* (reconstructed) in 4QJer^a before v 1, which is also the chapter division. All three medieval codices have a *setumah* at the end of v 10, marking the lower limit. In M^L a *setumah* after v 2 and in M^A a *setumah* after v 3 serve to set off the introductory narrative. The M^P and one MS in the Cambridge Genizah Collection (A 14.4) have no sections at either place.

Comparisons have been made between 21:1–7(10) and 37:1–10(11), since both report embassies sent by Zedekiah to Jeremiah when Jerusalem was being besieged by the Babylonians. Ewald and Stade (1892) argued that the two accounts were different versions of the same event, but their views were rejected early by Giesebrecht and Cornill, who believed that Zedekiah requested intercession from the prophet on two occasions. The present embassy occurs before the one in chap. 37. The siege was just beginning, according to Giesebrecht, and the crisis has nothing to do with promised Egyptian relief on the way, which is background for the embassy in chap. 37, as well as the slave manumission in chap. 34. Cornill says the question in chap. 21 is "Will the Chaldeans withdraw?" whereas the question in chap. 37 is "Will the Chaldeans, who have withdrawn, come back again?" The possibility then of doublets has been largely rejected (Peake; Streane; Volz; Condamin; Holladay; Jones), with H. Weippert (1973: 72) rejecting also the view of Duhm, Rudolph, and others that 21:1–7 is a secondary rewriting of 34:2–7 and 37:3–10. The narratives in 21:1–7 and 37:3–10 report separate embassies by Zedekiah to Jeremiah, both beginning major sections of the present book.

The oracle on the "two ways" in vv 8–9 bears a close resemblance to the sermon on the "two ways" in Deut 30:15–20. But there is no reason to believe that these verses have therefore passed through the hands of a "Deuteronomic redactor" (Berridge 1970: 204–5; *pace* Giesebrecht and others). They are Jeremiah's reinterpretation of preaching that is well known, developing a theme appearing elsewhere in the OT and throughout the literature of the ANE. So far as composition within the book of Jeremiah is concerned, this "surrender oracle" of vv 8–9 correlates with the narrative, preaching summary, and report of consequences in 38:1–6 (Volz), just as the "Temple Oracles" in 7:1–15 correlate with the narrative, preaching summary, and report of consequences in 26:1–19, and as the "Temple and Valley Oracles" in 7:30–8:3 correlate with the narrative, preaching summary, and report of consequences in 19:1–20:6 (see further Rhetoric and Composition for 19:1–13).

The following key word repetitions bind the four oracles together:

I	*Look I . . .*	*hinĕnî*	v 4
	the Chaldeans who are besieging you	*hakkaśdîm haṣṣārîm ʿălêkem*	
II	*. . . I will give*	*ʾettēn*	v 7
	from the pestilence, from the sword,	*min-haddeber min-haḥereb*	
	and from the famine	*ûmin-hārāʿāb*	
III	*Look I will set*	*hinĕnî nōtēn*	v 8
	by sword, and by famine, and by pestilence	*baḥereb ûbārāʿāb ûbaddāber*	v 9
	the Chaldeans who are besieging you	*hakkaśdîm haṣṣārîm ʿălêkem*	
IV	*. . . it shall be given*	*tinnātēn*	v 10

These oracles teem with *accumulatio*, as Calvin and others point out, although the phenomenon is evaluated negatively by Rudolph, who dubs it "verbosity of expression." H. Weippert (1973: 80) calls it *Kunstprosa* ("artistic prose"), which she evaluates more positively. The buildup of words and phrases is to drive the point home. Calvin says King Zedekiah needs to be awakened. In v 5:

> And I myself will fight against you with outstretched hand and with strong arm, yes, in anger and in wrath and in great fury.

In v 7 the *accumulatio* makes an abb'a' structure of four terms : three terms : three terms : four terms:

a Zedekiah . . . and his servants, and the people, and those remaining in this city
  b   from the pestilence, from the sword, and from the famine
  b' into the hand of Nebuchadrezzar . . . and into the hand of their enemies . . .
     and into the hand of those who seek their lives
a' And he will strike them down . . . he will not spare them, and he will not pity,
   and he will not have mercy

Some modern Versions (RSV; JB; NAB; NIV) follow T, which combines the last two categories of a) into one ("and the people in this city who remain" or the like), reducing the number from four to three. But other modern Versions (NEB; NJV; NRSV; REB; NJB) correctly translate four categories. In v 9 we find again the common

by sword, and by famine, and by pestilence.

All of these phrases are Jeremianic, the one familiar from Deuteronomy being "with outstretched hand and with strong arm" in v 5, although Jeremiah inverts the cliché, probably intentionally. The usual form is "(with) strong hand and (with) outstretched arm" (Deut 4:34; 5:15; 7:19; 11:2; 26:8).

The LXX has a fewer number of accumulated phrases than MT, which may mean, as Janzen (1973: 43–44; 205 n. 19) and McKane argue, that the Hebrew *Vorlage* to the LXX did not have them. But this makes neither the LXX nor its *Vorlage* the better and/or more original text. McKane's view of a later "editorial process of systematization and expansion" in MT is not the correct one, nor is there justification in his claim that rhetorical prose of the type found here is "far removed from the historical Jeremiah" (pp. 505–6). What has happened is that homiletical rhetoric—perfectly good homiletical rhetoric—has suffered both deliberate and accidental loss in the LXX text of Jeremiah.

Catchwords connecting to the following cluster of oracles:

v 10 *fire*   v 12 *fire*

NOTES

21:1. *The word that came to Jeremiah from Yahweh when King Zedekiah sent to him Pashhur son of Malchiah and Zephaniah son of Maaseiah, the priest.* Here for the first time in the book is third-person narrative prose documenting events in the reigns of either Jehoiakim or Zedekiah. Neither king is mentioned in the First Edition, except in the superscription of 1:1–3.

The word that came to Jeremiah from Yahweh. On this superscription, see Note for 7:1. Outside the First Edition, it appears variously in 21:1; 25:1; 30:1; 32:1; 34:1, 8; 35:1; 40:1; and 44:1. The T, as elsewhere, expands to "word of prophecy."

King Zedekiah. "Zedekiah" was the throne name given to Mattaniah by Nebuchadrezzar, who made him king after capturing Jerusalem and exiling Jehoiachin, the queen mother, and other leading citizens to Babylon in 597 B.C. (2 Kgs 24:17). An uncle to King Jehoiachin (not a brother, as stated in 2 Chr 36:10), Zedekiah became king at 21 and ruled for 11 years (597–586 B.C.), until Jerusalem fell a second time to Nebuchadrezzar, and Judahite nationhood was brought to an end (2 Kgs 24:18; cf. Jer 1:3). This king's weak personal character, a city now bereft of its most capable citizens, and a rival Judahite king held captive in faraway Babylon combined to create a near-chaotic existence all during Zedekiah's reign, and by the time the event reported here took place, which was 588 B.C., the die was cast for Jerusalem's fall. As far as Jeremiah was concerned, Zedekiah's reign was doomed before it began (24:8–10).

Pashhur son of Malchiah. Hebrew *pašḥûr ben-malkîyyâ.* This is not the Temple priest who placed Jeremiah in the stocks (20:1–6) but another Pashhur mentioned in connection with the events of 38:1–6, whose priestly family is recorded in Neh 11:12 and 1 Chr 9:12 as having survived into the postexilic period (Cheyne; Duhm). Because this Pashhur appears in 38:1–6 to be one of the princes (*śārîm*) calling for Jeremiah's death (v 4), and because the pit into which the prophet is subsequently thrown is said to belong to a certain "Malchiah, the king's son" (v 6), the argument has been put forth by certain commentators (Giesebrecht; Cornill; Rudolph; and others) that this Pashhur was not a priest but an appointee of the king, royal or otherwise. But such a view is difficult to maintain, particularly when the name and patronym of this priest correspond precisely to the name and patronym in the postexilic priestly lists and also when there is no clear indication in 38:1–6 that Pashhur son of Malchiah is one of the princes or that his father is "Malchiah, the king's son." Both may be true, but also not true. It may be that this individual was both prince and priest. Zephaniah, after all, was both prince and prophet (Zeph 1:1). Also, "the king's son" may simply designate a royal officer and not be someone in the royal family, which would mean that Malchiah need not be an actual son of the king, but this more general meaning for the term is not universally accepted (see Note for 36:26). If Pashhur is a priest, then it is odd that the title *hakkōhēn* ("the priest") is given only to Zephaniah, and not to both of them (although *Daath Mikra* maintains that it does apply to both; cf. Rosenberg). Regardless of what title or titles Pashhur holds, he is later in the company of princes who want Jeremiah put to death for preaching surrender to the Babylonians. This individual must then be a critic of the prophet. For the names "Pashhur" and "Malchiah," which have turned up on the Arad ostraca and on numerous seals and seal impressions, see Appendix I.

Zephaniah son of Maaseiah, the priest. An associate of Seraiah, the head priest (52:24; 2 Kgs 25:18), and possibly successor to Pashhur son of Immer who put Jeremiah in the stocks. As associate priest, Zephaniah assisted the head priest and was responsible for maintaining Temple order (29:25–26). After the fall of Jerusalem, both he and Seraiah were rounded up with others and brought before Nebuchadrezzar at Riblah, where they were executed (see Note for 52:24). Maaseiah, Zephaniah's father, was a Temple doorkeeper (35:4), the priest who gave Jeremiah access to the Temple when he went there with the Rechabites. Some years earlier, Zephaniah was criticized in a letter from Babylon for being "soft" on Jeremiah when the latter was preaching a long exile (29:25–28). This would seem to indicate that Zephaniah was a man of more restraint than his predecessor. Holladay and others have plausibly suggested that the Pashhur-Zephaniah team represented a pro-Egyptian group opposed to submitting to the Babylonians. But if Pashhur is a critic and enemy of

Jeremiah, as suggested above, and Zephaniah is sympathetic to the prophet, as appears likely, the king could be employing a "good cop, bad cop" strategy in sending the two together, which he seems to have done in sending Zephaniah with Jucal on a later embassy (see Note for 37:3). Malamat (1991b: 231–32) points out how in the Mari texts diviners are typically sent in pairs to the secret council of the king, most likely "to support the testimony emerging from the omens and to present it properly." The name "Zephaniah" occurs elsewhere in the OT and is well attested on contemporary nonbiblical artifacts. "Maaseiah," in its short form, "Maasai," is attested on one of the Arad ostraca, and appears in its long form on seals and seal impressions from Tell Beit Mirsim, Jerusalem, Hebron, and elsewhere. On both names, see further Appendix I.

2. *Seek would you Yahweh on our behalf.* The verb *drš* has the technical meaning of "seek by means of a divine oracle" (37:7; 1 Kgs 22:5; 2 Kgs 3:11). Earlier, Jeremiah cited foolish kings who failed to do this (10:21). In 37:3, the request is, "Pray (*hitpallel*) would you on our behalf to Yahweh our God," which means the same thing (Thelle 1998). Hezekiah's embassy to the prophet Isaiah in 2 Kgs 19:1–4 = Isa 37:1–4 came in response to a similar emergency. It was common practice in antiquity for kings to seek oracles from prophets or other intermediaries in times of war. In a Mari text the deity states:

> When you participate in a campaign, by no means set out without consulting an oracle. When I, in an oracle of mine, should be favorable, you will set out on a campaign. If it is not so, do not pass the gate [of the city?].
>
> (Malamat 1993: 238)

The Mari text's situation, however, differs from the present one in that the king is deciding whether to wage war, whereas Zedekiah, with an enemy outside Jerusalem preparing to besiege it, wonders whether he can defend the city or be delivered by miraculous intervention.

Seek would you. Hebrew *děrāš-nā'*. The particle *nā'*, which is emphatic (KB³) and forceful, occurs in 37:3 but not in 2 Kgs 19:4 = Isa 37:4.

Nebuchadrezzar, king of Babylon, is fighting against us. On the beginning of the final siege of Jerusalem, see 2 Kgs 25:1 and Note for 39:1.

Nebuchadrezzar, king of Babylon. The first mention of Nebuchadrezzar by name in the book. "Babylon" and "the king of Babylon" are first mentioned in 20:4. The LXX omits the name here, as it often does (Janzen 1973: 139–41). But Aq and Theod have it. Nebuchadrezzar II, oldest son of Nabopolassar, was king of Babylon from 604 to 562 B.C. These two kings, Nabopolassar and Nebuchadrezzar, brought Babylon to its zenith of power during the late seventh and early sixth centuries B.C., bringing down the mighty Assyrian Empire in 612 B.C., expelling the Egyptians from Syria and Palestine in 605 B.C., and keeping Egypt within its own boundaries thereafter — also, not incidentally, ending nationhood for Judah in 586 B.C. Nebuchadrezzar during his reign also effectively controlled the Trans-Jordan — Ammon, Moab, and possibly

Edom—extending his influence east of Edom into Kedar, which is in the Syrian-Arabian desert. The two kings embarked on an extensive building program, making Babylon one of the great cities—perhaps the greatest—in the ancient world (see Notes for 50:1 and 51:58).

The spelling of Nebuchadrezzar's name with an *r* instead of an *n* finds confirmation in the Babylonian Chronicle (BM 21946 obv. 1; Wiseman 1956: 66–67), where Akk *Nabū-kudurri-uṣur* is now agreed to mean "Nabu, protect the (eldest) son!" Earlier *kudurru* was taken to mean "boundary" (Tallqvist 1914: 152–53), but now it is translated "(eldest) son" (AHw 1: 500 *kudurru* III; CAD 8: 497 *kudurru* C). In Jeremiah 27–29, and only there in the book, the spelling "Nebuchadnezzar" (with an *n*) occurs 8 times (27:6, 8, 20; 28:3, 11, 14; 29:1, 3). This spelling occurs also in Daniel, while in Ezekiel it is with an *r*. In Jer 29:21, and 28 other times in the book (including the present verse), the spelling is with an *r*, which is older and doubtless correct. Spellings elsewhere in the OT vary, with variations occurring also in Heb MSS. Even in Akkadian texts the spellings vary. Van Selms (1974) thinks the spelling with an *n* comes from a nickname, since Akk *kudannu* means "mule" ("Nabu, protect the mule!"). For a good summary of Nebuchadrezzar's reign as known from the Bible and the Babylonian Chronicle, see Fensham 1982.

perhaps Yahweh will do for us according to all his extraordinary deeds, and he will go away from us. The LXX omits *'ôtānû*, "(for) us," which is the less common, *plene* form. Yahweh is known in Israel for his "extraordinary deeds" (*niplā'ōt*) in history (Exod 34:10; Pss 40:6[Eng 40:5]; 72:18; 78:4; 86:10; 96:3; and often in the Psalms), particularly in the Exodus (Pss 78:11; 106:22; cf. Exod 3:20). But in the back of Zedekiah's mind—and the minds of all devout people—was doubtless Hezekiah's embassy to Isaiah during the Sennacherib crisis (701 B.C.), the favorable answer then received, and Yahweh's miraculous deliverance of Jerusalem (2 Kings 19 = Isaiah 37). This is now the theme of the false prophets against whom Jeremiah has to contend.

perhaps. Hebrew *ûlay*. Hezekiah, too, was tentative about Yahweh's possible intervention in the crisis he faced: "Perhaps (*ûlay*) Yahweh your God heard (all) the words of the Rabshakeh, whom his master the king of Assyria has sent to mock the living God, and will rebuke with words that which Yahweh your God has heard" (2 Kgs 19:4 = Isa 37:4).

and he will go away. The verb *ʿlh* has the meaning "go away" in 8:18; 34:21; 37:5 and 11. See also 2 Kgs 12:18. Zedekiah is hoping that the Babylonians will lift the siege and go home.

3. *But Jeremiah said to them, Thus you shall say to Zedekiah.* Jeremiah does not go himself to the king but sends a message back through the messengers. Calvin thinks that this was an act of contempt on Jeremiah's part, but not necessarily. Jeremiah may not have been invited into the king's presence. Hebrew *tō'mĕrun* ("you shall say") has the final *nun* (*Nûn paragogicum*; GKC §47m), which occurs often (over 300 times) in older books of the OT. Here it is written defectively (usually it is *tō'mĕrûn*). The LXX adds "king of Judah" after "Zedekiah" (see v 7).

4. *Thus said Yahweh, God of Israel.* The LXX lacks "God of Israel." Rudolph thinks the LXX abbreviates; Janzen (1973: 43) disagrees, saying a prophetic cliché has been expanded.

I will turn around the weapons of war that are in your hand. The verb is *sbb,* which can also be translated "turn back." Yahweh will turn the weapons against those wielding them. Kimḥi says the fighters will have no power to wage war, making their weapons useless. The ANE treaties contain curses that call upon the gods to break and turn around the treaty-breaker's weapons, usually the bow (cf. Hos 1:5; Jer 49:35; Ezek 39:3). From a treaty of Esarhaddon (#543; Hillers 1964: 60):

May they break your bow . . .
May they reverse the direction of the bow in your hand.

Again, from an Esarhaddon treaty (#573–75; Wiseman 1958a: 71–72; Borger 1961: 193; *ANET*[3] 540; H. Weippert 1970: 402–8; 1973: 84–85), is this curse:

May they shatter your bow and cause you to sit beneath your enemy
May they cause the bow to come away from your hand
May they cause your chariots to be turned upside down.

In *ANET*[3] line #575 is translated: "May they turn backward your chariots" (so also Borger). Weippert sees the present situation as holy war in reverse, where Yahweh brings confusion to the ranks of Jerusalem's soldiers, and they are defeated (cf. Deut 28:20). From the Code of Hammurabi is a curse stating that the goddess Inanna will bring about confusion and defeat to fighting warriors (*ANET*[3] 179, rev. xxviii; *CS II* 353):

May she [i.e., Inanna] shatter his weapons on the field of battle and conflict
May she create confusion (and) revolt for him
May she strike down his warriors (and) water the earth with their blood!

that are in your hand. The LXX omits, which can be attributed to haplography (whole-word: *'šr . . . 'šr*). Here Janzen (1973: 43) agrees. The phrase is present in Symm.

the king of Babylon and. The LXX omits, which is doubtless more haplography (whole-word: *'t . . . 't*). The words are not MT expansion (*pace* Janzen 1973: 43; Holladay). Aquila, Symm, and Theod all have them.

Chaldeans. Chaldeans = Babylonians. On Chaldea and the Chaldeans, see Note for 50:1.

who are besieging you from outside the wall. The *lě* on *laḥômâ* ("wall") is a genitive: "of the wall" (GKC §129b). Some commentators (Ewald; Duhm; Peake; Streane; Volz; Bright; Thompson; Boadt) think that the Chaldeans are not yet up to the city wall but still in the open field. This mistaken interpretation appears to derive from the T (see below).

and I will gather them together into the midst of this city. I.e., the Chaldeans (Kimḥi; Volz), not the weapons of war (*pace* Rashi; Rudolph), and not the defenders of Jerusalem (*pace* Cheyne; Duhm; Peake). The view that Jerusalem's defenders are at this early stage engaging the enemy outside the walls of Jerusalem, after which they will be driven inside, is traceable to ʻIʼ, which has "I will gather *you* [i.e., the defenders of Jerusalem] together into this city." But the Babylonians have already begun their siege, which means they are outside the wall and the defenders all inside. Calvin has it right: the Chaldeans are fighting outside the city, and Yahweh will (later, after a breach is made) bring them inside, at which time they will occupy the heart of the city. This is how it happened (39:1–3).

and I will gather them together. Lacking in the LXX, but present in Symm (*kai sunaxō autous*). The words bring the thought to completion and should be retained.

5. *And I myself will fight against you with outstretched hand and with strong arm.* The pronoun *ʼănî* ("I") is emphatic: It is Yahweh himself who is taking up the fight against his covenant people, precisely the opposite of what Zedekiah wished for. Lam 2:5 states: "The Lord became like an enemy." Even without the precise wording of 22:7, the language here is nevertheless that of holy war (de Vaux 1956b: 264–65; Moran 1963a: 338). De Vaux points out that holy war traditions have their clearest and most complete expression in Deuteronomy, which he finds remarkable, since at the time, Israel's military triumphs were in the distant past. In the later years of nationhood, wars were less clearly religious in character, making Yahweh's statement here that he is fighting against Judah a sharp and unexpected reversal of ancient holy war ideology. On "holy war" in ancient Israel, see de Vaux 1956b: 258–67.

with outstretched hand and with strong arm. Hebrew *bĕyād nĕṭûyâ ûbizrôaʻ ḥăzāqâ*. This reversal of holy war ideology deeply penetrates the prophet's language, with the present phrase inverting the usual "(with) strong hand and (with) outstretched arm" cliché, signifying judgment here, not deliverance. In Deuteronomy, the standard cliché celebrates Yahweh's miraculous deliverance in the Exodus (Deut 4:34; 5:15; 7:19; 11:2; 26:8; cf. S. R. Driver 1902: lxxix, #12; Weinfeld 1972b: 329, #14), a sense in which Jeremiah also uses it (32:21). But "I will stretch out my hand" is a Jeremianic expression for divine judgment (6:12; 15:6), which may account for the reversal. The image of a flexed arm wielding the sword is well known from Egyptian literature, occuring in the Tell el-Amarna Letters (EA 286, 12; 287, 27; 288, 14, 34; cf. ANET[3] 487–89) and elsewhere. Rameses II is referred to as the "strong armed," the one "whose hand is outstretched" (Gaballa 1969). Pharaoh Apries (Hophra) took on the titulary name "possessed of a muscular arm"; and his father, Psammetichus II, gave himself the epithet "Mighty-armed" (Freedy and Redford 1970: 482–83; cf. Ezek 30:21–22).

yes, in anger and in wrath and in great fury. Hebrew *ûbĕʼap ûbĕḥēmâ ûbĕqeṣep gādôl*. Another cliché, occuring also in 32:37 and in Deut 29:27[Eng 29:28]. More common in Jeremiah is simply "(my) anger and (my) wrath"

(7:20; 32:31, 37; 33:5; 36:7; 42:18). The LXX omits "yes, in anger," which is not a MT expansion but another omission attributable to haplography (homoeo-arcton: *wb . . . wb*). Janzen (1973: 43, #44) in his evaluation of this reading is undecided.

6. *And I will strike down the inhabitants of this city—both human and beast; by a great pestilence they shall die.* The verb *nkh* can mean "strike down to kill" (26:23), but here probably means "strike down savagely"; death will come by pestilence (cf. 18:21). Yahweh's savage beating or striking down of his people is a recurring theme in the Jeremianic poetry (2:30; 5:3; 14:19; 30:14).

both human and beast. Hebrew *wĕ'et-hā'ādām wĕ'et-habbĕhēmâ*. Translating the *waws* "both . . . and" (so T; cf. KB³). The LXX and Vg omit the first *waw*, for which reason some delete (Giesebrecht; S. R. Driver; Ehrlich 1912: 296; Volz). The nouns here are to be taken as collectives: judgment will fall upon both humans and animals (7:20), another indication that Yahweh is carrying on holy war (cf. Deut 20:16–17; 1 Sam 15:3). In 27:6, Yahweh says he has given Nebuchadnezzar also the beasts of the field. The expression, "(hu)man and beast" occurs often in the Jeremiah prose (7:20; 21:6; 27:5; 31:27; 32:43; 33:10 [2×], 12; 36:29; 51:62) and once in the poetry (50:3).

7. *And after this . . . I will give Zedekiah, king of Judah, and his servants, and the people . . . into the hand of Nebuchadrezzar, king of Babylon. . . . And he will strike them down into the mouth of the sword . . . and he will not have mercy.* This will be after the siege has done its work, and Jerusalem's inhabitants are sick, wounded, or dead, as the enemy pours into the city. Yahweh says that he will give Zedekiah and survivors into the hands of Nebuchadrezzar and his army, who will then cut them down without mercy. In actual fact, while Zede-kiah was made to endure the horrible conditions of the siege, he did not him-self meet a violent death (cf. 34:5). His sons were killed by the sword, after which he was blinded, enchained, and carted off to Babylon (39:1–7; 52:4–11). It may then be said that he, like most of the others, was shown no mercy.

his servants. Hebrew *'ăbādāyw*. These are important people in the employ of the king, i.e., royal officials (cf. 22:2, 4; 25:19; 36:24, 31; 37:2, 18; 46:26). For "servants" of Yahweh, who figure in his rule over Israel and the rest of the world, see Note for 25:9.

and the people, and those remaining in this city from the pestilence, from the sword, and from the famine. A few Heb MSS, LXX, S, and T omit *wĕ'et* before *hannniš'ārîm* ("those remaining"), which gives a reduced reading: "and the people remaining in this city." Compressions of this sort are common in the LXX, but not in T. Many commentators (Giesebrecht, Duhm, Volz, Rudolph, Bright, Thompson, Holladay, McKane), in any case, delete the *nota accusativi*. Calvin says the copulative is to be taken as *even:* "even those remaining. . . ." A rhetorical structure in the verse argues in favor of a four-term *accumulatio*, not a three-term (see Rhetoric and Composition).

from the pestilence, from the sword, and from the famine. On this triad, usually in the form "sword . . . famine . . . pestilence" (v 9), see Note for 5:12. In the apocryphal book of Baruch it appears as "by famine, and sword, and pestilence"

(Bar 2:25 RSV). Many Heb MSS and the Vrs have "and from the sword," which is supported by 4QJer^c. But T supports MT. The Qumran text lacks "and from the famine," which could be attributed to haplography (homoeoteleuton: *h . . . h*).

into the hand of Nebuchadrezzar, king of Babylon, and. The phrase is lacking in the LXX, which is probably another loss due to haplography (whole-word: *byd . . . byd*). Some commentators (Giesebrecht; Duhm; Cornill; Holladay, who considers haplography; and Jones) go with the shorter LXX reading. Aquila, Symm, and Theod all contain the phrase. Read the MT. For occurrences of this stereotyped phrase in the Jeremiah prose, see Note for 22:25.

and into the hand of those who seek their lives. I.e., to kill them. The LXX omits "and into the hand," which does away entirely with the *accumulatio* in MT ("into the hand of Nebuchadrezzar" is a victim of haplography). Calvin does not find the repetition superfluous, saying that the enemy will not be content with plunder but will burn with rage and thirst for blood. Go then with the MT, whose longer reading also supports a rhetorical structure in the verse (see Rhetoric and Composition).

And he will strike them down. I.e., the Babylonian king will. The LXX and a Targum MS have "and they [i.e., the enemies] will strike them down." The LXX reading is consistent with its omission of the phrase naming Nebuchadrezzar, but because the latter is attributable to haplography, we cannot speak with Holladay about a shift of attention in MT to Nebuchadrezzar. The LXX is the defective text.

into the mouth of the sword. I.e., up to the hilt. Hebrew *lĕpî-ḥereb*. This ancient holy war expression (Josh 6:21; 8:24; 10:28, 35, 37, 39; 11:11, 12, 14) has been traditionally rendered "with the edge of the sword" (cf. BDB), the rendering appearing here in certain modern Versions (AV; RSV; NAB; NRSV). Akkadian has a comparable expression, *pî patrim* (AHw 2: 874 *pû[m]* I, F; cf. KB^3). The translation of *peh* as "edge" rather than "mouth" may derive from the Vg, which has *in ore gladii* ("to the edge of the sword"). Kimḥi says that "mouth" in this expression refers to the sword's sharp edge. The LXX's *ev stomati machairas* ("into the mouth of the dagger") literally translates the Hebrew. The inexactness of the Hebrew, noted by S. R. Driver and others, is reflected in other modern Versions (AmT; NEB; JB; NJV; NIV; REB; NJB), which render the expression together with the verb as "put them to the sword." While this preserves the general sense, it inadequately translates the Hebrew (except that the *lamed* on *lĕpî* is correctly rendered "to"). Meek (1951) says the phrase means "smite into the mouth of the sword," which is the plain meaning of the Hebrew and doubtless the correct rendering. Meek points out that swords (and axes) have turned up in excavations in northern Syria, northern Mesopotamia, and northwestern Iran where the blade is represented as a tongue sticking out of an open-mouthed lion or dragon carved into the hilt (see Meek 1951: 32 for drawings). Some swords and axes have two devouring animals, which helps clarify the "double-mouthed" (not "two-edged") swords of Judg 3:16; Prov 5:4; and Ps 149:6. The "double-mouthed" sword thrust by Ehud into Eglon, king of Moab, went in hilt and all (Judg 3:22), doing its full work of consuming the victim. The sword is commonly said to "consume" (*'kl*) its prey (Deut 32:42; 2 Sam 2:26; 11:25), i.e., flesh and blood of the victim enter the mouth of the sword at the hilt. Yadin (1963: 78–80, 206–7) thinks the sword used in Joshua's campaigns was the sickle sword, which had a long curved blade and was a "smiting" weapon. But the excavated swords with "mouths" include also the short, straight sword, which was a "thrusting" weapon. A weapon of this type was used against Eglon. On *lĕpî-ḥereb*, see also discussion in Keel 1974: 77–79 n. 1.

he will not spare them, and he will not pity, and he will not have mercy. This same triad occurs in 13:14. The LXX omits one of the expressions, probably "and he will not pity" (so *BHS*), which can be attributed to haplography (whole-word: *wl' . . . wl'*). It also has the first person for both verbs and adds another "them" at the end (*ou pheisomai ep' autois kai ou mē oiktirēsō autos*, "I will not be sparing of them, and I shall not have compassion upon them"). The first-person verbs are consistent with the LXX's omission of the phrase naming "Nebuchadrezzar."

8. *And to this people you shall say.* The verb *tō'mar* ("you shall say") is singular, which means Yahweh is speaking directly to Jeremiah, giving him the oracles to follow for delivery to the people. These oracles do not go to the messengers who are sent back to the king.

Look I will set before you. 4QJer^c has *hinnēh* with a conjugated form of the verb.

the way of life and the way of death. The "ways of life and death" expressed here give a new twist to the sermon in Deut 30:15–20, which, according to G. E. Wright (1953: 321), may have been recited at Josiah's covenant renewal festival (2 Kings 23). In Deuteronomy, the "way of life and good" consists in obeying the commandments; the "way of death and evil" consists in disobedience and the concomitant effrontery of chasing after other gods. The same basic idea is expressed in the blessing-and-curse passage of Deut 11:26–32, which Peake thinks served as a model for the preaching here. Jeremiah's preaching, in either case, presupposes a different reality entirely. People are on record as having disobeyed the commandments and gone after other gods; therefore, the covenant curses are about to fall upon them, with the result that the way of life has now become surrendering to the Babylonians; holding out in the city is the way of death. These oracles in vv 8–10 were preached by Jeremiah while he was in the court of the guard (38:2; Volz) and are what led to him being cast into a pit. Preaching surrender was not something new. Jeremiah preached it when the Babylonians came to Jerusalem in 597 B.C. (13:15–17). Volz cites also as background for the present oracles the decision made by the four lepers of Samaria to surrender to the Syrians, which promised life and ended up giving them life (2 Kgs 7:3–8). On the wisdom theme of the "two ways" in Jeremiah and elsewhere in the OT, see Note for 6:16.

9. *Whoever stays in this city shall die by sword, and by famine, and by pestilence, but whoever goes out and surrenders to the Chaldeans who are besieging you shall live, and his life will be his booty.* These words are repeated almost verbatim in the oracle of 38:2. The verb *yṣ'* (normally "to come/go out") has the

technical meaning here of "surrender" (38:2, 17–18; 1 Sam 11:3, 10; 2 Kgs 24:12; Isa 36:16 = 2 Kgs 18:31). The same is true with the following verb, *npl* (normally "to fall"), which can also mean "surrender/desert to the enemy" (37:13–14; 38:19; 39:9; and 52:15 = 2 Kgs 25:11), its meaning here. The S lacks the latter verb, bringing its reading into line with 38:2, where the verb docs not occur. The two verbs together make a redundancy, which could make 38:2 the preferred reading, and the reading here (in both MT and LXX) an expanded one (so Holladay). Surrender, shameful as it is, will not have come as a completely new idea to Zedekiah, even if he was hoping for a deliverance along the lines of what occurred when Sennacherib held Jerusalem under siege. In 597 B.C., Jehoiachin and the queen mother made the decision to surrender, and Zedekiah should also have remembered that Jehoiakim's policy of rebelling against Nebuchadrezzar proved to be a disaster. So while commentators point out here and in 38:1–6 that counseling surrender, as Jeremiah did, amounted to (high) treason, there are times when it is the only course of action to take. As things turned out, Zedekiah and his advisers did not correctly assess the situation, and the price they paid was high. The city was captured, and nationhood for Judah came to an end.

by sword, and by famine, and by pestilence. The LXX lacks "and by pestilence," which could be due to haplography (homoeoarcton: *w . . . w*). This same omission occurs in the LXX equivalents of 32:24[LXX 39:24]; 38:2[LXX 45:2], and elsewhere (see discussion in Note for 38:2). The term is present in Aq (*kai en loimō*).

and his life will be his booty. On this pithy remark, which was also spoken to Baruch (45:5) and Ebed-melech (39:18), see Note for 45:5. Those surrendering to the Babylonians will get the same preferential treatment that these two trusting souls are promised. A few Heb MSS and the LXX have after "booty" the word "and live" (*wāḥāy*), which could be an addition from 38:2.

10. *For I have set my face against this city for evil, and not for good. . . . Into the hand of the king of Babylon it shall be given, and he will burn it with fire.* Another version of the oracle in 38:3 and a portion of the oracle spoken to Zedekiah in 34:2. See also 32:3, 28–29.

For I have set my face against this city for evil, and not for good. On the idiom "to set the face against," see Note for 42:15. The expression "for evil and not for good" (*lĕrāʿâ wĕlōʾ lĕṭôbâ*) occurs elsewhere (39:16 and 44:27) and may derive from Amos (Amos 9:4). The "good and evil" duality is present also in Jeremiah's vision of the figs (chap. 24).

oracle of Yahweh. The LXX omits, which here could be due to haplography (homoeoteleuton: *h . . . h*). Aquila, Symm, and Theod all have it.

Into the hand. Hebrew *bĕyad*. The LXX has "hands" plural (*cheiras*).

MESSAGE AND AUDIENCE

The audience learns from the introductory narrative to the oracles here preserved that Yahweh's word came to Jeremiah when Zedekiah sent Pashhur son of Malchiah and Zephaniah son of Maaseiah to him. The request was that Jeremiah inquire of Yahweh, since Nebuchadrezzar had come to Jerusalem and was making war against the city. Zedekiah expressed the hope that Yahweh would perform another of his miraculous deeds and that Nebuchadrezzar would return home or depart for some other place. The audience will remember hearing about what happened when Sennacherib came to besiege Jerusalem and how Yahweh miraculously intervened, causing the Assyrian king to hurry home. And they will have recalled often enough and recited in worship the miracles associated with the Exodus and other grand deliverances of the past. But some may also recall Nebuchadrezzar's last visit to Jerusalem, when the city surrendered, and Jehoiachin, the queen mother, and many prominent citizens were shamefully marched off to Babylon.

To this embassy Jeremiah gives two oracles, which are to be brought back to the king. In the first, Yahweh says he will turn around the weapons currently in the hands of Jerusalem's defenders. What is more, he will bring the Babylonians now outside the wall into the city center. Yahweh, to everyone's horror, says he is warring against his own people with the same flexed hand and arm that once worked the grand deliverances they celebrate. Reversing a familiar metaphor will drive home the point that Yahweh is reversing the direction that the holy war is now taking. He will do this in a terrible fit of rage, striking down both humans and beasts in the city, leaving them to die by a pestilence that will race through every quarter once the dead bodies accumulate and there is nowhere to bury them.

In a second oracle, Yahweh says he will give Zedekiah, his servants, people of the city, and the survivors of the pestilence, sword, and famine into Nebuchadrezzar's hand and also into the hands of others who are seeking their lives. In a final merciless act, the enemy will finish off would-be survivors with the sword, which is consistent with the aims and purpose of holy war.

In connection with the present crisis, Yahweh tells Jeremiah to speak a second word directly to the people. In the first of two oracles, the people are presented with a way of life and a way of death. No longer will this have anything to do with obedience to the commandments. The choice is now to wait out the crisis with others and die by sword, famine, or pestilence or to surrender to the Chaldeans and gain the modest war booty of their own lives. In a second oracle, Yahweh says that he has set his face against the city for evil and not for good. The king of Babylon will capture it and burn it with fire.

All four oracles date to the time when the Babylonian army arrived in Jerusalem in 588 B.C. and began their siege of the city. The Egyptians have not yet made their move that forced a temporary lifting of the siege. Two oracles are sent with the messengers to King Zedekiah, who requested them, and two are spoken by Jeremiah directly to the people—if not in the Temple courtyard, then in some other public place. Anytime after this, the oracles and their introductions could have been written down by Baruch or some other scribe in the prophet's confidence.

2. Oracles to the Royal House (21:11–14)

a) Execute Justice in the Morning! (21:11–12)

21 [11]To[a] the house of the king of Judah: 'Hear the word of Yahweh, [12]house of
David.'
　　Thus said Yahweh:
　　Execute justice in the morning
　　　　and rescue the robbed from the oppressor's hand!
　　lest my wrath go forth like fire
　　　　and burn so none can quench it
　　　　　　on account of their[b] evil doings.

b) Indictment for Royal Pride (21:13)

[13]Look I am against you, sitting one of the valley
　　rock of the tableland—oracle of Yahweh
Those saying, 'Who can come down upon us
　　and who can enter into our habitations?'

c) Judgment on Royal Deeds (21:14)

[14]But I will reckon upon you
　　according to the fruit of your doings
　　　　—oracle of Yahweh
And I will kindle a fire in her forest
　　and it will consume everything around her.

RHETORIC AND COMPOSITION

The present verses contain three brief oracles delivered for the benefit of
Judah's royal house (v 12aβ–bc; v 13; v 14), preceded by an introduction to the
King Collection and a superscription to the three oracles (vv 11–12aα). Each
oracle has a messenger formula, which is to say that vv 13–14 are two oracles,
not one, as many commentators assume. Rudolph's omission of the formula in
v 12 (on metrical grounds) is to be rejected, and the omission of the formula in
v 14 by the LXX forms part of a larger loss attributable to haplography (see
Notes). Taken as a cluster, the three oracles show a progression from admonition to accusation to judgment, just as the three oracles of 7:3–14 do (see Rhetoric and Composition for 7:1–15):

I	Admonition to royal house about executing justice	v 12
II	Accusation against Jerusalem for boasting impregnability	v 13
III	Judgment on the royal house	v 14

---

[a]Deleting the copulative as a later addition (see Notes).
[b]Reading the Kt (cf. 26:3); Q has "your doings" (cf. 4:4b).

The unit as a whole is delimited at the top end by a *setumah* in M^A, M^L, and M^P prior to v 11, where also a shift from prose to poetry occurs. The three oracles are all poetry, two lines each. Delimitation at the bottom end is by a *setumah* in M^L (only) following v 14, after which comes the chapter division and a return to prose. The main medieval codices contain no sections after vv 12 or 13, but one MS in the Cambridge Genizah Collection (A 14.4) does have a section after v 12.

All three oracles have verbal similarities to other oracles, or portions of other oracles, in the book. Cornill (following Stade 1892: 278–79) and Volz took vv 11–12 to be a doublet of 22:1(2)–3; however, the beginning unit in chap. 22 is vv 1–5, which contains two oracles, one of greater length (vv 3–5), preceded by narrative that puts the oracle in context (vv 1–2). This narrative, providing a context for oracles that are similar, could point to 21:11–12 and 22:1–5 being doublets, just like 7:1–15 and 26:1–19; 7:30–8:3 and 19:1–20:6; and 21:8–10 and 38:1–6 (see Rhetoric and Composition for 21:1–10). Ideas about doublets in the case of 21:11–12 and 22:1–5, or secondary expansion in the case of 22:1–5, are found also in Duhm, Rudolph, and Thiel (1973: 238). But since the oracle in 22:3–4 is so much longer than the oracle here and has only the first line in common with the present oracle, the two may not be doublets at all but separate oracles delivered to different audiences on separate occasions (Weiser). In view of the dramatic quality of the oracles here (see below), this latter possibility seems more likely. The final line of v 12 is also precisely the same as the line in 4:4b. What we probably have are separate oracles with a single line in common. What does seem to be clear is that vv 11b–12 are not a "Deuteronomic addition" (Mowinckel 1914: 20; Jones; *pace* Giesebrecht, xxi). The language is Jeremianic, and the verses should therefore to be taken as a self-standing Jeremiah oracle.

The two oracles in vv 13–14 have similarities to the Babylon oracle in 50:31–32, where the latter could be a reworking of the former. But again, the Babylon oracle could simply be employing at beginning and end some of the same language occurring in the oracles here. The view that vv 13–14 are a "post-Deuteronomic" addition (Thiel 1973: 238 n. 21) should be rejected. The language here is also clearly Jeremianic, and these oracles, like the first, give every indication of being self-standing and authentic words of the prophet.

Oracles I and III contain the following link terms:

| I | . . . like fire . . . their doings | *kā'ēš . . . maʿălêhem* | v 12b |
| III | . . . your doings . . . fire | *maʿălêlêkem . . . 'ēš* | v 14a |

The term "fire" is called a recurring motif by Bright and a catchword by Thompson and Holladay.

The three oracles have a dramatic component typical of other Jeremianic oracles. In all three, the prophet addresses the royal house or Jerusalem in the first line; then, in the second line, he turns to address an audience not specified (apostrophe). This explains the many pronoun changes, one of which is eliminated by a Qere reading in v 12:

| I | Yahweh admonishes the royal house directly to execute justice | v 12a |
| | Yahweh warns of possible judgment to an unspecified audience | v 12b |

| II | Yahweh accuses Jerusalem directly of "sitting pretty" | v 13a |
| | Boast of impregnability is quoted to an unspecified audience | v 13b |

| III | Yahweh speaks directly to the royal house of coming judgment | v 14a |
| | Yahweh speaks judgment to an unspecified audience | v 14b |

It is doubtful whether Jeremiah spoke any of these oracles to the royal house in person. The dramatic element suggests, rather, a delivery to ordinary citizens in the Temple courtyard or at some other public place.

Within the King Collection is a collection of oracles to the royal house consisting of 21:11–22:5 (see Rhetoric and Composition for 21:1–10). This collection contains an inclusio, where the opening of Oracle I here in 21:12 balances the opening of Oracle I in 22:3–4:

21:12   Execute *justice* in the morning
           and rescue the robbed from the oppressor's hand

22:3   Do *justice* and righteousness
           and rescue the robbed from the oppressor's hand

It is possible that this beginning poetry in the King Collection was at some earlier time attached by catchword to the final poetry in chap. 20. Holladay suggests *bōqer* ("morning") as the catchword:

20:16   Let him hear a cry *in the morning (babbōqer)*
21:11   Execute justice *in the morning (labbōqer)*

Catchwords connecting to the previous unit:

v 12 *fire*   v 10 *fire*

Catchwords connecting to the unit following:

21:11 *the house of the king of Judah*   22:1 *the house of the king of Judah*

NOTES

21:11–12. *To the house of the king of Judah.* Hebrew *lĕbêt melek yĕhûdâ.* The MT has a copulative (*waw*) at the beginning, which appears to be a later add-on, creating continuity with what precedes (Rudolph). The words originally formed a superscription to the King Collection (21:11–23:8), just as "To the prophets" in 23:9 is now a superscription to the Prophet Collection (23:9–40). Foreign Nation Oracle Collections are similarly introduced (46:2; 48:1; 49:1, 7, 23, 28). The LXX lacks the copulative and reads the *lamed* as a vocative: *ho oikos basileōs Iouda* ("O house of the king of Judah"), which creates a redundancy with "(O) house of David" following, and is not the better reading (*pace* Stade 1892: 278; Cornill). Aquila and Symm (*kai tō oikō basileōs Iouda*) support the MT.

Hear the word of Yahweh, house of David. Hebrew *šimʿû* ("Hear") is a plural imperative, indicating that the entire royal house is being addressed, not just the king. The oracle introduced also contains plural imperatives (v 12: *dînû . . . wĕhaṣṣîlû*, "Execute . . . and rescue").

house of David. Hebrew *bêt dāwid.* A common dynastic name for the kingdom of Judah (2 Sam 3:1, 6; Isa 7:13). The phrase *bytdwd* ("house of David") in Aramaic has turned up on a ninth-century B.C. royal inscription from Tell Dan (Biran and Naveh 1993: 87; *CS II* 162). Kimḥi says David is mentioned because he administered justice and righteousness to all (cf. 2 Sam 8:15).

Execute justice in the morning, and rescue the robbed from the oppressor's hand! "Justice" (*mišpāṭ*) in the OT is something you do (5:1; 7:5; Gen 18:25; 1 Kgs 3:28b; Mic 6:8; Ps 9:17[Eng 9:16]). The verb here is *dîn*, "judge, execute," but in 22:3 the royal house is told to "Do justice!" *ʿăśû mišpāṭ.* The same applies to "righteousness" (*ṣĕdāqâ*), a term appearing often with "justice" and most closely associated with it (4:2; 9:23[Eng 9:24]; 22:3, 13, 15; 23:5 = 33:15; Ezek 18:5, 21; 33:14, 19; 2 Sam 8:15; 1 Kgs 10:9). The two terms are often used interchangeably in the OT. In the earliest books of the OT, *mišpāṭ* has the meaning of "manner" or "custom" (Gen 40:13; Josh 6:15; Judg 13:12; 1 Sam 2:13; 27:11; cf. O. Booth 1942: 105–7; Snaith 1983: 75–76; Berkovitz 1969: 198–99). Deriving from the root *špṭ*, "to judge," *mišpaṭ* is a judgment determined by custom or precedent (compare the role of "precedent" in English and American law). Later, *mišpaṭ* comes to mean largely proper administration of law and justice in the society. Justice in the present oracle refers to equitable and impartial action by the royal house in conformity with what is legally and morally right, where what is legally and morally right is defined ultimately by stipulations of the Sinai covenant. With regard to both legal cases and disputes of a more informal nature, doing justice consists of rendering right and fair decisions of punishment and vindication. In the OT, doing justice has much to do with eliminating oppression and satisfying the claims of society's poor, needy, and disenfranchised (22:3; cf. Exod 22:20–21[Eng 22:21–22]; 23:6–7; Isa 1:17; and Note for 7:5–6). In the absence of promulgated covenant law, justice consists of action conforming to self-evident norms of what is right and proper, which reverts back to *mišpāṭ* in the older sense of "custom" or "manner." The covenant people are expected to do justice because Yahweh does justice (Gen 18:25; Deut 32:4; Jer 9:23[24]; Psalms 82 and 146). Yahweh loves justice and hates robbery, particularly when the latter goes hand in hand with a burnt offering (Isa 61:8).

In the ANE generally, the king was both lawgiver and judge. In Israel, however, laws were not promulgated by the king but by Yahweh (de Vaux 1965b: 150–52; Boecker 1980: 41). But the king did possess judicial powers, as de Vaux points out, and was, in fact, a judge. In the capacity of judge, he had a solemn obligation to see that justice reigned in the land and was himself expected to execute justice (Psalm 72). Needless to say, this could only be carried out with help from royal officials (Hammershaimb 1966: 36). King David rendered judgments in the city gate (2 Sam 15:2; cf. Ps 101:8), his most famous decision being one that brought justice to himself (2 Sam 12:5–6). King Solomon is remembered for an even more famous judgment that determined the true mother of a baby claimed by feuding harlots (1 Kgs 3:16–28). Filled with divine wisdom, Solomon was acclaimed by all Israel "to have done justice" (la'ăśôt mišpāṭ; v 28). Jeremiah was spared death in a dreadful pit because Ebed-melech brought his plight to King Zedekiah, who, at the time was sitting as judge in the Benjamin Gate (Jer 38:7). The fact that Jehoiakim is scored by Jeremiah for not doing justice and righteousness as his father did (22:13–17) may indicate that he did not bother to sit as judge in the gate, as he should have. The present admonition to "execute justice" is doubtless spoken to Jehoiakim and his royal house. Because of a general breakdown in societal justice during Judah's last years, there arose the belief that justice and righteousness would characterize the reign of the Messiah (23:5–6; Isa 9:5–6[Eng 9:6–7]; 11:1–4). Justice was also expected from kings in neighboring cultures. The Prologue to the Code of Hammurabi (ca. 1700 B.C.) begins by stating that Hammurabi had been named by the gods Anum and Enlil

> to cause justice to prevail in the land
> to destroy the wicked and the evil
> that the strong might not oppress the weak . . .

At the end, Hammurabi states that he did precisely this (i 30–39; v 10–20; ANET³ 164–65; CS II 336–37). A Neo-Babylonian text tells similarly of a king contemporary with Jeremiah who restored justice when the social order was in complete collapse (see Note for 2:34). For further discussion of "justice" in the OT, also other relevant extrabiblical texts on societal justice, see Note for 5:28.

Execute justice . . . and rescue. Hebrew *dînû . . . mišpāṭ wĕhaṣṣîlû*. The LXX has *krinate . . . krima kai kateuthunate kai exelesthe*, "Judge a judgment . . . and act rightly and deliver," which adds a second verb (so Rahlfs). This verb could possibly translate a missing *ûṣĕdāqâ*, since the parallel clause in 22:3 reads *mišpāṭ ûṣĕdāqâ* ("justice and righteousness"), although there the LXX translates *krisin kai dikaiosunēn*. If *ûṣĕdāqâ* was originally in the text here, as it may well have been since "justice and righteousness" often occur together, its absence in MT could be due to haplography (homoeoarcton: *w . . . w*). Janzen (1973: 28) takes *kai kateuthunate* as a (variant) reading or misreading of Heb *wĕhaṣṣîlû* ("and rescue"), which it does not appear to be. McKane follows Ziegler (1957: 255), who omits *kai exelesthe* as a secondary reading.

in the morning. Hebrew *labbōqer* means "in the morning" or "until the morning" (Exod 34:2, 25; Deut 16:4; Amos 4:4; 5:8; Zeph 3:3; Ps 30:6[Eng 30:5]; Ezra 3:3; 1 Chr 9:27; and elsewhere), not "each morning" or "every morning," even though daily action in a given case may be implied. The idea of "each/every morning" is expressed by the idiom *babbōqer babbōqer* (Zeph 3:5), and by the plural *labbĕqārîm* (Isa 33:2; Pss 73:14; 101:8; Lam 3:23). Ziegler (1950: 286) translates "jeden Morgen" in the present verse, but his comparison is to a plural in Ps 101:8. Ehrlich (1912: 297) and Rudolph propose emending to a plural, but this should be rejected. The Versions all read "in the morning" (so also Kimḥi; AV; RSV; NRSV). The emphasis in the oracle is on executing justice, not when or how often to do it. Nor is the point that justice be rendered as quickly as possible (*pace* Giesebrecht; McKane; cf. NEB and REB: "betimes"), however desirable this might be. The royal house, king included, is simply being called upon to render judgments as it is supposed to do and see to it that justice is done. On the city gate as the place where judgments are rendered, see Köhler 1956a: 149–75. Doing it in the morning was a custom from early times, when people passed through the gate, and witnesses could readily be summoned (Ruth 3:13; 4:1–2).

and rescue the robbed from the oppressor's hand. Hebrew *wĕhaṣṣîlû gāzûl miyyad 'ōšēq.* Equitable decisions in the city gate included rescuing victims of robbery and other crimes. The defining act of grace in the OT is Yahweh's rescue of Israel from an oppressor in Egypt, for which reason the covenant people must also be about rescuing the oppressed. Justice in the OT therefore has a close association with rescue and deliverance (Num 35:24–25; Ps 76:10[Eng 76:9]; P. Ramsey 1949: 273–75; Berkovitz 1969: 190–97). Ramsey says that "True justice receives its decisive definition by reference to the standard of God's righteous judgment," and in biblical thought this righteousness is invaded by the "vocabulary of salvation" (cf. Snaith 1983: 69). The close association of *ḥesed* ("covenantal love"), *mišpaṭ* ("justice, judgment"), and *ṣĕdāqâ* ("righteousness, deliverance"), best seen in Jer 9:23[Eng 9:24], is not understood in modern Western thought, according to Berkovitz, where justice is usually thought to be opposed to acts of kindness and mercy. One either loves or judges. It is not so in the Bible, where the concepts are coordinated. The king and the royal house bear a particularly heavy responsibility for rescuing the oppressed, because often—quite often—help will not otherwise be forthcoming. If the royal house is not rescuing the oppressed, it is a good bet that they are engaged in oppression themselves, or in league with those practicing it (Isa 3:14–15; 10:1–2; Mic 3:9–11). Jehoiakim certainly fits the description of a king who practiced oppression (22:17). Robbery and oppression are closely associated in the OT (Deut 28:29; Lev 19:13; Ezek 18:18; and Ps 62:11[Eng 62:10]), where "oppression" (*'ōšeq*) may also mean "extortion." Extortion practiced by the royal house could be a confiscation of property (e.g., Naboth's vineyard in 1 Kgs 21:1–16; cf. Hos 5:10; Isa 5:8). The Qumran *Temple Scroll* (11QT 57:19–21) says regarding the king: "And he shall not pervert justice (*mšpṭ*), and he shall not take a bribe to pervert righteous judgment (*mšpṭ ṣdq*), and he shall not covet field and vineyard, and any wealth and house, and any thing of delight in Israel, nor rob" (Yadin 1983: 258–59).

from the oppressor's hand. Hebrew *miyyad ʿôšēq.* The infinitive *ʿašôq* in 22:3 also means "oppressor." On the occasional interchange of participle and infinitive in the OT, see Wernberg-Møller 1959: 58. The oppressor here is a robber who robs others (Rashi). The LXX, S, and T have "his oppressor" both here and in 22:3, which gives the same meaning.

lest my wrath go forth like fire, and burn so none can quench it, on account of their evil doings. The same tricolon (except with *"your* evil doings") occurs in 4:4b. For other variations of this phrase, see Note on 7:20. This outpouring of the divine wrath is what the Covenant Code promises to anyone who oppresses the sojourner, orphan, or widow (Exod 22:20–23[Eng 22:21–24]). While the application here is probably broader, society's poor and disenfranchised are of primary concern.

on account of their evil doings. A stereotyped expression appearing variously in Jeremianic poetry and prose (4:4b; 21:12; 23:2, 22; 25:5; 26:3; and 44:22; cf. Isa 1:16; Hos 8:15; Deut 28:20), which has turned up also in the Qumran *Temple Scroll* (11QT 59:7; cf. Yadin 1983: 267; Brooke 1997: 202). Lacking in the LXX, this phrase has been taken by many (Stade 1892: 278; Cornill; Rudolph; Weiser; Holladay; McKane) as an addition from 4:4b. But since the entire tricolon here matches the entire tricolon in 4:4b, this argument is less than persuasive. The phrase appears in G^L, Theod, T, S, and Vg, and should therefore be retained (Giesebrecht). Also, "their doings" (Kt) balances "your doings" in v 14; both terms, along with a repetition of "fire," serve to link Oracles I and III (see Rhetoric and Composition).

13. *Look I am against you.* Hebrew *hinĕnî ʾēlayik.* A stereotyped judgment phrase, here with *ʾel* but sometimes with *ʿal*, is called by Humbert (1933) a "challenge formula." Humbert claims it is the summons to a duel, but this remains unproved. Zimmerli (1979: 26, 175) takes it simply as an introduction to a divine threat (once in Ezek 36:9, a promise also), noting in addition that the phrase occurs six times in Jeremiah (21:13; 23:30, 31, 32; 50:31; 51:25), fourteen times in Ezekiel (Ezek 5:8; 13:8, 20; 21:8[Eng 21:3]; 26:3; 28:22; 29:3, 10; 30:22; 34:10; 35:3; 36:9; 38:3; 39:1), and twice in Nahum (Nah 2:14[Eng 2:13]; 3:5). Here a feminine singular suffix points to Lady Jerusalem as the addressee.

sitting one of the valley. Hebrew *yōšebet hāʿēmeq.* Weiser translates "enthroned over the valley," citing for comparison Yahweh's enthronement over the cherubim atop the ark (1 Sam 4:4; 2 Sam 6:2 = 1 Chr 13:6; Pss 80:2; 99:1). The LXX goes its own way with *ton katoikounta tēn koilada sor,* "who dwells in the valley of Sor (Tyre)," including in its translation the next word *ṣûr*, which it reads as *ṣōr* (cf. Ezek 27:3). Aquila similarly has *Tyros* ("Tyre"), but Symm *petra* ("rock"). The "sitting one" image occurs often in Jeremiah (see Note for 46:19). Reference here is to Jerusalem (Jerome; Rashi; Kimḥi; *yōšebet* is feminine), although questions have been raised about the city's being situated in a valley. Topography, however, is not at issue. Jerusalem is surrounded on three sides by deep valleys (cf. *hāʿēmeq* in 31:40; *ʿāmāqayik* in Isa 22:7), and its elevation high above these valleys gives the city a look of being secure, which is what this oracle is all about (Calvin).

rock of the tableland. Hebrew *ṣûr hammîšôr.* Although *mîšôr* can mean "level ground, plain," a better translation here is "tableland," as in 48:8 and 21, where the term denotes the Moab highlands. Jerusalem sits high in the hill country of Judah, remote and secure like a rock on the height.

Who can come down upon us. I.e., from the hills around about Jerusalem, particularly the Mount of Olives to the east, which looks down upon the city. Hebrew *yēḥat* is from the root *nḥt,* meaning "to descend, penetrate." The LXX (*tis ptoēsei hēmas,* "Who will frighten us?") and Vg (*quis percutiet nos,* "Who will pierce us?") appear to read an N-stem imperfect of the verb *ḥtt,* "be shattered, terrified" (cf. Isa 7:8; 30:31). The boast of the royal house is that Jerusalem is impervious to attack. Moab and Edom harbored a similar pride about their cities (48:28–30; 49:16).

and who can enter into our habitations? I.e., the royal buildings of the city. The T has "into our palaces." But Heb *mĕʿônôtênû* may carry the disparaging meaning, "our (hidden) dens" (NJV: "Who can get into our lairs?").

14. *But I will reckon upon you according to the fruit of your doings—oracle of Yahweh.* The LXX omits, which can be attributed to haplography (homoeoarcton: *w . . . w*). In such a brief oracle the line can hardly be an add-on (*pace* Rudolph; Janzen 1973: 44 #47; and Holladay, who take it as quarried from 23:2). The phrase is different in 23:2. Aquila and Theod have the line here. On the verb *pqd* ("to reckon, pay a visit, punish"), which occurs very often in Jeremiah, see Note for 5:9.

according to the fruit of your doings. The phrase (with *"his* doings") occurs in the poetry of 17:10 and the prose of 32:19, the only other occurrences in the OT (Holladay 1960: 355). The "fruit of your doings" refers here to miscarriages of justice, a theme upon which the OT prophets never ceased to vent their ire (Amos 5:10–13; Isa 1:15–17, 21–23; 5:22–23; Jer 2:34; 5:26–28; Ezek 22:29) and which was also voiced impassionedly in Temple Psalms (Ps 94:1–7). Injustice is commonplace during the reign of Jehoiakim (22:17; cf. 7:8–11). Unjust reigns in other societies similarly came under censure (see Neo-Babylonian and much earlier Ugaritic texts in Notes for 2:34 and 5:28).

And I will kindle a fire in her forest, and it will consume everything around her. For variations of this refrain in Jeremiah and elsewhere, see Note for 17:27. This "forest" (*yaʿar*) is not the wooded hills surrounding Jerusalem (*pace* McKane) but royal buildings within the city (Calvin). Because of a lavish use of cedar, one of the buildings of the royal palace was called "The House of the Forest of Lebanon" (1 Kgs 7:2–12; 10:17–21), whose destruction is again predicted in 22:5, 6–7, and 20–23.

MESSAGE AND AUDIENCE

In the first of these oracles, Yahweh begins by admonishing the royal house to carry out justice in the manner it is supposed to, one example being to rescue the oppressed from someone who has robbed him. If this is not done, says Yahweh to another audience listening in, the divine wrath will burn like an unquenchable fire. The reason: royal deeds are evil. On the face of it, this oracle with the possible exception of the concluding reference to "their evil doings" is little more than the sort of admonition that one would likely hear from the preacher in Deuteronomy. However, if injustices by the king and other royalty are a daily occurrence, then what we have here is a demand that things get turned around in a hurry, for failure to protect victims of oppression and other such evils to which the poor and needy continually fall prey, is a gross violation of covenant law.

In the second oracle, Yahweh indicts a proud Jerusalem, sitting securely as she does on a rocky plateau in the Judaean mountains. He tells the city he is against her. Then turning to address another audience, Yahweh makes his listeners privy to the talk currently going on in the royal palace. There the king and his princes are heard boasting that no one, surely no one, will be able to swoop down and enter their habitations. Or has Jeremiah said "enter their (hidden) lairs"?

In the third oracle, Yahweh says to Jerusalem's proud leaders that he will reckon with them according to the fruit of their deeds. The language is now judgment. Turning then to address his other audience, Yahweh says he will kindle a fire in the forest of which Jerusalem's royalty is so proud, and it will consume everything round about. This sounds as if the whole city will be ablaze. Will the audience know that their deeds have been bad deeds, and the fruit thus borne has been bad fruit?

When the three oracles are heard in sequence, v 14a will answer the rhetorical questions of v 13b (Calvin). Members of the royal house say, "Who can come down upon us, and who can enter into our habitations?" Yahweh answers, "I can, and I will!" But v 13b will not likely be heard as a cheeky response by the royal house to Yahweh's warning in v 12b, as Rudolph suggests, although those listening will be conscious of the shifts between speaker and audience. They may also perceive in the three oracles a progression from admonition to indictment to judgment, which occurred in the three Temple Oracles of 7:3–14. The two clusters cover some of the same ground: care for the needy and oppressed, robbery, and mistaken ideas about Jerusalem's inviolability, which is rooted ultimately in a costly misunderstanding of the conditional Sinai covenant. When all three oracles are heard in tandem, the "evil doings" of Oracle I will anticipate the "fruit of [their] doings" in Oracle III, giving the latter definition and pointing out the sad consequences in store for a nation when its royal house fails to carry out the mandate it has to execute justice.

To a later audience, the oracles to the house of David will supplement the prior oracles to Zedekiah (21:1–7) and the people (21:8–10) that were spoken some 15–20 years later. At this point the *waw* is added to the superscription in 21:11: "*And* to the house of the king of Judah." The present oracles will also help explain Jeremiah's uncompromising word to Zedekiah about Jerusalem's fate, picking up on words in 21:5–6 and 10 that Yahweh will fight against the city, and what is said in 21:10 about the king of Babylon's destroying the city by fire.

Volz dates Oracle I early in Jehoiakim's reign, i.e., 609–606 B.C. Oracles II and III are dated by him sometime prior to 588 B.C. when rebellion against Nebuchadnezzar was still possible. Holladay assigns all three oracles to Jehoiakim's reign: Oracle I to ca. 609–608; Oracle II to an unspecified date in Jehoiakim's reign; and Oracle III to a date before the siege of 598 B.C. In my view, all three oracles should probably be dated early in Jehoiakim's reign, i.e., 609–605 B.C., when Jeremiah was still speaking openly in public and trying to right the wrongs of a king wholly unsuited for office. Oracle III, which promises judgment, was not fulfilled in the Babylonian siege of 598 B.C. but, rather, when Jerusalem fell in 586 B.C. Volz suggested that Oracle I was recited before a large audience on festal days when people were assembled in Jerusalem. Possibly all three oracles were recited on such an occasion.

3. Once Again, O King: Do Justice and Righteousness! (22:1–5)

22 ¹Thus said Yahweh: Go down to the house of the king of Judah and you shall speak there this word. ²And you shall say, 'Hear the word of Yahweh, king of Judah, who sits on the throne of David—you, and your servants, and your people who come through these gates.'

³Thus said Yahweh:
Do justice and righteousness, and rescue the robbed from the oppressor's hand; and the sojourner, the orphan, and the widow do not wrong, do not treat violently; and the blood of the innocent do not shed in this place. ⁴For if you really do this word, then through the gates of this house shall come kings sitting for David on his throne, riding in chariots and with horses—he, and his servants,[a] and his people.

⁵But if you will not hear these words, I swear by myself—oracle of Yahweh—that this house will come to be a ruin.

RHETORIC AND COMPOSITION

These verses contain a directive from Yahweh that Jeremiah speak a word to the king at the gates of the royal palace (vv 1–2), after which come two oracles presumably delivered there (vv 3–5). The unit is prose, delimited on either side by poetry. The upper limit is marked additionally by a *setumah* in M^L (only) prior to v 1, where the chapter division also comes. The lower limit is marked by a *petuhah* in M^A and 4QJer^c and by a *setumah* in M^L and M^P after v 5. 4QJer^a has no section after v 5. The M^L and M^P also have a *setumah* after v 2,

---

[a]Reading the Q, which is supported by T and 4QJer^c; Kt has "his servant" (singular).

which sets off Oracle I from the introduction. In 4QJer^c there is a space after v 4, which Tov (1997: 189–90) thinks may be a *setumah*. If so, then v 5 with its "oracle of Yahweh" formula could be a separate oracle. However, there are no sections after v 4 in M^A, M^L, M^P, or 4QJer^a.

The discourse in vv 3–5 is taken here as two separate oracles, although in Jeremiah single oracles can have both an opening and a closing formula, e.g., 2:2–3, 5–9; 30:18–21. Also, single oracles can contain both a positive and negative protasis-apodosis, e.g., 17:24–27, or only one conditional, e.g., 7:3–7, which has only the positive, and 26:4–5, which has only the negative. In the present case, we have one oracle containing a positive conditional followed by another oracle containing a negative conditional. Since the two oracles will be heard in succession, the effect upon the audience will be no different from hearing one oracle with both positive and negative conditionals. Wording in the negative conditional of v 5 also indicates that there are two oracles here, not just one (see Notes).

Muilenburg (1959) has shown that the protasis-apodosis construction in prophetic covenantal speech (usually, but not always, expressed both positively and negatively: "If . . . then . . . if not . . . then") is a formal element in covenantal speech generally (Exod 19:5–6; Josh 24:15, 20; 1 Sam 12:14–15, 25), seen most prominently in Deuteronomy (Deut 11:26–28; 28:1–68), but found also in law codes and treaties of the ANE, where the formulations have their provenance in royal proclamations. In Jeremiah, covenant speeches of this type occur in 7:3–7; 17:24–27; 22:1–5; and 26:4–5.

Concerning whether the present verses are a doublet of 21:11–12 or a secondary expansion of the same, see Rhetoric and Composition for 21:11–14. Weiser rejects the idea of secondary expansion, saying that the present verses are a later word to the royal palace. Similar wording in 21:12 and 22:3 ("Execute/do justice . . . and rescue the robbed from the oppressor's hand"), on which the doublet and secondary expansion theories largely rest, makes an inclusio for the subcollection of oracles in 21:11–22:5 (see Rhetoric and Composition for 21:11–14).

Catchwords connecting to the preceding unit:

22:1 *the house of the king of Judah*   21:11 *the house of the king of Judah*

Catchwords connecting to the unit following:

22:1 *the house of the king of Judah*   22:6 *the house of the king of Judah*

These latter catchwords were noted by Mowinckel (1946: 49).

NOTES

22:1. *Thus said Yahweh: Go down to the house of the king of Judah and you shall speak there this word.* This directive compares with the one in 26:2, where Jeremiah is told to deliver his celebrated Temple Oracles of 609 B.C. Here the prophet is at the Temple, instructed to "go down" (*rēd*) because the palace is on lower ground (Kimḥi; J. D. Michaelis 1793: 174; Giesebrecht; Hyatt; and others; cf. 36:12; 2 Kgs 11:19). From the palace to the Temple, one "goes up" (26:10).

2. *And you shall say, 'Hear the word of Yahweh, king of Judah. . . .'* Although pertaining to the entire royal house, this word is to be addressed directly to the king. The king will probably not hear it, since Jeremiah goes only to the palace gates. The oracles in 21:11–14 address the royal house more broadly, being delivered before a general audience at some unspecified location.

who sits on the throne of David. The mention of David here and in v 4 has the same function as in 21:12, to refer indirectly but intentionally to a king of Israel who did justice (2 Sam 8:15). There is no allusion to the Davidic covenant of 2 Samuel 7 (*pace* Boadt; Jones); the covenant at issue is the Sinai covenant, which is conditional and concerned largely with land tenure.

and your servants. Hebrew *waʿăbādeykā*. The LXX has *kai ho oikos sou*, "and your house." Royal "servants" are important people in the employ of the king (see Note for 21:7).

and your people who come through these gates. The LXX has "and your people, and they who enter these gates," which introduces a redundant category of people. Since these are the gates to the palace (Giesebrecht; Cornill; Holladay), those passing through will only be members of the royal house or people having legitimate business with the royal house, both of whom could properly be called the king's people. The Temple Oracles were delivered at the gates of the Temple (7:2), which cannot be indicated here since, as Kimḥi points out, no one will likely ride a horse or chariot through these gates (cf. v 4).

3. *Do justice and righteousness, and rescue the robbed from the oppressor's hand.* A variation of the admonition in 21:12 (see Note there), adding to *mišpāṭ* ("justice") the correlative term *ṣĕdāqâ* ("righteousness"). Boadt notes that "justice and righteousness" are terms denoting covenant responsibility in Amos 5:7 and Isa 1:21; also Psalms 72 and 89. According to Snaith (1983: 72–73), both *ṣedeq* (masculine) and *ṣĕdāqâ* (feminine) originally meant "straightness," for which reason the terms came to be used "for what is or ought to be firmly established, successful, and enduring in human affairs." The terms can also mean deeds not obligatory upon the doer (Berkovitz 1969: 196), "rightness" as opposed to *rešaʿ*, "wickedness" (Ps 45:8[Eng 45:7]), and "rescue" or "salvation," as indicated here and elsewhere (Isa 51:5).

the sojourner, the orphan, and the widow. According to Deuteronomy, these individuals in society require special care (Deut 10:18–19; 14:29; 16:11), with the prophets issuing stern reminders should the mandate go unheeded, which it often did (Isa 1:17; 11:3–4; Jer 7:5–6). Psalm 72:4 places the burden of care squarely on the king. The motif of doing justice to the needy appears repeatedly in Ugaritic literature, e.g., in the Keret Legend, where Yaṣṣib upbraids his ailing father for not judging the cause of the widow, the orphan, and the poor

(*ANET*³ 149 vi 33–34, 46–50; *CS I* 342; Ginsberg 1945: 50–52); and in the Tale of Aqhat, which holds up the good Daniel as someone who did judge the cause of the widow and adjudicate the cause of the orphan (*ANET*³ 151 v 7–8; 153 i 24–25; *CS I* 346, 351). On justice toward the sojourner, orphan, and widow, see also Note for 5:28.

do not wrong. Hebrew *'al-tōnû.* The verb *ynh* occurs also in Exod 22:20[Eng 22:21] in a context similar to the present one. It means cheating or taking unfair economic advantage of another (Lev 25:14). Ezekiel says the righteous man wrongs no one and will live (Ezek 18:5–9).

and the blood of the innocent do not shed in this place. The idiom "to shed blood" means "to murder" (Milgrom 1991: 710). A warning to keep the sixth commandment is given in the first Temple Oracle of 7:6; in 22:17 Jehoiakim is judged for having grossly violated it. "This place" is not the Temple area (*pace* Craigie et al.), because the oracle is delivered at a gate near the palace. But reference could be more broadly to the city of Jerusalem.

4. *For if you really do this word, then through the gates of this house shall come kings sitting for David on his throne, riding in chariots and with horses—he, and his servants, and his people.* This same protasis-apodosis argument is used in Jeremiah's oracle about Sabbath observance (17:24–25), but there reference is made to gates of the city. Practicing justice, in any case, is necessary for maintaining the Davidic line on Judah's throne.

this house. The royal palace, not the Temple as in 7:10–14 (Giesebrecht).

kings sitting for David on his throne. Hebrew *mĕlākîm* ("kings") is probably to be taken as a plural intensive in view of the following "he" (see discussion in Note for 13:13).

he, and his servants, and his people. The LXX and Vg have plurals to go with the plural "kings": "they, and (their) servants, and their people." The T has singulars. Volz, Rudolph, Weiser, and Janzen (1973: 133) take the phrase as an expansionist gloss (Rudolph from v 2b) but without textual support. See a similar enumeration (using plurals) in 17:25. There is also no reason to take the singulars of MT as reflecting later messianic concerns (*pace* Duhm, Cornill, Volz, Holladay). These singulars balance the singulars of v 2.

5. *But if you will not hear these words.* I.e., "if you will not heed these words." Hebrew *wĕ'im lō' tišmĕ'û 'et-haddĕbārîm hā'ēlleh.* The LXX has *mē poiēsēte,* "you will not do," which creates a consistency with the verbs of vv 3–4. The use of different verbs in MT—"do" in vv 3–4 and "hear" in v 5—may be a further indication that v 5 is a separate oracle (see Rhetoric and Composition). In the single oracle of 17:24–27, "hear" appears in both the positive and negative conditionals. The phrase "these words" plural (in both MT and LXX) is also inconsistent with "this word" in vv 1 and 4, pointing once again to there being two oracles here and suggesting that the second oracle may be a later add-on.

I swear by myself. On Yahweh's swearing by his own name, see Note on 49:13.

that this house will come to be a ruin. Hebrew *kî-lĕḥorbâ yihyeh habbayit hazzeh.* Usually the land is said to become a ruin (7:34; 25:11; 44:22), otherwise Jerusalem and the cities of Judah (27:17; 44:2, 6). "This house" refers to the royal palace (Duhm; Cornill; cf. 17:27), not the "house of David." As in the prior oracle (v 2), reference here is to the Sinai covenant, not the Davidic covenant of 2 Samuel 7. Nevertheless, the king is being held responsible for upholding the Sinai covenant. If he and the royal house do not do justice and righteousness, then the covenant curses will fall upon the house in which they reside. Curses awaiting the king who fails to observe God's commandments are the focus of one column of the *Temple Scroll* (11QT 59), where vocabulary and phraseology from Deuteronomy and Jeremiah dominate (Yadin 1983: 265–70; Brooke 1997: 202).

MESSAGE AND AUDIENCE

The audience here is informed that Jeremiah was directed to go from the Temple precinct down to the royal palace and there speak a word to the king. Presumably this word was to be spoken at the palace gates, which are mentioned in the directive.

The first oracle is a command that the king and his house do justice and righteousness and rescue any and every victim of oppression coming to their attention. To the sojourner, orphan, and widow they are to do no wrong, no violence, and they are definitely not to shed innocent blood, which the king has power to do. Yahweh says that if they really do this, then the royal horses and chariots carrying the Davidic king and his retinue will continue on festival days and every ordinary day to pass through the palace gates. A second oracle follows with a conditional for noncompliance. If the royal house does not heed these words of warning, Yahweh swears that he will make the royal palace a ruin.

When the present oracles are heard in tandem with those preceding, the words "Do justice and righteousness, and rescue the robbed from the oppressor's hand" will echo words in 21:12, which are nearly the same. They will also anticipate Jeremiah's word in 22:13–17, in which judgment falls hard on one of Judah's last kings, who failed miserably in doing justice and righteousness, being known rather for his cheating, shedding of innocent blood, and acts of oppression.

These oracles and their introduction are best dated early in Jehoiakim's reign (Volz; Rudolph; Holladay), perhaps the very beginning, when the Temple Oracles were delivered (ca. 609–608 B.C.). They are similar also to the Sabbath Oracle in 17:24–27, which may have been delivered about the same time. Volz and Weiser imagine a grand festival occasion for the delivery, which is possible.

4. A Cutting in Lebanon South (22:6–9)

22 [6]For thus said Yahweh concerning the house of the king of Judah:
    Gilead you are to me
    .the top of Lebanon

> But I will surely make you a wilderness
>   cities that are uninhabited[a]

> [7]So I am sanctifying destroyers against you
>   each person with his axes
> And they will cut down your choicest cedars
>   and fell them upon the fire.

[8]And many nations will pass by this city, and they will say each person to his fellow, 'Why has Yahweh done thus to this great city?' [9]And they will say, 'Because they abandoned the covenant of Yahweh their God and worshiped other gods and served them.'

RHETORIC AND COMPOSITION

These verses consist of an oracle with expanded messenger formula (vv 6–7), followed by a wisdom comment later added (vv 8–9). The oracle is in poetry; the wisdom comment in prose. The upper limit of the unit is marked by a *petuhah* in M[A] and 4QJer[c] and a *setumah* in M[L] and M[P] before v 6. Marking the lower limit is a *petuhah* in 4QJer[a] and M[P] and a *setumah* in M[L] and M[A] after v 9. Shifts from prose to poetry in vv 6 and 10 corroborate this demarcation.

The oracle of vv 6–7 leads off a rhetorical structure in 22:6–23, which forms the core of the King Collection (see Rhetoric and Composition for 21:1–10). This core consists of three "Lebanon-cedar" poems, within which are interspersed an oracle and lament, and an oracle of nonlament. The poems are linked by key words, the whole forming a large chiasmus (Lundbom 1975: 101–4 [=1997: 133–36]):

> Gilead you are to me
>   the top of *Lebanon (hallĕbānôn)*
> A . . . .
>   . . . .
> And they will cut down your choicest *cedars (ʾărāzeykā)*
>   and fell them upon the fire
>
>   (22:6–7)

> Weep not for the dead . . . .
>   . . . . [Josiah]
> B   weep continually for the one who goes away
>   . . . . [Jehoahaz]
>
>   (22:10–12)

---

[a]Reading the Q, *nôšābû*, "they are (un)inhabited"; Kt is a third-feminine singular, "it is (un)inhabited," or "each one (un)inhabited" (see Notes).

Woe to him who builds his house . . .
....

C   And he frames for himself windows
      and panels *in cedar (bā᾽ārez)*

          ....

      Are you a king because you compete *in cedar? (bā᾽ārez)*

          ....
                                        (22:13–17)

      They shall not lament for him

B'   .... [Jehoiakim]
                                        (22:18–19)

Go up to *Lebanon* and scream *(hallĕbānôn)*
   and in the Bashan raise your voice!

      ....

A'   You who dwell *in Lebanon (ballĕbānôn)* . . .
      nested *in the cedars (bā᾽ărāzîm)*

      ....
                                        (22:20–23)

The present oracle has two stanzas, each of which is two bicolons in *qinah* (3:2) meter (Giesebrecht; Hyatt). The whole has this key word balance (Lundbom 1975: 48–49 [= 1997: 67–68]):

I   ....   v 6a
       .... *Lebanon*

II .... *cedars*   v 7b
       ....

The poetry also has assonance:

I   .... *᾽ăśîtĕkā* .... *I will make* ......   v 6b

II .... *maśḥitîm* .. *᾽îš* ...   . *destroyers* ... *person*   v 7a
       .... *hā᾽ēš*   .... *the fire*   v 7b

Yahweh is the speaking voice throughout, addressing directly the royal palace (apostrophe). Jeremiah, or else a later voice, is the speaker of the question-and-answer dialogue.

The prose comment is linked to the oracle by these key words:

v 6 *cities*   v 8 *city* (2×)
     each person   *᾽îš*   *each person*   *᾽îš*

Catchwords connecting to the preceding unit are the following (Mowinckel 1946: 49):

v 6 *the house of the king of Judah*   v 1 *the house of the king of Judah*

Catchwords connecting ahead are "Lebanon" and "cedars" in the present poem to "Lebanon" and "cedar(s)" in other poems of the core structure. Mowinckel (1946: 49) identified "Lebanon" as a catchword between vv 6–7 and vv 20–23, to which should be added "cedar(s)" in vv 7, 14–15, and 23.

NOTES

22:6. *the house of the king of Judah.* "House" (*bêt*) here refers to the royal palace (cf. v 13), not the Davidic royal line. This introductory formula is then eminently suitable to the oracle following, which is the first of three judgment words on the palace complex newly enlarged by King Jehoiakim. Reference is not to the Temple, Jerusalem, or the land of Judah (*pace* Jerome; Duhm; Ehrlich 1912: 297), although it goes without saying that these too will be destroyed.

Gilead you are to me, the top of Lebanon. An "obscure comparison," to quote J. D. Michaelis (1793: 175), which has been variously interpreted. The T takes "Lebanon" here and in vv 20 and 23 as referring to the Temple (Vermes 1958: 4; cf. 1 Kings 5–6), a tradition surviving in Jerome and the Church Fathers (Sparks 1959: 271; Hayward 1985b: 102–3). Boadt thinks Jeremiah is addressing the king (pronouns in the verse are masculine singular), but "Gilead" and "Lebanon" are more commonly metaphors (not similes) for the royal palace (Volz; Rudolph; Hyatt; Holladay). Both localities were richly forested in biblical times (Baly 1974: 221–23; P. J. King 1993: 153), making them suitable descriptions of palace buildings whose interiors were lavishly supplied with cedar and other choice woods. One building in the complex was called "The House of the Forest of Lebanon" (1 Kgs 7:2–5). On luxurious Gilead, known otherwise for its trees producing balm, see Note for 8:22. Lebanon's reputation for possessing cedar and cypress trees is alluded to often in the OT (Isa 37:24 = 2 Kgs 19:23; Ezek 31:3; Zech 11:1–2). Gilead and Lebanon are linked again in Zech 10:10, where, as here, the pairing may represent choice highland forests of east and west (Ottosson 1969: 244). In 22:20 and Isa 2:13, Lebanon and Bashan are paired, the latter located just north of Gilead in the Transjordanian highlands and famous for its stands of oak trees. The point being made here is that Yahweh thinks very highly of the royal palace, being just as proud and possessive of its extraordinary beauty as Solomon himself was; however, he will now destroy it because of a blatant disregard of covenant obligations by the king currently residing there, viz., Jehoiakim. This argument echoes one used by Yahweh against the covenant people in an earlier prophetic word from Amos: "You only have I known of all the families of the earth; therefore I will punish you for all your iniquities" (Amos 3:2). See also the arguments in Jer 11:16 and 12:7.

But I will surely make you a wilderness, cities that are uninhabited. The expression *'im lō'* has the force of an oath (Calvin; Brichto 1963: 123; cf. Note on 15:11). The NEB: "I swear that I will make you a wilderness." Here again, "wilderness" and "uninhabited cities" are metaphors for the palace (Hyatt), now envisioned as lying in ruins. The Kt *nôšābâ,* "it is (un)inhabited" is the more difficult reading (cf. 6:8), and if original, it may be taking "cities" in a distributive sense: "cities, each one uninhabited." See "destroyers . . . each person" in v 7. The Q would then be a correction to make the verb agree with the subject noun. The Versions all read a plural, "they are (un)inhabited." "Cities" plural is actually the problematic term, and some modern Versions (Moffatt, AmT, RSV, JB [but not NJB], NAB, and NRSV) read "city" or "town." J. D. Michaelis (1793: 175) suggested emending ʿārîm ("cities") to ʿeryâ ("bareness"), which requires the change of only one letter. His reading: "But will I not make you a wilderness, bareness, not inhabited." Another possibility would be to take ʿārîm as a "surface plural" (GKC §124b), where the meaning would be "a (flattened) city." The metaphor, in any event, is "language at a stretch" and may just as well be left "as is."

7. *So I am sanctifying destroyers against you.* Jeremiah's use of wĕqiddaštî ("So I am sanctifying") introduces holy war language (Weiser; Soggin 1975b), where the "destroyers" (mašḥitîm) are attacking forces of the Babylonian army (cf. 4:7). On the sanctifying of armies for holy war, and Yahweh's engagement now in a holy war against Judah, see Notes for 6:4 and 21:4–5. Weiser imagines that the destroyers are supernatural "angels of death," similar to those working evil in Exod 12:23 and 2 Sam 24:16, but Berridge (1970: 84) and Lindström (1983: 63) rightly reject this interpretation. The destroyers here are human agents.

each person . . . the fire. The Hebrew appears to have a wordplay between ʾîš and hāʾēš.

his axes. Hebrew kēlāyw. For the general word kēlîm, the present image requires tools used to fell trees, which will in fact be wielded by the enemy to wreck the palace's wooded interior. "His axes" is then a more suitable translation than "his weapons" (T has "his weapon" singular). In 21:4 kĕlê does mean "weapons." The LXX has *kai ton pelekun autou,* "and his axe" (singular). From Ps 74:5–7 we learn that the Babylonians wrecked the Temple with axes, hatchets, and hammers before setting it afire, and we may assume that they did the same to the royal palace.

your choicest cedars. I.e., the cedar interior of the palace. David resided in a house of cedar (2 Sam 7:2), and Solomon built "The House of the Forest of Lebanon," another grand building of cedar interior in the royal complex (1 Kings 7). Now more recently, Jehoiakim has planned, begun, or already had built for himself a spacious palace building with cedar interior (22:13–14). The "choicest cedars" then do not refer to chief men of state (*pace* Duhm; Streane), which can be traced to Jerome, who has "strong ones and princes of the city" (Hayward 1985b: 111), and ultimately to T, which has "the best of your strong men." On the palace of Baal, which is described as a "house of cedar" in the Baal and Anath Cycle, see Note for 22:14.

and fell them upon the fire. The king's palace was burned by Nebuzaradan after the city was taken in 586 B.C. (39:8; 52:13 = 2 Kgs 25:9).

8–9. These verses are an adaptation of Deut 29:23–25[Eng 29:24–26], which envisions the curses of the Sinai covenant as having fallen on the covenant

people, and the Promised Land as having been reduced to a burned-out waste.
The parallel texts:

Deut 29:23–25[Eng 29:24–26]	*Jer 22:8–9*
And all the nations	And many nations will pass by this city, and
will say,	they will say each person to his fellow,
'Why has Yahweh done thus to this land;	'Why has Yahweh done thus to this great city?'
what caused this great display of anger?'	
And they will say, 'Because they abandoned	And they will say, 'Because they abandoned
the covenant of Yahweh, the God of their fathers, which he made with	the covenant of Yahweh their God
them when he brought them from the land	
of Egypt, and they went and	and
served other gods, and worshiped them. . . .'	worshiped other gods and served them.'

For other question-and-answer forms in Jeremiah (5:19; 9:11–13[Eng 9:12–14];
16:10–13), and one of comparable nature in the Annals of Ashurbanipal, see
Note for 5:19. Compare also 1 Kgs 9:8–9 where, as in the present dialogue and
in Deut 29:23–25, the question will be asked not by Judahites but by people of
other nations. The envisioned question here deals with the fate of Jerusalem
(Rudolph; Weiser; Thiel 1973: 240), not just the palace and not the land as a
whole. But there is no reason (with Thiel) to date the dialogue after the fall of
Jerusalem. It could certainly have preceded the fall.

8. *And many nations*. The LXX omits "many," which can be attributed to
haplography (homoeoteleuton: *ym . . . ym*). The adjective need not be taken as
a borrowing from 25:14 (*pace* Janzen 1973: 44; and Holladay). Also to be rejected is the emendation by Volz and Rudolph to "many peoples" ("viele
Leute"). The source passage of Deut 29:23[Eng 29:24] has "all the nations."

each person to his fellow. 4QJer[a] has *ʿal rēʿēhû*, whereas MT has *ʾel rēʿēhû*.
Janzen (1973: 181) calls *ʿal* a copyist's error in anticipation of the next *ʿal*,
which it need not be. The interchange of *ʾel* and *ʿal* is found throughout the
book of Jeremiah (see Note for 11:2).

9. *Because*. Hebrew *ʿal ʾăšer*. A match for the preceding *ʿal-meh*, "Why?"
(Holladay), as also in Deut 29:23–24[Eng 29:24–25].

MESSAGE AND AUDIENCE

Yahweh in the present oracle addresses the royal palace, comparing its buildings to Gilead and the mountain ranges of Lebanon. Their beauty resides inside, where cedar beams resting on cedar pillars and cedar paneling from floor to ceiling are a sight to behold. Yahweh has unconcealed pride, also a sense of ownership in this show of splendor alongside his own house, comparably adorned; nevertheless, he swears that he will reduce it to a wilderness, an assemblage of cities uninhabited. Indeed, he has commissioned destroyers to wage holy war against the place. With axes in hand, they will cut down the cedar and burn it into nothingness.

Sometime later a question-and-answer dialogue is added (vv 8–9), which gives the audience a reason for the judgment that the oracle itself does not give. This need not be initially for a middle or late exilic audience, although it is suitable enough for audiences then as well as later. The imagined dialogue could precede the fall of Jerusalem and thus come from the same time as the oracle—otherwise soon afterward. Volz dates the oracle at about the same time as the oracle in vv 1–5, i.e., early in the reign of Jehoiakim. In his view, first comes a friendly either-or admonition; then, when that is not heeded, holy anger and judgment (cf. 7:3–14 and 21:11–14). The oracle cannot date from the very beginning of Jehoiakim's reign because some time must pass, allowing for this ambitious king to begin work on a new palace. A date of 607–605 B.C. is about right.

5. Lament Jehoahaz, Not Josiah! (22:10–12)

22 [10]Weep not for the dead[a]
　　and condole not for him
　　　　weep continually for him who goes away
Because he will not return again
　　and not see the land of his birth.

[11]For thus said Yahweh to Shallum son of Josiah, king of Judah, who reigned in place of Josiah his father, who departed from this place:
　　He will not return there again. [12]For in the place where they exiled him, he
　　will die, and this land he will not see again.

RHETORIC AND COMPOSITION

The present verses consist of a lament for Jehoahaz (v 10), followed by an oracle for the same (vv 11–12). In the latter, the young king of only three months is called by his given name, Shallum. The lament is in poetry; the oracle in prose. Berridge (1970: 100) takes the poetic verse, rather, as a "call to lament"

---

[a]Repointing MT *lĕmēt*, "for a dead (man)," to *lammēt*, "for the dead (man)" with LXX and S.

(cf. 4:8; 6:26; 25:34; Joel 1:5–14), saying it is no part of any liturgy. But Weiser calls it a lament. It is definitely not a judgment oracle (*pace* Holladay). Verses 11–12 are a judgment oracle, preceded by an expanded messenger formula similar to the one in v 18a. This formula should include the words, "who departed from this place" (*pace* Bright and NAB, who begin the oracle with these words). Because of the messenger formula, vv 11–12 cannot be taken as later comment on the lament, a view widely held among commentators and others (Duhm; Cornill; Rudolph; Hyatt; Thiel 1973: 240–41; Carroll; Holladay; Jones; McKane), some of whom attribute the lament to Jeremiah, and the comment to Baruch.

The unit as a whole is demarcated at the top end by a *petuḥah* in 4QJer^a and M^P and a *setumah* in M^L and M^A before v 10. Demarcation at the bottom end is by a reconstructed *petuḥah* in 4QJer^c (Tov 1997: 190) and a *setumah* in M^A, M^L, and M^P after v 12. 4QJer^a lacks a section after v 12. Separating the lament from the oracle is a reconstructed *petuḥah* in 4QJer^c (Tov 1997: 190) and a *setumah* in M^L and M^P after v 10. 4QJer^a and M^A both lack the section after v 10.

The lament is a tricolon followed by a bicolon (*BHS*). Contrasting terms, "for the dead" and "his birth," make an inclusio for the whole (Holladay).

```
. . . . . . . . . . . . . . . for the dead            v 10
   . . . . . . . . . . . . . . . . . . . . . . .
   . . . . . . . . . . . . . . . . . . . . . . . .
. . . . . . . . . . . . . . . . . . . . . . .
   . . . . . . . . . . . . . . . . . . his birth
```

Compare "cursed"/"blessed," and "cursed"/"making him very glad," in 20:14–15.

The prose oracle also has an inclusio made by the following repetition:

He will *not* return there *again* . . .	*lō* . . . *'ôd*	v 11b
and this land he will *not* see *again*	*lō* . . . *'ôd*	v 12

The oracle is linked to the lament by these key terms:

v 10 Because *he will not return again*	vv 11–12 *He will not return . . . again . . .*
and not see the land of his birth	*and this land he will not see again*

There are no catchwords connecting to poems preceding or following. On the rhetorical structure comprising all of 22:6–23, see Rhetoric and Composition for 22:6–9.

NOTES

22:10. *Weep not for the dead, and condole not for him; weep continually for him who goes away.* Calvin says this is a general declaration applicable to the whole people. Lamentation is not to be over the dead but over those taken away into exile. If this is a general declaration, then it would most likely reflect the exiles of 597 or 586 B.C. Calvin dates the lament to 597. The point about an anonymous utterance is made also by Roach (1941: 348). But the more common view is that Josiah is "the dead (king)," and the "(king) who goes away" is Jehoahaz, his son, referred to in v 11 as Shallum. Rashi and Kimḥi incorrectly identify the dead king as Jehoiakim and the king taken into (Babylonian) exile as Jehoiachin. The sad events of 609 B.C. are well known. Josiah was killed by Pharaoh Neco at Megiddo, and Jehoahaz, his son, was put on the throne. But after a reign of only three months, Jehoahaz was summoned by Neco to Riblah (in Syria on the Orontes), deposed, and taken prisoner to Egypt. If Josiah went to meet Neco in the spring or early summer of 609, which is likely (cf. 2 Sam 11:1), his reign would have ended and the reign of Jehoahaz begun at that time, with the reign of Jehoahaz terminating in the summer or early fall of that same year (Thiele 1956: 23). We should not conclude from the lament (or call to lament) that Jeremiah was unmoved by Josiah's death. What we have here is another "idiom of exaggerated contrast" (see Excursus II on 7:22–23), in which Jeremiah says not that people should refrain from weeping for Josiah, which they are presently doing, but that they should weep *more* for Jehoahaz (Shallum), who must languish in exile and will never return home. There is a fate worse than death (8:3), although people tend to think otherwise (Calvin). Also, according to 2 Chr 35:25, Jeremiah himself made public lamentation for Josiah at his funeral. Later tradition gives a mixed report on both kings. The outpouring of grief for Josiah was said by Josephus (*Ant* x 78) to have been very great and to have gone on for many days. A day of remembrance, in fact, was still being held for the fallen king in the second century B.C. (1 Esd 1:32). Nevertheless, Josiah was faulted for his "Megiddo adventure"—in 2 Chr 35:22 for not listening to Neco, who spoke from "the mouth of God," and 1 Esd 1:28 for not heeding the words of Jeremiah, who spoke from "the mouth of the Lord." Van der Kooij (1998: 102–6) thinks the author of 1 Esdras has in the back of his mind Jeremiah's prophecy concerning Egypt in 46:2–12, which predicts Neco's defeat. Had Josiah listened to the prophet, he would not have gone to engage the Pharaoh at Megiddo. Jehoahaz, for his part, gets a bad wrap-up in 2 Kgs 23:32, a judgment omitted by the Chronicler.

and condole not for him. On the verb *nûd*, which means to show grief by shaking the head to and fro, see Note on 15:5. Jeremiah was himself told to refrain from such activity in 16:5.

weep continually for him who goes away. To people apparently still mourning Josiah when Jehoahaz, three months later, was spirited away, Jeremiah says to weep continually (not "bitterly," as the RSV translates) for Jehoahaz. The Hebrew is *bĕkû bākô*, where the infinitive absolute after the imperative indicates repetition, not intensification. Jehoahaz's exile to Egypt and death there will be more grievous than Josiah's death and honorable burial in Jerusalem. Compare the oracle of Huldah in 2 Kgs 22:18–20, where Josiah's death and burial "in peace" is presented to him as preferable to being alive in future days when grievous evil will befall the nation (cf. 2 Kgs 20:16–19 = Isa 39:5–8). Ezekiel appears to lament Jehoahaz in Ezek 19:1–4, indicating that Jeremiah's advice was carried out; however, this emanates from a later time, when Zedekiah has become another "captured lion" brought before an alien king (19:8–9). Jehoahaz and Zedekiah had the same mother, Hamutal, daughter of Jeremiah of Libnah (2 Kgs 23:31; 24:18 = Jer 52:1), who is the "lioness . . . among lions" in Ezek 19:2 (Malamat 1975: 126).

Because he will not return again, and not see the land of his birth. The negative does double-duty for both verbs (cf. v 12). According to 2 Kgs 23:34, Jehoahaz did in fact die in Egypt. Volz and Rudolph combine the two verbs into one verbal idea: "see again" ("wiedersehen"), but precise wording and poetic scansion speak against this interpretation. The verbs belong in different colons (RSV; NEB; JB; NJV; NIV; Holladay; *pace BHS*), and an intervening ʿôd between them carries the meaning of "again," which precludes this meaning for an auxiliary *yāšûb*.

11a. *For thus said Yahweh to Shallum.* Hebrew *ʾel* = ʿal (see Note for 11:2). This is a divine word "concerning" Shallum.

Shallum son of Josiah, king of Judah, who reigned in place of Josiah his father, who departed from this place. Shallum is doubtless Jehoahaz (cf. 2 Kgs 23:30–34; 2 Chr 36:1–4), although different identifications are made by Jerome, Rashi, and Calvin. Jerome and Rashi think the reference is to Zedekiah, which it cannot be according to 1 Chr 3:15, and Calvin settles on Jehoiachin, who then has to be a grandson of Josiah. McKane notes that the Jehoahaz identification is rightly made by Ibn Ezra. "Shallum" is widely thought to be the king's name before he ascended the throne (Blayney; Cheyne; Duhm; Peake; Volz; Honeyman 1948: 20; Weiser; Rudolph; Hyatt; and others). Two subsequent Judahite kings took throne names upon accession: Eliakim, whose name was changed to Jehoiakim (2 Kgs 23:34 = 2 Chr 36:4), and Mattaniah, whose name was changed to Zedekiah (2 Kgs 24:17). The name "Shallum" may have been used here (and also in 1 Chr 3:15) because this brief claimant to the throne did not reign long enough to be considered a bona fide king or perhaps because he was no longer king (Volz). Jehoahaz is not listed in the superscription of 1:1–3. Also, as Malamat (1975: 127) points out, 2 Kgs 23:34 bypasses Jehoahaz in the royal succession, stating that Neco made Jehoiakim king "in place of Josiah his father." But here in v 11 it states that Shallum (Jehoahaz) "reigned in place of Josiah his father." The choice of Jehoahaz over his half-brother Jehoiakim, who was two years older, violated the principle of primogeniture. This may be attributed to an anti-Egyptian stance shared with his father or maybe because the "people of the land" put him on the throne, as they had done earlier with Josiah (2 Kgs 21:24; 23:30) or else both (Malamat 1956: 126; 1973: 271; Wilcoxen 1977: 152–53). Doubtless for his anti-Egyptian sympathies he was deposed by

Neco (Bewer; Malamat 1975: 126), and the pro-Egyptian Jehoiakim was made king. "Shallum" is a common OT name (32:7; 35:4; 1 Kgs 22:14; 2 Kgs 15:10), having turned up also on the Lachish and Arad ostraca, and on twenty or more contemporary seals, bullae, and jar handles (see Appendix I).

Josiah. 4QJer^a spells the name without the final *waw* in its first occurrence within the verse; 4QJer^c the same in its second cccurrence.

king of Judah. Hebrew *melek yĕhûdâ.* Lacking in the LXX but present in 4QJer^c. If "Josiah" was spelled without the final *waw* in the Heb *Vorlage* to the LXX, the omission could be attributed to haplography (homoeoteleuton: *h . . . h*), and not be secondary expansion, as suggested by G. Greenberg (2001: 233).

his father. Spelled *'ābîhû* in 4QJer^c.

11b–12. *He will not return there again. For in the place where they exiled him, he will die, and this land he will not see again.* This was stated also in the lament (v 10b).

For. Some Heb MSS, T, and the Versions heighten the contrast with an adversative, *kî-'im* ("But").

they exiled him. The LXX and Vg read "I exile him," which has Yahweh speaking in the first person. This reading, which need not be original, nevertheless supports the view that vv 11b–12 are a divine oracle.

MESSAGE AND AUDIENCE

This lament calls on people to weep not for the dead but for him who goes away. Specification is lacking, but the original audience would have known the referents. We, for our part, may reasonably take the dead to be Josiah and the one going away to be Jehoahaz. People at the time were still making lamentation over Josiah, but Jeremiah says they should be weeping more over Jehoahaz. A mere youth, he has gone away from Jerusalem and will never return to see the land of his birth.

The audience then hears an oracle having much the same message, introduced by an expanded messenger formula stating that the oracle concerns Shallum, i.e., Jehoahaz, who reigned briefly in place of his father but who has since departed Jerusalem. The lament can be dated to the late summer or early fall of 609 b.c. (Holladay), which was three months after the death of Josiah and just after Jehoahaz left Jerusalem to face Neco at Riblah. The oracle can be dated about the same time.

In the larger context, this lament and oracle will anticipate the oracle of non-lament over Jehoiakim in vv 18–19, the present expression being one of genuine grief, the expression in vv 18–19 being one of uncompromising judgment. The contrast is even sharper. Here people are told not to lament the good Josiah because a lamentation over Jehoahaz is more necessary. In v 18, people will not lament Jehoiakim because this king was unworthy of royal office, and his ignoble death and nonburial will not bring them to a state of grief.

6. A King with an Edifice Complex (22:13–17)

22 [13]Woe to him who builds his house without righteousness
    and his upper rooms without justice
He makes his fellow serve for nothing
    his wages he does not give to him
[14]Who says, 'I will build for myself a house of dimensions
    with spacious upper rooms'
And he frames for himself windows[a]
    and panels[b] in cedar
        and paints in vermilion

[15]Are you a king because you compete in cedar?
    Your father—Did not he eat and drink
and do justice and righteousness?
    Then it went well for him
[16]He prosecuted the case of the poor and needy
    then it went well
Is not that knowing me?
—oracle of Yahweh

[17]Indeed your eyes and your heart are on nothing
    except your cut
and for shedding innocent blood
    and for practicing oppression and running.

RHETORIC AND COMPOSITION

The present verses form the centerpiece oracle in a rhetorical structure comprising 22:6–23 (see Rhetoric and Composition for 22:6–9). Most commentators extend the unit to v 19, which includes Jehoiakim's judgment after the present indictment. However, vv 18–19 form a separate oracle (Duhm; Carroll). In the larger rhetorical structure the present oracle and the one following are intentionally juxtaposed, connected by the following catchwords:

v 13 *woe*   v 18 *woe* (4×)

The upper limit of the unit is marked by a *petuḥah* in 4QJer[c] (reconstructed; Tov 1997: 190) and a *setumah* in M[A], M[L], and M[P] before v 13. 4QJer[a] as reconstructed lacks this section. The lower limit is marked by a *setumah* in 4QJer[c] (reconstructed; Tov 1997: 191–92), M[A], and M[L] after v 17. After this verse, M[P] has a *petuḥah*.

---

[a]Reading MT *ḥallônāy* as an abbreviated plural (see Notes).
[b]Repointing the passive participle *sāpûn* to the infinitive absolute *sāpôn* (see Notes).

The oracle as presently constituted divides into three stanzas, having a line division of 4:4:2. The first two stanzas are nicely balanced by almost *verbatim* repetitions:

I   . . . . *who builds his house without righteousness*   v 13
       and his upper rooms without justice

      . . . . . *I will build for myself a house* . . . . . .   v 14
       . . . . *upper rooms*
       . . . . *for himself* . . . .
       . . . . *in cedar*

II   . . . . *in cedar*   v 15
       . . . . *Did not* . . . .
       . . . . *justice and righteousness*
       Then it went well . . . .
       . . . .   v 16
       then it went well
       Is not . . . .
       . . . .

Holladay notes the repeated *bĕlō'* ("without") in v 13; also the repeated *hălô'* ("Did not/Is not") in vv 15–16.

Stanza III has particularly nice repetition in the Hebrew:

III   *kî* . . . . *kā* . . . . *kā*   v 17
     kî . . . *'al* . . . . *kā*
     wĕ'al . . . . . . *ha* . . . . *li* . . . . . .
     wĕ'al . . *hā* . . . *we'al* . . *ha* . . . *la* . . .

Since v 17 adds nothing to the key word structure of vv 13–16, and since the "oracle of Yahweh" formula (present also in 4QJer^c) comes at the end of v 16, it could be that v 17 is a later add-on. Cornill takes this verse to be an isolated "four-line poem" linking vv 13–16 with vv 18–19.

The oracle alternates both speaking voices and addressees. In Stanza I, Yahweh speaks to an assembled audience about Jehoiakim, introducing the king's own boastful ambitions in v 14a. In Stanzas II and III, Yahweh addresses the king directly, referring first to the good deeds of Josiah, his father, and then unleashing a harsh rebuke to him for behavior both self-serving and inhumane.

NOTES

22:13. *Woe to him who builds his house without righteousness, and his upper rooms without justice.* For national well-being it is essential that the king practice righteousness and justice (see Notes for 21:11 and 22:3). The king under review here is Jehoiakim, whose disregard for both is seen in his building or enlarging of a palatial structure, where the use of forced labor would have made his Egyptian suzerain proud. Jehoiakim withheld wages from workers who had earned them, and as the indictment proceeds, we learn that this oriental despot was also remiss for not prosecuting cases of the poor and needy in court and for reprehensible behavior generally—being consumed with personal greed, shedding innocent blood, oppressing his subjects, and then running from responsibility as cowardly souls are wont to do. Jeremiah might have compared this king to the "partridge that brooded but did not bring forth," whom he likened to "one raking in riches but not by right" (17:11). Other prophets raised their voices in protest against such abuses of royal office (Mic 3:9–10; Isa 5:8; Hab 2:9–12). Ben-Barak (1975) has suggested that Jehoiakim's selfish luxury, exploitation of subjects, and disregard of covenant Law runs parallel to the admonition in Deut 17:14–20, which although having Solomon in mind, warns Israel's future king not to multiply horses, wives, or riches for himself, not to rise arrogantly above his brothers, and not to disregard the commandments. If the king heeds this warning, he will live long in the land. It does not follow, however, that this admonition must therefore postdate Jeremiah, as Ben-Barak alleges, for it could just as well predate the prophet, in which case it would have inspired oracles such as the present one. This denunciation of a king by a prophet is one of the sharpest in the Bible, ranking with Nathan's rebuke of David (1 Sam 12:1–15) and Micaiah's judgment oracle against Ahab (1 Kgs 22:15–23). Volz ranks Jehoiakim as Jeremiah's greatest enemy. Among Judah's kings he certainly was.

Woe to him who builds his house without. . . . The Heb has alliteration in *bōneh bētô bĕlō'*.

Woe. Hebrew *hôy* (and also the very similar *'ôy*) appear often in Jeremiah, sometimes as a genuine cry of lament (4:13, 31; 6:4; 10:19; 15:10; 22:18; 34:5; 45:2), sometimes as a prophetic invective (13:27; 22:13; 23:1), and sometimes as an outcry in which there is a little of both, particularly if used ironically or against a foreign nation (30:7; 47:6; 48:1, 46; 50:27). Here *hôy* is a prophetic invective. The term appears to have its origin in funeral laments (Clifford 1966: 459; W. Janzen 1972: 39). According to Janzen, *hôy* (also *'ôy*) originated in funerary laments but then underwent "a metamorphosis from grief and mourning to accusation, threat, and even curse." Thus, in oracles such as the present one and the one in 23:1, also in the preaching of certain other prophets (Amos 5:18; 6:1; Mic 2:1; Isa 5:8, 11, 18, 20, 21–22; Hab 2:6, 9, 12, 15, 19; Jer 48:1; 50:27; Ezek 13:3, 18; 34:2), *hôy* is an invective portending disaster. Gerstenberger (1962: 261) thinks *hôy* (like *'ôy*) contrasts with *'ašrê*, "happy," and that both terms originated in the wise man's reflections about conditions in the world. Only later did the prophets use *hôy* to unleash Yahweh-centered indictments for covenant apostasy. But Gerstenberger must emend to get the contrasting terms into his two parade examples, Ecc 10:16–17 and Isa 3:10–11, which considerably weakens his argument (Clifford 1966: 458–59). W. Janzen (1972: 62 n. 76) also discounts the Gerstenberger thesis because it assumes too much of a connection between covenant breaking and sapiental instruction.

his upper rooms. Hebrew *ʿălîyôtāyw.* S. R. Driver (p. 129a) describes these as "chamber[s] erected on the flat roof of an eastern house, with latticed windows, giving free circulation to the air, secluded and cool" (cf. Judg 3:20; 1 Kgs 17:19; Dan 6:10). King Ahaziah fell through an upper-room lattice of his palace in Samaria (2 Kgs 1:2).

He makes his fellow serve for nothing, his wages he does not give to him. Jehoiakim robbed his subjects to pay Neco (2 Kgs 23:35); now he robs again to build a sumptuous palace. It is assumed that this self-indulgent king got the job done by resorting to forced labor (corvée), widely used in Egypt, and instituted in Israel by David (2 Sam 20:24) and Solomon (1 Kgs 4:6; 5:28–29[Eng 5:13–14]; 11:28), the latter employing it on a grand scale to build the Temple in Jerusalem. Jehoiakim, then, had no intention of paying his workers anything. The whole enterprise had to be highly unpopular, being perhaps another penalty imposed on political opponents who supported Jehoahaz (Wilcoxen 1977: 159). A seventh-century B.C. seal of unknown provenance, belonging to an individual in charge of forced labor during the reigns of one of Judah's last kings, has been found. Inscribed on both sides, it reads on one side, which is the personal side: "Belonging to Pelaʾyahu (son of) Mattityahu." On the reverse, which is the official side, it reads: "Belonging to Pelaʾyahu who is over the corvée (*hms*)." Avigad (1980; 1997: 28–29, 56–57) published the seal, and suggests that perhaps its owner was in charge of the corvée during Jehoiakim's reign.

The claim is sometimes made that Jeremiah does not speak out against social injustice as much as certain other prophets do, e.g., Amos, Micah, and Isaiah. Holladay (II p. 595) says: "In contrast to the eighth-century prophets there is curiously little emphasis on social injustice in the words of accusation uttered by Jrm." However, social concerns—particularly those central to Deuteronomy—are well represented in Jeremiah's preaching (see, e.g., 2:34–35; 5:1, 26–28; 6:7, 13 = 8:10b; 7:8–11; 9:2–5[Eng 9:3–6]; 17:11; 21:11; and 22:3–4, 13–17). Wessels (1992) maintains that the concern for a just society is a major issue in the book. Drotts (1973: 197) compares Jeremiah's denunciation of King Jehoiakim for his perfidious treatment of slaves with Martin Luther King Jr.'s prophetic words and actions that served to bring "white backlash, unemployment, poverty, ignorance, and discrimination under the scrutiny of the moral will of God." It is not that Jeremiah said little about social injustice; rather, it is that we hear this prophet also addressing numerous other issues related to unbelief and covenant disregard: worship of other gods, idol-making, harlotry, adultery, stealing, murder, child sacrifice, lying, duplicity, empty oaths, Sabbath profanation, false prophecy, and so on. All of these, needless to say, contribute mightily to injustice and the breakdown of community well-being.

his fellow. Hebrew *rēʿēhû.* The term *rēaʿ* simply means "another (fellow)" in the present context (cf. KB[3]), where assumptions about friendship or social parity are not being made. Bright imagines an "extreme democracy" in which the king and carpenter are like "neighbors" (Jones too), but this is unconvincing. The person doing forced labor is a "fellow" of the king only in the sense that both are members of the same covenant community, nothing more.

his wages. Hebrew *pōʿălô.* The term *pōʿal* usually means "work, deed" (Isa 1:31) but here denotes "wages for work" (cf. Job 7:2). On the pointing, see GKC §93q.

14. *Who says, 'I will build for myself a house of dimensions, with spacious upper rooms.'* The "woe" of v 13 does double duty: The intended meaning here is then, "Woe to him who says. . . ." The main question regarding this confident boast is whether the king simply intends to build, has recently begun building, or has now finished building his palatial house. The LXX has *ōkodomēsas seautō,* "you have built for yourself," which eliminates the boast and begins the direct address here instead of in v 15. This reading also assumes that the palace is already built. In addition, the LXX omits *hāʾōmēr* ("who says"), which is present in Aq, Symm, and Theod. The MT reading is to be preferred. A royal palace was discovered in the 1950s by Aharoni at Ramat Raḥel, south of Jerusalem on the road to Bethlehem, and the suggestion was made that this may have been Jehoiakim's royal palace (Aharoni 1961; *NEAEHL* 4: 1261–63). Aharoni thought originally that this palace was built by Uzziah in the eighth century B.C., but he later abandoned the date for one in the late seventh century (1961: 118). This palace, still standing in 597 B.C., was destroyed at the same time Jerusalem was destroyed. But B. Mazar (1988: 4) has argued that Jehoiakim's palace, which he believes was a summer residence, is likely to have been built in the new "Upper City" of Jerusalem, the Mishneh, an expansion of the city on the western hill occurring during Hezekiah's time. P. J. King (1993: 123–24) also thinks that Jehoiakim's palace must have been in Jerusalem.

It has commonly been supposed (Duhm; Weiser; Bright 1981: 325; Thompson; Boadt; Jones) that Jehoiakim managed this building project in spite of the heavy tribute imposed on him by Neco. The tribute, as reported in 2 Kgs 23:33–35, was 100 talents of silver and one talent of gold, borne entirely by "the people of the land." Malamat (1975: 127 n. 8), however, says that this amount was relatively low compared with the 1,000 talents of silver imposed on Menahem by Pul of Assyria (2 Kgs 15:19), or the 300 talents of silver and 30 talents of gold imposed on Hezekiah by Sennacherib (2 Kgs 18:14–16), the latter requiring the king to dig deep into both the Temple and the palace treasuries. Neco is thought to have imposed the lower tribute in exchange for Jehoiakim's loyalty, which he doubtless received. Because of this low tribute, requiring no outlay of funds by Jehoiakim himself, the king early on had money enough in the coffers to build or enlarge his palace.

a house of dimensions. I.e., a house with large dimensions. Hebrew *bêt middôt.* We might say today, "a house of square footage," meaning extensive square footage. Compare *ʾanšê middôt,* "men of (huge) dimensions," in Num 13:32. The subsequent adjective, "spacious" (*mĕruwwāḥîm*), is a double-duty modifier covering "dimensions" (D. N. Freedman).

with spacious upper rooms. On the "upper rooms," see v 13 above. The Pual masculine participle *mĕruwwāḥîm* ("spacious") is odd after a feminine plural noun, but the basic meaning is not in doubt. There is little support for a repointing of the term, with Cornill and Rudolph, to an unattested plural noun, *merwāḥîm*. The rendering "spacious upper rooms" follows Aq and Symm (*hyperōa euruchōra*); also T and Vg (*coenacula spatiosa*). The LXX has *hyperōa hripista*, "airy upper rooms" (NEB: "airy roof-chambers"). These rooms on the roof were for summer use (Kimḥi; cf. Judg 3:20).

And he frames for himself windows, and panels in cedar. 4QJer^c has *qrw^c* (without a prefixed *waw*), supporting the LXX reading of a passive participle: *diestalmena*, "structured (for a window)." 4QJer^a reads the same as MT: *wqr^c*, "and he frames." The verb *qr^c* ("cut, make wide") means "to frame" the eyes with mascara in 4:30, and the T translates it "frames" in the present verse. Reference, in any case, is to the cutting open, not widening, of windows in the wall (Rashi; Kimḥi). In the Baal and Anath Cycle, Baal builds a palace with windows and panels the interior with cedar from Lebanon (*ANET*^3 134–35, v, vi, and vii; *CS I* 261–62). On Jerusalem's royal houses with cedar interior, see Notes for 22:6–7.

windows. Hebrew *ḥallônāy* is not "my windows," but may instead be an abbreviated plural (GKC §87g, although it opts for a redivision of consonants). It is taken so by the Versions and by Kimḥi, Blayney, and Volz. The reading *ḥallônāyw*, "his windows," which incorporates the *waw* from the following word, was proposed by J. D. Michaelis (1793: 178), and before him by a Dr. Durell known to Blayney, the latter saying that he knew of one MS with this reading. Although accepted by a number of commentators (Giesebrecht; Cheyne; Duhm; Cornill; Bright; Thompson; Holladay; Craigie et al.), this proposal has not been adopted by any of the modern Versions. D. N. Freedman suggests that a terminal *waw* on *ḥallônāyw* could have been lost by haplography, since the following word begins with *waw*. This explanation would similarly give the reading, "his windows."

and panels in cedar, and paints in vermilion. The MT points the first verb as a passive participle, *sāpûn*, but many read it along with the following verb as an infinitive absolute: *sāpôn . . . māšôaḥ* (Blayney; Volz; Rudolph; Holladay). The two infinitives substitute as finite verbs after a preceding finite verb (GKC §113yz). The LXX takes all three verbs in the line as passive participles: *diestalmena . . . exulōmena . . . kechrismena . . .* ("structured . . . paneled . . . painted . . ."). Rashi says Jehoiakim covered the palace roof with cedars; Calvin imagines cedar-covered walls. Sunken stone panels discovered in an eighth- or seventh-century B.C. burial chamber within the Monastery of St. Étienne (École Biblique) in Jerusalem, just north of the Damascus Gate, are thought to imitate the cedar-paneled walls of Judahite palaces at the time, as well as the Temple and House of the Forest of Lebanon built earlier by Solomon (Barkay and Kloner 1986: 27).

vermilion. Hebrew *šāšar* (Akk *šaršerru; CAD* 17/2: 124–25; *AHw* 3: 1191) is a red clay or paste used to make vermilion paint; also the (bright) red color itself. R. J. Forbes (1965: 221) says that vermilion was probably made from red lead. Chemical analyses of ancient paintings in vermilion indicate a natural compound of clay mixed with iron oxide or mercury. Babylonian wall paintings in vermilion are referred to in Ezek 23:14. In 1930–31, Thureau-Dangin uncovered an eighth- or seventh-century B.C. Assyrian provincial palace at Til Barsip (Tell Ahmar) whose wall decorations, in brilliant colors, had survived almost entirely intact. The red paint on them has since been analyzed as "an ochre pigment, a natural compound of clay and oxide of iron" (Parrot 1961: 263, 266). This was the ancient vermilion. The paintings celebrate the king's achievements as monarch, warrior, and big-game hunter. Along with scenes boasting successful battles and the subjugation of enemies, are more irenic portrayals of the king, with officials and servants performing appointed duties, entertaining foreign dignitaries, and receiving homage and tribute from subject peoples. On the Til Barsip paintings, see Parrot 1961: xvi–xvii; 100–111, pls. 109–20; 262–63, pls. 336–37; and 266–78, pls. 342–48. One wonders then if Jehoiakim's adventure in vermillion did not consist of having self-aggrandizing portrayals painted on his newly-built palace walls.

15. *Are you a king because you compete in cedar?* This question probes deeply into the essence of kingship: is building with cedar what makes one a king? Some commentators (Duhm; Cornill; Rudolph; Carroll; Holladay) emend the verb to an unattested Hithpael in order to get a judgment on play-acting (GKC §54e). Is Jehoiakim by his extravagant behavior simply "trying to be king"? Such condescension is improbable. Jehoiakim is not trying to be king; he is king, and has been so for some years! MT's *hătimlōk*, which is a Qal imperfect with *hē'* interrogative (BDB, 573), yields a more vigorous reading, questioning whether palace-building is what kingship is all about. The verse goes on to state that kingship is in fact about doing justice and righteousness. The participle *mĕtaḥăreh* ("compete") is a Tiphel form of *ḥrh*, "to be hot," on which see Note for 12:5. Jehoiakim is "hotly competing" in cedar acquisition and construction. Jones says this points to the universal human weakness of having to do more splendidly than others. Instead of "in cedar," the majority of LXX MSS have "with Ahaz" (*en Achaz*), and G^A reads "with Ahab" (*en Achaab*), which cannot be right. The MT's "in cedar" suits the context perfectly and is a key word in the larger structure to which the present oracle belongs (see Rhetoric and Composition for 22:6–9).

Your father—Did not he eat and drink? I.e., did not Josiah enjoy life? Jehoiakim's "father" is neither Solomon (*pace* Giesebrecht), nor Ahaz (*pace* Volz; cf. LXX). Yahweh shows himself here, as elsewhere, as unopposed to eating and drinking (cf. Ecc 2:24; Matt 11:19). Kings dine well as a matter of course. The point is that Josiah ate and drank but also practiced justice and righteousness; therefore, it went well with him. See the fragrant memory of Josiah in Sir 49:1–3.

and do justice and righteousness? The essence of kingship (see Notes for 21:12 and 22:3).

Then it went well for him. Hebrew *'āz ṭôb lô.* An unmistakable echo of Deuteronomy, where the fruit of covenant obedience is that it will "go well" (*yṭb*) with the people (Deut 4:40; 5:16, 29; 6:3, 18, 24; 10:13; 12:25, 28; 19:13; 22:7). Jeremiah repeats this evaluation of Josiah's kingship in v 16a.

16. *He prosecuted the case of the poor and needy; then it went well.* The Heb has a cognate accusative: *dān dîn* (lit., "He judged judgment"), on which see GKC §117p–r. Cognate accusatives occur frequently in Jeremianic discourse (5:28 [2×]; 7:13; 11:19; 18:11, 18; 22:16, 19; 23:5, 20, 31; 29:11, 14 ["I will restore your fortunes" occurs another 10×]; 30:13; 37:1; 46:5; 49:20, 30; 50:45), those in 5:28 and 30:13 employing the same verb as here. The point is that Josiah rendered just judgments. See again v 19. This is indirect approval, one would imagine, for the Josianic Reform. In 5:28, Jeremiah speaks out in protest because cases of the orphan and needy are not being prosecuted, which appears to reflect the same situation as here. On Deuteronomy's preaching about not perverting justice toward the sojourner, orphan, and widow, as well as the care expected and provided in neighboring societies for these same individuals, see Note for 5:28. In the Keret Legend, Yaṣṣib censures his father for neglecting the orphans, widows, and poor, telling him he should step down (*ANET*[3] 149; *CS I* 342). That father-son contrast is here reversed: Jehoiakim, the son, is upbraided for not judging the cause of the poor and needy as Josiah, his father, did.

then it went well. The LXX omits, but there is little justification for taking this to be an MT plus (*pace* Duhm; Cornill; Rudolph; Bright; Thompson). Aquila and Symm both translate (*tote kalōs ēn autō*, "then it was good for him"). The repetition is good Hebrew style and doubtless intentional.

Is not that knowing me? Hebrew *hălô'-hî' hadda'at 'ōtî.* 4QJer[a] supports K[OR], which reads the masculine *hû'*; MT and 4QJer[c] have the feminine *hî'*. "Knowing Yahweh" is here equated with doing justice and righteousness and prosecuting the cases of the poor and needy (Siqueira 1987: 15–17). Josiah did it; Jehoiakim is not doing it. Elsewhere in Jeremiah, "knowing Yahweh" means "knowing his way" (5:4–5) and "knowing his ordinances" (8:7). Jeremiah's counsel in 9:22–23[Eng 9:23–24] is that boasting ought not be of one's wisdom, strength, or riches but that one understands and *knows* Yahweh.

17. *Indeed your eyes and your heart are on nothing except your cut.* Reading the initial *kî* as an asseverative: "Indeed!" Jehoiakim shows himself to be blithely unaware of what goes into living the good life. Psalm 19:9[Eng 19:8] says that Yahweh's covenant demands bring gladness to the *heart* and light to the *eyes*. Yahweh's word brought gladness to the heart of Jeremiah (Jer 15:16). Volz compares Jehoiakim's greed to that of Ahab when the latter seized Naboth's vineyard, which brought forth from the prophet Elijah a censure no less sharp than the present one (1 Kings 21).

except your cut. Holladay's translation. Hebrew *kî 'im-'al-biṣ'ekā.* The root *bṣ'* means "to cut, sever," with the noun *beṣa'* meaning "(unlawful) gain" (cf. 6:13). Jehoiakim is cheating others by taking too much for himself (Kimḥi: "your thoughts are only on your desire to acquire wealth"). This judgment, although hyperbolic, is nevertheless deserving. Jehoiakim's view of kingship is perhaps that of the later Roman orator, Gaius Memmius, whose famous statement, *Nam impune quae lubet facere, id est regem esse*, "For to do with impunity whatever one fancies is to be a king" (Sallust,

Bellum Iugurthinum xxxi 26; Loeb), urged people on to exact vengeance from their enemies.

and for shedding innocent blood. Warnings about not shedding innocent blood are given by Jeremiah in 7:6 and 22:3, the latter issued specifically to the king. The charge of innocent blood is made against Jehoiakim in 2 Kgs 24:4, an example of which was his murder of Uriah the prophet (Jer 26:20–23). Innocent blood will also be shed by others when the reigning king sheds it with impunity. Reference is made elsewhere to murders of the innocent needy (2:34) and murders of the very young sacrificed on altars to Baal (19:4). Jeremiah saw fit to warn the court about shedding innocent blood when he himself was on trial, which, not surprisingly, was during Jehoiakim's reign (26:15).

and for practicing oppression and running. Hebrew *hā'ōšeq* is clear; it means "(the act of) oppression" (6:6), otherwise "(the act of) extortion" (NJV: "fraud"). The term *hammĕrûṣâ* is less certain, with little help being supplied by an embellished T reading ("what is your soul's good pleasure"), and by the reading of LXX (*phonon*, "slaughter, murder"). Jerome in his commentary has "murder" (*homicidium*). Cornill believes the LXX's *phonon* is derived from the verb *rṣṣ*, "to crush, oppress," a suggestion made earlier by Giesebrecht. However, "murder" may be a bit strong or, at the very least, an imprecise rendering of this root (KB³ has a *mĕrûṣâ* II meaning "exortion"; BDB, 954, a noun meaning "crushing, oppression"), and the likelihood is that this translation owes its derivation to what has just been said about "shedding innocent blood." The more common solution, which is also contextually derived, is to take *mĕrûṣâ* as a *hapax legomenon* in the OT and translate it with a synonym of "oppression," e.g., "violence," "extortion" or "tyranny" (Rashi; Kimhi; Calvin; also the majority of recent commentators and modern Versions). Rashi notes a pairing of the verbs *'šq* and *rṣṣ* in 1 Sam 12:3, saying that the reference here is to "the crushing of the poor." But Ehrlich (1912: 299) says *mĕrûṣâ* cannot mean "oppression" or "extortion" and must carry its usual meaning of "running" or "zeal" (from *rûṣ*; cf. BDB, 930). The term means "manner of running, course" in 8:6 (Q); 23:10; and 2 Sam 18:27. Aquila and Symm in the present text have *ton dromon*, "the running, fleeing," and Jerome in the Vg translates *cursum*, "running, course." I suggest therefore that *hammĕrûṣâ* be rendered "(the) manner of running," where reference is being made to the king's habit of running from responsibility for evil deeds he has done. On another occasion, Jeremiah faulted fellow prophets for running (*rûṣ*) on false errands (23:21). Particular notice should also be taken of 12:5, where the verbs "run" (*rûṣ*) and "hotly compete" (*ḥrh* Tiphel) occur together. This is precisely what we have here (*ḥrh* Tiphel occurs in v 15). Jeremiah is talking about a king continually on the run, one who "(hotly) competes" in cedar construction but after committing evil is in the habit of "running (away)." If there did exist a noun *mĕrûṣâ* meaning "oppression," then here at the end we might have a play on words.

MESSAGE AND AUDIENCE

Yahweh in the present oracle says woe to anyone who builds his house, complete with upper rooms, without regard for righteousness or justice. A curse has not fallen upon this individual, but it may just as well have, for the divine woe is laden with funerary overtones. Yahweh is talking about someone who makes others work for nothing, giving them no wages at all. Sounds a bit like forced labor, although other kings are on record as having used it, notably David and Solomon, the builder of builders. But Yahweh in the present instance is opposed to such exploitation. He is also less than impressed with all the boasting he hears. An ambitious king wants a palatial residence, spacious upper rooms, windows, cedar paneling, and vermilion adorning the interior, and Yahweh says "No."

It soon becomes clear that a royal palace is at issue, for Yahweh now turns to address the king directly. Does this scion of David think that competing in cedar makes him the king he is? Let him have another look at his father, the good King Josiah. Did not he wine and dine as king and yet do justice and righteousness? Yes, and it went well for him. What is more, he prosecuted cases of the poor and the needy, and this too made things go well, as Deuteronomy promised it would. Yahweh then asks the king rhetorically, "Is not that knowing me?" The king is left to answer this question for himself. And those listening will have to do the same.

In its present form, with v 17 as part of the oracle, the concluding words to the king are explicit and harsh. Yahweh says that this king cares about nothing except amassing wealth, which could not be said of Solomon, despite the riches he attained (1 Kgs 3:13), nor is he above shedding innocent blood, practicing oppression, and then running away. This indictment of Jehoiakim was probably not uttered in the king's presence but before another audience. The oracle does not name the king, but the audience will know it is Jehoiakim, disliked as he is not only by Jeremiah but by members of the royal house, leading citizens of Jerusalem, and the population at large, who had to dig deep to pay the tribute money to Neco.

This oracle is generally dated to the early years of Jehoiakim (Peake; Volz; Rudolph; Weiser; Holladay; Jones). A date of 606–605 B.C. is about right, which gives Jehoiakim time to build his new palace, and finds Jeremiah still walking the streets of Jerusalem, preaching his message unhindered. After 604, when the prophet's scroll had been read to the king and consigned to the flames in a burst of unconcealed rage, Jeremiah and his colleague Baruch were out of public view (36:19, 26).

President Mobutu Sese Seko of the former Zaire was a tribal chief, basically, who functioned in a manner reminiscent of antiquity's despotic kings. Like Jehoiakim, he lavished wealth on himself, family, and friends, while leaving the rest of the country in abject poverty. His hometown of Gbado Lite in the north he made into a modern city equipped with every convenience. It had paved streets with curbs, hydroelectric power, electric lights, modern hotels, and food by the truckload arriving steadily. Other Zairians, meanwhile, had little money and very little to eat. The Kinshasa airport was littered with inoperable planes that had been cannibalized for spare parts; not a single bus ran on the city streets—they were lined up, as far as the eye could see, in multiple junkyards— and not a single traffic light worked. The open market was a veritable war zone. Mobuto, however, rested comfortably in his plush presidential palace and for enjoyment had his own private zoo. Like King Jehoiakim, this self-indulgent leader came to a sad but deserving end. He knew nothing about justice and caring for the poor. On the abuse of power by other African political leaders, see Katho 2001: 156–58.

7. A Non-lament for Jehoiakim (22:18–19)

22 ¹⁸Therefore thus said Yahweh to Jehoiakim son of Josiah, king of Judah:
   They shall not lament for him
       'Woe, my brother!
         Woe sister!'
   They shall not lament for him
       'Woe lord!
         Woe his majesty!'
   ¹⁹The burial of an ass he will be buried
       dragged away and cast off
           beyond the gates of Jerusalem.

RHETORIC AND COMPOSITION

The present verses contain an oracle of non-lament for Jehoiakim, who is named in the expanded messenger formula of v 18a. Delimitation at the top end is indicated by a *setumah* in 4QJer^c (reconstructed; Tov 1997: 191–92), M^A, and M^L and a *petuḥah* in M^P prior to v 18. Delimitation at the bottom end is indicated by a *petuḥah* in 4QJer^c (reconstructed; Tov 1997: 181) and a *setumah* in M^A and M^L after v 19. The M^P has no section there.

The oracle is two lines with *verbatim* repetitions typical of the Jeremiah poetry (4:23–26; 5:4–5, 15, 17; 23:21; 50:35–38; 51:20–23). With *verbatim* repetitions, other terms in the poetic line must vary. Here the laments are reproduced so that only the first and last terms contain the possessive pronoun:

Woe *my* brother!	Woe sister!
Woe lord!	Woe *his* majesty!

Various attempts have been made, ancient and modern, to add or substract the pronouns of a given term, but these should be set aside and the present arrangement left intact (see Notes).

The "woe . . . therefore" (*hôy . . . lākēn*) sequence in vv 13–19 is an important prophetic speech form, occurring in Amos 6:1–7; Isa 5:8–25; Mic 2:1–5; and elsewhere (Jones). Jones says that the combination of terms, introducing first an indictment and then a judgment, occurs more than fifty times in the OT. But this combination does not argue for an original unity of vv 13–19. The present oracle is independent of the oracle in vv 13–17. Nevertheless, the "woe . . . therefore" collocation may still be intentional within the larger rhetorical structure of 22:6–23 (see Rhetoric and Composition for 22:6–9). This collocation occurs only one other time in Jeremiah, in 23:1–8, where it also is editorial.

These catchwords link the present oracle to the previous one:

v 18 *woe* (4×)   v 13 *woe*

NOTES

22:18. *Therefore thus said Yahweh to Jehoiakim son of Josiah, king of Judah.* The LXX adds *ouai epi ton andra touton*, "Woe upon this man," which some commentators (Cornill; Rudolph; Bright; Holladay) believe to be original. The lack in MT (*hwy ʿl ʾyš hzh*) could be due to haplography (homoeoteleuton: *h . . . h*).

son of Josiah. "Josiah" is spelled *yʾwšy[h]* in 4QJerᶜ; in MT the spelling is *yʾšyhw*.

They shall not lament for him. Hebrew *lōʾ-yispĕdû lô*. The MT repeats the same verb in the next line, while the LXX varies the verbs: *mē kopsōntai . . . mē klausontai*, "they shall not lament . . . they shall not weep" (Vg also varies the verbs). Compare the repeated *ṣʿq* ("scream") in 22:20. The LXX's second verb does not translate Heb *yiśrĕpû*, "they shall burn (spices)," as Holladay states (p. 592 n. 18b). Compare verbs in 34:5 in both MT and LXX. Jehoiakim's death is here anticipated, and he will not be mourned as Josiah was.

'Woe, my brother! Woe sister!' . . . 'Woe lord! Woe his majesty!' "Woe" (*hôy*) is here a cry of lament, as also in 34:5. "Woe, my brother!" occurs in 1 Kgs 13:30, where it is uttered at the burial of an unnamed Judahite prophet. For a discussion of the term, which in 22:13 and 23:1 is a prophetic invective, see Note on 22:13. The LXX in the present verse omits "Woe sister!" and "Woe his majesty!" but both appear to be present in 4QJerᶜ (reconstructed; Tov 1997: 192). Gᴼ and Gᴸ have different readings for "my brother": Gᴼ has *adelphe* ("brother" without "my"); Gᴸ has *kurie* ("lord"). The Vg too has simply "brother" (*frater*). Gᴼᴸ also read "brother" instead of "sister" (Heb *ʾāḥôt* is "sister" singular, not "sisters"), and "brother" instead of "his majesty." "His majesty" (*hōdōh*) may have confused the ancient translator(s) because of an uncommon third-masculine singular suffix, *ōh* (T; Kimḥi; cf. GKC §58a). Proposals by Dahood (1961) and Holladay to alter the terms in the interest of achieving greater symmetry should be set aside.

Questions have been raised about the cry "Woe sister!" Kimḥi suggests that it may have been for Jehoiakim's wife, an interpretation favored also by Blayney. The scene envisioned is a procession of mourners where one is condoling with the other, and the prophet, says Calvin, is imitating their words. Kimḥi views the laments in the first line as those uttered by the king's relatives, in the second those of the king's subjects. All the laments are stereotypical. Gaster (1969: 604) cites an ancient text of the Babylonian Akitu (New Year's) Festival where, at a certain point in the proceedings, wailing women begin parading around, crying, "Woe brother! Woe brother!" Also, in the *balag* laments of ancient Mesopotamia (M. E. Cohen 1988: 245, 335), which are even older, these lines appear:

> She who has a new spouse says, "My spouse!"
> She who has a newborn child says, "My child!"
> My young girl says, "My brother!"
> (In) the city my mother says, "My child!"
> The young child says, "My father!"

Other recurring lines in the *balag* laments (pp. 438, 590, 662, et passim):

> . . . "My house! . . . "My city!"
> . . . "My spouse!" . . . "My child!"
> . . . "My cella!" . . . "My treasure house!"
> . . . "My property!" . . . "O my possessions!"
> . . . "O my young maidservant!" . . . "My slave girl!"

See "Lamentations over the Destruction of Sumer and Ur" in *ANET*³ 460–61, 613; cf. *CS I* 537–38.

19. *The burial of an ass he will be buried.* On the cognate accusative, see Note for 22:16. The expression here is oxymoronic (Watson 1984: 312–13; cf. Chotzner 1883: 14), for as the verse goes on to state, dead asses receive no burial; they are dragged off and left on a dungheap. Jerome adds that unburial means being "torn by beasts and birds" (*a bestiis avibusque lacerandum*). Whether such a thing happened to Jehoiakim has been much debated, particularly in view of the LXX reading of 2 Chr 36:8 and the reading of G^L for 2 Kgs 24:6, both of which report a burial for Jehoiakim in the Garden of Uzza, where Manasseh and Amon were buried (2 Kgs 21:18, 26). The MT of 2 Kgs 24:6 and 2 Chr 36:8 says only that Jehoiakim "slept with his fathers," although this is the normal euphemism for burial in one's ancestral tomb. Judah's kings were entombed in the City of David, i.e., within the inner citadel of Jerusalem, probably at the southern end (Yeivin 1948). Ussishkin (1970) found some 50 tombs opposite the City of David, across the Kidron in the modern town of Silwan, which he thought were for "nobles and notables" of the kingdom of Judah. But it is unlikely that any of Judah's kings (including Hezekiah, Manasseh, Amon, and Josiah) were buried outside Jerusalem. According to Yeivin (1948: 38–39), biblical and postbiblical tradition are one in placing the burial of Judah's kings within the walls of the capital city, which was the custom also in neighboring countries. An eventual burial for Jehoiakim may have taken place, but we know nothing about how this king met his end and whether, in

fact, he was subject to the dishonorable treatment predicted here. Suspicions are many that his death was not a natural one. Albright (1932: 90–91), assuming that Jeremiah's prediction here and in 36:30 must have been approximately fulfilled, also that the compiler of Kings put Nebuchadnezzar's invasion of Judah *after* the death of Jehoiakim (2 Kgs 24:10), imagined a palace revolt in which Jehoiakim was slain and Jehoiachin, his son, was placed on the throne. The Annals of Ashurbanipal (Rassam Cylinder III 8–9) report the death of Aḫsheri, king of Mannai, who, after a popular rebellion in his country, was killed and suffered the further indignity of having his body thrown into the streets, where it was ripped into pieces (Streck 1916 II: 24–25). Bright (1981: 327), too, thinks Jehoiakim was assassinated just after the Babylonians began their westward march in December 598 B.C. The beginning of the march and death of Jehoiakim is placed by Tadmor (1956: 230) in Kislev 597 B.C. (on names of months in the Jewish calendar, see Appendix IX). However, this reconstruction is complicated by the report in 2 Chr 36:6 that Nebuchadnezzar came to Jerusalem and "bound [Jehoiakim] in chains to take him to Babylon." Josephus (*Ant* x 96–98) and the Rabbis thus develop various scenarios in which Jehoiakim is captured and then brought to a dishonorable end. Both appear to harmonize data in 2 Chr 36:6 with what is stated in the present verse (Begg 1996). The surrender of Jehoiakim (or his body) to Nebuchadnezzar is discussed in the Midrashim (Leviticus Rabbah 19:6; Genesis Rabbah 94:9), where a comparison to the rebellious Sheba and his fate is made (2 Sam 20:14–22). On the latter, see Daube 1965: 49–68. Reflecting this tradition, Kimḥi says that Jehoiakim died outside Jerusalem when being taken (a second time) into exile and that the Chaldeans would not permit his burial. Cornill imagines that Jehoiakim died a natural death and received an honorable burial, like all other kings. He and others (Giesebrecht; Rudolph; Weiser; Hyatt) think the body was later disinterred and dishonored—either by the Babylonians or by his own people (cf. 8:1–2), as happened to Martin Bucer and Oliver Cromwell in England. This explanation has not won much support, because disinterment cannot be inferred from the present passage or from any other biblical passage. Some commentators (Volz; Jones) who think Jehoiakim was buried say simply that Jeremiah's prophecy went unfulfilled. We really do not know how Jehoiakim died or to what extent the present prophecy was fulfilled. On the indignity of bodies lying unburied, about which Jeremiah says a great deal, see Note for 7:33.

dragged away and cast off beyond the gates of Jerusalem. The infinitive absolutes, *sāḥôb wĕhašlēk* ("dragged away and cast off"), describe more particularly the circumstances of the king's nonburial (GKC §113h). The same prediction, stated differently, is made in 36:30. Dead bodies are commonly dragged off (and torn) by wild dogs (15:3; 2 Kgs 9:35–37), but since Jehoiakim's corpse is to end up outside the city, it may be that people will drag it there. Hebrew *hašlēk*, normally "thrown, cast off," can in this case mean "leave unburied" (Cogan 1968; 1971: 33). Joüon (1937) cites a modern example of the indignity described here following a clan feud among Arabs at Palmyra (Syria). The chief of one clan, after slitting the throat of his rival, vowed that his victim would not be carried to his burial in the usual manner but dragged there by oxen, as dead sheep are dragged away.

beyond the gates of Jerusalem. If all previous kings of Judah were buried in Jerusalem, then it was an added indignity for Jehoiakim's corpse to end up outside the city gates.

MESSAGE AND AUDIENCE

The present oracle with its expanded messenger formula states that King Jehoiakim will not be lamented with customary cries of lament. Instead he will receive the burial of an ass, dragged away and left unburied beyond the gates of Jerusalem. Such a burial will be no burial.

In the larger context, this oracle will be heard as a much-needed judgment on Jehoiakim, who, in the previous oracle, was indicted for covenant violation and offending human sensibilities. The judgmental "woe" of v 13 makes up for the "woes" of lament this king will not receive when he dies. He treated others shamefully; now in death abundant shame will be heaped upon him. His grand building project will also be contrasted to his ignoble death (Volz), conveying an even harsher judgment than the one that is meted out in the NT parable about the rich man who builds large barns and then dies (Luke 12:16–21). This oracle will also hearken back to the lament and oracle for Jehoahaz in vv 10–12, which, by contrast, were sympathetic outpourings for one who never got to be king. And the audience will not likely miss another contrast between Jehoiakim and Josiah. In 22:10 Jeremiah had to tell people mourning Josiah to cease their laments; here the prophet envisions a situation where people will not be lamenting their king at all. This oracle of non-lament is to be dated during Jehoiakim's reign, possibly just before he died in December, 598 B.C., but possibly somewhat earlier, when the conflict between the king and Jeremiah was at its height, i.e., ca. 605–604 B.C.

8. Lebanon South to Be Strangely Favored (22:20–23)

22 ²⁰Go up to Lebanon and scream
 and in the Bashan raise your voice!
And scream from Abarim
 because all your lovers are broken
²¹I spoke to you in your good times
 you said, 'I will not listen'
This has been your way from your youth
 that you have not listened to my voice

²²All your shepherds the wind shall shepherd
 and your lovers into captivity shall go
Indeed then you will be ashamed and disgraced
 from all your wickedness

²³You who dwell^a in Lebanon
  you who are nested^b in the cedars
How you will be favored when pangs come upon you
  pain like a woman in labor.

RHETORIC AND COMPOSITION

There is little doubt that the present verses constitute a unit. The upper limit is indicated by a *petuḥah* in 4QJer^c (reconstructed; Tov 1997: 181) and a *setumah* in M^A and M^L before v 20. The M^P has no section there. After v 23 there are no section markings in any of the medieval codices or in 4QJer^c, but a shift from poetry to prose and the beginning of a new unit about Jehoiachin in v 24 makes a division between vv 23 and 24 virtually certain. Duhm noted that vv 20–23 speak generally about the destiny of Judah's kings and suggested that originally these verses may have concluded the sayings about Jehoahaz and Jehoiakim. The rhetorical structure delimiting 22:6–23 (see Rhetoric and Composition for 22:6–9), suggesting a one time independent collection, indicates much the same.

Commentators typically remark that this poetry seems to interrupt an otherwise focused attack on Judah's kings, for which reason it is said to be a later insertion. As for location, this is adequately explained by the larger rhetorical structure, for which it is the conclusion. Being a divine speech to Jerusalem, it complements 22:6–7, which is a divine speech to the royal palace. Both speeches are riveting judgments, and it is fitting that the whole of Jerusalem should be asked at the end to lament, for judgment against kings and royal buildings will inevitably mean judgment on the entire city, and following judgment will come the weeping of bitter tears.

There is no debate about whether the present poetry is Jeremianic. Both Giesebrecht (p. xxi) and Mowinckel (1914: 20) assign it to the prophet, and more recently Holladay (p. 601) and Jones (p. 292) have pointed out certain similarities in vocabulary and phraseology with the poetry in chaps. 2–3 (Holladay: chaps. 2–6). What we have here, basically, is a judgment oracle, even though there is no messenger formula. Yahweh is the speaker in v 21 ("I spoke to you in your good times") and without difficulty can be shown to speak the entire poem (Volz).

The poem has an inclusio made from "Lebanon" and "cedars" (Condamin notes "Lebanon"), the same key words that make an inclusio in 22:6–7. Both passages I analyzed earlier, although the present one with a slightly different interpretation (Lundbom 1975: 48–50, 57 [= 1997: 67–69, 77–78]):

I . . . . *Lebanon and scream*   v 20
  . . . . *your voice*

---

^aReading the Q *yōšabt*, or the more usual *yōšebet* (10:17; 46:19); the Kt with the *yod* is strange, perhaps attaching a second feminine singular perfect pronominal form to the participle (cf. GKC §90n).

^bReading the Q *mĕqunnant*; Kt and 4QJer^c again have the strange *yod* termination (see prior Footnote).

And scream . . . .
　　because all your lovers . . . .　　*kî* . . .
. . . .　　v 21
　　　. . . . . '*I will not listen*'

. . . .
　　that you have not listened to my voice　　*kî* . . .

II　*All* . . . .　　*kōl* . . .　　v 22
　　and your lovers . . . .

. . . .
　　from all . . . .　　*mikkōl* . . .
. . . . *Lebanon*　　　　　v 23
　　. . . . . *cedars*
　　. . . . .
　　　. . . . .

Stanza II with assonance makes another inclusio (Lundbom 1975: 57–58
[= 1997: 78]):

II　. . . . . *yēlēkû*　　　v 22
　　. . . . .
　　. . . . .　　v 23
　　. . . . . *kayyōlēdâ*

This poem, concluding as it does the core poetry to the King Collection, appears to have been connected at one time by catchword to the first poem of the
Prophet Collection (Lundbom 1975: 102–3 [= 1997: 135–36]). This shows the
Jehoiachin oracles in 22:24–30 and the messianic oracles in 23:1–8 to be a later
addition. There are no catchwords connecting the present poem to the Jehoiachin oracles. The concluding "king poem" begins:

　22:20　Go up to Lebanon and scream
　　　　　and in the Bashan raise your voice!
　　　　And scream from Abarim
　　　　　because all your lovers *are broken*　　*nišběrû*

And the first "prophet poem" begins:

　23:9　My heart *is broken* within me　　*nišbar*
　　　　all my bones shake

NOTES

22:20. *Go up to Lebanon and scream.* Hebrew *ʿălî hallěbānôn ûšěʿāqî.* Compare the call for a lament in 49:3: "scream (*šěʿaqnâ*), Rabbah's daughters!"
4QJer^c has "into (the) Lebanon" (*blbnwn*), which corresponds to the reading
in v 23. The reading of 4QJer^c is the *lectio facilior.* The MT varies the pre-

fixed particles for the three mountain sites: *hallĕbānôn . . . babbāšān . . . mēʿăbārîm*, which appears to be intentional. "Lebanon" usually has the article (22:6), although in poetry and in the Dead Sea Scrolls the article is often omitted (18:14; Hos 14:8[Eng 14:7]; Nah 1:4; cf. KB³). For the use of *ʿălî* without *ʾel*, see *ʿălî gilʿād* in 46:11. "Lebanon" refers here to the mountains of Lebanon in the far north, whereas in v 23 the term is a metaphor for the cedar-lined palace in Jerusalem. Reference is not to the Temple (*pace* T, which has "the house of the sanctuary"). Jerusalem, personified as a woman, is being told to ascend the mountains of Lebanon, as well as two other mountain ranges, Bashan and Abarim, and lament loudly so that everyone can hear. The reason: her "lovers" are destroyed. She may also be lamenting before the foreign gods she has been worshiping. She is definitely not going to the mountains to call for help from her allies (*pace* Blayney; McKane). For mountains and hills as places of lament, see 3:21; 7:29; Isa 15:2; and Judg 11:38. The directive is bitterly ironic (Calvin): Jerusalem is embarassed over her helpless state and will not want to do what she is asked. It would all be for nothing.

the Bashan. The name takes the article, as in German "die Schweiz" (for Switzerland). Bashan is located north of Gilead in the Transjordan highlands (50:19; 2 Kgs 10:33), where mountains also rise up (Ps 68:16[Eng 68:15]).

And scream from Abarim. Hebrew *wĕṣaʿăqî mēʿăbārîm*. The Hebrew repeats the verb *ṣĕʿāqî* ("scream") from the first line, whereas the LXX translates with two different verbs: *kraxon* ("scream") and *boāson* ("cry loudly"). Holladay (p. 600) disapproves of the repetition ("not appropriate . . . in parallelism") and chooses two different English equivalents. But the Hebrew is perfectly good poetry, and repetitions of this type, where words in one colon—often at the end—repeat at the beginning of a subsequent colon, occur often in Jeremiah (2:10, 13; 25:30; 31:9; 47:2; and 51:31). This is a bona fide rhetorical device, given the name *anadiplosis* by classical rhetoricians (see Rhetoric and Composition for 51:27–33). The LXX, as in v 18, shows itself to have an aversion to repetition.

from Abarim. Hebrew *mēʿăbārîm*. The Abarim is a Moabite mountain range that includes Mount Nebo (Num 27:12; 33:47–48; Deut 32:49). Van Zyl (1960: 51) says that the term was initially used as an appellative (common noun) but here has become a name designating the entire Moab highland. Thus we have three mountainous areas to which Jerusalem is directed: one in the north, one in the northeast, and one in the southeast. Jerusalem's lament will be heard everywhere. The Versions do not render *ʿăbārîm* as a proper noun. The LXX has *eis to peran tēs thalassēs* ("to the other side of the sea"), which could presuppose a Hebrew *Vorlage* that read *mēʿēber yām* (S: *mn ʿbrj jmʾ*; cf. Deut 30:13) or could be simply a misdivision of consonants.

because all your lovers are broken. McKane, assuming that the calamity in question has not yet occurred, says that the verb here has to be a prophetic perfect. But that is unnecessary. If the passage is dated just before 597 B.C., as is widely assumed, Assyria is no more and Egypt is back to defending its own borders. The years between 605 and 597 were chaotic, with Babylon now the undisputed power broker in the region. Most commentators say the "lovers" are nations with whom Judah has been allied (2:18, 36), who are now rendered helpless by Babylonian military might. Kimḥi and Calvin both name Assyria and Egypt. The term "your lovers," *mě'ahăbayik* (here in pausal *-bāyik*), occurs only in this verse, in v 22, and in 30:14. In 30:14, they are imagined friends turned foe, the case also in Ezek 23:5–9 and 22–23, where the Assyrians, Babylonians, and other nations are named. The "lovers" (*'ăhābîm*) of Hos 8:9–10 were similarly Assyria and other nations.

are broken. Hebrew *nišběrû.* The term can mean "broken" in a physical sense or "broken" in a psychological sense, i.e., "brokenhearted" (cf. 8:21; 23:9). Here both meanings have applicability: neighboring nations have been rendered incapable of fighting their own or other nations' wars. 4QJerᶜ has *nšpkw,* "they are poured out." The LXX's *sunetribēsan,* "they were broken, crushed," supports MT. Compare Egypt's own plight in the judgment of Ezek 30:8.

21. *I spoke to you in your good times; you said, 'I will not listen.'* Yahweh refers here to his word that came to the people via the prophets and their refusal to listen. The people's response is reported as being the same in 6:17 and 19. Adamant refusals by the people occur frequently in Jeremiah's early preaching: "I will not serve" in 2:20; "I am not defiled, after the Baals I have not gone" in 2:23; "I have not sinned" in 2:35; "We will not walk" in 6:16; and "We will not give heed" in 6:17. Jeremiah himself heard a refusal similar to the present one from exiles in Egypt. They said regarding a word he spoke to them in Yahweh's name: "We will not listen to you" (44:16). The charge that the people did not listen to Yahweh, particularly his oracles spoken by the prophets, is a major prose theme in the book (16:12; 25:3–4, 7, 8; 26:5; 29:19; 36:31; 37:2; 44:4–5). The reason is that they were listening to prophets, diviners, and workers of magic whom Yahweh had not sent (23:16; 27:14, 16; 29:8–9).

in your good times. I.e., when times were peaceful and secure. Hebrew *běšalôtayik.* Rashi translates "when you lived in peace" (Sir 47:13 so characterizes the reign of Solomon). The plural indicates that many such times existed. A few Heb MSS and the Vrs (LXX, Aq, Symm, S, Vg) have a singular (which omits the *yod*). The LXX's "in your transgression" (*en tē paraptōsei sou*) appears to be contextually derived (McKane). Aquila and Symm: (*en) tē euthēnia sou* ("in your abundance").

This has been your way from your youth, that you have not listened to my voice. The LXX omits the *kî* ("that"), which should be retained (see Rhetoric and Composition). D. N. Freedman suggests the possibility of LXX haplography if *mnʿwryk(y)* was spelled with the archaic suffix *ky* (cf. Ps 103:5). "This" (*zeh*) points back to the defiant "I will not listen" (Giesebrecht). Hebrew *šmʿ bě* means more precisely "to obey." The point about not listening to Yahweh in the early days of the covenant relationship is made elsewhere in 32:23 and 34:14—in the first case subsequent to settlement in the land, and in the second subsequent to Yahweh's making the covenant with Israel. There may or may not be a conflict here with the romantic portrayals in chap. 2, where Yahweh speaks of Israel's "bridal (*něʿûrîm*) devotion" in the Wilderness (2:2–3) and then of a refractory partner after her settlement in the land (see Notes for 2:2 and 2:7). But Kimḥi says reference here is to the wilderness generation, which would then reflect the traditions preserved in Exodus and Numbers; also in Deut 9:6–29; Jer 7:25–26; and Ezek 20:13–26. Compare also the confession in 3:24–25.

22. *All your shepherds the wind shall shepherd.* Hebrew *kol-rōʿayik tirʿeh-rûaḥ*. A wordplay on *rōʿayik tirʿeh*, "shall shepherd your shepherds." There is also irony, since shepherding implies "gathering," whereas the wind "scatters." The shift is now to the future. This wind will be the east wind off the desert, the sirocco, which will scatter Judah's shepherds in every direction (4:11–12; 18:17). "Shepherds" is a general term for "rulers" in the ANE (see Note for 2:8); here it refers first and foremost to "kings" (Rashi) but also to princes and other Judahite leaders. Jehoahaz has already been blown away to Egypt, and yet to come are the exiles of Jehoiachin and Zedekiah to Babylon. With both kings went also a goodly number of other prominent citizens. Aquila and Symm have "your companions" (*tous etairous sou*) for "your shepherds," which may be influenced by "your lovers" in the next colon, and misread *rōʿayik* ("your shepherds") as *rēʿayik* ("your companions"). NEB and REB thus translate "your friends," but this does away with the wordplay (Duhm; Rudolph; Jones).

and your lovers into captivity shall go. Who are these "lovers"? Are they Judah's (former) allies, as in v 20, or Jerusalem's "shepherds" referred to in the prior colon? One will note that Pashhur's "dear friends" (*ʾōhăbeykā*) in 20:4 and 6, who might also be called "loved ones," were other priests, prophets, and highly placed friends in Jerusalem (see Note for 20:4). In the present verse, then, the people's "lovers" are probably not former allies (who are already "broken") but the Jerusalem leadership destined for a coming exile (Rudolph; Thiel 1973: 242).

Indeed then you will be ashamed and disgraced. Hebrew *kî ʾāz tēbōšî wĕniklamt*. Dahood (1976a: 55) translates the initial *kî* as a vocative: "O then you will be ashamed and abashed," which is quoted with approval by Althann (1997: 103). The AV and NAB render the particle as an asseverative: "surely," which is how I have translated it here. Most modern Versions (RSV; NEB; NJV; NIV; NRSV; REB; NJB; NSB) do not translate it at all. The particle "then" (*ʾāz*) shows that the denouement is still to come. On the verbal combination "ashamed and disgraced," see 14:3 and 31:19. People were said earlier to be incapable of shame and disgrace (3:3; 6:15 [= 8:12]), but Jeremiah warned that shame would nevertheless come (2:36; 8:9), and it did (9:18[Eng 9:19]; 51:51). Shame came to Northern Israel (31:19; 48:13) and awaited other nations destined for defeat (46:24; 48:1, 20, 39; 49:23; 50:2). On shame in Jeremiah, the OT, and the ancient world in general, see Note for 2:26.

from all your wickedness. Hebrew *mikkōl rāʿātēk*. A wordplay with *kol-rōʿayik* ("all your shepherds") in the previous line. The LXX's "by all your friends" (*apo pantōn tōn philountōn se*) appears again to misread the Hebrew, as Aq and Symm did in the case of *rōʿayik*, "your shepherds" (see above). Shame and disgrace are the bitter fruit of evil behavior (3:25).

23. *You who dwell in Lebanon, you who are nested in the cedars.* Whereas "Lebanon" in v 20 meant the mountains of Lebanon, here the reference is to cedar-lined buildings atop Jerusalem, one of which was called "The House of the Forest of Lebanon." See also 22:6. The focus now is upon the king and his royal compatriots, who are nicely nested in their posh, protected Jerusalem palace (Rashi; Kimhi). The phrase "who are nested in the cedars" is an *abusio* (implied metaphor), on which see Note for 4:4. Compare also 49:16, where Edom mistakenly thinks that dwelling in a lofty, seemingly secure nest will put her out of enemy reach. Habakkuk says: "Woe to him who makes an evil profit for his house, to set his nest on high, to save himself from the reach of evil" (Hab 2:9).

How you will be favored when pangs come upon you. More irony, if one reads *nēhant* as an N-stem of *hnn*, meaning "you will be favored!" The AV translated the verb *hnn* ("How gracious thou shalt be"), which Blayney interpreted to mean that the inhabitant of Lebanon, once obstinate and inflexible in prosperity, will be changed by adversity and made gracious in temper and disposition. Such an interpretation hardly fits the context, which is one of judgment. The NJV translates "How much grace will you have, when pains come upon you . . . ," which is an improvement, but not a particularly compelling rendering of the Hebrew. Most commentators and modern Versions follow the LXX, S, and Vg, which translate an equivalent of "groan." The LXX has *katastenaxeis*, "you will groan," and the Vg *congemuisti*, "you have groaned." The context requires a future, but Volz says that a perfect verb with *mah* ("How") can indicate future tense. The usual explanation, then, is that the present verb does not derive from *hnn* ("to be favored"), since no other N-stems are attested in the OT, but rather from *'nh*, "to groan," where the *'aleph* has fallen away (*nēnahat* = *ne'ĕnahat*; KB³; GKC §23f n. 1 says the form is corrupt). Dahood (1962b: 70; 1965: 66 #1630a) arrives at "groan" by proposing a Hebrew root *nhn* based on Ugaritic. "Groan" admittedly fits the context, but an N-stem participle of *hnn* is attested on a Phoenician inscription from Sidon (*CIS* i 3, 12: *nhn*), which Cooke (1903: 30–31, 36) tentatively translated as "to be pitied." One may then propose that *nēhant* is, after all, an N-stem perfect of *hnn*, which besides requiring no change has the added advantage of preserving an additional ironic reading in what is already a highly ironic poem.

pain like a woman in labor. Hebrew *hîl kayyōlēdâ.* The phrase occurs also in 6:24 and 50:43. One of the curses of a defeated people, particularly the soldiers, was that they would become (weak like) women (see Notes for 4:31 and 6:24). But here, since the figure in the poem is already a woman, the point may be that Jerusalem's anguish will be comparable to the pain of childbirth without the compensation of gaining a child (D. N. Freedman).

MESSAGE AND AUDIENCE

This poem is totally lacking in specifics about speaker and addressee: no messenger formula to confirm that the "I" of v 21 is the divine "I" and no identification of the female addressee anywhere. The message is also less than transparent due to metaphors, wordplays, words changing referents, and a generous amount of irony. Only an audience knowing the background against which the poem was spoken could be sure of its message, and even then, the message would still prove difficult for some. For later audiences, and for us, the interpretation is based on what we know from other Jeremiah oracles.

It is generally agreed that Yahweh is addressing Jerusalem at the time of Nebuchadnezzar's expedition against the city in 597 B.C. Some think the city has not yet capitulated (Weiser; Boadt); others think it has (Volz; Rudolph). This dating is arrived at, to some extent, by the location of the poem between oracles against Jehoiakim (vv 18–19) and Jehoiachin (vv 24–30).

The divine speech can be interpreted as follows. Yahweh tells Lady Jerusalem to ascend three mountain ranges—Lebanon in the north, Bashan in the northeast, and Abarim in the southeast—and cry loudly from each over lovers who have been broken. Who are these lovers? Since Lady Jerusalem is on foreign mountains, the lovers are perhaps foreigners. Foreign gods were doubtless worshiped there. The directive is probably ironic, in which case the lamenting could all be in vain. Yahweh says he spoke to Jerusalem in her good times, but she said, "I will not listen." It became a habit with her from early times that she would not listen to Yahweh's voice. For this reason, Yahweh says, the wind shall shepherd her shepherds, and her lovers shall go into captivity. The shepherds are Jerusalem's rulers, and the lovers may now be the same; otherwise, they are the foreign peoples and their foreign gods or both. All, in any case, will go into captivity, with shame and disgrace becoming the bitter fruit of Jerusalem's wickedness. The poem closes by addressing the inhabitant of "Lebanon South," probably now Jerusalem's king and his royal entourage, who are comfortably nesting in their cedar-lined palace. Yahweh says that this elite group (and everyone else in the city) will be strangely favored when pangs come upon it like they come to a woman in labor.

This call to lament is an appropriate conclusion to the core collection of 22:6–23. There was judgment on the royal palace at the beginning (vv 6–7), an indictment of Jehoiakim in the center (vv 13–17), and now a judgment on all Jerusalem at the end, which will evoke grievous lamentation from everyone (vv 20–23). We recall that the early foe-lament collection in 4:5–9:21[Eng 9:22] was so ordered that laments followed words of judgment (see Rhetoric and Composition for 4:5–10).

9. Coniah: A Rejected Seal (22:24–27)

22 ²⁴As I live—oracle of Yahweh—even if Coniah son of Jehoiakim, king of Judah, be a seal on my right hand, surely from there I will tear you off. ²⁵And I will give you into the hand of those who seek your life and into the hand of those before whom you are in dread and into the hand of

Nebuchadrezzar, king of Babylon, and into the hand of the Chaldeans.
²⁶And I will throw you and your mother who bore you to another land
where you were not born, and there you shall die. ²⁷So to the land where
they will carry their great desire to return, there they shall not return.

RHETORIC AND COMPOSITION

The present oracle announces Yahweh's rejection of Jehoiachin and his banishment into exile. In the oracle following, vv 28–30, captivity has already occurred (Giesebrecht; Duhm; Peake; Rudolph; and others). The present oracle
is delimited by a shift to prose in v 24 and a shift back to poetry in v 28. There
is also a beginning "oracle of Yahweh" formula in v 24, which is present in
4QJerᶜ. The medieval codices and 4QJerᶜ have no sections before v 24, but
after v 27 Mᴸ has a *setumah*, and Mᴬ and Mᴾ have a *petuḥah*. 4QJerᶜ has no
section there.

Rudolph and Weiser make poetry out of v 24, but they have to delete in order to do it. The idea is much older (Giesebrecht; Duhm; Cornill; Volz) that
vv 25–27 expand upon v 24, two reasons being that v 25 has *accumulatio*, which
is thought to betray the work of a "Deuteronomic" editor, and v 27 shifts from
the second person to the third. Duhm takes vv 25–26 as an addition to v 24, and
then v 27 is called *ein Zusatz zum Zusatz* ("an addition to an addition"). All
these views are passé, and the tendency more recently has been simply to take
vv 24–27 as a prose oracle of singular integrity (Bright; Holladay; Craigie et al.;
Jones), which is correct. McKane continues to believe that v 24 is the kernel
out of which vv 25–27 are generated, but his view is to be rejected. The repetition in v 25 is a fine example of *exergasia* (Schoettgen 1733: 1249–63; English:
Lundbom 1975: 121–27 [= 1997: 155–63]), which Kimḥi says intensifies the
power of the sentence.

Although in prose, vv 25–27 contain impressive rhetorical features. In v 25
this repetition appears:

> v 25 And I will give you *into the hand* (*bĕyad*) of those who seek your life
> *and into the hand* (*ûbĕyad*) of those before whom you are in dread
> *and into the hand* (*ûbĕyad*) of Nebuchadrezzar, king of Babylon
> *and into the hand* (*ûbĕyad*) of the Chaldeans

The Hebrew of vv 26–27, whose pronouns translate only with difficulty into English, contains a word and syntactic chiasmus at the end of each verse: the
verbs are at the extremes, and *(wĕ)šām(â)*, "(and) there," repeats at the center.
The lines taken together also invert verbs with the negative particle:

v 26b *lō-yulladtem šām / wĕšām tāmûtû*
v 27b *hēm mĕnaśʾîm ʾet-napšām lāšûb šām / šāmā lō yāšûbû*
v 26b you were *not* born *there* / *and there* you shall die
v 27b they will carry their great desire to return *there* / *there* they shall *not* return

The beginning clauses of the verses make yet another inversion, rendering less likely the proposed deletion of the definite article on *hā'āreṣ* ("the earth") in v 26 (see Notes):

v 26a	. . . . *'al hā'āreṣ . . . 'ăšer*
v 27a	*wĕ'al-hā'āreṣ 'ăšer* . . . .
v 26a	. . . . *to the land . . . where*
v 27a	*So to the land where* . . . .

The change of audience at the beginning and end of the oracle has troubled commentators but should be taken here as elsewhere as a bit of drama added to the Jeremianic discourse. One sees the same thing happening again in the next oracle. Here Yahweh addresses the following audiences:

Yahweh speaks to an unidentified audience	v 24a
Yahweh speaks to Jehoiachin directly	vv 24b–26
Yahweh speaks to an unidentified audience	v 27

There are no catchwords to the poem preceding, confirming the view that v 23 was at one time the end of a collection (see Rhetoric and Composition for 22:20–23). Catchwords connecting to the next oracle are the following:

v 24	*Coniah*	v 28	*Coniah*
v 26	*I will throw you*		*are they thrown*
	land (2×)	vv 28–29	*land* (4×)

NOTES

22:24. *As I live . . . even if Coniah son of Jehoiakim, king of Judah, be a seal on my right hand, surely from there I will tear you off.* Coniah may or may not be the seal on Yahweh's hand; regardless, Yahweh will tear him off. Uncertainty stems from the fact that *kî 'im* is not usual in oath formulas, and one is also not entirely sure how to translate the oath when a subsequent *kî* occurs. Jeremiah uses a *kî 'im . . . kî* construction in his court defense (26:15), but that translates easily into a protasis-apodosis argument: "Only know for sure *that if* (*kî 'im*) you put me to death, *then* (*kî*) you will bring innocent blood upon yourselves." In the present verse the AV (following LXX, T, and Vg) takes the investiture of Jehoiachin as possible but not actual: "*though* . . . Coniah were the signet ring on my right hand, *yet* I would tear you off." More recent Versions and most commentators translate similarly. Exceptions are the NEB, which assumes that Jehoiachin is being rejected at the outset ("Coniah . . . shall be the signet-ring on my right hand no longer"), and Thompson, Holladay, and McKane, who follow NEB's interpretation. McKane explains *kî 'im* as a rare variant of *'im*, which in oath formulas means "certainly not" (GKC §149). But the REB changes the NEB's reading, assuming now that Jehoiachin currently is the signet ring on Yahweh's finger but will be torn off. Events behind this divine imprecation have their own ambiguity. Jehoiachin was made king after the death of Jehoiakim, and he together with the queen mother ruled Judah for only three months, after which they surrendered the city to Nebuchadrezzar. Jeremiah told them to do so (13:18–20). Jehoiachin and others were then exiled to Babylon, and Zedekiah was made king. Was then Jehoiachin king, or was he not? He is reckoned among Judah's last kings in 2 Kgs 24:8–15, portrayed as a king in exile in 2 Kgs 25:27–30, and placed securely in the Davidic line in later Jewish tradition (cf. 1 Chr 3:17–19, where he is followed by Zerubbabel, who, according to Hag 2:23, was a seal on the finger of Yahweh; also Matt 1:11–12 in the NT); however, like Jehoahaz, who also sat on the throne for a brief three months, Jehoiachin goes unmentioned in the superscription of Jer 1:1–3. Jehoiachin receives a harsh word in the present oracle, corresponding to the bad wrap-ups given in 2 Kgs 24:9 and 2 Chr 36:9.

As I live. Hebrew *ḥay-ʾānî*. This divine self-asseveration occurs also in 46:18; Zeph 2:9; and often in Ezekiel, e.g., Ezek 5:11; 14:16, 18, 20; et passim. In Deut 32:40 it appears in the form *ḥay ʾānōkî lĕʿōlām*, "As I live forever." Only Yahweh can swear by himself (see Note for 49:13).

Coniah. Hebrew *konyāhû*. A shortened form of Jehoiachin (2 Kgs 24:6, 12) occurring also in 37:1 and 1 Chr 3:1; not a pre-accession name or a name of disparagement (*pace* Kimḥi; Calvin). The king's name also appears in the OT as "Jeconiah" (*yĕkonyāhû* in 24:1; *yĕkonyâ* in 27:20 [Q]; 28:4; 29:2; Esth 2:6; and 1 Chr 3:16, 17). Honeyman (1948: 16) notes seven different spellings of the name in the Hebrew Bible. The name has turned up also on the Lachish and Arad ostraca (see Appendix I). For a "Coniah" mentioned in Lachish Letter #3, see Note for 37:5.

a seal on my right hand. Hebrew *ḥôtām ʿal-yad yĕmînî*. Seals were used throughout the ANE by kings, scribes, and other prominent citizens to authenticate letters, documents, and the like (32:10; 1 Kgs 21:8; Esth 8:9–10), being comparable to the seals of today's notaries public. One impressed them in wax or prepared clay (Job 38:14). Ancient seals were equivalent to one's signature, and also protected the sealed items from being tampered with. They could be hollowed-out cylinders hung on cords around the neck (Gen 38:18, 25; Song 8:6), as was the custom in Assyria and Babylonia, or stones fixed in rings worn on the finger, which was the practice in Egypt (cf. Gen 41:42) and later in Persia (Esth 3:10). The seal here is on a ring; therefore, it is a "signet" or "signet ring." If a king was wearing it, the ring was likely made of gold, on which was fixed an oval-shaped onyx, jasper, or other precious stone (Exod 39:6). Inscriptions on the stones were made by engravers (Exod 28:11). Seals could also be made from clay or scarabs (= dead dung beetles), the latter being the oldest type of seal common in Egypt. The king could himself wear the seal or give it to another to act on his behalf. In times of royal transition, the king's seal might also be given to an interim person until a new king was on the throne (1 Macc 6:15; Josephus, *Ant* xx 32). Pharaoh gave Joseph his signet ring (Gen 41:42). Similarly, the Persian king entrusted his signet ring to Haman, then later to Mordecai (Esth 3:10; 8:2). Both practices—the entrusting of a king's seal to another, and doing the same in a time of transition—have relevance to the present situation, even though the seal here has metaphorical meaning. In the post-exilic period, Zerubbabel, who was the grandson of Jehoiachin (1 Chr 3:16–19), was said to be chosen by Yahweh to become his signet ring (Hag 2:23; Sir 49:11). For a large collection of West Semitic seals with pictures, see Avigad 1997. Seals and scarabs are also discussed in Tufnell, "Seals and Scarabs" in *IDB* R–Z, 254–59.

I will tear you off. Hebrew *'etqenkā*. The verb *ntq*, "to tear away," points to violent action. On the *energic nun*, see GKC §58i. The shift here to direct address, present also in LXX and T, is doubtless intentional (see Rhetoric and Composition). The Vg has *evellam eum*, "I will tear him off."

25. *And I will give you into the hand of those who seek your life.* A stereotyped expression in the Jeremiah prose (19:7; 21:7; 22:25; 34:20, 21; 38:16; 44:30; 46:26). Holladay sees irony in Yahweh's tearing Jehoiachin off his own hand and then giving him into the hand of enemies. The fourfold repetition of "into the hand" in the verse reinforces this irony (see Rhetoric and Composition).

and into the hand of those before whom you are in dread. The same basic expression as in 39:17. The LXX lacks "into the hand," which has the effect of combining this phrase with the one preceding. The two should not be joined. What we have are four separate phrases, each beginning "into the hand," embellishing a single idea (see Rhetoric and Composition). The tendency with many commentators (Giesebrecht; Cornill; Volz; Rudolph; Weiser; Bright; Holladay; McKane) has been to take "into the hand" with the next phrase (also lacking in the LXX) as MT expansion.

and into the hand of Nebuchadrezzar, king of Babylon. Another stereotyped phrase in the Jeremiah prose (21:7; 22:25; 32:28; 44:30; 46:26), occurring sometimes without "Nebuchadrezzar" (20:4; 21:10; 22:25; 27:6; 29:21; 32:3, 4, 36; 34:2, 21 [expanded]; 37:17; and 38:3 [expanded]). The LXX omits the phrase, but this can be due to haplography (whole-word: *wbyd . . . wbyd*). Aquila and Theod have it.

and into the hand of the Chaldeans. This stereotyped expression occurs in 22:25; 32:24, 28, 43; 38:18; and 43:3. On Chaldea and the Chaldeans, see Note for 50:1.

26. *And I will throw you and your mother who bore you to another land where you were not born, and there you shall die.* The queen mother is Nehushta (see Note on 13:18). This prophecy was fulfilled (24:1; 29:2; 52:31–34; 2 Kgs 24:15; 25:27–30). On Nebuchadrezzar's capture of Jerusalem in 597 B.C. (including documentation in the Babylonian Chronicle), which led to the exile of Jehoiachin, his wives, the queen mother, and other leading citizens to Babylon, see Note for 29:2.

And I will throw you. Hebrew *hēṭaltî* makes for another violent image (16:13; cf. Isa 22:17). Yahweh will hurl as with a slingshot the young king and his mother into a foreign land.

another land. The LXX lacks *'aḥeret* ("another"), which could be more haplography (homoeoarcton: *'aleph . . . 'aleph*), since the word is present in

4QJer^c, Aq, and Theod (*eteran*). The LXX also fails to translate the article on *hā'āreṣ* ("the land"), which makes more sense because one would expect *'ereṣ 'aḥeret*. Some scholars (Ehrlich 1912: 300; Rudolph; Bright; Holladay) simply delete the article, but one wonders if a repetition might not be intended, with *hā'āreṣ* occurring again in v 27 (see Rhetoric and Composition).

and there you shall die. Dying in an unclean land is a curse (Kimḥi; see Note on 20:6).

27. *So to the land where they will carry their great desire to return, there they shall not return.* These same words, with only minor changes, were later spoken to Judahite exiles in Egypt (44:14). The expression, *hēm mĕnaśśĕ'îm 'etnapšām*, is lit., "they are lifting up their soul/desire." Rashi says it means "they are longing for," being an expression of consolation to one's inner soul that one will return again to one's land. For another use of *nepeš* meaning "desire," see 34:16. The LXX omits *lāšûb šām šammâ*, "to return there, there," which Janzen (1973: 119) notes can be attributed to haplography (homoeoarcton: *l . . . l*). 4QJer^c (by reconstruction) supports the reading of MT. The message then of these two final verses, unimpaired and maybe even enriched by a shift in audience, is this: "You will get what you don't want, and what you do want you won't get." King Jehoiachin and the queen mother, to their great horror, will be violently thrown into a strange *land*, and the *land* to which they long to return, they shall not return.

MESSAGE AND AUDIENCE

Yahweh begins this oracle by swearing an oath that Coniah, king of Judah, though he be Yahweh's signet ring, will nevertheless be torn off. The oath is spoken to an unspecified audience, the words of rejection to the king directly. Yahweh makes his words to the king even more severe by saying that the king will be given into the *hand* of his enemies. Four times this is repeated. Violent action will continue. The king and the queen mother will be thrown into a land where they were not born, and there they will die. An unmitigated curse. Turning in conclusion to the audience listening in, Yahweh says that the land to which they yearn to return, they shall not return.

The oracle can be confidently dated to 597 B.C., before Jehoiachin, the queen mother, and other Jerusalem citizens of note were exiled to Babylon. When heard following the divine utterance in vv 20–23, the mountain wailing will be followed by Yahweh's rejection of his king, which will be the cause for more wailing.

The "Chorus of the Hebrew Slaves" in Verdi's opera, *Nabucco* (1842), attempts to capture later longings of Jewish exiles in Babylon for home and the joys they once knew there:

Del Giordano le rive saluta	To the waters of Jordan bear greeting
Di Sionne le torri atterrate	To the down-fallen temples of Zion
Oh, mia patria si bella e perduta!	Oh, my country so fair and so wretched
Oh, membranza si cara e fatal!	Oh, remembrance of joy and of woe!

Arpa d'or dei fatidici vati	Golden harps of the Prophets Oh tell me
Perche muta dal salice pendi?	Why so silent ye hang from the willow?
Le memorie nel petto raccendi	Once again sing the songs of our homeland
Ci favella del tempo che fu!	Sing again of the days that are past
O simile di Solima ai fati	We have drunk from the cup of affliction
Traggi un suono di crudo lamento	And have shed bitter tears of repentance
O t'ispiri il Signore un concento	Oh, inspire us Lord Yahweh[a] with courage
Che ne infoda al patire virtu!	So that we may endure to the last
Va, pensiero, sull'alli dorate	Speed your journey, my thoughts and my longings
Va, ti posa sui clivi, sui colli	Speed your journey to mountain and valley
Ove olenzzano tepide e molli	Where the sweet-scented air breathes a fragrance
L 'aure dolci del suolo natal!	O'er the homes that we knew long ago!

(Libretto by Temistocle Solera; tr. Norman Tucker and Tom
Hammond; London: G. Ricordi, 1962)

10. Is Coniah a Throwaway Pot? (22:28–30)

22 [28]Is an unwanted, smashed pot
   this man Coniah?
     or a jar in which no one takes delight?
So why are he and his offspring thrown
   and cast away to a land that they do not know?

[29]Land, Land, Land
   Hear the word of Yahweh!

[30]Thus said Yahweh:
Write this man down childless
   a man who will not prosper in his days
Indeed there shall not prosper from his offspring
   a man to sit upon the throne of David
     and rule again in Judah.

RHETORIC AND COMPOSITION

These verses contain an oracle lamenting Jehoiachin's recent departure into exile. The limits are indicated by a return to poetry in v 28, then a shift back to prose in 23:1, which is the chapter division. This oracle has its "Thus said Yahweh" formula in the center, at v 30, but it may have been added later (see Notes). The upper limit is confirmed by a *setumah* in M^L and a *petuḥah* in M^A and M^P before v 28. 4QJer^c has no section there. The lower limit is confirmed by a *petuḥah* in M^A and a *setumah* in M^P after v 30, where M^L has no section.

---

[a] The translated version has "Jehovah."

Both M^L and M^P have another *setumah* after v 29, which is probably guided by the messenger formula in v 30 but does not further divide the oracle. J. W. Olley (1998: 115) in a study on Isaiah section markings concludes that their location is often guided by messenger formulas in the text (i.e., "Thus said Yahweh" and "oracle of Yahweh") or where Yahweh begins speaking in the first person, which corroborates my own judgments regarding the location of section markings in the book of Jeremiah. Olley suggests that these locations may relate to ancient liturgical usage, which is certainly a possibility.

The oracle here is generally agreed to be poetry (*pace BHS*, NEB, and REB), which divides into three stanzas forming a line count of: 2:1:2. For other Jeremiah oracles with short centers, see 5:15–17; 8:13–17; and 8:18–21. The key word structure of this oracle is the following:

I   . . . .   v 28
        this man . . . .

        . . . .
        . . . . . *he and his offspring* . . . .
        . . . . . *a land* . . . .

II   *Land, Land, Land*   v 29
        . . . .

III   . . . . *this man* . . . .   v 30
        . . . .
        . . . . . *from his offspring* . . . .
        a man . . . .

Here both speakers and audiences change, making another Jeremiah dialogue poem enriched by drama. Apostrophe is also in evidence, as the audiences in vv 29–30 are imaginary:

I   Jeremiah addresses an unidentified audience   v 28
II   Jeremiah addresses the "land"   v 29
III   Yahweh addresses imaginary scribes   v 30

Hyatt and Holladay think that v 28 is spoken by the people, but Berridge (1970: 179) takes the verse to be a lament of the prophet. In Berridge's view vv 29–30 are Yahweh's response, presumably because v 29 contains "Hear the word of Yahweh" and v 30 has an introductory "Thus said Yahweh." In my view v 30 with its messenger formula is Yahweh's word, but v 29 is the voice of Jeremiah.

Catchwords connecting to the oracle preceding:

v 28	*Coniah*	v 24	*Coniah*
	are they thrown	v 26	*I will throw you*
vv 28–29	*land* (4×)		*land* (2×)

Catchwords connecting to the unit following:

22:28–29 *land* (4×)   23:3 *lands*

NOTES

22:28. *Is an unwanted, smashed pot this man Coniah? or a jar in which no one takes delight? So why are he and his offspring thrown and cast away to a land that they do not know?* A threefold rhetorical question in the *hă . . . 'im . . . maddûaʿ* ("If . . . if . . . so why . . . ?") form, which is a signature of the prophet (see Note on 2:14). Jeremiah addresses the first two questions to people who will want to give "no" answers; this then sets up a final question posing the incongruity, i.e., "Why are the king and his offspring cast away into a foreign land?" Calvin thinks God is the speaker and says he is assuming here the character of a wonderer, so that people will cease to wonder. The LXX begins the verse by naming "Jehoiachin" (not "Coniah"); it has a much shorter reading, the Hebrew *Vorlage* of which is beyond reconstruction. A partial 4QJer^c reading supports MT. The LXX also does not translate the clauses as questions, perhaps because it lacks the first term with the *hē'* interrogative (Heb *haʿeṣeb* = "Is a pot?"). The T does not translate the clauses as questions either.

an unwanted, smashed pot. Hebrew *ʿeṣeb*, although an OT *hapax legomenon*, is generally taken to mean "pottery vessel" (KB^3; Rudolph; Weiser; Bright; and others), which follows Vg *vas fictile*. Honeyman (1939: 86) decides in favor of a pot because of the parallelism with *kĕlî* (here "jar") and because Jeremiah uses the broken pot image elsewhere (19:1–13; 48:12). See the "smashed wine jar" image in 13:12–14. But just what sort of pot this might be cannot be determined. Kelso (1948: 28 #66) says it is ceramic ware, probably a pottery vessel. Rashi translates the Heb as *ʿāṣāb*, "idol (image)," which carries over an interpretation given in Midrash Leviticus Rabbah 19:6. Calvin also has "statue." "Idol" is accepted by McKane, even though it fits poorly in the context. The NEB's "mere puppet," which survives in Thompson ("figurehead") and Holladay ("puppet"), is to be rejected. The LXX lacks "smashed" (*nāpûṣ*), which some commentators (Volz; Rudolph; Bright) delete. But together with the LXX omission of "this man" following, we have what is probably another loss due to haplography (homoeoteleuton: *h . . . h*). Holladay argues for the retention of "smashed" because it makes a wordplay with *ḥēpeṣ* ("delight") later in the line. The term "smashed" is also present in 4QJer^c and should be retained.

this man. Hebrew *hāʾîš hazzeh.* This LXX omission is also deleted by many commentators (Duhm; Cornill; Volz; Rudolph; Bright), but as we have just said, it is probably part of a three-word haplography. Holladay argues for its originality, finding a wordplay in *nibzeh* ("unwanted") and *hazzeh* ("this"). It too should be retained because it makes an important key word repetition in the poem (see Rhetoric and Composition). The partial 4QJer^c reading supports MT, as does Aq.

a jar in which no one takes delight? Hebrew *kĕlî ʾên ḥēpeṣ bô*. The phrase (in simile) occurs in a Moab oracle in 48:38b and also in Hos 8:8, from which it may derive (K. Gross 1930: 4).

So why are he and his offspring thrown and cast away to a land that they do not know? The LXX lacks "he and his offspring" and contains singular verbs: "he is thrown," "he is cast away," and "he does (not) know." Although once again many commentators delete (Giesebrecht; Duhm; Cornill; Volz; Rudolph; Weiser; Bright), this omission, as Holladay points out, can be due to haplography (homoeoteleuton: *w . . . w*). To show how biased modern scholarship is in favor of the shorter LXX text, we quote Wessels (1989: 239), who says: "The fact that something is lacking in the Septuagint, but appears in the Massoretic text, is an indication that it is a later addition." Bias has now become fact! If the expression is retained, as I think it should be, we can assume that Jehoiachin had children at the time he was exiled (Malamat 1951: 84). 2 Kings 24:15 mentions the king's wives but says nothing about children. There is also a chronological problem further complicating matters. 2 Chr 36:9 states that Jehoiachin was eight years old when he began his three-month reign, whereas 2 Kings 24:8 says he was eighteen years old when taken into exile. According to 2 Chr 3:17–18, Jehoiachin had seven sons, and the Babylonian cuneiform text listing his prison rations, which dates from the 10th to 35th year of Nebuchadnezzar II, lists rations also for five of his sons (*ANET*[3] 308). In the NT, see Matt 1:12. It is not necessary to argue that all of Jehoiachin's sons were born in captivity, as some do. He could have had one or more sons while still in Jerusalem. Jehoiachin was put on the throne in Dec 598 B.C., and reigned until March 597. Jerusalem surrendered on March 16, 597 B.C. (Bright 1981: 327; Tadmor 1956: 230). On Jehoiachin's capture, exile to Babylon, and later release from prison, see 2 Kgs 24:10–15; 25:27–30 = Jer 52:31–34. Lamentations for an exiled king are contained in two of the Mesopotamian city laments (Dobbs-Allsopp 1993: 72). See also Lam 2:9 and 4:20.

29. *Land, Land, Land.* The repetition is for emphasis (*geminatio*), similar to the threefold "temple of Yahweh" repetition in 7:4 (see Note there). Calvin says that in repetition "the hardness of iron is overcome by the repeated strokes of the hammer." The LXX has only two occurrences of "land," which could, as Janzen (1973: 117) notes, be due to haplography (whole-word). The same reduction from three terms to two occurs in the LXX of 7:4. It is also possible that in both cases the reduction is due simply to the LXX's aversion to repetition, which is well-attested in the book of Jeremiah. There is scant justification for the reduction to only one "land," as proposed by Volz. Reference is sometimes made to the "earth, earth, earth" repetition in the Gilgamesh Epic (Maqlû I 37: *irṣitum, irṣitum, irṣitum*; Meier 1937: 8; J. Herrmann 1949–50; Gaster 1969: 605, 707); however, since this is an incantation, the parallel is not particularly compelling. Jeremiah is here calling on the land to hear and be witness to the divine word spoken against Jehoiachin. By personifying the land, he engages in apostrophe. In 2:12 a personified heavens was summoned to witness against the apostasy of Judah, and more apostrophe appears in the verse following.

30. *Thus said Yahweh.* The LXX omits, for which reason some commentators (Giesebrecht; Cornill; Weiser; Rudolph; Bright; Janzen 1973: 85; Holladay) take this messenger formula to be a later addition. Giesebrecht says the formula is superfluous after "Hear the word of Yahweh" immediately preceding (v 29). But the omission can be attributed to haplography (homoeoarcton: *k . . . k* or whole-word: *yhwh . . . yhwh*). The T, Aq, Symm, Theod, and Vg all have the formula.

Write this man down childless. More apostrophe, with Yahweh now imagining scribes at his side, ready to take dictation. The singular imperative of the LXX imagines only one scribe. Some have suggested that Jehoiachin is being entered childless in a census list (Neh 12:22–23; cf. Isa 4:3), but we noted above that Jehoiachin did have sons, some of whom could have been born in Jerusalem. The Hebrew *'ărîrî* is clear: it means "childless" (Gen 15:2; Lev 20:20–21) and is rendered in the Vg as *sterilem* ("barren, sterile"). There is no reason to follow G. R. Driver (1937–38: 115), who thinks the real meaning of the Hebrew is "disgraced," i.e., stripped of honor (so NEB and REB). There is also little enthusiasm for the LXX's *ekkērukton anthrōpon* ("a man banished by public proclamation"), so most commentators stay with the MT. The LXX text is likely corrupt, translating as it does the next word, *geber*, with *anthrōpon* (*pace* BHS) and then omitting the rest of the phrase. What we have here is a bold metaphor meaning: "Jehoiachin may just as well be recorded as childless, for he will have no heir to sit on the throne of David." In the end it matters not whether he has one son, two sons, or five sons—in Jerusalem, in Babylon, or on the way to Babylon. Most of the modern Versions (but not the AV) get the basic meaning by translating a simile (i.e., with "as"), which the figure is not. Wessels (1989: 244) thinks that Jeremiah has overreached his judgment, i.e., the statement was hyperbole and consequently wrong. But the statement is not hyperbole; it is a bold metaphor that was fulfilled.

a man who will not prosper in his days. Hebrew *geber* can mean simply "man," although here it doubtless has overtones of a man who is young, strong, and eminently able. The LXX lacks "(he) who will not prosper in his days," probably, as was just mentioned, because of a corrupt text. Things have changed since Jeremiah lamented over wicked people prospering (12:1). Here the verb *ṣlḥ* means prosper in the sense of "succeed" via a royal heir.

Indeed there shall not prosper from his offspring a man to sit upon the throne of David and rule again in Judah. Taking the *kî* with Calvin as an emphatic "Indeed!" The same prophecy was given earlier to Jehoiakim (36:30). Malamat (1975: 138) is of the opinion that Jeremiah rejected the legitimacy of Jehoiachin, whom the false prophets were advocating in the last decade of Judah's existence, preferring Zedekiah instead, despite his drawbacks. And yet, while no son of Jehoiachin will reign in Judah, the Davidic line will survive, as the oracles in 23:5–6 and 33:17–18 declare. One may also note that Matt 1:11–12 has Jehoiachin and his son Shealtiel in the messianic line. The present verse was also put to use in the Dead Sea community. The Qumran *Temple Scroll* (11QT 59:14–15) says concerning the king who disregards God's commandments that "there shall not be found for him a man to sit upon the throne of his fathers all the days" (Yadin 1983: 268–69; Brooke 1997: 202).

MESSAGE AND AUDIENCE

Jeremiah begins here by asking if this man, Coniah, is a piece of throwaway pottery, and if not, why he and his offspring are hurled violently into a land they know not? Is no one listening? The prophet then turns to address the land—three times he calls to it, admonishing it to hear Yahweh's word. Then the divine voice is heard, addressing ready scribes with the words: "Write this man down childless," for he will not prosper in his days. Nor will his offspring prosper: Coniah will not have even one of his sons to sit upon the throne of David.

This dialogue poem can be dated to 597 B.C., just after Jehoiachin, his wives, and whatever family he had began the long walk to Babylon. Together with the oracle preceding, we have "before-and-after" utterances marking this sad event. Yahweh has the first and last word; Jeremiah speaks his lament in the middle. Here the prophet is heard to echo, with deep feeling, Yahweh's words about Jehoiachin and the royal family's being flung into a strange land.

11. The Call Is Out for New Shepherds (23:1–4)

23 ¹Woe to shepherds who destroy and who scatter the flock of my pasture—oracle of Yahweh.

²Therefore thus said Yahweh, God of Israel, against the shepherds who shepherd my people:
  You, you have scattered my flock and dispersed them, and you have not reckoned them. Look I will reckon upon you your evil doings—oracle of Yahweh.

³And I, I will gather the remnant of my flock from all the lands where I dispersed them, and I will bring them back to their pasture, and they shall be fruitful and multiply. ⁴And I will raise up over them shepherds who will shepherd them. And they shall not again be afraid, and they shall not be broken, and they shall not be reckoned with—oracle of Yahweh.

RHETORIC AND COMPOSITION

The King Collection is brought to a conclusion with the oracles of 23:1–8, which, together with the oracles and narrative prose of 21:1–10, make an outer frame for the whole. These oracles indict and judge Judah's shepherds, promising after the judgment meted out upon them Yahweh's selection of new shepherds who will do the job properly. These shepherds are the kings, primarily, although other leaders are included. However, in Yahweh's future the pastoral number will be reduced to a single Branch of Davidic stock, who will execute justice and righteousness in the land. The present indictment, judgment, and messianic promise are presented along lines similar to those in Ezekiel 34. The words of promise in 23:6 state that the future Davidic king will be named "Yahweh is our righteousness," a wordplay and reversal on the name of the reigning king, Zedekiah, which means "My righteousness is Yahweh" (see Rhetoric and Composition for 21:1–10). Yahweh's final word then to his covenant people is not judgment but future salvation. This grand and climactic end is witnessed in other prophetic books, particularly Isaiah, and is the way that the divine action is seen to culminate in the Song of Moses, Deuteronomy 32.

There are three distinct units in 23:1–8: 1) vv 1–4, which are three general oracles of indictment, judgment, and future hope, in prose; 2) vv 5–6, which are a "Look, days are coming" oracle in poetry; and 3) vv 7–8, which are another "Look, days are coming" oracle in prose. The latter two oracles appear with minor change elsewhere in the book. The LXX places the oracle of vv 7–8 inappropriately at the end of the chapter, i.e., after v 40.

The present oracle cluster is delimited at the top end by the return to prose at v 1, which is also the chapter division. Holladay at one time (1966b: 420–24) made poetry out of vv 1–4 but in his commentary gave that up. He now considers the verses *Kunstprosa*. Before v 1, M^A has a *petuḥah* and M^P a *setumah*. The M^L has no section here. Delimitation at the bottom end is aided by a return to poetry in v 5, which is corroborated by a *setumah* in M^A and M^L after v 4. The M^P has no section here. There is also a *setumah* in M^A (only) after v 1, which divides Oracles I and II and is probably guided by the expanded messenger formula beginning v 2.

All three oracles have "oracle of Yahweh" formulas. The LXX's omission of the formulas in vv 1 and 2 is not necessarily an indication of MT expansion, as Holladay alleges. All three are likely original. Aquila and Theo contain the formula in v 2. What may well be expansion is the embellished "Therefore thus said Yahweh, God of Israel, to the shepherds who shepherd my people" formula beginning v 2. It is certainly not needed, since an "oracle of Yahweh" formula ends the verse. One may compare the "Thus said Yahweh" formula beginning 22:30, which is also unnecessary. The introductory formula of v 2 apparently announces the judgment in Oracle II, beginning as it does with "Therefore" (*lākēn*). The "Woe . . . therefore" collocation is here an editorial device used to announce judgment after an indictment for wrongdoing (see Rhetoric and Composition for 22:18–19).

The recognition that 23:1–4 contain three separate oracles renders unnecessary the concern expressed by McKane and others that these verses lack internal coherence. It has been pointed out, for example, that in v 2 the shepherds drive the sheep away, whereas in v 3 it is Yahweh who does it. In separate oracles, such an inconsistency—if it is one—can stand. The view of some scholars (Cornill; Volz; Rudolph; Mendecki 1983) that v 3 is an exilic or postexilic gloss owing its inspiration to Ezekiel 34 should be rejected. The verse is entirely consistent with the thought of Jeremiah and fits in well with v 4. Lust (1981: 126) also points out that "gathering and return," which figures prominently in Jeremiah (and Ezekiel), is not a "Deuteronomistic" idea. Nothing in any of these oracles requires a post-586 B.C. date, a setting other than Jerusalem, or an attribution to someone other than Jeremiah (*pace* Duhm; Mowinckel 1914: 50; 1956: 167; Thiel 1973: 246–49; McKane). All can be said to reflect the aftermath of Jerusalem's capitulation to Nebuchadnezzar in 597, and the exile following. The oracles also give every indication of being genuine Jeremiah utterances (Weiser; Holladay). Giesebrecht (p. xxi) says they emanate from the hand of Baruch.

The three oracles are linked by key words, some of which progress like the locust parade in Joel 1:4. Key words are the following:

I	Woe to *shepherds . . . who scatter the flock . . .*	v 1
II	*You, you have scattered my flock and dispersed them*	v 2
	and you have not reckoned them	
	Look *I will reckon upon you . . .*	
III	*And I, I will gather . . . my flock . . . where I dispersed them . . .*	v 3
	And I will raise up . . . shepherds who will shepherd them . . .	v 4
	and they shall not be reckoned with	

Most of the key words are repetitions, but not to be missed is the contrast between "You, you have scattered," and "I, I will gather," made emphatic by the added pronouns "you," *'attem,* followed by "and I," *wa'ănî* (Holladay 1966b: 422–23).

There is also an audience shift evident when the three oracles are heard in sequence:

I	Yahweh speaks to an unidentified audience
II	Yahweh speaks directly to the shepherds
III	Yahweh speaks to an unidentified audience

Catchwords connecting to the oracle preceding:

23:3 *lands*		22:26–29 *land* (6×)

Catchwords connecting to the oracle following:

v 2	*Look I*	v 5 *Look*
v 4	*And I will raise up*	*when I will raise up*

These latter catchwords are noted by both Fishbane (1985: 472) and Parke-Taylor (2000: 56).

NOTES

23:1. *Woe to shepherds who destroy and who scatter the flock of my pasture.* Another oracle beginning like 22:13–17, where the "woe" (*hôy*) is not a lament but a prophetic invective (see Note for 22:13). "Shepherds" is a general term for leaders in the ANE (see Note for 2:8) but here refers primarily to Judah's kings (Rashi; Kimḥi). The indictment is kept general but focuses indirectly on the royal houses of Jehoiakim and Zedekiah. The claim has been made by Cornill (p. 265) and others that nowhere in the entire book does Jeremiah attack Zedekiah personally, which may need to be qualified in light of Jeremiah's rebuke to the Jerusalem hierarchy in chap. 34. There was nothing to admire in the man, weak soul that he was, and Jeremiah had reason enough to attack others in his royal house, some of whom wanted to put him to death. Cornill, Weiser, Rudolph, Hyatt, and others nevertheless think the present verse reflects conditions in the time of Zedekiah, which is probably on target. Volz and Holladay date it at the end of Zedekiah's reign, but I would prefer a date at the beginning, just after the exile of 597 B.C. The "scattering" refers to this exile (*pace* McKane), which would also make Jehoiakim the real villain. In 10:21 Jeremiah says that due to stupid shepherds the flocks of "their pasture" (*marʿîtām*) were scattered.

who destroy. Hebrew *mĕʾabbĕdîm.* Calvin finds a basic contradiction in the idea of pastors (= shepherds) who destroy, but it is nevertheless a well-documented fact that failed leadership reaps bitter fruit for those living under that leadership. Cheyne says: "If it is true of all sin that no one can calculate its issues, this is specially true of the sins of rulers" (cf. Isa 9:15[Eng 9:16]). Klein (1980: 171) also remarks that one lesson to be learned from this passage is that the leaders of God's people are particularly accountable, because their failures bring about failures in the people. Horace (*Epistles* i 2 14) is credited with a famous quotation: *Quidquid delirant reges, plectuntur Archivi* ("Whatever folly the kings commit, the Achaeans pay the penalty"). Here judgment comes because of the royal injustices warned against in 22:3–4 and said to have been committed in 22:13–17.

my pasture. Hebrew *marʿît* is a grazing place for sheep. The LXX has "their pasture" (cf. 10:21; 25:36), possibly because it omits the messenger formula and takes someone other than Yahweh to be the speaker. In 25:36, the shepherds are heard crying loudly because Yahweh is devastating their pasture. Either reading is acceptable here. The sheep belong to the shepherd (= king) and also to Yahweh, and the pasture too (= land) belongs to both. On people being "sheep of (Yahweh's) pasture," which is a recurring metaphor in the Psalms, see Pss 74:1; 79:13; 95:7; 100:3; Ezek 34:31.

2. *against the shepherds who shepherd my people.* Hebrew *ʿal-hārōʿîm hārōʿîm ʾet-ʿammî.* The LXX reads: *epi tous poimainontas ton laon mou,* "against those who feed my people," which omits the first *hārōʿîm,* "the shepherds," and translates the second as a participial "those who feed" (from *rʿh*). The omission, as Janzen (1973: 117) notes, can be attributed to haplography (whole-word). The Vg reads similarly: *qui pascunt populum meum,* "who feed my people." Calvin reads "feed," the translation carried over also into the AV. See again v 4. Influence may be from 3:15 and Ezekiel 34. Here, however, *hārōʿîm hārōʿîm* is a play on words: "the shepherds who shepherd" (NAB; NRSV; NJB).

You, you have scattered my flock and dispersed them. The verbs are plural. Kings, along with others in the royal house, are here held responsible for the exile that has just occurred.

and you have not reckoned them. Look, I will reckon upon you. . . . A wordplay in the Hebrew: *wĕlō' pĕqadtem 'ōtām . . . hinĕnî pōqēd 'ălêkem.* On the verb *pqd,* which occurs often in Jeremiah and means "to pay a visit, reckon (upon, with)," see Note for 5:9. Here the shepherds are indicted for not calling the sheep to account, for which reason Yahweh says that he will reckon with them. This visitation will result in punishment and exile (cf. 22:22). The punishment will befit the crime. Samuel delivered this word to the disobedient Saul: "Because *you have rejected (mā'astā)* the word of Yahweh, *he therefore has rejected you (wayyim'āsĕkā)* from being king" (1 Sam 15:23b).

your evil doings. Hebrew *rōa' ma'allêkem.* A stereotyped expression in Jeremiah poetry and prose, on which see Note for 21:12.

3. *And I, I will gather the remnant of my flock from all the lands where I dispersed them, and I will bring them back to their pasture, and they shall be fruitful and multiply.* This oracle focuses on divine initiative and divine action and shifts to a word of promise. Yahweh admits now to having dispersed the covenant people (cf. Deut 28:64) but says he will bring them back to "their pasture" *(nĕwēhen),* which is the land of Israel (Calvin; cf. 50:19), where they will be fruitful and multiply. The same message was conveyed to Judahite exiles in Babylon (29:10–14). In 31:10, Yahweh is celebrated among the nations as the God who scatters *(mĕzārēh)* but then gathers *(yĕqabbĕṣennû).*

The idea of a remnant, expressed often but not exclusively in the OT by the terms *šĕ'ār, šĕ'ērît,* does not originate with Jeremiah. It is at least as old as the Song of Moses (Deut 32:26–27, 36) and appears often in the eighth-century prophets, particularly Isaiah, in whose time Judah was nearly exterminated by Sennacherib's army (Isa 1:9; 4:3; 7:3; 10:20–23; 11:1–9; 37:4, 31–32; Mic 2:12; 4:6–7; 5:6–7[Eng 5:7–8]; 7:18). In Jeremiah, the remnant idea first appears with reference to Northern Israelites who survived the Assyrian destruction of 722 B.C., to whom Yahweh gave the hope of a return to Zion (31:7–9; cf. Isa 11:16). Jeremiah also uses "remnant of Israel" to include those who survived the Assyrian invasion of 701 B.C. (6:9; cf. 50:17). Judahites who survived Jerusalem's destruction in 586 B.C. and remained in the land (39:9–10; 40:6; 41:10) but then went to Egypt are called the "remnant of Judah" (40:11, 15; 42:15, 19; 43:5; 44:12). Jeremiah says most of these people will die in Egypt, though a small number will return to Judah (44:11–14, 27–28). Judahites exiled to Babylon were the favored remnant, according to Jeremiah, and to them was given an unqualified word about eventual return to their homeland (24:4–7; 29:10–14; 50:19–20).

from all the lands. The LXX has "from the whole earth," *apo pasēs tēs gēs;* Aq has "from all the nations," *apo pasōn tōn gaiōn* (cf. 29:14).

and they shall be fruitful and multiply. Hebrew *ûpārû wĕrābû.* The phrase is stock, appearing often in Genesis (Gen 1:22, 28; 8:17; 9:1, 7; and elsewhere) and in the so-called P material (Lev 26:9; cf. S. R. Driver 1913: 131). Having a central importance in the Creation account of Genesis 1, the phrase suggests here that nothing less than a new creation is in store for Israel (Boadt). The phrase appears also in 3:16 (inverted) and in Ezek 36:11. In Jeremiah's first letter to the exiles he told them in Yahweh's name to take wives and "multiply" (*rĕbû*) in Babylon (29:6).

4. *And I will raise up over them shepherds who will shepherd them.* A wordplay similar to the one in v 2a. The LXX, Vg, and AV again have "who will feed them."

And they shall not again be afraid, and they shall not be broken. Hebrew *wĕlō'-yîrĕ'û 'ôd wĕlō'-yēḥattû*. On the verb *ḥtt*, meaning "broken" in either a physical or psychological sense, or both, see Note for 1:17. The expression "do not be afraid, and do not be broken/dismayed" occurs elsewhere in 31:10 = 46:27; Deut 1:21 and 31:8. In Ezek 34:5, 8, negligence by shepherds has left the flock exposed to wild beasts, which in v 28 are identified as (foreign) nations. Ezekiel goes on to say that Yahweh in his promised future will make a covenant of peace with his people, at which time all wild beasts will be banished from the land. Upon the people will then fall showers of blessing (vv 25–26). Abarbanel[a] says this refers to the messianic era, when the Jews will no longer fear the nations.

and they shall not be reckoned with. I.e., for the purpose of being punished. Hebrew *wĕlō' yippāqēdû*. The more usual interpretation (AV; RSV; JB; NAB; NJV; NIV; NRSV; NJB) is "and there shall not be any unaccounted for," i.e., none shall be missing (cf. 1 Kgs 20:39), but the repeated use of *pqd* in these oracles suggests that the N-stem here means that judgment will be over and the covenant people will not require another painful visitation from Yahweh, resulting in a reckoning and punishment (Blayney; NEB; REB; cf. Prov 19:23; Isa 24:22). The LXX omits the phrase, a circumstance that can be attributed to haplography (homoeoteleuton: *w . . . w*). Aquila and Symm have the reading.

MESSAGE AND AUDIENCE

In the first of these oracles, Yahweh hurls a "Woe!" upon shepherds who destroy and scatter the flock of his pasture. In the second, prefaced now by an embellished messenger formula indicating judgment on these shepherds, Yahweh turns to address the culprits directly. Pointing the finger with his emphatic "you," he says that these would-be shepherds have not only scattered the flock, but failed to call them to account as good shepherds are supposed to do, for which reason Yahweh says he will call them to account. Their deeds have been evil. In Oracle III, Yahweh speaks his emphatic "I" to an unidentified audience, and tells them he will gather remaining sheep from the lands to where he—not the shepherds—have dispersed them, and will bring them back to

[a]Isaac Abarbanel (properly Abrabanel), 1437–1508, was a Jewish statesman, philosopher, and exegete, born in Lisbon, but who later lived in Spain and Italy, where he wrote commentaries on the Major and Minor Prophets. His Jeremiah commentary was written in Venice and published in 1504 (*EncJud* 2: 103–9).

their pasture, where their numbers will increase. It will be a new creation, for "they shall be fruitful and multiply." Yahweh promises also to raise up new shepherds who will do the job right. The sheep that remain will no longer be afraid, no longer be broken in body and spirit, and no longer be visited by Yahweh for a reckoning, which, to the careful listener will mean no more visitations for the purpose of punishment.

Since the oracles retain their metaphorical character throughout, it remains for the audience to determine that the shepherds are Judah's inattentive kings with inattentive officials under them, and the sheep are poor Judahites who have been carried off into exile. The audience will also have to see the return to pasture as a return to the Promised Land, and they should also discern in this image a new act of divine grace in store for the remnant, one that will exceed anything the covenant people have known in the past. When the oracles are heard in sequence, the audience can be expected to perceive a movement from indictment to judgment to future grace. In other oracle clusters (7:3–14; 21:11–14), movement has been from admonition to indictment to judgment. But now the time for admonition is past. What people need is a hope after the judgment, and this is what the audience is given. They are told once again that salvation is Yahweh's end game. All three oracles can be dated early in Zedekiah's reign, shortly after the exile of 597 B.C.

When these oracles are heard in their larger context, the "woe" of the first oracle will echo the "woe" to Jehoiakim in 22:13; the judgmental "therefore" introducing the second oracle will echo the judgmental "therefore" spoken against Jehoiakim in 22:18; and the indictment of the shepherds for scattering Yahweh's flock will give a reason for judgment against the same in 22:22, where it was stated ironically that the shepherds faced a scattering by the wind. On a more positive note, it will be evident that on the other side of judgment is a salvation that Yahweh, just now, is preparing for his covenant people.

12. For David: A Righteous Shoot (23:5–6)

23 ⁵Look, days are coming—oracle of Yahweh—
    when I will raise up for David a righteous Shoot
And he shall reign as king and shall succeed
    and do justice and righteousness in the land

⁶In his days Judah will be saved
    and Israel will dwell in security
And this is his name by which one will call him:
    'Yahweh is our righteousness.'

RHETORIC AND COMPOSITION

In the present verses is an oracle that reappears with only minor changes in 33:14–16. It is poetry (*pace* RSV; NJV; NRSV), which delimits it from the prose oracles preceding and the prose oracle following. The oracle is marked additionally at the top by a *setumah* in M^A and M^L before v 5. The M^P has no section there. At the bottom is a *petuḥah* in M^A and a *setumah* in M^L and M^P after v 6.

Some scholars (Duhm; Volz; Mowinckel 1956: 20 [a reverse from 1914: 20]; McKane) deny this oracle to Jeremiah, but most (Giesebrecht; Peake; Cornill; Gressmann 1929: 252; Rudolph; Weiser; Hyatt; Holladay) take it to be a genuine utterance of the prophet. The hesitation has largely to do with views about the oracle being messianic and whether or not Jeremiah is likely to have held messianic views or been concerned at all to affirm the survival of a Davidic line. That Jeremiah would have subscribed to the Davidic covenant as presented in 2 Samuel 7 is reasonable. He seems simply to have been unwilling to extend this eternal and unconditional covenant to include Zion and the Temple (see Note for 7:4). Other passages in the book contain ideas similar to those presented here (30:8–9; 33:14–16). Jeremiah spent his entire public ministry in Jerusalem, and there is evidence aplenty that his preaching appropriated tenets of Southern theology, rooted in the traditions associated with Abraham and David (see §Introduction: Sources for the Prophet's Theology).

The oracle is structured by the following key words, some of which have been noted by Volz:

I	. . . . days	*yāmîm*	v 5
	. . . . righteous	*ṣaddîq*	
	. . . .		
	. . . . and righteousness	*ûṣĕdāqâ*	
II	*In his days*	*bĕyāmāyw*	v 6
	. . . .		
	. . . . our righteousness	*ṣidqēnû*	

Catchwords connecting to the oracles preceding (Fishbane 1985: 472; Parke-Taylor 2000: 56):

v 5 *when I will raise up*   v 4 *And I will raise up*

Catchwords connecting to oracle following:

v 5 *Look, days are coming*   v 7 *Look . . . days are coming*

NOTES

23:5. *Look, days are coming.* The phrase is not eschatological (Weiser), i.e., it does not look ahead to the end of world history, at which time God will reward the righteous and punish the wicked. It simply points ahead, as do the other occurrences of the phrase in the book (see Note for 7:32), to an indefinite future after the collapse of the nation, when kingship will be reinstated.

when I will raise up for David a righteous Shoot. The phrase is given messianic interpretation in T ("when I will raise up for David an Anointed One [= Messiah] of righteousness"), as well as in Kimhi. Abarbanel says that, since the Hasmonean kings were not of the Davidic dynasty, the passage must refer to the Messianic Era. "Messianism" is the Jewish hope for a future golden age that will revive the golden age of the past, i.e., the kingdom ruled by David. Levey (1974: xix) gives this definition:

> Messianism is the predication of a future Golden Age in which the central figure is a king primarily of Davidic lineage appointed by God . . . it was believed that during the time of the Messiah the Hebrew people will be vindicated, its wrongs righted, the wicked purged from its midst, and its rightful place in the world secured. The Messiah will pronounce doom upon the enemies of Israel, will mete out reward and punishment in truth and in justice, and will serve as an ideal king ruling the entire world.

While Messianism has roots in preexilic prophecy, it flowers much later, for which reason messianic ideas must not be read back into the mind of Jeremiah as, for example, Calvin does when he says that the present prophecy speaks of (the) Christ. The term "Messiah" (*māšîaḥ*) is not used with reference to a future redeemer anywhere in the OT or Apocrypha (Klausner 1956: 8), and the term "Shoot" (*ṣemaḥ*), which appears here, assumes a technical meaning only in Zech 3:8 (= Zerubbabel originally; so Duhm) and 6:12 (= Joshua, the high priest). In the Tannaitic literature of ca. 50 B.C. to A.D. 200 (BT Sanhedrin 97a–98b) and in the NT Gospels (Matt 9:27; 15:22; 20:30–31 and parallels), "son of David" has come to mean "the Messiah." This having been said, however, the idea of Yahweh raising up an ideal king from Davidic stock can reasonably be attributed to Jeremiah, although it is not original with him. Isaiah gives eloquent expression to the idea of a renewed kingdom under Davidic rule in Isa 11:1–9, a passage with striking similarities to the present one. One also sees the hope of a restored Davidic rule in Amos 9:11; Mic 5:1[Eng 5:2] and Isa 9:6–7. Mowinckel (1956: 15–20) assigned all these passages except Isa 9:6–7 to the postexilic period, doing the same with the present verses, which he believed were dependent on Zech 3:8 and 6:12. But all the named passages are arguably preexilic, and few if any scholars today would claim that the verses here owe their inspiration to Zech 3:8 and 6:12. The idea of David's royal line continuing forever has its basis in the covenant promise to David in 2 Samuel 7, which is preexilic. Psalm 89:28–37 is a later echo.

when I will raise up. Hebrew *wahăqîmōtî.* In 33:15 it is "I will make sprout" (*'aṣmîaḥ*). The verb here functions as a catchword to the previous oracle cluster (see Rhetoric and Composition).

a righteous Shoot. Or "a rightful Shoot." Hebrew *ṣemaḥ ṣaddîq.* The term *ṣemaḥ* means "sprout, shoot," although most modern Versions follow the AV and translate "Branch." Comparable terms in Isa 11:1 are different: *ḥōṭer* ("rod") and *nēṣer* ("sprout, offshoot"); in Ps 132:17 it is a *qeren* ("horn") that will sprout for David (cf. Luke 1:69). More discussion, actually, has centered around the term *ṣaddîq*, whether it should be translated "righteous" or "rightful," the latter meaning supported now by readings from Phoenician and Ugaritic (Swetnam 1965). The most important of these is the Larnax Lapethos 2 (or Narnaka 2) Inscription, which is a third-century B.C. dedication to the god Melqart that turned up on the north coast of Cyprus in 1893 (Cooke 1903: 82–83, 86–87; Honeyman 1940; Widengren 1951: 51–53; Donner and Röllig 1962–64 I: 10, #43; II: 60; van den Branden 1964: 257–58; Beyerlin 1978: 232–34). In line 11 the same expression occurs as here, *wlṣmḥ ṣdq*, which is translated "and to the legitimate offspring" or the like (Widengren renders it "righteous offshoot"). The other inscription is from Sidon, dated to the fifth century B.C. or later, which describes an heir apparent to the king of Sidon (Donner and Röllig 1962–64 I: 3, #16; II: 25). Here the expression *wbn ṣdq* occurs, which is translated "and the legitimate son/heir." These readings (and others) raise the question whether the present expression ought not be translated "rightful shoot," particularly in light of the uncertainty in Judah over who was the rightful king, the exiled Jehoiachin, or the enthroned Zedekiah (Swetnam 1965: 39–40). If *ṣemaḥ ṣaddîq* is translated "rightful shoot," then Jeremiah is implying—if not saying outright—that neither Jehoiachin nor Zedekiah is legitimate; for a legitimate king, the people will have to wait until Yahweh raises up one in the future. This makes good sense, particularly in light of what has just been said about Jehoiachin being left without a son to occupy David's throne (22:30), and an unmistakable silence regarding Zedekiah in the present verses ending the King Collection (23:1–8), precisely where one would expect some word about him (see below, v 6). At the same time, "righteous Shoot" also fits the context well, for the following verse states that this future king will "do justice and righteousness in the land." See also Isa 32:1: "Look, a king shall reign in righteousness (*lĕṣedek*)." If "righteous Shoot" is read in the present verse, then Jeremiah is indirectly condemning Jehoiakim, who was the most unrighteous of kings (cf. 22:13–17), and v 6b is indirectly condemning Zedekiah, who did not live up to his name, "My righteousness is Yahweh." Perhaps Jeremiah is saying that the future king will be unlike either of them!

And he shall reign as king and shall succeed. This colon is absent in the parallel verse of 33:15. On the cognate accusative *mālak melek*, compare 37:1, where an imperfect form of *mlk* appears in prose. Cognate accusatives occur frequently in Jeremiah (see Note for 22:16).

and shall succeed. I.e., his reign shall prosper as the reigns of the last four Judahite kings have not. The H-stem of *śkl* can also mean "have insight, act prudently," which would be suitable here. The LXX has *kai sunēsei* ("and he shall perceive"), and Calvin says "right judgment" rather than "success" is meant, noting what follows about this king doing justice and righteousness. But other occurrences of the verb in Jeremiah carry the idea of success (10:21; 20:11; and 50:9 with repointing), and the T translates "and prosper." Compare

Isa 52:13: "Look, my servant shall succeed (*yaśkîl*)." On the success achieved by David while he was still in the employ of Saul, see 1 Sam 18:5.

and do justice and righteousness in the land. Another indication that the future king will be wholly unlike Jehoiakim. Kings are expected to do justice and righteousness (see Notes for 21:12 and 22:3). Again, David was remembered as doing both (2 Sam 8:15). See also Ps 72:1–2.

6. *In his days Judah will be saved, and Israel will dwell in security.* A syntactic chiasmus in the Hebrew, with "Judah" and "Israel" at the center. The parallel text of 33:16 has "Jerusalem" instead of "Israel," which occurs here in the reading of G^S. Mention of both Judah and Israel indicates that a united Israel—such as existed under David—will enjoy this future salvation and secure existence. Jeremiah's early preaching envisioned a return of Northern Israel to Zion (31:1–20). See also 3:18; 31:27–28, 31–34; 33:23–26. On the theme of Israel dwelling "in security," see 32:37; Deut 33:28; Isa 30:15; 32:17.

Some Old Babylonian and Assyrian texts from Nineveh and Assur have turned up purporting to predict the rise of unnamed rulers, stating how long the new king will reign, and promising for the country either safety and well-being or a period of major unrest (Grayson and Lambert 1964; *ANET*^{3} 606–7; Beyerlin 1978: 118–22). The texts are dated sometime prior to 650 B.C. (Lambert 1970: 176–77), and there is debate about whether they are genuine predictions or prophecies *ex eventu*; also whether they are omen apodoses or more similar to biblical prophecy and/or biblical apocalyptic, e.g., Dan 8:23–25; 11:3–45. Hallo (1966), who does not weigh heavily the predictive element in biblical prophecy, thinks they are "pretended" predictions, i.e., *vaticinium ex eventu*, but Lambert maintains that some, at least, were intended as detailed predictions of historical events, though not with any overall plan and not leading to a grand climax in history such as we find in biblical thought. One of the texts (Text A) from Assur reads:

> [A ruler will arise], he [will rule] for eighteen years
> The country will live safely, the interior of the country will be happy, the people will [have abun]dance
> The gods will make beneficial decisions for the country, favorable winds [will blow]
> . . . .
> That ruler will be killed in an uprising
>
> A ruler will arise, and he will rule for thirteen years
> There will be an attack of Elam against Akkad, and
> The booty of Akkad will be carried off
> The temples of the great gods will be destroyed, the defeat of Akkad will be decreed (by the gods)
> There will be confusion, disturbance, and unhappy events in the land, and

The reign will diminish (in power); another man, whose
name is not mentioned (as successor) will arise . . .
(ANET³ 606)

Lambert makes no attempt to name the rulers, but D. N. Freedman suggests
that the first ruler of 18 years may have been Sargon II, who reigned from ca.
722–705 B.C. and was killed in battle. For another dynastic prophecy of the
same type, one that refers to the fall of Assyria and the rise of the Chaldean dynasty, see Grayson 1975b: 24–37; *CS I* 481–82.

one will call him. Hebrew *yiqrĕ'ô*. A few Heb MSS, T, and Vg (*vocabunt
eum*) have "they will call him." The MT reading is called a mixed form in
GKC §60c; 74e. But the LXX has a singular verb and supplies *kurios* ("the
Lord") as subject, supposing that the Lord is giving the name. In the MT the
name will presumably be given by the people collectively. It will not, in any
case, be given by a foreign ruler, as happened with both Jehoiakim and Zedekiah (see Note for 22:11a).

'*Yahweh is our righteousness.*' Hebrew *yhwh ṣidqēnû*. A deliberate play and reversal on the name "Zedekiah," *ṣidqîyāhû*, which means "My righteousness is
Yahweh." The future king will be a turnaround from Zedekiah, embodying in
name and being the precious commodity of "righteousness," something the
present king has not! The King Collection as a whole is structured in such a
way as to make the same point (see Rhetoric and Composition for 21:1–7).
This collective confession is then a sharp censure of Judah's last king: not a
positive word about him. Klausner (1956: 104–6) made the suggestion, restated
along similar lines by Carroll, that the present verse is a positive word about
Zedekiah, spoken by Jeremiah about this "kindly and gentle son of a king" before he was put on the throne. The hope at the time was that he would be this
"righteous shoot," and so he was called by the name "Yahweh is our righteousness." When made king by Nebuchadnezzar, the young Mattaniah was given
the throne name "Zedekiah," which was similar. Klausner concedes that this
pious hope went unfulfilled, and suggests therefore that the prophecy had to be
set aside for a later fulfillment. This rather fantastic thesis is to be rejected.
Zedekiah is alluded to in the verse but indirectly and in an entirely negative
way. The LXX transliterates the present phrase as a proper name: *Iōsedek*.

MESSAGE AND AUDIENCE

Yahweh in the present oracle says that in future days he will raise up for
David a righteous Shoot, perhaps meaning a rightful Shoot, and that this king
shall enjoy a prosperous reign and do justice and righteousness in the land—
precisely what ought to happen. It is not said when this happy event will
come about, but the references to a "righteous" Shoot and "do[ing] justice
and righteous in the land" are unmistakable censures of King Jehoiakim,
which the audience might be expected to pick up. Yahweh goes on to say that

in the days of this king Judah and Israel will be delivered (from enemies) and will dwell in security. The mention of both Judah and Israel indicates that the kingdom will be reunited, as it was formerly under David. The name of the future king, "Yahweh is our righteousness," is an indirect censure of King Zedekiah, whose name is nearly the same in reverse. The audience must now realize that Judah's last two reigning kings are castoffs in Yahweh's eyes, no better than Jehoahaz and Jehoiachin, and that his sights are now set upon the future. Will they know that this future is a future on the other side of judgment? This oracle is best dated early in Zedekiah's reign (Bright), i.e., soon after 597 B.C.

When the present oracle is heard following the oracle in 23:3–4, it will be clear that the future king will reign after Yahweh has gathered a remnant of covenant people from countries far and near. This makes it clear that the coming days are indeed a ways off.

13. New Exodus, New Oath (23:7–8)

23 ⁷Look, hereafter, days are coming—oracle of Yahweh—when they will no longer say, 'As Yahweh lives who brought up the children of Israel from the land of Egypt,' ⁸but 'As Yahweh lives who brought up and who brought in the offspring of the house of Israel from a land to the north and from all the lands where I scattered them.' And they shall dwell on their own soil.

RHETORIC AND COMPOSITION

This oracle ends the King Collection, which began at 21:1. That the oracle is self-contained may be concluded by its duplication in 16:14–15 and by its ill-suited placement in the LXX after v 40 of the present chapter. The oracle is prose, separated from a previous oracle in poetry and from a confession and oracle beginning the Prophet Collection in v 9, which is also poetry. At the top end is a *petuḥah* in M^A and a *setumah* in M^L and M^P before v 7. At the bottom end is a *petuḥah* in M^A and a *setumah* in M^L and M^P after v 8.

The LXX omission of these verses after v 6 and their insertion after v 40 call for special comment. It is widely agreed that the placement after v 40 is ill chosen. The Hebrew *Vorlage* to the LXX obviously did not have the oracle after v 6, since the LXX combines the introductory words of v 9 with the last words of v 6, translating: "And this is his name which the Lord will call him, Iosedek among the prophets." The omission is best explained as another loss due to haplography (homoeoarcton: *l . . . l*). What seems to have happened is that in the Hebrew *Vorlage*, or else in the LXX text, the verses were later inserted after v 40, supplied perhaps from another Hebrew manuscript (Cheyne). The thesis of Janzen (1973: 93, 220–21 #17), quoted approvingly by Holladay, is that originally this oracle stood between vv 1–4 and vv 5–6, and that it fell out from here by haplography ("Look, days are coming" begins v 5 and v [7]). Then at a later time it was reinserted where it now appears in the

MT and LXX, respectively, at first vertically in the margins, then later in the text itself! This explanation should be rejected. It is too complicated, too conjectural, and totally unnecessary.

Whereas many commentators take the present oracle as being exilic or post-exilic, it fits the post-597 B.C. situation well and can certainly be assigned to Jeremiah (Weiser; Thompson; Jones).

Catchwords connecting to the oracle preceding (Craigie et al.):

v 7 *Look . . . days are coming*   v 5 *Look, days are coming*

NOTES

23:7–8. See exegesis for 16:14–15.

7. *the children of Israel.* The LXX has "the house of Israel"; however, in v 8 where MT has "house of Israel," it omits the phrase entirely.

8. *who brought up and who.* An omission in the LXX, doubtless due to haplography (whole-word: *'šr . . . 'šr*; or homoeoarcton: *h . . . h*).

who brought in the offspring of the house of Israel from a land to the north and from all the lands where I scattered them. Isaiah 43:5 looks ahead to the redemption of Israel's "offspring" (*zeraʿ*) from the east. Jones thinks that "offspring" in the present verse has a deeper theological meaning of Israel as a fulfillment of Yahweh's promise to Abraham (Gen 13:15–16; 15:5, 18).

where I scattered them. Or "where I dispersed them." The verb is *ndḥ.* The LXX has the reading of 16:15: "he scattered them." The shift to the divine "I" is awkward but can stand (Calvin). Yahweh is speaker of the oracle.

And they shall dwell. Hebrew *wĕyāšĕbû.* The LXX has *kai apekatestēsen autous,* "and I will restore them" (= *wahăšibōtîm* in 16:15). The LXX and 16:15 do not read "and I shall settle them" (*pace* Holladay, 621 g–g).

MESSAGE AND AUDIENCE

The oracle here, as in 16:14–15, gives a Judahite audience facing exile a new confession that will be greater than the one celebrating deliverance from Egypt. The oracle makes good sense any time after 597 B.C., when people are either exile-bound or already exiled to Babylon. It will assume even greater meaning after 586 B.C., when the Judahite population has been scattered in every direction.

In its present context the oracle builds on the words in v 3, where Yahweh speaks of gathering the remnant of his flock from distant places and returning them to pasture. The final reference about Israel dwelling in the land also confirms the words in v 6, which says that Judah will be saved and Israel will dwell in security.

B. SPEAKING OF PROPHETS (23:9–40)

1. Of Adulterers the Land Is Full! (23:9–12)

23 ⁹To the prophets:
   My heart is broken within me
      all my bones waver
   I have become like a drunken man
      and like a mighty man whom wine has overcome
         before Yahweh
         and before his holy words.

   ¹⁰Indeed of adulterers
      the land is full!

   Indeed before the curse the land mourns
      pastures of the wild are dried up
   Yes, their course has become evil
      and their might is not right

   ¹¹Indeed even prophet
      even priest—they are polluted!
   Even in my house
      I have found their evil
         —oracle of Yahweh.

   ¹²Therefore their way shall become to them
      like slippery ground in thick darkness
         they shall be pushed and fall upon it
   Indeed I will bring evil upon them
      in the year of their reckoning
         —oracle of Yahweh.

RHETORIC AND COMPOSITION

Here begins the Prophet Collection, 23:9–40, which forms the second part of the appendix to the First Edition. Containing an introductory *lannĕbi'îm* ("To the prophets"), it continues to the end of the chapter (see Rhetoric and Composition for 21:1–10). The verb "broken" (*nišbar*) in v 9 is a catchword to the verb "broken" (*nišbĕrû*) in 22:20 (Lundbom 1975: 103 [= 1997: 135]), showing that 22:24–23:8 is a later addition to the King Collection preceding.

   Oracles in the present collection come from different periods, although most, if not all, were probably delivered during the reigns of Jehoiakim and Zedekiah, at which time Jeremiah had a particularly difficult time with Jerusalem's priests and prophets. Doubts expressed by older scholars about the genuineness of this material are passé and should no longer be entertained. Duhm's view that vv 16–40 are a product of the second century B.C. is fanciful, and one can dismiss also the views of Cornill and Mowinckel (1914: 20), who say that little can be credited to Jeremiah after v 24. The entire section reflects accurately the prophet as he is otherwise known, also the last decades of Judah's existence when Jeremiah was in conflict with Yahweh prophets who were nevertheless false. The conflict reaches a dramatic climax at the Temple in 594/3, when Jeremiah meets the Yahweh prophet Hananiah son of Azzur and declares him to be ingenuine (chap. 28).

Some scholars (Volz; Rudolph; Weiser; Hyatt; Kraus 1964: 27–28) have suggested that the opening oracle in vv 9–12 was spoken early in Jeremiah's ministry, soon after his call, when he was young, naïve, and having his eyes opened for the first time to just how much evil existed in Jerusalem, lurking even within the Temple precincts. This view is a bit romantic and does not correspond to the facts as we know them. Berridge (1970: 182–83) has therefore called it into question, and rightly so. Jeremiah did battle with the men from Anathoth early in his career (11:18–23), which would have included priests from that village, but during this time he was not, so far as we know, in conflict with priests and prophets in Jerusalem. These came later in the reigns of Jehoiakim and Zedekiah. Furthermore, with Jeremiah's public career beginning in 622 B.C. or soon after, as I have argued, there cannot be in these verses a reaction to objectionable Temple practices that existed prior to the Josianic Reform (cf. v 11). Giesebrecht thinks these first verses come from the end of Jeremiah's ministry, which is more likely, although they need not be confined to Zedekiah's reign. Charges against the Jerusalem prophets—here and in chaps. 27–29—are basically two: 1) they are prophesying in Yahweh's name but are false; and 2) they are guilty of low moral character, engaging in adultery, lying, and strengthening the hand of evildoers (23:14). They are not prophesying by Baal, as were the prophets singled out for reproach in 2:8 (*pace* Hyatt). In 23:9–40 this forbidden practice is ascribed only to the prophets of Samaria (23:13). Baal worship is much remembered and probably still around (7:9; 9:13[Eng 9:14]; 11:13, 17; 12:16; 19:5; 23:27; 32:29, 35), but the prophets in this later period seem more to be Yahweh prophets who have a wrong message and are themselves of dubious character.

The first unit in this collection is vv 9–12, delimited at the top end by the introductory "To the prophets," before which is a *petuḥah* in M^A and a *setumah* in M^L and M^P. There are no sections in the medieval codexes after v 12, but an "oracle of Yahweh" formula does conclude the second oracle there. Some MSS of the LXX omit this formula, but it should be included, as should the formula at the end of v 11, which the LXX omits. *BHS* and most commentators take vv 9–12 as the unit, which it undoubtedly is.

The unit consists of a Jeremiah confession (v 9); an oracle of indictment (vv 10–11); and a second oracle of judgment introduced by "therefore" (v 12). All is poetry. The confession is in the style of a lament (Weiser; Kraus 1964: 26;

Berridge 1970: 181), of which there are many examples in chaps 11–20. Jeremiah then is speaker of the confession and Yahweh speaker of the two oracles (Weiser; Rudolph; Holladay). Yahweh is not the speaking voice in v 11 (*pace* Kraus 1964: 29; Bright; Boadt). The whole is a familiar Jeremiah-type dialogue, where Jeremiah unburdens himself to Yahweh, and Yahweh answers him by divine oracle—here two oracles, one indicting the prophets, the other judging them. Berridge (1970: 181–83) thinks the dialogue actually occurred in reverse order, i.e., Yahweh first gave his indictment and judgment, and then Jeremiah lamented in response to Yahweh's "holy words" (v 9c). But according to this view, the lament goes unanswered. This reconstruction appears to read more than is necessary into the "holy words" of the confession, which could refer to any divine pronouncement. The term "words" (*dibrê*) could even be the "words of the covenant" (*dibrê habběrît*) contained in Deuteronomy 1–28 (Deut 28:69[Eng 29:1]; cf. 1:1). Additionally, the usual order in Jeremianic discourse is first the confession, then the divine answer.

Jeremiah's confession is well ordered with repetitions, balancing terms, and a concluding couplet, similar to those appearing in 4:26 and 25:38:

I	My heart . . .	*libbî*	v 9
	all my bones . . .	*kol-ʿaṣmôtay*	
	. . . like a man . . .	*kěʾîš*	
	and like a mighty man . . .	*ûkěgeber*	
	before Yahweh	*mippěnê yhwh*	
	and before his holy words	*ûmippěnê dibrê qodšô*	

The oracle following is also nicely structured, having these repetitions and balancing key words:

II	Indeed . . .	v 10
	. . . the land	

III	Indeed . . . the land . . .
	. . . .
	. . . evil
	. . . .

IV	Indeed even . . .	v 11
	even . . .	
	Even . . .	
	. . . their evil	

The confession is linked to the first oracle by the following repetitions:

I	I have become . . .	*hāyîtî* . . .	v 9
	. . . and like a mighty man . . .	. . . *ûkěgeber*	
	before . . .	*mippěnê* . . .	
	and before . . .	*ûmippěnê* . . .	

III	. . . *before* . . .	. . . *mippĕnê* . . .	v 10
	Yes, it has become . . .	*wattĕhî* . . .	
	and their might . . .	*ûgĕbûrātām* . . .	

The two oracles are also linked by repetitions:

I	*Indeed* . . .	*kî* . . .	v 10a
	Indeed . . .	*kî* . . .	v 10b
	. . . . *evil*	. . . *rā'â*	v 10c
	Indeed . . .	*kî* . . .	v 11a
	. . . . *their evil*	. . . *rā'ātām*	v 11b
II	*Indeed . . . evil* . . .	*kî . . . . rā'â* . . .	v 12b

Rudolph identifies "evil" as a *Stichwort* in these verses, and McKane (p. 570) correctly takes the three occurrences of *kî* in vv 10–11 as asseveratives, i.e., as "indeed" or the like, but he does not render them as such in his translation. The *kî* in v 12b is also an asseverative.

Catchwords connecting to the following oracles (Condamin):

v 10	*adulterers*	*mĕnā'ăpîm*	v 14	*Committing adultery*	*nā'ōp*
v 11	*they are polluted*	*ḥānēpû*	v 15	*Therefore*	*lāken*
v 12	*Therefore*	*lāken*		*pollution*	*ḥănuppâ*

NOTES

23:9. *To the prophets.* Hebrew *lannĕbî'îm*. A superscription to the Prophet Collection, similar to the superscription of an early King Collection in 22:11 and superscriptions to various Foreign Nation Collections (see Note for 21:11). Compare also the oracles directed against prophets in Mic 3:5–8 and Ezek 13:1–16. The AV in the present verse incorrectly reads the superscription as part of the first colon: "Mine heart within me is broken because of the prophets." A similar joining exists in T, but the Vg (*Ad prophetas*) correctly takes *lannĕbî'îm* to be a superscription. The T also has "prophets of falsehood," as it does throughout the chapter and elsewhere in the book (see Note for 2:8). The reason T uses "prophets of falsehood" is that in Aramaic *nby'* carries the meaning "true prophet of the Lord," necessitating a differentiation betweeen true prophets and false prophets (Hayward 1985a: 210; cf. Churgin 1907: 118).

My heart is broken within me. Hebrew *nišbar libbî bĕqirbî*. The psalmist's heart is broken because of insults (Ps 69:21[Eng 69:20]), but here Jeremiah is overcome by Yahweh's holy words (cf. 6:11; 20:8–9). The language is not entirely emotive (Bright says Jeremiah is not "heartbroken"), but just as certainly it does not denote simply a state of mind. Jeremiah is comparing his condition to drunkenness, when one is reduced to physical, mental, and emotional weakness. Hillers (1965) points out that a weakened condition can result from hearing bad news (4:19–21; 8:18–21; see Note for 6:24).

all my bones waver. Hebrew *rāḥăpû kol-ʿaṣmôtay.* The Qal of *rḥp* does not otherwise occur in the OT, but the Versions all translate "tremble" or "shake," which is the meaning given the Qal in KB[3]. Rashi says the verb means "to sway like the wings of a bird hovering over its nest," a meaning that the Piel has in Gen 1:2 and Deut 32:11. The image here is one of weakness and instability. A drunk individual cannot hold a cup in hand or maintain balance while walking. Such a one staggers and falls.

I have become like a drunken man, and like a mighty man whom wine has overcome. Calvin says the prophet was stunned, all his senses taken from him. It is doubtful that Jeremiah is reporting the reception of a divine word while in a state of ecstasy, although this cannot be ruled out. Lindblom (1965: 216–17) says that in the great prophets one finds "elevated inspiration," not so much a state of ecstasy, and that Jeremiah's excited feelings upon receiving a revelation were caused more by the contents of the revelation than by any psychical experience that the prophet may have undergone. In the NT, men filled with the rush of the Holy Spirit on Pentecost were thought to be drunk on new wine (Acts 2:12–15).

before Yahweh, and before his holy words. Jeremiah, unlike the false prophets, has stood in Yahweh's council and heard his holy words (v 18), which, because of their immense power, have now overwhelmed him (6:11; 20:9; 23:29; cf. Rabinowitz 1972–73: 133–34). The LXX's final "and from before his beautiful glory" (*kai apo prosōpou euprepeias doxēs autou*) is not right (Rudolph).

10. *Indeed of adulterers the land is full!* This bicolon is lacking in the LXX and is probably another loss due to haplography (whole-word plus: *ky-m . . . ky-m*). Aquila and Theod have it. The bicolon is short if the scansion of BHS be accepted, and the stanza is also short compared with the two stanzas following. But if the confession be taken with only the first oracle as forming the original dialogue, then we could have a short center such as the ones that occur in other Jeremianic poems (see Rhetoric and Composition for 22:28–30). There is no need, in any case, to take 10a and 10b as textual variants and delete one or the other, whether because of alleged dittography in 10b or because 10b is thought to have intruded from another context, or for some other reason (*pace* Giesebrecht; Duhm; Cornill; Volz; Rudolph; Bright; Janzen 1973: 12; Holladay). The MT makes perfectly good sense, and its reading should be retained. Jeremiah states in 9:1[Eng 9:2] that the entire population consists of adulterers, where "adulterers" (*mĕnāʾăpîm*) appears to be a more general term for an apostate people. Blayney thinks the term here has general meaning. But it should probably be taken in a specific—and also hyperbolic—sense (Peake; Rudolph). False-speaking prophets in Babylon are commiting the real thing with their neighbors' wives (29:23). Adultery and lying commonly go together, and they are the chief acts of wrongdoing assigned to the (false) prophets in the book of Jeremiah (v 14). Compare also the indictment against Jerusalem's male population in 5:7–8.

Indeed before the curse the land mourns. In place of *ʾālâ* ("curse") a few Heb MSS, the LXX, and the S have *ʾēlleh* ("these"), which attributes a land in "mourning" (= drought) to the "adulterers." But there is assonance in *'ālâ* *'ābĕlâ*, "the curse, it mourns" (Cheyne), suggesting that the MT pointing is correct (Jones). Drought is one of the covenant curses (Deut 28:23–24), and Isaiah has no difficulty in seeing a connection between covenant infidelity and a mourning creation (Isa 24:4–7). On "the land mourning" in Jeremiah, which is an *abusio*, see Notes for 4:28 and 12:4. A causal connection between sexual impropriety and drought is assumed also in 3:1–5.

pastures of the wild are dried up. Hebrew *yābĕšû nĕ'ôt midbār.* Here *midbār* is not desert or wilderness but uncultivated meadows in the open country (see Note on 9:9[10]).

Yes, their course has become evil. Hebrew *mĕrûṣātām* is lit., "their running"; see 8:6 (Q). The subject can be either the "adulterers" in v 10a or the prophet and priest in v 11. It is probably the former, since the prophets and priests are only part of the adulterous company filling the land. Compare Isa 59:7 and Prov 6:18.

and their might is not right. Hebrew *ûgĕbûrātām lō'-kēn.* Jeremiah here reverts once again to military imagery, more specifically the behavior of battle-ready horses. The "course" of the wicked just mentioned is compared to that of a horse plunging headlong into battle in 8:6, and here *gĕbûrâ* can be an allusion to the "might" of horses (cf. Job 39:19 and Ps 147:10).

11. *Indeed even prophet, even priest—they are polluted!* The verb *ḥnp*, which the modern Versions translate "ungodly" or "godless" (cf. KB[3]), basically means "to be polluted" (3:1; Ps 106:38; cf. BDB). The Vg has *polluti sunt.* The basic idea is that Jerusalem's prophets and priests have defiled themselves and as a result have lost their holiness. The T has "scribe . . . and priest," as in 6:13 (= 8:10); 18:18; and elsewhere (see Note for 6:13). The unholy alliance between prophet and priest is elsewhere cited in 5:31; 6:13 (8:10); and 14:18. After Jeremiah preached his blistering Temple Oracles in 609 B.C., it was the prophets and priests who united in calling for his death (26:11).

Even in my house I have found their evil. "My house" is the Temple. Precisely what was happening there is not known, but a sacrilege of some sort is alluded to in 7:30; 11:15; and 32:34. See also Ezekiel 8. Jeremiah is not referring to pagan practices in the Temple before the Josianic Reform (2 Kgs 23:4–7) but to practices of like nature that were revived after Jehoiakim became king. Yet the former may give some indication of what is happening now—pagan worship, cult prostitution, etc.

12. *Therefore their way shall become to them like slippery ground in thick darkness.* Hebrew *'ăpēlâ* is "thick, deep darkness" (2:31; Exod 10:22; Deut 28:29). Duhm goes against the accent and puts "in thick darkness" with the next colon. BHS and many modern Versions follow suit. But the LXX and Vg support the Masoretic scansion, which is carried over into the translations of the AV, RSV, and NRSV. Slippery ground is dangerous; in deep darkness even more so because with a push one can easily fall. Jeremiah is thus describing the judgment in store for Jerusalem's unholy priests and prophets. "Darkness" is a common biblical metaphor for calamity and judgment (4:28; 13:16; 15:9; Mic 3:6; Isa 8:22; cf. Matt 22:13).

they shall be pushed and fall upon it. Hebrew *yiddaḥû* as pointed is an N-stem of *dḥḥ*, although a few MSS read *yiddāḥû* from *dḥḥ*, which has the same meaning: "to be pushed." In Ps 35:5–6 the angel of Yahweh "pushes" (*dôḥeh*) evildoers on a way "dark and slippery" (*ḥōšek waḥălaqlaqqôt*). Yahweh himself may be doing the pushing here; otherwise it would have been the enemy. See also Pss 36:13[Eng 36:12]; 73:18; and Prov 14:32.

Indeed I will bring evil upon them. Hebrew *kî-'ābî' 'ălêhem rā'â.* A Jeremianic expression, on which see Note for 6:19.

in the year of their reckoning. Hebrew *šĕnat pĕquddātām.* The phrase recurs in 11:23 and 48:44 and has other variations in Jeremiah (see Note for 6:15).

MESSAGE AND AUDIENCE

Jeremiah opens the present dialogue by lamenting his weakened condition before Yahweh and his holy words. His mind and all his senses have been rendered incapable, and his bones shake out of control. He compares himself to a man drunk on wine. Yahweh answers the prophet, saying he understands fully. Indeed, the land is full of adulterers. Because of this curse the land is bone dry. The course of these animal-like men is evil; their might is not right. Yahweh continues the indictment, saying that even prophet and priest have become polluted; even in his Temple their evil can be found. In a second oracle, Yahweh judges this adulterous population. Their way will prove to be a slippery slope in thick darkness, on which a push will easily bring them down. Yahweh says he will indeed bring evil upon them in the year of their reckoning.

These oracles can be dated anytime after Jehoiakim's reign begins in 609 B.C., when pagan rites have once again made entry into the Temple, and judgment is still a ways off.

2. Tale of the Evil Prophets (23:13–15)

23 [13]Now in the prophets of Samaria
    I have seen a foolish thing:
They prophesied away by Baal
    and led my people Israel astray

[14]But in the prophets of Jerusalem
    I have seen a horrible thing:
Committing adultery and walking by the lie
    they even strengthened the hands of evildoers
        so that no person turned from his evil
All of them have become to me like Sodom
    and her inhabitants like Gomorrah.

[15]Therefore thus said Yahweh of hosts concerning the prophets:
Look I will feed them wormwood

and will make them drink poisoned water
Because from the prophets of Jerusalem
pollution has gone forth to all the land.

RHETORIC AND COMPOSITION

The present verses contain two oracles (vv 13–14, v 15), both in poetry, which are delimited at the top end by a concluding messenger formula to the prior oracle in v 12. Verse 13b, with two occurrences of the *nota accusativi*, may be later prose expansion. Delimitation at the bottom end is by a *petuḥah* in M^A and M^L after v 15, where M^P has no section. Prior to v 15 is a *petuḥah* in M^A and M^P and a *setumah* in M^L separating the two oracles. Oracle II is also set off by the expanded messenger formula in 15a. The M^L (only) has another *setumah* after v 13, the purpose of which is unclear. Verses 13 and 14 must remain together if the prophets of Samaria and Jerusalem are to be contrasted (Calvin).

Although vv 13–14 contain no messenger formula, Yahweh must be the speaker on account of the first-person *lî* ("to me") in 14c (Holladay). What we have then is another two-oracle sequence of indictment and judgment, where the oracle of judgment begins with the often-used "therefore." A similar two-oracle sequence occurs in vv 10–12.

The first oracle is two stanzas, having the following repetitions and balancing key terms:

I	*Now in the prophets of Samaria*		v 13
	I have seen		
	. . . . *by Baal*	*babbaʿal*	
	. . . .		
II	*But in the prophets of Jerusalem*		v 14
	I have seen		
	. . . . *by the lie*	*baššeqer*	
	. . . . *evildoers*	*měrēʿîm*	
	. . . . *from his evil*	*mērāʿātô*	
	. . . . *like Sodom*		
	. . . . *like Gomorrah*		

The two oracles are linked by the following repetition:

I	. . . . *the prophets of Jerusalem*	v 14
II	. . . . *the prophets of Jerusalem*	v 15

Catchwords connecting to the preceding oracle (Condamin; Craigie et al.):

v 14	*Committing adultery*	*nāʾōp*	v 10	*adulterers*	*měnāʾăpîm*
v 15	*Therefore*	*lāken*	v 11	*they are polluted*	*ḥānēpû*
	pollution	*ḥănuppâ*	v 12	*Therefore*	*lāken*

Catchwords connecting to the oracle following:

v 14 *evildoers . . . from his evil*   v 17 *Evil*

NOTES

23:13–14. *Now . . . but.* The initial *waws* set up a contrast, not a comparison, as the AV translates ("and . . . also"). Coordinating *waws* commonly mean "both . . . and" (BDB; KB³), but here a contrast is intended between Samaria's bad prophets and Jerusalem's prophets, who are worse. Many of the modern Versions leave the *waw* of v 13 untranslated (Giesebrecht says it is an error), and Overholt (1970: 52) takes it to be a connective to the prior verse, which it is not. Holladay (following Calvin) translates the two *waws* as "Indeed . . . But," which gives the first *waw* an unusual asseverative meaning but produces the same effect as the translation here.

13. *Now in the prophets of Samaria I have seen a foolish thing: They prophesied away by Baal and led my people Israel astray.* Reference may be to the large number of Baal prophets residing in Samaria during Ahab's reign, who were undone by the contest on Mt. Carmel featuring Elijah, the great Yahweh prophet (1 Kings 18). These cannot be the prophets playacting before Ahab and Jehoshaphat in 1 Kings 22 (*pace* Overholt 1970: 53), who are Yahweh prophets.

I have seen a foolish thing. Hebrew *tiplâ* ("a foolish thing") means, lit., "something unseemly, lacking in (moral) taste" (Job 1:22; *tāpēl* in 6:6). The prophets of Samaria are belittled here, not censured, as are the prophets of Jerusalem. The REB translates "a lack of sense." Although the same term describes false prophetic visions in Lam 2:14, it is still weaker than the *ša'ărûrâ* ("horrible thing") of v 14 (Calvin; Giesebrecht). Calvin says the stronger *ša'ărûrâ* is reserved for Jerusalem's prophets, who thought themselves infinitely better. Further, the prophets of Samaria require no strong censure, since they were condemned long ago, and now no one would defend them.

They prophesied away by Baal. The verb *hinnabbĕ'û* is a contracted Hithpael (GKC §54c; cf. Ezek 37:10), which occurs uncontracted in some Heb MSS (Blayney). The term means "to rave on as a prophet" (see Note for 14:14). Jeremiah himself is charged with frenzied prophesy in 29:26–27, although this comes from someone who is trying to discredit him.

and led my people Israel astray. Hebrew *wayyat'û 'et-'ammî 'et-yiśrā'ēl.* Hosea leveled the same charge against the clergy of Northern Israel (Hos 4:12), which amounts to a breach of covenant. In Jerusalem, Yahweh prophets with their lying dreams are doing similarly (v 32) and along with other leaders have been misleading an indiscerning populace for a century or more (Mic 3:5; Isa 3:12; 9:14–15[Eng 9:15–16]). Duhm, Cornill, and Rudolph delete "Israel" as a gloss, for which there is no warrant. The term should be retained.

14. *But in the prophets of Jerusalem I have seen a horrible thing: Committing adultery and walking by the lie, they even strengthened the hands of evildoers.*

Jerusalem's immoral Yahweh prophets are *worse* than Samaria's prophets of Baal. In the allegory of 3:6–11, the whole of Israel comes off less guilty than self-assured Judah. Compare also Isa 28:7; Mic 3:11; and the allegories in Ezek 16:44–52 and 23:1–20. Jesus says that false prophets are known by their fruits (Matt 7:15–20).

I have seen a horrible thing. The LXX has *eōraka phrikta,* "I saw a bristling thing." The "horrible thing" (*ša'ărûrâ*) in 5:30 is clergy misrule and prophets prophesying by "The Lie," i.e., Baal. The "horrible thing" (*ša'ărûrît*) in 18:13 is burning incense to false gods, which appears to be the same covenant violation as that cited in Hos 6:10. Here the "horrible thing" could conceivably be walking after "The Lie," i.e., Baal, but more likely is walking by "the lie," which is false prophecy in the name of Yahweh. It is doubtful whether any prophets are still speaking for Baal in Zedekiah's reign. The problem in Zedekiah's reign was Yahweh prophets speaking "lies" (chaps. 27–28), which is probably what is indicated here. If we assume a more negative meaning for *ša'ărûrâ* than for *tiplâ* in v 13 (*pace* McKane), we have a *distributio* (see §Introduction: Rhetoric and Preaching: Argumentation). There are the bad Baal prophets of Samaria on the one hand, and the even worse prophets of Jerusalem on the other, who, if they are not all Yahweh prophets, are mostly so. The remaining verses in the Prophet Collection literally teem with *antitheses* and *distributios* (see vv 16, 21, 23, 28, 35–36, and 37–38), and we seem to have another example here. Yahweh, it should also be noted, has "seen" other disturbing sights in Jerusalem (7:11; 13:27b), there being no secret places where people can hide or where he is unable to see (16:17; 23:24).

Committing adultery and walking by the lie. Here two infinitive absolutes are combined: *nā'ôp wĕhālōk* ("committing adultery and walking"). In 7:9 is a string of six infinitive absolutes in one of Jeremiah's Temple Oracles. If kings are prone to injustice and inhumanity (21:12; 22:15–17), prophets and priests seem to have the occupational hazard of falling victim to adultery and lying (cf. 29:23). Adultery here is to be taken literally (Kimḥi; Rudolph; Bright; Holladay; McKane), as also in v 10; it is not a metaphor for religious apostasy (*pace* Berridge 1970: 34 n. 52). The mention of Sodom and Gomorrah in the verse also suggests sexual immorality (Loader 1990: 61; 1991: 13), where the names of the two cities are brought up, not because of the judgment they incurred, but rather to recall the evil that flourished there, which was considerable (Duhm; cf. Gen 18:20). This verse is an indictment, a point overlooked by Overholt (1970: 53); judgment does not come upon these prophets until v 15.

and walking by the lie. Hebrew *wĕhālōk baššeqer.* Here *šeqer* with the article appears to mean simply "the lie" (= false prophesy), not "The Lie" (= Baal), as in chaps. 1–20 (*pace* Thompson; Boadt; Holladay). On the latter, see Notes for 3:23 and 5:31. "The lie" is definitely required in 23:26, where Yahweh prophets (v 24: "speaking in my name") are being contrasted to earlier prophets of Baal (v 27). Prophesying the lie (*šeqer*) here, in vv 25–26, 32, and nine times in chaps. 27–29 (27:10, 14, 15, 16; 28:15; 29:9, 21, 23, 31) means prophesying peace and security for Judah, disobedience to Nebuchadnezzar, or a speedy end to the exile of 597 B.C. (Overholt 1970: 29). "Walking (in the way)" has ethical implications in the OT, referring to one's behavior or conduct, often routinely or over a period of time (see Note for 6:16). In the present case, the Yahweh prophets of Jerusalem are walking the way of false prophesy.

they even strengthened the hands of evildoers. If the prophets of Samaria led people astray, and they did, these prophets accelerate covenant disobedience by encouraging evildoers and making them stronger. Compare 2:33; also Ezek 13:22, where the same idiom occurs. On the idiom "to strengthen (weak) hand(s)," see also Judg 9:24 (for evil); 1 Sam 23:16 (for good); Isa 35:3 (for good); and Job 4:3 (for good).

so that no person turned from his evil. Hebrew *lĕbiltî-šābû* is grammatically dubious because of the perfect verb (so GKC §152x). Duhm therefore emends with LXX's *apostraphēnai* ("turned back") to the infinitive *šûb* (cf. Ezek 13:22); Ehrlich (1912: 303) emends to *yāšûbû*, supposing that a *yod* was lost through haplography. But see *lĕbiltî-bō'û* in 27:18 (cf. GKC §72o; 76g). Jeremiah is saying that the prophets are preventing the very thing they should be working to achieve, i.e., turning people away from evil. But instead they encourage evildoers, if not by word, then by example.

All of them. I.e., all people generally.

Sodom . . . Gomorrah. Reference is to the people of Sodom and the people of Gomorrah (Kimḥi), who are cited here because of wicked behavior that became proverbial (Genesis 18–19). The wicked cities actually numbered five: Sodom, Gomorrah, Admah, Zeboiim, and Zoar (Gen 14:2, 8; Wis Sol 10:6), with only Zoar escaping the divine wrath (Gen 19:21–22; cf. Deut 29:22[Eng 29:23]). Sodom and Gomorrah are referred to again in 49:18 and 50:40, another time by implication in 20:16, and they serve as background for Jeremiah's dialogue over the fate of Jerusalem in 5:1–8. Repeated mention of the cities by other prophets (Isa 1:9–10; 3:9; 13:19; Amos 4:11; Hos 11:8; Zeph 2:9; Ezek 16:46–52) and in the NT (Matt 10:15; 11:23–24; 2 Pet 2:6; Jude 7; Rev 11:8) indicates that just the mention of their names was tantamount to issuing a curse (Hillers 1964: 74–76). Not only was their wickedness proverbial, but so also was the fiery judgment meted out to them (see Note for 20:16).

and her inhabitants. I.e., Jerusalem's inhabitants.

15. *Yahweh of hosts.* The LXX lacks "of hosts," as it frequently does. Rofé (1991) thinks *ṣĕbā'ôt* ("hosts") is an LXX deletion in the Jeremiah book, but Janzen (1973) and others take it to be an MT expansion. The LXX does translate the term on occasion (see Appendix VI for the distribution).

concerning the prophets. I.e., the prophets of Jerusalem, on whom the judgment will fall. The LXX also omits these words; T expands to "prophets of falsehood," as elsewhere.

Look I will feed them wormwood and will make them drink poisoned water. The same food and drink will be served to the people as a whole in the coming judgment (see Note for 9:14[15]). A poisoned-water curse is included in an

Esarhaddon treaty (#521–22; Wiseman 1958a: 67–68; Hillers 1964: 63–64), on which see Note for 8:14. In Asia today, cholera comes through the drinking water.

Because from the prophets of Jerusalem pollution has gone forth to all the land. Hebrew *ḥănuppâ* ("pollution") is cognate to *ḥānēpû* ("they are polluted") in v 11, confirming what has been said about the prophets of Jerusalem being morally bankrupt.

MESSAGE AND AUDIENCE

Yahweh in this first divine speech intends a contrast between the prophets of Samaria and the prophets of Jerusalem. In the former, he saw foolish Baal prophecies leading people down the wrong path. The audience knows all about this, and heads will be nodding in approval. But then Yahweh says that in the prophets of Jerusalem he saw something really horrible. They compromised their holiness by committing adultery and living by lies, so much so that evildoers were strengthened and became unrepentant of their evil. Will the audience willingly hear this word, which strikes closer to home, and will they perceive that the prophets of their city should instead have been turning people away from evil? Yahweh says that Jerusalem has become like Sodom and Gomorrah, something the audience may already know if they heard Jeremiah's dialogue on the fate of Jerusalem (5:1–8). A follow-up oracle promises judgment on these prophets. As a reward for their celebrated living, he will set a table of wormwood and poisoned water for them and make sure they eat and drink to the full—a fitting punishment for clergy who have spread their pollution throughout the land.

These oracles can be dated early in Zedekiah's reign, i.e., in the years following the exile of 597 B.C. (Volz; Weiser; Rudolph). When heard after the oracles immediately preceding, Jerusalem's prophets (and priests), polluted as they are by adulteries and other immoralities, will get the emphasis in Yahweh's indictment (vv 10–11, 14–15). It is, alas, the "way" in which they "walk" (vv 12, 14). But in the end, Yahweh says, will be a judgment.

3. Prophets with a Vision of Their Own (23:16–17)

23 ¹⁶Thus said Yahweh of hosts:
Do not listen to the words of the prophets who prophesy to you; they make you nothing; a vision of their own heart they speak, not from the mouth of Yahweh, ¹⁷continually saying to those who spurn me, 'Yahweh has spoken, "It will be well for you"'; and to everyone who walks in the stubbornness of his heart they say, 'Evil will not come upon you.'

RHETORIC AND COMPOSITION

Delimitation of the present verses has been difficult for commentators and others, who seem not to know how far the unit extends. Many of them

(Giesebrecht, Rudolph, Weiser, Hyatt, Bright, Lipinski 1970a; Thompson, Boadt, Carroll, Craigie et al., Jones, McKane) take vv 16–22 as the unit; Holladay, vv 16–20. Neither grouping is correct. The upper limit is indicated by a *petuḥah* in M^A and M^L before v 16, but not in M^P. None of the medieval codices has a section after v 17. Clarity comes only with a proper delimitation of vv 18–22, into which has been inserted a separate oracle in vv 19–20. The primary poem there is vv 18 and 21–22 (see Rhetoric and Composition for 23:18–22). This leaves vv 16–17 as a self-standing oracle, in which Yahweh addresses people on the problem of false prophets and false prophecy.

The present oracle is prose (Cornill; RSV; NRSV), not poetry. Most commentators, with the modern Versions, scan it as poetry, but they do so only by making deletions, usually *metri causa*. However, in v 17 there are nicely balanced phrases with inversion:

> continually saying / to those who spurn me, Yahweh has spoken,
>   well / it will be for you,
> and to everyone who walks in the stubbornness of his heart / they say,
>   it will not come upon you / evil.

The oracle is Jeremianic (Mowinckel 1914: 21), not assignable to some "Deuteronomic" editor (*pace* Carroll), much less an editor of the second century (*pace* Duhm, who dates all of vv 16–40 then).

Catchwords connecting to the previous unit:

v 17 *Evil*   v 14 *evildoers . . . from his evil*

Catchwords connecting to the unit following, some of which are noted by Condamin:

v 16 *listen*   v 18 *and let him hear . . . and heard*
      the prophets who prophesy   v 20 *his heart*
      their own heart   v 21 *the prophets . . . they prophesied*
v 17 *his heart*   v 22 *caused to hear*
      Evil   *evil* (2×)

NOTES

23:16. *Thus said Yahweh of hosts.* Holladay (and before him Cornill) deletes, for which there is no textual warrant. The difficulty for Holladay appears to be delimitation: Jeremiah, he thinks, must be the speaker in vv 16–20. The LXX translates *ṣĕbā'ôt* ("of hosts") with *pantokratōr*, as it does occasionally elsewhere (see Appendix VI).

Do not listen to the words of the prophets who prophesy to you. Hebrew *'al* is equivalent here to *'el* (see Note for 11:2). This directive is heard repeatedly in chaps. 27–29 (27:9, 14, 16, 17; 29:8), countering prophets who are telling people not to submit to Nebuchadnezzar and that the Temple treasures taken to Babylon in 597 B.C. will be speedily returned. In the next verse this message is also said to be a comforting "It will be well for you."

who prophesy to you. Hebrew *hannibbĕ'îm lākem.* The phrase is lacking in the LXX and is likely another loss due to haplography (homoeoteleuton: *m . . . m*). Many commentators (Duhm; Volz; Rudolph; Weiser; Bright; Thompson; Carroll; Holladay; McKane) omit for metrical reasons (assuming this to be poetry); Janzen (1973: 44) says the phrase comes from 27:15–16; Thiel (1973: 250) attributes it to the "Deuteronomist" or a later hand.

they make you nothing. Hebrew *mahbīlîm hēmmâ 'etkem.* The verb is a denominative H-stem of *hebel,* the familiar Ecclesiastes word meaning "vanity" (see Note for 2:5; cf. BDB: "to cause to become vain"; KB³ "to delude"). In 2:5 Jeremiah said the fathers "went after The Nothing (i.e., Baal) and became nothing." Now Yahweh prophets are making others "nothing" by preaching "nothing," which comes down to entertaining hopes that will come to "nothing."

a vision of their own heart they speak, not from the mouth of Yahweh. One of many antitheses in these verses. Hebrew *lēb* ("heart") might better be rendered "mind," as in 7:31 and 14:14 (see Notes for 5:21 and 11:20), however the term repeats in v 17. The AV has "heart" in both verses; the RSV has "minds" in v 16 and "heart" in v 17. The same problem of translation recurs in v 20. We learn here also that visions can be spoken (Amos 1:1; Isa 2:1), and later from v 18 that prophets can "see" Yahweh's word. Jones calls this the technical vocabulary of Hebrew prophecy. These prophets, in any case, are not speaking from Yahweh's mouth, as Jeremiah is doing (1:9; 15:19).

17. *continually saying.* Hebrew *'ōmĕrîm 'āmôr.* The Versions omit the infinitive absolute, which can, however, follow a participle for purposes of intensification (Calvin; GKC §113r). In 41:6 the LXX omits an infinitive absolute in the *hōlēk hālōk* ("continued walking") construction. Rudolph omits the infinitive too, citing metrical excess. But the MT reading can stand. The idea here is that prophets are giving a false message without letup.

to those who spurn me. The verb *n's* ("spurn") is associated with covenant-breaking in 14:21 (Yahweh) and Deut 31:20 (people). In the latter, Yahweh worries that once his people taste good things in the Land of Promise they will turn to other gods, spurn him, and break the covenant he has with them. In 14:21 a sinful people, in confession, fear that Yahweh will spurn them and break his covenant with them.

Yahweh has spoken. Hebrew *dibber yhwh.* The LXX reads the Hebrew consonants as *dĕbar-yhwh,* translating the whole phrase "to those who spurn the word of the Lord." Many commentators (Giesebrecht; Duhm; Peake; Cornill; Volz; Rudolph; Bright; Holladay) adopt this reading (cf. Isa 5:24). The T follows MT. Either reading is acceptable. McKane's deletion of the words, however, is without basis and should be rejected.

It will be well for you. The same phrase occurs in 4:10. The Heb is *šālôm*, meaning "peace, well-being." On Jeremiah's difficulties with the "peace prophets," see 6:14 = 8:11; 14:13; and 28:9.

and to everyone who walks in the stubbornness of his heart they say, 'Evil will not come upon you.' The prefixed *lamed* on the previous *limna'ăṣay* ("to those who spurn me") does double duty for *wĕkōl*; thus: "and *to* everyone" (Holladay; see also the Vrs). The LXX has an expanded reading: *kai pasin tois poreuomenois tois thelēmasin autōn, panti tō poreuomenō planē kardias autou eipan,* "and to all those who walk in their own desires, to everyone who walks in the error of his heart, they said," which is explained by Ziegler (1957: 265) and Janzen (1973: 28) as a double reading. It is also possible that we may have a case of MT haplography (whole-word plus: *kl hlk . . . kl hlk*); however, the phrase "to all those who walk in their own desires" has no obvious parallel in Jeremiah. The phrase "in the stubbornness of his heart," which denotes irksome self-reliance, is Jeremianic (see Note for 3:17). In 5:12 the prophets are reported as saying, "Evil will not come upon us," which gives the same false sense of security as here. See also Mic 3:11 and Amos 9:10. Reinhold Niebuhr (1937: 94) says: "The mark of false prophecy is that it assures the sinner peace and security within terms of his sinful ambition." True prophecy reveals sin for what it is and calls for repentance.

they say. Hebrew *'āmĕrû.* Bright deletes the word *metri causa*, citing also its omission in some LXX MSS (G^A, G^S), the OL, and Arabic. But the omission is more likely due to haplography (homoeoteleuton: *w . . . w*). The word should be retained, because it appears in all of the other texts and has a function in the rhetorical prose of the verse (see Rhetoric and Composition).

MESSAGE AND AUDIENCE

Yahweh in this oracle tells people not to listen to the prophets who are prophesying to them, i.e., prophets currently enjoying the limelight and to whom they are listening. These prophets are only enhancing their vanity, articulating visions they have conjured up and not speaking words from Yahweh's mouth. They keep repeating them, telling them to people who in fact are spurning Yahweh and are stubbornly self-reliant, saying all will go well, and evil will not come.

This oracle can be dated early in Zedekiah's reign, ca. 594/3, at which time there is talk of rebellion against Babylon, and Jeremiah has his celebrated confrontation with Hananiah, prophet of Yahweh, from Gibeon (chaps. 27–28). When heard in tandem with the preceding oracles, Yahweh's present judgment will pick up on the "lie" that prophets are said to be "walking by" in v 14, which is adding to the people's wickedness, not bringing them deliverance from it.

4. Prophets without Portfolio (23:18–22)

23 [18]For who has stood in the council of Yahweh?
 then let him see and let him hear his word!
  who has hearkened to my word[a] and heard?

[19]Look! the tempest of Yahweh
 wrath goes forth
  yes, a whirling tempest
Upon the head of the wicked it whirls
 [20]the anger of Yahweh does not turn back
until it does and until it fulfills
 the purposes of his heart
In the days afterward
 you will consider the meaning in this.

[21]I did not send the prophets
 yet they, they ran
I did not speak to them
 yet they, they prophesied

[22]Now if they had stood in my council
 and caused my people to hear my words
Then they would have turned them from their evil way
 and from the evil of their doings.

RHETORIC AND COMPOSITION

Delimitation here has been a problem for commentators, not only because there is no section marking or other indicator of a break at the upper end, but also because vv 19–20 are duplicated in 30:23–24, suggesting to some that they intrude in the present context. Peake and Hyatt rightly note that vv 19–20 break the connection between vv 18 and 21. But others (Giesebrecht; Cornill; Volz; Condamin; Rudolph; Thiel 1974: 251; McKane) take v 18, with or without vv 19–20, as more supplementation, which it is not. This verse is also not prose (*pace* BHS; JB; NJB; NSB), even though it does contains the *nota accusativi* before *děbārô* ("his word"). Prose particles are known to appear in poetry, but less often (D. N. Freedman 1982). Clarification of these verses and a solution to the delimitation problem come once it is recognized that v 18 combines with vv 21–22 to form a nicely-balanced self-standing poem, into which has been inserted another self-standing poem, vv 19–20 (Lundbom 1975: 89–90 [= 1997: 118–20]). The upper limit of the present unit can then be set at v 18. The lower limit is marked by a *setumah* in M^A and M^L after v 22. The M^P has no section here.

---

[a]Reading the Kt "my word"; Q has "his word"; see Notes.

The main poem is three stanzas, its repetitions and balancing key terms being the following:

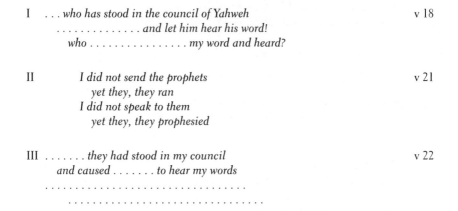

I   . . . who has stood in the council of Yahweh   v 18
     . . . . and let him hear his word!
     who . . . . my word and heard?

II   I did not send the prophets   v 21
              yet they, they ran
          I did not speak to them
              yet they, they prophesied

III . . . . they had stood in my council   v 22
     and caused . . . . to hear my words
     . . . .
          . . . .

For other tightly-balanced centers in the Jeremianic poems, see Rhetoric and Composition for 2:4–9.

Yahweh is the speaker throughout. His initial question in v 18 is posed in the third person, but with "my word" (Kt) comes a shift to the first person, which is then retained to the end of the poem. A similar shift of person occurs at the beginning of the divine speech to Coniah in 22:24. "His word" (Q) can be explained as an attempt to provide consistency in v 18, once vv 19–20 were inserted, at which point the continuity between vv 18 and 21 was broken.

The inserted poem of vv 19–20 begins with the familiar Jeremianic *hinnēh* ("Look"), on which see Note for 1:9. The speaker here is Jeremiah, who adds a word of judgment to Yahweh's word of indictment. Jeremiah's speech is a general condemnation of the wicked but in its present context becomes a condemnation of the uncredentialed prophets and their message, although the judgment is still slated for everyone. Why it breaks up the Yahweh speech is not clear. The usual explanation is that it announces Yahweh's true word of judgment spoken in council, which counters the false word of prophets who say (in v 17) that there will be peace (Cheyne; Rudolph; Bright; Thompson; Boadt; Craigie et al.; Jones). But the judgment would have gone much better after v 22.

Catchwords connecting to the previous unit:

v 18	and let him hear . . . and heard	v 16	listen
v 20	his heart		the prophets who prophesy
v 21	the prophets . . . they, they prophesied		their own heart
v 22	caused to hear	v 17	his heart
	evil (2×)		Evil

There are no catchwords connecting to the oracles following.

NOTES

23:18. *For who has stood in the council of Yahweh? then let him see and let him hear his word! who has hearkened to my word and heard?* The "who?" (*mî*) questions are rhetorical; however, they are not meant to evoke the answer "No one" (*pace* Duhm; Peake), as in 15:5. Job, it is true, claims not to have been present to hear the goings-on in the heavenly council (Job 15:8), but prophets are expected to have been there, as we learn from v 22. Jeremiah stood in council (18:20), and so did Isaiah when he heard another pair of "who?" questions coming from the heavenly throne, to which he gave a ready response (Isa 6:8). The questions posed here may be truly open-ended, i.e., they could be asking who, if anyone, has stood in Yahweh's council; but in view of what follows, they are more likely directed at prophets who have not been in council. Because uncredentialed prophets are targeted in the prior oracle (vv 16–17), some commentators (S. R. Driver; Weiser) and some modern Versions (Moffatt; AmT; RSV; NEB; NIV; REB; cf. *BHS*) add a qualifying "of/among them" to the first question (RSV: "For who among them has stood in the council of the Lord . . . ?"). But there is no textual warrant for this interpretive supplement, and it should be dropped (as it has been in the NRSV). Verse 18 begins a new divine speech, having no original connection to the oracle of vv 16–17.

stood in the council of Yahweh. Hebrew *ʿāmad bĕsôd yhwh.* To "stand" before Yahweh is to be in his service (see Note for 15:19); to "stand in council" is to stand ready as a royal messenger in the heavenly precincts, into which one has been transported by means of a vision (1 Kgs 22:19–23; Isa 6:1–8; cf. R. Brown 1958: 420). The prophet Isaiah reported his call in these words: "I saw (*ʾerʾeh*) the Lord sitting upon a throne, high and lifted up. . . . And I heard the voice of the Lord saying, 'Whom shall I send, and who will go for us?' Then I said, 'Here I am, send me'" (Isa 6:1, 8). Prophets, then, are members of the divine council only to the extent that they enter God's presence in the capacity of the royal messenger and receive messages from him to be delivered to the people. In this intercessory role they also bring requests from the people to God, which he either grants or refuses to grant. The term *sôd* means "council" or "counsel," where in both cases the idea of confidentiality or secrecy is assumed (Amos 3:7). All of God's great works begin in secret (Jer 33:3; Ps 139:13–16). Compare comments of the great NT scholar, Johannes Weiss (1959: 14), on the obscure beginnings of the nascent Church.

The idea of a divine council or assembly is very old, attested in Sumerian and Babylonian religion, and later in Syro-Phoenician religion, as is known from the Ugaritic texts of Ras Shamra (T. Jacobsen 1943: 167–72; H. W. Robinson 1944; Polley 1980; Mullen 1980; "Divine Assembly" in *ABD* 2: 214–17). It has also turned up in the Aramaic texts from Deir ʿAlla (I 8; Hoftijzer and van der Kooij 1976: 173, 179, 192–93; *CS II* 142), where reference is made to Shadday gods' having gathered in assembly. According to Jacobsen, the origins of the divine council are to be found in a "primitive democracy" among preliterate Sumerians, who projected terrestrial life into the heavenly realm, where it served to describe the life of the gods. From later Babylonian texts we know that these religious ideas outlived the democracy from which they came, continuing in Sumerian and Babylonian religion long after autocratic kingship had emerged in the early third millennium. On Mari prophets of the early second millennium who stood in secret councils of earthly—not heavenly—kings, see Malamat 1991b. There is no parallel, as far as we know, to the biblical idea of prophets' carrying messages from the divine assembly to people on earth (Polley 1980: 149; Mullen 1980: 218). But that Yahweh has a council of heavenly beings is attested throughout Scripture (Deut 32:8 ["sons of God" in LXX and 4QDeut]; 33:2; Ps 89:6–9[Eng 89:5–8]; Sir 24:2), where such beings assist in Creation and are present when judgment is meted out in Eden and at Babel (Gen 1:26; 3:22; and 11:7 ["Let us make . . ."; "like one of us"; "Let us go down . . ."]). They are also heard singing Yahweh's praises (Pss 29:1; 148:2; Job 38:7; Dan 7:9–22; Luke 2:13; Rev 4:1–11) and seen performing various acts of service (Isa 6:1–8), e.g., that of a prosecuting attorney ("the satan") and enticer (1 Kgs 22:19–22; Job 1:6–12; 2:1–7). These beings also suffer judgment themselves on account of moral lapses (Ps 82:1–8, which may have a Canaanite background and may presuppose a polytheistic world view). Psalm 82 and other biblical texts "point to the tendency in Israel to borrow the ancient Near Eastern myth of the assembly of the gods, to place Yahweh as head of the pantheon, and then to reduce the status of the 'gods' to spiritual beings which surround Yahweh's throne" (Polley 1980: 147). Yet these beings render homage to Yahweh, carry out his decrees, and in no way rival his power. Polley (p. 148) says they "enhance his glory by providing a court befitting his majesty." The divine council is also background to the call of Second Isaiah in Isa 40:1–11 (Cross 1953; Muilenburg 1956a: 422–23).

then let him see and let him hear his word! Hebrew *wĕyēre' wĕyišmaʿ 'et-dĕbārô*. The omission of "and let him hear" in the LXX is no reason to delete (*pace* Holladay; McKane). The term is present in Aq, Symm, Theod, T, and Vg. The LXX is perhaps avoiding a repetition, since the same verb occurs again at the end of the verse. Both verbs are jussives. The present colon then does not extend the first question but, rather, is an intervening exhortation between questions. The same sort of discourse is seen in vv 26–28, where two jussives in v 28, *yĕsappēr ḥălôm . . . yĕdabbēr dĕbārî* ("let him tell the dream . . . let him speak my word"), intervene between a pair of rhetorical questions. In the present verse, the LXX translates its single verb *kai eide* (= *wayyar'*, "and has seen"), which most commentators and modern Versions adopt. But the Masoretic pointing should be retained, posing as it does a particularly vigorous challenge to the opposition. "Seeing" Yahweh's word relates to the prophet's visionary experience. In 2:31 the people are told to "perceive" (*rĕ'û*) Yahweh's word.

who has hearkened to my word and heard? The Kt "my word," which the LXX omits, is probably original (Cornill; Peake). Yahweh is speaker and continues to be the speaking voice in vv 21–22 (see Rhetoric and Composition). The final "and heard" is this time an ordinary imperfect, meaning "really heard." Rashi says the first occurrence of the verb has to do with actual hearing, the second with acceptance (NEB: "and obeyed"). Some commentators (Giesebrecht; Duhm; Volz; Weiser; Rudolph) and some modern Versions (JB; NAB; NRSV) repoint the second occurrence to an H-stem, "so he may announce (it)," which wrongly assumes the same meaning as in v 22. Here the emphasis is on hearing, not preaching.

19. *Look! the tempest of Yahweh.* "Look" (*hinnēh*) is the most common beginning of a Jeremianic oracle (see Note for 1:9), except that here Jeremiah is the speaker, not Yahweh. Hebrew *sĕʿārâ* is not the legendary sirocco (on which see Note for 4:11) but a swirling tempest with rain, perhaps a tornado (Ezek 13:11, 13). Both winds are OT metaphors for coming destruction. The wind cited here occurs again in 25:32, where it describes Babylonian storm troops engulfing nation after nation. As a metaphor of Yahweh's judgment, see Amos 1:14. This same wind is the whirlwind that took Elijah up to heaven (2 Kgs 2:1, 11) and the whirlwind out of which Yahweh spoke to Job (Job 38:1; 40:6).

wrath goes forth. Hebrew *ḥēmâ yāṣĕʾâ*. A portion of the stereotypical threat occurring in 4:4 and 21:12 (see Note on 4:4). Some commentators (Volz; Rudolph; Weiser; Bright; McKane) delete *ḥēmâ* ("wrath") as a gloss, which is without basis. The line can be read as a tricolon. One also need not revocalize, with G. R. Driver (1950a: 413), to *ḥōmâ* ("hot"), an adjective modifying "the tempest of Yahweh" (cf. NEB and REB).

yes, a whirling tempest. The masculine *saʿar* ("tempest") may intentionally vary the feminine *saʿărat* used in the first colon (Holladay). Nouns in poetry usually match with respect to gender, but sometimes genders are switched for special effect (Watson 1980). The verb *ḥûl* means "(do a) dance, whirl," and *mitḥôlēl* (Hithpolel) anticipates *yāḥûl* (Qal) in the following colon.

Upon the head of the wicked it whirls. The LXX omits "head," as it does also in 30:23. The omission in this verse or the other in the LXX's Hebrew *Vorlage* can be attributed to haplography (homoeoarcton: *r . . . r*). Duhm and Holladay note the assonance in *rōʾš rĕšāʿîm* ("the head of the wicked"), another reason for retaining "head."

20. *the anger of Yahweh does not turn back until it does and until it fulfills the purposes of his heart.* See Note for 4:8. The anger of Yahweh is as sure as his word: it does not return empty (cf. Isa 55:11). The point here is not that Yahweh's anger cannot be averted, since it can be (18:7–8; 26:3), but that when the anger does pour forth, it will accomplish what it set out to do. "Heart" (*lēb*) refers here to the divine will.

In the days afterward. Hebrew *bĕʾaḥărît hayyāmîm*. On this expression, which means "in future days" or "in days to come," see also 30:24; 48:47; 49:39; Gen 49:1; Num 24:14; Deut 4:30; 31:29; Isa 2:2; and Ezek 38:16. Kimḥi thinks that reference here is to the Messianic Era, but the consensus otherwise is that eschatological meaning is not present in the preexilic use of this expression (Lipiński 1970a: 450), as, for example, one finds in Dan 2:28 and 10:14, where it has become a technical term for the End Times (Seebass, *TDOT* 1: 210–11).

A comparable Akk expression, *an(a) aḥ-rat ūmī*, means "in future days" or "for (all) the future" (*CAD* 1/1: 193–94; AHw 1: 21).

you will consider the meaning in this. The Hebrew *titbônĕnû bāh bînâ* employs a cognate accusative: "you will understand the understanding in it" (GKC §117p–r; see Note on 22:16). Calvin translates: "you shall know what this means." The LXX omission of *bînâ* ("understanding, meaning") can probably be attributed to haplography (homoeoteleuton: *h* . . . *h*), even though the term is also lacking in the duplicated verse of 30:24. Theodotion has the term here. The point being made is that only with the passage of time will people come to understand what this judgment will mean. There is a sense in which this bit of wisdom is a reversal of the rhetorical question of 5:31: "But what will you do at the end of it?" But people engaged in wrongdoing and all sorts of foolishness do not think about the ends to which these will bring them, and when those ends come, they are shocked, disillusioned, and unaccepting. But when truth is spoken and the wicked are punished, at a later time some—though not all—will consider, understand, and accept what has happened.

21. *I did not send the prophets, yet they, they ran; I did not speak to them, yet they, they prophesied*. The verbs "send" (*šlḥ*) and "speak" (*dbr*) are bedrock indicators that Yahweh views the prophet as a royal messenger (cf. 1:7; 26:12, 15). In one of the Mari texts (ARM X 8), a messenger to the king is told: "Now go, I have sent you! To Zimrilim you shall speak thus" (Beyerlin 1978: 125). Yahweh speaks to prophets in the heavenly council (v 18), after which they are sent forth with a message to be delivered to the people. Note that the divine actions here invert the normal sequence, which occurs elsewhere in the Jeremianic poetry and demonstrates once again how Hebrew rhetoric does not follow logical progression (see Note for 1:17). In actual fact, the speaking comes before the sending. This double antithesis contains the heart of the present indictment. Yahweh says prophets are running who have not been sent and prophesying without his having spoken to them. The repetition of the pronouns emphasizes the point. The text does not specify it, but these are the false prophets with whom Jeremiah and a confused population had to contend (Kimḥi). For prose versions of the present indictment, see 14:14 and 23:32.

22. *Now if they had stood in my council and caused my people to hear my words*. The protasis contains two conditionals, both of which went unmet by these would-be prophets. They had not stood in the divine council and had not brought Yahweh's word to this people. Here the verb *yašmiʿû* is correctly pointed as an H-stem, "(they) caused to hear." But it is not a jussive, "let them proclaim" (*pace* NEB, JB, and NJV; but abandoned in REB and NJB). The LXX's *eisēkousan* mistakenly takes the Hebrew verb as a Qal: "they heard" (Giesebrecht). The remainder of the verse tells what would have happened (or should have happened) had these prophets preached Yahweh's word of judgment. People would have been turned from their evil. As it was, they were lulled into believing that all was well and that no evil would come.

Then they would have turned them from their evil way and from the evil of their doings. The same judgment is made somewhat differently in 23:14. What these prophets were supposed to have been preaching is stated in 7:3; 18:11; 25:5; 26:3; 35:15; and 36:3, 7. The LXX omits *"them from their evil way and,"* which could be due to haplography (homoeoarcton: *m . . . m*). Janzen (1973: 117) and others do not take the final *mem* on *wîšîbûm*, "then they would have turned them," as part of the haplography, which it should be. The LXX reading is "then they would have turned my people."

and from the evil of their doings. A stereotyped expression appearing variously in Jeremianic poetry and prose (see Note for 21:12).

MESSAGE AND AUDIENCE

Yahweh begins the primary speech by asking who has stood in the heavenly council. Whoever has, let him see and hear Yahweh's word! In a follow-up question, he asks who has hearkened to his word and really heard? Before the audience can answer, or perhaps because it is unwilling to answer, Yahweh hastens to state emphatically that he did not send prophets, yet they ran; he did not speak to them, yet they prophesied. If they had stood in council, which these prophets had not, they would have brought Yahweh's true message to the people. Then, just maybe, they would have turned the refractory souls from their evil ways. Since the audience will be made up of these very people, the speech that began and has continued up till now as an indictment of the false prophets will end up being an indictment on them. The conclusion is roughly the same as that in 5:31: "And my people, they love it [misrule of prophets and priests] so! But what will you do at the end of it?"

Jeremiah in the intervening judgment speech directs audience attention to Yahweh's wrath, which, as a mighty storm goes forth to dance on the heads of the wicked. This anger, says the prophet, will not turn back until Yahweh has accomplished what he set out to do. The audience may not understand it now, but in future days there will be some that will.

The judgment speech, being a general condemnation of the wicked, could have been spoken any time before the destruction of Jerusalem. Weiser dates it to the time of Zedekiah, before the final destruction. Yahweh's indictment of prophets who have not been in council is most likely to come from Zedekiah's early years, when Jeremiah is known to have been in conflict with other prophets. Holladay's date of 600 B.C. is not possible, for then Jeremiah is out of public view. Sometime later, when the judgment speech had been inserted into the indictment speech, judgment comes upon the uncredentialed prophets and their message, although the storm will still engulf everyone.

When the indictment speech of vv 18, 21–22 is heard following the oracle of vv 16–17, the question of who has stood in Yahweh's council will be answered, although in the negative: Not those prophets who are prophesying "It will be well for you. . . . Evil will not come upon you."

5. Am I a God Nearby and Not a God Far Off? (23:23–24)

23 [23]Am I a God nearby
  —oracle of Yahweh—
   and not a God far off?

[24]If a person hides himself in secret places
  do I myself not see him?
   —oracle of Yahweh.

The heavens and the earth
  do I not fill?
   —oracle of Yahweh.

RHETORIC AND COMPOSITION

Here at the close of the King and Prophet Appendix is a collection of oracles, many of them very brief, like those in 3:12, which seem to derive from disputations between Jeremiah and other prophets. We note that in other collections within the book, e.g., 10:22–25 and 17:9–18, prophetic utterances of brief and miscellaneous character are brought together at the end. Then expounding two polemics against (lying) dreams and the phrase "the burden of Yahweh" are speeches by Yahweh and Jeremiah in highly repetitive prose, which begin the first polemic (vv 25–28a) and constitute all of the second (vv 33–40). In vv 23–40 there are no catchwords; were it not for the messenger formulas, of which there are quite a number in the MT, we would not know how to divide the units. Sections in the medieval codices (in M^A and M^L at v 29; in M^P at vv 30 and 38) are of no help. Divisions must be made largely on the basis of content, which fortunately in this case is not difficult. Commentators and the modern Versions all break between v 32 and v 33, the former discourse being the polemic against (lying) dreams, and the latter the polemic against "the burden of Yahweh." The only uncertainty is whether to group vv 23–24 with the polemic against (lying) dreams (Rudolph; Bright; Jones) or to keep them separate (Holladay; Carroll; McKane). The decision here has been to keep them separate; if they connect at all, it is secondarily with the "heavenly council" image in vv 18 and 21–22. The connection made by some commentators to the polemic against dreams (e.g., by Cornill and others, who discuss issues of immanence and transcendence, familiarity with the divine and holy respect) is nonexistent.

The unit here consists of three oracles in a cluster, all of them rhetorical questions. The messenger formula of Oracle II (v 24a) is lacking in the LXX but should be retained (Rudolph). The modern Versions (except RSV and NRSV) all take the verses, with BHS, as poetry, even though Oracle III (v 24b) has two occurrences of the *nota accusativi*.

NOTES

23:23. *Am I a God nearby . . . and not a God far off?* Hebrew *ha'ĕlōhê miqqārōb 'ānî . . . wĕlō' 'ĕlōhê mērāḥōq.* The twice-occuring construct form with a preposition following is unusual but no doubt an indication that the line is poetry. The terms are spatial (*qārōb* = "nearby" and *rāḥōq* = "far off"), not temporal, and the question is rhetorical, requiring a "No" answer. Yahweh is not *just* a God nearby, but a God *both* near and far (Ps 138:6). If the accent is anywhere, it is on Yahweh's distance from earth and the things of earth. The LXX, Theod, and S have a statement, "I am a God nearby . . . and not a God far off," which reverses the meaning. Yahweh is now simply a near God, which cannot be right, even though other OT texts do support the idea of Yahweh's nearness to his people (Lemke 1981: 551–53). If this oracle is taken together with the other two, particularly Oracle III affirming that God fills heaven and earth, the MT has to be read: God is *both* near and far (Calvin).

24. *If a person hides himself in secret places, do I myself not see him?* On the all-seeing eye of Yahweh, see 49:10 and Note for 7:11. Pharaoh Amenophis IV (= Akhenaten), in a mid-fourteenth-century B.C. hymn to Aten, praised his patron god, who saw all from the distant heavens ("The Hymn to Aton," *ANET*[3] 371; *CS I* 46):

> Thou hast made the distant sky in order to rise therein,
> in order to see all that thou dost make.

The heavens and the earth do I not fill? Yahweh says in Isa 66:1: "Heaven is my throne and the earth is my footstool." See also 1 Kgs 8:27; Ps 139:7–12; and Amos 9:2–4. From the library of Ashurbanipal (668–627 B.C.) comes a hymn to Shamash, the sun god, who was said by the worshiper to look over everything "above and below" ("Hymn to the Sun God," *ANET*[3] 387–88):

> The people of the world, all of them, thou dost watch over . . . those endowed with life, thou likewise dost tend; thou indeed art their shepherd both above and below. Faithfully thou dost continue to pass through the heavens. The broad earth thou dost visit daily.

MESSAGE AND AUDIENCE

These rhetorical questions are general and could have been uttered at any time. But as a group, and in their present context, they critique prophets whose God is too small, too localized, and who are themselves far distant from Yahweh God (Overholt 1970: 64). Yahweh is a God both near and far, one who sees in darkness and light, and who fills heaven and earth. In disputations with other prophets, Jeremiah probably uttered these oracles during the early years of Zedekiah's reign. That these questions, which are in fact affirmations, would have spoken to an exilic audience in Babylon goes without saying—when

Yahweh would have seemed distant to many Jews and it was more important than ever to perceive Yahweh as a God for whom all boundaries were non-existent (W. Herrmann 1983).

Taken in the larger context, the accent here on Yahweh being a God who fills the distant heavens serves to reinforce what is said in vv 18 and 21–22 about true prophets' having stood in the heavenly council and false prophets' not having been there.

Saint Cyprian, the bishop of Carthage (A.D. 249–58), who himself went into hiding during the third-century persecution of Decius, cited the present verses when addressing lapsed Christians who had secured *libelli* (certificates) for making sacrifices to gods of the Roman state. Quoting the LXX version of v 23, Cyprian said:

> [God] sees what is secret and hidden, He discerns what is concealed, and no man can evade the eyes of the God who says: "I am a God at hand, and not a God afar. If a man be hid in secret places, shall I not therefore see him?"
>
> (*De Lapsis* 27; English: Bévenot 1957: 35)

6. Speaking of Dreams . . . (23:25–32)

23 [25]I have heard what the prophets say who are prophesying a lie in my name: 'I have dreamed, I have dreamed.' [26]How long will there be in the mind of the prophets prophesying the lie—yes, prophets of their deceitful mind, [27]those who plan to make my people forget my name with their dreams, which they recount each person to his fellow, as their fathers forgot my name through Baal? [28]The prophet who has with him a dream, let him recount his dream; and the one who has my word with him, let him speak my word faithfully.

What is the grain to the straw?
— oracle of Yahweh.

[29]Is it not so—my word is like fire
—oracle of Yahweh—
and like a hammer shattering rock?

[30]Therefore look I am against the prophets
—oracle of Yahweh—
who steal my words each person from his fellow.

[31]Look I am against the prophets
—oracle of Yahweh—
who heed their own tongue and oracle an oracle.

³²Look I am against those prophesying lying dreams
  —oracle of Yahweh—
    yes, they recount them and lead my people astray
      with their lies and with their wantonness.

For I, I did not send them
  and I did not command them
    and they are no profit whatever to this people
      —oracle of Yahweh.

RHETORIC AND COMPOSITION

The present verses contain at the beginning a divine polemic against lying dreams (vv 25–28a), in support of which six brief oracles follow—two contrasting these dreams with Yahweh's true and all-powerful word (vv 28b–29) and four pronouncing judgment on prophets not in possession of Yahweh's word (vv 30–32). This unit is to be set apart from the three preceding oracles on the omnipresent Yahweh (vv 23–24) and from the polemic following, opposing the expression "the burden of Yahweh" (vv 33–40). Delimitation of the present verses is not by section markings but by content. Also v 32, after which all modern commentators and modern Versions break (also *BHS*), is a summary conclusion (Thiel 1973: 252–53). The M^A and M^L have a *setumah* after v 29 and M^P has a *setumah* after v 30, but neither v 29 nor v 30 gives any indication of being a break in the text.

The beginning speech (vv 25–28a), in highly repetitive prose and without a messenger formula, appears to develop from Oracle V (v 32a). Both censure prophets who are prophesying lying dreams. Oracle III (v 30) begins with a judgmental "therefore" (*lakēn*), which is discussed in Rhetoric and Composition for 22:18–19. This term occurs again (in duplicate) at the close of the polemic in vv 38–39, where it performs an even more condemnatory function than here. The six oracles in the present cluster are nicely structured, having the following repetitions and balancing key terms:

I	*What* . . . . ?	*mah*	v 28b
II	*Is it not so* . . . . ?	*hălô' kōh*	v 29
III	. . . . *look I am against the prophets*		v 30
IV	*Look I am against the prophets*		v 31
V	*Look I am against those prophesying* . . . . *my people*		v 32
VI	. . . . *this people*		

Volz takes all of vv 25–32 as poetry, although he concedes that the meter is not very clear. Holladay at one time also took vv 25–27 to be poetry (1966b: 424–32), but this is given up in his commentary, where he now agrees with H. Weippert (1973) that it is *Kunstprosa* ("structured prose"). This is perhaps as good a definition as can be given, although the stereotyped prose of vv 25–28a seems less rhythmic than the oracles. Nevertheless, in v 26 is this chiasmus (Zurro 1987: 201):

> . . . in the mind / of the prophets prophesying the lie   bĕlēb / hannĕbî'îm
> yes, prophets / of their deceitful mind   ûnĕbî'ê / libbām

And Holladay, in his earlier analysis, found this chiasmus in v 28a:

> . . . who has with him / a dream   'ăšer-'ittô / ḥălôm
> but the one who has my word / with him   wa'ăšer dĕbārî / 'ittô

In his commentary Holladay takes vv 28–29 as poetry (BHS takes only 28b–29) and vv 30–32 as more structured prose. He also says the entire passage is authentic to Jeremiah, which it gives every indication of being (pace Duhm; McKane). The LXX lacks the messenger formulas in vv 28b, 31, and 32, but there is no reason why these and three other formulas in vv 28b–32 should be regarded as secondary (pace Volz; Janzen 1973: 201 n. 76; McKane).

NOTES

23:25. I have heard what the prophets say who are prophesying a lie in my name: 'I have dreamed, I have dreamed.' Here and in the verses following, we find the strongest polemic anywhere in the Bible against dreams and dreamers of dreams. It is repeated more briefly in 27:9–10 and 29:8–9 against prophets, diviners, and dreamers who are opposing Nebuchadnezzar and his newly-emerging suzerainty in the region. Dreams, however, are generally viewed positively in the OT, where they are often a bona fide medium of divine revelation, e.g., in the so-called E document of the Pentateuch: Gen 20:3; 28:10–17; 31:24; 37:5–10; 40:5–11; also in Num 12:6; 1 Kgs 3:5; Joel 3:1[Eng 2:28]; and elsewhere. In Num 12:6–8, however, Yahweh's direct speech to Moses is ranked higher than revelations given to prophets in visions and dreams.

Dreams are basically what we think them to be today: visionary experiences while one is asleep or in an intermediary state between wakefulness and sleep, occurring usually but not always at night or in the early hours of the morning (Oppenheim 1956: 187, 225–26; Lindblom 1965: 84–85; Gen 28:11–12, 16; 1 Kgs 3:5; Isa 29:7; in the NT: Matt 1:20, 24). Dreams are well attested in the ancient world. Extrabiblical texts in sufficient quantity contain dream reports from Sumer (Sargon of Akkad; Gudea of Lagash); Old Babylonia (King Ammiditana; Gilgamesh; Uta-napishtim), Mari (a native of Sakka; a priest of the god Itur-Mer; the woman Addu-duri), the Hittites (the hunter Keshshi; King Hattushili III; his wife; King Murshili II); Ugarit (King Keret); Assyria (Prince Kumma; King Assurbanipal) Neo-Babylonia (King Nabonidus), and Egypt (Pharaohs Sesostris I, Amenophis II, Thutmosis IV, and Marniptah), to name some of the better-known examples. In the Deir 'Alla plaster text from the early eighth century B.C. (I 1), the gods are said to have come to

Balaam (in a dream) in the night (Hoftijzer and van der Kooij 1976: 173, 179, 186; *CS II* 142), which correlates nicely with the biblical account of a nocturnal visit to this same individual by God (Num 22:20). On dreams in the ANE, see Oppenheim (1956); Butler (1998); and Husser (1999); on dreams in the Mari letters, see Moran (1969a) and Sasson (1983). Dreams in the OT are discussed by E. L. Ehrlich (1953); and in the OT and later Judaism by Zeitlin (1975). Dreams and dreamers are also well documented in classical sources (see Oppenheim and Husser). In the Bible, Deut 13:2[Eng 13:1] legislates against (Canaanite) prophets and "dreamers of dreams" (*ḥōlēm ḥălôm*), stating that if such individuals, regardless of what success they have enjoyed, attempt to lead people in the direction of other gods, they are to be shunned and put to death. This legislation is repeated almost verbatim in the Qumran *Temple Scroll* (11QT 54:8–16; 55:17–18; Yadin 1983: 243–45).

Discussion of the present text has focused on whether dreams themselves are being discredited or whether dreams have become intolerable because they are lying dreams. Lindblom (1965: 201) points out that the classical prophets did not attach much value to dreams, and the present polemic, in his view, is against dreams vis-à-vis the divine word. The former is chaff, the latter grain. This is the view expressed also by Rudolph, Weiser, McKane, and the majority of commentators. But Kimḥi and Calvin both find nothing wrong with dreams per se, nor do they see the polemic here as a contrast of dreams to the divine word. For them the polemic is against dreams containing lies, which stand over against revealed words that are true. Overholt (1970: 66–68), noting no disparagement of dreams in v 28a, thinks the contrast made between dream and word is overdrawn and that "dreams mislead not because of what they *are*, but because of what they *contain*." Husser (1999: 142) says that, except for vv 28–29 and 32, Jeremiah's criticism is not of dreams as such but of dreams that lead people to forget Yahweh. But in a reading that includes vv 28–29 (he assumes a later redaction of the text), dreams are disqualified entirely when compared to the divine word.

Nevertheless, it is still the case that dreams are noticeably absent in revelations of the classical prophets, whereas these same prophets commonly report visions—Husser (p. 145) says there are 24 vision accounts in the prophetic corpus if one includes the two visions of Micaiah ben Imlah (1 Kgs 22:17, 19–23). Jeremiah himself experiences visions (1:9, 11–14; 24:1–3), although the "vision" (*ḥāzôn*), just like the dream, comes under censure by him for being a lie or being self-originating (14:14; 23:16). Compare Ezek 13:6–7, 23; 21:34[Eng 21:29]; 22:28; and Lam 2:14. And one can only wonder what lies behind Jeremiah's comment in 31:26, following an oracle predicting Judah's restoration: "At this I awoke and looked around, and my sleep was pleasant to me." One gets the impression, nevertheless, that ancient peoples could and did distinguish between "vision" and "dream" (Husser 1999: 28, 151), so when the terms occur together in biblical parallelism, as they often do (Num 12:6; Joel 3:1[Eng 2:28]; Job 20:8), one should not assume that they mean the same thing. Yet there is evidence that in the Hellenistic period, some in texts from

Qumran, that the distinction between the terms had become blurred (J. E. Miller 1990: 403–4). Dreams are distinguished from (words spoken by) prophets in 1 Sam 28:6 and 15.

In postexilic Judaism dreams fell into disrepute (Zech 10:2; Ecc 5:2, 6[Eng 5:3, 7]; Sir 34:1–8), doubtless because of attacks such as the present one and because prophets of dreams were held responsible for the destruction of the nation and the Temple. This did not continue, however. A dream of Judas Maccabeus, in which the prophet Jeremiah presents him with the sword to strike down his enemies, is said to be worthy of belief in 2 Macc 15:11. In Wis Sol 18:19 a dream also forewarns people of impending punishment. And in the NT dreams are again genuine vehicles of revelation, particularly in the Gospel of Matthew (Matt 1:20; 2:12, 13, 19, 22; 27:19). Josephus and Philo attached importance to dreams, even as the entire Hellenistic world did (Zeitlin 1975: 8–14).

the prophets . . . who are prophesying a lie in my name. A stereotyped expression appearing variously in the Jeremiah prose (14:14, 15; 23:25, 26; 27:10, 14, 15, 16; 29:9, 21), for which Holladay (1960: 354–55) finds a "prototype" in the poetry of 5:31: "The prophets, they prophesy by The Lie." There, however, *baššeqer* (with the article) has to be translated "by The Lie," i.e., "by Baal." Here and following, *šeqer* with or without the article means simply "lie, falsehood," i.e., the preaching of peace and security for Judah, disobedience to Nebuchadnezzar, and a quick end to the exile of 597 B.C. (see Note for 23:14). In v 27, Baal worship is referred to as a problem of the past.

'I have dreamed, I have dreamed.' Hebrew *ḥālamtî ḥālāmětî.* A taunt, where the repetition is for emphasis (Kimhi), whether or not the prophets are guilty of boasting. The repetition could also be to portray the giving of one dream report after another. For other repetitions of this type, called *geminatio* in the rhetorical handbooks, see "my innards, my innards" in 4:19; "came, came" in 46:20; and "will bend, will bend" in 51:3. On threefold repetitions, see Note for 7:4. There is no reason, with Duhm (and *BHS*), to emend the beginning of v 26 to get a threefold repetition here. The term "I have dreamed" (spoken once) may well be stereotyped. Gideon heard one of the Midianites saying to his fellow: "Look, I have dreamed (*ḥālamtî*) a dream . . ." (Judg 7:13). In the Mari texts, dream reports often begin *ina šuttiya . . .*, "In my dream . . ." (ARM X 50: "In my dream, I entered the temple . . . ; ARM X 51: "In my dream, Belet-biri stepped up to me . . ."), which Moran (1969a: 28) says is apparently a convention. On the Akkadian parallel to the Hebrew expression, see also Husser (1999: 142).

26–27. How long will there be in the mind of the prophets prophesying the lie—yes, prophets of their deceitful mind, those who plan to make my people forget my name with their dreams, which they recount each person to his fellow, as their fathers forgot my name through Baal? The question is rhetorical, pointing to a disputation currently taking place (Calvin); however, the long sentence dangles without a predicate nominative for the verb *hăyēš,* "will there be?" Commentators (Blayney; Duhm; Peake; Cornill; Volz; Rudolph; Holladay) resort therefore to emendation or a redivision of *hăyēš bĕlēb* ("will there be in the mind") beginning v 26, neither of which yields a happy solution. The general idea, however, is clear: Prophets with their lying dreams are causing people to forget Yahweh's name. Hebrew *haḥōšĕbîm* ("the ones planning") here denotes people who are devising evil plans (cf. 11:19; Ezek 11:2), whether or not they realize what they are doing.

26. *How long?* Hebrew *'ad-mātay* is a term of lament, appearing elsewhere in 4:14, 21; 12:4; 13:27; 31:22; 47:5; and with particular frequency in the Psalms (see Note for 4:21).

in the mind of the prophets. Hebrew has "in the heart" (*bĕlēb*), which in ancient thought is the seat of thought and the will (see Note for 11:20). In the NT, it is said that evil thoughts and evil speech issue from the heart (Matt 12:34–35; 15:18–19).

yes, prophets of their deceitful mind. Reading *ûnĕbî'ê tarmît libbām* with MT as a triple construct chain (cf. NJV), although emending and revocalizing with the T, S, and Vg to the participle *ûnibbĕ'ê*, which occurs in vv 26 and 32, would give the smoother reading: "yes, prophesying a deceit of their mind." Giesebrecht, Cornill, Rudolph, Weiser, and Holladay emend and revocalize. For *tarmît libbām* ("deceit of their mind") in a polemic much the same as the present one, see 14:14 (Q).

forget my name with their dreams. The LXX has "forget my law," although at the end of the verse it has "forgot my name." The T and Vg support MT with "my name" in both places. The LXX reading could be indebted to "they have forsaken my law" in 9:12[Eng 9:13], although there the verb is *'zb* ("forsake"); here it is *škḥ* ("forget"). The unstated assumption in the verse is that dreams conveying a false message result in people forgetting Yahweh.

they recount each person to his fellow. Hebrew *yĕsappĕrû 'îš lĕrē'ēhû.* The phraseology in Judg 7:13 is the same. The expression, "each person to his fellow," is common in Jeremiah (22:8; 23:27, 30, 35; 31:34; 34:15, 17; 46:16; cf. 7:5; 9:3, 4[Eng 9:4, 5]). In v 30, it means one prophet to another; here it means a prophet to anyone who will listen (Giesebrecht; Peake). In "The Epic of Gilgamesh" (VII 4:14; *ANET*[3] 87), Gilgamesh says to Enkidu after having dreamed a dream: "My friend, I saw a dream last night." Pharaoh's chief butler and baker related dreams to Joseph when the three of them were in prison (Gen 40:9–19).

as their fathers forgot my name through Baal. A comparison using *ka'ăšer*, on which see Note for 7:14. For the association of the "fathers" with Baal, see 2:5–8; 9:13[Eng 9:14]; and 19:3–5.

28. *The prophet who has with him a dream, let him recount his dream; and the one who has my word with him, let him speak my word faithfully.* A *distributio*, the purpose of which is to argue for faithful preachers of Yahweh's word. For other *distributios*, see 23:13–14 and 28:8–9. Jeremiah's willingness to let prophets recount their dreams is condescending irony (compare "They have their reward!" in Matt 6: 2, 5, 16). His point is that recounting dreams must not be

confused with faithful preaching of Yahweh's word. The shift to the singular sets forth a general principle, which is used here in defense of Jeremiah's preaching and maybe also to designate him "the prophet like Moses" (1:6–9; cf. Num 12:6–8). For another shift to the singular to state a general principle, see v 37. The LXX has "let him recount his dream," which some commentators (Cornill; Rudolph; Weiser; Bright; cf. *BHS*) adopt. The MT may have lost a *waw* through haplography (next word begins with *waw*).

faithfully. Or "truthfully." Hebrew *'ĕmet*. The term is an adverbial accusative (Giesebrecht; Cornill; cf. GKC §118m). On faithful preaching in the NT, see 2 Cor 2:17 and 2 Tim 2:15.

What is the grain to the straw? Hebrew *bar* is clean, threshed grain; *teben* the crushed stalks, i.e., "straw" or "chaff." This oracle may be an old proverb (Mc-Kane), here pressed into service to contrast the divine word with narrated dreams. The contrast is not, as Overholt (1970: 68) maintains, between dreams *and* words that call a wayward people to repentance, on the one hand, and dreams *and* words that lead people astray, on the other. It is between the true word of Yahweh and dreams that are false. The "grain and straw" image gets a different but not entirely contrary twist in the Talmud (Nedarim 8a–8b), where, in a discussion about how a ban placed upon one in a dream might be lifted, Rabbi Aḥa is said to have posed the question to Rabbi Ashi: "What if one was both banned and freed from the ban in a dream?" Rabbi Ashi answered: "Just as grain is impossible without straw, so is there no dream without meaningless matter."

oracle of Yahweh. The LXX omits this formula but then adds, "so are my words." This is probably from the *kh dbry* that begins the next oracle, which in the MT is pointed to read "so—my word." Here we seem to have a good case for dittography, since "my words" (but not "so") occurs in the LXX at the beginning of v 29. Janzen (1973: 12) proposes a double reading, conflated differently in MT and LXX. The suggestion by Polak (1984), who reads the verse as poetry, that the LXX with an "expanded colon" is the more original text, the MT being a secondary condensation, is unconvincing.

29. *Is it not so—my word is like fire . . . and like a hammer shattering rock?* Yahweh's words in the mouth of Jeremiah were to become like a fire that would consume people (5:14). Within him, the divine word was a fire he could not contain (20:8–9). Nahum spoke of Yahweh's wrath being poured out as a consuming fire and a force sufficient to shatter rocks (Nah 1:6). The ancient Hebrews, along with other peoples of preclassical antiquity, are said to have understood the spoken word as creative energy (Thornton 1945–46), i.e., words were invested with enormous power, enabling them to create and destroy, as well as to be self-fulfilling. Once spoken, words could not be called back. In support of this view it is pointed out that *dābār* means both "word" and "act," and it is said that a distinction between the two was not made by the ancient Hebrews. The latter point, however, has not gone unchallenged (Thiselton 1974: 287). Language of such a dynamic character is particularly in evidence when God speaks or when prophets speak on his behalf (Amos 3:8; Hos 6:5;

Grether 1934; 103–7; Dürr 1938: 92–114; Rabinowitz 1966: 316–21; 1972–73: 127–33). Yahweh speaks and the world comes into being (Gen 1:3; Ps 33:6); in Jeremiah's mouth, Yahweh's words destroy and recreate (Jer 1:9–10; 5:14; 23:29). Yahweh's word is also self-fulfilling (1:12; 4:28), and once spoken, it does not return to him void (Isa 55:10–11). Yet, Yahweh's word can be revoked when the human condition changes, as we know from Jer 18:8–10, and more dramatically from the tale about the prophet Jonah. Jeremiah attests to the power of the divine word more than any other prophet, at times providing rare glimpses into his inner self, where the word is said to have overcome him in his call (1:6–7), strongly affected his senses later on (23:9); when at one point he tried holding it in, he found he could not (20:8–9; Grether 1934: 105–6). This view of the power-laden divine word, albeit with changes, carried over into later Judaism (Sir 45:3; Wis Sol 18:15–16) and can be seen reflected in the Talmudic literature (Lauterbach 1939). One sees it reflected also in the pages of the NT (Matt 8:8, 26, 32; 9:22; 16:19; 18:18; 24:35).

hammer. Hebrew *paṭṭîš*. The hammer of a blacksmith (see Isa 41:7 and Note for Jer 50:23).

30. *Therefore look I am against the prophets . . . who steal my words each person from his fellow.* "Therefore" (*lākēn*) introduces judgment, although the judgment here is unspecified. Kimhi says that Yahweh is against these prophets, to destroy them. More difficult is an explanation of the charge being made. The verb "steal" (*gnb*) means that these prophets are appropriating something not rightfully theirs. That something, says Yahweh, is "my words." But how can prophets under indictment be speaking Yahweh's words? Rashi and Kimhi think that the prophets in question are stealing oracles from prophets who are genuine. Since Jeremiah and other genuine prophets occasionally prophesied salvation for Judah, also judgment on Judah's enemies, the peace prophets could have taken these oracles and used them improperly. Peace was not now in the offing for Judah. Prophets also should be reporting their own revelations, not the revelations of other prophets.

31. *Look I am against the prophets . . . who heed their own tongue and oracle an oracle.* Here is a derisive judgment against prophets who speak nonsense, emanating from themselves or others—in any case a message not from Yahweh. The verb *lqh*, usually "to take," is used in an unconventional way. Rashi interpreted it to mean "teach" in the sense of 9:4[Eng 9:5]: "They teach their tongue to speak a lie." Holladay says the prophets are "taking charge" of their own tongue. The verb could also mean "heed, obey," as in Prov 10:8. Whatever its precise meaning, prophets are beholden to their own tongues, not preaching from the mouth of Yahweh.

and oracle an oracle. Hebrew *wayyin'ămû nĕ'ūm*. Another cognate accusative (see Note for 22:16), where *yin'ămû* ("they oracle") may be Jeremiah's own coinage (Bright). The combination makes a wordplay. The verb is otherwise unattested in the OT, although Gelston (1993) suggests revocalizing the problematic *hinnām* ("behold them") in Isa 41:27 to a Qal participle of *nûm* with the definite article, *hannām* ("the speaker"). He notes that in 1QIs[a] the reading for this term is *hnwmh*. A verb *nûm* (denominative of *ně'ūm*), meaning "to speak, say," does appear in postbiblical Hebrew (*nûm* I in *Dict Talm*, 887). The LXX has "and sleep their sleep," which Giesebrecht notes renders the verb *nûm*, "to slumber." Giesebrecht thinks the LXX misunderstood the Hebrew, which it probably did, although it may also be associating sleeping with the dreaming of dreams. It should also be noted that at Mari dreams do produce oracles (Husser 1999: 44–46).

32. *Look I am against those prophesying lying dreams . . . yes, they recount them and lead my people astray with their lies and with their wantonness.* This oracle correlates closely with the opening discourse in vv 25–28a, which may develop from it. Some commentators (Giesebrecht; Cornill; Volz; Rudolph; Weiser; Bright; Thompson) add "the prophets" after "Look I am against," with the LXX and Vg, which brings the wording in line with the wording in vv 30 and 31. Precise parallelism, however, is not required in three successive oracles. Read therefore the MT.

and lead my people astray. In v 13 this charge was leveled, not surprisingly, against the prophets of Baal. But prophets of Yahweh also lead the covenant people astray when they traffic in lies and wanton behavior, which is what they are doing.

their wantonness. The noun *paḥăzût* is a *hapax legomenon* in the OT, but together with its cognate verb *pḥz*, it appears to denote immoral and reckless behavior, often of a sexual nature (Greenfield 1978). Greenfield suggests for the root a meaning of "wantonness" or "licentiousness," which supports the Qal definitions "be wanton, reckless" given in BDB. The noun *paḥăzût* he translates as "lewdness," pointing out that this meaning is well documented in Syriac and Palestinian Aramaic, as well as in passages in the Testament of Levi (Col. b II. 14–16), Sirach (19:2; 23:5; 41:17), and various texts from Qumran (Enoch; 4Q184). Akkadian *paḥāzu* means "behave arrogantly" (AHw 2: 811); and in postbiblical Hebrew, *pḥz* means "be blown up, be haughty, heedless" (*Dict Talm*, 1152), where the behavior is also judged to be sinful or preliminary to a fall. De Hoop (1997: 24) in a contextual analysis concludes that the verb means "to deceive" and that the noun in the present verse means "deceit." But the results of his contextual analysis are not compelling, and he is overly dismissive of the etymological evidence supporting traditional renderings. Here in the present verse and probably also in Zeph 3:4, where the participle *pōḥăzîm* occurs, we are most likely talking about prophets' wanton behavior, which in Jer 29:23 is seen to go hand in hand with trafficking in lies.

For I, I did not send them. This is a stereotyped disclaimer in the prose for prophets who prophesy a lie in Yahweh's name (14:14–15; 23:32; 27:15; 29:9, 31), echoing what is said in the poetry of v 21 (see Holladay 1960: 357; and H. Weippert 1973: 118–21).

and they are no profit whatever to this people. Hebrew *wĕhô'êl lō'-yô'îlû*. The language is Jeremianic; note the expressions "No Profit(s)" in 2:8 and 11; and "no profit" in 16:19, where reference is to Baal or the Baals. Here it is Yahweh prophets who profit the people nothing.

MESSAGE AND AUDIENCE

Yahweh in the opening discourse says that he has heard the lying prophecies uttered in his name by prophets who repeatedly say, "I have dreamed." How long must this continue—schemes of no good that make the covenant people forget his name, just as people earlier forgot his name because of Baal? If the prophet has a dream, let him tell his dream, but the prophet who has Yahweh's word, let him speak that word faithfully. Will the audience perceive that the problem now is with competing Yahweh prophets and their modes of revelation, some of them true and some of them false?

In the first two oracles following this discourse the audience is asked to have another look at the character of the divine word. Supporting a faithful proclamation of the word in contrast to lying dreams, Yahweh says, "What is grain compared to straw?" Also, do people not know that the word of Yahweh "is like a fire, and like a hammer shattering rock?"

In the judgment oracles, Yahweh says he is against prophets who do not have his word to speak, and who make up for their lack by stealing his words—or words alleged to be his—from other prophets. Yahweh is also against prophets who obey their own tongue and "oracle an oracle," who prophesy lying dreams and lead the covenant people astray by their lies and wanton behavior. In conclusion, Yahweh says he did not send these prophets, he did not command them; they are, in a word, no profit whatever to the covenant people.

The opening speech and the oracles following best reflect the early reign of Zedekiah, i.e., 597 to 594 B.C., when Jeremiah was in greatest conflict with other prophets (Volz).

When the opening polemic is heard following the divine council speech of vv 18 and 21–22, the audience will perhaps perceive an ironic contrast between prophets who have not "heard" Yahweh in council (v 18) and Yahweh's now having "heard" the lies that these dreamers are speaking in his name (v 25). Also reinforced will be the point that prophets of any earthly use must first have been present in the heavenly council to hear what Yahweh commanded and then been sent by him to correct people given to evil behavior. True prophets could not be more sharply distinguished from prophets who are false. The powerful divine word in the oracle of v 29 may also echo for the audience the powerful judgment pronounced by Jeremiah on the prophets in vv 19–20.

Mendelssohn in Aria #17 of his great oratorio "Elijah," after the descent of heavenly fire on Mt. Carmel, the confession of the people, and Elijah's command that the prophets of Baal be seized and killed by the Brook Kishon (1 Kgs 18:38–40), introduces these words from v 29:

Is not his word like a fire, and like a hammer that breaketh the rock, a hammer that breaketh the rock, that breaketh the rock into pieces? like a fire, like a fire! like a hammer that breaketh, that breaketh the rock? His word is like a fire; and like a hammer, a hammer that breaketh the rock. . . .

One can also hear the breaking of rock and incendiary lightning in Leonard Bernstein's "Jeremiah" (Symphony #1; 1942). In the first two movements, Prophecy and Profanation, dissonant strains from the strings and woodwinds are interrupted repeatedly by thunderous poundings on the drums and crashing sounds of the cymbals. The composer explains these movements as an attempt to parallel in feeling the intensive pleas of the prophet with his people (Prophecy) and to create a general sense of the destruction and chaos brought upon the nation by pagan corruption of the priesthood and among the people (Profanation). Bernstein's aim in the symphony as a whole was to deal with the crisis of faith, which, in his view, was the main crisis of the twentieth century.

7. Speaking of 'Burdens' . . . (23:33–40)

23 [33]Now when this people or the prophet or a priest asks you: 'What is the burden of Yahweh?' then you shall say to them: 'You are the burden,[a] and I will cast you off!' — oracle of Yahweh. [34]So the prophet or the priest or the people who says, 'the burden of Yahweh,' yes, I will reckon against that person and against his house.

[35]Thus you shall say each person to his fellow and each person to his brother, 'What has Yahweh answered?' or 'What has Yahweh spoken?' [36]But 'the burden of Yahweh' you shall not again remember, for the burden becomes to each person his own word, and you pervert the words of the living God, Yahweh of hosts, our God. [37]So you shall say to the prophet: 'What has Yahweh answered you?' or 'What has Yahweh spoken?' [38]But if 'the burden of Yahweh' you say:
Therefore thus said Yahweh:
Because you have said this word, 'the burden of Yahweh,' when I sent to you saying, you shall not say 'the burden of Yahweh': [39]Therefore look I, yes I will surely lift you up and cast you out — also the city that I gave to you and to your fathers — from my presence. [40]And I will put upon you an eternal reproach and an eternal disgrace that will not be forgotten.

RHETORIC AND COMPOSITION

In these concluding verses of the King and Prophet Collection, are two discourses having to do with the tired expression "the burden of Yahweh." The first is an oracle from Yahweh to Jeremiah containing a word for the people (vv 33–34); the second is Jeremiah preaching that word, after which a second oracle is delivered (vv 35–40). This second oracle, which conveys judgment, is strengthened by a double "therefore" (*lākēn*). In the LXX, vv 7–8 of the chapter have been placed after v 40.

---

[a]Redistributing the consonants of MT to read *'attem hammaśā'*, with the LXX, Vg, and most modern translations.

The present unit is separated from what precedes by content and a summary oracle in v 32 (see Rhetoric and Composition for 23:25–32). The lower limit is clear, indicated in M^A and M^P by a *petuḥah* and in M^L by a *setumah* after v 40, which is also the chapter division. The M^P also has a *petuḥah* after v 38, which may be to divide the two judgment statements introduced by "therefore."

There is a broad consensus that v 33 stems from Jeremiah but not vv 34–40, which are said to be a late (some would say a very late) addition (Volz; Rudolph; Weiser; Hyatt; Bright; Holladay; McKane). Duhm and Thiel (1973: 253) take all of vv 33–40 as the product of a late author. Lindblom (1965: 290) calls vv 34–40 one of the longest glosses in the OT, "a specimen of Talmudic learning, which has nothing at all to do with the prophecies of Jeremiah"—a real stretch, to say the least, of the term "gloss"! In any case, his point and the line generally taken is that v 33, with its wordplay on *maśśāʾ* and the retort by Jeremiah, has a ring of authenticity, whereas vv 34–40, which ban the expression "the burden of Yahweh," breathe a different spirit, one more akin to the debates of scribes and Rabbis in later Judaism. Holladay adds that the style, phraseology, and pronoun shifts in (the MT of) vv 34–40 betray scribal "carelessness." The verses are also said to lack subtlety and be without a trace of irony.

The "different spirit" argument for vv 34–40 will not stand up under scrutiny. Even McKane sees in these verses an attempt to recapture the conflict between "peace" and "doom" prophecy in the time of Jeremiah. The comments of Overholt (1970: 70–71) are along similar lines. Jones says that vv 34–40 are definitely more than scribal comment, coming either from Jeremiah or a prophet in the tradition of Jeremiah. Verse 36, in his view, lies at the very center of authentic prophetic tradition, and vv 39–40 are typical prophetic judgment. Holladay's appraisal of vv 34–40 as a "careless and overblown" text, except for a few infelicities of Hebrew grammar and style, is largely contrived. The MT makes better sense than Holladay is willing to admit. Once the repeated terms, "the burden of Yahweh," "What has Yahweh answered?" and "What has Yahweh spoken?" are set aside, everything remaining is familiar Jeremiah prose. The expression in v 35, "each person to his fellow and each person to his brother," is compared by Holladay to another usage in 31:34, but he says the phrase there has a place; here it is prolix. Why it is prolix here and not there is left unexplained.

What Holladay also fails to note is that "each person to his fellow," taken singly, is a very common phrase in Jeremiah, occurring slightly altered also in the poetry (see Note for 23:27). Other Jeremianic words and phrases, to which Holladay normally pays close attention, go unnoted. The verb *pqd* ("reckon, call to account") in v 34 occurs 60 times in Jeremiah (see Note for 5:9), and "you shall not again remember" in v 36 is a signature expression in the prose (see *lōʾ* + *zkr* + *ʿôd* in 3:16; 11:19; and 31:34; also *lōʾ* + other verbs + *ʿôd* in 3:16, 17; 31:29, 34, 39). The shame vocabulary in v 40 is all Jeremianic: 1) the phrase "an eternal disgrace that will not be forgotten" is a prosaic version of "eternal disgrace will not be forgotten" in the poetry of 20:11; and "will not be forgotten," by itself, occurs in the poetry of 50:5; 2) "reproach" (ḥerpâ) is a common Jeremianic term; and 3) "disgrace" (in the form kĕlimmâ) occurs three other times in Jeremianic poetry and prose (see Notes). There is no reason based on language to assign vv 34–40 to an author in the postexilic period. Further, alternation of speaker and audience occurs throughout the discourse of Jeremiah and is not to be wondered at. The only verb out of the ordinary here is the second person singular imperfect in v 37, tōʾmar, which can—and in this case should—be translated impersonally (see Notes). Other shifts between singular and plural verbs make perfectly good sense once the discourses are rightly assessed. As for the claim that vv 34–40 do not breathe the spirit of Jeremiah, this is "psychologizing" of the same sort used to deny the Sabbath day prophecy in 17:19–27 to Jeremiah (see Rhetoric and Composition there) and should not influence exegesis in the way that it has in the past.

The present unit consists of two basic discourses:

| I | Yahweh giving Jeremiah an oracle for the people | vv 33–34 |
| II | Jeremiah giving the people this oracle and another | vv 35–40 |

In Discourse I, Yahweh is seen to be the speaker on the basis of the judgment statements "and I will cast you off" (wĕnāṭaštî) and "yes, I will reckon (ûpāqadtî) against that person and against his house." Jeremiah is seen to be the addressee because of the singular verbal suffix on "asks you" (yišʾālĕkā) and the singular verb "then you shall say" (wĕʾāmartā). The oracle is destined for a multiple audience because of the plural pronouns "to them" (ʾălêhem) and "you" (ʾetkem).

In Discourse II, Jeremiah is the speaker because of the inclusive "our God" (ʾĕlōhênû) in v 36. A multiple audience is addressed because of the plural "you shall say" (tōʾmĕrû) in v 35; the plural "you shall not remember" (lōʾ tizkĕrû) and plural "you pervert" (hăpaktem) in v 36; and the plural "you say" (tōʾmērû) beginning v 38. Plural verbs and pronouns continue in the divine oracle of vv 38–40. The second-singular imperfect in v 37, tōʾmar, states a general principle: "you say" or "one shall say."

The first discourse (vv 33–34) contains this structured repetition:

I	Now when *this people or the prophet or a priest* asks you:	v 33
	'What is the burden of Yahweh?'	
	. . . .	
	So the prophet or the priest or the people who says,	v 34
	'the burden of Yahweh' . . .	

The second discourse (vv 35–40) also has a nicely balanced key word structure:

II	*Thus you shall say . . . 'What has Yahweh answered?' or*	v 35
	'What has Yahweh spoken?'	
	So you shall say . . . 'What has Yahweh answered you?' or	v 37
	'What has Yahweh spoken?'	

Therefore	*lākēn*	v 38b
Therefore	*lākēn*	v 39
. . . . *I gave to you* . . .	*nātattî lākem*	
And I will put upon you	*wĕnātattî ʿălêkem*	v 40

A single verb ties the two discourses together, making an inclusio for the whole:

I	*and I will cast you off*	*wĕnāṭaštî*	v 33
II	*and I will cast you out*	*wĕnāṭaštî*	v 39

NOTES

23:33. *Now when this people or the prophet or a priest asks you: 'What is the burden of Yahweh?' then you shall say to them: 'You are the burden, and I will cast you off!'* Yahweh in this oracle is telling Jeremiah what to say when ordinary people, prophets, and priests taunt him with the question "What is the burden of Yahweh?" Anticipated questions paired up with divine answers in readiness occur elsewhere in Jeremiah, as well as in Ezekiel (13:12–14; 15:1–4; 16:10–13; Ezek 21:12[Eng 21:7]; 37:18–19; cf. Long 1971: 134). Some questions and answers are for a later time (see Note for 5:19, with a parallel from the Annals of Ashurbanipal). The answer here is clarified by the readings of the LXX and Vg, which preserve Jeremiah's sharp reply, "You are the burden, and I will cast you off!"

You are the burden. J. D. Michaelis (1793: 200) saw already that the correct Hebrew reading was *'attem hammaśśāʾ*, "You are the burden!" which most commentators and modern Versions now adopt. Michaelis also considered that a long form of the pronoun with terminal *hēʾ* might be used in the expression, in which case the reading would be "You are a burden!" This suggestion has been made more recently by Wernberg-Møller (1956), who said after noting the long form in the Qumran scrolls that the form was in fact ancient. The MT has an incomprehensible *'et-mah-maśśāʾ* ("What burden?" preceded by *'et*), which may be a deliberate redivision and repointing of consonants to suppress a reading judged infelicitous (Walker 1957). The MT reading, in any case, is corrupt (GKC §117m note), and the translations of the AV ("What burden?"), NJV ("What is the burden?"), and NIV ("What oracle?") perpetuate the corruption. The reconstructed Hebrew preserves a wordplay on *maśśāʾ*, which literally and metaphorically means "burden" in the sense of a load and "burden" in the sense of a divine oracle (Casanowicz 1893: #234; Yellin 1933–34: 3). It is generally agreed that two separate nouns derive from the verb *nśʾ*, "to lift (up), carry" (BDB; KB³), which makes the terms homonyms (McKane). A *maśśāʾ* is something "lifted up" (2 Kgs 9:25: "Yahweh lifted up [*nāśāʾ*] this burden [*maśśāʾ*] against him"). The literal meaning, not used in the present verse, is the amount of weight a beast is able to carry (Exod 23:5; 2 Kgs 5:17;

8:9). In the Arad ostraca (#3 line 4) it is the load put upon a donkey (Aharoni 1981: 17–18). Jeremiah uses the term literally in his Sabbath day oracles (17:21–22, 24–27). For a metaphorical use of "burden" meaning "load," which is what appears here in Jeremiah's answer, see Job 7:20, where Job says to God: "[Why] have I become a burden to you?" Compare also Num 11:11, 17; and Deut 1:12. Many scholars (following J. D. Michaelis and Giesebrecht, D. FriedrichGraf) explain *maśśā'* as deriving from the expression "to lift up the voice," *nāśā' qôl* (Gen 21:16; 27:38; Isa 52:8; cf. H.-P. Müller, "maśśā'" in *TDOT* 9: 20–21). In its technical sense, meaning "oracle," *maśśā'* is employed widely in the prophetic books, often as a superscription (Isa 13:1; 14:28; 15:1; Nah 1:1; Hab 1:1; Ezek 12:10; Zech 9:1; 12:1; Mal 1:1; and often). In Jeremiah, the term meaning "oracle" occurs only here, where the connotation is nega-tive. This negativeness carries over into Lam 2:14, which states that prophets saw enticing but empty "burdens" (*maś'ôt*) for the people.

Much discussion has centered on whether *maśśā'* may in fact mean "oracle of disaster." The idea is present in Jerome, Calvin, and others (Blayney; Giese-brecht; Gehman 1940–41; de Boer 1948: 214; H.-P. Müller, "maśśā'" in *TDOT* 9: 23) that the "burden" spoken by the prophets is heavy because it contains divine judgment. Midrash Genesis Rabbah (44:6) says that the Rab-bis chose "burden" as the severest of ten designations for prophecy, citing as a prooftext "like a heavy burden" (*kĕmaśśā' kābēd*) in Ps 38:5[Eng 38:4]; cf. de Boer 1948: 206. But McKane (1980a: 37–38) says the idea of *maśśā'* being a doom prophecy was refuted by J. D. Michaelis, who claimed it was also used for oracles having nothing to do with doom. But the passages cited, Prov 31:1; Lam 2:14; and Zech 12:1, do not support his claim. The consensus seems to be that, while the idea of "disaster" is not inherent in *maśśā'*, the term does nevertheless connote disaster in prophetic contexts. This has a direct bearing on the present verse, for if "burden" means "oracle of disaster," then the people's question is likely asked in derision. They are saying, "Well now, Jere-miah, what disastrous burden do you have to unload today?" Rashi takes the question as one expressing derision; so also Kimḥi. Compare the mocking words put to Jeremiah in 17:15. So we are not talking here about a serious re-quest for a divine oracle, such as Zedekiah made during the final siege of Jerusalem (21:2; 37:3, 17), which is what Volz (also Rudolph and Weiser) imagines as background for a detached v 33, but rather a statement by people, prophets, and priests deriding Jeremiah's prophecies of doom or mocking their nonfulfillment.

the prophet or a priest. Some commentators (Cornill; Volz; Rudolph; Weiser; Holladay; and McKane) delete one or both terms, arguing that they are added from v 34. But there is no basis for the deletion, which appears simply to be a streamlining of the verse thought to be the genuine kernel of vv 33–40. There is, in fact, a chiasmus in the terms of vv 34–35: "people / prophet or priest // prophet or priest / people." McKane's argument (1980a: 52–53, also in his commentary) that "the people" (*hā'ām*) has an all-inclusive meaning of the Judahite community in v 33, thereby rendering "prophet or priest" superflu-

ous, but a reduced meaning of "laymen" in v 34, is spurious exegesis and
should be rejected. The whole of v 34 restates the judgment in straight talk via
the wordplay of v 33. The T here substitutes "scribe" for "prophet," as it does
elsewhere (see Note for 6:13).

And I will cast you off. Hebrew *wĕnāṭaštî.* A converted perfect, as also in v 39.
The verb *nṭš* means "to cast off, abandon" (7:29; 12:7). Here Yahweh readies
himself to throw off a troublesome burden (cf. Isa 1:14). But is not Yahweh the
God who carries his people like a long-suffering father and lifts them high on
eagle's wings (Exod 19:4; Deut 1:31; 32:11–12; Hos 11:3; Isa 46:3–4; 63:9)?

34. *So the prophet or the priest or the people who says, 'the burden of Yahweh,'*
yes, I will reckon against that person and against his house. Here the opaque
judgment of v 33 is restated in plain language. This rhetoric is seen often in
Jeremiah, where transparent restatements come immediately after metaphorical, hyperbolic, or ironic statements (in poetry, see the signature bicolon in
Note for 3:3). Yahweh's judgment here is in response to the abuse of a consecrated phrase (Cheyne). The phrase, therefore, must be taken out of service.
The oath "by Yahweh's life" was banned at an earlier time because of misuse
(see Note for 4:2, and compare Matt 5:33–37). Ezekiel censured the widely-
used "oracle of Yahweh" (*nĕʾūm yhwh*) formula, although stopping short of an
outright prohibition (Ezek 13:6–7). Whenever language suffers abuse, becomes empty by mindless repetition, or is compromised in some other way by
people not using it properly, there is justification for banning it and replacing
it with meaningful language. That is precisely what is happening here: the
question "What is the burden of Yahweh?" is to be banned and replaced by the
questions "What has Yahweh answered?" or "What has Yahweh spoken?"

yes, I will reckon against that person and against his house. Divine judgment
comes not only to errant individuals, but to their entire house (20:6). See retribution discussion in Note for 31:29.

35. *Thus you shall say each person to his fellow and each person to his brother.*
The plural *tōʾmĕrû* ("you shall say") indicates that Jeremiah, now the speaker,
is addressing a multiple audience (see Rhetoric and Composition). He is telling people how to inquire from anyone they meet—not just from himself or
from other prophets—concerning revelations that have come from Yahweh.

'What has Yahweh answered?' Hebrew *meh-ʿānâ yhwh.* The verb *ʿnh* ("to answer") occurs repeatedly in the OT to denote God's response to prayers offered
by prophets as well as other individuals, also denote a divine revelation, even
when a specific request has not been made (33:3; 42:4; 1 Sam 7:9; Mic 3:7;
Hab 2:2; Malamat 1966: 212–13). In 33:3, Yahweh says, "Call to me and I will
answer you (*wĕʾeʿĕnekā*)." The verb *ʿnh* appears in the eighth-century Zakir Inscription (A 11; Donner and Röllig 1962–64 I: 37; #202; II: 205; ANET[3] 655;
CS II 155), where King Zakir of Hamath says when ten kings, led by Ben-
hadad III, had come up against him: "Then I lifted up (*wʾšʾ*) my hand(s) to
Bĕʿēl Šĕmayin, and Bĕʿēl Šĕmayin answered me (*wyʿnny*)." In the celebrated
contest on Mt. Carmel between Elijah and the prophets of Baal, the prophets
of Baal were first to cry out to their god: "O Baal, answer us," but no one

answered. Elijah, when it came his turn, also cried out: "Answer me, Yahweh, answer me," and the fire of the Lord fell (1 Kgs 18:26, 37).

'What has Yahweh spoken?' Hebrew mah-dibber yhwh. This question employs the common verb dbr ("to speak"), which reports divine revelations throughout the book of Jeremiah (10:1; 11:17; 13:15; 16:10; 26:13, 19; 27:13; 30:4; and often). Balaam, as reported in Num 22:8, says to the elders of Moab: "I will bring back word to you as Yahweh speaks (yĕdabbēr) to me."

36–37. The LXX lacks the following words: "and you pervert the words of the living God, Yahweh of hosts, our God. So you shall say to the prophet: 'What has Yahweh answered you?'" This could be attributed to haplography (homoeoarcton: w . . . w), although the LXX may have been forced to translate a damaged or partly unreadable text. Cornill thought that the LXX had a corrupt text. Theodotion has the omitted words. Also, one will note that what remains of v 37 in the LXX has been expanded. It reads: kai dia ti elalāsen kurios ho theos hymōn ("and wherefore spoke the Lord our God?"). Where then did it get "our God," if not from the end of v 36? Janzen (1973: 99–100, 223–24), conceding that vv 36–38 in both MT and LXX have problems, says the present omission may result from the accidental loss of a line. This loss could then result from haplography, although one still wonders how the LXX managed to preserve "our God" from the missing words.

36. you shall not again remember. Another stereotyped phrase in the Jeremiah prose (see Rhetoric and Composition), for which reason the Qal tizkĕrû ("remember") need not be repointed, with some commentators (Giesebrecht; Duhm; Cornill; Volz; Rudolph; Bright; Holladay; McKane), to an H-stem tazkîrû ("mention"). They cite LXX's mē onomazete, "you shall not speak of" (cf. AV: "shall ye mention no more"). The expression shall no longer even be called to mind. It is to be forgotten.

for the burden becomes to each person his own word. The phrase is difficult, although like the earlier phrase of v 31, "who heed their own tongue and oracle an oracle," one can discern here a debunking of prophets who speak their own words and not the words of Yahweh. In v 16 the peace prophets were said to be speaking "a vision of their own heart, not from the mouth of Yahweh." Reference then is not to genuine prophecy (pace NEB; REB; McKane; Jones) but to prophecy that misconstrues words of the living God, Yahweh of hosts (RSV; NRSV). Nothing is gained by dropping the hē' on hammaśśā' ("the burden"), as proposed by Giesebrecht and Duhm, or by reading the article as a hē' interrogative, as proposed by Ehrlich (1912: 305), Rudolph, and Bright.

and you pervert the words of the living God, Yahweh of hosts, our God. The verb hpk means "to change, overturn, pervert." For the expression "living God" ('ĕlōhîm ḥayyîm), see 10:10. In 2:13 and 17:13 Yahweh is called "the spring of living water" (mĕqôr mayim ḥayyîm).

37. So you shall say to the prophet. The second-singular imperfect, tō'mar, is here an impersonal directive, such as we have in modern English; the verb could also be translated "one shall say" (Volz; Rudolph; cf. GKC §144h; Prov 19:25; Isa 7:25). Note how the singular imperfect intervenes to set forth a gen-

eral principle in 23:28 (see Note there). It is not necessary, then, to emend to a second plural with the LXX and S (*pace* Duhm; Cornill; Holladay).

38. *But if 'the burden of Yahweh' you say. Mezudath David*[b] paraphrases: "If after all these warnings, you still say . . ." (Rosenberg). The LXX omits these words, but most commentators retain. McKane deletes, saying that the LXX reads more easily. But this is debatable. After a statement of general principle, a phrase such as the present one is almost required to resume the direct address and introduce the oracle following, which states the consequences in the event of noncompliance. The omission could also be due to haplography, since the end of LXX v 37 has *ho theos hymōn* ("our God"), which presupposes Heb *'ĕlō-hênû* (homoeoteleuton: *w . . . w*).

39. *Therefore look I, yes I will surely lift you up.* Harsh judgment comes in subtle language, for which reason the Hebrew here is uncertain, and translation difficulties were experienced early. The MT takes the two verbs as coming from the root *nšh = nš'* (with a *shin*), which could be the verb meaning "to forget." The infinitive absolute, *nāšō'*, has a final *'aleph*, reflecting Aramaic and later Hebrew spelling (GKC §23 l). The words *wĕnāšîtî 'etkem nāšō'* might then translate, "yes, I will forget you continually," or "yes, I will forget you utterly" (the infinitive absolute after a verb can be to intensify; cf. GKC §113r). The former reading would scarcely have been acceptable in later Judaism. The latter is bad enough, which may be why the Mandelkern Lexicon does not list the verb under *nšh*, "to forget," but rather under *nšh*, "to lend" (Cornill, citing Hitzig, suggests the translation: "I will loan you out"). Kimḥi interprets the verb to mean "I will forget." The AV has "I will utterly forget you" and is followed by the NJV and NIV but by no other English translation. Most commentators and modern Versions read the first or both verbs as emanating from *nš'* (with a *śin*), "to lift up," which appear in a few Heb MSS and find support more or less in the translations of LXX, Aq, Symm, S, and Vg. The LXX translates the first verb with *lambanō* ("I will seize"), omitting "you" + the infinitive absolute. The advantage of this reading is that it repeats the play on *maśśā'* in v 33. We can, however, retain "you" + the infinitive absolute, simply repointing *nāšō'* ("forget") to *nāśō'* ("lift up").

and cast you out—also the city that I gave to you and to your fathers—from my presence. The verb *nṭš* ("cast out") is the same verb that occurs in v 33. Calvin thinks that reference here is to exile, although noting that the verb "cast out" ill suits stones of a city. His solution is to give the phrase figurative meaning: God will take away the city and its inhabitants as if they were driven away by the wind. But McKane points out that *nṭš* in the sense of "abandon" does fit the image of a city—i.e., Yahweh will abandon Jerusalem. We have then *nṭš* being used in two senses: the people will be "cast out (into exile)," and the city will be "abandoned." Kimḥi says that Yahweh will forsake the people and the

---

[b]*Mezudath David* ("Fortress of David") is the second part of a two-part commentary on the Prophets and Hagiographa written by the eighteenth-century Jewish biblical exegete David Altschuler of Jaworow, Galicia (modern Poland). It was completed and published by his son, Jehiel Hillel, in 1780–82 (*EncJud* 2: 783–84).

city. It is also possible that the phrase "also the city that I gave to you and to your fathers" is a later addition. But "city" can stand in the text (*pace* Volz, who substitutes "land"), which argues for retaining the entire phrase.

from my presence. Hebrew *mēʿal pānāy*. The LXX omits, but *apo prosōpou mou* is present in Aq, Symm, and Theod. Cain after his sin and banishment went out "from the presence of Yahweh" (Gen 4:16). David, too, after his sin asked that Yahweh not cast him away from his presence but restore him (Ps 51:13–14[Eng 51:11–12]).

40. *an eternal reproach and an eternal disgrace that will not be forgotten.* Hebrew *ḥerpat ʿôlām ûkĕlimmût ʿôlām ʾăšer lōʾ tiššākēaḥ*. This terminology of shame is all Jeremianic. Hebrew *kĕlimmût* ("disgrace") is a *hapax legomenon* in the OT, but the more common *kĕlimmâ* occurs in 3:25; 20:11; and 51:51. "Reproach" (*ḥerpâ*) is very common in Jeremiah (see Note for 24:9), appearing together with "disgrace" in 51:51. The expression "will not be forgotten" occurs also in 20:11 and 50:5; in the former almost the exact phrase appears as here: "eternal disgrace will not be forgotten." On shame in the ancient world, see Note for 2:26.

MESSAGE AND AUDIENCE

Yahweh in the first oracle tells Jeremiah how to answer anyone in conversation who says, "What is the burden of Yahweh?" He is to say, "You are the burden, and I will cast you off." Not covenant language exactly but having the sound, nevertheless, of a covenant curse. Yahweh restates his answer unambiguously: Whoever says "the burden of Yahweh" can expect punishment, and it will be carried out not only upon the errant individual but upon his entire house. This judgment seems unusually harsh for just using a disallowed expression, but in the background is doubtless a problem of greater magnitude. If the question put to Jeremiah is a taunt by clergy and people more attuned to prophecies of peace, the ban will have the greater purpose of censuring individuals who refuse to hear Yahweh's true word, and the judgment will have the greater purpose of punishing individuals who are putting their trust in a false word and are thereby becoming false themselves.

Jeremiah conveys this word to the people, emphasizing that by using this tired expression and by peddling burdens of their own making they are, in fact, perverting words of the living God, Yahweh of hosts. Not by accident does Jeremiah add "our God," which affirms a oneness with the people. If the people do not dispense with empty phrases and empty prophecies, a second oracle is given them. It spells out what will happen if the people disobey the word they have just heard. Yahweh will reward their disobedience and reckless disregard for his true word by lifting them up and casting them out from his presence. The city given to them and to their fathers he will also abandon. A people that revels in heaping abuse on Yahweh's messengers will, in the end, earn for themselves eternal reproach and eternal disgrace. Whereas the abuse they toss about will be forgotten, the shame they are destined to bear will endure.

These two discourses are probably to be dated to the reign of Zedekiah, though not necessarily during the final siege, which is when Volz dates v 33. They seem to reflect Jeremiah's conflict with the "peace" prophets early in Zedekiah's reign, i.e., 597–594 B.C. Nothing here emanates from the postexilic period, when the conflict and fuss about what precise language to use would be in the distant past. When the present words are heard after the divine words immediately preceding, the audience will perceive two polemics in tandem: one against lying dreams and one against the tired phrase "the burden of Yahweh."

II. Prepare for a Life in Exile
(24:1–29:32)

◆

A. Good Figs Gone for Export (24:1–10)

24 ¹Yahweh showed me, and there! two baskets of figs situated in front of the temple of Yahweh—after Nebuchadrezzar, king of Babylon, had exiled Jeconiah son of Jehoiakim, king of Judah, and the princes of Judah and the craftsmen and the smiths from Jerusalem and brought them to Babylon. ²The one basket had very good figs, like the early figs, and the other basket very bad figs, which could not be eaten because they were so bad. ³And Yahweh said to me: 'What do you see, Jeremiah?' And I said: 'Figs! The good figs are very good, and the bad ones very bad, which cannot be eaten because they are so bad.' ⁴And the word of Yahweh came to me:

⁵Thus said Yahweh, God of Israel: Like these good figs, so will I regard the exiles of Judah whom I sent away from this place to the land of the Chaldeans—for good; ⁶and I will keep my eye upon them for good, and I will bring them back to this land, and I will build them up and not overthrow, and I will plant them and not uproot. ⁷And I will give them a heart to know me, for I am Yahweh, and they will be a people to me, and I, I will be God to them, for they shall return to me with their whole heart.

⁸And like the bad figs, which could not be eaten because they were so bad, indeed thus said Yahweh: So will I make Zedekiah, king of Judah and his princes and the remnant of Jerusalem, the ones who remain in this land, and the ones who dwell in the land of Egypt. ⁹Yes, I will make them a fright, a calamity to all the kingdoms of the earth, a reproach and a proverb, a taunt and a swearword, in all the places where I shall disperse them. ¹⁰And I will send against them the sword, the famine, and the pestilence, until they are consumed from upon the soil that I gave to them and to their fathers.

RHETORIC AND COMPOSITION

Here, following the King and Prophet Appendix (chaps. 21–23), begins another major section in the book of Jeremiah, although the LXX is different in that the Foreign Nation Oracles are located after 25:13a. In the MT, a section comprising chaps. 24–36 contains: 1) "The Book of Restoration" (30–33), which is an independent collection still intact; 2) a pair of prose groupings sub-sequently broken up to form the present sequence: "The Jehoiakim Cluster" (25–26, 35–36) and "The Zedekiah Cluster" (24, 27–29); and 3) a single prose narrative (34), which has been inserted next to chap. 35 for polemical reasons. Some scholars (Bright; Boadt; Carroll; Rofé 1989: 393–95; Jones; Parke-Taylor 2000: 297) view chap. 24 as a conclusion, which it is not. Form, content, and location all point to its being a beginning. Like chap. 1 opening the Jeremiah book, in which one finds the almond branch and boiling pot visions (1:11–14), the present chapter with its vision of fig baskets (24:1–4) defines Judah's destiny after the humiliating events of 597 B.C., simultaneously marking Jeremiah's re-turn to ministry after a forced retirement. These two chapters, 1 and 24, are the only chapters of their kind in the book. Both contain vision reports in which Yahweh is in dialogue with the prophet, and the visions in both issue forth in divine oracles.

Chapter 24 anticipates some of the most important themes preached by Jere-miah before and after the fall of Jerusalem: a return from Babylon and rebuild-ing in the land; a new covenant; and judgment on those seeking refuge in Egypt. So far as placement is concerned, chap. 24 is not connected to the King and Prophet Appendix (Rudolph), nor does it form an inclusio with chap. 1 (*pace* Rofé 1989: 393–94). As Rofé himself recognizes, the flaw in his view is that it does not sufficiently account for the similar dates in 24:1 and 29:2, which point to a continuity between these chapters. Chapter 24 is then a be-ginning chapter that belongs with chaps. 27–29. Jerome began Book V of his commentary with chap. 24, and Mowinckel (1914: 5) too, made a major break between chaps. 23 and 24. For an explanation of how chaps. 24–36 may have achieved their present sequence, see "Excursus III: The Composition of Jere-miah 24–36," at the end of 25:1–14 below.

The present chapter at an earlier time was the first of four Zedekiah prose narratives arranged in a chiasmus. The chiasmus was made primarily from opening statements about date, which doubled as "catchlines" linking the nar-ratives (Lundbom 1975: 109–11[= 1997: 143–45]):

A   Chap. 24—after the exile of Jeconiah
  B   Chap. 27—beginning of Zedekiah's reign [4th year][a]
  B' Chap. 28—beginning of Zedekiah's reign (4th year)
A' Chap. 29—after the exile of Jeconiah

One notes in addition that common subject matter fills the middle chapters: preaching and symbolic action advocating subservience to the king of Baby-lon. The outer chapters, 24 and 29, also have thematic continuity, dividing as they do the Judahite community into good and bad remnants. Matching this "Zedekiah Cluster" (24, 27–29) is another four-chapter "Jehoiakim Cluster"

---

[a]MT's "Jehoiakim" is changed to "Zedekiah," and the fourth year is derived from the super-scription in 28:1, which reads, "in that same year" (see Notes).

(25–26, 35–36) structured similarly, on which see Rhetoric and Composition for 25:1–14.

The upper limit of the present unit is marked by a superscription and introduction in v 1, before which is a *petuḥah* in M^A and M^P and a *setumah* in M^L before verse 1. This is also the chapter division. The lower limit is marked by a *petuḥah* in M^A, M^L, and M^P after v 10, which is another chapter division. A new superscription and introduction come in 25:1–2. The M^A and M^P also have a *petuḥah* and the M^L a *setumah* after v 2, which separates the report of a vision received by Jeremiah and the divine-human dialogue occurring in that vision. The M^A and M^L also have a *petuḥah* and the M^P a *setumah* after v 3, which separates the dialogue from Oracle I. Both of these latter sections appear to be guided by first-person introductions: "And Yahweh said to me," beginning v 3 and "And the word of Yahweh came to me," beginning v 4. The M^A, M^L, and M^P all have a *setumah* after v 7, separating Oracle I from Oracle II.

The present narrative then consists of: 1) a vision report in the first person, dated in general terms, containing a dialogue between Yahweh and Jeremiah (vv 1–4); and 2) two prose oracles giving the vision an interpretation (vv 5–7 and vv 8–10). The date in v 1 seems parenthetical, but this does not mean that it is secondary, as some commentators allege (see Notes). This is simply one of many dating notices integrated into prose narratives in this part of the book, and as was mentioned, it doubles as a catchline linking chap. 24 to chap. 29 in an earlier rhetorical structure. The two oracles address two communities of people: Judahites recently spirited away to a Babylonian exile and a remnant of the same left in the land. Both communities are spoken of in the third person. Yahweh addresses neither of them directly, as he does Jeremiah in the opening dialogue.

Views vary considerably on the authenticity and provenance of this narrative, some attributing it to Jeremiah and dating all or part of it to Zedekiah's reign (Giesebrecht; Cornill; Mowinckel 1914: 21[?]; Volz; Rudolph; Weiser; Bright; Thompson; Holladay; Craigie et al.; Jones), others assigning the whole of it to a postexilic editor (Duhm; May 1942; Hyatt; Thiel 1973: 253–61; Pohlmann 1978: 20–31; Zimmerli 1982: 109–14; Carroll; Rofé 1989: 396; Beyerlin 1989: 58–67; McKane). Mowinckel was uncertain about the passage, and both Volz and Holladay are required to make considerable deletions to come up with an "original form." Duhm, Pohlmann, and McKane find not so much as a Jeremianic kernel in the chapter, McKane viewing it as a pastiche made from other passages in the Hebrew Bible.

Arguments for a late date and non-Jeremianic origin, together with counterviews in older and more recent scholarship, include the following:

• Verse 8 speaks of Jewish exiles already in Egypt; therefore, the narrative must postdate the fall of Jerusalem or be even later, when the Jewish people were divided in two—in Egypt and in Babylon (Duhm; Hyatt; Thiel; Zimmerli; McKane). Kimḥi also says the verse refers to those who went with Johanan son of Kareah to Egypt after the fall of Jerusalem (43:5–7), which may build on Midrash Song of Songs (7:14), where the bad figs already anticipate the captivity of Zedekiah. But a Jewish emigration to Egypt is placed during the reign of Jehoiakim (see Notes) by many scholars (Cornill; Rudolph; Bright; Jones), which means that in 597 B.C. Jews would have been living in Egypt. So the reference does not require a post-586 B.C. date for the passage, much less a later date.

- This passage is to be compared to the Sabbath Day Oracles in 17:19–27, which are thought to be postexilic in date (May; Hyatt). The Sabbath Day Oracles, however, are not postexilic, but are rather early Jeremianic preaching after 622 B.C. (see Rhetoric and Composition for 17:19–27).
- The reading of *et-gālût yĕhûdâ* in v 5 as "exiled Judahites" is interpreted by McKane to mean that the Jehoiachin group of exiles was the entire community of Jewish exiles in Babylon and that deportees of 586 B.C. were not part of the reckoning. Those remaining in Jerusalem, and perhaps those emigrating to Egypt, were doomed to extinction. This adventure in fantasy assumes then that chap. 24 does not record Jeremiah's activity between 597 and 586 B.C. Such an interpretation of *et-gālût yĕhûdâ* cannot be taken seriously.
- The passage has the vocabulary and phraseology of a postexilic "Deuteronomist" (Duhm; May; Thiel). Mowinckel (1914: 21) put chap. 24 in his Source A (= Jeremianic) material, although he did so with a question mark. Rudolph says the material is Source A. There are, after all, the same first-person superscriptions, "And Yahweh said to me" along with "And the word of Yahweh came to me," that appear in 1:4, 7, 9, 11–12, 13–14, about which questions of authenticity seldom, if ever, arise. Examples of diction in chap. 24 cited by May (1942: 154–55) in support of his late "Deuteronomic" biographer, for which no parallels outside Jeremiah are given, bear no resemblance to S. R. Driver's list of D phrases (1902: lxxviii–lxxxiii). Also, as the Notes below indicate, the vocabulary and phraseology of the chapter are precisely what one finds characterizing the Jeremiah prose and in some cases the Jeremiah poetry; e.g., "for good" in vv 5–6; "build up, overthrow, plant, uproot" in v 6; "to know me" in v 7; "in all the places where I shall disperse them" in v 9; and "the sword, the famine, and the pestilence" in v 10 (cf. H. Weippert 1973: 191). The covenant formula in v 7 occurs six other times in the book, twice in poetic contexts (30:22; 31:1); all the curse words of v 9, except two, are common stock in Jeremiah prose (H. Weippert 1973: 185); and "fathers" used in v 10 as an embellishing term is found often in the Jeremiah prose. The D phrase is "the God of your / our / their fathers" (S. R. Driver 1902: lxxx). This is not "Deuteronomic" prose early or late but, rather, prose indigenous to the book of Jeremiah.
- A conflict is said to exist between Jeremiah's round condemnation of the Jerusalem population in 5:1–8 and his positive view of those now going into Babylonian exile (May; Hyatt). This hardly needs comment, because

the passages in their respective contexts present no contradiction at all. Moreover, the approval given the exiles who went to Babylon pertains not at all to their moral character (Holladay; Jones).

• Another conflict is said to exist between Jeremiah's attitude in 34:1–5, where it is predicted that Zedekiah will die in peace, and here, where Zedekiah and others are promised expulsion from Jerusalem and destruction by sword, famine, and pestilence (May). This, again, is no conflict, since Zedekiah was not killed after being captured, and he along with others met the very fate of expulsion from the land that is described here (Holladay; Jones).

• The preaching of "alternatives" (good figs versus bad) is said to be a "Deuteronomistic" feature (Zimmerli, citing Thiel), which, even if it did characterize "Deuteronomic" preaching, would not be an argument against its appearing in bona fide Jeremiah discourse. Krašovec (1984: 89), who prefers to speak of "antithesis," points out that what occurs here is present also in the narrative that reports Jeremiah's visit to the potter's house (18:1–10). Moreover, there is the preaching of alternatives in 27:4b–8; 38:2, 17–18; 39:16–18; 42:9–12 and 15–18, and a better example yet is in 1:13–19, where, after a vision like the present one, Yahweh gives two oracles: one promising judgment upon Judah, the other promising salvation to Jeremiah. It would be a great surprise if Jeremiah did not manifest this very common mode of thinking.

The two oracles here have nicely-paired rhetorical structures, showing among other things that the numerous deletions by Volz, Niditch (1983: 53–70), and Holladay are wholly unnecessary. One notes collocated repetitions and key words, inversions, and alternating perfect and imperfect forms of the verb. The covenant formula in the second part of Oracle I appears strategically at the center:

I	Thus said Yahweh, God of Israel:	kōh-ʾāmar yhwh	v 5
	Like these good figs	kattěʾēnîm haṭṭōbôt	
	so will I regard the exiles of Judah		
	whom I sent away from this place	šillaḥtî	
	to the land of the Chaldeans—for good	lěṭôbâ	
	and I will keep my eye upon them for good	lěṭôbâ	v 6
	and I will bring them back to this land	wahăšîbōtîm	
	and I will build them up and not overthrow		
	and I will plant them and not uproot		
	And I will give them a heart to know me	lēb	v 7
	for I am Yahweh	kî	
	and they will be a people to me	wěhāyû-lî lěʿām	
	and I, I will be God to them	wěʾānōkî ʾehyeh lāhem lěʾlōhîm	
	for they shall return to me	kî	
	with their whole heart	libbām	

II *And like the bad figs . . .*   *wĕkattĕʾēnîm hārāʿôt*   v 8
    indeed *thus said Yahweh:*   *kōh ʾāmar yhwh*
    So *will I make* Zedekiah, king of Judah   *ʾettēn*
        and his princes
            and *the remnant* of Jerusalem   *šĕʾērît*
            the ones who remain in this land   *hanniš̆ʾārîm*
        and the ones who dwell in the land of Egypt

    Yes, I *will make them* a fright   *ûnĕtattîm*   v 9
        a calamity *to all* the kingdoms of the earth *lĕkōl*
            a reproach and a proverb
            a taunt and a swearword
        in all the places where   *bĕkōl*
    I shall disperse them

    And I will send against them   v 10
        the sword
        the famine
        and the pestilence
            until they are consumed from upon the soil
                that *I gave to them*   *nātattî lāhem*
                    and to their fathers

The messenger formulas in vv 5 and 8, one or both of which are deleted by certain commentators (Giesebrecht; Cornill; Volz; Rudolph; Weiser; Holladay; McKane) who believe that vv 5–10 are spoken only to Jeremiah, are integral to the structure and vary their positions at the beginning of each oracle:

I   Thus said Yahweh, God of Israel . . . .   v 5
II . . . . indeed thus said Yahweh v 8

Holladay and McKane say the formula in v 8 interrupts the comparison, which it does. But variation in repetitive discourse, even when—and sometimes because—it disrupts, is effective rhetorically. Both formulas should be retained, because they make it clear that the message to Jeremiah is for the people.

NOTES

24:1. *Yahweh showed me, and there! two baskets of figs.* The rhetorical particle *wĕhinnēh*, which the AV renders "and behold," goes untranslated in the more recent Versions, perhaps because it is lacking in the LXX. But its omission there, as Janzen (1973: 119) points out, could be attributed to haplography (homoeoteleuton: *h . . . h*). The term suggests that sudden awareness known to artists of something in the physical world that might go unnoticed by others. Rather than the usual "and look!" *wĕhinnēh* is here translated "and there!" meaning "and there, before my very eyes!" This statement with minor variation introduces visions seen by the prophet Amos (Amos 7:1, 4, 7; and

8:1). The expression "Yahweh showed me" occurs one other time in Jeremiah, in 38:21, and is found also in 2 Kgs 8:10, 13; and Ezek 11:25. The vision here and its accompanying divine word is said by Lindblom (1965: 140–41) to be a "symbolic perception," which is an observation of a real object in the real world. This vision then is no different from the "almond branch" and "boiling pot" visions of 1:11–14, and possibly Amos's vision of the basket of summer fruit (Amos 8:1–2). Two real baskets of figs are seen sitting in front of the Temple, but for the prophet they bring a sudden revelation from Yahweh. Yet since the good figs in one of the baskets are said in v 2 to be only "*like* early figs" (*kit̲ʾēnê habbakkūrôt*), it could be that Jeremiah is reporting a vision occurring solely in his mind, where things are not exactly as they are in the real world (Volz; Rudolph; Holladay). Otherwise we have to imagine a real basket of figs that were not early figs but figs that simply looked like early figs. Lindblom's "symbolic perception," it should be noted, precluded the figs' being a firstfruits offering, which they likely are.

two baskets of figs. On the *ʾaleph* in *dûdāʾê* ("baskets"), which appears to express the dual number, see GKC §93x. Hebrew *dûd* means "(cooking) pot" (1 Sam 2:14; 2 Chr 35:13) or "basket." Rashi's rendering is "pots"; Kimḥi follows T, with "baskets." The LXX (*kalathous*) and Vg (*calathi*) both have "(wicker hand)baskets." Dalman (1933: 204), Honeyman (1939: 80–81), and Kelso (1948: 18 #39) support the translation "baskets," Dalman saying that these were heavy baskets used to carry fruit. Kelso says the *dûd* is otherwise a deep, round-bottomed, two-handled cooking pot, varying in size from four inches to fourteen inches in diameter. Honeyman thinks it was single-handed. The basket, in any case, presumably had the same general shape as the cooking pot.

situated in front of the temple of Yahweh. Hebrew *mûʿādîm* means "situated" (M. Greenberg 1997: 426) or "arranged" (Bright; Holladay), i.e., set in their appointed place, which precludes the need that some scholars feel to emend. The T has "placed," which corresponds to LXX's *keimenous* ("set down") and Vg's *positi* ("set, placed"). The Hophal participle occurs one other time in Ezek 21:21[Eng 21:16], where Greenberg translates "wherever your blade (*pānayik*) has been assigned (*mûʿādôt*)." The figs in front of the Temple are presumably there as an offering of the firstfruits (Deut 26:1–11; cf. Exod 34:22; Deut 16:9–12), to be presented at the yearly Feast of Weeks (= Pentecost), seven weeks after Passover (Cheyne; Zimmerli 1982: 110). This is late May or early June when the first figs have just ripened (v 2). These figs awaited examination by the priest, who would judge on their worthiness as an offering. Some have wondered how the one basket of bad figs could show up as a Temple offering, for which reason they either delete the Temple reference (Cornill) or detach the incident from reality (Rudolph; Holladay). Neither remedy is necessary. A bad offering of figs is no strain on the imagination. Unworthy offerings were always a problem (Gen 4:3–4; Mal 1:6–9), and if the priests are inspecting, it stands to reason that some offerings will be rejected as unacceptable.

after Nebuchadrezzar, king of Babylon, had exiled Jeconiah son of Jehoiakim, king of Judah, and the princes of Judah, and the craftsmen and the smiths from Jerusalem and brought them to Babylon. For historical background, see 2 Kgs 24:10–17. Zedekiah's accession year was 597 B.C. (Tadmor 1956: 230). This contextual note and the one like it in 29:2 bind chaps. 24 and 29 together in an earlier "Zedekiah Cluster" of narrative prose (see Rhetoric and Composition), and the note here ought not be deleted as a gloss from 2 Kgs 24:14–15 (*pace* Ehrlich 1912: 306; Volz; Rudolph; Weiser; Bright; Holladay; McKane). Volz, however, does consider that the note might originate with Baruch.

Jeconiah. The spelling is *yĕkonyāhû*, which occurs only here. The king's name appears as "Jehoiachin" in 2 Kgs 24:6 and 12, and as "Coniah" in Jer 22:24, 28; 37:1; and 1 Chr 3:1. On other spellings in Jeremiah and the OT, see Note for 22:24.

the princes of Judah. Hebrew *wĕ'et-śārê yĕhûdâ*. Here, as elsewhere in the book, *śārîm* is rendered by the not-entirely-suitable term "princes," which reflects earlier English usage, when the term had broader meaning. The AV used "princes," and it was carried over into the RSV. Today "prince" means largely a "male member of the royal family," but earlier it also meant "principal person, chief, head man, commander" (*OED* 12: 490–92). Some recent English Versions (NEB, NJV, NIV, NRSV, REB) translate *śār* as "official" or "officer," but *śār* is more inclusive, meaning roughly "one of the king's men." These were individuals holding upper-level civil and military positions, which could be royal or nonroyal. Some were scribes (36:12) and others military commanders, palace guards, or members of the police force. The "princes of the troops" (*śārê haḥăyālîm*) assuming leadership at Mizpah in the post-586 B.C. resettlement were military or paramilitary figures, one of whom, Ishmael son of Nethaniah, was a royal figure (41:1). The others were probably not royalty. Jezaniah son of the Maacathite (40:8) was a foreigner. Princes of the king of Babylon were doubtless a mix of upper-level officers (39:3). Bright thinks that among the Judahite princes taken to Babylon were many who had intervened on Jeremiah's behalf (chaps. 26; 36), since we hear no more of them. Those remaining in Jerusalem were, almost without exception, hostile to Jeremiah.

the craftsmen. A *ḥārāš* is a craftsman in wood, metal, or stone; an engraver (T; 10:3; Exod 28:11; 1 Sam 13:19). The noun is a collective. The LXX has *technitas* ("craftsmen"). These skilled workers are also listed among exile-bound Judahites in 29:2 and 2 Kgs 24:14, 16. Such people would be useful to Nebuchadrezzar, and their loss to Judah would serve the Babylonian king additionally by depriving a subjugated nation of a valued asset in maintaining independence and a defense.

the smiths. Hebrew *hammasgēr*. Another collective noun occurring elsewhere in 29:2 and 2 Kgs 24:14, 16, probably meaning "metalworkers" or "locksmiths" (Giesebrecht; Condamin). The term in postbiblical Hebrew means "locksmith" (*Dict Talm*, 804), which is how T translates it here. The LXX has *tous desmōtas* ("the prisoners"), adding also another category of people, *tous plousious* ("the wealthy"). The former can be explained as a derivation from the verb *sgr*, "to shut someone in." The noun *masgēr* in the OT otherwise means "prison" (Isa 24:22; 42:7; Ps 142:8[Eng 142:7]). The Vg follows the LXX with *inclusorem*. D. N. Freedman suggests that the added LXX term could point to a loss of *wĕ'et-he'āšîr* ("and the rich") in the MT by haplography (ho-moeoteleuton: *r . . . r*). Hebrew *'āšîr*, another collective noun, occurs without the article in 9:22[Eng 9:23]. Smiths would also be useful to Nebuchadrezzar in Babylon, and their loss at home might prevent remaining Judahites from producing arms for a revolt.

to Babylon. Hebrew *bābel*. The preposition "to" is omitted by ellipsis. See again 28:3; also *'ereṣ kaśdîm* ("*to* the land of the Chaldeans") in v 5. Ellipsis in proper nouns that represent a point of destination occurs elsewhere in the Jeremianic prose, e.g., in 26:10 and 33:11 ("*to* the house of Yahweh"); in 31:6 ("*to* Zion"); in 31:38 ("*to* the Corner Gate"); in 43:7 ("*to* the land of Egypt"); and in 44:28 ("*to* the land of Judah").

2. *The one basket had very good figs, like the early figs.* Hebrew *tĕ'ēnê hab-bakkūrôt* are the first-ripe figs of late May or early June (Post 1932–33 II: 515; idem, "Figs" in *HDB* 3: 6), but since the good figs here are only *like* early figs, we cannot be sure whether they were early figs. Early figs, in any case, are referred to often in the OT (Hos 9:10; Isa 28:4; Mic 7:1; Nah 3:12) and were considered a special delicacy (Rashi; Cheyne). In the Near East, fig trees bear two, sometimes three crops, one a winter fruit, ripening as early as Passover on last year's branches (Post; Pliny, *Nat Hist* xv 19; cf. Matt 21:19; Mark 11:13; Rev 6:13). Summer figs turn ripe in late August or early September. The fig tree in the OT is a symbol of peace and prosperity (1 Kgs 4:25; Isa 36:16; Mic 4:4; Zech 3:10; 1 Macc 14:12). See further on figs and fig trees, P. J. King 1993: 148–49.

and the other basket very bad figs, which could not be eaten because they were so bad. The *mem* on *mērōa'* is causative: lit., "because of their being bad" (GKC §119z; cf. *mērōb* in Gen 16:10 and 1 Kgs 8:5). Figs need to be fully ripe for good eating, but these have become rotten. The point is stated more strongly in 29:17, where the expression "horrid figs" (*tĕ'ēnîm haššō'ārîm*) occurs.

3. *And Yahweh said to me: 'What do you see, Jeremiah?' And I said: 'Figs! The good figs are very good, and the bad ones very bad, which cannot be eaten because they are so bad.* The same question-and-answer form occurs in 1:11, 13, and elsewhere in vision narratives (see Note for 1:11). The LXX lacks the repeated "figs" (*tĕ'ēnîm*) in Jeremiah's answer, which Janzen (1973: 117) says may have been lost through haplography (whole-word).

4. *And the word of Yahweh came to me.* A superscription of the type found in 1:4, 11, and 13. See Note for 1:4.

5. *Thus said Yahweh, God of Israel.* This messenger formula should not be deleted (*pace* Volz; Rudolph; Weiser; Holladay; McKane). The LXX, T, and Vg all have it. The vision is not a private message for Jeremiah but a message for the entire Judahite community, at home as well as abroad.

Like these good figs, so will I regard the exiles of Judah. On the *kĕ . . . kēn* construction, here and again in v 8, see Note for 2:26. Already in 597 B.C., Jeremiah is beginning to offer hope to the Babylonian exiles. Ezekiel does the same in Ezek 11:14–21, an important parallel to the present passage. Commentators are divided over the precise meaning of *gālût yĕhûdâ*. Some give the term the meaning "the exile of Judah" or "exiled Judah" (Rashi; Giesebrecht; Duhm; Volz; Craigie et al.; McKane; cf. GKC §95t and LXX 28:4); others (S. R. Driver; Condamin; Bright; Thompson; Holladay; Jones; cf. BDB; KB³) take it as a collective: "the exiles of Judah." In 28:4 (MT) and 29:22 the term means the same as here: Judahites exiled to Babylon in 597 B.C., which are the "good figs" (Midrash Song of Songs 7:14; Jerome). If the term does mean "exiled Judah," what it does not imply, surely, is that the whole of Judah went to Babylon in 597 B.C., which is the end result of McKane's convoluted exegesis. From Calvin comes the oft-repeated point that good and bad figs do not ascribe moral character or lack of the same to the two groups of people but, rather, describe the fate of each group in the days ahead. Calvin says the oracle speaks not of persons but of punishment. Yet he does concede that those left behind were more wicked than those taken away, which could be his way of saying that the elect behave better than the non-elect. One can certainly speak of the "good figs" as those blessed and the "bad figs" as those unblessed. The oracle, in any case, turns on its head the popular notion that those left behind were the favored ones and those marched off to Babylon were the unfavored. But Yahweh says that in the divine economy those recently exiled will have a future, whereas those left behind will not (cf. Ezek 11:14–21; 17:1–21).

whom I sent away from this place to the land of the Chaldeans. Holladay (following Niditch 1980: 53, 60) takes this to be a gloss, but without textual basis. "I sent away" balances "I will bring them back" (v 6) in the larger rhetorical structure (see Rhetoric and Composition). In *'ereṣ kaśdîm* is another omission of the preposition "to" by ellipsis; read thus: "*to* the land of the Chaldeans."

for good. I.e., for the covenant people's welfare. Hebrew *lĕṭôbâ* appears in the covenant blessings of Deut 28:11; also again in Deut 30:9. But most of the other OT occurrences, as Jones points out, are in Jeremiah (14:11; 21:10; 39:16; 44:27).

6. *and I will keep my eye upon them for good, and I will bring them back to this land.* A few MSS, LXX, and Vg have "eyes" plural. The expression "to keep an eye on someone" means to look after them (see Note for 39:12). Here it is an anthropomorphism for the showing of divine favor. The AmT paraphrases: "I will look with friendly eyes upon them." At this time of national disaster, when a large segment of the nation has been exiled to a distant land, Jeremiah is delivering an oracle about returning (cf. 23:3). See also Ezek 11:16–17.

and I will build them up and not overthrow, and I will plant them and not uproot. These four verbs appear variously throughout the Jeremiah prose (see Note for 1:10). On the theme of "building and planting" in Jeremiah (1:10; 18:9; 24:6; 29:5, 28; 31:4–5, 28; 35:7; 42:10; 45:4), and elsewhere in the OT (Deut 6:10–11; 20:5–6; Amos 9:14; Zeph 1:13; Ezek 36:36), see Bach 1961.

7. *And I will give them a heart to know me, for I am Yahweh, and they will be a people to me, and I, I will be God to them, for they shall return to me with their*

whole heart. Jeremiah is anticipating his "new covenant" prophecy, when Yahweh promises to write his Torah on the human heart (31:31–34). Von Rad (1965: 212) says: "Here is [Jeremiah's] prophecy of the new covenant compressed into one sentence." The language is closer, however, to the "eternal covenant" passage of 32:38–40, also Ezekiel's oracle about Yahweh giving Israel a new heart and spirit when the covenant bond is again in force (Ezek 11:19–20; 36:26–28). M. Greenberg (1997: 736–37) cites this verse as an example of Jeremiah's oracles' vacillating between an affirmation that repentance is initiated on the human level and precedes forgiveness (cf. 36:3) and an affirmation that God's cooperation is required in the process of repentance. In his view, the change in human nature is not an act of grace. Zimmerli (1982: 111–13), too, stresses the conditional element in God's promise of salvation, saying that salvation here depends on the conversion of those exiled. But the idea that repentance is initiated on the human level and is a precondition for God's salvation comes from texts such as Ezek 18:30–31 and Deut 30:1–10, not Jeremiah. In Ezek 18:30–31 Israel is told to repent, rid itself of all sin, and get for itself a new heart and a new spirit. Nothing of that sort is implied here, nor in the Jeremiah new covenant passages, where the giving of a new heart and salvation for the covenant people are unconditional acts of divine grace. Calvin goes so far as to say that even human repentance is a gift of God (Jer 31:18–20; cf. Rom 2:4). God, in Calvin's view, is not simply the helper in repentance, he is the author of it and anticipates us by his grace. In giving people a new heart, God will change them inwardly, which Calvin says is a more excellent grace than restoring them to the land. The word "heart" (*lēb*), here as elsewhere, includes the mind, will, and understanding.

to know me. "Knowing Yahweh" is another key theme in Jeremiah (see Note on 4:22).

for I am Yahweh. Hebrew *kî 'ănî yhwh*. The expression occurs also in 9:23[Eng 9:24] and significantly in that context, as here, after a statement about "knowing Yahweh." The deletion by Volz and Holladay is without basis. On the similar phrase, *kî-šĕmî yhwh* ("that my name is Yahweh"), see Note for 16:21.

and they will be a people to me, and I, I will be God to them. The same covenant formula appears often in Jeremiah (7:23; 11:4; 24:7; 30:22; 31:1, 33; 32:38). See also Ezek 11:20 and 36:28.

for they shall return to me with their whole heart. If the initial *kî* were to be translated as a conditional "if," then one would have the conditional grace advocated for the passage by Zimmerli. But the Versions ancient and modern all render the particle "for" or "when," which is correct and is consistent with Jeremianic theology found elsewhere in the book. Jeremiah makes extensive use of the verb *šûb* ("turn, return, repent"). In the early chapters, calls for repentance are repeatedly made but go unheeded (5:3; 8:4–5). Foreseen here is a complete turnabout for the covenant people, with repentance taking place because of the new heart Yahweh promises to give them. The present phrase is deleted by Volz and Holladay but without textual support. It balances "and I will give them a heart to know me, for I am Yahweh" in the larger rhetorical structure and should be retained. Together these statements frame the covenant formula (see Rhetoric and Composition).

their whole heart. Complete and unreserved action.

8–10. These verses are repeated with variation in 29:17–19, where the judgment on Judah's king and the remnant left in Jerusalem after 597 B.C. is in response to their not having listened to Yahweh's word as it came via the prophets.

8. *And like the bad figs, which could not be eaten because they were so bad . . . So will I make Zedekiah, king of Judah. . . .* Another *kĕ . . . kēn* comparison, as in v 5. One can only wonder whether this oracle came to the ears of Zedekiah, and if it did, just when? It could have been received by Jeremiah early in Zedekiah's reign and then made public at a later time. There was, after all, a period of roughly seven years (594–588 B.C.) during which we know nothing of Jeremiah's activities. It could be that Jeremiah's delivery of this oracle made necessary his retirement from public view, which would have repeated what happened in 604 B.C. when the prophet's first scroll was read publicly and he became persona non grata with King Jehoiakim. The usual view of Zedekiah is that he was personally so weak that he could do little in the face of an oracle such as the present one. But would not others have been just as offended by this oracle, since, as we mentioned, they would likely have attributed their escape from exile to their own superiority?

indeed thus said Yahweh. Translating the *kî* as an asseverative: "indeed." The LXX and Vg omit the particle, but many commentators (Giesebrecht; Cornill; Volz; Rudolph; Weiser; Holladay; McKane) go further and delete the entire formula. The *kî* appears to be required because the formula here interrupts the opening words of the oracle. Its omission in the LXX could be due to haplography (homoeoarcton: *k . . . k*). The formula in its entirety should be retained, because it alternates nicely with the formula in v 5 (see Rhetoric and Composition).

the ones who remain in this land. Blayney says that one MS has "in this city," a reading that appears also in the S, Vg (*in urbe hac*), and G^A. The parallel oracle in chap. 29 is spoken to those who dwell "in this city," i.e., Jerusalem (29:16). But "land" here is the accepted reading.

and the ones who dwell in the land of Egypt. Already in 597 B.C. Jews are living in Egypt, and more will go there before and after the fall of Jerusalem. Jehoahaz was taken there over a decade ago, in 609 B.C., and others likely went with him. During the reign of Jehoiakim, Uriah the prophet fled to Egypt (26:21–23), which does not prove that he sought refuge with Jews living in the country but suggests it. Bright, along with others, favors a Jewish emigration to Egypt during Jehoiakim's reign, saying that, if it did not occur when Jehoiakim switched allegiance to Nebuchadrezzar ca. 604 B.C. (2 Kgs 24:1), it did when the Babylonian king invaded Judah in 598–597 B.C. More Jews doubtless went south during Zedekiah's reign, before the fall of Jerusalem. What is certain is that, by the time Johanan son of Kareah and his group arrived in Egypt ca. 581 B.C., entire communities of Jews were established in Migdol, Tahpanhes, Memphis, and the land of Pathros in the far south (44:1). There is no basis then for dating this passage in the middle-exilic or postexilic periods because of a reference here to Jews living in Egypt (see Rhetoric and Composition), nor is there justification for deleting the reference, as Volz and Holladay do.

9. *Yes, I will make them a fright, a calamity . . . a reproach and a proverb, a taunt and a swearword.* This indignity was anticipated in 18:16, and did in fact occur with the destruction of Jerusalem (Lam 2:15–17). Twice in the poetry (18:16; 51:37), and often in the prose (19:8; 24:9; 25:9, 11, 18; 29:18; 42:18; 44:6, 8, 12, 22; and 49:13), one comes upon strings of curse words such as the present one. The distribution of curse words in these strings is as follows:

> *a fright (zaʿăwâ* Q; *zĕwāʿâ* Kt): 24:9; 29:18; 34:17
> *a calamity (rāʿâ):* 24:9
> *a reproach (ḥerpâ):* 24:9; 29:18; 42:18; 44:8, 12; 49:13
> *a proverb (māšāl):* 24:9
> *a taunt (šĕnînâ):* 24:9
> *a swearword (qĕlālâ):* 24:9; 25:18; 42:18; 44:8, 12, 22; 49:13
> *a desolation (šammâ / šĕmāmâ):* 18:16 (poetry); 19:8; 25:9, 11, 18; 29:18;
>   42:18; 44:6, 12, 22; 49:13; 51:37 (poetry)
> *a curse (ʾālâ):* 29:18; 42:18; 44:12
> *(a) ruin(s) (ḥōreb / ḥorbâ / ḥorbôt):* 25:9, 11, 18; 44:6, 22; 49:13
> *(an) object(s) of hissing (šĕrēqâ / šĕrîqôt* Q): 18:16 (poetry); 19:8;
>   25:9, 18; 29:18; 51:37 (poetry)

This rhetoric of accumulation occurs also in Deut 28:37, where two of the present curse words appear: "proverb" (*māšāl*) and "taunt" (*šĕnînâ*). The pair is present also in 1 Kgs 9:7. The string here, with the exception of the two words just mentioned, are common stock in Jeremiah (H. Weippert 1973: 188), pointing neither to "Deuteronomic" authorship nor later interpolation (*pace* Volz; Thiel 1973: 257; Niditch 1980: 54, 62). Jones states: "In no sense can this section be ascribed to Deuteronomic origin. At most, one can say that in a verse not germane to the central image of the section [i.e., v 9], there is evidence that the Jeremiah tradition shows familiarity with a specific element within Deut. and has made it its own" (p. 318). In the Qumran *Temple Scroll* (11QT 59:2), one finds this string: "and they will become [a ho]rr[or] ([l]š[mh]), a proverb (*lmšl*), and a byword (*wlšnnyh*), and with a heavy yoke (*wbʿwl kbd*)." Again in 11QT 59:4 is this string: "a waste (*lšwmh*) and a hissing (*wlšrqh*) and a desolation (*wlḥwrbh*)" (Yadin 1983: 266).

a fright. Hebrew *zaʿăwâ* (Q). On the Q-Kt spelling, see the Note for 15:4. This term occurs in Deut 28:25 but most often in Jeremiah (15:4; 24:9; 29:18; 34:17).

a calamity. Hebrew *lĕrāʿâ.* This term occurs in a string of curse words only here. The LXX omits, and many scholars (Cornill; Ehrlich 1912: 307; Condamin; Rudolph; Bright; McKane) delete as a dittography of "fright." Volz, Weiser, and Holladay relocate the word to the end of v 8. Neither change is necessary; the LXX omission is likely due to haplography (homoeoarcton: *l* . . . *l*, or homoeoteleuton: *h* . . . *h*).

a reproach. Hebrew *ḥerpâ.* A very common term in Jeremiah (6:10; 15:15; 20:8; 23:40; 24:9; 29:18; 31:19; 42:18; 44:8, 12; 49:13; 51:51), appearing not only in curse-word strings of prose but also in poetry. In 15:15 and 20:8 the prophet laments the reproach he himself has endured. This term occurs nowhere in Deuteronomy.

a proverb, a taunt. Hebrew *māšāl* and *šĕnînâ.* Both terms occur in Jeremiah only here; "proverb" occurs eight times in Ezekiel.

a swearword. Heb *qĕlālâ.* Another term appearing very often in Jeremiah, both singly and in lists of curse words (24:9; 25:18; 26:6; 29:22; 42:18; 44:8, 12, 22; 49:13). It occurs frequently in Deuteronomy as well (Deut 11:26, 28, 29; 21:23; 23:6[Eng 23:5]; 27:13; 28:15, 45; 29:26[Eng 29:27]; 30:1, 19), although there, in every case except one (21:23), it is a general word for "curse" as opposed to "blessing" and does not appear in any list of curse words.

in all the places where I shall disperse them. This phrase, with or without the prior curse words, is taken as more expansion by certain commentators (Giesebrecht; Volz; Weiser; Rudolph; Holladay; McKane), but again without any textual support. Rudolph and Weiser take it to be an addition from Deut 28:37 and say it contradicts v 10. The contradiction to v 10 is largely contrived (some of those remaining in the land can reasonably expect to meet humiliation in a later dispersion), and Deut 28:37, with its different wording, is not likely to be the place from which the phrase has been quarried, particularly since the phrase and others like it employing *ndḥ* ("to disperse, scatter") are found all through the book of Jeremiah (8:3; 16:15; 23:3, 8; 24:9; 27:10, 15; 29:14, 18; 32:37; 40:12; 43:5; 46:28). They are, in fact, a signature phrase of the Jeremiah prose.

10. *the sword, the famine, and the pestilence.* On this triad, see Note for 5:12.

until they are consumed from upon the soil that I gave to them and to their fathers. An unusual formulation using *hā'ădāmâ* ("the soil, ground") instead of *hā'āreṣ* ("the land"). See also 12:14 and 27:10–11. The language here is likely intentional, indicating punishment for sin. Cain laments being driven "from (the face of) the ground" (*mē'al pĕnê hā'ădāmâ*) as punishment for his sin (Gen 4:14). In the present instance Yahweh is talking about his gift of the land. The LXX omits "and to their fathers" (*wĕla'ăbôtêhem*), which is another loss due to haplography (homoeoteleuton: *hm* . . . *hm*). Janzen (1973: 44) deletes as MT expansion, but Holladay retains; "fathers" is a common embellishing term in Jeremiah, occurring often in phrases such as the present one about Yahweh's gift of the land (3:25; 7:7, 14; 9:15[Eng 9:16]; 16:13; 19:4; 23:39; 24:10; 25:5; 35:15; 44: 3, 10, 17, 21).

MESSAGE AND AUDIENCE

Jeremiah reports here a vision received from Yahweh, perhaps reminding his audience of earlier visions received and reported that called him to be

Yahweh's prophet and commissioned him for prophetic service. This vision, we are told, came after a humiliating subjugation of Jerusalem by Nebuchadrezzar, king of Babylon, resulting in Judah's loss of its young king, Jehoiachin, other royalty, prominent people in government, and other valued citizens of the city—all to exile in a faraway land, from which probably none would ever return. In this vision, two baskets of figs were seen against the backdrop of the Temple. One was filled with good figs, the early-ripened variety; the other with bad figs, so bad that they could not be eaten. Yahweh asked the prophet what he saw, and he told him. Yahweh then interpreted the vision in two oracles following.

Yahweh will regard Judahites exiled to Babylon like these good figs, for his larger plan calls for a return to the land, where they will be built up. At that time, they will be given a new heart to know him, for he is Yahweh, and the covenant will once again be the bond it was meant to be. The covenant people, for their part, will return to Yahweh in this new situation with their whole heart.

Yahweh regards Zedekiah, his princes, and all those remaining in the land like the bad figs. This includes those left in Jerusalem, those living in Judah's cities and villages, and those who managed what they thought to be a timely escape to Egypt. All will be accursed. Sword, famine, and pestilence will consume all residing on the soil that Yahweh provided for them and their fathers.

The oracles in combination overturn popular notions about what has recently happened to the nation. Men, women, and children taken to Babylon are as good as lost, while those remaining—however few in number and however precarious their existence might be—are surely the favored ones. But Yahweh tells Jeremiah, and eventually Judahite audiences in both Judah and Babylon, that things are just the reverse: the exiles are his favored ones and those left behind the unfavored. A Jerusalem audience will scarcely believe this. But all the main themes of Jeremiah's preaching before and after the fall of Jerusalem are announced here: the return of exiles from Babylon, their rebuilding in the land, the making of a new covenant, and judgment on those who have fled to Egypt.

This is the first dated prose in the book, and while we are not told precisely when the vision and its accompanying oracles were received, we are told that they came following the exile of 597 B.C., when Zedekiah was already king. A date soon after 597 has broad support. Volz puts it closer to 588 B.C. The vision and the oracles, though coming directly to Jeremiah, were meant for the community at large, and we may assume that at some point people in Jerusalem and Judah, and eventually exiles in Babylon and Egypt, would hear them. During the final siege of Jerusalem and after the city's fall, all these ideas had become public knowledge.

B. INDICTMENT OF JUDAH AND THE NATIONS (25:1–38)

1. Nebuchadrezzar: Yahweh's Servant for a Time (25:1–14)

25 ¹The word that came to[a] Jeremiah concerning all the people of Judah in the fourth year of Jehoiakim son of Josiah, king of Judah (that was the first year of Nebuchadrezzar, king of Babylon), ²which Jeremiah the prophet spoke concerning all the people of Judah and to all the inhabitants of Jerusalem, saying: ³From the thirteenth year of Josiah son of Amon, king of Judah, yes, until this day—this is twenty-three years—the word of Yahweh has come to me, and I have spoken to you—constantly I spoke—but you have not listened; ⁴and Yahweh has repeatedly sent to you all his servants the prophets—constantly he sent—but you have not listened, indeed you have not bent your ear to listen. ⁵Return, would you, each person from his evil way and from your evil doings, and dwell on the soil that Yahweh gave to you and to your fathers for all time.

⁶Do not go after other gods to serve them and to worship them, and do not provoke me to anger with the work of your hands, and I will do you no hurt. ⁷But you have not listened to me—oracle of Yahweh—so as to provoke me to anger[b] with the work of your hands, to your own hurt.

⁸Therefore thus said Yahweh of hosts: 'Because you have not listened to my words':

⁹Look I am sending and I will take all the tribes of the north—oracle of Yahweh—also to Nebuchadrezzar, king of Babylon, my servant, and I will bring them against this land and against its inhabitants and against all these nations round about, and I will devote them to destruction, and I will make them a desolation, an object of hissing, and ruins forever. ¹⁰And I will banish from them the voice of joy and the voice of gladness, the voice of the groom and the voice of the bride, the sound of millstones and the light of the lamp. ¹¹And all this land will become a ruin and a desolation,[c] and these nations shall serve the king of Babylon seventy years.

¹²And it will happen when seventy years are fulfilled, I will reckon against the king of Babylon and against that nation—oracle of Yahweh—their iniquity; also against the land of the Chaldeans, and I will make it desolations

---

[a] Reading "to" for Heb *ʿal;* several MSS have *ʾel.* The two prepositions are used interchangeably in Jeremiah to mean "to" (see v 2 and Note for 11:2).

[b] Reading with T the infinitive of the Q, *hakʿisēnî* ("to provoke me to anger"); cf. 7:18 and 32:29. The Kt has an impossible *hikʿisûnî* ("they provoked me to anger"?).

[c] Reading *ûlĕḥorbâ* ("and a desolation") with many MSS, G^OL, Aq, Symm, Theod, S, T^MS, and Vg; MT lacks "and."

forever. [13]And I will bring[d] against that land all my words that I have spoken against it, everything written in this book, which Jeremiah prophesied against all the nations. [14]Indeed many nations and great kings shall make them serve—even them! And I will repay them according to their deeds and according to the work of their hands.

RHETORIC AND COMPOSITION

MT 25:1–13a = LXX 25:1–13a; MT 25:13b = LXX 32:13; MT 25:14 = LXX 0. Chapter 25 at an earlier time was the first of four Jehoiakim prose narratives, 25, 26, 35, and 36, arranged in a chiastic structure. Chronology was broken so that the first narrative would balance the last. This configuration we have called "the Jehoiakim Cluster," and it matches a similarly-structured "Zedekiah Cluster" comprising chaps. 24, 27, 28, and 29 (see Rhetoric and Composition for 24:1–10). On how chaps. 24–36 may have achieved their present sequence, see "Excursus III: The Composition of Jeremiah 24–36," at the end of the present unit. The chiasmus of the present cluster is created, as is the case also with the Zedekiah Cluster, primarily from introductory dates that double as "catchlines" linking the narratives (Lundbom 1975: 107–9 [= 1997: 140–43]):

A   Chap. 25—4th year of Jehoiakim
  B   Chap. 26—in the beginning of Jehoiakim's reign
  B′ Chap. 35—in the days of Jehoiakim
A′ Chap. 36—4th year of Jehoiakim

The correspondence between the beginning and ending chapters, 25 and 36, is exact; that of the center chapters, 26 and 35, inexact. However, as is true also in the Zedekiah Cluster, common subject matter unites the middle chapters: both are incidents occurring in the Temple.

Chapter 25 (or 25:1–13a) is not, then, a concluding narrative, so far as composition is concerned (*pace* Duhm; Birkeland 1939: 44–45; Rudolph; Weiser; Hyatt; Bright; Thompson; Boadt; Zimmerli 1982: 110; Holladay; Jones). Birkeland and Weiser took 25:1–13/14 as a conclusion to the *Urrolle* ("original scroll") of chap. 36. The entire chapter, as we have said, was once the lead narrative in a prose cluster that reported Jeremiah's preaching and activity during Jehoiakim's reign. For a different compositional view of chaps. 25–36 but one which takes chap. 25 as a beginning and not a conclusion, see Rofé 1989: 394–95. The idea that 25:1–13a (or the whole of chap. 25) concluded an early Jeremiah book develops from 1) a misinterpretation of "this book" in v 13, viz., that it refers *back* to a scroll of Jeremiah's collected preaching between 627 and 605, thought to be contained within 1:1–25:13a; 2) a disproportional emphasis on the divergence between the MT and LXX after 25:13a; and 3) an exaggerated

---

[d]Kt *whb'yty* is a scribal error for *wĕhēbē'tî* (Rudolph; cf. Num 14:31); Q is *wĕhēbē'tî*. M[A], M[C], and earlier Rabbinic Bibles have a *whb'wty* spelling for the Kt, which was the spelling carried over into *BH*[1].

connection between chaps. 25 and 36, both of which are dated in Jehoiakim's fourth year, and the latter of which reports the preparation of the *Urrolle*. "This book" in v 13 originally looked ahead (and still does look ahead) to a scroll originally containing only the Babylon oracles and later all the Foreign Nation Oracles, which even yet follow v 13a in the LXX (Blayney; Cheyne; Peake; McKane). In the MT the Foreign Nation Collection follows chap. 45, where it was subsequently relocated. So far as a connection to the *Urrolle* is concerned, McKane rightly says that "all the theories about the relation of 25.1–13 or 25.1–14 to the [original] scroll should be discounted" (p. 631). The only sense in which chap. 25 can be termed a conclusion, and this would apply also to chap. 36, is that it reports Jeremiah's activity just before he winds up an early stage of his public career. A year later he is sent into forced retirement (36:19, 26) and does not reemerge while Jehoiakim is king.

The whole of chap. 25 is commonly taken to consist of three sections: 1) vv 1–14; 2) vv 15–29; and 3) vv 30–38. With this division I am in basic agreement, except that I take vv 30–38 to be a three-oracle cluster against the nations. The first two sections are narrative prose; the third, except for v 33, is poetry. Giesebrecht takes vv 1–14 as emanating from Baruch (Source B), then later revised; Rudolph takes the verses as Source C. Mowinckel (1914: 31) takes vv 1–11a as Source C and vv 11b–14 as a later addition. The chapter has its own integrity, and can be taken, in the MT at least, as an essential unity (Peake). This does not, however, preclude subsequent expansion, although I would limit such to a minumum and do not believe the claims made for two editions (*pace* Schwally 1888; Duhm; Cornill; Thiel 1973; Tov 1985; Carroll; Holladay), which rest largely—but not exclusively—on divergencies between the MT and LXX and the supposition that the LXX preserves the better and more original text. The two-edition theory also builds on textual deletions and emendations, many of which are unsupported by manuscript evidence and are frequently made when both MT and LXX agree on the reading in question. The "fourth year of Jehoiakim" (25:1), however, will not cover the Babylon oracle in vv 12–14, the reason being that "this book" in v 13, which looks forward not backward, cannot precede the writing of the Babylon scroll to which it makes reference (51:60). The Babylon scroll was written a decade or more later in the reign of Zedekiah (594/3 B.C.). It is not necessary then to take (with Cornill) all of 25:1–13 as originally an introduction to the Foreign Nation Collection. This collection needs only to be prefaced by vv 12–13a of the Babylon oracle. Peake questioned whether 25:1–13 introduced the Foreign Nation Oracles, saying it was improbable that the LXX placement after v 13a was its original position. His objection was that this would tear chap. 25 in two, which he found unacceptable. The cup of wrath vision in vv 15–29, said Peake, could not have followed the detailed Foreign Nation Oracles, where its effect would be completely lost. In this he is quite right. But everything else in the chapter, except vv 12–14, is datable to Jehoiakim's fourth year, at which time anxiety would have been widespread that all nations—not just Judah—faced danger in the wake of Nebuchadrezzar's victory over the Egyptians at Carchemish.

The upper limit of the present unit is marked by a superscription and introduction in vv 1–2, before which there is a *petuḥah* in M^A, M^L, and M^P prior to
25:1. The lower limit is marked by a *petuḥah* in M^A and a *setumah* in M^L and
M^P after v 14. There are no sections in v 13, notably after v 13a, where the LXX
makes its celebrated divergence from MT. The M^A, M^P, and 4QJer^c have a
petuḥah and M^L a *setumah* after v 7, which are doubtless guided by the messenger formula in v 8 and serve to separate Oracle I from Oracle II.

The present unit consists of 1) a dated narrative reporting an address by Jeremiah to his people, in which he recalls 23 years of having received Yahweh's
word and having preached a message of reform, to which the people said a
resolute 'No' (vv 1–5); 2) a divine oracle stating Yahweh's call for reform and
an indictment for the people's same stubborn disregard (vv 6–7); 3) a second
divine oracle promising judgment on Judah and the nations (vv 8–11); and
4) a third divine oracle promising specific judgment on Babylon once 70 years
have elapsed (vv 12–14). Oracle I (vv 6–7) is demarcated by an unannounced
shift to Yahweh as speaker in v 6 ("Do not provoke me to anger . . . and I will do
you no harm") and an "oracle of Yahweh" formula in v 7. The speaker of vv 3–5
is Jeremiah (MT).

Oracle I has this nice balance:

I	. . . *and I will do you no hurt*	*wĕlō’ ’āraʿ lākem*	v 6
	. . . *to your own hurt*	*lĕraʿ lākem*	v 7

Oracle II has a chiastic structure made from the following key words and
phrases:

II	*king of Babylon*	*melek-bābel*	v 9
	this land . . . all these nations	*hā’āreṣ hazzō’t . . . kol haggôyim hā’ēlleh*	
	all this land . . . and these nations	*kol-hā’āreṣ hazzō’t . . . haggôyim hā’ēlleh*	v 11
	the king of Babylon	*’et-melek-bābel*	

Oracles I and II are linked by these catchwords (cf. Cassuto 1973c: 225):

I	*But you have not listened to me*	*wĕlō’-šĕmaʿtem ’ēlay*	v 7
II	*Because you have not listened to my words*	*. . . lō’-šĕmaʿtem ’et-dĕbāray*	v 8

Yahweh continues to be the speaking voice in Oracles II and III, even surprisingly in v 13, where Jeremiah's prophecies written in a book are cited. These
two oracles are also linked together by catchwords (cf. Cassuto 1973c: 225;
Keown et al.):

II	*seventy years*	*šibʿîm šānâ*	v 11
III	*seventy years*	*šibʿîm šānâ*	v 12

Oracle III in the LXX, as has been mentioned, introduces the Foreign Nation
Oracles, preeminently those against Babylon, which follow after v 13a. In the

MT these oracles have been relocated to chaps. 46–51 (see Rhetoric and Composition for 46:1).

Although I believe that the LXX placement of Foreign Nation Oracles after 25:13a is earlier, I also believe that these oracles, once an independent collection, are intrusive in their context and break up a chapter that otherwise hangs together. Rofé (1989: 397) has argued that the insertion of Foreign Nation Oracles in LXX after 25:13a represents a later reworking, and in this he is probably correct.

There is wide support for the view, here as elsewhere, that the LXX omissions in the chapter are actually MT plusses (Schwally 1888; Duhm; Cornill; Janzen 1973; Tov 1985; Holladay; Jones; McKane; and others). For some, this points to a revision of Jeremiah's original message in the MT. The view in its most radical form was formulated by Schwally, who took the entire chapter (as he did the entire Foreign Nation Collection) to be ingenuine. For him chap. 25 contained no legacy of the Jeremianic preaching—even in his core verses of 1–3, 8–11a, 13a or 12 (1888: 183). Although Schwally's negative appraisal of the chapter was dismissed as baseless by Giesebrecht and critiqued more sharply still by Cassuto (1973c: 204–14), it has affected subsequent interpretation, and even yet is quoted approvingly by McKane. Duhm considered a large part of 25:1–14 to be genuine, although he dated the verses to the postexilic period—after Zechariah but before 2 Chr 36:21 and Daniel 9.

I do not agree that the LXX omissions are largely MT plusses. Some may be, but many are not. We have, for example, seven arguable cases of LXX haplography in vv 1–14. Then there are the omitted LXX references to Nebuchadrezzar/the king of Babylon and Babylon/the Chaldeans (vv 1, 9, 11, 12), which are poorly explained as actually reflecting Jeremiah's preaching in 605 B.C. It makes much better sense if the Babylon and Nebuchadrezzar references are retained. Some scholars, in fact, argue that Jeremiah is revealing for the first time the identity of the foe from the north, now that Nebuchadrezzar has won a decisive victory at Carchemish (Giesebrecht; Rudolph; Bewer; Childs 1959: 194). Giesebrecht (p. 135) says:

> In the fourth year of Jehoiakim the battle of Carchemish was fought, and through it an important decision of historical proportions was brought about. The foe from the north, with which Jeremiah had continually threatened, now gained definite form.

If Jeremiah, then, is now announcing Babylon to be the foe from the north, the LXX, for whatever reason, has deleted the Babylonian references, and its text, instead of being the more original, is rather an impoverished secondary text because of the deletions. With these LXX omissions, and also deletions and emendations even when the MT and LXX agree, certain scholars (Schwally 1888; Cornill; Hyatt; Holladay) argue that Jeremiah's preaching here had only to do with Judah (cf. v 2) and that references to the nations enter later in a revision now preserved in MT (see Notes). But again, in 605 B.C. after Carchemish,

Babylon has become a threat to all nations, not just Judah, and the idea that Jeremiah's preaching at this time would have only to do with the fate of Judah is hardly credible. The conclusion here is one that has been reached with respect to other parts of the Jeremiah book, viz., that the longer MT is consistently the better and more original text and that the shorter LXX is impoverished because its Hebrew *Vorlage* suffered from an unusually large number of omissions due to haplography (Appendices III and V); additionally, in the translation from Hebrew to Greek it sometimes abridged or attempted simplification of its Hebrew *Vorlage* (Volz; Thiel 1973: 264–65; G. Fischer 1991). The clearest indications of abridgment or simplification are the LXX's dislike of repetition and its omission of duplicated passages the second time they occur (see Rhetoric and Composition for 30:8–11).

NOTES

25:1. *The word that came to Jeremiah concerning all the people of Judah.* On this particular superscription, which except for here and in 44:1 appears in the form "The word that came to Jeremiah from Yahweh," see Notes for 7:1 and 21:1. The T expands to "word of prophecy."

in the fourth year of Jehoiakim son of Josiah, king of Judah. The fourth year of Jehoiakim was 605 B.C., an important date in the ancient world because in this year the Babylonian army under Nebuchadrezzar defeated the Egyptians at Carchemish, bringing Syria and Palestine firmly within its grasp. In 605 Jeremiah delivered judgment oracles against Egypt (46:2), prepared a scroll of oracles and other prophetic utterances from the time his public ministry began (36:1), and delivered a personal oracle of salvation to Baruch ben Neriah, the scribe who wrote up the scroll (45:1).

(that was the first year of Nebuchadrezzar, king of Babylon). Other synchronisms of Judahite and Babylonian chronology are found in 32:1; 52:12; and 2 Kgs 25:8. The LXX omits the present synchronism and the one in 52:12 but not the ones in 32:1 and 2 Kgs 25:8. Many scholars (Schwally 1888: 178 n. 1; Giesebrecht; Duhm; Cornill; Bright; Janzen 1973: 100; Tov 1985: 221; Holladay; McKane) take the Babylonian date as a learned gloss, but this largely has to do with their bias in favor of the shorter LXX text. The synchronism could be original (Peake; Volz; Rudolph; Weiser). Aquila has it. Many of the later fifth-century Elephantine papyri, written by professional scribes, contain a double date, Babylonian and Egyptian (see Note for 32:1). There is a slight discrepancy in correlating the two dates. Nebuchadrezzar took the throne in September 605 upon the death of his father, Nabopolassar, but his first official year did not begin until April 604 (Tadmor 1956: 229; Bright 1981: 326). The problem seems to be that the Babylonian calendar reckoned an accession year from the time the king ascended the throne until the following New Year (= April), when his first regnal year began.

the first. The feminine singular adjective *ri'šōnît* is a *hapax legomenon* in the OT, but in the mind of the Judahite narrator most likely refers to the first regnal year of the king, not an accession year (Begrich 1929: 60–61 n. 2).

2. *which Jeremiah the prophet spoke concerning all the people of Judah and to all the inhabitants of Jerusalem.* Because Jeremiah is still moving freely about Jerusalem, this preaching must precede the scroll writing of chap. 36, which is dated in the same year (Streane; Jones). When the scroll is dictated, Jeremiah cannot enter the Temple area (36:5). The LXX omits *kol* ("all") in the phrase "and to all the inhabitants of Jerusalem," which may be due to haplography (homoeoteleuton: *l . . . l*). Cornill, Janzen (1973: 66), and Holladay take the particle as an MT plus. For a discussion of *kol*, which occurs over 500 times in the book of Jeremiah and is sometimes omitted and sometimes added, see Janzen 1973: 65–67.

Jeremiah the prophet. The LXX omits, as it does in 28:12; 38:9, 10, 14, and elsewhere (see Appendix VI B). Often it will retain "Jeremiah" and omit "the prophet," making it difficult to know if the title here is original. Schwally (1888: 178 n. 1), Giesebrecht, Duhm, Peake, Cornill, Bright, and Holladay omit it as an MT plus; Volz, Rudolph, Weiser, and McKane retain. The LXX omission has no effect on interpretation, since v 1 names Jeremiah as the subject for "which he spoke" (*hon elalēsen*).

3. *From the thirteenth year of Josiah son of Amon, king of Judah, yes, until this day—this is twenty-three years—the word of Yahweh has come to me, and I have spoken to you—constantly I spoke—but you have not listened.* It has been 23 years since Yahweh's word first came to Jeremiah in his call, which was 627 B.C. (1:2). Jeremiah is not claiming to have been preaching for 23 years, for the prophet's public ministry did not begin until 622 B.C., or soon after. For this revision of the traditional chronology, see §Introduction: Prophetic Ministry. It is then for a lesser number of years, say about 18, that Jeremiah has been preaching and the people not listening.

From the thirteenth year. Hebrew *min-šĕlōš ʿeśrēh šānâ*. The LXX has "in the thirteenth year" (*en triskaidekatō etei*); Aq and Symm "from the thirteenth year" (*apo triskaidekatou etous*).

the word of Yahweh has come to me. Hebrew *hāyâ dĕbar-yhwh ʾēlāy*. Compare the first-person superscriptions in 1:4, 11, 13; and elsewhere (see Note for 1:4). The LXX omits, and once again many take the words as an MT plus. Here the omission combines with other LXX readings in vv 3–5 to make Yahweh, not Jeremiah, the speaker. The omission may then be part of a larger editing. But this does not make the LXX the better or more original text. Aquila and Theod have the omitted words. Also, there is no messenger formula in vv 3–5 indicating a divine oracle. In fact, vv 1–2 introduce Jeremiah as addressing a Judahite audience, and the concluding *lēʾmōr* ("saying") in v 2 introduces his speech, not Yahweh's. More important, if LXX's omission of "the word of Yahweh has come to me" be accepted, the text will then read as if Jeremiah has been *preaching* for 23 years, which, as we have said, cannot be right. He has been preaching for 18 years at most. The omitted words should therefore be retained, with MT (Volz; Rudolph; Weiser).

and I have spoken to you—constantly I spoke—but you have not listened. Hebrew *wā'ădabbēr* ("and I have spoken") is a *waw consecutive* imperfect of the type found in Isa 6:1 (GKC §111b). The verb repeated with *škm* ("to rise early"), which recurs in v 4, is for emphasis (see Note on 7:13). Here in v 3 the form is an anomalous *'aškēm* (Q), "I rose early," instead of the usual *haškēm*, "rising early." Several MSS and T have *haškēm*, leading some scholars (Duhm; Cornill; Ehrlich 1912: 307; Rudolph; Holladay) to emend. But *'aškēm* can stand (Giesebrecht). The LXX lacks the concluding "but you have not listened" (*wĕlō' šĕma'tem*), which can be attributed to haplography (homoeoarcton: *w . . . w*). These words should not be deleted with Schwally (1888: 179) who imagines that the prior "I have spoken" introduces the repentance message of v 5 (all of v 4 is taken as interpolation). Aquila, Symm, and Theod have the words. More important, the indictment is incomplete without "but you have not listened" (cf. 7:13, 25–26; 11:7–8; 29:19; 35:14–16; 44:4–5). On the recurring theme of Yahweh speaking and people not hearing in the Baruch prose, see Note for 44:5.

4. *and Yahweh has repeatedly sent to you all his servants the prophets—constantly he sent—but you have not listened, indeed you have not bent your ear to listen.* On Yahweh's having sent prophets without success to the covenant people in times past, see Note for 7:25. Jeremiah cites these former prophets (of doom) in his speech to Hananiah in 28:8.

and Yahweh has repeatedly sent. Hebrew *wĕšālaḥ yhwh*. The perfect consecutive verb carries forth repeated action in the past (GKC §112e). The LXX omits "Yahweh" in the interest of keeping Yahweh as the speaker. Read the MT (so Ehrlich 1912: 307).

to listen. Hebrew *lišmōa'*. The LXX omission of this term can be attributed to haplography (homoeoarcton: *l . . . l*). The word is present in Aq and Theod.

5. *Return, would you, each person from his evil way and from your evil doings, and dwell on the soil that Yahweh gave to you and to your fathers for all time.* "Return!" (*šûbû*) is Jeremiah's recurring trumpet call (18:11; 35:15), said by Volz to be the *Kernwort* of the prophet's preaching. Volz compares it with the later preaching of John the Baptist. Prophetic preaching modifies in a significant way the preaching of Deuteronomy, which simply admonishes people to keep the covenant in order that they may live long in the land (Deut 5:32–33). Jeremiah, too, preached this message (11:4–5), and in his first Temple Oracle (7:3–7) told the people to "make good" (*hêṭîbû*) your ways and your doings," which is somewhere between a call to obedience and a call for conversion. In the call to return, tenure in the land is no longer assured; in fact, people are told that unless they change their evil behavior the land will be lost. Calvin notes a wordplay in the Hebrew on *šûbû* ("return") and *ûšĕbû* ("dwell"). The LXX has "I gave" (*edōka*) instead of "Yahweh gave," which is consistent with its shift to Yahweh as speaker. Yahweh's gift of the land to the fathers is a central theme both in Deuteronomy (Deut 6:10, 18; 8:1; 9:5; 10:11; cf. 32:7–9) and in Jeremiah (Jer 3:18; 7:7, 14; 11:5; 16:15; 24:10; 25:5; 30:3; 32:22; 35:15).

for all time. Hebrew *lĕmin-ʿôlām wĕʿad-ʿôlām.* On this idiom, see Note for 7:7. Yahweh may have given Israel the land for all time, but since the Sinai covenant is conditional in nature and contains a multitude of curses should the people disobey (Deuteronomy 28), one wonders if the Deuteronomic wording, "that you may live long in the land" (*wĕhaʾăraktem yāmîm bāʾāreṣ*), would not have been a better and more realistic articulation of the divine promise (cf. Deut 5:33).

6. *Do not go after other gods to serve them and to worship them, and do not provoke me to anger with the work of your hands, and I will do you no hurt.* This could be preaching out of Deuteronomy, but it is followed immediately with an indictment on the people for breaking the first and second commandments (cf. Exod 20:3–4; Deut 5:7–8), which makes it more like early Jeremiah reform preaching. See also 35:15.

the work of your hands. Hebrew *maʿăśēh yĕdêkem.* The LXX, T, and Vg have "works" plural; T and Vg have a plural also in vv 7 and 14. This stereotypical phrase has generally positive meaning in Deuteronomy (Deut 2:7; 14:29; 16:15; 24:19), although there and elsewhere it can refer disparagingly to idols (Deut 4:28; 31:29; Jer 1:16; 25:6, 7; 32:30; 44:8; cf. 2 Kgs 22:17). See further Note for 1:16.

And I will do you no hurt. Hebrew *wĕlōʾ ʾāraʿ lākem*, where *raʿ* can also be translated "evil." The LXX has *tou kakōsai hymas* ("to do you evil/hurt"), which is MT's reading at the end of v 7. The T: "and I will not do evil to you."

7. *oracle of Yahweh—so as to provoke me to anger with the work of your hands, to your own hurt.* The LXX once again omits, and many (Schwally 1888: 180; Giesebrecht; Cornill; Peake; Volz; Rudolph; Weiser; Tov 1985: 233) take the words as an MT plus. If the Hebrew *Vorlage* to the LXX lacked the messenger formula, as it sometimes does, this omission could be due to haplography (homoeoarcton: *l . . . l*). Jeremiah states often that Yahweh becomes provoked by people's worshiping false gods and their idols (7:18; 8:19; 11:17; 25:6–7; 32:29–30; 44:3, 8), a perspective he shares with the Song of Moses (Deut 32:16, 21). See also Huldah's oracle in 2 Kgs 22:17.

so as to provoke me to anger. Hebrew *lĕmaʿan hakʿisēnî* (Q). Here the conjunction *lĕmaʿan* ("so as to") indicates not purpose, but result. For other such usages, see Note on 27:10.

to your own hurt. Hebrew *lĕraʿ lākem.* An interesting rhetorical twist is that now it is not Yahweh who will bring hurt on the people for chasing after other gods but the people who, because of their adventurism, will bring hurt on themselves. See also 7:6, where the same expression occurs, and 7:19, where the same rhetoric is employed.

8. *Therefore thus said Yahweh of hosts: 'Because you have not listened to my words.'* The messenger formula in this introductory statement is not really needed, since the oracle following has an "oracle of Yahweh" formula (v 9). There is also somewhat of a problem in correlating "because you have not listened to my words" with the oracle following, since that oracle promises judgment not only for Judah but for other nations. Rudolph says: "für die Sünde

Judas . . . kann nur Judah gestraft werden" ("For the sins of Judah, only Judah can be punished"), a comment echoing those made by Schwally (1888: 181) and Cornill earlier. Rudolph's solution and that of others (Schwally; Duhm; Volz; Weiser; Thiel 1973: 271; Holladay) is to delete "and against all these nations round about" in v 9. There is no textual support for this deletion, since the LXX has "all the nations" (*panta ta ethnē*) in its text. The aim of the deletion apparently is to make the oracle one in which only Judah is addressed. But on balance it seems more likely that the nations were included in the judgment from the beginning. The entire chapter speaks of judgment on the nations. It must then be concluded that the reason given for the judgment in v 8, which may be a later addition providing linkage to the previous oracle (see Rhetoric and Composition), simply lacked precision in introducing the oracle, or else that it actually intended to say that Judah's sins were of such a great magnitude that they would bring about a worldwide judgment. Cassuto (1973c: 208) says that,

> if Judah's punishment can only come within the framework of a world catastrophe, which must necessarily overwhelm other peoples too, the prophet cannot differentiate between the two details of one event and assign two different causes to them, and the problem of the sources of the disaster that will trouble the gentiles will not even enter his mind.

Yahweh of hosts. The LXX lacks "of hosts," as elsewhere (see Appendix VI). Aquila, Symm, and Theod all have *tōn dunameōn*.

9. *Look I am sending and I will take all the tribes of the north . . . also to Nebuchadrezzar, king of Babylon, my servant.* Yahweh will summon the punishing agent, which at first will be tribes of the north, then Nebuchadrezzar and the army of Babylon. Within a few short years, in 599–597 B.C., this was precisely the sequence of events for Judah: Yahweh sent marauding bands from "the north" to ravage the land (2 Kgs 24:2), after which came Nebuchadrezzar in 597 to capture Jerusalem. And in 599–598, just before Nebuchadrezzar came to Jerusalem, the Babylonian king was raiding desert camps of Arabs from his base in Syria. One must keep in mind that Nebuchadrezzar's broader aim was to subjugate all nations in the west, not just Judah. As the present oracle was spoken, he was in Philistia destroying Ashkelon and Ekron. In 601 B.C., he was fighting Egypt on its own frontier and a couple decades later would be campaigning again in Egypt, as well as in Ammon and Moab. The aim of the Babylonian king was to destroy or subjugate all the nations of the former Assyrian Empire.

all the tribes of the north. Hebrew *kol-mišpĕḥôt ṣāpôn*. An enemy coalition (cf. 1:15). The LXX lacks "all" and has *patrian* singular ("clan, tribe"). The MT presupposes two separate though not mutually exclusive enemies, which is the better reading (Peake). The T has "all the kingdoms of the north." On the proverbial "north" where powers of disaster are bred, see Note for 1:14.

also to Nebuchadrezzar, king of Babylon, my servant. This bold metaphor occurs two other times in 27:6 and 43:10. It is an *oxymoron*, since "my servant" in the mouth of Yahweh is otherwise a term of endearment (e.g., "my servants the prophets" in 7:25; 26:5; 29:19; 35:15; 44:4; "Jacob my servant" in 30:10 [= 46:27]; and "David my servant" in 33:21, 22, 26). Smelik (1997) says the term means to be provocative. Never in the Bible except here is an enemy of Israel given this title. Cyrus is called "my shepherd" (*rōʿî*) in Isa 44:28, and "his [Yahweh's] anointed" (*mĕšîḥô*) in Isa 45:1, but the Persian king figures prominently in Israel's future salvation. The LXX omits the present phrase along with the "oracle of Yahweh" formula, which has led a train of scholars beginning with Graf and Kuenen to delete. In their view, the original text was without a reference to Nebuchadrezzar, who in being added to the MT becomes an adjunct to the tribes of the north. Hebrew *wĕʾel* ("also to") before Nebuchadrezzar does in fact read poorly after the two verbs beginning the verse. However, if the "oracle of Yahweh" formula was missing in the LXX's *Vorlage*, the loss of "also to Nebuchadrezzar the king of Babylon, my servant" could be attributed to haplography (homoeoarcton: *w . . . w*). The MT may then be the better text. Its two verbs and two objects form a chiasmus, where the first verb goes with the second object, and the second verb goes with the first object (D. N. Freedman):

> Look, I am sending
>   and I will take
>   all the tribes of the north
> also to Nebuchadrezzar, king of Babylon, my servant

Yahweh *is sending* to Nebuchadrezzar, and *will take* all the tribes of the north. Even with this unusual grammatical sequence, the tribes of the north should probably still be understood as coming into the land before Nebuchadrezzar. But reading the text in this fashion helps explain the difficult *ʾel* ("to") before "Nebuchadrezzar." On "my servant" having possible theological and political overtones in this present usage, see Note for 27:6.

against all these nations round about. As noted in v 8 above, this phrase ought not to be deleted simply to do away with "the nations." The LXX has "the nations," lacking only "these."

I will devote them to destruction. Hebrew *hahărамtîm.* The verb *ḥrm* (sacred ban = genocide) is unusually strong for use against Israel, even if other nations are included. The term derives from holy war, referring to the ban (*ḥērem*) placed on a captured city's inhabitants (sometimes also cattle and other spoil) for the purpose of devoting (= destroying) them as a gift to Yahweh (50:21, 26–27; 51:3; cf. Deut 2:34–35; 13:16–17[Eng 13:15–16]). Israel in taking the Promised Land carried on holy war against its enemies, but now Yahweh is turning the tables and will declare holy war on Israel, or what is left of Israel. But McKane says the verb here may mean nothing more than "destroy." The readings of the Versions vary. The LXX has *exerēmōsō autous* ("I will utterly desert them");

T: "I will consume them"; and Vg: "I will destroy them" (*interficiam eos*). But Aq and Symm both have a stronger "I will devote them," *anathemati(s)ō autous*.

a desolation, an object of hissing, and ruins forever. More *accumulatio*. On land and city curses in Jeremiah, which repeat in vv 11, 12, and 18, see Note for 48:9.

a desolation. Hebrew *šammâ*. A very common term in the poetry and prose of Jeremiah (see again vv 11, 18, and 38), occurring often in strings of curse words (see Note for 24:9).

an object of hissing. Hebrew *šĕrēqâ*. Another common Jeremiah curse word (18:16; 19:8; 25:9, 18; 29:19; 51:37), included often in curse-word strings (see Note for 24:9).

and ruins forever. Hebrew *ûlĕḥorbôt ʿôlām*. The singular *ḥorbâ* ("ruin") occurs in vv 11, 18, and often in Jeremiah (7:34; 22:5; 27:17; 44:2, 6, 22), frequently in strings of curses (see Note for 24:9). The plural is intensive (GKC §124e), such as we have in *šimmôt ʿôlām* ("desolations forever") of v 12. The LXX's *oneidismon* ("reproach") appears to presuppose Heb *ḥerpat*; cf. 23:40 (*ḥerpat ʿôlām*); 24:9; and 29:18. Holladay prefers the LXX reading, saying that the inhabitants of a city can hardly become rubble. But in support of MT's *ḥorbôt*, it should be noted that the coming destruction will be upon both inhabitants and the land. The term *ʿôlām* ("forever") is not meant in an absolute sense, for it is later qualified by a reference to "seventy years" of Babylonian suzerainty (Calvin; Brueggemann). Calvin says Jeremiah is correcting himself, thus mitigating his earlier judgment.

10. *And I will banish from them the voice of joy and the voice of gladness, the voice of the groom and the voice of the bride.* This curse ending joyful sounds in the land occurs elsewhere in 7:34 and 16:9. See also Bar 2:22–23. In Ezek 26:13 we read: "And I will stop the music of your songs, and the sound of your lyres shall be heard no more." All are standard treaty curses, having numerous Akkadian parallels (Hillers 1964: 57–58; Weinfeld 1972b: 141). An Esarhaddon inscription contains this curse: "No joyful man enters its streets, no musician is met." And in the older *balag* city laments of ancient Mesopotamia (M. E. Cohen 1988: 721, 723, et passim), these stereotyped lines appear:

That city, where its young girls are no longer happy!
That city, where its young men do not rejoice!

The dancing places are filled with ghosts
The street is not sated with its joy.

(pp. 245, 336)

In the Deir ʿAlla texts (Combination II 7) we find this line: "A traveller will not enter a house, neither will enter there a bridegroom a house," which appears to mean that in a devastated country no wedding will take place (Hoftijzer and van der Kooij 1976: 174, 180, 226; *CS II* 144). But the day will come when joyful sounds will again be heard in Jerusalem and other cities of Judah (33:11).

the sound of millstones and the light of the lamp. An expansion of the usual
Jeremianic list of joyful sounds, occurring only here. Hebrew *rēhayim* is a
dual, indicating a pair of millstones. The LXX's *osmēn murou* ("scent of
myrrh") in place of "sound of millstones" cannot be right (Cornill: an inner-
Greek confusion of *murou*, "of myrrh," and *mulou*, "of a millstone"). With
bread being baked every day, grinding is a daily activity, done in the early
morning by women (Isa 47:2; Job 31:10; cf. Homer, *Odyssey* xx 105–9). Two
women sit facing each other at the hand mill, both of them holding the handle
by which the upper stone is turned on the lower one (Matt 24:41; Luke 17:35).
Lamps are lit at the onset of darkness, and throughout the evening hours their
soft light can be seen. The two images symbolize domestic life. They are also
complementary: one is *heard* in the *morning*, the other *seen* in the *evening*. In
the Talmud (Sanhedrin 32b) the sound of the mill is said to refer to the time of
circumcision, the light of a lamp to a time of festival—both joyous occasions
(Morris 1929–33). On oil lamps in the time of Jeremiah, see R. H. Smith
(1964) and P. J. King (1993:178–79). The cessation of millstone sounds is another curse. An Esarhaddon treaty states (#443–45; Borger 1961: 188; Hillers
1964: 58; Weinfeld 1972b: 141–42; ANET³ 538):

> May there be no noise of millstone and oven in your houses
> May you experience a constant lack of grain for grinding.

In Rev 18:22–23, the curse on Babylon *redivivus* (= Rome) includes both the
cessation of millstone sounds and the light of a lamp.

11. *And all this land will become a ruin and a desolation.* Reference here is
to the land of Judah ("this land" means Judah also in v 9). The LXX omits
"this" and "(for) a ruin," but both words are present in Aq, Symm, Theod, T,
and Vg, which argues for their retention (*pace* Schwally 1888: 181 n. 2; Cornill; Rudolph; Bright; Janzen 1973: 45; Holladay). Ehrlich (1912: 308) supports the whole of v 11 as preserved in MT.

and these nations shall serve the king of Babylon seventy years. The 70 years
here and in 29:10 refer not to the length of Judah's exile or to "Jerusalem's desolations" but to Babylon's tenure as a world power (Duhm). Kimhi says that
Cyrus attacked Babylon after 70 years of Babylonian rule. The idea that Jerusalem and the Temple lay in ruins for 70 years is postexilic (Zech 1:12; 7:5;
2 Chr 36:21; Dan 9:2) and not implicit in Jeremiah's prophecies (Orr 1956:
304–6; Weinfeld 1972b: 144). The number 70 is stereotyped, thus no more
than an approximation. If it corresponds to anything, it is the conventional description of a full life-span (Ps 90:10). Tyre is forgotton for 70 years, then remembered (Isa 23:15–17). The Black Stone of Esarhaddon (d. 680 B.C.) makes
reference to an anticipated 70-year period of Babylon's desolation, which, however, was not carried out due to special favor shown by Marduk (Luckenbill
1924–25: 166–68; Weinfeld 1972b: 144–46). As far as Babylon's tenure as a
world power is concerned, 70 years turned out to be a good approximation:
From the fall of Nineveh (612 B.C.) to Babylon's capture by Cyrus (539 B.C.)

was 73 years; from the Battle of Carchemesh (605 B.C.—Nebuchadrezzar's first year; cf. 25:1) to Babylon's capture by Cyrus (539 B.C.) was 66 years; and from the actual end of the Assyrian Empire (609/8 B.C.) to Babylon's capture by Cyrus and the return of the exiles (539 B.C.) was almost precisely 70 years. The LXX here reads "and they [presumably Judah's inhabitants] shall serve among the nations seventy years." While this statement is true, the MT reading is still preferable (*pace* Schwally 1888: 181; Cornill; Holladay). Not only Judah but all nations would be under Babylonian suzerainty for 70 years.

12. *And it will happen when seventy years are fulfilled, I will reckon against the king of Babylon and against that nation—oracle of Yahweh—their iniquity; also against the land of the Chaldeans, and I will make it desolations forever.* Many commentators take all or part of this verse as secondary, some omitting (with LXX) the Babylonian references so as to leave a prophecy only against Judah (Bright; McKane), others omitting the entire verse for this reason and others; e.g., it is assumed that phrases in the verse have been quarried from 29:10; 51:26, and 62 (Rudolph; Weiser; Holladay). Older commentators, for an even greater assortment of reasons, took all or most all of vv 11–14 as secondary (Graf; Giesebrecht; Duhm; Cornill; Peake; Streane; S. R. Driver; Volz). Besides a stated preference for the shorter LXX text, these scholars argued that an oracle against Babylon was out of place in the present context. Many, it should be added, also denied Jeremianic authorship for a Babylon oracle, a position taken similarly with regard to the Babylon oracles in chaps. 50–51 (see Rhetoric and Composition for 46:1 and 50:1–3). Of the two LXX omissions in the present verse, 1) "against the king of Babylon and" and 2) "oracle of Yahweh[e] —their iniquity; also against the land of the Chaldeans," the former can be attributed to haplography (whole-word: *ʿl . . . ʿl*). As far as Jeremianic authorship of a Babylon oracle is concerned, the conclusion reached in chaps. 50–51 is that Jeremiah has authored most of these oracles, which makes it unnecessary to deny Jeremianic authorship to the Babylon oracle here. This oracle needs only to be dated after the fourth year of Jehoiakim, which would mean that it postdates the two oracles preceding. But it need not be later than Zedekiah's middle years, i.e., 594/3 B.C. (see Rhetoric and Composition). The anticipation of a 70-year Babylonian rule restates what is said in v 11b, with the one difference that now judgment is said to await Babylon at the end of this period. Babylon's 70-year rule is anticipated also in 29:10, except that there, in place of an eventual judgment for Babylon, a promise of eventual salvation for Yahweh's covenant people is given.

and I will make it desolations forever. Hebrew *wĕśamtî ʾōtô lĕšimmôt ʿôlām.* The expression "desolations forever" occurs also in 51:26, 62; and Ezek 35:9, where in each case the plural form is an intensive plural (see Note for 51:26). Compare the singular *šĕmāmâ ʿad-ʿôlām* in 49:33. This strong imprecation is more prophetic exaggeration, comparable to what the prophet predicts for

---

[e]The LXX text of Ziegler omits the messenger formula; the Rahlfs LXX text has *phēsin kurios* ("said the Lord"). The formula is lacking in G[BS], but other LXX MSS have it.

Judah in v 9. Calvin correctly recognized that Babylon, at least when taken by Cyrus in 539 B.C., was not reduced to a perpetual ruin. The city remained safe and for many ages was celebrated for its great splendor. Calvin said that here the prophet simply exceeded the limits of truth in this prophecy. A permanently desolated Babylon is predicted also in Isa 13:20. The masculine *'ōtô*, "it, him," refers back to "that nation" (Holladay). Emendation to the feminine *'ōtāh*, "it, her," which assumes the antecedent to be "the land of the Chaldeans" (*'ereṣ* is feminine), is unnecessary (*pace* Ehrlich 1912: 308; Rudolph). The LXX has a masculine plural, *autous* ("them").

13. *And I will bring against that land all my words that I have spoken against it, everything written in this book, which Jeremiah prophesied against all the nations.* The LXX concludes the verse with "everything written in this book," after which come the Foreign Nation Oracles (LXX 25:14–31:44). In the LXX arrangement, "this book" appears to have referred originally to the Babylon oracles only (Rashi), which were written on a separate scroll (51:59–64). Then later reference was to all the Foreign Nation Oracles (Kimhi), also probably written on a separate scroll. In the MT, where the Foreign Nation Oracles have been relocated to chaps. 46–51, "this book" refers to a Jeremiah book of 51 (and finally 52) chapters. In both cases "this book" is forward-looking; reference is not back to Jeremiah's collected Judah utterances in 1:1–25:13a (see Rhetoric and Composition). Furthermore, "that land," *hā'āreṣ hahî'*, in both MT and LXX refers to Babylon, not Judah (*pace* Hyatt) and ought not to be deleted (*pace* Holladay) or changed to "this land," *hā'āreṣ hazzō't* (*pace* Rudolph; Weiser; Bright). These are simply additional attempts to reinterpret the oracle as being only for Judah. "That land" refers clearly to "the land of the Chaldeans" mentioned in v 12 (G. Fischer 1991: 482).

which Jeremiah prophesied against all the nations. These words are lacking in G[BS], although in some LXX MSS *osa eprophēteusen Ieremias epi panta ta ethnē* appears as a subscription at the end of the Foreign Nation Collection (LXX 32:13; Rahlfs prints it in the main text; Ziegler lists it as a marginal reading). Holladay thinks that the LXX uses these words to introduce the Elam oracle, which according to its arrangement comes immediately after "all that is written in this book." But this is doubtful, since the Elam oracle has an introduction also in MT 49:34a, differing there only slightly from the introduction in the LXX. Birkeland (1939: 45–46) took the present words as a superscription to 25:15–38 (bound together by v 14), a view that found favor with E. Nielsen (1954: 76) and one that has found its way into the translations of JB and NJB. Whether the present words were part of the original oracle is unclear. It is surprising, surely, to hear Yahweh refer to Jeremiah by name in a divine oracle, which may indicate that the phrase is a later addition.

14. *Indeed many nations and great kings shall make them serve—even them! And I will repay them according to their deeds and according to the work of their hands.* The LXX omits, for which reason many commentators delete. But the loss can be attributed to haplography (homoeoarcton: *k . . . k* with *kōh*, not *kî*, or homoeoteleuton: *m . . . m*). Aquila, Theod, T, and Vg all have the verse;

Symm has v 14a. That many nations and great kings shall one day make Babylon serve is predicted also in 27:7.

shall make them serve. Reading an imperfect *ya'abdû*; where a *yod* on the prior word can be assumed to have been lost through haplography (Blayney; Ehrlich 1912: 308). The verse is prophecy (Rudolph), but MT *'ābĕdû* cannot be a prophetic perfect (Cornill). The verb *'bd* + *bĕ* in the Qal means "make serve" (22:13; 25:14; 27:7; 30:8; 34:9), a meaning the H-stem also has (cf. Exod 1:13, 14). The combination can mean "do work with (an animal)," as in Deut 15:19. Jeremiah is saying that many nations and great kings shall enslave the people of Babylon (Rashi), perhaps even that they will work the Babylonian people the way a farmer works his ox.

even them! Hebrew *gam-hēmmâ*. The pronoun gives emphasis to *bām*, "them" (GKC §135g). Servitude will be the lot of the Babylonians—even them! Note the emphatic "even he!" (*gam-hû'*) in the parallel verse of 27:7b.

And I will repay them. On Yahweh's repayment (*šlm* Piel) of Babylon, see also 50:29; 51:6, 24, 56. Judah's full repayment at the hand of Yahweh is discussed in the Note for 16:18.

according to their deeds and according to the work of their hands. A cliché, as we see from v 6, but here referring to Babylon's (evil) deeds and its worship of idols. Elsewhere it is said that Babylon will be punished by Yahweh because it is proud (50:31–32) and because it trusts in its own gods (50:38b; 51:47, 52).

MESSAGE AND AUDIENCE

The present narrative states that a word came to Jeremiah from Yahweh in Jehoiakim's fourth year, which, the audience is told, was also the first year of Nebuchadrezzar, the king of Babylon. Jeremiah is said on this occasion to have begun his address to a Jerusalem and Judahite audience with a personal word about his many years as prophet to this people. In this remarkable insight into a prophet's inner thoughts, in which he unburdens himself of a deep personal hurt, we are told that for 23 years Yahweh's word has come to him (beginning with the time he first received Yahweh's call to be a prophet), and for a lesser number of years he has spoken to these people, but they would not hear him. Jeremiah reminds these people that over the years Yahweh has sent—repeatedly sent—his servants, the prophets, but the people would not hear them either. No attempt even to bend the ear. Yahweh's message was simple: return from your evil ways and doings, and live in the land I gave to you and to your ancestors.

A divine oracle follows in which Yahweh, who is now the speaking voice, asks only that the people obey the first two commandments. If they do, Yahweh will do them no hurt. Then Yahweh says what Jeremiah has just said—namely, that the people have not listened to him, provoking him instead with handmade idols, to their own hurt. A second oracle follows, which is one of judgment. Because the people have not heeded Yahweh's covenant or his messengers who called them to return to the covenant demands, the whole world will pay a huge price. Yahweh will send for the tribes of the north and for Nebuchadrezzar, the king of Babylon, who, wonder of wonders, is now acting as his servant, and these combined forces of hostility will be brought against Judah and the surrounding nations. Yahweh in anger will devote them all to destruction. The language here, as the careful listener will be quick to recognize, is holy war language. The peoples suffering judgment will endure shameful reproach, and the lands they have inhabited will become rubble for all time. Glad sounds will vanish — the happy voices of bride and groom, the morning sound of grinding millstones; missing also will be the soft lamplight of evening. Judah, it is repeated, will become a ruin, and she along with other conquered nations can expect to be in the service of the king of Babylon 70 years.

In a third oracle, which is dated sometime later, Yahweh says that after 70 years he will reckon with the iniquity of the king of Babylon, the nation of Babylon, and the land of a proud Babylonian people. The land he will make desolations forever. The oracle goes on to say, in what may be a later add-on, that all the dire predictions contained in a book of oracles against this nation will fall on Babylon. At this time many nations and great kings will make the Babylonians serve — yes, even them! For Yahweh intends to repay Babylon for its evil deeds and for its handmade idols.

Jeremiah's speech and the first two divine oracles are datable to the fourth year of Jehoiakim, i.e., 605 B.C. Oracle III, because of v 13, must date to after 594/3 B.C., when Jeremiah is said to have written the Babylon collection of oracles into a book.

As I write (August 2001), an evening wedding celebration is taking place in East Jerusalem. Lights are on outside the St. George Hotel, and the sounds of honking cars and happy voices fill the street. But should violence and war come again to this city named for peace, sounds such as these will no longer be heard, and the soft lights now seen will no longer pierce the evening darkness.

EXCURSUS III: THE COMPOSITION OF JEREMIAH 24–36

Chapters 24–36 are manifestly out of chronological order, which does not make them unique in the book of Jeremiah, since prophetic utterances and narrative all throughout the book are assembled according to criteria other than chronology. It is just that a lack of chronological sequence is more noticeable in these chapters because many of the narratives are dated. The Book of Restoration in chaps. 30–33 has been inserted into the larger book we now possess (30:2), possibly to juxtapose the hope it contains with the hope in Jeremiah's letter to the exiles in chap. 29. This onetime independent book has undergone its own expansion, from a poetic core in 30:5–31:22 to a book comprising chaps. 30–31, and finally to a book comprising chaps. 30–33 (see Rhetoric and Composition for 30:1–3).

With the aid of rhetorical criticism, which, it should be noted, here functions as a *diachronic* method, we can identify two earlier clusters of narrative prose: a "Jehoiakim Cluster" (chaps. 25, 26, 35, 36), and a "Zedekiah Cluster" (24, 27, 28, 29). The one remaining chapter of Zedekiah prose in chaps. 24–36 is chap. 34, which has been inserted into the place it occupies for polemical purposes. Reporting on how Zedekiah and the people of Jerusalem reneged on a covenant made to release Hebrew slaves, it is juxtaposed to the report of faithful Rechabites in chap. 35. Together the two narratives make the single point that marginal Rechabites showed themselves to be more faithful to their covenant than Zedekiah and the people of Jerusalem showed themselves to be to theirs (Lundbom 1997b: 46–47).

The main question to be answered, then, is how such carefully-wrought clusters of Jehoiakim and Zedekiah prose could have been undone, leaving us with the disarray we now have? Why, we may ask, were not the clusters kept together when integrated into an expanded Jeremiah book, and placed one after the other? The answer given in my earlier work (Lundbom 1975: 110–11 [= 1997: 144–45]) is one I would still put forward as best explaining the material as we have it. When a decision was made to integrate the two clusters into a larger Jeremiah book, chap. 24 of the Zedekiah Cluster was chosen as a suitable beginning because it was programmatic for Zedekiah's reign and contained a vision account similar to the vision accounts in chap. 1, which began the existing book. The most suitable conclusion was chap. 36 of the Jehoiakim Cluster, vv 1–8 in particular, which served as a colophon reporting the role that Baruch played in writing down the first Jeremiah scroll (Lundbom 1986b: 104–6). If chap. 24 was the chosen beginning and chap. 36 the chosen conclusion, it was inevitable that the two clusters be undone and that the chronology be broken. This, I believe, is what happened, and it explains the present sequence of chaps. 24–29 and 34–36, where Zedekiah prose and Jehoiakim prose are interspersed. Even so, we should note that chaps. 25–26 and 35–36 of the Jehoiakim Cluster and chaps. 27–29 in the Zedekiah Cluster were left undisturbed. The work of compilation, both the preparation of narrative clusters and their partial undoing to create a larger Jeremiah book, was likely the work of Jeremiah's colleague and friend, Baruch the scribe.

2. A Wrath-Filled Cup of Wine for the Nations (25:15–29)

25 [15]For thus Yahweh, God of Israel, said to me: Take this wrath-filled cup of wine from my hand, and make all the nations to whom I am sending you drink it. [16]And they shall drink and retch and go mad before the sword that I am sending among them. [17]So I took the cup from the hand of Yahweh and made all the nations to whom Yahweh sent me drink: [18]Jerusalem and the cities of Judah, and its kings, its princes, to make them a ruin, a desolation, an object of hissing, and a swearword, as at this day; [19]Pharaoh, king of Egypt, and his ser-

vants, and his princes, and all his people, [20]and all the mixed races; and all the kings of the land of Uz, and all the kings of the land of the Philistines, that is, Ashkelon, and Gaza, and Ekron, and the remnant of Ashdod; [21]Edom, and Moab, and the Ammonites; [22]and all the kings of Tyre, and all the kings of Sidon, and the kings of the coastlands that are across the sea; [23]and Dedan, and Tema, and Buz, and all who crop the hair at the temples; [24]and all the kings of Arabia, and all the kings of the mixed races who dwell in the desert; [25] and all the kings of Zimri, and all the kings of Elam, and all the kings of Media; [26]and all the kings of the north, those near and those far, one to another; yes, all the world's kingdoms that are on the face of the earth. And the king of Sheshak shall drink after them.

[27]Then you shall say to them:

Thus said Yahweh of hosts, God of Israel:
Drink and be drunk, yes, vomit and fall, and you shall never rise before the sword that I am sending among you.

[28]And it will happen that they will refuse to take the cup from your hand to drink; then you shall say to them:

Thus said Yahweh of hosts:
You shall certainly drink! [29]For look, if I am beginning to work evil in the city upon which my name is called, then for you, shall you assuredly go unpunished?

You shall not go unpunished, for I am calling a sword upon all the inhabitants of the earth—oracle of Yahweh of hosts.

RHETORIC AND COMPOSITION

MT 25:15–29 = LXX 32:15–29. The present verses are delimited at the top end by the messenger formula in v 15, before which comes a *petuḥah* in M[A] and a *setumah* in M[L] and M[P]. At the bottom end delimitation is by an "oracle of Yahweh of hosts" formula at the end of v 29 (MT only) and a shift to poetry in v 30b, after a new introductory directive to Jeremiah in v 30a. There are no sections in the medieval codices after v 29. A space exists in 4QJer[c] after v 26, but Tov (1997: 181, 193) fails to identify it as a section. If the space is a section, it would mark a break between the end of the litany of nations, where Jeremiah is the speaker, and the divine oracle beginning in v 27. The *petuḥah* in M[A] and *setumah* in M[L] after "then you shall say to them" in v 27 appear to be misplaced.

The passage is entirely in prose (*pace* DeRoche 1978, who tries to make vv 15–19 and 26–29 into poetry), containing as it does an extraordinary number of prose particles (69 in 230 words, according to D. N. Freedman [*'ăšer*: 7; *'et*: 39; *ha-*: 23], which is 30%, significantly above the 20% benchmark set by Andersen and Forbes for prose in Jeremiah, Ezekiel, and the historical narratives of Kings and Chronicles; cf. Andersen and Forbes 1983: 166). Giesebrecht (p. xxi) and Rudolph, nevertheless, take this as genuine preaching from Jeremiah (Source A). Mowinckel (1914: 21) took only vv 15–16 and 27–29 as Source A. Its formal structure in outline is the following:

I   Directive to Jeremiah in a vision, serving also as a superscription (vv 15–16)
    Report saying that the directive has been fulfilled (vv 17–26)

II Directive to Jeremiah to speak a curse on the nations (v 27a)
       Oracle preceded by a "thus said Yahweh of hosts, God of Israel"
       messenger formula (v 27b)

III Directive to Jeremiah when the nations refuse the curse (v 28a)
       Oracle beginning ". . . look" (hinnēh), preceded by a "thus said Yahweh
       of hosts" messenger formula (vv 28b–29a)
       Oracle followed by an "oracle of Yahweh of hosts" messenger formula (v 29b)

This formal structure has similarities to the formal structure in the narrative of 18:1–12, where Yahweh sends Jeremiah to the potter's shop for an object lesson, and then follows with divine oracles. There, as here, a directive is given, and Jeremiah reports having carried it out. But the narrative here is a vision report, where Yahweh and Jeremiah are in dialogue about the latter serving up a cup of wrath to the nations (vv 15–17). In this respect, it is more like the dialogues in other visionary reports (1:11–12, 13–14; 24:1b–3). Weiser correctly points out that the oracles of vv 27–29 give the vision meaning. The same thing occurs in chaps. 1 and 24, where oracles give fuller meaning to the visions. In the present narrative Yahweh begins and ends the discourse; Jeremiah speaks in the middle:

Yahweh speaks to Jeremiah	vv 15–16
Jeremiah answers Yahweh	vv 17–26
Yahweh speaks to the nations	vv 27–29

Here, as in 25:1–14, many have argued that the passage has undergone substantial revision: e.g., that the list of nations in vv 18–26, with or without v 17, is a later insertion (Mowinckel 1914: 21; Volz; Bardtke 1935: 223; Weiser); that the oracles in vv 27–29 are a later expansion (Cornill; Rudolph; Holladay; Mc-Kane); and that the LXX omissions are in fact MT pluses of the revision. While it is possible that the list of nations could be a later addition, it is unlikely. The list is certainly not intrusive in the context, as argued by some. Such a list is already anticipated in v 15 (Rudolph). Cassuto (1973c: 218) says that only by naming the nations as he does can Jeremiah convey to his audience the dreadful punishment coming from the hand of the Lord. Here, as elsewhere, we can also set aside the fiction that Jeremiah is not a prophet to the nations, which was argued by Duhm and survives still in McKane. As far as differences between the MT and LXX are concerned, things here are little different from what we find in 25:1–14 and elsewhere. In the present verses there are nine arguable cases for LXX haplography, in addition to which are other clear cases in which the LXX has either misunderstood or misread the Hebrew. The shorter LXX text is once again not the better or more original text (*pace* Schwally 1888; Duhm; Peake; Cornill; Holladay; McKane; and others); rather, it is a seriously flawed text. For more on the authenticity or lack of the same in chap. 25, see Rhetoric and Composition for 25:1–14.

Yahweh's directive to Jeremiah links up with Oracle I to the nations by the following repetitions and balancing key words (cf. Cassuto 1973c: 224):

And they shall drink and retch and go mad
  before the sword that I am sending among them   v 16

Drink and be drunk, yes, vomit and fall . . .
  before the sword that I am sending among you   v 27b

The words "before the sword that I am sending among them" in v 16 should not be deleted (*pace* Cornill; Rudolph). The repetition gives every indication of being intentional, reverting as it does to what was stated at the beginning.

NOTES

25:15. *For thus Yahweh, God of Israel, said to me.* This first-person introduction expands the more usual "Thus Yahweh said to me," which appears in 13:1; 17:19; and 27:2. The LXX lacks the initial *kî* ("for"), which could be due to haplography (homoeoarcton: *k* . . . *k*). The particle need not be secondary (*pace* Rudolph; Holladay; McKane). The combination *kî kōh* occurs often in the book, e.g., in 22:6, 11; 27:19; 28:14; 29:8, 10, 16; 30:5, 12; 31:7; and elsewhere. The LXX also lacks the phrase "to me," which was probably in the original (Giesebrecht; cf. T: "to me").

Take this wrath-filled cup of wine from my hand, and make all the nations to whom I am sending you drink it. This is generally agreed to be the report of a vision (Kimhi; Calvin; Duhm; Cornill; and most modern commentators). In this vision, Jeremiah, the cupbearer (cf. Gen 40:11–13), takes from Yahweh's hand the wine of wrath and serves it to the nations. H. W. Robinson (1927: 12–13) says the vision implies no real cup and has no corresponding symbolic act. Nevertheless, it does have symbolic significance (Lindblom 1965: 130–31). The setting may be a banquet that Yahweh is hosting for the nations, which will take an unexpected turn (H. W. Robinson; Holladay; cf. Zeph 1:7–8; Jer 51:39). A painted pitcher from Ras Shamra depicts El sitting at a table, with goblet in hand, hosting what appears to be a sacrificial meal (Schaeffer 1963: 211, fig. 30; cf. Dahood 1966a: 70).

Take this wrath-filled cup of wine. Hebrew *qaḥ 'et-kôs hayyayin haḥēmâ hazzō't.* On the divine imperatives *qaḥ* and *qĕḥû* ("Take!") issued to the prophet, see Note for 43:9. The construction here is difficult because both "wine" and "wrath" have the definite article. Giesebrecht takes the two terms as being in apposition to one another ("the wine" = "the wrath"), which is accepted by Peake and explained as such in GKC §131k, although in the Grammar it is said that "the wrath" is probably a gloss. D. N. Freedman suggests taking *et-kôs hayyayin* as a construct chain, with *hahēmâ* and *hazzō't* both functioning as adjectives in the attributive position. Hebrew *hēmâ* ("wrath") is normally a noun; however, we may note that the LXX reads it as an adjective, going its own way with *to potērion tou oinou tou akratou toutou* ("the cup of this unmixed wine"). Aquila has *tēs orgēs* ("of wrath"); Symm and Theod *tou thumou* ("of passion"). Jerome in the Vg translates *calicem vini furoris huius* ("a cup of this wrathful wine"). Some commentators (Cornill; Rudolph; Holladay; McKane) delete *hahēmâ* as a gloss, which is too easy. The term occurs in 4QJer^c. Weiser translates: "diesen Becher voll Zornwein," which is similar to the translation adopted here. On wine and wine-making in antiquity, see Note on 48:11–12.

This type of cup (*kôs*) is a drinking vessel (Honeyman 1939: 82; Kelso 1948: 19–20 #43; cf. 16:7; 35:5; 49:12), usually made of clay but crafted or overlaid in silver or gold for royal households (51:7; Rev 17:4). Kelso says the term can also refer to a broad, shallow wine bowl. Either could be with or without handles. According to Honeyman, these cups had no handles and were about eight centimeters in diameter with a "lip" at the brim (1 Kgs 7:26). To "drink the cup" frequently takes on symbolic significance extending well beyond the act of drinking and may, in some cases, not include drinking at all. Drinking the "cup of consolation" with mourners (16:7) is to share a cup of wine with them, but more important it is to give them comfort. The "cup" symbolizes blessing and salvation in Pss 16:5; 23:5; and 116:13, but in the present case it symbolizes the divine wrath, as it does often in the OT (49:12; 51:7; Hab 2:16; Lam 4:21; Ezek 23:31–34; Isa 51:17, 22; Pss 11:6; 75:9[Eng 75:8]) and in the NT (Rev 14:10; 16:19; 18:6). In the Gospels, "the cup" signifies Jesus' entire experience of suffering and death (Mark 14:36 and parallels).

from my hand. Jeremiah sees Yahweh stretching forth his hand to give him the cup of death for the nations. When he received his call, Yahweh stretched forth a hand to put words into the prophet's mouth (1:9). Compare the anthropomorphic imagery in Isa 6:6–7 and Ezek 2:9–10.

and make all the nations to whom I am sending you drink it. The people of Judah underwent a similar forced drinking (13:12–14). Jeremiah, not just a prophet to Judah, gives the cup of destiny to all the nations (1:5, 10). Again we see him acting in the capacity of a royal messenger in Yahweh's employ, this time as the King's cupbearer. Note the verb *šlḥ*, "to send" (cf. 1:7; 26:12, 15). The images of the cupbearer and herald coalesce, for Jeremiah is not serving the nations a literal cup of wine but, rather, delivering them a message of divine judgment. In 5:14, Yahweh's words in the prophet's mouth will come to Judah like a consuming fire; in 23:29 they are this and also like a rock-shattering hammer. Yahweh says in Hos 6:5: "Therefore I have hewn them by the prophets, I have slain them by the words of my mouth." In the judgment here, Yahweh's word spoken by Jeremiah is a potent, yes lethal, cup of wine. Jeremiah himself became like a drunken man before Yahweh's holy words (23:9) but, not being under a curse, he lived to preach another day. The nations are under a divine curse. A vassal treaty of Esarhaddon (681–669 B.C.) contains this malediction:

> [Just as bread] and wine enter into the intestines, [so may they (the gods)] cause this curse to enter into your intestines [(and into) those of your sons] and your daughters.
>
> (Wiseman 1958a: 71–72, 560–62; *ANET*³ 539, #72)

and make . . . drink it Hebrew *wĕhišqîtâ* is an old second masculine singular, differing only orthographically from *wĕhišqîtā* (GKC §44g). The long form is original (it preserves the standard preexilic spelling with a vowel letter, in this case *hē'*) and is fairly rare in the OT, but it occurs often enough to show that it is not exceptional; cf. Cross and Freedman 1952: 65–67. The LXX lacks the pronoun "it" (*'ōtô*), which could be due to haplography (homoeoarcton: *'t . . . 't*). The T and Vg have "it"; Aq has "them" (*autous*).

16. *And they shall drink and retch and go mad.* Hebrew *wĕšātû wĕhitgōʿāšû wĕhithōlālû*. Here two important questions need to be asked: 1) Will the wine cause drunkenness simply because it is imbibed in large quantity, or will the resulting incapacity be due to poison in the wine? and 2) What precisely will be the effects on those drinking the wine? Will the victims stagger and fall, as drunkards typically do (Ps 60:5[Eng 60:3]), or will an inner turbulence cause them to vomit, as drunkards also typically do? BDB took the verb *gʿš* in the Hithpolel to mean "reel to and fro," a meaning it also assigned to the Hithpael (cf. 46:7–8). The meaning assigned to the Qal was "shake." This suggests a drunkard staggering about in the present case (AV; RSV; JB; NIV). The T reads all three verbs: "And they shall drink and be confused and tossed about." More recently, *gʿš* has been shown to mean "heave, retch, vomit" (G. R. Driver 1950a: 406; Greenfield 1958: 205–7, who cites evidence from Mishnaic Hebrew and compares with Akk *gešû*, "to belch, cough up"; CAD 5: 64; KB³; NEB; NJV), which supports LXX's *exemountai* ("vomit, be sick") and balances more precisely with "vomit" (*qĕyû*) in v 27. Brongers (1969: 190–91) thinks the wine has poison in it, which is possible but unnecessary. It is enough that the wine makes the banquet guests thoroughly drunk, which will leave them helpless before the sword that does the finishing work (cf. Jdt 13:1–8). McKane (1980: 487–92; 1986: 635–36) thinks there must be a proof of guilt and therefore imagines the ordeal ritual for a woman suspected of adultery in Num 5:11–31 as background. Aside from the fact that the adultery ritual of Num 5:11–31 has nothing to do with what is described here, at the present banquet table there is no ordeal taking place to determine innocence or guilt. Yahweh has already decided the nations' guilt and is simply carrying out sentences of death. Also, in the Jeremiah passages McKane cites for support, 8:14; 9:14[Eng 9:15]; and 23:15, it is "poisoned water" (*mê-rō'š*), not wine, that is offered as a drink. The verb *hll* in the Hithpolel is clear; it means "go mad/act madly" (BDB; KB³ *hll* III). Compare 46:9; 50:38b; and especially 51:7, where the verb

is again describing the effects of inebriation upon the nations. The Bible, it should be repeated, does not scruple in ascribing bad (or evil) happenings to Yahweh (Amos 3:6; 1 Sam 18:10; 1 Kgs 22:19–23; Isa 19:14).

And they shall drink. Hebrew *wĕšātû.* Ziegler's LXX text omits this verb (Rahlfs has *kai piontai*), but it is present in 4QJer^c. The omission may be due to haplography (homoeoarcton: *w . . . w*).

before the sword that I am sending among them. Once drunkenness ensues, madness follows, and the victims are made helpless before an oncoming sword. Death comes not from drinking the wine but from the sword. H. W. Robinson (1927: 12) says: "The drinking of the cup is obviously a figure of the Babylonian victories over the nations named." Duhm objects to the juxtaposed images of "wine" and "sword," wondering whether "before the sword that I am sending among them" should not be deleted. Cornill and Rudolph do delete, which is unwarranted (see Rhetoric and Composition). The images are not incompatible; in fact, they are necessary complements. Yahweh has a sword (47:6; Isa 27:1; 34:5–7), so do the Babylonians, and both will work as one in finishing off the nations that are now helpless because of drunkenness, vomiting, and madness.

I am sending. The MT has *'ānōkî* for the pronoun; 4QJer^c has *'ănî*.

17. *So I took the cup from the hand of Yahweh and made all the nations to whom Yahweh sent me drink.* Jeremiah is often characterized as the prophet of resistance (1:6), but he is much more the prophet of obedience, reporting as he does here and many times elsewhere that he did precisely what Yahweh commanded him to do (13:2, 5, 7; 18:3; 25:17; 32:9; 35:3–4; 36:4, 32).

all the nations. The LXX omits "all," as it does twice more in v 22. Other Versions have it.

18. *Jerusalem and the cities of Judah, and its kings, its princes, to make them a ruin, a desolation, an object of hissing, and a swearword, as at this day.* More *accumulatio.* On strings of curse words such as the present one, see Note for 24:9. Jerusalem and the cities of Judah, it should be noted, are first to drink. In God's economy, judgment begins at home (Matt 7:1–5; 1 Pet 4:17), a principle widely misunderstood by people who seem to find evil lurking everywhere except in their own midst. The LXX has "the kings of Judah"; T has just "her kings." Kimḥi says "kings" plural refer to Jehoiakim, Jehoiachin, and Zedekiah, which would make this a prophecy after the fact. But "its kings" may be an intensive plural, simply meaning "its king" (see Note on 13:13).

and a swearword, as at this day. The LXX omits, which may be attributed to haplography (homoeoteleuton: *h . . . h*). The concluding "as at this day" is familiar from Deuteronmy (Deut 2:30; 4:20, 38; 8:18; 10:15; 29:27[Eng 29:28]; cf. Jer 11:5; 32:30) and here is probably a later addition, as most take it (44:6, 23). Rashi dates the phrase post-586 B.C., because in his view Jeremiah wrote his book after the destruction of Jerusalem. The one adding the words is most likely Baruch. The phrase is present in Aq, Theod, and T.

19. *Pharaoh, king of Egypt, and his servants, and his princes, and all his people.* After Jerusalem and the cities of Judah, the next guests to receive Yahweh's cup of wrath are Pharaoh, his royal house, and all the people of Egypt.

That Egypt should drink first among other nations comes as no surprise in light of its defeat that very year at Carchemish. In the MT's Foreign Nation Collection, Egypt is first (46:1–26). Jeremiah also spoke against Egypt in 9:25[Eng 9:26]; 43:10–13; and 44:30.

his servants. Hebrew *'ăbādāyw.* These are important officials in the service of the king; see Gen 41:37–38, 46, and Note for 21:7.

20. *all the mixed races.* Hebrew *kol-hā'ereb.* The LXX: *pantas tous summiktous,* "all the mingled (peoples)." These are people of foreign origin or mixed race who reside in Egypt—mainly, colonists, mercenaries, and traders (Weiser). Jerome says they are *cunctusque qui non quidem est Aegyptius, sed in ejus regionibus commoratur* ("a body of people that is not Egyptian, but sojourns within that country"). We know Greek expatriates were living in Egypt at this time (46:9, 16, 21), and probably not a few Judahites were also settled there (cf. 44:1). At the time of the Exodus, people of mixed race joined the Israelites fleeing Egypt (Exod 12:38), and the same resided temporarily or permanently in Israel and Judah during all periods (Ruth 1:22; 2 Samuel 11; 15:18–22; 1 Kgs 10:15; Jer 38:7; Neh 13:3). A mixed and foreign population resided in Babylon (50:37), just as we find today in London, Stockholm, Nairobi, Chicago, Berlin, and other cities of the modern world.

and all the kings of the land of Uz. The LXX omits, and some commentators, following Graf and Kuenen, delete (so Giesebrecht; Duhm; Cornill; Rudolph; Holladay; McKane), but the omission, as Janzen (1973: 117) notes, is probably due to haplography (four-word: *w't kl-mlky 'rṣ . . . w't kl-mlky 'rṣ*). Aquila, Theod, T, and Vg all have the phrase. Uz, the home of Job (1:1), is in northwest Arabia, where also Tema and Dedan are located (Eph'al 1982: 88; *ABD* 6: 770–71). In the OT, Uz is associated geographically with Aram (= Syria) in Gen 10:23; 22:21; and 1 Chr 1:17; and with Edom or Seir (= Edom) in Gen 36:28; 1 Chr 1:42; and Lam 4:21. There is no oracle against Uz in the Foreign Nation Collection.

and all the kings of the land of the Philistines, that is, Ashkelon, and Gaza, and Ekron, and the remnant of Ashdod. Listed here are only four cities of the Philistine Pentapolis; missing is Gath, which was destroyed by Sargon II of Assyria in 711 B.C. (see Note for 47:5). Ashkelon and Ekron were both completely destroyed by Nebuchadrezzar in 604 B.C., at which time Gaza may have been attacked but not destroyed, since it was retaken by the Egyptians ca. 601–600 B.C. (see Notes for 47:1 and 47:5). Ashdod is said to be no more than a remnant, which could reflect its destruction at the hands of Psammetichus I (664–610 B.C.). According to Herodotus (ii 157), Psammetichus besieged Azotus (= Ashdod) for 29 years before taking it. Excavations at Tell Ashdod, carried out in the 1960s by Pittsburgh Theological Seminary and the Israel Department of Antiquities (D. N. Freedman 1963c; *NEAEHL* 1: 100), revealed Iron II destruction that may also have resulted from Nebuchadnezzar's campaign through Philistia in 604–601 B.C. (see Note for 47:5). Babylonian texts list Ashdod's king as receiving rations along with other Philistine prisoners (Weidner 1939: 928; *ANET*[3] 308). Ashdod was rebuilt in the postexilic period

(Neh 13:23). In Jeremiah's pronouncements against the Philistines in 47:1–7, only Ashkelon and Gaza are said to be awaiting their sad day of reckoning. During the 1980s and 1990s, major excavations were carried out at Tel Miqne-Ekron, directed by Seymour Gitin of the Albright Institute and Trude Dothan of The Hebrew University in Jerusalem (Gitin 1990; 1995; 1997; "Ekron" in *ABD* 2: 415–22; *NEAEHL* 3: 1051–59; P. J. King 1993: 20), and at Ashkelon, directed by Larry Stager and a team from Harvard (Stager 1991; 1996; "Ashkelon" in *ABD* 1: 487–90; *NEAEHL* 1: 103–12; P. J. King 1993: xxv, 23, 33–34). Tell eṣ-Ṣafi, currently thought to be ancient Gath, was excavated by F. J. Bliss and R. A. Macalister for the British Palestine Exploration Fund in 1899 (*NEAEHL* 4: 1522–24); in the late 1990s, new excavations were begun at the site by York University in Toronto and Bar Ilan University in Ramat Gan, Israel. Gaza, identified with Tell Kharubeh (= Tell ʿAzza) was partly excavated by W. J. Phythian-Adams in 1922, but its modest Iron II finds were inconclusive (*NEAEHL* 2: 464–67). Gaza has yet to be properly excavated, due to continuous occupation and unsettled conditions in the region.

the land of the Philistines. The LXX omits "land."

21. *Edom.* The high plateau country east of the ʿArabah Valley below the Dead Sea, from the River Zered (Wadi el-Ḥasā) to the Gulf of Aqaba. In the late seventh or early sixth century B.C., Edomites were threatening Judah's border in the eastern Negeb. On the history, geography, and archaeology of ancient Edom, see Note for 49:7. Jeremiah spoke a word against Edom in 9:25[Eng 9:26] but developed his judgment more fully in a number of oracles in 49:7–22.

Moab. The movement in Transjordan is from south to north. Moab was the high plateau country north of Edom, east of the Dead Sea. Its southern boundary was the River Zered (Wadi el-Ḥasā), and for many years its northern boundary was the River Arnon (Wadi al-Mūjib). From the eighth century on, it also controlled the plateau area north of the Arnon, as far as Heshbon. On the history, geography, and archaeology of ancient Moab, see Note for 48:1. Jeremiah spoke against Moab in 9:25[Eng 9:26], supplementing this with judgment oracles in the whole of chap. 48.

the Ammonites. Hebrew *bĕnê ʿammôn*, lit., "sons of Ammon," which is the usual designation for the Ammonites in the OT. Ammon was a small, tribal Transjordanian kingdom made up of Rabbah, its capital, and the surrounding towns, villages, and farmsteads. Its borders extended roughly from the Wadi Hesban in the south to the Jabbok River (Wadi Zerqa) in the north. On Ammonite geography and archaeology, see Note for 49:1; on Ammonite history in the late seventh and early sixth centuries B.C., see Note for 49:2. Jeremiah spoke against the Ammonites in 9:25[Eng 9:26] and in the oracles contained in 49:1–6.

22. *all the kings of Tyre, and all the kings of Sidon.* Tyre and Sidon were the southernmost coastal cities of Phoenicia (modern Lebanon), their modern sites being just a short distance south of Beirut. There are no oracles against either Tyre or Sidon in the Foreign Nation Collection, but their ties to Philistine

cities are cited in 47:4, where also the LXX and T say that they will be destroyed (see Note for 47:4). Both cities were represented at the Jerusalem conference in 594 B.C., at which time rebellion against Babylon was discussed (27:1–3). Sidon ended up submitting to Nebuchadnezzar before the destruction of Jerusalem; Tyre resisted and was besieged by the Babylonian king for 13 years (ca. 585–573 B.C.), at the end of which all but the island portion of the city had been taken. Classical sources tell of other attacks against Tyre and Sidon during the same period by Pharaoh Apries (= Hophra) of Egypt, who reigned from 589–570 B.C. Herodotus (ii 161) says that Apries suffered defeat in both campaigns, the naval battle at Tyre perhaps being an Egyptian attempt to help break the Babylonian siege. Diodorus of Sicily (i 68) reports that Apries took Sidon by storm, also terrifying other Phoenician cities into submission.

the kings of the coastlands that are across the sea. An extension of the judgment on Tyre and Sidon. The LXX: "the kings who were on the other side (*tous en tō peran*) of the sea." Aquila, Theod, and T have "of the island"; Vg has "of the islands" plural. Hebrew *ʾî* is a collective noun meaning either "island(s)" or "coastland(s)" (cf. 2:10). Reference here is to the Phoenician colonies in the western Mediterranean, of which Carthage in North Africa is the best known (Calvin; Giesebrecht; Cornill). Legend has it that Carthage (in modern Tunisia) was founded by settlers from Tyre in the late ninth century B.C. Modern archaeological work, however, dates Phoenician expansion in the western Mediterranean as beginning ca. 750 B.C., and it could be earlier. Other Phoenician colonies existed on the islands of Sicily and Sardinia, also along the coast of Spain (*OEANE* 4: 327). How judgment was to come upon kings of such distant colonies is unclear; it could hardly have been from Nebuchadnezzar and the Babylonians.

23. *Dedan.* A caravan center at an oasis in northwest Arabia, identified with the ruins of al-Khuraybah, just north of the modern village of al-ʿUlā. Dedan receives a word of judgment in one of Jeremiah's Edom oracles (see Note for 49:8), which may have been fulfilled when Nebuchadnezzar raided desert camps of the Arabs in 599–598 B.C. (see Note for 49:28).

Tema. Another caravan center and oasis in northwest Arabia (Job 6:19; Isa 21:14), on the trade route from Babylon to Dedan (Ephʿal 1982: 15), not to be confused with Teman, which is a northeast region of Edom (cf. 49:7, 20). The identification of Temaʾ with modern Taymāʾ (= Teima) is widely accepted. Temaʾ is where Nabonidus took up residence for ten years while exiled from Babylon (ca. 553–543 B.C.; cf. Isa 21:13–17), and it is mentioned in the earlier Calah Inscriptions of Tiglath-pileser III (745–727 B.C.) as one among many Arab tribes bringing tribute of gold, silver, camels, and spices to the Assyrian king (Tadmor 1994: 142–43 [4:27]; 168–69 [7:3 reverse]; Luckenbill 1926: 287 [#799]; 293 [#818]; *ANET*[3] 283–84; *CS II* 288–89). Four (of 45) inscriptions found on the summit of Jabal Ghunaym, about 14 kilometers south of Taymāʾ, correlate well with the Harran Inscription of Nabonidus in documenting Babylonian military activity against Dedan and other cities of the area (Winnett and Reed 1970: 88–92, 102–3). On Nabonidus's Harran Inscriptions, see Note on 49:8. On the king's sojourn in Tema' and its documentation, see Eph'al 1982: 179–91.

Buz. Another settlement or region in the Arabian Desert, whose location is unknown. Buz fits contextually in northwest Arabia with Dedan and Tema, for which reason the *Oxford Bible Atlas* (May 1962: 67) and other older atlases identify it as a region between Dedan and Kedar. Its association with Uz in the book of Job (Elihu is a Buzite; Job 32:2) supports this general location. But others (Weidner 1945–51; Albright 1953: 8 n. 2; Simons 1959: 15; Eph'al 1982: 137; E. Knauf in *ABD* 1: 794) place Buz in (north)east Arabia, Simons in the desert region of El-Ḥasa, east of modern Riyadh and opposite the island of Bahrain. In one of the Calah Inscriptions of Tiglath-pileser III that mentions Tema, there is mention also of a town Bâzu, which is said to be in a waterless region of Arabia (Luckenbill 1926: 293 [#817]; *ANET*[3] 284). But Luckenbill was unsure of the reading. Inscriptions of Esarhaddon (680–669 B.C.), however, leave no doubt about the Bâzu readings there, which the Assyrian king says is a faraway land, beyond a salt desert (Eph'al 1982: 130–37; cf. Luckenbill 1927: 274 [#710]; *ANET*[3] 290). Older scholars identified Bâzu with Buz (Delitzsch 1881: 307; Glaser 1890: 266–67; Montgomery 1934: 50, 63), but this is now rejected by Eph'al, who says Bûz in Hebrew would translate as Būzu in Akkadian, and Bâzu in Akkadian would translate into Hebrew as Bāz.

and all who crop the hair at the temples. These are desert Arabs who crop their hair in a particular way; see Note for 9:25[Eng 9:26]. Judgment is also said to be slated for these people in one of the Kedar-Hazor oracles (49:32).

24. *all the kings of Arabia.* Hebrew *kol-malkê ʿărāb.* These are the kings who brought gold to Solomon (1 Kgs 10:14–15), who must now drink Yahweh's cup of wrath with the other desert Arabs. See again the Kedar-Hazor oracles in 49:28–33. The LXX omits the phrase, leading many scholars (Giesebrecht; Duhm; Peake; Cornill; Rudolph; Bright; Janzen 1973: 13; Holladay; McKane) to delete because of an assumed dittography, conflated readings, or some other scribal infelicity caused by a similar phrase following. The loss, however, can also be attributable to haplography (three-word: *wʾt kl-mlky . . . wʾt kl-mlky*). Aquila, Theod, T, and Vg all have the phrase.

all the kings of the mixed races who dwell in the desert. Rashi says these are allies of the Arabs, although T translates *kol-malkê hāʿereb* as "all the kings of the Arabs" (cf. 1 Kgs 10:15). But here the phrase means "all the kings of the mixed races" (cf. v 20).

25. *all the kings of Zimri.* The LXX omits, which is probably another loss attributable to haplography (three-word: *wʾt kl-mlky . . . wʾt kl-mlky*). The T, Vg, and a reconstructed 4QJer[c] all contain the phrase. Zimri's location is unknown, and neither it nor any people of Zimri are mentioned in the Foreign Nation Oracles. Identifications with "Zimran" in Gen 25:1 (Kimḥi), with "Zamereni" in Pliny (*Nat Hist* vi 32), and with "Zimarra" in a text of Tiglath-pileser III (Luckenbill 1926: 292 [#815]; Tadmor 1994: 136–37 [4:2]; *ANET*[3] 283; *CS II* 287), all of which are associated at some point with Arabia, remain unsubstantiated.

all the kings of Elam. Elam was located east of the lower Tigris, opposite
southern Babylonia (Chaldea). To the north was Media and Assyria; to the
south the Persian Gulf. In the seventh and possibly early sixth centuries B.C.,
Elam was much involved in world affairs, which may explain Jeremiah's judgment on such a faraway nation here and in 49:34–39, where there are two oracles in the Foreign Nation Collection (see Note for 49:34).

all the kings of Media. Media was an ancient kingdom in what today is
northwest Iran, eastern Turkey, and Azerbaijan. The Medes, who were frequently associated with the Elamites (Isa 21:2), rose to power in the late seventh century, joining forces with Babylon to overthrow Nineveh in 612 B.C.
Thereafter, Media continued as a force to be reckoned with, annexing territory
north and east of Mesopotamia in 585 B.C., e.g., Ararat, Minni, and Ashkenaz
(51:27). But its predicted attack on Babylon (51:11, 28; Isa 13:17), as far as we
know, never materialized. Media was conquered by Cyrus in 550 B.C., after
which it became absorbed into the Persian Empire. From this point on, the
Medes and Persians became closely identified (Esth 10:2 and Dan 8:20: "kings
of Media and Persia"). The LXX translation here is "all the kings of the Persians." On the geography and history of Media, see Note for 51:28. There are
no oracles against Media in the Foreign Nation Collection, but "the kings of
Media" are mentioned in 51:11 and 28.

26. *all the kings of the north.* Not the "tribes of the north" in 1:15 and 25:9,
who formed an enemy coalition from the more immediate north and east
against Judah in 599–598 B.C. The kings referred to here would be primarily
those of Ararat (= Urartu), Minni (= Mannai), and Ashkenaz (= Ashguzai/
Scythians) in the far north, who are cited in 51:27. A confusion of peoples may
lie behind LXX's *pavtas basileis apo apēliōtou* ("all the kings of the east"),
which cannot be right.

those near and those far. Hebrew *haqqĕrōbîm wĕhārĕḥōqîm*, which has inverted assonance. Compare a similar expression in 48:24. The inclusiveness
may be within the far northern region; on the other hand, kings in Syria may
also be "those near," particularly since Damascus, which receives a judgment
oracle in 49:23–27, is not named in the present list.

one to another. Hebrew *'îš 'el-'āḥîw*, lit., "each (man) to his brother." In
25:32 it says that "evil shall go forth from nation to nation." Here each nation
passes the cup of wrath to the next. Compare the passing of the cup of blessing
in the Christian Eucharist, which is both death and life (1 Cor 10:16; cf. Mark
14:23–24 and parallels).

yes, all the world's kingdoms that are on the face of the earth. Reading *hā'āreṣ*
as "the world," with the AV and RSV, as the Hebrew is otherwise difficult to render into English. The NJV has "all the royal lands which are on the earth."
This is a summary statement intending to include any nation or region not
mentioned, excepting Babylon, which follows climactically. Judgment will be
worldwide (cf. Isa 24:1–13). The LXX and S lack *hā'āreṣ* ("the earth, world"),
which does appear to be out of place. The Masoretes, for their part, took *ham-
mamlĕkôt hā'āreṣ* as a construct chain, but that violates the rule of construct

terms' not taking the definite article. Still, emphasis is created by the use of two different Hebrew words: *hā'āreṣ* ("the earth, world"), and *hā'ădāmâ* ("the ground, earth"). 4QJer^c has *hā'āreṣ*, but most commentators and modern Versions delete, in the interests of a smoother reading.

And the king of Sheshak shall drink after them. This phrase is also lacking in the LXX, but present in 4QJer^c (reconstructed). Again, many delete, as a later add-on (Giesebrecht, citing Kuenen, Schwally, and Movers before him; Duhm; Cornill; Volz; Rudolph; Janzen 1973: 122; Tov 1985: 221; Holladay; McKane), but the loss could also be due to haplography (homoeoarcton: *w . . . w*). The king of Sheshak is the king of Babylon, and he is last to drink. Note also that the Babylon oracles conclude the Foreign Nation Collection in MT (chaps. 50–51) where, as here, they are climactic. Babylon, once the golden cup in Yahweh's hand, will suddenly fall and be shattered (51:7–8).

Sheshak. Hebrew *šēšak* is a cipher for Babylon, occurring again in 51:41. The Rabbis called this an *atbash*, because the last letter of the alphabet (ת) is substituted for the first (א), the penultimate (ש) for the second (ב), and so on. Thus, ששך yields בבל, Babylon. The *atbash* cipher is used for Chaldea/Chaldeans in 51:1. Noegel (1996) thinks the *atbash* functions simply as a wordplay, not being necessarily a cryptic device, which is how Jerome and others since have interpreted it. Since "Babylon" and the "the king of Babylon" are spoken about openly in the Pashhur oracle (20:4–6) and in the prior oracles of the present chapter (25:9, 11, 12), all of which are dated roughly to the same time as the utterance here, there is scarcely a reason not to write the name of Babylon. Steiner (1996: 81–84), nevertheless, favors a cryptic interpretation, arguing that the *atbash* served as a mock lament added later in Babylon. But a mock lament is just as possible in Jerusalem during the reign of Jehoiakim, when indeed there was no need to conceal Babylon's name.

27. *Yahweh of hosts.* The LXX translates *ṣĕbā'ôt* ("of hosts") *pantokratōr*, as it does occasionally in Jeremiah (see Appendix VI). In v 29, "of hosts" is omitted, and in v 30 it is omitted with the entire messenger formula.

Drink and be drunk, yes, vomit and fall, and you shall never rise. Five verbs in rapid succession make for *asyndeton*, on which see Note for 4:5. The imperative form, *qĕyû* ("vomit"), is discussed in GKC §76h. The *lō'* in *wĕlō' tāqûmû* is emphatic: "And you shall never rise!" (cf. GKC §107o). This fifth verb is an imperfect, since ancient Hebrew does not use a negative imperative. That the nations will fall and rise no more indicates that this is not ordinary drunkenness, the effects of which will wear off. However, this does not mean that the wine must be poisoned (*pace* McKane). In their drunken state, the nations become easy victims for attack by the sword. These words are spoken as the cup is given to each nation. Compare the spoken words uttered by celebrants of the Christian Eucharist as they offer another the wine: "Drink this cup, all of it. . . ." This cup makes one a participant in the death of Christ, whose death in contrast to the present death, becomes the way to life.

28. *And it will happen that they will refuse to take the cup from your hand to drink.* The particle *kî* is not a conditional "if," as the AV and most modern Ver-

sions translate, but the conjunction "that." Nations can be counted on to refuse the cup.

then you shall say to them. The LXX omits "to them," but it is present in T, S, and Vg.

You shall certainly drink! The command was that Jeremiah make them drink (v 15).

29. *For look, if I am beginning to work evil in the city upon which my name is called, then for you, shall you assuredly go unpunished?* An argument *a minori ad maius*; on which see Note for 3:1. A similar but not identical argument appears in 49:12. It is Yahweh's intention to begin the judgment with Jerusalem and the cities of Judah, which then becomes a reason for subsequent judgment on the nations. Here Yahweh is enraged at the nations for thinking that they will be declared innocent. The LXX lacks *hinnēh* ("look"), which is the most common beginning to the Jeremianic oracle (see Note for 1:9). The T and Vg have the term. The LXX misunderstood the argument, translating two statements instead of two questions (Giesebrecht). The translator could have been confused by the absence of an interrogative particle, which is nevertheless possible in questions (cf. Note for 3:1 and GKC §150a). The expression "the city upon which my name is called" occurs later in Dan 9:18 and is not otherwise found in the book of Jeremiah. The Jeremiah expression is "the house upon which my name is called," i.e., the Temple (7:10, 11, 14, 30; 32:34; 34:15).

You shall not go unpunished. Hebrew *lō' tinnāqû*. The LXX, in converting two questions into two statements, fails to account for these words. Their omission may then be an earlier loss due to haplography (whole-word: *tnqw . . . tnqw*). The (preceding) question form is not a secondary development in proto-MT (*pace* Stipp 1997: 197–98) but standard Hebrew discourse. See again 49:12. When the two oracles are heard together, the present statement becomes Yahweh's answer to his own rhetorical question, which in the classical rhetorical handbooks is called *hypophora* (see Note for 49:7).

oracle of Yahweh of hosts. The LXX omits; T and Vg have the formula.

MESSAGE AND AUDIENCE

Jeremiah here reports a vision in which he saw Yahweh hosting a banquet for the nations, and where he was appointed the server of wine. Yahweh told him to take the cup from his hand, a cup filled with the divine wrath, and make the nations round the table drink it. All would become thoroughly drunk, retch, and go mad, after which they would fall victim to a sword Yahweh is sending upon them.

Jeremiah says he took the cup and made the nations drink. First to receive the wine of wrath was Jerusalem and the cities of Judah, which were brought to ruin. Next to drink was Pharaoh of Egypt and with him high-ranking Egyptian officials, then all the people in Egypt—natives, foreigners, and folk of mixed race. To the kings of Uz the cup was passed next, and after them to all the kings of the Philistines—Ashkelon, Gaza, Ekron, and the remnant of

Ashdod. Next in line were Edom, Moab, and the Ammonites, then the kings of Tyre and Sidon, and with them all the kings of the Phoenician colonies across the Mediterranean. The cup was then passed to desert Arabs—Dedan, Tema, Buz, the people with strange haircuts, the kings of Arabia, and kings of mixed races inhabiting the desert. The kings of Zimri and the kings of Elam and Media were also given the cup; then kings of the north, far and near. One passed to the next, and in the end all nations on the face of the earth were made to drink. Last, but not least, Sheshak, whom the people will recognize as being Babylon, had to drink the cup.

The oracles following contain Yahweh's word to the nations as they are given the cup. Jeremiah speaks the word. Oracle I is a curse given as the wine is presented: "Drink and be drunk, yes, vomit and fall, and you shall never rise before the sword that I am sending among you." Yahweh then tells Jeremiah that the nations will refuse the cup. Not a surprise. But he is to say that they must drink. Yahweh says that if he begins to work harm in his own city, how can they expect to escape punishment? They will be unable to answer, so Yahweh himself will answer. They will not escape, for Yahweh is calling forth a sword against all peoples of the earth.

While Jeremiah's vision report and the divine oracles concern the nations of the world, his audience is primarily Judahite (Cassuto 1973c: 219) and only secondarily the distant nations who may or may not hear what is said. The entire passage fits well the date given in 25:1, Jehoiakim's fourth year, 605 B.C. The Battle of Carchemish, which was fought and won by Babylon in this year, will make it clear to many that a worldwide campaign against the nations is in the offing. The destruction of Ashkelon and Ekron by Nebuchadnezzar in the year following will convince some doubters but probably not all. How far things will go is anyone's guess. Jeremiah, however, is beginning to preach to the nations about this time. The Egypt oracles can be dated to 605; the Moab oracles to 604 or later, and the Babylon oracles to 597–594 B.C.

When the present passage is heard in tandem with what precedes, the point will be reinforced that Babylon is judging the nations of the world, but in the end it too will be judged.

3. Yahweh Will Roar from on High (25:30–31)

25 ³⁰And you, you shall prophesy to them all these words, and you shall say to them:
> Yahweh will roar from on high
> and from his holy abode he will utter his voice
> He will roar mightily against his pasture
> a shout like the treaders will ring out
> to all the inhabitants of the earth

> ³¹The uproar has reached the end of the earth
> for Yahweh has a case against the nations

He has entered into judgment with all flesh
  as for the wicked, he has given them over to the sword
  —oracle of Yahweh.

RHETORIC AND COMPOSITION

MT 25:30–31 = LXX 32:30–31. Here at the conclusion of the present chapter
are added judgments against the nations, all of which are poetry except v 33,
which is later prose comment (*pace* Condamin, Weiser, and Holladay, who
attempt to make it poetry). Duhm correctly discerns in the verses three separate units: vv 30–31; vv 32–33; and vv 34–38. The same divisions are made by
Castellino (1980: 404–6), but his progression from "the setting of the stage"
(vv 30–31) to "the threats" (vv 32–33) to "the carrying out of the punishment"
(vv 34–38) is contrived and does not find support in the text. More convincing
is Castellino's observation that the whole of vv 30–38 is bound together by images of Yahweh as a lion, which make this inclusio:

I	*Yahweh will roar from on high*	v 30
III	*Like a lion he has left his den*	v 38

At the beginning, the lion is identified indirectly by his roar; at the end he
makes his appearance. This tie-in between end and beginning is noted by
Cheyne, Cassuto (1973c: 226), and others.

There is a problem about the presumed speaker in vv 30–31. These verses
contain two references to Yahweh in the third person, yet at the conclusion is
an "oracle of Yahweh" formula, which would indicate Yahweh as the speaker.
Since Yahweh can be expected to speak in the first person in a divine oracle,
some commentators judge the messenger formula to be late and misplaced
(Duhm; Cornill; Volz; Rudolph; Holladay; McKane). McKane points out how
the Vg converts the final colon of v 31 into a first-person statement: *Impios tradidi gladio* ("The wicked I have handed over to the sword"), which accommo-
dates the "oracle of Yahweh" formula by making Yahweh the speaker.
However, Jeremiah oracles can contain the divine name, e.g., 2:3, 15–19; and
5:10–11; which means that vv 30–31 could be a divine oracle, even though Yahweh names himself. The speaking voices in the core poetry are then Yahweh in
vv 30–31 and v 32 and Jeremiah in vv 34–38. In v 33 Yahweh is again referred
to in the third person, but this is later expansion.

Here, as elsewhere in the chapter, questions have been asked about whether
this poetry can be attributed to Jeremiah. Schwally (1888), Giesebrecht (p. xxi),
and Cornill denied all of vv 30–38 to the prophet, saying that the tone was different and the content spurious. But Mowinckel (1914: 21) assigned the verses
to Jeremiah (Source A). Some commentators have talked too about this poetry
being eschatological or apocalyptic (e.g., Duhm; Peake; Cornill; Streane;
Hyatt; Carroll), which is wide of the mark. The language and ideas are what
we find throughout the book and very different from what is found in later

apocalyptic writings (Volz). Also, because vv 30–31 appear to echo earlier prophecy in Amos 1:2; Joel 4:16[Eng 3:16]; and Hos 4:1, the poet is alleged to be someone else. It is conceded that many Jeremianic expressions also occur, but for those doubting Jeremianic authorship (Peake; Hyatt), these and the echoes of other prophecy are said to be imitative. Other commentators appraise the material more positively. Rudolph, for example, denies vv 30–31 to Jeremiah, but credits him with v 32 and vv 34–37. Bright's position is similar. Holladay, noting Jeremianic expressions and echoes from elsewhere says that Jeremiah is perfectly capable of adapting older material, and he attributes the entire passage—including v 33—to Jeremiah. Jones, too, thinks that Jeremiah is taking older phrases and applying them more broadly to the nations.

The upper limit of the present unit is indicated by a new directive in v 30a, after which a shift to poetry occurs. The lower limit is indicated by a concluding "oracle of Yahweh" formula in v 31, after which comes a *setumah* in M^A, M^L, and M^P.

The oracle has two stanzas with the following repetitions and balancing key words:

I Yahweh will roar from on high	yhwh mimmārôm yiš'āg	v 30
and from his holy abode	ûmimmĕ'ôn qodšô	
He will roar mightily	šā'ōg yiš'ag	
. . . .		
to all the inhabitants of the earth	'el kol-yōšĕbê hā'āreṣ	
II . . . . the earth	. . . . hā'āreṣ	v 31
. . . Yahweh	yhwh	
. . . . with all flesh	. . . . lĕkol-bāśār	
. . . .		

Catchwords connecting to the oracle following:

v 31 to the end of the earth	v 32 nation to nation
the nations	from remote parts of the earth

NOTES

25:30. *And you, you shall prophesy to them all these words, and you shall say to them.* "These words" are what follow, not the divine words preceding. The LXX again omits "all."

Yahweh will roar from on high. . . . He will roar mightily. The verb š'g ("roar") ends the first colon and then repeats at the beginning of the third colon, which is commonly seen in Jeremianic poetry (see Note for 22:20). Yahweh has the roar of a lion also in Amos 1:2; 3:8; and Joel 4:16[Eng 3:16], which in classical rhetoric is an implied metaphor called the *abusio* (only lions "roar"; see further Note on 4:4). Calvin judged the lion metaphor unsuitable for God, concluding here that God had adopted a hyperbolic way of speaking. In Amos 1:2 and Joel 4:16[Eng 3:16], the lion's roar is from Zion; here it comes from Yahweh's heavenly abode. The Amos passage most likely lies behind the present one, since in both, Yahweh roars against his own people and also against other nations.

on high. Hebrew *mārôm*. This is Yahweh's dwelling place in the heavens (Ps 7:8[Eng 7:7]), where the "throne of glory" has been from the beginning (see Note for 17:12). But *mārôm* in 31:12 is the place of Yahweh's earthly Temple in Zion.

from his holy abode. Hebrew *mimmĕʿôn qodšû*. Again, Yahweh's heavenly sanctuary (Deut 26:15; Ps 68:6[Eng 68:5]; Isa 63:15; 2 Chr 30:27). The LXX has simply *apo tou agiou autou* ("from his sanctuary").

He will roar mightily against his pasture. Heaven's roar is against earth and the people of earth. Hebrew *nāweh* ("pasture") should not be confused with *naḥălâ*, which is "hereditary property" given by Yahweh to Israel and other nations (see Note for 2:7). The term *nāweh* simply means "pasture," where a shepherd grazes and rests his sheep (33:12; Ps 23:1–2). The pasture here is called Yahweh's because he, like a lion, will make it his own when attacking the sheep that reside there. This pasture is not confined to Judah, as in 10:25; 23:3; and 50:19 (*pace* Peake). It is pastures of the earth and nations of the earth. Compare 49:19–20 and 50:44–45, where Yahweh will come similarly against the pastures of Teman (Edom) and Babylon.

a shout like the treaders will ring out. The metaphor now shifts from a roaring lion to treaders in a wine press. Grapes were treaded by foot, and those doing the treading would typically sing or shout robustly as they worked. Musicians provided accompaniment and rhythm. Virgil (*Georgics* ii 417) says: "Now the last vine-dresser sings of his finished rows" (Loeb). For pictures of Egyptian men treading grapes, in some cases accompanied by musicians, see *ANEP*[2] 26 #90; 48 #155, #156; and Lesko 1977: 16; 1996: 217, 220. The same kind of singing was done in American cotton fields of the South, and it can be heard the world over where men and women join together in common labor. That the shouting of treaders will reach deafening proportions is clear from this verse. Yahweh's roar is also deafening when he speaks judgment. It is, then, the voice of Yahweh that we are hearing, not the voices of those suffering the divine fury. The LXX translates the Hebrew verb *ʿnh* as "answer," assuming that people on earth are doing the shouting. It translates: *kai aided ōsper trugōntes apokrithēsontai*, "And these, like men gathering grapes, shall answer." But this verb *ʿnh* does not mean "answer" (Rashi); it means "ring out, shout" (BDB *ʿnh* IV; KB[3] *ʿnh* IV), and it is Yahweh's voice that is ringing out. The NEB attempted to translate *ʿnh* as "answer," with Yahweh still being the speaking voice ("an echo comes back like the shout of men treading grapes"). Holladay accepts the "echo" interpretation, but the REB abandons the translation. Whereas a comparison is made here to the shout of men treading grapes, the shout is in fact a battle shout. The two meanings of *hêdād*, the shout of treaders and the shout of battle, appear together in Isa 16:9–10. The suggestion has also been made that there is an allusion to the Canaanite storm god, Hadad, in the present verse

(Weiser; de Moor and de Vries 1988). But it is unclear whether *hêdād* has any-thing to do here with thunder, as de Moor and de Vries claim, and it is virtually certain that the term cannot be rendered "thunderstorm." What we are talking about is a vigorous, all-consuming shout of divine judgment, one that will be followed by a decisive act of divine judgment. The image of Yahweh treading wicked nations the way men tread grapes is found elsewhere in the OT (Lam 1:15; Isa 63:1–6). In Isa 63:1–6, which is a judgment upon Edom, the red juice of the wine coalesces with the lifeblood of the victims, an association that Je-rome makes in the present verse. On the basis of the Isaiah text, Julia Ward Howe wrote her great "Battle Hymn of the Republic."

to all the inhabitants of the earth. Cassuto (1973c: 220–21) calls this hyper-bole, but it is nevertheless the case that the divine roar is going out to all nations.

31. *The uproar has reached the end of the earth.* A repetition of what has just been said, with the difference that now the sound has actually been heard. He-brew *šā'ôn* is "a roar, uproar," where reference once again is to the mighty voice of Yahweh. In Isa 13:4 and 17:12, *šā'ôn* is the tumult of a marching army. See also Amos 2:2 and Hos 10:14. Hebrew *bô'* + *'ad* means "comes to, reaches" (2 Kgs 9:20). The two images, Yahweh's roaring voice and the tumult of war, again coalesce. The LXX takes *bā' šā'ôn* ("the uproar comes") with the last co-lon of v 30, so the reading (according to Rudolph's scansion) becomes:

He will roar mightily against his pasture	v 30
a shout like the treaders will ring out	
To all the inhabitants of the earth	
the uproar has come	v 31
to the end of the earth	

The difference is slight, but the MT division is supported by T, S, and Vg.

for Yahweh has a case against the nations. Hebrew *rîb* is a legal term mean-ing "accusation, case" (cf. 11:20 = 20:12). Yahweh spoke of his ongoing litiga-tion against Judah in 2:9.

He has entered into judgment with all flesh. Hebrew *nišpāṭ hû' lĕkol-bāśār.* The language continues to be legal (Rashi; Kimhi). The N-stem participle *nišpāṭ* ("entered into judgment") has reciprocal force: Yahweh has taken the nations to court and sought a judgment against them. In Hos 4:1, court action was only against Israel (Heb *yôšĕbê hā'āreṣ* = "the inhabitants of the *land*"); and in Isa 3:13–14 and Jer 2:35, only against Judah. Here it is against "all flesh," i.e., everyone (cf. 12:12). The verdict in all such cases is predetermined, be-cause Yahweh is both prosecutor and judge.

as for the wicked, he has given them over to the sword. Hebrew *hārĕšā'îm nĕtānām laḥereb.* Here at the conclusion things become concrete. The judg-ment, for all practical purposes, has already taken place (the verbs in this final line are prophetic perfects). Here also is the only moral judgment in the clos-ing poems of the chapter: the nations are said to be wicked. Yahweh has given over the wicked to enemies who will kill them by the sword. Hebrew *nĕtānām* is not "he will put (them)," as the RSV, NIV, and NRSV translate. The term means "he has given them over," appearing often in the stereotyped expression about people being "given over into the hand" of their enemies (Josh 10:19; Judg 2:23; 1 Sam 14:10, 12). Isaiah 34:2 states that Yahweh has doomed the nations and given them over (*nĕtānām*) to slaughter. The LXX (*edothēsan*, "they were given over"), T ("he hands them over"), and Vg (*tradidi*, "I have handed over") are all different, but each preserves the idea of Yahweh surrendering the wicked to their enemies.

MESSAGE AND AUDIENCE

Yahweh states here in oblique fashion that he is about to roar from heaven against his pasture on earth. The audience will perceive that Yahweh is portraying himself as a lion but will not know what pasture his sights are set upon. Yahweh's voice will also be the loud shout of men treading grapes, except that his shout will be the shout of battle. Instead of red juice flowing from ripened grapes, blood of victims will be poured forth. These victims will be the inhabitants of earth, which means Yahweh's pasture will be the whole earth. Yahweh then says that the sound has already been heard worldwide, for his case is against the nations. With all of them he is entering into judgment, and the wicked are as good as dead before the sword of their enemy.

This oracle can be dated along with earlier material in the chapter to Jehoiakim's fourth year, 605 B.C.; otherwise to 604 or 597–594, when Jeremiah was preaching against foreign nations.

When this oracle is added to what precedes, "these words" in v 30 will supplement the divine words of vv 27–29, which accompany the passing of Yahweh's cup of wrath. The directive to prophesy against the nations in v 30a will also supplement earlier directives to address the nations in vv 27a and 28a, and the statement about the wicked having been given over to the sword in v 32 will reinforce earlier predictions of the same in vv 16, 27, and 29.

4. Evil Will Travel (25:32–33)

25 [32]Thus said Yahweh of hosts:
Look, evil shall go forth
    from nation to nation
A great tempest is roused
    from remote parts of the earth.

[33]And they shall be—the slain of Yahweh in that day—from the one end of the earth to the other end of the earth. They shall not be lamented, and they shall not be gathered, and they shall not be buried; for dung upon the surface of the ground they shall be.

RHETORIC AND COMPOSITION

MT 25:32–33 = LXX 32:32–33. These verses contain a brief oracle in poetry
(v 32), followed by a supplementary comment in prose (v 33). The oracle is at
the center of a three-poem cluster of judgmental utterances against the nations that concludes the chapter (see Rhetoric and Composition for 25:30–
31). The upper limit of the unit is marked by a messenger formula at the beginning of v 32, before which comes a *setumah* in M^A, M^L, and M^P. The lower
limit is marked by the prose comment in v 33.

The oracle recasts a stanza from an earlier Judah oracle in 6:22. The prose
comment is linked to the final bicolon of the oracle by catchphrases:

from remote parts of the earth	v 32b
from the one end of the earth to the other end of the earth	v 33a

The prose comment taken as a whole contains this inclusio:

And they shall be . . .	*wĕhāyû*	v 33
. . . they shall be.	*yihyû*	

Catchwords connecting to the previous oracle:

v 32	*nation to nation*		v 31	*to the end of the earth*
	from remote parts of the earth			*the nations*

Catchwords connecting to the oracle following are of similar sound, not
meaning:

v 32	*evil*	*rā'â*		v 34	*Wail*	*hêlîlû*
v 33	*the slain*	*ḥallê*			*shepherds*	*hārō'îm*

NOTES

25:32. *Yahweh of hosts.* The LXX omits "of hosts," as elsewhere (see Appendix
VI). Aquila, Symm, and Theo have *tōn dunameōn*.

Look, evil shall go forth from nation to nation. In 6:22 a people from the
north was said to be coming against Judah. Now the word from Yahweh is that
evil shall go forth from nation to nation. Duhm imagined one nation attacking
another here, an interpretation rejected earlier by Calvin. The idea seems,
rather, to be that Yahweh will bring judgment upon one nation, then another.
The more usual Jeremiah phrase, where Yahweh is the speaker, is "(Look) I am
bringing evil . . ." (see Note for 6:19). So far as the march of nations is concerned, Babylon for the present will continue to be Yahweh's agent of destruction, but in the end another evil will bring it down.

A great tempest is roused. The "great tempest" (*sa'ar gādôl*) is Yahweh's destroying wind (cf. 23:19 = 30:23). It is not the east wind off the desert (cf. 4:11)

but a swirling tempest with rain. The N-stem of *ʿwr* means "be roused, incited to activity"; see also 6:22 and 50:41.

from remote parts of the earth. Hebrew *mîyyarkĕtê-ʾāreṣ*. This expression occurs only in Jeremiah (6:22; 25:32; 31:8; and 50:41).

33. *the slain of Yahweh*. The *ḥălālîm* are "those pierced (by the sword)," in this case those who have been struck dead (see Note for 51:4). A sword of Yahweh was earlier promised against the nations in 25:16, 27, 29, and 32. On "the slain of Yahweh," see also Isa 66:16.

in that day. I.e., the Day of Yahweh, on which see Note for 4:9. The LXX has "in the day of the Lord." Holladay deletes the phrase *metri causa*; however, the verse is not poetry.

from the one end of the earth to the other end of the earth. The expression occurred earlier in 12:12, only there it was "the sword of Yahweh" that was doing the consuming work; also there *(hā)ʾereṣ* had to mean "(the) land," not "(the) earth." We see once again how Jeremianic expressions used originally with reference to Judah and the land of Judah take on broader meaning when applied to the nations.

They shall not be lamented, and they shall not be gathered, and they shall not be buried; for dung upon the surface of the ground they shall be. Compare the stereotyped phrases in 8:2 and 16:4; in the poetry, see 9:21[Eng 9:22]. The LXX omits "They shall not be lamented, and they shall not be gathered, and," which can be attributed to haplography (whole-word: *lʾ . . . lʾ*). Aquila and Theod have the words. On the indignity of bodies lying unburied, see Note for 7:33.

MESSAGE AND AUDIENCE

Yahweh in this brief oracle says that evil shall go forth from nation to nation. The theater of divine activity is now on earth, not in the heavens: the great tempest Yahweh is rousing will originate in the farthest reaches of the earth. The effect of all this is stated in the supplementary comment. The slain of Yahweh will cover the earth, their numbers being so great that they will not be lamented, gathered up, or buried. Like dung on the ground they will be.

In its present form this oracle, like the one preceding, can be dated anytime after 605 B.C., when Jeremiah was addressing oracles to the foreign nations. The same date suits the added comment.

When the oracle and comment are heard following the oracle that precedes, what is said about the "slain of Yahweh" extending from one end of the earth to the other (v 33) will pick up from what was said about Yahweh's giving over the wicked to the sword (v 32). These words will also fulfill what was said in the cup-of-wrath prophecy about Yahweh's sword being readied for the nations (vv 16, 27, 29). The oracle and comment together will be heard as an additional word spoken by Yahweh when the cup of wrath was passed to the nations.

5. Wail, O Shepherds, and Cry Out! (25:34–38)

25 ³⁴Wail, O shepherds, and cry out
and roll about, O nobles of the flock
Because your days for slaughter are fulfilled
and you will be scattered
and you will fall like a vessel of great value
³⁵Flight shall vanish from the shepherds
escape from the nobles of the flock

³⁶The sound of a scream of the shepherds
and the wailing of the nobles of the flock
because Yahweh is devastating their pasturage
³⁷Yes, the peaceful pastures lie silent
before the burning anger of Yahweh

³⁸Like a young lion he left his lair
indeed their land became a desolation
Before the oppressive burning
before his burning anger.

RHETORIC AND COMPOSITION

MT 25:34–38 = LXX 32:34–38. The present verses are delimited at the top end by a return to poetry in v 34. Verse 33 is add-on prose to the prior unit. Delimitation at the bottom end is by a *petuḥah* in M^A, M^L, and M^P after v 38, which is also the chapter division. For the relation of vv 34–38 to the whole of vv 30–38, see Rhetoric and Composition for 25:30–31.

This poem has no messenger formula and no first-person pronouns to identify it as a divine oracle. It may then be taken as a judgment utterance of the prophet, perhaps originally mocking the leaders of Judah and Jerusalem, and then later reused to mock leaders of all nations. No mention is made of the nations such as there is in the two preceding oracles (vv 31, 32). Calvin said he had no doubt but that the prophet was now turning to address his own nation. Jones has suggested also that the kings here might be Judah's kings, but he recognizes that the utterance in its present context must refer to the kings of the nations.

The poem has three stanzas with the following repetitions and balancing key words:

```
I    ......shepherds...                                       v 34
        ......nobles of the flock
     Because....................        kî
     ...........................
     ........the shepherds                                    v 35
     .......the nobles of the flock
```

II . . . . *the shepherds*   v 36
  . . . . . . *the nobles of the flock*
    because Yahweh . . . .   *kî*

. . . .
. . . .   v 37
    before the burning anger of Yahweh

III . . . .   v 38
  indeed . . . .   *kî*
  Before the oppressive burning
  before his burning anger

The poem also has a deliberate structure of cognate repetition and inversion, in which the nouns of v 36 echo the verbs of v 34 (Holladay):

I   *Wail* . . . . *and cry out* . . .   *hêlîlû . . . wĕzaʿăqû*   v 34
II . . . *a scream* . . . . . *and the wailing* . . .   *ṣaʿăqat . . . wîlĕlat*   v 36

Catchwords connecting to the prior oracle are similar in sound:

v 34 *Wail*   *hêlîlû*   v 32 *evil*   *rāʿâ*
      shepherds *hārōʿîm*   v 33 *the slain*   *ḥallê*

NOTES

25:34. *Wail, O shepherds, and cry out.* Hebrew *hêlîlû hārōʿîm wĕzaʿăqû.* The same two verbs are paired in 47:2; 48:20, 31, and occur elsewhere (Hos 7:14; Isa 14:31; Ezek 21:17[Eng 21:12]; Joel 1:13–14). The verb *yll* in the H-stem means "wail, howl," and *zʿq* means "cry out (for help)." See also 49:3, which pairs *hêlîlî* ("Wail!") and *ṣĕʿaqnâ* ("Scream!"). This call to lament is mockery, as it often is in the Foreign Nation Oracles (48:20, 31, 39; 49:3; 51:8).

shepherds. Hebrew *rōʿîm* is a general term for "rulers" in the ANE, but often it refers more specifically to "kings" or "kings and princes" (see Note for 2:8). Calvin interprets the term broadly, saying that it refers to kings, their advisers, priests, and other rulers. But here "shepherds" likely means just "kings" (Kimḥi), as it is the nation's kings who receive Yahweh's cup of wrath (vv 17–26).

and roll about, O nobles of the flock. The verb *plš* Hithpael means "roll about (in mourning)," where the rolling is done in dust or ashes (*bāʾēper,* "in ashes," is added in 6:26 and Ezek 27:30). The T has "cover your heads with ashes." The "nobles" (*ʾaddîrîm*) are, lit., "majestic ones" or "mighty ones" (T), who constitute the nation's ruling elite (14:3; 30:21). Calvin says they are the rich and those held in public esteem, but who hold no office. But Kimḥi thinks "nobles," like "shepherds," refer again to the kings, which may be correct, since they are designated "the nobles of the flock."

Because your days for slaughter are fulfilled. In the divine economy, as also in the economy of earth, things happen "in the fulfillment of days"

(Gen 15:16). The time has now come for the rulers of the nations to be slaughtered. In 51:40 Yahweh says he will bring down the lions of Babylon like lambs to the slaughter. And in 50:27, Babylon's "bulls" are consigned to the slaughter, although it is unclear in this verse whether reference is to actual bulls or the nation's leaders.

and you will be scattered. Hebrew *ûtĕpôṣôtîkem* is generally taken to be a mixed form of *pûṣ*, "to scatter, disperse," combining the Qal *tāpûṣû*, "you will be scattered," and the H-stem *hăpîṣôtîkem*, "I will scatter you" (GKC §91 l). The T has "and you will be scattered." Aquila, Symm, and Theod translate with a noun (*kai oi skorpismoi hymōn*, "and your scatterings"), as does Vg (*et dissipationes vestrae*, "and your scatterings"), but a feminine noun, *tĕpôṣâ*, is unattested and generally not accepted by commentators and the modern Versions—only the RSV and NRSV retain with slight change the translation of AV: "For the days of your slaughter and dispersion have come." The term is omitted by the LXX, for which reason a number of commentators (Cornill, Rudolph, Bright, Holladay, McKane) and numerous modern Versions (NEB; REB; JB [but not NJB]; NAB; NIV; NSB) omit. The view of Rudolph, Bright, and Holladay that the verb is *npṣ* or *pṣṣ*, both meaning "to shatter" (so Syriac), is predicated on the assumption that the MT is defective, which enables these scholars to delete the verb and go with the LXX's "rams" at the end of the line. This eliminates entirely the shattered vessel image. But most agree that the verb is a form of *pûṣ*, "to scatter." A case can be made for retaining the verb. As for the LXX omission, it can be attributed to haplography (homoeoarcton: *w . . . w*). The argument of Janzen (1973: 14), that two verbs overload the line and that therefore one must be secondary and deleted, can be set aside. The line is easily translated as a tricolon. And Holladay's claim that the "scattering" image goes poorly with the "slaughtering" image is unconvincing. For kings and nobles both images are eminently suitable: in war some kings and nobles are killed; others are scattered by virtue of being exiled. This happened not only to Judah's royal house but to royal houses of all nations.

and you will fall like a vessel of great value. Whether the kings and nobles are killed or taken into exile, their fall will leave them broken individuals. The metaphors change if MT is to be read, for the high and mighty are now compared to vessels fallen and broken, Humpty Dumpty style. The colon is incorrectly said by Janzen (1973: 194 n. 17) not to make sense. In fact, it makes very good sense. The construct *kĕlî* is a general noun meaning "vessel (of clay or precious metal), jar, weapon, baggage," and the absolute *ḥemdâ* is a noun meaning "precious, desirable thing," thus an item of great value. Reference then is to a precious pottery vessel capable of being broken (cf. 19:11; 22:28). The expression "vessel(s) of great value" occurs elsewhere in Hos 13:15; Nah 2:10[Eng 2:9]; 2 Chr 32:27; and 36:10. The LXX in the present verse has "like the chosen rams" (*ōsper hoi krioi hoi eklektoi*), also translating "nobles of the flock" as "rams of the flock" (*hoi krioi tōn probatōn*). The reading of LXX is that the rams of the flock are going to fall like choice rams. If the MT reading is difficult, this rendering has to be worse, which is perhaps why even Duhm and

McKane accept the LXX reading only reluctantly. Some of the more recent English Versions (NIV; NRSV; NJB) return to "precious vessel" (AV had "pleasant vessel"), which allows for a sudden change of metaphors. Both Rashi and Kimḥi (following T) read "precious vessel." The change of metaphors is not a problem; in v 30 they changed abruptly from a roaring lion to men treading grapes. The LXX's "rams" can perhaps be attributed to the misreading of Heb *kiklî* ("like a vessel") as *kĕ'êlê* ("like rams").

35. *Flight shall vanish from the shepherds.* This vivid expression occurs also in Amos 2:14; Job 11:20; and Ps 142:5[Eng 142:4]. Hebrew *mānôs* means "flight, place of escape." The shepherds, like the nobles of the flock, will find no place of refuge.

36. *The sound of a scream of the shepherds and the wailing of the nobles of the flock.* Taking Heb *qôl ṣa'ăqat hārō'îm* as a triple construct chain: "The sound of a scream of the shepherds" (cf. AV). Another possibility could be "A sound! a scream of the shepherds." But compare in 48:3: "The sound of a scream (*qôl ṣĕ'āqâ*) from Horonaim"; and 51:54: "The sound of a cry (*qôl zĕ'āqâ*) from Babylon." The parallel phrase is similarly a triple construct chain: "and the wailing of the nobles of the flock." The nouns are cognates of the verbs in v 34 (see Rhetoric and Composition). At the beginning, Jeremiah commanded the shepherds and nobles of the flock to wail and cry loudly; now he claims to hear them doing precisely that (Cheyne), which is a case of apostrophe. The screaming and wailing is because Yahweh is devastating flocks in their pasturelands (cf. Zech 11:3a).

because Yahweh is devastating their pasturage. The verb *šdd* ("devastate") occurs throughout the book of Jeremiah, appearing particularly often in the Foreign Nation Oracles (see Note for 48:8). In Zech 11:3 shepherds are said to be wailing because their splendor is devastated. Hebrew *mar'îtām* ("pasturage") is a metonymy for "flock," as it is also in 10:21 (Giesebrecht). The T: "for the Lord has plundered their people." Kimḥi explains *mar'îtām* as the nations over which kings exercise rule.

37. *Yes, the peaceful pastures lie silent.* Hebrew *wĕnādammû nĕ'ôt haššālôm.* The verb is a prophetic perfect. Yahweh's destructive work is portrayed as already having been accomplished. The once-peaceful pastures now lie deathly silent—an ironic transformation from one kind of tranquillity to another. Isaiah imagines Jerusalem's return to a "peaceful pasture" (*nĕwēh šālôm*) once Yahweh pours out his Spirit on a devastated land (Isa 32:18).

before the burning anger of Yahweh. Hebrew *mippĕnê ḥărôn 'ap-yhwh.* This phrase and those concluding v 38 are variations on a common climactic expression in Jeremiah, affirming the awesomeness of Yahweh's anger (see Note for 4:8). The LXX has "my anger," which may simply reproduce the expression as it occurs in v 38b (which the LXX omits), or, as some have suggested (Schwally 1888: 188 n. 1, citing Spohn earlier; Volz; G. R. Driver 1960: 119), be a misreading of "anger of Yahweh" in an abbreviated form (אף י). The phrase, in any case, is not misplaced; nor should it be deleted (*pace* Duhm; Bright; Janzen 1973: 14 n. 21). The various forms of the expression and their repetition are important rhetorically in the poem (see Rhetoric and Composition).

38. *Like a young lion he left his lair.* Here and in the next colon are more prophetic perfects. Interpretations of the present colon vary because the subject is unspecified, unless one takes "Yahweh" preceding to be the antecedent of the verb. Additionally, different reasons are given for the young lion leaving his lair. Some say he is leaving in search of prey; others say he is leaving because the lair has been destroyed. In my view, Yahweh is the subject of the verb (Ehrlich 1912: 309) and metaphorically the young lion. Here concluding a three-poem cluster is a return to the beginning (v 30), where Yahweh's roar is again the roar of a lion (see Rhetoric and Composition for 25:30–31). This tie-in precludes the interpretation of T, which has "a king has gone into exile from his fortified place." But one should remember that T commonly substitutes "king" for "lion" (see Note for 4:7). Reference here is not to a Judahite king or to any other king (*pace* McKane, who connects with the lion of 4:7, making the young lion here Nebuchadnezzar). Also, movement out of the lair has nothing to do with leaving a devastated abode (= land) or with exile. Yahweh is leaving his abode to devastate nations of the world (vv 30–31). He is not abandoning Jerusalem and the Temple (*pace* Jerome; Kimhi; Calvin), although this idea is vividly portrayed in Ezekiel (see Note on 12:7).

indeed their land became a desolation. Translating *kî* here as an asseverative: "indeed." If this poem was originally spoken against the kings of Judah, then "their land" could be the land of Judah (Rudolph). But in its present context, "their land" is land belonging to the kings of the nations.

Before the oppressive burning. Hebrew *mippĕnê hărôn hayyônâ*. This phrase is a variation of the similar phrases in vv 37–38; nevertheless, the translation of *hayyônâ* is difficult. Hebrew *yônâ* can be either the feminine participle of *ynh*, "to oppress," or the noun "dove." The Vg has "dove," but this cannot be right (Calvin; McKane). If the MT is to be read, *hayyônâ* must be the participle of *ynh*, in which the definite article functions as a relative pronoun. This yields "the burning that oppresses," or simply "the oppressive burning." The NJV has "the oppressive wrath," and the NJB "the devastating fury," both of which are an improvement over AV's "the fierceness of the oppressor." Most commentators and modern Versions adopt the reading of several MSS, the LXX, and T, which have "sword" (= *hereb*) in place of "burning" (*hărôn*), making the phrase the same as the one in 46:16 and 50:16: "before the oppressive sword." The present phrase, in any case, as well as the one following, refer to Yahweh's anger that has made the land a desolation.

before his burning anger. This expression is a duplicate of the one in 4:26. The LXX omits.

MESSAGE AND AUDIENCE

Jeremiah in the present poem calls upon shepherds to wail and nobles to roll in the dirt. Why? Because the days for their slaughter have come. Some will be scattered to God knows where. All will fall like a precious china vase, broken forever. Chances for the shepherds and nobles to escape will vanish. Jeremiah then says he hears the screaming and the wailing. Yahweh is now devastating the flocks. The work is complete. Once-peaceful pastures lie deathly silent before the burning anger of Yahweh. Like a lion, Yahweh left his lair, and the land became desolate before the divine anger.

This poem could have originally been spoken against the kings and nobility of Judah, but in its present context is a climactic word to the kings and nobility of nations, calling them to lament their people and their lands. It is unclear when such a poem could have been spoken to Judah. Against the nations, it fits in with other utterances of the chapter, which are dated to 605 B.C.; otherwise to 604 or 597–594 B.C., when Jeremiah is preaching his Foreign Nations Oracles.

When this poem is heard in tandem with what precedes, Jeremiah will be supplementing the divine word that accompanies the passing of the cup of wrath; and it will be the word one might expect to hear at the end of a judgment, a word about wailing, crying out, and rolling in the dirt. These will be the final sounds before the land becomes silent. The image of a lion coming against a pasture in vv 30–31 will also be broadened. The attack now is not on a few sheep, not even a larger flock. Shepherds, too, will be attacked and killed, which is what one can infer from the vision of Yahweh's cup of wrath, where, at a banquet table all the kings of the nations sat as invited guests.

C. THE COST OF PROPHETIC PREACHING (26:1–24)

1. The Temple Oracles and Jeremiah's Day in Court (26:1–19)

26 ¹In the beginning of the reign of Jehoiakim son of Josiah, king of Judah, this word came from Yahweh: ²Thus said Yahweh: Stand in the courtyard of the house of Yahweh, and you shall speak concerning all the cities of Judah who come to worship in the house of Yahweh all the words that I command you to speak to them. Do not hold back a word. ³Perhaps they will listen and return each person from his evil way and I will repent concerning[a] the evil that I am planning to do to them on account of their evil doings. ⁴And you shall say to them:
   Thus said Yahweh:
   If you do not listen to me to walk in my law that I have set before you,
   ⁵to listen to the words of my servants the prophets whom I am sending

---

[a] Reading *ʿal* ("concerning"), with many MSS; MT has *ʾel* ("to"); cf. v 13.

to you, constantly I am sending,[b] although you have not listened, [6]then I will make this house like Shiloh, and this city I will make a swearword for all the nations of the earth.

[7]And the priests and the prophets and all the people heard Jeremiah speaking these words in the house of Yahweh. [8]And it happened as Jeremiah finished speaking everything that Yahweh commanded him[c] to speak to all the people, the priests and the prophets and all the people then laid hold of him, saying, 'You shall surely die! [9]Why have you prophesied in the name of Yahweh saying, Like Shiloh this house shall become, and this city will dry up without inhabitant?' And all the people crowded up to Jeremiah in the house of Yahweh. [10]And the princes of Judah heard these things and came up from the house of the king to the house of Yahweh, and they sat at the entrance of the New Gate of the house[d] of Yahweh. [11]And the priests and the prophets said to the princes and to all the people: 'A sentence of death for this man! because he has prophesied to this city according to what you have heard with your ears.' [12]Then Jeremiah said to all the princes and to all the people:

Yahweh sent me to prophesy to this house and to this city all the words that you have heard. [13]And now, make good your ways and your doings, and obey the voice of Yahweh your God; and then Yahweh will repent concerning[e] the evil that he has spoken against you. [14]But I, look I am in your hands. Do to me as seems good and right in your eyes. [15]Only know for sure that if you put me to death, then you will bring innocent blood upon yourselves and to this city and to its inhabitants; for in truth, Yahweh sent me against you to speak in your ears all these words.

[16]Then the princes and all the people said to the priests and to the prophets, 'There should be no sentence of death for this man, because in the name of Yahweh our God he has spoken to us.' [17]And men from among the elders of the land stood up and said to the entire assembly of the people:

[18]'Micah, the Morashtite, was prophesying in the days of Hezekiah, king of Judah, and he said to all the people of Judah:

Thus said Yahweh of hosts:
Zion shall be plowed a field
    and Jerusalem shall become stone heaps
And the mountain of the House
    high places of a forest.

[19]Did Hezekiah, king of Judah, and all Judah indeed put him to death? Did he not fear Yahweh and soften the face of Yahweh? And did not Yah-

---

[b]Omitting the *waw* on *wĕhaškēm* ("rising early = constantly"), with some MSS and the Vrs.

[c]Adding the pronominal suffix "him" to the verb, with LXX, S, T, and Vg (cf. 36:8); MT has just "he commanded."

[d]Adding *bêt*, with many MSS and the Vrs.

[e]Reading *ʿal* ("concerning"), with many MSS; MT has *ʾel* ("to"); see footnote on v 3.

weh repent of the evil that he spoke against them? And we are doing great evil against ourselves!

2. Uriah of Kiriath-jearim: Prophet of Yahweh (26:20–24)

26 [20]Also, a man was prophesying mightily in the name of Yahweh — Uriah son of Shemaiah from Kiriath-jearim. And he prophesied against this city and against this land like all the words of Jeremiah. [21]And King Jehoiakim heard his words, also all his officers and all the princes, and the king sought to put him to death. But Uriah heard of it, and he was afraid and fled, and came to Egypt. [22]So King Jehoiakim sent men to Egypt — Elnathan son of Achbor and men with him to Egypt. [23]And they fetched Uriah from Egypt and brought him to King Jehoiakim, and he struck him down with the sword and cast his dead body into the graves of the common people.
[24]But the hand of Ahikam son of Shaphan was with Jeremiah, so as not to give him into the hand of the people to put him to death.

RHETORIC AND COMPOSITION

MT 26:1–24 = LXX 33:1–24. The present chapter is a self-contained narrative reporting a dramatic preaching event in the life of Jeremiah, followed by a trial, to which has been added the report of another prophet who preached the same judgment as Jeremiah but who paid for the truth with his life (vv 20–23). The narrative begins by dating the event in the beginning of Jehoiakim's reign (v 1) and ends by stating how Jeremiah survived this crisis because of protection received from Ahikam son of Shaphan (v 24). The structure of the narrative compares with that in chap. 28, which began by dating the event being reported (v 1) and ended with a summary statement telling how the crisis turned out — in that case, how Jeremiah's opponent paid for false prophecy with his life (v 17).

The present chapter is one of four chapters, 25, 26, 35, and 36, that originally comprised a "Jehoiakim Cluster" of dated prose (with chap. 25 having also supplemental poetry at the end), on which see Rhetoric and Composition for 25:1–13a. In the present sequence of chapters, where the Jehoiakim Cluster and a similarly constructed Zedekiah Cluster have been partially dismantled and Jehoiakim prose has been interspersed with Zedekiah prose (see "Excursus III: The Composition of Jeremiah 24–36," at the end of 25:1–14), chap. 26 likely owes its position preceding chaps. 27–29 to a common thread running through all four chapters: namely, Jeremiah's bitter conflict with the priests and prophets of Jerusalem (Rudolph; Hyatt; Jones).

The upper limit of this narrative unit is marked by a *petuḥah* in M[A], M[L], and M[P] before v 1, which is also the chapter division. In 26:1 there is also a return to prose after the concluding poetry of chap. 25. The lower limit of the narrative is marked by a *petuḥah* in M[A], M[L], and M[P] after v 24, which is also a chapter division. M^A has a *petuḥah* and M^L and M^P a *setumah* after v 6, which marks the conclusion of Jeremiah's oracle. M^P alone has a *setumah* after v 9, the purpose of which is unclear. The same can be said for a *setumah* that M^A and M^L have after v 10. M^P has no section there; nor does 4QJer^c upon reconstruction. M^A, M^L, and M^P all have another *setumah* after v 15, marking the conclusion of Jeremiah's defense before the court.

The present narrative has long been recognized as providing the background for Jeremiah's Temple preaching recorded in 7:1–15, as well as containing a summary of that preaching. In fact, it was these two passages' reporting of a single event that became a lead argument for there being different prose sources in the book. Chapter 26 was said to be Source B (biographical/Baruch) prose, and 7:1–15 Source C (sermonic) prose (see Rhetoric and Composition for 7:1–15). Giesebrecht attributed the narrative here to Baruch on the basis of the third-person references to Jeremiah, as well as to other features. Mowinckel (1914: 24) similarly assigned the narrative to Source B, which he later took to derive from Baruch. Others from this early period (Peake; Cornill; Volz) and some more recently (Rudolph; Weiser; Bright; H. Weippert 1973; Holladay; Jones) have also credited Baruch with the narrative, or at least affirmed that the narrative reports an authentic incident from the life of Jeremiah. Duhm, too, said that the narrative most likely builds on Baruch's life of Jeremiah, although he found "midrashic" elements present, particularly in vv 1–6, where he said not a single word could have come from Baruch. Duhm could not imagine that Jeremiah would make deliverance of the nation dependent upon obedience to the law. Volz said simply that Baruch's style in vv 1–6 was somewhat clumsy. More recent scholars have tended to disregard the source-critical distinction between early and late prose, assigning the chapter to a late "Deuteronomic" editor or editors (Hyatt; Nicholson; Thiel 1981: 3–4; Smelik 1989–90; McKane) or simply denying the historicity of the incidents reported (Carroll) or both (Hossfeld and Meyer 1974). These views, as I have stated elsewhere, 1) suffer from an unclear definition of the term "Deuteronomic"; 2) make a false dichotomy between protohistorical and protobiographical reporting on the one hand, and literary composition on the other (the two are not mutually exclusive); and 3) lack a clear methodology for working with the biblical text. Redaction criticism, for example, is too derivative from source criticism and too lacking in basic principles of its own. Duhm could never be accused of not working from basic assumptions or along clear methodological lines, whatever one thinks of his assumptions and the conclusions that he came to. Reventlow (1969) has seen the inadequacy of source criticism, but his form-critical views have led him to conclude that the chapter is a liturgical piece from a later age, not the biography of an eyewitness. Carroll's treatment of chap. 26 is largely fantasy and cannot be taken with any seriousness. In my view, we can dispense entirely with phantom "Deuteronomic" editors (unless Baruch or a contemporary be one) and with midexilic or postexilic redactions. The narrative should be taken as historical by and large (Holladay), written soon after the events it reports took place. As for vocabulary and phraseology, the narrative is written in typical Jeremianic prose, such as one finds elsewhere in the book (Jones).

Some commentators (Duhm; Volz; Weiser; Hyatt) have taken the Uriah incident in vv 20–23 as an attachment, but Holladay believes it is well integrated into the narrative, which it is. However, it is not integrated to the extent that it reports something more said at Jeremiah's trial. Uriah's prophecy and subsequent execution by Jehoiakim are not being cited by the elders who have just remembered the Micah prophecy, nor by a hostile element in the crowd that is responding with a "counterprecedent" (*pace* Rashi, who follows Midrash Sifre Numbers 11:7; Fishbane 1985: 246) but, rather, by the one who is narrating the whole. The Uriah segment is connected to what precedes by catchphrases:

in the name of Yahweh	v 9
in the name of Yahweh	v 16
in the name of Yahweh	v 20

The narrator brings in the Uriah incident to tell his audience about another prophet who spoke in Yahweh's name but who did not escape Jehoiakim's wrath as Jeremiah did. The closing word in v 24 contrasts this tragic outcome with Ahikam's protection of Jeremiah, serving also as a quiet reminder of the divine promise to Jeremiah—in his call, in his commission, and later on in ministry—that he would be delivered from all his enemies (1:8, 18–19; 15:20–21).

Jeremiah's speech to the court is tied together by this inclusio:

Yahweh sent me . . . all the words . . .	v 12
. . . Yahweh sent me . . . all these words.	v 15

NOTES

26:1. *In the beginning of the reign of Jehoiakim.* Hebrew *rēʾšît mamlĕkût* is used here in a nontechnical sense to mean "beginning of the reign"; it does not mean "accession year," as does the Akk term *rēš šarrūti* (M. Cogan, "Chronology, Hebrew Bible," *ABD* 1: 1006; cf. Althann 1988). Cogan points out that the equivalent of Akk *rēš šarrūti* is Heb *šĕnat molkô* (2 Kgs 25:27). This nontechnical meaning applies also to the comparable expressions in 27:1; 28:1; and 49:34. Mesopotamia employed an accession-year (postdating) system, whereby the elapsed time between a king's accession and the following New Year was counted as an "accession year," not the first year of his reign. Egypt for most of its history employed a non-accession-year (antedating) system, which did not reckon an accession year, but counted the first year of a king's reign from the time he actually took the throne. Early on, Israel and Judah employed the non-accession-year system, but toward the middle or end of the seventh century B.C., beginning with Manasseh or Amon, Judah appears to have adopted the accession-year system under Assyrian and Babylonian influence. The accession-year system would then have been in use at the present time, which means that the period from Jehoiakim's ascent to the throne in September 609, until April 608, would have been his "accession year." The king's first regnal year would have begun in April 608, which was New Year according to the Nisan calendar in use in Judah at the time (Tadmor 1956: 229; Bright). Begrich (1929: 91, 93) argued that in all four Jeremiah texts, which are the only ones of their kind in the OT, "beginning of the reign" meant "accession year," and a number of scholars have concurred with this judgment (Rudolph; Weiser; Hyatt 1966: 205–6; Bright; Sarna 1978: 91; Holladay). Nevertheless, according to Tadmor and Cogan, the term appears to have only general meaning in the Jeremiah superscriptions, especially in 28:1 (though this date has problems), which means that the event reported here in chap. 26 could have occurred in Jehoiakim's accession year but need not have. On ancient Israelite chronology, see further H. Tadmor, *EncMiqr* 4: 245–310 [Hebrew]; idem, "The Chronology of the First Temple Period" in *WHJP* 4/1: 44–60. For months of the Jewish calendar, see Appendix IX.

Since the following verse tells us that pilgrims from outlying cities were expected in Jerusalem when Jeremiah was instructed to speak at the Temple, it is likely that the occasion was one of some importance. One of the annual festivals has been suggested (Exod 23:14–17; Deut 16:1–13), perhaps the Feast of Booths, which took place in the fall (Blayney; Rudolph; Weiser; Holladay). Others have suggested a New Year coronation for Jehoiakim (Duhm; Volz; Morgenstern 1929: 20–22), although Peake says this would have been an inappropriate time for such preaching. Quite obviously, any time would have been inappropriate, judging from what transpired after these riveting oracles were spoken.

reign. Hebrew *mamlěkût.* This spelling occurs in Hos 1:4 and a few other places in the OT; the spelling in Jeremiah is otherwise *mamleket* (27:1; 28:1).

this word came from Yahweh. The S and OL add "to Jeremiah" after "this word" (cf. 27:1; 34:1; 36:1; and 49:34), which is not present in MT or any other ancient Version. But the shorter reading could be original (cf. Peake), since there is no reason why this formulation must precisely match the others.

2. *Thus said Yahweh: Stand in the courtyard of the house of Yahweh, and you shall speak concerning all the cities of Judah who come to worship in the house of Yahweh all the words that I command you to speak to them.* The Temple courtyard (*ḥāṣēr*) was the usual place for Jeremiah to speak his oracles (19:14). In 7:2, Jeremiah was told to stand at the gate of Yahweh's house, which may have been a gate to the inner courtyard, thought by some to have been the Eastern Gate (Kimḥi; Morgenstern 1929: 21–22; see Note for 7:2). On the term *ḥāṣēr* ("enclosure, court"), which occurs 15 times in Jeremiah and often in the phrase "court of the guard" (37:21; 38:13, 28; 39:14; et passim), see Orlinsky 1939. The "court of the guard" was in the royal palace (32:2).

all the cities of Judah. A metonymy for "all the people of the cities of Judah" (Blayney). The wording in 7:2 is "all Judah," and in 31:24 "Judah and all its cities." The LXX in the present verse has "the Judahites" (*tois Ioudaiois*). This will be an occasion when people from all the outlying cities will be coming to Jerusalem (cf. 36:6).

Do not hold back a word. I.e., do not in any way diminish the message. Hebrew *'al-tigraʿ dābār*. The expression occurs in Deut 4:2 and 13:1[Eng 12:32] as *lōʾ tigrĕʿû / tigraʿ mimmennû* ("Do not hold back from it"), which Weinfeld (1972b: 360, #14) lists among idioms of Deuteronomy that may have influenced Jeremiah. Compare in the NT, Rev 22:19. Yahweh issues this warning because Jeremiah may have been tempted not to speak the divine word in full (see Note for 50:2). Prophets of Yahweh must speak "the word, the whole word, and nothing but the word." The same holds for writing up a scroll of Yahweh's revelations ("all the words" in 30:2). The reason for wanting to scale down a word of judgment, needless to say, would be a fear of possible consequences. Jeremiah had been forewarned that this could happen (1:17). On a later occasion, King Zedekiah admonished Jeremiah not to keep a word from him (38:14). Then after Jeremiah did tell him the undiminished word from Yahweh, which he did not want to hear, Zedekiah, in fulfillment of an oath he had sworn to Jeremiah, arranged for the prophet to hold back part of their conversation when critics questioned him later (38:24–26). Once again after the fall of Jerusalem, when people asked Jeremiah to petition Yahweh about where they should go after leaving Mizpah, he promised to give them Yahweh's answer and keep nothing back (42:4). This message, too, was one the people did not want to hear, which means it took courage as well as commitment for Jeremiah to speak the whole of Yahweh's word.

3. *Perhaps they will listen and return each person from his evil way and I will repent concerning the evil that I am planning to do to them on account of their evil doings.* Bedrock Jeremiah preaching (18:11; 25:5; 35:15; 36:3, 7). Note the individualizing tendency in "*each person* (*'îš*) from his evil way and I will repent," which is common in Jeremiah and becomes even more pronounced in Ezekiel (Ezek 18:21–23, 27–28; 33:11–20). In the divine word given at the potter's house (18:1–12), Yahweh made it clear that if the people repented of evil, it would bring about a corresponding change in his plans to do evil (see Note on 18:8). The LXX, perhaps to avoid an anthropomorphism, translates "I will repent" with a euphemistic "I will cease," *pausomai* (see again vv 13, 19). Aquila has "I shall be encouraged concerning the evil" (*paraklēthēsomai peri tēs kakias*). After "I will repent," many MSS have *ʿal* instead of *'el*, particles that alternate throughout the chapter. On the frequent interchange of *'el* and *ʿal* in the book of Jeremiah, see Note for 11:2.

on account of their evil doings. A stereotyped phrase in Jeremiah, which has turned up in the Qumran *Temple Scroll* (see Note for 21:12).

4. *And you shall say to them.* Hebrew *wĕʾāmartā 'ălêhem*. The LXX omits "to them," which can be explained as an inner-Greek haplography of *pros autous* after *ereis* (homoeoteleuton: *s . . . s*). Aquila, Symm, and Theod all have *pros autous*.

If you do not listen to me. Hebrew *'im-lōʾ* begins the protasis; the apodosis comes in v 6. Compare the arguments in 12:17; 17:27; and 22:5. Oracle I in

7:3–7 is conditional like the present one (v 5), but positive, calling for concrete acts of obedience to the covenant as formulated in the book of Deuteronomy. Oracle II in 7:8–11 and Oracle III (the Shiloh Oracle) in 7:12–15 are unconditional, the former an indictment and the latter announcing judgment. The oracle here appears to be a paraphrased summary of the three oracles in 7:3–14, more negative than Oracle I but less provocative than Oracles II and III.

to walk in my law. Hebrew *lāleket bĕtôrātî.* The present idiom appears also in 32:23; 44:10, 23; 2 Kgs 10:31; and Ps 78:10, where individuals or people in general are faulted for not walking in Yahweh's law. See also Jer 9:12[Eng 9:13]; 16:11; and 31:33; in the poetry, see 6:19, where, as here, Yahweh's "law/teaching" balances Yahweh's "words" spoken by the prophets. In 6:16 "walking the ancient paths" means following the genuine ethical principles of the Mosaic covenant. The "law" here refers not simply to Deuteronomy, although Deuteronomy is not to be excluded, but to stipulations at the heart of the Sinai covenant that are spelled out with bold specificity in Oracle II of 7:8–11. For "walking" as an expression of ethical behavior or conduct, see Note on 23:14.

5. *to listen to the words of my servants the prophets whom I am sending to you, constantly I am sending, although you have not listened.* People hear about walking in Yahweh's law from the priests, but it is the prophets who call for a return to the law when the way has been lost. Jeremiah says here that the prophetic call is going out continually, but people are not listening. The urgent nature of this admonition is preserved in a present participial construction, *'ānōkî šōlēaḥ,* "I am sending," not the usual "I sent to you all my servants the prophets," which is past (see Note on 7:25). Similarly, the rhetorical idiom of a repeated verb used together with *škm* is also past tense: "I sent to you . . . constantly I sent" (see Note for 7:13). But here Jeremiah is confronting a current unwillingness by the people to hear the prophetic message. Others besides Jeremiah were preaching it. The chapter, in fact, will go on to tell us about one such prophet, Uriah of Kiriath-jearim, who preached Yahweh's word and paid for it with his life (vv 20–23).

6. *then I will make this house like Shiloh, and this city I will make a swearword for all the nations of the earth.* The verse contains a syntactic chiasmus: "I will make / this house . . . // this city / I will make. . . ." See also v 9. "House" and "city" are a common word pair, repeated in vv 9 and 12 and occurring elsewhere in the Bible (1 Kgs 8:44, 48; 2 Chr 6:34, 38; 2 Kgs 23:27; Ps 127:1), and found also in Sumerian and Babylonian literature (Fleming 1986). In the Babel story of Gen 11:1–9, "city" and "temple" (*migdāl*) are correlative terms (Lundbom 1983: 205). One should note also a wordplay here between *šōlēaḥ / šālôaḥ* ("sent") and *šīlōh* ("Shiloh"). Mention of the ruined Shiloh sanctuary touched a raw nerve and is doubtless what brought Jeremiah to trial. Shiloh was destroyed sometime after 1050 B.C. by the Philistines (see Note for 7:12). Oracle I in chap. 7 pointed with specificity to a false confidence in the Temple on the part of the people. Since the time of Isaiah, in light of the miraculous deliverance of the city from Sennacherib in 701 B.C., it had become virtual dogma that Jerusalem and the Temple would not be destroyed (see Note for

7:4). Another reason for such a hostile response to preaching Temple destruction was that now, since the Josianic Reform, this had become the sole place of legitimate Yahweh worship. Assuming that Jeremiah had supported the Reform, as I think we must, an oracle now of judgment against the Temple would constitute a major turnaround in his preaching (Wilcoxen 1977: 164–65).

this city. On the Kt reading of the demonstrative *hazzō'tâ* ("this"), see GKC §34b. The T follows the Q, *hazzō't*. The LXX has "the city."

a swearword. Hebrew *qĕlālâ*. One of many curse words in Jeremiah, occurring often in a string of curses (see Note for 24:9).

7. *the priests and the prophets.* LXX has *pseudoprophētai* ("false prophets"), as it does also in vv 8, 11, and 16 (for other occurrences in Jeremiah, see Note on 6:13). Aquila and Symm in these verses have simply "the prophets."

8. *And it happened as Jeremiah finished speaking everything that Yahweh commanded him to speak to all the people.* It appears as though Jeremiah was able to finish what he had to say, which corresponds to the account in chap. 7, where the word about Shiloh ends Oracle III.

the priests and the prophets and all the people then laid hold of him. The priests and prophets lead the attack on Jeremiah, and here the people are said to be with them. But "all the people"? Possibly many of the people; certainly some of the people. One Hebrew MS (H$_{1k}$) omits "all the people" (F. S. North 1956–57: 79–80), which is said to alleviate two problems: 1) since the people crowd up to Jeremiah later (v 9), they should not now be grabbing hold of him with the priests and prophets; and 2) since the people later side with the princes who want to acquit Jeremiah (v 16), why are they now joining the priests and prophets in the attack? Many commentators (Hitzig; Duhm; Peake; Cornill; Rudolph; Bright; Holladay; McKane) therefore take "(and) all the people" as a secondary intrusion from v 7, even though both MT and LXX have the words here. Volz retains. The problem about the people first grabbing hold of Jeremiah and only later crowding up to him is scarcely a problem in narrative writing, least of all in ancient Hebrew narrative writing, where reporting things in chronological sequence is not required. In Hebrew thought and in Hebrew rhetoric, as we have said many times, things do not necessarily follow in sequence or in logical progression (see Note on 1:15). The shifting allegiance of the people is even less a problem, for one of the sure things the narrator here wants to report, and a universal phenomenon amply documented at all times and places, is the fickleness of crowds. In Shakespeare's "Julius Caesar," after the assassination is carried out by Brutus and his fellow-conspirators, Brutus gives a speech justifying the action, which is accepted by the crowd. Then Marc Antony gives his speech, which turns the crowd around and has them wanting now to take vengeance against Brutus and his fellows. That the crowd in the present situation might have changed sides after Jeremiah's testimony is apparently not thought possible by Carroll, among others, who imagines instead a contrived complexity in the literary work. It is true that when the trial is over there were still hostile people from whom Jeremiah had to be protected (v 24), but this does not preclude a shift in the mood of the crowd once Jeremiah had been heard and the princes had shown that they were in favor of acquittal. Perhaps the problem is with the hyperbolic "all." At no time did the people speak with a unified voice, but the controlling mood of the people appears clearly to have changed as the trial progressed.

You shall surely die! Hebrew *môt tâmût*. The same expression occurs in 1 Sam 14:44 and 1 Kings 2:37, 42. In the Covenant Code, the formula for certain crimes is *môt yūmāt*, "he shall surely be put to death" (Exod 21:15, 16, 17; 22:18[Eng 22:19]). Jeremiah has not done anything deserving death, but what is one to say concerning Uriah, about whom we will hear shortly (vv 20–23), also years later concerning Jesus and Stephen (Mark 11:15–19 and parallels; Acts 6–7), who hit directly at gross evil and announced God's judgment on people, the land, and precious symbols of the faith?

9. *Why have you prophesied in the name of Yahweh?* Anger is expressed because Jeremiah's prophecy is spoken in the name of Yahweh. Ahab became angry over Micaiah's prophecy for the same reason (1 Kgs 21:16). But with only Yahweh prophets in the field and contrary words being spoken, truth as well as untruth will be spoken in Yahweh's name. Thus the need for a true-false prophecy test, such as we have in Deut 18:21–22. Compare the conflict between Jeremiah and the Yahweh prophet Hananiah in chap. 28. The LXX has a statement of rationale instead of a question, translating *maddûaʿ* ("Why?") with *hoti* ("because"). It reads "because you have prophesied in the name of the Lord," giving a reason for the opposition having said, "You shall surely die." Compare v 11, where a reason is given for the desired sentence of death.

Like Shiloh this house shall become, and this city will dry up without inhabitant? Another syntactic chiasmus: "It will become / this house // and this city / will dry up." See also v 6. Holladay notes that the paraphrase leaves out the protasis, "If you do not listen to me" (v 4), which he says transforms a covenant speech into an announcement of judgment. The opposition claims again to have heard unmitigated judgment from Jeremiah in its statement to the court (v 11), and Holladay finds another example in 36:29, only there the reduction occurs in a divine oracle (see Note there). One might easily explain this reduction as an angry response by people who did not hear the oracle as it was spoken, common enough in heated debate, or who gave it back only partially in order to bolster reckless and impassioned charges. On the other hand, if the word about Shiloh was spoken as it is recorded in Oracle III of 7:12–15, where it is unmitigated judgment, then the charges here and in v 11 are accurate, even if they remain unjustified.

And all the people crowded up to Jeremiah. A summary statement in good narrative style, referring to what happened at the conclusion of Jeremiah's oracle (vv 7–9a). Several MSS once again have *ʿal* for *ʾel*, which is presupposed in the Versions (see Note for 11:2). Here *ʾel* gives a forcible picture of people pressing up to the prophet. The verb *qhl* does not signify a formal gathering of any sort; it simply means "crowded."

10. *And the princes of Judah heard these things and came up from the house of the king to the house of Yahweh.* The princes were not present to hear what Jeremiah said and therefore had to be summoned (Calvin). What they heard now was either a report from the messengers who came to get them, or the commotion firsthand from the Temple area nearby. The LXX translates *ton logon touton* ("this word"), evidently assuming that the princes heard Jeremiah's preaching. But Heb *haddĕbārîm hā'ēlleh* should be translated "these things." The princes "came up" (*ya'ălû*) from the palace because the Temple stood on higher ground (see Note on 22:1).

the princes of Judah. I.e., the king's men, who were male members of the royal family as well as nonroyal officials (see Note for 24:1).

to the house of Yahweh. The Heb omits "to" by ellipsis; see v 2 and Note on 24:1.

and they sat at the entrance of the New Gate of the house of Yahweh. Justice in ancient times was carried out at the city gate (Köhler 1956a: 149–75), so court has here been called into session. The location of the New Gate, mentioned also in 36:10 as an upper Temple gate, is not known for certain. According to T this was an eastern Temple gate, the view that carried over into later Jewish tradition (Rashi; Morgenstern 1929: 22–23). Kimḥi identified it with the Upper Gate built by Jotham between the Temple and the palace (2 Kgs 15:35), which, because it was built long after the erection of the Temple, was called the "New Gate." In a reconstruction by Kurt Galling (1931), Jotham's Upper Gate is identified with the Upper Benjamin Gate, where Pashhur imprisoned Jeremiah (Jer 20:2), a gate that lay on the north side of the Temple. The New Gate lay to the south of the Temple, connecting the Temple area to the palace area. In Galling's drawing the New Gate could also be viewed as an eastern gate, since it lay south of the Temple but east of the palace. This latter possibility could clear up the confusion regarding the two Temple gates of Ezek 40:44, where MT has a north and east gate, and LXX has a north and south gate. It would also support Jewish tradition in making the New Gate an eastern gate. Galling's view, which is accepted by Rudolph, confirms earlier doubts that Giesebrecht had about identifying the Upper Benjamin Gate with the New Gate.

the New Gate of the house of Yahweh. The MT lacks *bêt* ("house"), which should be added here, with many Heb MSS, two Gk MSS (G^Q and G^{min}), ArB, S, T, and Vg. This brings the reading into line with 36:10. Ziegler includes *oikou* ("of the house") in his LXX text; Rahlfs does not.

11. *And the priests and the prophets said to the princes and to all the people: 'A sentence of death for this man!'* The priests and prophets come forward as plaintiffs in the trial, with the people now joining the princes in hearing the case. Fishbane (1985: 246) has the priests, Levites, and princes acting as plaintiffs, which is not what the text says. The princes are never plaintiffs in this trial. And where do the prophets (LXX: *pseudoprophētai*) come in? The priests and prophets accuse Jeremiah of prophesying destruction of the city, which may reflect the unmitigated judgment of the Shiloh Oracle in 7:12–14 (only there

"the place" [*māqôm*], not "the city"), but it does not reflect the judgment stated here (vv 4b–6), which is conditional. See Note on v 9.

A sentence of death for this man! I.e., this man *deserves* to die (Giesebrecht; Duhm; cf. Deut 19:6; 21:22; 22:26; 2 Sam 12:5). A formal sentence has not yet been issued.

because he has prophesied to this city according to what you have heard with your ears. Only the people heard Jeremiah; the princes were not present. Here a reason is given for the accusers' wanting a death sentence, which the LXX provided additionally in v 9.

12. *Then Jeremiah said to all the princes and to all the people.* The LXX omits "all" (*kol*) before "the princes," which could be due to haplography (homoeoteleuton: *l . . . l*). Jeremiah presents here his defense to the princes and the people. It has frequently been pointed out what exemplary behavior Jeremiah shows in making his defense: no heroics, no theatrical defiance, simply a humble testimony exuding confidence in what he has prophesied. Jerome saw humility in the statement, "Do to me as seems good and right in your eyes" and calmness in the words, "For in truth, Yahweh sent me." Peake writes: "It is a great scene which here passes before us."

Yahweh sent me to prophesy to this house and to this city all the words that you have heard. Jeremiah's claim is that Yahweh sent him—bedrock testimony that he is Yahweh's royal messenger (1:7; 25:15). In one of the Mari Letters, a man is instructed in a revelation from the god Dagan to deliver a message to King Zimri-lim. Dagan says: "Now go, I have sent you!" (Beyerlin 1978: 125). Jeremiah's words also pass the true prophecy test in Deut 13:2–6[Eng 13:1–5] and answer the first charge made against him, that he dared prophesy what he did in Yahweh's name (v 9). Blank (1955) says this testimony is Jeremiah's strongest argument and the source of his prophetic authority.

13. *And now, make good your ways and your doings, and obey the voice of Yahweh your God; and then Yahweh will repent concerning the evil that he has spoken against you.* The rhetorical particle *wěʿattâ* ("And now") signals a discourse shift from past to present (see Note for 2:18). Hebrew *wěšimʿû bě* means here not simply "hear" or "listen" but "obey." What we are hearing now is Jeremiah's reform message as presented in Oracle I of 7:3–7, with the one difference that Yahweh has promised to repent of the evil he has planned, if people amend their ways (cf. 18:6–8). The LXX lacks "your God" and has "evils" plural. "Your God" should be retained because it appears to be answered by the "our God" in v 16.

14. *But I, look I am in your hands. Do to me as seems good and right in your eyes.* Authority statements now cease, and Jeremiah turns his attention to earth and looks for truth in the audience gathered about him. He does not say that he is leaving himself in the hands of God but that his life is now in the hands of the court. This submission to the will of the court is actually a veiled argument, one that the classical rhetoricians called "surrender" (Gk *epitrope*; Lat *permissio*; *ad Herrenium* 4:29; cf. Lundbom 1991b: 18–19). An example of "surrender" from the *ad Herennium*:

Since only soul and body remain to me, now that I am deprived of everything else, even these, which alone of many goods are left me, I deliver up
to you and to your power. You may use and even abuse me in your own way
as you think best; with impunity make your decision upon me, whatever it
may be; speak and give a sign—I shall obey.

(ad Herennium 4:29; Loeb)

On the expression "right in your eyes" (*yāšār bĕʿênêkem*) and discussion on
shifts in Jeremianic discourse from abstractions or general principles to specific cases at hand, see Note for 27:5.

15. *Only know for sure that if you put me to death, then you will bring innocent blood upon yourselves and to this city and to its inhabitants*. On the heels
of one rhetorical argument comes another. Jeremiah's warning about the consequences of adverse court action is also an argumentative move, called *descriptio* by later classical rhetoricians (*ad Herennium* 4:39, 51; cf. Lundbom
1991b: 19–20), who said it could be used in both prosecution and defense. In
the former it works to provoke indignation; in the latter pity. The *ad Herennium* proposes this *descriptio* for a person's defense:

For if you inflict a heavy penalty upon the defendant, men of the jury, you
will at once by a single judgment have taken many lives. His aged father,
who has set the entire hope of his last years on this young man, will have no
reason for wishing to stay alive. His small children, deprived of their father's aid, will be exposed as objects of scorn and contempt to their father's
enemies. His entire household will collapse under this undeserved calamity. But his enemies, when once they have won the bloody palm by this
most cruel of victories, will exult over the miseries of these unfortunates,
and will be found insolent on the score of deeds as well as of words.

(ad Herennium 4:39; Loeb)

Only know for sure. Hebrew *ʾak yādōaʿ tēdĕʿû*. The expression "know for
sure" occurs also in 42:19 and 22; see additionally Josh 23:13. Note here the
strong adversative *ʾak* ("only").

in truth, Yahweh sent me. A reaffirmation of what Jeremiah stated at the beginning of his testimony, only with an added "in truth." The issue is now true
and false prophecy. What will the court decide? Calvin says Jeremiah has made
his hearers the judges.

16. *Then the princes and all the people said to the priests and to the prophets,
'There should be no sentence of death for this man, because in the name of Yahweh our God he has spoken to us.'* Jeremiah's moving testimony was not wasted
on the assembled. The people have now switched sides, joining with the
princes in calling for acquittal. They accept Jeremiah's testimony that he has
spoken in the name of Yahweh. And they accept his call for people to amend
their ways, so the judgment of Yahweh can be averted. It seems that there were

some credible people resident in the city—at least, at this moment there were. Virgil (*Aeneid* i 148–53) noted how, in a time of national turmoil, when base fellows rage angrily, the common people will listen respectfully to a man known for piety and good works. Josephus (*Ant* x 91) appears confused on how the trial progressed, reporting that a decision was made to punish Jeremiah and that supportive testimony of the elders was disregarded by the rulers, but he adds that in the end the will of the elders prevailed. For other confusions in Josephus's account of the trial, see Begg 1995. Compare the verdict here with Pilate's words about Jesus in Luke 23:22: "I have found no crime in him deserving death."

17. *And men from among the elders of the land stood up and said to the entire assembly of the people*. The "elders" (*zĕqēnîm*) are men of age rather than status, mature in years, whose words carry authority (Calvin). From very early times, elders joined the judges in deciding legal cases (Deut 21:2). Elders are able to put things in historical perspective; here they are the people who remember.

18. *Micah the Morashtite was prophesying in the days of Hezekiah, king of Judah*. The elders remember Micah the Morashtite, who prophesied more than 100 years ago. Active before the fall of Samaria (Mic 1:2–7), Micah according to the superscription of his book (Mic 1:1) is said to have prophesied during the reigns of Jotham (742–735 B.C.), Ahaz (735–715 B.C.), and Hezekiah (715–687/6 B.C.). Coming from a small town in Judah, Micah prophesied the destruction of both Samaria and Jerusalem. Some of the elders now rising to speak may also come from small towns and villages outside Jerusalem (v 2), where memories live long and biases tend to locate evil in urban centers rather than in the localities they inhabit. Micah's legacy may have been greater in the outlying areas than in Jerusalem, where the prophet towering above all others had been Isaiah. Isaiah prophesied that Jerusalem would not be taken by Sennacherib in 701 B.C., and it was not. People from outlying districts would then be less offended by a word against Jerusalem than would natives of the city, particularly priests and prophets in the orbit of the Temple. Among these pilgrims to Jerusalem may also have been some who deeply resented Josiah's centralization of worship in the capital city. In seeking to reconstruct the dynamic of the present situation, we must reckon not only with the obvious tension between priests and prophets on the one hand, and princes loyal to Jeremiah on the other, but with an unstated tension between elders from outlying areas where Yahweh worship was disallowed, and priests and prophets with vested interests in the "legitimate" worship of the Jerusalem Temple. These elders, in any case, were the ones who remembered Micah the Morashtite. Cornill points out that this is the only direct citation of another prophet's words in the whole of prophetic literature.

Micah, the Morashtite. The Kt spelling of "Micah" is *mîkāyâ*; the Q is *mîkâ*, a shorter form of the name occurring in Mic 1:1. Moresheth was a town near Gath (called Moresheth-Gath in Mic 1:14), which has been identified since the time of J. Jeremias (1933: 51–53) with Tell Judeideh, a site in the Shephe-lah about 10 kilometers northeast of Lachish and 40 kilometers southwest of Jerusalem. The site was excavated briefly in 1899–1900 by F. J. Bliss and R. A. Macalister for the British Palestine Exploration Fund, at which time Iron II re-mains were found (*ABD* 4: 904; *NEAEHL* 3: 837–38).

was prophesying. Hebrew *hāyâ nibbā'.* The LXX lacks the participle, trans-lating only *hāyâ* with *ēn* ("he lived"); Aq and Symm have "he prophesied."

Zion shall be plowed a field, and Jerusalem shall become stone heaps; And the mountain of the House high places of a forest. See Mic 3:12. A later Psalm (79:1) laments that Jerusalem did in fact become "stone heaps" (*'iyyîm*), which is how ruined cities looked. The "mountain of the House" is the Temple Mount, which Micah said will be "high places" (*bāmôt*) overgrown with trees. There is irony in his use of "high places," for it implies a return to worship sites that are no longer worship sites. Andersen and Freedman (2000: 385) point out that "high places" plural balances "stone heaps" plural, which means we are not to envision high elevations in Jerusalem's natural terrain but high places made from heaps of ruins. The LXX has *alsos drumou,* "a wooded grove."

19. *Did Hezekiah, king of Judah, and all Judah indeed put him to death? Did he not fear Yahweh and soften the face of Yahweh?* The LXX, S, and Vg predicate "Hezekiah" and "all Judah" with a singular verb and then follow with two plu-ral verbs. The difference in this reading is that *both* the king and the nation are said to have feared Yahweh and supplicated him, whereas in the Hebrew only Hezekiah fears and supplicates. The speech of the elders reaches a climax with rhetorical questions, which have even greater force than strongly worded asser-tions. We have no independent tradition informing us about Hezekiah's treat-ment of Micah, but we can assume that this king did not put him to death. Did Hezekiah as a result of Micah's preaching "soften the face of Yahweh," an anthropomorphism meaning "make supplication"? We do not know. What we do know is that Hezekiah supplicated Yahweh when Sennacherib threatened Jerusalem (2 Kgs 19:14–19; cf. Isa 37:14–20) and that he prayed again to Yah-weh when he himself took sick and was told by Isaiah that he would die (2 Kgs 20:1–3). This latter incident, as reported in 2 Chr 32:26, is cited by Kimhi as an example of Hezekiah's humbling himself. And from 2 Kgs 18:3–6 we learn that Hezekiah did institute certain religious reforms, which could have been in re-sponse to Micah's preaching.

and soften the face of Yahweh. Hebrew *wayĕḥal 'et-pĕnê yhwh.* This stark an-thropomorphism (Peake; Cornill) means to mollify, appease, or supplicate Yahweh (2 Kgs 13:4; Ps 119:58; Zech 7:2; 8:21–22; Mal 1:9; cf. *ḥlh* Piel). Rashi says it is an expression for prayer; Calvin the same.

And did not Yahweh repent of the evil that he spoke against them? Jeremiah said the same would happen now if the people changed their ways (v 13).

And we are doing great evil against ourselves! The elders confirm the verdict, recognizing that by condemning Jeremiah they would, in fact, be condemning themselves. The biblical expression is bringing "blood upon one's own head"

(Josh 2:19; 2 Sam 1:16; 1 Kgs 2:37; cf. Matt 27:25). The elders and others present could be found opposing God! (cf. Acts 5:39).

20. *Also, a man was prophesying mightily in the name of Yahweh—Uriah son of Shemaiah from Kiriath-jearim.* A contemporary of Jeremiah is here cited by the narrator because he too prophesied against Jerusalem in Yahweh's name but suffered a worse fate than the fates of Micah and Jeremiah. Uriah must have been a presence to be reckoned with, for it says he "prophesied mightily" (*mitnabbēʾ*) in Yahweh's name. The verb *nbʾ* in the Hithpael means "prophesy with zeal," although elsewhere in the book it has the negative meaning of "rave on as a prophet" (see Note for 14:14). Torczyner (1938: 62–73) in translating and interpreting the Lachish Letters argued that "the prophet" referred to in one of the letters (3:20) was Uriah of Kiriath-jearim. But his view was rejected almost immediately (Albright 1936: 11; 1938: 15; Hempel 1938: 127), one reason being that Torczyner dated the letters to Jehoiakim's reign. When they were shown later to date to Zedekiah's time (Ginsberg; cf. Albright 1936: 11), Torczyner argued that the king here in chap. 26 was not Jehoiakim, as the text clearly states, but Zedekiah (Ginsberg 1940: 11). The connection to Uriah was contrived, and any identification of this prophet with Uriah is now considered out of the question (D. W. Thomas 1946a; 1946b; 1961). For an English translation of the Lachish Letters, see *ANET*[3] 321–22.

Uriah son of Shemaiah. These names were common in Judah at the time, both showing up on the Arad ostraca: "Uriah" on 26:1 and 31:2, and Shemaiah on 27:2; 31:5; 39:2, 7–8 (Aharoni 1981). "Uriah" has also appeared on the "Ophel Ostracon," a Khirbet el-Qom tomb inscription, and numerous seals. The name "Shemaiah," which is borne by other individuals in the book of Jeremiah (29:24; 36:12), has turned up on the Lachish ostraca, the Wadi Murabbaʿat Papyrus, and other contemporary seals and bullae (see Appendix I on "Uriah ben Shemaiah").

Kiriath-jearim. A border city in Judah on the western boundary of Benjamin (Josh 15:9; 18:14, 28), first identified with Kuryet el-ʾEnab (Abu Ghosh) by Edward Robinson in 1838 (E. Robinson 1874 II: 11), but now thought to lie on a commanding hill just to the west, Tell el-Achar (Deir el-Azhar), which is about 13 kilometers west-northwest of Jerusalem on the ancient road to Joppa (Vincent 1907: 417; F. T. Cooke 1923–24; *ABD* 4: 84–85).

against this city and. The LXX omits, which is probably another loss due to haplography (whole-word: ʿl . . . ʿl). Janzen (1973: 119) agrees here about the haplography.

21. *And King Jehoiakim heard his words, also all his officers and all the princes, and the king sought to put him to death.* King Jehoiakim, who remains entirely in the background when Jeremiah is put on trial, is here the one wanting action against a troublesome prophet and troublesome prophecy. The princes and officers in the royal house heard Uriah's prophecy, but only the king sought to kill him. The LXX omits "also all his officers," which may again be due to haplography (whole-word: *wkl . . . wkl*). So also Janzen 1973: 119. The "officers" (*gibbôrîm*, lit., "mighty men") are here military men (46:9;

48:14) or palace police, fleet of foot (46:6) and fully capable of pursuing Uriah, should the king need them.

and the king sought to put him to death. The LXX omits *hammelek* ("the king") and has a plural verb; the omission, however, is probably more haplography (homoeoarcton: *hm . . . hm*).

But Uriah heard of it, and he was afraid and fled, and came to Egypt. The LXX omits "and he was afraid and fled" (*wayyirā' wayyibraḥ*), which may again be a loss attributable to haplography (homoeoarcton: *wy . . . wy*). Aquila and Theod have the words. Janzen (1973: 21–22, 119) suggests either LXX haplography or a conflated MT. Conflation here does not seem to be the answer.

22. *So King Jehoiakim sent men to Egypt—Elnathan son of Achbor and men with him to Egypt.* The LXX lacks "Elnathan son of Achbor and men with him to Egypt," which Cornill suggests may be due to haplography (whole-word: *mṣrym . . . mṣrym*). Theodotion has the words. Others take them as an MT gloss (Giesebrecht; Duhm: "could be Haggada"; Ehrlich 1912: 311) or as a conflate text in MT (Janzen 1973: 100–101; Holladay). A common solution is to delete the earlier *'ănāšîm miṣrāyim*, "men of / to Egypt" (Cornill; Volz; Rudolph; Weiser; Bright). Many modern Versions do this or else paraphrase with similar results (NEB; JB; NAB; NIV; NRSV). However, *miṣrāyim* can be read "to Egypt," as in v 21; the omission of a prefixed "to" before places of destination is a common ellipsis in Jeremiah prose (see simply "house of Yahweh" in vv 2 and 10, and Note for 24:1). The T has "and King Jehoiakim sent men to Egypt," which is adopted by Vg and AV. The Lachish Letters (3:14–16) report a decade later that one Coniah son of Elnathan, commander of the army, had been dispatched to Egypt on a mission, the nature of which is unclear. He could have gone to solicit Egyptian help in the face of a Babylonian advance or to fetch a certain Hodaviah son of Ahijah and his men (*ABD* 4: 127). This Coniah, in any case, could be another son of the Elnathan mentioned here (Ginsberg 1948).

Elnathan son of Achbor. This individual sent to fetch Uriah is the same person who was sitting among Jeremiah's friends in the palace library when Baruch's reading of Jeremiah's scroll in 604 B.C. was called to their attention, and who subsequently urged Jehoiakim not to burn the scroll (36:12, 25). It is possible that he is also the Elnathan of Jerusalem mentioned in 2 Kgs 24:8, who was the father-in-law of Jehoiakim. The names "Elnathan" and "Achbor" have turned up on numerous seals, ostraca, and inscriptions of the period (see Appendix I).

and men with him. I.e., men under his orders (see Note for 41:2).

23. *And they fetched Uriah from Egypt and brought him to King Jehoiakim, and he struck him down with the sword and cast his dead body into the graves of the common people.* If Egypt was the only place to flee, it was still the wrong place. With Jehoiakim tied politically to Egypt from the time Neco enthroned him, until 604 B.C. when Jehoiakim switched allegiance to Nebuchadnezzar, Uriah's extradition was a routine matter. While this incident need not have occurred at the same time as Jeremiah's trial, it would have to be dated early

in the reign of Jehoiakim, when Judah's treaties with Egypt were still in effect (Weiser; Holladay). A fifteenth-century B.C. treaty between Ir-Addu and Niqmepa, from Alalakh, makes provision for extradition (Wiseman 1953: 26–30; *CS II* 329–31); so also an Egyptian treaty between Ramses II and Hattusilis III of the Hittites (ca. 1280 B.C.), which contains a mutual extradition clause (Jirku 1921: 148; *ANET*[3] 200–201, 203).

and he struck him down with the sword. No trial here; no chance for sympathetic princes to intervene if they had wanted to. Documentation of a prophet being murdered is unusual in the OT (2 Chr 24:20–22), although we learn from later Jewish and Christian sources that it happened more than once. The killing of prophets is painfully recalled in the NT (Matt 23:37; Luke 11:47–51; Acts 7:52; Heb 11:37) and in later Jewish tradition, which contains legends about prophets who suffered martyrdom, e.g., *The Lives of the Prophets* (Torrey 1946; Charlesworth 1985: 379–99) and the *Martyrdom and Ascension of Isaiah* (Charlesworth 1985: 143–76).

King Jehoiakim . . . cast his dead body into the graves of the common people. An indignity surpassed only by what Jehoiakim himself would have to bear (22:18–19; 36:30). Whether Uriah was left unburied is unclear. He was, in any event, brought without ceremony to a burial ground ill suited for a true prophet of Yahweh. In 2 Kgs 23:6 the cemetery for the common people is said to be located in the Kidron Valley, between the Temple area and the Mount of Olives, which is an area containing graves even today. The LXX has "the tomb (*to mnēma*) of the sons of his people," which destroys the sense by implying a family grave (Giesebrecht; Duhm).

the common people. Hebrew *běnê hā'ām*, lit., "the sons of the people" (see Note for 17:19).

24. *But the hand of Ahikam son of Shaphan was with Jeremiah.* This concludes the narrator's report of Jeremiah's trial, stating the outcome in a way similar to the wrap-up of the Hananiah episode in 28:17. Other like summary statements occur in 36:8 and 32. Jeremiah presumably walked away from his trial. Ahikam, a member of the royal house under Josiah (2 Kgs 22:12, 14), was the son of Shaphan, the scribe who figured prominently in the finding of the law-book in the Temple (2 Kgs 22:3–20) and who was probably head of a scribal school located there. The Shaphan scribal family had lifelong ties with Jeremiah (Skinner 1926:107; Muilenburg 1970a: 227–28, 231). Ahikam is now serving Jehoiakim, in which capacity he is able to protect Jeremiah. He may have been one of the princes sitting at the New Gate who voted for Jeremiah's acquittal. Luria (1982) traces the Shaphan family back two generations to Meshullam, the grandfather, and Azaliah, the father (2 Kgs 22:3), citing also a Rabbinic tradition that Shaphan played a crucial role in preserving the Torah. A seal has turned up that may have belonged to Shaphan's father, Azaliah (Avigad 1997: 79, #90; Heltzer 2000: 105). It reads, "Belonging to Aṣalyāhû, the son of Mešullām," which corresponds to Shaphan's double patronym in 2 Kgs 22:3. On the Shaphan family of scribes, see the chart below.

Ahikam son of Shaphan. The name "Ahikam" has shown up on the Arad ostraca and bullae contemporary with Jeremiah; the name "Shaphan" has turned
up on a Jerusalem cave inscription and other contemporary finds (see Avigad
1986b: 34–35, #14–16, and Appendix I).

so as not to give him into the hand of the people to put him to death. Were the
people still ready to kill Jeremiah? This closing word suggests a residue of the
anger expressed earlier by the people (v 8), but it says as much or more about
the residual anger of those who wanted to give Jeremiah over to the people,
namely the priests and prophets.

THE SCRIBAL FAMILY OF SHAPHAN

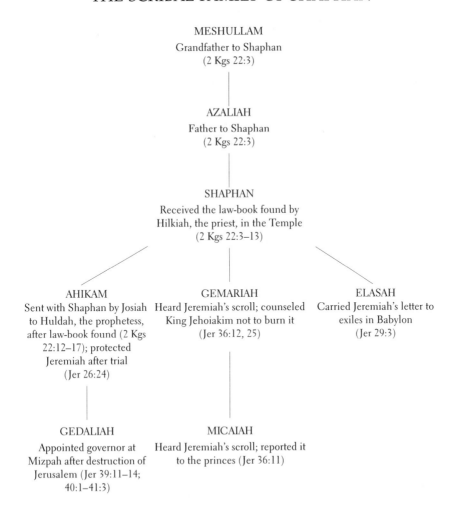

MESHULLAM
Grandfather to Shaphan
(2 Kgs 22:3)

AZALIAH
Father to Shaphan
(2 Kgs 22:3)

SHAPHAN
Received the law-book found by
Hilkiah, the priest, in the Temple
(2 Kgs 22:3–13)

AHIKAM
Sent with Shaphan by Josiah
to Huldah, the prophetess,
after law-book found (2 Kgs
22:12–17); protected
Jeremiah after trial
(Jer 26:24)

GEMARIAH
Heard Jeremiah's scroll; counseled
King Jehoiakim not to burn it
(Jer 36:12, 25)

ELASAH
Carried Jeremiah's letter to
exiles in Babylon
(Jer 29:3)

GEDALIAH
Appointed governor at
Mizpah after destruction of
Jerusalem (Jer 39:11–14;
40:1–41:3)

MICAIAH
Heard Jeremiah's scroll; reported it
to the princes (Jer 36:11)

MESSAGE AND AUDIENCE

This narrative reports that Jeremiah was told by Yahweh to stand in the Temple courtyard and speak his words to all who had come there to worship. It was an important occasion when people from outlying areas in Judah would have been present. Jeremiah was warned not to hold back so much as a word. Yahweh said that perhaps those assembled would listen and repent of their evil, in which case Yahweh would repent of the evil he was planning to do to them. Jeremiah is to say that if the people do not listen, do not walk according to covenant demands, or pay heed to the preaching of prophets sent over a considerable period of years, which they have not done, then he will make the Temple like the Shiloh ruin, and Jerusalem will become a curse word for all nations.

The priests, prophets, and assembled people heard Jeremiah preach this message, and when he finished, they seized him and said he must die for indulging in such a broadside attack. They asked him why he dared say such things in the name of Yahweh, repeating the threatened judgment without reference to the proviso about people repenting of their evil.

Once the princes in the nearby palace heard the uproar going on, or were apprised of it by others, they came up straightaway to the Temple and took their places in the New Gate. A trial was underway. The priests and the prophets called for Jeremiah's death because he had prophesied against Jerusalem. Turning to the people, who are now listening along with the princes to the charges, the priests and prophets say that the people have heard these words with their own ears. Jeremiah is then permitted to speak. Addressing the princes and the people, he says simply that Yahweh sent him with this word against Jerusalem and the Temple. Nevertheless, the prediction is not carved in stone. If the people make good their ways and their doings, Yahweh will repent of the evil that is planned. As far as he himself is concerned, Jeremiah surrenders his person to the will of the court. They can do with him what seems good and right in their eyes. But let those assembled beware. If they put him to death, they will bring innocent blood on themselves and everyone else in the city, for Yahweh has truly sent him to speak the words they have just heard.

The princes and the people accept Jeremiah's testimony that he has spoken true words in the name of Yahweh, and they reject the sentence of death. This verdict is confirmed by certain elders who stand up and recall a similar prophecy from Micah the Morashtite, who lived during Hezekiah's reign. Micah's words are quoted. He said that Jerusalem would be plowed as a field. And did Hezekiah put him to death, they ask? Did he not, rather, fear Yahweh and supplicate him? And did not Yahweh repent of evil, as Jeremiah says he will do now again? The elders conclude by saying that they and the others have come dangerously close to bringing great evil upon themselves.

The narrator then cites an incident concerning the Yahweh prophet Uriah, from Kiriath-jearim. He too prophesied against Jerusalem and Judah in words like those of Jeremiah, and when King Jehoiakim and others in the royal house heard of it, the king sought to kill him. Uriah got wind of the plot and fled to Egypt. It was the wrong place to go. Jehoiakim sent Elnathan son of Achbor and men with him to fetch Uriah, and they brought him to the king, who with dispatch had him cut down by the sword. As a final indignity, the king cast his body unceremoniously into the burial place of the common people. The narrator closes by saying that Ahikam son of Shaphan, however, gave Jeremiah protection after his trial, making sure that he was not delivered to the people to be put to death.

This narrative fits well the date to which it is assigned, i.e., the beginning of Jehoiakim's reign (609/8 B.C.). For those hearing it following the narrative and supplement in chap. 25, the focus will shift from a judgment on the nations to a judgment on Jerusalem and Judah, where chap. 26 will pick up once again on Yahweh's cup of wrath being given first to Jerusalem and Judah. For those hearing chap. 26 before chaps. 27–29, Jeremiah's conflict here with the prophets and priests will anticipate conflicts of a similar nature that will take place a decade or so later.

The NT Gospel writers drew clear parallels between this attack on Jeremiah and what happened to Jesus after he prophesied against Jerusalem and the Temple. Selwyn (1915) has pulled out parallels from all the Synoptics; what follows are parallels drawn only in the Gospel of Mark:

Jeremiah 26	Mark 13–15
. . . then I will make this house like Shiloh, and this city I will make a swearword for all the nations of the earth.	Do you see these great buildings? Not one stone will be left here upon another; all will be thrown down.
Jer 26:6	Mark 13:2
And the priests and the prophets . . . heard Jeremiah speaking these words in the house of Yahweh.	And the chief priests and the scribes were looking for a way to arrest him by stealth and kill him.
Jer 26:7	Mark 14:1
And it happened as Jeremiah finished speaking . . . the priests and the prophets and all the people then laid hold of him, saying, 'You shall surely die!'	And immediately, while he was still speaking, Judas arrived . . . and with him a crowd from the chief priests and the scribes and the elders. . . . And they laid hands on him and seized him.
Jer 26:8	Mark 14:43, 46
And the princes . . . came up from the house of the king . . . and they sat at the entrance of the New Gate of the house of Yahweh.	And they led Jesus to the high priest; and all the chief priests and the elders and the scribes were assembled.
Jer 26:10	Mark 14:53

Jeremiah 26	Mark 13–15
And the priests and the prophets said to the princes and to all the people, 'A sentence of death for this man! because he has prophesied to this city according to what you have heard with your ears.'	Now the chief priests and the whole council sought testimony against Jesus to put him to death. . . . And some . . . gave false testimony against him, saying, 'We heard him say, I will destroy this temple.'
Jer 26:11	Mark 14:55–58
Then Jeremiah said to all the princes and to all the people: 'Yahweh sent me . . . for in truth, Yahweh sent me. . . .	Again the high priest asked him, Are you the Christ . . . ? And Jesus said, 'I am. . . .'
Jer 26:12–15	Mark 14:61–62
Then the princes and all the people said . . . 'There should be no sentence of death for this man. . . .'	And they all condemned him as deserving death.
Jer 26:16	Mark 14:64
But the hand of Ahikam . . . was with Jeremiah, so as not to give him into the hand of the people to put him to death.	So Pilate, wishing to satisfy the crowd, . . . delivered him [to the people] to be crucified.
Jer 26:24	Mark 15:15

D. JEREMIAH AND THE YOKE BARS (27:1–22)

27 ¹In the beginning of the reign of Zedekiahᵃ son of Josiah, king of Judah, this word came to Jeremiah from Yahweh. ²Thus Yahweh said to me: Make for yourself straps and yoke bars; then you shall put them upon your neck. ³You shall also send them to the king of Edom, and to the king of Moab, and to the king of the Ammonites, and to the king of Tyre, and to the king of Sidon by the hand of messengers who are coming to Jerusalem, to Zedekiah, king of Judah. ⁴And you shall command them to their masters:

Thus said Yahweh of hosts, God of Israel:

Thus you shall say to your masters: ⁵I, I made the earth, human and beast that are on the face of the earth, with my great strength and with my outstretched arm, and I give it to whoever seems right in my eyes. ⁶And now I, I have given all these lands into the hand of Nebuchadnezzar, king of Babylon, my servant; and even the beasts of the field I

ᵃCorrection, following a few MSS and S (27:3 and 28:1); MT has "Jehoiakim."

have given to him, to serve him. ⁷So all the nations shall serve him and his son and his grandson until the time of his land comes—even he! Then many nations and great kings shall make him serve!

⁸And it shall be that the nation or the kingdom who does not serve him, that is, Nebuchadnezzar, king of Babylon, and who will not put its neck into the yoke of the king of Babylon, by sword and by famine and by pestilence I will reckon with that nation—oracle of Yahweh—until I have consumed them by his hand.

⁹And you, do not you listen to your prophets, and to your diviners, and to your dreamers,ᵇ and to your soothsayers, and to your sorcerers—they who are saying to you: 'You shall not serve the king of Babylon.' ¹⁰Indeed a lie they are prophesying to you, in order to remove you far from your soil, for I will disperse you and you will perish. ¹¹But the nation who does bring its neck into the yoke of the king of Babylon, and serves him, I will then leave it on its own soil—oracle of Yahweh—to work it and dwell upon it.

¹²And to Zedekiah, king of Judah, I spoke all these words: Bring your necks into the yoke of the king of Babylon, and serve him and his people, and live! ¹³Why should you die, you and your people, by sword, by famine, and by pestilence according to what Yahweh has spoken to the nation that will not serve the king of Babylon?

¹⁴And do not listen to the words of the prophets who are saying to you: 'You shall not serve the king of Babylon.' Indeed a lie they are prophesying to you, ¹⁵for I have not sent them—oracle of Yahweh—and they are prophesying the lie in my name in order that I should disperse you, and you will perish, you and the prophets who are prophesying to you.

¹⁶Then to the priests and to all this people I spoke:

Thus said Yahweh:

Do not listen to the words of your prophets who are prophesying to you, saying, 'Look, the vessels of the house of Yahweh will be brought back from Babylon now shortly.' Indeed a lie they are prophesying to you.

¹⁷Do not listen to them; serve the king of Babylon and live. Why should this city become a ruin? ¹⁸And if they are prophets and if the word of Yahweh is with them, do let them pressure Yahweh of hosts so that the vessels remaining in the house of Yahweh and the house of the king of Judah and in Jerusalem not go to Babylon.

¹⁹For thus said Yahweh of hosts concerning the pillars, and concerning the sea, and concerning the stands, and concerning the rest of the vessels remaining in this city, ²⁰which Nebuchadnezzar, king of Babylon, did not take when he exiled Jeconiah son of Jehoiakim, king of

---

ᵇEmend with the Vrs to *ḥōlĕmêkem*; MT has *ḥălōmōtêkem*, "your dreams."

Judah, from Jerusalem to Babylon, also all the nobles of Judah and Jerusalem: [21]Indeed, thus said Yahweh of hosts, God of Israel, concerning the vessels remaining in the house of Yahweh, and the house of the king of Judah, and Jerusalem:
[22]To Babylon they shall be brought, and there they shall be until the day I attend to them—oracle of Yahweh—and I bring them out and bring them back to this place.

RHETORIC AND COMPOSITION

MT 27:1–22 = LXX 34:2–22. Chapters 27–29 have been read together at least since the time of Hitzig (1841), there being in all three 1) distinctive linguistic features (Giesebrecht); and 2) a common background of Jeremiah in conflict with the optimistic prophets, the latter resulting from Judah's humiliation at the hands of Nebuchadnezzar in 597 B.C. Linguistic peculiarities include a preference for *yâ* rather than *yāhû* spellings of names compounded with "Yahweh," i.e.,"Jeremiah," "Jeconiah," "Zedekiah," and "Hananiah," although the long forms also occur. The short form of "Jeremiah" occurs nowhere else in the book. Also are unusual spellings of "Josiah" and "Jehoiakim" in the problematic superscription of 27:1, and the only spelling in the book of "Nebuchadnezzar" with an "n," although one spelling with "r" does occur in 29:21. Added to these are a frequency of titles following proper names: "Jeremiah, the prophet" (28:5, 10, 11, 12, 15; 29:1, 29); "Hananiah, the prophet" (28:1, 5, 12, 15, 17); "Jeremiah, the Anathothite (29:27); and Shemaiah, the Nehelamite (29:24, 31, 32). "Jeremiah, the prophet" occurs sporadically elsewhere, most often in superscriptions (45:1; 46:1, 13; 47:1; 49:34; 50:1; 51:59; see Appendix VI). Jeremiah's conflict with other prophets—both those in Jerusalem (chaps. 27–28) and in Babylon (chap. 29)—centers around the predictions these individuals are making that the humiliation of 597 B.C. will be speedily reversed; i.e., the exiles and Temple treasures taken away to Babylon will soon be returned to Jerusalem.

To chaps. 27–29 must also be added chap. 24, forming what I have called a "Zedekiah Cluster" of narrative prose. Whereas chaps. 27–28 combine to report the "yoke" prophecy of 594–593 B.C., chaps. 24 and 29 unite in reporting prophecies soon after the exile of 597 B.C., their common theme being a Judahite community divided into good and bad remnants (see Rhetoric and Composition for 24:1–10). Chapters 24, 27, and 28 include first-person narrations; chap. 29 is all third-person.

There has been no agreement on assigning chap. 27 to one of the so-called Jeremianic sources. Mowinckel (1914: 40) assigned the chapter to Source C, Giesebrecht (p. xxi) and Weiser to Source B, and Rudolph to Source A, leading H.-J. Kraus (1964: 59–60) to wonder if any of the sources really fit. Kraus correctly noted that the characteristic "Deuteronomistic mintings" of Source C were not present, a conclusion reached by Rudolph earlier. Rudolph said the only Source C phrase was "with my great strength and with my out-

stretched arm" (v 5), but even this phrase does not exactly reproduce Deuteronomy's "with strong hand and outstretched arm" (see Note for 21:5). The
claim that there is Deuteronomic language in the chapter is rejected also by
H. Weippert (1973: 107–21), Holladay, and Jones. What we are seeing here, in
scholars who follow the Source C assignment of Mowinckel, is the same unsubstantiated claim for postexilic prose encountered elsewhere—e.g., regarding chap. 18. Volz says we are in touch here with the historical Jeremiah, even
though he brackets out vv 19–22 as unoriginal. Actually, primary and secondary material are commonly distinguished here not so much on the basis of
vocabulary and phraseology as on the different readings of MT and LXX.

For more than a century and a half, scholars have viewed the MT as a
much reworked version of the LXX, which is quite a bit shorter. Early judgments against the MT were made by Movers (1837), Hitzig (1841), deWette
(1843), Kuenen (1863), and W. Robertson Smith (1892: 103–7, and these
carried over into the commentaries of Duhm and Cornill, somewhat less in
others. Giesebrecht believed that the LXX abbreviated MT, and together with
Hitzig recognized that at least a few LXX omissions were the result of scribal
error. More recently, scholars giving preference to the shorter LXX text of
chap. 27 include Rudolph, Bright, Janzen (1973); Tov (1975a; 1979), Holladay,
Goldman (1992: 123–88), and McKane, to name some of those more prominent in Jeremianic scholarship. Rudolph, Bright, Janzen, and Holladay admit
to some loss in LXX resulting from haplography, but not McKane. In the
present chapter, Thiel (1981: 9) takes the longer MT of vv 19–22 to be original,
and van der Kooij (1994) argues against Goldman that the MT of vv 5–15 is
earlier. In my view, the longer MT is a repetitious but perfectly coherent text
and the shorter LXX a victim of large-scale haplography. No less than 14 arguable cases for LXX haplography can be made in the chapter, as opposed to 3 arguable cases of MT haplography (see Notes and Appendix V). It is as apparent
here as elsewhere that the LXX is seriously flawed, translated from a badly-
copied Hebrew *Vorlage*, and all talk of *lectio brevior praeferenda est* must be
given up. McKane's cautionary word (p. 686) about scholarly over-reliance on
haplographic explanations in chap. 27 rings hollow, in that commentators who
do admit the phenomenon cite two, maybe three, examples, whereas McKane
himself admits not even one.

It should also be said that where commentators explain omitted LXX words
of hope as later supplements in MT: 1) this is largely a holdover from nine-
teenth-century source criticism, which was evolutionary in nature and deem-
phasized predictive prophecy, refusing to believe that prophets like Jeremiah
gave messages of hope; 2) words of hope here in chap. 27 are in fact well integrated into the oracles of judgment; and 3) Jeremiah preaches a future hope
for Judah also in chap. 24 (vv 4–7 on the "good figs") and chap. 29 (vv 10–14
in the main letter to the exiles), both of which are dated somewhat earlier than
the oracles here in chap. 27.

The upper limit of the present unit is marked by the superscription in v 1,
before which is a *petuḥah* in M^A, M^L, and M^P, and also the chapter division.

The lower limit is marked by a *petuḥah* in M^A, M^L, and M^P after v 22, which again is a chapter division. A new superscription is also present in 28:1. The M^L has a *petuḥah* after v 18, which separates Jeremiah's words to the priests and people from the first divine oracle to the same; M^A and M^P have no sections here. The M^L and M^P also have a *setumah* after v 20, which separates two messenger formulas preceding the final oracle to the priests and the people; M^A has no section here.

The chapter opens with a superscription supplying a date and a setting (v 1), after which there is a combination of narrative and divine oracles that report another circuit of preaching and symbolic action by the prophet. The narrative is first person, and the oracles number six, the same number as in chap. 28. Because Yahweh is referred to in the third person in vv 13 and 18, vv 12b–13 and vv 17–18 are assigned the speaking voice of Jeremiah.

The narrative has a carefully-wrought structure:

A	Jeremiah reports a divine directive to make a yoke and address foreign envoys		(vv 2–4a)
	Oracle I	Yahweh is giving lands to Nebuchadnezzar, his servant. Nations are *to serve him*; then in the future, nations *shall make him serve!*	(vv 4b–7)
	Oracle II	Nations not serving Nebuchadnezzar will be punished by Yahweh	(v 8)
	Oracle III	"*And you, do not you listen to your prophets, your diviners . . . they who are saying to you:* 'You shall not serve the king of Babylon.' *Indeed a lie they are prophesying to you, in order to* remove you far from your soil." Nations who serve the king of Babylon Yahweh will leave on their own soil *to work it* and dwell upon it	(vv 9–11)
B	Jeremiah reports having spoken similar words to King Zedekiah		(v 12a)
	Jeremiah:	"Bring your necks into the yoke of the king of Babylon, *and serve him and his people, and live!*"	(vv 12b–13)
	Oracle IV	"*And do not listen to the words of the prophets who are saying to you:* 'You shall not serve the king of Babylon.' *Indeed a lie they are prophesying to you . . . in order that*" [Yahweh] should disperse you, and you will perish."	(vv 14–15)
C	Jeremiah reports having spoken to the priests and to all the people		(v 16a)

Oracle V	"*Do not listen to the words of your prophets who are prophesying to you . . .* 'Look, the vessels of the house of Yahweh will be brought back from Babylon now shortly.' *Indeed a lie they are prophesying to you.*"	(v 16b)
Jeremiah:	"Do not listen to them; *serve the king of Babylon and live.*" If they are prophets, let them pressure Yahweh not to send Jerusalem's remaining treasures to Babylon	(vv 17–18)
Oracle VI	All remaining treasures in Jerusalem will go to Babylon until the day Yahweh brings them back	(vv 19–22)

The whole hangs together as a coherent discourse, with inversions to break the monotony of repetition and words of hope integrated into messages that are otherwise judgmental. One notes that in the message presented to Zedekiah, Jeremiah's own word comes first and the divine oracle second. This is reversed in the message presented to the priests and the people, where the divine oracle comes first; then comes Jeremiah's own word. Here, too, is a final oracle, making three oracles for the foreign kings and three oracles for the king and people of Jerusalem. Also to be noted are the balancing of judgment and hope themes in Oracles I and III, and again in Oracle VI.

The message to the priests and the people—Oracle V and Oracle VI with its prior superscription (v 21)—contains an inclusio, which is seen somewhat differently by Goldman (1992: 184):

V	*the vessels of the house of Yahweh* *will be brought back from Babylon . . .*	v 16
VI	*the vessels . . . in the house of Yahweh . . .*	v 21
	To Babylon . . . until . . . I bring them back . . .	v 22

NOTES

27:1. *In the beginning of the reign of Zedekiah son of Josiah, king of Judah, this word came to Jeremiah from Yahweh.* The MT reads "Jehoiakim," even though events of the chapter belong to Zedekiah's reign (vv 3, 12; 28:1). The T also has "Jehoiakim," for which reason medieval Jewish interpreters took the directive to Jeremiah from Yahweh as occurring before Zedekiah became king (Rosenberg). Calvin, too, took the divine word to Jeremiah as distantly anticipating the action to be carried out (Vg also has "Jehoiakim"). The "Jehoiakim" reading was carried over into the AV, but most modern Versions (except NAB, NJV, and NSB) correct to "Zedekiah." The LXX omits the verse, but it is present in Aq (with "Jehoiakim"). Some commentators, because of the LXX omission, judge v 1 to be secondary (Rudolph; Carroll; Jones; McKane) or delete (Giesebrecht; Duhm; Bright). Without v 1 the chapter begins, "Thus Yahweh said to me," which is how chap. 13, reporting the loincloth incident, begins (13:1). It is now generally agreed, in any case, that the superscription is in error and that the directive to Jeremiah belongs to Zedekiah's reign, most likely the king's fourth year (28:1). The usual explanation for the error is that a scribe carried the superscription of 26:1 over into 27:1 (Blayney; J. D. Michaelis 1793: 221; Hitzig; Giesebrecht; Cheyne; Duhm; and others), which is the same except that 26:1 lacks "to Jeremiah." A harmonizing attempt has been made with 28:1, which has a retrospective "in that year," and while 28:1 has its own problems, it is apparent that chaps. 27 and 28 belong together. It should also be noted that a "Zedekiah" reading in 27:1 has the support of a few Heb MSS, S, and the ArB.

In the beginning of the reign of Zedekiah. Hebrew *bĕrē'šît mamleket* does not appear to mean "in the accession year" in the book of Jeremiah (see Note for 26:1), where the accession year would be the period between the king's accession to the throne and the start of the New Year (2 Kgs 25:27). In 28:1, "in the beginning of the reign" is further designated as Zedekiah's fourth year, i.e., 594–593 B.C., also the date for the events here (Hyatt; Bright; Malamat 1975: 135–38; Holladay; McKane). The one problem with this reconstruction is that the conference is convened after a revolt in Babylon is already over. This revolt, which was quickly suppressed, is reported in the Babylonian Chronicle as having occurred in 595–594 B.C. (Wiseman 1956: 72–73; D. N. Freedman 1956: 58; Tadmor 1965: 230). Sarna (1978) therefore argues that the conference and Jeremiah's meeting with Hananiah should be placed two years before the revolt (cf. 28:3), which would enable the Jerusalem planning to anticipate events in Babylon and would coordinate Babylon's unrest at home with a simultaneous unrest in the western provinces. Sarna can also take *bĕrē'šît mamleket* as Zedekiah's "accession year," which he puts after 2 Adar (February/March) 597 B.C. This chronology has been adopted by Hayes and Hooker (1988: 95–96). But the "fourth year (of Zedekiah)" in 28:1 must then be disregarded or reinterpreted. Sarna and Hayes-Hooker take it as the fourth year in a sabbatical cycle, which makes the reference cryptic. Another difficulty with Sarna's 597 date is that planning a revolt so soon after Nebuchadnezzar's subjugation of Jerusalem is unlikely (Hyatt; Cogan and Tadmor 1988: 322 n. 6). A date of 594–593 makes more sense, allowing sufficient time for a pro-Egyptian faction in Jerusalem to gain the upper hand. Pharaoh Neco died in 594 B.C., and a rebellion could have had the support of his son, Psammetichos II, who was now on the throne. But since Egypt is not represented at the conference and is not mentioned anywhere as promising aid for the action under consideration, this point should not be pressed. Also to be factored in is the reported embassy by Zedekiah and Seraiah (or Seraiah without the king) to Babylon in 594–593 B.C., presumably to reaffirm Judah's loyalty to Nebuchadnezzar after the unrest at home and abroad (see Note for 51:59). But this embassy would be appropriate whether the Jerusalem conference took place in 597 or 594–593 B.C.

(Jehoiakim). The defective spelling, *yĕhôyāqîm*, occurs here (cf. 52:2).

Josiah. The Kt preserves a spelling with an added *waw: yᵓwšyhw*.

Jeremiah. Hebrew *yirmĕyâ*. This shortened spelling of the prophet's name occurs only in chaps. 27–29 of the book (27:1; 28:5, 6, 10, 11, 12, 15; 29:1); elsewhere it occurs in Ezra 1:1 and Dan 9:2. In Jer 29:27, 29, 30 is the long form, *yirmĕyahû*.

2. *Thus Yahweh said to me*. The LXX's omission of "to me" should not be deleted as an MT plus (*pace* Cornill; Holladay; McKane). Duhm eliminated the first-person reference by suggesting that *ᵓly* was an abbreviation for "to Jeremiah." But T and Vg have "to me," and so does 4QJerᶜ. This same introduction occurs in 13:1; 17:19; and 25:15 (expanded); in chaps. 1–20 the more common "and Yahweh said to me" occurs (see Note for 1:7). In the present chapter, first-person narration continues in vv 12 and 16, for which reason most commentators retain "to me."

Make for yourself straps and yoke bars. Hebrew *môṭâ* is a wooden carrying pole with bending action (1 Chr 15:15; cf. *môṭ* in Num 13:23) or else a wooden crossbar with similar flexibility used in the construction of a yoke (Lev 16:23; Ezek 34:27; cf. BDB). The term may also designate a yoke in its entirety, perhaps by synecdoche (Jer 28:10, 12; Isa 58:6, 9; cf. KB³). The Heb term for "yoke" is otherwise *ᶜōl* (28:11). Here Jeremiah is told to make multiple yoke bars (*môṭôt*), which may anticipate the additional yokes to be presented to the foreign envoys (v 3); otherwise, a single yoke with two bars for himself has to be assumed (Cheyne). The *môsērôt* are leather straps to secure the oxen in the yoke at the neck (2:20; 5:5; 30:8). The LXX has a somewhat different picture, translating *desmous kai kloious*, "chains and (wooden) collars." Zwickel (1991) argues, too, that the *môṭâ* is a yoke harness ("Jochhaken") used to attach the animal to the yoke. Modern yokes in use among Palestinian Arabs have a single crossbar ca. 4.5 feet in length, with ropes that tie under the animals' necks (Schumacher 1889; Turkowski 1969: 29–30). Holladay, noting that these yokes contain vertical pegs projecting downward in the crossbar, which along with ropes make collars around the neck of each animal, argues that the "yoke bars" (*môṭôt*) are in fact these smaller pegs. In his view, Jeremiah is simply directed to wear a collar of pegs and rope, not a full yoke, which would be far too cumbersome. It is reasonable that the yoke be either partial or minature if Jeremiah is to wear it for long, but whether the *môṭôt* can be these smaller pegs is doubtful. In Egyptian paintings we see yoke bars tied to the horns of oxen (Wilkinson 1878: 391–92, 420; BRL², 255; cf. Dalman 1932: 99–105). In antiquity the yoke symbolized servitude. In the Amarna Letters we read: "the yoke of the king my lord is upon my neck and I carry it" (EA 296: 38), and again, "my neck is placed in the yoke which I carry" (EA 257: 15; *ḫullu*, CAD 6: 230). In the OT, see also Gen 27:40; 1 Kgs 12:9–11; and Hos 11:7; in the NT, see 1 Tim 6:1. In both the OT and NT the yoke symbolizes the covenant bond (2:20; 5:5; Matt 11:29–30). In Isa 47:6,

Yahweh remembers how he gave his own people over to Babylon and how Babylon put them under a heavy yoke.

then you shall put them upon your neck. I.e., one yoke consisting of straps and a single crossbar, or one yoke consisting of straps and two crossbars. Of what size the yoke was we do not know. A minature replica is likely. Wearing the yoke was one of many symbolic acts that Yahweh commanded Jeremiah to perform (see Note on 13:1). Compare Zedekiah son of Chenaanah's spectacle with the horns of iron in 1 Kgs 22:11 and Isaiah's going naked and barefoot in Isa 20:2–6.

3. *You shall also send them to the king of Edom, and to the king of Moab, and to the king of the Ammonites, and to the king of Tyre, and to the king of Sidon by the hand of messengers who are coming to Jerusalem, to Zedekiah, king of Judah.* Envoys representing five neighboring kings have come to Jerusalem, or will arrive shortly, to talk rebellion against Nebuchadnezzar. Zedekiah will host the conference, but whether he presently is of a mind to rebel is unclear. As an appointee of Nebuchadnezzar, with presumably pro-Babylonian sympathies, he will likely have reservations about the wisdom of such action (Skinner 1926: 254). But Streane notes that in Ezek 17:15 Zedekiah is seen taking the initiative in negotiations with Egypt against Babylon. He could be doing the same here. It is significant that Egypt is not represented at the conference. Since the rebellion never took place, Cornill thinks it was because Egypt was not part of the plan. It could also be that Jeremiah's advice was heeded. Ashkelon and Ekron are not present because both were destroyed a decade earlier, in 604 B.C. Kida (1993: 179) thinks that Jeremiah's message to the kings may correlate with oracles spoken against foreign nations, which is possible. The kings appear here in the same order as in 25:21–22.

You shall also send them. Hebrew *wĕšillaḥtām*. I.e., the yokes duplicating the one Jeremiah has made for himself. Doubts have been expressed about Jeremiah's making six yokes, it being more likely that he made only one. But the LXX, T, and Vg all have "them." Nevertheless, numerous commentators (Hitzig; Giesebrecht; Duhm; Cornill; Peake; Streane; Rudolph; Weiser; Bright; McKane) omit the verbal suffix, with G^L, and simply read *wĕšālaḥtā*, "and you shall send," arguing that the verb by itself (pointed Qal) can refer to the sending of a message (29:31; 2 Sam 12:25). Some of the modern Versions interpret similarly: RSV, NRSV, JB [but not NJB], and NIV all read "send word"; NSB has "Skicka bud." But Volz, Holladay, and Jones maintain that Jeremiah could have presented each envoy with a yoke or the representation of a yoke. And the NJV and NJB retain "send them." The messengers, in any event, will report Jeremiah's symbolic act and its meaning to their kings upon return. How Jeremiah met the messengers we do not know, but we assume he did meet them.

the king of Edom. Edom's presence at the conference indicates that for the present, at least, it has common cause with Judah in opposing Babylonian suzerainty in the area. Edom will shift loyalty soon afterward, because the nation is remembered bitterly by the Jews for helping in the destruction of Jerusalem

(Obad 9–14; Ezek 25:12–14; 35:15; Ps 137:7; Joel 4:19[Eng 3:19]; 1 Esd 4:45). Edom appears to have escaped punitive action by Nebuchadnezzar in 588–586 B.C., also in 582 B.C. when both Ammon and Moab were attacked (see Note for 49:10). But at some point Edom will have to drink Yahweh's cup of wrath (25:21; cf. 9:24–25[Eng 9:25–26]), and Jeremiah thus delivers oracles of judgment against it (49:7–22). In the seventh–sixth centuries B.C., Edom is a kingdom to be reckoned with; currently it is threatening Judah on its southern front, although Bartlett (1999) thinks that Edom does not make substantial inroads into southern Judah and the Negeb until later.

the king of Moab. After the Battle of Carchemish (605 B.C.), Moab appears to have sworn alliegance to Nebuchadnezzar and remained loyal when Jehoiakim rebelled, for which reason it was not attacked in 597 B.C. Moab, in fact, aided Nebuchadnezzar against Judah at this time (2 Kgs 24:2). Yet now it is represented in Jerusalem when the talk is rebellion against Babylon. The nation was spared when Jerusalem fell in 586 B.C., but according to Josephus (*Ant* x 181–82), Moab was destroyed by Nebuchadnezzar in 582 B.C., at which time Ammon suffered a similar fate (see Note for 48:1). Jeremiah gives an unusually large number of judgment oracles against Moab (48:1–47), who sat at table with other nations to drink Yahweh's cup of wrath (25:21; cf. 9:24–25[Eng 9:25–26]).

the king of the Ammonites. This Ammonite king may have been Baalis, who plotted against Gedaliah after the fall of Jerusalem (40:13–41:15), or his predecessor, ʿAmminadab II. On the Ammonite King List and an Ammonite bulla from Tell el-ʿUmeiri naming Baalis, see Note for 40:14. The Ammonites, too, aided Babylon against Judah before Nebuchadnezzar came himself in 597 B.C. (2 Kgs 24:2) but, like Moab, is now talking rebellion against Babylon at the Jerusalem conference. Ammon continued in opposition to Babylon (unlike Edom, which shifted allegiance after the conference) and Nebuchadnezzar, when he entered the area in 588 B.C., threatened the nation on his way to attack Judah (Ezek 21:23–32[Eng 21:18–27]). According to Josephus (*Ant* x 181–82), Ammon was brought down by Nebuchadnezzar in 582 B.C., which would have been punishment for its present disloyalty and the role it played later in disrupting community life at Mizpah. The Ammonites were also destined to drink Yahweh's cup of wrath (25:21; cf. 9:24–25[Eng 9:25–26]), and Jeremiah spoke judgment oracles against the nation as well (49:1–6).

the king of Tyre . . . the king of Sidon. Here in 594–593 B.C. we see that the northern coastal city-states of Tyre and Sidon are still intact. Tyre survived Assyrian rule (738–627 B.C.) and the interim period between the Assyrian retreat and Nebuchadnezzar's campaigns into Syria and Palestine in 604 and 601 B.C., but soon afterward came under siege by Nebuchadnezzar in a battle that lasted 13 years (Josephus *Ant* x 228; *Against Apion* i 144). By 573 B.C., or perhaps earlier, all but the island portion of the city had been taken (see Note for 47:4). Sidon was destroyed by the Assyrians in ca. 677 B.C., but reestablished itself early in Nebuchadnezzar's reign, perhaps before (Elat 1991: 21) and had submitted to the Babylonian king by the time Jerusalem was destroyed. Kings of Tyre and Sidon are listed as imprisoned vassals in a "court list" of Nebuchadnezzar II (*ANET*³ 308), which dates to 570 B.C., according to Wiseman (1985: 73–75), but according to Elat (1991: 29–30) is earlier. Jeremiah lists both kings as having to drink Yahweh's cup of wrath (25:22). Tyre and Sidon do not receive separate oracles but are promised isolation from their southern allies in an oracle against the Philistines (47:4).

by the hand of messengers who are coming to Jerusalem. On *mal'ākîm* ("messengers") without the article, see GKC §126w. The LXX has "their messengers," expanding also its reading to "who are coming *to meet them* (*eis apantēsin autōn*) in Jerusalem." If the LXX's *Vorlage* read *liqrā'tām* (Hitzig; BHS), we could have an MT loss due to haplography (homoeoteleuton: *m . . . m*). Tov (1979: 82) leans in favor of the short reading of MT, taking the LXX reading as secondary. Hitzig said earlier that LXX's *apantēsatōsan* ("let them meet") in v 18 is not correct. On the messenger and his role in ANE society, see S. Meier (1988); also discussion in Notes for 2:2 and 23:18.

who are coming to Jerusalem. Hebrew *habbā'îm yĕrûšālayim.* For the omission of "to" before "Jerusalem," see Note for 24:2. The participle *habbā'îm* I have translated as present tense, viewing the arrival of the messengers as imminent. The rendering of AV ("which come") is not time specific; the more recent Versions translate a past perfect: "who have come." It could be that the messengers have already arrived, but if Jeremiah is to have sufficient time to make the yokes before meeting them, Yahweh's word may have to precede their arrival. In 32:7, which concerns Jeremiah's field purchase and is another symbolic action, the perfect *ba',* "(he) is coming," indicates future time.

4. *And you shall command them to their masters.* The verb *ṣwh* ("command") is forceful in the mouth of Jeremiah, but Jeremiah on other occasions issues commands (see Note for 36:5).

Yahweh of hosts. The LXX omits "of hosts," as elsewhere; see Appendix VI. Aquila and Theod have *tōn dunameōn.*

5. *I, I made the earth, human and beast that are on the face of the earth, with my great strength and with my outstretched arm, and I give it to whoever seems right in my eyes.* A grand statement of Yahweh as God of all creation, beginning with an emphatic "I." It is widely asserted that creation theology developed late in ancient Israel, the focus earlier being on Yahweh's redemption of Israel from Egyptian slavery. Von Rad (1962: 138) cites the present passage along with Isa 45:12–13 as expressing comparatively late ideas, seeing in them both Yahweh's power over history as deriving from his authority as Creator. It has also been usual to say that Jeremiah here anticipates the creation faith of Second Isaiah, yet there are differences as well as similarities between the two. For example, Yahweh's creation of earth and humans (*'ādām*) is mentioned only once in Isa 45:12, and his creation of the beasts (*bĕhēmâ*) is nowhere stated. The combination "human and beast," cited with reference to their lamented absence in the land and their joyful reappearance at a later time, is Jeremiah language (7:20; 21:6; 31:27; 32:43; 33:10, 12; 36:29; 50:3). Creation theology is well documented in Jeremiah (Saggs 1978: 42–43; H. Weippert 1981; Lang 1983), even

more so if we attribute to the prophet the liturgies and Aramaic pun in 10:1–16, which earlier scholars denied to Jeremiah but which fit perfectly into the Jeremianic thinking and the Jeremianic period. In Jeremiah's prayer after the purchase of the field, creation theology precedes redemption theology (32:17–23). See also 32:27, which contains a divine self-asseveration similar to the one here. The idea of Yahweh as Creator of the whole earth doubtless predates Jeremiah, the suggestion having been made that Jeremiah took over older claims advanced for Neo-Assyrian and Neo-Babylonian gods and applied them in new ways to Yahweh (Saggs 1978: 43–49; Lang 1983). A storage jar fragment found in excavations of late-eighth or early-seventh-century Jerusalem turned up an inscription reading "(God) Creator of Earth," (*'l*) *qn 'rṣ*. An eighth-century Phonecian inscription from Karatepe in Turkey contains the identical phrase (Avigad 1983: 41). Another carelessly written inscription in a burial cave at Khirbet Beit Lei, eight kilometers east of Lachish, which has been dated to the time of Hezekiah when Sennacherib was laying waste all of Judah (700 B.C.), or else to the time of Nebuchadnezzar's final destruction of Judah in 588–586 B.C., bears witness to Yahweh as God of the entire earth. It reads: "Yahweh (is) the God of the whole earth; the mountains of Judah belong to him, to the God of Jerusalem" (Naveh 1963: 84; Avigad 1979: 25; CS II 179–80; cf. Isa 54:5). Frank Cross (1970) gives only a slightly different translation (see Note for 34:7). J. A. Sanders (1977: 37–41) has argued that affirming Yahweh as God of all creation, which was part of the monotheizing process in ancient Israel, can be one criterion among others for true prophecy. He says:

> To stress the tradition of Yahweh as redeemer, provider, and sustainer and deny Yahweh as creator would be . . . to engage in "false prophecy." The so-called true prophets never *denied* that God was the God of Israel who had elected Israel and redeemed them from slavery in Egypt, guided them in the desert and given them a home, *and/or* had chosen David and established his throne and city. . . . But in addition to affirming God as redeemer and sustainer, the true prophets stressed that God was also creator of all peoples of all the earth.
>
> (Sanders 1977: 37)

human and beast that are on the face of the earth. Hebrew *'et-hā'ādām wě'et-habběhēmâ 'ăšer 'al-pěnê hā'āreṣ*. The LXX omits, and some scholars (Cornill; Tov 1979: 82; Holladay; Goldman 1992: 126–29; McKane) go with its shorter text, but a greater number support the embellished MT. Hitzig and others (Duhm; Peake; Rudolph; Janzen 1973: 118; Carroll) attribute the LXX omission to haplography (whole-word: *h'rṣ . . . h'rṣ*), which it probably is. Giesebrecht too retains, noting that Aq, Theod, G^L, S, T, and Vg all contain the omitted words. Ehrlich (1912: 312) says the phrase in question could be *epexegese* (= *exergasia*) on "the earth" and thus original. More recently Goldman has argued that the phrase is not essential to the theme, but van der Kooij (1994: 60–61) disagrees, saying that the phrase makes good sense contextually and is acceptable as an apposition. On the pairing of "human and beast" in the Jeremiah prose, see Note for 21:6.

with my great strength and with my outstretched arm. This stereotyped expression occurs also with reference to Yahweh's awesome creation in 32:17, which Martens (2001: 140–41) points out to be a peculiar usage in Jeremiah. In Deut 9:29 and 2 Kgs 17:36 the expression describes the Exodus deliverance (see again later in Bar 2:11). The more common cliché used in connection with the Exodus is "with outstretched hand and with strong arm" (see 32:21 and Note for 21:5).

and I give it to whoever seems right in my eyes. A statement of principle building on the Creation theology of Gen 1:28, which is given specific application in the verse following. See also Dan 4:14, 22, 29[Eng 4:17, 25, 32]; 5:21. A statement of principle is similarly injected in 18:7–10, where Yahweh's prerogative to judge or rescind judgment builds on the potter image in the J Creation account. Jeremiah elsewhere employs this same rhetoric—introducing abstractions or statements of principle—in 26:14–15 and 28:8–9. In 26:14 the expression "right in your eyes" (*yāšār bĕ'ênêkem*) also appears.

6. *And now I.* Hebrew *wĕ'attâ 'ānōkî.* Another occurrence of the emphatic divine "I." The rhetorical particle *wĕ'attâ* ("and now") facilitates the shift from an abstraction to the situation at hand (see Note for 2:18). The LXX omits both words, which could be due to haplography (homoeoteleuton: *y . . . y*). Janzen (1973: 119) notes haplography as being a likely possibility. G^L, Aq, and Theod all have *kai nun egō eimi.* Giesebrecht therefore retains. Van der Kooij (1994: 63), too, goes with the MT reading. The LXX reading is flat by comparison, lacking the emphasis of the Hebrew and the pivotal shift to Yahweh's choice of Nebuchadnezzar as servant and custodian of the land.

I have given all these lands into the hand of Nebuchadnezzar, king of Babylon, my servant; and even the beasts of the field I have given to him, to serve him. Shalmaneser III of Assyria (859–825 B.C.) boasted how the gods handed over to him all the wild animals, ordering him to hunt them (Michel 1947–52: 472–73; iv 40–42; *CAD* 2: 315 *būlu*). That Yahweh can give Nebuchadnezzar lordship even over the beasts is consistent with what is stated in Gen 1:26 and Ps 8:8[Eng 8:7].

all these lands. Hebrew *hā'ărāṣôt hā'ēlleh.* The LXX has "the earth" (*tēn gēn*), which carries over the wording and perhaps also the idea of v 5. Other Versions support the MT (T: "all these countries"; Aq and Symm: *pasas tas gaias [tautas]*; Vg: *omnes terras istas*), which is the better reading (*pace* Cornill; Janzen 1973: 66; Holladay; McKane). While Yahweh may be giving over the whole earth, as it were, to Nebuchadnezzar, of overriding importance here is that the nations represented at the present conference, and their lands, are being turned over to the Babylonian king. Van der Kooij (1994: 62–63) is right to link up "all these lands" with the nations of v 3, and one should add also "the nations" immediately following in v 7.

into the hand of. Hebrew *bĕyad.* I.e., "into the power of" (so T). See again v 8.

Nebuchadnezzar . . . my servant. On this bold metaphor, which occurs two other times in 25:9 and 43:10, see Note on 25:9. For the spelling of "Nebuchadnezzar" with an "n," see Note on 21:2. The LXX has "to serve him" (*douleuein autō*) instead of "my servant," which makes for parallelism with "to work for him" (*ergazesthai autō*) at the end of the verse. Holladay and McKane go with the LXX (cf. Janzen 1973: 54–57), but most commentators read "my servant" from the MT (so also T; cf. Tov 1979: 84). The translator(s) of the LXX may have found the juxtaposition offensive (Rudolph; Fensham 1982: 61), which would not be surprising since "my servant" as used here is an oxymoron. Because the LXX omits "my servant" in all three contexts and because "servant" is believed to carry theological overtones of obedience and dedication to Yahweh, Lemke (1966) argues that the term does not emanate from Jeremiah but is the result of an accidental transmissional error. This view does not carry conviction. The LXX, as we have seen, cannot be assumed to be the better or more original text. Furthermore, Nebuchadnezzar is surely not a worshiper of Yahweh, simply a servant doing (without his knowledge) the bidding of the One who has created the world and controls the history of all nations (Hyatt). Zevit (1969) has argued that "servant" simply means "vassal," which makes it more a political than a theological term. The expression, "Nebuchadrezzar . . . my servant," is eminently worthy of Jeremiah, whose discourse teems with robust and even shocking images.

the beasts of the field. Hebrew *ḥayyat haśśādeh*. These are the wild beasts (12:9; 28:14; Gen 2:19–20; 3:1; Exod 23:11; Hos 2:14[Eng 2:12]).

I have given to him. These words at the end of the verse are omitted in the LXX. Van der Kooij (1994: 64–65) thinks that the LXX has a simplified style, which is possible.

7. *So all the nations shall serve him and his son and his grandson until the time of his land comes—even he! Then many nations and great kings shall make him serve!* The entire verse and the *waw* beginning v 8 are lacking in the LXX, which may be attributed to haplography (homoeoarcton: *w . . . w*). The *waw* on *wĕhāyâ* (v 8) was apparently present in the LXX's *Vorlage*, but not *hāyâ*, which was also a victim of haplography (see below). The LXX of v 8 begins *kai to ethnos*, "and the nation." Movers (1837), Hitzig (1841), and Kuenen (1863) took v 7 as a later addition and were followed by Giesebrecht, Duhm, Peake, Cornill, Janzen (1973: 101–3), Tov (1979: 84–85), Holladay, and Goldman (1992: 136–46), among others. It is argued that the verse is a *vaticinium ex eventu*, said to break continuity between v 6 and v 8. Cornill thinks it is inappropriate to speak of Chaldean dominion being transitory, when Nebuchadnezzar's power ought, rather, be depicted as terribly as possible. The alleged source for the addition is 25:14a. The verse, however, should be retained (Volz; Rudolph; Weiser; Bright). Besides the argument for LXX haplography, it should be noted that v 7 is attested in T, S, and Vg. The other argument, that hope is incompatible with doom, is passé. The two are commonly juxtaposed in biblical discourse (e.g., in the Psalms), and here in chap. 27, hope enters two other oracles in vv 11 and 22 (see Rhetoric and Composition).

So all the nations shall serve him and his son and his grandson until the time of his land comes—even he! The expression "him and his son and his grandson" is not to be taken literally; it simply denotes three generations (cf. Exod 34:7), like the "70 years" of 25:11–12 and 29:10. And the time period is indefinite. Ehrlich (1912: 312) says "son and grandson" is an expression for descendants through all generations (cf. Judg 8:22), which goes too far. Nebuchadnezzar, as far as we know, did not have a grandson who ruled. When he died, in 562 B.C., he was succeeded by his son Evil-merodach (Amel-marduk), who reigned two years. After him, Neriglissar (560–556 B.C.) and Nabonidus (556–539 B.C.) occupied the throne until Babylon fell to Cyrus, the Persian, and neither was a blood relative of Nebuchadnezzar. The suggestion has thus been made that the present verse may have been omitted in the LXX because it was not literally fulfilled (Hyatt; Bright).

until the time of his land comes—even he! I.e., until judgment comes upon Nebuchdnezzar's land. The expression *'ad 'ēt* ("until the time") is again a limited but unspecified time (Dan 11:24; cf. Leviticus Rabbah 21:7). The final *gam-hû'*, "even he!" which the modern Versions do not translate, makes the point that even Nebuchadnezzar's land will come in for a day of reckoning. Compare *gam-hēmmâ* ("even them!"), referring to the Babylonians, in the parallel verse of 25:14a.

Then many nations and great kings shall make him serve! Service is a *leitmotiv* in the chapter, the verb *'bd* having just occurred at the beginning of the verse with its usual meaning. Now with *wĕ'ābĕdû* comes a wordplay and ironic understatement. The verb *'bd* + *bĕ* in the Qal can mean "make serve" (see Note for 25:14). Nations and kings will at some future time make the Babylonian king their servant, just as the Babylonian king is now making them his servant (T: "many nations and mighty kings shall enslave him"). The same prediction occurs in 25:14a, only there it is the king and the entire Babylonian nation that will be enslaved by "many nations and great kings." Cornill and others suggest emending *bô* ("with him") to *bāh* ("with it"), which anticipates judgment on the Babylonian nation, not on Nebuchadnezzar personally. But the context requires "with him," even though, as things turned out, it was Babylon, not Nebuchadnezzar (or a son or grandson), that reaped the judgment. One will note another play on *'bd* in v 11, where the meaning is "to work (the soil)."

8. *And it shall be that the nation or the kingdom who does not serve him, that is, Nebuchadnezzar, king of Babylon.* Here in vv 8–11 is an antithesis similar to those in chaps. 18 and 24: first, nations unwilling to serve the king of Babylon are told the outcome of their action; then, nations willing to serve are told the outcome of their action (Krašovec 1984: 89–90). Compare the antithesis in Bar 2:21–23.

And it shall be. Hebrew *wĕhāyâ*. The LXX omits the verb (without *waw*), which can be attributed to haplography (homoeoarcton: *h . . . h*). The T has the verb; so do Aq and Theod (*estai*). Tov (1979: 79) concurs that the LXX omission does not include the *waw*.

serve him, that is, Nebuchadnezzar, king of Babylon, and who will not. The LXX lacks these words also, and while some commentators delete, the loss is likely more haplography (two-word: *'šr l'* . . . *'šr l'*). See note in *BHS*. Aquila, Theod, T, and Vg have the words.

by sword and by famine and by pestilence I will reckon with that nation . . . until I have consumed them by his hand. The language is Jeremianic; see 14:15 and 24:10. On the triad "by sword and by famine and by pestilence," see Note for 5:12. The LXX lacks "and by pestilence," which it sometimes does (see Note for 38:2). But Aq and Symm both have the term (*en loimō*).

I will reckon with that nation. On the verb *pqd* ("to reckon, pay a visit") in Jeremiah, see Note for 5:9. The LXX omits "that nation," having simply "I will reckon with them." Since it reads "the nation and the kingdom" at the beginning of the verse, it may here be avoiding a repetition of "nation." At the same time, consistency is maintained by employing a plural pronoun for a plural antecedent.

until I have consumed them by his hand. T again "by his power" (cf. v 6). Commentators are troubled here by an infinitive, *tummî* ("I have consumed"), taking an object, since *tmm* in the Qal is usually intransitive (there is no Piel). The LXX translates *heōs eklipōsin* ("until they are abandoned"), leading H. Weippert (1973: 169 n. 275) to emend to *tummām*, "they are consumed"; cf. 24:10. But another transitive Qal of *tmm* is attested in Ps 64:7[Eng 64:6], which casts doubt on the wisdom of emending both texts, as BDB and KB³ suggest. To be rejected is the emendation by some to *tittî*, "I have given." Volz says, "(It) is too weak, and the corruption would not be explained."

9. *And you, do not you listen to your prophets, and to your diviners, and to your dreamers, and to your soothsayers, and to your sorcerers—they who are saying to you: 'You shall not serve the king of Babylon.'* An expanded form of the stereotyped directive in these chapters (see Note for 23:16). Note the *accumulatio*. These are prophets and clairvoyant types not residing in Jerusalem but in the countries represented, who are advising kings and fanning nationalistic sentiments there.

your prophets. Hebrew *nĕbî'êkem*. These countries have optimistic prophets like those inveighed against in 23:9–40 and elsewhere. The T has "prophets of falsehood"; the LXX *pseudoprophētōn* ("false prophets"), which never occurs in the MT of Jeremiah (see Note for 6:13).

your diviners. Hebrew *qōsĕmêkem*. Predicters of the future, basically, who shake arrows, cast lots, and examine livers for a fee (Ezek 21:26–27[Eng 21:21–22]; cf. Num 22:7). The divination practices of the medium of Endor, lit., "mistress of necromancy" (*ba'ălat-'ôb*), included calling up the dead (1 Sam 28:7–8). Balaam is called a "diviner" in Josh 13:22. According to the Bible, diviners were indigenous to Canaanite culture (Deut 18:9–14; 1 Sam 28:7–8), being present also among the Philistines (1 Sam 6:2) and the Babylonians (Ezek 21:26–27[Eng 21:21–22]). They and their secret arts are repudiated or forbidden outright in the OT (Deut 18:10; 1 Sam 15:23; 2 Kgs 17:17; Zech 10:2). Prophets, too, censure them in the strongest of terms, in Yahweh's name (Mic 3:6–7, 11; Isa 3:2; 44:25). Jeremiah knows prophets who are practicing divination in Jerusalem (Jer 14:14) and has a harsh word also for diviners in

Babylon who are speaking lies in Yahweh's name (29:8–9). Diviners and divination come under even stronger attack from Ezekiel, who brands both practitioners and the practice as false, pronouncing upon diviners and other like individuals—both men and women—Yahweh's sure judgment (Ezek 12:24, 28; 13:1–23).

your dreamers. The MT has *ḥălōmōtêkem* ("your dreams"), but commentators generally go with "dreamers," which is in the Versions and which must be the original reading (T has "the dreams of your dreamers"). Ehrlich (1912: 312–313) revocalizes to *ḥālōmōtêkem* ("your dreamers") on the basis of a Mishnaic parallel; Duhm achieves the same result by emending to *ḥōlĕmêkem*. See again 29:8. Oppenheim (1956: 240) says that these individuals, like the "master of dreams" (*baʿal hahălōmôt*) in Gen 37:19 and the "dreamer of dreams" (*ḥōlēm ḥălôm*) in Deut 13:2[Eng 13:1], habitually received dream-revelations. Jeremiah has the strongest polemic anywhere in the OT against dreamers in 23:25–32. For a broader discussion on dreams and dreamers in the OT and in the ANE, see Note for 23:25.

your soothsayers. Hebrew *ʿōnĕnêkem.* The term is a Polel participle of the verb *ʿnn,* whose meaning is uncertain. KB³ gives "to interpret signs" as a definition for the root. Arabic *ʿanna* means "to appear suddenly, show oneself, to intervene as a hindrance" (Kopf 1958: 190). An Ugaritic cognate *ʿnn* is also attested, but all that can be said here is that it appears in contexts concerning deities (*UT* 458 #1885). The secret art possessed by soothsaying men and women (Isa 57:3: "sons of a soothsaying woman") may have consisted of telling fortunes based on observations of natural phenomena (*ʿānān* means "clouds"), but this is unconfirmed. On astrology in Babylon, see Note for 10:2. According to the Bible, soothsayers were indigenous to Canaanite culture (Deut 18:14), being attested also among the Philistines (Isa 2:6). In Israel they were banned (Deut 18:10; Lev 19:26), but they existed anyway, particularly when legalized by King Manasseh (2 Kgs 21:6; 2 Chr 33:6).

your sorcerers. Hebrew *kaššāpêkem.* This noun is a *hapax legomenon* in the OT but comes from an attested verb, *kiššēp,* meaning "to practice sorcery." Another noun, *kešep,* "sorcery," also exists. Akkadian *kašāpu* (*CAD* 8: 284; AHw 1: 461) is probably close in meaning to the Hebrew verb: "to bewitch, cast an evil spell." Hebrew *kaššāp* also has a parallel in Akk *kaššāpu,* "sorcerer" (*CAD* 8: 292; AHw 1: 463). The Pharaoh of Egypt had sorcerers working magic at the time of the Exodus (Exod 7:11), and later in Dan 2:2 they are called upon in Babylon to interpret dreams. The Covenant Code specifies capital punishment for a sorceress (Exod 22:17[Eng 22:18]), and a ban on the dark practice exists also in Deut 18:10; nevertheless, sorcery was legalized in the North by Jezebel (2 Kgs 9:22) and in the South by Manasseh (2 Chr 33:6). Yahweh's judgment on such practitioners is not left in doubt by the prophets. A "mistress of sorcery" (*baʿălat kĕšāpîm*) will be blamed for all the dead bodies in Nineveh (Nah 3:4). Babylon, too, will fall, despite its many sorceries (Isa 47:9, 12). A bleak future for Judah's sorcerers and sorceries is predicted in Mic 5:11[Eng 5:12] and Mal 3:5.

they who are saying to you. Hebrew *'ăšer-hēm 'ōmĕrîm 'ălêkem.* The LXX omits *'ălêkem,* "to you," which van der Kooij (1994: 70) thinks simplifies a redundant Hebrew reading. But the loss is better explained as due to haplography (homoeoteleuton: *m . . . m*).

10. *Indeed a lie they are prophesying to you.* Hebrew *kî šeqer hēm nibbĕ'îm lākem.* On prophesying the "lie" (*šeqer*), which occurs three times here and nine times in chaps. 27–29, see Note for 23:14. The *kî* is taken here as an asseverative: "Indeed"; similarly in vv 14 and 16.

in order to remove you far from your soil, for I will disperse you and you will perish. See v 15, where the same future awaits Judah. The conjunction *lĕma'an* expresses the result as intent (BDB; KB³ *ma'an*). See again v 15; also 25:7. BDB (p. 775) calls the usage rhetorical, where "a line of action, though really undesigned, is represented . . . ironically as if it were designed" (cf. Deut 29:18). Prophets preaching rebellion against the king of Babylon have no idea that their prophecy will bring about their nation's exile, but it will. False prophecy and Yahweh's judgment will combine to bring both dispersion and death.

to remove you far from your soil. Hebrew *harḥîq 'etkem mē'al 'admatkem.* On the use of *'ădāmâ* ("soil, ground") instead of the more usual *'ereṣ* ("land"), which occurs also in the following verse, see Note for 24:10. The imagery bcomes bolder and more concrete: the neighboring nations will be exiled far from their native soil.

for I will disperse you and you will perish. The LXX omits, which appears to be more haplography (homoeoarcton: *wh . . . wh*, or homoeoteleuton: *m . . . m*). Aquila and Theo have the words. There is no need to propose a borrowing from v 15 (*pace* Giesebrecht). Yahweh here is prepared to disperse them among neighboring nations, where they will die.

11. *I will then leave it on its own soil . . . to work it and dwell upon it.* Here is another play on *'bd*, which means both "serve" and "work (soil or animals)." See the wordplay in v 7. For the meaning "work, till (the soil)," see Gen 2:5; 4:2, 12. Weiser points out that God's final word is a word of peace, but his way to peace does not go the way of political and religious freedom, which is what the leaders are urging. The same thing could be said to leaders in Jerusalem, and doubtless was.

oracle of Yahweh. The LXX lacks it, but the formula is present in Aq and Theo.

12. *And to Zedekiah, king of Judah, I spoke all these words.* Jones says: "the repetition serves to hammer home the message."

Zedekiah. Hebrew *ṣidqîyâ.* This shortened spelling of the king's name occurs also in 28:1; 29:3; 49:34; and 1 Chr 3:16. In 27:3 the longer form, *ṣidqîyāhû*, appears.

Bring your necks into the yoke of the king of Babylon. Plural verbs and "necks," plural, indicate that this word is not for the king alone but for others in the royal house (cf. 22:2) and perhaps for the entire nation. The LXX omits "into the yoke of the king of Babylon," which makes for an inferior reading (*pace* McKane). The point has been made that Jeremiah is not to be credited here with political adroitness; he is simply a prophet driven by the conviction that Yahweh is Lord of all history (Rudolph; Kraus 1964: 74–75). For a later variation of this same exhortation, see Bar 2:21.

and serve him and his people, and live! The priests and people are told the same thing in v 17. Reuven Yaron, in a lecture given at the University of California, Berkeley, on June 6, 1977, said that the expression "serve him and live" is probably very old, since it appears in the fourteenth century B.C. Amarna Letters (EA 162: 39; Knudtzon 1964: 656–57: *Unterwirf dich denn dem König, deinem Herrn! Dann lebst du* ["Submit yourself then to the king, your lord! Then you will live"]).

12b–14a. *him and his people, and live! Why should you die, you and your people, by sword, by famine, and by pestilence according to what Yahweh has spoken to the nation that will not serve the king of Babylon? And do not listen to the words of the prophets who are saying to you: 'You shall not serve.'* This large LXX omission is recognized by many (Hitzig; Peake; Cornill; Bright; Janzen 1973: 118; Tov 1979: 87; Carroll; Holladay[a]) as a loss due to haplography (whole-word: *'bdw . . . 'bdw*).

13. *Why should you die . . . ?* The king and his royal house are here given the way of life and the way of death, which Jeremiah laid before the people in 21:8–10.

14. *And do not listen to the words of the prophets who are saying to you: 'You shall not serve the king of Babylon.' Indeed a lie they are prophesying to you.* As Yahweh's messenger, the prophet must above all be true. Nothing less was expected of messengers generally, as S. Meier (1988: 22–24, 168–79) points out in his study of messengers throughout the ancient world. From the Bible he cites the example of Ahimaaz, a messenger sent to David after Absalom was killed, who was willing only to tell the king the good news, that his enemies had been defeated, and not the bad news, that Absalom had been killed (2 Sam 18:19–30). Meier cites also the following passage from the Amarna Letters (EA 1: 81–88), where the Egyptian Pharaoh complains to the Babylonian king about a breakdown in communication due to "apple-polishing" on the part of the king's messengers:

> Your messengers don't speak truly to you. . . . Don't listen to your messengers whose mouths are false. . . . I swear they have not served you and so they told lies in order to escape your punishment. (p. 169)

a lie. Hebrew *šeqer.* The LXX has *adika,* "a wrong," rather than *pseudos,* "a lie."

14–15. *prophets . . . prophets.* T: "prophets of falsehood" (2×); LXX: *prophētai* in v 15. These are the optimistic Jerusalem prophets.

15. *for I have not sent them.* A recurring disclaimer by Yahweh (see Note for 23:32).

---

[a]Holladay claims (p. 116) to support haplography but makes no mention of it in his textual notes (p. 113).

the lie. Hebrew *laššāqer.* The LXX has *ep' adikō,* "for wrong"; Aq: *psuedos,* "a lie."

in order that I should disperse you, and you will perish. On the conjunction *lĕma'an,* expressing ironic result, see v 10. The LXX omits the suffix on the infinitive *haddîḥî,* "I should disperse," which has the false preaching of the prophets causing the dispersion (cf. Vg). Also, at the end of the verse the LXX adds *ep adikō pseudē* ("for false wrong"), which has been variously explained as an inner Greek doublet (Janzen 1973: 26, 64; Tov 1979: 88; McKane). But none of the reconstructed readings inspires confidence, and the plus is best deleted, with Giesebrecht, as unoriginal.

16. *Then to the priests and to all this people I spoke.* The focus now is on the Temple treasures, which are of special concern to the priests. But priests and people are also told to serve the king of Babylon and live. The LXX reverses "priests" and "people" and adds an initial "to you" (*hymin*): "To you and to all this people, and to all the priests I spoke." The added pronoun may belong to the LXX plus at the end of v 15, which does not appear to be original. The LXX reverses "priests" and "people" also in 28:5.

Do not listen to the words of your prophets who are prophesying to you, saying, 'Look, the vessels of the house of Yahweh will be brought back from Babylon now shortly.' Indeed a lie they are prophesying to you. Nebuchadnezzar looted the Temple when he subjugated Jerusalem in 597 B.C. (2 Kgs 24:10–13), and prophets are now saying that these treasures (presumably the ones not cut into pieces) will be returned shortly. This is another lie. They will not be returned shortly. There is no reason to argue, as some do, that any discussion of Temple vessels' being returned from Babylon must emanate from the postexilic period, when the cult was being reestablished (*pace* Volz; Rudolph; Ackroyd 1972: 175–77; Carroll; Holladay; McKane; cf. Ezra 1:7–11; 1 Esd 4:43–46, 57). According to the apocryphal book of Baruch, which is Hellenistic, these vessels and others taken to Babylon in 586 B.C. were returned to Jerusalem by Baruch soon after Jerusalem's destruction (Bar 1:8–9). But there is no evidence that such a prophecy was fulfilled (C. A. Moore 1977: 271).

your prophets. The T again has "your prophets of falsehood"; LXX *tōn prophētōn.* A. R. Johnson (1962: 64) thinks that "your prophets" points to individuals enjoying official status in the Jerusalem cult, which is possible. One may surely say that the possessive "your" is to denigrate the prophets, as well as the people paying them heed.

now shortly. Hebrew *'attâ mĕhērâ.* The LXX omits, and commentators divide over whether to retain or delete. Giesebrecht retains; Duhm deletes. Cheyne suggests tht the omission could be linked to the LXX's other omission in v 22. The T and Vg (*nunc cito*) have the words. What we have here is probably another LXX loss due to haplography (homoeoteleuton: *h . . . h*).

Indeed a lie they are prophesying to you. The LXX again has *adika,* "a wrong"; Aq has *pseudē,* "a lie." The LXX also adds *ouk apesteila autous,* "I did not send them" (cf. 15), which is not present in T and Vg, but could nevertheless be an MT loss of *lō' šĕlaḥtîm* due to haplography (homoeoteleuton: *m . . . m*).

17. *Do not listen to them; serve the king of Babylon and live. Why should this city become a ruin?* The LXX omits the entire verse plus the *waw* beginning v 18, which can be attributed to haplography (homoeoarcton: *'aleph . . . 'aleph*). The T and Vg have v 17. Many commentators delete with Hitzig. Weiser and Holladay retain. The rhetorical question has the ring of authenticity (cf. v 13).

a ruin. Hebrew *ḥorbâ.* A common curse word in Jeremiah (see Note for 25:9), included often in stereotyped curse-word strings (see Note for 24:9).

18. *do let them pressure Yahweh of hosts.* Hebrew *yipgĕ'û nā' bayhwh ṣĕbā'ôt.* The verb *pg'* (Qal) here and in 7:16 denotes strident intercession, where pleading and other desperate acts are occurring. The LXX's *apantēsatōsan moi* ("let them meet me") may have the correct verb but does not give a proper reading and is rightly rejected by Hitzig and Giesebrecht. The LXX adds the same verb in v 3. H.-J. Kraus (1964: 80) points out that v 18 has an unmistakable ironic tone, "because it would be obvious that the principal duty of the *nebiim* [prophets] is to be worried about and to pray for the life of the people." Jeremiah is mocking them, just as Elijah mocked the prophets of Baal as they were calling upon their god to bring rain, telling them to cry louder (1 Kgs 18:28).

so that the vessels remaining in the house of Yahweh and the house of the king of Judah and in Jerusalem not go to Babylon. These words are omitted in the LXX, but present in Theod, T, and Vg. They should be retained (Giesebrecht; Peake).

so that . . . not go. Hebrew *lĕbiltî-bō'û* is problematic because a perfect form of the verb appears to have been pointed by the Masoretes as an imperfect, the form one would expect (GKC §72o; 76g). But see *lĕbiltî-šābû* in 23:14. If the verb is an original imperfect, the *yod* on *yb'w* has likely been lost because of haplography (prior word ends in *yod*).

19–20. *For thus said Yahweh of hosts concerning the pillars, and concerning the sea, and concerning the stands, and concerning the rest of the vessels remaining in this city, which Nebuchadnezzar, king of Babylon, did not take when he exiled Jeconiah son of Jehoiakim, king of Judah, from Jerusalem to Babylon.* These are the Temple treasures that were not taken by Nebuchadnezzar in 597 B.C. but were taken in 586 B.C. (cf. 52:17–23).

of hosts concerning the pillars, and concerning the sea, and concerning the stands. The LXX omits, and commentators again divide on whether to retain or delete. Giesebrecht retains; Duhm (following Hitzig, Movers, and Kuenen) deletes. The lack of *ṣĕbā'ôt* ("of hosts") can be explained separately, since the LXX commonly omits the term (see Appendix VI). If *ṣĕbā'ôt* was present in the *Vorlage*, the loss of the remaining words could be due to haplography (homoeoteleuton: *wt . . . wt*). Theodotion has everything, including *tōn dunameōn* ("of hosts"); T and Vg also have the words.

remaining in this city. Lacking in LXX but extant in the the other Versions. Giesebrecht retains. Stipp (1997: 197) argues that the verb *ytr* N-stem ("remain") occurs only in MT and that phrases containing this verb (see also v 18, 21; and 34:7) are proto-MT additions. The large omission in v 21, however, is due to haplography.

son of Jehoiakim, king of Judah. This LXX omission can be also be attributed to haplography (homoeoteleuton: *h . . . h*). Theodotion, T, and Vg have the words.

20b–22a. The LXX omits all of the following: "*also all the nobles of Judah and Jerusalem: Indeed, thus said Yahweh of hosts, God of Israel, concerning the vessels remaining in the house of Yahweh, and the house of the king of Judah, and Jerusalem: To Babylon*," which is clearly a loss due to haplography (four-word: *mlk-yhwdh myrwšlm bblh . . . mlk-yhwdh wyrwšlm bblh*). Theodotion, T, and Vg all have the words.

Jeconiah. Hebrew *yĕkonyâ* (Q). Another short spelling of Jehoiachin's name, occurring also in 28:4; 29:2; Esth 2:6; and 1 Chr 3:16, 17. For the many different spellings of this king's name in the OT, see Note for 22:24.

the nobles. Hebrew *ḥōrîm* are the freeborn or nobles of a city (1 Kgs 21:8, 11). These nobles fared better than those caught by the Babylonians in 586 B.C. (39:6).

21. *Indeed, thus said Yahweh of hosts*. Taking the *kî*, with Calvin, as an asseverative: "Indeed." Calvin says that emphasis is required because the messenger formula of v 19 is repeated

22. *To Babylon they shall be brought*. And they were, in 586 B.C. (52:17–23).

and there they shall be until the day I attend to them. The LXX omits. Retain with Theod, T, and Vg. Restoration is as integral to this oracle as to the earlier oracles given the foreign envoys (see Rhetoric and Composition). On the verb *pqd* in Jeremiah, otherwise translated "reckon (with)" in prophecies of judgment, see Note on 5:9.

and I bring them out and bring them back to this place. The LXX omits, which can be due to haplography (homoeoarcton: *w . . . w*, or homoeoteleuton: *h . . . h*). Theodotion, T, and Vg have the words.

MESSAGE AND AUDIENCE

In this narrative, Jeremiah begins by reporting how Yahweh told him to make for himself straps and yoke bars. One yoke consisting of a crossbar and two straps was then to be put upon his neck. Yokes of presumably the same type were to be sent to the kings of Edom, Moab, Ammon, Tyre, and Sidon via envoys coming now to Jerusalem for a conference with King Zedekiah. We are not told what the conference was about, but the oracles following will answer that question. Jeremiah is told to command the envoys that they report Yahweh's oracles to their masters.

Oracle I, enriched by symbolic action, has Yahweh announcing with great emphasis that he made the earth along with the humans and beasts that inhabit it. He did it with his awesome strength, and can give over control of it to anyone he chooses. Just now he has decided to give all the lands represented at the present conference to Nebuchadnezzar, king of Babylon, who, not incidentally has become his servant, and even the wild beasts are given to him and will serve him. All nations, in fact, will serve Nebuchadnezzar and two generations of kingly rule after him, until his own land comes to its appointed time—yes, it will happen even to him! Many nations and great kings shall then make him serve. Some in the audience, perhaps, will catch the *double entendre*.

In Oracle II, Yahweh says that any nation unwilling to serve Nebuchadnezzar, and unwilling to put its neck into the yoke of the Babylonian king, he will visit with sword, famine, and pestilence, until they have been consumed. Oracle III tells these powerless kings not to listen to their prophets, diviners, dreamers, soothsayers, and sorcerers who are all saying not to serve the king of Babylon. Their prophecies are a lie, and unbeknownst to them, this lie will serve to remove these nations far from their home soil. Yes, Yahweh will disperse them until they perish. The nation that does bring its neck under the yoke of the king of Babylon and does serve him will be left by Yahweh on its own soil to work it and dwell upon it. Another *double entendre* for the attentive listener.

Jeremiah then says that he conveyed the same message to Zedekiah. He begins with some of his own words to the king and the royal house. They were told to bring their necks into the yoke of the king of Babylon. By serving him and his people, they will live. Why should they all die, he asks the king, by sword, famine, and pestilence, since Yahweh has spoken thus about any nation that will not serve the king of Babylon? What follows is a divine oracle in which Yahweh tells the king and his house not to listen to the prophets who are telling them not to serve the king of Babylon, for what they are saying is a lie. Yahweh says he has not sent them, and the lie being spread, unbeknownst to them, will result in Yahweh's dispersing them, and they will perish with the prophets prophesying to them.

Jeremiah then reports what he said to the priests and all the people. He begins here with an oracle, in which Yahweh says that the priests and people are not to heed prophets who are predicting that the Temple treasures taken to Babylon will be returned shortly. It is a lie. Jeremiah follows this with a word of his own, in which he repeats what Yahweh said about not listening to the prophets talking about a return of the sacred vessels. The priest and people are to serve the king of Babylon, and live. To the assembled he asks rhetorically, "Why should this city become a ruin?" If these individuals are prophets, and Yahweh's word is with them, let them pressure Yahweh not to have the remaining treasures in Jerusalem—in the Temple, in the royal palace, and anywhere else—go to Babylon. A second oracle then gives a final word about these treasures. Yahweh says they shall all go to Babylon, and there they shall remain until he attends to them and brings them back to Jerusalem.

The (corrected) superscription dates this oracle early in the reign of Zedekiah. The exact year, which is determined by the superscription in 28:1, is 594–593 B.C.

Bonhoeffer (1971: 299), in a baptismal letter of May, 1944 to the son of Eberhard and Renate Bethge, reflected as follows on what life in Germany would be like after the war was over:

We may have to face events and changes that take no account of our wishes and our rights. But if so, we shall not give way to embittered and barren pride, but consciously submit to divine judgment, and so prove ourselves worthy to survive by identifying ourselves generously and unselfishly with the life of the community and the sufferings of our fellow-men. "But any nation which will bring its neck under the yoke of the king of Babylon and serve him, I will leave on its own land, to till it and dwell there, says the Lord" (Jer. 27:11).

E. JEREMIAH MEETS HANANIAH (28:1–17)

28 ¹And it happened in that year, in the beginning of the reign of Zedekiah, king of Judah, in the fourth year[a] in the fifth month, Hananiah son of Azzur, the prophet who was from Gibeon, said to me in the house of Yahweh in the presence of the priests and all the people:

²Thus said Yahweh of hosts, God of Israel:

I have broken the yoke of the king of Babylon. ³Within two years' time I will bring back to this place all the vessels of the house of Yahweh that Nebuchadnezzar, king of Babylon, took from this place and brought to Babylon.

⁴And Jeconiah son of Jehoiakim, king of Judah, and all the exiles of Judah who came to Babylon, I will bring back to this place—oracle of Yahweh— for I will break the yoke of the king of Babylon.

⁵Then Jeremiah the prophet said to Hananiah the prophet in the presence of the priests and in the presence of all the people who were standing in the house of Yahweh; ⁶and Jeremiah the prophet said:

Amen! So may Yahweh do! May Yahweh confirm your words that you have prophesied—to bring back the vessels of the house of Yahweh and all the exiles from Babylon to this place! ⁷But do hear this word that I speak in your ears and in the ears of all the people: ⁸"The prophets who were before me and before you, from ancient times, yes, they prophesied to many lands and against great kingdoms of war and evil and pestilence. ⁹The prophet who prophesies peace, when the word of the prophet comes to be, the prophet whom Yahweh has truly sent will be known.'

¹⁰Then Hananiah the prophet took the yoke bar from upon the neck of Jeremiah the prophet and broke it. ¹¹And Hananiah said in the presence of all the people:

Thus said Yahweh:

Even so will I break the yoke of Nebuchadnezzar, king of Babylon, within two years' time from upon the neck of all the nations.

---

[a]Q is *baššānâ*, as in the beginning of the verse; Kt is the construct *bišnat*; see 32:1; 46:2; 51:59; and elsewhere; cf. GKC §134p.

And Jeremiah the prophet went his way.

[12]Then the word of Yahweh came to Jeremiah after Hananiah the prophet broke the yoke bar from upon the neck of Jeremiah the prophet: [13]'Go and you shall say to Hananiah:

> Thus said Yahweh:
> Yoke bars of wood you have broken, but you have made in their place yoke bars of iron.

[14]For thus said Yahweh of hosts, God of Israel:

> A yoke of iron I have put upon the neck of all these nations to serve Nebuchadnezzar, king of Babylon, and they shall serve him; even the beasts of the field I have given to him.

[15]And Jeremiah the prophet said to Hananiah the prophet: Do listen, Hananiah, Yahweh has not sent you, and you, you have made this people trust in a lie.

[16]Therefore thus said Yahweh:

> Look I will send you away from off the face of the earth. This year you will die, for you have spoken rebellion concerning Yahweh.

[17]And Hananiah the prophet died in that year, in the seventh month.

RHETORIC AND COMPOSITION

MT chapter 28 = LXX chapter 35. This chapter is paired with chap. 27 in a "Zedekiah Cluster" of narrative prose consisting of 24 and 27–29 (see Rhetoric and Composition for 24:1–10). Its upper limit is marked by the superscription of v 1, before which is a *petuhah* in M^A, M^L, and M^P, also the chapter division. Its lower limit is marked by a *petuhah* in M^A and M^L and a *setumah* in M^P after v 17, which is also a chapter division. A new superscription and introduction follow in 29:1–3. The M^A and M^L have another *petuhah* and M^P another *setumah* after v 11, where the narrative breaks at Jeremiah's departure from the Temple and before he receives a final word regarding Hananiah.

The chapter has been widely attributed to Baruch or another intimate eyewitness and accepted as historically authentic. Scholars (Giesebrecht; Duhm; Mowinckel 1914: 24; Volz; Rudolph; Weiser; Bright) assign the narrative to Source B (= Baruch / biographical prose), which is further strengthened when the first-person "to me" in v 1 is eliminated or reinterpreted (see Notes). Actually, the shift from the first person in v 1 to the third person in v 5 is no problem, bearing little if at all on the judgment that the narrative emanates from Baruch (Weiser). Holladay, too, takes the narrative as historically trustworthy, and Jones says it stands squarely in the Jeremiah prose tradition. The literary genre is surely not "legend," such as we have in the traditions of Elijah and Elisha (Muilenburg 1970a: 233; *pace* Koch 1969: 201), much less a "story" without historical basis (*pace* Carroll). McKane sees in the chapter an interweaving of sources (vv 6–9 and 15–17 must be disengaged from the prophet Jeremiah) that in the end leaves us with a narrative scarcely more reliable than Carroll's "story." Once again, McKane finds ambiguities and discontinuities where there are none. There is no problem here with predictive prophecy, as in chap. 27. Duhm says that Jeremiah really did predict Hananiah's death and that Hananiah really did die.

Problems of text are much the same as in chap. 27, although here not so numerous. Older commentators, and some more recently, show a decided preference for the shorter LXX text. There are exceptions. Giesebrecht, noting that the other Versions often support MT, sees haplography as an explanation for the LXX omissions in vv 3 and 15. Volz thinks the LXX in places has been abridged. Rudolph, Weiser, and Bright sometimes read the MT and sometimes the LXX. Cornill, Holladay (following Janzen 1973), and McKane heavily favor the LXX. Nevertheless, we have six arguable cases for LXX haplography in the chapter. So instead of taking the shorter LXX with greater seriousness, as McKane (p. 715) advises, what we really need to do is take the longer MT with greater seriousness, particularly when it finds support in other Versions, a point curiously underweighed by McKane, in light of his exegetical method that claims to pay the Versions more attention. The Hebrew *Vorlage* to the LXX doubtless had many of the omissions we now see in the LXX. This *Vorlage* then did not preserve a purer and more original text but was an inferior text plagued by haplographic and other transmissional errors.

The present narrative contains a superscription, which in spite of minor problems (see Notes), is nevertheless fully integrated into the introduction (v 1). The narrative contains six divine oracles (three from Hananiah, three from Jeremiah) and reports also Jeremiah's own words to Hananiah and the Temple audience. The number of oracles is the same as in chap. 27. With the exception of "to me" in v 1 and Jeremiah's quoted words in vv 6–9 and 15, the narrative is all third person.

The narrative structure contains multiple repetitions and linking terms:

A	Jeremiah reports on a specific date, *in that year*, that Hananiah spoke to him before a Temple audience of priests and people		(v 1)
	Oracle I (Hananiah)	*I have broken the yoke of the king of Babylon. Withn two years' time I will bring back to this place* all the Temple vessels *brought to Babylon*	(vv 2–3)
	Oracle II (Hananiah)	Jeconiah and exiles of Judah who came to Babylon I will bring back to this place . . . for I will break the yoke of the king of Babylon	(v 4)
B	Narrator reports Jeremiah's reply; also Hananiah's oracle of response		(vv 5–11a)

Oracle III (Hananiah)	Even so *will I break the yoke of Nebuchadnezzar, king of Babylon, within two years' time* from upon the neck of all nations	(v 11b)
C	Narrator concludes: "And Jeremiah the prophet went his way"	(v 11c)
D	Narrator reports that the word of Yahweh came to Jeremiah at a later time; directive given to go and speak to Hananiah	(vv 12–13a)
Oracle IV (Jeremiah)	Yoke bars of wood you have broken, but you have made in their place *yoke bars of iron*	(v 13b)
Oracle V (Jeremiah)	*A yoke of iron* I have put upon the neck of all nations; they and the beasts will serve Nebuchadnezzar	(v 14)
E	Narrator reports Jeremiah's discreditation of Hananiah: "Yahweh *has not sent* you, and you, you have made this people trust in a lie"	(v 15)
Oracle VI (Jeremiah)	*I will send you away* from off the face of the earth; this year *you will die*	(v 16)
F	Narrator reports that Hananiah *died* two months later, *in that year*	(v 17)

Hananiah's first two oracles are tied together by an inclusio, noted by Weiser as a repetition at the beginning and end of his speech. The inclusio inverts its key phrases, as noted by Keown et al.:

I   *I have broken the yoke of the king of Babylon. Within two years' time I will bring back to this place* . . .   vv 2–3

II   *. . . I will bring back to this place . . . for I will break the yoke of the king of Babylon*   v 4

In Oracle III, Hananiah repeats with slight change the substance and wording of Oracle I:

III   *. . . will I break the yoke of Nebuchadnezzar, king of Babylon, within two years' time* . . .   v 11b

It has been widely noted that Hananiah uses the same messenger formula, some of the same language ("so will I break"), and the very same symbolic action used by Jeremiah. Now we see that the prophet from Gibeon employs the same rhetoric that Jeremiah employs.

Jeremiah's defense has an inclusio made up of cognate terms, which is noted but in a different manner by Lys (1979: 467–68):

Amen! . . .   *ʾāmēn*   v 6
. . . *truly*   *beʾĕmet*   v 9

Jeremiah's speech when he was on trial also contained an inclusio (see 26:12b–15).

The entire narrative contains an inclusio as well, which can be assigned to the narrating scribe, perhaps Baruch. It consists of the following repeated key words:

| In that year | *baššānâ hahî'* | v 1 |
| In that year | *baššānâ hahî'* | v 17 |

Lys adds to this the collocation of specific dates in the verses, which further links the end with the beginning, but his large chiasmus for the chapter cannot be sustained.

NOTES

28:1. *And it happened in that year, in the beginning of the reign of Zedekiah, king of Judah, in the fourth year in the fifth month.* This superscription is agreed to have undergone expansion, but just what its original form was we cannot say. The T supports MT in all essential respects, but the LXX has a shorter version: "And it happened in the fourth year of Zedekiah, king of Judah, in the fifth month." Omitted in the LXX is "in that year," which connects this chapter's events with those in chap. 27, in addition to making an inclusio with "in that year" of v 17 (see Rhetoric and Composition). Mowinckel (1914: 9) believes "in that year" to be original. The LXX also omits "in the beginning of the reign," which makes for more continuity with 27:1, although here the MT and LXX both correctly name "Zedekiah" as the reigning king (MT in 27:1 has "Jehoiakim"). Janzen (1973: 15) thinks MT is a conflated text. The LXX has both "the fourth year" and "the fifth month," which in MT concludes the superscriptional data and could be a latter add-on stating more correctly when the events of chap. 28 (and chap. 27) took place. However, since specific dates are given also in v 17, both dates may have been integrated into the narrative from the beginning. In any event, the fourth year of Zedekiah, which was 594–593 B.C., is taken by most scholars to be the correct date for events in both chapters. There is still a problem in harmonizing this rather late date with the phrase "in the beginning of the reign," even though the latter does not mean "in the accession year" (see Note for 26:1).

in the fifth month. The fifth month is Ab (July/August) and is no doubt mentioned because Hananiah's death occurred in the seventh month of the same year (v 17).

Hananiah son of Azzur, the prophet who was from Gibeon, said to me in the house of Yahweh in the presence of the priests and all the people. We are prepared for this confrontation after hearing Jeremiah's warning to the foreign envoys, King Zedekiah, and the priests and the people that they not listen to prophets and seers of other description who are preaching rebellion against Nebuchadnezzar (27:14–18). Hananiah now steps forward to represent Jerusalem's prophets in challenging Jeremiah's prophecy. The "priests and people" making up the audience were the last to be addressed in 27:16–22. It could be that the present confrontation occurs soon after the concluding address in chap. 27.

Hananiah son of Azzur. Hebrew *ḥănanyâ ben-ʿazzûr.* "Hananiah" was a common name in Judah, occurring often in the OT and confirmed now from numerous extrabiblical sources. In the book of Jeremiah two other individuals bear the name (36:12 [long form]; 37:13). The spelling here is the short form, *ḥănanyâ,* which occurs throughout the chapter. The name has turned up on the Arad ostraca and on seals, bullae, and jar handles from other archaeological sites (see Appendix I). Of particular interest is the inscription of the name on 22 jar handles found at Gibeon, which happens to be Hananiah's home village. "Hananiah" means "Yahweh is gracious," a fitting summary of the preaching of this Hananiah. On the correlation of names with the individuals who bear them, see Note for 1:1. The name "Azzur" (= "helper") occurs two other times in the OT, in Ezek 11:1 and Neh 10:18.

the prophet. The LXX has *pseudoprophētēs* ("false prophet") here and eight other times in the book, seven of which are in chaps. 26–29 (see Note for 6:13). In the rest of the chapter it omits "the prophet" as a title for both Jeremiah and Hananiah. In T, Hananiah is designated "the false prophet" throughout the chapter; Aq and Symm have simply *ho prophētēs,* "the prophet." A Dead Sea Scroll fragment has turned up (4Q339) on which are listed eight false prophets who arose in Israel (Broshi and Yardeni 1995: 33–37). The text is Aramaic, written on leather, and damaged. Although only two letters are preserved of the name "Hananiah son of Azzur," it seems fairly certain that this name is attested. The final name is in doubt, but all the other names are easily recognizable. The list reads:

1 [Fa]lse prophets who arose in [Israel]:
2 Balaam [son of] Beor
3 [And the] Old Man [who] was in Bethel
4 [And Zede]kiah son of Che[na]anah
5 [And Aha]b son of K[ola]iah
6 [And Zed]ekiah son of Ma[a]seiah
7 [And Shemaiah the Ne]helamite
8 [And Hananiah son of Azz]ur
9 [And Johanan son of Sim]eon

On the list are four false prophets featured here in chaps. 28–29: Ahab, Zedekiah, Shemaiah, and Hananiah. On Balaam, see Numbers 22–24; on the old prophet from Bethel, see 1 Kgs 13:11–32; and on Zedekiah son of Chenaanah, see 1 Kgs 22:11–28. Broshi and Yardeni point out too that this document is the earliest Semitic source to use the expression "false prophets" (*nbyʾy [š]qrʾ*).

The maligning of Hananiah reaches a feverish pitch in Calvin, who views him as a grand impostor. The man, he says, was given to lies and immorality and even conscious of his own wickedness. Although Hananiah used the same messenger formula as Jeremiah, it was easy for people to decide between the two, one announcing commands from God, the other courting applause and human favor. The contrast is considerably overdrawn. Correctives have thus been issued by more recent scholars, although these typically err in the opposite direction. Peake says that there is no reason to doubt Hananiah's sincerity. Quell (1952: 43–67) claims, too, that while Hananiah may have possessed a limited view, he was still a prophet of rank, a man of sincere belief, and an authority to be reckoned with. There is no evidence that he was immoral, as were the prophets Zedekiah and Ahab in Babylon (29:23), and he preached with the same boldness and confidence seen earlier in Isaiah, who said Zion would not fall. Rudolph, too, views the conflict here as one between two earnest men. See also Kraus (1964: 89–91) and Overholt (1967: 244–45; 1970: 38–45). The point about Hananiah's not being immoral is fair enough. There is no evidence that he was. And Calvin clearly read more into the text than he should in suggesting that Hananiah was conscious of his own wickedness. Even if he were a wicked soul, which is nowhere stated other than its being said that he was preaching a lie, how did Calvin know that he was conscious of his own mischief? People engaged in wrongdoings of all sorts, from lying to more grievous things, are often totally unaware of what they are doing. Liars often think they are being truthful.

Gibeon. A Benjaminite city from the time of the Conquest, identified with el-Jib, some five miles north of Jerusalem on the Nablus Road and only a short distance north and west of Anathoth, the home of Jeremiah. According to Josh 21:17 Gibeon was a priestly city, like Anathoth. It was also a major cultic site, because Solomon went there to sacrifice at a high place and received Yahweh's gift of wisdom in a dream on that occasion (1 Kgs 3:4). Edward Robinson had identified Gibeon with el-Jib already in 1838 (E. Robinson 1874 I: 455–56), recognizing that *Jib* in Arabic is merely an abridged form of Hebrew "Gibeon." The site was excavated by J. B. Pritchard in the 1950s and early 1960s, at which time it was learned that the city reached its peak of prosperity in Iron IIC (700–600 B.C.), when it was producing and trading wine (Pritchard 1964; *NEAEHL* 2: 512–13). An extensive water system was also uncovered, which included a tunnel and the pool made famous by the conflict between the men of Abner and the men of Joab, which is recorded in 2 Sam 2:12–17 (Pritchard 1956; 1959; for a picture of the pool, see *ANEP*[2] 367 #879). Since Pritchard's excavations, the identification of Gibeon with el-Jib has not been seriously questioned (Blenkinsopp 1972: 5–6).[b] Another skirmish between Johanan and Ishmael took place at Gibeon after the destruction of Jerusalem, which is recorded in Jer 41:11–15.

said to me. Hebrew *'āmar 'ēlay.* Although the first-person "to me" is well attested in the Versions, many scholars delete or emend it because of the third person in v 5. This change has Hananiah speaking not to Jeremiah but to the Temple audience. Others (Rudolph; G. R. Driver 1964: 79; Bright) suggest that *'ly* abbreviates "to Je[remiah]," which, if true, must be said to introduce a

---

[b]Carroll (p. 539) mistakenly quotes Blenkinsopp in support of his claim that the site of ancient Gibeon is disputed, but Blenkinsopp on pp. 98–100 of his book is referring to the dispute over ancient Mizpah. Blenkinsopp fully supports the el-Jib site for Gibeon.

troublesome ambiguity into the text, and it is a wonder that the full form should be nowhere attested in the book. Volz and Weiser retain "to me," which is a perfectly acceptable reading (cf. 27:2).

in the presence of the priests and all the people. See 27:16. This may have been a Sabbath or other occasion when a large number of people would be present at the Temple.

2. *Thus said Yahweh of hosts, God of Israel.* Hananiah, being a Yahweh prophet, uses the same messenger formula as Jeremiah. The LXX here and in v 14 omits "of hosts, God of Israel," as it does elsewhere (see Appendix VI).

I have broken the yoke of the king of Babylon. The verb is a prophetic perfect. When the prophecy is repeated in vv 4 and 11, an imperfect verb is used. Weiser says we now hear "God's word against God's word." Hananiah's preaching echoes the preaching of Isaiah:

> Indeed the yoke of his burden, and the bar on his shoulder, the rod of one oppressing him, you shattered as on the day of Midian.
>
> (Isa 9:3[Eng 9:4])

> And it will happen in that day: his burden will be removed from your shoulder, and his yoke from your neck will be destroyed.
>
> (Isa 10:27)

> And his yoke will be removed from them, and his burden from his shoulder removed.
>
> (Isa 14:25)

However right this message was coming from Isaiah, it is now wrong. Von Rad (1965: 129) points out that the prophetic message is not timeless truth but a "particular word relevant to a particular hour in history." When lifted from its context, it can become a lie (v 17). On Hananiah and the preaching tradition of Isaiah, see Quell (1952: 59–60), Kraus (1964: 90–91), Overholt (1967: 244–45; 1970: 40), Buber (1968: 168), and Zimmerli (1995: 420–21). Jeremiah met up with a similar opposition when his Temple Oracles questioned Zion theology and preaching from Isaiah (see Note for 7:4).

3. *Within two years' time I will bring back to this place all the vessels of the house of Yahweh that Nebuchadnezzar, king of Babylon, took from this place and brought to Babylon.* Another explicit contradiction of what Jeremiah said in 27:16. What Hananiah promises here did not happen.

Within two years' time. Hebrew *bĕʿôd šĕnātayim yāmîm.* Or "within two full years" (AV; cf. GKC §131d; Gen 41:1; 2 Sam 13:23). Prophecies stating a definite time of fulfillment are rare, yet Jeremiah is similarly specific in prophesying Hananiah's death (v 16: "This year you will die").

all the vessels. Hebrew *ʾet-kol-kĕlê.* The LXX omits "all," which could be attributed to haplography (homoeoarcton: *kl . . . kl*). Giesebrecht considers haplography a possibility, noting that G^L, Vg, S, and T all have the term. The LXX

omits "all" in "all the exiles" in v 4 but otherwise retains the term, having "all
the exiles" in v 6; "all the people" in vv 1, 5, 7, 10 (not in MT), and 11; and "all
the nations" in vv 11 and 14. Janzen (1973: 65–67) says the particle *kol* ("all")
occurs over 500 times in the book of Jeremiah, and while it is difficult to know
whether a given plus or minus is original, he generally views the pluses,
whether in the LXX or MT, as secondary. But none of the zero variants discussed by Janzen is said to result from haplography. Here in chap. 28, any conclusion that the particle represents an MT expansion is largely conjecture.

that Nebuchadnezzar, king of Babylon, took from this place and brought to
Babylon. Lacking in the LXX but present in T and Vg. Some commentators delete with Duhm and Cornill, but the phrase is best retained (Volz, Rudolph,
Weiser, Bright). D. N. Freedman points out that if the final *bābel* ("Babylon")
was originally *bābelâ* ("to Babylon"), which is what we would expect here (see
v 4 and eight other times in chaps. 27–29: 27:18, 20, 22; 29:1, 3, 4, 15, 20), the
loss of the entire phrase could then be attributed to haplography (homoeoteleuton: *h . . . h*).

4. *And Jeconiah son of Jehoiakim, king of Judah, and all the exiles of Judah*
who came to Babylon, I will bring back to this place. A direct contradiction of
Jeremiah's prophecy that (Je)coniah (= Jehoiachin) would die in a foreign land
(22:26–27). Calvin finds this a remarkable utterance with Zedekiah occupying
the throne, because if Jehoiachin returns, Zedekiah will be deposed. Perhaps
Zedekiah is too weak to override popular sentiment. Nebuchadnezzar's preferential treatment of Jehoiachin in exile, known from a cuneiform text roughly
contemporary (see Note for 52:34), was doubtless intended to divide people's
loyalties. That is precisely the situation here.

Jeconiah. This shortened spelling of Jehoiachin, *yĕkonyâ*, occurs also in
27:20 (Q) and 29:2. For other spellings of this king's name in the OT, see Note
for 22:24.

son of Jehoiakim, king of Judah. The LXX omits, which may be attributed to
haplography (homoeoteleuton: *h . . . h*). The T and Vg have the words.

who came to Babylon, I will bring back to this place—oracle of Yahweh. The
LXX omits, probably more loss due to haplography (homoeoteleuton: *h . . . h*).
The T and Vg have the words.

5. *Then Jeremiah the prophet said to Hananiah the prophet.* Jeremiah now
speaks directly to Hananiah; therefore, we may take Hananiah's oracles in
vv 2–4 as being directed to Jeremiah, which argues against deleting "to me"
in v 1. The priests and people are onlookers, although we note in v 7 that
Jeremiah has included "all the people" in his audience. With both Jeremiah
and Hananiah given the designation "the prophet," added weight is attached
to the confrontation. Both are prophets; more than that, both are Yahweh
prophets. There is also irony in the assumed parity (Bright). The LXX omits
both occurrences of "the prophet," which is a more impoverished reading.

in the presence of the priests and in the presence of all the people who were
standing in the house of Yahweh. The LXX inverts "priests" and "people," as it
does also in 27:16. It is pointed out by Duhm, and again more recently by

Renkema (1997), that with the LXX order the priests alone can be the subject of *hāʿōmĕdîm*, allowing the participle to be translated, "who were serving/officiating (in the house of Yahweh)." See Pss 134:1; 135:2; and Neh 12:44 for *ʿmd* meaning "serve/officiate." This would call attention to the official status of the priests who are present. But whether the LXX reading is more original appears doubtful. In the MT of chaps. 21–52, "priests" always precedes "people," even in poetry (31:14). And here in the present verse T and Vg support MT.

6. *Amen! So may Yahweh do! May Yahweh confirm your words that you have prophesied — to bring back the vessels of the house of Yahweh and all the exiles from Babylon to this place!* Jeremiah's response is highly ironic (*epitrope*; see Note for 7:21). Having recently said that the exiles and Temple vessels would not soon come back, he is not now agreeing with Hananiah. Even if he wished for their return, he knew it would not happen. Holladay says that Jeremiah is mocking Hananiah, comparing his words to those of Micaiah in 1 Kgs 22:15. Quell (1952: 46) thinks that Jeremiah shows here a lack of conviction in his own words of doom, but that is wide of the mark (Rudolph; Kraus 1964: 95). For well over a decade, Jeremiah has had dealings with these prophets of "shalom" and is not now suddenly fooled by preaching from one of their number. This is a confrontation that has been waiting to happen; the positions of each were decided some time ago.

Amen. Hebrew *ʾāmēn.* Literally, "it is true" (11:5; 1 Kgs 1:36; Ps 41:14[Eng 41:13]), but here, because of the optative imperfects and ironic tone, it means: "Be it true (even though it is not true)!"

So may Yahweh do! May Yahweh confirm your words. The imperfect verbs *yaʿăśeh* and *yāqēm* are jussives expressing a wish: "May (Yahweh) do! May (Yahweh) confirm" (GKC §109b). The LXX lacks the second "Yahweh," but T and Vg both have it. The H-stem of the root *qwm* ("to confirm") is lit. "to make stand" (29:10; 33:14; 35:16; Deut 9:5; 1 Sam 15:13; 1 Kgs 12:15). In the NT, see Rom 15:8. Jeremiah is pretending to wish a successful outcome to Hananiah's words. The LXX, some Heb MSS, and T have "your word," singular, which may have been influenced by "this word," singular, in v 7. The Vg has "your words," plural (*verba tua*).

7. *But do hear this word that I speak in your ears and in the ears of all the people.* Jeremiah directs his response not simply to Hananiah but also to the people assembled. It may be significant that the priests, who are also present and figure prominently in the audience, remain unacknowledged. Hebrew *ʾak* ("but") is a sharp adversative, introducing an idea of contrariness (see Note for 5:4).

this word. Hebrew *dābār* here means "witness," not the preached word per se. Volz says "word of reservation." The LXX incorrectly expands to *ton logon kuriou*, "the word of the Lord." The T and Vg (*verbum hoc*) have simply "this word."

8–9. *The prophets who . . . prophesied . . . war and evil and pestilence. . . . The prophet who prophesies peace. . . .* Jeremiah does not counter here with an oracle of his own, which he could have. Maybe it was unnecessary. Only recently had the priests and people heard his oracle that the Temple treasures would not be returning from Babylon. Jeremiah had told them also to serve the king of Babylon and live (27:16–17). So now, rather than repeat his earlier oracle, he makes a general point about true and false prophecy. Digressions of this sort occur elsewhere in the Jeremianic discourse (see Note for 27:5). The particular argument used here is called a *distributio* in the classical rhetorical handbooks (*ad Herennium* iv 35), a figure that not only compares but apportions (Brandt 1970: 133–35). The emphasis is placed on prophets and prophecies of peace. For this discourse as an example of Jeremiah's breakaway from authority preaching, see Lundbom 1991b: 21–22.

8. *The prophets who were before me and before you, from ancient times, yes, they prophesied to many lands and against great kingdoms of war and evil and pestilence.* Jeremiah doubtless has in mind prophets such as Amos, Micah, Isaiah, Zephaniah, and others in the classical tradition. He is not saying, however, that all true prophets in the past were prophets of doom (*pace* Volz). The question of doom prophecy should actually have been settled over a decade ago, when Jeremiah's harsh words about Jerusalem and the Temple were recognized as having a precedent in the preaching of Micah (26:18). Jeremiah has himself been preaching oracles of doom against foreign nations, including Babylon, for a decade or more. Hananiah's oracles, too, could certainly qualify as the preaching of war against Babylon. Viewed as such, Jeremiah's statement here may be seen as a skillful attempt to make common cause with his opponent. The general principle applies to them both.

before me and before you. Another rhetorical move in which Jeremiah, at least for the present, is treating Hananiah as an equal and a prophet the same as he.

from ancient times. Or "from time immemorial." Hebrew *min-hā'ôlām*. The term *'ôlām* is indeterminate past or future time (5:15b; 6:16).

yes, they prophesied to many lands and against great kingdoms. The *waw* on the converted imperfect *wayyinnābĕ'û* is here translated (following the LXX, T, and Vg): "yes, they prophesied," but as a *casus pendens* it can go untranslated (GKC §111h; 143d; cf. 6:19; 33:24), as it does in all modern Versions since the AV. Compare also "many nations and great kings" in 25:14 and 27:7.

of war and evil and pestilence. The same triad appears in T, but "and evil and pestilence" is lacking in the LXX, perhaps in the interest of contrasting just "war" with "peace" in the next verse. The usual triad is "sword, famine, and pestilence." Since the triad here is different, "evil" (*rā'â*) should not be replaced with "famine" (*rā'āb*), in spite of MS support for this reading.

9. *The prophet who prophesies peace, when the word of the prophet comes to be, the prophet whom Yahweh has truly sent will be known.* Since a general principle is still being expounded, the imperfect *yinnābē'* should be translated present tense: "prophesies" (*pace* Holladay). Jeremiah at first sight seems to be citing the test for true prophecy in Deut 18:21–22; however, there, prophecies of doom are at issue, since people are told that, when prophecies go unfulfilled, "*You need not be afraid* of him" (Crenshaw 1971: 53; Childs 1985: 133–34). Now Jeremiah extends the test of fulfillment or nonfulfillment to

prophecies of peace. The issue turns finally on whether Yahweh has truly "sent" the prophet, as we know from judgments elsewhere against the peace prophets (23:21, 32; 27:15), from Jeremiah's parting word to Hananiah (28:15), and from Jeremiah's trial, where his defense rested on the testimony that Yahweh had "sent" him (26:12–15). On Yahweh's disclaimer about not having "sent" the peace prophets, see Note for 23:32. The legislation of Deut 18:21–22, which probably does figure in here, is repeated in the Qumran *Temple Scroll* (11QT 61:2–5; Yadin 1983: 277).

when the word of the prophet comes to be. The LXX omits "the prophet," even though it is not a title here. The Vg also omits, but not T. Here the verb *bō'* means "comes to be, is fulfilled" (Rabinowitz 1972–73: 130).

10. *Then Hananiah the prophet took the yoke bar from upon the neck of Jeremiah the prophet and broke it.* Duhm says: "Kurz und bündig!" ("Short and decisive!"). Hananiah carries out a symbolic action just as Jeremiah does, and for those looking on, it may appear as though this has rendered Jeremiah's prophecy ineffective. On the other hand, symbolic action, however efficacious in bringing prophecy to pass, has no power if Yahweh is not behind it. We see symbolic action come to nothing when Zedekiah son of Chenaanah parades before Ahab and Jehoshaphat with his horns of iron and strikes the prophet Micaiah on the cheek for an opposing word from Yahweh (1 Kgs 22:11–12, 24–28); also when Jehoiakim burns the Jeremiah scroll (36:23). On symbolic action elsewhere in the book of Jeremiah, see Note for 13:1. The LXX and S have "yoke bars," plural, which is the reading in vv 12–13. The LXX also adds "in the sight of all the people" after "Hananiah," which is not present in T or Vg.

and broke it. Hebrew *wayyišbĕrēhû.* Some scholars (Cornill; Ehrlich 1912: 313; Rudolph) emend the masculine suffix *hû* to a feminine *hā*, which one expects in light of the feminine noun *môṭâ* ("yoke bar"). The final *waw* could be accidental dittography (D. N. Freedman). Rudolph wonders too whether the narrator may have had *'ōl* ("yoke") in mind.

11. *Even so will I break the yoke of Nebuchadnezzar, king of Babylon, within two years' time from upon the neck of all the nations.* The LXX omits "within two years' time," but Aq, Theod, T, and Vg all have the words. Malamat (1975: 137 n. 32) translates *bĕ'ôd šĕnātayim yāmîm* as "in another two years" (T: "at the end of two years"), which from the present would have been ca. 591 B.C. and would connect with the date given in Ezek 20:1 (1975: 138–39). Ezekiel 20 reports a visit of elders to Ezekiel, possibly to inquire of Yahweh about the release of exiles. Sarna (1978: 95–96) dates the Jerusalem conference and the incident here to 597 B.C., pointing out that two years would put Hananiah's prophecy at the actual date of the rebellion in Babylon, i.e., 595 B.C. Hananiah, in any case, is wrong to say "within two years," and it is the time factor that makes his prophecy false and Jeremiah's true. The exile would not end in two years. It is not that Hananiah held out hope for the covenant people whereas Jeremiah held no hope. Hananiah simply failed to see the dreadful fall of the nation to Nebuchadnezzar, whereas Jeremiah did see it. For Jere-

miah, hope was on the other side of judgment—after some 70 years of Babylonian rule, according to 25:11–12 and 29:10. Also, it is not coming up with a "time certain" that makes Hananiah a false prophet, since Jeremiah too set a "time certain" for Hananiah's death, and that was fulfilled.

Even so will I break. Hebrew *kākâ 'ešbōr*. Jeremiah uses precisely the same words when breaking his decanter in the Ben Hinnom Valley (19:11). For other dramatic comparisons using *kākâ* ("even so"), see 13:9 and 51:64.

And Jeremiah the prophet went his way. Questions have been raised why Jeremiah acted in this manner. Has the good prophet lost his resolve? Is Hananiah the victor now, with the yoke lying broken on the ground? Duhm says that "here no sensible words will help, [Jeremiah] cannot quarrel as a market-crier with rivals." But Elie Wiesel (1981: 116) says this about Jeremiah's departure:

> That was wrong, as many scholars agree. Jeremiah was duty-bound to speak up. Either he is sure of himself and of God, or he is not. If not, he has no right to demoralize an entire nation; if he is sure, he is obliged to confront Hananiah and tell him the truth: that his illusions are dangerous, as illusions always are. His "Amen" is out of place. From Jeremiah we expect words of truth, not clichés of compromise. The spokesman for God thus becomes an echo for a false prophet.

But what about the audience? Was it hostile, and if so, might not leaving the scene be the better part of wisdom? Jeremiah may have remembered his day in court (Weiser), at which time support came from the princes and certain elders in attendance, but angry priests also there were calling for his death. If the priests now in the audience are once again hostile, as well they might be, it makes very good sense for Jeremiah to "go his way." Having done so, he lives to preach another day. His departure says nothing about being unsure of his message, lacking resolve, or not knowing whether Hananiah is or is not an authentic spokesman of Yahweh (*pace* Crenshaw 1971: 73). For the present, he has gone as far as he can go, and by allowing his opponent the last word, even though it be a false word, he fares better than by making a rebuttal. The silence will have been damning. Let the foolishness of this prophet ring in the ears of the priests and the people, and also in his own ears! Martin Buber gives another explanation. He says that, although Jeremiah knew like no other prophet knew that he had been called by God, and now most recently was made to wear the yoke to show that God had given the nations over to Nebuchadnezzar, there were still things he did not know.

> God had, indeed, spoken to him only an hour before. But this was another hour. History is a dynamic process, and history means that one hour is never like the one that has gone before. . . . One must not rely on one's knowledge. One must go one's way and listen all over again.
>
> (Buber 1968: 166–67)

12. *Then the word of Yahweh came to Jeremiah.* Hebrew *wayĕhî dĕbar-yhwh ʾel-yirmĕyâ*. This third-person superscription, sometimes expanded, occurs eleven times in the book (28:12; 29:30; 32:26; 33:1, 19, 23; 34:12; 35:12; 36:27; 42:7; and 43:8). For the first-person form, see Note for 1:4. The AV adds "the prophet" after "Jeremiah," which occurs later in the verse, but not here. It happens again following the fall of Jerusalem (42:7) that Jeremiah is forced to endure an extremely difficult situation, where he is expected to speak directly to the people, yet must wait patiently and obediently for the word of Yahweh to come to him (Zimmerli 1982: 95).

from upon the neck of Jeremiah the prophet. The LXX has "from his neck," but Aq, S, T, and Vg all have "neck of Jeremiah," supporting MT.

13. *Go and you shall say to Hananiah.* Hebrew *hālôk wĕʾāmartā*. This construction, the infinitive absolute *hālôk* paired with a perfect verb used to command, appears frequently in the Jeremianic prose (2:2a; 3:12; 13:1; 17:19; 19:1; 28:13; 34:2; 35:2, 13; 39:16). How soon after Jeremiah's first encounter with Hananiah this directive came is not known. Was there still a Temple audience on hand to hear the prediction of Hananiah's death?

Yoke bars of wood you have broken, but you have made in their place yoke bars of iron. The line is a syntactic chiasmus. The LXX has "I will make," which may be influenced by what follows (v 14): "A yoke of iron I have put upon the neck." The T and Vg (*facies*) support MT, although with future verbs. The MT, which is the *lectio difficilior*, is generally read (Cheyne; Volz; Weiser; Rudolph; Bright; Holladay; McKane; cf. NRSV changing from RSV, and NJB changing from JB). It goes without saying that Hananiah will not himself make a yoke; the point is that by prophesying as he has Hananiah is shaping the future in a way that he does not know. It was said earlier regarding prophets and various seers of other nations that they too, by preaching a lie, were unwittingly bringing about the very thing they wanted most to avoid (27:10). False preaching is not a trifle; it aids in bringing about precisely what one wants not to happen.

yoke bars of iron. Hebrew *mōṭôt barzel*. The Hebrew term for "iron," *barzel*, is of foreign origin (cf. 15:12), having also pejorative associations in the OT (Sawyer 1983: 131–32). Regarding Ezek 27:19, where Tyre appears to be trading in polished iron from Uzal in the Anatolian mountains (= ancient Hittite Empire; modern-day Turkey), see Elat 1983.

14. *A yoke of iron I have put upon the neck of all these nations to serve Nebuchadnezzar.* Here "yoke of iron" (*ʿōl barzel*) is used, the term appearing in the curse of Deut 28:48. This is another indication that two "yoke bars" make up a "yoke." "I have put" is a prophetic perfect.

all these nations. The LXX lacks "these" but has the "all." The Vg (*gentium istarum*) has "these" but not "all." Aquila, Theod, and T read with MT. The inclusion of "these" bears on the interpretation, for it suggests that the foreign envoys are still in Jerusalem (Rudolph).

and they shall serve him; even the beasts of the field I have given to him. The LXX omits, which could be due to haplography (homoeoarcton: *w . . . w*). The T and Vg have the words. On "beasts of the field," see 27:6.

15. *the prophet: Do listen, Hananiah.* The LXX omits, which may be due to haplography even though the LXX—except for v 1, where it has *pseudoproph-ētēs*—otherwise omits "the prophet" as a title in the chapter (whole-word: *hnnyh . . . hnnyh*). Giesebrecht suggests haplography, noting that the words are present in G^L, S, T, and Vg. If "the prophet" was at one time present in the Hebrew *Vorlage* to the LXX, the term could be original and not MT expansion, as many assume.

Yahweh has not sent you. The defining judgment on Hananiah; see v 9, and Note for 23:32.

and you, you have made this people trust in a lie. The LXX has *ep' adikō*, "in a wrong"; Aq and Symm *epi pseudei*, "in a lie" (cf. 27:16). The expression "trust in (the words of) a lie / the Lie" appears frequently in Jeremianic prose (7:4, 8; 13:25; 28:15; and 29:31; Holladay 1960: 356). People are supposed to put their trust in Yahweh (17:7; 39:18), and prophets speaking the truth make this happen. From the charge here Hananiah becomes designated a false prophet in the LXX and T. What makes him false is a false message (Overholt 1970: 45, 75, 85; Childs 1985: 139). In Hebrew thought, authenticity or its lack does not reside within a person's being, even though it is true enough that prophets consistently prove to be genuine or ingenuine. But we must not think of prophets as having a "good essence" making them true, or a "bad essence" making them false. If that were the case, then true prophets would always be true and false prophets always false. The prophet proves true by authentic speech and authentic action and false by inauthentic speech and inauthentic action. Each word and deed comes from a specific inspiration or lack of the same, which we judge to be true or false (A. B. Davidson 1895: 1).

16. *Look I will send you away.* Hebrew *hinĕnî mĕšallēḥăkā*. The Piel of *šlḥ* is forceful: "send away." A wordplay is made with "Yahweh *has not sent you (lō'-šĕlāḥăkā)*" in v 15 (Hitzig). Yahweh has not *sent* Hananiah to prophesy, but now is *sending* him—off the earth. Hananiah will die. Compare similar wordplays on *qr' drwr*, "proclaim liberty," in 34:17; on *m's*, "reject," in 1 Sam 15:23; and on *yrd*, "come down," in 2 Kgs 1:9–10, 11–12 (Lundbom 1973: 46).

the face of the earth. Hebrew *pĕnê hā'ădāmâ*. See 25:26; 35:7; and 1 Kgs 13:34. The phrase can also translate as "the (surface of the) ground" (8:2; 16:4; 25:33; Gen 2:6; 4:14).

This year you will die, for you have spoken rebellion concerning Yahweh. Jeremiah too is capable of time-specific prophecy. The T reads: "This year you shall die, and in another year you shall be buried," but Kimḥi says the plain meaning is that Hananiah will die within a year of the prophecy, and indeed he did die, in the seventh month. This sentence of death falls under the provisions stated in Deut 18:20, although because it speaks of "rebellion" (*sārâ*) against Yahweh, it might also fall under the provisions of Deut 13:6[Eng 13:5]. However, this latter passage does not apply to false prophecy in Yahweh's name but to false prophecy in the name of other gods. Shemaiah, a prophet in Babylon, is given similar judgment for preaching "rebellion" against Yahweh (29:32). The words "for you have spoken rebellion against Yahweh" are lacking in the LXX but present in G^L, Aq, Theod, S, T, and Vg. They should therefore be retained (Volz; Weiser).

17. *And Hananiah the prophet died in that year, in the seventh month.* The style is laconic, similar to the summary statements in 26:24 and 36:8, 32. The seventh month is Tishri (September/October). Omitted in the LXX are the words, "Hananiah the prophet in that year," but as Giesebrecht notes, Aq, Symm, Theod, G^L, S, T, and Vg all have them. There is thus slim basis for their deletion (*pace* Cornill; Holladay; McKane). The T expands to "and was buried in the seventh month." Hananiah's death occurred just two months after his prophecy (v 1). Yahweh brought it about, and in so doing decided the question of truth and falsity. When Jeremiah was on trial, the outcome was determined by Jeremiah's own witness, the testimony of elders, the judgment of the princes, and the protection given after the trial by Ahikam son of Shaphan (chap. 26). One might speak, then, in the present situation about the power and efficacy of the prophetic word (Lindblom 1965: 200). Calvin says Hananiah was driven out of the world by the mere sound of Jeremiah's tongue. Malamat (1975: 139–40) suggests a connection between the death of Hananiah and the difficult verse in Ezek 14:9, where Yahweh says: "And if the prophet be deceived and speaks a word, I, Yahweh, I have deceived that prophet, and I will stretch out my hand against him, and will destroy him from the midst of my people Israel." See also in this connection 1 Kgs 22:19–22.

MESSAGE AND AUDIENCE

This narrative begins by quoting Jeremiah as saying that Hananiah ben Azzur, the prophet from Gibeon, spoke to him in the Temple precincts before an audience of priests and people. In an initial oracle, Hananiah reported Yahweh as saying that he had broken the yoke of the king of Babylon and that within two years all the Temple treasures taken to Babylon in the loot of 597 B.C. would be brought back to where the people now stand. In a second oracle, Hananiah reports Yahweh as saying that Jeconiah and all the exiles taken to Babylon would likewise be returned, for the yoke of the king of Babylon had indeed been broken.

What follows is Jeremiah's response to Hananiah and the people assembled. He relieves the tension, but only temporarily, by feigned agreement with his opposite number. He says "Amen!" Would that Yahweh confirm this word about the Temple vessels and exiles' returning from Babylon. However, the assembled would do well to hear a word he has to speak. The stage is set for Jeremiah to repeat his contrary word from Yahweh, which some, no doubt, have heard before. But Jeremiah counters with neither an old oracle nor a new one, preferring instead a general word on prophets and prophecy. He tells Hananiah that prophets before both of them have prophesied war, evil, and pestilence, against many lands and great kingdoms—not just against Israel and Judah, but against the nations of the world. Foreign envoys may still be in the city. As for the prophet prophesying peace, says Jeremiah, when that word has been fulfilled, then it will be known that Yahweh has truly sent that prophet. The wait could be a long one. Hananiah has set a limit of two years. Jeremiah's move is a deft one. He himself has been preaching against neighboring nations, and Hananiah now is preaching rebellion against Babylon. Who is the prophet of peace? And who is the prophet of war, evil, and pestilence? Jeremiah does not give an answer. Those in the audience must make up their own minds. If the crowd is hostile, it cannot resort to violent action on hearing such words. But Hananiah, who was probably angry before things began, now becomes physical, pulling the yoke bar off Jeremiah's neck and breaking it. He is ready also with a third oracle summarizing the other two: in two years the yoke of Nebuchadnezzar will be broken from the neck of all the nations. The nations are on his mind too. Is this Hananiah's answer to Jeremiah's test for the true prophet?

What will Jeremiah do next? His prophecy has been roundly contradicted; at the hands of Hananiah he has been publicly shamed. No mention is made of anyone intervening on Jeremiah's behalf. The narrator says simply that Jeremiah "went his way." There was probably little else he could do. That his decision was the right one can be assumed in that he was able to walk away. No one harmed him. Humiliated he was, but in no way forced to back down.

The audience then learns that Jeremiah received another word from Yahweh and is told what happened next. If Jeremiah failed to deliver an oracle when he and Hananiah first met, he is not without oracles now. In a first oracle, he is instructed to tell Hananiah: "Yoke bars of wood you have broken, but you have made in their place yoke bars of iron." In a second oracle, Yahweh says that he has put an iron yoke on all the nations, a veiled reference doubtless to the nations recently represented in Jerusalem, but also to other nations not represented. All will have to serve Nebuchadnezzar. Yahweh has given even the wild animals over to him! Jeremiah is not finished.

After telling Hananiah straight out that Yahweh has not sent him and that his prophecy is making the people trust in a lie, he says in a final oracle that Yahweh is sending Hananiah off the face of the earth. Once, a prophet not sent; now, a prophet who is being sent. This very year Hananiah will die, for he has spoken rebellion not simply against Nebuchadnezzar but against Yahweh. If Jeremiah was cautious, indirect, and willing to suffer abuse in his first encounter with Hananiah, he is none of these things now. One cannot imagine a more direct, a more stinging, and a more specific prophetic utterance. The narrator concludes in laconic style: "Hananiah the prophet died in that year, in the seventh month." Jeremiah's word was fulfilled in two months! The audience is thus brought back to the beginning, where it was told that this incident took place in the fourth year of Zedekiah, the fifth month. A date for this narrative, then, is anytime after 594–593 B.C.

When this incident took place, there had to be uncertainty in the minds of some about which word was Yahweh's word and which prophet was Yahweh's prophet. For later audiences who might have heard a report such as we have presently in the narrative, it was clear that Jeremiah had spoken the truth, even if it was not clear that Hananiah had spoken a lie. For post-586 audiences hearing the narrative as we have it before us, there was no longer any doubt that Jeremiah was the true prophet speaking a true word and Hananiah a false prophet speaking a lie (Childs 1985: 140–41).

An audience hearing this narrative following the narrative of chap. 27 would appreciate how things at the time were building to a grand climax. Jeremiah's word mandating submission to the king of Babylon is given first to foreign envoys visiting the city, then to King Zedekiah, and then to priests and the people of Jerusalem. When will it be spoken to the prophets? The audience knows that they were the ones most offended, because Jeremiah had been telling everyone not to listen to them. What comes now in chap. 28 is a face-to-face meeting between Jeremiah and a lead prophet of the opposition. This has to rank as one of the most extraordinary encounters between true and false prophets in the Bible, comparable only with the meeting of Elijah and the prophets of Baal on Mount Carmel, where Yahweh's word and truth itself shines forth with unbelievable clarity.

In the NT, in the Acts of the Apostles, the following incident is reported:

> But a man named Ananias, with the consent of his wife Sapphira, sold a piece of property; with his wife's knowledge, he kept back some of the proceeds, and brought only a part and laid it at the apostles' feet. "Ananias," Peter asked, "why has Satan filled your heart to lie to the Holy Spirit and to keep back part of the proceeds of the land?" . . . Now when Ananias heard these words, he fell down and died. And great fear seized all who heard of it. . . . After an interval of about three hours his wife came in, not knowing what had happened. . . . Then Peter said to her, "How is it that you have agreed together to put the Spirit of the Lord to the test? Look, the feet of those who have buried your husband are at the door, and they will carry you out." Immediately she fell down at his feet and died. . . . And great fear seized the whole church and all who heard of these things.
>
> (Acts 5:1–11, NRSV)

Savonarola, prophet-friar of the late fifteenth century, predicted from his pulpit in Florence that Fra Mariano, who had preached a vicious sermon against him and was presently in Rome conspiring for his downfall, would die. The following year he did die. Savonarola predicted other deaths, e.g., that of King Charles VIII of France in 1497, which came to pass a year later (Ridolfi 1959: 186–89).

F. LETTERS TO THE EXILES (29:1–32)

1. Bloom Where You Are Planted! (29:1–23)

29 ¹And these are the words of the letter that Jeremiah the prophet sent from Jerusalem to the remnant of the elders of the exile, and to the priests and to the prophets, and to all the people whom Nebuchadnezzar exiled

from Jerusalem to Babylon—[2]after Jeconiah, the king, and the queen
mother and the eunuchs, the princes of Judah and Jerusalem, and the
craftsmen and the smiths had gone out from Jerusalem—[3]by the hand of
Elasah son of Shaphan and Gemariah son of Hilkiah, whom Zedekiah,
king of Judah, sent to Nebuchadnezzar, king of Babylon, in Babylon:
   [4]Thus said Yahweh of hosts, God of Israel, to all the exiles whom I
exiled from Jerusalem to Babylon:
   [5]Build houses and live in them; and plant gardens and eat their fruit.
[6]Take wives and beget sons and daughters, and take for your sons
wives, and your daughters give to husbands, and let them bear sons
and daughters. Yes, multiply there, and do not decrease. [7]And seek the
welfare of the city where I have exiled you, and pray on its behalf to
Yahweh, for in its welfare will be welfare for you.

[8]For thus said Yahweh of hosts, God of Israel:
Do not let your prophets who are in your midst or your diviners deceive you; also do not listen to your dreamers[a] whom you cause to
dream. [9]For by a lie they are prophesying to you in my name. I have
not sent them—oracle of Yahweh.

[10]For thus said Yahweh:
When Babylon has completed seventy years before me, I will attend to
you and confirm upon you my good word to bring you back to this
place. [11]For I, I know the plans that I am planning concerning you—
oracle of Yahweh—plans of welfare and not for evil, to give to you a
future and a hope. [12]And you will call me and will come and pray to
me, and I will listen to you. [13]And you will search for me and will find
if you seek me with your whole heart.

   [14]And I will be found by you
      —oracle of Yahweh—
      and I will restore your fortunes.

And I will gather you from all the nations and from all the places
where I have dispersed you—oracle of Yahweh—and I will bring you
back to the place from which I exiled you.
[15]Because you have said, 'Yahweh has raised up for us prophets in
Babylon':
   [16]For thus said Yahweh concerning the king who sits on the throne of
David and concerning all the people who sit in this city—your brothers who did not go out with you into exile:

---

[a]Repointing MT's *hălōmōtêkem* ("your dreams") to *ḥalōmōtêkem* or emending to *ḥōlĕmêkem*
("your dreamers"), to achieve consistency with "your prophets" and "your diviners," as in 27:9
(see Notes).

[17]Thus said Yahweh of hosts:
Look I am sending against them sword, famine, and pestilence, and I will make them like horrid figs, which cannot be eaten they are so bad. [18]And I will pursue them by sword, by famine, and by pestilence, and I will make them a fright to all the kingdoms of the earth—a curse, and a desolation, and an object of hissing, and a reproach among all the nations where I have dispersed them—[19]inasmuch as they have not listened to my words—oracle of Yahweh—which I sent to them by my servants the prophets—constantly I sent—and you did not listen—oracle of Yahweh.
[20]Now you! Hear the word of Yahweh, all the exiles whom I sent away from Jerusalem to Babylon:
[21]Thus said Yahweh of hosts, God of Israel, concerning Ahab son of Kolaiah and concerning Zedekiah son of Maaseiah, who are prophesying a lie to you in my name:
Look I will give them into the hand of Nebuchadrezzar, king of Babylon, and he will strike them down before your eyes. [22]From them will be taken up a swearword for all the exiles of Judah who are in Babylon: 'Yahweh make you like Zedekiah and like Ahab, whom the king of Babylon roasted in the fire,' [23]because they did a scandalous thing in Israel, yes, they committed adultery with the wives of their fellows and have spoken a lying word in my name that I did not command them. But I am he who knows[b] and am witness—oracle of Yahweh.

RHETORIC AND COMPOSITION

MT 29:1–23 = LXX 36:1–23. The present chapter contains a letter sent by Jeremiah to the exiles in Babylon (vv 1–23), to which has been appended another letter fragment sent by the prophet later on (vv 24–28). That we have also a subsequent letter is clear in that v 28 quotes v 5 of the first letter. The chapter concludes by narrating the response in Jerusalem to letters that arrived from a prophet in Babylon, and Jeremiah's judgment on that prophet (vv 29–32). Chapter 29 balances chap. 24 in a rhetorical structure comprising 24, 27–29 (see Rhetoric and Composition for 24:1–10).

This main letter with its introduction is demarcated at the top end by the introduction (vv 1–3), before which is a *petuḥah* in M^A and M^L and a *setumah* in M^P before v 1. This is also a chapter division. At the bottom end, demarcation is by a *setumah* in M^L and a *petuḥah* in M^P after v 23. The M^A for 29:9b–31:35a is not extant; therefore, its sections after v 9b are not known. The M^L (only) has a *setumah* after v 3, setting off the introduction from the letter itself. After v 7, M^L has a *petuḥah* that separates the first two oracles in the letter. The M^A, M^P, and one MS in the Cambridge Genizah Collection (NS 58.46) have no section

---

[b]Reading the Kt as *hûʾ yōdēaʿ* ("he who knows") with J. D. Michaelis (see Notes); Q *hayyôdēaʿ* is "the one who knows."

here. The M^L, M^P, and one MS in the Cambridge Genizah Collection (NS 58.37) have a *setumah* after v 15, which is a problematic verse and may be out of place. The M^P (only) has a *setumah* after v 17, the purpose of which is unclear. The M^P has a *petuḥah* after v 19, marking the conclusion of Oracle VI. The M^L has a *setumah* and the M^P a *petuḥah* after v 20, which separates the introductory word of v 20 from the oracle following.

As with other chapters in the Zedekiah Cluster, particularly chap. 27, a great deal of discussion has centered on the shorter LXX text and the original form of the chapter as a whole. The main omission in the LXX is vv 16–20, which many scholars delete, even though some (Cornill; Rudolph; Hyatt) have conceded that the loss might be due to haplography (homoeoarcton: *k . . . k* or whole word plus: *m bblh . . . m bblh*). Janzen (1973: 118) prefers the haplography explantion, and so also does Holladay in his complicated reconstruction. G^L contains vv 16–20, but places v 15 after v 20. The main reason given for deleting vv 16–20 is that a judgment on Jerusalem is said to be of no relevance to the Babylonian community (Peake; Welch 1921a: 362; Carroll). But Peake adds: "It is difficult to see why a post-exilic editor should have inserted the passage, the distinction between the Jews in exile with Jehoiachin and those in Jerusalem with Zedekiah having lost all significance with the destruction of the Jewish State." It was surely of more than just passing interest to the Babylonian exiles what would happen in Jerusalem, since the future of one community was tied up inseparably with the other. The two communities were contrasted as good and bad figs in chap. 24. Furthermore, if Jeremiah could speak about Babylon in chap. 27 to a Jerusalem audience, why could he not speak about Jerusalem in chap. 29 to an audience in Babylon? The prophet Ezekiel, who was living in Babylon, had a lot more to say about Jerusalem than about what was going on in Babylon. Calvin says that Jeremiah's letter here has a twofold aim: 1) to comfort the exiles and 2) to break down the obstinacy of his own nation.

Another objection to the inclusion of vv 16–20 in the letter is that it raises the question of how Jeremiah could speak ill of a reigning king in a letter carried by royal messengers (Volz). One could always say that the king had no knowledge of the letter being sent, but surely he would learn about it at some point. More likely Zedekiah was powerless to intervene if he did know, particularly if he was newly enthroned. How could Zedekiah countenance the oracle on the bad figs (24:8–10) coming from Jeremiah or later oracles during a decade of rule that demeaned him and the people of Jerusalem (21:4–6, 7; 37:7, 9–10, 17; 38:2, 3, 17–18)? Verses 16–20 belong to this letter and must be retained. Their loss in the LXX is simply one of fifteen arguable cases of haplography in the chapter.

Most commentators (Giesebrecht; Duhm; Peake; Cornill; Volz; Rudolph; Weiser; Hyatt; Bright) assign the prose here to Baruch or Source B, although with the qualification that it has probably undergone a later editing. Peake is impressed with the detailed references to persons and events. Mowinckel (1914: 24) assigned vv 24–32 to Source B, but not vv 1–23, which he said were

Source C. One can understand the latter assignment, in that this narrative is largely comprised of prose oracles in which one finds the stereotyped and repetitive language said to characterize Source C.

The chapter is narrative, reporting oracles lifted from two Jeremianic letters, and a final oracle destined for a third letter. The letters are not preserved in their original form. Jeremiah's second letter, as I mentioned, is only part of an original letter that was larger. Also, these "letters" lack formal openings and closings common to letters of the period (Pardee 1978: 330; 1982: 177–78; Taatz 1991: 46–56). Instead, we are given an introduction telling us *about* the (first) letter—who sent it, who was to receive it, when it was sent, and who carried it under what conditions (vv 1–3). Even the introductory "and concerning Shemaiah, the Nehelamite, you shall say" in Letter II (v 24) is not a formal address but simply a directive within a larger letter telling the addressee to convey an oracle (now incomplete) to Shemaiah the Nehelamite. These words are not a directive from Yahweh to Jeremiah (*pace* Bright; Holladay). A letter from Elijah to King Jehoram, preserved in 2 Chr 21:12–15, is similarly a prophetic oracle in letter form, without opening or closing formulas (Pardee 1982: 181). The NT letters of Paul are comparable, in that the bodies *mutatis mutandis* contain preaching, although here and there, formal elements are present, i.e., with sender and sendee named, according to typical letter form, and with the customary greetings.

The seven oracles of the main letter with their messenger formulas are the following:

I   *Thus said Yahweh of hosts, God of Israel . . .*   vv 5–7
     Build houses, plant gardens, marry, and have families;
         pray for the welfare of your city

II   *For thus said Yahweh of hosts, God of Israel*   vv 8–9
     Do not listen to the prophets, diviners, and dreamers in your
         midst; they are prophesying a lie in my name
     oracle of Yahweh

III *For thus said Yahweh*   vv 10–13
     When Babylon has served me for 70 years, I will confirm my
         good word and bring you back to this place
     oracle of Yahweh
     You will pray to me and I will listen to you, if you seek me with
         your whole heart

IV   I will be found by you   v 14a
     oracle of Yahweh
     and I will restore your fortunes

V   I will gather you from all the places where I dispersed you   v 14b
     oracle of Yahweh
     I will bring you back to the place from which I exiled you

VI *For thus said Yahweh . . .*   vv 16–19
    Thus said Yahweh of hosts
    Against the king and remnant in Jerusalem, I will bring judgment;
       they will be a reproach among the nations because they
       did not listen to my words sent by my servants, the prophets
    oracle of Yahweh
    You also did not listen
    oracle of Yahweh

VII *Thus said Yahweh of hosts, God of Israel . . .*   vv 21–23
    Ahab and Zedekiah will be given over to Nebuchadrezzar, who
       will strike them down; they will become a swearword
       because of their adultery and lies
    oracle of Yahweh

Oracle I begins with an expanded "thus said Yahweh" messenger formula. Oracles II, III, and VII have two messenger formulas, an expanded "thus said Yahweh" formula at the beginning and an "oracle of Yahweh" formula at the end or near the end. For other Jeremianic oracles having double formulas, see 2:2b–3 and 2:5–9. Oracles IV and V have a center "oracle of Yahweh" formula, which can also occur (3:12; 23:23, 29, 30, 31, and 32), although it is not usual. Oracle VI has an unusual double "thus said Yahweh . . ." formula at the beginning and a double "oracle of Yahweh" formula at the end. The LXX omits "oracle of Yahweh" in Oracles II (v 9), III (v 11), IV (v 14a) due to haplography, V (v 14b), and VI (2× in v 19). It does, however, translate the concluding "oracle of Yahweh" in Oracle VII (v 23).

Looking at the overall structure of vv 1–23, we see that the narrative has an introduction (vv 1–3) and four thematic segments from the main letter: 1) vv 4–9; 2) vv 10–14; 3) vv 15–19; and 4) vv 20–23. The location of v 15 remains in some doubt. This verse could be left where it is, in which case it becomes a background statement for the judgment on the Jerusalem community, stating that judgment will occur, despite predictions to the contrary from prophets in Babylon. If the verse (following G^L) is placed prior to v 21, then it becomes a background statement for the judgment on Ahab and Zedekiah, putting to rest a boast of the Babylonian exiles that they are doing just fine, with prophets of their own. Taking the text as it currently stands (a slight change from my earlier analysis; cf. Lundbom 1975: 104–6 [= 1997: 137–39]), the four segments of Jeremiah's letter can be seen to form a chiasmus based on key words and theme:

   A   Welfare (*šělôm*) of *Babylon* (vv 4–9)
     B   Welfare (*šālôm*) of *Jerusalem* (vv 10–14)
     B′   Judgment in *Jerusalem* (vv 15–19)
   A′   Judgment in *Babylon* (vv 20–23)

The first half of the letter is about *shalom*: first the anticipated *shalom* of the Babylonian exiles (v 7); then the eventual *shalom* of Jerusalem (v 11). The remainder of the letter is judgment and, in apportioning the judgment, Jeremiah—or else Baruch—reverses the order of subjects from the *shalom* part of the letter. The remnant in Jerusalem is judged first; then prophets in Babylon who are preaching lies and romping with wives of their friends.

NOTES

29:1. *And these are the words.* Hebrew *wĕ'ēlleh dibrê.* The same words open and close Deuteronomy 1–28 (Deut 1:1; 28:69[Eng 29:1]; cf. Lundbom 1996a). See also the opening to an early edition of Jeremiah's Book of Restoration (30:4).

the letter that Jeremiah the prophet sent from Jerusalem to the remnant of the elders of the exile, and to the priests and to the prophets, and to all the people whom Nebuchadnezzar exiled from Jerusalem to Babylon. Hebrew *hassēper* is a letter written on papyrus, rolled into a scroll, and sealed. Jeremiah sent a general letter to the entire Judahite community in Babylon, the text of which will now be reported. This letter inspired the later "Epistle of Jeremiah," an apocryphal work from the Hellenistic period.

the remnant of the elders of the exile. Hebrew *yeter ziqnê haggôlâ.* These are the surviving elders among the exiles—a rather touching detail. Many elderly folk would have died in the siege and capture of Jerusalem (6:10–11) or else on the forced march to Babylon. The LXX omits *yeter* ("remnant"), but the term is best retained (Rudolph; Weiser; Bright; Holladay). Rudolph gives it the meaning "preeminent" (cf. Gen 49:3), but this makes for redundancy with "elders." Ezekiel, after his call to be a prophet in Babylon (593 B.C.), was sought out on various occasions by "the elders of Judah/Israel" (Ezek 8:1; 14:1; 20:1–3), which would have been an influential body similar to the one that existed earlier in Judah (1 Kgs 20:7; 2 Kgs 23:1; Jer 19:1; 26:17). The "elders of the Jews" continued to be influential in the later return to Palestine (Ezra 5:5, 9; 6:7, 8, 14). From the Bīt Murašû archive, discovered at Nippur, we know that an "assembly of Egyptian elders" was also present in Babylon in the sixth century B.C. (Eph'al 1978: 76–80).

to the priests and to the prophets. The LXX has *pseudoprophētas* ("false prophets"), a term appearing again in v 8 and six other times in chaps. 26–29 (see Note for 6:13).

whom Nebuchadnezzar exiled from Jerusalem to Babylon. The LXX omits, which can be attributed to haplography (homoeoarcton: *'aleph* . . . *'aleph*). G^L, Aq, Theod, T, S, and Vg all have the phrase, and it is retained by Volz, Rudolph, and Weiser. In its place the LXX has *epistolēn eis Babulōna tē apoikia* ("an epistle to Babylon for the exiles"), which looks like fill-in on a damaged MS. See "and every freeman and prisoner" for "the princes of Judah and Jerusalem" in v 2. Jerusalem's capture by Nebuchadnezzar in 597 B.C. goes unrecorded in the book, with the Babylonian king's replacement of Coniah (Jehoiachin) by Zedekiah getting only passing mention in 37:1. The disgrace is recorded in 2 Kgs 24:10–17 and more summarily yet in 2 Chr 36:10. But it is documented in the Babylonian Chronicle (BM 21946 Rev. 11–13; Wiseman 1956: 72–73; *ANET*³ 564), which says that Nebuchadnezzar seized the (main) city of Judah, captured its king, appointed a king of his own choosing, and took considerable tribute back to Babylon. For a picture of the cuneiform text now in the British Museum, see *ANEP*² 348 #804.

2. *after Jeconiah the king, and the queen mother and the eunuchs, the princes of Judah and Jerusalem, and the craftsmen and the smiths had gone out from Jerusalem.* A parenthetical statement but part of the introduction, like the statement containing similar information in 24:1. These contextual notes are what link chaps. 24 and 29 in a larger rhetorical structure (see Rhetoric and Composition for 24:1–10). The verse then need not be taken in part or in its entirety as a secondary addition from 2 Kgs 24:12–16, as many commentators propose (*pace* Giesebrecht; Duhm; Cornill; Volz; Rudolph; Weiser, Bright; Holladay). The Versions all have it. Since nothing more is said here by way of a date, it may be that these letters—and others—went to Babylon very soon after the exile of 597 B.C.

Jeconiah. This shortened spelling of Jehoiachin, *yĕkonyâ*, occurs also in 27:20 (Q) and 28:4. For other spellings of this king's name in the OT, see Note for 22:24.

the queen mother. Nehushta, the daughter of Elnathan (see Note for 13:18). Her exile along with that of Jehoiachin is predicted in 22:26.

the eunuchs. Hebrew *hassārîsîm.* Although eunuchs (= castrated men) performed domestic service in the royal palace (Ebed-melech being one such person, 38:7; cf. 41:16), the term referred also to high-ranking government and military officials (52:25; cf. 39:3). The eunuchs here, as also in 34:19, are doubtless high-ranking officials. The T translates "princes"; Calvin prefers "chiefs." On biblical *sārîs* meaning "eunuch," see Tadmor 1995.

the princes of Judah and Jerusalem. The LXX omits and in its place has *kai pantos eleutherou kai desmōtou*, "and every freeman and prisoner." Theodotion (*kai archontōn Iouda ex Ierousalēm*) supports the MT. On the more inclusive meaning of Heb *śārîm* ("princes"), see Note for 24:1. Because the phrase here is without the copulative, Cheyne thinks "the princes" stands in apposition to "the eunuchs," although he knows of no other passage where princes are so called. The T reads: "and the princes, the princes of Judah and Jerusalem." Several Heb MSS, along with Gᴸ, Theod, S, and Vg, have the *waw*. Assuming then that the *waw* was originally in the text, we have another LXX omission attributable to haplography (homoeoarcton: *w . . . w*).

and the craftsmen and the smiths. Hebrew *wĕhehārāš wĕhammasgēr.* The LXX translates "craftsmen" (*technitou*) but not "smiths," which it does also in 24:1. Symm has *architektona kai ton sungkleionta* ("chief builders and smiths"), supporting MT. On these two groups of skilled workers, see Note for 24:1. Cuneiform texts from the reigns of Esarhaddon (680–669 B.C.) and Assurbanipal (668–627 B.C.) list among Egyptian deportees to Mesopotamia the following skilled persons: physicians, veterinarians, diviners, dream interpreters, snake charmers, singers, goldsmiths, coppersmiths, black[smiths], cartwrights, shipwrights, carpet-makers(?), brewers, bakers, fishermen, sailors, clerks, boat-house-keepers, and scribes (Eph'al 1978: 78; cf. *ANET*[3] 293).

3. *by the hand of Elasah son of Shaphan and Gemariah son of Hilkiah, whom Zedekiah, king of Judah, sent to Nebuchadnezzar, king of Babylon, in Babylon.* Zedekiah is on the throne, but to what extent his rule is established is anyone's guess. The present embassy is sent on official business, probably to deliver tribute and reaffirm Judah's loyalty to the Babylonian king. During these years, revolts and rumors of revolt challenged Nebuchadnezzar's rule—both in Babylon and in the newly acquired western provinces (see Notes for 27:1 and 27:3). This letter, which is hand-carried by Elasah and Gemariah, is destined not for Nebuchadnezzar or anyone in Babylonian officialdom but for the community of Judahite exiles. Another embassy went to Babylon in Zedekiah's fourth year, i.e., 594/3, perhaps for the same purpose, and on this occasion Jeremiah availed himself of the opportunity to send along with Seraiah ben Neriah a scroll predicting Babylon's eventual demise (51:59–64).

Elasah son of Shaphan. A member of the important Shaphan scribal family (2 Kgs 22:8–20). Two brothers of Elasah held influential positions during Jehoiakim's reign: Ahikam, who protected Jeremiah after his trial of 609 b.c. (26:24), and Gemariah, who had a Temple chamber (library) and was one of those urging Jehoiakim not to burn Jeremiah's scroll (36:10–12, 25). A son of Gemariah, Micaiah, was also connected with the Temple library at this time (36:11–13). After the destruction of Jerusalem, Gedaliah son of Ahikam and grandson of Shaphan was appointed governor over Judah (40:5), and it was into his care that Jeremiah was entrusted once he had gained his freedom (39:11–14). Because of Jeremiah's close ties with the Shaphan family all during his life, it is not too much to suggest, as some have done (Peake; Muilenburg 1970a; Jones), that a friendship with Jeremiah played some part in Elasah's hand-carrying this letter to Babylon. For a line of the scribal family of Shaphan, see p. 299.

Gemariah son of Hilkiah. Of this Gemariah we know nothing other than what is reported here. There is no indication that he was a brother to Jeremiah, whose father was also named Hilkiah (1:1). Possibly he was a son of Hilkiah, the high priest, who found the Temple law-book in 622 b.c. and figured prominently in the Josianic Reform. This latter Hilkiah and Shaphan, the scribe, were contemporaries (2 Kings 22). On the name "Gemariah," see Appendix I.

Nebuchadnezzar. The LXX omits the name here and in v 21 (see Appendix VI).

4. *to all the exiles whom I exiled.* The LXX omits "all" (*kol*), which can perhaps be attributed to haplography (homoeoteleuton: *l . . . l*). Volz and Rudolph emend with the Syriac to a third-person verb, "who have been exiled," saying that the shift from third to first person is awkward. But in expanded "thus said Yahweh" formulas, a divine "I" is perfectly acceptable; see 23:2a: "who shepherd *my people*"; 25:8: "you have not listened to *my words*"; 29:21: "who are prophesying a lie to you *in my name*"; and 29:31: "*when I, I did not send him.*" A first-person verb occurs here in both the MT and LXX and should therefore be retained (Bright; Holladay; McKane).

from Jerusalem to Babylon. The LXX omits "to Babylon" (*bābelâ*), which can again be loss due to haplography (homoeoarcton: *b . . . b*). The term is present in G^L, S, T, and Vg and should be retained (Giesebrecht; Volz; Rudolph; Weiser).

5. *Build houses and live in them; and plant gardens and eat their fruit.* On the verbs "build" (*bĕnû*) and "plant" (*niṭʿû*), which are thematic in the book of Jeremiah (1:10), see Note for 24:6. The exiles have a measure of freedom; they are not prisoners of war (Hyatt). Jeremiah's word to them is "Settle in for a time; you will not be returning home in the near future." Second Isaiah promises the building of houses and planting of gardens on the exiles' return (Isa 65:21).

6. *Take wives and beget sons and daughters, and take for your sons wives, and your daughters give to husbands.* More indication that the return home will not be soon. Some of the exiles may be refusing to marry and have children, which goes with unsettled times. Jeremiah himself was denied marriage and a family because of the impending distress in Judah (16:1–4; cf. Mark 13:17–19; Luke 23:28–31; 1 Cor 7:25–26). The latter part of the present sentence is a syntactic chiasmus: "and take for your sons / wives // and your daughters / give to husbands" (Kilpp 1990: 47). On the imperatives *qaḥ* and *qĕḥû* ("Take!") in divine commands issued to the prophet, see Note for 43:9.

and let them bear sons and daughters. The LXX omits, which can be attributed to haplography (homoeoarcton: *w . . . w*). Janzen (1973: 103–4) suggests the possibility of inner Greek haplography. The words are present in S, T, and Vg and should be retained (Volz; Rudolph; Weiser; Bright).

Yes, multiply there, and do not decrease. Hebrew *ûrĕbû-šām wĕʾal-timʿāṭû*. An echo of the Egyptian sojourn, where, in a foreign land and under less than ideal conditions, Israel's numbers did in fact increase (Exodus 1; Deut 26:5). These words reaffirm God's command in Gen 1:28: "Be fruitful and multiply (*ûrĕbû*)." Yahweh promises that the covenant people will multiply and be fruitful once they return to Zion (3:16; 23:3; 30:19).

7. *And seek the welfare of the city where I have exiled you, and pray on its behalf to Yahweh.* "To seek" (*drš*) in the OT often means "to pray" (10:21; Deut 4:29; Isa 55:6), which is indicated here in the verb following (*pll* Hithpael). In Deut 23:7[Eng 23:6] the covenant people are told *not to seek the welfare* (*lōʾ-tidrōš šĕlōmām*) of the Ammonites and Moabites—for all time. The reference here more likely urges good conduct (Calvin). To seek the welfare (*šālôm*) of one's city would certainly mean not to engage in revolt. The point has been restated in the modern day by Villafane (1992: 374), who says that seeking the welfare of large urban areas such as New York City requires "critical engagement," not assimilation, revolution, or escapism.

the city. This is not necessarily Babylon or Uruk, but whatever city or town in which the exiles happen to be. Settlement was not all in one place (compare the situation Egypt in 44:1). From the Bible and also the Bīt Murašû archive, we know that some exiled Jews were settled in the vicinity of Nippur. The river Chebar of Ezek 3:15 is the Kabāru Canal running through the city of Nippur

(Ephʿal 1978: 81). The LXX achieves broader meaning with *tēs gēs* ("of the land"), which would presuppose *hā'āreṣ*. But emendation is not required (Holladay). Aquila and Symm both have *tēs poleōs* ("of the city"), and "city" is the reading in S, T, and Vg.

and pray on its behalf to Yahweh, for in its welfare will be welfare for you. What is good for your city in Babylonia will be good for you. The LXX has "pray concerning them," i.e., the people. Prayer for the welfare of a foreign (= heathen) nation is a radical idea in the OT, but Jeremiah shows himself once again to be an untiring man of prayer (Volz). In the apocryphal book of Baruch, the people are told to pray for the life of Nebuchadnezzar and his son (Bar 1:11). The present verse also stands behind a later statement in the Mishnah (Aboth 3:2): "Pray for the peace of the ruling power, since but for fear of it men would have swallowed up each other alive." In the NT one can cite Jesus' words in Matt 5:44 ("Pray for those who persecute you") and Paul's counsel regarding governing authorities in Romans 13. Calvin said that praying for the ruling power applied also to his day.

welfare. The Heb word is *šālôm*, which can also be translated "peace" or "well-being."

8. *Do not let your prophets who are in your midst or your diviners deceive you; also do not listen to your dreamers whom you cause to dream.* Duhm and Cornill delete vv 8–9, a decision that eliminates the repudiation of (false) prophets and diviners in the letter. This deletion finds favor with Thiel (1981: 11–19) and McKane but with few others. Volz says that the verses cannot be omitted if false prophecy is a main object of the letter. Also, we seem to have here the same message delivered to the Babylonian exiles that was earlier delivered in Jerusalem (chaps. 27–28). The deletion, then, is without textual basis and is to be rejected. Here is a self-contained oracle on false prophecy, fitting in perfectly well with other oracles in the letter, particularly Oracle VII (vv 21–23). Relocation of the verses after v 15 is also unnecessary (*pace* Rudolph; JB [but not NJB]; NAB).

your prophets. The LXX has *hoi pseudoprophētai*, "the false prophets" (see v 1), lacking also "your," which the reading it has does not require. Ezekiel could not have been numbered among these prophets, since his call came in 593 B.C.

your diviners. Hebrew *qōsĕmêkem*. Judahite prophets are said to be practicing divination (*qesem*) in 14:14 but only in the present verse are "diviners" said to be active in the Judahite community. Other references to diviners in the book of Jeremiah are in the context of foreign nations (27:9; *habbaddîm* in 50:36). Perhaps now in a foreign country Jewish diviners have new freedom to practice their secret arts. In Israel and Judah, they were officially outlawed (see Note for 27:9).

your dreamers whom you cause to dream. The MT's *hălōmōtêkem* ("your dreams"), which despite support from LXX and Vg, is best repointed to *hālō-mōtêkem* or emended to *hōlĕmêkem* ("your dreamers"), as in 27:9 (Ehrlich 1912: 314; Volz; Soggin 1975f; Holladay). The T has "your dreamers of dreams," which may come from Deut 13:2–6[Eng 13:1–5]. The H-stem participle, *maḥlĕmîm*, has also troubled commentators and led to more emendation, but with the other change it can be left intact and read simply "cause to dream" (Kimḥi, following T). Soggin (p. 240) says: "According to this text the dreamers and probably the prophets and diviners as well were subjected to a serious moral blackmail . . . : public opinion demanded a message from them which would announce imminent return to those who had been deported." On dreamers and dreams in the ancient world, see Note for 23:25.

9. *For by a lie they are prophesying to you in my name.* A recurring refrain in chaps. 23, 27, and 29, on which see Note for 23:25. Hebrew *bĕšeqer* ("by a lie") can also be translated "falsely" (cf. 3:10). A few Heb MSS, LXX, S, and T omit the *bĕ*. The LXX has *adika* ("a wrong").

I have not sent them. On this disclaimer by Yahweh, see Note for 23:32.

10. *When Babylon has completed seventy years before me.* I.e., when Babylon has served Yahweh as a world power for 70 years. The specified period, which is a round number and no more, refers neither to Judah's exile in Babylon nor to Jerusalem's uninhabitation, both of which were considerably shorter (see Note for 25:11). The number 70 takes on particular importance here, in that Hananiah predicted an end to Babylonian suzerainty within two years (28:3, 11). This was the real difference between his prophecy and that of Jeremiah. It is not that Jeremiah was a doom prophet and Hananiah with the other prophets championed peace, freedom, and hope. This is way too simplistic. Jeremiah's opponents were saying that Judah's exile would be brief; Jeremiah was saying it would be long. Jeremiah, after all, during this same period was delivering oracles of judgment against Babylon (51:59–64). Calvin is impressed here that God's thoughts are not always hidden: Babylon's status as a world power, says God quite openly, will be ended after 70 years.

When Babylon has completed. Hebrew *kî lĕpî mĕlō't lĕbābel* is, lit., "when according to the completion for Babylon." KB³ translates *lĕpî mĕlō't*: "as soon as the time has passed." On the infinitive *mĕlō't* in the feminine form, which occurs also in 25:12, see GKC §74h.

I will attend to you and confirm upon you my good word to bring you back to this place. For Yahweh to "confirm" (*qûm* H-stem) his good word means he will fulfill it. On the verb *pqd*, which here means "attend to, take account," in a positive sense (cf. 15:15; 27:22), see Note for 5:9.

my good word. I.e., my promise (Calvin). Hebrew *dĕbārî haṭṭôb*. The LXX has "my words," plural, and omits "good." The MT reading, which is supported by G^L, T, S, and Vg, is preferable to what is here a generally bad LXX text (Giesebrecht). Compare Ps 45:2[Eng 45:1]: "my heart is stirred with a good word (*dābār ṭôb*)."

11. *For I, I know the plans that I am planning concerning you . . . plans of welfare and not for evil.* Now Jeremiah is speaking of *shalom* for the city of *shalom*, but it will be some years off. The LXX omits "I know the plans that I" (*yāda'tî 'et-hammaḥăšābōt 'ăšer 'ānōkî*), which is an obvious loss due to haplography, as Rudolph, Janzen (1973: 118), and Carroll recognize

(whole-word: *'nky . . . 'nky*). Most other commentators follow Giesebrecht in preferring MT, which is supported by G^L, Aq, Theod, S, T, and Vg. The words, then, should not be deleted (*pace* Cornill, Holladay, McKane). The expression "the plans that I am planning" (*hammaḥăšābōt 'ăšer 'ānōkî ḥōšēb*) and variations are signature coinages (and wordplays) by Jeremiah (11:19b; 18:11, 18; 29:11; 49:20, 30; 50:45). For other cognate accusatives in Jeremiah, see Note on 22:16.

to give you a future and a hope. Hebrew *lātēt lākem 'aḥărît wĕtiqwâ.* A hendiadys: "the hoped-for future." The term *aḥărît* also means "(latter) end," which in Jeremiah's earlier preaching had negative meaning (5:31; 12:4; 17:11). Here the term means "future," as in 31:17. Also positive in later chapters of the book is the phrase "in the days afterward," *bĕ'aḥărît hayyāmîm* (23:20; 30:24; 48:47; 49:37), which announces the time when understanding will come to the covenant people and neighboring nations will have their fortunes restored. The LXX here has simply "these (things)" (*tauta*); but G^{OL} have "thereafter" (*ta meta tauta*), with Aq and Theod adding "and a hope" (*kai elpida*). The T and Vg support MT. For the combination "future and hope," see also Prov 23:18 and 24:14.

12. *And you will call me and will come and pray to me, and I will listen to you.* Yahweh asks that Jeremiah call to him when he is in the court of the guard (33:3). Prayers by the people will also be possible in a foreign land, without a Temple (1 Kgs 8:46–52). The LXX omits "and you will call me and will come," which could have been due to haplography (homoeoarcton: *w . . . w*). Some (Volz; Rudolph; Weiser; Holladay; McKane; G. Greenberg 2001: 235) delete "and you will come" (*wahălaktem*) with S, but Ehrlich (1912: 315) defends *hlk* as an auxiliary verb that is used frequently in Jeremiah to prepare for an action to follow. On Jeremiah's pairing of *hālôk* with verbs of command, see Note for 28:13. In the present verse, Aq and Theod (*kai poreuesthe*) support MT. After the return home, Yahweh promises his people restored communication, at which time they will also be building houses, planting gardens, and raising families (Isa 65:21–24; cf. Sommer 1999: 649–50).

13. *And you will search for me and will find if you seek me with your whole heart.* This echo of Deut 4:29 does not mean that there has been a Deuteronomic editing of the verse (*pace* Hyatt). See also Jer 24:7. To seek Yahweh "with all your heart" means to seek him with your whole being.

14. *And I will be found by you.* Hebrew *wĕnimṣē'tî lākem.* The LXX has "I will appear to you," *kai epiphanoumai hymin* (cf. 31:3), but the MT reading is preferable in light of Deut 4:29, "and you will find (him)," *ûmāṣā'tā.* See also subsequent formulations in Isa 55:6 and 65:1.

oracle of Yahweh—and I will restore your fortunes. And I will gather you from all the nations and from all the places where I have dispersed you—oracle of Yahweh—and I will bring you back to the place from which I exiled you. The LXX omits, which appears to be another loss due to haplography (homoeoteleuton: *m . . . m*). Commentators (except Holladay) generally imagine MT expansion. But the words are present in Theod, T, S, and Vg.

and I will restore your fortunes. Heb *wĕšabtî 'et-šĕbûtĕkem* (Q). The Kt *šĕbîtkem* is an alternate spelling. A sonorous expression of *šûb* with a cognate accusative (E. L. Dietrich 1925: 1; Fitzmyer 1958: 463; Holladay 1958: 110–14). On the cognate accusative, see Note for 22:16. The expression occurs eleven times in Jeremiah (29:14; 30:3, 18 [poetry]; 31:23; 32:44; 33:7, 11, 26(Q); 48:47 [Moab]; 49:6 [Ammon] and 39Q [Elam]), and often elsewhere, e.g., in Deut 30:3; Amos 9:14; Hos 6:11; Zeph 2:7; 3:20; Lam 2:14; and Ps 126:1. Of the Jeremiah occurrences, six are H-stem (32:44; 33:7, 11, 26[Q]; 49:6, 39[Q]), which may be for purposes of intensification: "I will surely restore the(ir) fortunes" (see Note on 2:26 for the internal H-stem). The expression becomes thematic in the Book of Restoration (see Rhetoric and Composition for 30:1–3). It has also turned up in a mid-eighth-century B.C. Aramaic Sefîre Treaty found near Aleppo, Syria in 1931 (Fitzmyer 1958: 449–51, 463–64; Greenfield 1981: 110–12; *CS II* 217). The inscription says: "the gods have brought about the return (*hšbw 'lhn šybt*) of my father's house" (Sefîre III 24). Here in the present verse, "fortunes" doubtless refer not simply to the Temple vessels carried off to Babylon, which were chiefly at issue in chaps. 27–28, but to the land and treasures left behind in the land. These would include houses and gardens in Judah, which building and planting in Babylon would seem to render a lost possession forever. Rubinger (1977: 89) points out that those exiled to Babylon represented the upper social and economic strata of society, the very people who left behind homes and gardens now taken over by others in Jerusalem (Ezek 11:15). But the promise here is that Yahweh will restore the exiles' fortunes; one day houses, fields, and vineyards will again be bought in the land (Jer 32:15, 43–44; Ezek 11:17). Words of restoration like those occurring here are commonly found in the ancient Mesopotamian city laments (see Note for 48:47). In modern times, Napoleon, after defeating Prussia and occupying Berlin in 1806–8, took the quadriga (a four-horse chariot of Victoria, the goddess of victory) atop the Brandenburg Gate and brought it to Paris. But after Waterloo, it was returned to Berlin. Similarly, the High Altar at St. Mary's Basilica in Cracow, Poland, was dismantled and hidden before August, 1939, but the Germans found it and transported it the next year to Germany. After the war, it was discovered in the Nuremberg Castle and in 1946 was returned to Cracow.

15. *Because you have said, 'Yahweh has raised up for us prophets in Babylon.'* On the uncertainty over the location of this line in the letter, see Rhetoric and Composition. This boast coming now from Babylon is more than what appears on the surface. The exilic community is claiming for itself bona fide Yahweh prophets, who are preaching a word contrary to the word Jeremiah is preaching. Two of these prophets are Ahab and Zedekiah, for whom Jeremiah has a harsh word in vv 21–23. The T has "the Lord has raised up teachers for us in Babylon," which reflects the view of postexilic Judaism that one of the most important duties of the prophets was to call Israel back to the teaching of the Torah (Hayward 1985a: 215). On the substitution of "scribe" for "prophet" in T, see Note for 6:13.

16. *concerning the king.* The translation "concerning" for the preposition *'el* is required here and again in vv 21, 24, and 31.

the king who sits on the throne of David. This must refer to the present king, Zedekiah (Rashi), which means the very one who has dispatched those who are carrying this letter is himself about to be judged. But Zedekiah is not named, and the judgment is actually on everyone in the city. Should Zedekiah have known about this judgment, which he probably did eventually, he could also have thought that the evil might come after his time. Recall Hezekiah's attitude to the judgment oracle on Jerusalem and his own sons, which is recorded in Isa 39:6–8 (= 2 Kgs 20:17–19), as well as the judgment oracle on Jerusalem given to Josiah by Huldah the prophetess (2 Kgs 22:14–20). We know that in the present case the end came for Judah in a little over a decade, but Zedekiah would not have known that.

17–18. A summary of the oracle in 24:8–10.

17. *Look I am sending against them sword, famine, and pestilence.* "Look I" (*hinĕnî*) is the most common beginning of the Jeremianic oracle; see again vv 21b and 32, also Note for 1:15. On the triad, "sword, famine, and pestilence," see Note for 5:12.

and I will make them like horrid figs, which cannot be eaten they are so bad. A near-quotation of the lines in 24:2, 3, and 8. The term *šōʿārîm* ("horrid") is a *hapax legomenon* in the OT, but its meaning is not in doubt. Cognate terms occur elsewhere in the book: *šaʿărûrâ*, "horrible thing," in 5:30 and 23:14, and *šaʿărûrît*, "horrible thing," in 18:13. Dotan (1991), however, questions the accepted etymological basis of *šōʿārîm*, proposing for the same Hebrew word a plural adjective derived from *šaʿar*, "gate." In his view, *kattĕʾēnîm haššōʿārîm* means "like figs at the gate," the gate being the gate of the Temple (cf. 24:1–2). But T, S, Vg, the modern Versions, and commentators both ancient and modern all follow the traditional meaning, rendering this novel suggestion unlikely. On the causative sense of the final *mērōaʿ* ("so bad"), see Note for 24:2.

18. *and I will make them a fright to all the kingdoms of the earth—a curse, and a desolation, and an object of hissing, and a reproach.* On curse-word strings such as the present one, see Note for 24:9.

a fright. Hebrew *zaʿăwâ* (Q); *zĕwāʿâ* (Kt). On this Q-Kt, see Note for 15:4. The present curse word occurs elsewhere in 15:4; 24:9; and 34:17; see also Deut 28:25.

a curse. Hebrew *'ālâ*. This term appears also in 23:10; 42:18; and 44:12.

a desolation. Hebrew *šammâ*. A very common term in Jeremiah poetry and prose, occurring often in curse-word strings (see Note for 24:9).

and an object of hissing. Hebrew *wĕlišrēqâ*; some MSS have *wĕliqlālâ*, "and (for) a curse." For occurrences of this curse word in Jeremiah, see Note for 25:9.

a reproach. Hebrew *ḥerpâ*. Another common curse word in Jeremiah (see Note for 24:9).

among all the nations where I have dispersed them. The verb is a prophetic perfect (Kimḥi; Giesebrecht; Cornill; McKane). The dispersion has not yet occurred.

19. *inasmuch as they have not listened to my words—oracle of Yahweh—which I sent to them by my servants the prophets—constantly I sent—and you did not listen.* A recurring theme in Jeremiah. People have been listening to prophets, but to those Yahweh has not sent. To the prophets Yahweh has sent, they have paid no heed. On the rhetorical idiom of a repeated verb used together with *škm* (here "I sent to them . . . constantly I sent"), see Note for 7:13. The expression, "I sent to you all my servants the prophets" is discussed in Note for 7:25.

inasmuch as. Or "because" (AV; RSV; NJV). The conjunctive expression *taḥat ʾăšer* has this meaning also in Num 25:13; Deut 21:14; and 2 Kgs 22:17.

I sent to them. Hebrew *šālaḥtî ʾălēhem.* Several MSS have the suffix *kem*, "to you," which anticipates the direct address immediately following. It is unclear precisely where the shift to direct address occurs.

and you did not listen. Giesebrecht takes this shift to the second person as a scribal mistake, which is too dismissive, even though G^{OL} and S have a third plural. Since the final phrase has an additional "oracle of Yahweh" formula, one wonders if the final words might be a later add-on. But this particular oracle appears to have two messenger formulas at the beginning and two at the end (see Rhetoric and Composition). Kimḥi says the second person is to apply the prophecy now to the exiles, which is probably right. These people, too, need to be reminded that they did not listen to Yahweh's word when they were still in Judah.

20. *Now you!* Hebrew *wĕʾattem.* This emphatic pronoun underscores the shift in discourse now directed to the exiles, following an oracle concerning the unfavored remnant in Jerusalem.

21. *Ahab son of Kolaiah and . . . Zedekiah son of Maaseiah.* The LXX omits the patronyms, which it occasionally does. It includes the patronym for Zephaniah the priest in v 25. The patronyms here should be read; they are present in G^L, Aq, Theod, S, T, and Vg. Also, "Kolaiah" (*qôlāyâ*) makes a wordplay with both "swearword" (*qĕlālâ*) and "roast" (*qālām*) in v 22. We know nothing about these men other than what is reported here. Zephaniah, the priest, mentioned in 21:1 and 37:3, is also a "son of Maaseiah," but whether he is a brother to Zedekiah cannot be said. "Ahab" and "Zedekiah" are both common biblical names. The name "Kolaiah," spelled *qôlîyāhû*, has turned up on a late-seventh–early-sixth-century seal of unknown provenance (see "Ahab ben Kolaiah" in Appendix I); "Maaseiah" has turned up in its short form, "Maasai," on one of the Arad ostraca and in its long form on a number of seals and bullae (see "Maaseiah ben Shallum" in Appendix I).

who are prophesying a lie to you in my name. See v 9. The LXX omits, which is another loss due to haplography, independent of the omission of Zedekiah's patronym (homoeoarcton: *hn . . . hn*). Aquila and Theod have the words. Because these individuals have been "prophesying" (*hannibbĕʾîm*), it is assumed that they are prophets.

Look I will give them into the hand of Nebuchadrezzar, king of Babylon, and he will strike them down before your eyes. This together with what follows in v 22 is a predictive word; judgment has not yet taken place (Calvin).

Here only in chaps. 27–29 is the name "Nebuchadrezzar" spelled with the "r" (see Note on 21:2).

22. *From them will be taken up a swearword for all the exiles of Judah who are in Babylon: 'Yahweh make you like Zedekiah and like Ahab, whom the king of Babylon roasted in the fire.'* Malamat (1975: 136–37) connects this ferment caused by prophets in Babylon, also the ferment back in Jerusalem, with the call of Ezekiel in July 593 B.C., wondering if it may not have been these events that aroused Ezekiel to his mission. Why Nebuchadnezzar should carry out such cruel punishment on two Jewish prophets is not known. It is usually imagined that they were involved directly or indirectly in revolt activities, although the reason given in the text here is that they had committed adultery and were speaking lies in Yahweh's name. Since this is a divine oracle, we may assume that Yahweh is giving his own reasons for the executions, not Nebuchadnezzar's. Death by burning was carried out in ancient Israel (Gen 38:24; Lev 20:14; 21:9; Josh 7:15, 25; 1 Kgs 13:2) and in other countries, but it was still rare. The Code of Hammurabi prescribed the burning of persons for thefts made from a burning house, for noncloistered nuns drinking wine, and for incest (Laws 25, 110, 157; *ANET*³ 167, 170, 172; *CS II* 338, 342, 345). The Philistines threatened Samson's wife with burning if she did not disclose Samson's riddle (Judg 14:15). And in the later story of Shadrach, Meshach, and Abednego (Daniel 3), punishment by burning is portrayed as being a Babylonian practice. That it was carried out in Hellenistic times we know from the martyrdoms in 2 Maccabees 7. The verb *qlh* ("roast") in the present verse is odd; we would expect rather *śrp* ("burn"), which is otherwise used of human burnings in the OT. Morla Asensio (1988: 249–50) suggests that *qlh* is a euphemism, which makes also for irony. Ahab son of Kolaiah and Zedekiah son of Maaseiah both appear on Dead Sea Scroll fragment 4Q339, which lists false prophets having arisen in Israel (see Note for 28:1).

Ahab. The spelling is *'eḥāb.* Q^Or has the usual *'aḥ'āb*, as in v 21 and elsewhere in the OT.

swearword. Or "curse." Hebrew *qĕlālâ*. The term occurs often in curse-word strings (see Note for 24:9).

23. *because they did a scandalous thing in Israel, yes, they committed adultery with the wives of their fellows and have spoken a lying word in my name that I did not command them.* For the pairing of adultery and lying in the prophets of Jerusalem, see particularly 23:14.

a scandalous thing. Hebrew *nĕbālâ* can also be translated "stupidity, outrage, wanton folly." The term is reserved for foolish, senseless, and unruly conduct, the very opposite of action showing wisdom (Phillips 1975: 237). The OT expression "to do a scandalous thing in Israel" means to act in a way, often sexually, that is greatly offensive to moral sensibilities (Gen 34:7; Deut 22:21; Josh 7:15; Judg 20:6, 10; 2 Sam 13:12–13).

a lying word. The LXX omits *šeqer* ("lying"), but G^L, Aq, Theod, S, T, and Vg all have the term. Dahood (1977a) takes *dābār bišmî šeqer* (lit., "a word in my name lying") as a broken construct chain (the normal construct chain, *dĕbar-*

šeqer, occurs in Prov 13:5), but his conclusion that this is a sure indication of poetry cannot be right, at least not here.

But I am he who knows and am witness. This climactic word concludes the letter. Yahweh witnesses things that others do not (7:11; 16:17; 23:24), although it appears here that others too have learned about the wrongdoing, which is what usually happens.

he who knows. The translation follows J. D. Michaelis (1793: 228–29), who redivides the Kt to read *hû' yōdēaʿ*, "But I am he who knows and am witness." The pronoun *hû* stands for *hû'*, where the *'aleph* has fallen away. This reading has been adopted by G. R. Driver (1960: 123) and others. The Q *hayyôdēaʿ* ("the one who knows") has roughly the same meaning. The LXX omits the word, but Aq and Theod have it (*kai egō eimi ho gnōstēs kai martus*).

MESSAGE AND AUDIENCE

An introduction here tells a Jerusalem audience that Jeremiah wrote to all the exiles in Babylon after their deportation from Jerusalem in 597 B.C. and that the words following are from this letter. They hear first an oracle in which Yahweh tells the exiles to build houses and live in them, plant gardens, and eat their fruit. Men are also to take wives and have families, and the sons and daughters are to marry and have families. It is a new creation. The exiles must be fruitful and multiply, just like their ancestors who were slaves in Egypt. Moreover, they are to seek the welfare of the city where they now reside, for in its welfare will be their welfare.

A second oracle repeats the message currently being preached in Jerusalem. People are not to listen to prophets and would-be prophets who are dreaming of a speedy return home. These visionaries are speaking lies in Yahweh's name, and Yahweh says he has not sent them.

A third oracle states that, when Babylon has completed 70 years in the service of Yahweh, Yahweh will fulfill his good word to return the covenant people to Judah—but not in two years or four years or ten years. The length of their punishment will be 70 years. Yahweh says he knows the plans he has for the covenant people—plans of shalom and not evil, which will give them a future and a hope. Then the people will pray to him and he will listen—something that has not happened of late. If the people seek Yahweh with all their heart, they will find him. Another brief oracle (v 14a) states that Yahweh will indeed be found by his people and will restore the fortunes recently lost. A fifth oracle (v 14b) states that Yahweh will gather the exiles from all the places where he has dispersed them, and he will bring them back to the place from which they were taken.

Jeremiah then quotes what the exiles are saying about Yahweh's having raised up for them prophets in Babylon. According to the text as it now stands, these prophets are making grand claims about how things will improve markedly in Jerusalem. To this incurable optimism Jeremiah responds with an oracle concerning the king and those remaining in Jerusalem. In it Yahweh says that he will send sword, famine, and pestilence against them, and they will be like horrid figs that cannot be eaten. Yahweh's relentless pursuit of this un-blessed remnant will be such that they will become a curse among all the king-doms of the earth. The situation at home is little changed. People have not listened to Yahweh's words sent continually by prophets who are real prophets. The exiles in Babylon are told they were no better.

Jeremiah now tells his exilic audience to hear an oracle from Yahweh. It has to do with two would-be prophets in Babylon, Ahab son of Kolaiah and Zede-kiah son of Maaseiah, both of whom are prophesying lies in Yahweh's name. Yahweh says he will give them into the hand of Nebuchadrezzar, who will fin-ish them off shamefully in the sight of all. As a result, the exiles (not the nations round about) will have this curse on their lips: "Yahweh make you like Zede-kiah and Ahab, whom the king of Babylon roasted in the fire." Yahweh gives his reason for this exemplary act: Ahab and Zedekiah have created a scandal by committing adultery with wives of their friends; they have also been preaching lies in Yahweh's name. Yahweh says he knows it all and is a witness to it all!

The introduction states that this letter was sent to Babylon after the exile of 597 B.C. I tend to agree with Calvin who thinks it went soon after the exile. Calvin also thinks it was when Zedekiah's kingship was not yet firmly estab-lished. It should then be dated roughly the same time as chap. 24, its balancing narrative in the Zedekiah Cluster. Others (Peake; Weiser; Bright) date it later, ca. 594–593 B.C., which correlates it with the preaching in chaps. 27–28 and the unrest in Jerusalem and Babylon.

The audience hearing the Zedekiah Cluster will perceive in v 17 continuity with the bad figs spoken of in chap. 24. And having also just heard chap. 28, it will compare the false prophet Hananiah in Jerusalem with the false prophets Ahab and Zedekiah in Babylon; and once the whole of chap. 29 is heard, it will link those with the false prophet Shemaiah in Babylon as well. Looking ahead, we see that hopeful indications here ("a future and a hope," "a good word") anticipate the hope contained in the Book of Restoration following (chaps. 30–33).

Dietrich Bonhoeffer (1971: 299), in his 1944 baptismal letter to the son of Eberhard and Renate Bethge, quoted v 7 of the present letter about seeking the welfare of the city and praying to the Lord on its behalf. He was looking ahead to community life after the war and sufferings that were now being brought upon his people. When the war was over, churches in Germany—most coura-geously, churches under Communism in the DDR—did precisely this during the foreign occupation of their country.

More recently, I was much surprised to learn from Arab Christians in a group I addressed at the Sabeel Ecumenical Center, Jerusalem, in December 2001, that the Palestinian Arabs who were forcibly evicted or who fled from their homes during the 1948 War and were now (with their children and grandchildren) refugees in neighboring Arab countries did not think of them-selves, nor did other Arabs think of them, as the "remnant" with a promised fu-ture. The "remnant" of importance consisted of those still in the land—once

Palestine, but now the modern state of Israel. Although on a political level Palestinians have argued for the right of return, still there does not appear to be a corresponding religious conviction that one day God, in his own time, will bring the Palestinian exiles back to their land. Yet this is precisely the claim being made here in Jeremiah's letter to Jewish exiles in Babylon.

Felix Mendelssohn used v 13 from Jeremiah's letter in Part I of his *Elijah* oratorio (1846), where Obadiah sings in the tenor solo:

"If with all your hearts ye truly seek me, ye shall ever surely find me." Thus saith our God. Oh! that I knew—where I might find Him, that I might even come before His presence!

The chorus then follows with words from v 14:

Thus saith our God: "Ye shall ever surely find me." Thus saith our God.
(Part I, #4 Air; #5 Chorus)

2. Concerning Shemaiah in Babylon (29:24–32)

29 ²⁴And concerning Shemaiah, the Nehelamite, you shall say:
   ²⁵Thus said Yahweh of hosts, God of Israel:
   Because you, you sent letters in your name to all the people who are in Jerusalem, and to Zephaniah son of Maaseiah, the priest, and to all the priests saying, ²⁶Yahweh made you priest under Jehoiada, the priest, to be overseers in the house of Yahweh concerning every madman and one prophesying away, and you are to put him into the stocks and into the collar. ²⁷And now, why have you not rebuked Jeremiah, the Anathothite, who is prophesying away to you? ²⁸seeing that he sent to us in Babylon saying, 'It will be long! Build houses and live in them; and plant gardens and eat their fruit.'
²⁹And Zephaniah, the priest, read this letter in the hearing of Jeremiah, the prophet. ³⁰And the word of Yahweh came to Jeremiah: ³¹Send to all the exiles saying: Thus said Yahweh concerning Shemaiah, the Nehelamite, because Shemaiah prophesied to you when I, I did not send him, and he has made you trust in a lie—
   ³²Therefore thus said Yahweh:
   Look I will reckon with Shemaiah, the Nehelamite, and with his offspring. There shall not be to him a man dwelling in the midst of this people, and he shall not see the good that I will do for my people— oracle of Yahweh—for he has spoken rebellion against Yahweh.

RHETORIC AND COMPOSITION

MT 29:24–32 = LXX 36:24–32. This segment of chap. 29 contains a mid-letter directive to the recipient of a second letter sent by Jeremiah to Babylon (v 24), after which comes a fragment of that letter, having an oracle similarly fragmented (vv 25–28). A brief narrative follows (vv 29–31), which introduces a concluding oracle destined for Shemaiah the Nehelamite (v 32). Delimitation at the top end is by a *setumah* in M^L and a *petuḥah* in M^P before v 24. At the bottom end is a *setumah* in M^L and a *petuḥah* in M^P after v 32, which is also a chapter division. An entirely new collection, the Book of Restoration, begins at 30:1. Section markings for M^A are not extant. The M^L and M^P have another *petuḥah* after v 29, which separates a brief narrative statement from the introduction to the oracle against Shemaiah. The M^P (only) has another *setumah* after v 31, separating the introduction to the Shemaiah oracle from the oracle itself.

On the type of narrative constituting the whole of chap. 29 and the various problems associated with the chapter's composition, see Rhetoric and Composition for 29:1–23. Here in vv 24–32, the texts of both MT and LXX present difficulties, but the LXX—particularly with Zephaniah taking a rebuke for having reviled Jeremiah in v 27—is particularly confused (Giesebrecht: "completely distorted"; Peake: "an incoherent jumble") and of no help in reconstructing a coherent text. Here, too, there are more LXX omissions, a number of which can be attributed to haplography.

The main problem with vv 25–28 in the MT is that Jeremiah recounts what has been said in letters sent by Shemaiah to Jerusalem, but then the text breaks off abruptly. We anticipate a response from Jeremiah, but none is forthcoming. Jeremiah's judgment on Shemaiah comes only later, when he is commanded by Yahweh to write the exiles a third letter (vv 30–31). The second letter must then be only part of a longer letter, and its oracle only part of a larger oracle. Letters in antiquity were often semi-public, containing messages for entire communities. They were like the modern missionary letter sent from the field to families and the churches back home. Jeremiah's first letter was intended for a broad audience ("to the remnant of the elders . . . to the priests and to the prophets, and to all the people"), and Letter III was also to be sent "to all the exiles" in Babylon. Similarly, Letter II in its entirety must have been for a broad audience, not just Shemaiah, with only part of it coming to be included in the biblical text. Other parts not deemed important were edited out. The sequence of events lying behind all of chap. 29 can then be reconstructed as follows:

1) Jeremiah wrote a letter to the exiles in Babylon, which we may have in full in vv 4–23. In it he told them to build houses, plant gardens, and have families, because the exile would be long.
2) Shemaiah, most likely a prophet in Babylon, then wrote a number of letters to influential people in Jerusalem, objecting to what Jeremiah had said in his letter. In these letters, he asked why Jeremiah had not been censured.
3) Jeremiah at some point heard about the content of these letters and sent a second letter to Babylon. A fragment of this letter, containing

only a quotation from Shemaiah's letter and then ending abruptly, is preserved in vv 25–28.

4) Zephaniah, the priest, then read Shemaiah's letter to Jeremiah, so that he could hear it for himself, after which Jeremiah is commanded by Yahweh to send another letter to Babylon cursing Shemaiah in a divine oracle. This is Jeremiah's third letter, and it is not extant.

The abrupt ending of the Letter II fragment (v 28) results from Baruch (or another compiler) wanting to make an inclusio with the beginning of the main letter, which Letter II quotes (Lundbom 1975: 106–7 [= 1997: 139–40]). The inclusio consists of this repetition:

Build houses and live in them; and plant gardens and eat their fruit.	v 5
Build houses and live in them; and plant gardens and eat their fruit.	v 28

The repeated words emphasize the point Jeremiah wants to get across to the exiles: "Settle down for what promises to be a long stay in Babylon."

NOTES

29:24. *And concerning Shemaiah, the Nehelamite, you shall say.* The LXX (also S and Vg) omits *lē'mōr*, "saying," which may be due to haplography (homoeoteleuton: *'mr . . . 'mr*). Theodotion has the word. Hebrew *tō'mar* ("you shall say") is singular, and some commentators (Giesebrecht; Bright; Holladay) take the directive, therefore, as a divine word to Jeremiah. But in my view, this is Jeremiah's directive to someone on the receiving end of a second letter that he has sent to the Babylonian exiles.

Shemaiah, the Nehelamite. "Nehelam" is probably a place-name (T: "who is from Helem"; Jerome: *de loco Neelami*; Cornill; Rudolph), whose location is unknown. The name and epithet are analogous to "Jeremiah, the Anathothite" in v 27. Shemaiah, the Nehelamite, appears on Dead Sea Scroll fragment 4Q339, which lists false prophets that arose in Israel (see Note for 28:1). "Shemaiah" as a name appears elsewhere in 26:20 and 36:12; also on various extrabiblical finds (see Note for 26:20 and Appendix I).

25. *Thus said Yahweh of hosts, God of Israel (saying).* The LXX omits, which can be attributed to haplography (whole-word: *l'mr . . . l'mr*). Theodotion, T, and Vg have the words.

Because you, you sent letters in your name. I.e., not on Yahweh's behalf (Giesebrecht). These letters may or may not have contained the (lying) oracles Shemaiah is later judged to have uttered (v 31). The LXX reading, "I did not send you in my name," is corrupt (*BHS*).

letters. Hebrew *sĕpārîm*. Letters were often—but not always—written on papyri, then rolled up and sealed. The LXX omits this term, but Theod (*ta biblia*), T, and Vg have it. The LXX omission, along with two others in the verse, are taken by many (Duhm; Cornill; Ehrlich 1912: 316; Rudolph; Weiser;

Bright; Jones; McKane) as an indication that Shemaiah sent only one letter to
Zephaniah, the priest. But the omission of "to all the people who are in Jerusalem and" is likely due to haplography. The MT, which states that multiple
letters were sent, should be read. The plural *sĕpārîm*, cited often in 2 Kgs 10:1;
19:14; and 20:12, denotes not a single letter (*pace* Holladay) but a single communication in multiple letters (Bright). Zephaniah, the priest, reads to Jeremiah from his own letter in v 29.

   to all the people who are in Jerusalem, and. The LXX omits, which is doubtless another loss due to haplography (whole word: *'l . . . 'l*). See also 34:8.
Theodotion, T, and Vg have the words.

   *25–26. to Zephaniah son of Maaseiah, the priest, and to all the priests saying,
Yahweh made you priest under Jehoiada, the priest, to be overseers in the house of
Yahweh.* Zephaniah is probably successor to Pashhur, the Temple's "chief overseer" (*pāqîd nāgîd*) who imprisoned Jeremiah for his Topheth oracle (20:1–6),
and may have been exiled to Babylon in 597 B.C. (cf. v 6). Zephaniah, being
newly installed, is more kindly disposed to the prophet than his predecessor,
extending the courtesy of reading to him Shemaiah's letter and not disciplin-
ing him, as Shemaiah would like. The Jehoiada referred to is the famous
Jehoiada, the priest, who set up the office of Temple overseer (*pĕquddôt*) after
Athaliah's infamous reign and a Temple cleansing after her death (2 Kgs
11:17–18; 2 Chr 23:16–18). On the function of the Temple "overseer," see
Note for 20:1. The phrase "Yahweh made you priest under (*taḥat*) Jehoiada,
the priest" means that Zephaniah follows in a line of priestly overseers begun
under Jehoiada (Kimḥi; Hitzig; Giesebrecht; Peake, and others). Jehoiada is
not an otherwise unknown predecessor of Zephaniah's (*pace* Calvin). In the
NT, a similar idea is expressed in Matt 23:2, where the scribes and Pharisees
are said to "sit on Moses' seat." See also "you are a priest forever, after the order
of Melchizedek" in Ps 110:4; cf. Heb 5:6, 10; 6:20; and elsewhere. On
Zephaniah son of Maaseiah, his role as associate priest, and his inglorious end
following the fall of Jerusalem, see Notes for 21:1 and 37:3. On the names
"Zedekiah" and "Maaseiah," see Appendix I.

   and to all the priests. The LXX omits, and many (Duhm; Peake; Cornill;
Volz; Rudolph; Weiser; Bright; Holladay; McKane) delete the words, with a
view to making Zephaniah the sole recipient of Shemaiah's letter. Giesebrecht
retains, with G^L, T, and Vg. Read the MT; the letters are multiple.

   26. overseers. Hebrew *pĕqîdîm.* The Versions have a singular. The plural may
exist because priests other than Zephaniah filled the office of overseer after it
was instituted by Jehoiada.

   in the house of Yahweh. The *bĕ* is omitted by ellipsis, but many Heb MSS and
the Vrs read *bĕbêt.* The preposition *lĕ* ("to") is often omitted by ellipsis in Jeremiah prose (see Note for 24:1).

   every madman and one prophesying away. Hölscher (1914: 294) believed
that ecstatic prophecy prevailed during the entire OT period and that Jeremiah
is described here as an ecstatic prophet, mad and disturbed, who because of

unruly behavior is subject to priestly discipline (cf. 20:1–6). But the consensus otherwise is that ecstatic prophecy, though present in early Israel (1 Sam 10:10–11; 19:23–24), did not survive in Amos, Hosea, Isaiah (Isa 28:7), Jeremiah, or other prophets of the later period (Heschel 1962b: 352). The idea that Jeremiah is here exceeding the bounds of acceptable prophetic behavior with ecstatic excesses rests to a large extent on the veracity of Shemaiah and others who wanted to discredit him, which cannot be taken for granted. Shemaiah is simply angry that Zephaniah has not acted as Pashhur did, when he put Jeremiah in the stocks. To portray Jeremiah as one who "raves on as a prophet" is a means of disparaging him, comparing him to earlier ecstatic prophets or prophets still around who show the old characteristics. S. Parker (1978: 282) says: "One prophet is trying to counter another by using abusive language. . . . Nothing in the context suggests abnormal behavior that could be indicative of actual 'madness' or possession trance." This caricature cannot be taken, then, as evidence that Jeremiah was an ecstatic prophet. It is because of Jeremiah's unwelcome message, preached without letup, that his opponents think him mad (Hyatt).

madman. Hebrew *'îš mĕšuggāʿ*. The Pual participle *mĕšuggāʿ* comes from the verb *šgʿ*, "to be mad." The term refers elsewhere to prophets behaving like "mad(men)" (2 Kgs 9:11; Hos 9:7).

one prophesying away. On the verb *nbʾ* in the Hithpael, see Note for 14:14.

the stocks. Hebrew *hammahpeket*. An instrument of punishment that apparently held the body in a bent or crooked position (see Note for 20:2). The LXX has *to apokleisma* ("the prison").

the collar. Hebrew *haṣṣînōq*. The term is a *hapax legomenon* in the OT. In Jewish Aramaic *ṣînôqāʾ* is a "neck-iron," which compares with Ar *zināq*, meaning "neckband" (KB³). But Kimḥi says this is an instrument for securing the hands. The LXX is not quite right with *ton katarakten* ("the dungeon"), which it used to translate *hammahpeket* ("the stocks") in 20:2.

27. *And now, why have you not rebuked Jeremiah, the Anathothite, who is prophesying away to you?* The LXX, which is in confusion here, has Shemaiah asking Zephaniah why he took to rebuking Jeremiah. In fact, the very opposite occurred! Zephaniah had *not* rebuked Jeremiah (the LXX omits the negative), and Shemaiah is berating him for "going soft" on discipline.

28. *seeing that.* Or "inasmuch as." Hebrew *kî ʿal-kēn* gives a reason (Gen 18:5; 19:8).

It will be long. On *'ărukkâ* ("long"), see 2 Sam 3:1.

Build houses and live in them; and plant gardens and eat their fruit. See 29:5.

29. *And Zephaniah, the priest, read this letter in the hearing of Jeremiah, the prophet.* Zephaniah has not disciplined Jeremiah and now is being charitable by letting him hear Shemaiah's letter for himself. The LXX omits "the priest" and "the prophet." The T and Vg have both terms.

this letter. Hebrew *hassēper hazzeh*. Reference here is to the (one) letter sent to Zephaniah. The LXX omits "this," which is present in T and Vg.

30. *And the word of Yahweh came to Jeremiah*. On this superscription, see Note for 28:12.

31. *Send to all the exiles*. The LXX and a few Heb MSS omit "all," a loss that could be attributed to haplography (homoeoteleuton: *l . . . l*). Aquila, Theod, T, and Vg all have the word. Jeremiah is now being told by Yahweh to write yet another letter to the exiles, the purpose of which is to convey an oracle of judgment against Shemaiah.

because Shemaiah prophesied to you when I, I did not send him, and he has made you trust in a lie—. Shemaiah is likely a prophet, since he has "prophesied" (*nibbā'*) to the exiles. Yet Pashhur, the priest, was also accused of false prophecy (20:6). Further indication that Shemaiah was a prophet is the fact that Dead Sea Scroll fragment 4Q339 includes him on its list of false prophets (see Note for 28:1). This indictment of Shemaiah is the same as that brought against Hananiah (28:15).

32. *Look I will reckon with Shemaiah, the Nehelamite*. Another Jeremiah oracle beginning with *hinĕnî*, "Look I" (see 29:17, 21, and Note for 1:15). On the verb *pqd* ("reckon, pay a visit") in Jeremiah, see Note on 5:9. The LXX and T omit "the Nehelamite," but the Vg has it.

There shall not be to him a man dwelling in the midst of this people. I.e., he shall not have a descendant dwelling in the midst of this people. Shemaiah is not given Hananiah's curse of death, but his line will be cut off (extirpation), which makes one wonder if this individual, like Jeremiah and Ezekiel, was not also a priest. The prophetic office was not progenitive, as were the offices of king and priest. "To sit" (*yšb*) can mean "to govern" (Judg 4:5; 1 Sam 1:9), and "to sit in the midst of the people" can similarly mean to occupy a governing position among them (Gen 23:10; 2 Kgs 4:13; Rosenberg). However, *yšb bĕtôk* elsewhere in the book, e.g., when referring to Jeremiah following his release by Nebuchadnezzar, means simply "he dwelt amidst the people" (39:14; 40:6). Shemaiah's curse is best compared to the one brought on Jehoiachin in 22:30. On the curse of no offspring, see also Deut 28:18. The LXX has "in the midst *of you . . .* to see the good that I will do *for you*."

and he shall not see the good that I will do for my people. I.e., the descendant shall not see the future good. Reference is not to Shemaiah, who is not likely to be around in 70 years. The LXX clarifies the ambiguity with, "There shall not be a man of them in the midst of you to see the good that I will do for you." This prophecy has distinct echoes of the prophecy given to Eli in 1 Sam 2:31–32.

oracle of Yahweh—for he has spoken rebellion against Yahweh. The LXX omits, but Theod, T, and Vg have the words. Assuming that *nĕ'ūm yhwh* was in the LXX's Heb *Vorlage*, the remainder of the omission can be attributed to haplography (whole-word: *yhwh . . . yhwh*). But in 28:16 the LXX omits the same phrase, which may mean another explanation is required (Stipp 1997: 194). Speaking "rebellion" (*sārâ*) against Yahweh, in any case, is also the charge leveled against Hananiah (28:16).

MESSAGE AND AUDIENCE

The audience now hears an oracle for Shemaiah, the Nehelamite, that Jeremiah instructs someone in a second letter to Babylon to deliver. The letter and oracle are not given in full. Reported only is what Shemaiah said in letters that he sent to Zephaniah, the priest, and others in Jerusalem. Shemaiah is angry, wanting to know why Zephaniah, whose responsibility it is to keep order in the Temple and to put raving madmen into the stocks and collar them, as his predecessors have done since Jehoiada set up the overseer office many years ago, has not done this with Jeremiah. Did not Pashhur discipline Jeremiah after his Topheth oracle? Shemaiah then wants to know why Zephaniah has not disciplined Jeremiah, seeing that Jeremiah sent a letter to Babylon saying the exile would be long. "Build houses and live in them; plant gardens and eat their fruit," he told them. What more the present oracle went on to say we do not know. But we do know, as earlier audiences were likely to know, that these concluding words intend to echo and put the emphasis on Jeremiah's opening words in the first letter sent to the exiles (v 5).

The audience then learns from the narrator that Zephaniah read Shemaiah's letter so Jeremiah could hear it. Yahweh's word was not long in coming. Jeremiah is told to send another letter to the exiles, in which an oracle against Shemaiah is to be included. Yahweh sees Shemaiah as simply another prophet without portfolio, one who is making the people trust in a lie. Yahweh says he will therefore reckon with Shemaiah, the Nehelamite, and with his offspring. Shemaiah will not have a man to dwell among his people, which is to say he will not have a descendant to see the good that Yahweh has planned for future days. The reason: Shemaiah has spoken rebellion against Yahweh. This segment carries the same date as the main letter in vv 1–23, which is soon after the exile in 597 B.C.

When the present judgment on Shemaiah is heard following the judgment on Hananiah in chap. 28, the audience will know two prophets by name — one in Jerusalem and one in Babylon — who have spoken rebellion against Yahweh. It will also know that Yahweh sent neither and that both are guilty of causing others to believe in a lie. Hananiah is cursed to die; Shemaiah is cursed to be without a descendant on hand to see Yahweh's future good. For an audience hearing a longer reading, reference to a future good will suitably form a transition to the Book of Restoration following (chaps. 30–33).

III. THE BOOK OF RESTORATION
(30:1–33:26)

◆

A. BOOK OF THE COVENANT (30:1–31:40)

1. Superscription and Introductory Oracle (30:1–3)

30 ¹The word that came to Jeremiah from Yahweh: ²Thus said Yahweh, God of Israel: 'Write for yourself all the words that I have spoken to you into a scroll.'

³For look, days are coming—oracle of Yahweh—when I will restore the fortunes of my people Israel and Judah, said Yahweh, and I will bring them back to the land that I gave to their fathers, and they shall possess it.

RHETORIC AND COMPOSITION

MT 30:1–3 = LXX 37:1–3. The present verses serve as an introduction to the "Book of Restoration," otherwise known as Jeremiah's "(Little) Book of Comfort" or "Book of Consolation." Originally a collection of largely hopeful prophecies comprising chaps. 30–31, this book was later expanded to include chaps. 32–33 in the larger Jeremiah book. The collection was once contained on a separate scroll (30:2); now it is a "book within a book."

The Book of Restoration is built around a core of judgment and hope poems (30:5–31:22), paired in such a way that judgment is answered by hope, and lament by divine promise (see Rhetoric and Composition for 30:4–7). Volz saw a dramatic presentation in this alternation, echoing an earlier remark by Erbt (1902: 291) that 31:18–20 was a liturgy comparable in style to liturgies in chaps. 3 and 14. Erbt saw in 31:18–20 a vision of Jeremiah (v 18), a lament by Ephraim (v 19), and an answer from Yahweh (v 20). A dramatic quality in the core poetry has been recognized more recently by Krašovec (1984: 90–91), who sees here an antithetical movement from judgment to salvation. The core poetry then contains also judgment and lament, but each poem is answered by a divine word of salvation or promise. In the added material of 31:23–40, in which the new covenant is the crowning promise, and in the even later supplementary material of chaps. 32–33, everything is future hope and salvation. The Book of Restoration preserves the bulk of Jeremiah's hopeful preaching, the dominant themes being: 1) a restoration of Israel and Judah's fortunes; 2) a return of Israelite and Judahite exiles from their captivities in the north; and

3) the covenant promises that bind Yahweh to Israel and Judah through the tragedy of 586 B.C. and ensure an even grander relationship in the days to come. The Book of Restoration is then an integral part of the completed Jeremiah book, fulfilling as nothing else does Yahweh's early promise to Jeremiah that his prophetic mission to Israel and the nations would be "to uproot and to break down . . . to build up and to plant" (1:10; cf. Childs 1979: 351).

The first Book of Restoration (30–31) frames the material it adds and the book as a whole with the key phrase "(For) look, days are coming," as well as verbs joined with "again" (*'ôd*) or "not again" (*lō' 'ôd*). The former is an opening formula; the latter a closing formula (see Rhetoric and Composition for 31:23–26). The opening formula here in the introduction makes an inclusio with the closing formula at the end of chap. 31 (Lundbom 1975: 35–36 [= 1997: 51]):

30:3   *For look, days are coming* . . .   *kî hinnēh yāmîm bā'îm*
31:40   *and it shall not again be overthrown* . . .   *wĕlō'-yēhārēs 'ôd*

The superscriptions in 30:1 and 32:1 (expanded), "The word that came to Jeremiah from Yahweh," also point to the conclusion that chaps. 30–31 are an original compositional unit (Bozak 1991: 18; Becking 1998: 3–4).

The enlarged Book of Restoration (30–33) is tied together by the key phrase "I will (surely) restore the(ir) fortunes," which functions as another inclusio:

30:3   *when I will restore the fortunes of my people*   *wĕšabtî 'et-šĕbût 'ammî*
33:26 (Q)   *for I will surely restore their fortunes* . . .   *kî-'āšîb 'et-šĕbûtām*

Here again the superscriptions in 30:1 and 34:1 (expanded), "The word that came to Jeremiah from Yahweh," point additionally to chaps. 30–33 being a compositional unit. Mowinckel (1914: 46) identified "I will restore their fortunes" as a *Stichwort* ("key word") in chaps. 30–31; Volz took the phrase in v 3 as being thematic for chaps. 30–31. On the basis of this phrase, which may have been lifted from the poetry in 30:18, the "Book of Restoration" is given its present name. The phrase occurs also in an oracle in 29:14 and at two other strategic points in chaps. 31 and 32:

1) At the beginning of the added material in chap. 31:
    when I restore their fortunes   31:23
2) At the conclusion of the narrative in chap. 32:
    for I will surely restore their fortunes   32:44

Other occurrences are in 33:7 and 11, making it a key word for all of chaps. 30–33.

Interpretation of the Book of Restoration has followed a path similar to the one taken in interpreting the Foreign Nation Oracles (chaps. 46–51), particularly the oracles against Babylon in chaps. 50–51. Critical scholars of the late eighteenth and nineteenth centuries denied the foreign nation oracles to

Jeremiah because they were deemed incompatible with his judgment preaching to Judah (see Rhetoric and Composition for 46:1 and 50:1–3). Here in the Book of Restoration, because of the overriding themes of hope and salvation, early critical opinion (Movers 1837; deWette 1843; Hitzig 1866) found this preaching more in line with Second Isaiah.[a] Although a "Second Isaiah" (or "Second Jeremiah") thesis for chaps. 30–31 was denied by Graf, later commentators (e.g., Giesebrecht; Duhm; Cornill) continued to be consumed by isolating authentic Jeremiah utterances from those deemed inauthentic, the latter being assigned to a later age. The enterprise continues into the present day, particularly among German scholars doing redaction criticism (Böhmer 1976; Lohfink 1981; and others).

It is generally agreed in light of verses such as 30:18 and 31:38 that the final composition of chaps. 30–31 must postdate the destruction of Jerusalem. But with Volz and Rudolph came a major change. These scholars restored much of the salvation preaching in 30–31 to Jeremiah, the reason being that it was now thought to emanate from Jeremiah's early career when he was calling for a return of Northern Israel (cf. 3:12–18). The idea that some of the preaching in 30–31 was originally directed to Northern Israel was present earlier in Duhm, Cornill, Peake, and others, but for Volz and Rudolph this preaching now supported Josiah's program to centralize worship in Jerusalem and the king's ambition to extend Judah's border northward after Assurbanipal's death (627 B.C.) and Assyria's departure from the region (Weiser). Herein lay the promise that "Virgin Israel" would again plant vineyards on the mountains of Samaria (31:4–5), that "the remnant of Israel" would be brought back from the north country (31:7–8), and that "Rachel's" tears would be dried because her lost sons would return (31:16). This early salvation preaching, so the argument went, was then later recycled to address newly exiled Judahites or else both Israelites and Judahites who, after 597 B.C., languished in their respective captivities "in the north."

More recently, but with a good deal less success, Lohfink (1981) and Holladay (1983) have claimed for Jeremiah certain preaching in chaps. 30–31 from the Josianic years. Lohfink finds a one-time unified composition in the poetry of 30–31, but like the earlier source critics, he comes up with this only by eliminating passages and judging selected redactional formulas as secondary, which becomes a highly subjective enterprise and one not particularly convincing (cf. Sweeney 1996: 570). Lohfink's alleged thought progression from "the North in its misery" (30:5–7, 12–15) to a "call for the return of exiles" (31:21–22) is also a problem, since the judgment poem of 30:5–7 cannot be directed to Northern Israel but must address a Judah currently under attack. Holladay appropriates the Lohfink thesis, but this only creates greater chronological difficulty for him in reconstructing Jeremiah's early career. In what is now his second attempt at a low chronology, where Jeremiah is said to receive

---

[a] For purposes of the present discussion, I am not deciding whether there is a Trito-Isaiah. "Second Isaiah" is taken to mean all the prophetic material in Isaiah 40–66.

his call in 615 B.C. at 12 years of age, we must imagine Jeremiah preaching in support of Josiah's reform while he was 12 to 18 years old, giving also his celebrated Temple oracles and standing trial at 18 years, which is simply too young an age for these activities (Lundbom 1993: 60–62).

Early Jeremianic preaching to Northern Israel was imagined also by Karl Gross (1930: 35–36), whose more important contribution was to show that in both language and ideas Jeremiah owed a substantial debt to Hosea. Evidence of this appears in the early chapters and in chaps. 30–31 (Gross 1930: 32–33; 1931). Since the time of Gross, it has become common therefore to look for parallels in language and thought between Jeremiah and Hosea, not simply between Jeremiah and Second Isaiah. With the latter, it boils down to a question of whether Second Isaiah was influenced by genuine poetry of Jeremiah or whether influence went the other way (Holladay II 156). Scholars have advanced both points of view, although today there is little inclination (except in the case of Carroll and McKane) to deny salvation preaching to Jeremiah. As was stated earlier, Jeremiah's mission is to be seen from the outset as one of "tearing down and building up." Most commentators since Volz have assumed a core of authentic Jeremianic preaching in chaps. 30–31, many even a substantial amount originating with Jeremiah (Eissfeldt 1965: 361).

A list of verbal parallels between chaps. 30–31 and Second Isaiah was compiled by Cassuto (1973b: 149–51), more extensive even than the earlier list of Movers. The most complete study of words, phrases, and themes common to chaps. 30–31 and Hosea continues to be that K. Gross (1930; 1931), whose work continues to be of value. More recently, a list of verbal parallels between chaps. 30–31 and other material in the book has been compiled by G. Fischer (1993: 143–47), a comparison that also needs to be made, since parallels external to the book of Jeremiah must be weighed against parallels within the book itself. The most important parallels in language and theme between chaps. 30–31 and Second Isaiah, Hosea, and other Jeremianic discourse are the following:

A. Jeremiah 30–31 and Second Isaiah
  1) 30:5: "and (there is) no peace" (*wě'ên šālôm*). See Isa 48:22 and 57:21, but the expression occurs also in Jeremiah (Jer 6:14 [= 8:11]; and 12:12).
  2) 30:10: "But you, do not you be afraid, Jacob my servant . . . and do not you be broken, Israel." Second Isaiah makes frequent use of "do not be afraid / fear not," *'al-tîrā'* (Isa 41:8, 10, 13–14; 43:1, 5; 44:2), but this reassuring divine command occurs also in Jeremianic poetry and prose (Jer 1:8; 42:11; 46:27, 28); the verb by itself is more common yet in Jeremiah. Found in Jeremiah often is also the verb *htt*, "be broken, be dismayed" (Jer 1:17; 8:9; 17:18; and elsewhere); *yr'* ("fear, be afraid") and *htt* ("be broken") occur together in Jer 23:4. "Servant" (*'ebed*) as an epithet for "Jacob/Israel" is found throughout Second Isaiah, with "Jacob my servant" occurring in Jeremiah only here and in 46:27–28. But "Jacob" referring to Yahweh's covenant people occurs often in Jeremiah

(Jer 2:4; 5:20; 9:3[Eng 9:4]; 10:16, 25; 30:7, 10 [2×], 18; 31:7, 11; 33:26; 46:27 [2×], 28; 51:19), where reference in some cases appears (originally) to have been only to Northern Israel and in some cases to "all Israel." In 30:7 and 18 "Jacob" denotes the "remnant of all Israel," i.e., Judah.

3) 30:11: "For I am with you." See Isa 43:5, but this preeminent biblical promise is found in Jeremiah (Jer 1:8, 19; 15:20; 42:11; 46:28) and throughout the OT.

4) 30:14, 15: "Because your iniquity was *much* (*rōb*), your sins *were numerous* ('*āṣĕmû*)." See Isa 47:9: "with your *many* (*bĕrōb*) sorceries and with the exceeding *greatness* (*bĕ'āṣĕmat*) of your enchantments."

5) 30:16: "into captivity (they) shall go." See Isa 46:2, but the expression occurs also in Jer 20:6 and 22:22.

6) 30:17: "For they have called you an outcast: 'That Zion Whom No One Cares About.'" The giving of embellished names in order to disparage occurs in Isa 60:14; 62:4, and 12 but also in Jer 46:17 ("Call the name of Pharaoh, king of Egypt: 'Loud Noise, Who Lets the Deadline Pass'").

7) 30:19: "From them thanksgiving (*tôdâ*) shall go forth and the sound (*wĕqôl*) of merrymakers." See Isa 51:3c.

8) 30:24: "the burning anger of Yahweh does not turn back (*lō' yāšûb*) until it does ('*ăśōtô*) and until it fulfills the purposes of his heart." See Isa 55:11.

9) 31:7: "Cry (*ronnû*) with gladness for Jacob and scream over The Head of the Nations." See Isa 44:23; 49:13; 52:9; and 54:1. The common term here is the verb *rnn* ("to cry out"), which appears elsewhere in Jeremiah (Jer 31:12; 51:48).

10) 31:8: "Look I will bring (*mēbî'*) them from the land of the north (*mē'ereṣ ṣāpôn*), And I will gather them from remote parts (*mîyyarkĕtê*) of the earth." Compare Isa 43:6 and 49:12. But the language here, "bring . . . (land of) the north . . . remote parts," is more likely that of Jeremiah, this statement being a reversal of the one in Jer 6:22. See also Jer 25:32 and 50:41.

11) 31:9: "I will bring them to streams of water." A similar image appears in Isa 49:10, but this too is more likely a reversal of the image used in Jeremiah's oracle against Philistia (Jer 47:2).

12) 31:10: "coastlands/islands" ('*îyyîm*). See Isa 41:1, 5; 42:4, 10, 12; 49:1; 51:5; although the term occurs also in Jeremiah (Jer 2:10; 25:22; and 47:4).

13) 31:10: "as a shepherd (keeps) his flock." See Isa 40:11. The image of "a shepherd and his flock (*'ēder*)" is found also in Jeremiah (Jer 6:3; 51:23).

14) 31:11–13: "ransom/redeem" (*pdh*), "be glad, make glad" (*śmḥ*), "joy" (*śāśôn*), and "sorrow" (*yāgôn*). See Isa 51:3, 11; 60:20; 61:3 (cf. Ludwig 1968: 537 n. 35). All, however, are well-attested Jeremiah words.

15) 31:11: "redeem" (*g'l*); a favorite Second Isaiah word but occurring also in Jer 50:34.

16) 31:12: "be radiant" (*nhr*). See the usage in Isa 60:5.

17) 31:12: "And their soul shall become like a saturated garden." See Isa 58:11, but the verb *rwh* ("to saturate") is attested elsewhere in Jeremiah (Jer 31:14, 25; 46:10).

18) 31:14: "And I will saturate the soul of the priests with abundance." Priestly restoration is present in Isa 61:6 and 66:21.

19) 31:14: "being sated (*śb'*) with Yahweh's goodness (*ṭûb*)." See Isa 58:11; 63:7; 66:11. But Yahweh's "goodness" is a theme found also in Hosea and Jeremiah (see below).

20) 31:16: "For there is a reward for your labor." See Isa 40:10 and 62:11.

21) 31:23: "O holy mountain." Compare "my holy mountain" in Isa 56:7; 57:13; 65:11, 25; 66:20. The expression "his holy abode" (*mĕ'ôn qodšô*) occurs in Jer 25:30.

22) 31:33: "I will put my law in their inward parts." "My law" (*tôrātî*) appears in Isa 51:7 but also occurs often in the Jeremiah prose (Jer 9:12[Eng 9:13]; 16:11; 26:4; 44:10). See also "law of Yahweh" in Jer 8:8.

23) 31:34: "and their sin I will not remember again." See Isa 43:25.

24) 31:35: "(The one) who stirs up the sea so its waves roar, Yahweh of hosts is his name." Duplicated exactly in Isa 51:15.

B. Jeremiah 30–31 and Hosea

1) 30:10 and elsewhere in chaps. 30–31: "return, repent" (*šûb*). The verb appears often in Hosea (22×) but is a signature verb in Jeremiah (111×), found throughout the book (K. Gross 1930: 18; Holladay 1958).

2) 30:13, 17: "heal, healing" (*rp'*). See Hos 5:13; 6:1; 7:1; 11:3; 14:5[Eng 14:4]. K. Gross (1930: 10, 16; 1931: 246–47) finds considerable language of sickness and healing in both Hosea and Jeremiah. See also Jer 4:19; 6:7, 24; 8:18, 21, 22; 10:19; 14:17, 19; 15:18; 17:14; 30:12–17; and 33:6 (cf. Muilenburg 1970b: 45–48).

3) 30:13: "sore/wound" (*māzôr*). See Hos 5:13 (2×).

4) 30:14: "your lovers" (*mĕ'ahăbayik*) with reference to a military foe; cf. Jer 22:20, 22. In Hos 2:7–15[Eng 2:5–13], "lovers" are the false gods; in 8:9–10, they are Assyria and other nations who will become Israel's military foes.

5) 30:18 and throughout chaps. 30–33: "I will (surely) restore the(ir) fortunes." See Hos 6:11, although this may be a later addition.

6) 31:2: the theme of God's grace (*ḥēn*) that come to the covenant people in the wilderness. See Hos 2:16[Eng 2:14]; 9:10; 13:5.

7) 31:3: the theme of God's love (*'ahăbâ*) for his people. See Hos 3:1; 11:1, 4; 14:5[Eng 14:4].

8) 31:3: the theme of "steadfast love/faithfulness" (*ḥesed*). Reference here is to God's "faithful" leading of Israel along, but usually in Hosea and

Jeremiah the concern is for Israel's "steadfast love/faithfulness" or lack of the same toward God. See Hos 4:1; 6:4, 6; 10:12; 12:7; cf. Jer 2:2.

9) 31:9, 18, 20: "Ephraim," meaning Northern Israel. The term is used throughout the book of Hosea (37×). See also Jer 7:15.

10) 31:9: the "father/son" metaphor used for Yahweh and his relation to Israel. See Hos 2:1[Eng 1:10]; 11:1; also Jer 3:4, 19.

11) 31:12, 14: the theme of Yahweh's "goodness" (ṭûb). See Hos 3:5; 10:11; cf. Jer 2:7.

12) 31:15: "bitterest weeping." See "bitterness" (tamrûr) in Hos 12:15; cf. Jer 6:26. The term "weeping" (bĕkî) occurs again in Jer 31:9, 15–16, and often elsewhere (Jer 3:21; 9:9[Eng 9:10]; 48:5; et passim).

13) 31:18–19: Ephraim's acknowledgment of sin and guilt. The same is anticipated or actualized in Hos 3:6; 5:15–6:3; 14:3–4[Eng 14:2–3]; cf. Jer 3:13, 23–25; 14:20.

14) 31:18: "like a young bull not trained." See Hos 10:11.

15) 31:20: "Is Ephraim my dear son? Is he the child of delight? For more than all my speaking against him, I will assuredly remember him still." On God's inner tension about giving Ephraim up and the decision finally not to do so but to show mercy, see Hos 11:8–9.

16) 31:27: "when I will sow the house of Israel and the house of Judah with the seed of human and the seed of beast." See Hos 2:25[Eng 2:23].

17) 31:34: "for I will forgive their iniquity, and their sin I will not remember again." A reversal of terminology and idea in Hos 8:13, also Jer 14:10. See in addition Jer 33:8.

C. Jeremiah 30–31 and other Jeremianic discourse

1) 30:3: "(For) look, days are coming." Common oracle introduction in the Jeremiah prose; see Note for 7:32.

2) 30:5: "A sound of fright we have heard." The use of qôl to denote "sounds" of war (4:19, 21; 6:17, 23; 8:16; and elsewhere), frightful human "sounds" during war, or persons weeping is found throughout Jeremiah (see Notes for 3:21 and 30:5).

3) 30:6: "Ask, would you, and see." Imperatives with "see" (r'h) occur often in Jeremiah (2:10, 19; 3:2; 5:1; 6:16; 7:12; 13:20).

4) 30:6: "Ask, would you, and see if a male can bear a child? So why do I see every man, his hands on his loins like a woman in labor?" Rhetorical questions with maddûaʿ, usually threefold questions, are a signature in Jeremiah found nowhere else (see Note for 2:14). The term "like a woman in labor" is also one of many like expressions typically found in Jeremiah (6:24; 22:23; 49:24; 50:43).

5) 30:11: "For I am with you . . . to save you." See Jer 1:8, 19; 15:20–21, although the verbs there for "salvation" are different.

6) 30:11: "(For) I will make a full end of all the nations. . . . But of you I will not make a full end." This is Jeremianic language; see Note for 4:27.

7) 30:12: "your blow (is) incurable"; 30:14: "for the blow of an enemy I have struck you"; 30:17: "and from your blows I will heal you." The term "blow" (*mkh*) occurs very often in Jeremiah (6:7; 10:19; 14:17; 15:18; 19:8; 49:17; 50:13).

8) 30:13: "There is none to diagnose your case" (lit., "there is none to judge your judgment") is one of many cognate accusatives in Jeremiah (see Note for 22:16). In 30:14 another one appears: "For the blow/ stroke of an enemy I have struck you"; also "(when) I will restore the fortunes" in 30:3 and throughout the Book of Restoration (see Note for 29:14).

9) 30:16: "Those who plunder you shall be for plunder, and all who despoil you I will give for spoil"; 31:4: "I will build you and you shall be built"; and 31:18: "You disciplined me and I was disciplined. . . . Bring me back so I may come back." Double-root repetitions are another signature of Jeremiah; see Note for 11:18.

10) 30:13, 17: "healing" (*rp'*). The verb and cognate noun occur very often in Jeremiah (3:22; 6:14; 8:11, 15, 22; 14:19; 15:18; 17:14; 19:11; 33:6; 46:11; 51:8–9). For language of sickness and healing in Hosea and Jeremiah, see above.

11) 31:4–5: "build . . . plant" are very common Jeremiah words; see Note for 1:10.

12) 31:4: "virgin Israel." See also 18:13 and 31:21. The term "virgin people" occurs in 14:17, and "virgin daughter Egypt" in 46:11.

13) 31:13b: "joy . . . make glad"; "joy and gladness" are a favorite Jeremiah word pair; see Note for 15:16.

14) 31:19: "I was ashamed and also disgraced." This verbal pair occurs also in 14:3. The verb *bôš* ("to be shamed, ashamed") occurs very often in Jeremiah.

While not all the words and ideas in these lists have the same value as evidence, the discourse in chaps. 30–31 does appear to betray influence from Hosea, an influence discernible also in the early chapters of Jeremiah. Diction in chaps. 30–31—in both poetry and prose—is also precisely what one finds elsewhere in the book, strengthening the impression that the oracles and other utterances in these chapters emanate from Jeremiah, not Second Isaiah or some unknown prophet before, during, or after the Exile (*pace* Mowinckel 1914: 47; Fohrer 1981b; Carroll). The parallels between chaps. 30–31 and Second Isaiah have clearly been overdrawn. Many are vitiated or else reduced as evidence by parallels existing within the book of Jeremiah itself. And when these parallels are set over against parallels between Jeremiah and Hosea, the most reasonable conclusion is that Second Isaiah drew inspiration from the preaching of Jeremiah, not the reverse (Graf; Cassuto 1973b; S. Paul 1969). Second Isaiah also appropriated words and concepts from First Isaiah, e.g., Yahweh as the "Holy One of Israel" (Muilenburg 1956a: 383, 400). The "Second Isaiah" thesis for material in chaps. 30–31 should therefore be abandoned.

The poetry and prose in these chapters is all arguably Jeremianic in origin, whereas hardly any can be convincingly claimed for Second Isaiah.

One may also conclude with Volz and Rudolph that some—though not all—of the material in 30–31 is early preaching by Jeremiah to Northern Israel during the reform years of Josiah, i.e., 622–609 B.C., after which it was recycled to address Judah or a united Israel-Judah. The first Book of Restoration was brought together after 586 B.C., but nothing requires a date in the middle- or postexilic periods for this composition (*pace* Smend 1899: 250–51 n.; Duhm; Peake; Mowinckel 1914: 46–47; Schmid 1996; and others). Jones (p. 372) says: "The conclusion that this is a late compilation is altogether too facile." This first Book of Restoration could have been prepared during the Mizpah sojourn, once thought to have lasted only a few months but now lengthened to four years, i.e., from 586 to 582 B.C., due to a revised chronology that places the 582 B.C. exile (52:30) in response to Gedaliah's murder. Erbt (1902: 287–91) expressed the view that 31:2–6, 15–17, and 18–20 could come from the period of the Mizpah sojourn, and it makes sense now for all of chaps. 30–31. During this sojourn—and even afterwards—Jeremiah counseled the restless remnant to remain in the land, perhaps thinking they could live there until Yahweh brought the exiles home.

On the relative merits of chaps. 30–31 in the MT and LXX, Becking (1994a: 169) says there is no indication that the LXX has intentionally abridged its *Vorlage* or that MT has expanded a superior text of earlier date. In his view it is not possible to decide which text is a deviation of the other, a refreshing evaluation in light of the current scholarly bias in favor of the shorter LXX text. G. Fischer (1995: 129) has argued that in chaps. 30–31 the MT is the more original text. Supporting this view are 20 arguable cases of LXX haplography in chaps. 30–31; another 18 occur in chaps. 32–33.

The present introduction is delimited at the upper end by a *setumah* in M^L and a *petuḥah* in M^P before v 1, which is also the chapter division. Jerome recognized a major break at 30:1 by beginning Book VI of his commentary there. Delimitation at the lower end is by a *petuḥah* in M^L and M^P after v 3. The M^A of 29:9b–31:35a is not extant. Based on these sections, one should not take vv 1–4 as the introduction, as some commentators do (e.g., Streane; Volz; Condamin; Rudolph; Weiser; Carroll; Keown et al.). This introduction is the typical prose found elsewhere in the book, likely the work of Baruch (Weiser), who perhaps wrote this scroll, as he did the slightly earlier one, in 605 B.C. (Holladay).

NOTES

30:1. *The word that came to Jeremiah from Yahweh.* On this superscription, see Notes for 7:1 and 21:1. The T expands to "word of prophecy."

2. *'Write for yourself all the words that I have spoken to you into a scroll.'* Jeremiah was directed to write up an earlier scroll of his prophecies, the purpose of which was to gain the people's repentance (36:2–3). Here, to judge from the oracle following, the purpose for writing a scroll seems to be to record for posterity Yahweh's promise that the fortunes of Israel and Judah will be restored and that exiles from both nations will be returned by Yahweh to the land. This will serve to keep the exiles' hope alive and will also confirm Yahweh's word when the day of fulfillment comes. One other time Jeremiah is said to have written a scroll of his prophecies—i.e., against Babylon (51:60).

for yourself. Hebrew *lĕkā*. The LXX omits. The command is given to Jeremiah, but the scroll is obviously not for him but for the larger dispirited community.

all the words. I.e., all the words of certain divine prophecies not otherwise specified. The directive is not as inclusive as the one in 36:2. Yahweh may also be telling the prophet to be sure and write down all the words in the collection that Yahweh has in mind and not leave out any. A cautionary word along these lines was given to him twice about the preached word (26:2; 50:2), although in both cases the words to be preached were words of judgment. Here the overriding message is one of hope for the future.

3. *look, days are coming.* A recurring phrase in the book, on which see Note for 7:32. Here in the Book of Restoration the phrase takes on a rhetorical function (see Rhetoric and Composition).

I will restore the fortunes. A sonorous expression of the verb *šûb* with a cognate accusative (see Note for 29:14), which also has a rhetorical function in the Book of Restoration (see Rhetoric and Composition). See also Deut 30:2–3, where the restoration of fortunes will come once the people have returned (= repented) to Yahweh. The "fortunes" are treasures taken as war booty to Babylon, as well as treasures in the land destroyed by the enemy. The LXX and T take *šĕbût* to mean "captives, captivity" (from *šbh*, "to take captive"), which is the meaning given to the term in the AV. The LXX reads *šbh* rather than *šûb* again in 31:19. But more recent modern Versions (except NIV) translate the Hebrew as "fortunes," which is correct. Becking (1994a: 158–59) thinks the LXX deliberately adapted its text to those living in a Hellenistic world.

Israel and Judah. Some commentators (Volz; Rudolph; Weiser; McKane) want to eliminate "and Judah" as later expansion, but most retain, which is correct since the verses are introducing the first Book of Restoration (chaps. 30–31), where the concern is for both Israel and Judah's future. The Versions all have "Israel and Judah." The term "Judah" occurs here, in the superscription of 30:4, and four other times in 31:23–40, all of which is expansionary material creating the first Book of Restoration. "Judah" occurs nowhere in the poetry of 30:5–31:22, some of which was originally preaching to Northern Israel only. During the final years of Zedekiah's reign and after, Jeremiah's focus was on a restored Judah-Israel.

said Yahweh. Hebrew *'āmar yhwh*. This appears superfluous after an earlier messenger formula in the verse, but the LXX, T, and Vg all have it.

and I will bring them back to the land that I gave to their fathers, and they shall possess it. Yahweh's gift of the land to the fathers is a central theme in

Deuteronomy and Jeremiah (see Note for 25:5). See particularly 3:18, which states that Judah and Israel will come from their respective exiles in the north and be reunited in the land given to the fathers.

and they shall possess it. Hebrew *wîrēšûhā*. The LXX has *kai kurieusousin autēs* ("and they shall rule over it"). The language of MT (*yrš*, "to possess") reproduces the language of Deuteronomy and is probably the better reading. Aquila and Symm have *kai klēronomēsousin (autēn)*, "and they shall possess (it)."

MESSAGE AND AUDIENCE

The audience is told here that Jeremiah received a divine word from Yahweh to write all the words now specified by him on a scroll. An oracle to the people follows, in which Yahweh says that days are coming when he will restore the fortunes of both Israel and Judah, here called "my people," and will bring them back to the land given to their ancestors, and they will possess it.

Since this divine directive with its lead oracle is made an introduction to the first Book of Restoration (chaps. 30–31), a date for both must be after the destruction of Jerusalem. Holladay's date of 588–587 B.C. is a bit early. I would suggest the time of the Mizpah sojourn, i.e., 586 to 582 B.C.

When the present oracle and other hopeful prophecies following are heard after the main letter to the exiles and the concluding oracle in chap. 29, the hope expressed in 29:10–14 and 32 will serve to lead into them.

2. Yahweh Waits to Be Gracious (30:4–31:22)

a) A Time of Distress for Jacob (30:4–7)

30 [4]And these are the words that Yahweh spoke to Israel and to Judah:
[5]For thus said Yahweh:
A sound of fright we have heard
    terror, and no peace
[6]Ask, would you, and see
    if a male can bear a child?

So why do I see every man
    his hands on his loins, like a woman in labor?
        and all faces turned deadly pale?

[7]Woe! For great is that day
    there is none like it
Yes, a time of distress it is for Jacob
    and from it shall he be saved?

RHETORIC AND COMPOSITION

MT 30:4–7 = LXX 37:4–7. Here in 30:5–31:22, the poetic core of the Book of Restoration begins (Lundbom 1975: 32–34 [= 1997: 47–49]), with only 30:8–9 being a mostly prose addition. This poetry combines judgment and hope, lament and promise, and at the center covenant formulas are balanced on either side of a judgment oracle. The whole is a moving dialogue, well suited for liturgical use:

Catchwords

a	Judgment (30:5–7) Hope (30:10–11)	Jacob / save(ed) (yšʿ) / fright(en) (ḥrd)
b	Judgment (30:12–15) Hope (30:16–17)	blow (mkh) / heal(ing) (rpʾ) / care about (drš)
c	Hope (30:18–21) Covenant Formula (30:22) Judgment (30:23–24) Covenant Formula (31:1) Hope (31:2–14)	Look (I) / restore–turn back (šûb) go forth (yṣʾ) go(es) forth (yṣʾ) / dance-whirls (ḥûl)
b′	Lament (31:15) Promise (31:16–17)	voice (qôl) / weeping (bky) / sons (bānîm)
a′	Lament (31:18–19) Promise (31:20–22)	Ephraim / return, bring back, come back turning away, turnable (šûb)

The judgment oracle at the center, 30:23–24, appears also in 23:19–20 where it has been inserted editorially. The covenant formulas on either side of this oracle are articulated in reverse order. In 30:22 the formula is spoken directly to its audience; in 31:1 the speech is indirect. This inversion and addressee alternation are added indications of an intentional structure for the poetic core.

While the controlling structure of the core is an alternation of judgment and hope, lament and promise, constituent parts of the collection alternate masculine and feminine forms of address (Holladay; Bozak 1991: 19–20). The nation—whether Northern Israel, Judah, or both—is addressed alternately as "Jacob," "Israel," or "Ephraim," then as "Virgin Israel" or "Rachel." When masculine address forms are used, the discourse is usually indirect (30:10–11 is an exception); when female address forms are used, the discourse is usually direct (31:15 is an exception):

30:5–7	Jacob's (masculine) lament told to unspecified audience
30:10–11	Jacob / Israel (masculine) told directly about his salvation
30:12–15	(Zion—feminine) addressed directly about her hurt
30:16–17	Zion (feminine) addressed directly about her healing
30:18–21	Jacob's (masculine) restoration told to unspecified audience
30:23–24	(Judah—masculine) told indirectly and directly about the divine wrath
31:2–6	Israel's (masculine) grace told to unspecified audience (vv 2–3a)
	Virgin Israel (feminine) told directly about restoration (vv 3b–6)
31:7–9	Jacob / Israel / Ephraim's (masculine) return told to unspecified audience
31:10–14	Israel / Jacob's (masculine) restoration told to the nations
31:15	Rachel's (feminine) lament told to unspecified audience
31:16–17	Rachel (feminine) told directly about the return of her sons
31:18–20	Ephraim's (masculine) repentance told to unspecified audience
31:21–22	Virgin Israel (feminine) told directly to mark way of return

Messenger formulas also aid in delimiting constituent parts of the collection (Duhm; Lohfink 1981; Bozak 1991; Sweeney 1996), but like gender alternation they are not the controlling structure. Messenger formulas alternate between "(For) thus said Yahweh" and "oracle of Yahweh":

30:5	For thus said Yahweh
30:10	oracle of Yahweh
30:11	oracle of Yahweh
30:12	For thus said Yahweh
30:17	oracle of Yahweh
30:18	Thus said Yahweh
30:21	oracle of Yahweh
31:1	oracle of Yahweh
31:2	Thus said Yahweh
31:7	For thus said Yahweh
31:14	oracle of Yahweh
31:15	Thus said Yahweh
31:16	Thus said Yahweh
31:16	oracle of Yahweh
31:17	oracle of Yahweh
31:20	oracle of Yahweh

The core of poetry is tied together by an inclusio made from repeated and balancing key words in 30:6 and 31:22b (Lundbom 1975: 32–34 [= 1997: 47–49]):

30:6   Ask, would you, and see
        if a *male* can bear a child?   *zākār*
     So why do I see every *man*   *geber*
        his hands on his loins like a woman in labor?

31:22b For Yahweh has created a new thing on earth:
      the *female* protects the *man*!   *nĕqēbâ . . . gāber*

In mood also, the end is a return to the beginning. The opening poem talks about battle-weary men acting like women in labor, whereas the closing line says that females must protect the men, an ironic reversal of how things should be—particularly in wartime. So, although the collection as a whole has an overriding theme of salvation, the beginning and end reflect the anguish of a more recent judgment.

The present poem is demarcated at the top end by a *petuḥah* in M^L and M^P before v 4. Neither codex has a section after v 7, but 4QJer^c does, marking the poem's conclusion with a *petuḥah*. The beginning of the unit is also marked by the superscription in v 4 and the messenger formula in v 5; at the end there is additionally a shift to prose in v 8. This poem and the one following in vv 10–11 have been deliberately juxtaposed, as the above structure indicates. In my view, vv 5–11—with or without vv 8–9—were not originally a unified composition (*pace* Boadt; Becking 1989). They, like the poems in 20:7–10 and 11–12 and other poems here in chaps. 30–31, were originally self-standing and have been brought together into a larger composition. Section markings after v 7 (4QJer^c) and v 9 (M^L and M^P) are a further indication that breaks belong at these two points.

The present poem has three stanzas with the following repetitions and balancing terms:

I . . . . v 5
          . . . . *and no* . . . .   *wĕ'ên*
        . . . . *and see*   *ûrĕ'û*   v 6
      . . . .

II . . . . *do I see every man*   *rā'îtî kol-geber*
      . . . .
        all faces . . . . *kol-pānîm*

III . . . .   v 7
      there is none . . . .   *mê'ayin* . . .
      . . . .
      . . . .

The structural significance of *'ên* ("no") and *mê'ayin* ("there is none") in I and III is noted by van der Wal (1996: 82), but vv 5–7 do not have the chiastic structure that he claims for them.

Jeremiah is the speaker of this poem, articulating as elsewhere the deep anguish of a defeated people before its enemy (Giesebrecht; Peake; Volz; Rudolph; Weiser; Bright; Thompson). The speaker is not Yahweh, as claimed by Calvin and more recently Holladay. The messenger formula in v 5 is responsible for the confusion (see Notes). The verses are in the style of a lament (Giesebrecht); they are not a divine oracle (Duhm).

The poem is linked to the inserted prose oracle in vv 8–10 by these key words (Condamin):

v 7 *that day*   v 8 *in that day*

Catchwords connecting to the companion poems in vv 10–11 are the following:

v 5 *fright*   *ḥărādâ*   v 10 *frighten*   *mahărîd*
and no   *wĕʾên*   *Jacob* (2x)
v 7 *Jacob*   *look I will save you*
shall he be saved   *and none*   *wĕʾên*
v 11 *to save you*

NOTES

30:4. *And these are the words that Yahweh spoke to Israel and to Judah.* This superscription introduces all the prophetic utterances in chaps. 30–31, not just the one following or a select number of utterances within the chapters. In form it is similar to the superscriptions in Deut 1:1 (*"These are the words* that Moses spoke to all Israel . . ."); Deut 28:69[Eng 29:1] (*"These are the words* of the covenant that Yahweh commanded Moses . . ."); and Jer 29:1 (*"And these are the words* of the letter that Jeremiah the prophet sent . . ."). If Baruch composed it, we see continuity not only with the report of Jeremiah's letters to the exiles in chap. 29 but also with the first edition of the book of Deuteronomy (chaps. 1–28), which was a completed book in Jeremiah's time (Lundbom 1996a: 314–15). Again, some commentators (Volz; Rudolph; Weiser; McKane) want to eliminate "Judah" here, but as we said earlier, the Book of Restoration is intended for both Israel and Judah (30:3). The Versions all have both Israel and Judah.

5. *For thus said Yahweh.* The LXX omits *kî* ("For"), but Aq, Symm, and Theod all have *hoti houtōs.* The omission could be attributed to haplography in the Hebrew *Vorlage* (homoeoarcton: *k . . . k*) or be an inner-Greek haplography (homoeoarcton: *ho . . . ho*). More problematic is the formula itself, which is ill suited for the poem following. The beginning "we have heard" has to be Jeremiah speaking for himself and the people (cf. 6:24). The speaker here, and throughout the poem, cannot be Yahweh (*pace* Calvin; Holladay). Rudolph takes the formula as a later redactional element; Weiser deletes. There are other instances in the book where messenger formulas introduce prophetic utterances not likely to be divine oracles (9:16[Eng 9:17]; 17:5). In the present case, it could be that the compiler took Jeremiah's poem in vv 5–7 and Yahweh's answer in vv 10–11 as a single divine word (so Bright). Many of the Jeremianic oracles are in fact dialogical in form, containing both the prophet's voice and the voice of Yahweh (e.g., 4:5–8, 13–17; 5:10–13; and 6:1–7). See also the prophet's complaint and Yahweh's answer in 4:19–22. So in the larger composition this messenger formula probably applies to the poems as a pair, one spoken by the prophet, the other spoken by Yahweh—this, despite two other "oracle of Yahweh" formulas in vv 10–11.

A sound of fright we have heard. Hebrew *qôl ḥărādâ šāmāʿnû.* The term *ḥărādâ* and its cognate verb in v 10 denote a state of deep fright (lit., "trembling"), the sort coming uninvited to a defeated people or a people fearing defeat at the hands of its enemies (1 Sam 14:15; Isa 21:4; Ezek 26:16; cf. Becking 1989: 65). The "sound" (*qôl*) is then of panic-stricken voices in the prophet's ears, heard on other occasions when a battle was raging or envisioned as raging (4:29, 31; 9:18[Eng 9:19]; 10:22; 25:36; 48:3; 49:21; 50:22, 42, 46; 51:54). The term *qôl* could be rendered "voice" (AV) or "cry/cries" (RSV; NEB; JB; NAB; NJV; NIV). Jeremiah is hearing battle-weary soldiers crying out like women giving birth. There is no warrant for emending "we have heard" to "I have heard" (*pace* Volz; Rudolph; Weiser; JB [but not in NJB]), which reproduces "I have heard" in 31:18 and creates an unneeded consistency with "I see" in v 6. The LXX's "you will hear" has not won adherents (Duhm and Volz: "based on a misunderstanding"). The NEB translated it, but this was abandoned in REB for the reading of MT. Aquila, T, and Vg all support MT, whose reading should be retained.

terror, and no peace. Hebrew *paḥad wĕʾên šālôm*, with *šālôm* having the fuller meaning of personal and community well-being. People generally, both good and bad, want for themselves peace and the fruits of peace (cf. 4:10; 5:12; 6:14; 8:11), but when Yahweh unleashes holy terror on wicked humanity, it matters not that the human desire is otherwise (Isa 48:22; 57:21). Jeremiah himself spoke about hoping for peace and seeing only terror (8:15; 14:19). Compare Isa 21:4: "My desired twilight turned for me into fright (*ḥărādâ*)." Hebrew *paḥad* ("terror") is an ancient term deriving from holy war (see Note on 49:5), promised now in later days to a disobedient covenant people (Deut 28:67; cf. Isa 2:10, 19, 21). On the language of horror and terror in Jeremiah, see Muilenburg 1970b: 50–54.

6. *Ask, would you, and see if a male can bear a child? So why do I see every man, his hands on his loins, like a woman in labor?* A variation of the familiar Jeremianic *hă . . . ʾim . . . maddûaʿ* ("If . . . if . . . so why . . . ?") argument, modified here by containing a directive in the first member instead of a rhetorical question. On the three-question form, see Note for 2:14. Ginsberg (1946: 35) argued that the *ʾim* ("if") beginning the second colon seemed to require a double rhetorical question, which would make the form here like others in Jeremiah and like the examples he observed in Ugaritic. He thus took the form here to be defective. Held (1969: 78–79) cited Ginsberg's proposal

with approval; however, reconstruction does not appear necessary. Nor is it necessary to translate the *'im* clause as a statement and only the *maddûaʿ* clause as a question, as the NJV does. The directive to make an investigation is Jeremianic (2:10: "Cross over to the Greek islands and see . . ."; 18:13: "Ask please (*ša'ălû-nā'*) among the nations, who has heard things like these?"), to which one may add the string of imperatives followed by *maddûaʿ* in 46:3–5 and 14–15 for comparison. The question about a male bearing a child is ironic, since it proposes an impossibility. Though the verb *yld* can also mean "beget" (16:3; Gen 4:18; 10:8; Prov 23:22), that meaning makes no sense here, as Calvin rightly points out, for the answer to the question would then be "yes," and the incongruity essential to the argument would be destroyed. Precluded similarly is a "yes and no" answer (*pace* Bozak 1991: 36–37). The statement and rhetorical question mean to set up Jeremiah's preferred question — i.e., why are soldiers bent over helpless, like women in labor? They are not giving birth, but they surely look as though they are! On the language of travail and anguish in Jeremiah, see Muilenburg 1970b: 48–50.

So why do I see every man, his hands on his loins, like a woman in labor? Compare the "so, why have I seen?" question in 46:5, where Jeremiah registers astonishment over Egyptian soldiers in defeat. Hebrew *geber* is a virile man, here a man fighting in Jerusalem's defense. Ehrlich (1912: 317) says *geber* is employed because giving birth is a feminine function. The term is used again ironically in 31:22b. The dual *ḥălāṣayim* means "loins," the part of the body between the ribs and the hip bones (KB³). This is the only occurrence of the word in the book. On the imagery of men behaving like women in labor, see also Isa 13 j:8 and 21:3. A curse upon defeated warriors is that they will become like (weak) women (see Notes on 4:31; 6:24; and 50:37).

like a woman in labor. Hebrew *kayyôlēdâ.* The LXX lacks the term and many delete with Duhm. But Giesebrecht retains, noting that the term is present in Aq, Symm, Theod, the Hexapla, Gᴸ, S, T, and Vg and is necessary for understanding the portrayal (cf. 6:24; 22:23; 49:24; 50:43).

and all faces turned deadly pale? Hebrew *yērāqôn* is a noun meaning "mildew," the sort that afflicts field crops (1 Kgs 8:37; Amos 4:9; Hag 2:17). On the root *yrq* and its various forms, see Brenner 1982: 100–102. Here the term refers to yellow-green paleness of face, brought about in Kimḥi's view from severe pain. See also A. R. Johnson 1964: 41. It is more the look of death (Moffatt: "deadly pallor"; NAB and NIV: "deathly pale"; REB: "deadly pale"; NSB: "dödsbleka"). For other descriptions of faces turning pale due to fright, see Isa 13:8; Nah 2:10; and Joel 2:6. The LXX omits "all" and reads the *hôy* beginning v 7 as *hāyû* (metathesis): "Faces are changed; they have become jaundiced (*eis ikteron egenēthē*)." This yields tolerable sense, and some scholars (Mowinckel 1946: 109 n. 95, appealing to meter; Volz; Rudolph; Weiser; Holladay) adopt the reading, but MT's *hôy* ("Woe!") is best retained (McKane). It is not incomprehensible (*pace* Becking 1994a: 152). Jerome's Vulgate has *Vae!* ("Woe!").

7. *Woe! For great is that day.* On the multiple uses of *hôy* ("Woe!") in Jeremiah, see Note for 22:13. The "day" referred to here is Yahweh's day of judg-

ment, which came climactically in Jerusalem's fall to the Babylonians. There is no way this poem could originally have been addressed to Northern Israel (*pace* Lohfink 1981), since its "Day of Yahweh" was in the distant past. On the "Day of Yahweh," see Note for 4:9. Medieval Jewish commentators (Rashi, Kimḥi, Abarbanel) interpreted the "day" eschatologically (cf. "Gog and Magog" in Ezekiel 38–39; Dan 12:1; BT Sanhedrin 98b). The original proclamation was surely without messianic ideas (Calvin; Volz), but we see the beginnings of such in the interpolated vv 8–9, where "that day" has become transformed (along with v 7b) into a future day of salvation, and David is once again reigning as king.

there is none like it. The MT reads *mē'ayin kāmôhû,* "from where is like it?" but if *mē'ayin* is repointed to *mē'ên,* the reading becomes "there is none like it" (cf. 10:6–7) or "without any like it" (cf. 4:7; 26:9; 46:19), which nicely balances *wĕ'ên* ("and no") in v 5 (see Rhetoric and Composition). The meaning is the same: the coming day of Yahweh will have nothing to which it may be compared.

Yes, a time of distress it is for Jacob. The expression "time of distress, trouble" (*'ēt ṣārâ*) occurs also in 14:8 and 15:11; in 16:19 it is "day of trouble" (*yôm ṣārâ*). "Distress" is associated with childbearing also in 4:31; 6:24; 49:24; and 50:43. While "Jacob" may have referred originally to just Northern Israel in 30:10 and 31:7, and 11, here and in 30:18 it means the entire covenant people, of which only Judah remains (Giesebrecht; Jones). It has the same broader meaning in 10:16, 25, and later in Second Isaiah (Isa 40:27; 41:8, 14, 21; 42:24 et passim). Northern Israel's distress occurred in 722 B.C. at the hands of the Assyrians.

and from it shall he be saved? This colon has been universally taken as a declaration of divine deliverance, being read this way in all the Versions, ancient and modern, and interpreted as such by most all commentators. Calvin saw the day of distress as Jerusalem's destruction; still, he maintained that here at the end of the verse the prophet gives the hope of divine mercy, even deliverance from the distress. This word of hope is also seen by many as making a fitting transition to vv 10–11, where salvation is promised in a divine oracle, and to the interpolated vv 8–9, where "that day" becomes the day when Yahweh will break the enemy's yoke of servitude. Giesebrecht, however, says that this sudden announcement of rescue together with the punishment is unprophetic, and he is right. This lament cannot end by announcing a miraculous deliverance such as Jerusalem experienced in 701 B.C. In 586 B.C. Jacob (= Judah) was not saved. The suggestion therefore put forth by Holladay (1962a: 53–54; 1974: 111–12; 1989: 172–73) that the words were originally posed as a question to which the answer was a resounding "No!" is clearly the right interpretation. There is no *hē'* interrogative here, but questions can be posed without one (Mitchell 1908). What we have then is another concluding question like "and would you return to me?" in 3:1, which originally required a "no" answer but over time came to be a statement celebrating Israel's repentance (see Note for 3:1).

MESSAGE AND AUDIENCE

In this poem of lament, Jeremiah articulates his own anguish and that of the people as Jerusalem teeters on the verge of destruction. Here is not a vision of what will happen at some future time but a report of something happening currently. The prophet hears with everyone else a frightful sound, one of anguish and terror, and asks those listening to inquire whether it is possible for a male to bear a child. It is not necessary to answer. Why then does Jeremiah see every man with his hands on his loins like a woman giving birth? Their faces have the look of death! The audience again need not answer. So Jeremiah must come out with a thundering "Woe!" There is nothing quite like the present day, a day belonging to Yahweh that brings distress upon poor Jacob. Will he be saved from it? The audience is left to answer this question. But will it?

This pathos-filled lament was probably spoken to a Judahite audience just prior to 586 B.C., at which time Jeremiah was in the court of the guard (Bright; Berridge 1970: 187). But once Jerusalem had been reduced to ruins, this poem to the survivors was joined with the salvation oracle in vv 10–11, and the two together answered the question about Jacob's being saved quite differently. Yes, Jacob would be saved, not from Nebuchadrezzar and the Babylonian army, but from its distant land of captivity. Salvation was now being promised to both Israel and Judah (v 4), and Jeremiah's lament along with Yahweh's answer had become a single divine word. And at an even later time, the question in v 7b became not a question at all but a statement anticipating Yahweh's salvation on the other side of judgment, which at this point had already been fulfilled.

b) Do Not You Be Afraid, Jacob (30:8–11)

30 ⁸And it will happen in that day—oracle of Yahweh of hosts:
    I will break his yoke from upon your neck
        and your straps I will tear away
So strangers shall not again make him serve; ⁹instead they shall serve Yahweh their God and David, their king, whom I will raise up for them.

    ¹⁰But you, do not you be afraid, Jacob my servant
        —oracle of Yahweh—
    and do not you be broken, Israel
For look I will save you from afar
    and your offspring from the land of their captivity
And Jacob will return and be undisturbed
    yes, be at ease and none will frighten

    ¹¹For I am with you
        —oracle of Yahweh—
    to save you
For I will make a full end of all the nations

among which I have scattered you
But of you I will not make a full end
Yes, I will correct you justly
but I will by no means leave you unpunished.

RHETORIC AND COMPOSITION

MT 30:8–11 = LXX 37:8–9. The present verses contain three oracles, the first in vv 8–9 being a subsequent addition to the core poetry meaning to reinterpret v 7. "That [judgment] day" of v 7 now becomes "that [salvation] day" of v 8. This added oracle, which is mostly but not entirely in prose, also attaches itself to the pair of oracles in vv 10–11 that promise a future salvation for Jacob. The oracle in vv 8–9 is delimited at the top end by a *petuhah* in 4QJer^c before v 8; The M^L and M^P have no section here, and the verses in M^A are not extant. Delimitation at the bottom end is by a *setumah* in M^L and a *petuhah* in M^P after v 9. 4QJer^c upon reconstruction appears not to have a section after v 9 (Tov 1997: 195). Oracles II and III, which in the core poetry become a single word of salvation, are delimited at the top end by a *setumah* in M^L and a *petuhah* in M^P before v 10 and at the bottom end by a *petuhah* in M^L, M^P, and 4QJer^c (reconstructed) after v 11.

Both vv 10 and 11 have "oracle of Yahweh" formulas, indicating two separate oracles. In the parallel passage of 46:27–28, however, the first formula is lacking. There is also no section marking after v 10, which is the case also after 46:27 in 2QJer, M^A, and M^P, although M^L does have a *setumah* after v 27. What we probably have here are two salvation oracles combined to answer Jeremiah's word of judgment in vv 5–7 (see Rhetoric and Composition for 30:4–7). Since the judgment in vv 5–7 is in the style of a lament, it is natural that it be answered by a salvation oracle (Begrich 1934: 82). Assurances of salvation following laments are well documented in the Psalms, and here too we likely have a liturgical form created for use in worship. While it is possible that the present salvation oracles were addressed originally to Northern Israel, as a companion piece to vv 5–7 they are likely to have been spoken from the start to Judah (Holladay), then later on applied to both Israel and Judah.

The LXX omits vv 10–11, perhaps because of a duplication in the Foreign Nation Collection (MT 46:27–28). Quite often, though not always, the LXX omits doublets the second time they occur in the book (first noted by G. L. Spohn in 1824; cf. Janzen 1973: 2–3). In the LXX, where the Foreign Nation Oracles come earlier, the second occurrence is here. The oracles, however, cannot be omitted in the present context without the larger structure being violated. Thus they are not a gloss on vv 7–9 (*pace* Janzen 1973: 94) or a further working out of vv 8–9 (*pace* Calvin; McKane). Verses 8–9 break the continuity between vv 5–7 and vv 10–11. It is unnecessary to decide which placement—the one here or the one in 46:27–28—is better or more original. The verses are suitable in both contexts, and questions about priority of place are largely irrelevant (Streane; Becking 1994a: 149–50).

Also a nonissue (except for Carroll and McKane) is whether vv 10–11 belong to the period of Second Isaiah. Graf argued long ago that the verses were authentic to Jeremiah, the language in both verses—particularly v 11—strongly supporting this claim (Bright; Holladay; Jones: "the resemblance [to Second Isaiah] is superficial"). The "do not you be afraid! / fear not!" of v 10, which was the parade example of those arguing a Second Isaiah provenance, is a divine command elsewhere in Jeremiah (1:8; 42:11) and, in fact, is a formula much older than either Jeremiah or Second Isaiah (see Notes). Also, its collocation here with the phrase "do not be broken" is clearly a Jeremianic construction (see Rhetoric and Composition for 30:1–3).

In the parallel verse of 46:28, an opening line similar to the opening line in v 27 is added:

I   *But you, do not you be afraid, Jacob my servant*   v 27 (= 30:10)

. . . .

II   *You, do not you be afraid, Jacob my servant*   v 28

. . . .

Some commentators (Volz; Rudolph; Bright; Holladay) thus restore what they think is a missing colon in 30:11a, although there is no textual warrant for doing so. The opening colon in v 11a adds "to save you," which is not present in 46:28, perhaps to function as a catchword with the oracle in v 10 and the companion poem in vv 5–7 (see below). The link between vv 10–11 is made with these key words:

I   *For look I will save you* from afar   *kî hinĕnî môšîʿăkā*   v 10b
II   *For I am with you . . . to save you*   *kî . . . lĕhôšîʿekā*   v 11a

Oracle II contains this balance of sound:

II   *For I am with you . . .*   *kî-ʾittĕkâ ʾănî . . .*   v 11a
     But of you . . .   *ʾak ʾōtĕkâ . . .*   v 11c

The inserted vv 8–9 are prose for the most part. The whole cannot be scanned as poetry (*pace* Thompson), nor can vv 8–9 be taken with Bozak (1991: 21) as a stanza of a unified poem in vv 5–11. However, the line "I will break his yoke from upon your neck, and your straps I will tear away" might be poetry, which would explain its otherwise troublesome second person suffixes (see Notes). We see again in 31:23 second person poetry embodied in a prose oracle. The oracle here could, but need not, derive from Jeremiah. A late date is also not required (Hertzberg 1952: 596–97). It could date from the same time as other supplemental material in the first Book of Restoration (30:1–3; 31:23–40), since it has a similar rhetorical structure: an introductory formula and a verb + "not again":

I   And it will happen *in that day* . . .   *. . . bayyôm hahûʾ*   v 8
     So strangers *shall not again make him serve* *. . . wĕlōʾ-yaʿabdû-bô ʿôd*

On the structured prose in the first Book of Restoration, see Rhetoric and Composition for 31:23–26.

Oracle I is linked to the prior poem in vv 5–7 by these catchwords:

v 8 *in that day*   v 7 *that day*

Oracles II and III are linked to their companion poem in vv 5–7 by these catchwords:

v 10	*frighten*	*mahărîd*	v 5	*fright*	*hărādâ*
	Jacob (2×)			*and no*	*wĕ'ên*
	look I will save you		v 7	*Jacob*	
	and none	*wĕ'ên*			*shall he be saved*	
v 11	*to save you*				

NOTES

30:8. *And it will happen in that day.* This formula introduced Judah's day of judgment in 4:9, but here things are reversed. The future day will now see Yahweh breaking the yoke placed on Jacob by his enemies. The day of distress spoken of in v 7 is past, and a remnant of Jacob has been saved. Anticipated also is the salvation promised in vv 10–11.

Yahweh of hosts. The LXX omits "of hosts," as elsewhere (see Appendix VI).

I will break his yoke from upon your neck, and your straps I will tear away. A syntactic chiasmus with the verbs at the extremes. The yoke and straps symbolize servitude—in international law, a suzerain-vassal relationship between nations (Becking 1989: 75–76). Earlier in Josiah's reign Judah was promised a breaking of the Assyrian "yoke" and "straps" that kept her subservient, and this did happen quite dramatically when Nineveh fell in 612 B.C. (Nah 1:13; cf. Isa 10:27). More recently Judah was placed under the yoke of Nebuchadrezzar and the Babylonians at Yahweh's command (27:2–15). But the promise now is that this yoke too will be broken, not in a short while, as the dreamer-prophet Hananiah predicted (28:2–4, 10–11), but in a day of Yahweh's own choosing. The salvation envisioned here is grander: the yoke of "nations" (plural) will be broken (T; Rashi). Kimḥi says this is the yoke of Gog and Magog or the yoke of every nation that exerted power over Israel in exile. But an eschatological interpretation is not required. That day of salvation actually came, and when it did it was remembered with songs of thanksgiving (Ps 107:14).

his yoke . . . your neck . . . your straps. Straps (*môsērôt*) made of leather were to secure the yoke to the oxen (2:20; 5:5; 27:2). On the yoke and its symbolism in the ancient world, see Note for 27:2. In the MT, Yahweh's initial words are direct: "I will break his yoke (i.e., the yoke of Babylon) from upon your neck, and your straps I will tear away." Compare Isa 10:27. Then in vv 8b–9 there is a shift to the third person. The LXX is all third person. There the initial words read: "I will break the yoke from upon their neck, and their fetters I will burst." 4QJer^c supports MT, and so basically do all the Versions except the Vg, which has "his straps." Nothing much is at stake. A day will come when Israel's servitude to Babylon will end. Becking (1994a: 159) says that, if the oracle ends with "I will burst," then the MT's shift of person at 8b can be explained. The LXX translation, in his view, is a later accommodation to facilitate audience understanding. Recognizing a break after 8b is important, but in my view the shift of person there is due to the oracle's having embodied a bicolon of poetry (see Rhetoric and Composition).

So strangers shall not again make him serve. Hebrew ʿbd + bĕ in the Qal means "make serve, enslave" (see Note for 25:14). The LXX's "and they shall no longer serve strangers" misses the causative meaning in the Qal and eliminates the indirect object "him" (bô) entirely. The omission of the indirect object can be attributed to haplography (homoeoteleuton: w . . . w). The promise given here reverses the judgment in 5:19; 25:14; and 27:7. "Strangers" (zārîm) are "foreigners," as in 5:19; 51:2, 51; and Ezek 7:21; 11:9; 28:7, 10; 30:12. In Jer 2:25 and 3:13 they are the "strange gods."

9. instead they shall serve Yahweh their God and David, their king, whom I will raise up for them. This verse or something like it is required after what precedes, since being freed from one's enemies is not enough. Calvin says order must be established; but more to the point, a new servitude must replace the old. Liberation in the biblical view is a change of masters (Daube 1963). Yahweh therefore breaks the yoke of foreign nations so that the people will once again serve him (cf. Exod 23:25; Deut 10:12), and here, also, a Davidic king whom Yahweh will raise up.

David, their king, whom I will raise up for them. This king will not simply be like David or be a king in the Davidic line; he will be a David redivivus (G. F. Moore 1927 II: 325–26). Beginning here and elsewhere in the OT are the messianic ideas seen flowering in later Judaism (Hos 3:5; Amos 9:11; Jer 23:5–6; 33:15–16, 17, 21–22; Ezek 34:23–24; 37:24–25; Isa 55:3–4; cf. BT Sanhedrin 98a), when there also emerged the idea of an Elijah redivivus (Mal 4:5; cf. Matt 11:11–15). Romantic longings for a "king like David" are present already in the Deuteronomic History (2 Kgs 14:3; 16:2; 18:3; 22:2). The reference in Hos 3:5 to people's seeking Yahweh and David, their king, is important background for the present verse and need not be dismissed as later Judahite interpolation (Andersen and Freedman 1980: 301; Emmerson 1984: 101–13). Emmerson points out that while Hosea opposed the Northern institution of kingship, he did not oppose kingship per se, and a future Davidic kingship in this prophet's thought was certainly possible. Jeremiah, too, appears to have supported the idea of a future Davidic king for Israel (23:5–6; 33:15–16), and the same is true for Second Isaiah (Isa 55:3–4).

10–11. But you, do not you be afraid, Jacob my servant . . . Israel. . . . I will save you from afar. . . . I am with you. Begrich (1934) argued that "do not be afraid" was the typical beginning of a "salvation oracle" spoken by priests in public worship (cf. Lam 3:57; Ps 35:3) and that the prophets, Second Isaiah in particular, borrowed the style in their preaching (Isa 41:8, 10, 13–14; 43:1, 5; 44:1–2). If Jeremiah appropriated such a genre, he definitely made it his own in this and other preaching. This is the first time "my servant" occurs as an honorific title for Jacob/Israel in the OT (S. R. Driver 1913: 261), a concept that becomes fully developed in Second Isaiah (Isa 41:8; 42:1, 19; 43:10; 44:1–2; 44:21). The title "Jacob, my servant," occurs also in Ezek 37:25. Becking (1989: 70) calls attention to prior Aramaic and Akkadian texts containing the "do not be afraid / fear not" injunction. In the eighth-century B.C. Zakkur (Zakir) Inscription, for example, the god says to the king of Hamath:

> Do not be afraid! Since I have made [you king, I will stand] beside you. I will save you from all [these kings who] have besieged you.
> (CS II 155; ANET³ 655; M. Weippert 1981: 102–3)

And in an oracle concerning Esarhaddon (680–669 B.C.), the Assyrian king is told:

> Fear not, Esarhaddon! I, the god Bel, am speaking to you. I watch over your inner heart as would your mother who brought you forth. Sixty great gods are standing together with me and protect you.
> (ANET³ 605)

Another oracle gives Ashurbanipal (688–627 B.C.) reassurance after a tearful supplication:

> The goddess Ishtar heard my anxious sighs and said, "Fear not!" and gave me confidence (saying), "Since you have lifted your hands in prayer and your eyes have filled with tears, I have had mercy."
> (ANET³ 606)

For other "do not be afraid / fear Not" assurances in Assyrian texts, see M. Weippert 1981: 96–98. Weiser also points out that the reassuring "do not be afraid" occurs earlier in biblical theophanies, spoken to individuals by either Yahweh or his angel (Gen 15:1; 21:17; 26:24; cf. Conrad 1985).

10. *and do not you be broken, Israel.* On the verb *ḥtt*, "be broken, dismayed," see Note for 1:17.

For look I will save you from afar. I.e., from exile. The word is spoken in Zion.

and your offspring from the land of their captivity. Calvin says that offspring are mentioned because the captivity will be long. While children sometimes pay for the sins of their parents, it is also true that sometimes only they receive the blessings promised to their parents (Gen 12:1–3, 7; 13:14–17).

And Jacob will return and be undisturbed. Hebrew *wĕšāb yaʿăqōb wĕšāqaṭ.* Calvin took *šāb* as coming from the verb *yšb*, "to dwell," but most commentators and Versions prefer *šûb*, "to return," some giving that verb the meaning "once more" or "again" (NEB; REB; JB [but NJB has "return"]; NAB; NJV).

Gordis (1933b: 157) proposed giving *šûb* the meaning "rest" (similarly in 4:1), but this is unnecessary, since "rest" and "quiet" are conveyed in the next two verbs. The idea of "returning and rest" is a familiar theme from First Isaiah (Isa 30:15; cf. 7:3–4).

yes, be at ease. Hebrew *ša'ănan* is a Palel form of *š'n*, meaning "be at ease, rest easily" (cf. GKC §55d). The verbs *š'n* and *šqṭ* occur together again in 48:11.

and none will frighten. Hebrew *wĕ'ên maḥărîd*. The metaphor of sheep lying peacefully in pasture is a common image used to describe a people unmolested by enemies (Zeph 3:13; Ezek 34:28; 39:26).

11. *For I am with you . . . to save you.* On the great "I am with you" promise in the Bible, see Note for 1:8.

For I will make a full end of all the nations. . . . But of you I will not make a full end. The word *kālâ* in Hebrew is strong, meaning "(full) end" or "completion." In 5:10, Yahweh indicated that he would make a "full end" of his people, but here he promises not to make a "full end of them." The "but" ('*ak*) beginning v 11c, which is not present in 46:28, strengthens the antithesis. Did Yahweh make a full end of Judah? Well, yes, the nation was destroyed. But was it a complete end? Well, no, a remnant survived. On the basis of this promise, earlier judgments regarding the covenant people (5:10, 18) had therefore to be amended, supplemented, or reinterpreted (see Notes for 4:27 and 5:10). The tension is similar when deciding whether a "full end" promised to the nations came about. It says here that a full end will be made of all the nations. Yet, the nations did not come to an absolute end—even Babylon, for whom no mitigating word is to be found in the oracles against it. Some nations are even promised restoration, their fortunes included (46:26; 48:47; 49:6, 39). While the language of the present verse is definitely Jeremiah, the idea that the covenant people will not be completely destroyed is clearly present in Deuteronomy 32, where Yahweh says that in meting out their punishment he will nevertheless stop short of making their rememberance cease altogether. The reason: this would send the wrong message to Israel's adversaries, who would then dishonor his name (Deut 32:26–27). A remnant is therefore preserved, after which Yahweh goes on finally to take vengeance on Israel's enemies (vv 34–43). Compare also the remnant theology in Isa 10:20–23.

among which I have scattered you. I.e., in exile (9:15[Eng 9:16]; 13:24; 18:17; cf. Deut 4:27; 28:64). Berridge (1970: 187) takes "I have scattered you" as a prophetic perfect, but the verb is better read as a simple past. After 597 B.C., a scattering of people to Babylon, Egypt, and other neighboring countries had already occurred, to which could be added Northern Israel's earlier scattering to Assyria.

Yes, I will correct you justly. Calvin: "with moderation." In 10:24 Jeremiah asked for correction "with justice" for himself—i.e., not with a full measure of the divine anger (see Note there).

but I will by no means leave you unpunished. Hebrew *wĕnaqqēh lō' 'ănaqqekā*. The verb *nqh* means "to clean, clear, leave unpunished" (Akk *zakû*; CAD 21: 25–32; cf. Cogan 2001: 174). Correction with justice does not translate into no punishment (Exod 20:7; 34:7; Num 14:18; Nah 1:3). Other nations are also told that they cannot hope to escape the divine punishment (Jer 25:29; 49:12).

MESSAGE AND AUDIENCE

Yahweh in Oracle II (v 10) emphatically tells the covenant people, who are now called "my servant," not to be afraid and not to be broken, which assuredly they are. He will save them and their offspring from the faraway places to which they have been taken captive. Jacob will return and live undisturbed in his land, with no one frightening him there. Oracle III (v 11) gives the grand "I will be with you" promise, with Yahweh saying once again that he will save his people. The nations to which they have been scattered will receive their "full end," but of the covenant people Yahweh will not make a "full end." Correction meted out to them will be just, but they will not go unpunished. In the past, Yahweh warned often enough that punishment would come if the covenant was not kept and, if the people do not remember those warnings, they will know now about punishment from personal experience.

Both oracles could have been spoken originally to a Northern Israelite audience during the reform years of Josiah, but in answering the judgment in vv 5–7 they now address both Israel and Judah—possibly before the destruction of Jerusalem (Berridge 1970: 187); otherwise, soon after. They were spoken in Jerusalem (v 10: "from afar . . . from the land of their captivity"), not in exile.

In Oracle I (vv 8–9), Yahweh says that on a future day he will break the Babylonian yoke from upon the nation's neck, and its straps of bondage will be torn away. No longer will strangers make them serve; instead the covenant people will serve Yahweh and a Davidic king Yahweh will raise up for them. This oracle is later, after the fall of Jerusalem when "that day" of v 7 has ceased to be a day of distress and is now an anticipated day of salvation. When all three salvation oracles are heard following the judgment word of vv 5–7, the final "and from it shall he be saved?" in 7b is changed in tone to mean "yet from it he shall be saved!"

c) Your Blow Is Incurable (30:12–15)

30 ^{12}For thus said Yahweh:
Your brokenness is desperate
   your blow incurable
^{13}There is none to diagnose your case of a sore
   a healing scar there is not for you
^{14}All your lovers have forgotten you
   you, they care not about

For the blow of an enemy I have struck you
   punishment of a cruel one
Because your iniquity was much
   your sins were numerous

¹⁵Why do you cry over your brokenness
  your desperate pain?
Because your iniquity was much
  your sins were numerous
    I did these things to you.

RHETORIC AND COMPOSITION

MT 30:12–15 = LXX 37:12–14. This poem is delimited at the top end by the messenger formula at v 12, before which comes a *petuḥah* in M^L, M^P, and 4QJer^c. The verses are not extant in M^A. The next section in all three texts follows v 17, strengthening the impression that vv 16–17 are meant to be joined with vv 12–15. The two are in fact companion poems but most likely at one time were independent of one another (see Rhetoric and Composition for 30:4–7). Some commentators take one or both as originally addressed to Northern Israel (Volz and Holladay: vv 12–15; Rudolph, Weiser, and Hertzberg 1952: 597, vv 12–17), but more likely both addressed Judah from the start, sometime around the fall of Jerusalem. The wounds of vv 12–15 are Zion's recent wounds, not ancient wounds sustained by Israel in its fall to the Assyrians in 722 B.C. Furthermore, "Zion" in v 17 identifies the addressee of vv 16–17 as Jerusalem. But in the poetic core the two poems expand their audience to both Israelite and Judahite exiles (30:4).

Almost all commentators (Duhm; Volz; Rudolph; Weiser; Hyatt; Bright; Holladay; and others) attribute the present poem to Jeremiah. Peake and Cornill were tentative about authenticity, but not McKane, who cites both in support of his view that the whole of vv 12–17 derives from a later imitator who plundered the Jeremiah vocabulary. McKane is driven to such an uneconomical view because he wants to keep vv 12–17 together and cannot attribute the salvation preaching of vv 16–17 to Jeremiah.

The poem comprises three stanzas, having the following repetitions and balancing terms (cf. Lundbom 1975: 58 [= 1997: 78–79]):

I	*Your brokenness is desperate*	*ʾānûš lĕšibrēk*	v 12
	your blow . . .	*makkātēk*	
	There is none	*ʾēn . . .*	v 13
	. . . . there is not . . .	*. . . ʾēn*	
II	*. . . the blow . . . I have struck you*	*makkat . . . hikkîtîk*	v 14
	. . . . .		
	Because your iniquity was much		
	your sins were numerous		
III	*. . . . . your brokenness*	*šibrēk*	v 15
	your desperate pain	*ʾānûš makʾōbēk*	
	Because your iniquity was much		

your sins were numerous

. . . .

Catchwords connecting to the companion poem in vv 16–17 (Condamin):

v 12	*blow*		v 17	*I will bring up . . .*	*ʾaʿăleh*
v 13	*healing scar*	*rĕpūʾôt tĕʿālâ*		*from your blows*	
v 14	*you, they care not about*			*I will heal you*	*ʾărūkâ lāk*
	blow . . . I have struck you			*Whom No One Cares About*	

NOTES

30:12. *Your brokenness is desperate, your blow incurable.* Hebrew *ʾānûš lĕšibrēk naḥlâ makkātēk.* Hebrew *ʾānûš* ("desperate") is a Jeremiah word (15:18; 17:9, 16), occurring here and in v 15 with reference to a terminal medical condition. The LXX misunderstood it (LXX: *anestēsa suntrimma*, "I have brought about a fracture"), as it did earlier in 17:9 and 16 (Becking 1994a: 154). The *lamed* on *lĕšibrēk* is emphatic: "*your* brokenness is desperate" (Haupt 1894; 1907; Nötscher 1953: 380; cf. GKC §143e). These two expressions compare with those in 10:19 and 14:17, where *šeber* ("brokenness, break, shatter") and *makkâ* ("blow, stroke") are again paired. The phrase "your blow (is) incurable" occurs also in Nah 3:19 with reference to the demise of Assyria. Jeremiah bewails his own brokenness in 10:19; in 14:17 it is the brokenness of his people. For him the two are inseparable; in 8:21 he says, "For the brokenness of my dear people, I am broken." In 15:18, Jeremiah complains again about ongoing sickness and pain, asking, "Why has my pain become continual and my blow desperate, refusing to be healed?" (see Note there). The imagery in all these texts is strong, indeed violent, portraying one who has sustained a vicious—perhaps mortal—blow and lies in a helpless state. It is not the ordinary hurt or injury, because recovery is very much in doubt. Yahweh is addressing his faithless wife, Zion (feminine pronouns), who lies battered, helpless, and alone on the ground. One-time lovers have forgotten her, and Yahweh, her husband and friend, is now the enemy (v 14). In today's world such a woman would be seen as an abused wife, but in the ancient world she is a faithless wife getting her due—shame, physical abuse, and death.

13. *There is none to diagnose your case of a sore.* Hebrew *ʾên dān dînēk* (lit., "there is none to judge your judgment") contains a wordplay and a cognate accusative construction, of which there are many in Jeremiah (see again v 14 and Note on 22:16). The same verb + cognate accusative appears in 5:28: "They would not prosecute a case" (*dîn lōʾ-dānû*), and in 22:16: "He prosecuted the case (*dān dîn*) of the poor and needy." Here, however, the phrase requires a medical equivalent. The AV's "there is none to plead thy cause," which is carried over into the RSV, NAB, NIV, NRSV, and NJB, cannot be right. The NEB and REB omit the phrase, as do some commentators (Duhm; Peake; Cornill; Volz; Weiser; Bright; Thompson). But it can be translated if *dîn* is simply

rendered "exercise judgment." What is lacking, says Jeremiah, is someone to diagnose Zion's case and bring about healing. The move at this point is from crushing blows and gaping wounds to infectious body tissue. Hebrew *māzôr*, here and in Hos 5:13, is a boil, cyst, or other sore containing matter to be pressed out (BDB; KB³; Andersen and Freedman 1980: 413: "an oozing infection"; cf. Isa 1:6). It is not a "dressed wound" (from *zûr*, "to press"), as assumed by older commentators (Rashi; Blayney; Giesebrecht; Peake; Streane), who made a connection with the next term, "healing." The Masoretic accent, which some want to move forward, should remain under *lĕmāzôr*. Those who place it under "healing" simply want to accommodate their deletion of "diagnose your case."

Although we may suppose that individuals with simple medical skills existed in ancient Israel, there is nevertheless no evidence from the OT that Israel had indigenous doctors. Ancient Hebrew, as far as we know, did not even have a noun for "doctor"; it simply used the participial forms *rōpē'* and *rōpĕ'îm* ("healer/healers"). And when these terms refer to human healers, they are always foreigners (Gen 50:2; Jer 8:22; 2 Chr 16:12; Job 13:4). Also, except for the doctor-embalmer in Gen 50:2, such individuals are spoken of disparagingly. The priest functions as a one-man health department when it comes to controlling the spread of maladies such as scale disease (leprosy); otherwise, he does not function in the role of doctor (C. Weiss 1940). According to Weiss, only the prophets practiced the art of healing, and then they did so only on occasion. Neufeld (1970: 428–29) thinks that ancient Israel's medical practitioners were apothecaries organized into guilds (cf. Neh 3:8). Actually, Yahweh is the only real healer of his people (3:22; 17:14; 30:17; 33:6; Gen 20:17; Exod 15:26; 23:25; Num 12:13; Deut 7:15; 32:39; 2 Kgs 20:5; Hos 6:1; 7:1; 11:3; 14:5[Eng 14:4]; Pss 103:2–3; 147:2–3), and not until the second century B.C. do we find a passage in Jewish tradition extolling the virtues of the human doctor (Sir 38:1–15). In Lam 2:13, a ruined Zion is asked, "Who can heal you?" The answer comes in v 17 of the following oracle, where Yahweh says, "and from your blows I will heal you."

a healing scar there is not for you. This colon is repeated verbatim in 46:11, supporting the MT's break in the present verse just before *rĕpu'ôt*, an abstract plural noun meaning "healing" (GKC §124d). The word *tĕ'ālâ* occurs only here and in 46:11 and is usually taken to mean "a coating of new flesh and skin over a wound" (BDB; KB³). But since another noun with the same spelling means "watercourse, canal," we may actually be talking here and in 46:11 about a scar. In 8:22, Jeremiah asks why "healing" (*'ărûkâ*) had not arisen on his wounded people, something Yahweh promises only later (30:17; 33:6). In either case, what we have here is an incurable wound, which was a traditional curse in the ancient world (Hillers 1964: 64–66). Hillers gives this example from the Code of Hammurabi (rev. xxviii 50–69):

May Ninkarrak, daughter of Amum, who speaks well of me in Ekur, bring on his limbs a severe malady, an evil plague, a festering wound, which does not get better, which no physician understands or can cure by bandages, and which, like the sting of death, cannot be got rid of. May he continue to lament over his (lost) manhood until his life is extinguished.

(Hillers 1964: 64; *ANET*³ 180; CS II 353)

In the curses of Deuteronomy 28, it is stated that a people guilty of covenant disobedience will be smitten with the same maladies suffered by the Egyptians at the time of the Exodus, and from these they will not be healed (Deut 28:27, 35, 59–61).

14. *All your lovers have forgotten you; you, they care not about.* This is the people's lament in Lam 1:2 and 19. "All your lovers" (*kol-mĕʾahăbayik*) are not the doctors but imagined friends who should be visiting Zion or sending someone on their behalf (cf. 2 Kgs 20:12 = Isa 39:1) but are doing neither. Political allies from the distant and more recent past (22:20, 22; cf. Hos 8:9–10; Ezek 23:5–9, 22–23; J. A. Thompson 1977), these nations have either come themselves to a miserable end or will come to one shortly; at the present time they care nothing about Zion. Egypt heads the list (37:5), and Assyria could be added if we go back some years (Kimḥi; Calvin), but its days as a world power are over, and presently it is visiting no one. One might also imagine the solicitous nations who were represented at the Jerusalem conference in 594 B.C. (27:3) but whose friendship was short-lived; they are now of no help to Zion. Edom, in fact, has allied itself with Babylon and become Zion's enemy (see Note for 27:3). Zion, to its great hurt, has forgotten the love shown by Yahweh to his people from earliest times (Deut 7:7–8; 10:15; 23:6[Eng 23:5]; Hos 11:1), but this love in 31:3 is nevertheless reaffirmed as an "eternal love," *ʾahăbat ʿôlâm* (cf. 1 Kgs 10:9; Isa 48:14).

you, they care not about. The LXX lacks "you" (*ʾôtāk*), which may be due to haplography (homoeoteleuton: *k . . . k*). The verb *drš*, usually "seek," can also mean "care for" (Deut 11:12; Ps 142:5[Eng 142:4]). See again v 17.

For the blow of an enemy I have struck you. Another cognate accusative (see above v 13). Here it becomes clear that the enemy behind the enemy is Yahweh. The verb *nkh* ("strike down") is strong, often meaning "strike to kill." Jeremiah says to Yahweh in 14:19: "So why have you struck us down, that there is no healing for us?" Earlier divine assaults on Judah were to no effect (2:30; 5:3).

punishment of a cruel one. Hebrew *mûsār* can also be translated "discipline" or "correction," which is what Yahweh attempted in times past but his people refused to accept (see Note on 2:30). Now it becomes punishment, and the people must accept it. The uncertainty here is whether Zion is victim of a cruel punishment or a cruel foe. If the latter, then reference is to Nebuchadrezzar or Yahweh, or both. The Babylonian enemy is described as "cruel" (*ʾakzārî*) in 6:23 and 50:42. Calvin was uncomfortable about Yahweh being the cruel foe; nevertheless, he conceded that this was in fact being said. This reading follows MT, where *mûsar ʾakzārî* is taken as a construct chain: "punishment of a cruel (one)." Note the construct chain *makkat ʾôyēb* ("blow of an

enemy") in the prior colon. But the LXX has *paideian sterean* ("cruel correction"). Commentators divide on the translation. Kimḥi follows MT, which has
the support of T. But Rashi takes *mûsar* as an absolute and *'akzārî* as an adjective, giving the LXX's translation of "cruel punishment." Others more recently
(Giesebrecht; Duhm; Cornill; Volz; Rudolph; Weiser; Bright; Thompson)
achieve the same result by repointing *mûsar* to the absolute *mûsār*. See also JB
and NJV. Either rendering is possible. In favor of the MT reading it may be
said that translating the "cruel (one)" gives a parallel to "enemy" (*'ôyēb*) in the
prior colon, where the verb "I have struck" does double duty for both colons.
Some prefer this reading (Holladay; Jones; Keown et al.; McKane), which was
adopted by the AV ("chastisement of a cruel one"), and retained by the RSV
and NRSV ("punishment of a merciless foe").

Because your iniquity was much, your sins were numerous. "Iniquity" (*'āwôn*)
and "sin(s)" (*haṭṭā't*) are a stereotyped pair in Jeremiah (see Note for 16:18).
Some commentators (Volz; Rudolph; Weiser; Bright; Holladay) delete the
present line as a mistaken repetition of v 15, which is unjustified. Nor is there
justification for deleting both lines as moralizing supplements, as Gerlach
(1986: 38) does. The repetition is part of the poem and doubtless intentional
(cf. 14:3–4). Yahweh's judgment is not capricious; it is done for a reason,
which is human sin (5:6; 8:14; 13:22; 14:10; 15:13; 16:10–13, 18; 17:1–4; 44:23;
50:7). This is stated at the very beginning of the Bible (Genesis 3–4) and is a
theme running through the entire Primary History from Genesis to Second
Kings (D. N. Freedman 2000). One also finds here another biblical idea—viz.,
that sickness results from sin (cf. 14:19–20; Isa 1:4–6; Matt 9:1–6).

15. *Why do you cry over your brokenness, your desperate pain?* The omission
of this verse in the LXX can be due to haplography (homoeoteleuton: *k . . . k*).
Some Gk MSS insert 15b after 16a, where it does not belong. The entire verse
is present in Aq and Theod. Hebrew *mah* in this case has to be translated
"Why?" The masculine verb *tiz'aq* ("do you cry") occurs here in place of the
second feminine singular (see also *watûkāl* for *watûkālî* in 3:5; cf. GKC §47k;
69r). Duhm emends to *tiz'āqî*.

your desperate pain? Hebrew *'ānûš mak'ōbēk*. Jeremiah complained about
his own personal pain (15:18: *kĕ'ēb*), and so did Baruch (43:5: *mak'ôb*). Pain
will later come upon Babylon (51:8).

*Because your iniquity was much, your sins were numerous, . . . I did these
things to you.* Yahweh answers his own rhetorical question, giving the reason
for the brokenness, the pain, and the punishment. Zion will not say why she
is crying. In classical rhetoric, giving an answer to one's own rhetorical question is called *hypophora* (see Note for 49:7). The figure occurs again in 31:20.
Yahweh has inflicted the punishment but remains guiltless. The fault is
Zion's own.

I did these things to you. The G^OL, Aq, and Theod have a third plural: "they
did these things to you." According to this reading, Zion's iniquity and sin
brought the punishment (cf. 4:18), or else her military foes did. According to
the reading of MT, Yahweh brought the punishment to Zion.

MESSAGE AND AUDIENCE

In language Jeremiah used to described his own broken condition and the broken condition of his people, Yahweh now portrays his bruised, sick, and abandoned wife, Zion, telling also why she has come to such a lamentable state. He speaks to her directly, pronouncing her brokenness desperate and her crushing blow incurable. She also has an undiagnosed infection, which either resists treatment or indicates a hopeless condition. The wished-for scar that would indicate healing does not appear. Yahweh notes also that Zion has no visitors. Posturing friends from the distant and recent past have all forgotton her. Now when she needs them most, they care nothing about her condition. Yahweh says he is the one who has struck Zion this cruel blow. But punishment has a reason. Zion's cup of iniquity is full, yes overfull. Yahweh concludes by asking Zion why she is crying. Zion cannot answer. So Yahweh answers his own question, repeating once again that because of her iniquity and sin he has done these things to her.

The present oracle could date from any time around the fall of Jerusalem, possibly just before the fall, when Egyptian help fizzled and Zion's situation became hopeless (Boadt); otherwise, just after the fall (Hyatt; Bright). Because of the immediacy of the poem, its audience can only be people of Jerusalem and Judah. An original audience of Northern Israel in Josiah's reign has to be ruled out.

d) But from Your Blows I Will Heal You (30:16–17)

30 ¹⁶Hereafter all who consume you shall be consumed
    and all your foes—all of them—into captivity shall go
Those who plunder you shall be for plunder
    and all who despoil you I will give for spoil

¹⁷For I will bring up new flesh for you
    and from your blows I will heal you
        —oracle of Yahweh—
For they have called you an outcast:
    'That Zion Whom No One Cares About'

RHETORIC AND COMPOSITION

MT 30:16–17 = LXX 37:16–17. The present poem has no section markings at the top end, but a messenger formula in v 17 suggests an oracle independent from vv 12–15, which has its own "thus said Yahweh" formula. Delimitation at the lower end is marked in M^P and 4QJer^c by a *petuḥah* and in M^L by a *setumah* after v 17. For the pairing of this poem and the poem in vv 12–15 in the larger poetic core, see Rhetoric and Composition for 30:4–7. Most commentators (except Duhm and McKane) credit this oracle to Jeremiah. Its vocabulary and style are Jeremianic, and so also is the *lex talionis* sequence in v 16 (Holladay). Rudolph and Weiser take the oracle to be early Jeremianic preaching to Northern Israel, but this means eliminating "Zion" from v 17 (see Notes). Alonso-Schökel (1979: 2, 8), taking the same view that this oracle addresses Northern Israel and that "Zion" in v 17b is a gloss, argues that the poem concludes with v 17a because the "oracle of Yahweh" formula is there. But there is no reason why a formula cannot be in the middle of the verse. Usually it comes at the very end of the oracle but not always (cf. 2:9). "Zion," too, should not be eliminated.

This poem has two stanzas, with the following repetitions and balancing key words:

I   . . . *all who consume you* . . . . .   *kol-ʾōkĕlayik*   v 16
         and all your foes—all of them . . . .   *wĕkol-ṣārayik kullām*
      Those who plunder you . . . . .   *šōʾsayik*
         and all who despoil you . . . . .   *wĕkol-bōzĕzayik*

II   *For* . . . .   *kî*   v 17
      . . . .
      For . . . .   *kî*
      . . . .

Catchwords connecting to the companion poem in vv 12–15:

v 17 *I will bring up*   *ʾaʿăleh*   v 12 *blow*
      from your blows   v 13 *healing scar*   *rĕpūʾōt tĕʿālâ*
      I will heal you   *ʾărūkâ lāk*   v 14 *you, they care not about*
      Whom No One Cares About   *blow . . . I have struck you*

NOTES

30:16. *Hereafter all who consume you shall be consumed.* Hebrew *lākēn kol-ʾōkĕlayik yēʾākēlû*. This first of three *lex talionis* phrases in the verse (cf. Isa 33:1; Ezek 39:10) varies the common double-root idiom in Jeremiah (see Note on 11:18). The present participles indicate a recent destruction by the enemy. But those who have brought judgment and ruin to Judah will be victims of the same. Then one will see a return to Yahweh's early care for his people, when Israel was holy and all who "ate" (*ʾkl*) of his "firstfruits" met up with evil (2:3). It has been something very different of late (5:17; 8:16; 10:25; 50:7, 17).

Hereafter. Commentators have been bothered by this *lākēn* since the term normally means "therefore," announcing judgment after an indictment (see Rhetoric and Composition for 22:18–19). Here in vv 12–15 the judgment is upon Zion, but now in v 16 comes judgment for the nations and salvation for Zion. Calvin said the logic was unsuitable, and others have agreed. The problem stems largely from a sequential reading of v 16 after vv 12–15, which is now required since the poems in vv 12–15 and vv 16–17 are combined in the larger poetic core. If the oracle in vv 16–17 stood by itself, *lākēn* could simply mean "after this" or "hereafter," as in the "Look, hereafter, days are coming" introduction (see Note on 16:14). Blayney gives *lākēn* that meaning here, which should be accepted.

and all your foes—all of them—into captivity shall go. Some commentators (Giesebrecht; Rudolph; Weiser; Bright; Holladay; McKane) eliminate "all of them," with one LXX MS (G[198]), S, and Vg, but the repetition can stand. The T has it. Dahood (1977b) repoints *kullām* to a defectively written participle of *'kl*, *kōlīm* ("consumed"), assuming a wordplay here with the previous *kol* ("all"). His translation: "and all your adversaries consumed." But this makes it necessary to posit a delayed subject ("all who despoil you") in the next line for "into captivity (they) shall go," which yields a less than satisfactory rendering. The LXX has: "they shall eat their own flesh" instead of "into captivity (they) shall go," which Becking (1994a: 160; 1998: 8) says is a deviation from MT, influenced perhaps by Isa 49:26: "And I will make your oppressors eat their own flesh." The MT should be read. Babylon is promised its own captivity in Isa 46:2.

Those who plunder you shall be for plunder. Hebrew *šō'sayik* ("Those who plunder you") is an Aramaic form of *šōsĕsayik* (GKC §67s). Some MSS have a Q reading of *šōsayik* (from *ššh* = *šss*, "to plunder"; BDB; KB³). Babylon is portrayed as the happy plunderer in 50:11, but in 50:15 the cry goes up that Yahweh should do to her as she has done (cf. 50:29). Van Selms (1971) cites a fourteenth-century B.C. Ugaritic text (CTA 32), which he calls a "prophecy of salvation," where a similar "turning of the tables" occurs. It states that when the people of Ugarit throw off their Hittite overlords, the Hittites will be the ones bringing tribute to Ugarit.

and all who despoil you I will give for spoil. Hebrew *wĕkol-bōzĕzayik 'ettēn lābaz.* The verb *bzz* means "despoil, take as booty." Booty is national treasure (15:13; 17:3; 49:32; 50:37). In 50:37 this curse on Babylon appears: "A sword to her treasures, that they become booty (*buzzāzû*)."

17. *For I will bring up new flesh for you, and from your blows I will heal you.* The bicolon is a syntactic chiasmus in Hebrew. The LXX has *apo plēgēs odunēras,* "from your grievous blow" (cf. 14:17). This is a stunning reversal of what before was taken to be a hopeless case (v 13 and 8:22). Yahweh, the "great healer" in Hosea and Jeremiah (K. Gross 1931: 246–47), is the only one who can heal his broken people (see Note on 30:13). Now he promises to do just that (cf. 33:6).

For they have called you an outcast: 'That Zion Whom No One Cares About.' "Zion" is not quite a vocative, as suggested by Ehrlich (1912: 318), but his insight helps clear up a muddle in the earlier interpretation of this line. It is now clear that detractors passing by the ruined city have coined a derisive name for Zion. Compare the derisive name given to Pharaoh in 46:7: "Loud Noise, Who Lets the Deadline Pass." The problematic words are *ṣiyyôn hî'* ("That Zion" or "she is Zion"), where the LXX equivalent (Rahlfs; Field 1875: 656), *thēreuma hymōn estin* ("she is your prey"), makes no sense in the context. Giesebrecht left his translation blank; Duhm omitted the Hebrew words as a gloss, and Cornill emended LXX's *hymōn* ("your") to *hēmōn* ("our"), which Ziegler incorporated into his LXX text (cf. Becking 1998: 8). This gives an LXX reading of "she is our prey," which is said to be a corruption of Heb *ṣêdēnû*. The end result is a sensible rendering (the detractors say about Zion: "she is our prey"), but the proposed corruption of the Heb is a stretch, to say the least. As a result, all subsequent commentators (except Holladay) and all modern Versions (except JB) have read MT's "Zion." And NJB abandoned "our booty" in the JB, restoring "Zion." The MT, which is now seen to make perfectly good sense and has the support of T and Vg, should be retained. Rudolph and Weiser eliminate "Zion" only to accommodate their view that the oracle was originally spoken to Northern Israel, but this too should be rejected. The oracle was spoken from the first to Zion and Judah. In it Yahweh says he will not hear of Zion's being called an outcast and will answer the taunt by punishing Zion's foes and restoring her to health in the days ahead.

an outcast. Hebrew *niddāḥâ* is the N-stem participle of *ndḥ*, "be scattered, dispersed." 4QJer^c has the spelling *ndḥt* (cf. Ezek 34:4, 16). Some take this as a disparaging name: "Outcast"; T has "The Exiled One." Zion is empty, and its survivors are dispersed to Babylon, Egypt, and elsewhere (40:12; 43:5; 46:28; 50:17).

Whom No One Cares About. Hebrew *dōrēš 'ên lāh.* For *drš* meaning "care about," see v 14. Yahweh finds this taunt offensive because it implies that he too cares nothing for Zion. The city is likely in ruins, so passersby are mocking its emptiness. Taunts can be expected not only in the lands where Judahites will be dispersed (24:9; 29:18) but now on the road passing Jerusalem. But this is reversed in Second Isaiah, who says that Zion will experience a future glory (Isaiah 60), at which time she will be called "Cared About (*děrûšâ*), a city not forsaken" (v 12; Halpern 1998: 639).

MESSAGE AND AUDIENCE

Yahweh says here that the days are coming when all those who consume the covenant people will themselves be consumed. Zion's foes — all of them — will go into captivity and, instead of plundering other people's treasures, they will become plunder. Poetic justice. Judgment on the foes means restoration for the covenant people, and Yahweh says that he will bring about the very healing that earlier was said to be impossible. The foes have called them an outcast, 'That Zion Whom No One Cares About.' The audience will perhaps realize that someone does care, and it is Yahweh.

This oracle by itself may have been spoken to Judahites who had witnessed the destruction of Jerusalem, at which time a future judgment on Judah's enemies would have been the main point. But when paired with Judah's judgment in vv 12–15, the message of future healing in v 17a will get the accent. A formerly hopeless condition now becomes hopeful. Judah's blow was judged incurable, but now Yahweh will heal it. The audience here will be both Israelite and Judahite exiles (30:4).

e) Rebuilt City, Return to Joy (30:18–22)

30 [18]Thus said Yahweh:
Look I will restore the fortunes of Jacob's tents
    and on his dwellings I will have pity
A city shall be built on its tell
    and a citadel on its rightful place shall sit

[19]And from them thanksgiving shall go forth
    and the sound of merrymakers
And I will multiply them, and they shall not decrease
    I will give them honor, and they shall not be insignificant

[20]His sons shall be as of old
    and his congregation before me established
I will reckon with all who oppress him
    [21]and his noble one shall be one of his own

And his ruler from his midst shall go forth
    and I will bring him near, and he will approach me
For who is he that would risk his life
    to approach me?
      —oracle of Yahweh.

[22]And you will be a people to me
    and I, I will be God to you.

RHETORIC AND COMPOSITION

MT 30:18–22 = LXX 37:18–21. The present verses consist of a salvation oracle (vv 18–21), to which has been appended a covenant formula by the compiler of the poetic core (v 22). There is a "thus said Yahweh" messenger formula at the beginning of v 18 and an "oracle of Yahweh" formula at the end of v 21. Some early Jeremiah oracles have formulas at beginning and end, for example, 2:2–3, 5–9, and there are double formulas in the oracles of 31:31–34 and 35–37, but as a rule only one formula per oracle occurs. My preference here is to take the present verses as one oracle, although it is possible that two smaller oracles have been combined into one. The covenant formula is omitted in the LXX, but that can be attributed to haplography (see Notes).

The unit as a whole is delimited at the top end by the messenger formula in v 18, before which comes a *petuhah* in M^P and 4QJer^c and a *setumah* in M^L. At the bottom end, delimitation is by a *petuhah* in 4QJer^c and M^P and a *setumah* in M^L after v 22. The oracle concludes with a messenger formula at the end of v 21, which is present in 4QJer^c. 4QJer^c, in addition, has a long space after the first word in v 19, but this cannot be a section, even though Tov (1997: 196) identifies it as such. Holladay (p. 179) does not think the last line of v 21 is poetry (he calls it a pious add-on), a view that is reflected also in the translations of JB and NJB. It does contain the *nota accusativi*, a recognized prose particle. But other modern Versions take the line to be poetry, which it can be. Since the line falls within the oracle proper, i.e., before the messenger formula, it probably is not later comment. Furthermore, v 21bc has a repetition of "(to) me" (see below), which is another indication that 21c is original.

Commentators are divided on questions about the date, authenticity, and provenance of this oracle. Duhm placed it in the Maccabean period, but other proponents of a postexilic date (Peake; Cornill; Hyatt; Carroll; McKane) regard this as too late. Many credit the oracle to Jeremiah (Volz; Rudolph; Weiser; Bright; Thompson; Holladay; Jones; Keown et al.), which is defensible in spite of priestly and messianic ideas seemingly present. The oracle cannot, however, be considered one-time preaching to Northern Israel (*pace* Volz; Rudolph; Hertzberg 1952: 597; Boadt; Holladay). It is unlikely that Jeremiah would support the rebuilding of Samaria and a restoration of political, social, and cultic life there, particularly if he was backing Josiah's program of centralized worship in Jerusalem. It is best to take the oracle as Jeremianic preaching to a Judahite audience just after the fall of Jerusalem (Bright). In the poetic core, this oracle and the covenant formula appended to it address an enlarged audience of Israelite and Judahite exiles (30:4).

The oracle has four stanzas with good parallelism and numerous syntactic inversions. These repetitions are also present in Stanzas II and IV:

II	. . . . . *and shall go forth*	*wĕyāṣā'*	v 19
IV	. . . . *shall go forth*	*yēṣē'*	v 21bc
	. . . . *(to) me*	*'elay*	
	. . . .		
	. . . . *(to) me*	*'ēlay*	

Catchwords connecting to the poem following (Keown et al.):

v 18	*Look I*	*hinĕnî*	v 23	*Look*	*hinnēh*
	restore	*šāb*		*goes forth*	*yāṣĕ'â*
v 19	*and shall go forth*	*wĕyāṣā'*	v 24	*does not turn back*	*lō' yāšûb*
v 21	*shall go forth*	*yēṣē'*			

NOTES

30:18. *Look I.* Hebrew *hinĕnî.* The very common beginning (with a participle) of a Jeremiah oracle (see Note for 1:15).

I will restore the fortunes of Jacob's tents. Other occurrences of the expression "I will (surely) restore the(ir) fortunes" are in prose (see Note for 29:14). For the importance of this phrase in the Book of Restoration, see Rhetoric and Composition for 30:1–3. The reference to "Jacob" is not an indication that the oracle is addressing Northern Israel. Here (and also in 30:7) "Jacob" denotes the entire covenant people, of which only Judah remains. Elsewhere in the book it has the inclusive meaning of "all Israel" (see Rhetoric and Composition for 30:1–3). The LXX lacks "tents," which may explain why it translates "his captives" (*aichmalōsian autou*) instead of "his dwellings" in the colon following (cf. Isa 49:13). The term appears to be present (upon reconstruction) in 4QJer[c] (Tov 1997: 196–97). "Tents" is an archaism for "dwellings" (cf. 4:30) and should be retained because of the parallelism (cf. Num 24:5; Ps 78:60; and Isa 54:2).

and on his dwellings I will have pity. This colon makes a syntactic chiasmus with the prior colon. Judah's houses and other buildings are now in ruins, but Yahweh cares about them (the verb is *rḥm*, "to have compassion, pity").

A city shall be built on its tell, and a citadel on its rightful place shall sit. Another syntactic chiasmus in Hebrew, with verbs at the extremes. Yahweh's caring is an active caring, which means that ruined cities and buildings will be rebuilt. Since "city" and "citadel" are indefinite nouns, they are commonly taken as collectives—i.e., cities and citadels generally (REB: "Every city will be rebuilt on its own mound, every mansion will occupy its traditional site"). Except for those who take this oracle as originally addressing Northern Israel, it is widely recognized that Jerusalem's prominent buildings are being called to mind. A Hittite treaty between Suppiluliumas I of Hatti (ca. 1350 B.C.) and Kurtiwaza (= Shattiwaza) of Mitanni concludes with a blessing promising full restoration to the vassal if it remains faithful to the treaty:

> If you, Kurtiwaza, the prince, and (you), the Hurrians, fulfill this treaty and (this) oath, may these gods protect you. . . . May the Mitanni country return to the place which it occupied before, may it thrive and expand. May you, Kurtiwaza, your sons, and your sons' sons (descended) from the daughter of the Great King of the Hatti land, and you, the Hurrians exercise kingship forever. May the throne of your father persist, may the Mitanni country persist.
>
> (ANET[3] 206; cf. Beckman 1996: 44, 48)

A city shall be built on its tell. Hebrew *wĕnibnĕtâ ʿîr ʿal-tillāh.* The masculine verb *wnbnh* in 4QJer[c] is permissible with collective and mixed subjects (*ʿîr*, "city," is feminine; *tēl*, "tell," is masculine; cf. GKC §145o). Another masculine verb, *wĕyāṣāʾ* ("and it shall go forth"), predicates a mixed subject in v 19a. Kimhi and Calvin follow T and take the city here to be Jerusalem. Judah's capital city is further indicated by the mention of rulers' being raised up in v 21 (Thompson). A "tell" is a mound of rubble left from a former occupation. Cities are thus rebuilt on the rubble of prior cities, though sometimes they are not rebuilt (49:2; Deut 13:17[Eng 13:16]; Josh 8:28; 11:13). At some point, a tell becomes abandoned (Jerusalem is an exception), giving archaeologists opportunities to excavate, such as they enjoy today throughout the Near East. For the rebuilding of Jerusalem and Judah's cities, see also 31:23–25, 38–40; Ezek 36:10, 33–36; 48:15–35; Isa 44:26–28; 49:16–17; 61:4.

and a citadel on its rightful place shall sit. I.e., where it belongs or where it stood previously (*mišpāṭô*). Hebrew *mišpāṭ* may also mean "plan, specification" (BDB, 1049; Exod 26:30; 1 Kgs 6:38); thus: "according to its (original) plan." The term *'armôn* means "citadel, fortress, palace" (6:5; 9:20[Eng 9:21]; 17:27; 49:27) and can also be a collective. But the structures here are commonly taken to be those that previously stood in Jerusalem. Rashi (following T) says *'armôn* refers to the Temple (Vg: *templum*); Kimḥi, the Temple and the king's palace (Lam 2:5, 7); and Calvin, simply the palace. Heawood (1911–12: 70) thinks *'armôn* may mean "layout of city streets" (see Note on 6:5), which would mean that city streets would once again be where they had been before the destruction. The Babylonians were eager to destroy all of Jerusalem's celebrated buildings (6:5), and when they captured the city, they did precisely this (39:8; 52:13 = 2 Kgs 25:9).

19. *And from them thanksgiving shall go forth and the sound of merrymakers.* Out of Jacob's cities and dwellings, large and small, grand and modest, will be heard songs of thanksgiving and the sounds of merrymakers. The "thanksgiving" (*tôdâ*) is here a song of thanksgiving, of which there are many in the Psalter (e.g., Psalms 92, 95, 100, 105–7, 118, 136, 138). One "song of ascent" contains these words:

When Yahweh restored the fortunes of Zion
  we were like those who dream
Then our mouth was filled with laughter (*śĕḥôq*)
  and our tongue with a ringing cry . . .
Yahweh has done great things with us
  we are glad.
                              (Ps 126:1–3)

"Merrymakers" (*mĕśaḥăqîm*) are happy folk singing and dancing to musical instruments (2 Sam 6:5), boys and girls frolicking in the streets (Zech 8:5). These are the very people Jeremiah shunned after accepting his prophetic call (15:17), and since then his ears have been flooded with terrible sounds, sounds of war, primarily—anxious messengers reporting an approaching enemy, the ominous trumpet sound, battle shouts, the neighings and stamping hooves of stallions, the clatter of chariots, their rumbling wheels, crashing noises of all kinds, people writhing like women in labor, others lamenting over their fallen houses—but these will be replaced by happy voices, singing and dancing, and the joys commensurate with a restoration of community life (31:4, 13; 33:11; cf. Isa 35:10; 51:3). Happy sounds will also break the silence that has pierced Jeremiah's ears—no joyful voices of bride and groom, no sound of grinding millstones in the morning, no sound of cattle on the hillsides; in the fields and on city streets are only an accumulation of bodies, lying silently.

and (it) shall go forth. Hebrew *wĕyāṣā'*. The masculine verb predicates a combined masculine and feminine subject. See v 18 above, where a masculine verb predicates a mixed subject in 4QJer^c. Emendation here to a feminine verb is therefore unnecessary (*pace* Duhm; Holladay).

And I will multiply them, and they shall not decrease; I will give them honor, and they shall not be insignificant. The verbs "multiply" (*rbh*) and "honor" (*kbd*) appear to be a fixed pair, as Kselman (1979) has pointed out after discovering the paired cognates *rabû* and *kabtu* in Akkadian poetry. The command to multiply and not decrease is given in Jeremiah's letter to the exiles (29:6), echoing the divine word at Creation (Gen 1:28) and recalling also Israel's experience as a slave people in Egypt, when its numbers increased from a few to many (Exodus 1; Deut 26:5). Now Yahweh promises that his remnant people will multiply and be fruitful upon their return to Zion (cf. 3:16; 23:3; Hos 1:10; Ezek 36:9–11; Isa 49:20–21; 54:1–3). The Hittite treaty cited above promised expansion for the Hurrians if they kept the terms of their treaty. The verb *ṣ^cr* in the second colon is rare, meaning the opposite of "come to honor" (Job 14:21). The LXX lacks this colon, "I will give them honor, and they shall not be insignificant," which could, as Janzen (1973: 119) recognizes, be due to haplography (homoeoarcton: *w . . . w*, or homoeoteleuton: *w . . . w*). The colon exists in 4QJer^c, Theod, T, and Vg.

20. *His sons shall be as of old.* I.e., Jacob's sons shall be as in ancient times (*qedem*; BDB, 869; GKC §118u). The reference here is not to David or the glories of the Davidic–Solomonic era (*pace* Calvin; Giesebrecht; Bright). The "sons" are Jacob's sons (Rudolph), and the anticipation is to a time when all the tribes of Israel (= Jacob) will be accounted for (cf. 31:1; Ezekiel 48). The LXX reads: "And their sons shall go in (*eiseleusontai*) as before," which may imagine priestly sons *going in* to the holy place (*bô'* in Exod 28:29). But this does not translate Heb *hāyû* ("they shall be").

and his congregation before me established. Another syntactic chiasmus with the prior colon, varying the normal parallelism of v 19b. Jacob's "congregation" (*'ēdâ*) is likely a worshiping congregation (1 Kgs 8:5), with "before me" (*lĕpānay*) having the technical meaning of "(standing) before Yahweh" in service and/or worship (see Note for 15:19). Dahood (1973: 83–84) citing a Ugaritic parallel thinks that "sons" and "congregation" break up a stereotyped phrase, strengthening the idea that the congregation is one in which all of Jacob's sons are present. The LXX has *ta marturia autōn* ("their testimonies"). Giesebrecht took this to be a misunderstanding, but it is now supported by the 4QJer^c reading, *w^cdwtw*, "his testimony" (Tov 1997: 196–97; Becking 1994a: 156).

I will reckon with all who oppress him. The LXX omits "all," which can be attributed to haplography (homoeoteleuton: *l . . . l*). Janzen (1973: 65–67) says the word is a common MT addition. On the verb *pqd* ("reckon, pay a visit, punish") in Jeremiah, see Note for 5:9. Earlier on, Yahweh promised a reckoning for Judah; now he will reckon with Judah's oppressors (*lōḥăṣāyw*).

21. *and his noble one shall be one of his own. And his ruler from his midst shall go forth.* The future leader of the restored community is here called an *'adîr*, "noble one, prince, majestic one" (14:3; 25:34–36) and a *mōšēl*, "ruler" (22:30;

33:26; 51:46). The term *melek* ("king") is not used. But T has "king" and "anointed one," with Kimḥi and Calvin interpreting the terms similarly. The usage has to be intentional, because the term "king" has doubtless been tarnished by Judah's last occupiers of the throne, Jehoiakim and Zedekiah. Jeremiah speaks about a future "king" (*melek*) only four times, twice saying that kings will continue to occupy David's throne, if people keep the Sabbath and present kings do justice and righteousness (17:25; 22:4), neither of which happened, and twice when specifying the future king as being a "king like David" (23:5; 30:9), the idea evolving into a later messianic hope. Things are much the same in Ezekiel, where the "prince" (*nāśîʾ*) and the "priest" are envisioned as joining forces in the restoration (Ezekiel 44–46), and a Davidic "king" or "prince" is promised for the future (Ezek 34:24; 37:24–25). In the case of Jeremiah, one might even say that the ancient idea of Yahweh being Israel's only real King dominates his thinking (Jer 8:19; 10:7, 10; 46:18; 48:15; 51:57). If so, the idea likely emanates from traditions passed on about Samuel (1 Sam 8:4–7), with which Jeremiah was familiar and which impacted his own prophetic self-understanding (see §Introduction: Early Life and Call to Be a Prophet). The emphasis here in the present verse is that the future ruler will come from within the people and not be a foreigner (cf. Deut 17:15). The idea is well attested in antiquity. The Hittite treaty just cited (v 18) gave its blessing to the longevity of the Hurrians' own royal line.

and (he) shall be. Hebrew *wĕhāyâ.* 4QJerᶜ has *wĕhāyû* ("and they shall be"), presumably taking "his noble one" and "his ruler" as a compound subject. The LXX also has a plural verb but with a plural subject: *kai esontai ischuroteroi autou* ("and his mighty ones will be").

and I will bring him near, and he will approach me. Holladay notes a wordplay in *miqqirbô* ("from his midst") and *wĕhiqrabtîw* ("and I will bring him near"). The future leader will have special access to Yahweh, perhaps as Moses did (Exod 24:2). But the usual interpretation is that he will combine royal and priestly offices as postexilic leaders later did (Zech 3:6–10). The LXX reads: "and I will gather them, and they shall return to me," which appears to be a misunderstanding (Jones).

For who is he that would risk his life to approach me? The pronoun *mî* with the enclitic *hûʾ-zeh* strengthens the interrogative: "Who is he . . . ?" (GKC §136c; BDB, 261 4b; cf. Ps 24:10; Esth 7:5). The expression "risk his life" is lit., "pledge his heart" (*ʿārab ʾet-libbô*). Coming near to Yahweh is a risk if one initiates the action, just as when someone comes uninvited into the presence of the king (Esth 4:11). Yahweh's unapproachableness stems basically from his holiness (Exod 3:5; 19:9–25).

22. *And you will be a people to me, and I, I will be God to you.* The LXX omission of this covenant formula might be explained as another abridgment to eliminate a repetition, since the formula occurs again in 31:1. Many commentators delete, citing also the comment of Volz that the changed address (second person plural) identifies the formula as an addition. The formula does not belong to the oracle; nevertheless, it connects to the oracle and fills out a

rhetorical structure for the poetic core (see Rhetoric and Composition for 30:4–7). Since *hinnēh* ("Look") beginning v 23 is also lacking in LXX, the larger omission is likely attributable to haplography (homoeoteleuton: *h . . . h*). The formula is present in 4QJer^c, Symm, Theod, T, and Vg, and *hinnēh* is translated by Aq, Symm, T, and Vg. The covenant formula undergirds Yahweh's promise of future restoration, a function it also has in 31:1. As was noted above, ANE treaties promise a restoration of national life, expansion, and indigenous rulers if the treaty is kept. A similar logic *mutatis mutandis* can be assumed to operate here. With the covenant between Yahweh and his people intact, a restoration of cities and buildings, indigenous rule, and a return to joyful community life will all occur. On the covenant formula in Jeremiah and elsewhere, see Note for 7:23.

MESSAGE AND AUDIENCE

Yahweh begins this oracle by saying that he intends to restore the fortunes of "Jacob's tents," the archaic language being an indication that things new will include things old. Yahweh says he cares about fallen buildings; therefore, a city will arise on its former ruins and a citadel will sit where it once did. Does Yahweh mean every city and every citadel, or is he talking simply about Jerusalem? Surely Jerusalem will be rebuilt. At this time there will also be a return of joyful sounds—people singing thanksgiving songs to Yahweh, happy dancers in the square, children playing in the streets. People will multiply in number and Yahweh will give them honor. Jacob's sons, all of them, will be as of old, with the congregation once again gathering for worship. Yahweh will now reckon with all who oppress Jacob, and a leader from within the ranks shall arise. Yahweh will bring this leader near him, as he did with Moses, for otherwise who will risk his life to approach Yahweh? To this oracle is added the covenant formula, for a restoration of this magnitude is unthinkable without there being a covenant between Yahweh and his people.

This oracle is spoken to a Judahite audience after the fall of Jerusalem in 586 B.C., perhaps soon after, at which time the hope is for a later rebuilding of Jerusalem. Later it will speak to an enlarged audience of Israelite and Judahite exiles, both of whom will be promised restoration in the Land of Promise. The accent now is on the fact that all the sons of Jacob will be accounted for. Northern exiles from Assyria will join southern exiles from Babylon, and together—with Yahweh's help—they will rebuild the land and see there a joyful return to the community life they once knew.

f) Yahweh's Desert Storm (30:23–24)

30 ^{23}Look! the tempest of Yahweh
  wrath goes forth
  a sweeping tempest
Upon the head of the wicked it whirls

²⁴the burning anger of Yahweh does not turn back
Until it does and until it fulfills
    the purposes of his heart
In the days afterward
    you will understand it.

RHETORIC AND COMPOSITION

MT 30:23–24 = LXX 37:23–24. This poem is duplicated in 23:19–20, and here the LXX has it in both places. Often the LXX omits the second occurrence of a duplication in the book. The poem is delimited at the top end by a *petuḥah* in 4QJerᶜ and Mᴾ and a *setumah* in Mᴸ before v 23. There are no section markings after v 24, but the chapter division delimits the poem here. The next section comes after 31:1, suggesting a joining of the covenant oracle in 31:1 to the present verses. But the two do not belong together (*pace* Giesebrecht; Volz; Hyatt; McKane); the covenant oracle in 31:1 goes, rather, with the salvation oracle in 31:2–6 (see Rhetoric and Composition for 31:1–6).

This poem is the center judgment of the poetic core (see Rhetoric and Composition for 30:4–7). In a collection otherwise dominated by future hope, it should be noted, nevertheless, that judgment words spoken by the prophet come at the beginning (30:5–7), middle (30:23–24), and end (31:22).

Catchwords connecting to the prior oracle:

v 23	*Look*	*hinnēh*	v 18	*Look I*	*hinĕnî*
	goes forth	*yāṣĕ'â*		*restore*	*šāb*
v 24	*does not turn back*	*lō' yāšûb*	v 19	*and shall go forth*	*wĕyāṣā'*
			v 21	*shall go forth*	*yēṣē'*

Catchwords connecting to the following poem in 31:2–6:

v 23	*goes forth*	*yāṣĕ'â*	v 4	*and go forth*	*wĕyāṣā't*
	whirls	*yāḥûl*		*dance*	*mĕḥôl*

NOTES

30:23–24. See exegesis for 23:19–20.

23. *sweeping.* Hebrew *mitgōrēr.* The Hithpolel participle in 23:19 is *mitḥôlēl* ("whirling"), which is more integrated into the poetry (see Note there).

Upon the head of the wicked. The LXX lacks "head," as also in 23:19, but it is partially extant in 4QJerᶜ. The omission could be due to haplography (see Note for 23:19).

24. *the burning anger of Yahweh does not turn back.* The term *ḥărôn* ("burning") is lacking in 23:19. For other variations of this Jeremianic phrase, see Note on 4:8.

In the days afterward. On this expression, see Note for 23:20.

you will understand it. Hebrew *titbônĕnû bāh.* The cognate accusative *bînâ* ("meaning, understanding") is added in 23:20. The reading here is supported by 4QJer[c] and Aq; Symm adds the accusative (*sunesei*). Bright suggests that *bînâ* may have been lost by haplography (homeoteleuton: *h . . . h*).

MESSAGE AND AUDIENCE

This general condemnation of the wicked, which was originally spoken to a pre-586 B.C. audience misled by uncredentialed prophets preaching a false message (23:19–20), in the context here addresses a remnant Judahite audience after the destruction of Jerusalem. This audience is being told about Yahweh's future salvation, but it is nevertheless reminded—as elsewhere in the collection—that Yahweh's wrath was poured out because of the people's wickedness. If people do not understand this now, they will one day in the future.

g) Grace Again in the Wilderness (31:1–6)

31 [1]At that time—oracle of Yahweh—I will be God to all the tribes of Israel, and they, they will be a people to me.

[2]Thus said Yahweh:
It found grace in the wilderness
   a people, survivors of the sword
      Going to find his rest is Israel
[3]From far off Yahweh appeared to me:
   'With an eternal love I have loved you
      therefore I draw you faithfully along

[4]Again I will build you and you shall be built
   virgin Israel
Again you'll deck yourself with your hand-drums
   and go forth in the dance of merrymakers
[5]Again you'll plant vineyards on Samaria's mountains
   planters shall plant and eat the fruit'

[6]For there shall be a day watchmen will call out
   on Mount Ephraim
'Up, let us go to Zion
   to Yahweh our God!'

RHETORIC AND COMPOSITION

MT 31:1–6 = LXX 38:1–6. The present verses contain the covenant formula, given as a prose oracle (v 1), and a salvation oracle in poetry (vv 2–6). The chapter division marks the upper limit of the unit, correctly joining the covenant oracle to the salvation oracle following. The latter may be thematic for all or part of what remains in the chapter (Weiser; Bright; Carroll; Jones). Weiser noted that it precedes the important new covenant promise in 31:31–34. Sections here in chap. 31 begin after v 1, where M^L and M^P have a *setumah* and 4QJer^c a *petuḥah*. These mark the upper limit of Oracle II, which has also an opening messenger formula in v 2. The unit as a whole is delimited at the bottom end by a *petuḥah* in M^L and a *setumah* in M^P and 4QJer^c (upon reconstruction) after v 6 (Tov 1997: 197–98). The M^A up to 31:35a is not extant.

Oracle I (v 1), where Yahweh is the speaker, is brief. An "at that time" introduction identifies it as prose. In the larger poetic core it balances the covenant formula in 30:22 (see Rhetoric and Composition for 30:4–7).

Oracle II (vv 2–6) is the first of three originally independent hope oracles making up a unit within the poetic core: 1) vv 2–6; 2) vv 7–9; and 3) vv 10–14 (Condamin). This oracle comprises three stanzas of poetry with the following repetitions and balancing key words:

I	. . . .		v 2
	. . . .		
	. . . .		
	. . . . . . *Yahweh*	yhwh	v 3
	. . . .		
	. . . .		
II	*Again*	ʿôd	v 4
	. . . .		
	Again	ʿôd	
	. . . .		
	Again you'll plant . . . on Samaria's mountains	ʿôd tiṭṭěʿî . . . běhārê šōměrôn	v 5
	planters shall plant	nāṭěʿû nōṭěʿîm	
III	. . . .		v 6
	on Mount Ephraim	běhar ʾeprāyim	
	. . . .		
	. . . . . *Yahweh our God*	yhwh	

Although this oracle has an opening "thus said Yahweh" messenger formula (v 2), it is widely recognized that Yahweh does not begin speaking until v 3b, and then he speaks only up through v 5 ("I" pronouns; "virgin Israel" being addressed with feminine singular pronouns). In v 6 Jeremiah brings in the voices of watchmen who will call people to worship Yahweh in Zion. Textual uncertainties create various problems within vv 2–3a, of which the speaker is only one (see Notes). These verses must be Jeremiah speaking, because Yahweh is referred to in the third person in v 3a. What we have then is another dialogue oracle, the speaker breakdown of which is the following:

I	Jeremiah speaks	vv 2–3a
I–II	Yahweh speaks	vv 3b–5
III	Jeremiah speaks	v 6

So understood, Jeremiah begins the oracle by remembering that Israel in the past, and now also more recently, found grace in the wilderness. He concludes by anticipating the day when watchmen will call people from the northern territories to make their pilgrimage to Zion. The words of the watchmen close the oracle, which is a common feature in Jeremianic discourse (4:31; 9:18[Eng 9:19]; 20:10; 30:17; 46:17). Yahweh in the center directly addresses virgin Israel, professing his eternal love for her and promising a renewal of community life in the northern homeland.

Oracle II is generally taken (except by Carroll and McKane) as a genuine Jeremiah utterance, a number of commentators and others dating it to the reign of Josiah and viewing it as early preaching to Northern Israel. People once again will be planting vineyards on the mountains of Samaria (v 5), and watchmen on Mount Ephraim will be calling people to make the pilgrimage to Zion (v 6), which make a northern focus for the oracle clear. The call for Northern Israel's restoration was already seen by Calvin, with early critical commentators (Giesebrecht; Duhm; Peake; Cornill) going on to connect it with the early Jeremianic preaching in 3:12–18. Influence from Hosea in vv 2–3 is also evident (K. Gross 1930: 5, 14; 1931: 245, 336, 343), pointing once more to early preaching. Scholars more recently (Volz; Rudolph; Hertzberg 1952: 597; Eissfeldt 1965: 361; Bright) have seen this early preaching against the background of Josiah's reform and the centralization of worship in Jerusalem. Some, however, date the passage after the fall of Jerusalem, in the period of Gedaliah's governorship (Skinner 1926: 303; Hyatt; Lindars 1979: 50–52). Carroll and McKane date the oracle considerably later: Carroll (like N. Schmidt 1901b: 2391), in the Persian period, and McKane, "deep in the post-exilic period." Neither can imagine a sour and isolated Jeremiah, elsewhere so critical of the cult, speaking here joyously in its support (so also Cornill on v 6). McKane's low chronology is another reason for his ruling out an early Jeremiah career in Josiah's reign, and he is unwilling also to assign any salvation preaching to the prophet. Such interpretations are flat and rightly rejected by a majority of today's Jeremiah scholars.

Catchwords connecting to the prior poem in 30:23–24:

v 4	and go forth	wĕyāṣā'̄t	v 23	goes forth	yāṣĕ'â
	dance	mĕḥôl		whirls	yāḥûl

Catchwords connecting to the poem following (cf. Condamin):

v 2	a people	v 7	your people
v 6	Ephraim	v 9	Ephraim

NOTES

31:1. *At that time.* On this phrase in the book of Jeremiah, see Note for 3:17.

I will be God to all the tribes of Israel, and they, they will be a people to me. An expanded version of the covenant formula found throughout the OT (see

Note for 7:23). This formula has also turned up in the Qumran *Temple Scroll* (11QT 59:13; Yadin 1983: 268).

to all the tribes of Israel. Hebrew *mišpĕḥôt* ("tribes") can also be translated "families" (10:25; 33:24); here it has the inclusive meaning of Israelites both North and South (see Note for 2:4). The LXX has "to the nation" singular (*tō genei*) and lacks "all." This could simply be a misreading (*mšpḥt*) or misunderstanding (Giesebrecht), but the absence of "all" is likely a loss attributable to haplography (homoeoteleuton: *l . . . l*). The term is present in 4QJer^c, Aq, T, and Vg.

2. *It found grace in the wilderness, a people, survivors of the sword.* The present bicolon translates without difficulty once it is recognized that *ʿam* ("people") is a delayed subject doing double duty for both colons. A construction of the same type is found in Hos 8:5, where a delayed *ʾappî* ("my anger") is subject for the entire bicolon (Lundbom 1975a). Here the masculine *ʿam* is predicated by the third masculine singular *māṣāʾ* ("it found"). An even more anticipated "Israel" is delayed to the very end of the verse. The LXX (*euron*) and Symm (*euriskō*) contain a first person singular verb, which may betray influence from Hos 9:10: "Like grapes in the wilderness I found Israel." But Yahweh here is not the speaker. The LXX continues with a series of mistranslations: "I found him warm (*thermon*) in the wilderness with (*meta*) those who were destroyed by the sword." Hebrew *ḥōm* ("heat, warm") is misread for *ḥēn* ("grace"), *ʿim* ("with") is misread for *ʿam* ("people"), and *śrd* ("escape") is turned into its opposite with *ollumi* ("destroy" = *šdd*?).

Hebrew *ḥēn* ("grace, favor") is an important theological term in the OT, denoting here Yahweh's freely bestowed favor on his people Israel (Freedman, Lundbom, "ḥnn" in *TDOT* 5: 30–35). This grace recalls the liberation from slavery in Egypt and anticipates a new covenant for the future when Yahweh will forgive the people's sins. Here also appear to be echoes of Exod 33:12–17, where the talk is about Moses and the people having "found favor" (*mṣʾ* + *ḥēn*) in the eyes of Yahweh (Rudolph). Duhm and K. Gross (1931: 334–36) see influence as well from Hos 2:16–17[Eng 2:14–15], where Yahweh says he will bring Israel back to the wilderness and there speak to her heart, and she, for her part, will answer him as in the days of her youth (cf. Jer 2:2). Echoes of the ancient Wilderness trek are evident enough in the verse (Rashi; Kimhi) but are being combined with Northern Israel's more recent "wilderness" experience in Assyrian exile (Giesebrecht; Streane; Skinner 1926: 304). Added later will be a company of Babylonian exiles who "escaped from the sword" (51:50), at which point the verb will become a prophetic perfect (= "shall find"; Moffatt; AmT; NIV). We see here the beginning of the "new Exodus" theme that so dominates the thought of Second Isaiah (Isa 40:3–5; 43:18–21; 48:20–21; 51:10–11).

Going to find his rest is Israel. Hebrew *hālôk lĕhargîʿô yiśrāʾēl.* "Israel" is another delayed subject—both for the colon and for the verse as a whole—and *rgʿ* is an internal H-stem meaning "to (find) rest" (GKC §53e; Deut 28:65; Isa 34:14). The H-stem usage of *rgʿ* in 50:34 is transitive: "to give rest." The infinitive absolute *hālôk* translates here as a conjugated verb, "is going" (Rashi and

Kimḥi focus on the Exodus and translate it past: "went"). The Hebrew then is, literally, "He is going to find his rest, i.e., Israel (is)." Some commentators (Rashi; Kimḥi; Calvin; Cheyne; Streane; Holladay; McKane) and some ancient as well as modern Versions (Aq; Symm; T; AV; REB; NIV) make God the subject and read a double accusative: "He (God) went to give Israel his rest." In earlier biblical sources Yahweh promised a "rest" (*nûaḥ* H-stem) to Israel, which meant settlement in the Promised Land and safety from enemies round about (Exod 33:14; Deut 3:20; 12:9–10; 25:19; Josh 1:13; 21:43; cf. von Rad 1966). Now, however, reference is primarily, though not exclusively, to an anticipated redemption of the ten Northern tribes from Assyrian exile and their return to the land of Israel, their resting place (Abarbanel). On another occasion, Jeremiah challenged the people of Judah to "find rest" by walking in "the good way," but they rejected it (6:16).

3. *From far off Yahweh appeared to me.* Interpretation here turns on the translation of *mērāḥôq*, which can mean either "from far off" or "from long ago," and on the translation of the indirect object as "to me" (MT) or "to him" (LXX). We can probably dismiss "from long ago" at the outset (*pace* Rashi; Kimḥi; Holladay; T; AV; NEB [but not REB]; NJV; NIV), even though a divine revelation—and a very important one—did occur at the time of the Exodus, the reason being that the oracle goes on to say that *again* Yahweh will build up Israel, *again* there will be drum-playing and dancing, and *again* vineyards will be planted and people will eat their fruit. This revelation is then a current one, which must mean that Yahweh is offering it from some distant location. A common interpretation among commentators (Peake; Cornill; Streane; Rudolph; McKane) who see the revelation as current and accept also the LXX's "to him" is that Yahweh is speaking from his dwelling place in Jerusalem to exiles afar off (cf. 30:10; 51:50). But the problem with reading "to him" is that the pronouns following are feminine, addressing "virgin Israel" (Cornill). Thus MT's "to me" appears to be preferable (Giesebrecht; Volz). Jeremiah, in any case, is the speaker, and he seems to be saying that Yahweh appeared to him from "far off" with hopeful words for a languishing Israel, and these now follow (cf. 31:26). Whether this revelation be from high heaven or some other distant location is not important. What does seem to be clear, at least from 23:23–24, is that Yahweh is very much a God "far off" (*mērāḥôq*).

With an eternal love I have loved you; therefore I draw you faithfully along. In the second colon, *ḥesed* is an adverbial accusative: "faithfully" (GKC §118m). The LXX has *eis oiktirēma*, "in compassion." God's "love" (*'aḥăbâ*) for his people is not as prominent a theme in the OT as it later becomes in the NT, but it is present, mainly in Hosea, Deuteronomy, and Jeremiah (K. Gross 1931: 243–46; Moran 1963b). See also Isa 43:4. Here in the present verse this love is said to stand behind Yahweh's "faithfulness" (*ḥesed*), which is a very important theological concept in the OT (see Note for 2:2) and nothing less than a divine attribute according to Yahweh's self-asseveration in Exod 34:6–7. The AV translated *ḥesed* as "lovingkindness"; the RSV translates as "steadfast love." The present verse is also extraordinary in that it speaks of Yahweh loving Israel with an "eternal love" (*'ahăbat 'ôlām*). The verb *mšk* means "draw, drag along," often being translated "continue" (Ps 36:11[Eng 36:10]). Yahweh's faithfulness continues by virtue of its ongoing drawing power. The same is true with Yahweh's "love" (Hos 11:4). In Second Isaiah Yahweh says: "In a flood of anger I hid my face for a moment from you, but with eternal faithfulness (*ûbĕhesed 'ôlām*) I will have compassion on you" (Isa 54:8).

4–5. *build . . . plant*. On these thematic verbs in Jeremiah, see 31:28 and Note for 24:6.

4. *Again I will build you and you shall be built*. A characteristic double-root repetition in Jeremiah, where the verb is strengthened by the addition of its passive. See again 31:18. The usage has been noted also in Ugaritic poetry (see Note for 11:18), and Gevirtz (1973) has turned up other examples from the Amarna Letters. The threefold "again" (*'ôd*) in vv 4–5 gives emphasis to Israel's future restoration (*anaphora*). The scattered nation is like a demolished building, whose stones and bricks are strewn all over the ground. But here Yahweh's building activity means increased population (30:19), prosperity, and a return to community life in the homeland. Kimhi takes this as referring to the Jewish people, which it does, but one should nevertheless note that others confessing Yahweh's name will similarly be built up in the future (12:16; cf. 1:10).

virgin Israel. Hebrew *bĕtûlat yiśrā'ēl*. One of the many personifications of the nation in the book of Jeremiah but without the irony expressed in 14:17 ("virgin people"); 18:13; and 31:21. In the three latter passages, Judah is personified, whereas here it was originally Northern Israel, as in Amos 5:2. Schmitt (1991) thinks the term refers only to the respective capital cities. In his view, "virgin Israel" personifies Samaria in Amos 5:2; Jer 31:14 and 21; and Jerusalem in Jer 18:13. But such an interpretation appears too restrictive, and the personifications are more likely of entire nations. Also, in Jer 31:21 "virgin Israel" refers to the remnant of old Israel, i.e., Judah, not Northern Israel.

Again you'll deck yourself with your hand-drums. Israel's maidens will again dress up in festive attire to play their drums at the dance. Cornill and Peake are happy to find here a Jeremiah not always gloomy and not opposed to merriment as such. A hint of this comes in 8:18, where the prophet laments a former joy that has left him. The verb *'dh* means "to deck oneself with ornaments" (4:30; cf. 2:32), and the *tōp*, which is a hand-drum made from animal skin stretched over a circular frame of wood or metal (C. Sachs 1940: 108–9; *ABD* 4: 936; cf. Mishnah Kinnim 3:6), is here part of the maidens' festival attire. Held usually in the left hand, the drum was struck with the palm or fingers of the right. No sticks were used. The instrument provided rhythm for song and dance and was played mostly, though not exclusively, by women (Gorali 1972: 71). The LXX translates with *tympanon*, a later Greek term denoting a hand- or kettle-drum. The Vg term is *tympanum*. Comparisons have been made to the *duff* in use among Arabs (Streane; Finesinger 1926: 66; KB³), which is a hand-drum of similar type, with small pieces of brass affixed to the rim. However, the hand-drum in use among the Israelites, Canaanites, Egyptians, Assyrians, and other ancient Near Eastern peoples had no jingling metal (C. Sachs

1940: 108–9; Sendrey 1969: 373; C. Meyers 1991: 18), which means it was not, strictly speaking, a tambourine or timbrel. Numerous depictions of ancient musicians holding hand-drums, most of them women, have come to light. For pictures of terra-cotta figurines and other artwork depicting ancient drummers, see *ANEP*[2] 63 #199, #202, #203; 64 #204, #211; cf. 272–73; and Meyers. None of these drums show dangling metal. Actually, tambourines and timbrels are not attested before the thirteenth century A.D. (C. Sachs 1940: 289). The hand-drum was a symbol of joy (Gen 31:27; Isa 24:8) and was played on a variety of occasions. In the biblical tradition, hand-drums and other instruments, played by both men and women, are said to have accompanied singing and dancing in sacred worship (2 Sam 6:5; 1 Chr 13:8; Ps 149:1–3; 150:4), prophetic ecstasies (1 Sam 10:5), victory celebrations where the women sang and played when the warriors returned from battle (Exod 15:20–21; Judg 11:34; 1 Sam 18:6; Ps 68:26[Eng 68:25]), late night parties (Isa 5:12; 24:8; Job 21:12), and yearly festivals (Isa 30:29–32; Ps 81:3–4[Eng 81:2–3]), which is what the present oracle anticipates (v 6). The festival here is likely the joyful harvest festival (Feast of Booths), because planting and reaping are mentioned. McKane is bothered by a lack of continuity (more properly a lack of sequentiality) in vv 2–5, then again in v 6, where the festival dancing and drum-playing come before the planting and ingathering, and the call to make the pilgrimage is mentioned last. But sequentiality or logical progression, as we have said repeatedly, is not required in Hebrew rhetorical discourse, especially poetry (see Note on 1:15). The oracle here has simply to be heard as a whole without regard to the verse-by-verse presentation of ideas. A similar lack of logical progression occurs in Ps 81:3–4[Eng 81:2–3]), where the call to sing and play instruments precedes the trumpet call announcing that the feast is at hand.

and go forth in the dance of merrymakers. See again v 13. Maidens playing the hand-drum are a sure indication that there will be singing and dancing. At the harvest festival young maidens are prominent; recall the "daughters of Shiloh" in Judg 21:19–21. On "merrymakers" (*měśaḥăqîm*), see Note for 30:19. The term for dance is *měḥôl* (from *ḥûl*, "to whirl"); thus dancing will be in a circle. The LXX (*meta synagōgēs*), S, and T have "with a community" instead of "in the dance." Becking (1994a: 157) thinks (in the case of LXX) that this could result from misreading *biqhal* for *bimḥôl*. The LXX makes the same substitution in v 13. Read the MT, with Snaith (1945: 24), supported now by 4QJer[c].

5. *Again you'll plant vineyards on Samaria's mountains.* Mention of "Samaria's mountains" is a clear indication that this oracle has Northern Israel in view. These are the mountains in and around Samaria (Amos 3:9), not just the mountain of Samaria itself. Vineyards will be planted as usual, in terraces on the mountain slopes (cf. Isa 5:1).

planters shall plant and eat the fruit. Hebrew *wěhillēlû* is lit., "and (they) will profane," which refers here to eating the fruit after it has been set aside as holy. According to Levitical law, fruit of newly planted trees (and vines) could not be eaten until the fifth year (Lev 19:23–25). The first three years, the fruit must not be eaten at all; the fourth year, it is set aside as a praise offering to Yahweh; and in the fifth year, the planter is free to eat it. It stands to reason, then, that one does not plant vineyards unless the chances are good that one will reap some benefit from them. In wartime, vineyards are planted, and others eat the fruit (5:17; Deut 20:6), which is one of the covenant curses (Deut 28:30; cf. Amos 5:11). But Jeremiah says here that the day will come when those who plant vineyards will enjoy their fruit (cf. Amos 9:14; Isa 65:21–22). The LXX omits "planters" and translates the verbs as imperatives: "Plant and praise!" The second imperative mistakes *hll*, "to praise," for *ḥll*, "to profane" (cf. Isa 62:9). The T also reads *nṭ'w* as an imperative and takes *nṭ'ym* as a plural noun: "Plant the plants, and eat them as common produce." Jerome in the Vg strangely expands and converts the promise into its negative: *plantabunt plantantes, et donec tempus veniat non vindemiabunt* ("they will plant plants, and when the time comes they will not gather"). But, as Kedar-Kopfstein (1969: 56–57) points out, Jerome changes his translation in the commentary to: *plantate plantaria et vindemiate* ("plant plants and gather!"), which approximates T. Janzen (1973: 118) takes the omission of "planters" as being due to haplography, which is possible in view of three successive consonants repeating in two words. 4QJer^c has "planters." Volz and Rudolph take the entire phrase as a gloss from Deut 28:30 (cf. JB and NJB). The MT reading, supported by 4QJer^c, should be retained.

6. *For there shall be a day when watchmen will call out on Mount Ephraim.* These "watchmen" (*nōṣĕrîm*) are individuals stationed at high elevations, calling the villagers to begin their pilgrimage to Jerusalem (Rashi; Kimḥi). Psalm 122:1 says: "I was glad when they said to me, let us go to the house of Yahweh." Watchmen ascend to elevated heights also to view the new moon, which signals the beginning of the festival (Cheyne; Duhm; cf. Ps 81:3–4[Eng 81:2–3]). Even today in Jerusalem, the festivals of Judaism and Islam (e.g., Ramadan) can begin only after the new moon has been sighted and announced. The LXX has *hoti estin hēmera klēseōs apologoumenōn en oresin Ephraim* ("for it is a day of those advocating a calling to the feast on the mountains of Ephraim"). Aquila and Symm read an imperative: *kalesate phulakas en orei Ephraim* ("call watchings on the mountain of Ephraim!").

on Mount Ephraim. "Mount Ephraim" here is not a general term for the region of Ephraim (see Note for 4:15) but a promontory on Ephraim's southern mountains where the watchmen ascend. In 4:15 a watchman announced the approach of an enemy from here. In this verse, he bears happier tidings.

Up, let us go to Zion. Hebrew *qûmû wěna'ăleh ṣiyyôn.* This formulation is similar to the negative "Up, let us attack at noon / at night" in 6:4–5. See also 49:38, 31. The language is elliptical: "let us go Zion" (people in the Upper Peninsula of Michigan say "Let's go Green Bay"). Omission of the preposition "to" is common in Jeremiah poetry and prose (see Note for 24:1). The LXX reads the cohortative as another imperative: *Anastēte kai anabēte eis Siōn,* "Up and go to Zion!" Northern Israelites are called here to worship Yahweh at Zion, supporting the view that this oracle endorses Josiah's program to unite

North and South (Bright; Jones). Jeremiah is not yet openly hostile to Temple worship. After 586 B.C., a reunited Israel and Judah with Jerusalem as the cultic center became a revived hope (3:14–18).

to Yahweh our God! This confession of Yahweh as Israel's God is climactic, coming as it does at the end of the oracle. On climactic asseverations of the divine name in Jeremiah and elsewhere in the OT, see Note for 10:16.

MESSAGE AND AUDIENCE

Jeremiah begins Oracle II by stating an ancient truth once again seen to be operative: a people has survived the sword only to find grace in the wilderness, and after a period of wandering they go to find their rest. It is Yahweh's revelation to Israel from long ago, now repeating itself in the exile of the Northern tribes to Assyria. Jeremiah says that Yahweh has appeared to him from afar with some very comforting words. Yahweh loves Israel with an eternal love, for which reason he has faithfully drawn the nation along. Speaking with unconcealed warmth and affection, Yahweh says he intends to build up virgin Israel so that she can once again dress for the festival and put nimble fingers to the drum, as people gather to sing and dance. Again she will plant vineyards on Samaria's mountains and be there to enjoy the fruit of the harvest. Jeremiah concludes the oracle by saying that the day will come when watchmen will ascend Mount Ephraim to call loudly for the people to begin their pilgrimage to Zion, and there they will worship Yahweh their God.

Oracle II can be dated to Jeremiah's early career, i.e., in 622 B.C. or afterward, when people from Northern Israel were being summoned to festivals in Jerusalem (2 Kgs 23:1–23), and Israelite exiles in faraway Assyria could look forward to the day when they too would be doing the same.

To this oracle has been attached Oracle I, reaffirming the covenant. After 586 B.C., the two oracles together addressed a broad audience of Israelite and Judahite exiles, assuring them that Yahweh in future days would be God to all the tribes of Israel, and they would all be his people.

h) Yahweh Will Return the Remnant of Israel (31:7–9)

31 ⁷For thus said Yahweh:
Cry with gladness for Jacob
 and scream over The Head of the Nations
Proclaim, praise, and say:
 'Yahweh has saved your people
  the remnant of Israel!'

⁸Look I will bring them
 from the land of the north
And I will gather them from remote parts of the earth
 among them the blind and the lame

the pregnant and woman in labor together
  a great assembly shall return here

⁹With weeping they shall come
  and with supplications I will lead them
I will bring them to streams of water
  on a level path, in which they will not stumble
For I am as a father to Israel
  and Ephraim, my firstborn is he.

RHETORIC AND COMPOSITION

MT 31:7–9 = LXX 38:7–9. The present verses consist of a single hope oracle, the second of three that form a unit within the poetic core (see Rhetoric and Composition for 30:4–7 and 31:1–6). The oracle is delimited at the top end by a "for thus said Yahweh" formula beginning v 7, prior to which is a *petuḥah* in M^L and a *setumah* in M^P. Upon reconstruction, 4QJer^c also has a *setumah* before v 7 (Tov 1997: 197–98). Delimitation at the bottom end is marked by a *setumah* in M^L and a *petuḥah* in M^P and 4QJer^c after v 9. Some commentators (Giesebrecht; Duhm; Hyatt; Thompson; Keown et al.; McKane) take all of vv 7–14 as a unit, which ignores this latter section. Verses 10–14 have their own "oracle of Yahweh" formula at the end. The present verses are then a self-contained oracle (Condamin; Rudolph; Weiser; Bright; Boadt; Carroll; Jones). There is no justification for selecting out v 9b and combining it with vv 2–6, as Volz and Holladay do (Duhm and Cornill had earlier biases regarding v 9b). It is the climactic line of the oracle, similar to 6b in vv 2–6.

Commentators and others are divided over questions of date, authorship, and provenance of these verses. Some, because of a similarity in ideas and phraseology to Second Isaiah, deny the verses to Jeremiah and date them in the postexilic period (Giesebrecht; Duhm; Peake; Cornill; Streane; Hyatt; Carroll; Mendecki 1988; McKane). Others attribute them to Jeremiah, dating them either in Josiah's reign or close to the fall of Jerusalem (Volz; Rudolph; Weiser; Bright; Thompson; Boadt; Holladay; Jones). The verses contain the "new Exodus" theme so prominent in Second Isaiah, but Halpern (1998) has recently argued that it is the prophet of the exile who builds on Jeremiah, not the other way around. This is the view also of Holladay, and I think the correct one. The diction here is very much that of Jeremiah, e.g., "gladness," "Look I will bring . . . from the land of the north," "from remote parts of the earth," and "they shall (not) stumble," to mention some of the most obvious examples. Also, as Holladay, Jones, and Halpern all point out, ideas of deliverance here invert the same ideas found in Jeremiah's earlier judgment preaching (compare vv 8–9 with 6:21–22; 18:15; 25:32; and 50:41).

This is another dialogue oracle. Jeremiah speaks first in v 7, calling people to cry out loudly and praise Yahweh for saving the remnant of Israel. Then Yahweh speaks in vv 8–9 (divine "I"), replying to this joyous acclamation (Calvin;

Streane). Recognizing this as a dialogue oracle resolves a concern raised by Weiser, who says that since the divine speech begins in v 8, the messenger formula should precede this verse instead of preceding v 7.

The oracle has three stanzas with repeated and balancing terms. The whole can be taken as an expanded key word chiasmus (Holladay), where Yahweh and his people ("Jacob and Israel; Ephraim") are named in I and III, and enumeration ("blind, lame, those pregnant, those in labor") occurs in II, which is the center (cf. Lund 1942: 57–58). In II and III the verb *bô*' ("bring, come") is also repeated:

I	. . . . *for Jacob*	*lĕyaʿăqōb*	v 7
	. . . .		
	. . . .		
	. . . . *Yahweh*		
	. . . . *Israel*		
II	*Look I will bring them*	*hinĕnî mēbî*' '*ôtām*	v 8
	. . . .		
	. . . .		
	. . . *the blind and the lame*		
	the pregnant and woman in labor . . .		
	. . . .		
III	. . . . *they shall come*	*yābō*'*û*	v 9
	. . . .		
	. . . . . *I am as a father to Israel*	*hāyîtî lĕyiśrā*'*ēl lĕ*'*āb*	
	. . . . *Ephraim*	'*eprayim*	

Catchwords connecting to the prior oracle (cf. Condamin):

v 7	*your people*	v 2	*a people*
v 9	*Ephraim*	v 6	*Ephraim*

A host of catchwords (not including the name of Yahweh) connect this oracle to the oracle following (cf. Carroll; Jones):

v 7	*cry (for joy)*	*ronnû*	v 10	*Hear*	*šimʿû*
	Jacob			*nations*	
	gladness	*śimḥâ*		*and say*	*wĕ*'*imrû*
	nations			*Israel*	
	Proclaim . . . and say	*hašmîʿû . . .*		*he will gather him*	*yĕqabbĕṣennû*
		wĕ'*imrû*			
	your people		v 11	*Jacob*	
	Israel		v 12	*And they shall come*	*ûbā*'*û*
v 8	*Look I will bring*	*hinĕnî mēbî*'		*and cry for joy*	*wĕrinnĕnû*
	And I will gather them	*wĕqibbaṣtîm*	v 13	*be glad*	*tiśmaḥ*
	together	*yaḥdaw*		*together*	*yaḥdaw*

v 9   *they shall come*   *yābō'û*   *and I will make*   *wĕśimmaḥtîm*
                                                     them glad
      Israel   v 14   *my people*

NOTES

31:7. *For thus said Yahweh: Cry with gladness for Jacob, and scream over The Head of the Nations.* The LXX expands the messenger formula, rearranges the two verbs, and omits *śimḥâ* ("gladness"), its translation being: "For thus said the Lord to Jacob: Rejoice and exult over the head of the nations." But Yahweh is not addressing Jacob. Jeremiah begins as speaker of the oracle by telling an unspecified audience to be joyful on Jacob's behalf. This directive to cry out in hymnic joy occurs often in the Psalms (Pss 5:12[Eng 5:11]; 33:1; 98:4, 8; 132:9; 149:5), as well as in Second Isaiah (Isa 44:23; 49:13; 52:9; 54:1). Isaiah 51:11 says that the ransomed of Yahweh will come with singing (*bĕrinnâ*) to Zion. See also Deut 32:43; Zeph 3:14; Isa 55:12; and Zech 2:14[Eng 2:10]. The two verbs, *rnn* ("cry for joy") and *ṣhl* ("shout, scream"), occur together in Isa 12:6 and 24:14.

Jacob. Here referring to just Northern Israel (Cornill), as is the case with "Ephraim" in v 9.

and scream over The Head of the Nations. Hebrew *wĕṣahălû bĕrō'š haggôyim.* The verb is *ṣhl*, which means "scream, make a shrilling cry," or with reference to horses, "neigh" (5:8; 13:27; 50:11). Here is it a human scream of joy (cf. Isa 24:14). Parallelism in the bicolon makes "The Head of the Nations" a boastful epithet for Jacob. This epithet could also be translated "The First of the Nations" (Weiser; Bright), which would go better with Ephraim the "firstborn" in v 9. In Amos 6:1 Jerusalem and Samaria's notables are ironically called "distinguished ones of the first of the nations (*rē'šît haggôyim*)." One of the covenant curses states that if the covenant is disobeyed the sojourner in Israel will become the "head" (*rō'š*) and the Israelite the "tail" (Deut 28:43–44). Now, with restoration in view, Israel will once again become "head (of the nations)." Babylon in her day of reckoning will become "last of the nations," *'aḥărît gôyim* (Jer 50:12). Rashi imagines the joyful scream here as being made from lofty towers so it can be heard. Duhm is thinking along similar lines in wanting to emend "the nations" (*haggôyim*) to "mountains" (*hārîm*). The scream in his view is made on the top (*rō'š*) of the mountains (cf. Isa 42:11). Some scholars (Giesebrecht; Peake; Cornill; Ehrlich 1912: 320; Snaith 1945: 25; Hyatt) have adopted this reading, but it is self-serving to the extent that it creates yet another parallel to Second Isaiah for those wanting to date the oracle in the postexilic period. As a matter of fact, the scream of joy, the proclamation, and the praise of Yahweh's salvation could occur anywhere.

Proclaim, praise, and say. Asyndeton, on which see Note on 4:5.

Yahweh has saved your people. The Masoretes pointed the verb as an imperative: *hôša'* ("Save!"), but T and LXX translate a perfect form, "(he) has saved."

"Your people" in T and LXX also becomes "his people." Most commentators therefore repoint the Heb to *hôšîaʿ* ("he has saved" written *defective*) and emend "your people" to "his people." Thus, the RSV (following Moffatt and AmT): "The LORD has saved his people," with most other modern Versions translating similarly. The AV had "O LORD, save thy people," which is retained by NJV and NIV and reappears in the NRSV. Kimḥi sees no problem with an imperative following an acclamation; nor does Bright, who although he goes with the LXX and T, concedes that the MT reading is not impossible. Nothing precludes a cry of gladness occurring simultaneously with a plea for salvation, because the human soul is fully capable of such a mixing when great moments occur. But new support for the LXX and T renderings comes from the reading *hwsyʿ* in 4QJer^c, which, if pointed *hôšîaʿ* (*scriptio plene*), yields "he has saved." 4QJer^c follows with "your people" (*ʿmk*), suggesting that the correct reading is probably "Yahweh has saved your people." Since these are words put into the mouths of the people, a shift to the second person is not a problem. Jeremiah is telling Judahites to address their kinfolk in the North with the words "Yahweh has saved your people!" The verb is a prophetic perfect, i.e., "Yahweh will (indeed) save your people" (Streane). Many of those arguing for a perfect verb form wanted a postexilic date for the oracle, assuming that a return had already taken place. But the return is still anticipated for the future.

the remnant of Israel. Hebrew *šĕʾērît yiśrāʾēl*. The term originally meant the remnant of Northern Israel (Cornill), then later the remnant of all Israel (= Judah), as in 6:9. The idea of a surviving "remnant" for Israel is given prominence in Isaiah (Isa 7:3 and elsewhere), but it appears also in Jeremiah, where *šĕʾērît* has multiple meanings (see Note for 23:3). The term in the present verse need not be taken as a late gloss (*pace* Giesebrecht; Duhm; Cornill; Rudolph; Carroll; McKane). The article by Heaton (1952) on the root's *šʾr* is valuable in showing how in the OT the term "primarily directs attention not forward to the residue, but *backwards* to the whole of which it had been a part" (p. 29), and that a doctrine of the Remnant such as one finds in the NT writings of Paul (Rom 9:27–29; 11:4–36) is nowhere present in the OT prophets. But Heaton dates far too many relevant passages in Isaiah 1–39, Micah, Zephaniah, and Jeremiah to the exilic or postexilic periods, which leads him to negative conclusions about there being seeds of later doctrine in the preexilic prophets. On the origin and development of the remnant idea in the OT, with parallels in other ANE literature, see Hasel 1972. On the "remnant of Israel" as it developed after the prophets, see de Vaux 1933.

8. *Look I will bring them from the land of the north, And I will gather them from remote parts of the earth*. The opening *hinĕnî mēbîʾ* ("Look I am bringing/ will bring") in the mouth of Yahweh is a signature expression of Jeremiah (see Note for 39:16). Yahweh now answers the joyful outburst over Israel's deliverance by disclosing his plan for dispersed Israel. He will bring the remnant home from their northern exile and also gather others from the distant places where he scattered them (cf. 31:10). The dispersion as described is extensive, but this is no proof that the passage is late (*pace* Duhm). In Jeremiah's

judgment preaching to Judah, Yahweh says he will bring an enemy from the land of the north (6:22) and like an east wind will scatter his people to faraway places (9:15[Eng 9:16]; 13:24; 18:17). But later, to dispersed Judah, he promises that he will gather them (3:18; 16:15; 23:3, 8; 29:14; 32:37; cf. Deut 30:3–4; Ezek 11:17; 20:34, 41; 28:25; Isa 41:9; 43:5–6).

from the land of the north. The LXX has just "from the north." 4QJer^c supports MT.

And I will gather them. Hebrew *wĕqibbaṣtîm.* 4QJer^c has an imperfect form of the verb.

among them the blind and the lame, the pregnant and woman in labor together. Anyone and everyone will make this journey. God, says Rashi, will not leave the staggering behind. Such people could not have made the walk to Assyria, or (excepting poor blind Zedekiah) the later walk to Babylon (cf. Mark 13:17–18). Calvin notes that the blind cannot take a step without stumbling or falling; nor can the lame make progress on such a journey. But God promises that both will be on the walk home, and such care will he provide the returning band that even pregnant women and those in labor will be able to journey with the rest. Calvin finds this a wonder, which is precisely the point. The promises of God exceed what is thought humanly possible. God has the power to make the blind see and the lame walk and enable the pregnant and those in labor to undertake arduous journeys. In the NT, note the conditions under which Jesus is born (Luke 2:1–7). In place of the present words, the LXX has "to the feast of the Passover, and they shall give birth" which is widely judged a corruption, although Becking (1994a: 161) has argued that, with retroversion, the Old Greek might be more original. This is doubtful. Jones thinks the LXX reading may have been intentionally doctored. Noting that the LXX adds "sons of Levi" in 31:14, he thinks that this reading along with the one here may represent a late orthodox editing of MT. The T, Vg, and 4QJer^c all support MT.

a great assembly shall return here. Hebrew *qāhāl gādôl yāšûbû hēnnâ.* The MT, LXX, T, and Vg all give the present reading; nevertheless, certain commentators (Blayney; Duhm; Volz; Rudolph; Weiser; Bright; Thompson; McKane) want to emend *hēnnâ* ("here") to *hinnēh* ("Look"), placing the latter at the beginning of v 9. The idea is attractive, since v 8 begins with *hinĕnî* ("Look I"), but there is really no justification for the emendation, and none of the modern Versions adopts it. The text reads perfectly well as is and should be retained. Yahweh makes the statement as if speaking in Jerusalem.

shall return. Hebrew *yāšûbû.* 4QJer^c is written *defective: yšbw.*

9. *With weeping they shall come, and with supplications I will lead them.* The assembly appears to be genuinely repentant, unlike the Judahites making "weeping supplications" to Baal in 3:21. Rashi says the people are coming home in prayer and repentance (cf. 31:19). Kimḥi says the weeping is for joy. Repentance and joy may certainly occur simultaneously, so emotional will be the return. The LXX, T, and Vg contrast the coming home with the earlier going away, presumably translating *yābō'û* "they shall go" rather than "they shall come." The LXX: "In weeping they went out (*exēlthon*), but in encouragement

(*paraklēsei*) I will direct them [home]." Calvin, in support of this interpretation, cites Ps 126:6: "He that surely goes forth with weeping . . . shall surely come in with a cry of joy." The exile, says Calvin, can be compared to sowing and the return to a joyful harvest. Other commentators, too, express a preference for this interpretation, but the MT rendering is more dynamic, with the returning throng weeping and supplicating Yahweh as he leads them along. Also, one should note that *bo'* in the perfect means "come (in)," not "go," in 31:12.

I will bring them to streams of water. The successive verbs "I will lead them, I will bring them" are sonorous in Hebrew: *'ôbîlēm 'ôlîkēm*. A *naḥal* is a "stream" or "brook" (Ar *wadi*), water flowing gently except in the rainy season when it becomes a virtual torrent (cf. 47:2). The Promised Land is filled with "streams of water" (Deut 8:7), and these will be a welcome sight to the returnees. For later Judahites coming home, these streams will contrast with the "rivers of Babylon" alongside which they sat down and wept (Ps 137:1). In Second Isaiah's "new Exodus," Yahweh's leading will bring the people to springs in the desert (Isa 35:6–7; 41:18; 43:19–20; 44:3–4; 48:21; 49:10). In the NT Apocalypse, the Lamb will lead survivors of the tribulation to springs of living water (Rev 7:17).

to streams of water. 4QJer^c has *'al* for MT's *'el*. On the interchange of *'al* and *'el* in Jeremiah, see again v 12 and Note for 11:2.

on a level path, in which they will not stumble. 4QJer^c has a *waw* prefixed to *lō'* ("and they shall not stumble"). The homeward trek will be "on a level path" (*bĕderek yāšār*). The AV, RSV, and NRSV translate *yāšār* as "straight" ("a straight way/path"), which does not really suit the context. The path must be "smooth" or "level" so that the blind and lame will not stumble and fall. The lame run the added risk of suffering dislocation (cf. Heb 12:13). In Jeremiah's judgment preaching, people are brought to stumbling either because of their own perverse ways (18:15; 20:11) or because Yahweh brings it about in judgment (6:15, 21; 8:12). For later Judahites returning from Babylon, the highway will also be on level ground, with low places being built up (Isa 40:3–4; 42:16; 45:2, 13; 49:11; 57:14; 62:10).

For I am as a father to Israel, and Ephraim, my firstborn is he. These concluding words are climactic, like the asseveration in 10:16. For "father-son" imagery elsewhere in Jeremiah (3:4, 19; 31:20) and its likely derivation from Hosea (Hos 2:1[Eng 1:10]; 11:1), see K. Gross 1930: 7. The imagery is present also in Deut 32:5–6. In 3:19, Yahweh expresses the desire to have treated his daughter-people as one of the sons, giving her an inheritance. "Father" is not a common designation for Yahweh in the OT, but it does occur (see Note for 3:4; cf. Muilenburg 1960). The declaration of Israel as Yahweh's "firstborn" (*bĕkōr*) has roots in the Exodus tradition (Exod 4:22), but here in the present verse the firstborn is Ephraim. Calvin says "Ephraim" is simply another name for the whole people of Israel, but it seems, rather, that reference here is only to Northern Israel (Hertzberg 1952: 597; *pace* McKane), as in Jeremiah elsewhere (7:15; 31:9, 18, 20) and all through the book of Hosea. Ephraim as Yahweh's "firstborn" finds biblical support in 1 Chr 5:1–3, where

Reuben's birthright is given to the sons of Joseph, Ephraim and Manasseh, and in Gen 48:8–20, where Ephraim is placed ahead of Manasseh by a grandfather (Jacob) who himself supplanted an older twin. Yahweh's rejection of "Ephraim" for "Judah" in Ps 78:67–68 is claimed in light of Northern Israel's destruction in 722 B.C.; and in Ps 89:27–28[Eng 89:26–27], where Yahweh is said to be "Father" to David, his firstborn, the meaning is that David is preeminent among the kings of the earth.

MESSAGE AND AUDIENCE

Jeremiah begins this oracle by telling a Judahite audience that they can cry loudly and joyfully for Jacob (their kinfolk from the North who are presently languishing in Assyrian and Median cities), for once again he will become head of the nations. In proclamation and praise, they are to address their brothers and sisters with the words "Yahweh has saved your people, the remnant of Israel!"

Yahweh then answers this acclamation by declaring that he will indeed return remnant Israel from its northern exile, gathering others as well from places hither and yon. Among the returnees will be the blind and the lame, pregnant women, and those ready to give birth. It will be a vast throng, and the walk home will go considerably better than the walk leaving home. Yahweh envisions them weeping as they walk, their tears communicating joy, repentance, and fresh supplication. He promises them streams of water and a level path on which they will not stumble. The oracle closes with Yahweh saying that he is indeed like a father to Israel, and Ephraim is his firstborn.

This oracle appears to have just Northern Israel in view, which means it is early Jeremianic preaching from the reign of Josiah (after 622 B.C.) and a sequel to the oracle in vv 2–6. At the time of Judah's destruction, it will have expanded application to Judahite exiles (30:4), anticipating for both remnant peoples the day when they will make a return together.

When this oracle is heard following the oracle in vv 2–6, Jeremiah's call for joyful cries in v 7 will continue the watchmen's joyful call of v 6, and Yahweh's promise of Israel's return to Zion will now be described in fuller detail (Calvin; Jones).

i) The One Who Scattered Will Gather (31:10–14)

31 [10]Hear the word of Yahweh, nations
    and declare among the distant coastlands, and say:
He who scattered Israel will gather him
    and will keep him as a shepherd his flock
[11]For Yahweh has ransomed Jacob
    and redeemed him from a hand stronger than his own

[12]And they shall come and cry for joy on the height of Zion
    and they shall be radiant over the goodness of Yahweh

Over the grain and over the wine and over the oil
   and over the young of the flocks and the herds
And their soul shall become like a saturated garden
   and they shall no longer languish any more
¹³Then shall the maiden be glad in the dance
   yes, young men and old men together

And I will turn their mourning into joy
   and I will comfort them
      and I will make them glad from their sorrow
¹⁴And I will saturate the soul of the priests with abundance
   and my people with my goodness will be sated
      —oracle of Yahweh.

RHETORIC AND COMPOSITION

MT 31:10–14 = LXX 38:10–14. These verses are delimited at the top end by a
setumah in M^L and a *petuḥah* in M^P and 4QJer^c before v 10. At the bottom end
delimitation is by a *setumah* in M^L and a *petuḥah* in M^P and 4QJer^c after v 14.
Prior to the latter markings is a concluding "oracle of Yahweh" formula. This
oracle is the third of three hope oracles that form a unit in the poetic core (see
Rhetoric and Composition for 30:4–7 and 31:1–6). The LXX lacks the messenger formula and some commentators delete, but it should be retained. It is
present in 4QJer^c. With reconstruction, 4QJer^c has a *setumah* after v 10 (Tov
1997: 197–98), which neither M^L nor M^P has. This could indicate that v 10 was
at one time independent, since the verse does not figure in the rhetorical
structure (see below), and 10b has a parallel in 23:3–4 with its successive "gathering" and "shepherding" images. Otherwise, v 10 fits well with the rest of the
oracle, announcing Yahweh's redeeming work to the nations.
   Judgments about date, authorship, and provenance are much the same
here as for vv 7–9, with some commentators taking vv 7–14 as a single unit
(see Rhetoric and Composition for 31:7–9). At issue once again is a similarity
of ideas and phraseology to Second Isaiah, to which is added here the reference in v 14 to good times awaiting the priests, which some commentators
(Giesebrecht; Volz; Rudolph; Hyatt; and others) find difficult to attribute to
Jeremiah. Volz deletes all of v 14. But the verses contain parallels in vocabulary and phraseology to other Jeremianic preaching, with the result that commentators are divided on interpretation, much as they are regarding vv 7–9,
except Holladay, who uncharacteristically dates this oracle to the Persian
period.
   The oracle has three stanzas, with Stanzas II and III inverting their balancing key words:

II	*the goodness of Yahweh*	*ṭûb yhwh*	v 12
	. . . their soul . . . saturated	*napšām . . . rāweh*	

III *And I will saturate the soul . . .*   *wĕriwwêtî nepeš . . .*   v 14
     . . . . my goodness . . . . .   *ṭûbî*

Stanza II, being the center, also has enumeration, "grain . . . wine . . . oil . . . the young of the flocks . . . the herds," as in the prior oracle (see Rhetoric and Composition for 31:7–9).

The present oracle is crafted as another dialogue, with Jeremiah speaking in Stanzas I and II (third-person references to Yahweh) and Yahweh speaking in Stanza III (divine "I" and "my people").

A host of catchwords—not including the name "Yahweh"—connect this oracle to the previous one. Some of the following are noted by Carroll and Jones:

v 10	Hear	šim'û	v 7	cry (for joy)	ronnû
	nations			Jacob	
	and say	wĕ'imrû		gladness	śimḥâ
	Israel			nations	
	he will gather	yĕqabbĕṣennû		Proclaim . . .	hašmî'û . . .
	him			and say	wĕ'imrû
v 11	Jacob			your people	
v 12	And they shall	ûbā'û		Israel	
	come				
	and cry for joy	wĕrinnĕnû	v 8	Look I will bring	hinĕnî mēbî'
v 13	be glad	tiśmaḥ		And I will gather	wĕqibbaṣtîm
				them	
	together	yaḥdaw		together	yaḥdaw
	and I will make	wĕśimmaḥtîm	v 9	they shall come	yābō'û
	them glad				
v 14	my people			Israel	

Catchwords connecting to the next oracle:

| v 10 | Hear | v 15 | is heard |
| v 13 | and I will comfort them | | to be comforted |

NOTES

31:10. *Hear the word of Yahweh, nations, and declare among the distant coastlands, and say.* Jacob's redemption is here announced to the nations, who in turn are to declare it to distant coastlands. The nations too must know of Yahweh's redemption (4:16; 33:9; 50:2). The "distant coastlands" (*'îyyîm mimmerḥāq*) are the Greek islands (2:10), Crete (47:4), and Phoenician colonies in the western Mediterranean as far away as Spain (see Note for 25:22). Second Isaiah says these same coastlands wait for Yahweh (Isa 42:4; 51:5; 60:9) and will sing his praises (Isa 42:10; 66:19).

and say. Hebrew *wĕ'imrû.* Some commentators (Giesebrecht; Duhm; Rudolph; Holladay) delete as (metrical) excess, but the same term appears in v 7.

He who scattered Israel will gather him. The verb *zrh* means "to winnow, scatter" and is used metaphorically in the OT to describe the separation and dispersion of people (see Note for 49:32). The reference here is to Northern Israel's dispersion, applied later to the dispersion of all Israel. On the theme of Yahweh's gathering the people that he scattered, see Note for 31:8.

and will keep him as a shepherd his flock. Shepherding is another widely used metaphor in the Bible and throughout the ancient world, describing the rule of kings and royal appointees (see Note for 2:8) and the rule of God or the gods. The last years of both Israel and Judah saw shepherds unfit for royal office, which led to the demise of the two nations. Jeremiah had harsh words for Judah's kings, through whose negligence the flock (= subjects) was scattered (10:21; 13:20; 23:1–2; 50:6; cf. Ezek 34:1–10). But Yahweh is the good shepherd, leading and watching his flock, feeding it, and gathering the lambs in his arms (Psalms 23; 77:21[Eng 77:20]; 80:2[Eng 80:1]; Isa 40:11). Here he promises to shepherd Northern Israel, a promise made later also to Judah (23:3–4; cf. Ezek 34:11–16). In the NT, Jesus is the good shepherd (John 10:1–18).

11. *For Yahweh has ransomed Jacob and redeemed him from a hand stronger than his own.* Here another great biblical theme occurs: God's redemption of people from slavery and every other form of oppression. In the OT it is mainly the redemption of Israel; in the NT it is the redemption of the world (Matt 20:28; 1 Tim 2:6; cf. John 3:16), which returns to pick up a theme from OT prehistory (Genesis 6–9). Now Yahweh declares as an accomplished fact his redemption of Jacob, i.e., Northern Israel. The two verbs, *pdh* ("ransom") and *g'l* ("redeem"), are used interchangeably in the OT (Hos 13:14; Ps 69:19[Eng 69:18]) and in theological contexts mean roughly the same thing. The verb *pdh* is more general, referring simply to the redemption of persons and other living beings; *g'l* has its origin in the sphere of law, where it denotes the collective responsibility to heal or restore balance within the kin-group. A *gō'ēl* is someone obligated to perpetuate the line of a deceased kinsman (levirate marriage), avenge the murder of a kinsman (Num 35:19–21), redeem a kinsman's forfeited property (Lev 25:25; Ruth 4:1–6; Jer 32:6–15), or redeem a kinsman himself if he has fallen into slavery (Lev 25:47–55; cf. A. R. Johnson 1953; Dentan, "Redeem, Redeemer, Redemption," *IDB* R–Z, 21). This redemption from slavery is what assumes such theological importance in the OT: Yahweh, as *gō'ēl*, takes it upon himself to redeem Israel, his firstborn, from Egyptian slavery (Exod 6:5; 15:13; Deut 7:8; 9:26; cf. Exod 4:22). Here in the present verse, Yahweh is redeeming the remnant of Northern Israel from its servitude in Assyria, and later on, he will redeem the remnant of Judah from its servitude in Babylon (50:34; Isa 41:14; 43:1, 14; 44:6, 22–23; 47:4; 48:17, 20; and often). There is nothing indicating that Israel's repentance is a determining condition for this redemption, as Unterman claims for the early Jeremianic preaching ("Redemption," *ABD* 5: 654). Repentance does seem to be present in 31:9, which he cites, but only by implication. Things are less clear with respect to the oracles in 31:15–22, where Ephraim asks for restoration (*šûb*) and is genuinely sorry (*nḥm*) about having turned away (vv 18–19). But there, nothing explicit is

said about redemption, making Israel's repentance a condition for the divine favor no more than an inference. On Yahweh as Israel's *gō'ēl* ("Redeemer"), see also the Note for 50:34.

a hand stronger than his own. Hebrew *mîyyad ḥāzāq mimmennû.* The Assyrians, like the Egyptians earlier, refused to let their captives go (50:33). But happily for Israel—and later for Judah—"their Redeemer is strong," *gō'ălām ḥāzāq* (v 34). The psalmist knew this same truth (Ps 35:10). By the time Jeremiah began preaching in 622 B.C, or shortly after, Assyrian troops had withdrawn from Philistia, Tyre, and Judah, and Nabopolassar was now king in Babylon (626 B.C.). By 616 B.C., Nabopolassar was fighting Assyria in the Upper Euphrates, and in 614 B.C., the Medes took Asshur (Bright 1981: 315–16). Nineveh fell in 612 B.C. In the years, then, between 622 and 612, hopes were high in Judah that Israelite exiles from Assyrian and Median cities would be returning home.

12. *And they shall come and cry for joy on the height of Zion.* The goal of these returnees will be Zion, as in 31:6. On the "height of Zion" (*mĕrôm-ṣîyyôn*) sits the Jerusalem Temple (Calvin; cf. Ezek 20:40), where Yahweh will be worshiped. The LXX's "on the mountain of Zion" does not require emending *bimrôm* to *behārîm* (*pace* Rudolph) or deleting "Zion" (*pace* Volz; Rudolph).

and they shall be radiant over the goodness of Yahweh. Yahweh's "goodness" (*ṭûb*) consists of bumper crops along with enlarged flocks and herds, resulting in an abundant food supply. For this same meaning of *ṭûb,* see v 14; also 2:7 and Hos 3:5. The verb *nhr* can mean "flow, stream" (51:44), which is what the AV chose to translate the present verse (cf. Rashi; Kimḥi), but it is now generally agreed that the verb here is another root meaning "to shine, be radiant" (KB³ *nhr* II; Ps 34:6[Eng 34:5]; Isa 60:5). The LXX has *kai hēxousin* ("and they shall abound"). 4QJerᶜ again has *'al* for MT's *'el* (see above v 9), which makes for consistency with the rest of the verse.

Over the grain and over the wine and over the oil. The principal crops of Palestine (cf. Deut 8:8), cited commonly in Deuteronomy in this triadic formula (Deut 7:13; 11:14; 12:17; 14:23; 18:4; 28:51). The formula appears only here in Jeremiah, for which reason Volz and Holladay delete v 12b as a gloss on the "goodness" of v 12a. But the line is better retained. The triad appears also in Hosea (Hos 2:10, 24[Eng 2:8, 22]), who has a great deal to say about Yahweh—not Baal—being the provider of Israel's crops. Also, embellishment in the center of the Jeremianic oracle is a phenomenon with parallels elsewhere (see Rhetoric and Composition). Hebrew *dāgān* ("grain") is a generic term for cereal grains, either wheat (*ḥiṭṭâ,* or *bar* after winnowing) or barley (P. J. King 1993: 145); *tîrōš* is new (unfermented) wine (KB³ *tîrōš*); and *yiṣhār* is fresh (olive) oil (BDB, 844). The LXX has "in a land of grain and wine and fruits."

and over the young of the flocks and the herds. I.e., the lambs and calves. Hebrew *wĕ'al-bĕnê-ṣ'ōn ûbāqâr.* "Flocks" and "herds" are another common pairing (3:24; 5:17), and the mention here of young animals suggests that both will be expanding. The LXX's *kai ktēnōn kai probatōn* ("and of flocks and of cattle") does not preserve this nuance.

And their soul shall become like a saturated garden. The adjective *rāweh* means "saturated, well watered"; the verb *rwh* occurs with similar meaning in vv 14 and 25. See also Isa 58:11. The LXX has *ōsper xulon egkarpon*, "like a fruitful tree," which appears to extend the "grain, wine, and oil" bounty of the prior line (Becking 1994a: 162). Read the MT (Snaith 1945: 26). The "soul" (*nepeš*) of the people is their whole being (cf. v 14).

and they shall no longer languish any more. Hebrew *wĕlō'-yôsîpû lĕda'ăbâ 'ôd.* The H-stem of *ysp* ("to add") followed by an infinitive means "continue." Here with a negative, the meaning is "do no longer." The verb *d'b* means "to become faint, languish." The Hebrew expression with *'ôd* is strong: since the weak and thirsty will be filled to overflowing, they will no longer languish *any more.*

13. *Then shall the maiden be glad in the dance, yes, young men and old men together.* The maidens will dance in a circle (31:4), and their own gladness will make the young men and old men glad. Their dancing will be accompanied by singing (v 12; Pss 149:3; 150:4). The T has everyone dancing, although the men and women will not be dancing together (Peake; Rosenberg). The LXX says nothing about dancing, but everyone is happy. It translates: "Then the maidens shall be happy in the assembly (*charēsontai . . . en synagōgē*) of young men, and the old men shall be happy (*charēsontai*)." This appears to read *biqhal* ("in the assembly") for *bĕmāḥôl* ("in the dance"), and *yiḥdû* ("shall rejoice") for *yaḥdāw* ("together"). Support is unanimous for MT's "in the dance," but some commentators (Duhm; Peake; Cornill; Streane; Weiser; Rudolph; Holladay; McKane) and some modern Versions (RSV; NEB; JB [but not NJB]; NRSV; REB) prefer LXX's repeated "be happy" over MT's "together." However, the entire colon in the MT is preferable (Ehrlich 1912: 321; Volz; Condamin; Bright) and has support in 4QJer^c, Aq, and Vg. The LXX's repeated verb is suspicious, with "together" precisely the word we would expect in the context. Jeremiah typically joins representative persons with "together" (6:11, 12, 21; 13:14; 31:8, 13; 46:12, 21; 48:7; 49:3).

maiden. Hebrew *bĕtûlâ* is, lit., "virgin," a young woman having had no sexual experience. Jeremiah uses the term elsewhere to mean "(young) maiden" (2:32; 51:22), also metaphorically and ironically to disparage Israel (= Judah) and other nations (14:17; 18:13; 31:4, 21; 46:11).

young men. Hebrew *baḥûrîm.* 4QJer^c spells with a full ḥolem vowel: [*b*]*ḥwrym.*

And I will turn their mourning into joy. Yahweh is now the speaker. 4QJer^c has "your mourning," which goes ill with remaining third-person references in the line, and which continue in v 14. This promised joy (*śāśôn*) and the gladness (*śimḥâ*) in the next colon are precisely what was lost in Judah (see Note for 7:34). When the nation fell, dancing was turned into mourning (Lam 5:15). But here for returning Israel the reverse is promised; cf. Ps 30:12[Eng 30:11]. Second Isaiah also speaks of a ransomed host singing with "joy and gladness" on their return to Zion (Isa 35:10; 51:11).

and I will comfort them. Hebrew *wĕniḥamtîm*. The LXX omits, but the term should not be deleted (*pace* Duhm; Cornill; Holladay) because the loss can be attributed to haplography (homoeoarcton: *w . . . w*). It is present in 4QJer^c. The root *nḥm* in the Piel means "to comfort, console" (16:7; cf. Parunak 1975: 516). Extending comfort is a disposition, action, and attribute of Yahweh, like "being gracious" (*ḥnn*), "professing love" (*'hb*), and "showing mercy, compassion" (*rḥm*), where the defining characteristics are divine initiative and unconditional action. Pastor John Rogers (1988: 283) says the following about the present verses and the collection to which they belong:

> God's compassion is unconditional; there is no Deuteronomic "if." God does not wait until his exiled children have repented of their pride and folly and have become worthy of his mercy. There is only God's gracious initiative echoing through the "Book of Consolation," like bells ringing out of control.

and I will make them glad from their sorrow. The maidens will be glad because Yahweh will replace everyone's sorrow with gladness. The LXX takes "and I will make them glad" with the previous colon and joins a second verb, *megalunō* ("I will exalt"), with the verb beginning v 14. The result is that the priests of v 14 are both exalted and given their fill. "From their sorrow" (*mîgônām*) is not translated. This reading has been explained in various ways, none of which is very convincing (cf. McKane, 795). Becking (1994a: 158) thinks the LXX failed to understand *mîgônām*, but this word could have been lost due to haplography (homoeoteleuton: *m . . . m*). The MT, in any case, should be read. Aquila has "and I will gladden them from their grief" (*kai euphranō autous apo tēs lypēs autōn*). The "sorrow" or "grief" (*yāgôn*) now about to vanish for the returnees is precisely what descended upon Jeremiah and Baruch as Judah plunged into ruinous darkness (8:18; 20:18; 45:3). See Isa 35:10; and compare in the NT, Rev 21:4.

14. *And I will saturate the soul of the priests with abundance.* Most of Northern Israel's priests are in exile, although one at least returned (2 Kgs 17:27–28), and those who were consecrated subsequently developed a Yahwism along syncretistic lines (vv 32–34). According to Deut 18:6–8, Levites from the Northern towns would have come south in the seventh century to serve at the altar in Jerusalem. There are Israelite priests, in any case, both in exile and in the northern territory to whom Yahweh now bids a welcome to come to Jerusalem, saying they will enjoy an abundance unlike any they have known. With the high places now shut down due to Hezekiah and Josiah's centralization programs (2 Kgs 18:22; 23:15–20; cf. Deuteronomy 12), many Levites are on welfare (Deut 12:12, 18–19; 14:27–29; 16:11, 14; 26:11–13), and a promise of food in abundance should speak to their condition. The verb *rwh* in the Piel means "to saturate," usually with an abundant supply of water (31:25), but here the priests are promised an abundance of "fat(ness)" (*dāšen*). This is not the fat of offerings, which goes to Yahweh by being burned on the altar

(Lev 7:31). The "fat(ness)" promised to the priests is food in abundance, or general prosperity (T; Calvin; Thompson; McKane; cf. Pss 36:9[Eng 38:8]; 65:12[Eng 65:11]; Isa 55:2). The LXX lacks "fat" and adds "sons of Levi," which is another inferior reading. 4QJer^c supports MT. The term *dāšen* is sonorous with *šāšôn* ("joy") in the prior line. Hebrew *nepeš* is best taken here as referring to the whole being, as in v 12c, although it might possibly be reduced to "appetite" since food is at issue (Streane). It is unlikely to have the more restricted meaning of "throat" (*pace* Gruber 1987: 365; KB³), although "throat" may translate *nepeš* in 31:25.

MESSAGE AND AUDIENCE

Jeremiah begins this oracle with an announcement to the nations, who in turn are to tell people on distant coastlands that the One who scattered Israel is now about to gather him and will care for him as a shepherd cares for his flock. The nations must know, as they doubtless already do, that Yahweh is redeeming Israel from a hand of considerable strength. They, too, know the mighty Assyrians. Israelite exiles together with people from the northern territories will come and sing joyfully on Zion's height, and there they will beam brightly over Yahweh's goodness, consisting of abundant crops with expanding flocks and herds. The returnees will be refreshed like a well-watered garden, and men young and old will be gladdend by maidens twirling in the dance.

Yahweh confirms this happy anticipation by saying that mourning will indeed be turned into joy. Yahweh will comfort them and replace their sorrow with gladness. Israelite priests—those from exile and those living to the north—will be filled to overflowing with Yahweh's abundance, and others too will experience the divine goodness in a way they have not known before.

This oracle should be dated to the reform years of Josiah, i.e., anytime after 622 b.c., when the call was being made for Northern Israel to make its way to Zion. After the fall of Jerusalem, the oracle became a call for all exiles to return at some future date to Zion's lofty height.

When heard following the oracle in vv 7–9, the present oracle will supplement Yahweh's word of salvation to Israel's remnant by an announcement of the same to the nations, and via the nations to people further distant. The whole world must know of Israel's redemption and of Israel's God who will bring about this redemption.

j) Rachel Weeping in Ramah (31:15)

31 ^15Thus said Yahweh:
The voice of lament is heard in Ramah
    bitterest weeping
Rachel is weeping over her sons
    she refuses to be comforted over her sons
        because they are not.

RHETORIC AND COMPOSITION

MT 31:15 = LXX 38:15. This brief poem is delimited at the top end by a "thus said Yahweh" formula beginning v 15, before which comes a *setumah* in M^L and a *petuḥah* in M^P and 4QJer^c. At the bottom end delimitation is by a *setumah* in M^L and a *petuḥah* in M^P after v 15. Upon reconstruction 4QJer^c also has a *petuḥah* after v 15 (Tov 1997: 199), while one MS in the Cambridge Genizah Collection (AS 53.47) lacks a section here. In 4QJer^c is another *petuḥah* (reconstructed) midway in v 15 (after "bitterest of weeping"), the purpose of which is unclear.

Many commentators and scholars take vv 15–22 as the literary unit (Duhm; Peake; Streane; Volz; Hyatt; Bright; Thompson; Boadt; Trible 1977: 271; 1978: 46; B. W. Anderson 1978: 470; Keown et al.), some only vv 15–20 (Giesebrecht; Condamin; Rudolph; Weiser; Carroll; Jones; McKane), which follows the older view that these verses—particularly vv 15–20—are authentic to Jeremiah. They also betray influence from Hosea in vocabulary ("Ephraim") and pathos (weeping, repenting, and Yahweh wavering over whether to give Israel up), and are said to represent preaching to Northern Israel early in the prophet's career. Rachel (v 15), after all, is ancestress of the Northern tribes. Also, the verses have no parallels to Second Isaiah. Trible (1977: 276; 1978: 46) and B. W. Anderson (1978: 475) argue for the unity of vv 15–22 on the basis of a repeated *tamrûmîm* in vv 15 and 21, the former meaning "bitter," the latter meaning "signposts." However, v 15 is self-standing and in the larger poetic core is paired with the hope oracles in vv 16–17 (see Rhetoric and Composition for 30:4–7). In v 15 Rachel makes her lament; in vv 16–17 Yahweh answers the lament with hope for the future.

Although I am not inclined to isolate vv 15–22—or vv 15–20—as a literary unit, it is nevertheless the case that here at the end of the poetic core is a noticeable shift in theme and mood. Setting aside for a moment the hope passages interspersed throughout the collection, we have, as a replacement for the beginning judgment (30:5–7, 12–15), weeping, repentance, and confession at the end (31:15, 18–19). Similar shifts occur in the two cycles of poetry appearing early in the book: 1) the cycle in 2:1–4:4 begins with indictment and judgment for apostasy (2:4–9, 10–13) and ends with calls for "returning/repentance" (3:1–5, 12–14, 19–20, 21–25; 4:1–2); and 2) the cycle in 4:5–9:25[26]—later 10:25—begins with judgment at the hands of the foe from the north (4:5–8, 13–17) and ends with confession and lamentation (8:18–21; 8:22–9:1[2]; 9:9–10[10–11], 16–18[17–19], 19–21[20–22]; 10:19–21, 23–24). These shifts are doubtless intentional in the book's composition and have as a theological correlative the belief that in the end judgment must issue in confession and repentance.

Lindblom (1965: 142–43) calls the poem here a "literary vision" in which sound dominates; others of the same type occur in 4:13; 6:22–26; and 46:3–12. Rachel is not the speaking voice; it is another who hears her weeping. Judging from the messenger formula, the speaker would appear to be Yahweh (Calvin;

Holladay), but some commentators (Duhm; Volz; Rudolph; Bright) take Jeremiah to be the speaker, which on the basis of content is likely. Jeremiah appears to be the one hearing Ephraim's lament in vv 18–19. What we have in the present case are companion poems forming a dialogue: Jeremiah hears Rachel's lament in v 15, then Yahweh answers the lament in vv 16–17. The messenger formula in v 15 can thus be retained (Rudolph), since dialogue oracles in which Jeremiah and Yahweh alternate as speakers often have messenger formulas at the beginning.

The present poem has nice repetition:

. . . .	
weeping	*bĕkî*
. . . . *weeping over her sons*	*mĕbakkâ ʿal-bāneyhā*
she refuses . . . . . . over her sons	*mēʾănâ . . . ʿal-bāneyhā*
. . . . *they are not*	*ʾênennû*

There is a chain effect in "weeping . . . weeping over her sons . . . over her sons" (called "stairlike parallelism"; see Note for 4:13), which precludes deleting the first "over her sons," with the LXX (*pace* Blayney; Cornill; Ehrlich 1912: 321).

Catchwords connecting to the prior oracle:

v 15	*is heard*	v 10 *Hear*
	to be comforted	v 13 *and I will comfort them*

This poem is the third in a row to begin with the verb *šmᶜ* ("hear").

Catchwords connecting to the companion oracle following:

v 15	*voice*	v 16	*your voice*
	weeping (2×)		*weeping*
	her sons (2×)	v 17	*sons*

NOTES

31:15. *The voice of lament is heard in Ramah.* "The voice/sound (*qôl*) is heard" is a signature expression of Jeremiah (see Note for 30:5). Also, the Jeremiah poem frequently begins with the word *qôl*, as is the case here (see Note for 3:21). The present colon contains a broken construct-chain, "voice . . . lament," leading some modern Versions (AV; RSV; JB; NJV; NIV) to join "lament" (*nĕhî*) with "bitterest weeping" in the second colon. Calvin sees here an example of the rhetorical figure "personification" (Gk: *prosōpopoiia*; Lat: *conformatio*), where the speaker represents an absent person as being present (*ad Herennium* iv 53). Making the dead speak was also called *eidōlopoiia* by the classical rhetoricians. The absent (dead) Rachel is here present to lament the loss of her sons.

in Ramah. Hebrew *běrāmâ*. This term has long been a problem, largely because T translates not as a place-name, but rather as "in the height." The Masoretes pointed the term *běrāmâ*, "on a height," since "Ramah" usually takes the article—i.e., *hārāmâ*, "the Ramah" (cf. 40:1). Compare "the Bashan" in Note for 22:20. Only in Neh 11:33 does the place-name Ramah occur without the article. But the LXX and S read "Ramah" here, and so does Matt 2:18, which quotes the verse in connection with Herod's slaughter of infants in and around Bethlehem at the time Jesus was born. It is a simple matter to repoint the Hebrew to *bārāmâ*, "in (the) Ramah," which is what Duhm and Rudolph do. Tsevat (1962), however, views any change in pointing with disfavor, comparing "a voice is heard on a height" with "a voice on the bare heights (*šěpāyîm*) is heard" in 3:21. This is in line with Jewish interpretation of the verse, which follows T and supports MT's *běrāmâ*. Jerome in the Vg also translates *in excelsio* ("on a height"), and Becking (1994b: 230) cites other ancient Greek witnesses (G^AS; Aq) that translate with *en (tē) hypsēlē*, "in (the) height." Non-Jewish commentators (except Holladay) read "Ramah," most of whom argue in addition that Ramah is the location of Rachel's tomb and where her weeping is now being heard (see below). Depending on the date of T, the LXX and Matt 2:18 may preserve the oldest tradition. The terminus ad quem for *Targum Jonathan* is ca. A.D. 300 (Hayward 1987: 12; Zatelli 1991: 482), but the work could contain accurate geographical information from an earlier period, perhaps even from before the destruction of Jerusalem in A.D. 70 (Zatelli). The T does not likely predate the LXX, and if it is later than Matthew, it could be countering a reading in Matthew and the LXX text upon which that Gospel rests. The Masoretic pointing of *běrāmâ*, probably following T, is much later. Ramah has been identified either with er-Ram, about seven kilometers north of Jerusalem, or Ramallah, about twelve kilometers north (see Note for 40:1).

bitterest weeping. Hebrew *běkî tamrûrîm*, lit., "weeping of bitterness." In 6:26 people are told to prepare for "bitterest mourning" (*mispad tamrûrîm*), as one does for the loss of an only son.

Rachel is weeping over her sons; she refuses to be comforted over her sons, because they are not. Rachel, wife of the patriarch Jacob and mother of Joseph and Benjamin (Gen 30:22–24; 35:16–20), is the ancestress of Northern Israel. In giving birth to Benjamin, Rachel died and was buried somewhere between Bethel and Ephrath, the latter said to be Bethlehem (Gen 35:16–20; 48:7). We last see Rachel, suffering in hard labor, and then in a final motherly act, naming her son *Ben-'ônî*, "Son of my sorrow." Now again the voice of Rachel is heard, this time weeping over her sons (= the people of the tribes of Joseph and Benjamin) who have been carried off into exile (vv 16b–17). The portrayal has stirred generations. The text here does not say that Rachel is weeping at the site of her tomb, but this assumption has nevertheless been made. Cuneiform texts in the British Museum give evidence for an ancient belief that mothers who died in childbirth became weeping ghosts (E. Burrows 1926–27: 185). Burrows says that Jeremiah may therefore be alluding to a popular belief in a weeping mother whose voice is heard around Ramah. Folk beliefs of a similar nature are attested throughout the world, some appearing in German fairy tales (Gunkel 1921: 90; R. C. Thompson 1908: 20–21; Gaster 1969: 605–6). In the Mesopotamian city laments, it is the goddess who weeps over a city's destruction, the loss of life, and the dispersement of people (Kramer 1982: 141; 1983; Dobbs-Allsopp 1993: 75–90). In Lamentations, a personified Jerusalem does the weeping (Lam 1:16). The present verse is quoted in Matt 2:18, where Rachel weeps once again over Herod's slaughter of the infants at the time Jesus was born.

If we assume that the present oracle originally had Northern Israel in focus and was spoken early in Jeremiah's career, then Rachel must be weeping over the people exiled to Assyria when Northern Israel was destroyed in 722 B.C. (Kimḥi; Calvin; Peake; Volz; Rudolph; Weiser; Holladay; Jones). But if the oracle postdates the Babylonian destruction of Jerusalem in 586 B.C. (Giesebrecht; Lindars 1979: 53), then Rachel is weeping for all of Jacob's children who were carried into exile. In 586 the connection with Ramah would be particularly fitting, since Ramah at that time was a holding area for exile-bound Judahites, one of whom was Jeremiah before his release (40:1; Genesis Rabbah 82:10).

The location of Rachel's tomb, assuming it is relevant to the portrayal here, poses yet another problem. The site presently venerated is located at the northern edge of Bethlehem, on the west side of the modern Jerusalem–Bethlehem road. This site has the support of Eusebius, Jerome, and other early Christian writers, and at least since the fourth century A.D. a monument there has marked the spot. The present structure dates to Crusader times. This site is also supported by Matt 2:18, which, in spite of locating Rachel's weeping at Ramah, makes its application to a slaughter occurring in and around Bethlehem. Jewish tradition (e.g., Midrash Genesis Rabbah 82:10) recognized a location problem early, noting that the tomb is placed within the border of Benjamin (*bigbûl binyāmīn*) in 1 Sam 10:2, but in other biblical references it is put on the way to Ephrath, i.e., Bethlehem (Gen 35:19; 48:7). The latter is in Judah (Mic 5:1[Eng 5:2]). Most modern scholars believe the tomb was located farther north in Benjaminite territory (1 Sam 10:2), probably in the vicinity of Ramah. Among other things, it is pointed out that "Ephrath" may not be the "Ephrathah" in which Bethlehem was located (Ruth 4:11; Mic 5:1[Eng 5:2]), which would make the glosses in Gen 35:19 and 48:7 incorrect (Volz; Rudolph; Hyatt). Supporting a more northerly location are also five ancient monuments discovered at Qubûr Běnê-Israîn, which is near er-Ram and Ḥizmēh (Macalister 1912: 81–82; Lombardi 1970; 1971). The view is then widely held that Rachel's tomb was originally in the vicinity of Ramah and that the site in Bethlehem developed later as a result of the glosses in Gen 35:19 and 48:7, confusing Ephrath with Ephrathah. Tsevat (1962) has argued with less success for a location of the tomb at Kiriath-jearim (cf. 1 Chr 2:50). For a discussion of Rachel's lament in the Targum and in Jewish interpretation generally, where it has a prominent place in the New Year's celebration, see Zatelli 1991 and Dresner 1994: 149–73. On Rachel's portrayal in music and the arts, see *EncJud* 13: 1490–91.

Rachel is weeping over her sons; she refuses to be comforted over her sons. Hebrew *bāneyhā* in this case is better translated "her sons" than "her children," because Jeremiah has in mind Rachel's sons Joseph and Benjamin and the tribes named after them. The LXX has a shorter text: *Rachēl apoklaiomenē ouk ēthelen pausasthai epi tois hyiois autēs* ("Rachel could not stop weeping over her sons"), which appears to omit only the first "over her sons." This omission could be due to its aversion to repetition (although this is not a second occurrence); more likely it is another loss due to haplography (homoeoteleuton: *h . . . h*). The repetition, in any case, is doubtless intentional and should be retained (Volz; Rudolph; cf. Rhetoric and Composition). On the language of grief and mourning in Jeremiah, see Muilenburg 1970b: 55–59.

she refuses to be comforted over her sons. The N-stem of *nhm*, elsewhere "to be sorry, repent," here means "to be comforted, consoled" (Parunak 1975: 520). The portrayal is of a woman who cannot be comforted, where Rachel is doing precisely what Jacob did upon hearing the news that Joseph was dead (Gen 37:35: "but he refused to be comforted," *wayĕmā'ēn lĕhitnahēm*).

because they are not. Hebrew *'ênennû* is a *distributive* singular: "he (= each one of the sons) is not" (GKC §145m). The Versions have a plural. Sons carried off into exile (so T; cf. Lam 1:5) are as good as dead. Rachel is grieving over all her children, none of whom remains (cf. Isa 49:15).

MESSAGE AND AUDIENCE

A Judahite audience is told here that Rachel's weeping voice has been heard at Ramah. It may already know this due to popular belief. Like Jacob after hearing that his favored son was not, and he could not be comforted, now Rachel too refuses to be comforted because her sons are not. This oracle may have been spoken originally to Northern Israel, and with it the comfort oracles that follow. Needless to say, it would also have had a profound impact on exile-bound Judahites in 597 and 586 B.C., particularly the latter as they sat enchained at the Ramah holding camp (40:1–4). For all Judahites, those exiled and those remaining in the land, the companion oracles in vv 16–17 give a divine response of comfort and hope.

Matthew applies this oracle to Herod's massacre of the infants in Bethlehem (Matt 2:17–18). More recently, this passage has had a profound impact on Jewish survivors of the Holocaust. Emil Fackenheim tells of a Polish guard who testified at the Nuremberg trials and said that women carrying their children were sent with them to the crematorium at Auschwitz. The children were then snatched from them and sent to the gas chambers separately. When the pogrom was at its height, children would be thrown alive into the furnaces, with their screams being heard in the camp. The report from Ravensbrueck was no less chilling. Fackenheim says,

> In 1942, the medical services of the Revier were required to perform abortions on all pregnant women. If a child happened to be born alive, it would

be smothered or drowned in a bucket, in the presence of the mother. Given a new-born child's natural resistance to drowning, a baby's agony might last for twenty or thirty minutes.

(Fackenheim 1990: 347–48)

k) Rachel, Don't You Weep No More! (31:16–17)

31 [16]Thus said Yahweh:
Restrain your voice from weeping
    and your eyes from tears

For there is a reward for your labor
    —oracle of Yahweh—
and they shall return from the land of the enemy

[17]And there is hope for your future
    —oracle of Yahweh—
and sons shall return to their territory.

RHETORIC AND COMPOSITION

MT 31:16–17 = LXX 38:16–17. These verses contain a cluster of very brief hope and comfort oracles that answer the weeping of Rachel in v 15. The cluster is delimited at the top end by a "thus said Yahweh" formula beginning v 16, before which is a *setumah* in M[L] and a *petuhah* in M[P]. Delimitation at the bottom end is by a *setumah* in M[L] (only) after v 17. 4QJer[c] upon reconstruction appears not to have a section here. The LXX lacks the "oracle of Yahweh" formulas in vv 16b and 17, leading some commentators (Duhm; Cornill; Volz; Rudolph; Weiser; Holladay; McKane) to delete them. But they are probably original, since brief oracles with formulas occur also in 3:12; 23:23–24, 28b–32.

Oracles II and III have these balancing repetitions:

II . . . *there is* . . . . . *for your*	*yēš . . . li . . . ēk*	v 16b
. . . .		
and they shall return	*wĕšābû*	
III . . . *there is* . . . . . . *for your*	*yēš . . . lĕ . . . ēk*	v 17
. . . .		
and they shall return	*wĕšābû*	

Catchwords connecting to the companion poem preceding:

v 16	*your voice*	v 15	*voice*
	weeping		*weeping* (2×)
v 17	*sons*		*her sons* (2×)

NOTES

31:16. *Restrain your voice from weeping.* The verb *mnʿ*, occurring often in Jeremiah, means "to hold back, restrain" (2:25; 3:3; 5:25; 42:4; 48:10). Yahweh is speaking here to Rachel, addressing the weeping heard in v 15. Since Rachel is dead, this is a case of apostrophe (see Appendix XII).

and your eyes from tears. Hebrew *dimʿâ* is a collective noun meaning "tears."

a reward for your labor. Bearing children is likened to the receiving of wages (*śākār*); it is the woman's reward (Gen 30:18; Ps 127:3). Leah says that with six sons she now has a good dowry (Gen 30:20). Here Yahweh tells Rachel that with the return of her sons her labor is rewarded.

and they shall return from the land of the enemy. It is made plain both here and in v 17b that Rachel's tears are for her sons in exile. But they shall return (cf. 24:6; 29:10–14; 30:3; 31:8–9).

17. *And there is hope for your future — oracle of Yahweh.* Hebrew *wĕyēš-tiqwâ lĕʾaḥărîtēk nĕʾūm-yhwh.* The LXX omits the colon along with the messenger formula, which can be attributed to haplography (homoeoarcton: *w . . . w*). The term *ʾaḥărît*, "(latter) end, future," suggests posterity (cf. Ps 109:13). In Jeremiah's letter to the exiles (29:11), Yahweh says to the seeming unfortunates that he is planning for them "a future and a hope."

and sons shall return to their territory. I.e., the land of Israel. Hebrew *gĕbûl* more accurately means "border" but can denote territory within a border. Calvin says the part is taken for the whole, i.e., the whole country is meant. The LXX has *monimon tois sois teknois*, "an abiding (place) for your children," which may be translating Heb *yšb* ("to dwell") rather than *šûb* ("return"). But without the previous colon, its Hebrew *Vorlage* is defective. Aquila and Theod translate the present colon in line with MT.

MESSAGE AND AUDIENCE

In these oracles Yahweh addresses Rachel with the comforting words that her weeping can stop, for her labor will be rewarded now that her sons are promised a return from enemy hands. There is hope for her future; the return will be to the land of Israel. All three oracles speak directly to the exiles of Northern Israel, and together with the companion oracle in v 15 may be early Jeremianic preaching. The oracles will also have an immediate impact on Judahite exiles who are leaving for exile in 597 and again 586. Like Jeremiah's letter to the exiles, these oracles will give them a hope of returning one day to the land that they have left.

1) Ephraim Heard Rockin' in Grief (31:18–19)

31 ¹⁸I can indeed hear
  Ephraim rockin' in grief
'You disciplined me and I was disciplined
  like a young bull not trained

Bring me back so I may come back
   for you are Yahweh my God

¹⁹For after my turning away
   I repented
And after I came to understand
   I hit upon my thigh
I was ashamed and also disgraced
   for I bore the reproach of my youth.'

RHETORIC AND COMPOSITION

MT 31:18–19 = LXX 38:18–19. The present verses are delimited at the top end by a *setumah* in M^L (only) before v 18. 4QJer^c upon reconstruction appears to lack a section here. There are no sections in the medieval codices following v 19, indicating that the poem was taken together with its companion piece in v 20. Both poems are generally attributed to Jeremiah, being seen by many as more early preaching to Northern Israel, at which time Hosea's influence was the greatest (see Rhetoric and Composition for 31:15). We have here another dialogue, with Jeremiah first hearing and then repeating Ephraim's mournful confession of sin and disgrace (vv 18–19) and Yahweh answering with an extraordinary outpouring of divine mercy (v 20). The proportions are reversed from vv 15–17, where the divine answer (in three oracles) was twice the length of the lament. Here the divine answer is half the length of the lament. Erbt (1902: 291) took vv 18–20 to be a liturgy, which probably it was.

   This poem has two stanzas with repetition and balancing grammatical forms:

I   . . . .   v 18

   . . . .

   You disciplined me and I was disciplined   *yissartanî wā'iwwāsēr*

   . . . .

   Bring me back so I may come back   *hăšîbēnî wĕ'ăšûbâ*
   for . . . .   *kî* . . .

II *For after my turning away*   *kî-'ahărē šûbî*   v 19

   . . . .

   And after . . . .   *wĕ'ahărē*

   . . . .

   for . . . .   *kî* . . .

Catchwords connecting to the companion poem following:

v 18 *Ephraim*   v 20 *Ephraim*

Catchwords derived from the verb *šûb* also connect not to the companion oracle (v 20), but to the concluding poetry in vv 21–22:

v 18 *Bring me back so I may come back* v 21 *Return* (2×)
v 19 *my turning away*   v 22 *turnable*

NOTES

31:18. *I can indeed hear Ephraim rockin' in grief.* Rachel's weeping was heard in v 15; now it is intense lamenting from Ephraim, who represents the sons of Rachel. Ephraim is lamenting his sin (Weiser), although T says it is because he is exiled. No doubt it is both. The Hithpolel of *nûd* is an intensive form meaning "to shake (the head) back and forth (in a lament)" (cf. H-stem in 18:16). The Qal means "waver" (4:1) and "console, condole" (15:5; 16:5; 22:10; and elsewhere; cf. Note for 15:5). The Vg follows T with *transmigrantem* ("wandering"), although in his commentary Jerome lists *lamentantem* ("lamenting") as an alternative reading.

You disciplined me and I was disciplined. This double occurrence of a root (*multiclinatum*) is a signature of Jeremiah (see Notes for 11:18 and 31:4). Another occurs in the next line. The verb *ysr* means "to correct, discipline, punish." Here Ephraim admits to having accepted discipline from Yahweh, which Kimḥi says came with many years in exile. Preaching discipline to Judah met with no success. In 6:8, Jerusalem was told to "correct yourself" (*hiwwāsĕrî*), but Jeremiah learned to his sorrow that people simply refused to take "correction" (*mûsār*; see Note for 2:30).

like a young bull not trained. An *ʿēgel* is a bull calf, here one as yet untrained to wear the yoke or who breaks the yoke (AV: "as a bullock unaccustomed to the yoke"). The imagery may derive from Hosea (Hos 4:16; 10:11; 11:4; cf. K. Gross 1930: 12). Ephraim has come around to confess its rebellion, and in light of v 19b ("the reproach of my youth") perhaps the nation's long-standing rebellion referred to in 2:20. Jerusalem—to the person—is said to have broken Yahweh's yoke in 5:5.

Bring me back so I may come back. Or "restore me so I may be restored." This double root occurrence is with the verb *šûb*—the first an H-stem and the second a Qal. Ephraim has already confessed and will confess some more, but for him to be restored, which is what this supplication is all about, Yahweh must act. But Yahweh is not necessarily being called upon to aid the process of repentance, however much this idea may be inferred from other texts. M. Greenberg (1997: 736) says that in Jeremiah there is a vacillation between affirming on the one hand that human repentance can precede and induce divine forgiveness (26:3; 36:3) and on the other that repentance is a process involving God's cooperation (24:7; 32:40). Here Greenberg recognizes that Ephraim is already contrite but says nevertheless that he is imploring God's help in repentance. The verb is *šûb*, which in its second (Qal) occurrence could be rendered "and I will repent." But that does not seem quite right if repentance has already occurred or if this is a plea for restoration, which it seems to be. Peake and Hyatt both note that repentance is already in evidence. But their point about the return being a return from exile is not as convincing, unless we assume for *šûb* a double meaning (Trible 1977: 273; 1978: 42). Ephraim admittedly wants to return to its land but is asking primarily to be restored to Yahweh's favor. The concluding plea in Lam 5:21 asks for the same: "Restore us (*hăšîbēnû*) to yourself, Yahweh, that we may be restored (*wĕnāšûbâ* Q)." Repentance in exile and subsequent restoration is anticipated in Deut 30:1–10.

for you are Yahweh my God. Or if we read "Yahweh" as a vocative: "for you, Yahweh, are my God." Compare the corporate confession in 3:22.

19. *For after my turning away I repented.* The verb *nḥm* appears to mean more than "being sorry," which is how it is sometimes translated (8:6). Repentance goes beyond being sorry. Hebrew *šûbî* ("my turning away") denotes rebellion. The LXX has *aichmalōsias mou* ("my captivity"), which appears to translate either the verb *šbh* ("to take captive") or the noun *šĕbî* ("captivity"); compare the LXX reading of *šbh* instead of *šûb* in 30:3. Becking (1994a: 162) says that the LXX may have had *šbyy* in its *Vorlage*, but the MT reading is supported by *šwby* in 4QJer[c]. Aquila has *to epistrepsai me*, "my turning (from error)," i.e., my returning. Ephraim here says that he was genuinely sorry for his rebellion. Jeremiah, however, complained that no one in Judah was sorry (*nḥm*) about his evil (8:6).

And after I came to understand, I hit upon my thigh. D. W. Thomas (1934: 304) thinks the verb *ydʿ* ("to know") in the N-stem means in this instance "to become quiet, submissive" (REB: "now that I am submissive"), but the usual rendering, "to be instructed, come to understand" (BDB; KB[3]; Volz), is perfectly acceptable, even preferable. Pastor David Bartlett (1978: 76) comments on the verse here: "Punishment is seen not just as punishment, but as instruction. Remorse ends not simply in guilt, but in a deeper self-understanding." Such a view belies the popular notion that punishment does no good. With some it does no good, but with others it brings new self-understanding. Hitting one or both thighs is an ancient expression of emotional pain or sorrow (Ezek 21:17[Eng 21:12]; Parunak 1975: 519), attested also in the Sumerian text "Descent of Ishtar to the Nether World" (reverse, line 21; ANET[3] 108; cf. Lipiński 1970b), and in Homer (*Iliad* xv 397–98; xvi 125; *Odyssey* xiii 198–99). The LXX does not reproduce the expression in a translation that takes in the following verb: *estenaxa eph' hēmeras aischunēs* ("I groaned during days of shame"). Read the MT.

I was ashamed and also disgraced. Hebrew *bōštî wĕgam-niklamtî*. Kimḥi says that the second verb (*klm*) denotes more intense shame, thus the *wĕgam* ("and also"). The verbs occur in combination also in 14:3 and 22:22. In 22:22 Judah is promised what Ephraim is now confessing, since in its brazenness it knows no shame (3:3; 6:15 [= 8:12]). But in Isa 54:4 the promise is reversed:

Do not be afraid, for you will not be ashamed
    and do not be humiliated, for you will not be abashed

for the shame of your youth you will forget
and the reproach of your widowhood you will not remember any more.

for I bore the reproach of my youth. Hebrew *ḥerpâ* ("reproach") is a common
Jeremiah term, appearing often in strings of curse words (see Note for 24:9).
Israel has accumulated both sin and shame from her youth (3:24–25; 22:21;
32:30; cf. Isa 48:8; 54:4).

MESSAGE AND AUDIENCE

Jeremiah here tells his Judahite audience that from the distant north the wim-
pering voice of Ephraim can be heard. It speaks words of contrition, and Jeremiah repeats them for all to hear. Ephraim admits to having accepted
Yahweh's discipline. He was, by his own admission, like a young bull unwilling
to bear the yoke. Now he asks that Yahweh restore him; without this, estrange-
ment will continue and he may remain forever in the land where he now resides. More confession follows. Ephraim says that after turning away he was
genuinely sorry and repented, and once he did some self-evaluation he reacted
with horror. He was ashamed and disgraced, for the reproach of his youth he
was forced to bear.

This may also be early preaching with a focus on Northern Israel; similarly,
Yahweh's response that follows. The Judahite audience hearing it can sense
its own need to confess sin and be restored to Yahweh's favor, but will it? After
the fall of Jerusalem, the poem and its companion oracle will be a timely
word for all the exiles, making it clear to them that the way back into Yahweh's favor and the way back to the Land of Promise is through repentance
and self-understanding.

m) But I Still Remember Ephraim (31:20)

31 [20]Is Ephraim my dear son?
  Is he the child of delight?
For more than all my speaking against him
  I will assuredly remember him still
Therefore my innards moan for him
  I will assuredly have mercy on him
    —oracle of Yahweh.

RHETORIC AND COMPOSITION

MT 31:20 = LXX 38:20. The present verse contains a divine oracle answering
Ephraim's confession in vv 18–19. Yahweh does not address Ephraim directly,
as he did Rachel in vv 16–17, but rather speaks to an unspecified audience.
There are no section markings separating this oracle from its companion
poem, but a *setumah* in 4QJer^c and M^L and a *petuḥah* in M^P follow the "oracle

of Yahweh" formula at the end of v 20. This formula should not be deleted (*pace* Giesebrecht; Volz).

Like its companion poem, this oracle is structured by parallel grammatical forms:

Is . . . . ?	*hă* . . .	v 20
Is . . . . ?	*'im* . . .	
. . . .		
I will assuredly remember him . . .	*zākōr 'ezkĕrennû*	
. . . .		
I will assuredly have mercy on him	*raḥēm 'ăraḥămennû*	

Catchwords connecting to the companion poem preceding:

v 20 *Ephraim*   v 18 *Ephraim*

NOTES

31:20. *Is Ephraim my dear son? Is he the child of delight? For more than all my speaking against him, I will assuredly remember him still.* Hebrew *yaqqîr* means "dear, very precious" (cf. *yāqār* in 15:19 and *yĕqār* in 20:5) The rhetorical questions feign surprise (Cheyne), conveying both distance and intimacy between Yahweh and Ephraim (Trible 1977: 274; 1978: 43). One is reminded here of Saul's tender words to David after David discovered him, spared his life, and upbraided him for wanting to take his life: "Is this your voice, my son David?" after which Saul began to weep (1 Sam 24:16). The questions posed here are answered by Yahweh himself, which classical rhetoricians called *hypophora* (see 30:15 and Note on 49:7). The entire verse echoes the divine pathos and love expressed earlier in Hosea (Hos 11:1, 8–9; K. Gross 1930: 13; 1931: 244–45; Ludwig 1968: 531–32). The LXX and Vg do not translate the *hē'* interrogative or the *'im* beginning the second colon. Omission of the latter in the LXX could be attributed to haplography (homoeoteleuton: *m . . . m*). Held (1969: 79) thinks that the *kî* colon should continue the question, as it does in Num 11:12; Amos 6:12; Mic 4:9; Hab 3:8; Jer 18:14–15; Isa 66:8; Job 7:12; and 10:5–6, proposing further that Hebrew had a fixed *hă . . . 'im . . . kî . . .* formula like the Jeremianic *ha . . . 'im . . . maddûa' . . .* (see Note for 2:14). This would yield the following translation:

Is (*hă*) Ephraim my dear son?
Is (*'im*) he the child of delight?
Then (*kî*) why so often do I speak of him
    and definitely remember him still?

But whether such a formula existed is questionable. In Amos 6:12 and Jer 18:14–15, the *kî* clause is better rendered as an affirmation preceded by "but."

Is he the child of delight? The noun *šaʿăšūʿîm* (a doubling from *šʿ* in the Pilpel) is another intensive form meaning the object of play or delight. Kimḥi says the portrayal is that of a father who plays with his son. In Isa 66:12 the Pulpal form of the verb means "rocked back and forth on the lap." The *lî* of the prior colon could do double duty here, which would yield "my delight."

For more than all my speaking against him, I will assuredly remember him still. This translation of the much-discussed first colon follows 48:27 ("For more than all your words against him . . ."), which is different only in that it employs the noun *děbārîm* instead of the verbal infinitive. Hebrew *bô* does not mean "with him" (*pace* Calvin); nor does it mean "of him" or "about him," the rendering of Duhm and a number of commentators since. Duhm thought the mere mention of Ephraim's name made Yahweh remember him. The term *bô* means "against him" (AV; RSV; NJV; NIV; REB; Giesebrecht; Rudolph; McKane), as in 48:27. Yahweh says that in spite of all his pronouncements against Ephraim he remembers him, and in the future will continue to remember him with deep affection. The LXX reads *hoti anth' ōn hoi logoi mou en autō* ("for because my words are in him"), which differs little from the embellished reading of T ("For at the time when I put the words of my Law upon his heart to do them"). The MT should be followed, although Hayward (1985b: 111–12) notes that Jerome in his commentary interprets God's words as being within Ephraim, which reflects the reading in T.

I will assuredly remember him still. Hebrew *zākōr 'ezkěrennû ʿôd*. The LXX lacks *ʿôd* ("still"), which can be attributed to haplography (homoeoarcton: *ʿayin . . . ʿayin*). The particle appears in Aq, Symm, T, and Vg and is necessary for the sense (Giesebrecht). Yahweh's remembrance implies providential care (Gen 8:1).

Therefore my innards moan for him. Hebrew *ʿal-kēn hāmû mēʿay lô*. A truly extraordinary anthropomorphism, with Yahweh's "innards" (*mēʿîm*) said to be in divine turmoil. The same expression is used by Yahweh with reference to Moab, only there with biting irony (48:36). Jeremiah confesses a similar turmoil within himself in 4:19, although for him it is an uninvited psychophysical experience. The verb *hmh* means "to roar, moan, growl," suggesting rumblings in the digestive track. Elsewhere in Jeremiah this verb denotes the "roar" of the sea (5:22; 6:23; 31:35; 50:42; 51:55). In traditional exegesis the portrayal here is viewed as the tender feelings of a father (Calvin; Cornill), but more recently it has been argued that the imagery is female (Trible; Holladay; Carroll), particularly since *mēʿîm* can refer to the "womb" in a woman's body (Gen 25:23; Isa 49:1; Ps 71:6). But such an interpretation is certainly not required, because the term can mean "bowels" or "innards" of a woman (Num 5:22; Song 5:4) or a man (Gen 15:4; 2 Sam 7:12; 16:11; Jer 4:19). In Gen 15:4 *mēʿîm* refers to the male reproductive organs, where the Hebrew says, lit., "What comes out from your innards will be your heir." The term has the same meaning in 2 Sam 7:12 and 16:11. One cannot conclude then with Trible (1977: 275; 1978: 44–45) that in the present passage "(exclusively) female imagery abounds." And it is a "quantum leap" to go from "innards" and the verb "to show mercy" (*rḥm*) in the next line to a conceptualization of "Mother Yahweh" in the mind of Jeremiah (so Trible and Carroll), which would have made the most irreverent of persons in ancient Israel blush. The LXX has "therefore I eagerly long for him" (*dia touto espeusa ep' autō*), which effectively does away with the anthropomorphism (Becking 1994a: 163). For other examples of passionate divine love in the Bible, where one also finds anthropomorphic language being used, see Schildenberger 1963.

I will assuredly have mercy on him. Here the verb is *rḥm*, which means simply "show mercy, compassion." It may indeed denote "mother love" (Trible), but is also love shown by a father (Ps 103:13). Showing mercy is nothing less than an attribute of Yahweh (Exod 34:6; D. N. Freedman 1955), and in future days Yahweh promises to display this attribute to his people (33:26).

MESSAGE AND AUDIENCE

Yahweh in this oracle asks an unspecified audience—though it may be Judahite—whether Ephraim is still his dear son, whether he is the child who once gave him such delight? Perhaps the audience will remember Saul's tender words to David. If so, it will know that here the roles are reversed: Yahweh is the gracious and innocent father; Ephraim is the guilty and contrite son. Yahweh continues by saying that however much he has spoken against Ephraim, he will nevertheless remember him and with human-like passion waits excitedly to show him mercy.

This oracle like its companion poem in vv 18–19 could have been directed to Northern Israelite exiles during Josiah's reign. A Judahite audience hearing it would then know that on the other side of judgment is a God of grace and mercy waiting expectantly to receive his wayward child back again.

When both poems in vv 18–20 are heard following the poems in vv 15–17, Rachel's weeping will be balanced by the tearful confession of Ephraim, and it will be understood that Rachel's sons are not gone but simply languishing in exile. Both laments receive comforting answers, with Yahweh making clear his intention to bring the exiles home and restore them to favor. In the NT, the contrite return of the wayward son and God's ready compassion are shown vividly in Jesus' parable of the Lost (Prodigal) Son (Luke 15:11–32).

William Cowper's great hymn, "God Moves in a Mysterious Way" (1774), contains this verse:

Judge not the Lord by feeble sense
But trust him for his grace
Behind a frowning providence
He hides a smiling face
(*HAMR* 1981 #181)

n) Return, Virgin Israel! (31:21–22)

31 [21]Set up road-markers for yourself
    make for yourself signposts
Fix your mind on the highway
    the way you have gone[a]
Return, virgin Israel
    return to these your cities

[22]How long will you waver
    O turnable daughter?
For Yahweh has created a new thing on earth:
    the female protects the man!

RHETORIC AND COMPOSITION

MT 31:21–22 = LXX 38:21–22. The present poetry is delimited at the top end by a *setumah* in 4QJer^c and M^L and a *petuhah* in M^P before v 21. Delimitation at the bottom end is by a *petuhah* in 4QJer^c and a *setumah* in M^L and M^P after v 22. In v 23 is also a shift to prose. There is a space in 4QJer^c before "new thing" in v 22a (Tov 1997: 199), but this cannot be a section marking. Tov suggests that a scribe left an open space because of a flaw in the leather or the stitching (p. 182).

Some commentators (Rudolph; Weiser; Carroll; Holladay; Jones; McKane) have assigned independence or semiindependence to vv 21–22, one reason being that the discourse now addresses "virgin Israel" (v 21) after being concerned about "son Ephraim" (vv 18–20). Jeremiah is the speaking voice (Cornill; Rudolph; Weiser; Hyatt; Boadt), indicated by an absence of messenger formulas and the third-person reference to Yahweh in v 22b. This poetry combines with the oracle in v 20 to conclude the poetic core on a note of promise (see Rhetoric and Composition for 30:4–7), although the promise is somewhat compromised by a parting word about Israel's waywardness and weakened state (v 22). This could suggest that at one time v 22 was independent of v 21. Now both verses address "virgin Israel," who is the remnant of old Israel, i.e., Judah (see Notes).

The poetry as presently constituted can be taken as a two-stanza poem with repetition and plays on the verb *šûb* ("return, turnable"):

I	*Return*	*šûbî* . . .	v 21c
	return	*šûbî* . . .	
II	. . . .		v 22a
	turnable	*haššôbēbâ*	

---

[a]The Kt spelling, *hālāktî*, is the archaic second person feminine singular perfect form: "you have gone" (see 2:20, 33b; et passim); this spelling occurs also in 4QJer^c.

This poetry concludes the poetic core, its final line in v 22b making a key word inclusio with 30:6 of the opening poem (Lundbom 1975: 32–34 [= 1997: 47–49]):

31:22b For Yahweh has created a new thing on earth:
      the *female* protects the *man*!   *něqēbâ . . . gāber*

30:6   Ask, would you, and see
        if a *male* can bear a child?   *zākār*
        So why do I see every *man*   *geber*
        his hands on his loins, like a woman in labor?

Catchwords from *šûb* link this poetry not to the oracle immediately preceding but to its companion poem in vv 18–19:

v 21 *Return* (2×)   v 18 *Bring me back so I may come back*
v 22 *turnable*   v 19 *my turning away*

Catchwords from *šûb* also link the poetry to the prose following:

Return . . . .   *šûbî* . . .   v 21c
return . . . .   *šūbî* . . .
turnable . . . .   *haššôbēbâ*   v 22

when I restore . . .   *běšûbî*   v 23

NOTES

31:21. *Set up road-markers for yourself.* The Hebrew is sonorous, with the first and third words sharing a dominant consonant and two long "i" vowels: *haṣṣîbî . . . ṣîyyūnîm*. Five imperatives in the verse also produce *asyndeton* (see Note for 4:5). The "road-markers" (*ṣîyyūnîm*) are stone pillars, which also serve as markers for burial places (2 Kgs 23:17; Ezek 39:15). The LXX misreads this term as *Siōn* ("Zion"), with Aq and Symm doing only slightly better with *skopian* ("watchtower"), the term carried over into the Vg (*speculam*). The partial 4QJer^c reading (*ṣyw*) supports MT, although with the spelling *ṣywnym*. "Virgin Israel" is being told here in "Hansel and Gretel" fashion to mark the way into exile so she may find the way home.

    make for yourself signposts. Hebrew *tamrûrîm*, translated "signposts," is an OT *hapax legomenon* whose derivation is unclear. A word with the same spelling means "bitterness" in 6:26 and 31:15, and the T in an embellished reading translates the term "bitterness." The LXX is a bit closer with *timōrian*, which can mean "vengeance," but also "help." However, this rendering may simply be a transliteration of the Hebrew (KB³). Giesebrecht emended to *timōrîm*, "(artificial) palm trees" (= signposts), being anticipated here by both Rashi and Blayney, who took the derivation to be from *tāmār*, "palm tree." The *tōmer* in 10:5 is a "post" or "scarecrow." The rendering "signposts," because of the parallelism with "road-markers" in the line, is now generally accepted.

Fix your mind on the highway, the way you have gone. Hebrew *libbēk* (lit. "your heart") is best translated "your mind" (see Note on 11:20). The "highway" (*měsillâ*) is a built-up road (18:15) on which the exiles will go to Babylon and will one day come back (Isa 35:8; 40:3; 49:11; 62:10).

Return virgin Israel, return to these your cities. Here and in the verse following, Jeremiah again rings the changes on the verb *šûb* ("return"), which one might well call a leitmotif for the poetic core, focusing as it does on the people's return to the land and resettlement there. In the expanded Book of Restoration (chaps. 30–33) the leitmotif is the nation's "restoration (*šûb*) of fortunes" (see Rhetoric and Composition for 30:1–3). This poetry exhibits more "stairlike parallelism," on which see 31:15 and Note for 4:13. A recognition of this particular type of parallelism is credited now to the twelfth-century Jewish exegete, Rabbi Samuel ben Meir (Rashbam), who explained it in his commentary on Ecc 1:2 (Japhet and Salters 1985: 23–24, 39 n. 97, 90–93).

virgin Israel. As in 18:13, this metaphor denotes the remnant of old Israel, or Judah, which is now leaving for exile in 597 or 586 B.C. Reference is not to "Northern Israel," as in 31:4 (*pace* Holladay), or to the old Northern capital of Samaria (*pace* Schmitt 1991: 385–86). Jeremiah is addressing Judahites; Northern Israelites left for exile more than 125 years ago. The balancing of this metaphor with "turnable daughter" in v 22 supports the view that "virgin Israel" is used here in an ironic sense.

return to these your cities. I.e., the cities of Judah. Jeremiah is speaking in Judah. For MT *'ēlleh* ("these") the LXX has *penthousa* ("mourning"), which appears to (mis)read Heb *'bl(h)* (cf. Becking 1994a: 158). In any case, the demonstrative should not be deleted with Giesebrecht (*metri causa*) and Volz; it is present in 4QJer^c. For the omission of the article on "these," see GKC §126y.

22. *How long?* Hebrew *'ad-mātay.* A term of lament (see Notes for 4:21 and 23:26), which must be read if not as full-blown irony at least as gentle chiding. In my view, commentators have commonly made two mistakes in the interpretation of this verse. First, the words are taken as if they were spoken in total seriousness or with unmitigated sympathy, which they are not. Second, they are thought to refer to a distant future, when in fact they address a lamentable and incongruous present.

will you waver. Hebrew *tithammāqîn.* The verb *ḥmq* is uncommon, but its meaning is not in doubt. This one OT occurrence of the Hithpael means "turn here and there, waver" (Qal: "turn away" in Song 5:6). Again irony. Jeremiah is saying to exile-bound Judahites: "How long must your wandering go on?" Compare 13:27, which in its larger context anticipates the exile of 597 B.C.: "Woe to you, Jerusalem; you are not clean—for how much longer (*mātay 'ōd*)?"

O turnable daughter. The article on *habbat* is a vocative. Hebrew *habbat haššôbēbâ* plays on the two occurrences of *šûb* in v 21 and embellishes the idea of virgin Israel as a people who turns here and turns there. This epithet occurs one other time, in 49:4, where reference is to Ammon. The LXX translates with *thugatēr ētimōmenē* ("dishonored daughter"). Aquila is closer to the Hebrew with *hē rembeuousa* ("the roaming woman"); also Symm with *hē hypostrephomenē* ("the turnable woman").

For Yahweh has created a new thing on earth: the female protects the man! Because the verb *br'* ("create") and the noun *nĕqēbâ* ("female") are found in the Genesis 1 account of creation, which according to source critics belonged to a postexilic P (priestly) source, Duhm took the present line to be a postexilic gloss. Neither term appears elsewhere in Jeremiah. Today, however, P material is believed by many to be older, and a date for the P document has been pushed back to preexilic times (Milgrom 1991: 12–13). All indications are that Jeremiah in his chaos vision of 4:23–26 was well acquainted with the Genesis 1 creation story. There is no reason, then, to take the line as a later add-on; it belongs with the rest of vv 21–22 and can be attributed to Jeremiah (Holladay 1966c: 236). The verb *bārā'* is a perfect form that should be translated "has created." Yahweh is not about to create something new in the future, as most commentators assume, but has created something presently that Jeremiah finds a wonderment.

the female protects the man. Hebrew *nĕqēbâ tĕsôbēb gāber.* The phrase is a *crux interpretum,* even though translation of the Hebrew poses no problem. 4QJer^c in a partial reading supports MT. There is also general agreement that what is stated here in some way points to a reversal of the natural order of things (Streane; Jones). The suggestion has been made that the climactic line is a proverb. The verb *tĕsôbēb* is a Polel of *sbb,* meaning "she surrounds, protects," the sense being basically what we have in Deut 32:10, where Yahweh is remembered as having protected Israel during the wilderness wanderings. The verb provides assonance with *haššôbēbâ* ("turnable") in the previous line (Holladay). Jeremiah says that the *nĕqēbâ* ("female") is protecting the *geber,* who is a "man," but more specifically a strong man, a warrior. The gender of the woman is emphasized (cf. Gen 1:27), though not to the extent imagined by Carroll, and the fighting ability of the man is the second thing that receives the accent. If the gender of the man were being emphasized, *zākār* ("male") would be used. A suggestion I made nearly thirty years ago (Lundbom 1975: 32–34 [= 1997: 47–49]) is the one I would still propose as yielding the best sense for this phrase in the immediate context: Jeremiah is expressing shock and surprise at the weakness of Judah's soldiers in defeat. He is saying, "My, a new thing on earth! the woman must protect the (fighting) man." Needless to say, it should be the other way around. But Jeremiah, being keen on inversions and expressions of incongruity, is simply exclaiming over a sight that results from Judah's defeat at the hands of the Babylonians in either 597 or 586 B.C. Also, and this is a key element in the interpretation, the line here in 22b is structurally connected to 30:6 (see Rhetoric and Composition), creating an associative link of similar ideas and recurring irony. In 30:6 Judah's defending soldier, who is male (*zākār*), has become so weakened that he is bent over helpless like a woman in travail. Here in 31:22b, the battle-weary soldier is so exhausted that a female (*nĕqēbâ*) must protect him. Women are the only ones left with strength. These women do not become men, as some have suggested; they remain women, but the roles have changed so that they end up protecting the men who can no longer protect them. Something similar happened in Germany at the end of World War II, where it was the *Trümmerfrauen* who took over the men's role in doing the hard work of cleaning up war damage in the country. More recently (February, 1997), a movie entitled *The Italian Girl in Algiers* was advertised on a San Diego bus with the words "In this one the girl rescues the boy."

Beginning early, this phrase was given a totally positive meaning, which is precisely what happened to the ironic questions in 3:1 and 30:7 (see Notes there). The LXX translated it *en sōtēria perieleusontai anthrōpoi* ("men shall go around in safety"); the T: "the people, the house of Israel, shall pursue the Law." Kimḥi said that the woman shall go after the man, which he interpreted to mean that the children of Israel shall return to the Lord their God, who will redeem them (cf. Hos 3:5). Jerome and the Church Fathers interpreted the phrase as anticipating the miraculous birth of Christ, i.e., the Virgin would be carrying Christ in her womb, a view that was still prevalent in Calvin's time. For a survey of various messianic interpretations, see Condamin 1897. Herder (1833 II: 119) acknowledged the hyperbole in the line but said that reference was to peaceful times in the future when "there shall be so much security round about that even the wife can give [the husband] protection." Most interpretations by modern commentators, if they make one (and often they do not), are similarily positive ones.

MESSAGE AND AUDIENCE

Jeremiah here tells Judahites being readied for exile to set up road-markers when they go, to make signposts, and take careful notice of the highway on which they have traveled. "Virgin Israel" will return one day to cities it is now leaving. The word following is bittersweet. Jeremiah asks the "turnable daughter" how long she will go here and go there, a tendency she had even before this trek was forced upon her. Then, in a parting word that must be taken as gentle irony, Jeremiah says that Yahweh has created something new on earth: the female is protecting the warrior! They all understand.

This poem could have been spoken to exiles leaving Judah in 597 B.C. or in 586, after Jerusalem had fallen. It is not addressed to Northern Israel (*pace* Holladay), whose departure to Assyria took place long ago. And Carroll's date in the Persian period is out of the question, although then, the words would surely take on renewed meaning. As for the poetic core as a whole (30:5–31:22), which these verses conclude, a date for its composition and reading must be assigned after the fall of Jerusalem. In my earlier work I suggested a date of 597 B.C., when the first group of exiles was leaving for Babylon, but that is too early since the poem in 31:2–6, which is part of the overall structure, presupposes the fall of Jerusalem. The ironic word in 31:22b underscores the somber mood at the time of both the 597 and 586 exiles; nevertheless, the collection gives departing Judahites a word of hope from Yahweh that after judgment will come a glorious salvation.

As we have noted, both Jewish and Christian traditions from earliest times gave the final line in v 22b a totally positive interpretation. An allusion to this line has also been found in the *Gospel of Thomas* (logion 4), where the idea is expressed that every woman must become a man. It states:

Simon Peter said to them: Let Mariham go away from us. For women are not worthy of life. Jesus said: Lo, I will draw her so that I will make her a man so that she too may become a living spirit which is like you men; for every woman who makes herself a man will enter into the kingdom of heaven.

(Bader 1961–62: 57)

3. Look, Days Are Coming! (31:23–40)

a) May Yahweh Bless You, O Holy Mountain! (31:23–26)

31 ²³Thus said Yahweh of hosts, God of Israel:
Again they shall say this word in the land of Judah and in its cities, when I restore their fortunes:
    May Yahweh bless you
      righteous pasture
        O holy mountain
²⁴And Judah and all its cities shall dwell in it together, the farmers and they who set out with the flock. ²⁵For I will saturate the thirsty soul, and every languishing soul I will fill.

²⁶At this I awoke and looked around, and my sleep was pleasant to me.

RHETORIC AND COMPOSITION

MT 31:23–26 = LXX 38:23–26. Here begins a new oracle collection, mostly but not entirely in prose, which expands the poetic core (30:5–31:22) to make the first Book of Restoration (chaps. 30–31). The poetic core contains many prophecies on the restoration of Northern Israel; here the focus is exclusively on the restoration of Judah, or a reunited Israel and Judah. In its first stage, the expansion consisted only of the prophetic utterances in vv 23–34. These utterances are structured by "look, days are coming" formulas giving future-oriented predictions, and by verbs coupled with "again" (*'ôd*) or "not again" (*lō' . . . 'ôd*), which indicate that Israel and Judah's future will contain both continuity and discontinuity with the past. Verbs with "again" in v 23 and "not again" in v 34b make an inclusio for the whole (Lundbom 1975: 34–36 [= 1997: 50–52]). The overall structure is then:

Again they shall say this word . . .	*ʿôd yōʾmĕrû* . . .	v 23
Look, days are coming . . . when I will sow . . .	*hinnēh yāmîm bāʾîm* . . .	v 27
they shall not again say . . .	*lōʾ-yōʾmĕrû ʿôd* . . .	v 29
Look, days are coming . . . when I will cut a new covenant . . .	*hinnēh yāmîm bāʾîm* . . .	v 31
And they shall not again instruct each person his fellow . . .	*wĕlōʾ yĕlammĕdû ʿôd* . . .	v 34a
. . . and their sin *I will not remember again*	. . . *lōʾ ʿezkār-ʿôd*	v 34b

In days to come, old sayings about Zion will again be spoken, old proverbs about accumulated sin will not be spoken, and most important of all, a new covenant will be cut with the house of Israel and the house of Judah, unlike the Mosaic covenant that the people broke and that ended tragically with Israel's loss of nationhood in 586 B.C. For antitheses of a similar type, see 3:16–17 and 16:14–15 [= 23:7–8]. Similar images of reversal and promised restoration are found in the ancient Mesopotamian city laments (Dobbs-Allsopp 1993: 38–41).

In a second stage, the poetry of vv 35–37 was added, and after it a prose prophecy (vv 38–40), the first part of which is framed in the same manner as the prophecies added in stage one:

Look, days are coming . . . when the city shall be rebuilt . . .	*hinnēh yāmîm bāʾîm* . . .	v 38
And the measuring line shall go out again . . .	*wĕyāṣāʾ ʿôd qāw hammiddâ* . . .	v 39

The second part of this prophecy (v 40) makes an inclusio with 30:3, bringing the first Book of Restoration to completion:

30:3	*For look, days are coming* . . .	*kî hinnēh yāmîm bāʾîm* . . .
31:40	*and it shall not again be overthrown* . . .	*wĕlōʾ-yēhārēs ʿôd*

The "new covenant" promise, instead of concluding the expansion, is now situated in the center (see Rhetoric and Composition for 31:31–34), and the expansion has new thematic continuity between beginning and end: the prophecies in vv 23–26 and vv 38–40 look ahead to a rebuilt and reconsecrated Jerusalem, with the key words *haqqōdeš* ("the holy") in v 23 and *qōdeš* ("holy") in v 40 creating the linkage. To this correspondence can be added another — namely, the prophecy about sowing Israel and Judah with seed in vv 27–30 and the covenant prophecies regarding the seed of Israel and Judah in vv 35–37. Here the linkage is created by "seed" (*zeraʿ*), which has been identified as a catchword between the two units (Jones). The expansion material, then, in its final form shows itself to be a large key word chiasmus (Keown et al., 126) — five oracle clusters prophesying on the following themes:

A Rebuilding *the holy* Jerusalem	*haqqōdeš*	vv 23–26
B Sowing *seed* of Israel and Judah	*zeraʿ*	vv 27–30
C New covenant with Israel and Judah		vv 31–34
B′ Preserving *seed* of Israel and Judah	*zeraʿ*	vv 35–37
A′ Rebuilding *holy* Jerusalem	*qōdeš*	vv 38–40

From Duhm comes the idea that 31:25 once marked the end of a collection that began with 30:4, and that the unusual v 26, "At this I awoke and looked around, and my sleep was pleasant to me," was a remark of some later reader incorporated into the text. A few scholars have accepted this view (Mowinckel 1914: 47; Jones; Leene 1992: 356–63), but it was rightly rejected by Hyatt. Verse 26, it is true, does conclude a column in 4QJer^c (Tov 1997: 178–81, 199) and could be secondary, as many take it (see Notes), but it is not the end of a collection. Its function is simply to give a response by Jeremiah to the oracle just received from Yahweh; thus, another dialogue.

The present unit is delimited at the top end by a *petuḥah* in 4QJer^c and a *setumah* in M^L and M^P before v 23. Delimitation at the bottom end is by a *petuḥah* in 4QJer^c and a *setumah* in M^L and M^P after v 26. Tov (1997: 199) records a space in 4QJer^c after v 24 but does not list it as a section, which it probably is not.

The scholarly consensus is that the present verses do not derive from Jeremiah. In support of this view it is said that the phrases "righteous pasture" and "holy mountain," referring to Jerusalem and the Temple (v 23), would be strange coming from the prophet's mouth (Cornill; Peake; Rudolph; Weiser; Hyatt). But Jones, who believes the metaphors are embodied in a quotation, thinks that they do not necessarily reflect a narrow priestly conception and need not therefore be "intrinsically foreign to the Jeremiah tradition in its final form" (pp. 396–97). We note also that the three honorific names for the Temple in 17:12, like the honorific names for Zion here, are thought by some to derive from a liturgy edited into the text (see Rhetoric and Composition for 17:12) and need not therefore be denied to Jeremiah. The usual argument, that a Jeremiah so critical of Temple worship and one who prophesied destruction of Jerusalem could not have uttered such words, is rendered invalid if, after Jerusalem and the Temple were destroyed, Jeremianic judgment gave way to Jeremianic prophecies of reversal for the future. One should therefore take the present verses in the same spirit as other Book of Restoration promises and allow for the possibility that Jeremiah could have envisioned a rebuilding of Jerusalem (and the Temple) later on. The concluding oracle in 31:38–40, in fact, looks ahead to a rebuilt and reconsecrated Jerusalem.

Catchwords from *šûb* link the expansion to the concluding verses of the poetic core:

when I restore . . .	*bĕšûbî*	v 23
turnable	*haššôbēbâ*	v 22
return	*šûbî* . . .	v 21c
Return	*šûbî* . . .	

I do not, however, agree with Leene (1992: 352–55) that vv 23–26 are to be interpreted in light of vv 21–22, i.e., that "the woman who surrounds the man" (v 22b) is Lady Zion encircling the population of Judah. The connection between the poetic core and the expansion is simply one of catchwords.

NOTES

31:23. *Thus said Yahweh of hosts, God of Israel.* The LXX omits "of hosts, God of Israel," as elsewhere in Jeremiah (see Appendix VI). 4QJer^c partially preserves "of hosts."

Again they shall say this word . . . when I restore their fortunes. With Jerusalem and the Temple in ruins, people cannot say the blessing that follows. But it will be said again one day in the future. For the "I will (surely) restore the(ir) fortunes" expression, see Note for 29:14; as a leitmotif for the Book of Restoration, see Rhetoric and Composition for 30:1–3.

May Yahweh bless you, righteous pasture, O holy mountain. Hebrew *yĕbā-rekkā yhwh nĕwēh-ṣedeq har haqqōdeš*. The LXX translates *eulogēmenos kurios epi dikaion oros to hagion autou* ("Blessed be the Lord on his righteous, holy mountain"), which bestows the blessing on Yahweh instead of on the holy mountain (cf. 50:7). It also omits Heb *nĕwēh* ("pasture"), an omission that can be attributed to haplography (homoeoteleuton: *h . . . h*). The MT is supported by Aq, Symm, T, and Vg. This was doubtless a well-known blessing that is here incorporated into the oracle. Compare the honorific names given to the Temple in 17:12, which may be from another well-known liturgy.

righteous pasture. Hebrew *nĕwēh-ṣedek*, where *nāweh* is normally the "pasture" in which sheep graze, but in certain cases is applied metaphorically to the land given to Israel as an inheritance from Yahweh (10:25; 23:3; 50:19). The pastoral imagery derives ultimately from poems and narrative about the Exodus and Wilderness Wanderings, especially Exod 15:13, where "your holy pasture" (*nĕwēh qodšekā*) is a reference to Yahweh's tabernacle. But the "righteous pasture" here is Jerusalem (Calvin), however much the imagery fails to suit an urban center (cf. Exod 15:17). In 50:7, "The Righteous Pasture" becomes an epithet of Yahweh.

O holy mountain. Or "mountain of the Holy One." Hebrew *har haqqōdeš*. Another honorific title for Jerusalem, the mountain on which Yahweh's holy Temple stands. This metaphor occurs often in the OT, particularly in First and Second Isaiah (Isa 11:9; 27:13; 56:7; 57:13; 65:11, 25; 66:20) and the Psalms

(Pss 2:6; 15:1; 43:3; 48:2[Eng 48:1]). For Jerusalem as the future "holy mountain," see also Zech 8:3. Further on in Jer 31:40, the valleys surrounding Jerusalem and the terraces on the city slopes are similarly envisioned as becoming "holy for Yahweh."

24. *And Judah and all its cities shall dwell in it together, the farmers and they who set out with the flock.* "Judah and all its cities," here a metonymy for "the people of Judah and all its cities" (Kimḥi; cf. 4:29; 7:2; 11:12; 26:2), as a phrase is the subject of the verb "dwell" (Giesebrecht; *pace* LXX; NEB; REB). The words need not be deleted as a gloss (*pace* Holladay; McKane; cf. Cornill). These people will dwell again in the land of Judah, not in the "righteous pasture" of Mount Zion (Heb *bāh*, "in it," refers back to the feminine *'ereṣ*, "land"). Repeated and balancing words frame the blessing on Jerusalem:

> ... *in the land / of Judah and its cities*   v 23
> May Yahweh bless you . . .
> *And they shall dwell in it / Judah and all its cities* . . .   v 24

farmers. Hebrew *'ikkārîm*, lit., "plowmen." These are tenant farmers who work the land but do not own it (14:4; 51:23).

and they who set out with the flock. I.e., the shepherds (51:23). Farmers and shepherds will one day return to the land and live there together in harmony (cf. Isa 30:23), reversing the legendary tension between the two groups in ANE society (cf. the Cain and Abel story in Gen 4:1–16). The verb *nsʿ* means, lit., "to pull up stakes, set out" (4:7), here "to migrate." Giesebrecht says the awkward *wĕnāsĕʿû baʿēder* can be taken with T as an abbreviated relative construction: "they (who) set out with the flock," or else the conjugated verb can be emended to a participle construct (*wĕnōsĕʿê*) with Aq, Symm, S, and Vg (GKC §130a), giving a similar result. The *pathaḥ* vowel under the *beth* is unusual. Some MSS have *bāʿēder*: ("with *the* flock"), which is a better reading.

25. *For I will saturate the thirsty soul, and every languishing soul I will fill.* The line is a syntactic chiasmus with verbs at the extremes. The verbs are also prophetic perfects, anticipating action already completed. The *kol* ("all") in the second colon does double duty for the first colon: "For I will saturate *every* thirsty soul" (Ringgren 1982: 101). The imagery here is the same as in 31:12 and 14, where Yahweh in the restoration promises to more than satisfy the hungry and thirsty with his goodness. Gruber (1987) suggests translating *nepeš* as "throat" ("For I shall fill up the parched throat, and every dry throat I shall replenish"), which is possible for the first *nepeš* but not the second, which requires a more holistic interpretation—i.e., a whole being filled with food.

thirsty soul. Hebrew *nepeš ʿăyēpâ*. The psalmist addresses Yahweh with the words: "I have stretched out my hands to you, my soul as thirsty land (*napšî kĕ'ereṣ-ʿăyēpâ*) to you" (Ps 143:6).

and every languishing soul. Hebrew *wĕkol-nepeš dā'ăbâ*. This could be another abbreviated relative construction: "and every soul (that) languishes"; otherwise MT *dā'ăbâ* ("it languishes" or Aramaic participle? cf. Giesebrecht) is better repointed to the adjective, *dĕʾēbâ* (Hitzig; Rudolph; McKane; cf. BDB, 178).

26. *At this I awoke and looked around, and my sleep was pleasant to me.* This verse is singular in the book and taken by many to be a later add-on (Duhm; Peake; Cornill; Volz; Weiser; Rudolph; Hyatt; Bright; Holladay). Perhaps it means to echo the sentiments of Ps 126:1: "When Yahweh restored the fortunes of Zion, we became like those who dream." The prophet has to be the speaker (Rashi; Kimhi; Calvin; T adds "The prophet said"), although this creates a problem since Jeremiah elsewhere expresses himself strongly against revelations mediated through dreams (23:25–32). One might get around the problem by saying that this was a nocturnal "vision" (Jones; cf. Zech 4:1), but since it comes during sleep, for all practical purposes it is a dream. The verse has interesting parallels in extrabiblical sources. Oppenheim (1956: 229) cites an Assyrian text (Cyl. A X: 70–71) in which Ashurbanipal, after hearing good news from all battle fronts, says: "(When I was) in (my) bed my dreams were very pleasant, and, in the morning, I overheard only nice words (said by other persons)." In other texts Oppenheim points out how evil dreams oppress and frighten individuals, so much so that they pray to their god, "Make my dream pleasant" (1956: 230). He says that in the dream report, which appears in a strictly conventionalized frame, there is often a section at the end referring to the reaction of the dreaming person (1956: 187). Here in the present verse, whatever its provenance, the point seems to be that the dream of a restored Jerusalem and Judah was a pleasant one, and upon waking, Jeremiah was faced with a harsher reality, making the dream all the more sweet. It is also Jeremiah's response to the word from Yahweh. Bonhoeffer found this verse meaningful, quoting it in his *Letters and Papers from Prison* (1971: 131).

and my sleep was pleasant to me. Hebrew *ûšĕnātî ʿārĕbâ lî*. The verb *ʿrb* means "to be pleasing" (6:20).

MESSAGE AND AUDIENCE

In the present oracle, Yahweh tells a remnant audience in Judah—also Judahites abroad—that when the nation's fortunes are restored people will again say of Jerusalem, "May Yahweh bless you, righteous pasture, O holy mountain." The audience if it knows these words will wonder if they will ever be spoken again. Yahweh says that Judahites in this future time shall reinhabit the land, farmers and shepherds together. Yahweh will saturate the thirsty and fill the hungry with food in abundance.

This audience, or a later one, then hears a word of response from Jeremiah. He says that after hearing these heavenly words he awoke, looked around, and his sleep seemed particularly pleasant. Small wonder! This ideal future compared to present reality was doubtless as unbelievable to him as to everyone else.

The oracle can be dated any time after the destruction of Jerusalem in 586 B.C. Jeremiah's response could date from the same time, or later. Nothing, however, supports a date for either one in the Persian period (*pace* Carroll; Holladay), when these would no longer be a promise for the future.

b) Planting, Building, and Accountability (31:27–30)

31 [27]Look, days are coming — oracle of Yahweh — when I will sow the house of Israel and the house of Judah with the seed of human and the seed of beast.

[28]And it will be, as I have watched over them to uproot and to break down and to overthrow and to destroy, also to bring evil, so I will watch over them to build and to plant — oracle of Yahweh.

[29]In those days they shall not again say:
    Fathers have eaten sour grapes
        and children's teeth become set on edge
[30]But each person in his iniquity shall die. Every human who eats the sour grapes, his teeth shall become set on edge.

RHETORIC AND COMPOSITION

MT 31:27–30 = LXX 38:27–30. The present verses contain three future-oriented prophecies: 1) an oracle promising the repopulation of a united Israel and Judah (v 27); 2) an oracle promising rebuilding and replanting in the land; and 3) a promise that in future days the retribution doctrine of Yahweh will be based on individual accountability (vv 29–30). These prophecies constitute a rhetorical unit in the first Book of Restoration, where they are made to balance the covenant promises in vv 35–37 (see Rhetoric and Composition for 31:23–26). The "latter day" promise of vv 29–30 may also be a divine oracle; however, it lacks a messenger formula. The unit is delimited at the top end by a *petuḥah* in 4QJer[c] and a *setumah* in M[L] and M[P] before v 27. Delimitation at the bottom end is by a *setumah* in M[L] and what appears to be a *petuḥah* in M[P] after v 30. In M[P] an omitted v 30 has been inserted into the open section in small writing.

The oracles in vv 27–28 are generally attributed — by a few scholars, cautiously — to Jeremiah (Giesebrecht; Weiser; Hyatt; Bright; Holladay), although Duhm assigned them to his postexilic editor. Volz preserves for Jeremiah only v 27b, and Rudolph says that v 27 can be saved for the prophet if "and the house of Judah" is deleted. Such a deletion is to be rejected, since the present expansion is directed to Judah or a united Israel and Judah. Verses 29–30 are more often assigned a later date, since commentators (Duhm; Peake; Cornill; Volz; Rudolph; Hyatt; Holladay) see in the discrediting of the "sour grapes" proverb a dependence upon Ezekiel 18. This, however, is at best uncertain. All three prophecies can be attributed to Jeremiah (Giesebrecht; Weiser; Bright) or taken to reflect an authentic Jeremiah tradition (Jones).

The first and last prophecies are linked together by the word *'ādām* ("man, human"):

I   . . . the seed of *human* (*'ādām*) and the seed of beast . . .   v 27
III   *Every human* (*kol-hā'ādām*) who eats the sour grapes . . .   v 30

These catchwords connect to the following oracle:

v 29   *fathers*   v 32   *fathers*
v 30   *in his iniquity*   *ba'ăwônô*   v 34   *their iniquity*   *la'ăwônām*

NOTES

31:27. *Look, days are coming.* On this stereotypical phrase in Jeremiah, see Note for 7:32. The LXX adds *dia touto* (= Heb *lākēn*, "therefore"); cf. 35:18 (LXX 42:18).

when I will sow the house of Israel and the house of Judah with the seed of human and the seed of beast. The verb *zr'* ("sow") takes a double accusative (GKC §117ee). The land presently is a ruin and its population decimated, but Yahweh repeats a promise made elsewhere that in future days he will repopulate a united Israel and Judah (see Note for 30:19). The metaphor used to describe the restoration ("I will sow . . . seed," *zāra'tî . . . zera'*) is unusual and open to misunderstanding, e.g., in Carroll's infelicitous talk of "semen." The imagery may derive from Hos 2:25[Eng 2:23], where Yahweh speaks similarly about a restoration of land and people. There the verb *zr'* ("sow") is chosen to make a play on *yizrě'e'l* ("Jezreel"). Yahweh's judgment in Jeremiah is promised for both humans and beasts (7:20; 21:6), and it came upon both (32:43; 33:10, 12; 36:29). Now both will enjoy an increase in the new creation. On the pairing of "human and beast" in Jeremiah, see Note for 21:6.

the house of Israel and the house of Judah. The LXX reduces to "Israel and Judah," but the MT reading is supported by Aq, Symm, T, and Vg. This prophecy is given to a united Israel and Judah, which is true also of the "new covenant" prophecy coming next (v 31). On Israel and Judah as a united entity in future days, see also 3:18; 50:4–5; Ezek 37:15–23; and Hos 1:11.

28. *And it will be, as I have watched over . . . so I will watch over.* A comparison of the *ka'ăšer . . . kēn* type, occurring again in 32:42 (see also Note for 13:11). When Yahweh "watches over" (*šqd*) his word, it means he will fulfill a promise (1:12).

to uproot and to break down and to overthrow and to destroy, also to bring evil. The LXX has only two verbs: *kathairein kai kakoun*, which appear to translate MT's *lahărōs . . . ûlěhārēa'* ("to overthrow . . . and to bring evil"). Cornill and Holladay select the wrong equivalents—Cornill the first and last verbs; Holladay the first two verbs. Elsewhere in Jeremiah the LXX translates Heb *hrs* with *kathaireō* (24:6; 31:40[LXX 38:40]; 42:10[LXX 49:10]; and 45:4[LXX 51:34]). Janzen (1973: 35) and McKane, who select the right equivalents, take the other three verbs to be MT expansion, but Becking (1994a: 151) thinks the LXX has contracted four standard Jeremiah verbs, "to uproot, to pull down, to overthrow, to destroy," into one verb *kathairein*, "to destroy." But the LXX is probably shorter as a result of two haplographies: 1) the loss of *lintôš wĕlintôṣ wĕ*, "to uproot and to break down, and" (homoeoarcton: *l . . . l*); and 2) the loss of *ûlĕha'ăbîd*, "and to destroy" (homoeoarcton: *wlh . . . wlh*). On the six common verbs of destruction and restoration in Jeremiah, see Note for 1:10. The Jeremianic theme of "building and planting" is discussed in Note for 24:6.

29. *In those days they shall not again say.* This antithesis usually appears with a messenger formula (see Note for 3:16). Jeremiah's prophecy on retribution is future oriented; the comparable prophecy in Ezekiel 18 has immediate application (May 1961: 114–16).

Fathers have eaten sour grapes, and children's teeth become set on edge. An existing proverb being quoted widely in Judah and in Babylon among the exiles following the 586 B.C. disaster (Lam 5:7; Ezek 18:2). A striking parallel exists in a Neo-Assyrian prayer from one who has a disease that may have come from a wrong he did not commit but that someone else committed. It too shows that sin can be punished to the second or third generation. The petitioner prays:

> Loosen my disgrace, the guilt of my wickedness; remove
> My disease; drive away my sickness; a sin I know (or)
>   know not I have committed;
> On account of a sin of my father (or) my grandfather, a
>   sin of my mother (or) my grandmother,
> On account of a sin of an elder brother (or) an elder
>   sister, on account of a sin of my family,
> Of my kinsfolk (or) of my clan . . .
> The wrath of god and goddess have pressed upon me.
>   (Mullo-Weir 1929b: 765; Sigerist 1951: 445)

In another expiation ritual, the petitioner prays for deliverance from a sin any number of possible individuals close to him may have committed, possibly one of his children or a friend:

> Make thou the angered god and angered goddess to
>   be at peace with me
> The wrath of god and goddess relax for me;
> The sin of the wrongdoing of father, mother, brother,
>   sister, son, daughter, man-servant, or maid-servant,
> Of comrade, associate, male friend, female friend, or . . .
> . . . . and I will sing thy praises.
>   (Mullo-Weir 1929a: 282)

The proverb here in Jer 31:29 had obvious currency at the time (Kilpp 1985; Waldman 1989–90: 1), just as it did whenever the need arose to explain Israel's corporate responsiblity for sin (Josh 7:24–26; 1 Sam 22:16–19; 2 Sam 21:1–9) or related ideas of inherited guilt and punishment, otherwise termed "delayed retribution" (Exod 20:5; 34:7; Num 14:18; Deut 5:9; Pss 79:8; 109:14; Job 21:19). These ideas are all present in Jeremiah (2:5–9; 5:1–8; 18:21; 32:18), where one encounters also the more official view that judgment finally came upon Judah because of the sins of Manasseh (15:4; cf. 2 Kgs 21:10–15; 23:26–27; 24:3–4). But continued use of this proverb was not now possible, since the present generation might have concluded, and did conclude, that as children of transgressors they were not themselves responsible for the sin in question. A corrective would therefore be necessary, so Jeremiah stated that in days to come this proverb about fathers eating sour grapes and children's teeth being set on edge would no longer be spoken. All would die for their own iniquity. Ezekiel makes the point even more emphatically to the exiles, with the one difference that they are told to change their way of thinking now (Ezekiel 18). Moreover, unless the wicked repent, they will be punished just as the previous generation was. Ezekiel develops the subject of individual responsibility at some length (Ezek 3:17–21; 14:12–23; 33:1–20). For the Babylonian exiles, the question of theodicy also arose: people were saying that Yahweh's ways were unjust (Ezek 18:25–29). But Ezekiel said "No," stating for the individual the same doctrine of divine retribution that Jeremiah gave for the nation after his visit to the potter's shop (Jer 18:5–10). The later Rabbis took the view that the sins of the fathers would fall upon the children (only) when the children continued in their fathers' way (Waldman).

sour grapes. Hebrew *bōser.* The term is a collective meaning "unripe fruit" (Rashi) or "unripe grapes" (Job 15:33).

and children's teeth become set on edge. The verb *qhh* in the Piel means "become blunt, dull" (Ecc 10:10, of an iron tool), the meaning also of the Qal here and in Ezek 18:2 (BDB; KB³), where reference is to a condition of the teeth. The LXX verb *aimōdeō* denotes a sensation in the teeth caused by acidic food. (In Ezek 18:2 the LXX translated *qhh* with *gomphiazō,* "to gnash, suffer pain in the teeth.") The Vg has *obstupuerunt* ("become senseless, numb"). The AV's expression, "teeth . . . set on edge," occurs earlier in John Wyclif's fourteenth-century Bible translation (*OED* 5: 69; M. Greenberg 1983: 327–28), although there it is used to render "cleanness of teeth" (= hunger) in Amos 4:6. The T paraphrases with "but the children are punished," which is what the proverb means to convey (v 30).

30. *But each person in his iniquity shall die.* The principle is stated in Deut 24:16: "The fathers shall not be put to death for the children, nor shall the children be put to death for the fathers; every man shall be put to death for his own sin." According to Boecker (1980: 37), this law was promulgated in order to put an end to blood revenge. It was put into practice by King Amaziah of Judah, who, in avenging the death of his father, put the conspirators to death but spared their children (2 Kgs 14:5–6; 2 Chr 25:1–4). Ezekiel states as a principle: "The soul that sins shall die" (Ezek 18:4, 20). The Hebrew here in the present verse may be elliptical—i.e., the *kî 'im* ("but") may intend a repe-

tition of the *yō'mĕrû* ("they shall say") in v 29 (Schoneveld 1963: 341; Kaminsky 1995: 147–49), since *kî 'im* constructions introduce new declarations in 7:32; 16:14–15 [= 23:7–8]; and 19:6. Schoneveld's reading here is, "But they will say, 'Each person in his own iniquity shall die.'" According to this interpretation, people in future days will speak a new proverb in place of the old one. See also 3:16b–17, where another new declaration will replace an old one in future days.

Every human who eats sour grapes. The LXX omits "every human" (*kol-hā'ādām*); however, the phrase is well attested in the Vrs (Aq, Theod, Symm, G^L, S, T, Vg) and should be retained (Giesebrecht). It links the first and last prophecies together (see Rhetoric and Composition).

MESSAGE AND AUDIENCE

Yahweh in this first oracle says that he will sow a united Israel and Judah in the future with the seed of humans and the seed of beasts. In a second oracle, this promise of a population increase is supplemented by a promise that the land too will be restored—new plantings and new buildings. The third promise, probably also a divine oracle, is that the future will differ from the past and present, in that people will no longer speak the proverb about fathers eating sour grapes and the children's teeth being set on edge. Instead, each person will die in his own iniquity, which is to say, the one who eats sour grapes will have his own teeth set on edge.

These oracles postdate the fall of Jerusalem, because people are currently using the cited proverb to explain the catastrophe of 586 B.C. But they are spoken soon after, since vv 29–30 are directed to the future. The Persian period is too late for the final prophecy (*pace* Carroll; Holladay), because its subject matter has already become a current issue for Ezekiel and the Babylonian exiles.

The mention of iniquity in v 30 will introduce to an audience hearing the first Book of Restoration the "new covenant" oracle coming next, where the act of grace said to undergird the new covenant is the forgiveness of sins (v 34). In the present verses, however, sin will be punished, not forgiven. These verses then, vv 29–30, are a foil for the new covenant prophecy. Similarly, Ezekiel's teaching about "the soul that sins shall die" concludes with an exhortation that Israel get itself a new heart and a new spirit (Ezek 18:31).

The Roman poet Horace (65–68 B.C.) believed that sin multiplied with the generations, yet he expressed this hope in Augustus, whose rule promised stability and good government (*Odes* iii 6):

Delicta maiorum immeritus lues
Romane, donec templa refeceris
    aedesque labentes deorum et
    foeda nigro simulacra fumo

Thy fathers' sins, O Roman, thou,
though guiltless, shalt expiate, till thou
dost restore the crumbling temples
and shrines of the gods and their
statues soiled with grimy smoke.

(Loeb)

c) The New Covenant (31:31–34)

31 [31]Look, days are coming—oracle of Yahweh—when I will cut with the house of Israel and with the house of Judah a new covenant, [32]not like the covenant that I cut with their fathers in the day I took them by the hand to bring them out from the land of Egypt, my covenant that they, they broke, though I, I was their master—oracle of Yahweh.

[33]But this is the covenant that I will cut with the house of Israel after those days—oracle of Yahweh: I will put my law in their inward parts, and upon their hearts I will write it. And I will be God to them, and they, they will be a people to me. [34]And they shall not again instruct each person his fellow and each person his brother, saying, 'Know Yahweh,' for they, all of them, shall know me, from the least of them to the greatest of them—oracle of Yahweh—for I will forgive their iniquity, and their sin I will not remember again.

RHETORIC AND COMPOSITION

MT 31:31–34 = LXX 38:31–34. The present verses, which give Yahweh's promise of a new covenant to Israel and Judah, are delimited at the top end by a *setumah* in M^L and a *petuhah* in M^P before v 31.[a] Delimitation at the bottom end is by a *setumah* in M^L and a *petuhah* in M^P after v 34. There are four "oracle of Yahweh" formulas here, although the LXX with its lack of a formula in v 34 has only three. Since vv 31–32 cannot be divided we must have two oracles with double formulas, which does occasionally happen (e.g., 2:2–3, 5–9; 30:18–21; 31:35–37). Oracle I states what the new covenant will *not* be (vv 31–32), and Oracle II states what it will be (vv 33–34). With this division a nice syntactical variation also shows up in the two beginnings:

I   *Look, days are coming / oracle of Yahweh / when I will cut . . . a new covenant*   v 31
. . . oracle of Yahweh   v 32

II   *But this is the covenant that I will cut . . . / after those days / oracle of Yahweh:*   v 33
. . . oracle of Yahweh . . .   v 34

---

[a]In M^P omitted words are written into the open section in small letters.

In the first Book of Restoration these oracles climactically ended the expansion material of 31:23–34. After vv 35–40 were added, vv 31–34 became situated at the center of the expansion of vv 23–40, where again they assumed a climactic position (see Rhetoric and Composition for 31:23–26). To show this center position of vv 31–34 currently, one only need measure the amount of expansion text on either side. A line count in M^L (Freedman et al. 1998: 537) turns up 24 lines of text for vv 23–30 (with liberal spacing) and 22 lines of text for vv 35–40 (with constricted spacing). In *BHS* there are 11+ lines of text for vv 23–30, and 12+ lines of text (some of it poetry) for vv 35–40. A word count, however, shows near-perfect symmetry: 101 words in vv 23–30, and 101(2)[b] words in vv 35–40. In vv 31–34 there are 92 words, just slightly less than the number in each passage creating the frame.

These new covenant oracles are widely attributed to Jeremiah and said by some to be his greatest preaching (Hyatt). This assessment derives largely from Christian scholars who see the importance of this prophecy in the NT and for the early Christian Church (see Excursus V). Some earlier critical scholars (Movers, Stade, Smend, Schmidt) denied the prophecy to Jeremiah, as they did other hopeful prophecies, arguing that such were more in the spirit of Second Isaiah. But Giesebrecht took the passage as emanating from Baruch, and thus a vestige of Jeremianic preaching. Things went in a different direction with Duhm, who reduced the passage to the pedestrian teaching of a postexilic scribe, an assessment that has failed to win acceptance except with Carroll and McKane. Duhm's view was refuted early on by Cornill and W. J. Moulton (1906). Hyatt also rightly pointed out that the new covenant promise does not promote the ideal of a scribe but the ideal of a prophet. Since Jeremiah in his call is portrayed as "the prophet like Moses" (see Note for 1:7), and Moses is the one who gave Israel the Sinai covenant, it is only natural now that Jeremiah be the one to give Israel a new covenant.

Catchwords connecting to the prior unit:

| v 32 | *fathers* | | v 29 | *fathers* | |
| v 34 | *their iniquity* | *la'ăwônām* | v 30 | *in his iniquity* | *ba'ăwônô* |

NOTES

31:31. *Look, days are coming.* On this phrase in Jeremiah, see Note for 7:32. The new covenant is announced for future days.

31–32. *when I will cut with the house of Israel and with the house of Judah a new covenant, not like the covenant that I cut with their fathers in the day I took them by the hand to bring them out from the land of Egypt, my covenant that they, they broke, though I, I was their master.* Discontinuity gets the accent in the new covenant promise. The term "new covenant" (*běrît ḥădāšâ*) occurs only here in the OT, denoting the basis on which a future relation between

---

[b] A word count of 102 results from adding *bā'îm* ("are coming"), with the Q, in v 38.

God and his people will rest following the collapse of the Mosaic covenant and Israel's loss of nationhood in 586 B.C. This new relationship, which Yahweh himself will create, is anticipated in other terms by Jeremiah (24:7; 32:38–40; 50:5) and also by Ezekiel (Ezek 16:60; 34:25; 36:27–28; 37:26), Second Isaiah (Isa 42:6; 49:8; 54:10; 55:1–5; 59:21; 61:8), and Malachi (Mal 3:1; cf. 2:1–9). The new covenant forms the centerpiece of a larger hope that includes a new act of salvation, a new Zion, and a new Davidic king.

Scholars have considered two related questions when discussing the concept of a new covenant: 1) whether this covenant really is "new," and 2) whether the Mosaic covenant over against which the new covenant stands continues to be viable. Some think the new covenant is a renewal of the Mosaic (= Sinai) covenant and nothing more (Duhm; Levin 1985: 140–41; Lohfink 1991b: 45; Rendtorff 1993: 198; Holmgren 1999: 75–95), while others believe that Jeremiah announces the end of the Mosaic covenant and presents here a covenant that is really new (B. W. Anderson 1964: 232; Zimmerli 1965a: 80; von Rad 1965: 212–13; Wolff 1983: 53, 60). Von Rad agrees that the Mosaic covenant really was broken and that there is no attempt here, as in Deuteronomy, to reestablish it on the old bases; nevertheless, the revelation it contained is not nullified in whole or in part. So far as content goes, the new covenant neither alters nor expands the old. Marconcini (1993) says the new covenant renews the old, but on entirely different grounds. What may certainly be said is that for Jeremiah the gulf between the new covenant and the Mosaic covenant is greater than for any who preceded him. In my view, the new covenant cannot be reduced to a renewed Sinai covenant such as took place on the plains of Moab (Deut 5:2–3; 28:69[Eng 29:1]), at Shechem (Joshua 24), or in Jerusalem at the climax of the Josianic Reform (2 Kings 23). Although this new covenant will have admitted continuity with the Sinai covenant, it will still be a genuinely new covenant, one that marks a new beginning in the divine-human relationship because 1) it is given without conditions; 2) it will be written in the hearts of people in a way the Sinai covenant was not (v 33); and 3) it will be grounded in a wholly new act of divine grace, i.e., the forgiveness of sins (v 34). On the unconditional nature of the "eternal covenant" (*běrît 'ôlām*), which is another name for the new covenant, see Note for 32:40.

with the house of Israel and with the house of Judah. Some commentators and other scholars (Giesebrecht; Cornill; Peake; Streane; Volz; Rudolph; Weiser; Hyatt; Bright; Wolff 1983: 50–51) want to eliminate "and with the house of Judah" as a gloss, since "Judah" does not appear in v 33, but there is no textual support for the deletion. Actually, a minority reading in v 33 has *běnê yiśrā'ēl* ("children of Israel") for *bēt yiśrā'ēl* ("house of Israel"), which would include both Israel and Judah (see below). Moreover, the Book of Restoration prophecies—of which this is one—are intended for both Israel and Judah (30:3–4). In the unit immediately preceding, Yahweh sows "the house of Israel and the house of Judah" (v 27). In v 33, then, "Israel" means all Israel, including Judah. But there is nothing to suggest that this new covenant will be made with an expanded Israel, including Gentiles. It was so interpreted by the Christian Church, but the promise as given is not that inclusive.

not like the covenant that I cut with their fathers. The "fathers" here are the Exodus generation, making this the Sinai covenant. In the Qumran *Temple Scroll* (11QT 29:10) is the phrase "according to the covenant which I have made with Jacob at Bethel," which is thought by some to give the phrase here a positive but different interpretation. The Qumran covenant, according to members of that community, was to be just like the covenant made with the patriarchs (Yadin 1983: 129; Swanson 1994; Brooke 1997: 202–3).

I took them by the hand. A metaphor of parental guidance derived perhaps from Hos 11:3 but not otherwise used to describe the Exodus deliverance. See later Isa 40:11b; 41:13; and 42:6.

my covenant that they, they broke, though I, I was their master. The added pronouns here and elsewhere in the passage are for emphasis. The people have broken the covenant, not Yahweh who was their master or husband (Heb *b'l* can mean "be master over" or "be husband"—terms largely interchangeable in ancient culture, especially when used metaphorically). The metaphors have now shifted from father-son to husband-wife (cf. 3:19–20). The seeds of destruction for the Sinai covenant were sown at the very beginning, when the people made a golden calf in the Wilderness (Exodus 32) and Moses, in his anger, broke (*šbr*) the tablets on which the Ten Commandments were written (v 19). The verb *prr* H-stem here in the present verse is strong ("break, render ineffectual"), occurring elsewhere in the OT with reference to a breaking of the Mosaic covenant (11:10; Deut 31:16, 20; Lev 26:15; Ezek 16:59; 44:7). In Hos 8:1, Yahweh says the people "have transgressed my covenant" (*'āběrû běrîtî*), which is not quite as strong (but see RSV: "they have broken my covenant"). A phrase corresponding to the present one has turned up in the Qumran *Temple Scroll* (11QT 59:8): *'šr hprw bryty*, "according to which they broke my covenant" (Yadin 1983: 267; Brooke 1997: 202). The LXX reads the present phrase differently: *hoti autoi ouk enemeinan en tē diathēkē mou, kai egō ēmelēsa autōn* ("because they did not continue in my covenant, and I neglected them"), which gives a reason for making the new covenant and states that disregard of the old resulted in divine neglect. This translation carries over into Heb 8:9 of the NT. Some suggest reading *'ăšer* as a conjunction instead of as a relative pronoun (Aq also *hoti*), and emending *bā'altî* ("I was master") to *gā'altî* ("I abhorred"; cf. 14:19), but the LXX translation is still not vindicated and is rightly rejected by both commentators and the modern Versions. Moreover, the expression, "for I, I am your master" (*kî 'ānōkî bā'altî*) occurs in 3:14, supporting the MT (Renaud 1999).

33. *But this is the covenant that I will cut with the house of Israel after those days . . . I will put my law in their inward parts, and upon their hearts I will write it.* The law (*tôrâ*) will remain in the new covenant and the obligation to comply with its demands will still exist; nevertheless, conditions will be vastly improved because Yahweh promises to write the law on the human heart. Jeremiah does not specify what this law will consist of, but it is only reasonable

to assume that it will be the law at the heart of the Sinai covenant (Kimḥi: "There will never be a new Torah"), which at minumim would be the Ten Commandments, but doubtless somethng more (B. W. Anderson 1964: 236–37). Jewish and Christian valuations of the law differ, even as valuations differ within both traditions. Pharisaic Judaism counted 613 commandments to be obeyed, which, by any measure is radically reduced by Christians. But Christians do not reject a core of Sinaitic Law being at the heart of the new covenant, as is sometimes alleged. Jesus holds the Ten Commandments in high regard (Matt 19:17–19; 22:36–40), claiming also to fulfill the law, not do away with it (Matt 5:17–18). Paul, too, for all his polemic against the Law, considers the Law holy and claims to uphold it (Rom 3:31; 7:12; see Excursus V). But already at the Jerusalem Conference reported in Acts 15, compromises had to be made. There it was agreed that while Gentiles did not have to be circumcised, they should nevertheless abstain from eating food offered to idols, blood and meat from strangled animals, and also from sexual immorality.

The new covenant is new because Yahweh's *torah* will be written on the human heart (von Rad 1965: 213–14; Weinfeld 1976: 28; Wolff 1983: 54). The Sinai covenant was written on tablets of stone (Exod 24:12; 31:18; et passim). In the homiletical rhetoric of Deuteronomy, however, the *torah* was supposed to find its way into the human heart (Deut 6:6; 11:18). But Deuteronomy knows—as does Jeremiah—that the heart is deceitful and layered with evil (Deut 10:16; 11:16; Jer 4:4). Jeremiah is the more negative in assessing the human condition. He says the heart is evil, stubborn, and rebellious (5:23; see Note for 3:17), that sin is "engraved" on the tablet of the heart (17:1), and that the heart "is deceitful above all things" (17:9). In addition, he believes that the people have not the ability within themselves to make their relationship with Yahweh right again (2:25; 13:23; von Rad 1965: 216–17; B. Robinson 2001: 204). Nevertheless, prior "heart talk" in Deuteronomy and Jeremiah is background for and determines the articulation of the new covenant promise (H. Weippert 1979). If the law did not penetrate the human heart before, and this might still be debated (Ps 119:11), it will with the new covenant in place, because Yahweh promises to make it happen (cf. Isa 51:7). Even in the later chapters of Deuteronomy, which may be contemporary with Jeremiah, the law is said to reside in human mouths and hearts, enabling people to carry it out without difficulty:

> Indeed this commandment that I am commanding you today, it is not too difficult for you, and it is not far off; it is not in heaven that one should say, 'Who will go up for us to the heaven and get it for us that we may hear it and do it?' And it is not from across the sea that one should say, 'Who will cross over for us to the other side of the sea and get it for us that we may hear it and do it?' Indeed the word is very near you, in your mouth and in your heart to do it.

(Deut 30:11–14)

Jeremiah, on another occasion, says that Yahweh will give Israel a (new) heart to know him (24:7; cf. Deut 30:6). Ezekiel, on his part, expects for Israel a new heart and a new spirit (Ezek 11:19; 18:31; 36:26), although in 18:31 people are told to make both for themselves—a demand, needless to say, incapable of fulfillment. Ezekiel alone imagines that human beings have such a capacity (M. Greenberg 1983: 341). The new heart and new spirit are otherwise understood to be gifts of divine grace.

the house of Israel. Hebrew *bēt yiśrā'ēl*. A few MSS read *běnê yiśrā'ēl* ("children of Israel"), which is less ambiguous because it includes both Israel and Judah.

I will put my law in their inward parts, and upon their hearts I will write it. Another syntactic chiasmus with verbs at the extremes. Hebrew *nātattî* is a perfect form, which Weinfeld (1976: 27) says is usual in grant-type covenants. Even though the new covenant is announced for the future, Yahweh has already carried out the action, just as he did when calling Jeremiah to be a prophet (1:5) and designating him for ministry (1:10). Many Heb MSS have a *waw conversive* on the verb, making it future: "And I will put." But the LXX (and Heb 8:10 in the NT) are without a conjunction.

in their inward parts. Hebrew *běqirbām*. The LXX: "in their mind" (*eis tēn dianoian autōn*).

and upon their hearts I will write it. In ANE religion, oracles were inscribed on the hearts and livers of both humans and animals (Hogg 1911: 60). Here the new covenant will be written on hearts previously inscribed with sin (17:1). Yahweh's future covenant action will be more individualized than it was in the past (Giesebrecht; Peake; Hyatt), similar to what will occur in divine retribution, where each person will die for his own sin (31:30). Hyatt says that while this new covenant is made with the nation, it nevertheless carries weighty implications for personal religion. Sin and covenant become even more individualized in the Qumran *Manual of Discipline* and in the NT Letter to the Hebrews (see Excurses IV and V).

And I will be God to them, and they, they will be a people to me. The same formula used to describe the Sinai covenant. On its occurrence in Jeremiah and elsewhere, see Note for 7:23.

34. *And they shall not again instruct each person his fellow and each person his brother, saying, 'Know Yahweh,' for they, all of them, shall know me, from the least of them to the greatest of them.* In ancient Hebrew thinking, the "will" took up residence in the heart (A. R. Johnson 1964: 77–79), so if the *tôrâ* is to be written on the human heart, people will have the will to obey it. Moreover, they will no longer have to admonish one another to "Know Yahweh!" for everyone will know him. "Knowing Yahweh" here as elsewhere requires the expanded meaning of "knowing and doing the *tôrâ*" (Hos 4:1–2; Jer 5:4–5). In Deuteronomy, people had to be continually told: "Be careful to do (the commands)" (5:1, 32; 6:3, 25; et passim), "Take heed . . . lest you forget the covenant / Yahweh" (4:23; 6:12; 8:11; et passim), the liturgical injunctions in 6:6–9

and 11:18–20 admonishing them also to keep Yahweh's words in their hearts as well as in more conspicuous places. But now Yahweh will inscribe the law on the human heart, which is thought by some to be the genuinely new element in the new covenant (Hyatt; B. W. Anderson 1964: 234–35; von Rad 1965: 213–14; Potter 1983: 353). Von Rad says that in the old covenant God spoke and the people listened, but now this will be dropped; God will put the law straight into Israel's heart, and obedience will no longer be a problem. Very well, but can Christians claim that this has happened with the dawn of the Kingdom? Jewish interpretation, too, interprets the promise literally, but it looks forward to fulfillment in the Messianic Age, which has not yet come. Because the verb *lmd* (Piel: "teach, instruct") occurs here, it is assumed by many that "teaching" is at issue and that with the new covenant in place there will no longer be a need for instruction. Some say God alone will be teacher of the people (Isa 54:13; Matt 23:8–10; cf. Derrett 1981: 377). Potter thinks the new covenant will no longer be mediated by now-discredited scribes and elitists (cf. 2:8; 8:8) but will be apprehended by all. But this is largely a holdover from Duhm's idea that the passage promoted a scribal ideal: "*dass all Juden Schriftgelehrte sind* ("that all Jews shall be scribes"). Formal teaching is not at issue. "Know Yahweh!" is instruction from a prophet, which is to say that Jeremiah envisions a day when people the likes of himself will be out of a job. Volz recalls Moses' hearing about unauthorized prophesying in the wilderness camp and exclaiming to Joshua, "Would that all Yahweh's people were prophets!" (Num 11:29). But in this future day, things will be even grander, for not only will a leveling have occurred, but no one will need to admonish another to "Know Yahweh!" for everyone will know him. Here we must also allow for some hyperbole, similar to what occurs in 50:20, where it says that in the days to come no sin will be found in Judah.

for they, all of them, shall know me. Anticipated in 24:7. See also Hos 2:22[Eng 2:20].

from the least of them to the greatest of them. The gamut here in this stereotypical expression is not age but social standing (see Note on 6:13). Jeremiah discovered earlier that neither the poor nor the great knew Yahweh's way (5:4–5). The prefixed *lěmin* on *lěmiqtannām* indicates the starting point; thus: "from the least of them . . ." (GKC §119c n. 2).

for I will forgive their iniquity, and their sin I will not remember again. Another syntactic chiasmus like the one in v 33, reversing the wording and thought of 14:10; also Hos 8:13 (K. Gross 1930: 4). This is the really new element in the new covenant (Skinner 1926: 329; B. W. Anderson 1964: 235–36; Römer 1991; Krašovec 1993), finding expression elsewhere in Jeremiah and the prophets after him (33:8; 50:20; Ezek 36:22–32; Isa 43:25; 44:22; 55:7). Yahweh is merciful and gracious, according to the divine self-asseveration of Exod 34:6–7, and one who forgives iniquity, transgression, and sin, yet at the same time a God who will not clear the guilty, punishing offenders to the third and fourth generation (cf. Jer 32:18). Only recently Yahweh offered to pardon (*slḥ*) Jerusalem if just one righteous man could be found (5:1, 7) or if people would repent and turn from their evil way (36:3), but the offers came to nothing. Yahweh then does forgive sin; nevertheless, forgiveness of sins is not what undergirded the Sinai covenant; in fact, it played no part at all in that covenant's earliest formulation or in the formulation of Deuteronomy (Exod 32:32–34; Deut 31:16–29; cf. Wolff 1983: 59; P. D. Miller, 812). The act of divine grace undergirding the Sinai covenant was the deliverance from Egypt (Exod 20:2; Deut 5:6). In Deuteronomy, the nation is promised life if it obeys the covenant; if it does not obey, Yahweh will rain down a multitude of curses, the most serious of which will be the loss of the land. The first edition of Deuteronomy (chaps. 1–28; Lundbom 1996a: 314–15) makes no provision for a restored divine-human relationship once the covenant is broken and the curses have fallen (Deut 4:29–31 bases Yahweh's mercy on a remembrance of the covenant with the fathers—i.e., the Abrahamic covenant). Disobedience, says von Rad (1965: 270), is not the problem for Deuteronomy that it later became for Jeremiah and Ezekiel. Deuteronomic theology is best summed up in Joshua's words to the people at Shechem: if you disobey the covenant, Yahweh will *not* forgive your sins; instead he will punish you (Josh 24:19–20). This theology is carried over into the Holiness Code (Lev 26:14–20), although there, provisions are made for the forgiveness of sins, after which Yahweh will begin again with Israel on the basis of his covenant with Abraham (Isaac and Jacob) and his remembrance of the land (26:40–45).

MESSAGE AND AUDIENCE

Yahweh in the present oracles says that in future days he will cut a new covenant with the house of Israel and the house of Judah. It will not be like the covenant cut earlier with the generation delivered from Egypt, the covenant that the people broke, though Yahweh was their master. Added pronouns emphasize who was master and who did the breaking. In this future covenant Yahweh will put his law into the people's inward parts, inscribing it on their hearts. Then, once again, he will be God to them, and they will be a people to him. It will not be necessary for one to instruct the other to "know Yahweh," for everyone will know him, from the lowliest to the greatest. The most important feature of this new covenant is saved for last: Yahweh will forgive the people's iniquity and forget their sin. An extraordinary act of divine grace! No threat of punishment for violating the covenant; instead, a promise to forgive sins!

This new covenant was announced to a Judahite audience probably just prior to the destruction of Jerusalem, at which time Jeremiah was confined to the court of the guard. At this time Jeremiah also gave his prophecy on the eternal covenant (32:38–40). Seeds of both appear earlier in oracles spoken at the beginning of Zedekiah's reign (24:7). It is unlikely, however, that this prophecy was given originally to exiles of the Northern Kingdom in Josiah's reign (*pace* Rudolph; von Rad 1965: 212). More unlikely still is a date for the prophecy in the postexilic period (*pace* Duhm; Carroll).

Robert Bellah (1975: 139–51), writing in the early 1970s, had come to the conclusion that the covenant between God and the Puritan founders of America—which had much the character of the Deuteronomy covenant—was broken through and through. What was needed, in his view, was a reaffirming of this outward covenant and its remaking into an internal covenant, which America had done earlier in its religious and ethical revivals.

Martin Luther King Jr. during this same period in American history saw himself as being "the prophet like Moses," leading his people out of the Wilderness and showing them from a distance the Promised Land. In his "Moses on the Mountain" speech" given April 3, 1968, just prior to his death, King said:

> We've got some difficult days ahead. But it really doesn't matter with me now. Because I've been to the mountaintop. I won't mind. Like anybody, I would like to live a long life. Longevity has its place. But I'm not concerned about that now. I just want to do God's will. And he's allowed me to go up to the mountain. And I've looked over, and I've seen the Promised Land. I may not get there with you, but I want you to know tonight that we as a people will get to the Promised Land. So I'm happy tonight. I'm not worried about anything. I'm not fearing any man. "Mine eyes have seen the glory of the coming of the Lord."
>
> (M. L. King 1959: 63)

For other comparisons between Jeremiah and Martin Luther King Jr., see Drotts 1973.

EXCURSUS IV: THE NEW COVENANT IN THE LITERATURE OF JUDAISM, INCLUDING QUMRAN

In postexilic Judaism the covenant idea contains all the ambiguities chracterizing the larger eschatological hope generally. National life has been reconstructed along the old lines, which is to say, the Mosaic covenant is again central and the Law (Torah) occupies a position of supremacy. In Nehemiah 9–10 a "faith covenant" (ʾămānâ in 10:1[Eng 9:38]) is made to walk according to Yahweh's tôrâ given through Moses. Ezra prays that the people will thereby return to the "faithful heart" of Abraham (9:7–8). At the same time a new covenant is looked for in the future, at which time the Messianic Age will dawn. Baruch 2:35 speaks of an eternal covenant that will secure Israel's tenure in the land. In Jubilees, where the Law has eternal validity and the Messianic Age is thought to have already begun, an eternal covenant is described in which the people on their part will confess sin, and God on his part will create a holy spirit in the people and will cleanse them (Jub 1:22–24).

Among the Essenes at Qumran, the new covenant finds fulfillment in a separated community (*yḥd*) that believes it is living in the "last days." This community has important similarities to the early Church. Members of the Qumran community swore an oath to uphold a covenant variously described as a "covenant of God," an "eternal covenant," a "covenant of repentance," a "covenant of steadfast love" (*ḥsd*), and a "new covenant." Essene covenant theology is contained in two sectarian documents found among the Dead Sea Scrolls: the *Manual of Discipline* (1QS), and the *Damascus Document* (CD), which also goes by the name of the *Zadokite Document*. The latter was known before the Dead Sea discoveries, two fragmentary medieval codices having been found in the genizah of the Cairo Synagogue in 1896, which were published in 1910 (*APOT* II 785–834; Rabin 1958). The *Damascus Document* contains three references to a "new covenant" that people have entered into "in the land of Damascus," a cryptonym for their place of exile in the Qumran desert (cf. Amos 5:26–27). The "new covenant" references are CD 6:19; 8:21 = 19:33/34; and 20:12 in Rabin (also Gaster 1976), and 8:15; 9:28, 37 in *APOT* II. Seven MSS of the *Damascus Document* were found in Cave 4, some tiny fragments also in Caves 5 and 6 (Cross 1995: 72; *IDB Supp* 210). Also, in the *Pesher on Habakkuk* found at Qumran (1QpHab), there may originally have been a "new covenant" reference in 2:3; however, the MS has a lacuna where scholars think "covenant" once stood, leaving the reading uncertain and opinions about it divided.

The Essene Jews who separated themselves from the rest of Judaism and relocated in the Qumran desert did so in order to be reborn as the New Israel. According to Cross (1995: 71), the word "community" (*yḥd*) as used in the *Manual of Discipline* is eschatological—i.e., it means "Israel of the New Covenant." People entering this new covenant were required to return to a serious study of the Mosaic Law; required also of each member was strict obedience to the Law's demands as understood in light of interpretations given by the priestly hierarchy. At the top of this hierarchy was the Teacher of Righteousness, the original leader of the sect and also the author, perhaps, of the *Manual of Discipline*. The *Damascus Document* is from a later period, after the Teacher's death (Cross 1995: 96). The community bore an unmistakable stamp of legalism; nevertheless, that legalism was informed by the prophets, whose great legacy at Qumran was the conviction that sin lay deep within the human soul and only through repentance and purification was a restored relationship with God possible. The *Damascus Document* in 19:16 (*APOT* II 9.15B) called the Qumran covenant a "covenant of repentance" (*bryt hšwbh*). Repentance had to precede purification, which was accomplished in the initiatory baptismal rite (M. Black 1961: 94).

This new covenant was to be eternal. Whatever else this signified, it at least meant that anyone entering the covenant was expected to remain within it for life (1QS 3:11–12). The covenant was renewed annually, at which time all members underwent evaluation. This covenant had its obligations, and like the Mosaic covenant these obligations were fortified with blessings and curses

(1QS 2:1–18). The *Manual* reads much like Deuteronomy. The main difference between the two is that in the *Manual* the older corporate sense is gone;
the blessings and curses, for example, now fall upon individuals. The *Manual*
does not foresee any abrogation of the covenant as a whole, nor does it imagine
that noncompliance might lead to the whole community being destroyed. The
same can also be said of the Church (see Excursus V). On the other hand, the
individual responsibility presupposed in the *Manual* appears not to result from
any inner motivation, at least not of the sort that Jeremiah envisioned in his
new covenant prophecy. God is said to have placed a holy spirit in the people
of Qumran (1QS 3:7), but they still need admonitions to obey, as both the
Manual and the *Damascus Document* make clear.

The new covenant idea undergoes no further development in Judaism. The
Midrashim contain merely a few citations of Jer 31:33 for purposes of focusing
on the old problem of remembering the Torah. Midrash Song of Songs 8:14
interprets the phrase about God writing the Torah on the people's hearts to
mean that God recalls for the people what they themselves have forgotten and
what has led them into error. More often in the midrashic literature, the Jeremiah verse is given a meaning closer to the one it had originally: that forgetting the Torah can be expected in the Present World, and only in the World to
Come, when the Torah is (truly) written on the heart, will people no longer
forget it (Midrashim Ecclesiastes 2:1; Song of Songs 1:2; Pesiqta 107a; Yalqut
on Jer 31:33; cf. St.-B. 3: 89–90, 704). Medieval Jewish writers cited the Jer
31:31–34 passage largely to refute Christological interpretations, e.g., arguing
that the Mosaic Torah was not abrogated by Jesus and the Christian Gospel,
but that in the Messianic Age it will be renewed and internalized in a new
covenant lasting forever (Sarason 1988: 103–9). In the modern *Encyclopaedia
Judaica* (1971–73), there are no articles on "new covenant" or "eternal covenant," and in the article on "covenant" (M. Weinfeld), neither of these covenants is mentioned.

EXCURSUS V: THE NEW COVENANT IN THE NEW TES-
TAMENT AND PATRISTIC LITERATURE TO a.d. 325

A. New Testament

The Christian Church, from earliest times, claimed the promise of Jer 31:31–
34 and understood itself to be the people of the new covenant. It also thought
of itself as a new people (1 Pet 2:1–10): Israel reborn—but a more inclusive Israel to which Gentiles now belong. It comes as somewhat of a surprise then to
find so little said in the NT about a new covenant. G. E. Wright (1971: 986) attributes the paucity of references to legalistic connotations that the term "covenant" had in the NT period. He says that "covenant" had come to mean almost

exclusively obedience to the law; for this reason NT writers were uncomfortable with the term, using it only to point out that in Christ the covenant was not law but faith or life in the Spirit. NT rhetoric at this point contrasts sharply with Jewish rhetoric and Essene rhetoric as contained in the sectarian documents from Qumran, where the law is central.

The words "new covenant" are placed on the lips of Jesus only in the longer text of Luke 22:20, where, at the Last Supper, Jesus passes the wine and says, "This cup . . . is the new covenant in my blood." Scholarly opinion is divided about the originality of this reading, though the longer text does enjoy wide support (RSV and NEB omit; JB, NAB, and AB retain). This Lucan text, in any case, depends most likely upon 1 Cor 11:25 where Paul cites a Last Supper tradition antedating him, perhaps reflecting usage within the Antioch Church (J. Jeremias 1955: 127–31): "This cup is the new covenant in my blood." Mark 14:24 records Jesus' words as, "This is my blood of the covenant," a modification in the direction of Exod 24:8 (*TDNT* 2: 133; Richardson 1958: 230; cf. Heb 9:20). Matthew 26:28 adds "for the forgiveness of sins," which is new covenant language from Jer 31:34 (Dodd 1952: 45). In some ancient MSS both the Mark and Matthew texts have the word "new" added. Some form critics conclude that neither "new" nor "covenant" was spoken by Jesus (Bultmann 1951: 146; J. Jeremias 1955: 110–15), which is to say that the Last Supper liturgy was originally briefer and in the Synoptic passages has undergone expansion. But even in its most radical reconstruction the Last Supper liturgy clearly conveys the idea that Jesus' death, or his shedding of blood, seals the new covenant now made by God with humankind. Sacrificial terminology from Exod 24:3–8, almost entirely absent in the Prophets (but see Zech 9:11), has come to dominate the covenant idea, where it takes on fresh new meaning.

Paul refers to himself and the Corinthian laity as "ministers of a new covenant" (2 Cor 3:6), where Jer 31:31–34 appears to be in the back of his mind. This covenant has found expression in the *hearts* of the Corinthians, wherein the "Spirit of the living God" resides (vv 2–3). It therefore contrasts with the "old covenant" of Moses (vv 14–15), which was written on stone (v 3).

Paul might have said more about the new covenant were it not for his concern to establish a more ancient base than Jer 31:31–34 for the new faith in Christ. The important promise for Paul is the one given to Abraham, that through him all the families of the earth would be blessed. Paul grounds the blessings through Christ in the Abrahamic covenant so they may apply equally to Jews and Gentiles (Gal 3:14). Paul must short-circuit the Mosaic covenant if he is to realize his goal of evangelizing the Gentiles, for the Mosaic covenant was made only with Israel (cf. Rom 9:4; Eph 2:11–13). Moreover, the Mosaic covenant contains the law, which is now a burden to everybody—Jew and Gentile. In Paul's view the law only brings people under its curses. But Christ, by dying on the cross, becomes himself a curse redeeming those under the law who have faith in him (Gal 3:10–14). The new covenant, therefore, contains only blessings, making it just like the Abrahamic covenant. The Mosaic covenant serves Paul only for the purpose of making a contrast with the Abrahamic covenant. In his allegory in Gal 4:21–31, Paul sees the Abrahamic covenant (fulfilled through Sarah) leading to freedom, sonship, and the Jerusalem above; the covenant made at Sinai (called Hagar) leads to present Jerusalem — i.e., the Jews and Judaizers, and thus slavery.

As a Christian, Paul has a major problem knowing what to do with the law (Torah). The law is supposed to belong to the new covenant, but the coming of Christ has eclipsed the law. Paul resolves this problem to some extent by seeing a development in the covenants. Among the former covenants, the Abrahamic covenant is primary and is not annulled by the Mosaic covenant coming later (Gal 3:17). Paul exploits the dual meaning of *diathēkē* as "covenant" and "will" (or "testament") in Gal 3:15–18 in order to make this point. The Mosaic covenant when originally given was accompanied with great splendor, though it was a splendor that faded (cf. Exod 34:29–35); now there is no splendor at all associated with the Mosaic covenant because of the surpassing splendor of Christ, whose new covenant is eternal (2 Cor 3:7–11). Paul also sees a development in the covenants when he views the Mosaic law as a schoolmaster that must discipline a people not yet mature (Gal 3:23–24). With the coming of Christ, however, those having faith are no longer subject to their former schoolmaster (vv 25–26). In Romans, Paul says that Christians are discharged from the law (Rom 7:6), that Christ is the end of the law (10:4). Yet Paul does not want to dispense with the law; in fact, he calls it holy (7:12) and claims to uphold it (3:31). His other statements, however, distance him irrevocably from Judaism, for whom the law is central and eternally binding. For Paul, Christ is central, and the new covenant written by his life-giving Spirit surpasses all other covenants and is eternal.

Paul's law and grace dichotomy (Rom 6:14) stems from the lack of a typology in his thinking between the new covenant in Christ and the Mosaic covenant. Were such a typology made, Paul would have to concede that the Mosaic covenant/law had its own accompanying act of divine grace, which was the Exodus from Egypt.

Paul's views on sin and reconciliation in Romans lack covenant language per se; nevertheless, they rest almost certainly on broad-based assumptions about the new covenant existing in the early Church. According to Paul's gospel, both Jew and Gentile are under the power of sin, both stand in need of forgiveness, and both are reconciled to God by Jesus' death on the cross. In Ephesians too (whether or not it is Pauline), the blood of Christ is said to bring Gentiles near to God, even though formerly they were strangers to the covenants of promise (Eph 2:12–13).

In Rom 2:14–15, Paul seeks parity between Jew and Gentile by stating that upright Gentiles not possessing the Jewish law show, nevertheless, "that what the law requires is written on their hearts." Such people also possess a "conscience" (*syneidēsis*). The first remark about a law-equivalent "written on the heart" appears to be a borrowing from Jer 31:33 (cf. St.-B. 3: 89–90); the following remark about a "conscience that bears witness" derives most likely from Stoic or Jewish-Hellenistic philosophy. Paul's precise understanding of how the new covenant manifests itself among the Gentiles is by no means transparent in these verses, but one should note that his thinking nevertheless runs parallel to Jeremiah's new covenant passage, where the promise of a law written on the heart is followed by the promise of a new inner motivation to know and do the Law (Jer 31:34).

In Rom 11:25–32 the new covenant prophecy is given a most extraordinary interpretation, unlike any other in the NT and certainly unlike any made subsequently by the Church Fathers. Elsewhere the referent for the new covenant is the Church, which is the New Israel; here the referent is the Israel that remains hardened to the gospel (Dodd 1932: 182). Paul says that at some future time, when the full number of Gentiles has come in and the Parousia of Jesus occurs, *all* Israel will be saved. Isaiah 59:20 is quoted in support of the Parousia (Rom 11:26); next comes the new covenant prophecy: "And this will be my covenant with them, when I will take away their sins" (v 27). The OT passage or passages here quoted cannot be identified with certainty. The first part of v 27, "And this will be my covenant with them," is thought to be a continuation of the previous quotation of Isa 59:20 into v 21a. The second part of the verse, however, "when I will take away their sins," has to be from somewhere else. Some suggest that this phrase comes from Isa 27:9b, which in the LXX compares nicely, except for the singular "his sin." The plural "their sins" concludes the new covenant passage of Jeremiah (LXX 38:34), where also in v 33 the beginning words are "For this is the covenant." Paul could then be giving a freely rendered abridgment of Jer 31:33–34 (Dodd 1932: 182). An abridgment of this same Jeremiah passage is found in Heb 10:16–17. Regardless of what precise passages make up this florilegium, Paul gives the new covenant promise its most inclusive meaning possible: he believes this covenant really is for everyone. He concludes by saying, "For the gifts and the call of God are irrevocable" (Rom 11:29), by which he means not just the covenant promise to Abraham but also the new covenant promise. Both covenants are unconditional, eternal, and given for the salvation of all.

Paul's lack of a typology between the Mosaic covenant and the new covenant in Christ is compensated for, to some extent, by theology contained in the Gospels of Matthew and John. Indirectly, and in different ways, both gospel writers draw a parallel between Jesus and Moses. Matthew depicts Jesus as the "new Moses" leading a "new Exodus," the Sermon on the Mount being Jesus' "new Torah" (W. D. Davies 1969: 10–32). Although the new Torah is significantly less burdensome than the old (Matt 11:28–30), no antithesis is intended between the two; the new comes to complete the old (5:17). Matthew does, however, intend an antithesis between the new people of God and the old. Jesus pronounces his "blessings" on the new people (5:3–11), but on the old people he pronounces "woes" (23:13–36). These blessings and woes are structurally balanced in the Gospel, most likely an adaptation of the old treaty form found in Deuteronomy and elsewhere (Deut 11:26–32; 28). But the language is toned down. The words *makarioi* (blessed) and *ouai* (woe) translate the Hebrew *'ašrê* and *hôy*, both milder than the covenant words *bārûk* (blessed) and

ʾārûr (cursed). Jesus does not go so far as to curse the scribes and Pharisees. Also, with blessings and woes spoken to different audiences, the new people of God receive neither woes nor curses, only blessings. Matthew believes that there can be no abrogation of the new covenant and no destruction of the Church (cf. Matt 16:18).

John in a different way presents Jesus as the "new Moses" (Glasson 1963). But for this Gospel writer, Jesus gives no new Torah, unless one identifies such in the new commandment to "love one another" (John 13:34). Jesus himself is the Logos. John therefore makes a law/grace dichotomy similar to Paul's: "For the law was given through Moses; grace and truth came through Jesus Christ" (1:17). The Holy Spirit is John's answer to the new inner motivation required to know and do the Torah. He dwells within the believer (14:17) and in Jesus' absence will bring his teachings (Torah) to remembrance (14:26). He will also convince the rest of the world of sin, righteousness, and judgment (16:7–11).

In the letter to the Hebrews, the new covenant is given its most prominent place in the NT. The new covenant passage from Jeremiah is quoted twice, once in its entirety (Heb 8:8–12) and once in abridged form (10:16–17). For this NT writer, Christ is the great high priest of the heavenly sanctuary (7:26), one who "has obtained a ministry which is as much more excellent than the old as the covenant he mediates is better, since it is enacted on better promises" (8:6). The Mosaic covenant, here called the "first covenant," was shown to be faulty because people under it turned up faulty (8:7–8a; cf. Hals 1988: 91). Reference is presumably being made to the first covenant's provisions for noncompliance—i.e., the curses. The new covenant prophesied by Jeremiah has better promises: it contains an unconditional commitment by God to forgive sins; it is eternal (9:15; 13:20); and Jesus is the covenant's surety (7:22). According to Hebrews, Jeremiah in announcing this new covenant treats the Mosaic covenant as obsolete. That obsolescence is just now being seen as the first covenant is ready to vanish away (8:13).

Jesus is the "mediator of the new covenant" (Heb 9:15; "better covenant" in 8:6; "fresh covenant" in 12:24; cf. 1 Tim 2:5–6; Isa 42:6; 49:8). In Judaism the covenant mediator was Moses (cf. Gal 3:19), and after his death the high priest (Richardson 1958: 229). Jesus becomes mediator of the new covenant by virtue of his death on the cross, which the author of Hebrews explains in priestly and sacrificial categories understood within Judaism (9:1–14). Special appropriation is made of the Day of Atonement ritual (Leviticus 16). As the high priest who enters once and once only the Holy Place with his own sacrificial blood, Jesus secures for God's elect their eternal redemption (9:11–12, 24–28; cf. 7:27). This death purifies human consciences (9:14; 10:22; cf. Rom 2:15), something not possible with the earlier sacrifices (9:9).

The Holy Place—or Heavenly Sanctuary (9:24)—is for the elect also the Promised Land of rest and inheritance (4:9–11; 9:15). In raising the subject of inheritance, the author of Hebrews uses both meanings of diathēkē: "covenant" and "will" (9:15–22; cf. Gal 3:15–18). A will does not take effect until the death of the one who makes it—i.e., the testator. Jesus is therefore the testator of the new covenant. At his death the elect receive their inheritance, which is redemption from transgressions under the first covenant. The blood performs the same function of ratification in the new covenant as it did in the old (9:18–21; cf. Exod 24:6–8). The author echoes a common rabbinic theme when he says that without the shedding of blood there is no forgiveness of sins, or no atonement with God (9:22; cf. Lev 17:11).

In the abridged quotation from Jeremiah in Heb 10:16–17 the accent is on the concluding words of the new covenant promise—i.e., that God will no longer remember the peoples' sins. Earlier in chap. 10 the author maintained that yearly sacrifices on the Day of Atonement—as well as daily sin offerings—were ineffectual because they had to be repeated. Jewish teachers would find such an argument unconvincing; indeed it is flatly contradicted in *Jub* 5:17–18. Nevertheless, for the writer of Hebrews Jesus makes the single offering of his body, which for all time perfects the sanctified elect (10:10, 14). Once the forgiveness of sins is granted, there is no longer any sin offering that can be made (10:18, 26).

The "once for all" view of Jesus' sacrifice is matched in Hebrews with a "once for all" view of repentance, enlightenment (baptism), and sanctification of the believer. If one deliberately sins after coming to a knowledge of the truth, that person profanes the blood of the new covenant and has only God's vengeance to look forward to (10:26–31). This exaggerated view of Christian sanctification has the effect of recasting the new covenant in terms of the old, and it also qualifies the "blessings only" promise made to the Church. Although curses are not explicitly placed on individuals who lapse under the new covenant, they are implied (6:1–8; 10:26–31; cf. Gen 17:13–14). The idea that deliberate sin makes a sin offering inefficacious is found in Num 15:30–31 (Mishnah Yoma 8:9 applies the same principle to the Day of Atonement ritual). But in a closing benediction the author of Hebrews prays that the Lord Jesus, "by the blood of the eternal covenant," will equip the elect to do God's will (13:20–21).

B. Patristic Literature to A.D. 325

The Church of the second and third centuries carried on a polemic against two major opponents, one external to the Church, the other internal. The external opponent was the Jews, from whom an all-Gentile Church had now been completely cut off. The Fathers saw the Jews as a rejected people, one that the Church had supplanted in God's economy of salvation. In arguing against the Jews, they contrasted the new and old covenants, or the new and old "laws," if topics such as circumcision happened to be at issue (Tertullian, *adv. Jud.* 3). By the end of the second century, "New Testament" (= "New Covenant") was the name given to the Gospels and other apostolic writings that the Church took to be Scripture (Irenaeus, *haer.* iv 15.2). The Hebrew Scriptures were called the "Old Testament" (Melito of Sardis *frag.* 4; Irenaeus *haer.* iv 15.2), a designation found already in 2 Cor 3:14, where Paul alludes to the *reading* of the "Old Covenant" in the synagogue.

The internal threat to the Church was heresy, above all Gnosticism, which peaked in the mid–second century. The most serious aberration of Christian thought to have an impact on covenant understanding came from Marcion (A.D. 100–160), a Gnostic in the minds of some, but for others one who merely had affinities with Gnosticism. Marcion wanted to cut off Christianity from Judaism—completely and for all time. Against Marcion, and others such as Valentinus, who was a true Gnostic, the Fathers fought to preserve Christianity's Jewish roots, arguing that the God of the NT was not distinct from the God of the OT, that the Holy Spirit in the NT was the same Holy Spirit at work in the OT, and that NT Scripture itself was inextricably bound to OT Scripture—indeed, it was a fulfillment of it. Gnostics minimized the historical foundations of Christianity, being more concerned with creation than with covenant, which perhaps explains the noticeable absence of discussion about the covenant in Gnostic treatises, including the texts now available from Nag Hammadi. In a rare quotation of the words of Institution for the wine in *Pistis Sophia* (iv 141), the wine and/or blood—along with fire and water—are mysteries possessing the ability to purify from sin (C. Schmidt 1978: 366–69).

The Fathers explained the rejection of the Jews by citing the "calf incident" in the Wilderness, at which time the Mosaic covenant was promulgated (*Ep. Barn.* 4; 14; Irenaeus *haer.* iv 15.2; Tertullian, *adv. Jud.* 3; cf. Exodus 32). Origen (*contra Cels.* ii 74–75) typed the Jews on the basis of this incident; i.e., the incident explained how it happened that the Jews rejected Jesus.

The *Epistle of Barnabas* does not mention the new covenant but, rather, "the new law of our Lord Jesus Christ," which contrasts with the older law of sacrifice in that it is "without the yoke of necessity" (*Ep. Barn.* 2). The Christian has forgiveness from sins through Jesus' blood (chap. 5). For Barnabas there was only one covenant, received by Moses, but immediately lost due to the sin of the calf. In reality, Israel never had a covenant with God. Christians are heirs to this one covenant through Christ, in whom it is sealed upon their hearts. Barnabas thus argues that one covenant cannot belong to both Jews and Christians (*Ep. Barn.* 4; 13–14; cf. Bultmann 1951: 98, 110–11). Promises of a future covenant cited from the OT are Ezek 11:19; 36:26 (chap. 6); and Isa 42:6–7 (chap. 14).

Justin Martyr in his *Dialogue with Trypho the Jew* recognizes two laws or covenants (*dial.* 10–12, 67, 118, 122–23). The old through Moses has been abrogated and remains only for the Jews, although Justin asks rhetorically if even this is so, since the Jews do not believe their own Scriptures *dial.* 29). The new law and covenant through Christ in any case replaces the old; it does not require circumcision along with lesser observances, and it is final, eternal, and universal in scope (*dial.* 11). Jeremiah 31:31–32 and Isa 51:4–5 point to Christ as the new law and covenant, also to Christians, who are the true spiritual Israel (*dial.* 11; cf. 123). Isaiah 42:6–7 likewise points to Christ, and its promise of a covenant that will be a "light to the nations" finds fulfillment in illumined Gentiles, who under the new covenant are the true proselytes (*dial*. 122).

Irenaeus (*haer.* iv 15.1) says that when the Israelites made the calf they decided in favor of slavery. This did not cut them off from God, but it did subject them to a state of servitude for the future (cf. Gal 4:21–31). Stephen in Acts 7:38a–43a referred to the calf incident and God's decision to give up the Jews to slavery, and is cited (iv 15.1). The old covenant, under which the Jews lived until the coming of Christ, is law; the new covenant under which Christians live, promised in Jer 31:31–32 and Ezek 11:19; 36:26 (iv 33.14) and not fulfilled by Zerubbabel when Temple worship was restored after the Exile (iv 34.4), is gospel, or a "covenant of liberty" (iv 9.1–2; 16.5; 33.14; 34.3–4). It was fulfilled in Christ. Both old and new covenants were prefigured in Abraham (iv 25.1, 3). The older law predicted the new covenant, which in turn became a fulfillment of it (iv 34.2). The new covenant also canceled the old covenant (iv 16.5). Irenaeus reflects the typological thinking of Hebrews when he says the old covenant was a *type* of heavenly things—things now existing in the Church (iv 32.2). The Bishop of Lyons, however, was also capable of some process thinking. In his view, divine grace multiplies over time, and Christian living is a process of maturation. God's new covenant of liberty bestowed more grace than the old covenant of bondage. Then, as the Christian's love toward God increases, God bestows more and greater gifts (iv 9.2–3). Life under the new covenant also calls for greater faith, which means a higher quality of living (iv 16.5; 28:2). Since the new covenant grants real liberty, the Christian is more significantly tested in doing what God requires (iv 16.5).

Tertullian cites the new covenant promise of Jeremiah to show the Jews that circumcision is replaced by a new law unlike any previously given (*adv. Jud.* 3). The old law made customary the *lex talionis*; the new urges mercy and converts one to peace (cf. Iren., *haer.* iv 34.4 on the new covenant bringing peace). Gentiles are admitted under this new law. In fact, a curious reversal has taken place: the Jews, who were known by God and made the recipients of his many benefits, forgot him and turned to idolatry, i.e., the calf; the Gentiles originally did not know God; nevertheless, they forsook their idols and converted to him by accepting the new law in Christ. Jeremiah 31:31–32 is quoted against Marcionism to show that the old covenant was only temporary, since it needed changing. Isaiah 55:3 promises in addition that the old covenant will be replaced by an eternal covenant that will run its course in Christ (*adv. Marc.* iv 1; cf. Justin, *dial.* 12; 118 on the new covenant as an eternal covenant).

Clement of Alexandria, who was a Christian philosopher, saw in Jer 31:33–34 an indication that God had implanted his heavenly teaching, or laws, into human minds and hearts. These laws enable all people to know him and to be the recipients of his grace (*Protr.* 11 [PG 8: 233–34]). Clement says the old covenant disciplined people with fear, but in the new covenant fear is turned into love (*paed.* i 7; cf. Just., *dial.* 67, who says the new covenant no longer builds on "fear and trembling"). Clement does recognize that the law given through Moses was an ancient grace, but it was only temporary; eternal grace and truth came through Jesus Christ.

Origen (*contra Cels.* ii 74–75) says the Jews fashioned the calf because they did not believe the marvels of Egypt, the Sea, and the Wilderness. In keeping with their character of disbelief, they refused to accept the coming of Jesus and the "second covenant," which were equally marvelous. Christian preachers, says Origen, like the Apostles are to be "ministers of the new covenant" (2 Cor 3:6), i.e., messengers who ascend high mountains by preaching good news to the poor (*comm. Jo.* i 11; cf. Isa 52:6–7; 40:9). Paul was a "minister of the new covenant," distinguished not by voluminous writings but by the preaching done under the power of the Spirit (*comm. Jo.* v 3; cf. Rom 15:19). Origen therefore wonders if he himself will qualify as a "minister of the new covenant" with all the writing he is doing (*comm. Jo.* v 4).

Lactantius (*Div. Inst.* iv 20) reiterates themes developed by the earlier Fathers. Jeremiah 31:31–32 shows that Jews are disinherited and that Christians, thanks to the death of Jesus, are now heirs to the Kingdom. The "house of Judah" in v 31 refers to those called out from among the Gentiles. There are two testaments: the old, which is used by the Jews, and the new, which is used by Christians. The new fulfills the old and is more complete than the old. As a result of being adopted under the new covenant, the Gentiles are freed from their chains and brought into the light of wisdom (Isa 42:6–7).

Against Marcion and others, the Fathers argued that although there were two covenants (and two peoples), there was but one God (Irenaeus, *haer.* iv 9, 15, 32–33; Tertullian, *adv. Marc.* i 20; iv 1; Origen, *comm. Jo.* i 14). Clement of Alexandria argued against the Valentinians that the Holy Spirit operating in the Church was the same Holy Spirit that operated in the OT (*exc. Thdot.* 24 [*PG* 9: 671–72]). Irenaeus saw in both Testaments the same righteousness of God when God takes vengeance, although he believed that in the NT vengeance was more real, more enduring, and more rigid (*haer.* iv 28.1).

The Marcionite heresy required also from the Fathers a defense of the unity of Scripture. Origen did this with eloquence. He said that all the sacred writings were in fact one book (*comm. Jo.* v 4; *comm. Mt.* ii 15), "one perfect and harmonized instrument of God" (*comm. Mt.* ii 1). The OT was the beginning of the gospel of Jesus Christ; from another point of view, John the Baptist was a *type* of OT (*comm. Jo.* i 14–15). If Origen was the most eloquent in defending the unity of Scripture, Tertullian was the most open in acknowledging Scripture's diversity, but he said that amidst all the diversity, there was still no inconsistency with one and the same God (*adv. Marc.* iv 1).

d) Ongoing Creation, Ongoing Covenant (31:35–37)

31 [35]Thus said Yahweh
   who gives the sun for light by day
statutes of the moon and stars
   for light by night

who stirs up the sea so its waves roar
  Yahweh of hosts is his name:

³⁶If these statutes depart
  from before me—oracle of Yahweh
Then the seed of Israel shall cease
  from being a nation before me—all the days.

³⁷Thus said Yahweh:
If the heavens above can be measured
  and the foundations of the earth explored to the depths
Then I, I will reject all the seed of Israel
  because of all that they have done
    —oracle of Yahweh.

RHETORIC AND COMPOSITION

MT 31:35–37 = LXX 38:35–37. The present verses contain two oracles (vv 35–36; v 37), the first preceded by an expanded messenger formula that doubles as a hymnic introduction (v 35). This division is confirmed by section markings, which delimit the unit at the top by a *setumah* in M^L and a *petuḥah* in M^P before v 35 and at the bottom by a *setumah* in M^A, M^L, and M^P after v 37. The medieval codices also divide after v 36, where M^A and M^L have a *setumah*, and M^P has a *petuḥah*.

The unit also appears to be delimited within its context by being poetry, although this judgment is not unanimous. Some commentators (Condamin; Volz; Rudolph; Weiser; Bright; Thompson) and most of the modern Versions take all three verses as poetry, but McKane and Keown et al. follow the REB and take only v 35 as poetry; vv 36–37 are taken as prose. The NEB took v 36 as poetry, and vv 35 and 37 as prose. The NJV takes vv 35–36 as poetry and v 37 as prose. Holladay judges all three verses to be postexilic prose. Those taking v 37 as prose may be influenced by the prose particle *ʾăšer* ("that") in that verse.

Older commentators (Hitzig; Giesebrecht; Peake; Duhm; Cornill; Hyatt; and others) denied these verses to Jeremiah, assigning them to a postexilic author. The reasons: 1) similarity in style and thought to Second Isaiah; 2) restoration preaching, here said to be a strident "nationalism" unlikely to emanate from Jeremiah; and 3) a less-elevated prophecy coming after the "new covenant" oracle, which was viewed as anticlimactic. Added to these were lesser arguments about the verses being un-metrical, and v 37 being perhaps a marginal gloss since in the LXX it comes before v 35. None of the arguments carries much weight. Similarities to Second Isaiah boil down to one verse, Isa 51:15, about which influence can be argued either way. Rudolph thinks that Isa 51:15 imitates Jeremiah. Alleged "creation" parallels to Second Isaiah (Isa 40:12, 26; 42:5; 44:24; 45:7, 18) are also indecisive (so Peake), since material of the same sort is found in Jeremiah (5:22; 10:12–16 [= 51:15–19]). The argument about "nationalism" in the passage, whether or not it discredits Jeremiah, is the weakest of all. The passage is not about nationalism but about the status of Yahweh's covenant with Israel, which is on another level entirely. Many, therefore, have discounted the arguments for anonymity and a late date and attributed the verses to Jeremiah (Volz; Rudolph; Weiser; Boadt) or at least see no reason why the verses cannot be attributed to the prophet (Streane; Bright; Thompson; Jones).

The unusual combining of a "thus said Yahweh" oracle formula with a confessional "Yahweh of hosts is his name" in v 35 can be explained as resulting from the entire verse being an expanded oracle formula, of which there are any number in the book of Jeremiah (11:21; 12:14; 14:15; 22:11; 23:2; 27:19–21; 29:16, 21, 31; 32:36; 42:9). But this one is different; the only other one like it occurs in 33:2, which reads:

> Thus said Yahweh who made it
> Yahweh who formed it to establish it
> Yahweh is his name!

Both formulas may be hymnic fragments (Weiser), where the repeated divine name makes an inclusio.

The two oracles then have double formulas, such as we have in the prior oracles of vv 31–34:

I	*Thus said Yahweh . . . Yahweh of hosts is his name:*	v 35
	. . . oracle of Yahweh . . .	v 36

II	*Thus said Yahweh:*	v 37
	. . . oracle of Yahweh	

The LXX omits "thus said Yahweh" in v 37 but adds an "oracle of Yahweh" after the first colon in the verse, thus retaining a double formula. The LXX reordering, where v 37 is placed before vv 35–36, matters little since both oracles are kept intact, simply put in reverse order. Becking (1994a: 165–67) sees in the LXX ordering a concentric symmetry whereby the hymnic fragment is placed in the center, but he agrees that one cannot decide here which text is more authentic.

The two oracles are bound together by an array of repetitions and balancing key words (cf. Lundbom 1975: 58–59 [= 1997: 79–80]):

I	. . . . *for light by day*	. . . *lĕʾôr yômām*	v 35
	statutes	*ḥuqqōt*	
	for light by night	*lĕʾôr lāyĕlâ*	
	If these statutes	*ʾim . . . haḥuqqîm hāʾēlleh*	v 36
	from before me	*millĕpānay . . .*	

| Then the seed of Israel . . . . | gam zeraʿ yiśrāʾēl . . . | |
| from . . . before me—all the days | mi . . . lĕpānay kol-hayyāmîm | |

II	If the heavens	ʾim . . . šāmayim	v 37
	. . . . . the earth	. . . ʾereṣ	
	Then . . . all the seed of Israel . . .	gam . . . kol-zeraʿ yiśrāʾēl	
	. . . . . all	. . . kol . . .	

The feminine and masculine terms for "statutes," ḥuqqōt and ḥuqqîm, link Oracle I to its introduction. The use of masculine and feminine forms of the same noun results in a *merismus*, indicating totality. For another *merismus* using the same Hebrew word, see Psalm 119, where the feminine plural in v 16 balances off the masculine plurals used throughout the rest of the psalm (D. N. Freedman). The word "seed" (*zeraʿ*) links Oracles I and II. "Seed" is also a catchword back to v 27, balancing the present oracles and the oracles in vv 27–30 in a chiastic structure within the first Book of Restoration (see Rhetoric and Composition for 31:23–26).

Catchwords connecting to the final oracle:

v 37 *be measured*   *yimmaddû*   v 39 *measuring*   *hammiddâ*

NOTES

31:35. *who gives the sun for light by day.* Yahweh is the God of Creation, the one who placed (*ntn*) the sun in the heavens to give light upon the earth (Gen 1:14–18). In Gen 1:17 the verb *ntn* is also used (Thompson; H. Weippert 1981: 38). Compare Pss 19:2–7[Eng 19:1–6]; 136:8.

statutes of the moon and stars for light by night. Continuing Yahweh's work of placing night lights in the heavens, acknowledged here as one of Yahweh's statutes within the created order (cf. 5:24; 33:20, 25), for which praise is due (cf. Ps 136:9). With a mention of "statutes" (*ḥuqqōt*), the emphasis is not on creation as such, but on Yahweh's orderly regulation of the universe. The term "statutes" is lacking in one Hebrew MS and in the LXX. Some delete *metri causa* (Giesebrecht; Duhm; Cornill; Bright; Janzen 1973: 49; Holladay; McKane; cf. NEB [but changed in REB]); others emend to the participle *ḥōqēq*, "who decrees" (Volz; Rudolph; Keown et al.), which then balances *nōtēn*, "who gives," in the prior colon. The latter adjustment does not improve the sense, since according to Gen 1:16–17 Yahweh "makes" (*ʿśh*) the moon and stars and "places" (*ntn*) them in the heavens; he does not "decree" them. And deletion *metri causa* is a dubious solution. "Statutes" is well represented in the Vrs (Aq, G^L, S, T, Vg) and recurs in a similar context in 33:25. Here the term is a link to *haḥuqqîm hāʾēlleh* ("these statutes") in the oracle (see Rhetoric and Composition) and should be retained.

who stirs up the sea so its waves roar, Yahweh of hosts is his name. The line recurs in a divine self-asseveration in Isa 51:15, where "Yahweh of hosts is his name" is said by some to be a later addition (Levin 1985: 199). The verb *rgʿ* here and in Isa 51:15 means "stir up, disturb" (Rashi; cf. LXX in Isa 51:5: *ho tarassōn tēn thalassan*, "the one who stirs up the sea"; here in Jer 31:35: *kai kraugēn en thalassē*, "and a roaring in the sea"), a meaning it may also have in Job 26:12 (but there the RSV translates another root meaning "to still, bring to rest"; BDB *rgʿ* II). In the present verse this latter meaning is found in T ("rebuking the sea") and Aq (*katastellei tēn thalassan*, "he keeps down the sea"). The verb *hmh* ("to roar, moan") occurs often in Jeremiah, referring to a low-pitched moan (4:19; 31:20; 48:36) or the roar of the sea (5:22; 6:23; 31:35; 50:42; 51:55). The imperfect verb with *waw consecutive* after a participle yields a frequentative (iterative) present—i.e., a calm sea being periodically disturbed by roaring waves (GKC §111u; cf. Ps 107:25). Kimḥi and other Jewish interpreters see an allusion here to Yahweh's deliverance at the Sea of Reeds (Job 26:12), but this was probably not in the prophet's mind (Calvin).

the sea. Hebrew *hayyām*. There may be a wordplay here with *yômām* ("by day") in v 35a.

Yahweh of hosts is his name. The LXX translates *ṣĕbāʾôt* ("of hosts") with *pantokratōr*, as it does occasionally (see Appendix VI). On this climactic doxology, see Note for 10:16.

36. *If these statutes depart from before me . . . Then the seed of Israel shall cease from being a nation before me—all the days.* A protasis-apodosis argument, on which see Note for 4:1–2. The hymnic introduction has announced Yahweh as the God of Creation, whose fixed statutes control movements of the sun, moon, and stars in the heavens. See Psalm 93. Yahweh now says that if these fixed statutes depart (*yāmūšû*) from before him, then the seed of Israel shall cease (*yišbĕtû*) from being a nation before him. Since the former will not happen, neither will the latter. The mention of Israel's "seed" (*zeraʿ*) in connection with the stars calls to mind Yahweh's covenant with Abraham (Gen 15:5; 22:17; 26:4), which is doubtless being reaffirmed here (Jones; Huffmon 1999: 175). Huffmon points out that the protasis-apodosis arguments in these verses have only three close biblical parallels: Gen 13:16 (the promise to Abraham and his seed); Jer 33:20–21; and 33:25–26 (mention again of Abraham, Isaac, and Jacob's seed). The Abrahamic covenant is eternal and cannot be broken (Gen 17:13–14; Judg 2:1; Lev 26:44–45) as could the Mosaic covenant (v 32). It therefore preserves Israel until the new covenant takes effect. One may see also in this oracle an allusion to God's covenant with Noah in Gen 9:8–17 (Weiser), which follows a promise that "day and night shall not cease (*lōʾ yišbōtû*)" (8:22). See also 33:20 and 25. But the Noachian covenant is more inclusive, seeing that it is made with the "seed" of every living creature on earth. On Jeremiah and natural law, see 5:22; 8:7; and 18:14.

all the days. Hebrew *kol-hayyāmîm*. For this expression, see also 32:39; 33:18; and 35:19.

37. *Thus said Yahweh.* The LXX omits, but the formula is present in Aq, Symm, T, and Vg.

If the heavens above can be measured, and the foundations of the earth explored to the depths, then I, I will reject all the seed of Israel. Another protasis-apodosis form stating two impossibilities: the creation being scoped out, and Yahweh rejecting all of Israel's seed. The LXX adds a negative ("I shall *not* reject the seed of Israel"), which arrives at the right conclusion but destroys the argument. Job could only repent in dust and ashes after God put to him the big questions about the vastness and mystery of his creation (Job 38–39), asking where he was when the foundations of the earth were laid, and who determined their measurements (38:4–5). Job, in spite of his wisdom, knows nothing about the secrets of the heavens and the deep (Job 11:7–9; cf. Isa 40:12–31; Ps 8:4–5[Eng 8:3–4]). Only from Enoch do we later get answers (*1 Enoch*). The LXX reading of the present verse, "If the heaven was raised into the heights . . . and if the base of the earth was lowered down" (*ean hypsōthē ho ouranos eis to meteōron . . . kai ean tapeinōthē to edaphos tēs gēs katō*), makes little sense and is widely dismissed by commentators. The LXX's *hypsōthē* ("is raised") in place of MT's *yimmaddû* ("be measured") can be explained as a rendering of *yrmw* in its Hebrew *Vorlage*, instead of *ymdw* (*BHS*). The translation of Aq supports MT: *ei metrēthēsontai hoi ouranoi anōthen, kai exichniasthēsontai ta themelia tēs gēs katō* ("If the heavens above will be measured, and the foundations of the earth below be tracked out").

all the seed of Israel. Hebrew *kol-zeraʿ yiśrāʾēl*. The LXX omits "all," which should be retained (*pace* Volz; Holladay); it balances "all" in the next colon, and more important it implies a remnant theology (Calvin; cf. Isa 10:22; Rom 9:27). Much of Israel's seed was destroyed, but not all, and from what remains Yahweh will honor his covenant to preserve Israel. Once again, the covenant here is with Abraham, which is the covenant picked up by Paul in the NT (Rom 11:1, 28–29).

because of all that they have done. I.e., all the sin they have committed (T; Calvin; cf. 7:13), which would be reason enough for rejection.

MESSAGE AND AUDIENCE

Jeremiah in introducing the first oracle reminds his audience that the one now speaking has put the sun, moon, and stars in the heavens and that their regulated movements light both day and night. He is also the one who raises a tumult in the sea with great waves. Yahweh of hosts is his name! In the oracle Yahweh says that if these statutes governing the heavenly bodies depart from before him, then will Israel's seed (continuing as a nation) cease from before him. Forever. The audience can decide for itself whether either might happen. A second oracle argues similarly. If the heavens and the foundations of the deep can be examined by anyone, then will Yahweh reject Israel's seed because of what the covenant people have done. The issue of sin is raised but not directly. Some in the audience will know what they and others have done and will probably know too that there is reason enough for Yahweh's rejection. But since conditions for rejection cannot be met, there is more reason for hope.

For audiences hearing the present oracles after the oracles on the new covenant, Yahweh's continued care over Israel will be assured. The Mosaic covenant was broken, and the new covenant must await a fulfillment in the future. What sustains Israel until the new covenant is realized? Answer: the covenant made with Abraham, which is eternal and cannot be broken.

These oracles probably postdate the new covenant oracles, which would put them after the fall of Jerusalem. There is no reason to assign them a postexilic date, although it goes without saying that the postexilic community will be sustained by them, just as survivors of the 586 B.C. disaster were.

e) Rebuilt City, Reconsecrated Valley (31:38–40)

31 [38]Look, days are coming[a]—oracle of Yahweh—when the city shall be rebuilt for Yahweh from the Tower of Hananel to the Corner Gate. [39]And the measuring line shall go out again, straight over Gareb Hill and turn to Goah. [40]And all the valley land, the corpses and the ashes, and all the terraces[b] up to the Brook Kidron, up to the corner of the Horse Gate toward the east, shall be holy for Yahweh. It shall not be uprooted, and it shall not again be overthrown—forever.

RHETORIC AND COMPOSITION

MT 31:38–40 = LXX 38:38–40. This concluding oracle in the first Book of Restoration is delimited at the top by a *setumah* in M^A, M^L, and M^P before v 38. Delimitation at the bottom is by a *setumah* in M^L and M^P and a *petuḥah* in M^A after v 40, which is also the chapter division.

Commentators generally deny this oracle to Jeremiah, dating it in the postexilic period where it is said to support Nehemiah's rebuilding program and parallel the topographical survey of Zech 14:10. This precludes it from being a prediction, despite the "look, days are coming" introduction. McKane, who thinks a Jerusalem rebuilding program is already in progress, views the prediction as contrived. Since the city to be rebuilt is Jerusalem, Volz and Rudolph also date the passage late; for them it stands apart from the genuine "Ephraim" prophecies within chaps. 30–31. The consensus then regarding this oracle is much the same as with Yahweh's promise of Jerusalem's restoration in 31:23–26. Here the expression "holy for Yahweh" is also said to breathe a priestly spirit foreign to Jeremiah (Weiser).

Another argument heard in support of a late date, which applies also to the oracles in vv 35–37, is that an oracle on rebuilding Jerusalem comes as an anticlimax after the "new covenant" promise of vv 31–34 (Peake; Hyatt). McKane says it is unskillfully "tagged on." Yet how could anything coming after the new covenant oracles help but be anticlimactic? More important, statements such

---

[a]Insert *bā'îm* ("are coming"), with Q; omission due to haplography (see Notes).

[b]Reading the Q *šĕdēmôt*, "terraces"; Kt *šĕrēmôt* is of unknown meaning (see Notes).

as these misunderstand the nature of Hebrew composition, assuming as they do that bona fide compilations must always have their climax at the end. This sometimes happens, as, for example, when the Book of Restoration was expanded to include 31:23–34 and the new covenant oracles were put last. But when the oracles in 31:35–40 were added, the new covenant oracles found themselves in the center of the expansion; nevertheless, in this position too they were climactic, since they came at the midpoint of a chiastic structure in which the climax is not at the end but at the center (see Rhetoric and Composition for 31:23–26). The present oracle then simply balances off the oracle beginning the expansion (31:23–26), the two promising a rebuilding and reconsecration of Jerusalem.

Bright thinks that Jeremiah could well have spoken the sentiments expressed in these verses, and I would agree (cf. 30:18). The oracle postdates—not predates (*pace* Calvin)—the fall of Jerusalem, and with the city now a heap of rubble, its terraces destroyed and its valleys more a dumping ground than ever, the promise of a rebuilt and reconsecrated Jerusalem comes as a radical word from Yahweh and more daring preaching on the part of Jeremiah. Everyone, surely, has concluded by now that this was the end of things. In this prophecy, then, Jeremiah shows himself once again to be out ahead of the people in hearing the divine word, speaking words they can scarcely believe, and being the prophet of reversals that he has always been. This prophecy may not kindle the imagination as the new covenant prophecy does, but it is powerful and eminently worthy of a prophet like Jeremiah.

The main point of this oracle is that lofty Jerusalem, together with its terraces and surrounding valleys, shall be rebuilt and reconsecrated "for Yahweh." The key word is *lyhwh*, which occurs at the beginning of the oracle and is repeated at the end (Cheyne; Cornill):

. . . the city shall be rebuilt *for Yahweh*	*lyhwh*	v 38
. . . the valley . . . and the terraces . . . shall be holy *for Yahweh*	*lyhwh*	v 40

The word *qōdeš* ("holy") links this oracle with the oracle in vv 23–26 (see Rhetoric and Composition for 31:23–26).

Catchwords connecting to the previous oracles:

v 39 *measuring*	*hammiddâ*	v 37 *be measured*	*yimmaddû*

NOTES

31:38. *Look, days are coming.* On this phrase, see Note for 7:32. The MT omission of *bā'îm* ("are coming"), which is remedied by a Q reading, is generally attributed to haplography (homoeoteleuton: *ym . . . ym*). Many MSS and the Vrs have the word. *BHS* has the haplography wrong, connecting the omitted word with *n'm* instead of with the preceding *ymym*. If there was a skipping of the eye to *n'm* , the omitted word would have to begin with *nun*, not *beth*, and the haplography would be homoeoarcton, not homoeoteleuton.

the city shall be rebuilt for Yahweh from the Tower of Hananel to the Corner Gate. The city is Jerusalem (T; Kimḥi), and the verb *bnh* in this case means "rebuild" (cf. Josh 6:26; Amos 9:14; Ezek 36:36). Jerusalem will be rebuilt, not for Israel, but for Yahweh. What follows is a walking tour of the city's boundaries before its destruction, beginning in the northeast quadrant and proceeding in counterclockwise fashion until it ends up near where it began. Kimḥi thinks the description is of a Jerusalem larger than before, but this is probably not the case.

The Tower of Hananel was located at the northwest corner of the Temple complex, not far from the Fish Gate (Weiser; Simons 1952: 231; Bahat and Rubinstein 1990: 30–31; cf. Neh 12:39). The citadel of 1 Macc 13:52, also the Antonia Fortress of Herod (Josephus, *Wars* v 238–47), may correspond to this tower or at least mark the spot where it stood (Vincent 1934–35: v; Benoit 1975; Bahat and Rubenstein 1990: 47, 55). The Corner Gate was Jerusalem's westernmost boundary, situated approximately where the present Jaffa Gate is located. It was 400 cubits (180+ meters) west of the Ephraim Gate (Vincent 1934–35: vi; Mazar, *EncMiqr* 3: 818; cf. 2 Kgs 14:13; 2 Chr 25:23), known also as the Benjamin Gate (Press 1953: 127; see Note for 37:13), through which Jeremiah tried to exit the city on his way to Anathoth when the Babylonian siege was lifted. According to 2 Chr 26:9, King Uzziah provided the Corner Gate with a watchtower. This gate, referred to also in Zech 14:10, may mark the spot of the later Hippicus Tower (T: "tower of Piqqus"; present-day "David's Tower"), which is mentioned often by Josephus in his description of Jerusalem's walls (*Wars* ii 439; v 144–47, 161–65; cf. Simons 1952: 234).

The location of the Corner Gate near the present Jaffa Gate assumes an eighth-century B.C. city expansion and settlement on the Western Hill, which was argued by some scholars already in the mid–twentieth century (Simons 1952: 226–81), and now appears certain in light of Avigad's 1968–71 excavations. These excavations uncovered not only a section of the so-called "Broad Wall" but numerous artifacts dating from the eighth and seventh centuries (Avigad 1970a; 1970b; 1972; 1975; 1983: 23–60; Geva 1979). Other excavations in the Armenian Garden (on the Ben-Hinnom Valley ridge) also confirm a late-eighth or early-seventh-century settlement on the Western Hill, which ended with the Babylonian destruction of the city (Gibson 1987). The description of the Potsherd Gate at the edge of the Ben-Hinnom Valley in Jer 19:2 makes it clear that Jerusalem's city wall had a gate on the Southwestern Hill (Simons 1952: 230). Other predictions of Jerusalem's rebuilding are found in 3:17; 30:18; 33:4–9; cf. Ezekiel 40–43. Topographical and structural details of preexilic Jerusalem are fully discussed in M. Burrows, "Jerusalem," *IDB* E–J, 843–66 (see p. 853 for the city plan). Other city plans are contained in Bahat and Rubinstein 1990: 30–31. For surveys of recent archaeological work in Jerusalem, including tomb discoveries in the Ben-Hinnom and Kidron Valleys, see Mazar et al., "Jerusalem: Early Periods and the First Temple Period," *NEAEHL* 2: 698–716; also Avigad and Geva, "Jerusalem: The Second Temple Period," *NEAEHL* 2: 717–57.

to the Corner Gate. Hebrew *ša'ar happinnâ*. The expression without *'ad* is elliptical (cf. v 40), although a preposition is supplied in LXX (*heōs*), S, T, and Vg. For other examples of this type of ellipsis in Jeremiah prose, see Note on 24:1. It is possible that the final *hē'* could double here as a *hē' locale* (G. R. Driver 1937–38: 120; note the *hē' locale* on *gō'ātâ*, "to Goah," in v 39), or one could suppose with Rudolph that a prefixed *lamed* was lost by haplography (double *lamed* in succession).

39. *And the measuring line shall go out again, straight over Gareb Hill and turn to Goah*. At the Corner Gate the measuring line turns south to follow Jerusalem's western boundary (the "Broad Wall") bordering on the Ben-Hinnom Valley. The locations of Gareb Hill and Goah are not known. It is generally agreed, however, that Gareb Hill must be at the southwestern corner of the city, where it is either a portion of the Southwestern Hill, or the hill itself (Duhm; Simons 1952: 232). "Gareb Hill," which may mean "Leper's Hill" (Hitzig; Cheyne; cf. KB[3] *gārāb*, "leprosy"), has also been identified with the hill above the Ben-Hinnom cited in the boundary listings of Josh 15:8 and 18:16, or else the hill called "Bezetha" cited by Josephus (*Wars* v 149). Goah would then be somewhere on the southern boundary, along the east–west course of the Ben-Hinnom. Barkay and Kloner (1986: 39) put Gareb Hill and Goah north of the present-day Damascus Gate (where the burial chambers of St. Étienne Monastery are located), but this is the wrong direction entirely, regardless of whether the rebuilt city is believed to be larger or more expansive than the city that was destroyed.

the measuring line. The Kt, *qĕwēh*, is a by-form construct of the Q, *qāw* (cf. 1 Kgs 7:23; Zech 1:16). The LXX translation (*hē diametrēsis autēs*, "her measuring line") misreads the final *hē'* as a *hē' mappiq* (Becking 1994a: 152). For other surveys of rebuilt Jerusalem using a measuring line, see Ezekiel 40–48 and Zech 2:5–9[Eng 2:1–5]. The eschatological vision of the New Jerusalem in Revelation 21–22 also contains measurements for the city, its gates, and its walls (21:15).

straight. Or "straightforward." Hebrew *negdô* is lit., "in front of itself," in which the third-person suffix used together with a verb of motion becomes a reflexive (BDB, 617; cf. Josh 6:5, 20; Amos 4:3; Neh 12:37). Calvin translates "before him," thinking that the measuring line goes forth in the presence of Yahweh. The LXX reading, *apenanti autōn*, "opposite them," has the line going forward in a direction opposite the Tower of Hananel and the Corner Gate. It is unnecessary to emend with Giesebrecht, McKane, and others to *negbâ*, "southward," even though the line is going south.

over Gareb Hill. Hebrew *'al gib'at gārēb*. Giesebrecht and Cornill want to read *'ad* ("up to") for *'al* ("over"), with some MSS, the LXX, G[L], and T. This reading is possible, but S and Vg (*super*) read "over Gareb Hill," which is better.

and turn to Goah. Hebrew *wĕnāsab gō'ātâ*. The LXX omits, which can be attributed to haplography (homoeoarcton: *w . . . w*). Other Versions did not understand "Goah." The T has "calf pool," and Aq simply transliterates with *gaatha.* The LXX, perhaps to fill a lacuna in its *Vorlage,* adds a city detail about which no one would argue, *kai perikuklōthēsetai kuklō ex eklektōn li-thōn,* "and it shall be enclosed with a circle of choice stones," but where it gets this supplement one cannot say. Snaith (1945: 32) suggests Rev 21:19–20.

40. *And all the valley land, the corpses and the ashes, and all the terraces up to the Brook Kidron, up to the corner of the Horse Gate toward the east, shall be holy for Yahweh.* Both valleys, the Ben-Hinnom and the Kidron, also the terraces above them on the city slopes, shall be holy for Yahweh, just as the city itself shall be (v 23). "All the valley land" refers not just to the Ben-Hinnom (*pace* Giesebrecht; Cornill; Rudolph; Weiser) but to both valleys. The word translated "valley land" is *'ēmeq,* not *gê',* as used in "Valley of Ben-Hinnom" (7:31–32). The term "Kidron Valley" does not occur in the OT, only *naḥal qidrôn* ("Brook Kidron") and in 2 Kgs 23:4, *šadmôt qidrôn* ("terraces of the Kidron"). Neither valley is here named; *'ēmeq* simply balances *šĕdēmôt* ("terraces"), the two areas outside and below the city wall needing reconsecration. The Ben Hinnom has suffered defilement on account of the Topheth (19:13; 2 Kgs 23:10), which is where child sacrifices to Molek occurred (2:23; 19:4–5; 32:35). The Kidron had been a dumping area for fat-soaked Temple ashes (Lev 1:16; 4:12; cf. Milgrom 1991: 240; Theod: *tēn spodian,* "the ashes") and destroyed cult images; it was also a burial place for the common people (1 Kgs 15:13; 2 Kgs 23:4, 6, 12). Milgrom says that sectaries at Qumran required that the ash dump lie not simply outside the Temple (Ezek 43:21) but outside the confines of Jerusalem. A large ash dump from later times has been found north of the present-day old city (near the former Mandelbaum Gate), which puts it beyond the Herodian "third wall." This dump contained the remains of animal flesh, bones, and teeth. Also, with the Babylonian slaughter of Jerusalem's population having just recently occurred, the Ben-Hinnom suffered a further indignity by being heaped with corpses (cf. 7:32; 19:6, 11). The T recalls that the valleys around Jerusalem were filled earlier with the bodies of Sennacherib's army, which is mentioned in this connection by both Rashi and Calvin (cf. 2 Kgs 19:35). Burials of a more dignified nature (some as early as the seventh and sixth centuries B.C., and some from the first century A.D. and later) have been found in the Kidron and Ben-Hinnom Valleys, most recently on the eastern slope below Mount Zion and on the Western Hill below the Scottish Church (Galling 1936, with map; Kloner 1982–83: 37–38; Barkay 1986, with pictures of finds; *NEAEHL* 2: 706–7, with map). A modern graveyard exists in the terraced area above the Kidron outside the old city wall and another on the southwestern hill above the Ben-Hinnon, where a number of well-known people are buried.

And all the valley land, the corpses and the ashes. Hebrew *wĕkol-hā'ēmeq happĕgārîm wĕhaddešen.* The LXX omission, as Barthélemy (1986: 692) has noted, is doubtless another loss due to haplography (whole-word plus: *wkl-h . . . wkl-h*). These words, or just "the corpses and the ashes," should therefore not be deleted (*pace* Duhm; Volz; Weiser; Bright; Holladay; McKane; NEB;

REB). Giesebrecht translates the MT, noting that the words are well attested in the Vrs (Aq, Symm, Theod, G^L, T, S, and Vg). The article on "the valley land" (*hā'ēmeq*) requires that "the corpses and the ashes" be terms of apposition (not part of a construct chain; *pace* AV; RSV; NRSV; NAB; NJV). They specify what has defiled the valleys in days past and also more recently.

and all the terraces. Sense can only be made of the Q, *haššĕdēmôt* ("the terraces"); the Kt *haššĕrēmôt* appears simply to be a scribal error, writing *r* for *d* (LXX transliterates Kt as a proper noun). Aquila translates *kai panta ta proasteia* ("and all the environs"), and Symm *kai sumpan kata ton chōron tōn taphōn* ("and all throughout the place of burial"). The Vg supports Symm with *regionem mortis* ("area of death"), dividing the Heb into two words: *śĕdēh māwet*, the first apparently being the common *śādeh* ("field") with a *śin*, not a *šin*. In any case, what are being referred to are the terraced fields on the slopes of Jerusalem, above the Ben-Hinnom and Kidron Valleys. The question is whether they were used for agriculture or burials, or for both. Lehmann (1953) accepts the renderings of Symm and Vg, and takes "field of Death" or "field of Mot" (the Canaanite god of death) as evidence for a Canaanite death cult in the Kidron, in connection with which was a burial area for (human) sacrificial victims. See also Croatto and Soggin 1962. The relevant Ugaritic texts employ a noun *šdmt*, meaning "field(s)" (*UM* 327 #1811; *UT* 488 #2388), which could explain Heb *šĕdēmôt* (with a *šin*) here and in 2 Kgs 23:4. It should be remembered that in all ancient inscriptions and MSS, no distinction is made between the *śin* and *šin*. But a "field of Mot" in the Kidron is by no means proved. The terraces may have been nothing more than agricultural plots. Excavations by Kenyon and Shiloh above the Kidron show agricultural terracing there from the fourteenth century B.C. until the Babylonian destruction of Jerusalem in 586 B.C. (Stager 1982; P. J. King 1993: 157–59).

up to the Brook Kidron. Hebrew *'ad-naḥal qidrôn.* One Heb MS reads *'al* ("above") for *'ad* ("up to"), and some commentators therefore want to emend (Volz; Rudolph; Bright; Holladay). This would put the terraces "above" the Brook Kidron, where some are located, but the narrator may still be wanting to delineate the boundary as he does in what follows: "up to (*'ad*) the corner of the Horse Gate."

up to the corner of the Horse Gate toward the east. We are now on the eastern boundary of Jerusalem, where the Horse Gate is located. This gate is usually placed at the southeastern corner of the Temple complex (Cornill; Weiser; Simons 1952: 232; Bahat and Rubinstein 1990: 30–31), where it served both the Temple and the palace quarter (Avi-Yonah 1954: 247). This would be south of the East (Golden) Gate, close to Ophel (Dalman's map in Bahat and Rubinstein 1990: 31; Vincent 1934–35: x; cf. Neh 3:28). Horses would have come into the palace through this gate, and it was where the infamous Athaliah was killed (2 Kgs 11:16; 2 Chr 23:15).

holy for Yahweh. Hebrew *qōdeš layhwh.* The most unclean areas surrounding the city must be made holy for Yahweh. The words "holy for Yahweh" were inscribed on a gold plate worn on the priest's forehead (Exod 28:36; 39:30), indicating that his person was sacred. The expression is then a priestly one, which makes one wonder if Jeremiah, now that Jerusalem's destruction and his battles with the priesthood are things of the past, may not be appropriating a term familiar from his priestly upbringing (cf. 1:1). From the usage here comes Jerusalem's later designation as "the Holy City" (Isa 48:2; 52:1), a designation that is also used for the New Jerusalem in Rev 21:2, 10. Silver shekels minted by Titus in the last years before Jerusalem's destruction (A.D. 67–70) bore the inscription "Jerusalem, the Holy" (*EncJud* 9: 1399). The name that the Arabs today use for Jerusalem is *al-Quds* ("the Holy").

It shall not be uprooted, and it shall not again be overthrown—forever. I.e., Jerusalem shall not be uprooted or overthrown (v 38). On the familiar Jeremianic verbs "uprooted" and "overthrown," see earlier v 28 and Note for 1:10. This prophecy has not been fulfilled—at least not in a literal sense. The city, although it was rebuilt by Nehemiah (Nehemiah 1–6) and achieved an even greater splendor from Herod the Great (37–4 B.C.), experienced subsequent indignities, including complete destruction at the hands of Titus and the Romans in A.D. 70, after which it lay in ruins for over 60 years. Despite other attacks since, the city nevertheless remains. In Revelation's New Jerusalem, the servants of God are promised a reign with God and the Lamb forever (Rev 22:3–5).

MESSAGE AND AUDIENCE

In this oracle a dispirited Judahite audience is told that in days to come the city of Jerusalem will be rebuilt for Yahweh. The measuring line will go out from the Tower of Hananel to the Corner Gate, and from there it will turn south and go straight over Gareb Hill, turn again, and follow the southern boundary to Goah. All the valley land surrounding the city, defiled by corpses and sacrificial ashes, and all the ruined terraces on the city slopes up to the Brook Kidron, up to the Horse Gate on the east, shall be made holy for Yahweh. The city will not be uprooted or again be overthrown—forever. But will it really be inviolable for all time?

This oracle addresses a remnant Judahite audience—in Judah and in exile—after the fall of Jerusalem. The first Book of Restoration (chaps. 30–31), which it concludes, is best dated during Jeremiah's Mizpah sojourn (586–582 B.C.). Its message to remnant Israel and Judah is that exiles will return to Zion, and their future in the city and in the land will have both continuity and discontinuity with the past. This final oracle returns the audience to the oracle in 31:23–26, which promises a reconsecration of Jerusalem's holy hill. The oracle also provides a transition into chap. 32 and its symbolic prophecy on Israel's repossession of the land.

EXCURSUS VI: THE EXPANSION OF JERUSALEM IN THE EIGHTH AND SEVENTH CENTURIES B.C.

Jerusalem grew from a city of 130–80 dunams (33.5 to 45 acres)[c] in the eighth century to a city of 500–600 dunams (125–50 acres) in the seventh century, making it a very large city (Broshi 1974: 23; 1978: 12). Broshi, who assumes a settlement on the Western Hill (= Upper City) beginning in the eighth century, puts the seventh-century population of walled Jerusalem at 24,000/ 25,000, a figure based on an average of 40–50 people per dunam. But Stager (1975: 243–44), who acknowledges an eighth-century expansion onto the Western Hill, says these figures are too high. Accepting Broshi's proportional increase of acreage and population, with a large expansion coming after Samaria's fall in 722 B.C. and another expansion coming after Sennacherib's Judah campaign in 701 B.C., when Judah's western provinces were given by Sennacherib to the Philistines, Stager says a more realistic population for the seventh century would be 7,500–12,000 people. Stager and Broshi's statistics on the size and population of Jerusalem in Iron II (900–586 B.C.) are the following:

	size in dumans (acres)	population (Broshi)	population (Stager)
10th c. B.C.	44 (11)	—	600–900
8th c. B.C.	130–80 (33.5–45)	6,000–8,000	2,000–3,600
7th c. B.C.	500–600 (125–50)	24,000 / 25,000	7,500–12,000

In a subsequent publication, Stager (1982: 121) puts the expanded eighth to seventh century population at 10,000 to 12,000 inhabitants. For more general population estimates in Western Palestine during Iron II, see Broshi 1993.[d]

---

[c]The dunam is a land measure equal to 1000 square meters, about 1/4 of an acre.
[d]Broshi's article is contained in the *Pre-Congress Symposium Supplement*.

B. JEREMIAH BUYS LAND IN ANATHOTH (32:1–44)

1. Why Are You Prophesying Thus? (32:1–5)

32 [1]The word that came to Jeremiah from Yahweh in the tenth year[a] of Zedekiah, king of Judah (that was the eighteenth year of Nebuchadrezzar).

---

[a]Q is *baššānâ*; Kt is the construct *bišnat*; see 28:1; 46:2; 51:59; and elsewhere; cf. GKC §134p.

[2]At that time the army of the king of Babylon was besieging Jerusalem, and Jeremiah, the prophet, was confined in the court of the guard, which was in the house of the king of Judah, [3]because Zedekiah, king of Judah, confined him saying: 'Why are you prophesying:

"Thus said Yahweh:

"Look I am giving this city into the hand of the king of Babylon, and he shall take it; [4]And Zedekiah, king of Judah, will not escape from the hand of the Chaldeans—indeed he will surely be given into the hand of the king of Babylon, and his mouth shall speak with his mouth and his eyes shall see his eyes.[b]

[5]"And to Babylon he shall make Zedekiah walk, and there he will be until I reckon with him—oracle of Yahweh—for though you fight the Chaldeans, you shall not succeed?"

2. The Right of Redemption Is Yours (32:6–15)

[6]And Jeremiah said, the word of Yahweh came to me: [7]Look, Hanamel son of Shallum, your uncle, is coming to you to say: 'Buy for yourself my field that is in Anathoth, for the right of redemption to buy is yours.' [8]And Hanamel, son of my uncle, came to me—according to the word of Yahweh—to the court of the guard, and he said to me, 'Buy, would you, my field that is in Anathoth, that is in the land of Benjamin, for the right of possession is yours and the redemption is yours. Buy it for yourself!' Then I knew that this was the word of Yahweh. [9]So I bought the field from Hanamel, son of my uncle, that was in Anathoth, and I weighed for him the silver—seventeen shekels of silver. [10]Then I wrote in the deed, and I sealed it, and I called for witnesses, and I weighed the silver on the two scales. [11]And I took the sealed deed of purchase—the contract and the conditions—also the open copy, [12]and I gave the deed of purchase to Baruch son of Neriah, son of Mahseiah, in the presence of Hanamel, son of[c] my uncle, and in the presence of the witnesses who had written on the deed of purchase, and[d] in the presence of all the Judahites who were sitting in the court of the guard. [13]And I commanded Baruch in their presence, saying:

[14]Thus said Yahweh of hosts, God of Israel:

Take these deeds—this sealed deed of purchase and this open deed—and you shall put them in an earthenware jar in order that they may last many days.

[15]For thus said Yahweh of hosts, God of Israel:

Again houses and fields and vineyards shall be bought in this land.

---

[b]Reading the Q "his eyes"; Kt has a singular "his eye," which is a scribal error.
[c]Add "son of" with several MSS, LXX, S, and T[MS]; MT omits (see Notes).
[d]Add the copulative with many MSS, LXX, S, and Vg.

3. Just Why Did I Buy This Field? (32:16–25)

[16]Then I prayed to Yahweh after I had given the deed of purchase to Baruch son of Neriah: [17]Ah, Lord Yahweh! Look, you, you have made the heavens and the earth with your great strength and with your outstretched arm. Nothing is too difficult for you, [18]who shows steadfast love to thousands but who repays the iniquity of the fathers into the lap of their children after them, the great God, the mighty, Yahweh of hosts is his name, [19]great in counsel and mighty in deed, so that your eyes are open upon all the ways of humanity's children, to give to each person according to his ways and according to the fruit of his doings; [20]so that you have shown signs and wonders, in the land of Egypt—up to this day— and in Israel and among humankind, and you made for yourself a name, as at this day. [21]And you brought your people Israel out from the land of Egypt with signs and with wonders and with a strong hand and with an outstretched arm and with great terror; [22]and you gave to them this land that you swore to their fathers to give to them, a land flowing with milk and honey. [23]And they came in and took possession of it, but they did not obey your voice and in your law[e] did not walk; everything that you commanded them to do, they did not do, so you made them meet up with all this evil. [24]Look, the siege ramps have come to the city to take it, and the city has been given into the hand of the Chaldeans who are fighting against it, because of the sword and the famine and the pestilence; and what you have spoken has happened. So look, you are watching! [25]Yet you, you have said to me, O Lord Yahweh, 'Buy for yourself the field with silver and call for witnesses,' but the city has been given into the hand of the Chaldeans!

4. Yahweh's Promised Judgment (32:26–35)

a) Is Anything Too Difficult for Me? (32:26–29)

[26]And the word of Yahweh came to Jeremiah: [27]'Look I am Yahweh, God of all flesh. Is anything too difficult for me?'

[28]Therefore thus said Yahweh:

Look I am giving this city into the hand of the Chaldeans and into the hand of Nebuchadrezzar, king of Babylon, and he shall take it. [29]And the Chaldeans who are fighting against this city shall come in and set this city on fire and burn it, including the houses on whose roofs they burned incense to Baal, and poured out drink offerings to other gods, in order to provoke me to anger.

---

[e]Reading the Q *ûbĕtôrātĕkâ* ("and in your law"), which is supported by many MSS, G[L], Aq, S, T, and Vg; Kt is a plural, *ûbĕtôrôtĕkâ* ("and in your laws"), which is read by the LXX.

b) Away with This City! (32:30–35)

[30]Indeed, the children of Israel and the children of Judah have been doing only what is evil in my eyes from their youth. Indeed, the children of Israel have only provoked me to anger with the work of their hands—oracle of Yahweh. [31]Indeed, with respect to my anger and my wrath, this city has become to me—from the day that they built it up until this day—in order to remove it from my presence, [32]on account of all the evil of the children of Israel and the children of Judah, which they did to provoke me to anger—they, their kings, their princes, their priests, and their prophets, also the men of Judah and the inhabitants of Jerusalem. [33]They faced me with the back of the neck, and not the face, although I taught them—constantly taught—but they did not listen to take correction. [34]And they set up their wretched things in the house upon which my name is called to defile it. [35]And they built the high places of Baal that are in the Valley of Ben-Hinnom to give over their sons and their daughters to Molech—which I did not command them, nor did it enter my mind for them to do this abomination—in order to make Judah sin.[f]

5. Yahweh's Promised Salvation (32:36–44)

a) The Eternal Covenant (32:36–41)

[36]But now after this, thus said Yahweh, God of Israel, to this city of which you are saying, 'It has been given into the hand of the king of Babylon by sword and by famine and by pestilence':

[37]Look I am going to gather them from all the lands where I dispersed them in my anger and in my wrath and in great fury, and I will bring them back to this place and settle them in security. [38]And they will be a people to me, and I, I will be God to them. [39]And I will give them one heart and one way to fear me all the days, for their own good and for their children after them. [40]And I will cut for them an eternal covenant, in which I will not turn away from them to do good to them; and the fear of me I will put in their hearts so they may not turn away from me. [41]And I will rejoice over them to do them good, and I will truly plant them in this land, with all my heart and with all my soul.

b) Fields Will Again Be Bought and Sold (32:42–44)

[42]For thus said Yahweh:

Even as I brought to this people all this great evil, so I am going to bring upon them all the good that I am speaking concerning them. [43]The field shall be bought in this land, of which you are saying, 'It is a desolation, without human or beast; it has been given into the hand of the Chal-

---

[f]Reading the Q *haḥăṭî*' (see Notes).

deans.' [44]Fields shall be bought with silver, also writing in the deed and sealing and the summoning of witnesses to witness, in the land of Benjamin, and in the regions around Jerusalem and in the cities of Judah, in the cities of the hill country and in the cities of the Shephelah and in the cities of the Negeb; for I will surely restore their fortunes—oracle of Yahweh.

RHETORIC AND COMPOSITION

MT Chapter 32 = LXX Chapter 39. The original Book of Restoration (chaps. 30–31) was at some point enlarged to include chaps. 32 and 33, each of which is a self-standing compilation on the same themes appearing in 30–31: 1) the return of Israelite and Judahite exiles; 2) resettlement of exiles and restored community life in Judah; and 3) new and ongoing covenants between Yahweh and Israel-Judah. The present chapter marks the end of Jerome's unfinished commentary.

Chapter 32 reports Jeremiah's purchase of a family plot at Anathoth, which is preceded by two judgment oracles given earlier to Zedekiah, and followed by Jeremiah's long prayer to Yahweh and Yahweh's answer in four divine oracles. Chronologically the chapter belongs with chaps. 37–38, which narrate events taking place during Jeremiah's confinement in the court of the guard (37:21; 38:28). The narrative here was doubtless included in the Book of Restoration because its message of hope fit more suitably here than in chaps. 37–38. Its two judgment oracles given to Zedekiah in vv 3b–5 largely repeat a similar oracle in 34:2b–3. That chap. 32 is essentially one piece can be seen by the final oracle's returning to pick up the main theme of the narrative, i.e., that fields will again be bought in the land (v 43; cf. v 15). The two concluding oracles parallel the two concluding oracles in chap. 31:

Oracle on the New Covenant	31:31–34
Oracle on the Rebuilding of Jerusalem	31:38–40
Oracle on the Eternal Covenant	32:36–41
Oracle on Renewed Field Purchases in Benjamin and Judah	32:42–44

A key phrase in the final verse of the chapter, "for I will surely restore their fortunes" (v 44) is repeated at the end of chap. 33 (v 26Q). In the enlarged Book of Restoration (chaps. 30–33), Israel and Judah's restored fortunes become a key theme (see Rhetoric and Composition for 30:1–3).

The present verses are delimited at the top end by a *setumah* in M[L] and M[P] and a *petuḥah* in M[A] before v 1, which is also the chapter division. Delimitation at the bottom end is by a *petuḥah* in M[A], M[L], and M[P] after the "oracle of Yahweh" formula in v 44, which is another chapter division. The messenger formula of v 44 is omitted in the LXX.

The chapter also has the following section markings, some of which set off divine oracles. Markings in M^A for a portion of 32:3–25 are unavailable because the text is not extant.

1) after v 5: M^A, M^L, and M^P have a *petuḥah*
2) after v 6: M^P only has a *setumah*
3) after v 14: M^L has a *setumah*; M^P a *petuḥah*; M^A has no section
4) after v 15: M^L and M^P have a *petuḥah*; M^A has no section
5) after v 25: M^A and M^P have a *setumah*; M^L has no section; two MSS in the Cambridge Genizah Collection (NS 58.32; AS 2.208) have a section
6) after v 27: M^P only has a *setumah*
7) after v 35: M^A and M^L have a *setumah*; M^P has no section
8) after v 41: M^A and M^L have a *setumah*; M^P has a *petuḥah*
9) after v 42: M^P only has a *petuḥah*.

Variations between the MT and LXX, which include here a large number of LXX omissions, are treated by commentators much the same as elsewhere. Giesebrecht is more evenhanded, noting versional support for MT even when an LXX reading is preferred. Duhm and Cornill consistently prefer the shorter LXX text, a *Tendenz* that becomes almost mechanical with Holladay (following Janzen) and McKane. In my judgment, the MT is much the better text, there being 18 arguable cases of LXX loss by haplography in the chapter. A recent work by Shead (1999) concludes also that the present chapter contains more LXX loss by haplography than is generally recognized. For this reason, and also for others, I would judge the LXX a very poor text from which to try and reconstruct original readings.

Critical scholars (except Carroll and McKane) accept this report of Jeremiah's buying the field at Anathoth (vv 6–15) as historical. However, some or all of the remaining material in the chapter is considered secondary by a majority of scholars. Views vary considerably, and nothing approaching a consensus exists on questions relating to the material's authenticity or provenance. Stade (1883: 15; 1885: 175) questioned the authenticity of vv 17–23 just in passing, a judgment cited with approval by Giesebrecht. Jeremiah's prayer was thus reduced to vv 16, 24–25. Duhm believed that vv 1–15 were definitely from Baruch's book but had been moved from chaps. 37–38 to their present position, where they underwent expansion by a later editor. In his view, all of vv 16–44 derived from a later editor. Cornill agreed, placing vv 16–44 with material in chap. 33 that was judged to be later. The issues here were the same as elsewhere: stereotyped prose and salvation oracles judged to be postexilic, and here in the present case a Jeremiah prayer that looked suspiciously like the prayer of Ezra in Neh 9:6–37, where Israel's redemption history is prefaced by Creation history. It was also argued that such a liturgical-sounding prayer was inappropriate in the context. Weiser, however, found it difficult to believe that Jeremiah, the son of a priest, would not know the liturgical tradition, and so he concluded that the secondary nature of vv 17–23 had not been proved to his satisfaction. It seems to me that this prayer, even more than the report of the field purchase, has all the marks of a genuine eye-witness account. The doubt and uncertainty expressed here would surely have been smoothed out in later narrative, where real-life complexities are subsequently overshadowed or forgotton once the symbolic action is fulfilled. But here Jeremiah seems not to have grasped the significance of what he has just done.

Older and also more recent attempts to show sources or redaction in the chapter must be judged unsuccessful; the same goes for attempts to date portions of the chapter in the postexilic period. While it is clear that the narrative and the oracles are brought together here by a compiler—most likely Baruch, who figures prominently in the transaction and is entrusted with the safekeeping of the prophecy (cf. chap. 36)—it is just as clear that the chapter contains a structure that has gone unrecognized by those dividing it into sources. The chapter, to be read properly, must be seen as a unified composition:

Superscription	v 1
Narrative and prior oracles to Zedekiah	vv 2–5
Oracle I—Judgment on Zedekiah	vv 3b–4
Oracle II—Judgment on Zedekiah	v 5
Narrative and oracles on the field purchase	vv 6–15
Oracle III—Salvation for the nation	v 14
Oracle IV—Salvation for the nation	v 15
Jeremiah's prayer to Yahweh	vv 16–25
Yahweh's answer to Jeremiah	vv 26–44
Oracle V—Judgment on the nation	vv 26–29
Oracle VI—Judgment on the nation	vv 30–35
Oracle VII—Salvation for the nation	vv 36–41
Oracle VIII—Salvation for the nation	vv 42–44

Jeremiah's prayer to Yahweh is at the center, on either side of which are placed four oracles. There are eight oracles in all: two judgment oracles for Zedekiah (I and II) balancing two salvation oracles for the nation (III and IV); and in Yahweh's answer, two judgment oracles for the nation (V and VI) balancing two salvation oracles for the nation (VII and VIII). We noted earlier in the poetic core that two judgment oracles (30:5–7, 12–15) had two balancing salvation oracles (30:10–11, 16–17). Some commentators (Volz; Rudolph; Bright; McKane) have failed to recognize v 14 as a separate oracle (III), deleting or judging inappropriate the messenger formula in v 14a. There is no warrant for this deletion. In the view of Gevaryahu (1970: 370–72; 1973: 211–13), the narrative in vv 6–15 is an expanded colophon attached to the document Baruch put away for safekeeping.

Three of the oracles begin with the familiar "Look I" plus a participle (see Note for 1:15):

I	*Look I*	*hinĕnî*	v 3b
V	*Look I*	*hinĕnî*	v 28
VII	*Look I*	*hinĕnî*	v 37

In the narrative, *hinnēh* ("look") occurs in vv 7, 17, 24, and 27; *hinněkā* ("look you!") in v 24.

The two judgment oracles for the nation contain an inversion in which the phrases about Yahweh being "provoked to anger" first follow and then precede the evils causing the provocation:

V the houses on whose roofs they burned incense to Baal, and poured out drink offerings to other gods		v 29
in order *to provoke me to anger*	*hak'isēnî*	
VI the children of Israel have only *provoked me to anger* with the work of their hands . . .	*mak'isîm 'ōtî*	v 30b
which they did *to provoke me to anger*	*lěhak'isēnî*	v 32
And they set up their wretched things in the house upon which my name is called to defile it. And they built the high places of Baal that are in the Valley of Ben-Hinnom to give over their sons and their daughters to Molech		vv 34–35

NOTES

32:1. *The word that came to Jeremiah from Yahweh.* On this superscription, see Notes for 7:1 and 21:1. The T expands to "word of prophecy." The "word" here is not the oracles of vv 3b–5 that came earlier to the prophet (cf. 34:2–3) but "the word" of v 6 given fully in v 7 (Kimḥi).

in the tenth year of Zedekiah, king of Judah (that was the eighteenth year of Nebuchadrezzar). The tenth year of Zedekiah and eighteenth year of Nebuchadrezzar was 587 B.C. (Tadmor 1956: 230). In Zedekiah's eleventh year the city was taken (1:3). Synchronistic chronology, to be expected now with the Babylonians dominating world affairs, occurs elsewhere in the book (see Note for 25:1). Many of the Elephantine legal papyri contain a double date, Babylonian and Egyptian (Kraeling 1953: 51; Horn and Wood 1954: 1; Porten, "Elephantine Papyri" in *ABD* 2: 450). The term *šānâ* ("year") repeats in the Babylonian date because of the compound number (GKC §134o).

2. *At that time the army of the king of Babylon was besieging Jerusalem, and Jeremiah, the prophet, was confined in the court of the guard, which was in the house of the king of Judah.* The LXX omits "at that time" (*wě'āz*), but it is translated in T, S, and Vg and is best retained (Giesebrecht). The LXX also omits "the prophet" after "Jeremiah," which it does elsewhere in the book (see Appendix VI); but here the ommission could be attributed to haplography (homoeoarcton: *h . . . h*). This is the second and final siege of Jerusalem, after Jeremiah was remanded to the court of the guard (37:21) and after the Egyptian advance forcing a temporary lifting of the siege (37:5). The resumption of the siege took place on First Adar 1 (February 24), 587 B.C. The incident reported here did not take place during the Babylonian withdrawal (*pace* Holladay); rather, during the summer of 587 B.C., a year before the city fell.

the court of the guard. Jeremiah's final place of confinement in the royal palace (see Note for 37:21), where he enjoyed a measure of freedom (see v 8 below).

3. *because Zedekiah . . . confined him saying: 'Why are you prophesying . . . ?'* The oracles to follow (vv 3b–5) were spoken earlier; they are brought in here to explain Jeremiah's confinement in the court of the guard. The account in chap. 37 states things a bit differently, although there an unhopeful word to the king (v 17) does precede Jeremiah's being remanded to the court of the guard (v 21). The oracles here compare with the oracle given earlier to Zedekiah in 34:2–3.

Look I am giving this city into the hand of the king of Babylon, and he shall take it. A prediction made by the prophet on many occasions (see Note for 34:2).

4. *And Zedekiah, king of Judah, will not escape from the hand of the Chaldeans—indeed he will surely be given into the hand of the king of Babylon, and his mouth shall speak with his mouth and his eyes shall see his eyes.* It is Nebuchadrezzar's mouth that will speak to Zedekiah's mouth, and the eyes of the Babylonian king that will look into the eyes of Judah's beaten king. Zedekiah may or may not be given an opportunity to speak, and he would probably just as soon avoid eye contact with Nebuchadrezzar if at all possible. The expression is rhetorically a synecdoche (the encounter will be more than eye to eye and mouth to mouth) and grammatically a syntactic chiasmus ("and it shall speak / his mouth with his mouth // and his eye his eye / shall see"). This "mouth to mouth" and "eye to eye" encounter, predicted also in 34:3, did in fact happen (39:5; 52:9).

5. *And to Babylon he shall make Zedekiah walk, and there he will be until I reckon with him.* Zedekiah is promised a Babylonian exile also in 34:3, which was fulfilled (39:7; 52:11). But what does Yahweh mean when he says that "there [Zedekiah] will be" (LXX: "dwell there") until he "reckons with" him? The verb *pqd* ("visit, attend to, reckon with") occurs frequently in Jeremiah (see Note for 5:9), its usage often yielding an understatement or a statement having deliberate ambiguity. The verb can mean "visit to deliver" (15:15; 29:10) but more often means "visit to punish." The T in this case has "until his memorial comes in before me," which points to Zedekiah's death (cf. Rashi; Kimḥi; G^A: *apothaneitai*, "to die"). Death in a foreign land, whether for a king or any other person, is neither a desired nor an honorable end (20:6; 22:12, 26). But Calvin thinks that Yahweh intends to reckon favorably with Zedekiah, since he will at least get a burial.

And to Babylon. The preposition "to" is omitted by ellipsis (see Note for 24:1).

5–6. *until I reckon with him—oracle of Yahweh—for though you fight the Chaldeans, you shall not succeed? And Jeremiah said.* The LXX omits the concluding words of v 5 and, except for the final *waw* on the name "Jeremiah," omits the words "and Jeremia[h] said" that begin v 6. Commentators are divided over whether the words in question are an MT plus (Cornill;

Janzen 1973: 104; Holladay; McKane) or an LXX loss due to abridgment (Giesebrecht; Rudolph). If the LXX omission is looked at in its entirety, we have another arguable case for LXX loss through haplography (homoeoteleu-ton: *h . . . h*). The omitted words are translated in Theod, S, T, and Vg and should therefore be retained.

for though you fight the Chaldeans, you shall not succeed. These direct words at the end of the oracle are addressed to all the people of Jerusalem (plural forms), not just to the king.

6. *And Jeremiah said, the word of Yahweh came to me.* The narrative picks up here from v 1 after the parenthetical words of vv 2–5. This lengthy digression makes necessary "and Jeremiah said," which should not be deleted with the LXX and S (*pace* Holladay). Its omission in the LXX, as we just noted, is due to haplography. Jeremiah, then, is not answering Zedekiah's question (Rashi; Ru-dolph; Weiser), which was posed earlier and here serves only as introductory background, but is addressing an assembly of people in the court of the guard (Kimḥi). The LXX has "and the word of the Lord came to Jeremiah," which is the same introductory formula as in v 26. But MT's "the word of Yahweh came to me" makes a better introduction to the first-person language in vv 8–25.

7. *Look, Hanamel son of Shallum, your uncle, is coming to you to say: 'Buy for yourself my field that is in Anathoth.'* Lindblom (1965: 200) and others speak here about presentiment, the sort that everyone experiences at one time or an-other. But the text says that Jeremiah learns of Hanamel's coming through a word from Yahweh, which is confirmed when the cousin comes (v 8).

for the right of redemption to buy is yours. The term *mišpaṭ* here means "right" or "due" (as established by custom), a meaning it has also in Deut 18:3 (Snaith 1983: 76). The LXX omits the term here and in v 8, but Giesebrecht notes that it is nevertheless translated in G^L, S, T, and Vg.

son of Shallum. "Shallum" was the preaccession name of King Jehoahaz (see Note on 22:11a).

8. *And Hanamel, son of my uncle, came to me—according to the word of Yah-weh.* This confirmation of an earlier word from Yahweh (vv 6–7), according to Rabinowitz (1966: 319–20; 1972–73: 123), is the essence of prophecy. The LXX omits "according to the word of Yahweh," but the words are translated in other Vrs (G^L, S, T, Vg) and should be retained (Giesebrecht). The loss here could be due to an inner-Greek haplography (homoeoteleuton: *patros mou kata ton logon kuriou*). The LXX adds "Shallum" after "son (of)," which may be a later addition; cf. vv 9 and 12.

to the court of the guard. In this place of confinement Jeremiah is able to re-ceive visitors, preach, and now to carry on a business transaction in the com-pany of witnesses. Calvin remarks that although Jeremiah was confined to the court of the guard, the Word of God was not bound (cf. Acts 28:16–31; 2 Tim 2:9). From an old Assyrian text we learn that prisoners were not always com-pletely isolated and could carry on business while in prison (Riemschneider 1977: 116). But one wonders how Hanamel got into a city under siege. He could have entered before the siege began; otherwise one must assume that he managed somehow to enter while the siege was in process, which would have been achieved at considerable risk (D. N. Freedman).

'*Buy, would you, my field that is in Anathoth, that is in the land of Benjamin, for the right of possession is yours and the redemption is yours. Buy it for yourself!*' The request is at once both ordinary and extraordinary. Hanamel has become poor and is forced to sell property that he owns. Belonging to the same priestly family as Jeremiah, he can and does own land. According to Num 18:23, the Levitical priests did not receive an inheritance (= share of territory, *naḥălâ*) in the Promised Land, but they did have cities and pastureland outside the cities (Num 35:1–8; Lev 25:34). Abiathar the priest had land (*śādeh*) in Anathoth (1 Kgs 2:26), and now, three and one-half centuries later, priestly families in Anathoth have land holdings there (Cogan 2001: 177). The law states that when someone becomes poor and is forced to sell land, the next of kin has the duty to redeem it, i.e., purchase the land for himself (Lev 25:25; de Vaux 1965b: 166–67). It is taken for granted in the OT that no one sells his land without being forced to do so (J. Pedersen 1964 I–II: 83–85). Jeremiah is thus acting as a *gōʾēl* ("redeemer"), exercising his right and obligation to buy the cousin's land (on the term *gōʾēl* and the obligations of "next of kin" to redeem, see Note for 31:11). Here, however, the city is under siege, and the time to buy land is hardly right. Reuven Yaron pointed out some years go in a lecture given at the University of California, Berkeley (June 6, 1977), that land, compared with movables, has the advantage of being a lasting commodity. Its main disadvantage is that in time of war it cannot be moved, which is precisely the situation here. When Hannibal was fighting the Romans (211 B.C.), the land on which he was encamped was put up for sale in Rome at public auction, and a Roman purchased it at full price. Not to be outdone, Hannibal imitated this confidence by putting up for sale all the banking establishments in the Roman Forum, but no bidder came forward (Florus i 22; Livy xxvi 11.6–7). Hannibal, as it turned out, failed in his attempt to take Rome. The situation here is quite different. Nebuchadrezzar is encamped on land now being sold in Jerusalem, and the purchaser is convinced that the Babylonian king will take the city, which he does.

that is in the land of Benjamin. The LXX places this phrase before "in Anathoth," leading some scholars (Giesebrecht; Duhm; Cornill; Janzen 1973: 133; and others) to omit the phrase as secondary. This explanation appears too simple (so Holladay, who retains). Both phrases are present in T and Vg. In the next verse, the LXX omits "that was in Anathoth."

for the right of possession is yours and the redemption is yours. Buy it for yourself! We do not know if Jeremiah was offered the land because he had seniority over other kinsmen. It is possible that other kinsmen were offered the land but declined. The LXX answers this question with the reading: "for yours is the right to possess it, and you are the oldest (*kai su presbuteros*)," omitting "Buy it for yourself!" The MT verb *gʾl*, "to redeem," appears to have been misread here as *gdl*, "to grow up" (Hitzig). But the urgent "Buy it for yourself!" is translated in Aq, G^L, S, T, and Vg (paraphrase), and should be retained (Giesebrecht).

Then I knew that this was the word of Yahweh. A singular confession by the prophet, showing that Yahweh's word in this case needed confirmation by subsequent events. Compare 1 Sam 10:2–10; also Gen 24:1–27.

9. *So I bought the field from Hanamel, son of my uncle, that was in Anathoth, and I weighed for him the silver—seventeen shekels of silver.* The LXX omits "that was in Anathoth" and "the silver" in its first occurrence, probably because both terms occur in both verses (Giesebrecht). "The silver" (*hakkesep*) should not be deleted; in its first occurrence it simply means "the price" or "the money" (Ehrlich 1912: 324–25; cf. Gen 23:9, 13; 31:15). Jeremiah here places a quantity of cut silver on one scale, which weighs in at 17 shekels according to stone weights on the other. Someone present with a pair of scales suspended from a bar does the weighing (cf. Zeph 1:11). The widespread use of silver to supplement traditional modes of payment is well documented in the seventh century B.C., at which time throughout the Assyrian Empire—also in Judah— it was weighed out on scales, as it had been for centuries. Silver was a more common currency than gold. Excavated hoards of silver from this period contain stamped or unstamped silver ingots, cut silver (*Hacksilber*), and silver jewelry (bracelets, earrings, nose-rings). Stamped ingots were of predetermined weight, which prepared the way for coinage coming later. Tel Miqne– Ekron produced a number of silver hoards, reflecting Ekron's status as a major olive oil and textile center during this period (Gitin 1995: 61, 69; 1997: 92–93; 1998: 282–84; Gitin and Golani 2001). A jar dating to the seventh century was found at En-Gedi (Stratum V) containing a hoard of silver ingots, some of them scored, which were doubtless used as currency (Meshorer 1978: 129–31; *NEAEHL* 2: 402; P. J. King 1993: 92). A number of other silver hoards from the late seventh and early sixth centuries B.C. have turned up at various ANE sites (Gitin and Golani 2001: 38–40).

Coins were minted for the first time in the late seventh century B.C. at Sardis, capital of Lydia in Asia Minor (Herr 1997: 159; Meshorer 1998: 33; P. J. King 1999: 104). Coinage spread into other parts of the Greek world and into Persia by the mid–sixth century B.C. By the late fifth century, foreign currency was circulating in Tyre, Sidon, Gaza, and Jerusalem. But even after coins came into use, people continued to pay for goods with ingots of precious metals, and in doubtful cases weighed the coins. Weights used on the scales were commonly made of stone, occasionally of bronze, and in preexilic Israel and Judah were shaped like round loaves of bread. The weights were inscribed with numbers and a symbol for the shekel, or just numbers, or some other term indicating a fraction of a shekel, e.g., two-sixths shekel, one-half shekel (*beqaʿ*; cf. Exod 38:26), one shekel, two shekels, four shekels, and eight shekels (Meshorer 1978: 131–33—with pictures). They also came in sets, so that fine differences could be weighed out. The first known coins from Judah were found in a cave in the Ben-Hinnom Valley and date to the sixth century B.C. They were Greek. Coins began to be minted in Judah about 400 B.C. On currencies, weights, and the development of coinage in the ancient world, see Meshorer 1978; 1998; and P. J. King 1999: 104.

seventeen shekels of silver. Since we do not know how much land was sold, nor do we know current values, this purchase price cannot be assessed as to worth. Biblical comparisons have only limited value. Joseph was sold to the Midianite traders for 20 (shekels of) silver (Gen 37:28), and David bought a threshing floor and oxen from Araunah the Jebusite for 50 shekels of silver (2 Sam 24:24). Presumably, Jeremiah bought the field at market value, although land values now would surely be depressed. It should be noted that Jeremiah did have the money to make the purchase. We do know how much silver changed hands. One shekel was equivalent to 11.4 grams in weight (Meshorer 1978: 131; 1998: 21; P. J. King 1999: 105), which means that 17 shekels of silver would have weighed 193.8 grams, or 6.78 ounces (Appendix IV), just less than half a pound. For pictures of a silver jewelry hoard, *Hacksilber*, and a silver ingot excavated at Tel Miqne–Ekron (Hoard 2), dating to Nebuchadrezzar's destruction of the city in 604 B.C. and weighing 259.4 grams, see Gitin and Golani 2001: 31, 33 + pls. 2.3 and 2.4. The T sets Jeremiah's purchase price at "seven manas and ten selas of silver," where the *mana* (Heb *maneh*) is now said to equal 25 usual shekels, and the *sela* one shekel (Rosenberg, 260). This would total 185 shekels, which looks to be an inflationary figure, but we have to be cautious since values and standards changed over time, and at a given time could even differ in regions of the same country. The Mishnah, for example, states that the *maneh* of Jerusalem differed in weight from the *maneh* in Tsippori (Meshorer 1978: 131). There is some doubt over an apparent reference to this verse in Matt 27:9–10, where it states that the 30 pieces of silver returned by Judas were used to buy a burial place for strangers. Quesnel (1989) says that while most exegetes think the Matthew passage alludes to Zech 11:12–13, he thinks the allusion is rather to Lam 4:1–2, noting that ancient Jewish tradition ascribed Lamentations to Jeremiah. But the Zechariah text and its reference to 30 shekels of silver is a better fit, which would mean that Matthew's citation of Jeremiah is in error. If reference is being made to Jeremiah's purchase here, then we have to settle for a very loose fulfillment of this prophetic act by the Gospel writer.

10. *Then I wrote in the deed, and I sealed it, and I called for witnesses, and I weighed the silver on the two scales.* This verse, repeating as it does the weighing of the money, is simply a listing of all the actions necessary to complete the transaction. Hebrew *wā'ektōb bassēper* ("Then I wrote in the deed") is translated in some of the modern Versions (JB; NAB; NJV) to mean that Jeremiah drew up the deed, but more likely it means that the deed was drawn up at his instruction and he simply signed it (RSV; NEB; NIV). The same expression is used of the witnesses in v 12, and they only affix their signatures. Baruch, the scribe, is present and would be the one writing up the deed (Avigad 1987: 202). From the Elephantine papyri we know that professional scribes were required to draw up legal documents (Porten 1968: 192–93). Avigad thinks that Baruch would also have sealed it. We know from seal impressions found with Baruch's name on it that he had his own seal (see Note for 36:4). But Jeremiah could have affixed his name to the deed, since he was a party to the transaction.

11. *And I took the sealed deed of purchase—the contract and the conditions—also the open copy.* We now know a good deal about how documents such as the present one were drawn up, also how they were stored and kept for future reference. The deed would have been written in duplicate on a single piece of papyrus, with a couple of blank lines in the center separating the two texts. The document on the top half would be the sealed copy and the duplicate below, the open copy, kept accessible for reference when needed. The sealed copy guaranteed that the text would not be tampered with and would remain as it was when written up (Yadin 1962a: 236; Avigad 1986b: 124–27). Avigad says the practice of writing two copies was ancient, known already in early Mesopotamia. The top copy would then be rolled up, holes made in the blank lines, and tied tightly with string. Clay seals would secure the string. If the papyrus was wide, a cut would be made in the blank lines of the center, but only up to the middle, and then the divided portions would be folded over the undivided portion, and the top deed would be sealed in the same manner as an unfolded document. The bottom part of the deed would also be rolled up, perhaps tied with string, but not sealed, so as to be accessible. Legal documents prepared in this fashion have turned up among the fourth- and fifth-century papyri found at Elephantine in Egypt (Rubensohn 1907: 5–9). In Greek papyri of the collection, open copies are exact duplicates of the sealed copies; they are not abstracts (L. Fischer 1910: 141). The Aramaic papyri from Elephantine were not written in duplicate (Rubensohn 1907: 8; Kraeling 1953: 51), but they do contain memoranda on the outside of the rolls identifying their contents, e.g., "document of a house," "document of sale," or "document of marriage" (Kraeling 1953: 50; ABD 2: 450). The same is true for the most part of the Bar Kochba (A.D. 132–35) contracts found in the so-called "Cave of the Letters" in Nahal Seelim, west of the Dead Sea, near En-Gedi. Yadin (1962a: 236–37) says that only occasionally did these documents give an abstract of the subject matter; usually the wording of the exterior was identical with that in the interior. The first-century B.C. Greek documents from Avroman in Kurdistan, written on parchment, were also done in duplicate and rolled up like the Elephantine papyri, except that halves were not folded over (Minns 1915, with a drawing). On the Elephantine legal papyri in Greek and Aramaic, their writing, tying, and sealing, see L. Fischer 1910; Kraeling 1953: 49–51; Porten 1968: 191–99; 1979; idem, "Elephantine Papyri" in ABD 2: 445–55. For pictures of sealed papyrus documents from Elephantine, see G. E. Wright 1957: 206; Porten 1979: 74; ANEP² 82 ##265, 279. On the Bar Kochba documents, see Yadin 1962a. For the large corpus of West Semitic seals, including pictures, see Avigad 1997.

the contract and the conditions. Hebrew *hammiṣwâ wĕhaḥuqqîm* is a stereotyped phrase in Deuteronomy, where it is translated "the commandment (and) the statutes" (Deut 5:31; 6:1), but just what it means here has been disputed since antiquity. The LXX omits the phrase, and some therefore delete it as a gloss (Giesebrecht; Cornill; Holladay; McKane; cf. NEB and REB, which reverse G. R. Driver 1937–38: 120). But the omission can be attributed to haplography (homoeoteleuton: *m . . . m*). The reading of T ("according to the

halakah and according to what is right") has a phrase that cites the legal re-
quirements in the closed and open copies, an interpretation that is carried over
into the AV ("according to the law and custom"), the JB [but not NJB], and the
NJV. Jerome assumed that the phrase was specifying the conditions of the contract (Vg: *stipulationes et rata*, "stipulations and legal [matters]"), an interpretation carried over into the AmT ("the terms and conditions") and other
English translations (RSV; NAB; NIV; NRSV; NJB). Bright has "the contract
and the conditions," which is as good a translation as any. The syntax is unusual since the phrase modifies both "the sealed deed of purchase" and "the
open copy" (Tsumura 1983: 477). See similar syntax in v 20.

   12. *and I gave the deed of purchase to Baruch son of Neriah, son of Mahseiah,
in the presence of Hanamel, son of my uncle, and in the presence of the witnesses
who had written on the deed of purchase, and in the presence of all the Judahites
who were sitting in the court of the guard.* Already we are beginning to see that
this is more than just a land purchase with seller, buyer, an accredited scribe,
and witnesses present to verify the transfer and have their names affixed to the
deed. Other Judahites are here to see Jeremiah entrust the deed to Baruch and
hear the oracles that follow (vv 14–15). What we have here is another symbolic
action by the prophet, and symbolic actions since they extend the prophetic
preaching require for posterity a greater audience able to witness the greater
significance of what might otherwise be an occurrence to which little or no importance is attached (see Note for 13:1).

   the deed of purchase. Hebrew *’et-hassēper hammiqnâ.* The Q^{OR} readings
omit the definite article on the construct term, which is required if this is to be
a construct chain (cf. vv 11, 14). The second term must otherwise stand in
apposition to the first: "the deed, the purchase (one)" (cf. GKC §127h).

   Baruch son of Neriah, son of Mahseiah. This is the first mention of Baruch in
the book, although he appeared earlier in time to write up Jeremiah's first
scroll (36:4). Here Baruch has written, tied up, and sealed Jeremiah's deed of
purchase, making him the natural person to receive it for safekeeping. Baruch
is a professional scribe, indicated by "the scribe" added to his name in 36:26
and 32 and by seal impressions with his name and title that have turned up (see
Note for 36:4). His name appears here with a double patronym, which is what
we find similarly after the name of Seraiah, Baruch's brother, in 51:59. In the
apocryphal book of Baruch, an even more-expanded patronym is given: "the
son of Neriah, son of Mahseiah, son of Zedekiah, son of Hasadiah, son of
Hilkiah" (Bar 1:1). Baruch belongs to a prominent scribal family. The names
"Mahseiah," "Neriah," and "Baruch" are all well attested in the period, having
turned up on the Arad ostraca and on various seals and seal impressions (see
"Baruch ben Neriah ben Mahseiah" in Appendix I).

   Hanamel, son of my uncle. The word *ben* ("son") appears to have been acci-
dently omitted in MT (Albrektson 1994: 37–38), being present in many Heb
MSS, LXX, S, and MSS of T. Hanamel is the cousin, not the uncle, of Jeremiah.

   the witnesses who had written on the deed of purchase. The witnesses
"who had written" (*hakkōtĕbîm*) on the deed of purchase simply affixed their

signatures, as Jeremiah did his (v 10). Witnesses normally signed the documents themselves (Kimḥi; cf. Mishnah Baba Bathra 10:1); the scribe in attendance did not sign for them. Witnesses of the Elephantine legal papyri signed for themselves in person (Kraeling 1953: 50; Porten 1968: 197–99; ABD 2: 450–51), the same being true for the witnesses of the documents from Avroman (Minns 1915: 25). On the Bar Kochba contracts, witnesses signed in their own language, writing down the back side of the open copy, each next to a different tie (Yadin 1962a: 236–38). The LXX supports MT's *hakkōtĕbîm* with *graphontōn*, but many Heb MSS and numerous other Vrs (Aq, Symm, S, T, Vg) have "who were inscribed," which contains or presupposes the passive participle, *hakkĕtûbîm*. According to this reading, the witnesses had their names inscribed on the deed, either because they had written it themselves or because someone else had written it for them.

the witnesses. Hebrew *hā'ēdîm*. The LXX reads "those who stood" (*tōn estēkotōn*). But Aq and Symm support MT with *tōn marturōn* ("the witnesses"); the same goes for T and Vg (*testium*).

all the Judahites. The LXX omits "all."

who were sitting in the court of the guard. The LXX omits "who were sitting" (*hayyōšĕbîm*), which can be attributed to haplography (homoeoteleuton: *ym* . . . *ym*). The term is translated in G^L, S, T, and Vg and should be retained (Giesebrecht).

13. *And I commanded Baruch in their presence*. Hebrew *wā'ăṣawweh* ("And I commanded") is strong, but since Baruch is in Jeremiah's employ, Jeremiah can command him (cf. 32:13; 36:5, 8). Jeremiah also commands Seraiah, Baruch's brother, concerning the scroll going to Babylon (51:59).

14. *Thus said Yahweh of hosts, God of Israel*. Jeremiah's command to Baruch takes the form of a divine oracle. The LXX translates *ṣĕbā'ôt* ("of hosts") with *pantokratōr*, as it does occasionally in the book (see Appendix VI). It also omits "God of Israel."

Take these deeds—this sealed deed of purchase and this open deed—and you shall put them in an earthenware jar in order that they may last many days. Jars of baked clay (earthenware pottery) were the usual containers for storing documents, wine, silver, gold, and other treasures (2 Cor 4:7). Like modern-day plastic, baked clay does not decompose. Cuneiform tablets from the eighteenth century B.C. in Babylon have been found stored in earthenware jars, their covers sealed with asphalt (Weidner 1956: 112). The documents from Elephantine, the Bar Kochbah caves, and Khirbet Qumran (Dead Sea Scrolls) were all found sealed in earthenware jars. Baruch is told here to put the complete document—the sealed copy and the open copy—into an earthenware jar, seal it, and probably bury it, since these are uncertain times. Jars containing stored items have been found under house floors and in open fields. On the use of earthenware jars for storing texts throughout the ANE, see O. Pedersén 1998: 243. One may well imagine that Hanamel also put some of his 17 shekels of silver into an earthenware jar and hid it for safekeeping.

Take these deeds. Hebrew *lāqôaḥ 'et-hassĕpārîm hā'ēlleh*. On the imperatives *qaḥ* and *qĕḥû* ("Take!") in divine commands issued to the prophet, see
Note for 43:9. The form of the verb here is the infinitive absolute, *lāqôaḥ*,
which can function as an emphatic imperative (D. N. Freedman, who cites
zākôr, "Remember!" and *šāmôr*, "Keep!" beginning the commandments on
Sabbath observance in Exod 20:8 and Deut 5:12, respectively). The LXX omits
"these deeds," which can be attributed to haplography (whole word: *'t . . . 't*).
This omission explains the subsequent singular pronouns in the LXX, which
make for an awkward reading.

this sealed deed of purchase. The LXX omits "the sealed," which can also be
attributed to haplography (whole-word: *w't . . . w't*).

many days. Hebrew *yāmîm rabbîm.* I.e., a long time.

15. *For thus said Yahweh of hosts, God of Israel.* The LXX again omits "God
of Israel."

Again houses and fields and vineyards shall be bought in this land. The LXX
has a different sequence: "fields and houses and vineyards." We now get the
larger message of Jeremiah's action. The purchase of the field was a symbolic
prophecy, another of many that Jeremiah carried out during his public ministry (see Note for 13:1). With Jerusalem and all Judah about to be given over to
an enemy, Yahweh says that houses, fields, and vineyards will again be bought
in the land. The term "again" (*'ôd*) occurs often in the Book of Restoration
(31:4–5, 23–40). We see here as clearly as anywhere in the book that Jeremiah
did in fact hold out hope for the future. He told the exiles in Babylon to build
houses and plant gardens (29:5, 28), which could easily have been interpreted
as abandoning all hope for the land of Judah. But these words, though spoken
to a Judahite audience, nevertheless send a strong message to exiles in Babylon
that the stay there will be temporary and that the day will come when houses,
fields, and vineyards will again be bought by Judahites in Judah (Rubinger
1977: 90–91). Dietrich Bonhoeffer (1971: 15, 415), another such person with
hope in a hopeless time, quoted this verse in his *Letters and Papers from Prison*.

16. *Then I prayed to Yahweh after I had given the deed of purchase to Baruch
son of Neriah.* Jeremiah is a man of prayer, combining here the reverence and
questioning so familiar from his earlier confessions. Jeremiah is otherwise
questioning Yahweh (12:1–3; 15:15–18; 20:14–18), complaining of unjust
treatment by friend and foe (11:18–20; 15:10; 18:18–23; 20:7–10), and interced-
ing for others (37:3; 42:2–4, 20); but this prayer is motivated by misgivings
about what he himself has just done (v 25).

17. *Ah, Lord Yahweh! Look, you, you have made the heavens and the earth
with your great strength and with your outstretched arm. Nothing is too difficult
for you.* Antecedent creation theology (v 17) in confessions of Israel's own redemption theology (vv 20–23) suggested to earlier scholars an exilic or postexilic date for the prayer, comparisons usually being made to Second Isaiah
(Isa 45:12–13) and Ezra's prayer in Neh 9:6–37 (von Rad 1962: 124, 136–39).
But creation theology begins an oracle in 27:5, which is not late, as von Rad
claims, and is well documented elsewhere in Jeremiah (see Note for 27:5). The

dedicatory prayer of Solomon in 1 Kgs 8:23 and Hezekiah's prayer for deliverance in 2 Kgs 19:15, neither of which is as late as the Exile, begin similarly with creation.

Ah, Lord Yahweh! Look. On this Jeremianic expression, see Note for 1:6. The LXX omits *hinnēh* ("look"), which Janzen (1973: 118) and Migsch (1996: 354 n. 94) correctly take to be a loss due to haplography (homoeoteleuton: *h . . . h*).

with your great strength and with your outstretched arm. On this expression, referring here not to the Exodus deliverance but to Yahweh's work of Creation, see Note for 27:5.

Nothing is too difficult for you. Hebrew *lō'-yippālē' mimmĕkā kol-dābār.* Yahweh says the same about himself in v 27. The verb *pl'* means "to be wonderful, extraordinary," where the sense can also be "too difficult" (Gen 18:14) or "too wonderful to understand" (Job 42:3). The idea of "hiddenness" is present in the readings of T ("nothing is hidden from before you") and LXX (*ou mē apokrubē apo sou outhen,* "but nothing can be hidden from you"), whereas "too difficult" is the sense preserved in Aq and Symm (*ouk adunatēsei apo sou/soi,* "is not wanting in ability from you/for you), and in the Vg (*non erit tibi difficile,* "will not be difficult for you").

18. *who shows steadfast love to thousands but who repays the iniquity of the fathers into the lap of their children after them.* A summary version of the divine retribution formula in Exod 20:5–6; 34:7; and Deut 5:9–10. Compare also Solomon's prayer in 1 Kgs 8:23. According to Jer 31:30, however, this principle will be modified in the future. The discourse shifts here to the third person, then back again to second person in v 19, which is acceptable in prayers (Calvin; cf. 1 Kgs 8:27).

into the lap of their children. Hebrew *'el-ḥêq bĕnêhem.* The term *ḥêq* ("lap, bosom") refers here to the fold in a robe above the midsection where the hands are placed and one's property can be kept (Exod 4:6; Prov 21:14). Large enough for carrying infants or lambs (Num 11:12; Isa 40:11), this pocket-like fold makes a purse or basket unnecessary. Here, as elsewhere, the term occurs in a figure of recompense (Ps 79:12; Isa 65:6–7).

the great God, the mighty, Yahweh of hosts is his name. This acclamation, "the great God, the mighty," reduces the threefold acclamation (omitting "the terrible") in Deut 10:17 and Neh 9:32. The RSV, NRSV, NAB, and NJV translate the definite article on "God" as a vocative ("O God"), but this assumes direct speech to God, which the present words are not (see above). A shift to third-person speech occurred at the beginning of the verse, and second person speech does not resume until v 19. Note also "Yahweh of hosts is *his* name." This word of acclamation should then be translated third person, like the acclamation in Deut 10:17. In Neh 9:32, the acclamation is made directly to Yahweh. Compare the parenthetical homage-rendering statements to God in the NT letters of Paul (Rom 1:25; 9:5; 11:33–36), found also routinely in the Talmud and other rabbinic writings. "Yahweh is his name" is an old climactic shout (Exod 15:3), whereas "Yahweh of hosts is his name" is a doxology occurring only in Jeremiah and Second Isaiah (see Note on 10:16). The LXX omits "of hosts is his name," as it often does (see Appendix VI).

19. *great in counsel and mighty in deed.* Hebrew *gĕdōl hā'ēṣâ wĕrab hā'ălîlîyyâ.* The only phrase of its kind in the OT (Holladay). "Counsel" (*'ēṣâ*) is given by the wise and the clever (18:18, 23; 49:7; 2 Sam 16:23), but Yahweh surpasses everyone in wise counsel and wise planning—both for good and for evil (49:20 [= 50:45]; Isa 25:1; 28:29; 46:10; Ps 33:11; Prov 19:21). The spelling of "deed" (*'ălîlîyyâ*) is a *hapax legomenon* in the OT (normally *'ălîlâ*). Rudolph says *iyyâ* is an abstract ending; cf. *pĕlîlîyyâ* ("judgment") in Isa 28:7.

so that your eyes are open upon all the ways of humanity's children. Yahweh has an all-seeing eye (7:11; 13:27; 16:17; 23:24; 29:23; 49:10). The LXX omits "all," which Migsch (1996: 355) notes can be attributed to haplography (homoeoteleuton: *l . . . l*). The verb "open" (*pĕqūḥôt*), also omitted in the LXX, is translated in Aq, Theod, G^L, S, T, and Vg (Giesebrecht) and should be retained.

and according to the fruit of his doings. The LXX omits, which is probably another loss due to haplography (homoeoteleuton: *yw . . . yw*). See also Migsch 1996: 355 n. 100. The phrase is Jeremianic (see Note for 17:10) and is translated in Theod, G^L, S, T, and Vg (Giesebrecht).

20. *so that you have shown signs and wonders, in the land of Egypt—up to this day—and in Israel and among humankind.* The implications of Yahweh's great counsel and mighty deeds are still being drawn out, with the prophet turning now to Israel's redemption history (Deut 6:22; cf. Neh 9:10). Yahweh's signs and wonders are even brought up to the present day. Is Jeremiah thinking about Jerusalem's surrender but preservation in 597 B.C.? We can be sure he does not anticipate a deliverance from Nebuchadrezzar now. In any case, these continuous wonders of Yahweh are being set over against Israel's continuous provocation in v 31. The syntax here, as in v 11, is unusual in that "up to this day" modifies both "in the land of Egypt" and "in Israel and among humankind" (Tsumura (1983: 478–79). The point is that Yahweh has given signs and wonders in all places and among all peoples from earliest times up to the present day.

and in Israel and among humankind. The LXX reads "and among the sons of earth" (*kai en tois gēgenesin*) for "and among humankind," which G. R. Driver (1964: 90) thinks reflects *w(b)bny (h)'dmh*, a forgotten Hebrew phrase. Yet there is little reason to emend; T and Vg support MT.

and you made for yourself a name, as at this day. See 2 Sam 7:23 [= 1 Chr 17:21]; Isa 63:12; Neh 9:10; and Dan 9:15. Here, "as at this day" comes expectedly at the end.

21. *And you brought your people Israel out from the land of Egypt with signs and with wonders and with a strong hand and with an outstretched arm and with great terror.* The verse has striking similarities to Deut 4:34 and 26:8. "Signs and wonders" were seen preeminently in the Exodus (Exod 7:3; Deut 6:22; 7:19; 29:2[Eng 29:3]; Pss 78:43; 105:27), and "with a strong hand and outstretched arm" is another cliché associated with the Exodus deliverance (see Note for 21:5).

and with great terror. Hebrew *ûbĕmôrā' gādôl.* The LXX (*kai en opamasin megalois,* "and with great sights"), T ("and with the great vision"), and Symm (*en tois phainomenois,* "with the revelations") all appear to have read *môrā'* as "sight" or "revelation" (Rosenberg says T read *môrā'* like *mar'eh*). But Aq has *(kai) ev phobemati megalo,* "(and) with great terror," and Vg *et in terrore magno,* "and in great terror," both supporting MT.

22. *this land that you swore to their fathers to give to them.* On Yahweh's promise of the land to the fathers, i.e., Abraham, Isaac, and Jacob, see Note for 11:5. The LXX omits "to give to them," which can be attributed to haplography (homoeoteleuton: *m . . . m*). See also Migsch 1996: 355.

23. *And they came in and took possession of it, but they did not obey your voice and in your law did not walk; everything that you commanded them to do, they did not do, so you made them meet up with all this evil.* Jeremiah's 35 years of preaching is summed up in this one verse. In his view, things began to go bad after Israel's settlement in the land (see Note for 2:7).

but they did not obey your voice and in your law did not walk. A syntactic chiasmus with the verbs at the extremes. For people not walking in Yahweh's law (*tôrâ*), see 6:16 (= "ancient paths"), 19; 8:8; 9:12[Eng 9:13]; 26:4–6; 44:10, 23; also 2 Kgs 10:31.

everything that you commanded them to do, they did not do. The LXX omits "to do" (*la'ăśôt*), which can be attributed to haplography (homoeoarcton: *l . . . l*).

so you made them meet up with all this evil. A fulfillment of what is stated in Deut 31:29 and repeated to the exiles in Egypt in Jer 44:23.

24. *Look, the siege ramps have come to the city to take it.* A metonymy (the army will take the city). This is lost in the translation of the LXX, which substitutes "a throng" (*ochlos*) for "the siege ramps" (*hassōlĕlôt*). On siege warfare, see Note for 6:6. The verb *bā'û* ("have come") is a prophetic perfect (Giesebrecht): Jeremiah is certain that the siege will be successful (v 25).

because of the sword and the famine and the pestilence. On this stereotyped triad in Jeremiah, see Note for 5:12. The LXX omits "and the pestilence," as it does occasionally (see Note for 38:2), although the omission here could also be due to haplography (homoeoarcton: *w . . . w*).

So look, you are watching! Hebrew *wĕhinnĕkā rō'eh.* The form *hinnĕkā* with the participle is a continual present. Jeremiah is saying to Yahweh: "Look! you see it happening before your very eyes!" The LXX omits, which some commentators (Giesebrecht; Rudolph; Holladay) think may be due to the anthropomorphism. But the loss can also be attributed to haplography (homoeoarcton: *w . . . w,* or homoeoteleuton: *h . . . h*), as Migsch (1996: 358 n. 118) has noted. The phrase is translated in G^L, S, T, and Vg (Giesebrecht).

25. *Yet you, you have said to me, O Lord Yahweh, 'Buy for yourself the field with silver and call for witnesses,' but the city has been given into the hand of the Chaldeans!* Here at the end of the prayer Jeremiah gets around to stating what is really on his mind, and it comes forth with a sense of urgency. The Chaldeans are outside the city, soon to take it, so why then has Yahweh told him to buy the field? We learn only here that Yahweh had actually instructed him

to buy the field and call for witnesses; it was not mentioned in v 7, which said only that Hanamel would come and ask Jeremiah to make the purchase. But Hanamel's word must have been for Jeremiah the word of Yahweh (cf. v 8). The answer to the prophet's vexation, one would imagine, is contained in the second oracle to Baruch (v 15), where the symbolism of the purchase is explained. This is not narrative from a later time; it is a reporting soon after the event, at which time Jeremiah is still uncertain about what he has just done.

O Lord Yahweh. The LXX omits, which Migsch (1996: 359 n. 119) explains as an inner-Greek haplography (homoeoteleuton: *me . . . kurie*).

with silver. The LXX adds after this word, "and I wrote a deed, and I sealed it, and I called witnesses" (*kai egrapsa biblion kai esphragisamēn kai epemarturamēn marturas*), which Janzen (1973: 64) thinks is expansion from v 10. But the addition changes the meaning, because Jeremiah now tells Yahweh only that he had directed him to buy the field with silver; after that, he carried this directive out by writing up a deed, sealing it, and calling for witnesses. The T and Vg support MT, which gives the better reading.

the city has been given into the hand of the Chaldeans. The verb *nittĕnâ* ("has been given")—here and throughout the narrative—is a prophetic perfect, i.e., the city is as good as captured.

26. *And the word of Yahweh came to Jeremiah.* On this third-person superscriptional form, see Note for 28:12. The T expands to "the word of prophecy." For MT's "to Jeremiah," the LXX has "to me," which G. R. Driver (1960: 121) says is another misread abbreviation: אלי for אל י (= אל־ירמיהו). The LXX has the same reading in 35:12 and 36:1. The MT reading is preferable (so Aq, Symm, T, Vg), since the superscription does not introduce first-person speech, as in v 6, but divine oracles on through to the end of the chapter.

27. *Look I am Yahweh, God of all flesh.* Yahweh is speaking now, and he prefaces his first oracle with a self-asseveration echoing Jeremiah's acclamation at the beginning of his prayer (v 17).

Is anything too difficult for me? On the different nuances of the verb *pl'* ("to be wonderful, extraordinary, too difficult"), see v 17. The LXX and T again translate the verb as "hidden," which may anticipate Yahweh's word in 33:3: "Call to me and I will answer you, and I will tell you great things and hidden things (*bĕṣūrôt*) you have not known."

28. *Therefore thus said Yahweh.* Here the LXX adds "the God of Israel."

Look I am giving this city into the hand of the Chaldeans and into the hand of Nebuchadrezzar, king of Babylon, and he shall take it. Jeremiah has heard Yahweh say this before and has been preaching this message a long while (see Note for 34:2). Perhaps now he needs to hear it again. In this oracle and the one following, which are the last recorded judgment oracles given to a Jerusalem audience, we have what sounds like an aged Jeremiah compressing into single oracles the preaching of 35 years, a florilegium, if you will, of quotations or main points contained in earlier oracles.

Look I am giving. Hebrew *hinĕnî nōtēn.* A bona fide Jeremianic construction (32:3; 34:2) not translated by the LXX, which omits *hinĕnî* and has *dotheisa paradothēsetai* for the verb ("will surely be given over"? cf. 38:3). The readings of Aq, Symm, T, and Vg support MT.

the Chaldeans and into the hand of Nebuchadrezzar. The LXX omits, but the words are translated in Theod, T, and Vg.

29. *And the Chaldeans who are fighting against this city shall come in and set this city on fire and burn it.* The verb *ûbā'û* is a perfect with *waw consecutive*: "and they shall come." The prediction that the Babylonians will burn Jerusalem has been made repeatedly (see Note for 34:2).

the houses on whose roofs they burned incense to Baal, and poured out drink offerings to other gods. This illicit worship was condemned in an oracle spoken by Jeremiah when he broke the decanter in the Ben-Hinnom Valley (19:13) and is a theme recurring throughout the book (see Note for 1:16). Remnants of incense burners were found on house roofs in Ashkelon dating to Nebuchadrezzar's destruction of that city in 604 B.C. (see Note for 19:13).

in order to provoke me to anger. Yahweh is "provoked to anger" (*k's* H-stem) by idols and the worship of other gods (see Notes for 7:18–19). The point is made again in v 32.

30. *Indeed, the children of Israel and the children of Judah have been doing only what is evil in my eyes from their youth.* Hyperbole. The expression "to do what is evil in the eyes of Yahweh" is stock in Deuteronomy, Judges, and Kings (Weinfeld 1972b: 339). The charge that the people have been disobedient "from their youth" is found elsewhere in Jeremiah (3:24–25; 22:21) and in Ezekiel (Ezek 20:5–26).

Indeed, the children of Israel have only provoked me to anger with the work of their hands—oracle of Yahweh. The LXX omits, which can be attributed to haplography (whole-word: *ky . . . ky*). See also Migsch 1996: 359 n. 123. The words are present in Aq, Symm, T, and Vg. On "the work of one's hands," meaning idols, see Note for 25:6.

31. *Indeed, with respect to my anger and my wrath, this city has become to me—from the day that they built it up until this day—in order to remove it from my presence.* Yahweh can cast the city away with a clear conscience because it has accumulated so much evil. Calvin sees this as a parade example of divine predestination, but what we may have is simply divine hyperbole. Reference, in any case, is not to the founding of Jerusalem, which occurred long before David made the city his own, but to building that occurred after Jerusalem became a Judahite city. Rashi says that Jerusalem became a provocation to God "from the day the Temple was built." Kimḥi's view is similar.

my anger and my wrath. On this expression in Jeremiah, see again v 37 and Note for 21:5.

this city has become to me. The verb *hāyĕtâ* ("has become") intentionally repeats *hāyû* ("have been") from v 30, balancing the two statements of divine hyperbole. The LXX lacks "to me."

in order to remove it from my presence. The prefixed *lamed* on *lahăsîrāh* means "in order to." On this expression, see 2 Kgs 17:18, 23; 23:27; 24:3.

32. *on account of all the evil . . . which they did to provoke me to anger.* The "evil" is doubtless making idols and worshiping other gods (v 29), which is specified in vv 34–35.

they, their kings, their princes, their priests, and their prophets. Accumulatio. See 2:26 and 4:9. The T again has "prophets of falsehood."

the men of Judah and the inhabitants of Jerusalem. A stereotypical phrase in the Jeremiah prose (see Note for 4:3), found elsewhere only in 2 Kgs 23:2 = 2 Chr 34:30 (S. R. Driver 1913: 276).

33. *They faced me with the back of the neck, and not the face.* This expression with reference to the people of Judah occurs earlier in 2:27. On the body language for showing contempt, see Note for 7:24.

although I taught them—constantly taught. Hebrew *wĕlammēd 'ōtām haškēm wĕlammēd.* For the rhetorical idiom of a repeated verb used together with *škm*, see Note for 7:13. The grammar here is different from what we are accustomed to, in that the first verb—like the verb of the idiom—is not a conjugated form but the infinitive absolute, *lammēd* ("to teach"). Since in every other occurrence of the idiom it is Yahweh who acts continually and persistently to correct his wayward people, the Versions ancient and modern all translate the first infinitive as a first person, "and I (have) taught," which is most likely correct. Giesebrecht (and others) emend the first infinitive to *wā'ălammēd* ("and I taught"). So read, the people are seen to be treating Yahweh with contempt despite his teaching them to act otherwise, with the result that they have not listened to take correction.

but they did not listen to take correction. A recurring theme in Jeremiah's preaching (2:30; 5:3; 7:28; 17:23; 32:33; 35:13). Hebrew *mûsār* means "instruction, discipline, correction," and "to take instruction/discipline" is a recurring theme in Proverbs (Prov 1:3; 8:10; 24:32).

34. *And they set up their wretched things in the house upon which my name is called to defile it.* "Their wretched things" (*šiqqûṣêhem*) are the disgusting idols introduced into the Temple (see Note for 7:30). In the seventh century B.C., the idea developed that idolatry pollutes (Milgrom 1998: 4–5).

35. *And they built the high places of Baal that are in the Valley of Ben-Hinnom to give over their sons and their daughters to Molech—which I did not command them, nor did it enter my mind for them to do this abomination—in order to make Judah sin.* See 7:31 and 19:5; Molech (Molek) worship is discussed in Note for 7:31. The verb *'br* in the H-stem means lit., "let pass through (the fire)," thus "give over (in sacrifice)" (Deut 18:10; Lev 18:21; 2 Kgs 16:3; 17:17; 21:6; Ezek 20:31).

which I did not command them, nor did it enter my mind for them to do this abomination. Milgrom (1998: 5) says that the reason for such a strong disclaimer (a *correctio*), which occurs also in 7:31 and 19:5, is that people believed Molek worship was compatible with Yahweh worship. The expression "to enter the mind" (lit., "to come up to the heart") is stereotypical in the Jeremiah prose (see Note for 7:31), with rare occurrences also in 2 Kgs 12:5 and Isa 65:17 (S. R. Driver 1913: 276).

for them to do this abomination. Hebrew *laʿăśôt hattôʿēbâ hazzōʾt*, where "for them" is added in translation to make it clear that the people, not Yahweh, has been doing the abomination. On this phrase, see Note for 2:7. The designation of idolatry as an "abomination" (*tôʿēbâ*) is the common language of Deuteronomy (Deut 7:25, 26; 13:15[Eng 13:14]; 17:4; 18:9; 20:18), appearing here and elsewhere in Jeremiah (16:18; 44:2, 22). The first occurrence is in Deut 32:16 (Weinfeld 1972b: 323).

to make . . . sin. Q: *haḥăṭîʾ*; the Kt lost an *ʾaleph* by haplography (double *ʾaleph* in succession).

36. *But now after this.* Hebrew *wĕʿattâ lākēn*, where *wĕʿattâ* signals a discourse shift (see Note for 2:18), in this case from present to future. In this oracle and the one following, Yahweh announces his future plans for an eternal covenant and a resumption of land purchases in Judah. For the translation of *lākēn* as "after this" in oracles of salvation, see Note on 16:14. The LXX and S omit *lākēn*, but it is translated in Aq, T, and Vg.

to this city of which you are saying, 'It has been given into the hand of the king of Babylon by sword and by famine and by pestilence.' The LXX omits the demonstrative on "this city," has a singular "you say" (*su legeis*), and has "by sword and by famine and by exile (*kai en apostolē*)." Aquila and Symm both have the demontrative pronoun (*tautēn*) and "by pestilence" (*en loimō*), and the other Vrs have the plural verb, *hymeis legete* (Field 1875: 667). A singular verb assumes that Yahweh is answering what Jeremiah stated in his prayer (v 24), but a plural verb assumes that others have joined Jeremiah in saying that the city will be taken by the Babylonians. Compare the LXX's singular "you say" in v 43, which precedes a quotation not in Jeremiah's prayer. In both cases Yahweh is addressing a plaint made by the people of Jerusalem. Another "you say," plural, occurs in 33:10.

37. *Look I am going to gather them from all the lands where I dispersed them in my anger and in my wrath and in great fury, and I will bring them back to this place and settle them in security.* On Yahweh's gathering the people that he scattered and returning them to the land of Judah, see Note for 31:8.

in my anger and in my wrath and in great fury. On this triad, see Note for 21:5. Yahweh's "fury" (*qeṣep*) makes the earth quake, leaving it a desolate wasteland (10:10; 50:13).

in security. Hebrew *lābeṭaḥ*. See 23:6 [= 33:16]; and Isa 32:17. Yahweh's original promise to Israel of settlement in the land was so that the people would live in security (Deut 12:10).

38. *And they will be a people to me, and I, I will be God to them.* The standard covenant formula (see Note for 7:23), included also in the "new covenant" oracle (31:33). The repetition of the pronoun "I" puts the emphasis here on Yahweh, as happens also in the formulas of 11:4; 24:7; and 30:22. But in the formulas of 7:23; 31:1, and 33, a repeated "they" puts the emphasis on the people.

39. *And I will give them one heart and one way to fear me all the days, for their own good and for their children after them.* Yahweh promises here to give the

people "one heart" and "one way" so they may fear him only. Bright translates: "singleness of mind and of purpose." It was duplicity in worship that led to a breakdown of the Sinai covenant and the crisis that the people are now in. Kierkegaard said: "Purity of heart is to will one thing." On Yahweh's gift of a new heart (and a new spirit) to his people, see Note for 31:33. The LXX reads "another way and another heart" (*hodon eteran kai kardian eteran*), which appears simply to misread the Hebrew (*'ahēr* for *'ehād*).

to fear me all the days. Hebrew *lĕyir'â 'ôtî kol-hayyāmîm*. The phrase, "to fear Yahweh/me all the days" is stock in Deuteronomy (Deut 4:10; 6:2; 14:23; 31:13) and has parallels in the Akkadian treaties (Zunz 1873: 670; Weinfeld 1972b: 332–33). For the expression "a heart to fear me [i.e., Yahweh]," see Deut 5:29. On the expression "all the days" in Jeremiah, see Note for 31:36.

for their own good and for their children after them. One fears God because of his awesome creation, his deliverance from evil, also because he is worthy of reverent fear. But the point here is that fear of God is for the people's own good (Deut 6:24) and the good of their children (Deut 4:10; 6:2). This rhetoric reverses the rhetoric of 7:19 about the worship of other gods' provoking not only Yahweh but the people themselves, to their own shame. See also "to your own hurt" in 7:6 and 25:7.

40. *And I will cut for them an eternal covenant, in which I will not turn away from them to do good to them; and the fear of me I will put in their hearts so they may not turn away from me.* It is generally agreed that this "eternal covenant" (*bĕrît 'ôlām*), cited again in 50:5, is the "new covenant" (*bĕrît hădāšâ*) promised by Yahweh in 31:31–34 (Calvin; von Rad 1965: 214–15), to be cut in the future with Israel and Judah as a replacement for the now-broken Sinai (Mosaic) covenant. The Sinai covenant with its blessings and curses was never guaranteed to be eternal. This covenant and the new covenant are both without conditions; thus, they really are new and are for all time (B. W. Anderson 1964: 231; see Note for 31:31). Second Isaiah's covenant for the new age will likewise last forever and will be a relationship of pure grace (Muilenburg 1956a: 399, 401).

The idea of an eternal covenant was neither new nor unique to Israelite religion. On a seventh-century B.C. amulet from Arslan Tash in northern Syria (ancient Hadattu), an "eternal sworn covenant" (*'lt 'lm*) cut among lesser divine beings, but established by the god Ashshur, was invoked to ward off child-stealing vampires (Torczyner 1947; Gaster 1947; *ANET*[3] 658; *CS* II 222–23; for a picture of the amulet, see *ANEP*[2] #662; cf. 328). In Israelite religion, covenants of an unconditional nature were given earlier to Noah, Abraham, Phinehas, and David (D. N. Freedman 1964; Weinfeld 1970; idem, "bᵉrîth," *TDOT* 2: 270–72), and these were meant to be for all time. Unconditional covenants were at home in Southern theology, i.e., in P traditions (Gen 9:16; 17:7, 13, 19; Exod 31:16; Lev 24:8; Num 18:19; 25:13) and psalms from the Jerusalem Temple (Pss 89:20–38[Eng 89:19–37]; 111:5, 9; cf. 2 Sam 23:5). Jeremiah, whose entire ministry was carried on in the Southern capital, was as familiar with these covenants as with the Sinai covenant, which was at home in Northern theology (Wang 1972: 9–11). The promise given to the Rechabites was unconditional (see Note for 35:19). At some point before the Exile, the covenants to Abraham and David were expanded to cover Jerusalem and the Temple (Isa 37:33–35 [= 2 Kgs 19:32–34]; Pss 105:8–11 [= 1 Chr 16:15–18]; 132:11–18; cf. Isa 31:4–5; Jer 7:1–15). Ezekiel and Second Isaiah look ahead to an "eternal covenant" between Yahweh and the nation (Ezek 16:60; Isa 55:3; 61:8; Renaud 1986), decribed elsewhere as a covenant of "peace" (Ezek 34:25; 37:26; Isa 54:10), or one in which Yahweh's Spirit will indwell the people (Ezek 36:27–28; Isa 59:21). These varied descriptions of a future covenant were part of a larger messianic hope taking shape at the time. The servant figure of Second Isaiah will personally embody the new covenant (Isa 42:6; 49:8), and through this servant other nations will be brought into covenant relation (Isa 55:1–5; Muilenburg 1956a: 405). Malachi's "messenger of the covenant," finally, is cast as a priestly figure (Mal 3:1; cf. 2:1–9). The idea of an "eternal covenant" survives in postexilic Judaism, including the Essenes, and the Christian Church, which claims to be a fulfillment of this prophecy. See Excursus IV: "The New Covenant in the Literature of Judaism, Including Qumran," and Excursus V: "The New Covenant in the New Testament and Patristic Literature to A.D. 325," at the end of 31:31–34.

in which I will not turn away from them to do good to them. The Hebrew actually reads, "I will not turn away from *after* them (*lō'-'āšûb mē'aḥărêhem*)," which is strange because of an assumed anthromorphism. The idea seems to be that Yahweh, in times past, has followed behind his covenant people and seen detestable sights, e.g., disgusting idols, and turned to walk away. But in the future, Yahweh says he will not do this. The same imagery, basically, is present in Deut 23:15[Eng 23:14], where it says that excrement in the camp must be covered up because Yahweh on a walk through the camp might come upon it, in which case the people are warned: "He will turn away from after you" (*šāb mē'aḥăreykā*). Calvin says that the *'ăšer* should not be translated here as the relative pronoun, but as "because." However, it makes better sense for Yahweh to say that he will not turn away from his people because of the eternal covenant, rather than to state things the other way around.

to do good to them. The LXX omits, doubtless again due to haplography (homoeoteleuton: *m . . . m*). See also Migsch 1996: 360 n. 127.

and the fear of me I will put in their hearts so they may not turn away from me. This repetition of what has already been stated in v 39 may be for the purpose of juxtaposing correlative ideas—not wording—in the phrases, "I will not turn away from them," and "so they may not turn away from me." The covenant people "turned away" (*sûr*) from Yahweh in the wilderness when they made the golden calf (Exod 32:8; Deut 9:12). Compare the admonitions in 1 Sam 12:20 and Deut 11:16–17.

41. *And I will rejoice over them to do them good.* A disposition on the part of Yahweh when he was building up his people (Deut 28:63), now promised to return in their restoration. See also Deut 30:9; Zeph 3:17; Isa 62:5; and 65:19. The LXX has "and I will watch over (*episkepsomai*) to do them good," which

may follow 31:28. The MT reading is supported by G^L, S, T, and Vg and should be followed (Giesebrecht).

and I will truly plant them in this land, with all my heart and with all my soul. On Yahweh "planting" (*nt'*) his people once again in the land, see 24:6 and 31:27–28. Hebrew *be'ĕmet* means "in truth, in (good) faith," referring here to Yahweh's act of planting. Yahweh is using language normally reserved for the people and their commitment to Yahweh (Deut 4:29; 6:5; 10:12; 1 Kgs 2:4; 2 Kgs 23:3). Only here in the OT is the expression "with all my heart and with all my soul" used in reference to God (S. R. Driver 1913: 101; Weinfeld 1972b: 334).

42. *Even as I brought to this people all this great evil, so I am going to bring upon them all the good that I am speaking concerning them.* Yahweh's good gifts are just as sure as his awesome judgment. A comparison using the *ka'ăšer . . . kēn* construction, on which see Note for 13:11. The same construction expresses the same idea in 31:28.

43. *The field shall be bought in this land, of which you are saying, 'It is a desolation, without human or beast; it has been given into the hand of the Chaldeans.'* The LXX again omits the demonstrative pronoun on "in this land," and has the singular "you say" (*su legeis*); cf. v 36. The plural verb is better, since the oracle is spoken to a larger Judahite audience. The LXX and the Vrs also appear to be missing the *hē'* before *śādeh* ("field"), which could be attributed to haplography (double consonants in succession). This final oracle, with its promise of fields once again being bought and sold in Judah, returns to the symbolic action that the chapter is basically about (v 15).

It is a desolation, without human or beast. The whole of Judah, that is, except Jerusalem, which has not yet been captured and destroyed. Anathoth, where the property that Jeremiah has just redeemed lies, is probably already in the possession of the Babylonians. On the expression "human or beast," see Note for 21:6.

44. *Fields shall be bought with silver, also writing in the deed and sealing and the summoning of witnesses to witness, in the land of Benjamin.* Benjamin is mentioned first because the field Jeremiah purchased was in Benjamin. After the fall of Jerusalem, a remnant community was formed at Mizpah in Benjamin (40:6), and some land transactions—under Babylonian supervision—doubtless occurred there while this community was in existence. We are told that the poorest of people were given fields and vineyards by Nebuzaradan (39:10). But this cannot be a fulfillment of the present prophecy, for Jeremiah doubtless has in mind a time when the land will be free from foreign occupation, and Judahites will be able to conduct their affairs in traditional ways.

and in the regions around Jerusalem and in the cities of Judah, in the cities of the hill country and in the cities of the Shephelah and in the cities of the Negeb. Compare the sweep of Judahite territory in 17:26 and 33:13. On the various territories, see Note for 17:26. The whole of Judah is envisioned here as being repopulated, with people once again making land purchases such as the one Jeremiah just made.

for I will surely restore their fortunes. Hebrew *kî-ʾāšîb ʾet-šĕbûtām*. The theme of the completed Book of Restoration, on which see Rhetoric and Composition for 30:1–3. For the expression elsewhere and those occurrences in Jeremiah employing an internal H-stem as here, see Note for 29:14.

MESSAGE AND AUDIENCE

A small Judahite audience assembled in the court of the guard witnessed the unusual land purchase reported here, and sometime later another audience, perhaps a bit larger, heard this report along with eight oracles and a prayer by Jeremiah, which make up the narrative as we now have it. This later audience is told that in the tenth year of Zedekiah, when Nebuchadrezzar was besieging Jerusalem, Jeremiah received a word from Yahweh while he was in the court of the guard. The reason for his confinement is explained. He was put there by Zedekiah, who wanted to know why Jeremiah was prophesying evil for Jerusalem and himself. The two oracles that follow were presumably spoken to the king before Jeremiah was put into the court of the guard. In the first, Yahweh says he is giving Jerusalem into the hand of the king of Babylon. Zedekiah too will be given into his hand, and he can expect to be mouth to mouth and eye to eye before the great king. Nebuchadrezzar will do the talking, roundly denouncing the enchained Zedekiah for breaking an oath he had sworn to him. In a second oracle, Yahweh says that Nebuchadrezzar will take Zedekiah to Babylon, and there he will remain until Yahweh visits him. A Judahite audience is then told directly that although they are fighting the Chaldeans, it is a lost cause and they will not succeed.

Following this background, the audience is told what came to Jeremiah as a present word from Yahweh. The account comes as a first-person report. Yahweh told Jeremiah that his cousin Hanamel would come and ask him to buy his field in Anathoth. The cousin had evidently fallen on hard times and needed to sell. The right of redemption belonged to Jeremiah. Things happened just as Yahweh said. Hanamel came to the court of the guard and asked Jeremiah to buy his field. Jeremiah says that then he knew this was a word from Yahweh. So he bought the field, weighed out 17 shekels of silver, signed the deed, had it sealed, and called for witnesses. Once the transaction was completed, Jeremiah took the deed—both the sealed and the open copy containing the contract and the conditions—and gave them to Baruch in the presence of Hanamel, the witnesses, and others who were present.

Two oracles were then spoken to Baruch in the presence of those assembled. In the first, Baruch was commanded to take the deeds and put them in an earthenware jar for safekeeping. He would probably bury them. In a second oracle, Yahweh gave the larger meaning of what had just transpired: once again, houses, fields, and vineyards would be bought in the land of Judah.

With the land purchase completed, a prayer to Yahweh by Jeremiah is then reported. It is not known whether those assembled in the court of the guard heard this prayer. It may have been prayed later. But the audience now hearing the narrative is made privy to Jeremiah's baring of his soul to Yahweh. The prayer begins by acclaiming Yahweh's mighty work of creation. Nothing is too difficult for Yahweh. What is more, Yahweh is a God of steadfast love but one who nevertheless lets fall the iniquity of fathers into the laps of their children. A great and mighty God is Yahweh of hosts! Yahweh is further extolled for being excellent in counsel, mighty in deed, and for being watchful over everything that happens, so justice is rendered to each person. Yahweh is the God who showed signs and wonders in the Exodus, and these miraculous works have continued up to the present day. Was 597 a deliverance? Was the siege-lifting, brief as it was, a deliverance? It is difficult to say. But there is no doubt that Yahweh gave Israel the good land promised to the fathers or that, after the settlement, rebellion set in, Yahweh's law was not obeyed, and now the people have met up with this unimaginable evil. Siege ramps are outside Jerusalem, and the city is as good as conquered by the Chaldeans. Sword, famine, and pestilence are everywhere taking their toll. Yahweh said this would happen, and it has. Jeremiah says Yahweh is watching things as they occur. So why now has Yahweh told Jeremiah to buy this field with silver and bring in witnesses? The prayer ends with the question Jeremiah wanted to ask at the beginning.

Yahweh answers this prayer with four oracles. The first two are directed to Jeremiah, although we can imagine a larger audience listening in. The first is preceded by a direct word to Jeremiah, in which Yahweh simply repeats what Jeremiah said at the opening of his prayer. Yahweh says he is indeed the God of all flesh, and he asks rhetorically if anything is too difficult for him. Yahweh knows the answer. So does Jeremiah. The first oracle is one of indictment and judgment, repeating much of what Yahweh has been saying to Jeremiah and to Judah over a period of years. The city will be given into the hand of the Chaldeans, after which they will set it on fire and burn, among other things, the houses on whose roofs the people have burned incense to Baal and poured out drink offerings to other gods. Yahweh says it again: This has provoked him no end! In the second oracle, Israel and Judah both are cited for coming to him in later days only to do evil. It began in their youth. Yahweh says again how idols have provoked him. Indeed, it is as if the city has come to him now—from the day it was built up—only so that he might banish it from his sight. This unhappy end has come about because of provocation by everyone—kings, princes, priests, prophets, and people of Jerusalem and all Judah. They have all treated Yahweh with contempt, disregarding his teaching and not listening to take needed words of correction. Abominable idols were set up in the Temple called by Yahweh's name! And things were no better in the Valley, where high places to Baal were set up and people did the unthinkable by offering their sons and daughters to Molech. Yahweh, needless to say, did not command such a thing; indeed, it never entered his mind!

Following this blistering attack, which explains once again the horrible fix the people are in, Yahweh turns to the more distant future, where his plans are of a different nature. The two oracles here address a larger Judahite audience. People have been asking the same question that Jeremiah has asked, and the first oracle speaks to their concern about Jerusalem being given over to the king of Babylon. But Yahweh says he intends to gather people from all the lands where his divine anger has driven them, and he will bring them back to this very place, where they will dwell in security. Once again they will be a people to him, and he will be God to them. Yahweh promises also to the returnees one heart and one path so they will fear him always—for their own good and for the good of their children after them. Yahweh will cut with them an eternal covenant, in which he will not turn away—as he is doing now—and good will be done for them. The fear of himself he will put in their hearts, so they too will not turn away—as they have now done. This will be a grand day of rejoicing, for Yahweh will take great pleasure in doing the people good. He will plant them in the land in all truth, showing resolve and singleness of purpose in everything he does.

In his final oracle to the people of Judah and Jerusalem, Yahweh says he can bring good just as well as evil, and the good is what he has planned for the people's future. Fields will once again be bought in the land, the land they are now lamenting because an enemy has overrun it and made it a ruin. The day will come when fields will be bought with silver, deeds will be signed and sealed, and witnesses will be summoned for land transactions in Benjamin and every other region of Judah, for Yahweh says he fully intends to restore the people's fortunes.

This narrative reflects the period of the final siege, a year before the fall of Jerusalem. The two oracles regarding Zedekiah were spoken earlier; the two oracles following the land purchase on the occasion itself; and the four final oracles on the same occasion or later. Jeremiah's prayer could also have been spoken on the occasion, or else later. A date for the narrative as a whole is sometime after the summer of 587 B.C. When this narrative is heard following chap. 31, the oracles on the eternal covenant (32:36–41) and renewed field transactions (32:42–44) will supplement the oracles on the new covenant (31:31–34) and the rebuilding of Jerusalem (31:38–40).

To Martin Luther are attributed the following words:

Und wenn ich wüßte, das morgen die Welt unterginge
So würde ich doch heute mein Apfelbäumchen pflanzen.

And if I knew that tomorrow the world would come to an end
I would still plant my apple trees today.
                    (Inscribed outside the Christengemeinschaft,
                              10 Lutherplatz, Eisenach, Germany)

        In the midst of the chaos and carnage
        That accompanies the siege of Jerusalem
        Jeremiah buys a farm outside the city
        Land now occupied by Babylonian troops

It is foolish in terms of dollars
For the land has no economic value
But as a sign of Jeremiah's hope in the New Covenant
The action makes great sense
The prophet puts his money
Where his mouth is.

(Steele 1985–86: 476)

C. MORE ON RESTORATION AND COVENANTS (33:1–26)

1. I Will Tell You Great and Hidden Things! (33:1–3)

33 ¹And the word of Yahweh came to Jeremiah a second time, while he was still confined in the court of the guard:

²Thus said Yahweh who made it
Yahweh who formed it to establish it
Yahweh is his name!

³Call to me and I will answer you
and let me tell you great things and hidden things
you have not known.

RHETORIC AND COMPOSITION

MT 33:1–3 = LXX 40:1–3. In chap. 33 are eight oracles, the same number as in chap. 32; however, here there is no narrative but simply expanded oracle formulas and brief introductions that provide the oracles with background (vv 1, 4–5, 19, 23–24). Oracle I (vv 2–3) addresses Jeremiah (singular suffixes) and is introductory: first to Oracle II (vv 6–9), then later to all the oracles in the chapter. Oracles II through VIII address a broader audience of Judahites facing a destruction of the city in which they are now imprisoned and, afterwards, a remnant of the same, who remain in the land or have been taken into exile.

This collection is linked to chap. 32 by the phrase, "And the word of Yahweh came to Jeremiah *a second time*, while he was still confined in the court of the guard" (v 1; cf. 32:1–2). A first revelation came to Jeremiah when Hanamel approached him with the request to buy his field. A second comes now when Yahweh promises to unveil hidden things to Jeremiah if he will but call upon him (vv 2–3). Both revelations came when Jeremiah was shut up in the court of the guard. There is no reason to view this linking statement as simply a "literary device" without historical value (*pace* Volz; Carroll; McKane). This prejudges chap. 33 as "an imitation and secondary elaboration of chap 32" (McKane, citing Thiel 1981: 37, who says chap. 33 is "post-deuteronomic"). Weiser and Holladay take v 1 as a serious historical notice, which it must be. A statement of the same sort occurs in 1:13, which does not make an artificial connection. Compare also 13:3. Chapter 33 completes the Book of Restoration (30–33) with the phrase, "I will surely restore their fortunes" (v 26Q), which makes an inclusio with a matching phrase in 30:3.

The eight oracles are arranged in two groups of four, just as in chap. 32. In the first group are two single oracles, vv 2–3 and vv 6–9, then a pair of similarly-structured oracles, vv 10–11 and vv 12–13. Oracles I and II are received prior to the fall of Jerusalem; Oracles III and IV after the fall. In the second group are two single oracles, vv 14–16 and vv 17–18, then a pair of similarly-structured oracles concluding the collection and also the enlarged Book of Restoration, vv 20–22 and 25–26. Oracle V in vv 14–16 repeats the oracle in 23:5–6 with little change. The eight oracles with their balancing formulas and key phrases are the following:

I	Expect Great and Hidden Things	vv 1–3
	And the word of Yahweh came to Jeremiah	v 1
	a second time . . .	
	Thus said Yahweh . . .	v 2
II	Healed City, Healed People	vv 4–9
	For thus said Yahweh, God of Israel . . .	v 4
	Look I am going to bring . . .	v 6
III	The Return of Joyful Sounds	vv 10–11
	Thus said Yahweh:	v 10
	Again it shall be heard in this place . . . 'It is a	
	waste, without human and . . . beast' . . .	
	. . . said Yahweh	v 11
IV	The Return of Pastureland	vv 12–13
	Thus said Yahweh of hosts:	v 12
	Again there shall be in this place of waste,	
	without human or beast . . .	
	. . . said Yahweh	v 13
V	A Righteous King in a Righteous City	vv 14–16
	Look, days are coming—oracle of Yahweh . . .	v 14
	In those days and at that time . . .	v 15
	a Shoot of righteousness . . . and righteousness . . .	
	In those days . . .	v 16
	'Yahweh is our righteousness'	
VI	Davidic and Levitical Lines to Continue	vv 17–18
	For thus said Yahweh:	
	There shall not be cut off for David a man . . .	v 17
	And for the Levitical priests, there shall not	v 18
	be cut off a man . . .	

VII   Covenants with David and Levi Remain Intact   vv 19–22
    And the word of Yahweh came to Jeremiah: v 19
    Thus said Yahweh: v 20
    If you could break my covenant of the day
       and my covenant of the night . . .
    then could my covenant be broken with David . . .   v 21
       also with the Levitical priests . . .

VIII   Seed of Jacob and David to Continue   vv 23–26
    And the word of Yahweh came to Jeremiah . . .   v 23
    Thus said Yahweh: v 25
    If indeed I have not established my covenant of
       daytime and night . . .
    then the seed of Jacob and David, my servant,   v 26
       I will reject . . .

The main break in the chapter, so far as oracles are concerned, comes after v 13, where the LXX omission begins. But this is not necessarily the point at which a later expansion occurs. If there are later expansions, and this is still a debatable point, they are best correlated with the superscriptions in vv 19 and 23. From a compositional point of view, there are three identifiable segments in the chapter (Parunak 1994: 514) introduced by three superscriptions:

1) vv 1–18   "And the word of Yahweh came to Jeremiah a second time"   (v 1)
2) vv 19–22   "And the word of Yahweh came to Jeremiah"   (v 19)
3) vv 23–26   "And the word of Yahweh came to Jeremiah"   (v 23)

Although some early and more-recent critical opinions deny the whole of chap. 33 to Jeremiah, dating it in the exilic or postexilic periods (Duhm; Cornill; Volz; Thiel 1981: 37; Carroll; McKane), Giesebrecht did assign v 1 and vv 4–13 to his Baruch source. Verses 2–3 were attributed by Movers and Hitzig to Second Isaiah because of supposed "Deutero-Isaianic phraseology." Streane agreed that vv 1–13 appear to have a considerable amount of editorial addition; however, he said that the case against these verses was far from proved, and more recent scholars have agreed. Rudolph, Weiser, Bright, Boadt, Holladay, and others have restored part or all of vv 1–13 to Jeremiah. Rudolph says that most of vv 1–13 is prophetic, not apocalyptic, as Duhm alleged. In his view, vv 10–12 presuppose the fall of Jerusalem but can be dated shortly after. Weiser does not think any of vv 1–13 presupposes the fall of Jerusalem and takes the verses to emanate from Jeremiah. Bright says vv 1–13 are similar in tone to chap. 32, developing further the theme of 32:15. However, most scholars take vv 14–26 to be a later addition, largely because the verses are lacking in the LXX. Yet vv 14–16 repeat with little change the prophecy in 23:5–6, which the majority of scholars credit to Jeremiah.

The present verses are prose, although NJV prints vv 2–3 as poetry. Delimitation at the top is by an introductory formula and a *petuḥah* in M^A, M^L, and

M^P before v 1, which is also the chapter division. At the bottom, delimitation is by a *petuḥah* in M^A and a *setumah* in M^L and M^P after v 3.

NOTES

33:1. *And the word of Yahweh came to Jeremiah a second time.* On this general third-person superscriptional form, see again vv 19, 23, and also Note for 28:12. Abarbanel thought "a second time" referred to a revelation concerning the messianic redemption, whereas the revelation in the preceding passage (chap. 32) referred to the redemption from Babylon.

while he was still confined in the court of the guard. On the present confinement, see 37:21. The adverbial *ʿôdenû* is discussed in Note for 40:5. The passive participle *ʿāṣûr* is to be translated the same as *kālûʾ* in 32:2: "confined" (Rashi; cf. 39:15). In 36:5 the term simply means "under restraint," i.e., under surveillance. Only the first two oracles in the chapter, vv 2–3 and 6–9, are received during this confinement. The two oracles following, vv 10–11 and 12–13, come after the fall of Jerusalem.

2. *Thus said Yahweh who made it, Yahweh who formed it to establish it, Yahweh is his name!* A divine self-asseveration similar to the confessions made by worshipers in 10:16 [= 51:19] and by Jeremiah in 32:17. Note also the expanded messenger formula in 31:35, which is similar to the present one. Weiser thinks both may be hymnic fragments.

Yahweh who made it, Yahweh who formed it. Reference is to "the earth," which in the RSV and most modern Versions is added after the first verb, with the LXX (*poiōn gēn*). Compare Isa 45:18. Aquila reads with the MT: *poiōn auto*, "who made it" (cf. AV; NJV). Calvin prefers just the pronoun, saying it is more forceful. Weiser and Holladay agree. But Calvin thinks "it" refers to Jerusalem, which cannot be right (cf. 32:31). The verbs here are *ʿśh* ("make") and *yṣr* ("form"), which appear in the Yahwist's account of Creation (Gen 2:4b, 7–8, 19; 3:1). Several Heb MSS, the LXX, S, and Vg omit the second "Yahweh," but this can be attributed to haplography (homoeoarcton: *y . . . y* or homoeoteleuton: *h . . . h*). The repetition is good poetry and gives emphasis to the divine name.

Yahweh is his name. On this old climactic shout, which usually appears in Jeremiah and Second Isaiah in the form "Yahweh of hosts is his name," see 32:18 and Note for 10:16. Yahweh uses the acclamation here to pledge fidelity to his promise (Cheyne).

3. *Call to me and I will answer you, and let me tell you great things and hidden things you have not known.* In this dark hour, Yahweh wants communication to be open with his prophet because he has great things to tell him about future days. Prayers from Jeremiah are thus being solicited, which Yahweh promises to answer. Calvin says that while Yahweh's words are to Jeremiah, they are for all people to hear so they too will pray. See 29:12.

great things and hidden things. Hebrew *gĕdōlôt ûbĕṣūrôt.* Zunz (1873: 670) and Weinfeld (1972b: 358 #20) both note that this is a variation on the stereotyped Deuteronomic phrase "great cities fortified sky-high" (Deut 1:28; 9:1). A few MSS, K^{OR}, and T have *ûnĕṣūrôt* (from *nṣr*), which translates as "and guarded, secret things" (cf. Isa 48:6). The two meanings are not that different. The term *bĕṣūrôt* can also mean "inaccessible things," and the question therefore is whether any secret or inaccessible things come in the oracles that follow. If we expect something extraordinary, for example, something similar to the new covenant promises of 31:31–34 and 32:37–41, the answer will probably be in the negative. However, there is no reason why anything above and beyond the more usual promises in the Book of Restoration must be anticipated. The oracle of restoration in vv 6–9 might easily suffice (Thompson; Holladay). All genuine prophecy is hidden or inaccessible until Yahweh reveals it to his prophet. On prophets' hearing the hidden things of God in divine council, see Note for 23:18.

MESSAGE AND AUDIENCE

Yahweh in the present oracle announces himself as the one responsible for the entire creation, telling Jeremiah therefore to call upon him so he can tell him great and previously hidden things he has not known. The oracle will doubtless be shared with a Judahite audience during the dark days of the siege, and they too, perhaps, will want to be privy to these marvelous things. Audiences after the fall of Jerusalem will also be in need of something hopeful to cling to, and so they are invited along with Jeremiah and others to call upon Yahweh in their moment of great need.

As the editorial note states, this oracle comes to Jeremiah while he is confined to the court of the guard. It follows, therefore, the directive that Jeremiah buy his cousin's field at Anathoth (chap. 32). If the field purchase is in the summer of 587, this revelation comes between then and the summer of 586 B.C., when Jerusalem falls.

2. Healed City, Healed People (33:4–9)

33 ⁴For thus said Yahweh, God of Israel, concerning the houses of this city and concerning the houses of the kings of Judah that were broken down toward the siege ramps and toward the sword, ⁵those coming to fight the Chaldeans only to fill them with the corpses of men whom I struck down in my anger and my wrath, and because I hid my face from this city on account of all their evil:

⁶Look I am going to bring to it new flesh and healing, and I will heal them and I will reveal to them the sweet smell of peace and security. ⁷And I will surely restore the fortunes of Judah and the fortunes of Israel, and I will build them as at first. ⁸And I will cleanse them from all their iniquity by which they sinned against me, and I will forgive all[a] their iniquities by which they sinned against me and by which they

---

[a] Reading the Q *lĕkol* ("for all"); Kt has a longer form, *lĕkôl*.

rebelled against me. ⁹And it shall be to me a joyful name, a praise, and a glorious decoration before all the nations of the earth who shall hear all the good that I am doing to them; they shall tremble and they shall shake on account of all the good and on account of all the peace that I am doing for it.

RHETORIC AND COMPOSITION

MT 33:4–9 = LXX 40:4–9. The present verses contain a restoration oracle for Israel and Judah focusing on Jerusalem and its inhabitants (vv 6–9). Preceding it is an expanded messenger formula giving background for the oracle (vv 4–5). The unit is delimited at the top end by a *petuḥah* in M^A and a *setumah* in M^L and M^P before v 4. Delimitation at the bottom end is by a *setumah* in M^A and M^L and a *petuḥah* in M^P after v 9.

The oracle can be assigned to Jeremiah, who received it while confined to the court of the guard (see Rhetoric and Composition for 33:1–3). The oracle begins with the familiar Jeremianic *hinĕnî* ("look I") with a participle (see Note for 1:15) and is structured in such a way that Jerusalem and its inhabitants are spoken of at beginning and end. In the center is a promise to Israel and Judah that their fortunes will be restored and that a remnant of each will be built up and cleansed of its sin:

City of Jerusalem:	Look I am going to bring *to it (lāh)* new flesh and healing	v 6
Jerusalem's People:	*and I will heal them (ûrĕpaʾtîm)* and I will reveal *to them (lāhem)* the sweet smell of peace and security	
Fortunes of Israel and Judah:	And I will surely restore the fortunes of Judah and the fortunes of Israel	v 7
Israel and Judah's People:	*and I will build them (ûbĕnitîm)* as at first. And *I will cleanse them (wĕṭihartîm)* from all *their* iniquity (*ʿăwōnām*) . . . and I will forgive all *their* iniquities (*ʿăwōnôtêhem*) by which *they sinned* (*ḥāṭĕʾû*) against me and by which *they rebelled* (*pāšĕʿû*) against me	v 8
City of Jerusalem:	And it shall be (*wĕhāyĕtâ*) to me a joyful name . . .	v 9
Jerusalem's People:	. . . all the good that I am doing *to them (ʾōtām)*	
City of Jerusalem	. . . all the peace that I am doing *for it (lāh)*	

The term "peace," which is desired particularly for Jerusalem, the "city of peace," makes an inclusio for the oracle:

. . . the sweet smell of *peace (šālôm)* and security	v 6
. . . all *the peace (haššālôm)* that I am doing for it	v 9

The term "this city" also makes an inclusio for the expanded messenger formula:

. . . concerning the houses of *this city* (*hāʿîr hazzōʾt*)   v 4
. . . I hid my face *from this city* (*mēhāʿîr hazzōʾt*)   v 5

NOTES

33:4. *concerning the houses of this city and concerning the houses of the kings of Judah that were broken down toward the siege ramps and toward the sword.* Houses near or attached to the wall of the city had to be torn down to defend against siege ramps and enemy swords outside the wall (the two prepositions *ʾel* must be translated "toward" or "in the direction of"). The inside of the city wall had to be fortified (LXX, T; Rashi; cf. Isa 22:10). Those tearing down the houses are the Judahite defenders. The siege is mentioned earlier, in 21:4, and the siege ramps in 32:24. "The sword" is a metonymy for the Chaldeans wielding the sword. The LXX reads *eis charakas kai promachōnas* ("for palisades and ramparts"), apparently misunderstanding the usage of "sword." Emendation of the Hebrew is unnecessary (*pace* Volz; Holladay). On siege warfare, see further Note for 6:6.

the houses of the kings of Judah. The royal palace consisted of multiple buildings. The LXX and Vg have "king" singular, but a plural is acceptable (cf. 19:13 and Note on 17:19).

5. *those coming to fight the Chaldeans.* Hebrew *bāʾîm lĕhillāhēm ʾet-hakkaśdîm.* This phrase has caused difficulty from earliest times, largely because of a sudden shift from the houses of Jerusalem (without conjunctive *waw*) to the defenders of the city. See a similar *mĕbîʾîm* ("those bringing") in v 11, which also lacks the conjunctive *waw*. The LXX perhaps for this reason omits *bāʾîm* ("those coming"), and Symm and Theod translate 4b–5a as "the sword of those coming" (*tēn machairan tōn erchomenōn*), which cannot be right. As v 6 of the oracle makes clear, both Jerusalem the city and the inhabitants of Jerusalem are being spoken of (see Rhetoric and Composition); here in the background notice the same is true. The oracle is in response to 1) houses being torn down; and 2) Judahite men fighting the Chaldeans and filling the demolished houses with dead bodies. The participle should therefore be given its normal translation of "those coming," where reference is to Judahites defending the city. "The Chaldeans" are the object (T; AV; and most modern Versions), not the subject (*pace* Cornill; RSV; NEB; NRSV; REB). The Judahites are fighting against the Chaldeans (Giesebrecht).

only to fill them with the corpses of men whom I struck down in my anger and my wrath. The conjunctive *waw* on *ûlĕmalʾām* has to be translated as an adversative: "but" or "only"; thus, "only to fill them. . . ." The Judahites have torn down houses to better defend the inner wall of the city, but the demolished houses have ended up being depositories for bodies of Judahite war victims (Rashi). For the expression "in my anger and my wrath," see 32:31, 37, and Note for 21:5.

and because I hid my face from this city on account of all their evil. The LXX has "from them" for "from this city." The people of the city are meant. Yahweh in his wrath hides his face, and the people are then punished (18:17; Deut 31:17).

6. *Look I am going to bring to it new flesh and healing, and I will heal them and I will reveal to them the sweet smell of peace and security.* This "new flesh" (*'ărūkâ*) and "healing" are precisely what the people did not experience earlier (8:22; 30:13). But now, after judgment, it will come (see also 30:17). M. Greenberg (1997: 736) says that here Jeremiah is announcing healing and rebuilding without the precondition of repentance, also without a prior statement about divine forgiveness. But pardon is announced in v 8, and repentance too may occur even though it is not stated.

to bring to it. I.e., the city of Jerusalem. Hebrew *ma'ăleh-lāh*. G^A, T, and Vg read "to them," but reference here is to the city (see Rhetoric and Composition).

sweet smell. Hebrew *'ăteret* is a *hapax legomenon* in the OT, about which one gets no help from the Vrs. The term has traditionally been taken as an Aramaic loanword (BDB), cognate to Heb *'šr* ("wealth") meaning "abundance" or the like (Kimḥi; AV; RSV; JB; NAB; NJV; NIV; cf. Prov 27:6; Ezek 35:13). But another noun construct in Ezek 8:11,*'ătar*, is commonly translated "smell (of incense)," which would be suitable here. Yahweh, with the sweet smell of peace and security, will reverse the present stench that is emanating from the corpses (Holladay). In the NT, see 2 Cor 2:15–16.

peace and security. Hebrew *šālôm we'ĕmet*. A hendiadys meaning "true peace" or "lasting peace" (Giesebrecht), occurring also in 2 Kgs 20:19. See in addition *šĕlôm 'ĕmet* in Jer 14:13.

7. *And I will surely restore the fortunes of Judah and the fortunes of Israel.* On the expression "restore the fortunes," which occurs again as an intensive H-stem in vv 11 and 26 (Q) as it does here, see Note for 29:14. For its thematic importance in the Book of Restoration, see Rhetoric and Composition for 33:1–3. Some LXX MSS have "Jerusalem" for "Israel," which makes sense in that the present oracle is focused on Jerusalem. But the majority reading may nevertheless be better, since the expression as used in the Book of Restoration promises restoration to both Israel and Judah, not simply a Jerusalemite or Judahite remnant.

and I will build them as at first. It is the people who will be built up (cf. 30:19; 31:27).

8. *And I will cleanse them from all their iniquity by which they sinned against me, and I will forgive all their iniquities by which they sinned against me and by which they rebelled against me.* This repeats the promise of the new covenant (31:34). See also 50:20 and Ezek 36:25. Restoration to divine favor requires cleansing.

9. *And it shall be to me a joyful name, a praise, and a glorious decoration before all the nations of the earth.* I.e., Jerusalem will be, not the covenant people, as in 13:11 (cf. T: "And they shall become before me . . ."). The LXX has "and it shall be for joy and praise," omitting the pronominal suffix "to me" and

"name." The shorter reading could result from two scribal haplographies, the first a loss of *lî*, "to me" (homoeoarction: *l* . . . *l*), and the second a loss of *šēm*, "name" (homoeoarcton: *š* . . . *š*). The MT reading is supported by Aq, Symm, T, and Vg and should be retained. Bonhoeffer quoted this verse in his *Letters and Papers from Prison* (1971: 300).

a glorious decoration. Hebrew *tip'eret*. On this term denoting beautification, see Note for 13:11.

all the good that I am doing to them. "Them" means the "Jerusalemites" here (Rudolph). The term is omitted in the LXX but present in Aq, Symm, T, and Vg. Yahweh refers first and last to the city; here in the middle, it is to the people of the city (see Rhetoric and Composition). The term *haṭṭôbâ* ("the good") has treaty overtones, as we know from the Mari Letters and Aramaic Sefire treaties where it means "friendship, good relations" (Moran 1963c; Fox 1973a). So when Yahweh talks in this verse about "the good" he will do for Jerusalem and its people, he is anticipating the time when he will cut a new covenant with them.

they shall tremble. I.e., the nations (Kimḥi). Calvin thinks that this extraordinary goodness of God will bring about the conversion of the Gentiles. Compare Ps 40:4[Eng 40:3].

that I am doing for it. Again confusion with the pronouns: one MS and the Vrs have "for them," but "the good" and "the peace" are promises to Jerusalem here (Kimḥi).

MESSAGE AND AUDIENCE

Yahweh begins this oracle by promising new flesh and healing to Jerusalem and its people. To replace the current stench of corpses will be the sweet smell of peace and security. This will come about when Yahweh restores the fortunes of Israel and Judah and builds up its people. Yahweh will also cleanse the people and forgive them their iniquity. In this future day the city of Jerusalem will be to Yahweh a joyful name, a praise, and a glorious decoration proudly displayed to the nations, who will hear of Yahweh's goodness toward the covenant people. On account of this goodness and peace, the nations will tremble—so much so that they may even come themselves to worship Yahweh.

An expanded messenger formula provides background, and in it the compiler has Yahweh call attention to the fact that houses of Jerusalem—including those belonging to the royal palace—have been torn down to fortify the city wall against Chaldean attackers, also that men defending the city are filling the ruins with corpses of Judahite war victims. Yahweh says that the people have been struck down as a result of his anger and a face turned the other way, because of all the evil the nation has committed.

This oracle, like the one prior to it, comes to Jeremiah while he is confined to the court of the guard. It may well have been delivered to a Judahite audience at this time. Jerusalem has not yet fallen. When heard following the oracle in vv 1–3, the goodness and peace will be what Yahweh promised to reveal to Jeremiah if he but called upon him, which the prophet presumably did.

3. Two Promises of Return (33:10–13)

a) The Return of Joyful Sounds (33:10–11)

33 [10]Thus said Yahweh:
Again it shall be heard in this place—of which you are saying, 'It is a waste, without human and without beast,' in the cities of Judah and in the streets of Jerusalem that are deserted without human and without inhabitant and without beast— [11]the voice of joy and the voice of gladness, the voice of the groom and the voice of the bride, the voice of those saying,

> Give thanks to Yahweh of hosts
> > for Yahweh is good
> > > for his steadfast love is eternal

and[a] those bringing a thank offering to the house of Yahweh, for I will surely restore the fortunes of the land as at first—said Yahweh.

b) The Return of Pasture Land (33:12–13)

33 [12]Thus said Yahweh of hosts:
Again there shall be in this place of waste, without human or beast, and in all its cities, pasture for shepherds resting the flock. [13]In the cities of the hill country, in the cities of the Shephelah, and in the cities of the Negeb, and in the land of Benjamin, and in the regions around Jerusalem, and in the cities of Judah, again the flock shall pass under the hands of the one who counts it—said Yahweh.

RHETORIC AND COMPOSITION

MT 33:10–13 = LXX 40:10–13. The present verses contain two similarly-structured restoration oracles: 1) one promising the return of joyful human sounds to the streets of Jerusalem and other Judahite cities now deathly silent (vv 10–11); and 2) one promising the return of pastureland in now-despoiled Judah, in which shepherds will again keep flocks (vv 12–13). Oracle I is delimited at the top by a *setumah* in M[A] and M[L] and a *petuhah* in M[P] before v 10; at the bottom, delimitation is by a *setumah* in M[A] and M[L] and a *petuhah* in M[P] after v 11. Oracle II is delimited at the top by a *setumah* in M[A] and M[L] and a *petuhah* in M[P] before v 12, and at the bottom by a *setumah* in M[A] and M[L] and a *petuhah* in M[P] after v 13.

The oracles have similar beginnings, both employing (along with other Jeremianic phraseology) the key word "again," which occurs prominently in the poetry and prose of the Book of Restoration (31:4–5, 23–40):

---

[a]Reading a conjunctive *waw* on MT *mĕbi'îm*, "and those bringing," with LXX, S, and Vg (see Notes).

I   *Again* it shall be heard *in this place*—of   *'ôd . . . bammāqôm-hazzeh*   v 10
    which you are saying, '*It is a waste,*   *. . . ḥārēb hû'*
    without human and without beast . . .'   *mē'ên 'ādām ûmē'ēn běhēmâ*

II *Again* there shall be *in this place*   *'ôd . . . bammāqôm hazzeh*   v 12
    of waste,   *heḥārēb*
    without human or beast . . .   *mē'ên-'ādām wě'ad-běhēmâ*

In both oracles, the concluding "said Yahweh" makes an inclusio with the opening "thus said Yahweh (of hosts)":

I   *Thus said Yahweh:*   *kōh 'āmar yhwh*   v 10
    . . . said Yahweh   *. . . 'āmar yhwh*   v 11

II *Thus said Yahweh of hosts:*   *kōh 'āmar yhwh ṣěbā'ôt*   v 12
    . . . said Yahweh   *. . . 'āmar yhwh*   v 13

Condamin, who scans the verses as poetry, which they are not, nevertheless notes all these repetitions.

Oracle II has, in addition, this key word inclusio:

II *Again ('ôd)* there shall be . . .   v 12
    again ('ôd) the flock shall pass . . .   v 13

NOTES

33:10. *in this place*. Another common term in the Jeremiah prose (see Note for 7:3), clarified in what follows about the desolate streets of Jerusalem and other Judahite cities (*Mezudath David*).

without human and without beast. See Note for 21:6.

in the cities of Judah and in the streets of Jerusalem that are deserted without human and without inhabitant and without beast. This looks like a later interpolation intended to clarify "this place." "Cities of Judah and streets of Jerusalem" is a stereotyped expression in Jeremiah (see Note for 11:6) not used by other prophets (S. R. Driver 1913: 276). The LXX omits "and without inhabitant," reducing the expression to the more normal "without human and without beast." The loss, however, could be attributed to haplography (whole-word: *wm'yn . . . wm'yn*). The Hebrew rendering "without human and without inhabitant" is a hendiadys, connecting with "and without beast."

11. *the voice of joy and the voice of gladness, the voice of the groom and the voice of the bride*. In earlier judgments (7:34; 16:9; 25:10) the absence of human voices was a curse (see Note for 7:34), but now the phrase takes on new meaning. The silent streets of Judah's cities will once again come alive with happy voices. On the return of joy to the city, see also 30:19; 31:4, 5, 12–14.

the voice of those saying, Give thanks to Yahweh of hosts, for Yahweh is good, for his steadfast love is eternal, and those bringing a thank offering to the house of Yahweh. Joyful worship will also return to Jerusalem (cf. 30:19). Temple thank offerings were earlier promised continuance if people kept the Sabbath (17:26), but they did not. But in the restoration these will be resumed.

Yahweh of hosts. The LXX translates *şĕbā'ôt* ("of hosts") with *pantokratori*, as it occasionally does in Jeremiah (see Appendix VI).

for Yahweh is good, for his steadfast love is eternal. A slightly altered refrain lifted from the Psalms (cf. Pss 100:5; 106:1; 107:1; 136:1), much used in Second Temple worship (1 Chr 16:34; 2 Chr 5:13; 7:3; Ezra 3:11), but one that could nevertheless be ancient (Peake).

and those bringing. The LXX, S, and Vg translate a conjunctive *waw* on *mĕbî'îm*, which MT does not have. Ehrlich (1912: 328) thinks the *waw* was lost in the MT by haplography (double *waw* in succession), which is probably right. But note the similar lack of a *waw* on *bā'îm* ("those coming") in v 5 (see Note there).

thank offering. Hebrew *tôdâ*. See Lev 7:11–15; 22:29. This offering was highly esteemed in later Judaism. The Talmud states: "In the time to come all sacrifices will cease, but the sacrifice of thanksgiving will not cease" (Kimḥi; H. Freedman).

to the house of Yahweh. The preposition "to" is omitted by ellipsis; see Note for 24:1.

for I will surely restore the fortunes of the land as at first. On the expression "restore the fortunes," which occurs in vv 7 and 26 (Q) as an internal H-stem as it does here, see Note for 29:14. For its importance in the Book of Restoration, see Rhetoric and Composition for 33:1–3.

12. *Yahweh of hosts.* The LXX translates *şĕbā'ôt* ("of hosts") with *tōn dynameōn*, which it does nowhere else in the book of Jeremiah (see Appendix VI).

Again there shall be . . . pasture for shepherds resting the flock. It is a sure sign of peace when flocks and herds can be brought securely into pasture (Calvin).

13. *In the cities of the hill country, in the cities of the Shephelah, and in the cities of the Negeb, and in the land of Benjamin, and in the regions around Jerusalem, and in the cities of Judah.* Compare the sweep in 17:26 and 32:44. On the location of the various territories, see Note for 17:26.

again the flock shall pass under the hands of the one who counts it. The shepherd counts the sheep as they pass under his rod, to make sure none is lost (Lev 27:32; Ezek 20:37). Virgil (*Eclogues* iii 34) too says: *Bisque die numerant ambo pecus, alter et haedos,* "twice a day both count the flock, and one of them the kids as well" (Loeb). The T substitutes "Messiah" for "the one who counts it."

MESSAGE AND AUDIENCE

In Oracle I Yahweh says that in the place people now call a wasteland, devoid of people and animals, glad sounds will again be heard—the voices of the groom and the bride, and the voices of grateful worshipers bringing thank offerings to the Temple, for Yahweh promises to restore the people's fortunes to what they were in prior times. In Oracle II Yahweh says that in the present wasteland there will again be pastures for shepherds to rest their flock. All throughout Judah flocks will be seen passing under the rod of the shepherd who counts them.

Both oracles appear to postdate the fall of Jerusalem, as the land is a complete ruin. When heard in tandem with the prior oracle (vv 4–9), the noise of houses being torn down, fighters shouting at the wall, and women wailing over fallen comrades heaped without ceremony in demolished houses will be followed here by an eerie silence. But Yahweh promises to replace both the unpleasant sounds and the deathly silence with the glad sounds of joy and thanksgiving, signifying health and new life.

4. A Righteous King in a Righteous City (33:14–16)

33 ¹⁴Look, days are coming—oracle of Yahweh—when I will confirm the good word that I spoke to the house of Israel and concerning the house of Judah:

¹⁵In those days and at that time
     I will make sprout for David a Shoot of righteousness
         and he will do justice and righteousness in the land

¹⁶In those days Judah will be saved
     and Jerusalem will dwell in security
And this is what one will call her:
     'Yahweh is our righteousness.'

RHETORIC AND COMPOSITION

MT 33:14–16 = LXX 0. Here at the end of chap. 33, four oracles invoking the name of David (vv 14–16, 17–18, 19–22, and 23–26) bring the expanded Book of Restoration to a close. These oracles (vv 14–26) are usually taken to be quite late (postexilic), largely because they are lacking in the LXX. See most recently Lust 1994. Other reasons for non-Jeremianic authorship and a late date have also been advanced: 1) oddities or carelessness of Hebrew style; 2) a repetition of material found earlier in the book (Peake; Ferry 1998); and 3) the infusion of ideas said to be foreign to Jeremiah, viz., covenant promises to the Davidic royal line and especially the line of Levitical priests. According to Buber (1949: 175), Jeremiah had nothing to say about the future of the priesthood.

All of these arguments, many of which date back to or echo earlier source-critical work, are less than conclusive. The present oracle only slightly modifies a messianic oracle in 23:5–6, which is widely taken to be Jeremianic. Also, a restored priesthood is assumed in 31:14, which can be dated originally to the reform years of Josiah, but at the very least takes on fresh importance after the fall of Jerusalem. Once the city is destroyed and the priesthood from Jehoiakim and Zedekiah's reigns is fully discredited, there is no reason why Jeremiah might not say something positive about this fundamental institution in Judahite society. He, after all, was himself of priestly stock. Giesebrecht said the phrase "Levitical priests" (*hakkōhănîm halewiyîm*) was suitable to Jeremiah's time (see Note for 33:18), but since he decided against the verses, he explained the phrase as an archaism employed by a later writer. McKane (p. 862) repeats this same uneconomical argument.

The argument about the repetition of material that occurs earlier in the book must be discounted. Vocabulary, phraseology, and whole passages are repeated all throughout the book, and repetitions are no more indicative of a late date here than elsewhere. The style too, except for some rare usages and unusual grammar, is largely what we find elsewhere. Holladay has restated the older view that the style here is careless, therefore indicating a postexilic (late-fifth-century) date for the material. But this judgment will not stand scrutiny, as his examples—singly or in the aggregate—are unconvincing. Here in the present oracle, he cites an interchange of *ʿal* and *ʾel* in v 14 and the omission of "name" in some form in v 16 (cf. 23:6: "his name"). As for the interchange of *ʿal* and *ʾel*, this is common throughout the book and cannot be written off as careless Hebrew, much less a mark of lateness (see Notes). As for a possible omission of *šĕmāh* ("her name"), which is present in T, this could be explained as a loss due to haplography (see Notes).

The omission of vv 14–26 in the LXX is the main issue. It has been argued recently that this omission was intentional, being dropped by an editor who was uninterested in the material (Grothe 1981). Grothe cites for comparison Sirach, where the discovery of Hebrew MSS showed that in at least two places the Greek translation altered or omitted materials. The best explanation for the LXX omission of vv 14–26, however, is that the verses were lost by (vertical) haplography (homoeoarcton: *h . . . h*), an explanation Holladay considers but rejects. Theodotion includes the verses in his Version. His rendering in Greek is preserved in the margin of G^Q and can be read in Swete 1914: 44–45. It should also be noted that vv 16–20 are extant in 4QJer^c (Tov 1997: 200).

Two other cases of vertical haplography (where the eye of the scribe skips inadvertently down the column rather than ahead in the line) should be noted in this connection. A long omission at the end of 1 Sam 10:27 in both MT and LXX is now apparent with the discovery of a longer text in 4QSam^a, the added words being present also in the Greek text used by Josephus (*Ant* vi 68–71; cf. McCarter 1980: 198–99). McCarter does not take the omission as haplographic, saying it is simply an extraordinary skipping of a paragraph. But the omission can be haplographic, since the omitted section begins [*wn*]*ḥš*, "and Nahash," and MT 11:1 begins *wyʿl nḥš*, "and Nahash went up" (homoeoarcton: *w . . . w*). MT's second word "Nahash" may also have facilitated the error. In Ezek 36:23b–38 another large omission occurs in Papyrus 967, the oldest Greek (LXX) manuscript of Ezekiel (second to third century A.D.). Filson (1943: 31–32) and M. Greenberg (1997: 738–40) argue that this is an inner-

Greek haplography, Filson saying that the omission most likely is a loss occurring in columns of a codex, where the scribe's eye jumped from *hoti egō eimi Kurios* ("that I am the Lord") in v 23a to *hoti egō (eimi)*[a] *Kurios* ("that I am the Lord") ending v 38 (homoeoteleuton).

The present oracle both expands and modifies the messianic oracle of 23:5–6. At the top end it is delimited by a messenger formula in v 14, which is preceded by a *setumah* in M[A] and M[L] and a *petuḥah* in M[P] before the verse. Delimitation at the bottom end is by a *setumah* in M[A], M[L], and M[P] after v 16. Also, 4QJer[c] upon reconstruction has a *setumah* after v 16 (Tov 1997: 181, 200).

The oracle in 23:5–6 is poetry, divided into two equal stanzas. Here the first colon has been expanded into a prosaic introduction (v 14), leaving two unequal stanzas of poetry. But these stanzas are balanced by the following repetition not present in 23:5–6:

I	*In those days . . .*	*bayyāmîm hāhēm*	v 15
II	*In those days . . .*	*bayyāmîm hāhēm*	v 16

Fishbane (1985: 471–74) thinks the oracle in its form here has been transformed by the exile, which is possible. But the destruction of Jerusalem alone is enough to account for the transformation, which means it could be dated anytime after 586 B.C.

NOTES

33:14. *Look, days are coming—oracle of Yahweh—when I will confirm the good word that I spoke to the house of Israel and concerning the house of Judah.* The formulaic "look, days are coming" introduction is Jeremianic (see Note for 7:32), assuming also structural importance in the first Book of Restoration (see "Rhetoric and Composition" for 30:1–3 and 31:23–26). It begins the poetic oracle in 23:5, but here is expanded into a prosaic statement about Yahweh confirming a good word spoken to Israel and Judah about their future (cf. 29:10). The particles *'el* and *'al* are used interchangeably, which is not carelessness or a mark of lateness, as Holladay claims (II 228–29), but something found throughout the Jeremiah prose (see Note for 11:2). Blayney calls it stylistic "elegance."

15–16. See exegesis for 23:5–6.

15. *In those days and at that time.* This combined formula, which is absent in 23:5, occurs elsewhere in 50:4 and 20. For "in those days" and "at that time," see Notes for 3:16 and 17.

I will make sprout for David a Shoot of righteousness. Hebrew *'aṣmîaḥ lĕdāwid ṣemaḥ ṣĕdāqâ.* In 23:5 the wording is "when I will raise up (*wahăqimōtî*) for David a righteous Shoot (*ṣemaḥ ṣaddîq*)," where the verb "I will raise

---

[a] G[A] adds *eimi*; G[B] and G[Q] omit.

up" functions as a catchword in the context, and the adjective ṣaddîq, which may mean "right" or "legitimate," is likely an indirect criticism of Zedekiah (Lust 1994: 38). The name of Zedekiah is played upon in the new name given to the messianic king, "Yahweh is our righteousness" (see Note for 23:6). Both here and in 23:5, T gives the prophecy a messianic interpretation ("I will raise for David an Anointed One [= Messiah] of righteousness"). But G^{OL}, Theod, and Symm support MT with anatolēn ("Shoot").

16. *In those days.* In 23:6 it is "in his days," i.e., in the days of the future Davidic king.

and Jerusalem will dwell in security. A change from "Israel will dwell in security" in 23:6. The oracle here makes the Davidic promise apply to Jerusalem.

And this is what one will call her: 'Yahweh is our righteousness.' The name "Yahweh is our righteousness" applies here to Jerusalem. In 23:6 it applies to the future Davidic king. A few MSS and S add "his name"; G^{OL}, Theod, and Vg add "the name"; and T adds "her name" after the initial "and this," which reflects "and this is his name" in 23:6. If the text originally contained "her name" (šĕmāh), its loss in MT could be explained by haplography (homoeoteleuton: h . . . h). In Isa 1:26, Jerusalem is said to become "the city of righteousness," and the closing verse to the book of Ezekiel says that the name of Jerusalem in future days will be "Yahweh is there," yhwh šāmmâ (Ezek 48:35).

MESSAGE AND AUDIENCE

Yahweh in this oracle says the days are coming when he will confirm good things spoken earlier to Israel and Judah. He will make sprout for David a Shoot of righteousness, one who will do justice and righteousness as kings are supposed to do. In those days Judah will be saved and Jerusalem will be secure. In fact, the city will be named "Yahweh is our righteousness."

When this oracle is heard in tandem with the two prior oracles, the focus will narrow from Israel and Judah, who are mentioned in the introduction, to Judah and Jerusalem—particularly the latter. Jerusalem is now presented with a new name: "Yahweh is our righteousness." The present oracle also begins a concluding cluster of oracles that supplement the oracles in vv 4–13. The oracles in vv 4–13 refer to the nation and its people in general; the oracles in vv 14–26 refer to royal and priestly offices in particular (Cheyne).

5. Davidic and Levitical Lines to Continue (33:17–18)

33 ¹⁷For thus said Yahweh:
There shall not be cut off for David a man who sits upon the throne of the house of Israel. ¹⁸And for the Levitical priests, there shall not be cut off a man from before me who brings up the burnt offering and who burns the cereal offering and who makes sacrifice—all the days.

RHETORIC AND COMPOSITION

MT 33:17–18 = LXX 0. This oracle is delimited at the top end by an opening messenger formula in v 17, before which comes a *setumah* in M^A, M^L, and M^P. 4QJer^c, upon reconstruction, also has a *setumah* there (Tov 1997: 181, 200). Delimitation at the bottom end is by a *petuhah* in M^A, M^P, and 4QJer^c upon reconstruction (Tov 1997: 200) and a *setumah* in M^L after v 18. On the absence of these verses in the LXX, see Rhetoric and Composition for 33:14–16.

This oracle promises a continuation of Judah's royal and priestly lines, for which reason many commentators deny it to Jeremiah and date it in the postexilic period (see Rhetoric and Composition for 33:14–16). But a postexilic date is not required; the oracle need only postdate the fall of Jerusalem. If Jeremiah did not speak it, then someone else has announced in Yahweh's name that these lines would continue despite the calamity of 586 B.C.

NOTES

33:17. *There shall not be cut off for David a man who sits upon the throne of the house of Israel.* The wording of this promise and the one following in v 18 is virtually the same as in the promise to the Rechabites in 35:19. The two promises are rooted in the unconditional covenants given to David (2 Sam 7:12–16) and Phinehas (Num 25:11–13). See also Sir 45:23–26. On the Davidic covenant, see also 1 Kgs 2:4; 8:25; and 9:4–9, where it is made conditional on Solomon's obedience to the commandments. The various OT covenants are discussed in Notes for 11:2 and 32:40.

18. *And for the Levitical priests, there shall not be cut off a man from before me who brings up the burnt offering and who burns the cereal offering and who makes sacrifice—all the days.* This is a stark reversal of Jeremiah's earlier words in 6:20; 7:21–22; and 14:12. But in the Restoration, Yahweh "will saturate the soul of the priests with abundance" (31:14), and the whole people shall be called "priests of Yahweh" (Isa 61:6). The "(whole) burnt offering," or "holocaust" (*'ōlâ*), is one in which the entire animal is consumed on the altar (6:20; 7:21); the "cereal offering" (*minhâ*) is a gift offering, typically of grain, flour, or cakes (see Note for 14:12).

the Levitical priests. The expression *hakkōhănîm halĕwiyyîm*, "the priests, the Levites" (= the Levitical priests), appears in Deuteronomy (Deut 17:9, 18; 18:1; 24:8; 27:9; cf. S. R. Driver 1913: 101) and other literature earlier than Nehemiah (Josh 3:3; 8:33; Ezek 43:19; 44:15). It need not, therefore, be taken as an archaism by someone writing in the postexilic period. Peake points out that making the Levitical priests coextensive with other priests was in conformity with Deuteronomic legislation (Deut 17:9, 18), something no longer recognized in Nehemiah's time.

all the days. On this expression, see Note for 31:36.

MESSAGE AND AUDIENCE

In this oracle, Yahweh affirms the earlier covenants made to David and Phinehas, that David's royal line and the priestly line of Aaron would continue in perpetuity. A post-586 audience, no doubt, will wonder how such can be fulfilled with kingship gone and the Temple in ruins. But the priestly line did survive the exile, and as for the promise to David that his line would continue, this met a postexilic disappointment in Zerubbabel, surviving thereafter as a messianic hope in Judaism and finding fulfillment in claims made for Jesus by the Christian Church (Matt 1:1–17; Luke 3:23–38).

This oracle is to be dated sometime following the destruction of Jerusalem. When heard in tandem with the oracle in vv 14–16, the focus will now be not so much on Jerusalem, but on the Davidic Shoot that Yahweh will cause to sprout in coming days, to which is added a promise about the continuation of the Levitical priesthood.

6. Two Covenant Promises (33:19–26)

a) Covenants with David and Levi Remain Intact (33:19–22)

33 ¹⁹And the word of Yahweh came to Jeremiah: ²⁰Thus said Yahweh:
If you could break my covenant of the day and my covenant of the night, so daytime and night would not come at their appointed time, ²¹then could my covenant be broken with David, my servant, so there would not be for him a son reigning on his throne, also with the Levitical priests, my ministers. ²²As the host of heaven cannot be numbered and the sand of the sea cannot be measured, so I will multiply the seed of David, my servant, also the Levites who minister to me.

b) Seed of Jacob and David to Continue (33:23–26)

33 ²³And the word of Yahweh came to Jeremiah: ²⁴'Have you not seen what this people has said: "The two families that Yahweh chose—now he has rejected them," so they have spurned my people from being any longer a nation before them?'
²⁵Thus said Yahweh:
If indeed I have not established my covenant of daytime and night— statutes of heaven and earth—²⁶then the seed of Jacob and David, my servant, I will reject, not taking from his seed rulers unto the seed of Abraham, Isaac, and Jacob, for I will surely restoreᵃ their fortunes, and I will show them mercy.

ᵃReading the Q, which is the H-stem ʾāšîb, with 32:44; 33:11; 49:6, and 39; the Kt both here and in 49:39 is the Qal ʾāšûb.

RHETORIC AND COMPOSITION

MT 33:19–26 = LXX 0. These concluding verses to the Book of Restoration contain a pair of similarly structured oracles affirming the eternal covenants to Abraham, David, and Phinehas, stating also that Yahweh has made a covenant with creation that people cannot break (vv 20–22, 25–26). Each oracle is preceded by a formula of introduction (vv 19, 23–24), the latter expanded in order to provide background for the oracle.

Oracle I and its introduction are delimited at the top end by a *petuḥah* in M^A and M^P and a *setumah* in M^L before v 19. 4QJer^c upon reconstruction also has a *petuḥah* before v 19 (Tov 1997: 200). Delimitation at the bottom end is by a *setumah* in M^A and M^L and a *petuḥah* in M^P after v 22. 4QJer^c ends at v 20. Oracle II and its introduction are delimited at the top by a *setumah* in M^A and M^L and a *petuḥah* in M^P before v 23. Delimitation at the bottom is by a *petuḥah* in M^A and M^P and a *setumah* in M^L after v 26, which is the chapter division. In M^A and M^L there is also a *setumah* and in M^P a *petuḥah* after v 24, separating the introduction from the oracle. On the omission of these verses in the LXX, see Rhetoric and Composition for 33:14–16.

It has been noted widely that these oracles parallel both in form and in content the two oracles in 31:35–36, which come near the close of the first Book of Restoration. All these oracles employ a protasis-apodosis form of argument and assume an eternal covenant between Yahweh and creation, which may be the Noachian covenant in Gen 9:8–17.

Oracle I reiterates the promise of the prior oracle in vv 17–18, which guarantees the continuance of both the Davidic royal line and the Levitical line of priests. Oracle II focuses on the covenant given to David and then uses this to affirm the eternal covenant given to Abraham (cf. 31:36–37).

Oracles I and II are balanced by the following key words (Condamin):

I	*If . . .*	*ʾim*	v 20
	my covenant of the day and my covenant of the night		
	then . . .	*gam . . .*	v 21
	David, my servant		
	the seed of David, my servant		v 22
II	*If . . . surely . . .*	*ʾim-lōʾ . . .*	v 25
	my covenant of daytime and night		
	then . . .	*gam*	v 26
	seed . . . of David, my servant		

NOTES

33:19. *And the word of Yahweh came to Jeremiah.* On this third-person superscriptional form, occurring in v 1 and again in v 23, see Note for 28:12.

20–21. *If you could break my covenant of the day and my covenant of the night, so daytime and night would not come at their appointed time, then could* *my covenant be broken with David, my servant, so there would not be for him a son reigning on his throne.* On the protasis-apodosis argumentative form ("If . . . then . . ."), which recurs in vv 25–26, see Note for 4:1–2. Day and night were established on the first day of Creation (Gen 1:5), and here Yahweh states that he is in covenant with them. Reference must be to Gen 8:22 (Rashi) and the Noachian covenant following in Gen 9:8–17. The continuance of the Davidic covenant (2 Sam 7:12–16) is argued on the basis of Yahweh's (prior) covenant with creation in Ps 89:20–38[Eng 89:19–37].

you could break. Hebrew *tāpērû*. G^L (*diaskedasthēsetai*), T, and Vg translate a singular Hophal passive (= *tûpar*, "it could be broken"), which is what appears in v 21. But Aq, Symm, and Theod have active plural forms. The assumption here is that people are unable to break the Creation covenant, but they could break and did break the Sinai covenant (11:10; 31:32).

my covenant of the day. Hebrew *běrîtî hayyôm*. A construct chain with the construct form taking a suffix, which is unusual (cf. Lev 26:42; Num 25:12; and GKC §128d). See again v 25.

daytime. Hebrew *yômām*. This rare substantive form, which occurs again in v 25, was used in the poetry of 15:9. The adverbial *yômām* ("by day") occurs in 31:35.

also with the Levitical priests, my ministers. The covenant made with the Levitical priests (Num 25:11–13) is here added to the Davidic covenant, which occurred also in the prior oracle (vv 17–18). The term "Levitical priests" is a reversal of the usual order: *halwîyyîm hakkōhănîm*, "the Levites, the priests" (see Note for 33:18).

22. *As . . . so.* Hebrew *'ăšer . . . kēn*. The use of *'ăšer* instead of *ka'ăšer* for the comparison was noted already by D. N. Lord (1854: 22). See also Isa 54:9. For the more usual *ka'ăšer . . . kēn* construction, see Jer 13:11; 31:28; and 32:42.

As the host of heaven cannot be numbered and the sand of the sea cannot be measured. These comparisons of magnitude are familiar from the promise to Abraham about his descendants (Gen 15:5; 22:17; 26:4; 32:12) but strange when applied to the descendants of David and Aaron (Lust 1994: 43). The "host of heaven" (*şěbā' haššāmayim*) refers to the sun, moon, and stars (8:2; Deut 4:19; 17:3).

who minister to me. Hebrew *měšārětê 'ōtî*. This rendering of a participle in the construct state before an accusative is more unusual grammar (cf. GKC §116g).

23. *And the word of Yahweh came to Jeremiah.* See v 19 for this superscriptional form.

24. *'Have you not seen what this people has said: "The two families that Yahweh chose—now he has rejected them," so they have spurned my people from being any longer a nation before them?'* It is unclear whether the quotation is self-reproach or a reproach from some other nation. "This people" (*hā'ām hazzeh*) probably refers to the people of Judah (cf. 4:10–11; 5:14, 23; 6:19; 7:33). But note the plural verb, "they have said" (*dibběrû*). With Jerusalem now in ruins,

it will appear to many that Yahweh has rejected (*m's*) both Israel and Judah (cf. 6:30; 7:29). But the answer in vv 25–26, also the answer earlier in 31:37, is that Yahweh has not rejected them. On Yahweh's election (*bḥr*) of Israel, see Deut 7:6–7; 14:2; 1 Kgs 3:8; and Ps 33:12.

Have you not seen? Hebrew *hălô' rā'îtā*. The same expression less the negative occurs in 3:6. Yahweh is addressing Jeremiah (the verb is singular).

The two families. I.e., Israel and Judah (Calvin; Giesebrecht; Peake; Streane; Rudolph; Bright; Holladay; cf. Isa 8:14; Ezek 35:10). Some commentators (Rashi; Kimḥi; Volz) take "the two families" (*hammišpāḥôt*) to be those of the royalty and the priesthood, which would carry over from vv 17–22 and could be supported by the later usage of *mišpāḥôt* in Zech 12:12–13. See Lust 1994: 43–44. On *mišpĕḥôt* meaning "tribes (of Israel)," see Note for 2:4.

so they have spurned my people from being any longer a nation before them. Yahweh is now speaking, saying that other nations have spurned his people from being a nation among the nations of the world. These other nations spurn the covenant people because they have been rejected by Yahweh. G^L, Theod, and S read "before me," but MT's "before them" (i.e., the other nations) is better (Volz). The verb *n's* ("spurn") is associated with covenant-breaking in 14:21 (Yahweh); 23:17 (people); and Deut 31:20 (people). The *waw* on the converted imperfect, "so they spurn," is a *casus pendens* (GKC §111h; 143d; cf. 6:19; 28:8).

25–26. If indeed I have not established my covenant of daytime and night—statutes of heaven and earth—then the seed of Jacob and David, my servant, I will reject, not taking from his seed rulers unto the seed of Abraham, Isaac, and Jacob. Another reaffirmation of the Abrahamic and Davidic covenants, both of which are eternal. With the Sinai covenant broken, it is the Abrahamic covenant—and also by implication the Davidic covenant—that will preserve Israel until the new and eternal covenant takes effect (see Note for 31:36). On the protasis-apodosis ("If . . . then . . .") form, see vv 20–21.

daytime. Another use of the rare substantive *yômām*; see above v 20.

rulers. Hebrew *mōšĕlîm*. G^{OL}, Theod, and S have a singular (cf. vv 17–18).

I will surely restore their fortunes. On the expression "restore the fortunes," which occurs also in vv 7 and 11 as an internal H-stem as it does here in the Q, see Note for 29:14. For its structural importance in the Book of Restoration, see Rhetoric and Composition for 30:1–3.

and I will show them mercy. The Book of Restoration appropriately closes with Yahweh saying that in coming days he will show his chastened people divine mercy (*rḥm*). See also 31:20.

MESSAGE AND AUDIENCE

In Oracle I, Yahweh builds again on an assumed covenant that he has with creation, arguing that if this covenant can be broken (and it cannot), then his covenants with David and the Levitical priests can also be broken. Then, in language familiar from the covenant promise to Abraham, Yahweh says that the descendants of David and Levi in future days will be such that no one will be able to number them.

Oracle II is introduced by Yahweh asking Jeremiah if he has heard what people are now saying in light of Judah's national catastrophe? No doubt he has. The two families Yahweh chose have been rejected, and this has earned them a reproach from the Gentiles, who reckon them no longer a nation among nations of the world. But Yahweh in the oracle says once again that if his covenant with Creation has not been established (and it has been), then he will reject the seed of Jacob and David and not take from the latter anyone to rule over the seed of the former. Yahweh closes the oracle, and also the collected promises of the Book of Restoration, with the repeated promise that he will restore people's fortunes. More important, in the days ahead he will show them his infinite store of divine mercy.

These two covenant promises date to after the fall of Jerusalem, and, while they may be later than the promises in 31:35–37 (Lust 1994: 42–43), they still do not require a postexilic date.

Concluding the Book of Restoration with these covenants to David and Phinehas confirms to a post-586 audience promises made in the oracles of vv 14–18, and together the four oracles in vv 14–26 make specific the more-general promises to the nation in the four oracles of vv 1–13. The focus on Yahweh's covenants with his people also establishes continuity with the new covenant and eternal covenant promises in 31:31–34 and 32:38–40 — one covenant only — for Israel and Judah in future days.

IV. False Covenants, True Covenants (34:1–36:32)

◆

A. Zedekiah's Covenant (34:1–22)

1. A Word on the King's Personal Fate (34:1–7)

34 ¹The word that came to Jeremiah from Yahweh when Nebuchadrezzar, king of Babylon, and all his army, and all the kingdoms of the earth under his dominion, and all the peoples were fighting against Jerusalem and against all its cities: ²Thus said Yahweh, God of Israel: Go, and you shall say to Zedekiah, king of Judah, and you shall say to him:

Thus said Yahweh:

Look I am giving this city into the hand of the king of Babylon, and he will take it and will burn it with fire. ³And you, you will not escape from his hand, but you will surely be captured and into his hand you will be given. And your eyes shall see the eyes of the king of Babylon, and his mouth shall speak to your mouth, and to Babylon you shall go.

⁴But hear the word of Yahweh, Zedekiah, king of Judah:

Thus said Yahweh concerning you:

You shall not die by the sword; ⁵in peace you shall die; and like the burnings for your fathers, the former kings who were before you, so shall they burn for you, and "Woe, lord!" they shall lament for you, for the word I, I have spoken—oracle of Yahweh.

⁶So Jeremiah, the prophet, spoke to Zedekiah, king of Judah, all these words in Jerusalem. ⁷And the army of the king of Babylon was fighting against Jerusalem and against all the cities of Judah, the ones remaining to Lachish and to Azekah, for they still remained among the cities of Judah, cities of fortification.

RHETORIC AND COMPOSITION

MT 34:1–7 = LXX 41:1–7. The present chapter is a self-contained narrative reporting first a word brought to King Zedekiah about his personal fate in the war with Babylon (vv 1–7), after which comes a harsh judgment on the king and the people of Jerusalem for reneging on a covenant Zedekiah made to release Hebrew slaves (vv 8–22). This narrative does not belong to the "Zedekiah Cluster" of narrative prose located prior to the Book of Restoration (see Note for

24:1–10). It is an independent piece, brought in and placed next to chap. 35 in order to contrast the unfaithfulness of Zedekiah and the people of Jerusalem in reneging on their covenant with the faithfulness shown by the Rechabites in keeping a covenant made with their father, Jonadab the Rechabite, not to drink wine (Lundbom 1975: 111 [= 1997: 145]; 1997b: 46–47). The whole of chap. 34 is tied together by this inclusio:

> Look I am giving this city into the hand of the king of Babylon,   v 2
> and he will take it and will burn it with fire.

> Look . . . I will bring them back to this city, and they will fight   v 22
> against it and take it, and they will burn it with fire.

This present portion of narrative is delimited at the top end by a superscription in v 1, before which comes a *petuḥah* in M^A and M^P and a *setumah* in M^L. This is also a chapter division. At the bottom end, delimitation is by a *petuḥah* in M^A, M^L, and M^P after v 7. Verse 8 begins the second portion of narrative with a new superscription. M^A and M^L also have a *setumah* and M^P a *petuḥah* after v 5, which separates Oracle II from the closing summary.

Although Mowinckel (1914: 31) took these verses to be Source C, the consensus among commentators expressing themselves on genre, composition, and authorship is that the prose derives ultimately from Baruch and can be taken to be historically reliable (Giesebrecht; N. Schmidt 1901b: 2387; Peake; Streane; Rudolph; Weiser). Even Duhm, Hyatt, and Thiel (1981: 38) find "Deuteronomic" editing to be minimal, perhaps just v 1. The one dissenting voice is McKane, who doubts Baruch's authorship and the narrative's historicity on his "lack of coherence" principle, manifesting itself here as an unresolved tension between vv 2–3 and vv 4–5. The tension is only apparent. Verses 2b–3 and vv 4b–5 are separate oracles and need only complement one another, which they do. All the verses are prose, not poetry (*pace* Lipinski 1974; Thompson).

The first portion of the narrative has this tie-in between beginning and end:

> The word that came to Jeremiah from Yahweh when Nebuchadrezzar,   v 1
> *king of Babylon, and all his army . . . were fighting against Jerusalem*
> *and against all its cities.*

> *And the army of the king of Babylon was fighting against Jerusalem*   v 7
> *and against all the cities of Judah,* the ones remaining to Lachish and
> to Azekah. . . .

NOTES

34:1. *The word that came to Jeremiah from Yahweh.* On this superscription, which occurs again in 34:8, see Notes for 7:1 and 21:1. The T expands to "word of prophecy."

when Nebuchadrezzar, king of Babylon, and all his army, and all the kingdoms of the earth under his dominion, and all the peoples were fighting against Jerusalem and against all its cities. Giesebrecht wants to take this chronological notice as secondary, even though he admits it is accurate. Holladay the same. But textual support for its omission is lacking, and there is really no reason why it should not be taken along with other documentary notices as belonging to the original narrative. A siege of Jerusalem is in progress, which according to the higher chronology, began in Tebet (January) 588 B.C. (see Note for 39:1). The question is whether the event reported here occurred before or after the Egyptian advance (37:5), which led to a lifting of the siege and a Babylonian withdrawal (dated by Bright to the summer of 588 B.C.). Zedekiah's first embassy to Jeremiah was at the beginning of the siege, before the Egyptian advance (21:1–7). His second was after the Babylonian withdrawal, at which time he was moving freely about the city (37:3–5). The report following (34:8–22), about the release of the Hebrew slaves and their reclamation, is after the Egyptian threat failed to materialize and the Babylonians resumed their siege that would bring about a final surrender. The event reported here may then have taken place before the reclamation, if, as some commentators maintain, Jeremiah's visit to Zedekiah was while he was still moving freely in the city. But he may not have been. It is possible that he could have gone to see the king from his place of confinement in the court of the guard, which was in the palace precinct. The word given here to the king bears its closest resemblance to the word given in 32:3b–5, which was when Jeremiah was confined to the court of the guard (32:2). So, while the present event cannot be dated with certainty, indications are that it (together with the event that follows, vv 8–22) belongs to the final stage of the siege, when the situation for Zedekiah and the nation had become desperate.

and all the kingdoms of the earth under his dominion, and all the peoples. The LXX has a reduced reading, eliminating at least "and all the peoples." G^L, S, T, and Vg support MT. It sounds as though a coalition of vassal states is joining Nebuchadrezzar's army in the fight. Contingents from other nations did Nebuchadrezzar's bidding prior to his own arrival in Judah in 597 B.C. (2 Kgs 24:2). Note also a plurality of anticipated attackers in 1:15 and 25:9. Vassal kings were required to swear loyalty to their sovereigns, one of the clauses in the treaties binding the two being that the vassal king would provide military assistance if needed. A treaty between Hittite King Mursilis II and Duppi-Tessub of Amurru (14th century B.C.) provides for military assistance from vassal kings in time of war (*ANET*[3] 204 ##9, 10; *CS II* 97 "Military Clauses"). Weinfeld (1976a) cites other examples from the ancient world, one being a vassal treaty drawn up by Esarhaddon, king of Assyria (680–669 B.C.), which contained a clause requiring Median vassal kings to be loyal to Esarhaddon's designated successor, Ashurbanipal. They must be prepared to fight and even die for him (lines 49–50, 229–31; Wiseman 1958a: 31–34, 45–46; *ANET*[3] 535–36). Military assistance clauses existed also in Greek and Roman treaties and are common as well in treaties of the modern world. In the present case, we must assume that kings and soldiers from other nations were fighting alongside Nebuchadrezzar in his war against Judah. Edom may have been one such nation, since it was later gleeful at the destruction of Jerusalem (Ps 137:7) and appears to have escaped punitive action by Nebuchadrezzar when he campaigned in the area in 588–586 and 582 B.C. (see Note for 49:10).

2. *Go, and you shall say to Zedekiah, king of Judah, and you shall say to him.* The LXX omits the first "and you shall say," which should be retained since it belongs to the command formula (the infinitive absolute *hālôk* paired with a perfect verb) occurring often in Jeremiah (see Note for 28:13). The verb is present in S, T, and Vg. The second *wĕʾāmartâ* ("and you shall say") is better omitted since it is redundant, but it could also be original. Duhm did not think that Jeremiah had ready access to the king, but others (Giesebrecht; Peake; Volz) assume that he did. If he did go to see Zedekiah, he must have been at liberty to move about, although he could have approached the king from the court of the guard, which was in the royal palace. From there he went to see Ebed-melech (39:15–18), and there people visited him to carry on business and hear him preach (32:1–15; 38:1–4). Volz is impressed that Jeremiah went, not to a public place, but to the palace to speak with the king alone.

Look I am giving this city into the hand of the king of Babylon, and he will take it and will burn it with fire. The MT lacks "and he will take it" (*ûlĕkādāh*), which is probably a loss due to haplography (homoeoarcton: *w . . . w*), since the term fills out a standard idiom in royal inscriptions of the ANE. The LXX has the term. This same prophecy, reported elsewhere (21:10; 32:3, 28–29; 34:22; 37:8–10; 38:3, 18, 23), was fulfilled (39:1–3, 8; 52:12–14). The words are repeated almost verbatim in 32:3, with the one difference that instead of "and he will burn it with fire," the prediction concludes with "and he will take it." Rudolph and Holladay want to delete "and he shall burn it with fire" as prophecy after the event (cf. 39:8), but this is unnecessary and there is no textual warrant for doing so. If Nebuchadrezzar is coming to put down resistance for good, he will undoubtedly burn Jerusalem, as he did other cities.

3. *And you, you will not escape from his hand, but you will surely be captured and into his hand you will be given.* Zedekiah was given the same word about his own fate on other occasions (21:7; 32:4; 34:21; 37:17; 38:21–23), and it too was fulfilled (39:5; 52:8–9; 2 Kgs 25:5–6).

And your eyes shall see the eyes of the king of Babylon, and his mouth shall speak to your mouth, and to Babylon you shall go. The Hebrew has a syntactic chiasmus: your eyes / the eyes of the king of Babylon // his mouth / your mouth. Ezekiel, too, predicted Zedekiah's capture and exile to Babylon (Ezek 12:13), but added ironically that the king would never "see" the faraway land. The words even here may have an ominous tone, for as things turned out, Zedekiah was blinded after his capture (39:7), and the last thing he saw before being carted away was the eyes of the Babylonian king, and with cruel finality was made to witness the extirpation of his dynastic line (his sons were killed). This prophecy, then, was fulfilled: Zedekiah did meet the king of Babylon face to face, and did go to Babylon where, in prison, he died (39:5–7; 52:9–11;

2 Kgs 25:6–7). Once again, Rudolph and Holladay want to delete "and to Baby-lon you shall go" as prophecy after the event (cf. 39:7). But if Zedekiah is not to die, as the next oracle states, it stands to reason that he will be exiled to Baby-lon. As a rebellious vassal, this king can expect no mercy from Nebuchadrez-zar, and the sparing of his life under the conditions reported is scarcely a merciful act. See also in this connection Ezek 17:11–21.

and his mouth shall speak to your mouth. I.e., he shall *speak* to you "face to face." Zedekiah will not be speaking to the king (*pace* RSV); the king will be speaking to him (AV; NEB). The LXX text of Ziegler omits these words (they are lacking in G^B and other ancient witnesses), but the Rahlfs text includes them (they are present in G^A). The loss can be attributed to haplography (ho-moeoarcton: *w . . . w*). Giesebrecht, noting their presence in T and Vg, says their inclusion is supported by 32:4 and that G^B appears to be faulty. Cornill and others retain.

4. *But hear the word of Yahweh, Zedekiah, king of Judah.* Hebrew *'ak* is a strong "but," which mitigates the consequences of Zedekiah's encounter with Nebuchadrezzar, but only slightly (Kimḥi; Calvin). The consolation promised Zedekiah may even be spoken with a tinge of irony, with Jeremiah pretending that things will go well for the king when they will not. Zedekiah will survive his capture and be given a burial, but the circumstances leave much to be de-sired, particularly when the prior oracle has been heard. Also, it is something less than high praise to be promised a fate better than what was promised Je-hoiakim (22:18–19; 36:30). Some commentators want a conditional word here, making the oracle like the one in 38:17–18. They therefore imagine a loss of words expressing a condition (Peake; Volz; Hyatt), or they interpret *'ak* as "if only" (Weiser; Boadt) or *šĕma'* as a strong "obey!" (Rudolph; Bright; Holladay). But this introductory word is not "if (only) you will hear . . ."; it is "but hear . . . !" The oracle following is straightforward judgment (McKane).

Thus said Yahweh concerning you. The LXX omits *'āleykā* ("concerning you"), which is redundant in view of the second person verb following. But T and Vg have the pronoun.

4–5. *You shall not die by the sword; in peace you shall die.* Another syntactic chi-asmus in the Hebrew. That Zedekiah will die "in peace" (*bĕšālôm*) means that he will not die by the sword (Kimḥi; Calvin; Giesebrecht; Ehrlich 1912: 329; cf. 1 Kgs 2:5–6). Calvin notes that Zedekiah's fate is less grim than what was pre-dicted for Jehoiakim, who could expect no burial. As things turned out, Zede-kiah did not die by violent means; instead he was required to make the long walk to Babylon, where he languished, a blind man, in prison until the day of his death. The prophecy regarding Josiah's death turned out differently. Huldah told Josiah that he would go to his grave "in peace" (*bĕšālôm*), but according to the Deuteronomic account, he was killed in battle (2 Kgs 23:29–30). The Chroni-cler modifies this slightly, having him wounded at Megiddo and dying in Jerusa-lem, after which he was buried in the tombs of his fathers (2 Chr 35:23–24).

You shall not die by the sword. The LXX omits, which eliminates the explicit contrast. The T and Vg have the words, which are best retained with MT.

5. *and like the burnings for your fathers . . . so shall they burn for you.* A comparison using the *kĕ . . . kēn* construction, on which see Note for 2:26. The Hebrew is awkward, with no verb in the first part of the comparison. The LXX has "and as they lamented your fathers . . . , they will lament also you," which leads naturally into the tearful cry of "Woe, lord!" Reference here is not to cremation, which was not practiced in ancient Israel, but to a burning of spices, incense, and perfumes near the body (de Vaux 1965b: 57). This was an honor bestowed on some kings, but not all (2 Chr 16:14; 21:19). The practice of royal burnings seems to be corroborated by excavated tumuli (grave mounds) west of Jerusalem, which are now thought to have been for burnings on behalf of the Jerusalem aristocracy (so G. Barkay; cf. Aharoni 1982: 238–39; P. J. King 1993: 141–42; Amiran 1958). Coming on the heels of an oracle that just predicted the burning of Jerusalem (v 2), the mention here of burnings on behalf of the king may be an added irony. However, according to Josephus (*Ant* x 154) Nebuchadrezzar buried Zedekiah royally.

the former kings who were before you. The LXX abbreviates; Aq, S, T, and Vg support the MT.

"Woe, lord!" they shall lament for you. Hebrew *hôy* is cry of lament, as in 22:18. For a discussion of this term, which can also be a prophetic invective, see Note on 22:13.

6. *So Jeremiah, the prophet, spoke to Zedekiah, king of Judah.* The LXX lacks "the prophet" and "king of Judah," eliminating titles at it commonly does (see Appendix VI).

7. *all the cities of Judah.* The LXX lacks "all," which could be attributed to haplography (homoeoteleuton: *l . . . l*). Frequent use of the hyperbolic "all" precludes any serious problem with the context (*pace* Janzen 1973: 66; Holladay). See also "all its cities" in v 1.

the ones remaining to Lachish and to Azekah, for they still remained among the cities of Judah, cities of fortification. The LXX omits "the ones remaining," on which see Note for 27:19–20. It appears that Nebuchadrezzar was in the process of taking daughter cities belonging to Lachish and Azekah (cf. Neh 11:30), which were the only fortified cities remaining in Judah, other than Jerusalem. Lachish and Azekah were fortified by Rehoboam (2 Chr 11:8), and although the former suffered major destruction at the hands of Sennacherib in 701 B.C., both were now surrounded by walls. The Babylonians, who followed the Assyrian practice of taking minor towns before the capital (Albright 1936: 15), doubtless took towns and villages belonging to fortified cities before the fortified cities themselves were attacked. In one of the Lachish Letters (4:10–13), an officer from some nearby outpost writes to Yaosh, garrison commander at Lachish, saying: "And let (my lord) know that we are watching for the signals of Lachish, according to all the indications which my lord hath given, for we cannot see Azekah" (*ANET*³ 322; Torczyner 1938: 78–79, 83–84; Tufnell 1953: 333). This is usually interpreted to mean that the officer had been looking for fire signals from Azekah, and since he could not see them, it meant that Azekah had fallen. Another town of Beth-haraphid, according to one interpretation, was also without inhabitants (4:4–6). The suggestion has been made that the outpost sending the letters was Mareshah (Marisa), identified with Tell es-sandahanna (*NEAEHL* 3: 948–51; *OEANE* 3: 412–13), five kilometers north-east of Lachish and one kilometer south of Beth Guvrin (Begin and Grushka 1999; Begin 2002). Begin argues that the commander is unable to see Aze-kah because it is not in his field of vision, therefore he is awaiting signals from Lachish, which is in his field of vision. One cannot therefore conclude that Azekah has fallen. Mareshah, also fortified by Rehoboam, figured prominently in the Hasmonean wars (2 Chr 11:8–9; cf. 1 Macc 5:66; 2 Macc 12:35). For a report on the discovery of the Lachish Letters, with early translation and com-ment, see Albright 1936; 1938; 1941b. Albright dated the Lachish Letters to the summer of 589 B.C. and the destruction of Lachish to the fall, after the autumn olive harvest (1936: 15). But the dates may have been a year or two later. Aze-kah presumably also fell before Jerusalem did in 586 B.C.

In a burial cave at Khirbet Beit Lei, eight kilometers east of Lachish, a care-lessly incised inscription was discovered that may date to Nebuchadrezzar's final destruction of Judah in 588–586 B.C. (Avigad 1979: 25). Naveh (1963: 84) translates the inscription: "Yahweh (is) the God of the whole earth; the moun-tains of Judah belong to him, to the God of Jerusalem." If this translation is cor-rect, we have a confession similar to the divine self-asseveration in 27:5 (see Note there). Cross (1970: 299–302) gives a somewhat different reading: "I am Yahweh thy God; I will accept the cities of Judah and will redeem Jerusalem." It appears, in any case, that refugees hiding near Lachish in this dark hour were expressing faith in Yahweh, the God to whom Jerusalem ultimately belongs.

Lachish. During the seventh and early sixth centuries B.C., the second most important city in Judah after Jerusalem (Stern 2001: 143). Lachish is now identified with Tell ed-Duweir (Tel Lachish), an imposing 30-acre site in the Shephelah some 23 miles southwest of Jerusalem, situated near the Wadi Ghafr, along which a main route in antiquity passed between the coastal plain and the Hebron hills. Tell ed-Duweir was excavated by J. L. Starkey and the Wellcome-Marston Research Expedition from 1932 to 1938, confirming Albright's identi-fication of the site. Prior to this time, Lachish was thought to be Tell el-Hesi. Excavations at Tell ed-Duweir turned up evidence of Iron II occupation, as well as the city's destruction by Sennacherib in 701 B.C. and by Nebuchadrez-zar in 589–587 B.C. In 1935, Starkey found the sensational Lachish Letters bur-ied in the city gate. For a history of biblical Lachish and a summary of the early archaeological work at Tell ed-Duweir, see G. E. Wright 1938b. For a more comprehensive report of archaeological work at the site during the past cen-tury, including the excavations of Y. Aharoni in 1966 and 1968 and the exten-sive excavations of Tel Aviv University directed by D. Ussishkin from 1973 to 1987, see Ussishkin 1978; 1983; idem, *NEAEHL* 3: 897–911; *OEANE* 3: 317–23; *ABD* 4: 114–26.

Azekah. Ancient Azekah has long been identified with Tell Zakariya at the northern end of a high ridge about 5.5 miles northeast of Beth Guvrin, in the Judean Shephelah (Alt 1929: 23–24). The site is due west of Bethlehem, 11 miles north of Lachish and 18 miles southwest of Jerusalem. King Sargon II of Assyria (721–705 B.C.), who campaigned in Philistia in 712 B.C., refers in his Annals to Azaqâ, a stronghold situated in the midst of the mountains, virtually inaccessible (Tadmor 1958: 81). The famous Madeba mosaic map (sixth century A.D.) refers to the area as "Bethzakar." Tell Zakariya was excavated by F. J. Bliss and R. A. Macalister for the Palestine Exploration Fund in 1898–99. A fortress with towers was then uncovered, which in its latest phase is thought now to belong to Rehoboam's fortification (2 Chr 11:9). On archaeological work carried out at Tell Zakariya, see J. D. Seger in *OEANE* 1: 243; and E. Stern in *NEAEHL* 1: 123; also *ABD* 1: 537–39. When the Jews returned from exile, families settled in both Lachish and Azekah (Neh 11:30).

MESSAGE AND AUDIENCE

This narrative segment reports a divine word that came to Jeremiah when Nebuchadrezzar and a coalition of other kings and peoples were fighting against Jerusalem and Judah's other cities. The prophet was told to go directly to King Zedekiah with an oracle. It stated that Yahweh was giving the city into the hands of Nebuchadrezzar, who would burn it with fire. As for the king himself, he had no chance of escape, and could expect capture. What is more, he would have the dubious honor of meeting the Babylonian king face to face, after which he would be taken to Babylon.

A second oracle mitigates this judgment, or so it seems. Zedekiah will not die by the sword but rather in peace. There will be burnings in his honor and people will lament him with the usual cries of "Woe, lord!" The narrator says that Jeremiah told this to Zedekiah in Jerusalem. The segment then concludes by repeating that the army of the king of Babylon was presently fighting against Jerusalem and the cities of Judah, now attacking daughter cities of Lachish and Azekah, for they alone remained of Judah's fortified cities, except for Jerusalem.

When the two oracles are heard together, the mitigation of Oracle II will be lessened and an ironic tone will be discerned. Zedekiah may die in peace, but it will be in faraway Babylon. Burnings in the king's honor will also be seen now against the backdrop of Jerusalem's dishonorable burning, and the cries of woe made for the king will be set over against the woeful cries of an entire nation that perished. It now becomes clear to the audience that people in Babylon will not mourn Zedekiah in the way that they mourned other kings of Judah, whether good or bad.

The narrative fits well into the period of which its superscription speaks, when the king of Babylon was into the last phase of his subjugation of Judah, 588–586 B.C. Cities around Lachish and Azekah were being taken, and Lachish and Azekah would be next. Jerusalem would be last.

When this narrative segment is heard together with the segment that follows, which reports Zedekiah's breaking of the covenant made to release Hebrew slaves, the audience will realize that the judgment given here to Zedekiah personally comes because he broke the oath made to Nebuchadrezzar when the latter installed him as a vassal king. Zedekiah was an oath-breaker.

2. The Covenant of Liberty: On Again, Off Again (34:8–22)

34 [8]The word that came to Jeremiah from Yahweh after King Zedekiah cut a covenant with all the people who were in Jerusalem to proclaim liberty to them, [9]to send away free each person his male slave and each person his female slave, Hebrew and Hebrewess, so that no person should make them serve a Judahite, his kin. [10]And all the princes and all the people who entered into the covenant gave heed to send away free each person his male slave and each person his female slave, so that he should not make them serve again; and they gave heed and sent them away. [11]Then they turned around after this and took back the male slaves and female slaves that they had sent away free, and subjugated them to being male slaves and female slaves. [12]And the word of Yahweh came to Jeremiah from Yahweh:

[13]Thus said Yahweh, God of Israel:

I, I cut a covenant with your fathers in the day I brought them out from the land of Egypt, from the house of slavery, saying, [14]After seven years' time you shall send away each person his Hebrew kin who was sold to you and served you six years, yes, you shall send him away free from your midst. But your fathers did not listen to me and did not bend their ear. [15]And you, you turned around one day and you did what is right in my eyes, to proclaim liberty each person to his fellow, and you cut a covenant before me in the house upon which my name is called; [16]then you turned around and profaned my name and took back each person his male slave and each person his female slave whom you sent away free according to their desire, and you subjugated them to be for you male slaves and female slaves.

[17]Therefore thus said Yahweh:

You, you have not listened to me to proclaim liberty each person to his kin and each person to his fellow.

Look I am proclaiming liberty to you—oracle of Yahweh—to the sword, to the pestilence, and to the famine, and I will make you a fright to all the kingdoms of the earth. [18]And I will make the men who walked over my covenant, who did not carry out the words of the covenant that they cut before me, the calf that they cut in two and walked between its parts—[19]the princes of Judah and the princes of Jerusalem, the eunuchs and the priests, and all the people of the land who walked between the parts of the calf. [20]And I will give them into the hand of their enemies and into the hand of those who seek their life, and their dead bodies shall become food for the birds of the skies and the beasts of the earth. [21]And Zedekiah, king of Judah, and his princes, I will give into the hand of their enemies and into the hand of those who seek their life, into the hand of the army of the king of Babylon, who have withdrawn from you.

[22]Look I am commanding—oracle of Yahweh—and I will bring them back to this city, and they will fight against it and take it, and they will burn it with fire; and the cities of Judah I will make a desolation without inhabitant.

RHETORIC AND COMPOSITION

MT 34:8–22 = LXX 41:8–22. This second portion of narrative in the chapter begins by reporting a covenant that Zedekiah made with the people of Jerusalem to release their Hebrew slaves, and then how they reneged on that covenant (vv 8–11). What follows are four divine oracles delivered to the king and the people of Jerusalem (vv 12–22). The event took place before the personal judgment on Zedekiah in vv 1–7. Delimitation at the top end is by a *petuhah* in M^A, M^L, and M^P before v 8 and at the bottom end by a *petuhah* in M^A, M^L, and M^P after v 22, which is also the chapter division. After v 11, M^A and M^P have another *petuhah* and M^L a *setumah*, which separate the opening narrative from Oracle I. After v 16, M^A, M^L, and M^P have a *setumah* separating Oracle I from Oracle II.

The oracles are taken to be four in number, although v 17a is admittedly brief and could be combined with vv 17b–21 into a single oracle. The reason for taking 17a as a separate oracle is that it has a separate messenger formula, "Therefore thus said Yahweh," and that it is an indictment, unlike vv 17b–21, which are a judgment. The four oracles are introduced by these four messenger formulas:

I	*Thus said Yahweh, God of Israel*	v 13
II	*Therefore thus said Yahweh*	v 17a
III	*oracle of Yahweh*	v 17b
IV	*oracle of Yahweh*	v 22

Oracles I and II (vv 13–16, 17a) are indictment; Oracles III and IV (vv 17b–21, 22) are judgment. Oracle III judges the king and the people of Jerusalem; Oracle IV judges Jerusalem and the cities of Judah.

Oracle I contains a contrast made explicit by emphatic pronouns ("I" and "you") and key words ("your fathers" and "you"). Oracles I and II, in a similar way, are linked and contrasted by emphatic pronouns ("I" and "you") and key word phrases ("did/have not listen(ed) to me"):

I	I (*’ānōkî*), I cut a covenant *with your fathers* (*’et-’ăbôtêkem*) . . .	vv 13–14
	But your fathers did not listen to me (*wĕlō’-šāmĕʿû ’ăbôtêkem ’ēlay*) . . .	

And you, you turned around (*wattāšūbû ʾattem*) one day and you did   vv 15–16
what is right in my eyes . . . *then you turned around* (*wattāšūbû*) and
profaned my name *and took back* (*wattāšîbû*) . . .

II   You (*ʾattem*), you have not listened to me (*lōʾ-šěmaʿtem ʾēlay*) . . .   v 17a

Verses 15–16 of Oracle I also ring the changes on the verb *šûb* ("turned around /
took back").

Oracles III and IV both begin with the familiar Jeremianic "look I":

III   *Look I . . .*   *hiněnî*   v 17b
IV   *Look I . . .*   *hiněnî*   v 22

The opening narrative and oracles following bristle with wordplays:

Narr	"they turned around" (*yāšûbû*) . . . and "took back" (*yāšîbû*)	v 11
I	"you turned around" (*tāšûbû*) in repentance, "then you turned around" (*tāšûbû*) . . ."and took back" (*wattāšîbû*) the slaves you set free	vv 15–16
III	"you have not listened to me to proclaim liberty (*liqrōʾ děrôr*) . . . Look I am proclaiming liberty to you (*hiněnî qōrē lākem děrôr*) . . ."	v 17
	"And I will make the men who walked over (*hāʿōběrîm*) my covenant . . . that they cut (*kārětû*) before me, the calf that they cut (*kārětû*) in two and walked (*wayyaʿabrû*) between its parts."	v 18
I–IV	"and you took back" (*wattāšîbû*) the slaves you set free . . . "and I will bring them [the Babylonians] back (*wahăšîbōtîm*) to this city"	vv 16, 22

Because this prose combines narrative (vv 8–11) and oracular preaching
(vv 12–22), the latter having the usual *accumulatio* and stereotyped phrases, es-
timations regarding authorship, date, and genre differ. Some commentators
(Giesebrecht; Peake; Weiser; Bright; Holladay) take these verses as continuing
the biographical (Baruch) prose that resumes at 34:1. According to this view,
the narrative and preaching authentically report an event from the end of
Zedekiah's reign. Duhm believes the verses to have a historical core going
back to Baruch, but v 1 and the long preaching in vv 12–22 he takes to emanate
from later editors, whom he does not hesitate to disparage, calling the manumission and its interpretation a distortion of history, theological fantasy, and
late midrash. Cornill tempers Duhm's assessment, but only slightly, judging
vv 12–22 to be late sermonizing, yet refusing to reduce the manumission and
reclamation to a political act, as Duhm does.

The argument is turned around in Wijesinghe (1997: 307), who thinks vv 8–11
are a secondary introduction to vv 12–22. He finds an elaborate concentric (=
chiastic) structure of key words in vv 8–22, leading him to conclude that the

narrative summary in vv 8–11 has been carefully constructed to introduce vv 12–22. While his structural scheme may have some merit, it is still open to question. Certain key words are selected for inclusion in the structure, while other occurrences are left out. For example, where does *qr' drwr* ("to proclaim liberty") in v 15 fit in, which appears in *both* MT and LXX? Even if the scheme be accepted, it is no sure indicator of primary and secondary sources. The main difference between vv 8–11 and 12–22 is that the former is narrative and the latter a cluster of divine oracles, and nothing precludes both of them being written up at the same time. Wijesinghe also has not demonstrated that the shorter text represented by the LXX is expanded by a later redactor. His conclusion (p. 324) that the narrative need have no connection with the reign of Zedekiah and the Babylonian invasion goes far beyond the evidence he himself adduces. Rudolph takes the verses as Source C (also Mowinckel 1914: 31) but says they provide access to preexilic events. Hyatt's position is similar. Thiel (1981: 39) finds in the verses more Deuteronomic editing than in vv 1–7, while McKane and Carroll revert to Duhm's radical assessment: McKane finds nothing in vv 12–22 attributable to Jeremiah, and Carroll calls everything midrash from the Persian period.

The reasons for a late dating, exilic or postexilic authorship, and doubts about historicity are the same here as elsewhere: 1) the existence of heavy prose in vv 12–22, which Duhm and older source critics attributed to later ("Deuteronomic") editors; and 2) a longer MT text, thought by many to contain expanded readings of late date. However, Holladay points out that the stereotyped vocabulary and phraseology of the oracles are precisely what one finds elsewhere in the prose of Jeremiah, agreeing with H. Weippert (1973: 86–106) that the verses represent an authentic Jeremiah tradition, and are not to be attributed to later "Deuteronomists." As far as the longer MT is concerned, it is not glossed to the extent that Janzen (1973), Holladay, and McKane allege. There are ten arguable cases of LXX haplography in the verses (Duhm, Janzen [1973: 118–19], Holladay, and McKane find none), and as Giesebrecht pointed out long ago, other ancient Greek witnesses, e.g., G^L, Aq, Symm, and Theod, along with the S, T, and Vg, support in a number of cases, not the shorter text of LXX, but the longer MT. Here, then, as elsewhere, the LXX has to be considered a defective and inferior text.

NOTES

34:8. *The word that came to Jeremiah from Yahweh.* On this superscription, which occurs also in 34:1, see Notes for 7:1 and 21:1. The T expands to "word of prophecy."

8–9. *after King Zedekiah cut a covenant with all the people who were in Jerusalem to proclaim liberty to them, to send away free each person his male slave and each person his female slave, Hebrew and Hebrewess, so that no person should make them serve a Judahite, his kin.* The king initiates this covenant with the people of Jerusalem; the action, so far as we know, was not in response to any prophetic word from Jeremiah. The ceremony, which included oath-taking, the cutting of a calf in two, and people processing solemnly between its parts (v 19), took place at the Temple (v 15). The release was a general release for all Hebrew slaves, corresponding to the Jubilee Year release (Lev 25:39–46) and releases known to have occurred throughout the ANE, also later in classical times. King Ammisaduqa of Babylonia (1646–1626 B.C.), for example, issued an edict of *mišarum* at the beginning of his reign, allowing people who had been enslaved because of debt to be released together with their families (*ANET*[3] 528 §20; cf. Weinfeld 1990; Milgrom 2001: 2167). Slaves were also released en masse in times of national emergencies, such as the present one. Since slaves were not normally subject to military duty, if they were free, they could be drafted into the army. Also, slave owners were obligated to feed and house their slaves, which in time of siege and food scarcity could be difficult. If the slaves were set free, they would have to find food and shelter on their own. A Mari Letter (XXVI 363), dated to 1765/4 B.C., refers to a general release of merchants and slaves by Hammurabi when his country was under threat of enemy attack, the purpose being to strengthen his army (Charpin et al. 1988: 164–65 #363; Anbar 1999). Diodorus of Sicily (xxxvi 4.8) reports, too, an offer by Salvius to free the slaves of Morgantina, a city he was besieging, but their masters countered with a like offer if the slaves would join in the city's defense, which they accepted, and the siege was repelled. But later the emancipation was rescinded, and a majority of the slaves deserted to the rebels.

Hebrews were permitted to have other Hebrews as slaves, the OT containing legislation both limiting and safeguarding what was apparently a long-standing practice (Exod 21:2–11; Deut 15:12–18; and Lev 25:39–46). In Israel, as in other nations, people belonging to the internal population were reduced to slavery for two main reasons: hunger and debt. Debts, whether personal or state-caused, reduced people and family members into slavery. Famine, whether due to natural causes or to war, forced people to sell children and even themselves into slavery in order that one or both might stay alive. Oppenheim (1955) published a collection of Neo-Babylonian texts from Nippur (656–617 B.C.) that deals with parents' selling small children into slavery. In two of the texts, small girls were sold when Nippur was under siege, the parents needing the money and at the same time wanting to see their children kept alive. Indebtedness could be incurred for a variety of reasons. Kings taxed people for defense, war, and other ambitious programs of state, occasionally having to tax them again in order to meet tribute demands from foreign rulers. The latter had happened just recently, when Neco demanded tribute money from Jehoiakim, who raised it from the people (2 Kgs 23:35). Nobles, landowners, and other people of means also charged excessive interest on loans, just one example of how the rich preyed on the poor (Neh 5:1–13). In Babylonia, Assyria, and Syria, interest rates on loans were a chief cause of insolvency: 20–25 percent on silver, and 33-1/3 percent on grain (Mendelsohn 1949: 23; idem, *IDB* R–Z, 385). What they were in Israel and Judah, one can only guess. Proverbs 22:7 says: "The borrower is a slave to the person who lends."

Amos knew people in Israel willing to "sell the righteous for silver, and the needy for a pair of shoes" (Amos 2:6; cf. 8:6). Sarna (1973: 148) says that insolvency was the prime cause of Hebrew slavery.

But ANE laws also set limits on slavery. The Code of Hammurabi (§117) states that when a seignior, because of debt, was forced to sell his wife, son, or daughter into slavery, this slavery could only last for three years; in the fourth year they must go free (*ANET*³ 170–71; *CS II* 343; Driver and Miles 1955: 46–49). The Bible too put limits and safeguards on keeping Hebrews slaves. After working six years, these slaves went free in the seventh, unless they desired to remain with their master, in which case they became slaves for life (Exod 21:2–6; Deut 15:12–18). The law in Lev 25:39–46 states that Hebrews who bought other debt-ridden Hebrews should not treat them as slaves but, rather, as hired servants or sojourners, who received more-benevolent treatment. Then at the Jubilee, they and their families went free, regardless of how long they had served. According to the Targum, even slaves who elected to remain with their masters for life went free in the year of Jubilee. On slavery in the ANE and the OT, see I. Mendelsohn 1949; idem, "Slavery in the OT," *IDB* R–Z, 383–91; R. de Vaux 1965b: 82–83; and M. Dandamayev, "Slavery (ANE and Old Testament)," *ABD* 4: 58–65.

cut a covenant. Hebrew *kĕrōt . . . bĕrît.* A literal rendering of the Hebrew is needed to appreciate the judgment in v 18. Compare Greek *horkia temnein* and Latin *foedus icere.* In English we say "cut a deal." Albright (1951) noted in fourteenth-century cuneiform texts from Qaṭna, which is southeast of Hamath in Syria, the expression, *TAR be-ri-ti,* which he translated "to cut a covenant."

all the people who were in Jerusalem. The LXX omits "all," which is present in T and Vg. It also omits "who were in Jerusalem," which may have been due to haplography (homoeoteleuton: *m . . . m*). The phrase is victim to a larger LXX haplography in 29:25, its only other occurrence in the book, making it unlikely that the reference to Jerusalem is a tendentious MT addition (*pace* Stipp 1997: 195).

to proclaim liberty to them. Hebrew *liqrō' lāhem dĕrôr.* The LXX omits "to them," which refers ahead to the male and female slaves. The expression "to proclaim liberty" (*liqrō' dĕrôr*) occurs also in Isa 61:1, but as a *terminus technicus* it refers to the release of slaves in the Jubilee (Lev 25:10), which in Ezek 46:17 is called the "year of liberty" (*šĕnat haddĕrôr*). Akkadian synonyms *durāru* and *andurāru* ("freedom, release") are also used with reference to debt remission and the manumission of slaves (*CAD* 1/2: 115; *AHw* 1: 50–51; Lewy 1958: 21–23). Since the term *dĕrôr* does not occur in Deut 15:12–18, and the present release is a general release as the release of Deut 15:12–18 is not, questions have been raised about the appropriateness of linking the present manumission to the Sabbatical release, which the oracle does explicitly in vv 13–14 and many scholars do as well in interpreting the passage. Some of the confusion may result from the two Sabbatical releases being placed one after the other in Deut 15:1–11 and 12–18. The release of debts (*šĕmiṭṭâ*) in Deut 15:1–11 follows the regular calendar: it is a general release every seven years — i.e., it applies to everyone at the same time. In the law following on the release of slaves, Deut 15:12–18, each slave goes free whenever his or her six years are up. This is no general release, nor is a general release of slaves mandated anywhere else in the OT, except in the Law of the Jubilee. How then does the reference to the Sabbatical release in vv 13–14 connect with the present release, which must be a Jubilee release? The seeming inconsistency—a general release here and a term release in Deut 15:12–18—is usually explained as the result of the Sabbatical release not having been obeyed, which is implied in the people's reported "turning around" (= repentance) in v 15. The Sabbatical release had certainly been disregarded, but the text is given a fuller and more reasonable explanation by Fried and Freedman (2001: 2257–58). In their view,

> All that Jeremiah says is that even though the fathers had not released their slaves after their individual six years of servitude in the past, as they ought to have (Exod 21:2; Deut 15:12), they still did what was right this time and had released their slaves during the year of the *děrôr*, the only occasion demanding universal manumission.

Zedekiah's release was, then, a Jubilee Year release, its purpose being to remedy past and present disregard of the Sabbatical release law (D. N. Freedman 1993: 251–52). All Hebrew slaves, in any case, went free, those who worked longer than the law required, and others whose terms had not yet expired. Weinfeld (1990: 41–42 n. 10) offers another explanation. Citing a view put forward by Rabbi Meir Loeb ben Jehiel Michael (Malbim),[a] Weinfeld argues that the present release was not in response to any law, either the Sabbatical law or the Law of the Jubilee, but was rather meant to be an absolute abolition of slavery for all time. Needless to say, the release was not understood this way by the narrator of chap. 34, and it is doubtful whether Jeremiah would have understood it as such. This view reads too much into the statement in v 9 "that no person should make them serve a Judahite, his kin." Also, in vv 13–16, explicit mention is made of people disregarding the Sabbatical law, which Weinfeld (and Malbim) seem to overlook. The view of Rudolph, Lemche (1976: 51–53), and others, that the association here with Deuteronomic law is secondary, is to be rejected (Bright; Sarna 1973: 148 n. 23). The integration of Deut 15:12 into the oracle is too complete for it to be secondary.

to send away free each person his male slave and each person his female slave, Hebrew and Hebrewess. The verb *šlḥ* + *ḥpšy(m)* means "send away free" (Deut 15:12, 13, 18; Isa 58:6), here broken up syntactically so that the terms frame the clause at either end. Both male and female Hebrew slaves are to be released. Compare the inclusive nature of the law as promulgated in Deut 15:12. The Covenant Code (Exod 21:2–3) provides only for the release of male Hebrew slaves after six years, although it states that, if the slave came in married, then his wife can go out free with him. The terms "Hebrew" and "Hebrewess" are

---

[a]Malbim (1809–79) was a rabbi, preacher, and biblical exegete from Bucharest who published commentaries on the Bible during the years 1867–76 (*EncJud* 11: 821–24).

unusual, although they do occur in Deut 15:12. The designation "Hebrew" (*'ibrî*) appears only seldom in the OT, and when it does, it retains its older association with slavery and occurs chiefly in the mouths of foreigners or when an Israelite is identifying himself to a foreigner (Gen 39:14, 17; 40:15; 1 Sam 4:6; 14:21; cf. de Vaux 1965b: 83; Bright 1981: 93–95).

so that no person should make them serve a Judahite, his kin. Hebrew *'bd + bĕ* means "make serve, enslave" (see Note for 25:14).

10. *And all the princes and all the people who entered into the covenant gave heed to send away free each person his male slave and each person his female slave, so that he should not make them serve again; and they gave heed and sent them away.* Duhm argued that this acceptance was simply a political move, having nothing to do with laws of religion. During the siege, slaves would be of no use to their owners, their work being in fields outside the city and the feeding of them being a burden the owners could well do without. That the slave owners may have acted from selfish motives is plausible enough, but there is no reason why, at the same time, they might not have sought to remedy a breach in covenant law. Duhm's view, reducing this incident to a strictly political action, has met with little enthusiasm. More than likely motives were mixed (Hyatt; Bright; Holladay).

all the princes. I.e., all the king's men. On *śārîm* meaning "princes," see Note for 24:1.

gave heed. Hebrew *yišmĕ'û*. The LXX has *epestraphēsan* ("they turned around"), which results from the loss of 10b and 11a in its text.

free . . . so that he should not make them serve again; and they gave heed and sent them away. The LXX omits, which can be attributed to haplography (homoeoteleuton: *w . . . w*), assuming that another loss in v 11a was independent of the present loss (see BHS). The T and Vg have the words.

11. *Then they turned around after this and took back the male slaves and female slaves that they had sent away free.* Another LXX omission attributable to haplography (homoeoarcton: *wy . . . wy*), if the loss is separate from the loss in v 10b. The T and Vg have the words. The first *yāšûbû* is "they turned around"; the second *yāšîbû* is "they took back." See another play on *šûb* in vv 15–16, where Jeremiah says "you turned around" (*tāšûbû*) in repentance, then "you turned around (*tāšûbû*) . . . and took back (*wattāšîbû*)" the slaves you set free. The slaves were probably reclaimed once the siege was lifted since they were needed in the fields.

and subjugated them. I.e., back into slavery. The Kt is an H-stem, *yakbîšûm*, which occurs only here in the OT. The Q is a Qal, *yikbĕšûm*, having the same meaning (cf. v 16; Neh 5:5; 2 Chr 28:10).

12. *And the word of Yahweh came to Jeremiah from Yahweh.* The introductory word of v 8 needs repeating because of intervening narrative (so *Mezudath David*). The LXX, S, and an edition of T omit "from Yahweh" (*mē'ēt yhwh*), but it is present in Aq. Since other third-person superscriptions in this form lack "from Yahweh" (see Note for 28:12), the words here are probably secondary, added perhaps from v 8 (Janzen 1973: 51; Holladay). Yahweh's word, in any

case, came to Jeremiah *after* Zedekiah cut the covenant and *after* the people reneged on it (vv 8, 11).

13. *Thus said Yahweh, God of Israel*. The LXX omits "God of Israel," which could be an abridgment, but could also be another loss due to haplography (homoeoarcton: *'aleph . . . 'aleph*).

I, I cut a covenant with your fathers in the day I brought them out from the land of Egypt, from the house of slavery. While references to Israel's former "house of slavery" (*bêt ʿăbādîm*) in recalling the Exodus are found in the early sources (Exod 13:3, 14; 20:2), they occur with greater frequency in Deuteronomy (Deut 5:6; 6:12; 7:8; 8:14; 13:6, 11[Eng 13:5, 10]). Mention of this slavery in the context of the Sinai covenant, which is precisely what occurs in Deut 5:6, sets the stage for what Yahweh will say next.

14. *After seven years' time you shall send away each person his Hebrew kin who was sold to you and served you six years, yes you shall send him away free from your midst*. This is the law from Exod 21:2 and Deut 15:12.

After seven years' time. Hebrew *miqqēṣ šebaʿ šānîm*, where *qēṣ* means not "end," but "period of time" (Wallenstein 1954: 211–13, who cites later Qumran usage; cf. NJV n.). The same expression occurs in Deut 15:1. In Hebrew reckoning, both the first and last years are counted. So, for example, circumcision occurs on the eighth day, which is the seventh day after birth; Jesus' resurrection is on the third day, the second day after his death. The Sabbatical law states that Hebrew slaves work for six years, then in the seventh they go free (Exod 21:2; Deut 15:12). The LXX in the present verse has "six years" (cf. LXX "sixth day" in Gen 2:2), which Giesebrecht takes to be a deliberate change by the LXX translator. The reading "six" was adopted by the RSV, but changed to "seven" in the NRSV. Aquila, Symm, T, S, and Vg all have "seven."

from your midst. Hebrew *mēʿimmāk*. The LXX omits, but Giesebrecht notes that other ancient witnesses have the term (G^L, Vg, S, T). It is present also in Deut 15:12–13.

But your fathers did not listen to me and did not bend their ear. It appears that previous generations also neglected to implement the Sabbatical release. The LXX omits "your fathers" (cf. 11:8; 35:15), which can be attributed to haplography (homoeoarcton: *'aleph . . . 'aleph*). The omission is of no consequence, however, since "your fathers" in the LXX carries over as the subject from v 13.

15. *And you, you turned around*. Hebrew *wattāšūbû 'attem*. The assumption here is that Jerusalem's present population has failed to obey the Sabbatical law, although now they have turned around (i.e., repented) and done right by releasing their Hebrew slaves. The emphatic pronoun "you" plural (*'attem*), contrasts with the emphatic "I" (*'ānōkî*) in v 13 and should not be omitted with the LXX (*pace* Janzen 1973: 51; Holladay). The LXX carries on in the verse with third-person verbs from the end of v 14, which eliminates the direct speech to the people of Jerusalem. Read the MT.

one day. Hebrew *hayyôm*, which could also be translated "recently" (Ehrlich 1912: 331).

and you did what is right in my eyes. Even though the release may have been done with mixed motives, it is said here to have been a right action.

and you cut a covenant before me in the house upon which my name is called. The covenant was made in the Temple, at which time the Law of the Jubilee was solemnly proclaimed. For the expression "the house upon which my name is called," see Note for 7:10.

16. *then you turned around.* Hebrew *wattāšūbû.* Another play on *šûb,* which meant "you repented" in v 15. Here people are said to have turned in the wrong direction, violating the covenant they had just made to release the Hebrew slaves. See the earlier play on *šûb* in v 11.

and profaned my name. Hebrew *wattĕhallĕlû 'et-šĕmî.* On the profanation of Yahweh's name, see also Amos 2:7 and Mal 1:11–12. In Jer 16:18, idols are said to have profaned Yahweh's land.

according to their desire. On *nepeš* meaning "desire," see 22:27 and Deut 21:14.

and you subjugated them to be for you male slaves and female slaves. The LXX texts of both Rahlfs and Ziegler omit "and you subjugated them to be," relegating the inclusion of the articular infinitive, *tou einai* ("to be"), to a minority reading. But Field (1875: 675) in his critical work on Origen's Hexapla takes the omission to be only "and you subjugated them," noting also that Aq and Theod have the words. They are present also in T and Vg. The smaller omission can be attributed to haplography (homoeoteleuton: *m . . . m*), and a loss of the remaining *lihyôt* (to be") can also be explained by haplography (homoeoarcton: *l . . . l*). There is no reason, in any case, to delete the words as an MT addition taken from v 11 (*pace* Janzen 1973: 51; Holladay).

17. *You, you have not listened to me to proclaim liberty each person to his kin and each person to his fellow.* The fact that the king and the people reneged on the covenant makes it seem as if they did not listen to Yahweh at all, putting their disobedience on the same level as that of earlier generations (v 14b). The LXX omits "each person to his kin and," which is likely (*pace* G. Greenberg 2001: 235) due to haplography (whole-word plus: *'yš l . . . 'yš l*).

You, you have not listened to me to proclaim liberty. . . . Look I am proclaiming liberty to you . . . to the sword, to the pestilence, and to the famine. The two oracles together play on "proclaim liberty," the second usage of which is bitter irony, since the people will not attain liberty but instead will be reduced to slavery (Chotzner 1883: 13–14). See a similar irony in 15:2–3. The punishment here will fit the crime (Calvin; Giesebrecht; P. D. Miller 1984: "poetic justice"). On the triad, "sword, famine, and pestilence," see Note for 5:12.

a fright. Hebrew *za'ăwâ* (Q); *zĕwā'â* (Kt). On the Q-Kt, see Note for 15:4.

18. *And I will make the men who walked over my covenant, who did not carry out the words of the covenant that they cut before me, the calf that they cut in two and walked between its parts.* Here is a double wordplay on the verbs *'br,* "walked (over)," and *krt,* "cut." The LXX not only misses the wordplays but gets the whole sense wrong. According to its translation, the men who transgressed the covenant are given the calf they had prepared for the sacrifice. The curse

meted out by Yahweh is stated in metaphorical terms: the men will become the calf cut in two because they violated the covenant. It is not necessary to render the curse as a comparison, which requires emendation to "like a calf" (*pace* Ehrlich 1912: 331; Volz; Rudolph). The difference is slight. In an Akkadian Treaty between Ashurnirari V of Assyria (753–746 B.C.) and Matiʾilu of Arpad, which was ratified by a lamb sacrifice, both simile and metaphor occur. The curse begins with this simile:

> If Matiʾilu sins against (this) treaty made under oath by the gods, then, just as this spring lamb, brought from its fold, will not return to its fold . . . Matiʾilu, together with his sons, daughters, officials, and people of his land . . . will not return to his country.

Then comes a shift to metaphor:

> This head is not the head of a lamb, it is the head of Matiʾilu, it is the head of his sons, his officials, and the people of his land.
> (*ANET*³ 532; cf. Luckenbill 1926: 266 ##752, 753)

A number of ANE treaties corroborate the ceremony here described (D. McCarthy 1963: 51–79). In another eighth-century treaty, this one in Aramaic between Bar-gaya of Katak and Matiʾilu of Arpad (Sefire I A 40), the curse attending the rite states: "[As] this calf is cut up, thus Mattiʿel and his nobles shall be cut up" (*ANET*³ 660; *CS II* 214; Fitzmyer 1961: 181, 185; Beyerlin 1978: 260). See also, from the same general period, clauses in the Vassal Treaties of Esarhaddon (*ANET*³ 539 #70; Wiseman 1958a: 69–72 ##551–54). A millennium earlier, in a letter sent to King Zimri-lim of Mari (1730–1697 B.C.), we hear of a treaty involving the symbolic rite of slaying a she-ass (Noth 1966a: 108–17; Malamat 1995). From this earlier period is also the Abban-Iarimlim Treaty from Alalakh (modern Acana, Turkey), dated to the eighteenth century B.C., where the slaying of a sheep accompanies a self-imprecation oath (Wiseman 1958b; D. McCarthy 1963: 52–53). The text (lines 49–43) reads: "Abban placed himself under oath to Iarimlim, and had cut the neck of a sheep (saying), '(Let me so die) if I take back that which I gave you!' "

The oath ratified the treaty, and we can assume that an oath was taken at the covenant ceremony here (Calvin; McCarthy 1963: 55–57; Weinfeld 1990: 57; idem, "*bᵉrîth*," *TDOT* 2: 256, 259–61). The people, by walking between the severed parts of the animal, consented to similar treatment should they break the covenant. Classical sources, too, attest to self-imprecation oaths in ceremonies of this type. Livy (xxi 45) reports a situation where Hannibal, in order to get his troops to fight an upcoming battle, promised among other things freedom for slaves who had come with their masters. To fortify this promise, he took hold of a lamb, swore an oath to the effect that the gods could slay him even as he was now about to slay this lamb, then killed the lamb with a stone to the head. See also another ceremony described in Livy i 24.

The biblical precedent for what occurs here is the ritual accompanying a covenant Yahweh makes with Abraham that Abraham's descendants will inherit the land of promise (Gen 15:7–21). There, animals were cut in two, and in the darkness "a smoking fire pot and a flaming torch passed between the pieces" (v 17), symbolizing the divine presence. Abraham was not a party to this covenant in the way that Zedekiah and the people of Jerusalem were party to the covenant of slave manumission. The covenant Yahweh made with Abraham was unconditional, with no demands being placed on Abraham and no chance for either noncompliance or abrogation. On the covenant of divine commitment, see D. N. Freedman 1964. A calf was slaughtered for the covenant ceremony presided over by Zedekiah, for as v 19 states, the people of Jerusalem and Judah walked in procession between the severed parts.

who did not carry out the words of the covenant. I.e., who did not keep the terms as stated in v 14. Hebrew *'ăšer lō'-hēqîmû 'et-dibrê habbĕrît.* The LXX omits "words (of)," which are present in Theod, T, and Vg. But Theod follows the LXX in reading "my covenant."

19. *and the princes of Jerusalem.* The LXX omits, which can be explained as an inner-Greek haplography, since the word immediately following in the LXX is *kai* (whole-word: *kai . . . kai*). Aquila, T, and Vg have the omitted words.

the eunuchs. Here high-ranking officials (Calvin: chief men); see Note for 29:2.

and all the people of the land who walked between the parts of the calf. The LXX has only "and the people" (*kai ton laon*), but Aq, T, and Vg have the omitted words.

20. *and into the hand of those who seek their life.* The LXX omits, which can be attributed to haplography (homoeoarcton: *w . . . w* or homoeoteleuton: *m . . . m*). Giesebrecht notes that the words are present in all the Hexapla codices, G^L, S, T, and Vg.

and their dead bodies shall become food for the birds of the skies and the beasts of the earth. Upon the men of Jerusalem who violated the covenant will come a curse of nonburial (see Note for 7:33). Death and nonburial are not promised to Zedekiah and his princes (v 21), which, at least in the case of Zedekiah, is consistent with the burial promised him in vv 4–5.

21. *And Zedekiah, king of Judah, and his princes, I will give into the hand of their enemies and into the hand of those who seek their life.* This is how it happened; see 39:4–5; 52:7–9. The LXX again omits "and into the hand of those who seek their life," which can be another loss attributed to haplography (whole-word: *wbyd . . . wbyd* or homoeoteleuton: *m . . . m*).

into the hand of the army of the king of Babylon, who have withdrawn from you. A reference to the Babylonian withdrawal from Jerusalem puts the incident early in the siege (Sarna [1973: 144–45] says between January and April 587 B.C.), when Pharaoh Apries (Hophra) and the Egyptians made a move out of Egypt, forcing the Babylonians to lift the siege (37:5). The LXX reading, *kai dunamis basileōs Babulōnos tois apotrechousin ap' autōn* ("and the forces of the king of Babylon to whom they are running away from them"?), is clearly defective (so also Janzen 1973: 42; McKane).

22. *and I will bring them back to this city.* This same prediction is made to the king in 37:7–10. For the prophecy of Jerusalem's destruction elsewhere in Jeremiah's preaching, see Note on 34:2. Here is another wordplay: as the people "took back" (*tāšibû*) their slaves (v 16), so also will Yahweh "bring back" (*hăšibōtîm*) the Babylonian army to Jerusalem. More punishment to fit the crime. The LXX has "land" instead of "city," which is not right (Giesebrecht). It is the city that will be attacked, taken, and burned with fire.

and they will burn it with fire; and the cities of Judah I will make a desolation without inhabitant. For a list of land and city curses in Jeremiah, see Note on 48:9.

MESSAGE AND AUDIENCE

The audience is told here about a word that came to Jeremiah from Yahweh after Zedekiah and the people of Jerusalem made a solemn covenant to liberate their Hebrew slaves, male and female both. The narrator ascribes a lofty aim to the action: "that no person should make them serve a Judahite, his kin." The princes and people followed through on their promise and released their slaves. But soon afterward, they turned around and subjugated them again to slavery.

Yahweh speaks to this perfidy in four oracles. In the first, presumably addressed to a broad Jerusalem audience, he begins with a poignant reminder that he cut a covenant with the ancestors when he delivered them out of Egypt, which, as they all know, was a house of slavery. That covenant contained provisions for the people to release their Hebrew slaves after six years of work. Previous generations conveniently ignored this command, and as for the present generation, well, they ignored it too, but Yahweh says they nevertheless had the good sense now to turn around and do what was right. They released their Hebrew slaves, which was the slaves' desire and what the Law of Jubilee required, but then they profaned Yahweh's name by reclaiming the slaves. In a second brief oracle, Yahweh sums up the indictment: "You, you have not listened to me to proclaim liberty each person to his kin and each person to his fellow."

The two oracles following are riveting judgment. In Oracle III, Yahweh tells those who failed to proclaim liberty to their slaves that he is proclaiming a dubious liberty to them: they can have their choice of sword, famine, or pestilence. Whichever they choose, Yahweh will make them a fright to every kingdom of the earth. Those participating in the covenant recently cut will become the calf cut in two, between which the princes of Jerusalem and Judah, eunuchs and priests, and people of the land walked in solemn procession. Yahweh says he will give them all into the hand of those seeking their lives. What is more, their dead bodies will be food for the birds of the skies and the beasts of the earth. As for Zedekiah and his princes, they too will be given into the hands of their enemies, namely, the army of Babylon currently on another errand. The audience may perceive that Zedekiah and the princes will not die or suffer the added indignity of nonburial, such as Jehoiakim was promised. What then will their fate be? Yahweh says in a final oracle that he has issued a command to bring the Babylonian army back to Jerusalem. They will besiege the city, take it, and burn it with fire. The cities of Judah will also be made desolate of inhabitants.

The event here described took place at the time of the Babylonian withdrawal from Jerusalem, when it is possible to look ahead to the army's return (v 22). This would be in Zedekiah's tenth year, early in 587 B.C. Fried and Freedman (2001: 2260) date the lifting of the siege between December 29, 588 and February 24, 587 B.C. Jeremiah's personal word to Zedekiah in vv 1–7 is later, spoken during the last stage of the siege (587–586 B.C.). When the two narrative segments are heard in sequence, the liberation of slaves and their reclamation will give added reason for the judgment on Judah's king. But this later judgment (vv 4–5) will also amplify an earlier judgment (vv 21–22) in which nothing is said about the king dying or being left unburied. The oracle in vv 4–5 makes it clear that Zedekiah will be given a burial, however unpleasant, in a foreign land. The narrative in v 7 also fulfills the divine word of v 22, since the Babylonians are now back, fighting the final battles against Jerusalem and the cities of Judah.

B. WHAT ABOUT THOSE RECHABITES? (35:1–19)

1. A Lesson on Obedience (35:1–11)

35 ¹The word that came to Jeremiah from Yahweh in the days of Jehoiakim son of Josiah, king of Judah: ²Go to the house of the Rechabites, and you shall speak to them and bring them to the house of Yahweh, to one of the chambers, and you shall offer them wine to drink. ³So I took Jaazaniah son of Jeremiah, son of Habazziniah, and his brothers and all his sons, indeed the entire house of the Rechabites, ⁴and I brought them to the house of Yahweh, to the chamber of the sons of Hanan son of Igdaliah, the man of God, which was next to the chamber of the princes, which was above the chamber of Maaseiah son of Shallum, the keeper of the threshold. ⁵Then I set before the sons of the house of Rechabites pitchers full of wine and cups, and I said to them, 'Drink wine.' ⁶But they said, 'We will not drink wine, for Jonadab son of Rechab, our father, commanded us saying, "You shall not drink wine—you or your sons—forever, ⁷and a house you shall not build, and seed you shall not sow, and a vineyard you shall not plant, nor shall it belong to you, for in tents you shall dwell all your days, in order that you may live many days on the face of the earth where you are sojourning." ⁸And we have obeyed the voice of Jonadab son of Rechab, our father, in all that he commanded us, so as not to drink wine all our days—we, our wives, our sons, and our daughters, ⁹also so as not to build houses for our

dwellings, and vineyard or field or seed not to have for ourselves. ¹⁰So we dwell in tents, and we have heeded and done according to everything that Jonadab, our father, commanded us. ¹¹But it happened when Nebucha-drezzar, king of Babylon, came up into the land, then we said, "Come, and let us enter Jerusalem because of the army of the Chaldeans and because of the army of the Aramaeans." So we are dwelling in Jerusalem.'

2. Oracles for the Obedient and Disobedient (35:12–19)

¹²And the word of Yahweh came to Jeremiah: ¹³Thus said Yahweh of hosts, God of Israel: Go, and you shall say to the men of Judah and to the inhabi-tants of Jerusalem:

Will you not take correction to listen to my words—oracle of Yahweh? ¹⁴The words of Jonadab son of Rechab, which he commanded his sons so as not to drink wine have been carried out, and they have not drunk to this day because they have heeded the command of their father. But I, I have spoken to you—constantly I have spoken—and you have not listened to me. ¹⁵And I have sent to you all my servants the prophets—constantly I sent—saying: Return, would you, each person from his evil way and make good your doings and do not go after other gods to serve them and dwell on the soil that I gave to you and your fathers. But you have not bent your ear, and you have not lis-tened to me. ¹⁶Indeed the sons of Jonadab son of Rechab have carried out the command of their father which he commanded them, but this people have not listened to me.

¹⁷Therefore thus said Yahweh, God of hosts, God of Israel:
Look I am bringing to Judah and to all the inhabitants of Jerusalem all the evil that I spoke concerning them, because I have spoken to them and they have not listened, and I have called to them and they have not answered.
¹⁸But to the house of the Rechabites Jeremiah said, Thus said Yahweh of hosts, God of Israel: Because you have listened to the command of Jonadab, your father, and you have kept all his commands and you have done according to all that he commanded you,
¹⁹Therefore thus said Yahweh of hosts, God of Israel:
There shall not be cut off a man belonging to Jonadab son of Rechab who stands before me all the days.

RHETORIC AND COMPOSITION

MT Chapter 35 = LXX Chapter 42. The present verses are a self-standing narrative reporting a symbolic act carried out by Jeremiah with the Rechabites (vv 1–11), after which come three divine oracles based on the encounter, two delivered to the people of Judah and Jerusalem, and one delivered to the Rechabites (vv 12–19). In the concluding narration of v 18, no command is given to Jeremiah to address the Rechabites, but we can assume that one must have been given; otherwise the command in v 2 has to cover this action. Whether or not the latter is intended, the narrative taken as a whole begins and ends with Jeremiah addressing the Rechabites. The Rechabites were probably on hand when Oracles I and II were spoken to the people of Judah and Jerusalem, perhaps in the outer courtyard of the Temple, although a location is not specified. But it can be assumed from the separate command in v 13 and by the larger audience now being addressed that the action has moved outside of the Temple chamber.

The narrative is delimited at the top end by a superscription in v 1, before which is a *petuḥah* in M^A, M^L, and M^P and also the chapter division. Delimitation at the bottom end is by a *petuḥah* in M^A and M^L and a *setumah* in M^P after v 19, which is another chapter division. The M^L and M^P separate Oracle I from Oracle II with a *setumah* after v 16. The M^A and Cambridge Genizah fragment A 14.2 lack this section. The M^L has another *setumah* after v 18, which separates the narrative from Oracle III. The M^A, M^P, and two MSS in the Cambridge Genizah Collection (A 14.2; NS 58.13) lack this section.

This narrative belongs to an original "Jehoiakim Cluster," comprising chaps. 25, 26, 35, and 36. In that structure it balances another Temple incident in chap. 26 (see Rhetoric and Composition for 25:1–14). The present sequence of narratives in the book is not, in my view, "something of a mistake," as alleged by Knights (1997–98: 208); it is a later arrangement made with another purpose in mind (Lundbom 1975: 110–11 [= 1997: 144–45]; see also "Excursus III: The Composition of Jeremiah 24–36" at the end of 25:1–14). On the juxtaposition of the present chapter with chap. 34, see Rhetoric and Composition for 34:1–7.

The historical character of the incident reported is generally admitted, with only Carroll and McKane repeating the earlier doubts of N. Schmidt (1901b: 2387), who, among other things, could not imagine Jeremiah praising the Rechabites when their entrance into Jerusalem was in violation of the command laid upon them by their ancestor. Schmidt suggested for chap. 35 a date in the Persian period (1901b: 2391). This view was dismissed early on by Peake, who simply pointed out that tents could have been pitched inside the city. No one since has much questioned the Rechabite presence in Jerusalem, which came about for obvious reasons. The detail that the chapter provides, which will be seen again in chap. 36, is either the report of someone who had intimate knowledge of what went on or else a fabrication. It can be said with confidence that this is not the stuff of which legend is made, where the field of vision admits no more than two persons at any one time, and single persons become bigger than life (Olrik 1908). Here we are told exact locations within the Temple, chambers next to and below the one that Jeremiah and the Rechabites entered, the names and patronyms of two of the chambers' occupants, one of whom was the doorkeeper of the Temple, and the name and patronym of the Rechabite leader.

Many commentators (Giesebrecht; Cornill; Peake; Streane; Rudolph; Weiser; Bright) have cited the first-person narrative as an indication of authenticity. Even those arguing for a "Deuteronomic" editing in vv 12–19 (Duhm; Rudolph, who takes the whole chapter to be Source C; cf. Mowinckel 1914: 31, 58–59; and Hyatt), believe the narrative goes back ultimately to Baruch and is basically authentic. The argument for a "Deuteronomic" editing—here as elsewhere—rests largely on Duhm's late dating of the heavy prose, i.e., prose having *accumulatio* and stereotyped phraseology. Thiel (1981: 44–48) and Migsch (1997), who build on earlier source criticism, are thus occupied with later "Deuteronomic" redactions. The heavy prose belongs to the authentic Jeremiah tradition (H. Weippert 1973: 121–48; Holladay) and can no longer be taken as a mark of exilic or postexilic authorship/editing.

The LXX text is again shorter than MT, but not the better text by a wide margin (*pace* Cornill; Janzen 1973; Holladay; McKane). Many of its readings are inferior, confused, or just plain wrong, in addition to which are nine arguable cases for LXX haplography in the chapter, some not noted as LXX omissions in *BHS* and none treated as haplographic loss by Cornill, Janzen, Holladay, or McKane. As Giesebrecht once again points out, readings in the other Versions usually support MT.

NOTES

35:1. *The word that came to Jeremiah from Yahweh.* On this superscription, see Notes for 7:1 and 21:1. The T expands to "word of prophecy."

in the days of Jehoiakim son of Josiah, king of Judah. The LXX omits "son of Josiah," which is present in S, T, and Vg. The date here ("in the days of Jehoiakim") is general, leaving us uncertain about precisely when the reported event took place. Blayney dated it in the fourth year of Jehoiakim, 605 B.C., associating it with Nebuchadrezzar's campaign against the Philistines. Cheyne, too, put it before the first arrival of Nebuchadrezzar, in the summer of 606 B.C. In my earlier work (Lundbom 1975: 107–8 [= 1997: 141]), I also dated the event before 605 B.C., noting that in this year Jeremiah was debarred from entering the Temple (36:5) and that a year later both he and Baruch went into hiding (36:19, 26). I had doubts about Jeremiah making any more public appearances, much less one in the Temple, while Jehoiakim was still on the throne. Jeremiah reenters public life just before Jerusalem's surrender to Nebuchadrezzar in 597 B.C., at which time we find him advising the newly-enthroned Jehoiachin and the queen mother to give themselves up (13:15–23). So if a date preceding Jerusalem's surrender to Nebuchadrezzar in 597 is to be assigned to the event here, it would have to be at the very end of Jehoiakim's life. This is the conclusion of Rudolph, who says a date of 605 is not possible because the Syrians were not then an ally of Nebuchadrezzar. Yet they may have been. Following Carchemish Syria belonged to Nebuchadrezzar, and a Syrian contingent could certainly have accompanied him on his march to Philistia in 604 B.C. A more pressing question in attempting to correlate this early date with the present event is whether Nebuchadrezzar, already in 604, was threatening Judah. Doubtless he was, since about this time 2 Kgs 24:1 reports that the king of Babylon "came up" ('ālâ), presumably against Jerusalem, and Jehoiakim became his servant for three years. But most commentators (Giesebrecht; Peake; Streane; Weiser; Hyatt; Bright; Thompson; Holladay) date the present event with the Rechabites to ca. 599–598 B.C. or earlier, correlating the Syrian reference in v 11 with 2 Kgs 24:2, which says that bands of Syrians joined bands of Chaldeans in overunning Judah. But v 11 also mentions Nebuchadrezzar, who was not present in the raids of 599–598 but came later with the full Babylonian army (Bright 1981: 327). The problem is noted by Rudolph. We must conclude, then, that the event here occurred either prior to 605 B.C., when Jeremiah had ready access to the Temple, or else early in 597 B.C., after Jehoiakim was dead, making a Temple visit by Jeremiah again possible.

2. *Go to the house of the Rechabites, and you shall speak to them . . . and you shall offer them wine to drink.* Here is another divine directive that Jeremiah carry out a symbolic act, similar to the directives given him to bury a loincloth in Parah (13:1) and break a jug in the Ben-Hinnom Valley (19:1). For other symbolic acts in the book of Jeremiah, see Note on 13:1. Jeremiah knows in this case that the Rechabites will not drink the wine, which proves to be the case (v 6).

Go . . . and you shall speak to them. The LXX omits "and you shall speak to them," which can be attributed to haplography (homoeoarcton: *w . . . w* or homoeoteleuton: *m . . . m*). Aquila, Theod, S, T, and Vg all have the words. The infinitive absolute *hālôk* paired with a perfect verb mandating action is a common construction in the Jeremianic prose (see Note for 28:13), arguing for the retention of "and you shall speak" (*pace* Holladay). De Vaux (1965b: 330) thinks that Jeremiah must first speak to the Rechabites in order to persuade them to enter the Temple, as their disavowal of permanent structures might cause them to resist entering a Temple building. But such a scruple is by no means assured.

the house of the Rechabites. Hebrew *bêt hārēkābîm.* "House" here means family or clan.

Rechabites. These people formed a subculture (perhaps even resident aliens; see v 7) within Israel and Judah, tracing their clan back to Jonadab son of Rechab (v 6). Jonadab lived in Northern Israel in the ninth century B.C., emerging there from the shadows when the zealous Jehu invited him to witness the final extermination of Ahab's royal house and a decisive purge of Baal worship (2 Kgs 10:15–27). According to 1 Chr 2:55, the Rechabites decended from the Kenites, which puts their origins back in the Mosaic Age. The Kenites are thought by some to have been the original worshipers of Yahweh (the so-called "Kenite Hypothesis"), with Jethro, Moses' father-in-law, having introduced Moses to his God. Calvin, Rashi, and *Mezudath David* all link up the Rechabites to Jethro. The Kenites (and Midianites) attached themselves to Israel in the wilderness and entered Canaan with them, continuing their semi-nomadic existence in the Negeb and on Judah's southern border (Judg 1:16;

1 Sam 15:6; 27:10; 30:29). Some found their way north to the territory of Naphtali, for example, near Kedesh, where Heber, the Kenite, pitched his tent (Judg 4:11), and his more famous wife, Jael, put one of the pegs through the head of Sisera (Judg 4:17–22; 5:24–27). It is generally assumed that since the Kenites and Rechabites lived in tents and did not till the soil, they were shepherds, pasturing flocks in the marginal areas of Northern Israel and southern Judah (Calvin; Pope in *IDB* R–Z, 15; Abramsky 1967). They also rejected settled life to the point that they did not drink wine. Pope says the rule imposed by Jonadab was the essence of nomadism, and that the conflict between nomadic and settled ways of life is well-nigh universal. In abstaining from wine, the Rechabites were like the Nazirites (Num 6:1–4), with whom the prophet Amos had sympathy (Amos 2:11–12). Rechabite seminomadism was assumed by Calvin and Blayney and developed fully in an essay by Karl Budde entitled "The Nomadic Ideal in the Old Testament" (1895). This anticultural, antisettlement way of life for the Rechabites has become an accepted view of scholars for more than a century (Cheyne; Duhm; Peake; Cornill; Streane; Weiser; Rudolph; Hyatt; Bright; Thompson; Boadt; Jones).

A few dissenting voices have arisen, however, reflecting the trend in recent biblical scholarship to downplay Israel's seminomadic origins and overlook a romantic impulse in late preexilic Israel that idealized the Mosaic Age (see Note for 2:2). Abramsky (1967) argued on slender evidence that the Rechabites resided in permanent settlements in the Judean Hills south of Jerusalem. Frick (1971; "Rechab," *ABD* 5: 630–32) followed with a theory that the Rechabites were a guild of itinerant craftsmen who made chariotry and weaponry. This theory hung on minority readings of G^{BL} in 1 Chr 4:12, where certain craftsmen are named "the men of Rechab" rather than "the men of Repha" (MT: "men of Recah"). The MT and LXX consistently read two separate names: 1) in 2 Kgs 10:15 and Jer 35:6[LXX 42:6] MT reads *rēkāb* and LXX *rēchab*; and 2) in 1 Chr 4:12 MT reads *rēkâ* and LXX *rēpha*. The Rechabites are not "the men of Recah" and thus not the guild of craftsmen mentioned in 1 Chr 4:11–14. Knights (1995–96; 1996–97) also dismisses the idea of a nomadic origin for the Rechabites, arguing that the Rechabites were prophets linking up with the itinerant lifestyle of Elijah. Cummings (1979: 124), too, has Jonadab a rival to Elisha in succeeding Elijah. Knights argues that the expression "to stand before Yahweh," which appears in the promise to the Rechabites in v 19, must indicate that the Rechabites were prophets (1996–97: 42), which, needless to say, is a reduction of evidence that he himself has produced. Anyone—priest, prophet, or ordinary person (7:10)—could "stand before Yahweh" in worship and service (see Note on 15:19).

The Rechabites were a conservative Judahite subculture that rejected basic tenets of the settled life. Jeremiah lifts them up, not because he espouses their lifestyle or because he thinks they are more true to Yahweh, though they may well have been more true. He may extend them sympathy because of romantic leanings, but the whole point of the symbolism here acted out is that the Rechabites are shown to be faithful to Jonadab, their father, in a way that

Judah has not been faithful to Yahweh. For this reason, and only for this reason, Jeremiah commends the Rechabites and gives them a promise for the
future. The Rechabites survived the exile, for a descendant is reported as helping in the rebuilding of Jerusalem (Neh 3:14). On the Rechabites, see further
the article by Pope in *IDB* R–Z, 14–16.

one of the chambers. In the Temple building, surrounding the holy place
(*hêkāl*) and the holy of holies (*dĕbîr*), there was an outer structure of (side)
chambers (*lĕšākôt; ṣĕlā'ôt*) built in three levels (1 Kgs 6:5–6), over which the
Levitical priests had jurisdiction (1 Chr 23:27–28). These chambers were living and working areas for priests in charge of the Temple (Ezek 40:45), priests
in charge of the altar (Ezek 40:46), singers (1 Chr 9:33), stewards (2 Kgs 23:11),
and Temple doorkeepers (Jer 35:4; 1 Chr 9:26–27). One chamber was apparently set aside for the princes (Jer 35:4). Some chambers were storage facilities
for Temple vessels and other treasures, for frankincense, cereal offerings, and
incoming tithes (1 Chr 28:12; 2 Chr 31:11–12), the latter consisting of fruit,
grain, wine, and oil (Neh 10:38–40[Eng 10:37–39]; 13:4–9). One might compare these to the side rooms in the Church of the Holy Sepulcher in Jerusalem
or in any other house of worship. We can imagine that Jeremiah took the Rechabites into the chamber of the sons of Hanan because a store of wine was there.
Regarding the side chambers in a reconstructed Solomonic Temple, including
a discussion about whether the doors led to the Temple interior or to the outside, see Garber 1951: 17–18; 1958: 127–33. This outer Temple structure is
described also in de Vaux 1965b: 315.

*3–4. So I took Jaazaniah son of Jeremiah, son of Habazziniah, and his broth-
ers and all his sons, indeed the entire house of the Rechabites, and I brought them
to the house of Yahweh.* Narratives of this type commonly contain a command
from Yahweh that Jeremiah carry out a specific action, followed by a first-
person report that the action was carried out (see Note on 25:17). If the entire
clan of Rechabites entered a single chamber there could not have been many
of them. According to Abarbanel, the whole family was taken to show that not
one of them would drink the wine.

Jaazaniah son of Jeremiah. On the name "Jaazaniah," see Note for 40:8.

and all his sons. The LXX omits "all"; see again v 15 and discussion in Janzen 1973: 65–67.

indeed the entire house of the Rechabites. Migsch (2001) argues that this
phrase, being general and prefixed by a *waw*, must be supplied with an adjective "remnant" (*yeter* or *šĕ'ārît*) after "all," giving the reading: "the whole remaining house of the Rechabites" (= all the other Rechabites). But there is no
textual basis for such an addition and no reason, basically, why the present
company must be the only Rechabites remaining. The phrase appears simply
to be a "catchall" following the specific mention of Jaazaniah's family. The text
is saying that all the Rechabites who had entered Jerusalem for safety were
brought. A few other individuals may also have been invited as witnesses, as we
assume happened when Jeremiah buried the loincloth in Parah, and broke the
jug in Ben-Hinnom.

4. *Hanan son of Igdaliah, the man of God.* The "man of God" is Hanan, not his father. Rashi and *Mezudath David* say the appellation means "prophet," a meaning found elsewhere in the OT (1 Sam 9:6–10 [Samuel]; 2 Kgs 1:9–13 [Elijah]; 4:7, 9, 16; et passim [Elisha]). The T has "the prophet of the Lord," and Hayward (1985a: 210, citing P. Churgin) says this translation is made because Aramaic *nby*' always signifies a true prophet of the Lord. The name *Hanan* has turned up on the Samaria and Arad ostraca, as well as on seals, bullae, and other artifacts of the period; the name *Igdaliah* has turned up on a seventh-century seal of unknown provenance (see Appendix I). The LXX and S read "Gedaliah" instead of "Igdaliah."

the chamber of the princes. On the meaning of *śārîm* ("princes"), see Note for 24:1.

Maaseiah son of Shallum, the keeper of the threshold. A priest who is likely the father of Zephaniah (21:1; 29:25; 37:3), the associate priest (52:24 = 2 Kgs 25:18). As "keeper of the threshold" or "doorkeeper" (*šōmēr hassap*), this individual is a high-ranking Levitical priest (2 Chr 34:9). Three "keepers of the threshold" watched over the three entrances to the Temple and helped with other Temple duties (2 Kgs 22:4; 23:4). Maaseiah may have given Jeremiah and the Rechabites Temple access. After Jerusalem was taken, the three keepers of the threshold were taken along with the high priest Seraiah, Zephaniah, and other high-ranking people of Jerusalem to face Nebuchadrezzar, who executed them (see Note for 52:24). Both of the names "Maaseiah" and "Shallum" appear on the Arad ostraca and other contemporary finds (see Appendix I). On the Temple doors, doorways, and stone thresholds, see Paul and Dever 1973: 35–36.

5. *Then I set before the sons of the house of Rechabites.* The LXX: "And I set before them."

pitchers full of wine and cups The LXX has "(pottery) jug" singular (*keramion*) and lacks "full," which can be attributed to haplography (homoeoteleuton: *ym . . . ym*). The T and Vg have "full." Hebrew *gĕbiʿîm* are serving vessels, which Honeyman (1939: 80) says were probably one-handled jugs with a pinched spout. Kelso (1948: 17 #37) says they were the common ceramic pitchers used to hold wine or water. Hebrew *kōsôt* are drinking vessels, larger than modern cups and more like bowls. On the "cup" and its metaphorical uses, see Note for 25:15.

and I said to them. The LXX omits "to them." The T and Vg have the term.

6–7. *But they said, 'We will not drink wine, for Jonadab son of Rechab, our father, commanded us saying, "You shall not drink wine—you or your sons—forever, and a house you shall not build, and seed you shall not sow, and a vineyard you shall not plant, nor shall it belong to you, for in tents you shall dwell all your days."'* The apodictic *lōʾ* could render the disclaimers, "We will never drink wine . . . you shall never drink wine . . . and a house you shall never build," and so on (Bright 1973: 197). The Rechabite vow has all the marks of desert life, rejecting as it does agrarian and urban culture. Cheyne said the Rechabites were like typical Arabs, reminding him in certain respects of the

Wahhabis, a puritanical movement in Islam that began in the mid–eighteenth century and flourished into the nineteenth and early twentieth centuries (cf. *EncIs* 11: 39–47). A comparison has also been made to the Nabataeans, about whom Diodorus of Sicily (xix 94) writes in the first century B.C.:

> They live in the open air, claiming as native land a wilderness that has neither rivers nor abundant springs from which it is possible for a hostile army to obtain water. It is their custom neither to plant grain, set out any fruitbearing tree, use wine, nor construct any house.

> (Loeb)

Parallels between the two groups have been overdrawn (cf. Knights 1993); nevertheless, the two ways of life are in many ways similar.

Jonadab son of Rechab, our father. Jonadab may be a distant ancestor of the Rechabite clan, although "father" (*'āb*) could simply mean "founder" of the movement (Hyatt; Abramsky 1967), as the prophet becomes "father" to the "sons of the prophets" (2 Kings 2). "Father" is also used in the OT as a strictly honorific title (2 Kgs 5:13; 6:21).

you shall not plant, nor. The LXX omits, which can be attributed to haplography (whole word: *l' . . . l'*). Giesebrecht says the omission is wrong.

in order that you may live many days on the face of the earth where you are sojourning. This represents an interesting twist on Deuteronomic theology, in which obeying the Sinai covenant means long life and continued settlement in the land (Deut 4:40; 5:16, 33). The Rechabites, however, see themselves as sojourners in the land, which may mean they are resident aliens (so Calvin).

on the face of the earth. Hebrew *'al-pĕnê hā'ădāmâ.* The LXX omits "face," which is present in T and Vg. For the full idiom, see elsewhere 25:26, 33; and 28:16.

8. *Jonadab son of Rechab, our father.* The LXX omits "son of Rechab," which is probably another loss due to haplography (homoeoteleuton: *b . . . b*). The T and Vg have the patronym. The LXX otherwise has the patronym in the chapter, except in v 10, where it is lacking in both MT and LXX. In v 18, where LXX and MT readings vary, the LXX even adds the patronym! There is no reason then to omit "son of Rechab" in the verse (*pace* Holladay).

in all that he commanded us. The LXX omits, which can be another loss due to haplography (homoeoteleuton: *nw . . . nw*). The T and Vg have the words.

10. *So we dwell in tents.* The Rechabites may now be living in tents within the city.

11. *But it happened when Nebuchadrezzar, king of Babylon, came up into the land, then we said, "Come, and let us enter Jerusalem because of the army of the Chaldeans and because of the army of the Aramaeans." So we are dwelling in Jerusalem.* Wherever the Rechabites had been living before, they are now residing in Jerusalem because of the military threat posed by Nebuchadrezzar and the allied "Aramaeans" (= Syrians, which is the modern name for this ancient people). Following the Battle of Carchemish, Syria was doubtless re-

quired to do Nebuchadrezzar's bidding. We know that a combined force of Chaldeans, Syrians, Moabites, and Ammonites ravaged Judah in 599–598 B.C. (2 Kgs 24:2), but whether this pillaging represents the threat here remains unclear (see Note on v 1). The LXX omits "king of Babylon," which it sometimes does (see Appendix VI). It also has *Assyriōn* ("Assyrians") instead of *Syrias* ("Syrians), which is not quite right (*pace* Rudolph; LXX translations in 2:18 and 2 Kgs 24:2 are both correct). Aquila and Symm (both *Syrias*), as well as T and Vg have "Syrians." The S has "Edom," which appears to misread a *dalet* for a *resh* (*'dm* for *'rm*).

So we are dwelling in Jerusalem. The LXX has "and we dwelt there" (*kai ōkoumen ekei*). Aquila, Symm, Theod, T, and Vg all support MT.

12. *And the word of Yahweh came to Jeremiah.* The T again has "word of prophecy." The testing of the Rechabites has concluded and Jeremiah is now said to have received a further word from Yahweh. The LXX has "to me" instead of "to Jeremiah," a change it makes also in 32:26 and 36:1. G. R. Driver (1960: 121) explains "to me" (אלי) as a misread abbreviation (אל־ירמיהו = אל י). Bright thinks the LXX is conforming to the autobiographical style of prior verses. "To Jeremiah" should be read (*pace* Giesebrecht; Duhm; Cornill; Holladay); the introduction parallels the one in v 1.

13. *Yahweh of hosts, God of Israel.* The LXX omits; it also omits "of hosts" in vv 17, 18, and 19 (see Appendix VI).

Go, and you shall say to the men of Judah and to the inhabitants of Jerusalem. Jeremiah is now sent to address a larger audience, which may have gathered in the outer court of the Temple (Cheyne). On the stereotyped phrase "men of Judah and inhabitants of Jerusalem," see Note for 4:3.

Will you not take correction to listen to my words? This is not so much another call to reform as an expression of frustration over the people's inability to reform (vv 14b–15). A recurring theme in Jeremiah's preaching is that people have refused to take "correction," *mûsār* (see Note for 2:30). But a cruel form of correction came finally in the end (30:14).

oracle of Yahweh. Omitted in the LXX, perhaps because of the messenger formula (which it reduces) at the beginning the verse.

14. *The words of Jonadab son of Rechab, which he commanded his sons so as not to drink wine have been carried out, and they have not drunk to this day because they have heeded the command of their father.* Here we see that abstinence from wine is not the issue; what Yahweh deems important is that the Rechabites have heeded the command of Jonadab, their father.

The words of Jonadab . . . have been carried out. A plural object (with *'et*) following a passive verb becomes the subject (GKC §121b; cf. Gen 4:18). The Hophal verb is singular (LXX translates with a plural). Compare a similar construction (without *'et*) in 36:32b.

to this day because they have heeded the command of their father. The LXX omits, but G^L, Aq, Theod, S, T, and Vg all have the words.

But I, I have spoken to you—constantly I have spoken—and you have not listened to me. See 7:13 and 25:3. For the idiom of a repeated verb with *škm*, which occurs again in the next verse, see Note for 7:13. The LXX has only *orthrou* ("in the morning" = "constantly"), but the whole idiom is present in Aq, T, and Vg. The LXX also omits "to me" (cf. 25:3), which is present in T and Vg.

15. *And I have sent to you all my servants the prophets—constantly I sent.* This verse is filled with stereotyped expressions commonly occurring in the Jeremiah prose. Cornill (1895: 59) found the prolixity here in the last half of the chapter "positively intolerable," and proceeded to cut out vv 15–16, even though he noted that all the Versions had them. On the expression, "I have sent to you all my servants the prophets," see Note for 7:25. This second use of the idiom with *škm*, "constantly I sent," underscores the divine frustration at not being able, over a period of years, to get the covenant people to obey Yahweh's commands. Jonadab, on the other hand, has registered astonishing success with his clan, which has obeyed his commands over a period of two and one-half centuries. The LXX lacks "all" (see v 3) and "constantly I sent." The T and Vg support the MT at both points.

Return, would you, each person from his evil way and make good your doings and do not go after other gods to serve them and dwell on the soil that I gave to you and your fathers. This was Jeremiah's basic reform message, which rested on Deuteronomy but moved beyond Deuteronomy by calling people to "return." Should they return, i.e., repent, they could hope to remain in the land given to Israel by Yahweh. Compare the first Temple Oracle in 7:3–7.

Return, would you, each person from his evil way. See Note for 18:11.

make good your doings. A variation of the standard "make good your ways and your doings," on which see Note for 7:3.

and do not go after other gods to serve them. See Note for 7:6.

and dwell on the soil that I gave to you and your fathers. On this expression and Yahweh's gift of the land, see Note for 25:5. The *'al* before *hā'ădāmâ* ("the soil") in 25:5 is preferable to *'el* used here, but the particles interchange (see Note for 11:2).

But you have not bent your ear, and you have not listened to me. Another stereotyped expression in the Jeremiah prose (7:24, 26; 11:8; 17:23; 25:4; 34:14; 44:5). The LXX omits "to me" as in v 14, but has "to me" in v 16.

16. *Indeed the sons of Jonadab son of Rechab have carried out the command of their father which he commanded them, but this people have not listened to me.* This is why the dramatization took place. Calvin says it was to shame the Judahites. An asseverative meaning for *kî* ("indeed") is required (the AV's "because" is not right). The verse is an emphatic recapitulation of what has preceded (Cheyne).

which he commanded them. The LXX omits, which can be attributed to haplography (homoeoteleuton: *m . . . m*). Giesebrecht retains, noting that the words are present in G^L, S, T, and Vg.

17. *Therefore thus said Yahweh, God of hosts, God of Israel.* The LXX omits "God of hosts, God of Israel" (see Appendix VI). The T has the full complement of divine names; the Vg has "Lord of hosts, God of Israel," as it does also in vv 13, 18, and 19.

Look I am bringing . . . all the evil. On this Jeremianic expression, see Note for 6:19.

to Judah and to all the inhabitants of Jerusalem. See above v 13. The LXX omits "all."

because I have spoken to them and they have not listened, and I have called to them and they have not answered. The LXX omits, but G^L, Theod, S, T, and Vg all have the words. Giesebrecht says this is Jeremiah's way of speaking, which it is (7:13, 27). There is an unhappy consequence to blatant contempt: when the people call, Yahweh will not answer (11:11, 14). Yahweh refuses also the intercessions of Jeremiah (7:16; 11:14; 14:11; 15:1). But in future days things will be better (33:3).

18. *But to the house of the Rechabites Jeremiah said, Thus said Yahweh of hosts, God of Israel.* After addressing the people of Judah and Jerusalem, Jeremiah turns now to address the Rechabites, who are apparently present at the larger gathering. The LXX omits "but to the house of the Rechabites Jeremiah said," which can be attributed to haplography (homoeoteleuton: *w . . . w*). It begins the verse with an abbreviated messenger formula but precedes it with an added *dia touto* (= Heb *lākēn*, "therefore"; cf. 31:27), after which its reading is somewhat different than in MT but with little change in meaning. One alteration it makes is from second person to third-person speech, which does away with the direct address to the Rechabites. Some scholars (Duhm; Cornill; Janzen 1973: 105–6; Holladay) prefer the LXX; others (Giesebrecht; Volz; Rudolph; Bright) prefer MT, saying that the LXX has abbreviated. But with two arguable cases of LXX haplography in the verse, the shorter LXX text is probably due to a defective Hebrew *Vorlage*. The Versions support MT.

and you have kept all his commands. The LXX omits, which can be attributed to haplography (homoeoarcton: *wt . . . wt*).

19. *Therefore thus said Yahweh of hosts, God of Israel.* The LXX omits, which can be attributed to haplography (homoeoarcton: *l . . . l*). The T and Vg have the formula.

There shall not be cut off a man belonging to Jonadab son of Rechab who stands before me all the days. In this dark hour the Rechabites receive a promising word from Yahweh, just as Baruch and Ebed-melech did (45:4–6; 39:16–18). Promises similar to the present one are made concerning the lines of David and the Levitical priests in 33:17–18, giving support to the view that this is an unconditional "covenant of divine commitment" (D. N. Freedman 1964), or what Weinfeld (1970) and Levenson (1976) call a "covenant of grant." Compare also the bittersweet prophecy to Eli in 1 Sam 2:33. "To stand before Yahweh" can mean to worship, intercede, receive a word from, or be in the service of Yahweh, and the one so standing may be a prophet, priest, or ordinary individual (see Notes for 15:1 and 15:19). Calvin rejected the view of certain Rabbis that the Rechabites were destined to become priests or Levites. The Rechabite clan reportedly survived into the New Testament period, with references to them occurring in the Mishnah, Talmud, and Midrashim (Abramsky 1967). The Mishnah (Taanith 4:5), for example, states that it was the family of Jonadab the son of Rechab who brought up the wood offering of the priests and the people on the 7th of Ab. Eusebius (*Ecc Hist* ii 23; ANF 8: 763), too, preserves an account by Hegesippus that one of the priests of the sons of Rechab protested the martyrdom of James, the brother of the Lord (= James the Just).

all the days. Hebrew *kol-hayyāmîm*. On this expression, see Note for 31:36. The LXX expands to "all the days of the earth" (cf. Gen 8:22).

MESSAGE AND AUDIENCE

The audience is told in this narrative that Yahweh by divine word instructed Jeremiah to go to the clan of the Rechabites, speak with them, and bring them into one of the Temple chambers, where he was to offer them wine to drink. Presumably the audience knew what Jeremiah knew, that these people, conservative as they were and living in somewhat of a time warp, would certainly refuse the wine. Jeremiah says that he carried out the directive, taking Jaazaniah with his brothers and all his sons, indeed the whole clan of Rechabites, to the Temple, where they proceeded to the chamber of the sons of Hanan, which was next to the chamber of the princes and above the chamber of Maaseiah, the keeper of the threshold, who probably provided them the Temple access.

Jeremiah says he set before the Rechabites full pitchers of wine and cups and bid them to drink wine. They refused, saying that Jonadab son of Rechab, their father, commanded his descendants not to drink wine then or in the future, and not to build houses, sow seed, plant or keep vineyards, but to live in tents. In so doing, they could hope to live long in the land where they were sojourning. The Rechabites announced with satisfaction that they had obeyed Jonadab and done as he commanded. They were living in tents and had entered Jerusalem now because Nebuchadrezzar had come into the land, and there was danger in outlying areas from the Chaldean and Aramaean armies.

With the demonstration now over, Yahweh spoke a second time to Jeremiah, perhaps right away or sometime later, and told him to go and speak to the people of Judah and Jerusalem. This would have been a more public setting, perhaps in the outer court of the Temple. Jeremiah in an oracle was to say to those assembled: "Will you not take correction and listen to my words?" The command by Jonadab to his descendants had been carried out, as those present in the chamber saw with their own eyes when the Rechabites refused the wine. Yahweh, however, has spoken to the covenant people continually and they have not listened; he has sent prophets with a message that they return from their evil ways and make good their doings and thus continue on the soil given to them and their ancestors, but they have not so much as bent an ear. The point is clear: the sons of Jonadab carried out their father's command, while the covenant people have not heeded Yahweh and the commands he has given them.

Jeremiah then speaks a divine word of judgment to the people of Judah and Jerusalem. Not addressing them directly, he says that Yahweh will bring upon them all the evil he promised to bring. The reason: he called to them, but they did not answer. An oracle of a different sort is given to the Rechabites. Speaking to them directly, Yahweh says that because they have kept the commands of Jonadab their father, a man from among them will stand before Yahweh all the days.

This incident took place sometime during the reign of Jehoiakim—exactly when, we cannot say. It could have been prior to 605 B.C., before Jeremiah was debarred from the Temple, or else in 597 B.C., after Jehoiakim was dead and Jeremiah had come out of hiding to address the nation, just before Jerusalem's surrender to Nebuchadrezzar.

When this narrative is heard following the narrative reporting Jerusalem's reneging on the covenant to liberate Hebrew slaves, an incident happening under another king and a decade or more later, the audience is presented with a contrast between the marginal Rechabites, who carried out an oath made to Jonadab their father, and a disobedient Zedekiah and slave-owning population of Jerusalem that did not carry out an oath solemnly made before Yahweh their God.

Like Baruch and Ebed-melech, the Rechabites took on a subsequent literary life of their own. An early Christian apocryphon, "The History of the Blessed Sons of the Rechabites," which overlays an earlier Jewish work with Hellenistic lore, is a highly embellished exegesis of the present chapter (Charlesworth, OTP II: 443–61). Charlesworth dates the work between the first and fourth centuries A.D., though in its present form it could be as late as the sixth century. The Blessed Ones of the Rechabites dwell now with angels in a place like the Paradise of God, where they pray to God day and night; it is in fact their occupation (§11). Intercessory prayers are made for the wicked of earth, about whom they hear from angels that have visited earth (§12). On this work and influences that may have shaped it, see Charlesworth 1982; 1986; and "Rechabites, History of," in ABD 5: 632–33.

C. A SCROLL FOR FUTURE DAYS (36:1–32)

1. Baruch and the First Jeremiah Scroll (36:1–8)

36 ¹And it happened in the fourth year of Jehoiakim son of Josiah, king of Judah, this word came to Jeremiah from Yahweh: ²Take for yourself a writing-scroll, and you shall write on it all the words that I have spoken to you concerning Israel and concerning Judah and concerning all the nations, from the day I spoke to you, from the days of Josiah, until this day. ³Perhaps the house of Judah will listen to all the evil that I am planning to do to them, in order that they may turn each person from his evil way, and I will forgive their iniquity and their sin. ⁴So Jeremiah called Baruch son of Neriah, and Baruch wrote from the dictation of Jeremiah all the words of

Yahweh that he had spoken to him upon a writing-scroll. [5]And Jeremiah commanded Baruch, saying: 'I am under restraint; I am not able to enter the house of Yahweh. [6]So you, you shall enter, and you shall read aloud from the roll that you have written from my dictation the words of Yahweh in the hearing of the people in the house of Yahweh on a fast day, yes, also in the hearing of all Judah who come from their cities, you shall read them aloud. [7]Perhaps their petition will be laid before Yahweh, and they will turn each person from his evil way, for great is the anger and wrath that Yahweh has spoken toward this people.' [8]And Baruch son of Neriah did according to all that Jeremiah, the prophet, commanded him, to read aloud the scroll of the words of Yahweh in the house of Yahweh.

RHETORIC AND COMPOSITION

MT 36:1–8 = LXX 43:1–8. The present chapter contains a core narrative of vv 1–8, to which have been added two supplementary narratives: vv 9–26 and vv 27–32. This division is rightly seen by E. Nielsen (1954: 65), who points out that while the three narrative segments are independent, they are also interdependent. An inclusio with inversion, which contrasts Yahweh's desire to forgive if the people will listen (v 3), with a decision finally to punish because they have not listened (v 31), ties the three segments together (Abrego 1983a: 7; 1983b: 31):

v 3 *Perhaps they will listen . . .*	*'ûlay yišmĕ'û*
all the evil that I am planning . . .	*'ēt kol-hārā'â 'ăšer 'ānōkî ḥōšēb*
and I will forgive their iniquity . . .	*wĕsālaḥtî la'ăwōnām*
v 31 *and I will reckon . . . their iniquity*	*ûpāqadtî . . . 'et-'ăwōnām*
and I will bring . . . all the evil that	*wĕhēbē'tî . . . 'ēt kol-hārā'â 'ăšer*
and they did not listen	*wĕlō' šāmē'û*

The three segments report three separate events, the first two being dated in the fourth and fifth years of Jehoiakim respectively, and the third documented more generally: "after the king burned the roll." The first and last segments report divine revelations to Jeremiah; the middle segment reports a reading of the Jeremiah scroll in the Temple by Baruch, the scribe. All three segments begin with the narrative *wayĕhî*, "and it happened / and it came" (Abrego 1983a: 3).

I	And it happened (*wayĕhî*) . . . this word came to Jeremiah from Yahweh . . .	v 1
II	And it happened (*wayĕhî*) . . .	v 9
III	And the word of Yahweh came (*wayĕhî*) to Jeremiah . . .	v 27

Two other occurrences of *wayĕhî* in the chapter, in vv 16 and 23, do not signal major breaks.

Chapter 36 is a concluding chapter (Engnell 1962; Kessler 1966: 389; Muilenburg 1970a: 223–24; Lundbom 1975: 107–9 [= 1997: 140–43]; Holladay), not a beginning chapter as argued by some (Rudolph; Rietzschel 1966: 17; Abrego 1983a; 1983b). The final prose collection in the Jeremiah book begins with chap. 37. Chapter 36 at one time concluded a "Jehoiakim Cluster" of narrative prose consisting of chaps. 25, 26, 35, and 36 (see Rhetoric and Composition for 25:1–14); in the present book—now including also the Book of Restoration in chaps. 30–33—it concludes a mixed assemblage of prose narratives from Jehoiakim and Zedekiah's reigns, beginning with chap. 24, not chap. 26 (see "Excursus III: The Composition of Jeremiah 24–36," at the end of 25:1–14). In the Jehoiakim Cluster—and also in the mixed assemblage—36 has its greatest affinity with 25, as others have noted (Jones; McKane).

The present segment (vv 1–8), which I have called the chapter's core narrative, at one time doubled as an expanded colophon for the Jehoiakim Cluster, also for the larger collection of chaps. 24–36 if these narratives ever had a separate existence (Lundbom 1986b: 104–6). Baruch in 36:1–8 presents himself as the scribe who figured prominently in preserving the Jeremiah legacy, something he does again in chap. 45, which later becomes the colophon concluding his book of 51 chapters (LXX). The standard colophonic elements identified by Leichty (1964) are present to a greater or lesser degree in 36:1–8; 45; and 51:59–64, but since all have embellishment more than what one finds in the standard colophon, we have designated them "expanded colophons." If then vv 1–8 are an early colophon for an assemblage of Jeremiah narrative, Baruch has to be the scribe writing the text to which the colophon is affixed, giving yet another reason for ascribing to Baruch this and other prose in the book of Jeremiah. The two remaining narrative segments in vv 9–26 and 27–32 are later additions to vv 1–8. In both, Baruch continues as a major figure and the scribe of record in the events that are taking place: in vv 9–26 he reads the scroll twice in the Temple, and in vv 27–32 he writes a second scroll after the first one is destroyed; then at a later time he adds more words from the prophet. For more discussion on the expanded colophon in the book of Jeremiah, including the Leichty criteria for colophons generally, see Lundbom 1986b, and Rhetoric and Composition for chap. 45.

Among older scholars there was little debate over the genre, provenance, and historical nature of the present chapter. It was taken to be biographical prose (Giesebrecht, xxi; and Mowinckel 1914: 24: Source B), with most everyone (including Mowinckel later on) viewing it as a composition written by Baruch having a high degree of historical trustworthiness. Even Duhm could say of chap. 36: "This important report about Jeremiah's literary activity stems in the main from Baruch's book." Duhm ascribed only vv 27–31 to a later editor, with v 32 again being credited to Baruch. Hyatt held a similar view. Other commentators more recently, e.g., Rudolph, Weiser, Bright, Thompson, Boadt, Holladay, and Jones, have affirmed the earlier consensus without Duhm's proviso regarding vv 27–31. Rudolph finds phrases reminiscent of Source C in vv 3, 7, and 31, but H. Weippert (1973: 141) and Holladay say these belong to the diction of Jeremiah. Nicholson's view that the entire chapter contains large-scale Deuteronomic editing is simply not borne out by the evidence, being dismissed even by Thiel (1981: 50 n. 3). The chapter is assuredly not legend, as Muilenburg (1970a: 233–34) correctly points out (*pace* Kessler 1966: 390; cf. Koch 1969: 201). Other late twentieth-century views, e.g., those of Wanke 1971: 59–74; Carroll; and McKane, that chap. 36 is "story" or a literary work with minimal historical concerns, build either on a mistaken genre assessment or genre confusion. It is as if a narrative having literary quality and expressing theological concerns cannot also report a historical event. Zimmerli (1995: 428) says: "With the account of Jeremiah 36, we enter historically secure territory," and there is scant reason to doubt that this is the case. As has often been pointed out, the chapter is filled with precise times and locations, numerous names and patronyms, and other circumstantial details that only an eyewitness or someone having spoken to an eyewitness could report (so Peake; Rudolph; Bright; Thompson; Boadt; Holladay). Baruch is said to have read the scroll "in the chamber of Gemariah son of Shaphan, the scribe, in the upper court at the opening of the New Gate in the house of Yahweh" (v 10). Then when the narrator has us accompany Micaiah son of Gemariah, son of Shaphan, into the palace chamber, we see sitting there Elishama, the scribe, Delaiah son of Shemaiah, Elnathan son of Achbor, Gemariah son of Shaphan, and Zedekiah son of Hananiah (v 12). Similarly, when we enter the king's winter quarters, Elnathan, Delaiah, and Gemariah are standing next to the king and urging him not to burn the scroll, after which we hear Jehoiakim command Jerahmeel, the king's son, Seraiah son of Azriel, and Shelemiah son of Abdeel to seize Baruch and Jeremiah (vv 25–26). The narrative throughout is brief, concise, and teeming with detail.

The MT and LXX diverge here as elsewhere, with the LXX in all but a few cases being the shorter text. These divergences are a minor issue to most everyone except McKane, who, along with Holladay, supports the shorter LXX with predictable consistency. Yet there are twelve arguable cases for LXX haplography in the chapter, which means the respective merits of the MT and LXX must be reevaluated. Of these twelve haplographies, only two are listed by Janzen (1973: 118–19).

The present narrative segment is delimited at the top end by a dated superscription in v 1, before which is a *petuḥah* in M^A and M^L and a *setumah* in M^P. This is also a chapter division. Delimitation at the lower end is by *petuḥah* in M^A and M^P and a *setumah* in M^L after the summary statement in v 8. A new superscription, also with a date, begins the next narrative segment in v 9. After v 3 is another *setumah* in M^A and M^L and a *petuḥah* in M^P, which for some reason separate Yahweh's command to Jeremiah that he write up a scroll and Jeremiah's fulfillment of that command.

Structure is given to the present segment by repetition and the balancing of key words and phrases (Abrego 1983a: 3–4; 1983b: 22):

> v 3 *Perhaps* (*'ûlay*) the house of Judah will listen to all the evil that I am planning
>   to do to them, in order that *they may turn each person from his evil*
>   *way*, and I will forgive their iniquity and their sin.

v 7 *Perhaps* (*'ûlay*) their petition will be laid before Yahweh, *and they will turn
each person from his evil way,* for great is the anger and wrath that
Yahweh has spoken toward this people.

NOTES

36:1. *the fourth year of Jehoiakim.* I.e., 605 B.C. This date had far-reaching significance in the ancient world. It was Nebuchadnezzar's first year as king of
Babylon (25:1) and the year in which he delivered to Neco and the Egyptians
a crushing defeat at Carchemish, then soon after, another defeat at Hamath,
leaving the way open to Syria and Palestine, which, within a year came under
his control (cf. 2 Kgs 24:7). In this year Jeremiah issued a blistering attack on
the nations (chap. 25), singling out Egypt for specific judgment (46:2–26). But
to his scribe, Baruch, the prophet gave a word of personal deliverance (chap.
45). In this defining moment, Jeremiah also received a divine word to write up
oracles and other utterances made over a period of years. On the slight chronological discrepancy between the Babylonian Chronicle and Jehoiakim's fourth
year, as well as discussion of the historical background for events occurring in
this year, see Note for 46:2.

this word came to Jeremiah from Yahweh. The LXX lacks "this" but expands to
"the word of the Lord." It also has "to me" instead of "to Jeremiah," the former
widely judged to be an inferior reading (Giesebrecht; Duhm; Rudolph; Holladay; McKane). Giesebrecht notes that Aq, Symm, S, T, and Vg all support the
reading of MT. Duhm takes "to me" (אלי) as a misread abbreviation for "to
Jeremiah" (אל־ירמיהו for אל י). The LXX mistakenly reads "to me" also in 32:26
and 35:12.

2. *Take for yourself a writing-scroll, and you shall write on it all the words that
I have spoken to you concerning Israel and concerning Judah and concerning all
the nations.* Although the OT refers elsewhere to a writing down of prophetic
utterances, or to prophetic utterances being disseminated in written form—in
Jeremiah: 29:1; 30:2; 51:60; and elsewhere: Isa 8:1, 16; 30:8; Hab 2:2—here is
an actual report of prophetic words being written on a scroll for public reading,
the only one of its kind in the entire OT. The question naturally arises, Was
this the first time Jeremiah's revelations and preaching were committed to writing, or were the same—or some of the same—written down earlier? Graf
(p. 442) believed that prior to this year Jeremiah had no need to write down his
prophecies, a view expressed later by Birkeland (1939: 43) and Mowinckel
(1946: 61). But Duhm thought that Jeremiah's prophecies must have existed
earlier in writing, a view cited with approval by Peake and one that has been es-
poused recently by McKane. McKane thinks that Jeremiah had been dictating
to Baruch all along and that Baruch is now simply collecting oracles already
written on a single scroll for public reading. This contradicts what is said in v 4
about Jeremiah dictating to Baruch, as McKane realizes, although this could
be remedied by taking v 2—which gives the command to write a scroll of oracles

from Josiah's days to the present—with Thiel, as a "post-Deuteronomic insertion." McKane (pp. 4–5), one should remember, favors the low chronology of Horst (1923), which puts the beginning of Jeremiah's public career at 609 B.C., or shortly thereafter, so we are talking about a master-disciple relationship of four years at most. McKane's contradiction is contrived, and the Horst chronology, as I have argued elsewhere (Lundbom 1993), is unacceptable. One must therefore go with a plain reading of the verse, viz., that this scroll contained revelations received over a long period—23 years according to 25:3—that Jeremiah is now dictating to Baruch. For a discussion on the progression from oral proclamation to written message in the prophetic tradition, see Zimmerli 1995: 422–31.

Take for yourself. Hebrew *qaḥ-lĕkā*. On the imperatives *qaḥ* and *qĕḥû* ("take!") occurring in divine commands to the prophet, see Note for 43:9.

a writing-scroll. Hebrew *mĕgillat-sēper*. Aside from the references here and in v 4, this two-word expression appears elsewhere only in Ps 40:8[Eng 40:7] and Ezek 2:9. A "writing-scroll" was pasted papyrus or sewn skins made into a roll for purposes of writing (cf. Isa 34:4). Although papyrus and tanned skins (leather) were both well known in ancient Israel, there are no references in the Hebrew OT to the use of either material for scrolls. However, the present verse in LXX 43:2 reads *chartion bibliou*, "a papyrus scroll," and again in v 23, *ho chartēs*, "the papyrus." The first mention of prophecy written on papyrus is otherwise 2 Esd 15:2. In the ANE generally, papyrus and animal skins were both used for writing and had been so for centuries—in Egypt since the early third millenium B.C. (G. R. Driver 1976: 81–82). The replacement of tanned skins with improved parchment (sheepskin or goatskin with the hair removed, smoothed with lime), and later vellum (high-grade calfskin), began ca. 200 B.C. (Hyatt 1943: 75; Lemaire in *ABD* 6: 1003). True paper (invented in China) began to replace papyrus in ca. the seventh or eighth century A.D. (R. J. Williams in *IDB* R–Z, 918).

Some think the present scroll would have been made of skins (Joseph Kara;[a] Kimḥi; Streane; Hicks 1983: 57–61), but most think it was made from papyrus (Duhm; Hyatt 1943: 72–73; Weiser; D. W. Thomas 1950: 5; Haran 1980–81; 1982; Holladay; and others), which Egypt had been exporting to countries in the north beginning at least in 1100 B.C. The Tale of Wen-Amon (ii 40) mentions "500 [rolls of] finished papyrus" enroute to Gebal (Gk: Byblos = "pith of papyrus"; later "book" and "Bible") in Phoenicia (*ANET*[3] 28; cf. Haran 1982: 164; *CS I* 92 translates "five hundred smooth linen mats," which may nevertheless be finished papyrus readied for writing). That papyrus was being used as writing material in Judah in the eighth to sixth centuries B.C. is attested by the seventh-century Wadi Murabbaʿat papyrus, also by fiber impressions on clay bullae found at Jerusalem, Lachish, and elsewhere (A. Lemaire in *ABD* 6: 1003). One of these bullae with the inscription "belonging to Berechiah, son of

---

[a]Joseph Kara (b. ca. 1060–70), a medieval Jewish Bible commentator from northern France, was a student and colleague of Rashi (*EncJud* 10: 759–60).

Neriah, the scribe," doubtless the Baruch mentioned here, had traces of papyrus on the reverse (Avigad 1978a: 52–53).

The papyrus plant (*cyperus papyrus*), harvested in abundance in the Nile Delta (cf. Isa 18:2), is known in the OT as *gōme'* (AV: "bulrushes" in Exod 2:3). Driver (p. 82) explains how the plant was processed into an early type of paper:

> The part of the plant used was the pith cut vertically into slices. In order to make a sheet of paper, these slices were laid crosswise, some vertically and others horizontally, pressed together and dried in the sun; uneven patches were then smoothed or pressed away and the sheets glued into a long strip which was cut to the required length and then rolled up.

An ancient account of the way papyrus was made into various grades of paper appears in Pliny (*Nat Hist* xiii 23–26). A relatively inexpensive material, papyrus was used for most scrolls in ancient Israel. Haran (1980–81; 1982: 168–72) also points out that writing could be done on both sides (Ezek 2:9–10), and when necessary, could be easily erased (Heb *mḥh*, "wash, wipe clean" in Exod 32:32–33; Num 5:23; Ps 69:29[Eng 69:28]). Writing on skins was the exception, done only for more important or official documents (Haran; Driver). The questions might then be asked, How important or how official was this scroll of Jeremiah's prophecies? Was it still at this point mainly Jeremiah's personal property? Haran (1982: 168) says that it was Jeremiah's personal property. The point is also made that a papyrus scroll would more easily be cut with a penknife and would burn more easily in the fire, which was the fate of this scroll once it came into the hands of Jehoiakim (v 23).

In the NT period, the standard material for copying sacred books was parchment. Most of the biblical books found at Qumran were written on parchment. There were strictures in the Talmud about using only skins for scrolls containing the Law (Haran 1985c); the *Megilloth* (Ruth, Song of Songs, Ecclesiastes, Lamentations, and Esther), however, could be written on papyrus. Other similar documents of the period were written on papyrus, e.g., the Nash Papyrus (Albright: first century B.C.), which contains a Hebrew text of the Decalogue and part of the Shema' (Deut 6:4–5); some — maybe all — the letters of the NT (cf. 2 John 12); and the Chester Beatty Biblical Papyri (second to fourth centuries A.D.), which contains most of the Greek OT and some passages from the NT. See further G. R. Driver 1976: 82–83; also "Chester Beatty Papyri," *ABD* 1: 901–3. On the use of papyrus and skins for writing in antiquity, see "Writing and Writing Materials," *IDB* R–Z, 918; and in *ABD* 6: 1003–4. For pictures of the Aramaic papyri from Elephantine, some of which have writing on both sides, and diagrams of how papyrus documents were prepared, see Porten 1979.

Israel . . . Judah. The LXX[BS] have "Jerusalem" instead of "Israel." The former is preferred by some commentators (Giesebrecht; Duhm; Peake; Cornill; Rudolph; Hyatt; McKane; cf. Isa 1:1), the MT reading by others (Volz; Weiser; Bright; Holladay; Jones), who note that the LXX witness is not unanimous, that other Vrs (G[L], S, T, and Vg) support MT, and that "all the nations" coming next indicates a perspective broader than Judah alone. The issue seems to be whether the scroll could have contained indictment and judgment against (Northern) Israel, or whether it would have restricted itself to judgment on Judah alone. It is true that v 3 hopes for a conversion of only the "house of Judah" and that Jeremiah's promise to the Northern tribes in 31:1 is one of hope; nevertheless, it is also the case that indictment and judgment fall upon "all the tribes of the house of Israel" in Jeremiah's early preaching (2:4; Calvin). Bright cites also the judgment in 3:6–11, to which one could add the indictments in 11:10 and 32:32. Actually, Jeremiah's doom preaching is corporate and inclusive throughout. Time and again he says it was the "fathers" who did not listen to the divine word (7:22–26; 11:7–8; 34:14), the "fathers" who chased the Baals and committed evils in violation of the covenant (2:5–9; 11:10; 23:27; 31:32), and the "fathers" who, with the present generation, must now bear the punishment for breaking the covenant (16:11–13; 23:39; 24:10; 32:18). An inclusive judgment on "Israel and Judah" is certainly possible here. The reference in v 3 to the "house of Judah" poses no difficulty: only Judah now is in a position to change its ways.

all the nations. Duhm takes the phrase as a later addition, which only serves to support his view that Jeremiah is not a prophet to the nations. There is no textual evidence supporting a deletion of the words. Thiel (1981: 49 n. 1) and McKane take the same line, Thiel saying that judgment on the nations implies salvation for Judah. All three views reduce the grand scope of biblical theology to earth-centered politics, where the assumption is that Jeremiah could not pronounce judgment on both Judah *and* the nations. The scroll mandated by Yahweh is to contain prophetic utterances against the nations. Jeremiah was called to be a prophet to the nations (1:5, 10), and that he was throughout his long career.

The question occupying the minds of many is what prophecies might have been included on this first scroll, called by the Germans the *Urrolle*, and which ones would have targeted the nations for judgment. We do not know what was written on the *Urrolle*; at the same time, speculation about its probable contents fills the commentaries and other works on Jeremiah. The *Urrolle* is assuredly not chaps. 1–6 (*pace* Rudolph; Bright; Rietzschel 1966: 136; Carroll; Holladay; Jones), which is not a self-standing composition (see Rhetoric and Composition for 6:27–30). It is also not 1–25:13a, for this same reason and for others (see Rhetoric and Composition for 25:1–14). I suggested earlier (1975: 30 [= 1997: 44]) that the *Urrolle* ought to be looked for within chaps. 1–20, since this is the earliest identifiable composition in the present book. None of these proposals, needless to say, will include the "cup of wrath" vision in 25:15–29, or the foreign nation oracles in chaps. 46–51. Chapters 1–20 do contain some utterances against the nations, e.g., 1:10; 9:24–25[Eng 9:25–26]; 10:1–10, 25; 14:22; and indirectly 18:7–9. This is not to say that any of these appeared on the *Urrolle*, only that judgments against nations of the world can be found in chaps. 1–20. It is probably best simply to stay with what is said here about the scroll's containing Yahweh's words against his own people and other nations, those which had been spoken up to the present time. The *Urrolle* could not have been too long, since it was read aloud three times in one day.

from the day I spoke to you. I.e., from the day I *first* spoke to you (AmT; Holladay).

from the days of Josiah, until this day. In 25:3 the elapsed time between the 13th year of Josiah and the 4th year of Jehoiakim is 23 years. After "Josiah" here, the LXX adds a "king of Judah" title. The T and Vg read with MT.

3. *Perhaps the house of Judah will listen to all the evil that I am planning to do to them, in order that they may turn each person from his evil way, and I will forgive their iniquity and their sin.* The reason for preparing the scroll and reading it publicly is the same as for prophesying generally: that people might hear Yahweh's word, turn from their evil ways, and receive Yahweh's forgiveness. The way things stand now, iniquity and sins have kept away the good (5:25), and in the end the people will be punished (14:10; 16:18). Zimmerli (1995: 428) says that this word was designed to shake the people into returning to Yahweh. The "perhaps" sounds optimistic (Duhm), as it did earlier when Yahweh sent Jeremiah to speak his Temple Oracles (26:3), but one wonders if Yahweh is really any more hopeful now than when he dispatched Jeremiah and others to find a righteous soul in Jerusalem (5:1). Still, the divine offer is genuine: Judah can return and be forgiven. Here, however, divine forgiveness is dependent upon a decisive return from evil (cf. Ezek 33:10–16; Isa 59:20). With the new covenant, forgiveness will be a unilateral act of divine grace (31:34; 33:8; 50:20; cf. Ezek 36:25–29; also Mic 7:18–20, which bases divine pardoning on the covenant with Abraham).

4. *So Jeremiah called Baruch son of Neriah, and Baruch wrote from the dictation of Jeremiah all the words of Yahweh that he had spoken to him upon a writing-scroll.* Jeremiah summons for the task of preparing a scroll a certain Baruch son of Neriah, who writes from Jeremiah's dictation. This is our introduction to the scribe who became Jeremiah's associate and friend to the end of his life. We know nothing about any prior relationship between the two. With the biographical prose of the book beginning just about this time, particularly the dated prose of chaps. 21–45, it seems likely that Baruch entered the scene now in the early years of Jehoiakim's reign and began working with Jeremiah from this point on (T. H. Robinson 1924: 220). Small amounts of prose and a virtual absence of dates in chaps. 1–20 (there is the superscription of 1:1–3 and a general "in the days of Josiah the king" in 3:6) point to the same conclusion, viz., that Baruch may have written small amounts of prose and done some editing of material in 1–20, but only in later chapters, particularly 24 to 45, can his more substantial contribution to the Jeremiah book be seen. Baruch was present when Jeremiah purchased the field at Anathoth, assisting him in executing the deed and affixing the seal (Avigad 1978a: 55). When the transaction was concluded, Baruch was given custody of the open and closed deeds and instructed by Jeremiah to preserve them for posterity (32:9–15). In the same year as now, Baruch himself received from Jeremiah a word of hope for the future (chap. 45). Finally, it was Baruch who accompanied Jeremiah on the journey to

Egypt (43:6–7), and he is arguably the one to whom we owe the report of events and prophecies occurring there.

It has long been assumed that Baruch was a scribe of high social standing (Cheyne; Peake). Josephus (*Ant* x 158) says he came from a distinguished family and was exceptionally able in his native tongue. In 32:12, he is introduced with a double patronym, "son of Neriah, son of Mahseiah," which for a scribe would indicate descent from an established scribal family. Scribes in antiquity came in families (Lambert 1957: 2–3; Rainey 1969: 128) and took great pride in their professional status (see "In Praise of Learned Scribes" and "The Satire on the Trades," both dating to the fourteenth or thirteenth century B.C., in *ANET*[3] 431–34). Baruch's brother, Seraiah, who held an important government post under Zedekiah and was the one responsible for the colophon in 51:59–64 (MT), was also a trained scribe (Gevaryahu 1973: 209). A seal impression from a royal archive of undisclosed location, but probably in Jerusalem, has turned up with the inscription, "Belonging to Berechiah, son of Neriah, the scribe." This seal doubtless belonged to the Baruch mentioned here (Avigad 1978a; 1986b: 28–29 #9; 1997: 175 #417). "Baruch" is the short form of "Berechiah" (*berekyāhû*) and the name by which the scribe presumably went. The seal has both a patronym and title "the scribe." Baruch is called "the scribe" later in vv 26 and 32. Millard (1999: 132) says that, among the seals found on cuneiform tablets, a minority have professions or occupations appended to their names. These include a mayor, goldsmiths, blacksmiths, seal-cutters, gate-keepers, a bird-catcher, a weaver, a baker, a granary-officer, and scribes. Since Baruch's seal impression was found among bullae belonging to royal officials, Avigad (1978a: 55; 1986b: 130) concludes that Baruch was not simply Jeremiah's personal scribe but an official scribe who perhaps left his position to join Jeremiah in his struggle. Muilenburg (1970a: 231) thought that Baruch was a royal scribe. If Baruch did have official status in Jerusalem, he could qualify as one of the otherwise elusive "Deuteronomic" scribes, with the one difference that he is a contemporary of Jeremiah, not an exilic or postexilic figure. A second bulla with the same inscription and a fingerprint turned up subsequently on the antiquities market and is in the possession of a London collector (*ArOd* 2/2 [1999] 31). The names "Baruch/Berekiah" and "Neriah" were common in the period and have been found on seals, bullae, and ostraca from Jerusalem, Arad, Lachish, and elsewhere (see Appendix I). On Baruch, the scribe, see articles by Muilenburg 1970a; Gevaryahu 1973; and Lundbom, "Baruch [Person]," *ABD* 1: 617. On owners and users of Hebrew seals, see most recently Millard 1999.

Malamat (1991a) has called attention to an interesting parallel in the Mari documents (ARM 26/2 #414) to the incident described here. A high official of Zimri-Lim, named Yasim-El, wrote to his lord about a certain Atamrum, a type of prophet called a "respondent," who requested a scribe to take down a message from the god Shamash for the king. He responded by getting Uto-kam, the scribe, who then wrote up the tablet. The relevant portion of the letter reads:

Another matter: Atamrum, the respondent of the god Shamash, came here and thus he spoke to me as follows: 'Send me a competent and discrete scribe that I have (him) write down the message of Shamash to the king.' That is what he told me. I have sent Utu-kam and he wrote this tablet; that man has appointed witnesses. Thus he (the prophet) said to me as follows: 'Send this tablet urgently and the exact wording of the tablet let him (the king) carry out.' Now, I have sent this tablet to my lord.

Malamat points out that this scribe, an expert in his craft, apparently had official status. The scribe would also have served as a confidant of the prophet, as Baruch served Jeremiah. Based on what is known elsewhere about prophetic activity at Mari, we assume that the prophet delivered his message orally, and the scribe wrote it down from dictation.

With Baruch being the writing scribe of the first Jeremiah scroll, it has been argued for more than a century that he was the one who authored the biographical prose in the book. Now with a distinction no longer being made between biographical and homiletical prose in the book (Sources B and C), e.g., in the works of H. Weippert (1973) and Holladay but anticipated one-half century earlier by T. H. Robinson (1924: 219), Baruch can be credited with all the prose. That family members and other professionally trained scribes might have assisted him need not be precluded. Needless to say, there is no proof for any of this, but the twin assumptions that Baruch authored the prose and assisted in the compilation of the Jeremiah book make even more sense if 36:1–8 and chap. 45 are colophons introducing him as the (primary) scribe responsible for preserving the Jeremiah legacy. That Baruch was introducing himself in chap. 45 was recognized earlier by Mowinckel (1946: 61–62), who as a result changed his mind about an anonymous biographer and accepted the view that Baruch was the author of the biographical (Source B) prose.

and Baruch wrote from the dictation of Jeremiah. The LXX simplifies to "and he wrote," since Baruch's name has just been used. The LXX usually gives the name (cf. Janzen 1973: 148–49). This is the only explicit reference in the OT to a scroll's being written from dictation (lit., "from the mouth," *mippî*), although the practice was common enough in the ancient scribal schools (Widengren 1948: 64, 90–91; Gadd 1956: 39; Rainey 1969: 127; G. R. Driver 1976: 69). This detail shows up occasionally in colophons. Hunger (1968: 8, 134) cites a colophon on a cuneiform text (#486) in which the scribe says that he had written his tablet from dictation, not having seen the old copy. On one of the Aramaic papyri from Elephantine (427 B.C.), the colophon to a legal document authorizing the release of a woman and her daughter from slavery begins: "Written by Haggai the scribe at Elephantine, at the dictation of Meshullam son of Zakkur" (ANET[3] 548). On another of these papyri, this one the marriage contract of a former slave girl, the colophon states that the document was written from dictation (ANET[3] 548–49). In the NT, a certain Tertius identifies himself as the writer of Paul's letter to the Romans (Rom 16:22), and one may assume that Tertius also wrote from dictation. On writing in antiquity and in ancient Israel, see Hyatt 1943; G. R. Driver 1976; and the articles "Writing and Writing Materials" in *IDB* R–Z, 909–21; and *ABD* 6: 999–1008. Egyptian scribes are pictured seated or squatting, with a sheet of papyrus or other writing material in one hand and a pen in the other; some are shown writing at desks (Hyatt 1943: 71; J. A. Wilson 1965: fig. 5c; *ANEP*[2] 72–73 ##230–32, 275–76; *IDB* R–Z, 920). An Assyrian scribe on an early eighth-century b.c. wall painting is seen writing in a standing position with a brush on skin or papyrus (*ANEP*[2] 74 ##235, 276; *IDB* R–Z, 919). And a relief of Tiglath-pileser III from Calah depicts two Assyrian scribes writing while standing as an Assyrian officer reads a list of war booty from a tablet. The one scribe holds a roll of papyrus or leather in his left hand, and in his right hand is a pen (Hyatt 1943: 73; G. R. Driver 1976: plate 23 #2).

5. *And Jeremiah commanded Baruch, saying: 'I am under restraint; I am not able to enter the house of Yahweh.'* It is usually assumed that Jeremiah is prevented, probably by Temple priests, from entering the Temple area because of his earlier preaching that necessitated a trial (chap. 26), or because of the incident with Pashhur, which landed him overnight in the stocks (20:1–6). Duhm's suggestion that he was ritually impure should be discounted. Hebrew *ʾănî ʿāṣûr* ("I am under restraint"), the LXX rendering *egō phulassomai* ("I am under guard"), and the rendering of Aq and Symm, *sunechomai* ("I am constrained"), could all mean that Jeremiah deems a Temple visit unwise because he will be under surveillance. The T has "I am shut up," which was carried over into the AV but is widely rejected. Rashi, no doubt also following T, thinks Jeremiah is in jail (cf. 33:1; 39:15), a view that does not find favor with Calvin. The "I am in hiding" of NJV is also dubious, for Jeremiah is not known to have gone into hiding until the next year (36:19, 26). Calvin believes that Jeremiah was prevented from entering the Temple by God, though he admits that human impediments may still have existed. He compares the restraint here to what was later imposed on Paul and his traveling party when they were forbidden to go to Bithynia (Acts 16:7). So whether the restraint comes from God or the Temple authorities, whether imposed by others or self-imposed—the point is that Jeremiah finds himself unable to go to the Temple. Baruch, therefore, must go in his stead.

And Jeremiah commanded Baruch. The verb *ṣwh* ("command"), which occurs again in v 8, is strong, but Jeremiah can and does command action from others (51:59; cf. 27:4). Baruch here is in Jeremiah's employ, as also in 32:13, so Jeremiah has the right to give him orders.

6. *So you, you shall enter.* Hebrew *ûbāʾtā ʾattâ*. The LXX omits, which is likely due to haplography (homoeoarcton: *w . . . w*, or homoeoteleuton: *h . . . h*). Janzen (1973: 119) takes the minus as a possible haplography. Giesebrecht too says the LXX omission is unjustified, noting that the words are present in G[L], S, T, and Vg. They should therefore be retained with MT (*pace* McKane).

and you shall read aloud . . . you shall read them aloud. The prose has a chiasmus in the Hebrew where, as in much of the Jeremiah poetry, the verbs are at the extremes:

and you shall read aloud . . . in the hearing of the people in the house of
Yahweh
. . . yes, also in the hearing of all Judah . . . you shall read them aloud

The LXX, perhaps because it omits "the words of Yahweh" earlier in the verse, reads at the end: "you shall read to them (*autois*)." But McKane points out that the Vg, which otherwise follows MT, also ends with *leges eis* ("you shall read to them"). On a later occasion Jeremiah commands Seraiah, Baruch's brother, that when he arrives in Babylon on a state visit he is to "read aloud" (*qr'*) a scroll he has brought with him (51:60–61) containing judgment oracles against that nation.

that you have written from my dictation the words of Yahweh. The LXX omits, having only "read aloud in this roll" (*avagnōsē en to chartio touto*). The omission can be attributed to haplography (homoeoteleuton: *h* . . . *h*).

on a fast day. Hebrew *běyôm ṣôm*. Jeremiah is anticipating a fast day, which raises the question of whether he had a fixed day in mind. There is no clear evidence for fixed days of fasting in preexilic Israel or Judah, except possibly the Day of Atonement, where the paraphrastic "afflict oneself" (*'nh* + *nepeš*) in P legislation (Lev 16:29, 31; 23:27, 32) is thought to be a technical term for "carry out fasting." Fixed days of fasting came in the postexilic period, when the destruction of Jerusalem was remembered (Zech 7:3, 5; 8:19; Esth 9:31). Then the Day of Atonement called for fasting and other privations (Mishnah Yoma 8). Public fasts in preexilic times seem to have been in response to national emergencies, e.g., the death of a king (1 Sam 31:13; 2 Sam 1:12), a military defeat or a military threat (Judg 20:26; 2 Chr 20:3), a plague (Joel 1:14), or a drought (Jer 14:12). Jeremiah in the present case appears to be anticipating a fast in response to the military threat posed by Babylon following its victory at Carchemish (see below v 9). The reason for selecting a fast day to read the scroll would be that many people would be present in Jerusalem, and a fast would likely render them more receptive to a chastening word; it might even lead them to repentance (Calvin; cf. 1 Sam 7:6; Jonah 3:5; Joel 2:12–13; Ecc 7:2).

yes, also in the hearing of all Judah who come from their cities, you shall read them aloud. People from the outlying areas will be in Jerusalem for this important occasion; cf. 26:2.

7. *Perhaps their petition will be laid before Yahweh, and they will turn each person from his evil way, for great is the anger and wrath that Yahweh has spoken toward this people.* The same hope is expressed in v 3, only now Jeremiah conveys it to Baruch. Jeremiah is hoping for prayer and repentance on the day of fasting. On the expression "to lay one's petition before" someone, see Note for 37:20.

for great is the anger and wrath that Yahweh has spoken toward this people. Compare Josiah's words after hearing the newly found law-book being read (2 Kgs 22:13). On the cliché "anger and wrath," see Note for 21:5.

8. *And Baruch son of Neriah did according to all that Jeremiah, the prophet, commanded him.* A summary statement similar to those in 26:24; 28:17; and 36:32. The LXX omits Baruch's patronym and Jeremiah's title.

MESSAGE AND AUDIENCE

The audience is told here about a word that came to Jeremiah from Yahweh in the fourth year of Jehoiakim. Their attention will have been quickened, since this year was a particularly anxious one for Judah and neighboring nations round about. Jeremiah was told to take a scroll and write on it all the words that Yahweh had spoken to him concerning Israel, Judah, and the nations, from the time he first addressed the prophet in the days of Josiah, until the present day. Yahweh's hope was that Judah might listen carefully to the evil being planned for it, with the result that the people would turn from their evil so Yahweh could forgive their sin.

Jeremiah does as he was instructed, calling a certain Baruch son of Neriah, who then wrote from dictation all of Yahweh's words on a scroll. Baruch may or may not have been a scribe of reputation at the time. In either case, the people will note that this individual is now identified with Jeremiah and his struggle. After the writing is concluded, Jeremiah tells Baruch that he cannot himself go to the Temple, for which reason Baruch must go and read the scroll on a fast day when, he is told, people from outlying areas will also be present in the city. Repeating to Baruch what Yahweh has told him, Jeremiah says that perhaps on this solemn occasion people will turn from their evil, for Yahweh's anger against them is great.

The narrative closes by saying that Baruch did as commanded. The audience hearing this narrative segment will know only that Baruch carried out Jeremiah's directive to read the scroll in the Temple, nothing more. Details will have to be supplied from other sources; some were probably already available, since the reading was public. But will they not want to know what happened behind the scenes, what the reaction was among the princes and the priests, and how the king responded to what he heard? They will remember how Josiah responded when he heard the newly-found Temple law-book, how he rent his clothes, sought an oracle from the prophetess Huldah, and then carried out a reform that turned the nation upside down, for the good. This king may have responded differently. What did he do? They certainly need to know more.

As the superscription states, this narrative reports an event that occurred in 605 B.C. But the narrative could not have been written up until at least a year after, since v 8 states that the scroll had been read, and this took place the following year. For the audience hearing a reading of the entire Jehoiakim Cluster, also the whole of chaps. 24–36, the present narrative will introduce Baruch as the scribe who figured prominently in preserving the Jeremiah legacy.

2. More on the Scroll's First Reading (36:9–26)

36 ⁹And it happened in the fifth year of Jehoiakim son of Josiah, king of Judah, in the ninth month, they called a fast before Yahweh—all the people in Jerusalem and all the people who had come in from the cities of Judah—in Jerusalem. ¹⁰And Baruch read aloud from the scroll the words

of Jeremiah in the house of Yahweh—in the chamber of Gemariah son of Shaphan, the scribe, in the upper court at the opening of the New Gate in the house of Yahweh—in the hearing of all the people. [11]And Micaiah son of Gemariah, son of Shaphan, heard all the words of Yahweh from the scroll. [12]And he went down to the house of the king, to the chamber of the scribe, and look! there all the princes were sitting: Elishama, the scribe, and Delaiah son of Shemaiah, and Elnathan son of Achbor, and Gemariah son of Shaphan, and Zedekiah son of Hananiah, yes, all the princes. [13]And Micaiah told them all the words that he had heard when Baruch read aloud the scroll in the hearing of the people. [14]And all the princes sent Jehudi son of Nethaniah, son of Shelemiah, son of Cushi, to Baruch, saying, 'The roll that you read aloud in the hearing of the people—take it in your hand and come.' So Baruch son of Neriah took the roll in his hand and came in to them. [15]And they said to him, 'Do sit down, and read it aloud in our hearing.' And Baruch read it aloud in their hearing. [16]And it happened when they heard all the words, they turned trembling one to another and said to Baruch, 'We must surely tell the king all these words.' [17]And they asked Baruch: 'Tell us, would you, how did you write all these words, from his dictation?' [18]And Baruch said to them, 'From his dictation; he would proclaim all these words to me and I would write upon the scroll in ink.' [19]And the princes said to Baruch, 'Go, hide yourself, you and Jeremiah, so that no one may know where you are!' [20]And they went in to the king, to the court, but the roll they deposited in the chamber of Elishama, the scribe. And they told in the hearing of the king all these words. [21]And the king sent Jehudi to take the roll, and he took it from the chamber of Elishama, the scribe, and Jehudi read it aloud in the hearing of the king and in the hearing of all the princes who were standing beside the king. [22]And the king was sitting in the winter house, in the ninth month, and a fire[a] in the stove was burning before him. [23]And it happened as Jehudi proclaimed three or four columns, he would tear it with the scribe's knife and would throw it into the fire that was in the stove, until the entire roll was consumed on the fire that was in the stove. [24]And they did not tremble, and they did not tear their garments—the king and all his servants who were hearing all these words. [25]However, Elnathan and Delaiah and Gemariah strongly urged the king not to burn the roll, but he did not listen to them. [26]And the king commanded Jerahmeel, the king's son, and Seraiah the son of Azriel and Shelemiah son of Abdeel to seize Baruch, the scribe, and Jeremiah, the prophet, but Yahweh hid them.

RHETORIC AND COMPOSITION

MT 36:9–26 = LXX 43:9–26. This narrative segment is delimited at the top end by a new superscription in v 9, before which is a *petuḥah* in M[A] and M[P]

---

[a] Reading *wĕʾēš* ("and a fire") for the *nota accusativi*, with the LXX, S, and T.

and a *setumah* in M^L. Delimitation at the bottom end is by a *setumah* in M^A and M^L and a *petuḥah* in M^P after v 26. Another *setumah* exists in M^A and a *petuḥah* in M^L and M^P after v 18, the purpose of which is unclear.

Volz put v 9 before v 5 of the previous segment, which makes everything in vv 5–8 — most importantly, v 8 — occur in the fifth year of Jehoiakim. The same transposition is made in the JB [but reversed in NJB] and the NAB. This transposition should be rejected, however, because it fails to recognize vv 1–8 as originally an independent narrative with a concluding summary statement. Verses 9–26 are another independent narrative detailing Baruch's reading of the scroll and what happened afterwards. This narrative, having its own date, was added to vv 1–8 later (see Rhetoric and Composition for 36:1–8).

The present narrative segment is given its structure by action statements that repeat the verb *qr᾽* + *bĕ᾽oznê(nû/hem)*, "read aloud + in the hearing of / our hearing / their hearing" (cf. Abrego 1983a: 4; 1983b: 25):

And Baruch read aloud the scroll . . . in the hearing of all the people	v 10
. . . and read it aloud in our hearing	v 15
And Baruch read it aloud in their hearing	
. . . and Jehudi read it aloud in the hearing of the king and in the hearing of all the princes	v 21

NOTES

36:9. *in the fifth year of Jehoiakim son of Josiah, king of Judah.* The LXX adds "King" before Jehoiakim but lacks the patronym and "king of Judah." The omission of "son of Josiah, king of Judah" can be attributed to haplography (homoeoarcton: *b . . . b*). Perhaps "King" was added before the name to compensate for the omission (cf. 26:21–23). The fifth year of Jehoiakim was 604 B.C. The LXX^{BS} have "the eighth year" of Jehoiakim, i.e., 601 B.C., a reading with nothing to commend it. The "fifth year" is supported by the other Versions, Josephus (Ant x 93), and virtually all commentators, many of whom point out that a four-year interval between the preparation of the scroll and its reading is too long. Only Holladay (following Lohfink) accepts an "eighth year" date, since it fits into his dubious scheme of Jeremiah making counter-proclamations to a public reading of Deuteronomy every seven years at the Feast of Booths (cf. Deut 31:10–13). The Deuteronomy reading and these counter-proclamations, according to Holladay (1983; 1985), would have occurred in the years 608, 601, 594, and 587 B.C. The idea is totally unsupportable and should be abandoned.

in the ninth month. I.e., the month of Kislev (November/December). By then the first rains will have come, and the weather in Jerusalem is probably cold and wet (cf. Ezra 10:9).

they called a fast before Yahweh — all the people in Jerusalem and all the people who had come in from the cities of Judah — in Jerusalem. The Hebrew reads as if the people in Jerusalem and those entering the city from outlying areas have called the fast (LXX; T; RSV; NEB; NJV). But some commentators (Rudolph; Bright; Jones) think that the leaders will have called the fast, not the people. Rudolph says "all the people" is not the subject but the object and takes the verb *qrʾ* as having a double accusative (cf. GKC §117gg). In his view, the authorities are calling 1) a fast; and 2) people from everywhere to come into Jerusalem. The Hebrew is admittedly awkward, but Rudolph's translation is open to question. Not a whole lot is at stake. A national emergency will call forth a broadly-based decision to proclaim a fast.

The present fast was most likely called in response to a military threat posed by the Babylonians, or else to a drought (Calvin; Duhm). Some think that Judah was experiencing a drought (so Ehrlich 1912: 334; Rudolph), in which case a mandate is cited in the Mishnah (Taanith 1:5) calling for three days of fasting if no rain has fallen by the first day of Kislev (November/December). We know that the liturgy in 14:1–10 was said in response to a drought, and the mention of fasting in 14:11 could relate to this same emergency. But it seems more likely here that the fast is called in response to the military threat now posed by the Babylonians (Zimmerli 1995: 428), who in 604 B.C. are already in Philistia destroying Ashkelon and Ekron. Since Jeremiah anticipated this fast a year earlier, it is more likely that he envisioned a military threat following the Babylonian victories at Carchemish and Hamath than a weather condition and its damaging effects, unless, of course, it had already not rained for some time. The fast, in any case, was a spontaneous response to some crisis facing the nation. In the United States, for example, spontaneous services of prayer took place in New York (Yankee Stadium) and Washington (the National Cathedral) following the terrorist tragedy of September 11, 2001.

and all the people who had come in from the cities of Judah—in Jerusalem. The LXX has only "the house of Judah" in what appears to be a defective text. Here McKane cannot give either MT or LXX a vote of confidence. If the Hebrew Vorlage to the LXX lacked the entire phrase, the omission could be attributed to haplography (whole word: *byrwšlm . . . byrwšlm* or *homoeoarcton: w . . . w*).

10. *And Baruch read aloud from the scroll the words of Jeremiah in the house of Yahweh.* Duhm says this had to be the greatest day in Baruch's life. Here the scroll is said to contain "the words of Jeremiah"; in v 11 it is "the words of Yahweh." In prophecy the two become one.

in the chamber of Gemariah son of Shaphan, the scribe. "The scribe" identifies Shaphan, not Gemariah, although the latter is also trained in the profession, since he comes from a family of scribes (see "The Scribal Family of Shaphan" following the Notes to 26:1–24) and has his own seal (see below). Shaphan served as scribe for King Josiah, a high position comparable to the modern-day "secretary of state." He is also the logical person to have headed a scribal school in Jerusalem. The current state scribe is Elishama (Giesebrecht; Peake; Rudolph; Bright; McKane), who in the next verse is reported as sitting in his palace chamber with other royal officials. Gemariah appears not to have succeeded his father, being simply a member of the council of princes (Peake).

The fact that Elishama's name is given without a patronym may indicate that he was not from a prominent scribal family, perhaps having received the appointment over someone who was. The Shaphan family had pro-Babylonian sympathies, and Jehoiakim was an appointee of Egypt ("Gemariah" in *ABD* 2: 929). In Judah's later remnant community at Mizpah, a power struggle took place between an heir to the royal line, namely, Ishmael son of Nethaniah, son of Elishama; and a descendant of the Shaphan family, viz., Gedaliah son of Ahikam, son of Shaphan. This ended tragically in the murder of Gedaliah by Ishmael (see Note for 41:1). If the two persons named Elishama are in fact one, then the fight to rule Judah's remnant community can be traced to tensions now existing between two prominent families. But in Cheyne's view, Gemariah is also a high-positioned scribe in Jehoiakim's administration. Cheyne notes that in Solomon's cabinet there were two scribes, one having civil and one having military duties (1 Kgs 4:3; cf. Jer 52:25). Gemariah, in any case, has his own Temple chamber, and it is here that Baruch gives a first reading of the Jeremiah scroll. Baruch's use of Gemariah's chamber shows not only that Baruch had access to restricted Temple areas, but that Gemariah supported Jeremiah's efforts to call the nation to reform. Later, Gemariah is one of those urging the king not to burn the scroll (v 25). It is gratuitous for McKane (p. 917) to say that Gemariah's representation as an ally of Jeremiah is an idea that should be given up. For what reason? There are indications aplenty in the book, explicit and otherwise, that Jeremiah had good relations with the scribal family of Shaphan throughout his career (Rudolph; Weiser; Bright; Muilenburg 1970a). See further Note for 26:24.

In the so-called "House of the Bullae" uncovered in Shiloh's City of David excavations, 51 seal impressions originally attached to papyri turned up in the 586 B.C. destruction level of Jerusalem. One of these was of particular importance (Shiloh 1984: 19–20). It contained the inscription "Belonging to Gemariah, [son of] Shaphan" (Shiloh 1985: 80–83 #2, 68; 1986: 28–29 #2, 33–34; Shiloh and Tarler 1986: 204–5; Bieberstein and Bloedhorn 1994 III: 134; Avigad 1997: 191 #470) and doubtless belonged to the individual named here. So we know that Gemariah was a professionally trained scribe, authorized to seal official documents and other records. The name "Gemariah" has shown up on other bullae and on the Arad and Lachish ostraca (see Appendix I).

Temple chambers were used for a variety of purposes (see Note for 35:2). Muilenburg (1970a: 229–30) thinks the present chamber (*liškâ*) was a library, belonging as it does to Gemariah. Since it is now clear that Gemariah was a scribe acting in some capacity within Jehoiakim's government, it is reasonable that a chamber belonging to him would contain stored documents. Here then is where the Jeremiah scroll should have ended up (see criterion #10 for a colophon in Leichty 1964; cf. Lundbom 1986b: 90; O. Pedersén 1998: 241). Instead it was consigned to the flames (v 23). The same might also be said about Jeremiah's scroll of Babylon oracles, which Seraiah wrapped with a stone and threw into the Euphrates (51:63–64). On archives and libraries in the ANE, see O. Pedersén 1998.

in the upper court at the opening of the New Gate in the house of Yahweh—in the hearing of all the people. Another precise description in the narrative, although for us the locations of the New Gate, the upper court, and Gemariah's chamber remain uncertain. According to the reconstruction of Galling (1931), the New Gate lay on the south side of the Temple, connecting the Temple to the palace area (see Note for 26:10). The "upper court" (*ḥāṣēr hāʿelyôn*) appears to have been an extension of the "inner court" enclosing the Temple (1 Kgs 6:36), an area reserved for the priests (2 Chr 4:9). In 2 Chr 20:5, mention is made of a "new court" existing in the time of King Jehoshaphat (873–849 B.C.). The "great court" (1 Kgs 7:12) was an expansive "outer court" of lower elevation, common to both Temple and palace and open to all (Rudolph; de Vaux 1965b: 316–17). Gemariah's chamber must have provided access to the "great court," since from this chamber Baruch read the scroll "in the hearing of all the people." Some have suggested that Gemariah's chamber had a window or balcony above the lower court (Blayney; Boadt). Compare the Pope's window at St. Peter's in Rome, which opens to the courtyard below.

11. *And Micaiah son of Gemariah, son of Shaphan, heard all the words of Yahweh from the scroll.* Micaiah had apparently been left in charge of his father's chamber while the latter was down at the palace with the princes (v 12). He heard the public reading and knew that others must be apprised of it. The name "Micaiah" in the Bible is associated primarily with the prophet who spoke boldly before Ahab and Jehoshaphat (1 Kings 22). In extrabiblical sources, the name is known from Jerusalem ostraca and various seals and seal impressions of unknown provenance (see Appendix I).

12. *And he went down to the house of the king, to the chamber of the scribe.* This scribal chamber (*liškat hassōpēr*) is in the royal palace, probably belonging to Elishama, the scribe. It is mentioned again in vv 20–21 (Galling 1931: 55). Like the chamber belonging to Gemariah, it too may have been a library (Muilenburg 1970a: 225). Micaiah "goes down" to the palace because the palace lies on lower ground than the Temple (see Note for 22:1).

and look! there all the princes were sitting: Elishama the scribe, and Delaiah son of Shemaiah, and Elnathan son of Achbor, and Gemariah son of Shaphan, and Zedekiah son of Hananiah, yes, all the princes. More circumstantial detail, showing that the narrative is not legend but a reporting by someone on the scene. We are told precisely who is sitting around the table. Baruch is not present, but he will enter the room shortly (v 14). On the meaning of the word *śārîm* ("princes"), which here includes individuals who are also trained scribes, see Note for 24:1.

Elishama, the scribe. The apparent successor to Shaphan, the scribe (see v 10), about whom nothing more is said in the narrative other than it was in his chamber that the scroll was left when the group went to inform the king. Elishama probably accompanied the group and may have gone back with Jehudi to collect the scroll after the king asked for it (vv 20–21). But he was silent when others urged the king not to burn the scroll (v 25), which may mean that he was more loyal to Jehoiakim. The name "Elishama," which belongs to six different people in the Bible, has shown up on numerous Judahite bullae, also bullae of Ammonite origin (see Note for 41:1). One of the former reads "(belonging) to Elishama, servant of the king," but Avigad (1986b: 23–24 #4) says he is probably not the same individual as here because his title is different. Ishmael, a Judahite royal family member who later plotted against Gedaliah and murdered him, is the grandson of an Elishama (41:1; 2 Kgs 25:25). We do not know if this Elishama is the same Elishama as here, but it is possible. Another excavated bulla, found over a century ago, could support a royal connection. It contains the inscription: "belonging to Elishama, the king's son" (Torrey 1923: 108; Avigad 1997: 53 #11). See discussion in Note for 41:1.

Delaiah son of Shemaiah. Delaiah is later present at the reading before the king and is one of those urging the king not to burn the scroll (v 25). He is thus a partisan of Jeremiah and Baruch. The name "Delaiah" has turned up on an ostracon from the Lachish "Solar Shrine" and on a Judahite seal and seal impression. On the name "Shemaiah," see Note for 26:20 and "Uriah ben Shemaiah" in Appendix I. The LXX here reads "Shelemiah."

Elnathan son of Achbor. This individual, who is a son of one of the reformers (2 Kgs 22:12), belongs to the group urging the king not to burn the scroll. Yet he was the one sent by Jehoiakim to extradite Uriah from Egypt (26:22–23). If the "Elnathan of Jerusalem" mentioned in 2 Kgs 24:8 is the same Elnathan as here, then a daughter of this individual was married to Jehoiakim. The LXX has "Jonathan" for "Elnathan." It is difficult to make a judgment on this man's sympathies; he could be one of those individuals, found in every age, who somehow manages to be on both sides of a conflict. The names "Elnathan" and "Achbor" have turned up on numerous ostraca, jar handles, seal impressions, and inscriptions of the period (see "Elnathan ben Achbor" in Appendix I).

Gemariah son of Shaphan. On Gemariah, see above, v 10.

Zedekiah son of Hananiah. Nothing more is known about this individual. "Zedekiah" was a common name of the period, given as a throne name to Mattaniah, who later succeeded Jehoiakim (2 Kgs 24:17). On the name "Hananiah," see Note for 28:1 and "Hananiah ben Azzur" in Appendix I.

yes, all the princes. The phrase repeats from the beginning of the verse and, because its function here is to emphasize, the waw on *wĕkol* should be translated as an asseverative: "yes" or "indeed." The phrase also denotes other princes in the room not mentioned by name.

13. *And Micaiah told them all the words that he had heard when Baruch read aloud the scroll in the hearing of the people.* I.e., he summarized the scroll for them. The LXX omits "(aloud) the scroll" (*bassēper*), which can be attributed to haplography (homoeoarcton: *b . . . b*).

14. *Jehudi son of Nethaniah, son of Shelemiah, son of Cushi.* It is highly unusual when someone in a narrative has his ancestry traced back three generations, but here there appears to be a reason. The present individual, who is a Judahite, had a Cushite (= Ethiopian) great-grandfather (Hitzig; Rice 1975: 104–9). But his father and grandfather's names are compounded with Yahweh. Jehudi is a trusted palace functionary, sent now to fetch Baruch and sent

later by the king to take the scroll from Elishama's chamber and then to read it before the king (vv 21–23). Ebed-melech, the palace eunuch who saved Jeremiah's life and received an oracle from Jeremiah promising his own deliverance (38:7–13; 39:15–18), was also a Cushite. Rice thinks that an Ethiopian presence in Judah goes back a century to when Egypt was ruled by an Ethiopian dynasty, and Judah had close relations with Egypt (2 Kgs 18:13–19:37). On the Cushites, see Note for 13:23. Some eliminate a four-generation genealogy by emending the text to read "Jehudi son of Nethaniah and Shelemiah son of Cushi" (Cornill; Rudolph; Hyatt), or by eliminating the name "Jehudi" here but retaining it in vv 21–23 (Volz). Both changes should be rejected; the four-generation genealogy is intentional. The names "Nethaniah" and "Shelemiah" have turned up on various extrabiblical ostraca, seals, and inscriptions (see Appendix I).

to Baruch. Here the LXX adds the patronym, "son of Neriah."

take it in your hand and come. Hebrew *wālēk* must either mean "and go (with us)" or "and come" (Judg 18:19 and 1 Sam 23:27, although in both cases the *waw* is pointed with a *shewa*, not a *qameṣ*; cf. G. R. Driver 1937–38: 122).

So Baruch son of Neriah took the roll in his hand and came in to them. The LXX omits Baruch's patronym and "in his hand"; for the verb, it has "went down." The T and Vg read with the MT.

15. *Do sit down.* Hebrew *šēb nā'*. The LXX's *palin* translates the verb *šub* ("again"), which is to be rejected even though *šûb* does have this meaning in v 28 (Giesebrecht; Duhm; Peake; Cornill; Rudolph; Weiser; Bright; McKane; *pace* Volz and Holladay, who repoint). Aquila (*epistrepson dē*, "turn now") and Symm (*analabe*, "take up again") read with the LXX; T, S, and Vg read with the MT. Calvin notes the courteous treatment accorded Baruch. He is with colleagues in familiar surroundings. Some of those present are obviously his friends.

And Baruch read it aloud in their hearing. Baruch's second reading of the scroll is to the princes, who, except for Micaiah, were not present to hear the public reading. The LXX omits the final "in their hearing," which may simply be to eliminate a repetition.

16. *And it happened when they heard all the words, they turned trembling one to another and said to Baruch, 'We must surely tell the king all these words.'* The verb *pḥd* means "to tremble, be in dread." The LXX omits "to Baruch," which means that the princes are simply telling one another that they must inform the king. According to the MT, the princes tell Baruch that informing the king will be necessary. The MT reading is not "inappropriate," as McKane (p. 905) alleges. It goes without saying that the princes have now decided among themselves that the king must know what has happened, but it is just as obvious that Baruch too must be told of their decision. All are presently sitting in the palace, where the king is not far away, and Baruch has much to lose if the king's wrath is kindled, which it likely will be. Baruch's own life may be in jeopardy. The princes anticipate this, and after asking him a final question, they tell him to go hide with Jeremiah. The text then need not to be emended with the LXX, as many commentators do.

17. *And they asked Baruch, 'Tell us, would you, how did you write all these words, from his dictation?'* The questions seem perfunctory, but the princes need to know something about the scroll's preparation in case the king should ask them. The LXX omits "tell us, would you," and "from his dictation." It also translates the interrogative as "from where?" (*pothen*). The LXX reading is also perfunctory: "From where did you get these words?" Did they really not know where Baruch got the words? Did they think Baruch was the prophet? The LXX deletions should certainly not be defended because "from his dictation" is repeated in Baruch's answer (v 18). Repetitions of this sort are precisely what we expect in Hebrew discourse, in which questions are not answered by a simple "Yes" or "No." Jones says that the repetition gives emphasis; H. Weippert (1989: 101 n. 6) believes this double question elicits the double answer in v 18. The MT should then be read.

18. *And Baruch said to them, 'From his dictation; he would proclaim all these words to me and I would write upon the scroll in ink.'* Here the LXX omits "to them" after "and Baruch said" and adds the name "Jeremiah" at the beginning of the answer. The imperfect verb *yiqrāʾ* and the participial construction *waʾănî kōtēb* are used here with frequentative (iterative) force, which expresses repeated action in the past; thus: "he would (repeatedly) proclaim . . . and I would (repeatedly) write" (GKC §107b; §112e). For this frequentative verbal usage, see again v 23.

I would write upon the scroll in ink. The term for "ink," *děyô*, is a *hapax legomenon* in the OT. The LXX omits. Proposals to emend *badděyô*, "in ink," to *běyād(î)*, "with (my) hand" (Giesebrecht; Ehrlich 1912: 334), or to take the term as later expansion (Duhm; McKane) are entirely unnecessary, for which reason most commentators stay with the MT (Peake; Cornill; Volz; Rudolph; Weiser; Bright; Holladay; and others). Lambdin (1953: 149) thinks the Hebrew word may be a graphic error for *rěyô*, which he says can be equated with Egyptian *ry. (t)*, meaning "ink." Black ink for writing was made from carbon, usually being soot scraped from cooking vessels or else specially prepared, and then mixed with a solution of gum and water and dried into cakes. Chemical tests on the Lachish Letters turned up traces of iron, which A. Lewis believed was an early constituent of ink (Torczyner 1938: 190–93). This would make the color red or reddish-brown. Early ink did not penetrate deeply into papyrus or skin so could be washed off easily (Exod 32:33; Num 5:23). Pens were made from a piece of thin rush (*Phragmites communis*), cut at one end on the bias and then frayed to form a brush. A rush pen (*ʿēṭ*) is referred to in 8:8 and would have been the type of pen used here by Baruch. Reed (*Juncus maritimus*) pens with a split nib came later in the Greco-Roman period, beginning about the end of the third century B.C. (cf. *kalamos*, "reed pen," in 3 John 13). Completing the scribal kit of Egyptian design was a palette with one or two hollowed-out cups (usually circular) to hold the dried ink. Palettes having two cups were for red and black ink. Some scribal kits also had small water jugs attached. For a rush pen pictured in its holder with an attached slate palette and water jug, see J. A. Wilson 1951: fig. 4c; ANEP[2] 73 #234; *IDB* R–Z, 919.

Other scribal kits were palettes of pencil-box shape, some with a sliding lid, which had recesses for pens and ink. Very ornate palettes of this design have been found in Egypt, and an eighth-century B.C. relief shows a Syrian scribe with one in hand, indicating usage outside Egypt (G. R. Driver 1976: 87). For a picture of this scribe standing before King Bar Rakab, see *ANEP*² 158 #460, 302; and Driver 1976: plate 33 #1. For pictures of other palettes, see one from the reign of Ah-moses I (1570–1545 B.C.) in *ANEP*² 73 #233, 276; and some of alabaster and ivory in Driver 1976: plate #32. Baruch would likely have possessed a writing palette of this type. The Hebrew word for palette, *qeset*, is an Egyptian loanword (Lambdin 1953: 154). The AV translated the term "inkhorn" in Ezek 9:2, 3, and 11, but this was changed to "writing case" in the RSV. Separate receptacles for holding ink may also have been used in Judah (Kelso 1948: 39 thinks they were made from the horns of an animal), since they are known to have existed in Egypt (Lucas 1934: 312). The scribe, in any event, would dip his rush pen into water and then rub it on a cake of ink, much as modern artists do with watercolors (Lucas 1934: 307). On pens, ink, and scribal palettes, see Lucas 1934: 307–12; A. Lewis on Lachish Letter ink in Torczyner 1938: 188–93; Hyatt 1943: 77–79; R. J. Forbes 1965: 236–39; G. R. Driver 1976: 85–87; R. J. Williams in *IDB* R–Z, 919; and A. Lemaire in *ABD* 6: 1003–4.

19. *And the princes said to Baruch, 'Go, hide yourself, you and Jeremiah, so that no one may know where you are!'* The princes wish to protect Baruch and Jeremiah, having little doubt about the king's response to what has just transpired and knowing full well what happened earlier to Uriah (26:20–23). This king was known for violent action (22:17). Their advice is that Jeremiah and Baruch tell no one of their whereabouts. It does happen that high-profile individuals, simply by retiring from public view, sometimes satisfy persecuting monarchs. It is said of St. Cyprian, Bishop of Carthage, who fled Carthage during the persecutions of Emperor Decius (A.D. 250–51) and went into hiding, that he continued to direct the affairs of the Church from where he was, without Roman interference. The authorities could have sought him out if they so wished (messengers could have been followed), but they did not and were content simply to confiscate his property (Raven 1984: 168). The likelihood here is that Jeremiah and Baruch remained in hiding during the rest of Jehoiakim's reign.

20. *And they went in to the king, to the court.* The court was an inner palace court where royal apartments were located (cf. 1 Kgs 7:8).

but the roll they deposited in the chamber of Elishama, the scribe. The verb is *hipqîdû*. The H-stem of this often-used Jeremiah verb (see Note for 5:9) means here "to hand over, deposit, commit" (cf. 37:21). The princes probably gave the scroll to someone in the chamber for safekeeping. Perhaps they were hoping that the king might not ask for it.

Elishama, the scribe. The LXX omits "the scribe."

And they told in the hearing of the king all these words. I.e., they summarized for him the scroll's contents. Many Heb MSS, G^AOLC, S, and T have "these" (*hā'ēlleh*), which should be added to the reading of the MT. The LXX omits "in the hearing."

21. *And the king sent Jehudi to take the roll, and he took it from the chamber of Elishama, the scribe.* Jehudi is the one sent earlier by the princes to fetch Baruch (v 14). He may just be a palace servant rather than one of the princes, but still an important person. Duhm thinks that he was a scribe. Jehudi is able to read, and the scribe's knife used to cut the scroll may have been his. The LXX again omits "the scribe" after Elishama.

and Jehudi read it aloud in the hearing of the king and in the hearing of all the princes who were standing beside the king. This is the third reading of the scroll in one day. Duhm wonders if the reading could have taken more than an hour.

22. *And the king was sitting in the winter house.* The "winter house" (*bêt haḥōrep*) may simply be palace quarters exposed to winter sun but more sheltered than the airy summer quarters (Harper 1905: 78; Hyatt; Holladay). See "the winter house" and "the summer house" in Amos 3:15. But Paul (1978; 1991: 125–26) argues for the older view, that the winter house is a separate building. This finds support in extrabiblical texts, among which is the Inscription of Barrakub, the Aramaean King of Sam'al (ca. 730 B.C.), who says that the old palace of Kilamu had to suffice for both a summer and winter house, but now Barrakub has built an additional abode (*ANET*[3] 655; CS II 161).

in the ninth month. I.e., Kislev (November/December); cf. v 9. The LXX omits the reference. Many commentators (Giesebrecht; Duhm; Peake; Cornill; Holladay; McKane) therefore delete, but its presence in other Vrs (G[L], S, T, and Vg) argues for retention. Duhm does not like the repetition after v 9. The reference can certainly be retained (so Volz; Rudolph; Weiser; Bright).

and a fire in the stove was burning before him. This reading follows the LXX (see footnote), except for its omission of "was burning." The T also omits the participle. In defense of MT's *'et*, it is possible for an accusative to depend on a preceding verbal idea; the reading could therefore be "and he had the brazier before him" (GKC §117 l).

the stove. Hebrew *hā'āḥ*. The noun *'āḥ* is another loanword from Egyptian *'ḥ*, meaning "brazier" (Kelso 1948: 16 #34; Lambdin 1953: 146; cf. KB[3]). Kelso says that these stoves were either metal or ceramic ware, but since this one was being used by a king in the palace, it was probably made of metal.

23. *And it happened as Jehudi proclaimed three or four columns, he would tear it with the scribe's knife and would throw it into the fire that was in the stove, until the entire roll was consumed on the fire that was in the stove.* The Hebrew imperfect and perfect with *waw consecutive* are both used here with frequentative (iterative) force to express repeated action in the past, thus: "he would (repeatedly) tear it . . . he would (repeatedly) throw" (GKC §107b; §112e). For the same usage, see v 18. Rashi notes too that the imperfect verb must be translated past tense. It is not specified who tears the scroll and throws it into the fire. It could have been the king, but it could also have been Jehudi on orders from the king. In either case, the king is carrying out a symbolic action, on which see Note for 13:1. The intent, as Blank (1950–51: 93) points out, is to neutralize the words of

curse on the scroll. This explains why the king and those with him do not tear their garments: The threat is now removed. But the king's action, like Hananiah's breaking the yoke off Jeremiah's neck (28:10–11), will come to nothing because Yahweh is not behind it.

three or four columns. Hebrew *šālōš dĕlātôt wĕ'arbā'â.* In one of the Lachish Letters (4:3) *delet,* lit., "door," is employed for the "column" of a scroll (Torczyner 1938: 79–80), a usage that may go back to writing boards having panels. On the Assyrian writing boards found at Nimrud, see D. J. Wiseman (1955) and M. Howard (1955). Albright (1970: 39 n. 5), commenting on the use of *dlt* in the Amman Citadel Inscription (line 5), said the word there, probably at Lachish, and also in Hebrew meant "announcement board," and he agreed after earlier doubts that it could mean "column of a scroll" in the present verse (cf. Hicks 1983: 54–55). If Jehudi is doing the reading and Jehoiakim the cutting, which is the usual assumption, then after Jehudi has read three or four columns and they fall to the ground, the king cuts them off and throws them into the fire. The process continues until the entire scroll is read and destroyed. Hicks, who thinks the scroll was made of skins, argues that the king is cutting sutures holding the skins together (p. 61). Cutting animal skins with a penknife is possible but would be more difficult. It makes more sense if papyrus is being cut. Also, even an angry king is not likely to have submitted himself to the smoke and stench of skins burning indoors.

he would tear it. Hebrew *yiqrā'ehā.* Calvin notes a wordplay with the prior *kiqrô'* ("as he proclaimed"). Another wordplay is evident in the repetition of this same verb in v 24, where it says that those hearing the scroll being read "did not tear" (*lō' qārĕ'û*) their garments. The subject of the verbs, as we mentioned, is unclear; it could be either Jehudi or the king.

the scribe's knife. Hebrew *ta'ar hassōpēr.* A penknife used for cutting papyrus. Most likely it belongs to Jehudi, which means he is seen to be a ready scribe. The LXX again omits "the scribe."

and would throw it into the fire. On the singular "he would throw (it)" after the plural "columns," see GKC §135p. In the Vassal Treaties of Esarhaddon (410–11) there is a solemn warning not to consign the tablet containing the treaty stipulations to the fire or to destroy it by other means (Wiseman 1958a: 59–60; *ANET*³ 538). A string of curses follows, showing what will happen if the vassal king does this. The words of the present scroll deal with a covenant between Yahweh and his people, and consigning it to the flames will bring to pass the curses on this king and his nation.

the entire roll. The LXX has *pas ho chartēs* ("the entire papyrus"); see Note on v 2.

24. *And they did not tremble, and they did not tear their garments—the king and all his servants who were hearing all these words.* For "and they did not tremble," the LXX has *kai ouk ezētēsan* ("and they did not examine"). At the earlier reading of the scroll before the princes (v 16), three of whom are present here, there was holy fear. Other contrasts of an indirect nature are also being made. The narrator is telling us that the king tore (*qr'*) the scroll instead of

tearing (qrˁ) his garments. There is a clear allusion here to what happened when the newly found law-book was read before King Josiah: great alarm over the impending wrath of Yahweh and the king tearing (qrˁ) his garments straightaway (2 Kgs 22:11–13). No such response from this king!

all his servants. Hebrew *wěkol-ˁăbādāyw.* "Servants" of the king are important royal officials (see Note for 21:7). The LXX lacks "and all."

25. *However, Elnathan and Delaiah and Gemariah strongly urged the king not to burn the roll.* Hebrew *wěgam* is an adversative meaning "however" or "nevertheless" (Calvin; Giesebrecht; Ehrlich 1912: 336). Three individuals among those present urge the king not to burn the scroll. The LXX text is defective, omitting "and Gemariah," which can be attributed to haplography (homoeoteleuton: *yhw . . . yhw*), and misreading Delaiah as *Godolias* (= Gedaliah). The two individuals here are urging the king to burn the scroll. Holladay in support of the LXX imagines a division of the house: Elnathan and Gedaliah urging the king to burn; Delaiah and Gemariah urging him not to burn. But such a reconstruction is too hypothetical, and one should stay with the MT (Duhm; Cornill; *pace* McKane).

but he did not listen to them. The LXX omits, which can probably also be attributed to haplography (homoeoarcton: *w . . . w*).

26. *And the king commanded Jerahmeel, the king's son, and Seraiah the son of Azriel and Shelemiah son of Abdeel to seize Baruch, the scribe, and Jeremiah, the prophet, but Yahweh hid them.* Jehoiakim acted similarly in response to the preaching of Uriah, whose extradition from Egypt was a simple matter (26:20–23). Here Yahweh hides the prophet and his friend.

Jerahmeel, the king's son. Hebrew *hammelek* should be translated "the king," not as a personal name (Vg and AV rendered *ben-hammelek* as "son of Hammelech"). A seal impression from the same hoard as the one naming Baruch contained the inscription, "Belonging to Jerahme'el, the king's son" (Avigad 1978a; 1986b: 27–28 #8; 1997: 175 #414; cf. *ABD* 3: 684). This impression probably belonged to the royal officer mentioned here, and if so we have three individuals in the chapter whose actual seal impressions have been found: Baruch son of Neriah, Gemariah son of Shaphan, and now Jerahmeel, the king's son. Numerous other seal impressions have turned up with "the king's son" after the name (Avigad 1986a: 51; 1986b: 25–26 ##6–7; 1997: 174–75 ##412–15), and in 38:6 there is mention of a certain "Malchiah, the king's son." In ancient Sumer, Kramer (1951: 241) reports that no scribe was ever designated "son of the king." These recent bullae finds have also revived the old debate as to whether "the king's son" means a son of the reigning king, a son of another king, or simply an officer in the king's employ. It has been argued that "the king's son" may simply designate a low-rank officer not of royal blood (de Vaux 1965b: 119–20). Görg (1985) says similar titles for court functionaries appear in Egyptian chronicles. Jerahmeel, because he is assigned police duties, could argue for a broader interpretation of the term. But many have rejected the broader interpretation, arguing that "son of the king" means just what it says, a member of the royal family (Torrey 1923: 108; Rainey 1975; Lemaire 1979; Avigad 1986b: 28). Jerahmeel could not be a grown son of Jehoiakim, who is only 30 years old at the time (2 Kgs 23:36; Jer 36:9), but he could belong to the royal family, as kings had large harems and thus, many sons.

Seraiah the son of Azriel. For the inscriptional evidence on both names, see Appendix I.

and Shelemiah son of Abdeel. The LXX omits, which is likely another loss attributable to haplography (homoeoteleuton: *'l . . . 'l*). Rudolph and Janzen (1973: 118) both agree. On the name "Shelemiah," see Appendix I.

Baruch, the scribe, and Jeremiah the prophet. The LXX again omits the titles. Baruch is called "the scribe" here and in v 32, and Stipp (1997: 191) points out that the LXX has the title in neither place. The omission in v 32, however, is likely due to a larger loss by haplography. On Baruch's professional standing and his descent from a distinguished scribal family, see Note for 36:4.

but Yahweh hid them. A rare statement of explicit theology in the Jeremiah narrative (see §Introduction: Theology in the Prose). The LXX has "but they were hidden," which is considered the original reading by many commentators (Duhm; Volz; Rudolph; Holladay; McKane). Perhaps it is (cf. v 19; 26:24; 28:17), although it is less dramatic. Giesebrecht notes that G^L, Aq, Symm, T, S, and Vg all support MT. About the closest we come to the present statement is in 32:8, where the narrator quotes Jeremiah as saying, after Hanamel comes to him about buying the field: "Then I knew that this was the word of Yahweh."

MESSAGE AND AUDIENCE

In this narrative segment the audience is told that a fast was called in Jehoiakim's fifth year, in the ninth month, that brought people throughout Judah to Jerusalem. Why the fast was called is not said, but the audience will know. On this occasion, Baruch read a scroll from Jeremiah in the Temple, in the chamber of Gemariah son of Shaphan, where he was able to address a large assembly, perhaps in the court below. Micaiah son of Gemariah was on hand to hear the reading, and when it was over he went down to the palace to inform the princes assembled in Elishama's chamber. Present were Elishama the scribe, Delaiah son of Shemaiah, Elnathan son of Achbor, Gemariah son of Shaphan, and Zedekiah son of Hananiah, among others. Micaiah told them what he had just heard, at which point the princes dispatched Jehudi, whom the audience is told was of Cushite ancestry, to bring Baruch to the palace with scroll in hand. Baruch came with the scroll. The princes then told him to sit down and read the scroll, which he did, and they were visibly moved. In fact, they were shaken and told Baruch that the king would have to be informed, but before going to the king they asked him how the scroll was written. Did he take it from dictation? Yes, he did. Jeremiah dictated the words and he wrote them in ink on the scroll. The princes then told Baruch to go with Jeremiah into hiding and to tell no one where they were. The princes were obviously concerned about their safety.

After leaving the scroll in Elishama's chamber, the princes went to the king and reported to him what had been read to an assembly over at the Temple. The king then sent Jehudi to fetch the scroll, which he did, and once back in the king's presence, Jehudi read the scroll to the king with the princes standing by. The audience is told that the king was sitting in his winter house, in the ninth month, warming himself before a fire in the stove. As Jehudi read three or four columns of the scroll, the king cut what had fallen to the ground with a scribal knife, probably belonging to Jehudi, and threw it into the fire. This continued until the entire scroll was consumed. No one trembled, not the king, not his servants, not even the princes who had anxious faces moments earlier, and no one tore their garments. Elnathan, Delaiah, and Gemariah, however, had urged the king strongly not to burn the scroll. But he would not listen. The audience will perhaps have remembered what took place when Josiah had read to him a newly found law-book some 18 years earlier, one with judgment written all over it, and how this good king rent his clothes and carried out in all haste a solemn ceremony of covenant renewal. Nothing like this happened now. Jehoiakim dispatched Jerahmeel, the king's son, and two others to seize Baruch and Jeremiah. But the audience is told that Yahweh hid them.

When this narrative is heard after the segment preceding, the summary statement of v 8 will be an introduction to the detailed account that now follows (Duhm). The audience needed to know more about what happened when Baruch read the scroll. Now it finds out. Some in the audience may have heard about the public reading from other sources, but they will not know what went on behind the scenes. Now, with an extraordinary walking tour through the libraries and inner chambers of the Temple and the palace, places to which none in the audience had direct access, they find out that Baruch was among friends in the inner sanctums and that the princes acted to protect Baruch and Jeremiah when they perceived that their lives were in danger. The visit to the king's winter house also shows the people just how arrogant and defiant this king was, not only toward Baruch and Jeremiah, but more importantly toward a message that had come to him and the nation from Yahweh God.

John Milton's portrayal of the underworld council following Satan's speech in *Paradise Lost* (ii 420–23) might well describe the princes here when they heard the words of Jeremiah's scroll:

> But all sat mute
> Pondering the danger with deep thoughts; and each
> In other's countenance read his own dismay
> Astonished.
>
> (Carey and Fowler 1968: 527)

3. The Scroll Is Rewritten (36:27–32)

36 ²⁷And the word of Yahweh came to Jeremiah after the king burned the roll, that is, the words that Baruch wrote from the dictation of Jeremiah: ²⁸Once again, take for yourself another roll and write on it all the former words that were contained on the first roll, which Jehoiakim, king of Judah, burned.

²⁹And concerning Jehoiakim, king of Judah, you shall say, Thus said Yahweh: You, you have burned this roll, saying, 'Why have you written on it "the king of Babylon will surely come and destroy this land and make to cease from it human and beast"?'

³⁰Therefore thus said Yahweh concerning Jehoiakim, king of Judah: He shall not have one to sit upon the throne of David, and his dead body shall be thrown out to the heat by day and the frost by night. ³¹And I will reckon upon him and upon his offspring and upon his servants their iniquity; and I will bring upon them and upon the inhabitants of Jerusalem and to the men of Judah all the evil that I spoke to them, but they did not listen.

³²So Jeremiah took another roll and gave it to Baruch son of Neriah, the scribe, and he wrote upon it from the dictation of Jeremiah all the words of the scroll that Jehoiakim, king of Judah, burned in the fire. And besides, many words like these were added to them.

RHETORIC AND COMPOSITION

MT 36:27–32 = LXX 43:27–32. The upper limit of this narrative segment, which has continuity with the prior segments in vv 1–8 and vv 9–26 but is nevertheless a separate accounting in its own right, is marked by a *setumah* in M^A and M^L and a *petuhah* in M^P before v 27. Its lower limit is marked by a *petuhah* in M^A and M^P and a *setumah* in M^L after v 32, which is also the chapter division. The M^A, M^L, and M^P all have a *setumah* after v 29, which separates the two oracles. The M^L and M^P have another *setumah* after v 31, separating Oracle II from the narrative conclusion.

This segment reports a final directive from Yahweh to Jeremiah at the end of his early career (vv 27–28) and Jeremiah's execution of this directive (v 32). Usually the directive and execution appear together (13:1–2, 3–5, 6–7; 18:2–3; 25:15–17; 35:2–4; 36:2–4), but here they are broken up in order to frame two oracles that come in the center. The LXX similarly divides a superscription to frame the Elam Oracle (see Rhetoric and Composition for 49:34–39). Oracle I indicts King Jehoiakim and is addressed directly to him (v 29). Oracle II judges the king, his offspring and servants, and the rest of the people for not heeding Yahweh's word (vv 30–31). This oracle appears to be addressed to a Judahite audience, but not directly, because its main concern is to render judgment on the king.

The present narrative follows the other narrative segments in the chapter naturally; it is not the contribution of a later redactor (*pace* Duhm, who is influenced by homiletical prose in the oracles). Verse 31 of Oracle II makes an inclusio with v 3 of the first narrative segment (see Rhetoric and Composition for 36:1–8). While the present segment reports a revelation to Jeremiah after the first scroll was burned, the date in v 9, the fifth year of Jehoiakim, appears to apply to it also.

The expanded formulas to the two oracles have this inversion:

I   *And concerning Jehoiakim, king of Judah . . . Thus said Yahweh:*   v 29
II   *. . . thus said Yahweh concerning Jehoiakim, king of Judah:*   v 30

NOTES

36:27. *And the word of Yahweh came to Jeremiah after the king burned the roll.* On this third-person superscriptional form, see Note for 28:12. The present revelation must have come after Jeremiah went with Baruch into hiding.

the words. The LXX has "all the words."

28. *Once again, take for yourself another roll and write on it all the former words that were contained on the first roll, which Jehoiakim, king of Judah, burned.* Weiser says the contempt of kings cannot deter the might of God. On this common divine command using *qaḥ* ("take!"), see 36:2 and Note for 43:9. The verb *šûb* is an auxiliary, meaning "(once) again." The LXX contains four omissions: "on it" after "and write," "the former" and "the first," and "king of Judah" after "Jehoiakim." The omission of "the former" can be attributed to haplography (homoeoteleuton: *ym . . . ym*), so also the omission of "the first" (homoeoteleuton: *m . . . m*); however, the omission of similar, but not identical, words in close proximity may require another explanation.

29. *And concerning Jehoiakim, king of Judah.* Another LXX omission, doubtless due to haplography (three-word: *yhwyqym mlk-yhwdh . . . yhwyqym mlk-yhwdh*). Haplography is considered possible by Rudolph, Holladay, and Keown et al. The words are present in T and Vg.

You, you have burned this roll. The added pronoun has the usual function of giving emphasis, whether or not Jehoiakim himself burned the scroll.

'*Why have you written on it "the king of Babylon will surely come and destroy this land and make to cease from it human and beast"?*' Here is the reason for Jehoiakim's destruction of the scroll, which the earlier narrative does not provide. On the expression "human and beast" in Jeremiah prose, see Note for 21:6.

30. *He shall not have one to sit upon the throne of David.* Jehoiachin did succeed Jehoiakim but was deposed almost immediately and taken to Babylon. Kimḥi says that since Jehoiachin reigned only three months he was not regarded as having sat on the throne. Calvin the same thing. Yet Jehoiachin does carry on the messianic line according to Matt 1:11–12 (Jechoniah = Jehoiachin).

and his dead body shall be thrown out to the heat by day and the frost by night.
The non-lament for Jehoiakim in 22:18–19 says as much. On the indignity of a
nonburial, see Note on 7:33. There is an irony here: Jehoiakim in the cold of
winter is sitting by a warm fire, but his dead body will be left to the dry heat of
day (*ḥōreb*) and the frost of night. When the two narrative segments are heard
together, a wordplay will also emerge on the verb *šlk*, "to throw": when the
scroll was read, Jehoiakim "would throw" (*hašlēk*) pieces into the fire (v 23);
now his dead body "shall be thrown" (*mušleket*) on open ground, where it will
be exposed to the elements (Kessler 1966: 398). For more discussion on how
Jehoiakim met his end, see Note for 22:19.

31. *And I will reckon upon him and upon his offspring and upon his servants
their iniquity.* On the Jeremianic verb *pqd* ("reckon, attend to"), see Note for
5:9. The LXX omits "their iniquity."

*and I will bring upon them and upon the inhabitants of Jerusalem and to the
men of Judah all the evil that I spoke to them, but they did not listen.* Judgment
comes because Yahweh spoke evil against the people and they would not listen. The LXX has "and I will bring upon him" singular (i.e., the king), "upon
the land of Judah," and "all the evils" plural.

32. *So Jeremiah took another roll.* The entire verse is a summary statement
like the one in v 8. The LXX has "and Baruch took another roll," followed by a
number of omissions. The MT reading is supported by G^L, S, T, and Vg. Giesebrecht thinks the LXX has abridged; Volz says that Jeremiah must remain the
key figure, which is probably right (so also Rudolph).

and gave it to Baruch son of Neriah, the scribe. The LXX omits, which can be
attributed to haplography (homoeoarcton: *wy . . . wy*). "The scribe" refers to
Baruch, since in compound names the title applies to the person with two
names rather than to one person or the other. The father, Neriah, was also
doubtless a scribe.

Jehoiakim, king of Judah. The LXX omits "king of Judah."

burned in the fire. The LXX omits "in the fire."

And besides, many words like these were added to them. On a plural object
after a passive verb, see Note for 35:14. This rewritten scroll—or a subsequent
version of it, I have called the First Edition of chaps. 1–20 (see §Introduction:
The First Edition of the Book of Jeremiah). The expression *nôsap ʿălêhem
dĕbārîm rabbîm kāhēmmâ*, "many words like these were added to them," refers
mainly to what was written by Baruch, not to later additions made by others
(E. Nielson 1954: 78).

MESSAGE AND AUDIENCE

The audience is informed in this concluding narrative segment that Yahweh's
word came again to Jeremiah after the scroll dictated to Baruch was burned by
Jehoiakim in the fire. The king's action was not the end of the matter. Jeremiah
is now directed to get another roll and write up everything contained on the
first roll. He is also given two divine oracles to proclaim. The first indicts

Jehoiakim for burning the first roll, giving also a reason for his having done what he did, which the audience has not heard before. Jehoiakim, it turns out, was unwilling to accept Yahweh's word that the king of Babylon could come and destroy Judah. No surprise. The king is also the subject of a second oracle spoken to an unspecified audience. Jehoiakim will not have a son to occupy David's throne. What is more, he will be denied a proper burial. His dead body will be thrown out on open land, where it will be exposed to the day heat and the night cold. Yahweh will reckon with this wicked and unrepentant king, as well as his offspring and servants. As for the others who remain in Judah and Jerusalem, Yahweh will bring upon them the promised evil about which they have already heard, but to which they would not listen. Following the oracles, the narrator tells us that Jeremiah replaced the destroyed scroll as directed. He took another writing-scroll, gave it to Baruch, and Baruch wrote on it all the words appearing on the scroll that Jehoiakim burned. To this scroll, the audience is also told, many similar words were added.

Although Oracle I is addressed directly to the king, it assuredly would not have been spoken in his hearing, since Jeremiah and Baruch are now at an undisclosed location. The same is true with Oracle II, which is addressed to an unspecified audience and concerns all of Judah, but is a judgment, nevertheless, targeting Jehoiakim. Both oracles are probably to be dated in Jehoiakim's fifth year (v 9), and what the narrative reports can also be dated then. The final statement that many similar words were added to the original collection comes from a later time—exactly when, we do not know.

When this concluding narrative segment is heard following the earlier segments, it will become apparent to the audience that Yahweh is more powerful than Judah's strident king. Jehoiakim sought to discredit Jeremiah's prophecy; Yahweh answered by confirming it. In fact, Yahweh said a good deal more than what was written on the first scroll, and now this also will be preserved.

INDEX OF AUTHORS

◆

INDEX OF SCRIPTURE

◆

THE ANCHOR BIBLE

Commentaries (C) and Reference Library (RL) volumes on the Old and New
Testaments and Apocrypha

THE CONTRIBUTORS

Susan Ackerman, Dartmouth College. RL17

William F. Albright, Johns Hopkins University. C26

Francis I. Andersen, Professorial Fellow, Classics and Archaeology, University of Melbourne. C24, C24A, C24E

Markus Barth, University of Basel. C34, C34A, C34B

Adele Berlin, University of Maryland. C25A

Helmut Blanke, Doctor of Theology from the University of Basel. C34B

Joseph Blenkinsopp, University of Notre Dame. C19, C19A, C19B, RL5

Robert G. Boling, McCormick Theological Seminary. C6, C6A

Raymond E. Brown, S.S., Union Theological Seminary, New York (Emeritus). C29, C29A, C30, RL1, RL7, RL15, RL22

George W. Buchanan, Wesley Theological Seminary. C36

Edward F. Campbell, Jr., McCormick Theological Seminary. C7

James H. Charlesworth, Princeton Theological Seminary. RL4, RL13, RL14

Mordechai Cogan, Hebrew University, Jerusalem. C10, C11

John J. Collins, University of Chicago. RL10

James L. Crenshaw, Duke Divinity School. C24C, RL16

Mitchell Dahood, S.J., The Pontifical Biblical Institute. C16, C17, C17A

Alexander A. Di Lella, O.F.M., Catholic University of America. C23, C39

David L. Dungan, University of Tennessee, Knoxville. RL18

John H. Elliott, University of San Francisco. C37B

Joseph A. Fitzmyer, S.J., Catholic University of America. C28, C28A, C31, C33, C34C

J. Massyngberde Ford, University of Notre Dame. C38

Michael V. Fox, University of Wisconsin, Madison. C18A

David Noel Freedman, University of Michigan (Emeritus) and University of California, San Diego. General Editor. C24, C24A, C24E

Victor P. Furnish, Perkins School of Theology, Southern Methodist University. C32A

Jonathan A. Goldstein, University of Iowa. C41, C41A, RL21

Moshe Greenberg, Hebrew University, Jerusalem. C22, C22A

Louis F. Hartman, C.SS.R., Catholic University of America. C23

Andrew E. Hill, Wheaton College. C25D

Delbert R. Hillers, Johns Hopkins University. C7A

Luke Timothy Johnson, Candler School of Theology, Emory University. C35A, C37A

Gary Knoppers, Penn State University. C12

Craig R. Koester, Luther Seminary. C36

Bentley Layton, Yale University. RL11

Baruch A. Levine, New York University. C4, C4A

Jack R. Lundbom, Clare Hall, Cambridge University. C21A, C21B

P. Kyle McCarter, Jr., Johns Hopkins University. C8, C9

John L. McKenzie, De Paul University. C20

Abraham J. Malherbe, Yale University (Emeritus). C32B

C. S. Mann, formerly Coppin State College. C26

Joel Marcus, Boston University. C27

J. Louis Martyn, Union Theological Seminary, New York. C33A

Amihai Mazar, Institute of Archaeology of Hebrew University, Jerusalem. RL2

John P. Meier, Catholic University of America. RL3, RL9, RL20

Carol L. Meyers, Duke University. C25B, C25C

Eric M. Meyers, Duke University. C25B, C25C

Jacob Milgrom, University of California, Berkeley (Emeritus). C3, C3A, C3B

Carey A. Moore, Gettysburg College. C7B, C40, C40A, C44

Jacob M. Myers, Lutheran Theological Seminary, Gettysburg. C12, C13, C14, C42

Jacob Neusner, University of South Florida at Tampa. RL8

Jerome H. Neyrey, University of Notre Dame. C37C

William F. Orr, Pittsburgh Theological Seminary. C32

Brian Peckham, Regis College, Toronto University. RL6

Marvin H. Pope, Yale University (Emeritus). C7C, C15

William H. C. Propp, University of California, San Diego. C2

Jerome D. Quinn, St. Paul Seminary. C35

Paul R. Raabe, Concordia Seminary, St. Louis. C24D

Bo Ivar Reicke, University of Basel. C37

Jack M. Sasson, University of North Carolina at Chapel Hill. C24B

Lawrence H. Schiffman, New York University. RL12

R. B. Y. Scott, Princeton University. C18

Choon-Leong Seow, Princeton Theological Seminary. C18C

Patrick W. Skehan, Catholic University of America. C39

Ephraim A. Speiser, University of Pennsylvania. C1

Ephraim Stern, Hebrew University, Jerusalem. RL19

Hayim Tadmor, Hebrew University, Jerusalem. C11

James Arthur Walther, Pittsburgh Theological Seminary (Emeritus). C32

Moshe Weinfeld, Hebrew University, Jerusalem. C5

David Winston, Graduate Theological Union, Berkeley (Emeritus). C43

G. Ernest Wright, Semitic Museum, Harvard University. C6